The Encyclopedia of Auto Racing Greats

THE ENCYCLOPEDIA OF AUTO RACING GREATS .. by
ROBERT CUTTER
and
BOB FENDELL

Prentice-Hall, Inc.,
Englewood Cliffs, N. J.

The Encyclopedia of Auto Racing Greats by Robert Cutter
and Bob Fendell
Copyright © 1973 by Prentice-Hall, Inc.

Printed in the United States of America

Prentice-Hall International, Inc., London
Prentice-Hall of Australia, Pty. Ltd., North Sydney
Prentice-Hall of Canada, Ltd., Toronto
Prentice-Hall of India Private Ltd., New Delhi
Prentice-Hall of Japan, Inc., Tokyo

10 9 8 7 6 5 4 3 2 1

Library of Congress Cataloging in Publication Data

Cutter, Bob.
The encyclopedia of auto racing greats.

1. Automobile racing—Biography.   I.   Fendell,
Bob,   joint author.   II.   Title.
GVI032.A1C87   796.7'2'0922 [B]   73–7541
ISBN 0-13-275206-9

FOREWORD

This book started out as something entirely different from what you now will read. Originally—some eight years ago when this project started—the men and women of motor racing were to have been just a part of a major encyclopedic work on the sport as a whole. Sharing equal attention with the people were to have been the cars, courses, engines, races, trophies, sponsors, governing bodies and all the elements that make up the colorful collage that has been motor sports for the past eight decades or so. But very early we began to reshape our efforts.

First, it was easy to gather information about the machines and places of racing, about the organizations and the prizes. What wasn't so easy was gathering material about the people of racing. Second, something we should have known all along became dominant in our thinking. Without the human element little of the data made sense. At a point now difficult to pin down, we decided to reshape this book into one dealing solely with people. Perhaps later another volume will cover the inanimate elements of motor sports.

There are about 550 individuals detailed in these pages; some articles cover families or natural groups. This book is a reference work, a pioneering one whose sins we devoutly hope will be forgiven by our professional readers, since the authors have tried to make it as accurate as humanly possible. But it also is a collection of interesting stories, each someone's life or part of it. Hopefully this book will be read as much for that as for the facts each article contains.

There are errors in this book. None of them was committed knowingly, but in preparing 550 or more articles, even over a span of years, errors will creep in. By crosschecking each other, the authors hope that the most glaring mistakes have been identified and eliminated. Motor sports—unlike baseball, football or many other American sports—suffers from a lack of accurate records, especially in early years. In researching this book, we have built up a rather extensive library of books, and magazine and newspaper clippings, on our subject. Often the details of a race, even the distances covered and times recorded, the speeds of the winners and the reasons non-finishers dropped out, vary according to the account one is reading.

In all cases we have tried to check with living participants or have taken a consensus of reliable reports. The same situation applies to such routine things as birth and death dates, places of these occurrences, early races of well-known drivers and the like. Again, we have tried to verify our facts or at least arrive at an acceptable consensus.

We should explain our method of working so that credits and charges can clearly be awarded. Basically one author was responsible for American personalities, the other for international personalities. This did not hold true in all cases, however. Moreover, both authors not only checked on the other's work, but regularly rewrote, cut or expanded it.

v

In the truest sense, then, both are responsible for the whole book.

We also are responsible for which personalities you find in this book and which ones have been omitted. We tried to include all major race or series victors. All World Champions, of course. Most Indianapolis victors. Most USAC and NASCAR victors. Most drivers who ever scored a World Championship point whether or not they ever won a title. Most major stock car and single-seater racers here and abroad.

Most of the major Land Speed Record drivers, including all of the successful holders of that special crown. But there are few rallyists, fewer still drag racers. Only a handful of amateurs or semi-professionals have made this book, and these only because of their prominence in establishing motor sports or because of their inherent color.

There are more than a few individuals in these pages who are here only because they attracted the authors' attention by a glorious failure or a fun-filled career that enlivened motor sports. And there are representative stories of some of the people behind racing—designers, car builders, mechanics, promoters, publicists, scorers, broadcasters.

There is even one non-human racer in here, and we challenge you to find him.

No significance should be read into the length of a particular biography. Our goal was to produce a readable, accurate magazine-type article on our subject. The longer the career, the greater the accomplishment, the more likely an article was to be long, but that was not always so. We have tried to avoid fiction, and thus some personalities have shorter articles than we would have liked because there was a lack of verifiable facts about them.

One day, perhaps, this reference book will be reissued in a revised, and hopefully expanded, form. For that reason we would welcome any comments, corrections, additions or suggestions for new subjects to be included in that future edition.

In closing, we should record for posterity that not once in the eight years that have gone into this book was a blow struck, a fist clenched or a voice raised between the two protagonists who conceived and produced it. If we have achieved nothing else, that in itself is quite an achievement.

Robert Cutter
Bob Fendell

GLOSSARY

Some knowledgeability on the part of the reader has been assumed, but a basic list of abbreviations, acronyms, and specialized terms is included here to make sure that the random reader, or one from one side of the Atlantic or the other, may pick his way through these pages. We have not attempted to list all the manufacturers' acronyms.

AAA American Automobile Association, which while not involved with racing today, once was, through its Contest Board.

ACA Automobile Club of America.

ACCUS Automobile Competition Committee for the United States, the U.S. arm of the FIA-CSI organization, and as such, the overall governing body for all U.S. motor sports.

ACF Automobile Club de France, a combination AAA and ACCUS for that nation.

AHRA American Hot Rod Association.

ARCA Automobile Racing Club of America. Midwest stock car group.

ARCF Automobile Racing Club of Florida.

ARDC American Racing Drivers Club.

ARRC American Road Race of Champions, an SCCA championship event.

black flag A signal used to call in a driver, whether to eliminate him from a race, inspect his car, or even to delay him (as a penalty) for improper or annoying conduct.

blown car In British usage, a supercharged car. The supercharger is sometimes called a blower.

blown engine An engine that has become inoperative, usually in rather spectacular fashion.

BRDC British Racing Drivers Club.

cam Camshaft.

CanAm Canadian-American Challenge Cup, an SCCA professional series for sports/prototype cars; in the late sixties and early seventies, for FIA's Group 7 machines.

c.c. Cubic centimeter(s), 1,000 of which make one litre, or about 61 cubic inches. Used to describe an engine's displacement.

checker, or checkered flag The symbol of victory, a flag of black and white squares waved at the winner and at each car that finishes the race behind him.

Chevvy Chevrolet

CRA California Racing Association.

CSI Commission Sportive Internationale, the motor sports section of FIA.

cu. in. Cubic inch(es), about 61 of which equal one litre or 1,000 cubic centimeters.

dice A battle between two or more cars for position, not necessarily for the lead.

displacement The size of an engine, expressed in cubic centimeters, cubic inches, or litres.

DNF Did not finish, as it usually is written in race charts.

d.o.h.c. Double overhead camshaft.

drafting Using a car in front as an air buffer by closely following him and getting into his slipstream. A racer may draft as close as a few inches behind the man in front, which takes steady nerves and confidence in the leading driver. See also slingshotting.

F1, F2, etc. Formula 1, Formula 2, etc.

FIA Federation Internationale de l'Automobile, which, through CSI, governs motor sports worldwide from its Paris headquarters.

FL Formula Libre, or fastest lap, whatever its context.

Formula As in Formula 1, etc., a detailed set of specifications that categorizes racing cars and thus sets up an equalized class for the championship of which cars compete. Current formulae include: 1, 2, 3, Vee, SuperVee (both the Vee categories for Volkswagen-powered cars), Ford (sometimes known as 100), A (also known as 5000), B (also known as Atlantic), C, and Libre, meaning anything goes.

GP Grand Prix, strictly speaking, a *grande épreuve* race, with points leading toward the World Championship in Formula 1; but loosely, any single-seater race, and occasionally other forms of racing as well.

GPDA Grand Prix Drivers Association.

Group As in Group 2, 5, 7, etc., a detailed set of specifications that categorizes racing cars, as the Formula does for single-seaters, and thus sets up equalized classes for its championships. Often Group cars from several categories will race together, unlike Formula racing where such joint racing is fairly rare.

GT Grand Touring, category of sedans in racing. Latterly adopted by U.S. passenger car builders to sell products by slapping a "GT" on anything with four wheels.

IMCA International Motor Contest Association, an AAA Contest Board rival superseded in the main by USAC, NASCAR, etc., except at fair dates in the Midwest and Southern U.S.

IMSA International Motor Sports Association.

Indy Indianapolis, sometimes used derisively to demonstrate the writer's distaste for the type of racing, course, or individuals associated with this classic American race. Not used in that sense in this book, however.

litre(s) A measure of engine displacement equal to 1,000 cubic centimeters, or about 61 cubic inches. The British spelling is preferred here because it is usually used in international racing as opposed to strictly U.S. racing where cu. in. prevails.

monocoque A type of aircraft construction adopted by European carbuilders and now pretty much international; the chassis of the monocoque car forms its frame rather than putting these two pieces together as was the rule. This type of construction makes for weight-saving, profile-cutting, and rather tricky problems on occasion.

m.p.g. Miles per gallon.

m.p.h. Miles per hour.

NASCAR National Association for Stock Car Auto Racing, sometimes also known as Bill France.

NHRA National Hot Rod Association, sometimes also known as Wally Parks.

Offy Offenhauser, a type of Indianapolis racing car power plant derived from a World War I airplane engine built under U.S. license from a French design, making it a wonder of the ancient world still with us today.

o.h.c. Overhead camshaft

PDA Professional Drivers Association, NASCAR driver organization.

pole The lead position at the start of the race, that is, next to the fence on the inside, theoretically an advantage, although not necessarily so. Capturing the pole (by turning the fastest qualifying lap) usually means extra money.

RAC Royal Automobile Club, the United Kingdom's combined AAA-ACCUS.

r.p.m. Revolutions per minute.

SCCA Sports Car Club of America.

slingshot Used as verb as well as noun. To slingshot is to pull out of the slipstream of a car one is drafting and shoot past.

spoiler An air deflector or airfoil mounted on a car, front or back, to aid in road-holding.

sucker car A British term for a ground-effects machine such as the 1970 Chapparal 2J, referring to the sucking effect of the auxiliary engine that helps the car stick to the ground.

TransAm Trans-American Manufacturers Championship, an SCCA professional series for larger sedans, unlike stock-car racing because it is contested on road courses rather than ovals.

2.5 Challenge A professional SCCA series for smaller sedans, referring to engine displacement (not to exceed 2.5 litres).

U2L Under 2 Litre, a predecessor to the 2.5 Challenge as an SCCA professional series for small sedans, again referring to engine displacement.

yellow flag, or yellow light A caution signal in all racing; cars cannot change positions under the yellow, although in some forms of racing they may close up on each other, giving drivers who are trailing others by wide margins one or more mid-race advantages to make up lost ground.

Contents

Bobby Grim
Bob Grossman
Guinness Brothers (Algernon and Kenelm)
Dan Gurney
Janet Guthrie
Albert Guyot
Mike Hailwood
Ted Halibrand
Jim Hall
Duncan Hamilton
Pete Hamilton
Ralph Hankinson
Sam Hanks
Walter Hansgen
Huschke von Hanstein
Fred Harb
Harry Harkness
Ron Harris
Ray Harroun
Harry Hartz
Wally Hassan
Paul Hawkins
Mike Hawthorn
Charlie Hayes
Donald Healey
George Heath
Tony Hegbourne
Cotton Henning
Hans Herrmann
Harry Heuer
Graham Hill
Phil Hill
Tommy Hinnershitz
Chick Hirashima
Mike Hiss
David Hobbs
Bob Holbert
Holman-Moody (John Holman and Ralph Moody)
Paddy Hopkirk
Ted Horn
Ronnie Householder
Earl Howe
Tony Hulman, Jr.
Denis Hulme
Jim Hurtubise
Dick Hutcherson
James Hylton
Jacky Ickx
Innes Ireland
Chris Irwin
Bobby Isaac
Alec Issigonis
Peter Jackson
Dick Jacobs
Vittorio Jano
Ned Jarrett
Charles Jarrott
Charles Jeantaud
Camille Jenatzy
Ab Jenkins
Gordon Johncock
Bobby Johns
Bob Johnson
Eddie Johnson
Junior Johnson
Parnelli Jones
Elizabetta Junek
Kas Kastner
Hiroshi Kazato
Foxhall Keene
Mel Kenyon
Leo Kinnunen
Rene de Knyff
Dave Koetzla
Frank Kurtis
Eddie Kuzma
Jim Lamb
Ferruccio Lamborghini
Tony Lanfranchi
Hermann Lang
Gerard Larrousse
Jud Larson

Niki Lauda
Christian Lautenschlager
Dave Laycock
François Lecot
Joe Leonard
Pierre Levegh
Guy Ligier
Frank Lockhart
Larry Lopatin
Fred Lorenzen
John Love
Tiny Lund
Brett Lunger
Dave MacDonald
Doc MacKenzie
Tony Maggs
Umberto Maglioli
Willy Mairesse
Timo Makinen
Jean Marcenac
Marchese Brothers
Onofre Marimon
Helmut Marko
Bobby Marshman
Lionel Martin
Maserati Brothers (Carlo, Bindo, Alfieri, Ettore and Ernesto)
Jochen Mass
Steve Matchett
Frank Matich
Banjo Matthews
Teddy Mayer
Tim Mayer
Raymond Mays
Rex Mays
Denise McCluggage
Roger McCluskey
Jimmy McElreath
Jack McGrath
Bruce McLaren
Hollingsworth McMillion
Francis McNamara
Sam McQuagg
Graham McRae
John Mecom
Major Melton
Arturo Merzario
Louis Meyer
Roberto Mieres
John Miles
Ken Miles
Harry Miller
Tommy Milton
Donna Mae Mims
Gerhard Mitter
Guy Moll
Alfred Momo
Bob Montgomery
Bud Moore
Lou Moore
Silvio Moser
Mike Mosley
Stirling Moss
Lothar Motschenbacher
Ralph Mulford
Herbert Muller
Frank Mundy
Jimmy Murphy
Paula Murphy
Luigi Musso
Herb Nab
Felice Nazzaro
Jochen Neerpasch
Norm Nelson
Alfred Neubauer
Ulf Norinder
Sam Nunis
Tazio Nuvolari
Barney Oldfield
Jack Oliver
Ernie Olson
Paul O'Shea
Nathan Ostich
Cotton Owens

Augie Pabst
Carlos Pace
Marvin Panch
Jim Pardue
Mike Parkes
Wally Parks
Reg Parnell
Benny Parsons
Chuck Parsons
Johnnie Parsons
Jim Paschal
Jas Patterson
David Pearson
Roger Penske
Bill Perkins
Henri Pescarolo
Ronnie Peterson
Kelly Petillo
Lee Petty
Richard Petty
Maurice Phillippe
Roy Pike
David Piper
Art Pollard
Ferdinand Porsche
Alfonso de Portago
Sam Posey
Pat Purcell
Dieter Quester
Ian Raby
Reid Railton
Jim Rathmann
Brian Redman
Alan Rees
Clay Regazzoni
Dario Resta
Carlos Reutemann
Lance Reventlow
Peter Revson
Bill Rexford
Eddie Rickenbacker
Jochen Rindt
Fireball Roberts
Floyd Roberts
George Robertson
George Robson
Pedro Rodriguez
Ricardo Rodriguez
Georges Roesch
Alan Rollinson
Mauri Rose
Bernd Rosemeyer
Lloyd Ruby
Paul Russo
Johnny Rutherford
Troy Ruttman
Eddie Sachs
Bill Sadler
Bob Said
Roy Salvadori
Frankie Sands
Roscoe Sarles
Swede Savage
Everitt Saylor
Jack Scales
Ludovico Scarfiotti
Harry Schell
Tim Schenken
Bill Schindler
Joe Schlesser
Louie Schneider
Benny Scott
Richard Scott
Wendell Scott
Archie Scott-Brown
Dick Seaman
Jack Sears
Henry Segrave
Johnny Servoz-Gavin
Wilbur Shaw
Carroll Shelby
Jo Siffert
Dick Simon
Jigger Sirois

J. Alex Sloan
Clay Smith
Louis Smith
Bill Smyth
Moises Solana
Raymond Sommer
Gober Sosebee
Tony Southgate
Art Sparks
Mike Spence
Chuck Stevenson
Jackie Stewart
Rolf Stommelen
Whitney Straight
Lewis Strang
Bill Stroppe
Hans Stuck
Summers Brothers
John Surtees
Len Sutton
Bob Swanson
Al Sweeney
Bob Sweikert
Piero Taruffi
Ron Tauranac
Anita Taylor
Geoffrey Taylor
Trevor Taylor
Marshall Teague
Len Terry
Herb Thomas
Larry Thomas
Parry Thomas
René Thomas

Alfred Speedy Thompson
Dick Thompson
Mickey Thompson
Joel Thorne
Jerry Titus
Floyd Trevis
Maurice Trintignant
Ernie Triplett
Wolfgang von Trips
Picko Troberg
C. F. Trossi
Bob Tullius
Curtis Turner
Stuart Turner
Ken Tyrrell
Rudi Uhlenhaut
Alec Ulmann
Al Unser
Bobby Unser
Nino Vaccarella
Ira Vail
Tony Vandervell
Gijs van Lennep
C. W. van Ranst
Achille Varzi
Frank Verbeck
Leo Villa
Luigi Villoresi
Red Vogt
Bill Vukovich
Billy Vukovich
Billy Wade
Louis Wagner
Dave Walker

Mike Walker
Rob Walker
Lee Wallard
Phil Walters
Rodger Ward
Bentley Warren
A. J. Watson
Joe Weatherly
John Webb
Edoardo Weber
Bill Weightman
Bob Welborn
Lou Welch
Christian Werner
Harry Weslake
Peter Westbury
Derrick White
Rex White
Sir John Whitmore
Robin Widdows
"Williams"
Frank Williams
Jonathan Williams
Jean-Pierre Wimille
Reine Wisell
Spencer Wishart
Wood Brothers
John Wyer
Cale Yarborough
Lee Roy Yarbrough
Count Louis Zborowski
Denny Zimmerman
John Zink
Paul Zuccarelli

RAUNO AALTONEN

In Europe, where rallyists are full time professionals and not weekend amateurs, Rauno Aaltonen was acknowledged to be one of the best in the exacting business of arriving where you are supposed to be at a certain time and more or less in one piece. The high spot to date of the career of the "Flying Finn" came in 1965, when he scored 6 outright victories in the 13 world class rallies that make up the European Rally Championship series. More than 30 factory teams compete, as well as countless independents who don't have too much chance against the factories, but who try anyway, in the more than 100 events held in Europe and Africa. The 6 outrights for Rauno's Mini-Cooper S stand as an all-time record, and included victories at Geneva, Czechoslovakia, Poland, Munich-Vienna-Budapest, Britain's RAC, and the Monte Carlo Rally.

The slightly built Aaltonen was born in 1938 near Turku, Finland, where his family still has a flourishing garage and auto sales business, offering BMC, Mercedes, and Saab cars. At the age of 7 he was given a motor boat, and first showed his competitive instincts by winning the Speedboat Championships of Finland and Scandinavia early in his teens. Aaltonen was only 16 when he took up automobile rallying in 1954, about the same time he began motorcycle racing. He was good enough in the latter sport to become a regular member of the Finnish Speedway Championship Team and to win the 1957 championship in the 125-c.c. class of the Swedish Motorcycle Grand Prix.

In the 4-wheeled world, Rauno drove in ice races, Formula Junior races, the European equivalents of American stock car races, and, of course, international rallies, in which he has gained his greatest fame outside of Europe. The Finn was considered a driving stylist, and he also knew quite a bit about the mechanical side of an automobile. At one time, in fact, he was thought to know too much about the automobile, in that he liked to fiddle with his mount, even during the course of a rally. He overcame that tendency and became a better driver for it. Like all Scandinavians, Rauno learned to deal with ice and snow early and is used to loose, unpaved roads, which made him the ideal rallyist for international events in which paved roads and good driving conditions are the exception rather than the rule.

Aaltonen won the Finnish rally championship in 1961, using both Saabs and a Mercedes. The next season he switched to a Mini on occasion, almost was killed in the Monte Carlo. Rauno became a BMC team driver in 1963, and his first great rally success came the next year in a Healey when Aaltonen won the Liège-Sofia-Liège Rally outright. After winning his 2nd Finnish championship in 1964, he concentrated on major European rallies in 1965, winning the Geneva, Polish, Czech, and RAC contests among others. It meant Aaltonen's initial European title.

In 1966 Rauno won the Tulip Rally and repeated in the Czech contest. He also entered major enduros in an Austin Healey Sprite, scoring class victories (with Clive Baker) at Sebring, Le Mans, and in the Targa Florio. The next year the Monte Carlo fell to Aaltonen's BMC car, and when the Britons stopped competing, he went to Lancia, then to BMW and Datsun. In 1970 Aaltonen signed with Ford.

CARLO ABARTH

There are many people who come close to hating Carlo Abarth, one of Italy's great car builders, and many more who merely were annoyed by the big man. But there are few who would deny he was an automotive engineering genius. Born November 15, 1908, in Vienna, Austria, Abarth took as his personal symbol the 8th sign of the Zodiac, Scorpio, under which he was born. It appears on everything he owns or produces, from his shirts to the gates of his Turin factories and from his black-crackle exhaust systems to the latest Abarth car.

In his early days, Abarth was a motorcycle champion, winning the Austrian title in that favored European sport 5 times with a Belgian FN-1600. At 20 he built his first car and designed his first muffler for his motorcycle. As he grew older, the Austrian's interests shifted more and more to cars, but World War II interrupted Abarth's transformation into an auto designer. Abarth had fled Austria before Hitler's takeover in 1938, but finally was overtaken in Yugoslavia by the widening German occupation of the Continent. He spent the war years as a machinist in Yugoslavia, but visited Italy frequently and grew to love that country. He also saw a future for his automotive ambitions there.

Late in the war, the Austrian became interested in the plight of Dr. Ferdinand Porsche, creator of the Volkswagen and the Porsche, who had been imprisoned by the French on war crimes charges. He spent much time and effort in the campaign to free Porsche, his family, and his co-workers. Abarth and another Austrian, Rudolf Hruschka, were subsequently given the first post-war Porsche franchise in Italy. Soon the two were acting as agents for Porsche as well with the Cisitalia company, which had been formed in Turin to turn out small racing cars. The two Austrians were eventually hired by Cisitalia to assist in the production of a full-sized Grand Prix car based on young Ferry Porsche's designs. Six cars were originally scheduled for production, but only one was completed. It competed just once, in Argentina, as an Autoar—it was slated to be the Argentine vehicle for a Peronist GP team—and now it reposes in the Porsche Museum in Stuttgart.

Abarth was racing director of Cisitalia, supervising such drivers as Nuvolari, Taruffi, Farina and a young man named Carlo Scagliarini. When the company was dissolved for lack of financing in 1948, Scagliarini approached Abarth and suggested that he take over the smaller Cisitalia cars as a private stable, with the backing of Scagliarini's father. All the drivers but Nuvolari agreed; they would race the 2 sports cars and a Formula 2 machine. Abarth & Co. was formed in 1949 to build these cars, to do a few engine conversions for special customers, and to produce mufflers—about 1,200 that first year. This was the beginning of Carlo Abarth's empire.

Carlo Abarth is a bundle of paradoxes, according to those who know him. To many, he was an egotist; yet a man who went out of his way not to talk about himself or to allow too many details of his life to be revealed. To others, Abarth was a scheming, thorough Teuton; yet a man apparently faithful to his friends, and happiest when surrounded by the frenzied confusion characteristic of the Italian temperament. Abarth cars carried his name all over the world, yet the man was rarely seen in public and almost never outside Italy. He rarely answered his mail, and when he did, it was in a flurry of dictated replies—not really answers—to an accumulation of several months. He once refused to ship some parts to Team Roosevelt because he didn't like the tone of the order; their association was thus broken. Another time he refused to acknowledge that one of his factories had mistakenly installed some exhaust system mounting brackets on the wrong side, and came close to severing relations with the Jaguar importer who had gently complained of the mistake. Still another time an American Abarth owner who inquired about the probable cause of a broken piston ring in his engine was told that Abarth & Co. couldn't be of any help because its piston rings didn't break.

Big businessmen are appalled by such things; yet if any of the world's limited-production builders are to survive the onslaughts of the giant corporations, Abarth would be one, it was believed, if only because of his close association with Fiat and his unique approach to business. Since he was still a relatively young man, Abarth himself was expected to be around for many a year, turning out some of the fastest cars ever built. But, in 1971, Carlo sold out his tuning business to Fiat, and his eminently successful sports cars to a favorite Abarth dealer. The scorpion was losing some of its sting.

GEORGE ABECASSIS

With Britain so competitive in international motor racing in recent years, it probably is hard for younger enthusiasts to realize that this was not always the case. In fact, there were long years of drought for British Racing Green, including the years just before and just after World War II. Not that there weren't good British drivers—men like George Abecassis.

Born in 1913, Abecassis started racing in 1935 at Donington and Brooklands with a rather staid Austin 7. But 2 years later he acquired a more competitive car, a 1.5-litre Alta, rebuilt after its previous owner, P. F. Jucker, was killed in practice on the Isle of Man. Abecassis was successful with this car in the remaining 3 seasons before the war. In 1938 George won the Crystal Palace Imperial Trophy and the Cup with 52.1 m.p.h. and 56.69 m.p.h. respectively, was 2nd to Arthur Dobson in the Palace Plate race and to A. F. P. Fane in the Imperial Plate. That same season Abecassis also won the Prescott hillclimb just to demonstrate his versatility.

After RAF service in World War II, George came back racing with an ERA. In Britain's initial airport race, the Gransden Lodge meeting, Abecassis came in second in a 3.3-litre Bugatti. In the ERA his best finish was a 3rd in the Uster Trophy at Ballyclare, Ireland. That same year he journeyed to Italy and ran in the all-Cisitalia Circuit of the Baths of Caracalla race, finishing 2nd to Piero Taruffi. In May, 1958, Abecassis took possession of the first Grand Prix Alta ever built, but the car lasted only 3 laps in its debut at the British Empire Trophy at Douglas on the Isle of Man. Perhaps George already was disenchanted with the car, for he drove a Maserati in the Formula 1 Jersey International road race at St. Helier. Bob Gerard won it for ERA, with Abecassis 2nd.

George's mind undoubtedly was on his garage business at Walton-on-Thames, and the Hersham and Walter Motors company that he had founded with John Heath. Shortened to HWM, it became a car marque, first as a twin-seater in 1950, then as a single-seater in 1951 when HWM went into Formula 2.

It took a couple of years to get HWM's bugs out, and in that time Abecassis's best racing effort came not in Britain but Le Mans in 1950, when he shared a class victory with Lance Macklin. The initial big HWM victory with George driving came in 1951 at Castle Combe, when he won a 2-litre race at 77.69 m.p.h. A couple of Goodwood 3rds, including one that a young fellow named Stirling Moss won in another HWM, and a 3rd at Winfield, Scotland, to Reg Parnell and Moss were other highlights of Abecassis's season. In 1952 Moss, Parnell, and Abecassis were 1st, 2nd, and 3rd in the Silverstone sports car race, and George was 3rd again in the Jersey International road race—this one also redesignated a sports car start.

The year 1953 saw a victory at Goodwood at 84.37 m.p.h. in the HWM and 2nd at the first international running (and 2nd start) of the Sebring 12-hour race. In the latter Abecassis shared a 2.9-litre Aston Martin with Parnell, and they won the 3-litre class, the John Fitch/Phil Walters Cunningham overall winner being a kick up in classification. A Jaguar power plant for the HWM produced some interesting times for George, including a 2nd to Jose Gonzalez in a Ferrari at the major Goodwood sports car race in 1954 and an 82.10-m.p.h. victory at Castle Combe's only Redex Trophy race in 1955.

2

For variety, Abecassis took a showroom Austin Healey 100S to the Mille Miglia that same season and finished 11th overall with no special preparation.

A variety of things caused Abecassis to retire midway through the 1956 season, after an imposing 2nd to Ron Flockhart in the Snetterton sports car race. There was his age for one thing, the responsibilities of HW Motors for another (because John Heath was killed in the Mille Miglia), and finally, George's marriage to the daughter of Aston Martin's David Brown.

TONY ADAMOWICZ

Tony Adamowicz and Sam Posey are both about the same age and both from Connecticut. Sam is voluble, Tony quiet. Posey has more or less unlimited funds to back his racing; Adamowicz has to scrape up his. Both ranged through single-seaters in lower racing classifications to TransAm cars to enduros with Ferrari at places like Le Mans and Daytona. They occasionally clashed, occasionally shared rides.

In the only real head-to-head competition between the two, Tony won the SCCA's Formula A Continental Championship in 1969, driving an Eagle-Chevy and holding off a challenge by Posey, who finished 3rd in the series. And Tony qualified at Indianapolis in 1970—the only man in history to do so under a yellow light up to that time—something that eluded Posey right through 1971 despite Sam's intense desire for a spot on the grid.

The fact that Adamowicz later was bumped by a faster car didn't diminish his feat.

Born in Torrance, Calif., May 2, 1941, Adamowicz started as an SCCA amateur in sports cars for silverware. After an Army hitch and a stint as a White House communications technician, Tony went back to the SCCA, then turned professional—or at least semipro—in 1968 when he drove in the Under-2-Litre section of the Trans-American Championship, pushing a Porsche to 1st place in the standings. Things weren't quite as cutthroat in those days as they were later, after Tony had moved on to the Continental series. This again was a less competitive race series in 1969 than it became in 1971 when L&M cigarette money transformed the Formula A card into a dog-eat-dog series called the L&M Continental Formula 5000 Championship, attracting international talent like David Hobbs and Frank Matich, as well as most second-line American single-seater talents. Only the Posey-Adamowicz battle in 1969 kept the series interesting. Both moved on in 1970, Sam to the senior portion of the TransAm and NART Ferrari drives, Tony to Indy and also to NART drives (including a 10th at Le Mans).

In 1971 Sam was trying to create his own breaks, running in the revitalized Continental, but Tony was still waiting for his career to move into high gear. The year started well. Adamowicz almost won the 24-hour endurance race at Daytona sharing a car with codriver Ronnie Bucknum. But their NART Ferrari 512S, which took over the lead when the John Wyer Porsche 917 of Pedro Rodriguez and Jackie Oliver pitted with mechanical troubles, couldn't hold off Rodriguez when the Mexican ace retook the road. Aided by rain, his special thing, Pedro regained the lead. Tony and Ronnie were able to hold on to 2nd place, thus posting one of the most important victories of Tony's career.

Adamowicz and Posey shared a NART Ferrari 512M at Le Mans and finished a strong third, and then Oscar Koveleski offered his old McLaren to Tony for the rich Canadian-American Challenge Cup series. Against the likes of Team McLaren and Jackie Stewart's L&M Lola, Tony's chances were slim indeed, especially with the old car; but he did surprisingly well, with a 4th at Road Atlanta, 5th at Watkins Glen and 3rd at Mid-Ohio. Maybe that was high gear, at last for the vice-president of the Polish Racing Drivers Association. Tony co-drove with Sam Posey in 1971 and 1972 at Le Mans and both times finished as highest placed American—6th overall in '72.

FRED AGABASHIAN

Golden voiced Fred Agabashian, heard on motor sports shows as a supersalesman for Champion Spark Plugs, is a handsome man with curly graying hair who used to be called the motor medic. Known as "Doc" among the racing brethren for his uncanny knack of diagnosing a race car's troubles on the basis of a few quick laps, Fred concentrated on the little cars with enough success to marry and live reasonably well. He was a man so good at midget racing during its heyday that he never even bothered with the Indianapolis 500 until he was 34. Born August 21, 1913, at Modesto in the heart of the California wine country, Agabashian began racing at the age of 21. Those were the hard times of the Depression, when purses were peanuts and racing was fiercely competitive. It was an era of nascent champions in California—Agabashian, Bill Vukovich, Johnny Parsons.

In 1947 Agabashian made his debut at Indianapolis in the Ross Page car, starting 23rd and finishing 9th. In 1948 he started next to last in the Ross Page car, but had supercharger trouble and finished 23rd. In 1949 he finished 27th when the engine overheated; but in 1950 he put his Wynn's Special in the front row, only to succumb to mysterious engine woes. Later he drove relief for Henry Banks. His teammate, Parsons, won that year.

When the Cummins Diesel Company came to the Speedway for the second time in 1952 with a $500,000 budget for what they called a racing laboratory, they chose Freddie as their driver because of the technical advice he could give on their wide, low car's performance. He gave them something else as well. He put the huge red and yellow diesel on the pole, with a short-lived track record of 138.010 m.p.h. Poor weight distribution, however, had worn one tire to ribbons during his 4-lap qualifying run.

In the actual race, Agabashian was in 8th place after the first 2 laps, then pushed forward to 5th, where he rode for 100 miles. On the 44th lap, Fred pitted for 2 new right side tires. Back in the race after a minute and 22 seconds, Agabashian was far back in the field, but gained ground steadily at his predetermined pace. But on the 70th lap, when the Cummins Special was again 5th, a smudge of black smoke belched from the exhaust pipe, and on the next lap, a heavy black cloud followed the car. On the 72nd lap Agabashian pulled to a stop. Dirt and rubber chunks from the tires of other cars had clogged the Special's turbo-supercharger intake. The car was placed 27th at the race's end.

The big 402-cu. in. Diesel engine seemed capable of much faster speeds, but the following year the AAA reduced allowable volume on diesels and Cummins didn't return. Instead, Fred codrove with Paul Russo to 4th place in Andy Granatelli's Grancor Elgin car. His best solo finish was 6th, in 1954, in the Merz Engineering car. Fred never followed the Championship Trail with regularity. The veteran won only one Trail race, at Sacramento in 1949, and drove only a couple of races a year on the Trail. In 11 Indianapolis races he completed 1,216 laps. Then he retired to travel for Champion.

J. C. AGAJANIAN

He wore a cowboy hat, high-heeled boots made specially for him in Spain, and clothes cut strictly to his own design. From 1948 through 1964 his cars won the pole position at Indianapolis 3 times, set 4 track records, and won the race twice. J. C. Agajanian never touched the wheel of a race car in competition, but his efforts at discovering drivers, building cars, and promoting races made him one of the most important men in this generation of American racing people.

As Aggie said when he first began to haunt the pits around Southern California, "We are in the used food business." Freely translated, this meant that Joshua James Agajanian (the "C" is adopted) is the scion of a fortune built on garbage collection and pig farming. Agajanian's father had fled his native Armenia under the threat of being drafted into the Czar's army. Having learned English by comparing English and Armenian Bibles, he came to Los Angeles, where he terminated his employment as a dishwasher on the day he learned that the hotel restaurant paid to have garbage hauled away to slop hogs. On such seemingly wasteful bits of knowledge are fortunes founded.

J. C. never became a race driver. As the legend goes —and he doesn't deny it—he became carried away one night with the beauty of one of the cars; he bought it. Second thoughts prompted him to hide it in the family garage. "What is that?" asked his father several days later. "Some kind of special dump truck? And where is the rest of it?" Told it was a race car, he declared, "Either it goes or you do!" (freely translated from the much more colorful Armenian). Aggie, however, achieved a compromise by promising never to drive it, but to hire a driver at no cost to the family.

Aggie subsequently became a promoter of major races, a member of the USAC executive board, and the owner of a succession of successful cars. He was partial to the number 98 on his Indianapolis and sprint cars; it was the number on his first money-making Indy vehicle. He was always one of the thinking men in the sport, and bankrolled the development of the air jack for faster tire changes at Indy. It was a J. C. Agajanian car with Johnny Mantz at the helm that last went nonstop (1949), finishing 7th. J. C. took Troy Ruttman out of the California midget ranks and won Indy in 1952 with the large Boy Wonder. Johnny Parsons was among many others who drove for him, but his most successful driver liason was with Parnelli Jones, whom he allegedly spotted in a Los Angeles jalopy race.

Agajanian used to act as finish flag waver at the annual Mobil Economy Run; his flag waving technique is impeccable. And he had the pleasure of seeing Papa Agajanian in the pits at Indy. There were definitely no dump trucks or pigs in the Agajanian corner those days. But that is telling only half the tales possible about "Jacie." That's what an aunt used to call him, and Aggie chose the to use the initials after a teacher assumed "Jacie" was a girl's name. He didn't publicize the fact, but in high school J. C. won honors as a tennis player and ran the 440 in 53.8 seconds. He had 2 younger brothers, Eli and Ben, the latter who had lost 4 toes, a professional football kicking star for more than a decade.

Lester Spangler, a West Coast driver of some repute, was the one who made Aggie act on his early mania for motor sports, kidding him about becoming a driver. In 1932, with his father away on a business trip, J. C. withdrew $1,500 from his savings account and bought an old 2-port Cragar racer. He was 19 at the time. The showdown with his father followed. Aggie's next crisis came 5 years later. Deaths and the Depression had spelled the demise of AAA racing on the West Coast; Legion Ascot Speedway in Los Angeles folded. A new track, Southern Ascot, also floundered, and the local drivers were racing roadsters in an effort to draw fans. In 1937 Agajanian stepped in to help organize the Western Racing Association.

WRA had an $1,100 deficit the first year, but the members elected J. C. treasurer, gave him a free hand in the sanction area, and Aggie blossomed into a promoter overnight. He promoted or co-promoted successful big car races at Ascot, Oakland, and Phoenix—without AAA aid. That his own cars often won helped matters along; he poured all his own profits into building better ones. He was WRA's president as well as treasurer in

1939. AAA came to him in 1947 to induce him to join its fold. He delayed a year, then brought the first number 98 Indy car East, with Mantz driving and Clay Smith—promoted when Al Henley quit—as chief mechanic. It was good experience for 1949 and the nonstop run.

On November 15, 1948, Aggie chose Carroll Speedway in Gardena, Calif., as the site for his "Welcome Home, AAA" program. In celebration he carved up a 400-pound hog for the men in the pits. After that he promoted as many as 6 tracks in the west, always taking time to follow his cars east to Indianapolis and even Trenton, N. J. In 1964 he bankrolled the presentation of the closed-circuit telecast of the Indy 500 at the 20,000-seat Los Angeles Arena. He did not make much money on the race with his car, but he packed them in at the pioneering telecast.

The Agajanian brood included daughter Joan, married to sports star Chuck Essigian, and sons Cary, J. C. Jr. and Chris. None exhibited any interest in becoming a race driver, or promoter for that matter, but J. C. Sr. would not have been surprised if he found a strange "dump truck" in the garage one day.

Besides Jones and Ruttman, Agajanian's drivers have included Walt Faulkner, Duane Carter, Gene Hartley, Chuck Stevenson, Johnny Parsons, Johnny Mantz, and Lloyd Ruby. Car owning was his strong point, although financially he probably just broke even. Promoting and real estate investments were much kinder.

Agajanian, more than any other single man, kept the Pikes Peak Hillclimb from becoming history. He also kept alive the dirt track at Sacramento, Calif., and the circuit at Gardena, which some say the Agajanians own.

The old ways have kept falling away. Dirt tracks, front-engined cars, and even the Mobil run have become history. Agajanian had to face a new generation of promoters and racing officials who were mainly businessmen, accountants, real estate tycoons, and public relations people. But one thing about racing doesn't ever change. Someone has to own the winning car and someone has to prepare it and someone has to drive it. He kept hoping that someday it would be number 98.

GIACOMO AGOSTINI

For a man who, through 1971, officially had never driven a racing car, Giacomo Agostini, a 10-time World Champion in the world of motorcycle racing, was as well known to automobile racing buffs as to fans of the 2-wheeled world. That was because every year, several times each year in the late Sixties and early Seventies, "Ago" was reported to be switching to auto racing.

But his motorcycle sponsors, the sponsors who made the life of a matinee idol possible for Agostini, had each time been successful in talking the young Italian out of making the switch. Successful, that is, until he wrapped up that 10th cycle title in 1971, making him the all-time top title-holder in the motorcycle world—better even than Mike Hailwood or Italy's own Ubbiali, each of whom managed 9 titles. Most of Ago's titles were won on MV Agustas, which were the hobby of Count Domenico Agusta, the autocratic Italian helicopter tycoon. Agusta paid Agostini as much as Grand Prix racing drivers could make, but expected unquestioning concentration on his bikes as a result.

Agostini, a finely featured, compact man who looked more like a film star than one of the world's more fearless, better coordinated athletes, was a man who saved his money, despite the apparently playboy life he led in his motorcycle racing years. At age 28 he could afford to flirt very seriously with the idea of quitting the bikes to go auto racing, or of combining the two. Meanwhile, the money would go, Jacky Ickx fashion, into apartment houses that would guarantee their owner an income long after he'd seen his last victory checker.

Agostini started with motorcycles at 15; even in Italy he couldn't go out on the roads in a car until 18. He had been riding scarcely a week when he determined that he must race it. By 1965, at age 22, he had a long string of successes, and three world titles, on a 250-c.c. Morini. An offer came from Count Agusta, and Ago accepted with alacrity, even though it was only to be number 2 to Hailwood. But by a stroke of good fortune, Hailwood left Agusta for Honda that same season, and Ago started winning the first of 5 World Championships in a row. And as fast and spectacular as Hailwood was on a bike, Ago was even more hair-raising and fan-pleasing.

He thrived on hero worship, and on skiing, performing gymnastics and squiring a succession of beauties. But he was also a full-blown professional, and drinking or late hours before a meet were out. Practice was in, even if Agostini knew the course like the back of his hand. Discipline and physical conditioning were needed to do "wheelies"—riding on the rear wheel only—at 140 m.p.h., which Ago was capable of at any given moment. Small wonder that Italian and other European promoters were prepared to shovel out appearance money, starting money, and usually top prize money to Agostini to get him to their meets. In the world of European cycle racing, where there are 2 or 3 times as many non-title as championship races, Giacomo's Agusta contract covered only the title starts; he was free to race or not to race in the non-title matches, hence the need for an extra financial inducement.

Agostini loved racing, however, and it was the rare promoter who was not able to lure him to a race. It was also not unusual to find Ago making side trips to auto racing tracks to test this car or that. Ferrari, Maserati, and Alfa Romeo all had their shots at him, and so did other racing teams, notably in Britain. More and more often Ago was found at Goodwood or Silverstone, testing a Lotus or a McLaren. But he never

signed; never, that is, until late in 1971 when Frank Williams, the independent Formula 1 racing manager, onetime manager of Piers Courage, and sponsor of Henri Pescarolo's 1971 March ride, announced that if Ago did go 4-wheeling, it would be aboard a Williams-inspired new F1 car, possibly to be co-sponsored by Politoys, an Italian toy company that already was co-sponsoring Ago's cycle rides.

The dazzling courage, the lightning reflexes, the color and glamor that were Giacomo Agostini might finally be ready to make the auto racing scene.

AHRENS FAMILY (KURT and KURT JR.)

Kurt Ahrens was one of the top German speedway motorcyclists in the years following 1947, winning the 250-c.c. championship in 1950. The following year the senior Ahrens took to the 4-wheeled variety of competition, driving a Formula 3 500-c.c. Cooper, Porsche Spyder, Mercedes 300SL, Alfa Romeo Veloce, and Lotus-Ford 22 before retiring in 1963 to run a chain of garages, service stations, and scrap-metal firms. On April 19, 1940 Kurt Ahrens, Jr., was born in Braunschweig, Brunswick, and 18 years later he was ready to do battle with his talented father. In his first race in Kiel, he came in 2nd in a Cooper behind the older man. Two weeks later, however, the roles were reversed in an international event in Leipzig. Kurt Jr. continued to drive the Cooper in 1959, earning a dozen wins in the 2 years, some of these in Formula Libre races.

He then purchased a Formula Junior Cooper for 1960, but spent most of the year sorting out his car. That winter he won the Australian FJ title, and the following year he won the German FJ championship from Gerhard Mitter. A highlight of the season was the FJ race at Brno, Czechoslovakia, in which he beat Mitter's Lotus-DKW across the line by 2.1 seconds, followed by Curt Lincoln and Kurt Sr. In 1962, the youngster fared far less successfully, the only bright spots being a couple of 2nd place finishes at the Vienna Grand Prix and in the Eifelrennen. At season's end he was slapped with a 6-month suspension for protesting the result of a race at the Nurburgring, considered an infraction of the rigid German racing rules.

When Kurt Jr. returned to racing in mid-1963, he scored 3 victories in a row in the Budapest, Vienna, and Cidonio Grands Prix. Later in the season, Ahrens won at the Eifelrennen and took the Tyrol GP. All told, Kurt had 14 FJ victories and enough F3 victories to win the German championship in that racing division.

Ahrens tried an experiment in 1964, dropping an F2 Cosworth engine into his faithful Cooper, but the combination failed in mid-race at Rheims, Crystal Palace, Zolder, and Avus. He also drove for the Abarth team, but the year was mostly a lost cause. The next season was as bright as the previous one had been dismal, however. Kurt won the German racing championship and was second in the 1000-c.c. class of the European Touring Car Championship. In 1967 he moved on to F2 proper in a Brabham, concentrated on sports cars after 1969 with the Porsche Salzburg 917 and 908/3 team. A high spot in this part of his career was a victory he shared in the 917 with Jo Siffert at the Austrian 1000 in 1969, Ahrens and Hans Herrmann shared a 908 at Monza that same season for a 2nd, and he and Vic Elford took 3rd in the 908 at the Spa and Nurburgring 1000s. In 1970 Ahrens and Elford won the Nurburgring race, and he shared a 3rd in the Spa 1000, but in 1971 Ahrens retired to work with his father in the scrap metal business.

JOHNNY AITKEN

Johnny Aitken, one of the early heroes of American racing, came from a substantial Indianapolis family. He did much of his competition in a National, one of many new American marques built in Indianapolis and struggling to establish a reputation. But his finest hours came as a pit manager at Indy, this though he ranked 4th in the 1910 AAA championship standings and was first across the line in that year's renewal of the Vanderbilt Cup.

Aitken's racing career was dogged by accidents. In the first Indianapolis program in 1909, he was making a tire test at 65 m.p.h. when a rock smashed his goggles. Luckily, the glass slivers missed his eyes. Bandaged, he won the 3rd event on the inaugural program in his National, then led the featured Wheeler-Shebler Trophy 300 for 105 miles until sidelined with a cracked head gasket. He is said to have wiped his brow and declared, "I'm glad to be out of that race. The track is so rough you couldn't plant corn in it." In December he was back, driving with a stocking cap over his face and his goggles over the stocking cap, but failed again to finish.

On September 5, 1910, he won an Indianapolis 80-lap race for stock-chassis cars with up to 600-cu. in. engines, having survived crashes at the inaugural of the new Atlanta Speedway and elsewhere. The 1910 Vanderbilt Cup on Long Island might have been an outright Aitken victory but for a spectator who winged his riding mechanic with an empty wine bottle. Johnny slowed to look after his partner and lost the race on handicap; the difference in time between 1st and 3rd was a mere 90 seconds.

After the first Indy 500, in which his car was retired with mechanical trouble, Aitken quit driving to become director of racing for National. Now began the more illustrious part of his career in terms of victories earned. He literally engineered himself out of a job when he directed Joe Dawson's triumph in a National over Ralph DePalma in 1912 at the 500. The firm finally had the competition victory it wanted and promptly quit racing to publicize its durability and speed.

But Aitken was back at Indy the next year as coach and pit manager for the Peugeot team. First he taught Jules Goux et Cie. the quick way around Indianapolis, then directed preparation of the cars, and finally worked out the strategy of the 1913 Goux victory. It was, however, a bit of a struggle. A gay little fellow, Goux was exuberant no matter where he was—even behind the wheel of a race car. He liked to charge for the sake of the competition, and that was not always compatible with winning what was then an endurance race. Aitken finally got him to obey orders by promising wine at every pit stop which he obtained from the Alliance Francaise people sitting in a box nearby. It was a 4-bottle victory, and the irrepressible Jules downed another magnum in celebration.

Johnny came out of retirement in 1916 to take the pole of the only scheduled Indy 300 (except for those early races) for the Speedway's own racing team, after helping repair the management's Peugeots and Premiers to fill out a field cut by the war. He led the race for 7 laps before dropping out. On Labor Day that same year, he won all 3 features on a new board track in Cincinnati, Ohio. It was his last notable achievement, for he died in the great Spanish influenza epidemic of 1918.

PIETRO ALBERTI

Pietro Alberti never drove a Ferrari in his life. In fact, he probably would have thought Nuvolari was a new kind of pasta. Pete was an American who inherited the Kinsey Special, formerly piloted by IMCA dirt champ Gus Schrader, and campaigned in the Midwest and East for about 15 years with little success. But this East St. Louis, Ill., driver was always a crowd pleaser, stomping on the accelerator with almost maniacal single-mindedness.

He stands out from the pack for one reason. Alberti was the favored chauffeur of the St. Louis Cardinals when the Gas House Gang was terrorizing baseball. He piloted a car owned by Pepper Martin, who at one time could have run for mayor of St. Louis on a vegetarian platform and won. Martin, whose *raison d'être* was baseball, found that watching Pete drive was substitute gratification for a desire to drive himself. The Dean brothers, Dizzy and Paul, and the rest of the pack occasionally could be seen clowning in Alberti's pits.

Pete was nearly at the end of his career when he started driving for Martin, and after he went through the fence at a small dirt track in rural Missouri the next year, he virtually quit. By then Martin had cooled a bit on racing, too. But if you pick up an American paper of the day, the chances are good that you would see a picture of the Gas House Gang clowning around a car. This kind of liaison did racing a great deal of good in the U.S. sports world.

SYDNEY ALLARD

For more than 40 years Sydney Herbert Allard was among the leaders in British automotive circles, despite the fact that he headed a rather small car-building company, had strange ideas about the relative importance of the automobile, and was intimately associated with Americans in days when the former Colonials were still viewed with suspicion.

Allard was born in June, 1910, in Wandsworth, London, and was educated at St. Saviour's College. On leaving school, he was handed the directorship of Adlards Motors Ltd. of Putney, a family-owned garage and sales operation. At this time, the young man was a motorcycle enthusiast, as were his 2 brothers and sister, despite a permanently damaged left eye. In 1927 he bought his first car, which qualified as a motorcycle because it was a 3-wheeled Morgan Super Sports, and won his first competitive try at Dartmoor that year. Later, this machine was converted to 4 wheels, and raced at Brooklands and other courses.

After unsuccessful experiments with a Talbot Special and other cars, he purchased a 1934 ex-Tourist Trophy Ford with which he grabbed fastest time of day honors for unsupercharged sports cars at the 1935 Brighton Speed Trials. Sydney used this car as the basis for his initial Allard Special, a Bugatti-tailed 2-seater, introduced in 1936, that was so successful he was asked to built replicas for fellow enthusiasts. World War II interrupted this operation, and during the conflict Allard equipped, staffed, and managed a 250-man Army Auxiliary Workshop at Fulham. In 1946 he founded the Allard Motor Company Ltd. and established himself as chairman, a position he already held with Adlards, Hilton Brothers, Ltd. and Encom Motors, Ltd.

The initial production Allard sports car appeared at the Bristol Club Speed Trials. In Britain's "Export or Die" drive in postwar Europe, Allards were important bidders for American and Canadian dollars. Sydney always had been an admirer of American ways, and he soon developed strong ties with America, although he visited its shores infrequently. In 1950 Allard and America's Tom Cole shared a 3rd-place finish at Le Mans in a 4374-c.c. Cadillac-engined J2 Allard. Working with Zora Arkus-Duntov, later of Corvette fame, Sydney developed a special chassis in which a wide variety of other big American powerlants could be dropped, including Ford, Mercury and Chrysler engines.

Allard had many other personal competition triumphs, despite his advancing years. In 1949 he won the British Hillclimb Championship, and in 1952 he was outright victor in the Monte Carlo Rally, starting from Glasgow and reaching Monaco without a single penalty point. This performance earned him the Rainier Cup and the RAC's Sir Malcolm Campbell Trophy. It was the first British victory in the prestigious rally in 21 years. In all, he competed in 14 Monte Carlos. His last run was in 1964, when his Ford Cortina crashed at a railroad crossing near Prague and was brushed by an express train before he could get out. He was unhurt.

In 1963 while on a visit to the United States, Allard, who had built some sprint cars in years past, became interested in the American sport of drag racing. He came back to England not only a convert but a leading apostle of quarter-mile competition. He helped organize Britain's first Drag Racing Festival in 1964, sponsoring the appearance of 10 top U.S. drivers and their unusual mounts. At that meet he unveiled his own car, the Allard DragStar Dragon, driven by his son Alan. This 1.5-litre, Ford Classic-engined dragster, the original British-designed car of this kind, achieved about 150 m.p.h., far below the American entries, but a good start for European dragging. Allard himself founded and became the first president of the British Drag Racing Association. He also designed and built a more powerful dragster powered by a 5700-c.c. Dodge engine.

Many British commentators were slow to take to the dragging sport, considering Allard's espousal of it something akin to his chairmanship of the Railway Conversion League. This latter organization called for the closing down of Britain's railways and conversion of their roadbeds to automobile highways, and was founded, in all seriousness, in 1957. But by the time of the 2nd British Drag Racing Festival in 1965, the American sport had become firmly established on the British racing scene. Illness struck Allard that same year, and April 12, 1966, he died at his home in Surrey. He was survived by his wife, the former Eleanor May (whom he interested enough in cars for her to become a leading rally driver), his son, and 2 daughters.

LESLIE ALLEN

Leslie (Bugs) Allen was among the many drivers in history who have had success in a couple of years and then have faded from the scene. A friend and protege of Cliff Woodbury, Leslie's magic years were 1926 and 1927 when he won AAA championships at Roby Speedway near Chicago and at Detroit in Frontenacs powered by 300-cu. in. Chevrolet engines. Bugs and Cliff, another AAA hero of the twenties, were favorites in the Midwest on dirt tracks, sharing a car at times. Allen tasted success at Indianapolis once, finishing 9th in a Miller in 1930. He never made the top 10 again.

BOBBY ALLISON

The year 1971 may have been a poor year economically for most Americans, but in 1971 Robert Arthur Allison got the chance to put it all together—talent, experience, desire, and a superb car—and he did. He won 7 NASCAR superspeedway victories and more money than he had seen in a decade or more of modified racing

and independent entries on the Grand National circuit.

There are those who say luck is an essential ingredient in any race driver's winning streak. May be happenstance is a better word. When David Pearson left the giant Holman-Moody operation to sign a 3-year contract to run Pontiacs for Chris Vello, a "millionaire" Greek from Indiana, Bobby took his place at the wheel of the 1969 Mercury. In the Winston 500 at Talladega, Ala., he lost a duel of Mercuries to his younger brother Donnie. In the World 600 at Charlotte, N. C., Bobby turned the tables on his brother, then proceeded to win the Dover, Del., 500, the Motor State 500 at Michigan International Speedway, and the Riverside, Calif., 400 (this race in a Dodge) before Richard Petty edged him at Atlanta's Dixie 500.

Bobby then defeated Petty at both the Michigan 500 and the Talladega 500, then won the Southern 500 at Darlington, S. C., and the National 500 at Charlotte. In one glorious season he almost doubled his previous decade's earnings, and that included a $131,000 season in 1970 in the Mario Rossi Dodge.

Allison was born in Miami, Fla., December 3, 1937, the 4th of 10 children of an automotive jobber. He owned a driver's license at the minimum age for that state, and well before that was practicing spins, turns and restarts in empty fields. He had his own car in high school, and argued his parents into allowing him to compete with it at Hialeah Speedway during his senior year. He finished 10th out of 55 in his first race. But after 2 flips, his father put a temporary end to his racing career.

Had Karl Kiekhaefer, who campaigned Dodges and the fabulous Chrysler 300s in an earlier era of stock-car competition, been less autocratic, Allison might have eventually turned into a contented resident of Oshkosh, Wis. as an employe of Mercury Outboard. His uncle, an executive with the firm, got Bobby a job there after his graduation from high school. The job suited him: testing engines involved running boats at top speed. Eventually he managed to swamp one, which did not sit well with Kiekhaefer. However, during the year he worked with Karl, Bobby became familiar with the racing operation. "Karl wasn't easy to get along with, but he sure knew what he was doing. I learned that preventive maintenance was as important to winning as a fast car. For the first time, I saw racing as a business," Allison declared.

Speedy Thompson, Herb Thomas, Buck Baker, Frank Mundy, and Jimmy Thompson campaigned a huge team of six Dodges and four Chryslers. There was no specific mechanic for any car, but each man signed for his work making him "very careful about the work you did."

It was only a matter of time before Bobby was out of boat engine testing and NASCAR Grand National mechanic work. He spent 2 unsuccessful years as a garage owner before deciding to drive again. He lived at home and competed under an assumed name (Bob Sunderman), but after his younger brother, Tommy, inadvertently betrayed him at the supper table, he parted company with his parents and began running the NASCAR sportsman circuit. He lied about his age to John Bruner, who was to become chief steward. Bruner later said, "That kid was 21 for more years than anyone else I knew, but he was a nice kid and a tremendous competitor."

His initial major victory came June 1, 1959, at Montgomery, Ala., his second late in October of the same year. A shop accident provided the stimulus that turned Bobby into a full-time pro. His fingers were crushed when an automatic transmission slipped from a hoist; during the 9 weeks of recuperation Bobby decided that "if I was going to get hurt, it might as well be at something I liked."

Allison's wife, Judy, whom he met one night when his jalopy crashed and burned, had full knowledge of his passion for racing when they were wed. They moved to Alabama to be closer to the most lucrative modified competition—a circuit that stretches from northern Louisiana through the Carolinas to Virginia—but the rise to success was slow. Allison won 2 features in Florida in 1959, 7 in 1960; then he began to travel and won 33 in 1961. He won his initial National title in 1962 when NASCAR subdivided modified racing to offer a modified special crown. He won again in 1963, and finally in 1964 won the modified crown itself.

Modified stock-car racing is the backbone of American oval track competition or was so for the generation of its growth after World War II. These cars, with older bodies but well-prepared engines, still make up the weekly programs at most tracks, although they have offshoots like super modifieds. Allison was king of modified racing in 1964 and 1965, towing his rig from track to track to race 5 or 6 nights a week. When the area covered is larger than from Scotland to southern France, the constant driving to get from track to track becomes a problem in itself. And on top of this there is the necessity of preparing the car. It literally can be a 24-hour a day job.

Modified racing is a rough training ground, too. Local drivers have been known to gang up on a touring pro, to spin him out or wreck him or just box him in so that he cannot win. Allison was known to take this treatment very unkindly, using his greater experience to create new piles of junk. And he taught his techniques to Donnie as well.

Allison tried a few Grand National races in 1961, but until it became evident that the only way to make a large amount of money was to gamble on the Grand National circuit, he was content in the modified ranks. In 1965 he drove 8 of the Grand Nationals; his family was growing—there were now 4 little Allisons—and the costs of campaigning even the modified were increasing. So when Mrs. Betty Lilly, a wheelchair-ridden Georgian, offered him a ride in her Ford for the 1966 season, Allison decided to try it. The arrangement did not work out, and Bobby had to take an even bigger financial gamble or go back to the modifieds.

It reportedly took him just 384 hours and $8,000 to turn a Chevelle into a Grand National car. He campaigned the lesser Grand Nationals extensively, winning his first 2 championship races on the annual NASCAR northern tour at the clay half-miler in Oxford Beach, Me., and a tiny quarter-mile at Islip, N.Y. In that one 1966 season, he carved out a reputation for fearlessness, tangling with the likes of Curtis Turner and Lee Roy Yarbrough in epic bumping and bashing duels calculated to impress upon all that this was not a man to be satisfied with also-ran money. In one race, after a bash by Turner that took him out, Allison restarted his car and belted Curtis broadside—on a safety lap, no less. It brought him a fine and the friendship of Turner who respected Bobby's audacity.

By 1967 Allison seemed to be over the hump. He had sponsorship for both the Grand National circuit and the SCCA's TransAm series, in a Chevelle and a Camaro respectively. Although not a factory deal, it was just about as good. There would be no more scrounging for vital parts, no more discoveries that over-the-counter parts were not what quality control should have made them. He need only prepare for and drive in the big races. A man could even see his family with so much time on his hands.

The independent Chevelle deal was dropped for a ride in a Bud Moore Mercury Comet, and when, in April 1967, the chance came to replace David Pearson in the Cotton Owens Dodge came, Bobby grabbed it.

However, things didn't go smoothly and late in 1967 Allison moved again into a factory Ford. He came back to the Dodge entourage in 1968 to drive a Mario Rossi-prepared car.

Allison's rivalry on the track with his younger brother Donnie now became intense. Bobby had encouraged Donnie; in 1960 he had given his modified to his brother Eddie, who promptly put Donnie in as driver. "Those guys gave me fits all year. Sometimes we'd be 10 or 20 laps ahead of the field and we'd be up there banging fenders," Bobby recalled. At Rockingham in 1968, Bobby drove his independent Chevelle to a distant second behind his factory-mounted brother.

Both brothers must have thought of their early rivalries when they clashed in the 1969 National 500 at Charlotte, where Donnie won a stirring duel.

Allison went into 1970 with a Grand National career average of better than 35 per cent finishes in the top 5. In the 11th annual Atlanta 500 that year, he not only broke (by 5.408 m.p.h.) a record average speed of 134.146 that had been set in 1964 by Fred Lorenzen, but also nipped favorite Cale Yarborough's Mercury by about 50 feet for the victory. Yarborough, who was out to add the victory to a record pole position run, was also trying to become the first man ever to win 4 Atlanta 500s (Lorenzen also had won 3). As the leaders made their final pit stops, Cale had an advantage of more than a lap. But Allison got out of the pits more quickly, and closed up the gap when the caution flag went out for oil on the track. When the green flag came out with about 8 miles remaining, Allison won a trophy dash to the wire, to the cheers of some 44,000 fans. He won over $22,000.

Bobby was one of the leaders in the Professional Drivers Association, comprised of most of NASCAR's Grand National regulars. According to contemporaries, he pressed hard for formalization of the organization and was one of its most effective recruiters.

In 1972 Bobby continued his ascendancy and he was mostly mounted on Chevrolet. He and the Junior Johnson Coca Cola Chevrolet were the GM part of a tripartite battle among Richard Petty (Plymouth) and David Pearson (Wood Bros. Mercury). He held his own and more, winning the Mason-Dixon 500 at Dover Downs, winning the Dixie 500 at Atlanta after edging A. J. Foyt in the Atlanta 500 and winning both Bristol, Tenn., races. In all, there were 10 victories in 31 starts, with total earnings of $271,395. There were 3 more 500 victories—the American, National, and Southern races. Small wonder he was the Driver of the Year.

CLIFF ALLISON

In every sport there are men who are quietly capable. In motor racing there always have been men who have looked unhurried, but have been fast, men who performed unspectacularly, yet managed to be among the finishers, high up in the standings. One of these was Britain's Henry Clifford Allison, born February 8, 1932.

Allison was 20 when he entered his initial race at Charterhall in a Formula 3 Cooper-Norton in 1952. Cliff raced this same car into 1956, his first victory coming in 1954. His switch from Cooper was to a factory ride with the then-new Lotus marque. With Colin Chapman's effort, in fact, Cliff scored perhaps the first major Lotus victory, a 750-c.c. class and index of performance victory at Le Mans in 1957 (and 14th overall in the power-packed field). The car was shared with second-string driver Keith Hall, which meant that the burden fell squarely on Allison's shoulders.

That same season Allison was 2nd in an Oulton Formula 2 race, won at Rouen. In 1958 he gave Lotus its initial major Grand Prix placing, a 4th, in the Belgian GP. One more lap to that race and Cliff might well have won overall, as the 3 cars ahead of him died in the final few hundred feet of the race just before and after the checker. That year saw Allison and Chapman appear at Sebring and score a 6th. This kind of driving was impressive enough to Enzo Ferrari to cause the Italian car-builder to offer a factory berth to Allison, an offer no driver could resist in those days.

It was with Ferrari sports cars that Allison scored a 3rd in the Nurburgring 1000 (shared with Willy Mairesse) and 2nd at Sebring (with Jean Behra). In the Italian GP that same season of 1959 Cliff scored a 5th, but it was the following season that seemed to suggest that Allison was on the threshold of real greatness. In 1960 he was 2nd in the Argentine GP to Bruce McLaren's Cooper, won the Buenos Aires 1000 with Phil Hill in sports cars. Then Allison and Hill shared the winning Ferrari at Le Mans. But 1960 also was the season that the Briton had a serious F2 practice accident at Monaco, curtailing his racing for much of the year.

In 1961 Allison seemed to have recovered. At Snetterton he was 2nd in the Glover Trophy; at Oulton, Aintree and Silverstone third—all these races in a Lotus Monte Carlo in UDT Laystall colors. But at Spa Allison again had a serious accident, and after this one he never seriously raced again, retiring to his wife, 4 children, farm, and garage.

DONNIE ALLISON

Donnie Allison wanted to be a jockey. He used to sneak away from school sometimes to get into the stable area of the track nearest his Florida home. He loved horses. But wheels got in the way. "It was a secret passion, mostly," he said. "But it ended after I gained 30 pounds in the hospital." That was in 1956, soon after Donnie had acquired his first motorcycle. He almost lost a leg by bouncing off a truck into the path of an oncoming car. It took him 4 months to recover.

Donnie Joseph Allison was born September 7, 1939, in Miami. At 15, he held Florida AAU swimming and

diving championships and had little interest in racing until his older brother Bobby got involved in it.

He accompanied Bobby and Eddie, another older brother, to the track, and it was inevitable that he would be offered a ride. One night at Hialeah Raceway, a one-third-mile oval, he taunted the owner-driver of a 1941 Ford into offering a turn at the wheel, to let Donnie see if he could make the car go faster. Donnie did. The following week he repeated the performance. The owner gave the car to Donnie on the spot.

Allison broke an axle on the next heat, but wasn't discouraged. He began to drive regularly in what were called amateur races. Finally there came the night when friends talked Bobby into letting his younger brother drive in a feature, since Bobby already had won his feature for the night. Donnie promptly drove into the fence, destroying the car. Bobby raced to the wreck, but once he had assured himself that his brother's injuries were nothing a week in the hospital couldn't mend, he screamed that Donnie was a no-talent race driver.

The challenge decided Donnie's career. He got his initial modified professional ride in 1959, went on to register track championships in Montgomery, Birmingham, and Huntsville, Ala., and Chattanooga, Tenn. Bobby helped eventually by giving Donnie his own old modified. Donnie was still riding the modified circuit even when he had begun to earn bigger money in the major leagues of Grand National racing.

Donnie moved up to a Grand National car in 1966, after finishing 9th at the smallest of the NASCAR super-tracks, the mile-long Rockingham (N.C.) Speedway. That finish was enough to earn him a ride in one of the better independent cars, Jon Thorne's Holman-Moody-prepared Ford Fairlane, for the 1967 season. In 20 races that year Donnie 7 times made the top 10 and was nominated Rookie of the Year. In 1968 he had a Ford factory ride in a Banjo Matthews-prepared Torino, and took his initial major victory, the Carolina 500 at Rockingham. In 13 GN races he finished 5 times in the top 5. Running what was then called the Grand Touring circuit, and later became the Grand American Challenge, Donnie added 5 victories and finished in the top 5 in 10 out of 12 races, His total NASCAR winnings were over $61,000, which was $8,000 more than brother Bobby won that year.

The two had locked wheels on minor tracks in smaller races, and even on the major tracks but never in contention for the lead at the same time. It finally happened at Charlotte Speedway in October 1969. The event was the National 500; there were 57,000 stock car fans in the stands and $116,000 in the prize fund. The race also provided the first real confrontation between the Boss 429 Ford Talladega and the new Dodge Daytona. Donnie was in the Ford, Bobby in the Daytona Charger.

Practice indicated that Donnie had the fastest car on the track, even though he only qualified 3rd, and on the very 1st lap of the race he took the lead. He held it until the first of his 11 pit stops; the Allison driving style was helping to consume 20 tires. In all, 6 drivers held the lead at various times, with 26 lead changes. Richard Petty, who led twice, was finally sidelined with a blown head gasket in his Ford. Buddy Baker, in a Dodge Daytona, was the most serious non-Allison threat, but he gambled and lost just 5 laps from the finish when he ran out of gas.

That left Bobby and Donnie in contention for the lead. Donnie had about 6 seconds in hand from a speedier final pit stop some 12 laps from the finish, but Bobby closed the gap after Baker fell out. Soon it was Allison vs. Allison, Ford vs. Dodge, nose to tail and side by side. The Talladega clearly was the faster car, yet the Daytona seemed to eat up distance in the turns. The two raced this way lap after lap, Bobby able to pull briefly alongside his younger brother but not quite able to pass. They went over the finish line as close as Damon and Pythias, but this time it was Donnie who won the 1st place check of more than $20,000. Their mother was sitting in the stands that day; fortunately no one asked her how she felt with two sons riding fender to fender at more than 160 m.p.h.

In 1970 Donnie added a new dimension to his career. He qualified for the Indianapolis 500 the first weekend in an A. J. Foyt-owned Coyote at 165.662 m.p.h. Donnie finished 6th at Indianapolis in 1971, moving up steadily in the late stages of the race after acting as backup to A. J. until he got the "go" signal. But at Pocono and Ontario, the other events of the USAC Triple Crown, mechanical trouble sidelined him.

When Foyt vacated the Wood Brothers NASCAR ride, Donnie inherited it and promptly won the Winston 500 at Talladega. It was another Donnie and Bobby show—for a lap—and one of the great NASCAR finishes of all time. The Allisons, in Mercuries, and Buddy Baker and Dave Marcis, in Dodges, had swapped the lead for 500 miles, interrupted only by lesser competitors crashing or spinning in the attempt to equal their breakneck speed. There were 7 caution periods, and the 80,000 fans needed them almost as much as the competitors. In the last 70 miles all 4 had held the lead and then, while leading 8 laps from the end, Marcis blew his engine in flaming splendor and he spun his car deliberately to extinguish the flames. That brought 5 laps of caution.

Now Donnie was leading, but only by a few car lengths over Buddy and Bobby. Over the next 2 laps they closed to within inches. The race would be decided on how the trio set up for the final lap; it was a $30,450 drag race. Donnie stayed right in the groove around the first 3 turns, bracketed by Bobby and Baker. On the final turn he accelerated an instant before the others and caught the benefit of the banking perfectly. Bobby and Buddy actually closed down the short home stretch, but Donnie won by a car length, with Baker about a yard back. That Bobby was to be the year's NASCAR superspeedway hero was bearable. Donnie Allison knew he could be the hero, too, on any given day.

GEORGE AMICK

A pall hung over big new Daytona International Speedway on April 9, 1959, as the Indianapolis cars prepared for their initial official race there. The stands were less than half filled, and the pit area was quieter than usual. The death of Marshall Teague during practice had been ominous. The big stock car veteran, a favorite at Indy, had been barrelling through a turn when, for no apparent reason, he lost control.

The drivers were like men facing an unknown menace, a menace as invisible as the wind. And that was it—wind currents strong enough to hold the heavy stock cars in invisible lanes. What, asked some of the drivers when no outsiders were present, would it do with the much lighter, much faster Indianapolis cars?

George Amick wasn't afraid. The 5-foot 5-inch pepper pot from Rhinelander, Wisc., had a foot as heavy as an elephant's, and he used it, secure in the knowledge that his skill could tame the speed and make it yield up fame and fortune. He had confidence, he had guts; but he knew when to charge and when to hold back. He had a natural talent for rating a race, picking his time to strike. Yet he, too, had spun on the high banks of this Dixie track in practice. He and the others knew that this was a challenge as tough as Indy, made doubly dangerous by its unknown aspects.

Dick Rathmann had the pole, although Amick was

fastest qualifier at 176.887. Brother Jim Rathmann, Rodger Ward, Amick, and Don Branson were among the top contenders. When the green flag waved, Jim Rathmann leaped into the lead, followed by Ward and Dick Rathmann. Elmer George in the HOW Special jumped into a surprising 4th, with Eddie Sachs in his slipstream. They came around in an incredibly short time, the brothers Rathmann dueling for first with Ward. It was like a model racing set, the cars circled the big speedway so fast—5 laps in less than 5 minutes on a 2.5-mile oval. Suddenly a car belched smoke, trailing it like a skywriter plane along the outer rim of the speedway down through the pit turn. It was Len Sutton; he made it into the pits, followed soon after by Tony Bettenhausen and Sachs.

Meanwhile, Ward dove off the turn to take the Rathmanns on the inside and hurtle down the straight into the lead with little room to spare. Five cars bunched up in front, Amick and Bob Christie steaming after the big 3 in cars which obviously didn't have the innards to get the lead. On the 12th lap, Jim Rathmann took the lead back and Amick fell before the onslaught of Elmer George. Three laps later, Jimmy Davies, in the new Greenman-Casale design, had been lapped by the top 3; Rathman's average speed of 169.205 might be compared with his 166.72 in what had once been the world's fastest single race, the 1958 Race of Two Worlds at Monza, Italy.

Halfway home it was still Jim, Rodger, Dick, George, and Bob Christie; the sparse crowd was out-shouting announcer Chris Economaki. Suddenly Jimmy Thomp-

son spun as he tried to overtake A. J. Foyt farther back in the pack. He looped off the track without harm, but it was a harbinger of trouble. The leaders were closing on the main part of the pack; traffic was going to be heavy. Amick's Bowes Seal Fast roadster began to make its move. He passed Christie and found Elmer George and young Jim Packard engaged in a duel for position too, high up on the rim of the bank, like 2 men in a log-rolling contest.

Then Dempsey Wilson's ancient Hoyt Special spun on the second turn, hit the rail and dropped to the lip of the track, its tires smoking. Wilson was unhurt. The yellow flag was out, but Jim Rathmann didn't seem to know it. He continued to speed until the black flag warning came out for him. When the green waved again, the first Daytona 100 was only 8 laps from completion and the speed average had risen, thanks to Jim, to 172.25 m.p.h. Rathmann was 8 seconds ahead of brother Dick, with Ward sandwiched in second place. Amick was 4th, with a shot at third, but Christie was close behind him.

The announcer saw the duel for third shaping up and concentrated on it; Amick and Christie slipped past Dick Rathmann but Christie nosed into third as they charged into the final lap. Then came the dreaded words: "There's a bad crash on the back straight. It looks like George Amick."

Amick was dead, killed instantly when the wind currents in the 2nd turn had their chance at him at 190 m.p.h., almost at the moment Jim Rathmann was being waved over the finish line as winner. Amick's car jammed its nose under the outer rail, sheering 9 huge fence anchors before flipping and sliding upside down for more than 300 yards to the infield grass. Bill Cheesbourg who spun behind him, said later, "There were wheels and pieces of car all over the track. I had no place to go." It was the end of a career that had once seemed headed straight for immortality.

Born October 24, 1924, at Vernonia, Ore., George Amick began racing jalopies around nearby Portland about 1946. He gravitated toward midget cars and, by the time he decided to make the move toward Indianapolis and the Championship Trail in 1955, he had won a reputation as a midget car ace. He finished 9th in USAC standings in 1955, then 4th, 3rd, and 2nd in 1958. He won at Atlanta's Lakeside Park in 1957 and at Langhorne and Phoenix in 1956. He had 3 second-place finishes in 1958—Indianapolis, Atlanta, and Syracuse.

While he passed his rookie test at Indy in 1957, Amick didn't get into the race until the following year, when he won Rookie of the Year honors in the Demler Special. He went from 25th grid position to 2nd, led at the 30- and 40-lap mark, and then, after pit woes, worked his way back up behind winner Jim Bryan in a tragic race which saw Pat O'Connor die. George drove for some of the best—Pete Schmidt, Leader Card, Lindsay Hopkins—and he had just switched to a Joe

Epperly-built Bowes Special that he hoped would bring him victory at Indianapolis 1959. Needless to say, the Bowes car never made it to Indianapolis either.

RICHARD AMICK

When Red Amick, no relation to George, qualified at Indianapolis at 143.084 m.p.h. in 1960, he must have hoped for a shot at the real big money—if the hot dogs had problems. The car was a few years older than when it won for Sam Hanks and Jimmy Bryan, and it was called the King O'Lawn Special now. It had new paint and a driver a little bit hungrier for some of that Indianapolis money. Amick drove a good steady race and finished 11th; it looked as if the 5-foot 10-inch ex-Hollywood native might be on the same path to fame as many graduates of the California roadster circuit.

But Amick became inactive in 1961 and 1962 because of personal problems, then had to start back up the ladder in IMCA sprint car racing in 1963. When he saw he still had it, Dick switched to USAC sprints again late in the season and tried for the 1964 Indianapolis 500. He didn't make it.

Amick began racing in 1948 when he was 19. He eventually established himself as a competent sprint car driver on independent circuits and in USAC where he campaigned in 1958. In 1959 he qualified for the Indy race as a rookie, but was involved in a 4-car crash in the 45th lap. Amick drove every kind of racing car that runs on the oval tracks, as well as late model stocks for NASCAR. But, though he was competent, and not lacking in courage, the brass ring never came his way. In his forties, with a family to support, he turned to the service station business finally.

What had been the difference? Cars just a little bit too tired? Some win even then. Luck? Or was it that the men who were trained on the dirt tracks may actually be at a disadvantage because of their technique now? Racing, American style, was never more lucrative. Nor had it ever been more competitive. Red Amick kept competing when he could, one of many hands reaching for the brass ring, still hoping to find it was made of gold.

CHRIS AMON

"Do I want to be the best racing driver in the world? Yes, I do want to be that, but I don't want to be doing that for the next ten years. I'd like to win a driving championship, then I'd like to do it again—to convince myself—and then I'd like to stop. But if I don't win the title through circumstances, at least I'd like to prove to myself that I'm the fastest driver around."

These were the sentiments Chris Amon, a 6-season Grand Prix veteran at age 25, expressed in 1969 when he still had yet to win a Formula 1 championship race.

In an increasingly nervous quest for that first GP victory, he would transfer from Ferrari of Italy to March of England to Matra of France, all within 3 years, and still the garland and 9 championship points would elude him. What would not elude him were a reputation for bad luck, coupled with the general esteem of his fellows. Like Jackie Stewart and Jacky Ickx, they knew he belonged right up there with them as one of the fastest racers in the series. As Chris Amon grew older, though, being fast wasn't nearly enough; being a winner was becoming obsessive.

"Spa in 1970 was a good race," said Amon in retrospect. "I held on to (Pedro) Rodriguez's BRM right to the finish and was 2nd. But 2nd place is no good. I've been doing that for a long time now, often finishing 2nd or 3rd and getting onto the front row of the grid, but it's all not good enough. Frankly, in 1969 I found that I was beginning to lose my edge. I was becoming interested in other things, like running my own CanAm car and searching for sponsors, and it all detracted from my driving.

"Because I didn't have a Ferrari F1 car after the British GP, I was losing my competitive urge. So I had to get back into F1 quickly, and I wasn't convinced Ferrari was going to become competitive again very soon. I had tested the flat 12 engine in private, and it was always breaking down in 4 or 5 laps. So I left Ferrari, even though I still had a good relationship with them and I liked it there. Sure, I've kicked myself in retrospect for leaving them, but if the situation were the same today, I'd probably do exactly the same thing."

F1 has always been most important for Chris Amon. All other forms of motor sport, much as he might like them and excel in them, were merely ways to prepare or to maintain form for the GP series. "I had wanted to drive a single-seater ever since I could remember," the wiry, smallish, longhaired New Zealander said. "That's why when everyone said I should start off in a sports car or a saloon, I just shook my head. It was my firm conviction that if you were going to be a GP driver, then you should drive nothing but single-seat racing cars, providing you could keep your head and work your way up slowly in them—but not too slowly. I was convinced that racing drivers can learn an awful lot of bad habits through racing other types of cars first, but I guess I was wrong."

Christopher Arthur Amon may or may not have been wrong on that point, but he was an authority on how to get started racing early. His start came very early in a unique single-seater: a tractor on his father's sheep ranch at Bulls, near Wanganui, where Amon was born July 20, 1943. When Chris was 16 and wanted to go racing more formally, his family had the means to allow him to do it. His first real car was an Austin-engined special, a sort of Down Under midget for dirt-track racing, in which he won 2 or 3 races before his 17th birthday. He sold that car for a 4-year-old 1.5-litre Formula 2 Cooper-Climax, which was driven in just one race at Levin. Amon was beaten there by a man in an experimental Piccolo Maserati 250F that had somehow gotten to New Zealand. Chris's Cooper, plus some cash, went toward the car; it was a rather brutish machine for a novice to control, but Amon did well with it throughout 1961.

The following year, at 18, he had the Maserati extensively rebuilt by Bruce Wilson, a well-known Kiwi mechanic, and proceeded to astonish Australian and New Zealand crowds. "That car taught me more about racing than any other car I have ever driven," Amon said, "but I was not so foolish as to limit myself to it alone." That same year he drove—and drove well by all reports—such other machinery as a Super Squalo Ferrari and a rear-engined 2.5-litre Cooper. Chris liked the Cooper and immediately set out to buy it from Australian Dave McKay's Scuderia Veloce team. It is always nice to have money. McKay offered the youngster a team berth, which gave him valuable discipline. He collected a 2nd, and a pair of 3rds.

The following year Reg Parnell approached Amon to drive his ex-Bowmaker Lola-BRM V-8 in Europe in 1963, replacing none other than John Surtees, who had left for Ferrari. Amon was 7th, in the French and British Grands Prix in his first formal F1 season, and his 20th birthday came on the day of the British race. A Le Mans drive was in the offing, but French officials claimed he was too young for such an endurance test. Since the 24-hour enduro wasn't single-seater competition, the decision didn't really bother the fair-haired New Zealander.

For 1964 Parnell planned to have Amon and motorcycle star Mike Hailwood in F1 Lotus-Climax 25 cars, but Parnell died before the season started. Reg's son, Tim, took over with the vastly underpowered Lotus-BRM, and a 5th at Zandvoort in the Dutch GP earned Amon exactly 2 points in the World Driver's Championship quest. Not much, but more than his roommates of the day—Hailwood and American Peter Revson. Chris also was 4th in the non-championship Mediterranean GP, and 5th at Snetterton, Syracuse (Italy), and Silverstone in the Lotus-BRM. In a Cobra sports car, furnished by Tommy Atkins for the Brands Hatch Guards Trophy, Amon finished 2nd to the experienced Jack Sears after a wheel-to-wheel duel. In 1965 Chris joined the senior racing Kiwi, Bruce McLaren, as a test driver and a 2-litre sports car pilot, the best offer he had gotten after his disappointing previous year.

The patient and mature McLaren taught Amon what it meant to be a true professional. Chris drove hundreds of miles testing Firestone tires on the McLaren-Elva, then on the prototype McLaren F1 car. He substituted for an injured Bruce at the Silverstone Martini Trophy and won, after starting from the back of the grid. He also won the Canadian-American Challenge Cup race at St. Jovite, and finished 6th in the series. McLaren arranged a place for Amon—now old enough for the French officials—on the Ford Le Mans team, and Chris shared a 7-litre GT with Phil Hill until transmission trouble eliminated the car. Amon actually did most of the driving while Hill commented on the race for American television, and the Kiwi even led for a while.

In 1966 the F1 McLaren-Ford had engine teething troubles, and Amon's best rides came in sports, prototype, and GT competition. He won again in the CanAm with a McLaren-Elva, copped a 3rd later in the season at St. Jovite, and finished 2nd behind Dan Gurney at Bridgehampton. At Le Mans, Amon and McLaren won with a Ford GT and spent 3 hours drinking champagne before falling into a hot bath. Despite his McLaren successes, in 1967 Amon signed with Ferrari, for he wanted a F1 victory badly, and driving for Ferrari had been a childhood dream. His first big success with the Italian marque came at the Daytona Continental when Chris and Lorenzo Bandini shared a P4 prototype and the victory in a 1st, 2nd, 3rd Ferrari sweep of the 24-hour race. The pair repeated at the Monza 1000, and Jackie Stewart shared the seat with Amon to clinch the manufacturers title in the Brands Hatch 500.

Driving the new three-litre V-12 Ferrari F1 car, Amon was 3rd four times—in the Monaco, Belgian, British, and German Grands Prix—and was 4th in the Dutch race, 6th in Canada, 7th in Italy, and 9th in Mexico. Added up, it totalled 20 points and a tie for 4th place in the 1967 championship rating with Surtees. By the season's end Chris also was Ferrari's team leader, not entirely due to his driving. In the Kiwi's first GP for Ferrari, Lorenzo Bandini had been killed, and in his 2nd race, he had had to avoid Mike Parkes's wreck. If

Amon was not doing well, it was understandable. Gloom characterized the Modena marque's pits.

The season's new Ferraris were having their problems in mechanical areas, too. In 1968 Amon slipped to 10th in the standings, his best finish a 2nd in the British GP, despite fast qualifying rounds at many circuits. He was 4th at South Africa, 6th in the Netherlands GP and 10th in France. Mechanical ills and 2 accidents knocked Amon out of 7 other starts. Nor were Ferrari's problems solved the following season, Amon managing only a 3rd in the Dutch GP for 4 points and 12th place in the standings at year's end. It was really frustrating to lead, as he did at Spain, through much of a race, only to have his engine blow or his steering fail. A first championship GP victory was as elusive as ever. Only victories in his native New Zealand GP 2 years in a row, his Tasman Championship title in 1968–69, and those splendid sports car and endurance race victories at places like Le Mans kept him going, and trying, especially after Ferrari all but quit GP racing while trying to speed up development of the new flat 12 powered F1 car that would be introduced in 1970.

In 1970 Amon came to a crossroads. He had to decide whether to remain with Ferrari and battle not only the other drivers out on the course but an aggressive team partner, Jacky Ickx, who had charged into the picture like a bull in the china shop. Chris agonized over what to do. There were offers galore: from the new March marque, from BRM, even from Matra, now established as a force in the GP world. In the end, Amon effected a compromise of sorts. For F1 he would drive as leader of the March team, partnered by Jo Siffert. He signed for an Indianapolis ride with Team McLaren. March agreed to ready a car for Chris in the rich Canadian-American Challenge Cup series. And, suprisingly, Ferrari agreed to use Amon for a few long-distance events in its new 512S sports car. He summed up his 3 F1 seasons with Ferrari this way: "The potential for success was there, but there was no success. They had the manpower, but not the organization to follow it through, and there was a constant engine problem in all classes. I went there with the impression that Ferrari had the best engines and the worst chassis, but more often than not it was the other way round."

Amon's decision paid off April 26, 1970, when his new March-Ford won the Silverstone International Trophy for F1 cars in a 2-heat race. It was a non-title contest, to be sure, but an important one, and Chris's initial F1 victory. Amon won the opening heat and was 2nd to Jackie Stewart in the second after a wheel-to-wheel battle, which gave him enough points to secure top ranking. The next goal was a championship F1 victory, which surely would prove more elusive until man and March-Ford meshed as one, but was possible in Amon's view. During the 13-race GP season, Amon came close to victory a couple of times, but the prize still eluded him. After retirements at South Africa, Spain, and Monaco, Chris was 2nd by 1.1 seconds to

Rodriguez's BRM in the Belgian GP. He set the fastest lap of the day, and, as it turned out, the fastest lap of any F1 race in 1970: 152.07 m.p.h. on the speedy Spa circuit.

In the Dutch GP, Amon's March again retired, this time in the opening lap; but in the French race, Amon finished 2nd, just over 7 seconds behind winner Jo Rindt, who was on his way to the World Championship. Britain came next, and a 5th place finish for Chris; then another retirement in Germany, an 8th in Austria, and a 7th in Italy. In the Canadian GP, Amon finished 3rd, behind the Ferraris of Ickx and Clay Regazzoni. He was 5th in the United States GP, 4th in Mexico. When the scorecard was tallied, Amon had 23 championship points and was tied with Rodriguez for 7th place.

Outside of the regular GP wars, Amon won the Silverstone Daily Express F1 race but retired from the F1 Race of Champions–both of these non-title races–and appeared for the final races of the CanAm series in a March 707. He was 5th at Brainerd, Minn., 4th at both Monterey and Riverside. These races were under the STP banner, and Amon's work encouraged Andy Granatelli to furnish him a car for the 1971 Tasman series of 7 races in Australia and New Zealand.

Amon had already signed for a new GP drive in 1971 with the French Matra team. "My decision to join March in 1970 came because I felt that I had to have the same engine as Stewart, Rindt, and the others," Amon recalled. "They were all going so quickly that I decided it must be the Cosworth-Ford engined car for me. March achieved more in a year than any builder has a right to expect, not only in F1, but in F2, F3, and CanAm, right from scratch. It was a tremendous achievement, but it was also their downfall. I really believe that if they had built just two or three F1 cars, even though the design was about 4 years old in comparison to everyone else's, they might have achieved some really startling GP successes. Around mid-season they were running out of money, and the car I was racing at season's end was virtually the same as it was at season's begining. You can't stand still in GP racing; you must modify as you go along, picking up things from others' successes, or you get slower and slower in comparison to them.

"And to top it all, the very reason I had made the switch—the engine—wasn't working out at all. Cosworth denies that anyone gets a better engine than anyone else, but I was convinced that March wasn't getting the same engine and service as the other teams. I can understand it if a team isn't free with its cash and isn't ready to let the engine builder make changes that he deems necessary to make the engine truly competitive, but the situation was a bad one for the driver, me. I believe that until the Belgian GP my engines were as good as anyone's, but after that I started going slower, and there wasn't any physical reason, just a mechanical one. I never had an engine like the one Rindt was running on his way to the World Championship." (Amon's infatuation with his engine problems led him finally, in 1972, to start his own engine company in conjunction with Aubrey Woods. F2 was first, but the ultimate goal had to be F1.)

So the switch to Matra was inevitable, and Amon, as was his custom, made his Matra debut an auspicious one, easily winning the 2-heat Buenos Aires Argentine GP for F1 and Formula 5000 cars combined. The race didn't prove all that much, but hopefully would introduce a successful 1971. But it was not to be. In another non-title race for F1 and F5000 cars, the so-called Questor GP at Ontario, Calif., Amon was 4th. In South Africa he was 5th. In the championship opener for Europe, raced in Spain and won by Stewart, Chris was 3rd. Amon's Matra was retired at both Monaco and Holland, finished 5th in the French GP, retired again in the Woolmark British GP and in Germany.

Matra skipped the Austrian GP in an effort to improve its cars. Amon was fast in the Italian GP, led for a while, and finished just 32 seconds behind Peter Gethin, the surprise winner. But this was an F1 race the likes of which hadn't been seen for years, the first 5 cars covered by a blanket of just one second! A smashed face visor had slowed Amon just enough. In Canada he was 10th, in the USGP 12th. The season's work totaled just 9 championship points, tying him with 4 others for 9th place in the standings.

"I didn't join Matra with the idea that the year would be fabulously successful," Amon said. "The car is very good. It compared favorably with the best car I had driven, the 1968 Ferrari V-12, but it also suffered from the same problem—lack of urge, power. It was getting better toward the year's end, but still had a way to go. But Matra is a tremendous team. They are young in motor racing and very enthusiastic. They have no great old traditions to hang on to like Ferrari has, and that can be a good thing. There are people at Ferrari who know about modern racing, and are attuned to making fast changes, but there also are too many people from 30 years ago who know only how it used to be done. But Matra left GP racing after the 1972 season. After a brief "return" to March, Amon left before the 1973 opener. The season started without him, although he had a contract to drive the new Tecno F1 cars if they appeared in time.

If Amon lacked one winning quality in his GP career, it was the so-called "killer instinct" seemingly present in so many sports champions. "This business of getting into a race and saying, 'I hate this fellow's guts, and I'm going to beat him', doesn't work for me," he said. "You could so easily hurt yourself by getting into a temper. A big part of the job, to my mind, is being steady. You can't afford to be too steady—you have to have a bit of fire. But it should be fire, not temper." Drawing that distinction sharply enough apparently eluded Amon, and with it that initial, wonderful championship GP victory.

BOB ANDERSON

Londoner Bob Anderson was that scarcest of creatures, a privately entered Grand Prix driver who occasionally found his way to a World Driver's Championship point or two despite the fact that his mount was usually the oldest and slowest on the grid. Anderson could go fast enough to win a championship, as he proved on Britain's motorcycle circuit, but his chances in a racing car steadily diminished each year. He just did not have the equipment, whether in Formula 1, in which he operated his own 2.7-litre, 4-cylinder Brabham-Climax, or in other types of auto racing, in which he would have loved to participate.

"I can't afford more than the Brabham," he said sadly near the end. "With support from component, fuel, and tire people, and with some starting money— although it is not enough, to be truthful about it—my wife and I, who really make up DWR Racing Enterprises, just make ends meet. If anything too drastic ever happens, I will have had it as far as racing goes. And I don't see how the situation will improve. Too much money–prize money as well as starting money– goes to the top, and very little falls down to the rest of the field. Promoters apparently can't see that with a more equitable distribution of starting and prize money, they would get far better fields."

Anderson fought a losing battle, not only on the GP circuits but in other forms of racing, too. He would have liked to drive at Indianapolis, for example, and

17

made no bones about it, but no owner would entrust a car to a relatively unknown driver, even if that man had shown amazing courage and endurance in sustaining his private effort for more than 3 years. And it didn't help that Anderson was nearly 40, nor that his early reputation was as a tiger and his later one as a car saver. Winning drivers lie somewhere between those two generalizations.

Robert Hugh Fearson Anderson was born in Hendon, a London suburb, about 1929, and lived quietly in Haynes, Bedfordshire, with his French wife, Marie-Edmée, and their son and daughter when not trucking off his GP racer on a revamped Volkswagen panel truck. Anderson first gained a reputation in the 2-wheeled world with victories on his own cycle at places like the Nurburgring, Mallory, Castle Combe, and Silverstone. In 1961 he tried auto racing for the first time, entering a Formula Junior race at Snetterton in a borrowed front-engined Lola-Ford. His 3rd place was good enough to encourage him to continue. The following year he joined Colin Chapman's Lotus factory FJ team, but in 1963 he struck off on his own. He knew that with 19-year-olds like Chris Amon popping up in Britain it would be hard for a 33-year-old comparative novice to get a F1 ride. Bob bought a ex-Bowmaker Lola-Climax, and with it he won the Rome Grand Prix, was 3rd at Imola, and finished 4th at Syracuse, Italy.

In 1964, Anderson swaped his Lola for a Brabham-Climax BT11 and scored his initial World Championship point with a 6th in the Dutch GP. He was 3rd in the non-championship Austrian GP and also in the Solitude race. Anderson was 11th in the season's final standings. The Grand Prix Drivers Association recognized his effort by awarding him its Von Trips Memorial Trophy as the year's most successful private entrant. The following year, the final one for the 1.5-litre F1, he ran the same car but didn't score a point. He qualified for, but retired from, the South African British and Dutch Grands Prix, was 9th at Monaco and in the French GP, and 6th at Syracuse.

For the new 3-litre season in 1966, Anderson acquired a 2.7-litre Climax engine ("all I could afford") for a spare Brabham chassis he was able to buy relatively cheaply. Sorting out that car was no fun either, but Anderson got back into the championship standings with a single point and a 4-way tie for 13th place. He was 6th in the Italian GP, then went to Africa. There he won the Rhodesian race, came in 5th in the South African GP, and was 2nd overall (after winning 1 heat and placing in the other) in the Capetown GP. He and Denis Hulme had a tangle at the Silverstone International Trophy, but Bob regained the course and finished 8th. The year's big disappointment was the French GP, which also was the European GP in 1966. Bob was running a strong 4th with 4 laps to go when a differential housing snapped. The car was awarded 7th.

Life can be heartbreaking for a private entry. In the opening 1967 race, for example, Anderson and his 3-year-old mount set a faster practice lap pace than such team drivers as Amon (Ferrari), Jo Rindt (Cooper-Maserati) and Pedro Rodriquez (Cooper-Maserati), yet failed to make the starting grid because there were just 5 berths for the 8 drivers who were not guaranteed places on the grid because of their factory status and 1966 standings. Monaco, Bob's favorite course was the one place where the far more powerful factory entries were brought down to his level. The twisting, demanding Monte Carlo streets are a great equalizer.

Anderson was considering quitting big time racing after the 1967 season, because of the rising costs that had eliminated just about every independent except Rob Walker, Jo Bonnier and himself from the GP scene. But he was determined to go all out to the very last. On a rainy August 14, 1967, he was testing new 15-inch wheels on his ancient Brabham-Climax at Silverstone prior to the first-ever championship Canadian GP when his road ran out. On his 6th lap of the empty track, the car swerved off the straightaway and crashed into an empty marshal's box. In a few hours, despite all modern medicine could do, Bob Anderson was dead. He was buried in St. Mary's Churchyard, Herndon, quite near where he was born.

GIL ANDERSON

It was 1910 and the farmers around Crown Point, Ind., knew only too well there was going to be an automobile race. All the competitors had been curdling the milk and scaring the chickens with huge cars which made enough noise to double for a thunderstorm. Some even went out to see what it was all about—cars going as fast as their drivers could force them over the twisting roads, while the riding mechanic tended the pumps and gauges. But one mechanic was otherwise engaged; he was hanging on to the front of the car for dear life. He seemed to be holding the radiator on!

It was Gilbert Anderson's racing debut and brought him fame immediately. Anderson was the riding mechanic for Adolph Monson and when, with about 60 miles to go, the radiator decided to detach itself, Gil cakewalked out to the front of the car and held it in place while Monson went full tilt at leader Louis Chevrolet. Louis beat them nevertheless, but Gil was famous.

In fact, Harry Stutz tapped him to drive his new car in a new 500-mile sweepstakes at Indianapolis May 30, 1911, forerunner of today's Memorial Day classic. Gil finished 11th under trying circumstances—the car had been put together barely in time for the race and had to pit 10 times for tire changes—but it was good enough for Stutz to open his famous national advertising campaign on "The Car That Made Good in a Day."

Anderson thus became a teammate of Earl Cooper

...easons. Mario was still free, when his ...edule would permit, to race for Fer... possibly, in the Canadian-American ...eries, if the Italian marque went that ...Andretti didn't do well starting in 1972, ...r lack of equipment or opportunity. But ...o plays a part. At Indy he was 8th when ...uel 3 laps from the finish. At Pocono he ...e gear trouble. At Ontario he blew the ...ctories in 1972. Oh, well, 1973 was an- ...th a new Parnelli car.

...ONS BROTHERS

...e 2 of them, heroes both, and they each held ...Land Speed Record. It never happened be- ...probably never will happen again: 2 brothers ...or this strange record in two competing efforts, ...ilding a machine that did the job.

...elder of the 2 Arfons brothers was Walter, born ...7, and the younger, by 9 years, was Arthur Eu- ...They were the sons of a chicken feed miller and ...time electrical contractor who lived near Akron, ...o. Neither distinguished himself in school, and up ...l 1953 when both were in the family business, nei- ...r showed any interest in land speed. Both, however, ...re avid private flyers. According to Art himself, he ...ppened on drag racing while taking his family for a ...unday ride to the airport.

He found the airport road blocked off and, down the ...road, a gathering of people. Thinking there had been a ...plane accident, he ran to investigate. The sight of these ...strange machines with their wondrous performance ...made an instant disciple of him. He went home and told Walt about it. For the following Sunday's meet they built a car, painted green with surplus tractor paint. The first Green Monster, sitting on one airplane wheel and 2 wheels from a Packard, with a '40 Olds engine and part of the frame of an Allis Chalmers tractor, soared down the quarter mile at 85 m.p.h., to the amusement of the experienced rodders.

Arfons says the ribbing they took made them deter- mined to build a more sophisticated car. Green Monster number 2 acquitted itself admirably in ATAA competi- tion near Akron. Eventually, there was a succession of Monsters, each more sophisticated than the last, as mechanical skills increased and experience taught the necessary ingredients of a winning dragster.

By 1960 Art Arfons was touring the country with a jet dragster giving exhibition runs at drag meets, and that fall he went to Bonneville, turning 342 m.p.h. in his jet car. The run gave Arthur and Walt their initial first- hand look at the problems of running the Salt Flats at speed. The brothers subsequently split, for reasons nei-

ther was interested in discussing publicly, but each had determined to return for a try at the record.

Art, meanwhile, continued his regular drag racing ef- forts. In 1961 he had shattered the 200 m.p.h. mark for a quarter-mile standing start, at Fort Worth, Tex., with a 209 m.p.h. run. In 1963 at Wingdale, N.Y., he topped this with 238 m.p.h. Two Bonneville efforts (over the short rodders' course) saw him go 270 and 313 m.p.h.

When the year of the Land Speed Record came, both Arthur and Walt were ready. On October 2, 1964, Tom Green drove the Wingfoot Express, named for its Good- year tires, to 413.2 m.p.h. to break the FIM (Fédération Internationale de la Motorcycliste) mark of Craig Breed- love (407.45). (Breedlove's car, a 3-wheeler, was tech- nically a motorcycle at this time.) But Walt hadn't even made it back to his motel when Art climbed into the latest Green Monster for a shakedown run. He had never run it at speed before; the car felt so good that the very next day, October 5, Art upped the record to 434.

Then Breedlove almost killed himself, wrecking his Spirit of America on October 16 while setting a new mark of 526.28 m.p.h. But the year was not over, for Art, already back in Akron, pointed his converted school bus-trailer west again and returned the Monster to Bonneville. On October 27, 1964, he did one leg at 571 m.p.h. and averaged 536.71 m.p.h. for the mile to recapture the record.

Breedlove returned to the salts the following year, on November 3, 1965, averaged 555.127 m.p.h. The stage appeared to be set for another round robin of rec- ord smashings when Art retook the course 4 days later,

and the original Howdy Wilcox. He finished in a dead heat with Earl in the only Indy 300, but after much in- decision the judges awarded the prize to Cooper. In No- vember, Anderson placed 4th in the Vanderbilt Cup at Milwaukee, then took 3rd in the 409-mile Milwaukee Grand Prix three days later. His was the only American car to finish, and the smallest machine of American manufacture ever to place in a GP race. In the Indy 500 of 1913, Anderson led briefly before 5 pit stops for tires dropped him to third. October 9, 1915, Anderson's Stutz crossed the finish line at the new Sheepshead Bay Speedway in Brooklyn, N. Y., taking the victory in the inaugural 350-mile Astor Cup race. His average speed was 102.60 m.p.h., the fastest time up until then for a race of that length.

Anderson raced in 1919 on the Indy Speedway- owned Premier racing team, but retired soon after to become an engineer for the Stutz Motor Co. and later for Revere Motors of Logansport, Ind.

EMIL ANDRES

The long-time USAC stock-car supervisor was a grizzled veteran of the racing wars who couldn't abide the idea of working at anything else. Born July 22, 1911, in Chicago, Emil Andres began racing stock cars at the old Evanston Motor Speedway in the depths of the Depression. It was one way to make money, and better than just hanging around like other 20-year-olds. The purses were woefully small though the fields were large. Within a year, Andres switched successfully to sprint cars, winning 17 consecutive features.

At the age of 23 Emil entered AAA competition, finishing 8th for the season and becoming a favorite throughout the Midwest for his daring driving tactics. Contemporaries say Andres would rather risk his life than move over an inch to let another driver get through. He learned better at Indianapolis in 1935, when he ruined his car in a trophy dash. The following year he finished 12th. But his best finish came in the 1946 run, when he was nosed out for 3rd by Ted Horn. He competed for 5 seasons after the war, finish- ing in the top 5 in 17 of 33 races.

Andres later went into race promotion and eventually became an official of USAC, when it began crowning stock car champs. He was known as a stickler for safety, allowing nothing of a questionable nature to get past his experienced eye.

MARIO ANDRETTI

Luigi Chinetti leaned over the wide desk in his Ferrari showroom in Connecticut and asked in his Italian ac- cent, polished through years of speaking broken En- glish to millionaires and American race drivers, "This

Andretti, what do you think of him? I have heard he drives American racers well. Do you think we could trust him with a Ferrari?" The answer was unequivocal. The old Le Mans hero's North American Racing Team would be getting a man with great potential. And Mario Andretti, all 5 feet 3 inches of him, was happy to ac- cept the ride, just as he was happy to get his first modi- fied stock-car ride or his first sprint ride or his first championship single-seater. It was only a year later that Luigi said, "Mario will show the world if he will drive in sports cars and Grand Prix. He can be the best."

Mario Gabriele Andretti was born in the village of Montana on the Adriatic Sea February 28, 1940. His father, Alvise, had owned several farms in the area, and there had been bishops named Andretti but no race drivers. After the war, that part of the Istrian Peninsula was ceded to Yugoslavia. After time in a displaced per- sons camp, the family moved to Lucca, outside Florence. Here Mario and twin brother Aldo learned that there was such a thing as automobile racing. "We lived across the street from a garage," Andretti recalled. "We hung around and watched the men work on cars, sometimes for races. We heard about Monza and the Mille Miglia, and one year the garage owners promised to take us to see both races. There was one long straight near Flor- ence in the Mille Miglia where the cars would come up in a wide sweep toward the turn where we stood. It was the most exciting thing to me since I had seen my family cheering and yelling when they heard the war was over. Those fast cars and the noise and the people yelling the name of the driver when he drove past. Aldo and I thought it was great. My hero was Alberto Ascari."

It wasn't long after this that the twins were intro-

duced to driving. There was one motorcycle, and there was a sort of Formula racing, with cars based on the Fiat Topolino. Mario and Aldo shared the motorcycle and the car. "My brother was better then, I think, because he was braver, and he was the one who tried harder. The family didn't like it when we came home all skinned up. They thought we should have more serious things to do. The only person I told that the bruises were from racing was my priest, and he couldn't tell on me because I told him in confessional." In 1955, Papa Andretti brought his boys to Nazareth, Pa., courtesy of his wife's relatives, and there they discovered modified racing. The pair worked in their uncle's gas station where they thought only of getting their own car. Aldo's edge lasted for 4 races after the boys pooled resources to buy a modified 1948 Hudson—Mario won 2 of them and Aldo 2. Aldo was running his 3rd race when the car flipped at Hatfield, Pa., fracturing his skull so badly he was in a coma for about a week. When he woke up he is supposed to have said, "Considering everything, I'm sure glad you were the guy to have had to tell Dad."

Mario had been frightened stiff. He called his mother after the accident and told her Aldo had fallen off the top of a truck while watching him race and had been knocked out. He slept in the hospital that night, finally telling his family the truth only after the police threatened to contact his home. Yet the boys bought another modified the following year, and for a while their father would not speak to them. Aldo has tried racing several times since, with little success to date. He married and the boys eventually drifted apart, Aldo moving to Indianapolis and the tire business. Mario, meanwhile, rose through three-quarter midgets, midgets, and modifieds over the next few years, working in the day as a mechanic and driving nights and weekends. "I remember the day I decided to give it a full shot, once and for all," Andretti reminisced. "It was Labor Day, 1963. I had won 3 out of 4 at Flemington, N.J.; then we hauled to Hatfield that night and I won 4 straight in my midget. I knew then that 1964 was going to be it. I had to hustle up a ride."

The unique thing about native American oval track racing is the willingness to gamble on a rookie if there are any credentials at all. This is especially so the further below USAC championship-type cars one goes. Mario had impeccable credentials. He got his initial championship ride at Trenton and spun out. He still had a sprint car ride, and he was resigned to trying for the sprint championship first, then moving on.

But at New Bremen, Ohio, a dangerous bullring of a track, Chuck Hulse, the contract driver for Dean Van Lines, was injured, leaving their Indy ride open. So Mario asked Rufe Grey, his sprint car owner, to get him in to see Clint Brawner, Dean's chief mechanic. He saw Brawner, but nothing happened; the car was kept out of the 500. However, Andretti impressed

Brawner in a sprint at Terra Haute, Ind., and Clint gave him the call. "Clint is the greatest guy to have in the pits. He told me when I climbed into the Dean Van Lines Special for that first race: 'Take it easy and learn. We got time,'" Mario said. "He knew I was going to go out there and go as fast as I could. But it took the pressure off me." Driving the front-engine Offy roadster, Mario led 2 late season races, but didn't win. He was still considered a rookie for the 1965 season, but he was on his way.

That winter Brawner joined the funny-car forces with his Hawk-Ford, based on Jack Brabham's chassis design for oilman John Zink and powered by the d.o.h.c. Ford. The car wasn't finished until May, and Mario took his first ride ever in a rear-engine car at Indianapolis. "The car felt so secure, it scared me. I felt as if I could do anything with it and I wondered if it would give warning if it was breaking away," Andretti said. He went out and set marks on the first day of qualifying, ending 4th fastest because Jim Clark, Dan Gurney, and A. J. Foyt broke his marks that very day. His 3rd-place finish in the race started him on the way to the season point title with a record of 1 victory at Indianapolis Raceway Park—and 10 finishes in the top 4 out of 17 races. He was the first rookie champion in decades. He repeated in 1966 without benefit of Indy points, though he sat on the pole for the Big One. He set a record by leading 500 consecutive miles of Championship Trail racing in annexing the Milwaukee 100, the Langhorne 100 and the Atlanta 300, ending with 8 victories in 15 events.

We come back to that conversation in Luigi Chinetti's office in the summer of 1965. It put Andretti at the wheel of a blue Ferrari for the Double 500 World Championship GT race at Bridgehampton that September, his initial ride in a car of this type. Unfamiliar with a 5-speed box, Mario missed shift after shift. He eventually went out with clutch trouble, but not before improving his lap times by 27 seconds. "I used to dream about this when I was a kid back in Italy," he said. "It's as scary as I thought then, but it's great. These cars go like crazy if you hit the loud pedal. They're a real challenge and I think I'm getting the hang of it." Andretti paired with Pedro Rodriguez to take 4th in a Ford sweep at the 1966 Daytona Continental 24-Hour race. It was then that Chinetti spoke of his potential. After winning Sebring, Mario went to Le Mans in 1967 with the Ford team and suffered a hairline fracture of a rib when his mount swerved into the wall and teammate Jo Schlesser hit him. But he set a new lap mark (equalled by Denis Hulme) of 3:23.6, 7 seconds faster than Gurney's old mark. The crash slowed his USAC defense, but he was set to go road racing again for Ford in the CanAm series.

There was another event that gave Andretti great satisfaction—the 1967 Daytona 500, big daddy of the stock car races. "In 1965 I had that Smokey Yunick

20

Chevelle for the 500," Mario said. "It would go good for awhile but it was too new to have all the bugs out. I'll race anything on four wheels, but this was special—all that money for winning and the chance to beat those NASCAR drivers in their own kind of racing. But it was the money, too, and my pride."

Daytona's 500-mile race is an atavistic fantasy. The good ol' boys of stock-car racing have acquired a veneer of modernity; the veneer has been polished with bags of greenbacks. But underneath is an element of clawing competition that erupts occasionally on the track when drivers feud with fenders, oblivious of the result of the "sporting spectacle." Andretti had a Holman-Moody Fairlane 427 and 12th place on a 50-car starting grid. Curtis Turner's Chevelle was on the pole and all the panoply, pulchritude and passion of the spectacle had peaked into the pulsating tension of the pace laps with the pounding roar of 50 unmuffled racers ready to erupt when the green flag fell.

The leaders were bunched like lemmings when it fell, running within a foot of one another at 180 m.p.h. But the caution flag—one of 9 displayed—fell quickly, too, after only 15 miles and a Chevvy spinout. It came out again after 60 miles when a Ford spun. Most of the leaders pitted for gas. Not Mario; he gambled and took the lead for the 10 caution laps. Paul Goldsmith's Plymouth grabbed it back on the green, lost it almost at once. Mario was riverboat gambling on gasoline fumes. In the backstretch he motioned Goldsmith by, preparing to dive down for his pit stop. Buddy Baker's Dodge proved 3 was a crowd and Cale Yarborough in a Ford was right behind. Baker broke the draft, diving for the lead on turn 3; the air shock sent Goldsmith into a long lazy spin, Yarborough spinning too. Both dropped back and eventually dropped out. Baker and teammate Innes Ireland were both to blow their engines.

Meanwhile, the 100-mile dice for the lead was drawing to a close and Mario was not among the top 5. He was 6th at 200 miles, with Curtis Turner making the pace and Freddy Lorenzen charging. Soon after, Turner's Chevelle blew its engine, and Richard Petty dropped out along with Don White, Ramo Stott, and Dick Hutcherson. Then Lee Roy Yarbrough spun, and suddenly it was Andretti and Lorenzen versus David Pearson. And since Fearless Freddie was following his long-time practice of slipstreaming, that meant Mario against Pearson. When Pearson retired on lap 159, the pit stops became all-important and Mario came in like clockwork, was refuelled and charged out again. He led at 300 miles, at 400 miles and at that long-awaited checker, with only Lorenzen in the same lap. The early gamble had paid off and Mario Andretti, USAC, joined the sparse list of drivers who had beaten the NASCAR heroes at their own game.

An era came to an end in Mario's life when Al Dean died. Andretti bought the Dean racing equipment and sponsored himself, with Brawner and co-chief mechanic

21

Jimmy ... was ... was ... win un... USAC s...

The er... season wh... time to lea... STP oil addi... the entire An... son, and the co... race but also th... the 1965–69 peric... 27 championship ... $750,000 in that tin...

A winner at Sebrin... reached in 1970 for th... in an earlier era. He ex... Formula 1, CanAm, and ... plane schedules. The plan... crashed his new Indianapo... trucking strike, and was forc... Indianapolis also proved a w... never in contention for the lead... approach to F1, signing with Sc...

He began 1971 in rather auspi... the South African GP at 112.36... race for Ferrari, in rather easy fashio... seconds ahead of Stewart, who would... Champion. He won the next race, th... GP in Ontario, Calif., a 2-heat combi... and Formula 5000 cars. Stewart was th... tion again. Jackie drew even with Mario's... points—the first time an American had led... early season—at Spain, as Andretti's Ferrar... the 51st lap. Monaco was passed up, and so w... and Britain after a 4-lap Dutch GP. Andretti... few more points with a 4th in the German GP, th... ped Austria and Italy. He was 13th in Canada an... to forego the U.S. GP for a postponed Trenton... USAC race. His 12 points earned him 8th place in... standings. Not so auspicious after all.

Nor were Mario's USAC races any better. His be... finish in 1971 was a 2nd, worse even than the solitary... victory of 1970. The McNamara-Fords had teething... problems, and Andretti and Granatelli were not happy... STP and Andretti parted company in October, 1971, the... agreement finally being made on the grounds of the... White House as President Richard Nixon was honoring... motor racing. It was as amicable as a thing could be in... the circumstances. Andretti wasn't unemployed for long... Within the week an announcement came from Torrance, Calif., and Mario Andretti, national champion of 1969, became the teammate of Al Unser, national champion of 1970, and Joe Leonard, national champion of 1971, all together on the Vel-Parnelli Jones USAC team. Between them, the trio had won 4 of the 6 USAC 500-mile races

held over those 3 s... 17-race USAC sc... rari in F1 and... Challenge Cup o... way as well. If... it wouldn't be f... racing luck als... he ran out of... was 7th desp... engine. No ... other year w...

but disaster waited in the wings. On his first run, Arfons was clocked at 575.72. On the second run, he clocked 577.386—averaged out to a new LSR of 576.553 m.p.h.—before a right rear tire exploded. Art was almost asphyxiated in the Monster's smoke-filled cockpit before he loosed the housing to clear his cockpit. Fiber glass parts shattered, the car careened from side to side and finally came lurching to a halt, but Arfons emerged unscarred, if stunned.

Arfons's mishap lifted a lot of pressure off Breedlove, of course, so that he was afforded the luxury of waiting for just the right conditions. On November 15, 1965, his 2 runs—one at better than 608 m.p.h.—added up to a new record of 600.6, a mark that was to last until 1970 when Gary Gabelich would go 622.407 in a rocket car that put the jet cars of Arfons and Breedlove to shame.

Art Arfons had one last crack at the Salt and the LSR in 1966. In that trial, November 17, he crashed at better than 600 m.p.h., yet lived. Testing had gone well, and the run was in good order until Arfons neared the measured mile mark (his off-course run having been better than 3 miles). Without warning, a front wheel came off. The car nosed down, then rebounded. More wheels came flying off, and the body might have somersaulted, but Art had already reacted by releasing the parachute. The opening chute helped right the car momentarily; it settled on one side and slid a mile or more along the salt, still enclosing—and, as it turned out, protecting—Arfons.

All that was left when the car finally stopped was the driver's compartment, its plexiglass shield blown away. Arfons was sandblasted raw, had a few cuts, and the retina of one eye was scratched. Otherwise, he was unharmed. He said he would return to the Salts again, but he never did, for one reason or another. He talked of going after the water speed record in a jet or rocket boat, but he didn't do that either. And who could blame him? But he did return periodically to the drag exhibition circuit until his out-of-control, crashing car killed three people in 1971. Art quit on the spot.

CAMERON ARGETSINGER

Watkins Glen, N.Y., is the site of the U.S. Grand Prix, and seems likely to remain so for many years to come. The rolling countryside of central New York, however, would never have housed one of the premier Formula 1 courses in the world had it not happened that a Youngstown, Ohio, lad named Cameron Argetsinger, born in 1921, spent his summers in the adjoining village of Burdett.

Argetsinger loved the area, and he loved the sports cars that echoed through the streets of the Glen even before the first round-the-town race. He was among the pioneers who founded the Watkins Glen Grand Prix

Corporation, and almost from the beginning, his was the executive talent behind it. He even drove in some of the early races. From the time when tragedy forced the end of street racing, through the abortive first closed courses, and on into the 2.3-mile closed course of the seventies, Argetsinger was a guiding force.

Father of 9 children, Argetsinger spent many years building the prestige of the Glen. It was he who made sure that most of the profits were plowed back into some facet of course improvement or spectator improvement or—failing these—into prize money. It was he who made Watkins Glen the first $100,000 GP race in the world. Independently wealthy, Cameron eventually tried to buy the non-profit corporation from his fellow villagers as a personal investment. They declined to sell, and Argetsinger resigned, effective May 1, 1970. Meanwhile, he accepted the task of expanding Chaparral Cars, Inc., Jim Hall's enterprise in Midland, Tex., a job he left to become director of pro racing for SCCA at the beginning of 1972.

ZORA ARKUS-DUNTOV

It was 1960, and a big, businesslike racing car was touring the country, making its appearance at the U.S. Grand Prix, at Pikes Peak, at Daytona, and at Riverside, where Stirling Moss took it around the International Speedway and pronounced it "a really big banger" of a car. The CERV-1, standing for the first Chevrolet Experimental Research Vehicle, was the brainchild of a slight, silverhaired gentleman who didn't look like a racer, but who lapped Daytona in his creation at better than 167 m.p.h., and who talked the language of the racing crowd, from Dr. Ferdinand Porsche to Briggs Cunningham.

This was Zora Arkus-Duntov, born in Belgium about 1911, raised in Russia, educated in Germany, a racer on 2 continents before and after World War II. Much of Arkus-Duntov's life story is shadowy, in spite of the easy access people have had to him since he joined Chevrolet in May 1953, after General Motors management had been impressed by a technical paper he contributed to *Automotive Engineer*. One finds scraps of information here and there, such as the story that he learned to drive in Russia as a chauffeur's assistant. His German education was capped by an engineering degree from the Institute of Charlottenburg in Berlin (1934), and he joined Dr. Porsche on the prewar Auto Union racing car development.

When Arkus-Duntov joined Chevvy he still had ties to Porsche, driving the silver German cars at Le Mans in 1954 and 1955, and scoring class victories each year, although Ferrari and Jaguar took the big overall crowns. In 1956, Zorro, as he was sometimes affectionately called, scored a stock car record behind the wheel of a

Chevvy at Pikes Peak; he also set a world's record for the flying mile in a Corvette at Daytona Beach. The following year at Sebring, he supervised Corvette's effort in the 12-hour race.

Arkus-Duntov's last official competitive ride was in a Maserati in a Formula Libre race at Lime Rock, Conn., in 1960. There was talk the following year of his attempting to qualify for the Indianapolis 500, but discretion prevailed (perhaps some of it his own), and his highspeed driving was subsequently limited to the test tracks.

His personal racing career was perhaps not the most spectacular, but the success of the Corvette as the first American sports car, the competition work of Chevrolet (despite its continuing "unofficial" status), and his influence on American automotive design generally have made Arkus-Duntov an integral part of the motor sport scene.

BILLY ARNOLD

There never was a gamer driver than Billy Arnold. He was a product of Chicago's tough South Side, and he learned to look out for himself the hard way. Arnold began racing in the twenties, the Golden Era of sports in America, at Roby Speedway. He barnstormed the Midwest for several years, earning the reputation of being a hard driver: hard on himself, hard on his competitors, and hard on the cars. Billy naturally gravitated toward the Indianapolis Speedway; it was the normal thing to do. The most money at one shot was there, and the best drivers, and above all, the best cars.

For example, the Boyle Valve Special. Millionaire Pete Boyle gave it to Billy for his rookie start at Indy in 1928. Billy pushed the car to a 7th-place finish, following directions scrupulously in order to make sure he was around at the end. In 1929, he won 8th-place money, again under orders to finish. For 1930 he was offered 2 rides in semi-stocks, but he wanted a Miller-engined mount; he was convinced that one of these would be the winning car. Harry Hartz owned one of them, but he expected to drive it himself if he recovered from injuries sustained in a crash at Salem, N.H., board track. When Harry didn't quite make it, he looked for a pilot.

Hartz's choice, Ralph Hepburn, wanted the car changed to his own specifications, which Hartz was unwilling to do except as a last resort. Meanwhile, Arnold, only partly through sheer admiration for the Miller, had become a fixture at the Hartz garage space. It was almost qualifying time, and Hartz had almost determined to run himself. The stop watch told him the bitter truth —he wasn't ready to stand on it. But there was the ubiquitous Arnold, playing one-man admiration society. Hartz let him try the car out, then asked what he thought of it.

"I wouldn't change a single thing. It's perfect," Arnold said. These were the magic words, and the result was an Indianapolis 500 champion. After putting it on the pole at 113.268 m.p.h., the 23-year-old, stubby, round-faced Billy took over the lead on the 3rd lap and ran to a 4-lap lead by the halfway point, despite big signs of "E-Z" and "SLOWER" from Hartz. Billy was having a ball out there, and though it must have been a joy to the fans, the speed was no comedy to Hartz, who feared for the engine. Arnold didn't slacken his pace even when Harry put up a sign saying "10 MILES" with an arrow pointing back.

Finally Hartz, in a blue rage, jumped onto the pit wall and shook his first at Billy each time he passed. When Arnold finally pitted for fuel and tires on his 111th lap, Hartz informed him that the prize money was the same no matter how great a lead he built up, unsympathetic to the plea that the car felt "real good at speed." Since Hartz was still lighting up like a mobile Christmas tree, Billy followed orders and won by 7.5 minutes, the first man to win without relief at over 100 m.p.h. average (100.448). The feat made him one of a dozen charter members of the Champion 100 Mile-an-Hour Club, founded in May, 1934.

Arnold's wide-open style made him a favorite on the dirt and board circuits, but it robbed him of a repeat victory at Indy in 1931. He was again far in the lead on the 162nd lap, with 87 miles to go, when his rear axle snapped on the northwest turn. He hit the wall; the right rear wheel flew 200 feet into the air, cleared a fence, and killed an 11-year-old playing a quarter of a mile away.

In 1932 Billy was belting along in the lead, 1:18 ahead at the 100-mile mark, when he again belted the retaining wall and sailed over it, landing upside down. That apparently put the fear of destiny in him, for he retired not long afterward, turning down Hartz's $2,500 offer for 1933 to become a sales promotion man for a car company. He later earned fame as an Army Air Force officer in World War II, and found his fortune as an Oklahoma City contractor and real estate man.

PETER ARUNDELL

If you were a betting man, there was a fair-haired, well-built athlete on whom several years ago you would have wagered more than a few dollars that he would make it big in Grand Prix racing. But that was before the years, and a terrible crash that nearly ended his life, caught up with Peter Arundell of England. He last raced in 1969, not in a Formula 1 car, but in a Formula Vee. Since then, Arundell has stuck to flying and selling cars, not racing them.

Arundell was born November 8, 1933, at Ilford, Essex. "I drove my first car at 11," he recalled, "but it was in 1954, at 20, that I really began to compete, and that was in club races in an MG TC. That car carried me a long way the next three years; all the way, in fact, to my first major race at Goodwood." Arundell was in the Royal Air Force in those days (1952–55) and, despite the fact that his father, who operated a one-man garage, had given him early exposure to cars, he was expected to become an industrial chemist.

He was casting about for something to do after he left the RAF when his amateur racing successes sparked the idea of driving professionally. Driving his own Lotus 11 and the cars of Jack Wescott (Lotus) and Frank Nichols (Elva), Arundell attracted the attention of Colin Chapman, who signed him to drive for his Lotus Formula Junior factory team in 1960. Peter scored his initial victory for Lotus at Snetterton late that season.

For 2 years Arundell played 2nd fiddle to Trevor Taylor on the Lotus FJ team, then took over as team leader when Taylor was moved up to the Lotus F1 squad. Peter, too, was slated for a GP drive whenever a 3rd Lotus was entered in international competition, but the shifting plans of Chapman failed to provide that opportunity. The Lotus 22 FJ car was a demanding car as well as a successful one, and Arundell placed first 18 times in 25 starts. He won the FJ title for Lotus, as had Jim Clark and Taylor the 2 previous seasons.

Of these days, Arundell recalled most vividly his one-man "race" of December 2, 1962. "Richard von Frankenberg, the former driver and now a motor sport journalist, wrote an article in which he accused our team, among others, of using oversize engines in order to win as many races as we did. He challenged Colin to run an inspected, standard Lotus 22 at Monza, to prove I could lap it at the same speed as when I won there a few months before. We did it, of course, and we won."

All Arundell did was drive 30 laps around the high-speed oval at an 115.99 m.p.h. average, easily beating his race-recorded mark of 113.47 m.p.h. Not only that, but in a 3-lap bit of extra relish, Peter averaged a spectacular 117.14 m.p.h. despite patches of ice on the track. The "victory" was worth almost $3,000 to Chapman, which covered his expenses for the demonstration of the prowess of both car and driver.

In 1963 Arundell again won the British FJ crown in the Lotus and cemented his unofficial title as the uncrowned king of that class. The same season, he finished 2nd in 2 non-championship F1 races, in one trailing John Surtees at Enna. In 1964, with FJ racing virtually at an end, Chapman finally moved Arundell up to bigger mounts as the teammate of defending World Champion Clark.

In his first F1 championship year, Peter started and finished 4 races and came in tied for 8th in the standings. He was 3rd at Monaco and Zandvoort, site of the Dutch GP; 9th at Spa in the Belgian GP; and 4th at Rouen in the French GP. But Arundell's season came to an end in July when he was driving in the Formula 2 chase at Rheims. His Lotus spun in front of Richie Ginther's car, which hit it broadside, and carried Jo Rindt's mount with it to the sidelines. Thrown clear as his car flipped, Arundell suffered a broken collarbone, broken arm, broken thigh, severe concussions, and a bruised hip.

It was a full 18 months before Arundell essayed a test drive in a Lotus 41 Formula Three car at Brands Hatch. A few laps after he started that December 9, 1965, test, Peter's lap times were only 3 seconds above the course record, and half an hour later he was a fraction of a second away from that mark. On January 1, 1966, the recovered driver started his first race since July, 1964, the non-championship South African GP. He finished 3rd in this opening race of the new 3-litre F1 series, in a 1965 1.5-litre Lotus-Climax.

The bigger Lotus-BRM put in an appearance the first time at the Belgian race, but Peter's car dropped a valve and failed to start. In the French race, at Rheims, his car lasted 3 laps before falling out with gearbox trouble. The same thing that got him at the British GP 2 weeks later after 32 laps, ignition trouble, sidelined Peter at Zandvoort. He finally completed a championship race at Nurburgring in the German GP, where he was 12th. Arundell didn't finish the Italian race, but was classified 8th. At Watkins Glen, Peter finished 6th, and in the Mexican finale he was 7th. All of this added up to a single World Championship point; Arundell had his health back, but his skills had not been regained. In 1967, Graham Hill replaced Arundell on the Lotus team, and 2 years later Hill won his 2nd World Championship in that post. It must have been a bitter moment for Peter Arundell.

ALBERTO ASCARI

Alberto Ascari was born July 13, 1918, when his father, Antonio, was still a relatively unknown mechanic and car salesman. He was only 7 when Antonio died in the French Grand Prix at the height of his racing career, yet all his life Alberto retained vivid memories of his father. Antonio had taken his young son for rides in his Alfas in those waning days of side-by-side seating for drivers and mechanics.

Four years later, Alberto had his first taste of competition when, as any 11-year-old son of a racing great might do, he borrowed a neighbor's motorcycle and "raced" around a previously quiet Italian piazza. In the years that followed, the young Ascari raced rented cycles, building up his confidence and skills. In 1936, after he left the umpteenth private school because schoolwork was boring, Alberto's mother finally gave up and helped him buy a 500-c.c. Sertum.

On June 28, 1936, Alberto Ascari made his racing debut in 2-wheeled competition; like his father, he failed to finish his initial race. But 6 days later, in a repaired and finely tuned machine, he won at Lario. Ascari gained some renown over the next 3 years as a cycle ace. He was a factory cyclist with Bianchi and the head of a fuel-transporting firm to North Africa (which was to gain him exemption from Mussolini's armies). On April 28, 1940, in the closed-circuit Mille Miglia of that year, Ascari entered his initial 4-wheel competition in a new marque's new car.

Alberto's 1.5-litre, 8-cylinder 815, Enzo Ferrari's first car away from Alfa Romeo, took the lead in the race, but fell by the wayside with a seized valve. The same year, Ascari was 9th in a 6CM Maserati in the last Tripoli GP. He failed to finish in the Targa Florio. But by now, Italy was at war, and it was 1947 before Ascari raced again.

He started with the new Cisitalia marque, but did not do well until he left them. His initial victory came on September 28, 1947, when he took a Modena sports car race in a Maserati. In his first full season, Alberto, or Ciccio as he was nicknamed, won the San Remo GP and the Pescara sports car race, and was runner-up in the British GP. In 1949 Ascari joined Ferrari's factory team and won the Bari, Italian and Swiss Grands Prix and the Silverstone International Trophy Race, among others. Travelling to South America, he drove a Maserati and won the Peron GP at Buenos Aires. The year 1952 brought Alberto's first World Championship title; before that he had scored in 2 German Grands Prix, the Italian GP and more than a dozen other major races, plus accumulating a hatful of 2nds and 3rds. In his 1st championship year, Ciccio won Grands Prix in Belgium, Britain, France, Germany, Holland and Italy. The following season he repeated his championship with victories in the Argentine, Belgian, British, Dutch and Swiss Grands Prix. Then he left Ferrari for Lancia, although the driver and Enzo remained friends.

In 1954, Ascari's only victory was the Mille Miglia, for Lancia was not yet ready for the Formula 1 grind, even if they did have the world's best driver. Vittorio Jano, in whose Alfa Romeo P.2 Alberto's father had died in 1925, was Lancia's chief engineer and had another good machine ready for 1955. It was in this car that Ascari scored Lancia's initial GP victory on March 27, in the Valentino GP. He quickly produced another victory in the Naples GP, then entered the important Monaco GP, which that year was also the European GP. On the 81st lap of Monaco, just as Ascari was about to take over the lead, his wheels locked and he was thrown into the harbor.

Ciccio emerged from the incident with only a broken nose, despite his 110 m.p.h. takeoff. But he was shaken; he withdrew from the Monza 1000 sports car race scheduled a week later. Back in Modena Ascari felt better and decided he needed a short, speedy drive to settle his nerves still more. His old employer, Ferrari, was only too glad to lend the seemingly recovered champion a car for a few laps on the Autodrome on May 26, 1955. On his third lap of the high-speed circuit, as he approached the circuit's 3rd curve—now called Curva Ascari—he braked, and the Ferrari's wheels locked.

Car and driver hurtled along the course; Ascari was finally thrown from the machine just as his father had been, years before. He died in the ambulance on the way to the hospital just as his father had. And he left a wife, a daughter, and a son, who was destined to try his hand at racing, just as his father; Antonio Ascari, or Tonino, born in 1942, raced single-seaters with limited success.

In all, Alberto Ascari won 47 international races in 56 starts in his 9 years of top-flight racing. He displayed virtuoso skill, coupled with great self-control, an engaging personality and inherent modesty despite his accomplishments. His two World Championships attest to the junior Ascari's ranking as one of the greatest of Italian drivers.

ANTONIO ASCARI

Antonio Ascari lit the way for his son in the world of automotive competition. Born September 15, 1888, in Bonferro di Sorga, a tiny village in Italy's province of Verona, Antonio was about 12 when the family moved to Milan. He found himself swept up in the Italian industrial revolution.

Like many another driver of his day, Antonio started as a bicycle mechanic. He graduated to automobiles with the short-lived De Vecchi firm, which gave its young foreman his competitive opportunity in the Modena 6 Days endurance race in 1911. Ascari's factory entry failed to win, nor did his driving skill electrify observers of the race, although in later years—by hindsight—it was recalled with such adjectives as "acrobatic" and "spectacular." When De Vecchi closed its doors, Antonio was fortunate enough to find a place with Alfa Romeo. His racing career, however meager, became even more so after the outbreak of World War I.

It was 1919 before Ascari—now married and the father of a 1-year old son, Alberto—returned to racing, some say at the encouragement of famed driver-singer Giuseppe Campari. The 31-year-old was a frugal man and had managed to save enough money to buy a 4.5-litre Fiat destined originally for Indianapolis but sidetracked by the war. In this mount, Ascari won both the Parma-Poggio di Berceto and Coppa della Consuma hillclimbs, important races in that day. But a crash in the Targa Florio put him on the sidelines for nearly 2 years.

Alfa Romeo cashed in on Ascari's competition reputation by making him a sales agent, but he returned to the Italian national driving scene in 1921. Soon he was a factory driver, teamed with Campari and Ugo Sivocci.

In 1923, the first of his big years, Antonio won the initial Cremona race in a 3-litre car, finished 2nd in the Targa Florio, and was 3rd in the Circuit of Mugello.

In 1924 the man and a new machine that was to become legendary came together: in Ascari's hands the Alfa Romeo P.2, designed by Vittorio Jano, set a fast pace throughout the season. Antonio came within 2 laps of the finish line in the lead of the French Grand Prix—his first race outside of Italy—when his engine quit (Campari won in a sister car); then endured similar fate in the Targa Florio within 50 yards of the flag. That autumn Ascari won the Italian GP—the initial one held at Monza—followed by codrivers Louis Wagner and Campari. His winning speed was 98.79 m.p.h. for the 497 miles.

In 1925 Ascari's victory in the European GP at Spa-Francorchamps at 74.56 m.p.h. signalled the start of a seemingly great season. But disaster was only a race away. In a light rain on July 26, 1925, at Montlhéry, France, with about 150 miles of the French GP gone and Ascari 4 minutes in the lead, his P.2 crashed. Antonio was coming out of a slightly uphill turn; what happened is pure conjecture, for no one was close enough to say for sure.

The belief is that Ascari's car skidded into a wire fence; normally he would have been able to recover from that, but a strand of wire from the fence entwined itself in the Alfa's wheel and locked it, making the vehicle uncontrollable. The car tore up the fence posts and spun down the track, throwing Antonio to the ground with great force. He died in an ambulance on the way to the hospital. Alfa withdrew from the race, although Campari had taken over Ascari's lead.

How far Antonio would have gone is something that no man ever will be able to say. His teammates and contemporaries in the racing field believe that he, like Juan Fangio, still had great years ahead of him despite his age (he was just shy of 37 at his death). One thing is sure. Unlike most drivers, Antonio left racing a future World Champion—his son.

RICHARD ATTWOOD

When Graham Hill won the World Driver's Championship in 1968, one of his key victories was the challenging race through the streets of Monaco. It was a scene of automotive carnage; only 5 of the 16 starters were running at the finish. But Hill could not coast home, for he was pressed hard and very unexpectedly by a BRM driven by Richard Attwood. It was the first time this young man had driven this particular type of car, and he had not competed at Monaco in any sort of car for 3 years. Yet he pressed Hill to the limit, ran the fastest lap of the day at 79.86 m.p.h. around the twisting course to set a record, and finished a mere 2.2 seconds behind

the champion after 2½ hours of racing.

Best of all, perhaps, Attwood was driving the BRM by default. He was given the mount (with a warning from the team managers not to drive over his head) at the last moment, grudgingly. In the early part of the race, in fact, he was subject to being called in at any sign of faltering; particularly after the regular team drivers, Piers Courage and Pedro Rodriquez, banged out their cars at 13 and 16 laps respectively.

His near-victory convinced the racing world that Attwood could successfully drive Formula 1 cars, even for an uncompetitive team, but BRM was as dubious as ever. Again, grudgingly, Richard was given some starts. A cracked water pipe knocked him out of the Belgian Grand Prix; he was 7th in the Dutch and French races; a leaking cooling system stopped him in the British GP; and he was 14th and last in the German battle. BRM then dropped him unceremoniously in favor of American Indy driver Bobby Unser—no doubt spurred on by Goodyear Tire money, for the U.S. manufacturer was pushing Unser at that moment. Unser was a disaster. He failed to start at Italy after a rules squabble, didn't appear for the Canadian GP, and blew 6 engines—5 in practice and the 6th in the race—in the U.S. GP. On top of that, he wrecked the car the last time the engine blew. Any grin on a certain British driver's face at his replacement's record was understandable.

Richard James David Attwood was born in Wolverhampton, Staffordshire, April 4, 1940, the younger son of a garage owner, auto dealer, and one-time Brooklands competitor. After graduating from Harrow, Attwood served a 4-year apprenticeship with Jaguar in Coventry, then moved into the family business as an assistant sales manager. He had started racing against his parents' wishes in BARC races in a Standard Eight at the age of 19. After that, he drove a Triumph TR-3 without a victory in more than 15 starts, but obtained his father's approval.

In 1961 Richard switched to the growing Formula Junior circuit and helped found the Midland Racing Partnership with 4 friends. His first season with the Cooper FJ was not too successful with only 1 win, but in 1962 he won 4 top British races—Silverstone, Snetterton, Aintree and Oulton Park—and finished 2nd at Goodwood, Rheims, and Monte Carlo in a qualifying heat. When MRP switched to Lola-Ford the next season, Attwood displayed even better form, including a victory at the FJ Monaco GP, and he took the Irish FJ crown despite a serious accident at Albi, in which he suffered a broken leg. Britain's automotive writers voted the schoolboyish-looking driver Rookie of the Year.

Taller than most top drivers, lean, and fair-haired (what was left of it), Attwood had his initial F1 drive in the Goodwood GP on Easter Monday, 1964, for BRM; he was 4th in a 2-year-old car. But the year really was auspicious for Dick in that he moved into Formula 2 in MRP's machines, which had been converted with Cosworth SCA powerplants. Attwood was 2nd to Jim Clark at Pau, then won the Vienna GP. He was also 2nd at the Albi GP and in the Eifelrennen, and 3rd at Aintree, but a converted FJ was no real match for regular F2 mounts. In 1965, Eric Broadley caught up with the Ford GT program, producing his new Lola-Cosworth car for the F2 wars. MRP stocked up with these, and Richard won the Rome GP, was 2nd again at Pau, 3rd at Crystal Palace, 4th at Snetterton, 5th at Karlsloga, and 6th at Brands Hatch.

In F1, driving for Tim Parnell's Lotus-BRM team, Attwood survived a crash at Monaco to score a 6th in the Italian GP for his initial World Championship points, but was far down in other championship races—12th at Zandvoort, 13th in the British GP, 10th in the Belgian race. His other drives included a 4.7-litre Ford GT at the Mallory Whitsun meet (2nd aggregate) and a Ferrari 250LM at the Rheims 12-hour race (4th shared with David Piper). In 1965, too, Attwood shared a Ferrari with Piper in the Kyalami 9-hour race in South Africa, scoring his initial victory of 3 (others: 1966 and 1969). The previous season Richard had pushed a Cobra to a class victory in the Nurburgring 1000 race; so his long distance, GT, prototype and sports car career was well launched, even if F1 was proving a problem.

In the Tasman Championship series in Australia and New Zealand at the start of 1966, Attwood and Jackie Stewart starred. The former nipped the latter in the Levin GP one week, then Stewart beat Attwood in the Lady Wigram Trophy the next. Both Britons were driving 2-litre BRM's Attwood filling in for Graham Hill, who took over the Australian races after Dick's fine New Zealand showings. The regular year was not a good one for Attwood; a 2nd in the Rheims GP and a 6th in the Albi GP were about the only F2 high spots. At Spa, co-driving a Dino 206 Ferrari for Maranello Concessionaires, he shared 6th place.

After 1966 Attwood's single-seater drives were few and far between. His only championship start in 1967 was in a Cooper-Maserati in the Canadian GP when he substituted for Rodriguez. He finished 10th. That winter, in the Tasman series in New Zealand and Australia, Richard again represented BRM in the early going, with Stewart taking over in the latter half of the series. Attwood was 3rd behind Clark and Stewart in the New Zealand GP and again in the Levin International. He was 2nd to Clark in the Teretonga race. There was nothing, really, to presage his surprising Monaco drive in 1968. In 1969, on the strength of the previous season's showing there, he got another Monaco ride, this time filling in for an injured Jochen Rindt in a Lotus 49. He finished 4th, earning 3 championship points.

In endurance racing, however, Attwood was doing rather well. In 1968 he codrove a 3-litre Porsche 908 with Hans Herrmann and Tatso Ikusawa to 6th place in the Watkins Glen 6-hour race. The following season he was 4th in the Nurburgring 1000 with Rudi Lins, 2nd with Vic Elford in the BOAC 500 at Brands Hatch, and 2nd again with Elford at the Glen 6-hour. These rides were all in the 908. With a new 4.5-litre Porsche 917 for the Austrian GP at Zeltweg—a prototype/sports car race despite its name—Richard and Brian Redman came in 3rd.

The year 1970 brought victory at Le Mans, where Attwood and Herrmann won in a 917. The same pair finished 3rd in the BOAC 1000 in a 917 and 2nd in the Nurburgring 1000 in 908. In the Targa Florio, Attwood and a little known codriver were 5th in a 908; in the Glen 6-hour he and Kurt Ahrens were 6th in a 917. The next day, Richard scored a 3rd in the Glen's Canadian-American Challenge Cup. Attwood and Herrmann teamed up at the Spa 1000 for a 6th, and he and Elford joined for the Austrian GP for a 4th, both rides in the 917.

Porsche repeated as champion in 1971, with Attwood again contributing important points. With Jo Bonnier, Dickie shared a Lola-FVC T212 in the Targa Florio, finishing 3rd. Teamed with Herbert Muller, Attwood appeared at Le Mans to seek a repeat of his 1970 feat. He came close, but not close enough. The 917K finished 2nd. In the Austrian 1000, Dickie was paired with Pedro Rodriguez and shared victory there. With Derek Bell at the Watkins Glen 6-hour, he was 3rd again in the last championship race for the big, beautiful 5-litre cars.

In November 1971, Attwood took the occasion of the

Kyalami race to announce his retirement from racing to tend the family business in Wolverhampton.

GIANCARLO BAGHETTI

Big things were expected of Giancarlo Baghetti, a short stocky Milanese who did not look Italian at all, except for his clothing, which was very much in the style of his native land. Every inch a professional driver, Carlo was the scion of a wealthy industrial family, and he became so involved in its financial transactions that his competition took on the coloration of the era of the playboy drivers.

Born December 25, 1934, Baghetti went into the family industrial empire at 18. He drove competitively for the first time just before his 22nd birthday; his car broke down, and the "season" ended almost as soon as it had started. In 1957 he used 2 Alfa Romeos—a Sprint Veloce and a Gulietta—to good advantage, starting in March with a second-place finish in the Coppa Vigorelli at Monza. The following season, Baghetti concentrated on the Veloce and again had a fine year in hill climbs, rallies, and the like. The Mille Miglia was a rally for the first time that year, and Baghetti, driving with his brother, Marco, was a surprise 2nd.

In 1959 Giancarlo switched to a Fiat Abarth 750 for pure racing purposes. He attracted enough attention for the factory to invite him to the Monza Autodrome

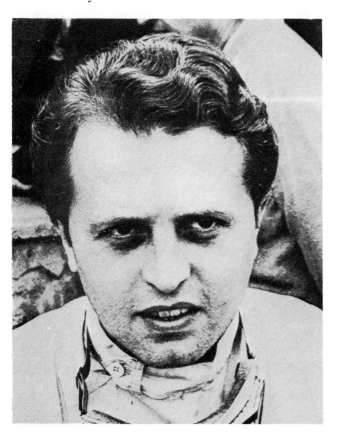

to help establish records for 7-day, 48-hour and 24-hour runs in an Abarth 1000. The following year Baghetti purchased a Dagrada Formula Junior (power by Lancia) and started single-seater competition, winning the Coppa Crivellari, the Fina, and the Vigorelli, all at Monza. The following season he was nominated by the organization of Italian racing stables as the most promising Italian driver in single-seater competition—a selection disputed by Lorenzo Bandini supporters. Enzo Ferrari, however, chose Baghetti as a team driver.

The Commendatore first put Baghetti in sports car events, starting at Sebring where he shared a V-12 with Belgium's Willy Mairesse until the car was taken over by Richie Ginther and Wolfgang von Trips; eventually it finished 2nd overall. He made his debut in Formula 1 at Syracuse (Italy), driving to an unexpected victory over a strong Porsche factory team. Almost at the heels of this victory came another in the Naples GP. After Nurburgring and Le Mans, Giancarlo was handed a rear-engined Ferrari for the French GP, his first World Championship event. Baghetti won the race, the first *grande épreuve* victory for an Italian-born driver since 1956 when Luigi Musso had shared such an honor with Juan Fangio in the Argentine GP. Baghetti's 4th victory of the year came toward the end of the season at Vallelunga in the Coppa Italia, and he was crowned Italian National Driving Champion.

In 1962 Baghetti was a regular Ferrari team member, and though the Maranello stable went nowhere that year, he finished with 5 World Championship points—11th on the list, or 1 better than teammate Bandini. Despite that, Bandini was retained and Baghetti was fired in a Ferrari purge of the competition department. Giancarlo signed with ATS, a new marque, which employed Phil Hill as well.

The season was a disaster for Baghetti, and he never regained the momentum of those startling few weeks in 1961. ATS cars were completely unsuccessful, and by the time Giancarlo abandoned the marque, he had been bypassed, much as Hill was. He had a dismal season driving Centro-Sud BRMs in 1964. Although he participated in some Italian Formula 3 and sports car events, the family business occupied most of his attention. He retired for good after the 1968 season.

LEN BAILEY

Born in Stratford-on-Avon in July 1928, Len Bailey could have been an accountant, as his family envisioned, but it would not have been as much fun as being a freelance automotive designer. Bailey decided early on his choice of career, and at 16 he was apprenticed to BMC in the Longbridge factory.

Bailey moved about BMC, first to the Coventry factory of Daimler (later taken over by Jaguar), then very

briefly to Rover—"pretty stodgy bunch," Len recalled—and finally back to the parent BMC as a member of its general engine department. In 1955, a 26-year-old Bailey took a plane to America and a job with American Motors. "They had few designers in those days," Len said, "but fairly unlimited budgets, despite the company's problems. I joined the research department and was part of the group that produced AMC's first V8 engine. It was still running the last time I looked in Roger Penske's 1972 Matadors in NASCAR racing."

It was while he was at AMC that Bailey started his long association with chassis design, as well as the power-train. By 1958 a better offer was at hand from the Ford Motor Co., and Len moved to Dearborn to work in its advanced engines department, but really he never made it. "I literally was highjacked as I walked down the corridor there by a chap I knew from my BMC days. He asked me to come into the experimental department where he worked, and the next thing I knew I was transferred there without ever working a day officially in engines."

Bailey had some interesting times at Ford, like slipping turbines in Thunderbirds and Fairlanes. "Took off like jet fighters, they did," he laughed. He also was involved in developing the Cardinal, which became the German Ford Taunus 12M, although it was strictly Detroit iron. Another project, this one with Roy Lunn, was the Mustang 1 prototype.

The time was about 1961. Bailey next was involved in one of the more exciting Ford projects of modern times. Because the Mustang prototype was so impressive, he was chosen to go with Lunn and some assistants back to England. Ford had just arranged to take over Eric Broadley's Bromley operation, to tie in with Broadley's Lola GT work and to develop a new car that was to become the Ford GT. Bailey still was there when the Ford Advanced Vehicles Operation was established at Slough with John Wyer, fresh from Aston Martin, as its head.

The basic GT40 was developed during the 1965-66 period, with Len involved in certain components and Lunn producing the car itself back in the States with KarKraft. Both closed coupes and open versions were produced, and Ford won at Le Mans, of course, in 1966 and also mounted up some private teams such as Alan Mann, Essex Wire and Holman-Moody. In 1967 another Bailey derivation of the basic car was introduced as the Gulf Mirage M1, with Wyer establishing JW Engineering, acquiring Slough and hiring Bailey for development of the design.

Ford's racing program was contracting, and Bailey took on other freelance assignments, including development of a replacement for the Cobra. "Shelby wanted a kind of American Lotus Super 7," said Len, "so I designed a car that was similar to my recent GT70. One prototype was built, but right then Shelby parted from Ford and the U.S. safety people really killed the project." Alan Mann got Bailey's services through Ford (Bailey was on their payroll steadily after 1958 as a consultant), and a CanAm car and later the F3L Cosworth V8-powered Ford prototype were produced. Len started work on the latter in November 1967, and the car rolled out the next March.

"We took two cars to the BOAC 500 at Brands Hatch, but we had only one decent engine. Mike Spence was leading when the bonding on a rubber driveshaft coupling failed. Then Chris Irwin was badly injured in practice at Nurburgring," said Bailey. "It was really a bad scene. But at the Martini Trophy at Silverstone, it was a last straw. Frank Gardner was taking the car through the backmarkers with Denis Hulme in hot pursuit in a big Lola when the F3L's camshaft failed. Later, we found out a bearing had been left out in assembly."

Funding was short so that project failed, as did the Ford P69, remembered in Britain as the 1969 BOAC 500 star with its twin-boom aerodynamics, a tail-mounted radiator and automatically operated aerofoils, not to mention its almost invisible cockpit; there was only a hole big enough to let the driver's head through once the car was buttoned up. On the side, meanwhile, Len developed a Tasman car for Gardner on a minimal budget. The Mildren-Alfa Romeo was not immediately successful, but it was still going strong in the 1972 Tasman three years later.

Other projects around the time were the very successful Alan Mann Escorts, virtually unbeatable in Gardner's hands, and a 1969 CanAm car that proved to be Ford's swansong in road racing for a time. When Ford withdrew, Mann went back to his aircraft maintenance business, which put Gardner and Bailey in business for themselves at Fairoaks Aerodrome. They raced an ex-TransAm Mustang, winning 9 of 11 British races, while Len was evolving the World Cup Rally Escorts that won the big event and the GT70 rally and road racing cars.

In November 1970 Bailey established himself at Gomm Metal Developments in Old Working, still working on an occasional Ford project and on freelance assignments like designing Frank Williams's Politoys Formula 1 car, introduced in 1972, and the Gulf Mirage M6 for John Wyer, born the same year. Versatile, prolific, imaginative, they all applied to Len Bailey.

BUCK BAKER

"It's like a century ago," said Elzie Wylie Baker, Sr. "It was a race in Greenville, S.C., and I was scared to death when I got out on that track. I don't remember when I couldn't drive a car, but this was different, although I didn't think it would be before I saw those other drivers. I realized they wanted to win that money —I don't remember how much it was—just as much as I did. I didn't have to worry. A tire came off my car and I was lucky I got it off the track."

It wasn't a century ago; it was 1939, and Buck Baker, born March 4, 1919, in Hartville, S.C., was just beginning a career that spanned the history of major-league American stock car racing. He became the grandfather of the NASCAR heroes—a feared and respected grandfather at that. For example, he won the Southern 500 at Darlington for the 3rd time in 1964. Only 1 other man in history had ever done that. Baker was champion of NASCAR twice (1956 and 1957), second twice (1955 and 1958) and 4 other times in the top 5. When he had really competitive machinery he was next to no one, but there were many years when he rode the ghost of a Chrysler legend or was otherwise ensnared in ill-founded hopes.

Buck drove modifieds upon occasion and even had a short fling at Indianapolis-type cars, but he always returned to the stockers. He set a new longevity record with every racing mile, a record not fully compiled because in the old outlaw days tracks sometimes disappeared as fast as the drivers got out of town.

"This track is like a teenage girl," he said at Darlington before the Southern 500 in 1964. "It changes face a hundred times a day. I never want to practice on this track any more than I have to. You can hit a greasy spot and wipe out your ride doing 90." He paused. "I want to win this one." He looked toward his white Dodge where Ray Fox, the master mechanic from Daytona Beach, was checking the innards, as if to indicate he had

the mount to do the job.

At that time Buck didn't look like the father of a 23-year-old son, Buddy, also a racing driver. There was hardly any gray in his luxuriant black hair and the little boy playing nearby, about 6, was a son by a second marriage. He didn't look like a man old enough to have been a sailor in World War II, a man who had once driven Greyhound buses.

He had started the season with one racing team, switched to another, then went with Fox in mid-season. He had won just 2 races in the past 3 years, in almost 100 starts, but one of them was in Fox's 1964 Dodge at Valdosta, Ga.

Back in 1953 Baker had won the Southern 500 in an Oldsmobile 88 at a record speed of 92.78. And in 1960 he entered the winner's circle again in a 1960 Pontiac at an average speed of 105.901. In 1964 the hot dogs were going 130, and Buck knew what he had to beat. But it would be done his way. "Those youngsters go out there to set a record and clinch the pole position," he said, "but what do you do if you wreck your car? That record doesn't spend too well."

Now it was race day, with Confederate flags waving, beauty queens by the score, and all those fans—some 80,000 of them—laughing, drinking, watching, eating, talking. The largest cook-out and camp-out in Dixie was in full swing in the infield, where more than 20,000 fans had been living for up to a week.

Baker had posted 135.162 m.p.h., against pole sitter Richard Petty's 136.815, and started 6th. When the pace cars pulled off the track and the race began, Buck stayed with the hard-charging blue Petty Plymouth, never out of the top 5, but never forcing matters. He let the track do the job for him. Of the 44 starters, 9 went out due to wrecks, 6 blew engines, 16 went out with mechanical trouble. Thirteen cars were running when Buck took the white flag 2 laps to the good of Jim Paschal in a Plymouth and 4 laps ahead of Petty. Baker had driven a steady race, respecting the 1.38-mile track, but remaining its consummate master. His winning average of 117.757 was slower than those of the previous 3 Southern 500 races but he, not the hot dogs, was the one with the $21,230 check in his pocket. When they asked him afterward if he was ever going to quit, Buck grinned. "When I think there are others who can do the job better, then I'll quit," he said.

He virtually retired from GN after 1967; most of his driving was in Grand American, capping a career that transcended the number of victories and the estimated $400,000 that he claimed to have won. Back in the early fifties, Bill France was in open warfare with AAA Contest Board. He convinced fellow NASCAR promoters that Indianapolis-type racing could provide an extra payoff data for them; thus the Speedway division was formed in 1952. The idea was good, but the cars were not—mostly old AAA machines or IMCA refugees fitted with stock passenger car engines. Nor were the tracks suitable because at that time, tracks as long as a mile were the exception, not the rule.

Baker won the division in a 7-race schedule in a Cadillac-engined car he had built largely to his own design. He won the May 10 Darlington classic, which carried a $10,000 purse, and the straightaway speed trials on the beach at Daytona, where his mount went 142 m.p.h. Other races were held at Martinsville, Va., Rochester, N.Y. (where NASCAR vice-president Ed Otto Sr. promoted), Heidelberg, Pa., Atlanta, and at Langhorne. The Speedway division later declined, with only 4 events in 1953 and none in 1954.

During the early years of NASCAR, Baker had run modified cars. "In 1950, I had one streak of 10 straight and another of 12 out of 14 victories," he said. After the demise of the Speedway series, he returned to Grand National racing, mostly as an independent. He carved out a career that saw him drive virtually every American marque that ever was run in NASCAR, compiling 46 official Grand National victories. And he enjoyed himself before, during and after each race.

In Grand American racing, Buck started in a Camaro, then switched to Pontiac Firebird. Through 1972 he won 8 races in 109 starts, but was in the top 10 sixty-three times, 44 of these in the top 5. In his fifties, Buck was still looking 15 years younger. He was still in good condition, still squeezing rubber balls to strengthen his grip, and still watching TV at home in a bucket seat with a steering wheel mounted in front. Randy Baker, his small

son by his second wife, used the seat, too, but there were several years yet before still another Baker might join Buck on the NASCAR circuits.

BUDDY BAKER

There was a time when the biggest victory posted by Elzie Wylie Baker, Jr., was in his class at the Pure Union Economy and Performance Trials. In his first 3 years of Grand National racing in the big NASCAR machines, he made the top 5 finishers twice out of 41 starts, earning the munificent total of 61 cents per racing mile. In his first 8 years, he did not gain a single victory, and in 326 races over 14 years he had but 6 victories. However, the earnings per racing mile rose appreciably, thanks to Charlotte Speedway and to Buddy's reputation as one of the great qualifiers of history. Vast, empty superspeedways with few if any fans in the stands seemed to motivate this 6 foot 5 inch, 240-pound giant.

It was Tuesday, March 24, 1970, at Alabama International Speedway in Talladega. It was late in the afternoon, and Baker was testing his blue droop-nosed Dodge Daytona Charger for the forthcoming first running of the Alabama 500. It had been raining that morning and the day had not brightened when the rain stopped.

Both the Charger and Baker were obviously in fine form, however. The average speeds kept climbing, lap after lap, until Buddy had cranked out 200.096, then a world closed-course record for the kind of machinery. The Dodge engineers in the pits told him about it and Buddy told them he could go faster. He did—200.447 m.p.h. around the 2.66-mile layout, a record that would likely stand for a while because engine size was being cut from 430 to 366 cu. in. for 1971 and all side-window glass was being eliminated.

The Alabama 500 should have been Buddy's initial big victory since the World 600 in 1968 at Charlotte, N. C. Certainly he was among the favorites; and he seemed sure to win when, 14 laps from the finish, right in front of the main grandstands, the Charger's engine exploded. Flames surged into the driver's compartment when the oil hit the hot exhaust manifold. Baker broadslid the car down the banking to a halt in the dirt next to the track and contorted his huge frame through the driver's side window in seconds. He suffered second-degree burns on the face and legs and a first-order scare. But his cool driving, according to NASCAR veterans, prevented a much greater holocaust. He was back racing soon after.

Buddy Baker was always Buck's boy. As a child he played in the pits; his first race was in 1958, when he was 17. By that time he had gotten his schooling, at Camden (S.C.) Military Academy and Central High School in Charlotte, where he played some football and

was a multi-event entry in track; but he always wanted to race. Buddy always had a ride, because when Buck didn't have an older car for him, some other friendly competitor would let him run a backup or obsolete stocker. The quality of the machinery may account for his record in the early years, when Buddy was learning by following his father in races, trying to corner and set up like the old master. But there was always one big difference. Buck was a man who always tried to finish; Buddy charged.

In 1965 Baker finished 2nd to A. J. Foyt at the Daytona 500, and 2nd to Ned Jarrett in the Southern 500. In 1966 he was in the top 5 only once out of 41 starts, running 2nd to Richard Petty at Atlanta. Then, in 1967, he led 14 out of 15 in one streak, but salvaged only a single victory, his initial one ever. It came at the National 500, and it came because he out-fought 6 other drivers, among them old A. J., David Pearson, Dick Hutcherson, Cale Yarborough, Bobby Isaac and Darel Dieringer. Each of these stars held the lead in a 44-car field, which included no less than six USAC aces. Baker's victory ended a Richard Petty Plymouth streak of victories at 10, and shamed a Ford superspeedway effort that boasted no less than 8 factory drivers.

In 1967, master mechanic Ray Fox predicted that Buddy would make it at Charlotte in a Fox-prepared car. Buddy had been a bridesmaid all year, but he proved his mettle as he survived 22 lead changes. It was like a game of musical chairs. One by one the contenders dropped out or dropped back, until the contest was be-tween pole-sitter Yarborough and Baker. Buddy grabbed the lead on the 201st lap; Cale nailed him on lap 219 and seemed to be pulling away, until suddenly he began to slow. Buddy had forced a pace which the Ford could not take. Cale never gave up, holding on to second, but his engine did 33 laps from the finish. Buddy won by a lap over Dodge team mate Isaac.

Victory came again at Charlotte in 1968. Poor pit crew work in mid-race had cost Buddy the Darlington Rebel 400 after he led 90 laps, but the engine had been strong. The Charlotte World 600 was shortened by rain to 382.5 miles, and only Donnie Allison (Ford) was in the same lap when Baker took the checkered flag.

Automobile racing is not a sport for giants. An ideal driver might be more like a spider monkey than someone who puts 240 pounds on one side of the car. Yet in 1969, Buddy Baker managed to win himself $63,510 in 18 starts without finishing in the top 5 once. Charging does pay. On Labor Day 1970 Buddy made it pay even more, when he won the Southern 500 at Darlington, thus becoming the first man to follow his father's footsteps there. For 1971 he was designated the official "Dodge Boy" in Chrysler's reduced factory support program, which was centered at Petty Engineering. He finished 2nd to Richard in the Daytona 500, then 3rd in the Winston 500, Southern 500 and Yankee 400. At the Rebel 400 at Darlington, Buddy won by 13 laps over Dick Brooks after the man with whom he had dueled most of the way, Donnie Allison, suffered engine failure 10 laps from the end.

He remained the Petty team Dodge for the early 1972 races, but the big man was limiting himself to the big ones. A 3rd in the Winston 500 at Talladega, Ala., was his early best until the World 600 at Charlotte. There he outdueled Bobby Allison to take a well-deserved 3rd victory on this rugged track.

CANNON BALL BAKER

Erwin George Baker was born near Lawrenceburg, Ind., March 12, 1882, and died of a heart attack May 10, 1960, in Indianapolis. In between those cold dates he set more different records on more different kinds of motor transport than any man is ever likely to match. Baker would try to set a record for any company in any vehicle, if the money were right. Somehow he usually succeeded.

Baker was not just a speed demon. His last appearance in competition showed he could be a featherfoot, too. In 1949, with three passengers, he drove from Boston to Miami in a Nash Ambassador at an average of 26.5 miles per gallon for the non-superhighway trip. But, then, no man ever drove across America more than Baker. He set 143 distance records, most of them across the country, in every kind of conveyance, from a tiny

motorcycle to a loaded medium truck. His powers of endurance were legendary, yet he had been a sickly child whose family had moved to Indianapolis to be near better medical aid.

He survived and through hard work (10 hours a day at the Indianapolis Drop Forge Company for 88 cents) and hard play (acrobatic workouts at a Turners Hall) he built himself up. In 1900 he went to Atlantic City with an acrobatic group to give an exhibition and there saw his first automobile. It didn't send him into immediate paroxysms of joy or desire. Almost 5 years later, Baker left Indy again as part of a travelling vaudeville act in which he battered punching bags with his hands, feet and head simultaneously. He got homesick in San Francisco and left the city the day before the famous earthquake; the hotel he had just vacated was demolished and only one guest survived.

In 1906 Baker bought an Indian motorcycle and for 2 years was content to drive it as transportation. Then, at a Fourth of July Elks picnic, he volunteered for a race to fill out the field at Crawfordsville, Ind. He won, then came in 2nd in another race. He was a natural racing driver, and he was hooked. Within a year the future Cannon Ball was a member of the Indian factory team, becoming a close friend of its founder and president, George A. Hendee. In 1909 he helped open the new Indianapolis track, winning the national 10-mile title, and in 1912 he went on a goodwill tour through Cuba, Jamaica, and Panama, logging 14,000 miles on a 7 h.p. motorcycle. He also made his first transcontinental run on this Indian bike.

In May 1915, Harry Stutz asked Baker to try to set a new crosscountry mark in the famed Bearcat. Baker installed double shocks, taped the springs, put on a bug screen over the radiator, and took off from San Diego with an AAA observer aboard on May 6. Twice the Stutz almost sank in Texas quicksand, and it almost mired in Okie and Jayhawk mud, too, but Baker set a new mark: 11 days, 7 hours, and 15 minutes to New York. There he was dubbed Cannon Ball, a name he liked so much he copyrighted it.

Baker chopped his own mark a year later, rolling into New York in 7 days, 11 hours, and 52 minutes from Los Angeles. Rain had held him a day in Kansas City. This run, in a Cadillac, added even more to his reputation, for he had had only 19 hours sleep the entire time. He began to offer manufacturers the slogan, "No record —no pay" In 1916 he gave Marmon a Detroit–Indianapolis record of 7 hours and 10 minutes, and Lexington a Chicago–Indianapolis mark of 8 hours and 50 minutes. He went to Australia to set FIM marks up to 24 hours for Indian. If a firm named 2 cities, Baker would set a record between them. In a Cleveland-built car called the Templar, a small but well-made and expensive vehicle, he set New York–Chicago and New York–Los Angeles records despite police harassment. The cross-country trip was made in 101 hours and 45 minutes, and the shorter run was 10 minutes short of 26 hours.

He also did stunts, like driving an Oldsmobile cross country in high gear, low and second having been removed from the car. His only Indianapolis appearance came about through the urging of Henry Ford. He drove a Frontenac into 11th place in 1922 with Shorty Hanson as his driving mechanic, but Baker found such activities rather boring. Besides, he felt the chance of cash remuneration was not good enough.

Baker said in later years that his toughest run across country came in the winter of 1924, in a make of car that has long since vanished, the Gardner. It was built by a buggy manufacturer who had seen the handwriting on the wall and wanted to diversify. The firm's president, Russel E. Gardner, reasoned that a winter record would open up sales of the vehicle with good publicity. Baker made a short test drive with the car, then announced he thought he could do the job, even though the car's top speed of 64 m.p.h. was only reached downhill with a tailwind. The Gardner's Lycoming engine was a good unit, but for its size it was carting a great deal of wood, steel, and rubber around.

But the vehicle must have been durable; if it had not been, it would not have survived. Baker headed out of New York during a thaw, although he might have preferred blizzard conditions. He encountered slush and melting ice through Pennsylvania and fog in the Midwest but battled through to St. Louis in just over 30 hours. The car had chains on all 4 wheels when he headed across Missouri and Kansas toward New Mexico. The roads were thick mud garnished with potholes and wagon ruts. But Cannon Ball came through with a 110-hour-and-15-minute effort, the first man ever to cross the American continent in the dead of winter in a car. About 1,400 miles of the route he had used chains.

Later, as chief test driver for the Rickenbacker Car Company, he beat this time with a winter mark of 71½ hours, driving time only. He performed all sorts of feats in this car, setting a new San Francisco–Los Angeles time of 8 hours, 57 minutes, and driving from El Paso to Los Angeles in 21 hours, 33 minutes. A famous jaunt of "three flags" from Vancouver, Canada, to Tijauana, Mexico, was made in 3 minutes shy of 41 hours. There were innumerable short trips and a few notable hillclimbs, too. At one time he held the stock-car record for Pikes Peak and for Summit Mountain, a 3-mile, 23-turn, 9 percent grade road located just outside of Uniontown, Pa. That one he scooted up in 2:57 in the wee hours of one morning, then raced the Pennsylvania state police to the border. Soon after Rickenbacker went into receivership in 1926, Baker made on epic run in a Buick-powered 2-ton tank truck, fully loaded with Atlantic sea water for San Francisco's edification, in 5 days 17 hours and 36 miuntes.

In retrospect, his career proved that, while people marvel at the durability of record-setting cars or their speeds, they do not necessarily buy them. Most of the cars he drove—Willys St. Claire, Stutz, Rickenbacker, Templar, Gardner, Olds, Graham-Paige, Nash—were among the finest obtainable in their day, but most didn't survive even as brand names.

Baker's favorite car was the air-cooled Franklin, a logically planned, well-built, durable vehicle that was among the best dollar values available. In it he set a host of new records, starting in 1928. In a Franklin Airman Speedster he beat the pride of the railroad industry, the 20th Century Limited, from New York to Chicago. The car had a top speed of just 70 miles per hour, yet he took it coast to coast at an average speed of almost 46 m.p.h. He averaged 54.7 m.p.h. in a 452-minute run from San Francisco to Los Angeles in a stock 135 sedan. And, as a kicker, he regained the transcontinental mark at 69½ hours in a 1930 Series 14 Franklin. His fastest cross-country trip—although unofficial—was 53½ hours in a 1933 Graham. That more than beat his own best official time of 60 hours, 31 minutes in a 1930 Stutz Versailles.

In 1948 Baker was appointed the first NASCAR commissioner. He was little more than window dressing, although he ostensibly had full jurisdiction over rules administration. Near the end he did not even appear at NASCAR events. The last record he set was a 15-minute, 12.75-second run up Mount Washington in a Nash 600 Airflyte in 1948. But, just as his career helped open the roads of America to more and more auto travel, his presence lent NASCAR the prestige it needed in its fledgling days.

MAURICE BALLOT

It is not for the hundreds of thousands of stationary and automobile engines or thousands of staid cars built by Etablissements Ballot that the brothers Ballot are remembered, but rather for the few swift cars they raced in Europe and America from 1919 to 1922. They had produced 4-cylinder auto engines both before and after World War I, and built cars from 1919 to 1929, when they were absorbed by Hispano-Suiza. The name disappeared 2 years later.

On Christmas Eve, 6 weeks after the 1918 Armistice, a one-time marine engineer named Maurice Ballot decided that France should be represented by a national team at the next year's Indianapolis 500 in America, which at that time was run to a 300 cu. in. formula. With much of France in ruins, its resources—both men and materials—near exhaustion, and its financial structure riddled by wartime inflation, this was an ambitious goal. Ballot was undaunted. He located a "secret" factory about 12 miles outside of Paris, then induced 2 top men to become part of his crash production team.

The first was René Thomas, who had won the Indy 500 in 1914 in a Peugeot. He knew the course, he knew the competition—since most of the cars that the Ballot would face would be holdovers from pre-war races—and he knew the needs of the driver-mechanic team that would have to cover the 500 miles. The second man was Ernest Henry, the famed Swiss engineer who had designed Thomas' winning d.o.h.c. Peugeot, like the successful Grand Prix cars just before the war. These two men and three assistant draftsmen isolated themselves in the rural factory, much as did Raymond Loewy and his design staff many years later in designing the American Avanti.

Just 101 days later, on April 17, 1919, the first car took to the roads around the factory by night, to keep the secret that a Ballot racing car existed. Even many of the workers who had contributed to the effort did not know at this point that their work was intended for competition instead of for an ordinary passenger car. A week later the cars were trucked to Le Havre and on April 26 they sailed for New York. Henry's design was not merely an extension of his 1912 Peugeot, but incorporated many things he had learned during the war while working with the straight-8 s.o.h.c. Bugatti airplane engines. The Ballot powerplant was a d.o.h.c. straight-8 of 4,917 c.c.

When unveiled at Indianapolis, the Ballots proved to be lean-looking vehicles with fairly primitive bodies, a large bolster tank behind the seats, and spare wheels mounted behind the tank. They contrasted greatly with their more streamlined, boat-tailed competitors; perhaps time had run out on the factory before such refinements could be made. Surprisingly, there was an American-made straight-8 at Indy in 1919, too, the Duesenberg.

René Thomas led the drivers of the Ballot team, backed by Louis Wagner, Albert Guyot, Paul Bablot, and Jean Chassagne, who was relief driver for all 4 cars. René himself took the pole position after qualifying at 104.78 m.p.h. the first man to exceed 100 m.p.h. at the Brickyard. All the Ballots demonstrated similar speed capabilities; the team was undoubtedly the fastest on the track. But Thomas, in charge of the team in America, felt that the cars were overgeared and that even higher lap speeds could be recorded with lower axle ratios. He cabled Ballot in France for permission to switch to smaller American-made wheels and tires.

Ballot did not want the change made, yet hesitated to deny Thomas anything he thought he needed for victory. He hesitated too long. After he had finally sent word that Thomas's own car could be changed to the smaller wheels but not the others, a cablegram came from René saying that he was making the switch on all cars because he had not heard otherwise from the factory. The move proved to be the Ballot team's downfall. The 1919 Indy 500 was a nightmare, not only for the Frenchmen, but for all the entries. Three drivers and mechanics were killed; tire troubles plagued all the cars; 3 of the Ballots suffered wheel collapses, Wagner going into a wall as the result of one. Guyot's was the only car to finish (in 4th place) behind the winner, Edward Howdy Wilcox, whose prewar, Henry-designed Peugeot averaged a lackluster 88.05 m.p.h.

The Ballot team returned to France, where the cars were fitted with high, slender, long-tailed bodies. Thomas, forgiven by Ballot, set a new 104-m.p.h. record for the Gaillon hill climb. In the same year's Targa Florio, Thomas crashed, after having driven the car 1,000 miles between Paris and Sicily. The race was not the ideal test of the powerful machine; Georges Boillot won with an average of just 34.19 m.p.h.

The 1920 Indianapolis formula was reduced to 183 cu. in., or 3 litres, and Ballot entered a 2-car factory team, outgrowths of the previous season's 5-litre machines. A 3rd car of the same type was sold to Ralph DePalma, much to René Thomas' disgust; he felt it was a reflection upon his ability and that of Chassagne who seconded him. Trying to show up DePalma in practice, Thomas crashed, knocking out Art Chevrolet in a Frontenac, but Thomas was able to answer the starting flag on race day itself. DePalma was penalized by a flat on the pace lap, caused by a sharp piece of metal on the track. Fast pit work put him back in the race and, by the 100th lap, he was challenging Joe Boyer for the lead, with Gaston Chevrolet's Monero and Thomas' Ballot behind him.

DePalma was in front with 14 laps to go when misfortune hit in the form of magneto trouble. Emergency repairs enabled him to finish 5th, with more than $11,000 in lap prizes. Chevrolet had won at 88.62 m.p.h., Thomas' Ballot was second, and a Duesenberg driven by Tommy Milton and Jimmy Murphy finished 3rd. Chassagne, after hurtling off the track, had finished 7th.

Thomas' feelings were still ruffled despite his finish over DePalma; he quit Ballot and signed with the Sunbeam forces. Ballot, who felt he should have won, was glad to see the Frenchman go. DePalma now became the team leader. At Elgin, Ill., soon after the Indy battle, he won the road races, edging Milton and Murphy.

In 1921, Grand Prix racing was revived on a full scale, with the Indianapolis 500 considered an integral part of the schedule. The 500 started as a DePalma benefit; he roared into the lead and piled up more than $20,000 in lap prizes, averaging 93.66 for the first 200 miles. Soon after, however, on the 111th lap, a connecting rod snapped, and Ballot was through for the day. Milton's winning time was a mere 89.62 m.p.h. DePalma toured the board circuits with the car before heading for the European GP races.

The French race came first, July 25, 1921, with unexpected and dramatic results—America's Jimmy Murphy, driving a Duesenberg, won at 78.10 m.p.h. He was followed by DePalma, who already had fallen out of Ballot's favor. It seems that DePalma and Pete DePaolo, his riding mechanic, had worked out a system whereby the mechanic shifted gears while the driver concentrated on the wheel, signalling for a shift by merely raising his thumb off the wheel. It worked well; DePalma found he could save as much as 6 minutes of time in 300 miles. Ballot was outraged, however, for he felt that he was being cheated by his driver. He insisted that DePalma shift gears for himself, and had the shift lever put back on the car's right from the center position to which DePalma had had it transfered to enable De-Paolo to perform the function.

However, DePalma stayed with Ballot until the end of the season, the Italian GP in September, which was won by Jules Goux at an average of 90.4 m.p.h. Goux drove the 326 miles on the Brescia course non-stop, the fastest long-distance race up to that time. Jean Chassagne was second and DePalma, who made the only pit stop of the three, was far back.

In addition to the 3-litre cars, Ballot raced a model of 1,986 c.c. Goux finished 3rd in the French Automobile Club's GP at Le Mans in this model in 1921, and a 2-car team finished 2nd and 3rd in the Targa Florio in the so-called bolster-tank form in 1922. The 3-litre cars were sold off and did well through succeeding years, notably in the hands of Malcolm Campbell, Jack Dufee and the Zborowski stable in England.

The following year was Ballot's last in racing, Two cars prepared by Goux entered the Indy 500; Goux himself, newly married to an American girl, fell out after only 25 laps. Eddie Hearne finished 3rd, far behind Murphy who won at 98.48 m.p.h. In a curious spare-tire-in-front form with a streamlined, barrel body, these models were not impressive. American single-seaters of the day were actually far more advanced than European efforts, and only the lucrative U.S. racing kept them from bothering to campaign overseas.

With the factory out of competition, attention was turned to production cars, the anchor badges of which symbolized Ballot's marine background. The 2LS in 1922 and the 2LT, both based on the GP models, were marketed as sports and touring cars respectively. In 1925 there was a 2LTS hemispherical version. In 1928, just before the company's absorption by Hispano-Suiza, the straight-8 RH model was produced, followed quickly by the RH2, a high-powered version of the same car, and the PH3, which was up to 3 litres. None of these could be considered sports cars. But later Ballots could take nothing away from the earlier racing automobiles which had provided so many thrills in America as well as Europe.

EARL BALMER

Earl Franklin (Bomber) Balmer, the flying brick mason from Floyd Knobs, Ind., was for a time one of the bright young stars of late model stock car racing. Born December 13, 1935, the future Bomber started racing

in 1957 on a quarter-mile track at Jeffersonville, Ind. He spun out on the 1st lap of his initial race; but by the end of the season he was a top contender. He raced with ARCA and MARC before making the switch to NASCAR and more full-time racing.

Balmer admitted he never even thought of NASCAR until ARCA scheduled its 250-mile race at Daytona International Speedway in 1964. Earl, always a charger, came into his own on the big 2.5-mile track. He started on the pole, topping 165 m.p.h. in a Plymouth set up under the more restrictive ARCA rules—a significant achievement. And he led the race until the poor overworked stock engine blew up. But the experience gave him confidence, he says, and made him wonder if he couldn't make it as a full-time racing driver with NASCAR, which pays much better purses. He had posted 2 MARC 100-miler victories in 1963, 5 in 1964, before his chance to switch came.

In June 1964 he signed to run a factory Dodge with Cotton Owen. His initial Grand National race was the Dixie 400 on June 7, where he blew the engine on the 12th lap. He started about 10 NASCAR races in all, finishing 4th at Nashville, Tenn.—a tight half-mile track more like the ARCA circuits—and 5th at Huntington International Speedway in West Virginia. In the Firecracker 400 at Daytona on July 4, Earl ran 8th.

After the great Chrysler-NASCAR controversy of 1964, Balmer's driving days were numbered. He quit the cockpit for the garage, becoming a top-flight mechanic. It was better than brick-laying.

37

LORENZO BANDINI

Italy's Lorenzo Bandini was both an excellent and a successful driver, but his fame almost until the year he died was unfortunately flavored not by a spectacular success but, rather, by an incident that may have deprived one man of a World Driver's Championship and given it to another. At Mexico City in 1964, Bandini's Ferrari bumped a BRM driven by England's Graham Hill and sent it into a guard rail, ending for Hill the race in which the mustachioed Britisher might have regained his 1962 world title. Instead, Lorenzo's Ferrari teammate, John Surtees, was 2nd and won the title.

It was not the first time the Italian had displayed the fiery traits often associated with Latins, nor was it the last. Bandini was considered a comer in Grand Prix racing, though he seemed to have less experience than many of his peers. Yet his "inexperience" was more reputed than real, for the young Italian had been driving since 1957. And he had raced for the Maranello marque since 1961, despite his youth.

Bandini was born December 21, 1936, in Barce, Cyrenaica, North Africa. The family returned to Italy 3 years later and settled near Florence. When Lorenzo was 15 his father died, and he was apprenticed to a local garageman to learn the mechanic's trade. Employer and employee did well by each other, and in 5 years Lorenzo was ready to open his own garage. He remained in this business even though he had surrendered almost full time to his great passion—auto racing. "I always wanted

to be a driver," he recalled. "But I had to wait and wait. It was like being madly in love with a beautiful girl and holding one's emotions in check, without being able to explain to her."

He had first competed late in 1957, in a Fiat 1100 borrowed from a friendly customer, at a hillclimb at Emilia, Italy. Bandini came in 15th in his class—an inauspicious beginning. Nevertheless, he was happy; he finally had begun the life he had wanted for so many years. His former employer knew of his passion, and lent him a hotter version of the same car for his next event. He finished 3rd and was offered a Fiat V-8; he made better showings with the better equipment, and at the beginning of 1958, arrangements were made for Bandini to drive a Lancia Appia Zagato. It was in this car that he first attracted national attention, by winning the 2-litre class in the Mille Miglia.

Late in 1958 Lorenzo purchased a Volpini Formula Junior—a scaled-down version of the then-current Italian GP designs—in which he debuted as a single-seater driver September 28, 1958, in Sicily's first FJ race, the 7th annual Sicilian Gold Cup. He finished 3rd in both heats and in the general aggregate. "A new world beckons to me," he told a friend after the day's exhausting action, "a terrible new world." For the next 2 years, Bandini concentrated on racing in the Volpini and in Stanguellini FJ cars, and generally attracted favorable comment. In fact, he and Giancarlo Baghetti were accepted as natural successors to such late greats as Alberto Ascari and Eugenio Castelotti, especially after Luigi Musso's untimely death.

Mimmo Dei, patron of Scuderia Centro-Sud, provided Bandini with his first Formula 1 ride in a 1.5-litre Cooper-Maserati at the 1961 Pau GP on Easter Sunday. It was a race, in retrospect, that had many significant portents; not the least of these was the victory of Jim Clark, his 1st in racing. Jo Bonnier was 2nd, Bandini 3rd. The rest of the season scarcely provided any encouragement for Bandini or the underpowered Centro-Sud cars. That winter Lorenzo campaigned in Australia and New Zealand with a 2.9-litre Cooper-Maserati, with limited success; he had previously driven FJ races in Cuba, and was becoming a world traveler while still a young man.

Centro-Sud was disbanded just before the 1962 season, but Enzo Ferrari was sufficiently impressed with Bandini to sign the Florentine to a factory ride behind Phil Hill, Baghetti, Ricardo Rodriguez, and Willy Mairesse. Lorenzo made his first start for Maranello at the Monaco GP and finished 3rd. Ferrari forces were in disarray that year, however, and save for 2 other championship GP drives (German and Italian) and the Enna GP in Sicily, which Bandini won, Lorenzo was relegated mainly to sports car events; the following year, Surtees and Mairesse were given the GP chores, and the 2 young Italians the sports car duties. Dei came to the rescue, however, by reviving Centro-Sud and purchasing the BRM in which Graham Hill had won the World Championship.

Bandini first drove this car in the 1963 French GP at Rheims in July, later competing in the British, Solitude and German events with the same mount. Finally Ferrari called on Lorenzo's F1 services for the Italian GP at Monza, and he remained on the team as the number 2 driver from that point until Surtees departure in 1966 elevated Bandini to the top spot. The wiry, dark Italian was a steady driver, occasionally hard on his mounts, and especially good at races like Le Mans (which he won in 1963), Clermont-Ferrand, and the Targa Florio (won in 1965). He was happy-go-lucky in many ways and loved to clown with his fellow drivers. Despite his brush with Graham Hill and similar incidents with other pilots, Bandini was well-liked by his peers as well as by the fans.

In 1964, he won the Austrian GP and was 3rd in the German, Italian and Mexican races. The following year he was 2nd at Monaco, and he narrowly missed GP victories in the Monaco and French F1 races in 1966. The year 1967 seemed to be shaping up as Bandini's best. He won both the Daytona and Monza sports car races in the Ferrari P4, codriving with Chris Amon, and was 2nd at the Brands Hatch non-title F1 Race of Champions. At Monaco in May, Bandini was running 2nd to Denis Hulme when his Ferrari hit a guard rail, bounced off a light pole, planed over the protective straw bales, and overturned. The car caught fire with Bandini trapped inside, and it was 4 minutes before he could be extracted. Suffering from third-degree burns over most of his body, Lorenzo fought for life for 3 days before succumbing May 10, 1967, and plunging Italy into deep mourning. Bandini was survived by his wife of 4 years, Margherita, who was carrying their child at the time of the driver's death.

HENRY BANKS

For many years, USAC was in the hands of the British: competition director Henry Banks was born June 14, 1913, in London, England. (Six months later, however, he was living in Royal Oak, Mich.) Banks's qualifications for this sensitive position included an illustrious racing career conducted entirely within the confines of the United States. He began at the age of 18, at the VFW track in Detroit, and ultimately became a protege of the great Ralph DePalma at Indianapolis. This was no surprise; the blood of auto racing pioneers flowed through Banks's veins. His father, William, was a member of the (French) Dietrich team from 1904 through 1908, and certainly did nothing to discourage his son from a racing career. In fact, William Banks traveled coast to coast with his son when Henry finally was established in the AAA circuit.

Henry won his initial race at 19 at Davison, Mich., then campaigned on the old Michigan-Ohio circuit in stock-engined sprint cars. His early hero was Bob Carey, who was AAA national champion in 1932. Banks subsequently went East as a teammate of Bill Schindler and Paul Russo in the Caruso equipe on the ARDC midget circuit, winning the ARDC title in 1941.

From the beginning, consistency was Banks's trademark—no flash, no derring-do (though there were accidents nevertheless.) His first car was a special, built by members of a car club, that was powered by an o.h.v. Model T Ford engine. Henry sent it through the fence in his initial race, but competed with greater success as he gained experience. During the week, he worked as a test driver for Pontiac on the General Motors Proving Grounds. When AAA began sanctioning races at Detroit, Banks joined the organization and finished third behind his idol, Carey, in the big race of the season. But he went independent the following year.

His career was not free of untoward incidents. During his Detroit competition he flew a hundred feet through the air, slicing off the tip of his nose on the car's visor. An unnamed physician sewed it right back on, and it healed so well you could hardly see the scar. And during his midget competition, he flipped on several occasions, the worst at Cedarhurst, N.Y., where he went end-over-end. Banks was still smiling when he was lifted from a large mass of debris.

It is something of an irony that Henry should have had jurisdiction for so long over USAC, which sanctions the Indianapolis 500. His own racing seemingly was jinxed there, despite the fact that DePalma chose him in 1936 to try to qualify a Miller 183. Banks was the first man ever to pass the Indy rookie driver test, instituted that year. But all he could do with the old car was first alternate and it was indicative of his luck that, when a car dropped out, no one thought to inform him to fire up his mount. In 1937 Charlie Voelker designed a V-12 for the DePalma Miller car. Banks couldn't qualify this one either—a broken rear end thwarted him.

In 1938 he finally qualified, in the Kimmel Special, in 31st grid position. He lasted 108 laps for 21st place before a connecting rod bearing gave. In 1939 and 1940 he was slated for a supercharged Maserati V-8, and both times the beast overheated during qualification. But as a relief driver he figured in both races. Billy DeVore's 10th-place Barbasol Special had Henry in the cockpit for 44 laps in 1939, and so did Chet Miller's Alfa Romeo for 100 laps the following year. That one was flagged in 17th position. The year Henry won the ARDC, he concentrated on midgets, dropping most of his occasional sorties onto the Championship Trail.

During World War II, Banks became Ford's top troubleshooter on the Pratt & Whitney aircraft engine, a career he never completely left until he went full time with USAC. Indy resumed after the war, and Banks qualified 21st in 1946. But he had to spin his car to avoid his old ARDC teammate, Paul Russo, who had hit the wall on lap 17. The result was axle damage for Banks's Auto Shippers mount, and retirement after 32 laps. The next year Henry made 36 laps in the Federal Engineering car. And so it went; in the 1950 Memorial Day race he had to hand over his Maserati Special to Fred Agabashian when cockpit fumes sickened him in the 72nd lap.

In spite of this inauspicious start, 1950 was to be Banks's championship year. Banks learned that Lou Moore was selling his Blue Crown Spark Plug car, which had dominated Indy. The prospective buyer was Murrell Belanger and the prospective driver was Tony Bettenhausen, but the deal was not yet consummated. Henry appealed to industrialist Lindsey Hopkins, whose cars he had driven for years, and Lindsey outbid Belanger. With the car, thanks to Moore, came Blue Crown sponsorship.

For the 1st time, Banks was going to run the full Championship Trail. He was 6th in the Milwaukee 100 on June 11, which Tony Bettenhausen won. On June 25, a day which was so hot that younger drivers needed relief, Banks held on to finish 2nd behind Jack McGrath. Banks didn't even qualify for the Springfield, Ill., 100 because the car was unsuitable, but on August 27, in the Milwaukee 200, he finished 2nd behind Walt Faulkner and moved into 4th place in the series, behind Parsons, Russo, and Faulkner. He didn't make the field at Syracuse September 9, but the next day, on the Detroit track where he had run as a youth, he gave the home folks something to cheer. Sixth after 40 laps, he began moving up on the leaders, taking over on lap 88 and going on to win 200 points. This was enough to give him 3rd place in the season standings.

Banks now had a real chance for the AAA title, although no one except Pete DePaolo ever had won the crown without at least a few Indy points. At Springfield's next race, Banks lasted only 13 laps, Banks was now 176 points behind the series leader. Sacramento was next. Though the California 100 was a rough race (won by Duke Dinsmore), Henry finished 3rd to Walt's 9th and cut the gap to 77 points. Paul Russo was sandwiched between the two, with 3 races to go.

November 12 on the old Phoenix track, a 4-car pileup took Russo out and sent Henry through the wooden fence. But Banks came back to the pits, worked frantically on the car, and returned for 12th place and 10 points, enough to surpass Russo. At Bay Meadows, Calif., on November 26, Tony Bettenhausen won, Banks finished 4th and Faulkner 6th. Walt still led by 107 points. Only a single run was left: the 200-miler at Darlington, S.C., on December 10.

The AAA boys had never run on this mecca of NASCAR, so there was no advantage to anyone. Six drivers still had a mathematical chance at the AAA title, but Faulkner in the Agajanian Special and Banks both would have to lose it. It was a humid gray day, and there was a threat of rain as the cars were sent off. It became a race within a race; for nearly 40 laps Faulkner led Banks by mere yards. Just past halfway, Henry made his move and only the 2 leaders, John Parsons and Bill Schindler, were ahead of him. The clouds were getting darker, and Henry was praying—just as he had in every one of the last few races. For a 37-year-old race driver the chance at a National Championship doesn't usually come again. He increased his pace, and soon had put 2 cars between himself and Faulkner. He didn't know that Walt was virtually out of contention with faulty steering. The rain came, and Banks pushed harder, though he could feel the rear end going. Then the caution flag came out: Julie Schaaff, who had once crewed for Henry, had crashed. Banks nursed his car along until the checker fell on Parsons. He knew he had won the title. Agajanian beat the crowd to him to congratulate him.

In 1951 Henry finished 2nd on the Trail, taking 6th at Indianapolis after qualifying 17th. He finished in the top of 10 in 11 of 13 races, but Tony Bettenhausen beat him to the title. From there on, it was downhill. In 1952's 500 he qualified 12th, finished 19th, and could make only 700 points for 10th place on the Trail. Henry was seriously thinking of quitting, but decided to give it one more try. He broke a crankshaft trying to qualify for Indy; he qualified for Milwaukee but never ran. That was the end. He went home to California to work for Ford Aircraft Division, supervising military engine requirements for 7 Western states. Under him were drivers Duke Nalon, Paul Russo and George Connor.

At Indy in 1954, he watched practice awhile, then retired officially to the life of Ford middle management. But in 1959 a call came that returned Henry to the sport he always loved. Duane Carter, another old racing champion, had just been fired by USAC's board of directors because he wanted to move too fast and too expensively toward complete domination of American auto sport. Tom Binford, President of USAC, asked Henry to take over as Director of Competition. He accepted. Under Banks the growth of USAC was slower, but surer. He brought to the job an ability absolutely necessary—he could work with Binford to keep one of the world's most democratic major racing organizations from flying apart at the seams.

Banks also worked as an extra in many movies; his tour de force was *To Please A Lady,* in which he lost the big race to Clark Gable. In 1970, after the retirement of Binford and the beginning of the Bill Smyth era in USAC, Henry became Director of Industrial Relations and Safety Certification. His tough-mindedness toward the preparation of cars has been credited with substantial improvements in competition safety.

SKIP BARBER

Can a man jump from SCCA amateur races directly into international Grand Prix racing? Apparently so, if we can judge from the case of Skip Barber of Carlisle, Pa., in 1971. Barber, no youngster at 34, went over to Europe to pick up a new single-seater, a March, to bring back to the United States for the Formula A series, newly redubbed the L&M Continental 5000.

Up to that point, Barber's total experience in single-seaters was limited to 2 seasons. In 1969 he drove exactly 3 Formula B races (winning 2 of them, at Mosport and Thompson) in the SCCA, as well as some Formula Ford appearances. Skip knew what he was doing, and proceeded to win the FF title in a Caldwell D-9 at the ARRC championship week at Daytona Beach, Fla., that winter, despite totalling the car in practice. Rebuilt overnight, the car started last but finished 1st. In 1970 he repeated the feat in FF, and also won the FB title, in two different Tecnos.

Gene Mason Racing, a group of Philadelphia businessmen, sponsored his 1971 racing, and with their money he went to Britain to buy the March. Instead of heading back immediately, Barber entered the Monaco GP. But a balky gearbox and rains that eliminated any chance for real practice ended that bid.

At Hockenheim, Germany, however, Barber made the starting field of the non-championship Jochen Rindt Memorial race. And Skip not only finished but scored a creditable 6th place. And in the next official GP at Zandvoort, Holland, he again made the field and finished 14th, "just trying to keep out of the way." In the Canadian GP Barber retired after 13 laps, but in the USGP he finished 18th. In 1972 in the L&M series, Barber returned to the Mason team. He set qualifying records at Road America, Wis., and gained a 3rd in one race with the refurbished March. What might have happened if Barber had started 5 or 10 years sooner? It's fun to think about it.

WOOLF BARNATO

He was a great bear of a man, with an unruly shock of hair that he covered with a yachting cap for racing—until it blew away. He was rich, a millionaire in the days when a million meant something. He was the boss in financial circles, but as a driver he took team orders better than most, and far better than anyone else in the group of individualists that formed the Bentley racing team.

Captain Woolf Barnato, often called Babe by his friends, already had a wide knowledge of cars and of racing them when he appeared in the Bentley showroom early in 1925. A natural athlete, good at all kinds of

games and sports, Barnato had become interested in racing early. With his resources based on South African diamonds and gold, acquiring cars was no problem, and starting in 1921 he had become a familiar figure at the Brooklands course—that great, paved bowl—in a wide variety of racing machines, including Talbots, Ansaldos, Calthorpes, Wolseleys, Enfield-Alldays and Bugattis. In November 1924, Babe had driven a Boulogne-model Hispano-Suiza for 300 miles at Brooklands at an average speed of 148.34 m.p.h. He captured new 2- and 3-hour records, a 200-mile record, and 200-, 300-, 400-, and 450-kilometer records, all in Class H.

It was only natural that Barnato would eventually buy a Bentley, a true sports car. His choice, back in 1925, was a 3-litre Super Sports on which he had fitted a special Jarvis body. Minus its fenders, headlights, windscreen, and other appendages, this car was a regular Brooklands racer for 2 years. But Babe also grew accustomed to using the fully-equipped car as his street machine. And in 1926, he acquired a few more. Bentley was in financial trouble, and a combine, formed and headed by Barnato, took over control of the company, with Woolf (who was the principal investor) as chairman.

He became more than just another customer, more than an executive with the company. He became one of the driving forces behind Bentley's racing efforts. He became, in fact, a Bentley team driver. They were a strange bag, with only Frank Clement a true professional—a man who depended upon his racing for his livelihood. The rest were like Barnato, wealthy or at

41

least well-fixed, youngish, venturesome. Tim Birkin, or more formally, Sir Henry T. S. Birkin, Bart.; Glen Kidston; Australian millionaire Bernard Rubin; bacteriologist Dr. J. D. Benjafield. Individualists all, hard to control, hard to get to take team orders, eager to charge, As chairman, Barnato could have thrown his weight, which was considerable, around and been the most bothersome of the bunch. Instead, he was one of the boys and the perfect team driver. If the game plan called for his car to run 3rd as a reserve to the lead car (and he rarely, if ever, drove the lead car), 3rd it would be, come hell or high water.

At this point in his career, almost everyone must have underrated Woolf. After all, he was mostly a club racer and a record setter under controlled conditions. In 1925 he had been 3rd in a 100-miler at Brooklands, in 1927 3rd in another 150-miler there. Yet the Bentley Boys themselves, though they rated Birkin fastest among them, also rated Barnato as the best road racer, not only in their company or in Britain, but perhaps in all of Europe. Their private opinion was about to be put to the test and proven out at Le Mans. The 24-hour race of the late Twenties or early Thirties was far different than the modern race. The course was narrower and more twisty. The paving was little better than ordinary country roads. Facilities for everyone, whether spectator or participant, were primitive by any standards.

Into the arena came Bentley for another try at the prestigious race it had won in 1925 and 1927. Barnato and his friend, Rubin, shared a 4.4 Bentley in 1928. The battle eventually became one between the British forces and those of the American Stutz company. The Stutz Black Hawks were 5 litres, the most powerful Bentley was Barnato's. The strategy was for him to wear down the Americans, aided by at least one of the other Bentleys, so that the 3rd one could be conserved for the final dash to the checker. But by dawn, Barnato's Bentley was the only one left. It was all up to him. With meticulous care, he drove the race exactly as he planned. At the right moment Babe took the lead and then held off any rushes by Stutz or Chrysler, also a Le Mans competitor that year.

Barnato won 1,658.6 miles from the start at an average speed of 69.108 m.p.h. The Stutz and 2 Chryslers followed him across the line. In 1929, it was much the same story, only this time Barnato shared his 6.6-litre car with Birkin. In daylight, other cars were as fast or faster than the Bentley, but at night the others slacked off while Babe maintained virtually the same pace. He virtually ran the wheels off his opponents, winning his second straight Le Mans at an average speed of 73.627 m.p.h. The distance in 1929 was 1,767.07 miles. The Barnato Bentley led 3 of its fellows across the line for a sweep of the top placings. It was a high-water mark for British racing.

The Bentley marque was expected to repeat in 1930. Their contender was Mercedes, but they outnumbered the white German car 6 to 1. But 3 of the Bentleys were still unperfected supercharged models that would not last the gruelling 24 hours. There were two 6.6's, one driven by Barnato and a new partner, Kidston, who proceeded to sit at the German car's tail hour after hour. Whenever the Germans looked back, there was the green Bentley, effortlessly staying up with the 7-litre Mercedes—or so it seemed.

Actually it was taking every last bit of the car and of its drivers' stamina, to keep up with the Mercedes. And the Germans were pushing equally as hard to stay ahead. The second 6.6 dropped out after running into a bank. Another Bentley, a mere 4.4, charged up to the leaders in a bid to help keep the pressure on the Mercedes entry and did so for a time until its tires gave out. The Germans were tiring, though, and Woolf pulled ahead, then dropped back and let the white car ahead once more. They took the challenge several times, surely realizing that Babe's strategy was to have the powerful car over-tax itself but unwilling to let the opportunity go. There was always the chance that the Bentley might fail as Barnato pushed ahead.

But the German car failed first, and it was only left for Woolf to nurse his battered machine to the end of the 24 hours. At the checker, 1,821.02 miles later, he had won his 3rd consecutive Le Mans at an average speed of 75.878 m.p.h. The physical beating that man and machine took was well worth while at that price. And Barnato's strength and courage were such that he often willingly took on such conditions if it meant victory. Winner of the Brooklands 6-Hour in 1929, Babe determined to run the Double 12-Hour race there the following season. In the midst of the race, with Barnato leading, a sudden hailstorm pelted the track. In the open Bentley, the driver was completely exposed to the weather, and Barnato's face and hands were cut raw.

But on he plunged, never reducing speed, even as other cars crashed behind him. He won at an average speed of 86.68 m.p.h. That winter Barnato was awarded the British Racing Drivers Club Gold Star. Almost as if it was a fitting way to cap a racing career, Woolf quit the courses as a competitor, though he did sponsor some cars in later years at Brooklands under the marque name of Barnato-Hassan. Underneath that name of course, they were Bentleys. After investing about $500,000, Barnato withdrew his financial support in June 1931, and Bentley died soon after as an independent company. Woolf lived until 1948.

CHUCK BARNES

Charles McLean Barnes, Jr., used to be one of the main attractions at a restaurant bar in South Daytona Beach, Fla., during Speed Weeks. That was when he was a public relations and special events man for the Firestone Tire and Rubber Company. The organist/pianist or the owner or the bartender or even some of the Speed Weeks patrons would ask Chuck to sing something, and the quiet, easy-going Barnes would unlimber a surprisingly good tenor voice for a song or two.

Appearances are deceiving, however. Barnes was about as easy-going as a Cummins Deisel tractor pulling a tandem trailer load of steel components, and he was just as efficient. But he inspired confidence in his word and deed in all kinds of people from all geographic areas. This is important for a public relations man; it is life or death for a business management representative and Barnes was one of the first of the modern era. He remained one of the most successful, too. Barnes has been business manager for Mario Andretti, A. J. Foyt, Parnelli Jones, Fred Lorenzen, and Rodger Ward. He represented Jackie Stewart, Jim Clark, Graham Hill, Chris Amon, and Jochen Rindt during certain facets of their careers, getting them American dollars for advertising, consulting, speaking, or just posing, and protecting them from friendly feelings toward business acquaintances. This has made him much wealthier than if he had stayed with Firestone because his fees range from 10 percent to 40 percent of parts of a client's income.

The function of a Chuck Barnes is to take the headaches out of making as much money as possible from racing (or other sports). A young man named O. J. Simpson left his fortunes up to Barnes and his associate, David Lockton. The Buffalo Bills football team and Chevrolet, among others, will make sure that O. J. will never want for money, the twosome did their work so well.

What Barnes does is match up money-making opportunities with his clients; to do that he has to be imaginative. When Rodger Ward retired as a driver, Barnes contacted a broadcasting network and offered him as a commentator on auto racing broadcasts, for example. But most of it is salesmanship. Barnes convinces companies they can sell their product or products better through affiliation with racing—in particular, through his clients—than otherwise.

His success bred a spate of competitors, none of them quite as successful so far. Barnes was a symptom of the development of American-style commercialization of the sport. It is entirely likely that within the Seventies, non-auto-related companies will be the major sponsors of automobile racing. Thank Chuck Barnes for helping start the trend.

EDGAR BARTH

Wilfried Edgar Barth was one of those drivers who deserved to be well-known outside of Europe, but never really achieved the status. A likeable personality, Barth was nearly 30 when he first took up auto racing in postwar Germany. Born January 26, 1917, at Herold-

Erzgeberge, now part of the German Democratic Republic, or East Germany, Barth graduated from high school in 1933 and was lucky enough to find a job with Auto Union. Within 3 years he was a test driver there, but not in the famed cars; rather, Edy became a distinguished motorcycle racer, winning some 25 medals before being drafted into the Army in 1938.

Barth's army career was cut short in 1940 when he was riding in a motorcycle side-car that was sideswiped by a truck. Edy suffered 7 broken bones and was declared unfit for front-line duty. He spent the rest of World War II in a motorcycle shop back in Germany. Out of the army, Barth tried to rejoin his old factory, now DKW, but there was no job. Instead he worked in a small textile factory started by his mother, racing cycles on weekends; this led to a job with the East German EMW factory both in cycles and in cars. In 1952 Barth started his auto racing career, and he concentrated on cars alone after 1953.

Edy's initial German are victory came around 1955 in the 1.5-litre EMW sports car, and it was in this car that he also won his initial big international race, the Prix de Paris, in 1956. The EMW clearly was outclassed by the Porsche, but Barth made it at least competitive. The following year Porsche invited Barth to drive one of its cars for a single race, the famed Nurburgring 1000. The East Germans didn't say he couldn't go to the Nurburgring, they merely said he couldn't race. But once he was there and testing the car, Barth became an international citizen, so to speak. It was unthinkable for him not to race this wonderful machine.

He raced and won. And as the band struck up the West German national anthem, Edgar Barth knew the die had been cast. He now was tied for better or for worse to the German Federal Republic. To return to East Germany would mean imprisonment certainly, and possibly death. Things were not all black, for Porsche promptly offered him a job—as a mechanic and some-time driver—at its factory, and his wife and son made it safely out of East Germany one dark night. The mechanic soon receded and the racing driver dominated, with Barth winning many national contests, particularly hillclimbs.

In 1959, 1963, and 1964 Edy won the European Mountain Championship in silver Porsches, and occasionally there were endurance race starts as well. In 1959 Barth won the demanding Targa Florio outright, a high spot of his enduro career. There were single-seater starts, and he drove both factory Formula 2 races and Formula 1 for Rob Walker's Cooper-Climax equipped private team in the 1964 German Grand Prix. That season was his last, for already the first signs of an illness that was to take his life were setting in. Edgar Barth, 48, father of two, died in a Ludwigsburg clinic on May 16, 1965. To his East German *Meister des Sports* title, the West Germans already had added their *Silberlorbeen des Bundesprosidenten* award, the only example of both Germanies honoring the same motor racer.

AL BARTZ

The hamlet of Mountain, Wis. has contributed an exceptional engine builder to the world of automobile racing. Born there in 1939, Al Bartz may have been Mountain's lone contribution to America's prowess in engine design. In any case, he did not tarry there long. He went where the action was—southern California.

Bartz managed to survive mechanical engineering courses at Santa Monica City College, then went to work for Hilborn Engineering assembling fuel injection components. He was among the pioneer hot rodders, although he didn't think of himself as such. It was the height of enjoyment to pilot a roadster 130 m.p.h. across the Mojave Desert's El Mirage dry lake. It was inevitable that a Hilborn employee so oriented would eventually try sprint and midget car racing; Al's home track was Ascot Park's unfriendly dirt oval in South Los Angeles. He was voted rookie of the year there in 1962. The driving career was cut short when, in 1963, he flipped end over end; nerve-tingling to the spectators but hard on machinery and driver. No race car, no ride, so he went to work for Jim Travers and Frank Coon, engine rebuilding masters.

He later decided to drive again, this time in a sprint car hand-built by himself. Taking a leave of absence from Travers-Coon, Bartz completed the racer. As the completion day approached, Bartz thought more and more about the flip. Thinking like that is not good for Ascot sprint car drivers; it turned Bartz into a car owner with Billy Wilkerson as his pilot. There was not enough money to sustain this relationship so he sold the car to Wilkerson and went back to the Travers-Coon fold.

He left them in May 1966 with no intention of opening a rival engine-building business. He had vague thoughts of going to Europe or getting out of the racing business entirely. "I was also thinking of building dry-sump systems, and Bruce McLaren wanted me to go to England to work there for him on the Canadian-American Challenge Cup Chevrolet engines. I really was in no hurry to make up my mind. I had a little cash, and I like the beach." Then the telephone began to ring. George Follmer needed an engine for the western part of the CanAm swing; Bartz assembled a 333 cu. in. Chevvy for George. Then Lothar Motschenbacher wanted an engine, and after that, there were the Mc-Laren team, Peter Revson, Chuck Parsons, Skip Scott, Jerry Hansen, and many others. Things got so busy that Bartz stopped taking orders (at $4,600 and up per engine). One day he looked around and "realized I was in business, for good or bad."

The famous Flower Power McLaren Chevrolets were prepared by Bartz, then assembled by team mechanic Gary Knudsen. These engines were among the most successful in racing history, completely dominating the CanAm series. They made a bit of trouble for Bartz because other customers would ask how come the McLarens were so much faster. Bartz would then pull out dyno figures that showed a maximum difference of 6 horsepower or around one percent.

The work of an engine rebuilder or blueprinter is much misunderstood, especially that of an independent operator like Bartz. Bartz uses parts available either stock or at one of many speed shops. He farms out magnafluxing, cylinder head porting, line boring, and the like. His job is to set the specifications for the porting and boring, pick the parts, and make sure that the assembled engine meets his current opinion of how much horsepower and torque are obtainable. Bartz engines tend to withstand high r.p.m. well, but, for CanAm at least, don't pull many foot-pounds of torque at the low end. He claims that the 5-speed gearboxes are suited by these characteristics.

As stock components get more precise and more reliable—as they inevitably are under the growing pressures of consumerism, government interest, and more automated manufacturing techniques—the need for an Al Bartz or a Travers-Coon lessens. Or does it? Bartz and others were turning into theorists, calling on their know-how and training to find more horsepower in the old stock block. It was inevitable that, should the piston engine survive for passenger car use, anti-pollution requirements would move it toward long-stroke designs. Then it would be a whole new game for the engine rebuilder, one almost exactly the opposite of current racing practice. That's when the masters and the mechanics separate.

NORMAN BATTEN

He was born to be a hero, even though it was in Brooklyn, N.Y. Norman Batten drove the Eastern dirt tracks in the early Twenties with some success. When he won the New York State Fair AAA 100-miler at Syracuse in 1924, he decided that the time had come to move on to bigger things. In 1925 he drove Pete DePaolo's Duesenberg Special at Indianapolis while Pete was having blistered hands cared for; and Pete went on to a blistering record Indianapolis average of 101.13 m.p.h. In 1926 Batten was ready to strike out on his own with a competitive car, a Miller. He finished a close 7th and he hit the board circuit as one of the favorites.

Then he became a hero. In 1927 his car caught fire, and no one would have blamed him if he had halted and jumped to safety. But he chose to remain in the car and drive it to the end of the pits were it would not ignite gasoline stores. The heroism left him with burns so severe it took almost a year for him to recover. But the following year Batten was back at Indy, driving hard. He finished 5th with the usual problems of poor pit work costing him one if not 2 positions. He continued to race the boards and continued to build his fame. When the chance came to race in Brazil and Argentina during the winter, Batten and Earl Devore decided to go. The *Vestris*, the British liner on which they were passengers, foundered in a storm November 12, 1928. Batten, a hero to the end, lost his life saving that of a woman.

HERMAN BEAM

Seven years a professional, Herman Beam competed in more than 200 races. Not only did he lose all of these, but there is no record of his ever leading one. Yet in the first 5 years of the life of what has become the mecca of the American stock car, Beam clocked more racing miles on the Daytona International Speedway than any other competitor.

Herman, a chemistry graduate of the University of North Carolina, was a pudgy, bespectacled man who stood 5 feet 7 inches tall. During his racing years he earned a special nickname—"The Turtle"—because he may have been auto racing's all-time loser. When he quit at the end of the 1963 season, it was not only because he was still losing, but because he could no longer maintain what for him was an expensive vice. Yet Beam entered more races than any other NASCAR driver,

and finished more. That fact, plus his uncanny ability to find the slowest groove in any race track and stay there, earned him almost enough to make a profit because NASCAR prize money descends down to the 20th position.

Being an intelligent and wryly witty man, Herman learned his limitations quickly and compiled a casebook in how to survive without any driving talent. His basic premise was, "I don't know what it takes to be a good racing driver but whatever it is, I haven't got it." Premise number 2 was, "I've lasted as long as I have by not trying to do the things I couldn't do. Some of my slowest races were when I was trying hardest." Premise number 3 was, "I have to make sure the car is under perfect control. I'm slow in everything I do. My reactions are slow and getting slower."

The only recorded time in 7 years that Herman came out of the slow groove was in the 1962 Atlanta 500 when he had to avoid a wreck. Instantly he found his car crowded up against the outside rail and he was clobbered. As he crawled out he uttered the immortal *mot juste*: "Oh well, you can't finish them all." (The records show he started in 51 races that year, and this was his only DNF.)

There were other notes in the Beam casebook of surviving with nothing but determination. For example, one should show up at the track as late as possible since living away from Johnson City, Tenn., cost money. One also should turn teetotaler and go on a hamburger diet. And one should head back home as quickly as possible after a race. Of course, going slow had other compensations—tires don't wear as fast, engines don't blow, and the body work is seldom scuffed. This was another Beam trademark—his cars were always among the prettiest in the race, for he repaired the merest scratch immediately. Strange as it may seem, he kept the vehicle in top racing condition mechanically. Throughout all the 7 years, he always had one of the fastest cars—potentially, that is—on the track.

Herman's first race was at Greensboro, N.C., in October 1957. He lost. His top finish in a major event came in the Volunteer 500 April 29, 1962. He started 22nd, finished 6 but was 31 laps behind the winner. Beam tried letting others drive his cars but he found that the hotshots raised his expenses so that it was as bad as if he had driven—except even they couldn't beat the factory people. It was the factories that drove Herman out of racing. Once he noted sadly: "If you're a close last that's not so bad, but when you're a bad last that's no good. The factory teams have driven all the independents out. I can't go on like I have been." Few fans noticed when Herman quit, but the drivers did. With the Turtle gone, the others had to take turns being last.

JOHNNY BEAUCHAMP

Though remembered as the man who came in 2nd in the closest 500-mile stock car race in American history, John Beauchamp was a stock-car champion with IMCA and was next to none in the department of sheer courage. When, in 1961, Beauchamp and Lee Petty hurtled out of Daytona Speedway during a qualifying race, their bumpers locked, it was like a horrifying replay of their epic duel in the first Daytona 500. They both recovered, Johnny to race again back in the Midwest, and it still seems a miracle after viewing the twisted wreckage of the 2 cars that day.

Perhaps it was no more of a miracle than separating Petty and Beauchamp in the 1959 race. Beauchamp, declared unofficial winner, got the kisses from the beauty queens and the pictures in the paper. Petty got the money after Bill France scoured hundreds of pictures including the famous movie film sequence before making the final decision. Beauchamp had come to Daytona as a 2-time IMCA stock car champion. He had started racing 11 years before with jalopies in his native Iowa and neighboring Nebraska. He was 35 at the time of Daytona, and what lured him was all that Daytona money.

In 1956 he had written the IMCA record book over with his Chevrolet and amassed 4,075 points compared to 2,274 for Sonny Morgan of Beaumont, Tex., his nearest competitor. He won 38 features compared with 32 for the rest of the field. He held 8 of the 17 recognized marks for the half-mile dirt ovals which constitute most of the IMCA circuit. In 1957, he repeated with his fuel-injected Chevvy, scoring 4,376 points; but he won only 32 features while the rest won 36. He added another record, too. Dethroned in 1958 by Don White, Johnny hoped for a career in NASCAR. Besides his Daytona 2nd place in a Thunderbird, he won at Atlanta March 22; then finished high at Martinsville, Va. After that he headed home to Iowa. He came back for the Daytona 500 twice, receiving head injuries in the 100-mile late model qualifyng event February 24, 1961, as he hooked his Chevvy's front bumper into Petty's rear when Petty's Plymouth hit the guard rail on the 37th lap of a 40-lap race. Joe Weatherly won the race. After that Beauchamp still raced, but not frequently, in IMCA.

CAREL DE BEAUFORT

Jonkheer Carel Pieter Anthonie Jan Hubertus Godin De Beaufort, a Dutch count whose home was Maarsbergen Castle, may have been the end of the line of true amateur Grand Prix drivers when he succumbed to injuries suffered in practice at Nurburgring for the 1964 German GP. Tall, broad-shouldered, perpetually sunny, he lived for auto racing and never failed to make known his pleasure at being able to compete with the greats of the driving world on equal footing. His smiles and handwaving at spectators, fellow drivers, and the world in general whenever his relatively ancient Porsche appeared on a course had become almost a tradition.

Born April 10, 1934, Carel was 22 when he first took up auto racing in his native Holland. This made him 30 when he died on August 8, 1964, 3 days after his Nurburgring crash, but in those 8 years he packed in a lifetime of racing and the type of fun that he obviously found satisfying. De Beaufort drove in Formula 2 competition for the first time in 1960 in a soon-familiar orange-colored Porsche, and the transition was an unusual one. (It was said that only the Porsche family and a few friends could get this shade of orange from the factory in those days. It is a color Frau Porsche liked.)

At first the drivers had no use for the Dutchman; he was a hazard to himself and others until he applied himself more diligently. The pros remember a sports car race at Avus in August 1959, when De Beaufort nearly killed himself, losing control of a Porsche at high speed, flying off the top of the 30-foot-high banking, and crashing into trees and bushes on the street below. Carel shook off a daze and drove back onto the circuit through the paddock, but was black-flagged. Jean Behra died in almost the same spot an hour later in a similar accident. Undaunted, De Beaufort returned with a cameraman and had his photograph taken there with a jaunty smile on his face. The remarks of some drivers about this incident are still unprintable.

Carel learned from that incident, however. The following year he was seen to be more intent, more cautious, yet still brave on the courses; and he started a

physical training regimen that was to transform his roly-poly frame to more pleasing proportions, although he never really was small enough to be comfortable in his tiny GP Porsche cockpit. His former detractors grew to like him in the main, and there were few unkind words said about him at the time of his death.

The car in which the Count was killed was surely one of GP history's most raced. It started life as a Rob Walker Team car in 1960 and was bought by De Beaufort late in the year for his new Ecurie Maarsbergen. The next season he raced it in the Belgian, French, British, Solitude, German, Italian, and Zeltweg GP races, as well as some others, finishing all of them. Lent to Giancarlo Baghetti for the Rome GP, it was the winner there in 1961, and the following year he lent it to Wolfgang Seidel to drive in the Brussels GP and in the Lombank Trophy, Lavant Cup, Glover Trophy, and Aintree 200 races in England. Back in Carel's hands, the car, still in Seidel's silver colors, was driven in the Dutch, Monegasque, Belgian, French, and Rheims Grands Prix, then received an orange nose for the British and Solitude races, and finally reached its all-orange state for the German GP.

"Old Fatty Porsche" as the car now was being called, also saw action with De Beaufort in the Italian and United States Grands Prix and at Karlskoga, Oulton Park, Roskildring, and Pau. Other races leading up to 1963, De Beaufort's greatest year in the car, included the Imola, Syracuse, Rome, Solitude, Zeltweg, Mediterranean, and Mexican events. In 1963 Carel's skills permitted him to make his best showing, 2nds in the Ger-

man and Rome Grands Prix and 3rd at Zeltweg. The next season he drove "Old Fatty" in the British International Trophy, Dutch, and Solitude races leading up to the fatal one at Nurburgring. De Beaufort also had a 1.5-litre Porsche in 1962, the year he first made the World Driver's Championship tables. He drove this car in that year's South African season, then had it driven in many other races by friends. In 1962, except for the United States GP which he entered with "Old Fatty" and earned the accolade of most improved driver of the year, De Beaufort finished every race in the 1.5-litre car.

To the end, Carel drove in his stocking feet, maintaining that with his shoes on he had trouble manipulating the foot pedals. He expected, he told friends, to step on a nail one day and die from blood-poisoning. His prediction did not come true.

FRANK BEEDER

Frankie Beeder's claim to fame is that he won the inaugural race at Langhorne Speedway. He drove relief in the Vanderbilt Cup race of 1936 and was one of the top early midget drivers in the East. Born in St. Louis, Beeder was a small man with a flare for the dramatic. He waved at the crowd, sometimes to the detriment of his position in the race, much like the latter-day Carel de Beaufort of Holland in Grand Prix racing.

JEAN BEHRA

There was a time after World War II when France had no champions, automotive or otherwise. Jean Behra, born in Nice on February 16, 1921, changed all that when he took up motorcycling, then switched to auto racing. A classical driver in the old sense, a contemporary of Stirling Moss and Juan Manuel Fangio, he was overshadowed by those greats and, despite his own color, by even more colorful second-line drivers like Harry Schell and Alfonso de Portago.

Driving a red Moto Guzzi motorcycle, Behra was 4 times Champion of France on 2-wheelers; and in 1951 Amedée Gordini signed the 30-year-old to his first auto racing contract. Now, 30 is an age when race drivers are thinking about retiring if they haven't reached the top, but Jean was just starting out with a marque that wasn't going anywhere. Yet he persevered to become one of the mainstays of postwar Grand Prix racing. Behra started his 4-wheeler competition forays in 1950 with a 1500-c.c. Maserati 4CLT and a 4.5-litre Talbot at places like Mont Ventoux and Montlhéry. Gordini gave him his initial ride for the Simca Gordini Team at the 1950 Bol d'Or at St. Germain merely as a test; and while Jean didn't place, he did perform well enough to be signed for 1951 as a member of a team that already included Maurice Trintignant, Robert Manzon and

André Simon. In his initial offical team ride Behra brought his light blue Formula 2 mount home 3rd in Les Sables d'Olonne GP.

But these early years were mainly ones of frustration for Behra and other Gordini drivers. Mechanical troubles abounded, and spare parts, new engines, and expert mechanical help all were lacking at times. The 1952 Swiss GP was a prime example. The top 3 of 4 cars always stayed bunched within 10 seconds or so of each other. Behra was consistently in the 3rd spot, Manzon in 4th, with Piero Taruffi's Ferrari in the lead. Then Jean limped into the pits with his exhaust pipe broken in such a way that he was being roasted alive. But Manzon pitted as well with water pouring from a cracked radiator. Gordini poured a bucket of water on Behra and his exhaust pipe and sent him out to continue the battle while Manzon's radiator was replaced.

Behra made another 2 laps and came in again, hotter than ever and now suffering from fume inhalation as well, choking and fighting for breath. But the only extra radiator Gordini had wouldn't fit Manzon's car. He poured another bucket of water on Behra and sent him back to the race. The plucky Frenchman finished 3rd, fighting off a number of challengers. Behra had guts. In the Pan-American Road Race that same year, he was driving a 2.3-litre Gordini, the smallest capacity car in the race, yet he won the initial—some said most difficult—leg of the race from Tuxtla to Oaxaca over faster, more powerful opposition like Mercedes-Benz, Ferrari, and others. On the next lap, he led again, only to have a tire blow—a tire that should have been re-

placed but was not because the Gordini team didn't seem to have one available. The car slid down a 60-foot ravine, and Behra spent considerable time in the hospital as a result.

The year 1952 was the season, too, of what many people considered Behra's finest race. It was in the Rheims GP, which had been expected to be another romp for Alberto Ascari (who would be the year's World Champion) and his all-conquering Ferrari. The flag dropped, and a little blue car leaped into the lead. There was momentary glory, but everyone thought the next time the cars came past, the blue car—Behra—would be buried in a sea of red. But no, time after time, the blue car streaked past the wildly cheering French stands inches ahead of its pursuers, who were dropping back, one by one, except for Ascari. The future champion dogged Behra's car, waiting, watching for an opening, trying desperately to get past somehow. Behra held on until Ascari's engine finally gave up.

Then he eased off, for no one else was close, and he won that GP at an average speed of 105.3 m.p.h., fast for those days. It was the greatest victory in the history of the Gordini marque, and until the advent of Matra in the late Sixties it was France's greatest postwar racing day.

Behra's association with Gordini continued through 1954, and he scored other victories for his national team, including an especially rewarding one at Pau that season when he dueled Trintignant (who had gone with Ferrari) wheel-to-wheel for much of the 3-hour race and crossed the finish line a scant 60 yards ahead. In the same season he won the Salon Cup at Montlhéry. But it was clear that the Italian marques were to dominate racing over the next few seasons, battled all the way by Mercedes-Benz and the British.

In the fall of 1954, at Orsi Maserati's request, Behra appeared at Monza to try out a Maser. After a few laps, he signaled that he would do one for time. The clock registered 1:59. Ascari was watching, and when Behra came in, he took the same car out and tried to beat Jean's time. He could do no better than match it. Convinced, Maserati signed Behra that day for the Italian team.

In 1955 Fangio, Moss, and Mercedes dominated Grand Prix racing, and while Behra demonstrated on several occasions he could keep up with them in the right machinery, he failed to win any championship races. In non-title racing, however, Jean took the Bordeaux, Pau, and Bari GP. The following season Mercedes quit the GP scene, and Moss came over to Maserati as team leader, with Behra his partner. Jean was 2nd in the Argentine GP opener to Fangio and Luigi Musso co-driving a Ferrari; he was 3rd at Monaco behind Moss and Fangio with Peter Collins co-driving; and he was 3rd again at the French GP behind the Ferraris of Collins and Eugenio Castellotti. In the British GP Behra again scored a 3rd behind Fangio and

48

Collins with Portago; in the German GP he took 3rd once more behind Fangio and Moss. In the non-title Australian GP, Behra was 2nd to Moss. In sports car racing he was 3rd in the Argentine 1000, shared the Nurburgring 1000 victory with Moss, Taruffi and Schell. He was 3rd in the Venezuelan GP behind Moss and Fangio. Behra and Louis Rosier shared the Paris 1000.

Moss deserted to Vanwall in 1957, and Behra thought he would team leader for Maserati, but Fangio appeared for that spot, and Jean could hardly complain about the Argentinian's right to the berth. Fangio went on to win his 5th World Championship that season. Behra suffered a series of mechanical breakdowns in his GP racing efforts, his best showing coming in the Argentine race where he scored a 2nd. At Aintree, for the British GP, he was leading them all—Fangio, Mike Hawthorne, Collins, Luigi Musso, Moss—when the his clutch disintegrated. But in other Masers he had better luck. At Sebring, Fla., he and Fangio won the 12-hour race, in the Argentine 1000 he was second, and in the Swedish 6-hour race he and Moss shared victory. Behra won the super-fast Moroccan GP all by himself.

Late in the 1957 season Behra was offered a ride by BRM, the struggling British effort, and in the Silverstone International Trophy Race he scored a 99.95 m.p.h. victory over Schell and Ron Flockhart of the same team. Just before that he tried out the BRM in the Caen GP and won that one at 92.8 m.p.h. The following season he raced BRM's, was 3rd in the Dutch GP, and 4th in Portugal. For other forms of racing, he drove Porsches and won the Rheims F2 race, was 3rd (in a car shared with Moss) in the Argentine 1000, 3rd (with Hans Herrmann) in the Le Mans 24-Hour, and 2nd in the Targa Florio. He won at Avus and Rouen in Porsches.

It was in a Porsche that Jean Behra, champion of France in motorcycles and cars, met his death at Avus August 1, 1959, while speeding on the high banking at about 130 m.p.h. Death called on the 4th lap of the German GP's sports car race in a rainstorm. Flung out of the car, he hit a flagpole, dying instantly. If a BRM had been ready, Behra would not have been in the lesser race, but he hadn't wanted to sit the weekend out.

DEREK BELL

The racing biography of Britain's Derek Bell reads like a classic driver's story. He started in club racing, moved up quickly to Formula 3 in which he starred, graduated to Formula 2, and was finally signed—by Ferrari, who has a liking for British drivers—for Formula 1, all within 5 years.

A war baby, born October 31, 1941, at Pinner, Middlesex, Bell was raised on a farm at Pagham, near Bognor Regis, in Sussex (near where he later set up his own family in a 17th century cottage). His stepfather

saw to it that Derek graduated from Cirencester Agricultural College before encouraging the youngster's racing desires, nurtured by visits to Goodwood, near Pagham, and to the 1959 Italian Grand Prix. Bell also began learning how to manage a 1,000-unit trailer park (caravan site, in Britain) on the side. Once he had earned his degree, however, it was full speed ahead on auto racing via the Jim Russell Driver's School, with a 1st in the Clubman's Formula with the old reliable Lotus 7 (purchased by selling his Austin-Healey road car). He missed winning the national championship by a single point.

In 1965 Bell switched to a more powerful car, a Lotus 31, for F3 racing. This, in turn, was followed in 1966 by a Lotus 41. Both seasons were trying ones, for Derek's privately maintained and entered cars had little chance against the factory and well-financed private teams that dominated F3. He won occasionally and always drove well, so that for 1967 he was offered a team ride by Peter Westbury of Felday. In a competitive Brabham BT21, Bell won 3 of the initial 4 races he entered, including the Coupe de l'Avenue at Zolder. At Albi he was 2nd, and he won at Silverstone, despite the domination of F3 that season by the French national marque, Matra. In the most prestigious of the F3 races, Monaco, he managed a creditable 3rd behind the Matras.

F2 beckoned Bell in 1968, initially with the Church Farm Racing Team in a Brabham BT23C, then in a Ferrari Dino 166 after a switch to a berth with the Commendatore's forces. In his initial start in the red cars, at Monza for the Lottery GP, Derek grabbed the pole in qualifying, but had the misfortune of spinning on some oil as the race started, causing a 7-car crash that eliminated 3 of the 4 Ferraris in the race The Ferraris did not win often, but in the hands of Bell, were always in the money, and his driving skills were quickly recognized. Cooper offered him a 3-year F1 driver's pact, but Bell stuck with Ferrari, which signed the Briton for F1 and F2 drives starting in the Tasman series with a 2.4-litre F2 car, as well as a 5 litre sports car. He was 4th in the New Zealand GP, 5th in the Lady Wigram Trophy and Teretonga International, 2nd to teammate Chris Amon in the Australian GP and to Jochen Rindt in the Warwick Farm race, and 5th in the Sandown Park International. Amon won the Tasman title, with Bell 4th in the final standings, a point behind 3rd-place Piers Courage.

The Ferrari F1 rides never materialized, however, and Derek's sole GP start in 1969 was in the British race in a 4-wheel-drive McLaren-Ford. He was retired with a broken suspension. In 1970 he managed 2 GP starts, retiring in the 2nd lap of the Belgian race in a Brabham BT26 and finishing 6th at the United States GP in a Surtees-Ford TS7. The single point that finish earned him tied Derek for 22nd on the World Championship standings with Dan Gurney, Francois Cevert, and Peter Gethin. But in 1971, a new road opened up, a spot with JW Automotive, driving 7-litre Porsches that were defending their world sports car championship.

The JW Porsche drives started well, with Derek and Jo Siffert teaming up for an inaugural championship victory in the Buenos Aires 1000 at 115.722 m.p.h. The pair were 5th at Sebring, 3rd in the BOAC 1000, and 2nd in the Monza 1000 to Pedro Rodriguez and Jackie Oliver, their teammates. The 1-2 finish for the JW pairings was the same for the Spa 1000, but at Le Mans, Bell and Siffert retired. For the Watkins Glen 6-hour race, Derek was teamed with Dickie Attwood, a veteran, and they finished 3rd. That John Wyer was satisfied with Derek's driving was evident when Wyer created his new Gulf Mirage, M6 effort to replace the Porsche for 1972; Bell was the development driver.

The enduro starts were always sandwiched in with F2. In 1970 Derek's Tasman and F2 starts had been sponsored by Tom Wheatcroft, the millionaire British builder, who also collected single-seat racing cars and was building a museum to house them. Bell's F2 starts were good but not great in 1970, and he won only at Barcelona, although there were 2nds at Nurburgring and Zolder, and 3rds at Thruxton, Hockenheim and Imola. In 7 other starts he failed to finish only twice, one of these an accident at Paul Ricard. In 1971 Wheatcroft concentrated on the museum, but Frank Williams came forward with a March-FVA 712M. Bell was 3rd at Thuxton, retired at Nurburgring while leading, and was 2nd at Monza by less than a second to winner Dieter Quester. It was a high spot in his F2 racing season. In

Derek's only F1 start, the British GP, he retired in the 24th lap.

Bell was as fast as ever, and in 1972 he faced one of the more active seasons of his career: Abarth 2-litre sports car drivers and the World Manufacturers Championship series with Wyer's Gulf-Mirage team, usually partnered by Holland's Gijs Van Lennep. It was a season of sorting out in all areas, with better days expected in 1973, when Lothar Motschenbacher would sign Derek for the Formula 5000 L&M Championship series.

JEAN-PIERRE BELTOISE

Matra, the French national marque, employed Jean-Pierre Beltoise as its lead driver, and it was he who won the Formula 3 Rheims Grand Prix on July 4, 1965, at 113.45 m.p.h., the initial major GP victory for a French car since 1952 and major French race victory for a French car since 1949. It was not a Formula 1 GP, of course, but Beltoise's achievement immediately made him a national hero. He became France's premier driver in all forms of racing up to F1.

The faith and backing of his fellow Frenchmen—even after a later sports car tragedy—paid off May 14, 1972, when Jean-Pierre, driving brillantly through the rain-swept and fog-shrouded streets of Monte Carlo, won his initial championship race, the Monaco GP, in a Marlboro BRM, with only Jacky Ickx able to stay near the Gallic driver. It was the slowest time for a Monaco

race since 1952, a mere 63.85 m.p.h., but considering the course and the weather conditions, it was as fast as sensible—and fast enough to win.

Beltoise had given clear portents of his feat in the qualifying session by making the grid's 2nd row. At the flag he got a fine start, taking a lead that he never relinquished. Even the incredible Jackie Stewart, who made a mid-race challenge, was unable to come up to Beltoise, and the Scot finished 4th behind Emerson Fittipaldi, who was a lap down to Jean-Pierre at race's end. There were moments that the BRM also went its own way, but Beltoise always proved its master. Perhaps the only regret was that the race, although driven on the coast of France, technically was outside the Republic and in the Monaco enclave. But the crowd was predominantly French and reacted as any Gallic throng might.

Born April 26, 1937, in Paris, Jean-Pierre Maurice Georges Beltoise was destined for a life in his father's butcher shop except that Père Beltoise became unnerved at the way Jean-Pierre drove the delivery truck through the thronged streets of the French capital. Asked if he wouldn't like another career, he agreed to try engineering school. At school he took up motorcycle racing. "I was in about 10 races," he recalled, "and won one. Most of the others I didn't finish, and in a few I didn't even get to start because my old machine was always breaking down." School and racing were interrupted by a 30-month stint in the French Army, he was even in the Sahara for a time. While in the service he wrote a motorcycle column for a cyclist's magazine; it gained him a reputation for expertise.

When Beltoise was released from the army, he worked a while at the Bonnet factory as a mechanic, then left when he couldn't get a racing ride. Eric Offenstadt offered him a motorcycle, and the young Frenchman took it. That was the beginning of a 2-wheel competition career that lasted 3 years and brought Jean-Pierre no less than 11 national titles on 3 different machines. "I loved racing motorcycles," he said, "but I always regarded them as second-best. My real ambition was to race cars, and the only reason I wasn't doing that was that I didn't have the money." Bonnet, who wouldn't give his own mechanic a ride, did offer the cycle champion a Targa Florio car in 1963, however. The 1000-c.c. Renault-Bonnet sports/prototype felt comfortable in practice, but the car was out of the race before Jean-Pierre actually got to drive in it. Another bid at Nurburgring's 1000 was a little better; he led for 4 laps until the Renault engine packed up. At Le Mans, codriving with Claude Bobrowski, Beltoise's Bonnet finished 11th overall, led the 1-litre class and was awarded Index of Thermal Efficiency honors, despite a last hour in the pits for repairs after Bobrowski banged up the car.

René Bonnet signed Beltoise as an F3 driver after that performance. At the Pau GP, the car's initial outing, it turned out to be overgeared and underbraked, and its steering wheel broke in Jean-Pierre's hands. Brake troubles ended a bid at Nurburgring, and Le Mans flopped when Beltoise's codriver ran out of fuel on the back of the course. Then came the Rheims 12-hour race and as close a brush with death as any driver is likely to have. Beltoise's Bonnet hit some petrol spewed in his path by a passing Ferrari, spun off the track and split open, catching fire. "I lost a lot of things in that crash," said Jean-Pierre. "I lost the full use of my left arm and leg. I lost the possibility of a good Japanese motorcycling contract that was pending. I lost another cycle championship and a lot of money." (He had won more than 20 cycle races that year in addition to his auto racing.)

It was 6 months before Beltoise could even walk again, but as soon as he could, he appeared on crutches at the Bonnet factory, now known as the Matra competition department, and was delighted to be told that a team berth awaited him as soon as he was able to drive. In June 1965 at La Châtre he started his first race since the accident and set a lap record before a steering cable broke. At Clermont-Ferrand he spun off with more steering problems, but then came Rheims and his great victory. A victory at the Cognac meet and 2nds at Rouen and Magny-Cours for the French F3 championship followed. Both the Matra F3 car and Jean-Pierre were improved in 1966, but Beltoise's participation in this class was limited. In the Monaco GP, the most prestigious of the formula's races, he won at 125.8 m.p.h., and at Brands Hatch late in that year he was 4th.

The year 1966 was the first for the Matra marque in Formula 2, and Matra was the only constructor to chalk up a non-Brabham victory when Beltoise won the F2 section of the German GP. Jean-Pierre's boxy car retired at Pau after an encounter with another car. The following week at Barcelona he was holding 2nd place behind Stewart in a driving rain until bumped from behind by Brabham, a shunt that ruptured the Frenchman's fuel pump and sidelined the car. The bad luck held at Zolder, but it changed at Rheims when he copped 3rd. Beltoise was running 4th at Montlhéry until his Matra ran out of fuel, a common managing fault with French teams apparently, but he managed to capture 6th place there. Denis Hulme and Jim Clark had their hands full with Jean-Pierre at Le Mans, but he finished 2nd to Denny. At Albi he led at one point and was in 2nd when his throttle cable broke and dropped him to 8th at the finish. At Brands Hatch Beltoise finished 5th.

The following season, Beltoise closed out his F3 career by sweeping the Argentine Temporada series, taking the 2 Buenos Aires races and those at Cordoba and at Mar del Plata. Jean-Pierre's efforts now concentrated on F2, and, while he did not win any of the major races, he was the best of the non-F1 drivers participating. At the Limborg GP Beltoise was 2nd overall, finishing the initial heat behind Clark, the next behind John Surtees and Jack Brabham. Stewart led him across the line at Enna in the Mediterranean GP, and Ickx edged Jean-Pierre in the Rome race. At Tulln he was 3rd to Jo Rindt and Brabham.

The year 1968 saw Beltoise's F2 successes continue, the Frenchman winning the European championship. In the major races he continued to do well, taking both heats in the Deutschland Trophy meet at Hockenheim, for example, coming in 2nd to Rindt in the Truxton Trophy and at Tulln, and capturing the Madrid and Zandvoort Grands Prix. The big news of 1968 was Beltoise's entry into major GP racing with Matra, starting with the South African GP behind the wheel of a ballasted F2 car. Jean-Pierre was 6th there. In Spain, replacing an injured Stewart in Ken Tyrrell's private Matra MS10, he set a lap record of 86.25 m.p.h. for Jarama, venue for the initial championship race on Spanish soil since 1964. But an extra stop forced by inattentive pit work earlier in the race made Beltoise 5th.

The car as set up for Spain needed modifications for Belgium, but there were strikes in France, so Beltoise ran with the unchanged car and finished 8th. The next race, with the cars properly changed to suit Zandvoort's conditions, including last-minute switches for the rain, saw Stewart and Beltoise 1–2 in the Dutch GP, Jean-Pierre driving the fastest lap once more of 88.56 m.p.h. on the slick track. After a 9th in France, he was 5th in Italy, one of 6 cars to finish out of 20 starters, despite constant misfires at high revs. At Monaco, in Britain, Canada, the United States, and Mexico, the still unstable Matras failed Beltoise, and in Germany both he and Vic Elford were blinded by spray from a skidding car in heavy rain and left the road. By the end of the 1968 season, Jean-Pierre was tied for 9th in the standings. That 1st Beltoise championship victory was proving elusive, but he was still young; and the Seventies were even more promising after he finished 5th in the championship standings in 1969, with a 2nd in the French GP, a couple of 3rds, and other placings for 21 points (a single digit behind Rindt).

The year 1970 saw victory, but only in sports cars. Sharing a Matra V12 630/650 with Henri Pescarolo, Beltoise won the Buenos Aires 1000, and driving alone at Magny Cours in a Lola-Chevrolet V-8, he took that race. Jean-Pierre and Pescarolo also were 3rd at another Buenos Aires race. But GP racing in the Matra MS120 was another disappointment. The best Beltoise could do all year were 3rd at the Belgian and Italian GP races. He also was 4th in South Africa, 5th in Holland and Mexico, 6th in Austria. An 8th in Canada and 13th in France completed his card. There were 5 frustrating retirements—Spain, Monaco, Britain, Germany, and the U.S. GP. The 12 points Jean-Pierre earned gave him 9th place in the World Championship standings.

Tragedy struck Jean-Pierre in the Argentine 1000 sports car race, the opening round of the 1971 World Manufacturers Championship series. Beltoise's Matra died on the fast Buenos Aires course, and he hopped

out and began to push the car toward the pit area. At least twice the rest of the field rushed past. But he had to cross the course, so after looking several times and gauging that he could give the racers room, he started to push the car across the track.

He was in mid-course, with room to pass on both sides—several cars, in fact, had already done that—when 2 cars roared out of the turn and bore down on the Matra. One cut right, and the other seemed ready to pass left, then tried to follow the first car through. Beltoise already had breathed a sigh of relief, thinking, he said later, "Okay, they'll both get through." But in an instant Beltoise saw the second car, a Ferrari driven by Ignazio Giunti, would not make it. Jean-Pierre jumped for his life, but the Ferrari plowed into the Matra and exploded. Giunti died.

Argentina held Beltoise responsible. Article 16 of the racing code forbade pushing a stalled car on the track. Charges were levelled. The French Automobile Sport Federation suspended Beltoise for 3 months pending an investigation. No one seemed concerned that the officials at the race had ignored the alleged violation for at least 2 laps, and hadn't even bothered to display yellow caution flags or lights. Jean-Pierre said simply: "I am distressed, I am sickened, I am undecided as to what to do. I affirm once again that I do not consider myself responsible for the accident at Buenos Aires." Whatever else others might decide, his fate as a driver was really the terrible concern of Jean-Pierre Beltoise himself.

The rest of 1971 came as an anticlimax to the Buenos Aires tragedy. What with license suspensions, hearings, and the like, it was no year for a man to drive high-speed machinery under the most demanding of conditions. Yet Beltoise tried. In GP racing he managed 6 starts and accumulated a single point in the standings. That came in the Spanish GP where he was 6th. Retired at Monaco, Jean-Pierre was 9th in Holland, 7th in both France and Britain. An accident knocked him out of the Canadian GP, but he was 8th in the U.S. race. It was no true test of his driving, only of his courage.

In 1973, Beltoise continued with BRM once again and again was active in F2 and sports car racing.

ROBERT BENOIST

The life of Robert Benoist, unvarnished by the lightest attempt at embellishment, reads like an Ian Fleming novel. A World War I fighter pilot, Benoist became a racing driver, won an unofficial World Championship, became an underground agent in World War II and, after several hair's breadth escapes from the Nazis—including one in a Bugatti—he was captured and executed because even under torture he refused to give his captors the slightest bit of information.

Benoist was born in March 1895, in Auffargis,

France, near Versailles. Although he had an early passion for things mechanical, Robert was very much a country person and was acknowledged to be one of the best rifle shots in his area. Benoist's racing career, like that of Barney Oldfield and many other drivers of that period, started with bicycles. By the time World War I started, he was an apprentice garage mechanic, and his skill brought him into the French Flying Corps in 1915. He emerged from the war a skilled pilot with a renewed taste for speed.

The confident young Frenchman walked into the offices of the de Marcay marque in 1921 and announced he was ready to drive one of its 1100-c.c. cyclecars in the Paris-to-Nice Trial, which included acceleration tests, a flying kilometer and a hillclimb in addition to what today would be called a rally. Benoist's performance was good enough for him to be offered a factory berth by Salmson. When Salmson disbanded its competition department 2 years later, Robert had a string of successes that included a victory in the Avenue des Aracais speed trials in Paris and a 2nd in the first Bal d'Or in 1922.

Louis Delage immediately offered Benoist a spot. The driver's initial starts were in hillclimbs in whch he quickly improved Delage's reputation. Under René Thomas' able direction—Thomas was Delage's lead driver—Benoist learned the fine points of racing, gaining a 3rd in the 2-litre French Grand Prix (also that season's European GP). The following season, 1925, Benoist won his initial major GP, the French race at Montlhéry, the same race in which Antonio Ascari was killed. Not since 1913 had a French driver won this most important of all French races; Benoist and Albert Divo, his codriver, were officially received by the President of France as a mark of esteem.

There was no formal World Driver's Championship in those days, but if there had been, Benoist would have been World Champion in 1927. He won the French, Spanish, Italian (and European), and British GP in a 1.5-litre Delage. But the following year Robert found himself without a ride; Delage had overextended himself financially and had to end his competition efforts and merge with Delahaye. He received occasional drives with Itala and Alfa Romeo, but his only real success was a 2nd in the San Sebastian GP with a Bugatti. This led to a job with the latter as manager of its Paris sales organization, later as supervisor of its occasional racing activities.

Like all French drivers, Benoist wanted to win the Le Mans 24-hour race, finally succeeding in 1937 in a 3.3-litre Bugatti Type 57. His winning speed was 85.13 m.p.h. in a race marred by a 6-car crackup and 2 driver deaths. The victory was sweet, though, because it was Robert's last race. The following year Benoist was recalled to military service, but he was not allowed to fly (to his disgust). With the fall of France, Benoist determined to reach England, via Spain, but was captured enroute in his 57S by a German armored column.

Robert was told to fall into the middle of the column, under the watchful eyes of a motorcycle machine gunner, and did so. At a crossroads he saw a chance to get away, however, and sped off before the startled Nazis knew what was happening.

It was the first of a score of escapes as Benoist handled contact between the Anglo-French forces and the French underground, taking over from Captain William Grover of British Intelligence—another prewar racing driver under the pseudonym of "Williams"—who had disappeared and was never found. This dangerous life continued until June 18, 1944, soon after D-Day, when Benoist was betrayed and captured by the Gestapo in Paris. Tortured, he refused to betray his contacts. In August, Benoist was transferred to the dreaded Buchenwald concentration camp. On the night of September 12, 1944, one of France's racing greats and 35 of his fellow Allied Intelligence officers were strangled to death.

W. O. BENTLEY

The Bentley marque is one of the world's most familiar today, yet the famous British company lasted only a dozen years as an independent producer of automobiles before becoming part of Rolls-Royce. For all of its short, independent life, Bentley was easily the most successful sporting car of its time. In fact, it was literally a car that was too good for its own good. In the major decade of the original Bentley firm, designer Walter O. Bentley built less than 6,000 cars—1,600 of the original 3-litre, 4-cylinder design, then a 4500-c.c., a 6,500-c.c. 6 and, finally, a fabulous 8-litre model with dual gas pedals. Then he was forced out of business, partly because his touring car was so successful against sports cars that the average British driver was afraid to drive it.

Bentley—successively a motorcycle racer, railroad shop apprentice, dealer in French cars, and aircraft designer—decided that everyone else was wrong in building fast touring cars on light chassis with engines that looked like the first attempts of a novice California hot-rod builder (and performed as unreliably). He proposed to make his dream car reliable, yet capable of performing with equal ease at 8 or 98 m.p.h. Into his first Bentley went know-how coming from experiments with a new French 4-cylinder side-valve called the DFB (Doriot, Flanerin et Parant), which he and his brother sold. He had put aluminum alloy pistons and a special camshaft into this car and gotten almost 90 m.p.h., fantastic for such a small engine in 1914. It was at the Tourist Trophy that year where he apparently met F. T. Burgess of Humber, with whom he went into business 5 years later. There also was the background during World War I of developing—from the French Clerget rotary aircraft engine—the Bentley rotary series.

The Bentley made its debut at the November 1919

Olympic Auto Show in London. It was a 2,996-c.c., 4-cylinder design with 4 valves per cylinder, monobloc cast without a separate head. It had a wheelbase of 112 inches and a track of 54 inches. When—before a select gathering of backers—W. O. gave it its first bench test in the cramped loft of his shop next door to a convalescent home, the engine wouldn't turn over. It was only when a red-faced Bentley substituted benzol for gasoline that the engine coughed to a deep roar. The story goes that a nurse from the convalescent home appeared at once, imploring W. O. to halt his engine because a patient was in the process of expiring. But W. O. refused, not being sure that his engine wouldn't expire if he cut it off. The first production Bentley didn't appear until 1921; it had triple cams with separate rockers, wet sump lubrication, and a 3.92 rear axle. It went faster than the claimed 80 m.p.h., and its immediate success bolstered Bentley's confidence immeasurably.

This was reflected in the modest competition program that W. O. undertook in 1922. His marque's 1st competition appearance, perhaps out of sentiment, perhaps through conviction that it was the best possible way to get attention for his car, was in the RAC's Tourist Trophy that year. A 3-car Bentley team came in 2nd, 4th and 5th in the Isle of Man grind in a pouring rain. The same year W. D. Hawkes drove a Bentley pseudo-racer at the Indianapolis 500-miler, finishing 20th and averaging over 80 m.p.h. in the 3-litre, streamlined car. Bentley built a T.T. replica with a higher compression ratio and a power output of 80 b.h.p. in 1923, but he did not offer an Indianapolis replica at the same time.

Although it was never officially adopted as a guide by the company itself, Bentley enthusiasts—and their number was large and growing, even in the early years—noticed that all cars produced prior to 1925 and all 3-litre models carried a blue radiator badge; these were quickly dubbed the "blue label" cars. It was a blue label T.T. Replica that was driven to 4th place in the first Le Mans 24-Hour Race in 1923 by private entrants John Duff and Frank C. Clement. The 3-litre car remained in regular production until 1927, and even after that year could be specially ordered. Constant refinements eventually brought the car's power output up to 88 b.h.p. and the 1924 introduction of front-wheel brakes gave it an even more impressive performance. Dr. J. D. Benjafield raced a special version of this car at Brooklands between 1923 and 1925, but it crashed at Montlhéry in 1926.

The Duff and Clement team won the marque's first honors at Le Mans in 1924 by covering 1,291 miles at a 53.78 m.p.h. average. That year the red-label cars made their appearance, the first called the Speed Model 3-litre, giving an even better performance than its predecessors due to twin carburetion among other things. In 1925 the "100 Mile Per Hour" model with a slightly shorter wheelbase (9 feet instead of 9 feet 9½ inches) appeared and was dubbed a "green label" car when en-

thusiasts noted that the firm had switched to that color for the radiator badge. The radiator was a further distinguishing mark for it was the first time a Bentley was offered with one that was narrower at the base than at the top. Only 15 genuine "100 M.P.H." Models were ever made, although the older, longer models sometimes were shortened in the wheelbase in later years and the engines brought up to "green label" specifications and offered as originals.

In 1926 the 3-litre engine was modified a great deal, an integral sump being added as well as a modified camshaft. In all, something like 1,600 3-litre cars were made by Bentley by the time regular production stopped in 1927; better than 300 of these survive today as prized possessions all over the world. By then the model had been somewhat superseded by the Standard 6, which had debuted at the Olympia Auto Show of 1925. This was a 6-cylinder car offering its purchaser a 6,597-c.c. engine and an 8-bearing crankshaft. It developed 140 b.h.p. at 3,500 r.p.m.'s and had a maximum speed of about 80 m.p.h. In truth it was the first non-sporting Bentley and should have been a competitor for the Phantom 1 Rolls, for example, but Bentley and sports cars had been too firmly fixed in the public mind for it to succeed.

Unfortunately, the 3-litre Bentleys already were being outclassed by other sports cars such as the Twin Cam Sunbeam. W. O. was equal to the problem, however, and quickly designed and introduced a 4.5-litre, 4-cylinder design that was recognizable by its black radiator badge. This car developed 110 b.h.p. at 3,500 r.p.m. and a maximum speed of 85 m.p.h. During its production life, which lasted until 1931 or so, 668 of these 4.5 models were made, including 6 constructed from parts on hand after the Bentley firm had been liquidated.

Meanwhile, the competition life of the marque had brightened considerably. Three-car teams were entered at Le Mans in 1926 and 1927, all 3 falling by the wayside that 1st year with various mechanical problems. In 1927, however, things were a lot different for Bentley. At about 9:30 P.M. with darkness already falling, the 3 Bentleys were involved in an accident that seemed to end the team's chances. With a 4.5 in the lead and the S. C. H. (Sammy) Davis and Benjafield 3-litre in 2nd, both cars came full tilt into the White House turn to find a traffic jam there that included their other team member. They couldn't stop, but Davis braked hard and deliberately skidded sideways into the melee rather than head-on. His car was wrecked externally but upon inspection he found it still could continue. He and Benjafield went on to win the 24-hour grind at an average speed of 61.35 m.p.h.

Although the marque's successes at Brooklands and elsewhere were great, it was performances like this one at Le Mans that made its great reputation. Between 1924 and 1930 Bentleys won the French classic no less than 5 times, the last 4 victories coming in a row. In 1928 it had to beat out an American Stutz. In 1929 Woolf Barnato and Tim Birkin won in the new Speed 6 model—a short-wheelbase 6.5-litre model—at 73.63 m.p.h. Three 4.5-litre Bentleys were in the next 3 places. Barnato won in the exact same car in 1930, partnered by Glen Kidston, with a replica in 2nd place.

In 1929 Sir Henry Birkin and the appropriately-named Colonel Clive Gallop developed a large, Roots-type supercharger that pepped up the Bentley 4.5 still more. About 50 "Blower Bentleys" were made altogether, including that in which Tim Birkin finished 2nd in the 1930 French GP against the lighter Bugattis and Delages of that day. The same car lapped Brooklands at 137.37 m.p.h.

W. O.'s final design for the marque that bore his name was an 8-litre, 7983-cc. luxury car that was announced in 1930. One of the first British cars to use the new hypoid bevel rear axle, the new model was offered in either 12- or 13-foot versions. It was capable of any speed from 5 to 105 m.p.h. without the slightest effort. Most of the 100 copies of this model produced were heavy saloons, but a notable exception was the 8-litre purchased by Forrest Lycett and greatly modified and developed by him and a friend, L. C. Mackenzie. Apart from its extensive mechanical reworking, this car was fitted with a sleek 2-seater body and as late as 1959 was setting records. That year it covered a flying mile at the Antwerp Motorway at no less than 140.845 m.p.h., not bad for a 29-year-old automoblie, and took a number of Belgian national class records.

The last independent Bentley, a 4-litre engine set in an 8-litre chassis (which resulted in a rather slow and lackluster car) was also introduced in 1930, but W. O. was not responsible for it. Rather, an outside consultant, H. R. Ricardo, gave the company's directors what they wanted rather than what he thought was best. Barnato, one of the group that had controlled the Bentley finances since 1926, withdrew his support; Bentley Motors Limited went into liquidation in 1931. Napier was ready to take over the company, but Rolls-Royce stepped in and acquired its assets for a mere $650,000.

W. O. stayed with Rolls to develop the Silent Sports Car model, first under its management, and it duly appeared at the 1933 Motor Show. It closely resembled the Rolls engine in its 20/25 model and offered the driver 3669 c.c. Most of the cars were fitted with heavy bodywork, however, and few passed 90 m.p.h. even with Vanden Plas sporting coachwork. In 1936, as the car had been modified and constantly grown heavier, a new 4257 c.c. engine was offered, first optionally, then as standard equipment. Bentley himself left Rolls in 1935 to go with Lagonda, but his name was continued, first on a separate line of cars, later on Rolls-Royce models with the only difference being in the radiator and a slightly lower price.

From 1935 to 1946 Bentley worked at Lagonda,

producing its 4.5- and 2.5-litre designs. Later he moved to Armstrong Siddeley as a consultant. Born in 1888, W. O. was retired when he visited Le Mans, scene of his great glories, in 1969 as Rolls celebrated the Golden Jubilee of the Bentley division. On August 13, 1971, W. O. Bentley died in a Woking nursing home in South London. His name and his handiwork will keep his memory as green as the Bentley racing cars that so dominated Le Mans in the Thirties.

CLIFF BERGERE

With a racing career spanning 4 decades, Cliff Bergere became an Indianapolis immortal, though he never won. The fabulous promoter Bill Pickens had him tour the hustings as a French flying ace of World War I, though he was born in New York City in 1897, son of one of the founders of the Title Guarantee and Trust Company. He left home after his family moved West, to live a life of adventure. First there was a short stint as a cowboy, then odd jobs around San Francisco, one of which was selling tickets for an airplane ride from the site of the San Francisco Exposition and keeping the 2 Curtis Jennies fueled and oiled. According to Bergere, he became an airplane stuntman because he wanted a full-length leather coat. A wing-walker and stunt pilot named Owen Locklear was the possessor of this bit of finery and if stunting was how Locklear got the coat, that's what Clifford wanted to do.

Bergere subsequently met Isadore Bernsteen, a motion picture executive. Bergere coyly remarked that he was really a stunt man; Bernsteen said he had a little stunt to be done—a leap off the mast of a schooner 75 feet into the water. Cliff accepted, then went to a local pool to practice. But he could not jump from the 15-foot board until the swimming instructor led him off into the water. Luckily the stunt was modified into a leap from deck height.

Cliff got his second stunt job some months later when he migrated to Hollywood. It was a plane-to-train leap which had killed a veteran acrobat a few days before. Cliff didn't know this, of course, as he dropped seat first onto a train going 55 m.p.h. and hung on. He credits the pilot with a perfect pass to deposit him from the swinging ladder onto the train. But he learned from the experience. Later he did plane-to-plane, horse-to-plane, plane-to-car, plane-to-boat, motorcycle-to-plane, and boat-to-plane switches—most of them firsts. Once, in what was to have been a transfer to a car, the plane hit an air pocket and dropped suddenly. Cliff swept West Pico Street, Los Angeles, with the seat of his pants. Another time propwash from the camera plane blew him off a wing, and he hung by a strut 4,100 feet in the air.

Bergere doubled for men like Reginald Denny, Richard Dix, Red Grange, 3 different O'Briens (Pat, George, and Edmund), James Cagney, Gary Cooper, Clark Gable, Wallace Beery, George Murphy, and George Sanders. Later, as a result of his racing career, he became the official crasher in auto race and gangster pictures. He even wrecked chariots in the Cecil B. DeMille silent epic *The Ten Commandments*.

Cliff entered racing about 1924 as a result of his stunt career, in a Duesenberg race car which was one of several he rented to movie studios. He beat Leon Duray and came to the attention of Bill Pickens. The great promoter saw in this 6 foot 2 inch young man with the carefully waxed mustache and the French-sounding name a valuable property, and "French flying ace" Clifford Bergere (Ber-ger-ee) was born.

From the Pickens fiction mill, Cliff learned that he had conquered Vail in the East for the dirt track championship and had come West to defeat his former compatriot, Duray, and the great Western hero, Frank Lockhart. Bergere made this come true in the Jack Dempsey Sweepstakes at Bakersfield, Calif., when Duray's engine quit and Cliff won after lapping Lockhart. Bergere raced Sundays in the IMCA programs at Ascot and did sensationally well. He eventually caused the break between Pickens and Duray when he won from Leon the fantastically rococco Italian Colony helmet, made originally at a cost of $2,500 for Ralph DePalma. Pickens was so sure even then that Lockhart would win the Indy 500 and, incidentally, capture the helmet from Cliff that he posed Frank in the thing be-

fore he gave it over. He was wrong only on the latter count.

Bergere was learning in his Duesenberg by doing. He spun and skidded so much that IMCA drivers finally petitioned to remove him from racing as a menace. Pickens told the truth when he intimated that their concern was because Cliff was winning most of the races. IMCA ruled that Cliff would have to demonstrate he could run a full lap without skidding or spinning, which of course he did with ease.

Still winning, Cliff began ranging farther afield into the Southwest; but he had taken notice of the growth of the board tracks. This and the prospect of much bigger purses brought him into the AAA fold. He raced all through the board track era, finishing high on occasion but never winning a really important race, and participating in some spectacular mishaps. In the closing days of the Salem, N.H., board track in 1929, for instance, his Miller race car spun when a wheel dropped into a hole in the track. Rotting boards gave way as parts of the car flew into the air after hitting the rim rail. The drivers' seat was plainly empty as the disintegrating vehicle careened to a halt. Had he been thrown to his death outside the track? When the vehicle stopped, Bergere emerged from beneath the car. He imperiously waved track officials aside and strode against traffic around the track until he stood opposite the grandstand. He gave the fans a victorious salute and then blew a kiss. The crowd went wild. This was showmanship in the heroic tradition!

Another time he was driving an old Frontenac in a minor race. The car's cockpit was much too small for him, and he wedged himself into it, commenting on the dire possibilities if the car caught fire. And it did. But when the dust and smoke settled, there was Cliff sitting Indian fashion on the car's tail. He steered it to a halt on the infield and with smoldering gloves and stockings walked across the track without looking either way to take his wife in his arms. She fainted while the crowd screamed in joy and incredulity.

It was inevitable that Bergere would eventually get to Indianapolis. He did it at the age of 30 in a green Miller racer, it was at Indy more than any other place that he stamped himself as an all-time great. He drove in 16 Indy races in all, his last at the age of 50, finished 9 times among the top 10, compiled 6,545 racing miles on the track and became the initial driver to run the full distance nonstop in a gas-fueled car, a feat that cost him victory for he drove the final laps so ill from fumes and so fatigued that he retched continually. In his first Indy he locked wheels with a relief driver named Henry Kohlert, watched the Kohlert car flip and pass 4 feet over his head, pitted to change 3 wheels and, despite 9 pit stops from spilling oil, finished 9th overall.

Cliff finished 3rd in 1932 in a Studebaker and in 1937 in an Offy. In 1941, as before every race, he calculated the average speed needed to win and drove to that average. But there was a difference this time. At 119 m.p.h. he felt the tires and fuel could be made to last for a nonstop run. So did Floyd Davis, but Moore, who owned both cars, pulled him in to give Mauri Rose the car. Rose won with it by default.

At 75 miles Cliff was 6th, at 100 he was 8th, at 150 he was 6th again and by 175 he had taken over 3rd place. Finally, at 300 miles, he went into the runner-up spot behind Wilbur Shaw. When Shaw crashed at the 380-mile mark, Bergere was in the lead (and at his pre-calculated average speed, too). But the stand-up Offen-hauser was belching fumes into the cockpit; Bergere was soon ill. Dizzy, he slowed down, dropping to 2nd, to 3rd, to 4th. All but overcome by fumes, he finished in 5th place and had to be lifted from the car and revived in the hospital. "I drove that last 50 miles on instinct," he said years later. "If I had made even one stop for water and to clear my head I think I could have won."

In 1940 Bergere had made history of another sort when on July 22 and 23 he teamed with Ab Jenkins in the Mormon Meteor to set a host of national and international unlimited marks up to 24 hours. Among those that lasted into 1965 were the 24-hour mark of 161.18 m.p.h., the 12-hour mark of 170.21 m.p.h. and the 6-hour mark of 172.38 m.p.h.

In the twilight of his racing career, which after World War II was confined to Indianapolis, Bergere found new glory with the Novi. He knew as well as anyone how to tame this beast, which was plagued through its early life by unimaginative engineering and poor racing luck. One of the great racing performances of all time was Cliff's in a race in 1947 which turned out to be his last. He had trained for this contest as arduously as ever. Wives all over Indianapolis were startled when the tall, nattily-dressed man with the graying mustache and sideburns asked if he could cut their lawns for free. Cliff was supposed to be the rabbit of a 2-car Novi threat. He was to run the opposition into the ground, with Herb Ardinger, a last-minute replacement for Doc Williams, to move up if and when Cliff's car burned it-self out.

Cliff pulled away easily from the leaders on the 1st lap. By the 4th he was lapping tail-enders; by the 23rd he was so far in front he seemingly had the race won. But then he pulled into the pits; his right front tire was worn through. With bad pit work Cliff came back in 7th, a lap behind leader Bill Holland. Again he started up the ladder and in less than 40 laps he was 2nd, on the same lap as Holland and gaining fast. But, just past the 150-mile mark, the Novi unaccountably stalled and Cliff rode in on a tow truck as Holland was setting a new record for 200 miles. Ardinger was called in, 9 laps behind Holland with an incredibly ill-handling car. Bergere took over and, before the 300-mile mark, entered the top 10. When he stopped for fuel just be-fore the 400-mile mark he was 5th. He lost it to Rex Mays on the stop, took it back within a lap and then took 4th place from Jimmy Jackson. When the check-ered flag fell on the winner he had made up 7 laps of his original 9-lap deficit and was closing on 3rd—this with a car which had 4 faulty wheels.

Bergere signed for the 1948 race but never ran. During practice he complained that oil leaking from the right front universal was soaking the brake lining. The complaint was ignored for the moment as engine de-signer Bud Winfield asked him to warm the car up at not over 3,000 r.p.m. Winfield would then take over to check out the engine. Bergere did as asked, but when he cut the engine and pulled the hand brake, the brakes grabbed. The car went into a sensational spin. When he came back to the garage, he heard owner Lew Welch saying, "Bergere must have been fooling around." Cliff went into a rage and quit on the spot. Two days later Ralph Hepburn, his best friend, was killed practicing in the same car.

Bergere tried other cars but had no heart for racing after that. He sat out 1949 but seemed ready to make a comeback in 1950 when he acquired the Cotton Hen-ning Maserati driven previously by Wilbur Shaw and Ted Horn. He cut a few hot laps and felt good but then his wife stopped it all. Shirley Bergere always had joked that she felt safer when Cliff was on a race track than when he was flying a plane. But this time she said she didn't feel good about the race. Cliff always followed her hunches. The next rainy day—when he knew he could get the headlines—he announced he was retired from racing.

Bergere became perhaps the best of the Champion Spark Plug lecturers. He would arrange to drive through a city industriously violating every traffic regulation in order to make time, with a dignitary in the back seat calculating the fines. Then he would drive the same route, follow every law to the letter and arriving only seconds later or sometimes just as fast. This preceded a safety lecture with illustrations on the futility of violating laws. He got headlines, but that was normal for Cliff Bergere. He had been a headliner all his life.

GARY BETTENHAUSEN

The offspring of famous people face a special obstacle when they choose the same profession. Gary Betten-hausen did. He was very close to his father, Tough Tony, and—by his own admission—thought Tony was indestructible. When Tony met his death at Indianapolis in 1961 at the age of 44, Gary would not really admit to himself that Tony died this way. He felt he had to follow in Tough Tony's footsteps as number one son, yet his desire to race had been diminished by the tragedy.

He started in go-karts, then moved to USAC stock cars. In his first time out in a sprint car he admitted he was terrified of all that Ford power, yet he finished 2nd. From 1961, when he began driving professionally, through 1965 there was little improvement in his driving or in his desire: he used the same No. 99, painted his cars black, but there seemed to be an ingredient missing —aggressiveness. Things were little better in 1966 except for some flashes of brilliance.

In 1967 Gary concentrated on midgets, winning 5 of 36 starts and finishing 3rd behind Mel Kenyon and Mike McGreevy in the USAC rolls. He began to remind people of Tough Tony—the walk in long strides with arms swinging, the piercing eyes, the broad muscular back. In 1968, he teamed with Willie Davis to drive the City of Syracuse Special sprint car. In his initial full sprint season, he won 7, and finished 2nd to Larry Dickson. He made his first Indy field and lasted 43 laps. On the season, he earned $40,000. Now there was a difference; Gary was beginning to enjoy racing and winning, enjoy beating anyone who was even momentarily in front of him on a race track. Maturity and unremitting practice had turned an essentially shy youth into what contemporaries call a carbon copy of Tough Tony. And Gary had to go one step further than his famous father. The small dirt tracks where the USAC sprint cars competed used to be called "bull rings." Racing on them took a special kind of skill that was important to American Championship racing, for it led to competition on the mile dirt ovals. There are few mile dirt tracks left; the sprint car championship has become a sport unto

itself. The tracks are dusty despite the best efforts of USAC; chancy because ruts often develop during the race; and the cars are entirely different from the rear-engined Championship cars. It is often a test of nerves and recklessness: the man who drives deeper into the corners and closer to the outside rail wins; the man who chops slower cars off and risks elimination himself to intimidate faster ones wins.

In 1969 Gary Bettenhausen was prepared to be that man. He was prepared to challenge the old king of the mountain, Larry Dickson. He was prepared to push him into the wall to win, or so Dickson felt. Bettenhausen broke into one of his rare trackside grins when he heard of Dickson's complaint. Next race, there was a picture of Dickson pasted to Gary's instrument panel, as if Larry were a marked man. This further annoyed Dickson. If such a psychological ploy had ever been used in sprint racing before, no one on the circuit knew it. Gary won the 1969 sprint championship, 8 late-season victories to 3 for Dickson. Such a title means an instant ride on the Championship Trail, but that was something Bettenhausen already had. Fred Gerhardt, the trailer body builder from California who also has become a race car builder, sponsored Bettenhausen, courtesy of Thermo-King truck trailer refrigeration.

Gary won his first Championship Trail race in uncharacteristic fashion at Phoenix International Raceway. It was his 27th birthday (November 18, 1968), and he had qualified only 14th. Perhaps this was all to the good because this Phoenix 200 developed into a demolition derby as crashes delayed the race almost 42 minutes. First A. J. Foyt's car skidded on an oil slick and bounced off the wall into a 250-foot slide before being struck in the fuel tank by Mario Andretti's car. The tangled wreckage burst into flames as it slid to a halt in the infield, Andretti and Foyt jumping out (A. J. with some burns). Soon after, Bud Tinglestad and Jim Malloy tangled in the 1st turn, Malloy's car bursting into flames. That shunt halted the race momentarily. Gary slowly improved his position until, on the 183rd lap, he had the lead. If he had enough fuel to last the remaining 17 miles, he seemed a sure winner. But on the 189th lap he spun, dropping down to the infield as the crowd began to stand up. The spin was over as quickly as it had begun. Gary caught the car and straightened it out before Ruby could do much more than unlap himself. Bettenhausen drove the final 11 miles with unprecedented caution for his first checkered flag in Championship racing.

The 2nd victory he also inherited. It was the Championship segment of the first Michigan Speedway Twin 200 on July 4, 1970. Gary won the pole position but Gordon Johncock whipped past him and led until, 22 miles from the end, he lost control on the high-banked first turn of the 2-mile oval and crashed. Bettenhausen took over and easily held off 1968 Indy winner Bobby Unser. At Indianapolis for Gerhardt, Gary lasted 35

58

laps in 1969 before a broken piston forced him out; during that stretch he had gained 5 positions and temporary 4th place. In 1970, again driving for Gerhardt, Gary lasted 55 laps before a dropped valve finished him. He was not in contention. In 1972 Bettenhausen joined Roger Penske as partner to Mark Donohue in USAC racing. He became team leader when Donohue was injured, but this was a strange year for him. He won his 3rd Championship Trail victory by 4 laps at Trenton, led the Indy 500 for 138 of its 200 laps only to suffer ignition troubles and finished 14th and then finished 19th at Pocono's Schaefer 500. Later in the season he broke an arm in a race honoring his father, soon after his brother, Merle, lost an arm in a USAC accident.

TONY BETTENHAUSEN

"The Tinley Park Express" was his nickname, but Melvin (Tony) Bettenhausen liked to think of himself as a man who was thrice blessed. He owned land (a soybean farm in northern Illinois), he had a fine family, and he raced for a living. If there was a more friendly, helpful man who won the USAC National Championship, he is not in the records. Tony died testing a car for a friend; he died when, for the second time, he was thinking of retiring. He had wanted just one more thing out of racing, a victory in the 500. That he never got his wish dims his luster not at all.

Born September 12, 1916, at Tinley Park, Ill., Bettenhausen raced for the first time in the Chicago Armory at the age of 22. But he was 35 before he won the national championship, and he won his next one at 42 (the first man ever to do it without winning a single race). The name Tony was a relic of his boyhood in the Chicago area. Any kid named Melvin in America has to fight to preserve his self-respect. And Bettenhausen entered such frays with a verve that would have made his Teutonic ancestors proud. He was nicknamed Tunney, after the heavyweight boxing champion, and this eventually became Tony. Not only was he a competitive little guy, he had confidence in his ability.

Bettenhausen saw experienced performers like Jimmy Snyder perform in the midget races in the Chicago Armory, and he decided he could do as well. He tried—and learned the hard way that this racing business was not all that easy. Early accounts refer to him as Flip Bettenhausen. There is a story that he walked into race car owner Murrell Bellanger's auto agency one day in 1938 and announced he would be willing to drive his championship car. Belanger brushed Tony off, but the kid predicted before leaving that Belanger would plead with him to drive one day. Tony's initial big car ride, at Syracuse, was a 2nd behind Rex Mays. Then came the war and Navy service. Tony came back determined to make his mark in racing, and passed his Indianapolis

rookie test in 1946 when he lasted 47 laps before a con rod gave. He never finished a 500 until 1958 when he earned 4th-place money.

But he did a bit better on the Championship Trail. In 1946 he won his initial major race at Goshen, N.Y. The following year Belanger offered him a ride and the combination was good for record victories at Springfield and Goshen. In 1949 he won at DuQuoin and at Detroit. In 1950 he won Milwaukee, Springfield, and Bay Meadows, Calif. The year of B & B, Bettenhausen and Belanger, was 1951. With only a 9th at Indianapolis for 200 points, Tony took Belanger's No. 99 and dominated the AAA circuit as no one had before. With Indy winner Lee Wallard out of competition. Tony amassed a record 2,556 points with 8 victories and a pair of 2nds out of 14 races. He failed to score points only at the Phoenix Fairgrounds.

And though Belanger's No. 99—driven by winner Lee Wallard at Indy—became one of the great money-winning cars of AAA history, it did not outclass the opposition except for preparation and the man behind the wheel. The clincher came that year at San Jose, Calif. on October 21 at the Santa Clara Country Fairgrounds. Tony needed only a 9th place finish there or at the 2 subsequent races, but he drove to win. He qualified at 36.41 seconds on the mile dirt track, which was 0.47 seconds better than Jim Rigsby in the Bob Estes Special. Rigsby jumped him for the 1st-lap lead, held it for 4 caution laps courtesy of a Bill Vukovich 1st-lap spin, then watched Tony charge by and never let up. He charged so hard that exactly at the halfway mark he had lapped every car in the field. Only then did he ease up, winning by 47 seconds or almost a lap and a half.

It was big news the next week when Bettenhausen failed even to finish at Phoenix after qualifying 4th fastest. Before the race Belanger (the Lowell, Ind., auto dealer and industrialist who made a profitable thing out of his hobby), explained that he was using this race to test modifications on his unbeatable No. 99. These modifications worked fine. After 1950 Phoenix winner Jimmy Davies led the 1st two laps, Tony took the lead on the 3rd and on the 20th lap enjoyed a 12-second advantage. It looked like another Tinley Park Express runaway when, on the 86th lap, a huge blister developed on Tony's right rear tire. His crew noticed it and frantically hoisted the "E-Z" sign while deciding whether to gamble or pull him in. The decision was made for them soon after when the tread ripped off the tire and, wrapping itself around the wheelhub, stalled the engine. Johnny Parsons in the Blue Crown Special won. He won also at the Bay Meadows 150 in the Ed Walsh Wynn Oil Special when Bettenhausen pitted after 97 laps of front running to make a precautionary tire change. The margin of victory was just the length of that extra pit stop. After winning the 1951 crown, the Tinley Park Express announced his retirement from all but Indianapolis competition. He owned a Chrysler agency in his home town, and his wife, Valerie, was in favor of the move. He also had 4 children whom he wanted to see more often. He took time out to sweep to a class victory in the 1951 Mexican Road Race and is said to have refused a ride with Ferrari.

The fact that he had never been able to finish Indy rankled, however, or his wife might have gotten a full retirement out of him. He failed to finish again in 1952, his engine stalling after 92 laps. Retirement didn't sit well with Tony. He went to almost all the races as a spectator, insisting he was retired, but you could see that the it wouldn't stick when you watched him look at the race cars. It was like a boy with his nose against the window of a bakery. Failure again at Indianapolis only whetted his appetite to drive once more, and he climbed back behind the wheel of Belanger's No. 99 at DuQuoin. He was running away from the field until a drive shaft snapped. He did win Syracuse the next week and also Phoenix.

In 1954 misfortune struck. He had accumulated his usual DNF at Indy and was preparing for a full season of Championship racing when, during a midget race in Chicago, his brakes failed in traffic. Riding over the wheel of another car, he flipped into a concrete wall, suffering head injuries. In critical condition for days, he pulled through and was back watching and planning for 1955 by the season's end. There was a 2nd place at Indy, but he had to share the ride with Paul Russo. He finished 4th for the season, without a victory. In 1956 he suffered a broken shoulder blade when he hit the wall at the Brickyard. He recovered and returned to win at

Syracuse again. In 1957 he drove the Novi at Indy, finishing 15th when he was flagged 5 laps shy of his goal. He skipped the first 4 Trail stops in another effort to stay away from racing, but returned to very disappointing finishes. It looked like time was going to do what Tony refused to do—retire him.

But the 1958 national championship season found Tony using his experience and consistency to defeat a new generation of chargers like Johnny Thomson and George Amick. Len Sutton won Trenton; Tony was 2nd. Jimmy Bryan won Indy; Tony was 4th in the Jones & Maley Offy, finally finishing an entire race. Art Bisch won Milwaukee; Tony was 2nd. Eddie Sachs won Langhorne; Tony was 5th. Then came 3 no-points races in a row—Atlanta, Springfield, and the Milwaukee 200. Suddenly, Thomson looked like the challenger to Amick, winning at DuQuoin and Syracuse, but he needed a sweep of the final 3 races to luck through. He didn't get it. Sachs won the Indy Fairgrounds race, Thomson 2nd, Amick DNF and Tony 5th (driving one-handed after a flying rock injured his right elbow). And Rodger Ward won the next Trenton race with Thomson 2nd, Amick DNF, and Tony was 3rd. That gave Bettenhausen the point-lead for the first time. When Thomson won Sacramento with Tony 5th, everything rode on Phoenix. The score read Bettenhausen 1,670, Amick 1,640 and Thomson 1,520.

It rained early the day of the race but the clouds disappeared, leaving the dirt well-packed and lightning fast. Bettenhausen had shifted from the Hardwood Door Special to the John Zink Special, both conventional Offies, in mid-season. He qualified for the outside of the 2nd row ahead of Rodger Ward, A. J. Foyt, Thomson, Sachs, and a rookie debuting in Championship racing, Lloyd Ruby. Starter Jimmy Jackson's green flag waved down and Larson jumped Rex Easton who was on the pole, taking the lead with Tony in hot pursuit. Bettenhausen scooted past the long way around, then drove down for a 2-car-length margin. The early laps of a 100-miler see the sorting out of who shall contend and who shall not. Amick's car was not handling; his only chance was merely to finish. But Thomson, Tony, Larson, and Sachs were all in contention.

The old veteran held Larson off for 10 laps as they pulled away from the pack. When 15 laps passed, Thomson and Sachs were moving up on Easton. The one-quarter mark, and it was Bettenhausen, Larson, Easton, Thomson, and Sachs. Then Eddie made his move in the red Pete Schmidt Special, running higher into the banks than Thomson. Sachs took the ultimate risk, scraping the outer guard rail with the tail of his car and diving at Thomson, forcing him down and back. He then passed Easton, followed a few laps later by Johnny. Then the real war began. Sachs and Thomson were closing on Tony and Larson as the crowd strained in excitement. Jud looked back at the fast-closing Sachs and pushed his black and white Bowes Seal Fast Special harder than he wanted to. He closed on Bettenhausen, running nose-to-tail for 3 laps, then took him on the 30th lap. Larson was in front to stay, but by a margin so close that he had to charge the entire race.

A battle remained for 2nd, Sachs and Thomson taking dead aim on Tony. Race-wise Bettenhausen dove for the inside, the shortest way around, and the 2 followed him. For 12 laps they rode almost 3 abreast—Bettenhausen down low, Thomson in the middle, and Sachs up top. Once Sachs managed to get into second but Tony, refusing to give an inch, fought him off. Almost unnoticed, George Amick rolled behind the pit wall, his hopes for the Championship finished.

Then Thomson found a hole and blasted into second. Tony fought him back, too, but Johnny, not to be denied, screamed through. On the 70th lap Bettenhausen once more took back the position. Something had to give, and it was Sachs. Eddie spun off the rail, caught his car and tore after the leaders again, but the caution lights flashed on, freezing positions for a lap. Sachs was out of contention. The caution came on at the 83rd lap for another spin, forcing a 3-lap slowdown. When the green signal flashed, the 3 men floored their accelerators for a 14-mile dash. During the caution, spectators in the pits had noticed oil spraying on Tony. Was this to be the end of a gallant title effort?

Larson took the lead again and Bettenhausen followed almost by instinct, a film of oil spreading across his goggles. Now Thomson made his move. The D-A Lubricant Special pulled even with the Zink car, moved slightly ahead, and then began unaccountably to drop back. On the next lap Thomson pitted, his motor finished for the day. The Championship Trail point battle was over. Tony didn't need to run any more, but he never stopped trying to catch Larson even if it was a herculean task with oil spraying and the outside world a blur of speed and merging colors. Bettenhausen finished 2nd with Sachs 3rd. He wheeled into the winner's circle next to Larson with his wife and the Zink crew—John Zink, chief mechanic Denny Moore, and the rest—crowding happily about him.

In 1959 Tony finished 2nd to Rodger Ward for the national title, winning at Trenton and Phoenix and finishing 4th at Indianapolis. He seemed about to go on forever. The next season he finished 5th for the season in the Dowgard car, running 2nd at Trenton and 4th at the Milwaukee 100, then leading the Milwaukee 200 for the 123 laps preceding a breakdown on the 182nd mile. He came in 2nd at DuQuoin and Syracuse and in the Hoosier Hundred at Indy Fairgrounds, but the rest of his season was a bust. In total points amassed during the postwar era, Tony was far in the lead. The only thing he had not done was win the 500. In 1961 the Tinley Park Express pushed the Autolite Special into the lead for the first 30 laps of the Trenton 100 before being forced out. But 5 weeks later he was dead. He crashed trying to find out how to improve the handling of a car listed for Paul Russo, his longtime competitor and friend.

MIKE BEUTTLER

There was an "Egyptian" driver in Formula 1 in 1971 —at least that's what the programs and press information kits said at the Hockenheim Jochen Rindt Memorial race, a non-championship Grand Prix contest early in the season. Actually Michael Beuttler wasn't an Egyptian, just a trim, experienced Englishman who was born in Cairo because his mother and Army father happened to be there on April 13, 1943.

The experience that had earned Beuttler his shot at F1 was fairly extensive. He had been racing since 1960 with the Chequered Flag team, and a group of British stockbrokers and financial whizzes had been backing Mike's single-seater efforts since 1968 when he entered the Formula 3 scene as a one-man team. It was first known simply as the Clarke-Mordant Racing team; then in 1971 was joined by a third man, Alistair Guthrie. After winning the Grovewood Award in 1970, Beuttler and his sponsors set their sights on Formula 2 with a March 712, but that turned out disastrously as the car continually came apart. He got into F1 simply by having generous sponsors and with an assist from March's Max Mosley, who arranged—perhaps to make amends for Beuttler's faulty F2 March—for his team to acquire the 711 that Ronnie Peterson had used to capture a 2nd at Monaco.

Mike already had gotten some F1 time in non-championship races such as the Brands Hatch Race of Champions (retired), the spring Oulton meet (retired) and that Rindt Memorial at Hockenheim (13th) when he took over the Peterson car for the Woolmark British GP as a late entry. He lasted 22 laps in his GP debut. In Germany for the real F1 race he lasted 4 laps. At Austria he finished 13th but was unclassified, and the story was similar in Canada (17th and running but unclassified) after another retirement in the Italian GP. Not a very auspicious beginning, but a beginning nonetheless.

In 1972 Beuttler's City sponsorship continued—with the addition of Jack Durlacher (once a partner of Rob Walker)—in both F1 and F2 with Marches.

LUCIEN BIANCHI

Le Mans and Lucien Bianchi just seemed to go together. His 13th ride in the world-famous French race was his greatest triumph, a victory shared with Pedro Rodriguez in a Ford GT-40 in 1968. His 14th ride there —or, actually, his preparation for his 14th—resulted in his death. Bianchi was born in Milan, Italy, in 1934, the son of an Alfa Romeo mechanic, but the youngster grew up in Belgium where his father was a mechanic for

Belgium's Johnny Claes. Lucien started rallying about the age of 18 and grew particularly adept at it and at long-distance racing.

Quiet, almost shy despite his red hair and mustache, Bianchi was a perfect codriver for either more extroverted drivers or other introverted ones. His rally and racing mates ranged from youngsters like Jacky Ickx to veterans like Jo Bonnier. After a string of consistently high placings in the Tour de France (including 3 class victories) and other rallies, Bianchi won the Liège-Sofia-Liège Rally outright in 1961, his initial big victory. The following year, he and Bonnier shared a winning ride at Sebring's 12-Hour for Ferrari.

In 1964 Bianchi shared a Daytona 2nd, a Nurburgring 1000 4th, and a Paris 1000 5th; then in 1965 he and his brother Mauro won the Nurburgring 500. He also came to America and tried unsuccessfully to qualify for the Indianapolis 500, but made some USAC starts. Certainly Bianchi's most successful year was 1968, since he not only won Le Mans but shared a Watkins Glen 6-hour victory with Ickx and broke into Grand Prix racing with a 3rd place at Monaco and a 6th at Spa, both with uncompetitive Cooper-BRM. Sixth at Daytona in sports car racing, Bianchi was 3rd in the Targa Florio—both in Alfas—and won the Watkins Glen 6-hour race in a GT-40 shared by Ickx. He was on his way to almost certain victory in that year's London-Sydney Marathon when his Citroen was struck by another car and Lucien suffered a skull fracture. On March 30, 1969, in the 2nd day of practice at Le Mans, Bianchi's Alfa Romeo T33 failed to clear the Mulsanne Straight and crashed at top speed into a telephone pole and small exchange building, killing him instantly.

GEORGE BIGNOTTI

The mechanic really rules the racing world. That alone would make this bespectacled San Francisco Bay area master mechanic one of the most important men in the American racing world, for he has supervised the wrench-twisting for such drivers as A. J. Foyt and Al Unser. The single-season record for victories on the USA Championship Trail is 10 and is held by both of these men. George was the mechanic each time.

There were two older Bignotti brothers, both racing mechanics, George (born in 1918 in San Francisco) cut his eye teeth on a pinion ring. When the boys finally grew up and bought a midget, they raced the car as often as 5 nights a week. George was the relief or substitute driver. When the regular driver didn't show, he jumped into the car and, in his best year, went for 14 victories in 18 starts. But he decided soon after that his place was in the mechanical end of the business or at home with wife and daughter. In 1954 Freddie Agabashian, who had driven the Bignotti midget, phoned George to come to Indianapolis and straighten out his car. Freddie finished 6th, and George's horizons expanded.

Working with Frank Kurtis in 1956, Bignotti was credited with the first Indy roadster, the lightweight car with the low silhouette and offset engine that started a trend. Foyt and Bignotti first were tossed together in 1960 under the Ansted Rotary colors. "I needed nerve pills before the first season was over," Bignotti recalled, "but he's great." The pair won the Indianapolis 500 in 1961 and 1964, won the USAC championship 3 times in 4 years, and were each other's biggest—and richest—boosters until one day in 1965 when they finally split. In 1962 Bignotti was named USAC Mechanic of the Year. He staged a repeat performance in 1970 after Al Unser won the Indianapolis 500.

Bignotti gained international fame in 1965 as the man who accomplished "the Americanization of Lotus," although his first efforts were not exactly crowned with success. The Sheraton Thompson people, Foyt's car sponsor, purchased one of Colin Chapman's British beauties in December 1964. The car had been back-up at Indianapolis earlier that year and later scored an impressive victory at Trenton in the hands of Parnelli Jones. Foyt and Bignotti had some ideas on curing what they considered weaknesses in the basic Lotus design (at least for United States racing) in the front and rear suspension, engine mounts and oil lines. With Lugi Lesovsky, a body expert, they tore the racer apart and started from scratch with the pieces.

Bignotti designed a heavier monocoque body for the car, had California's Douglas Aircraft build a set of stronger rear radius arms for it, then changed all the vehicle's suspension components to heat-treated chrome moly. A larger oil cooler that gave about 50 percent better cooling was installed and 3 aluminum plates were placed near the troublesome motor mounts in the 495 h.p. racer. "The whole conversion added about 50 pounds to the original machine," Bignotti said later in describing the conversion. "There wasn't too much left of the original car except the steering arms, magnesium wheels, Girling discs, the box, rear end, and the sway bar brackets in back. But we figured we had all the bugs ironed out."

Foyt took the Bignotti Lotus-Ford to Phoenix International Raceway in Arizona, site of the memorial Jimmy Bryan 150. The initial qualifying attempt (at 117.496 m.p.h.) took the pole for the April 1965 race. The time was just a fraction off Jones's lap record for the 1-mile oval set in November 1964 in a brand-new factory Lotus. In the race Foyt blasted the red and white Lotus into the lead early, heading Rodger Ward and Mario Andretti for the first 29 laps. On the 30th, he slowed, however, and by lap 41 he was parked and out of the race with a hose clamp failure that had led to overheating and falling oil pressure and, more importantly, a snapped rear sway bar.

"That damned bracket," Bignotti reflected. "It was one of the few Lotus parts I didn't bother to replace and that's what I got for it." Back to the pits went the car. "By the time George is through," cracked A. J. later, "that car may be more Foyt than Lotus, but by that same time we gonna get it into a going machine." Bignotti wasn't talking, just banging away, as always.

When George went to work for the John Mecom team in 1966 he was exposed to, and played nursemaid to, a succession of Lola chassis. It was here that he and Al Unser came together, and it was here that he began to think about how he could combine features from both the Lola and the Lotus into something better than either. When Mecom called it quits in 1968, George had already thought about the subject, and he and Unser ran a season with the wedge-shaped, part-Lola, part-Lotus, part-Bignotti car. Then in 1969 came the affiliation with Parnelli Jones and the ideas went into the so-called Colt chassis—another derivation from Lola/Lotus practice. For 1970 the important addition was a new body shell designed to minimize crosswind effects and improve downthrust. It had a curved underbelly. The success of the car proved that other people besides McLaren could stay ahead of the pack in design.

"What it comes down to is that you must go with your theories and your experience," Bignotti said late in 1970. "Racing is a matter of taking every legal edge you can. You try to set up the cars as best you know how, and then hope yours is the best there is. When Graham Hill won the 1966 Indianapolis 500 he got a car that I felt was the best in the light of my experience then. Even two years later I knew things I could have

done to make that car better. In making the body shell changes for 1970, I checked with friends of mine in the aircraft industry on the soundness of my theories. I have always tried to check out my theories before putting them into motion. I imagine I always will."

In 1971 Bignotti went with Al Unser and the Vel-Parnelli Jones team as chief mechanic. That meant he had ultimate responsibility for Joe Leonard's winning cars too. In 1972, more of his theories were put to the test with a "dream" trio of Unser, Leonard, and Andretti. Second at Indy and a winner at the Schaefer 500 in Pocono is not a bad testimonial but George tipped early that he had a new team and new things to check out in 1973.

CLEMENTE BIONDETTI

They called him "King of the Mille Miglia," and well they might, for Clemente Biondetti won that 1,000-mile Italian endurance race 4 times—3 of those times consecutively. Not only that, he won the 600-mile Tour of Sicily twice in a row. He was just as competitive in regular circuit racing, and he kept racing until he was 56 years old.

Biondetti was born August 18, 1898, and grew up in Tuscany. In 1923 he took up motorcycle racing with a 500-c.c. Motor Galloni, but soon switched to the more familar and successful marques like Norton, Excelsior, and AJS. Clemente's initial auto race came when he was 29 on an 1100-c.c. Salmson, and that season he won Italy's 1100 c.c. championship. High spots of those early years were the Tripoli voiturette races: he was 2nd in 1928, then won in 1929 at 66.04 m.p.h. It was at Tripoli, too, that he made his major race debut in the African nation's Grand Prix of 1930, coming in 3rd in a Talbot. In 1931 Clemente joined the Maserati factory team and finished 3rd in the Rome and French GP.

But it was with Alfa Romeo that Biondetti scored most of his great triumphs. In 1937 he was 2nd to Nino Farina in the Naples GP. In Tripoli his was the only Alfa that could run with the powerful Mercedes cars of Hermann Lang, Rudi Caracciola, and Manfred von Brauchitsch, but he retired when the Alfa blew up. In 1938–39 he was 3rd in the Ciano Cup at Leghorn. The year 1938 saw Biondetti's initial Mille Miglia victory. At age 40 in a 2.9 litre Alfa, he set a record 84.1 m.p.h. pace over the twisting up-and-down Mille Miglia route that stood until 1953 when a 4.1-litre Ferrari finally was able to top it. War was clearly imminent by then but there were 2 more seasons of racing left, and Clemente was at his peak. In 1939 he won the Acerbo Cup at Pescara at 83.61 m.p.h., was 2nd to Farina in the Prix de Berne and 2nd again in the 932-mile Tobruk-to-Tripoli race across North Africa. In 1940 he placed to Farina in the Tripoli GP.

63

When racing resumed, Biondetti was hardly considered a factor because he was 49 years old. But great things were still ahead of him. Beginning in 1947 he won the Mille Miglia 3 consecutive times, first in an Alfa, then in Ferraris. Each year his winning speed increased—68.63 m.p.h. to 75.16 m.p.h. to 81.53 m.p.h. In 1948 and 1949 he won the Tour of Sicily (and the Targa Florio designation, since that prize was awarded for the Tour those years instead of being run separately) in Ferraris at 55.50 m.p.h. and 51.29 m.p.h. In 1952 he was 2nd in the 12-hour Acerbo Cup, 3rd in the Monaco GP for sports cars and in the Villa Real race in Portugal. In 1954 he won the Bari 3-hour for sports cars in a Ferrari at 76.31 m.p.h., then was given an old 2.7-litre Ferrari for the Mille Miglia and placed 4th in the driving rain. With Masten Gregory, the young American, he was 4th at the 12-hour race at Rheims. But it was apparent that he was not well. Biondetti had known he had cancer for several years. When he felt it would be dangerous to others if he kept racing, he retired. A year later, in 1955, he was dead.

PRINCE BIRA

The programs always listed him simply as "B. Bira," but his real name was Birabongse Bhanudej Bhanubandh, Prince of Siam. Born in 1914, Prince Bira was sent to England for his education, and upon the completion of his work at Eton in 1933, he began racing a Riley, then a K3 MG Magnette. Two years later Bira acquired an ERA 1500-c.c. supercharged racing car that was the most successful type in its class. Driving on a British license, since Siam was not yet affiliated with the sanctioning FIA, Bira soon was winning more than his share of races, and he was awarded the coveted British Racing Drivers Club Gold Star 3 years in a row (1936–38). With Richard Seaman he became the favorite racing driver of the day in Britain, and his successes included ERA victories over the factory team itself. With a countryman named Prince Chula, an *équipe*, or racing team, was formed and was successful not only with the ERA, but with Maserati, Delahaye, and BMW. The Maser, formerly Whitney Straight's car, ran the initial 100-m.p.h. lap at Phoenix Park in Ireland. In a BMW, Bira won his class and was 3rd overall in the Tourist Trophy in 1937.

Racing was suspended during World War II, of course, but the Chula-Bira *équipe* was back in business as soon as racing resumed. Towards the end of 1948, the partnership dissolved, but Bira continued on his own, driving for Scuderia Plate in a 4CLT Maserati, for the British HWM team, and for himself with a little white mouse badge as his insignia in his own Maser and in a 4.5-litre unsupercharged OSCA with which he set a lap record and won at Goodwood in 1951. The OSCA, however, proved a disappointment, and Bira

began cutting back his auto racing for another one of his passions, yacht racing. In 1954, he was back in Grand Prix circles with a 250F Maserati, and his most brilliant postwar drive probably came in the French GP at Rheims, when he seemed a cinch to finish 3rd behind the superfactory team of Juan Fangio and Karl Kling in Mercedes racers, only to suffer a fuel line blockage as he switched to a reserve tank on the last lap. He lost 3rd place to a Ferrari. It was a final annoyance to the proud Prince, and soon after he quit the courses for good.

He was an outstanding amateur who felt the pinch of the factory teams and bowed to the inevitable. As a driver Bira was among the better ones of his day, both professional and amateur, and he was a fast man in the right kind of machine.

TIM BIRKIN

Sir Henry R. S. Birkin, Baronet, was courageous and talented behind the wheel of the monster cars (by modern standards) of the Twenties and Thirties. Perhaps too courageous, especially about his own welfare. Born in 1896, Birkin first started racing in 1921 at Brooklands with a French DFP, a small 2-litre turned out by Doriot, Flandrim et Parent. The chances are Birkin wasn't overly impressed by the old, underpowered French car. At any rate, he left racing for the next 6 years to get his Nottingham lace business firmly established.

In 1927 the man and the right car came together. The

64

car was the Bentley with which Tim Birkin is so intimately associated, although Alfa Romeo might equally have claimed the distinction. In a Brooklands 6-hour race, Tim was 8th in his initial Bentley start. The following year he brought a 3-litre home 3rd in the Essex 6 Hours, was 5th 3 times—at Le Mans with Jean Chassagne, in the Boillot Cup at Boulogne, and in the Tourist Trophy at Ards—and finished 8th in the German Grand Prix.

Birkin's initial big victory came in 1929, by which time he was a fully established member of the Bentley Boys (Birkin, millionaire Woolf Barnato, theatrical agent Jack Dunfee, bacteriologist Dr. J. D. Benjafield, and newspaperman S. C. H. Davis). Tim and Barnato codrove a Bentley Speed Six that year at Le Mans and won at an average speed of 73.6 m.p.h. It was the 2nd of 3 victories at Le Mans for Woolf, the 1st of 2 for Birkin. In 1929 Birkin also scored a 3rd in the Irish GP at Phoenix Park and an 11th in the gruelling Tourist Trophy.

The following year Tim had his own stable of Bentleys, financed by the Honorable Dorothy Paget (more famous for her equine racing stables). It was a great year for Tim. Mercedes was a serious challenger in the 24 Hours of Le Mans that year with a massive 7-litre supercharged SS that would be driven by Rudi Caracciola and Christian Werner. Before the race, Birkin and Barnato, who was chairman of Bentley as well as a chief driver, agreed to race their cars as a team. The strategy was for Birkin to drive to the limit of his car—which was his normal procedure anyway—and wear down Caracciola by making him use the supercharger more than he wanted to.

W. O. Bentley himself took the mechanic's seat in his car and spent a good part of the race peeling oranges for Birkin and himself, as Tim and Caracciola duelled through the afternoon. They passed and repassed and passed again all afternoon and into the night; both cars eventually broke, leaving the way clear for Barnato's victory. A month later, the duel was repeated in Dublin's Phoenix Park in Caracciola-type weather: a driving rain. Birkin hung on for most of the race, but a broken oil pipe dropped him to 4th by the finish of that Irish GP.

That September Tim drove what many consider to be his finest race. The French openly snickered when he appeared with an open 4-seater Le Mans Bentley sports car for the French GP. The snickers quickly disappeared as Birkin passed car after car. With his dotted scarf flowing behind him like a World War I pilot, Birkin overtook every competitor but Philippe Etancelin's Bugatti by the end of the 247-mile race. His 2nd-place finish brought him an ovation from the French crowd. At the close of the 1930 season, Tim was awarded the coveted British Racing Drivers Club Gold Star.

Nothing was doing with Bentley in 1931, and Tim switched to Alfa Romeo and Maserati. In the former he

won his 2nd Le Mans, codriving with Earl Howe, at an average speed of 78.15 m.p.h., and later won the Eire-ann Cup Irish GP at Dublin at 83.73 m.p.h. In the latter car, he took the 15-lap Mountain Circuit Championship at Brooklands and recorded a 4th in the Spa 24-hour race. Tim's great driving days were about over, although no one anticipated it at the time. He continued to drive a Bentley single-seater at Brooklands without much success.

The end came in the Tripoli Grand Prix in which Birkin was 3rd in a Maserati behind Achille Varzi in a Bugatti and Tazio Nuvolari in an Alfa Romeo. During the race Birkin drove as usual in a blue open-necked jersey with the sleeves pushed up over his elbows. The bare arm touched the exhaust pipe, burning his arm; Birkin ignored the wound and in his usual way failed to tell anyone about it. (A stammerer, he was often uncommunicative.) But when blood poisoning set in, Tim went to his old Bentley Boys teammate, Dr. Benjafield, because he wanted to be in good shape for an impending race.

For 3 weeks Benjafield and several other London specialists fought for Tim Birkin's life. With today's modern drugs, the fight would have been won; in 1933 it was lost, and the racing world lost a colorful personality.

GIOTTI BIZZARRINI

Giotti Bizzarrini was a handsome, lightly built Tuscan, a graduate engineer from the University of Pisa who served on the staffs of Alfa Romeo and Ferrari and then set forth as a free-lance designer for such new Italian marques as Lamborghini and Iso. Bizzarrini was with Alfa from the time he left the university in 1953 until 1957, when he joined Ferrari and was involved in the design and development of the 3-litre Testa Rossa, the original GT 2/2, and the Berlinetta GTO. In 1961, along with 4 others, he became involved in a dispute with the Commendatore Ferrari and left. Bizzarrini quickly was hired by Ferrari's emerging rival for the luxury Grand Touring market, Lamborghini, and was responsible for developing the d.o.h.c. V-12 for Lamborghini's 3500 GT. During the same period Bizzarrini designed and developed several cars for Iso, including 2 Chevrolet-powered designs—the Iso-Rivolta and the Iso Grifo 2-seat coupe—both bodied by Bertone. Bizzarrini himself liked to drive fast, and began racing a special version of the Grifo. At the 1965 Le Mans race, for example, he was 9th overall and 1st in class (over 5 litres).

Eventually Bizzarrini decided to build the competition Grifo as a GT car that would be marketed under his own name (in Europe the design was called the Strada 5300, but in the United States it was known as the GT America). Where the Grifo had been a road car with deluxe appointments and a refined look, the Strada America was a businesslike competition machine, available in several optional forms according to how serious the buyer was about racing and how much his pocketbook held. The basic car wasn't cheap, costing $11,000 or so on average. A Corvette 327 engine was standard, and a top speed of about 145 m.p.h. at 6,000 r.p.m. possible; the Bizzarrini could reach 60 m.p.h. from a standing start in about 6.4 seconds. And you knew you were travelling fast, for the car sat just 43 inches off the ground. These and other models made the marque a favorite of film and pop recording stars, and a few athletes and businessmen.

BUNKIE BLACKBURN

The footnotes of history are filled with might-have-beens who miss their moments of glory by the proverbial hair's breadth. Such a man was James R. (Bunkie) Blackburn, born April 22, 1936. His missed moment was in the 1961 Dixie 400 at Atlanta International Raceway, when Bunkie was pouring it on in a Pontiac that seemed to have wings. The personable young man, then in the 8th year of a racing career that would continue long afterwards, suffered the ultimate embarrassment. While leading, he ran out of gas.

A magnificent driver in modified and sportsman stock cars, Blackburn never quite made it in the NASCAR big time, perhaps because of fidelity to General Motors machinery long after Chevrolet, Pontiac, and Oldsmobile officially had ended their stock-car support. Blackburn was still running Pontiacs at Daytona and other superspeedways long after that brand traded in its Indian symbol for wide-track youth image. In fact, Blackburn was involved in one of the Union 76-Pure Performance Trials' little trickeries in 1966 when his Pontiac was found to have illegal reserves of gasoline built in so ingeniously the eagle-eyed inspectors had been completely fooled.

Originally from Fayetteville, N.C., Blackburn moved to Daytona Beach where he opened a bar. Later he became a regional distributor for Firestone Racing Tires. He left Grand National racing in 1968 with the announcement that he liked competition, but not at the speed necessary to be competitive at that time. He returned to late-model sportsman competition and was still campaigning a 1965 Chevelle as 1970 began.

BILL BLAIR

One of the underrated drivers of NASCAR's early years, Bill Blair was 35 when the group was founded. The 5-foot 6-inch veteran from High Point, N.C., managed to accomplish a number of notable feats nonetheless, before he disappeared from the racing scene in the mid-

Fifties. Driving Mercuries, he finished 4th in the strictly stock division in 1949 and 10th in 1950, winning the Vernon, N.Y., 200-lapper. In 1951 he finished 16th and decided something had to be done about Hudson Hornets. The following year at Atlanta's Lakeside Park, he stormed his No. 12 Olds 88 into the lead and held on to break a string of 7 straight Hudson Grand National victories. He finished 6th for the season, however, because he was skipping races.

Blair was present with a brand-new Olds 88 when 1953 Speed Weeks rolled around. The races then were held on the beach-road course, a 4.1-mile test completely different from anything now in existence. By 1953 NASCAR was well-established and so was its leading driver list. Blair won the 160-mile race in record time, then—as if he were proving this was no fluke—qualified on the new Raleigh mile track in a record 73.43 seconds. By then Olds' potential was well known; in fact, a new era of Chrysler hemis was approaching. Blair finished 13th in 1954 before he stopped racing. On that windy Sunday at Daytona, Bob Pronger on the pole and Fonty Flock next to him were the 88s to watch. The Mexican Road Race Lincolns were there, too, with Tom Cherry, Buck Baker, Curtis Turner, and Don Oldenburg. And the Hudson threat was strong with Herb Thomas, Tim Flock, Joe Eubanks, and Dick Rathmann. The field paraded once around the track before a bomb and starter John Bruner's green flag sent the 57 cars off from a standing start as 20,000 fans howled.

Fonty took the lead as the field gunned for the treacherous north turn. Second by a few car-lengths, Pronger swooped to the outside while track-wise Flock shut off and dived inside. Pronger didn't make the turn; his red and black 88 hurtled through the outer guard rail and rolled down the embankment. Shaken but unhurt, he resumed the chase in a battered car. After three laps, Fonty had a 30-second lead, while his brother Tim and Rathmann fought for 2nd. Herb Thomas had moved to 4th and one of the Lincolns, Tommy Thomson mounted, was 5th ahead of Blair. Three laps later the battle was for 3rd. Fonty was well ahead, out of traffic, and Rathmann was safely in 2nd, but Thomas had moved to challenge Tim Flock. Blair rode steadily in 6th.

A quarter of the way through the race it was Fonty, Rathmann, Thomas, Flock, Thomson, and Blair. But then Blair began to move. On the 12th lap he passed Tim Flock for 5th, a few laps later he took Thomson and closed on Thomas's Hudson. Herb saw him coming and began pressing, going high on the South turn bank and sliding through the North turn. When Rathmann had to pit on lap 23 for fuel and repairs, the two moved up a slot. But Fonty was still rolling along. On the 26th lap Blair inherited 2nd, about a minute behind Fonty. With 13 laps to go Fonty Flock looked like a cinch, even though the North Carolina vet chasing him began to increase his speed slightly. Fonty merely held his pace, but that would have been enough. Then, a lap and a half from the checkered flag, the Flock Olds began to sputter. He rolled to a stop on the North turn —out of gas. Fonty sat disgustedly by the side of the course as his friends in the stands moaned. He was about to abandon the car when Ebanezer Slick Smith, riding 8th in an Oldsmobile, pulled up behind him and began to push. Smith pushed him to his pit and then rode off to the crowd's cheers. But as Fonty's crew refueled the car, Blair roared past. Fonty took off after him, but it was too late; Blair took the checker.

Blair had gone the entire race non-stop while Flock and the rest of the top 5 each pitted once. His 89.50 m.p.h. race average was a new record, and Bill said that crew chief Harry Payne found 3 gallons of his 23 still left after the race. Blair declared the fantastic economy came because he dropped to 2nd gear only in the turns and stayed in high on the straights. He relied on his years of driving experience to find the quickest way to drift into the corners before powering out. Incidentally, Blair's No. 2 car looked like a passenger Olds that had gotten lost. Except for the number and 2 small sponsoring firm decals on the rear fender, he didn't even paint his name on it.

BOILLOT BROTHERS (GEORGES and ANDRE)

There were 3 Boillot brothers, although only 2 of them ever raced. The elder of the racers was Georges, born in 1885, who had a meteoric career, then died a hero in World War I. This set a standard for André that was perhaps cruel, and after one great race, the youngest of the Boillots never again excelled.

Georges, identifiable by his bristling handlebar mustache, raced mostly Peugeots. His initial major appearances were in the Targa Florio voiturette race, in which he retired in 1908 and 1909, then won in 1910, earning the Sicilian Cup by averaging 34.85 m.p.h. That year, too, he was 2nd to teammate Jules Goux in the Catalan Cup. But Georges wanted to race the big cars, and he had the talent and desire that wins races, as he demonstrated. In 1912 Boillot won the Mont Ventoux hillclimb, then captured the 2-day French Grand Prix at Dieppe with a 68.45-m.p.h. average, defeating Louis Wagner in a 16-litre Fiat (Georges's Peugeot engine measured half that). In 1913 Boillot won the Coupe de l'Auto, then took his 2nd straight French GP, this time at Amiens with a 71.12 m.p.h. clocking. Goux was 2nd. In 1914, Boillot came close to winning the premier French race a 3rd time, retiring just a lap from its end with engine problems. The same year, he travelled to America for the Indianapolis 500. He lasted 141 of the 200 laps before the Peugeot's frame snapped, setting the day's fastest lap at 99.5 m.p.h. The car was placed 14th in the final standings.

With the drums of war rolling, Georges enlisted in the French Air Service as a pilot. On April 21, 1916, somewhere over Verdun, he was shot down by 3 German fighters.

André picked up the mantle in 1919. His own greatest racing victory came that year in the twisting tortuous Targa Florio in Sicily. Driving a 5-year-old 2.5-litre Peugeot, André battled the roads as well as his opponents for 8 dramatic hours to win at an average speed of 34.19 m.p.h. At Indianapolis the same year, André raced a Baby Peugeot for 195 laps and finished 15th. He was back at Indy the following 2 seasons, finishing neither time, a 16th-lap engine failure getting his Peugeot in 1920, a broken connecting rod knocking out his Talbot-Darracq in 1921.

His luck was little better in many other races. In the 1921 French GP, for example, Andre was running 5th at Le Mans when he retired; in the 1923 Targa the story was the same. In 1924's Targa, Andre was 5th, the following season 3rd. There were mostly retirements in 1926, but then a 4th in the Targa in 1927 and a 2nd to "Williams" (William Grover-Williams of Britain) in the French GP. He did manage to win the Coppa Florio in 1922 and 1925, the Touring Car GP in 1923 and 1925, and the Belgian 24-hour race for touring cars in 1926, codriving with Louis Rigal in the latter. All these victories were scored in Peugeots. Racing was only occasional after that, but as late as 1931, racing under the pseudonym "Dribus," Boillot was at the Monaco GP with an antique Peugeot, its 1922 engine mounted in a 1920 chassis. He finished 6th.

BOB BONDURANT

When Shelby American won the World Manufacturers Championship in 1965, driver Bob Bondurant had a lot to do with that victory. A dark, handsome man in his early thirties, Bob had curly hair and flashing eyes. He drove his first formula car that same year in a race at Monaco, and there was talk of a Formula 1 ride soon in his future. Bondurant never made it to F1, but he was able to operate at speed nonetheless. He also managed to overcome physical injuries that laid him on the sidelines for almost 3 years to return as a competitive driver in the powerful Group 7 CanAm Challenge Cup machinery that sometimes went faster than the F1 cars.

Robert Bondurant was born in 1934 in Evanston, Ill., but always was listed as a Californian. Like Dan Gurney, he had headed out for the sun and the speeds of the West Coast early. Bob started as a mechanic and sometime Indian motorcycle racer, graduated to a Morgan Plus 4 in 1956 and proceeded to finish 3rd in his initial auto race at Santa Barbara. Soon after he did postgraduate work in the big, tricky Corvette, and it must be said that he performed with honors. He was West

Coast champion in 1959 and had a national reputation, but like many an amateur he reached a sticking point. Some amateurs stay there, big fish in small ponds, plugging away just for the fun of it. Bondurant continued to fool with West Coast amateur racing, but he also devoted a growing share of his time to helicopter mechanics and to earning a helicopter pilot's license in a day when these were unusual. It was 1963 before he got a real racing chance, which was provided by a friend named Carroll Shelby who had an Anglo-American car called the Cobra that needed racing. Like Corvettes, they were big and hairy, Bondurant's kind of car. The first race for Bob came at Continental Divide Raceway near Denver in August. Bondy won the GT class his first time out in the car.

There were 2 more races in 1963, then Bondurant signed a full-time professional road racing contract with Shelby. At Sebring he shared a Cobra with Lew Spencer and finished 5th overall and 2nd in class. At the Targa Florio he and Phil Hill codrove a Cobra to 2nd in class after several major repairs—more like rebuilds—on the road. The best of the European Cobra starts was at Le Mans where Bondy and Gurney won the GT class and finished 4th overall in the Cobra Daytona Shelby. In the USRRC fall series Bob had a Cooper-Cobra for Riverside (5th) and Laguna Seca (3rd).

For him, 1965 was the championship year. At Sebring he shared the winning Daytona coupe, repeated at the Monza 1000, the Nurburgring 1000 and the Rheims 12-hour race. At Spa's Grand Prix the Bondurant coupe was 2nd. At the Rossfeld hillclimb Bondy won the GT

class. At Daytona, too, he codrove a Ford GT40 with Richie Ginther and finished 3rd. In the Targa he crashed; at Le Mans the car suffered a mechanical failure and was retired. That year he was planning to visit Monaco as a race spectator when Ken Tyrrell (a good judge of talent) popped him into a Formula 3 Cooper-BMC at Goodwood for a test drive and decided the performance was good. He offered Bondy a ride for the F3 race that preceded the F1 race. Bob accepted and found himself sitting on the pole for the 2nd heat. There were some familiar faces around him, too—Roy Pike and Peter Revson.

At the flag Bondurant found himself outgunned by the more experienced F3 drivers, but he got away 4th. Dicing with Revson, he won the battle and set out after Pike in the lead. They dueled until Pike suddenly spun, and Bondurant broadsided his machine rather than hit Pike head on. Both cars were wiped out and Peter Revson went on to win it, his initial important race (the race that led to all the good things that happened to Revson after that).

Bondurant kept racing sports cars and an occasional F3 or even Formula 2 car for a couple of years. In 1967, at Watkins Glen, he met with a bad accident in the highly competitive USRRC race there that seemed to spell the end of Bob Bondurant, race driver. But 3 years later, at Road America in the USRRC's successor, the CanAm, who should finish 2nd to England's Peter Gethin but Bondy in a Lola-Chevvy T160. The comeback trail got started at St. Jovite where he retired, at the Glen where he was 14th, at Edmonton and Mid-Ohio where he retired again. Next came Elkhart Lake.

After Elkhart came Road Atlanta and another retirement, and more at Monterey and Riverside. In 1971 he had a McLaren M8E and started off with a 4th at Mosport. Suspension problems dropped him back to 16th at St. Jovite, his engine gave out at Road Atlanta. At the Glen he was 16th. After that he let his sponsor, movie actor Paul Newman, put another man into the car. The Newman tie-in had been a natural for Bondurant who had worked with the actor in *Winning* and in TV specials through the Bob Bondurant School of High-Performance Driving. He had acted as a technical advisor on other films too, notably *Grand Prix*. As usual, Bondy had found a way to work at what he liked and get paid well for it.

FELICE BONETTO

The Grand Prix of Bari was a wheel-to-wheel, nose-to-tail battle in 1948 between 45-year-old Felice Bonetto in a Cisitalia and Chico Landi in a Ferrari. With 10 laps to go Bonetto was leading when Landi tried to pass him in a corner. Bonetto's front wheels were caught between Landi's rear wheels and a hedge, flipping the car. Bonetto was thrown clear and knocked unconscious.

68

Solicitous spectators carried him into a nearby house, but he came to his senses quickly and tried to get back to his car. A doctor and a spectator attempted to restrain the still groggy driver, but were knocked down for their interference. Through sheer muscle he righted the car, pushed it to restart, jumped in as the motor caught, and rejoined the race.

Bonetto didn't win, but he was 2nd, such was his competitiveness. Enzo Ferrari had learned about this driver much earlier than 1948, in a Mille Miglia in the late Thirties. In those days Ferrari was team manager for Alfa Romeo, and in this race he was personally directing operations at an important refueling station. Ferrari awaited his aces—Nuvolari, Varzi, Chiron—who seemed sure to dominate the race. In the distance an Alfa hove into view, but he was not slowing, and Ferrari was afraid the driver would overshoot the station. He leaped into the road and waved his arms to direct the driver into the fueling area, but the car never slowed, and Ferrari had to leap for his life. It was a private Alfa 2.3 entered by Bonetto, and he was leading the race. (Bonetto later ended in a patch of water that spun the car and caused a bent front axle.)

It was 1947 before Bonetto got a decent ride, this time with Cisitalia, and it was a full season after that before the marque was fully competitive, but then, vitally aided by Bonetto, it won the Italian Formula 2 championship. Third in the Acerbo Cup in 1947, the following season Bonetto won at Mantua at 67.1 m.p.h. and at Vigevano at 50.83 m.p.h. He even got a call from Ferrari himself. Bonetto joined the Commedatore

a short time later but not before he scored a 2nd in the Mille Miglia of 1949 and another in the Naples GP. On his own, Felice bought a Formula 1 Maserati and an old 4.5-litre Alfa sports car. It was with the latter that he won at Oporto at 72.30 m.p.h. and led Juan Manuel Fangio and the rest of the Mille Miglia field in 1950 as far as Pescara. Then his car died because the mechanics had forgotten to refill it with oil. Alfa offered him a team berth, but Bonetto was considered number 3 and had to defer to his teammates. Thus he never won, only placed and showed, as at the Italian GP when he shared 3rd with Farina in 1951.

In 1952 he was offered the top spot on the Lancia team and jumped to it immediately. In that season's Targa Florio Bonetto scored his greatest personal triumph, demonstrating again his fierce competitiveness. Leading the Targa near the race's end, his Lancia ran out of fuel on a steep uphill some 300 meters from the finish line. Despite gruelling heat, but aided by the shouts of the Sicilian spectators, he pushed the Lancia up the hill and across the line before collapsing, a 49.70-m.p.h. victor. He was 2nd in the Tour of Sicily that season, too, and 3rd in the Monaco GP for sports cars in a 2.7-litre Ferrari sweep of the event. In 1953 Bonetto was 3rd in the Mille Miglia in a Lancia, 3rd in the Dutch GP in a Maserati shared with José Gonzalez, and won the Lisbon GP in a Lancia at 82.73 m.p.h. over Stirling Moss in a Jaguar.

Felice was in a Lancia for the 1953 Pan-American Road Race. Dueling with Piero Taruffi for the lead midway in the demanding test, Bonetto crashed near the village of Silao and was killed.

JO BONNIER

It was 1959, and the Dutch Grand Prix again was being held at Zandvoort. BRM, the once extremely popular British marque, no longer was expected to do well. In 13 seasons of competition it had never won an important race. It had started first in postwar Britain but had been passed by the late-comers, Jaguar, Cooper, Aston Martin, and even Vanwall. This season 2 BRMs appeared for the GP, one driven by Harry Schell, an American expatriate; the other by a virtual unknown from Sweden, Joakim Bonnier. Neither man had ever won a major GP race for any marque.

Masten Gregory's Cooper led for 7 laps while Bonnier hung on for second. Then the leader's car faltered and Bonnier led—for all of 15 minutes—until Jack Brabham, who would be the World Champion that year and the next, moved his Cooper into the lead. But Jo managed to stick to him like a shadow for 5 laps. Gaining confidence in himself and in his machine, Bonnier moved past Brabham into the lead once more. The sole BRM (Schell having fallen out with mechanical troubles) now

had to hold off 5 Coopers, 5 Ferraris and 2 Aston Martins. On the 50th lap Stirling Moss's car, previously far back, began to move up under the master's hand. On the 59th lap he took over the lead, and the race seemed to be over. But, like an American stock car driver, Jo found that he could slipstream Moss; with 16 laps to go, if he could stay close, perhaps something would happen to the Briton's car. It did. Moss's gearbox seized on the 62nd lap, and Bonnier was in front once more.

Brabham and Gregory were still in the race, and they moved up to challenge this Swedish upstart. Jo himself did not trust his car completely, and slowed almost to a crawl at the Zandvoort turns to conserve his brakes, ensure a smooth gearshift, and avoid taxing his suspension. Brabham gained steadily. Three laps to go and Jack was just 15 seconds behind Bonnier. Closer and closer. On the final lap, the BRM disappeared behind the sand dunes on the opposite side of the circuit, and the British pit crew spent long minutes waiting for its reappearance. Then Bonnier came around the last curve and into view; directly behind him was Brabham's Cooper. The BRM built up its revs and crossed the line at 170 m.p.h.; Bonnier's fist was raised in salute to acknowledge the roars of the crowd and the delirium of the British pit crew. In a few minutes, Bonnier was being pummeled and hugged in a rather un-British way. He was tired and absolutely filthy, he later recalled. But he also recalled that moment as one of the proudest in his life. For from the loudspeakers came a national anthem never before heard on a major international circuit, Sweden's. Those who were there that day said

that Jo Bonnier was crying before the strains of the anthem faded.

Jo looked fierce, but he was as reserved and soft-spoken as an English schoolmaster. Perhaps if Bonnier had been more of a Viking, he would have gone further than he did in the international auto racing scene. He was nevertheless an important part of the GP and sports car ranks for almost 20 years. More than that, he was an articulate spokesman for other drivers and one of the most popular.

Bonnier was born January 31, 1930, 2nd son of a famous genetics teacher and scion of a powerful publishing family, Bonniers Aktiebolag. Jo grew into a powerful man with a good mind. After education in Stockholm, at Oxford (where he learned to speak impeccable English), and Paris (where he learned equally impressive French), Jo was given the opportunity to join the traditional family business. Like his father, however, he did not find it challenging and he gave it up to choose a profession of his own.

Bonnier first competed in an auto race in 1948, in a Scandinavian rally across the rugged roads of Sweden. He had raced a Harley-Davidson motorcycle a year earlier. Over the next 5 years, he limited himself exclusively to rallying in a Citroen, an MG TC, and a Simca, when he had the chance. For 3 of those years, Jo was in the Swedish Navy on a destroyer, reaching the rank of Lieutenant. In 1953 he began ice racing in an HRG. For 2 years he won nearly every race he started, initially driving an ex-Juan Fangio 4.5-litre Talbot, then switching to an Alfa Romeo 3.5 Disco Volante, becoming the "King of the Ice" to Europe's motoring writers.

His successes with the Alfa opened doors at the Italian auto builder, and Bonnier was offered an Alfa distributorship in his native land. In 1955 Alfa gave him a new 2-litre car for the Mille Miglia, following his victory in the Swedish GP in an earlier model. Later that year he had an Alfa at Oulton Park in England to win his initial race there. He returned the same season to win the Tourist Trophy's 2-litre class, finishing 18th overall. In 1956 Bonnier continued with Alfa (though he sold his distributorship), but also started competing in a 1500-c.c. Maserati single-seater. His best showings that year included a triumph at Silverstone, a class victory in the Sardinian road race, another in the Nurburgring 1000, a 3rd in class and 15th overall in the Mille Miglia (starting from 174th place), and victories at Avus and in the Gran Premia di Roma.

He had a serious crash in an Imola sports car race in September, 1956. "Somebody got in my way, and my Maserati flipped," Jo recalled later. "I was flung out and hit a telegraph post head on. Really. I was asleep for some little time." In addition, a vertebra and several ribs were cracked. "I felt terrible, but I flew to Rome for the next series of races the following week. There were 3 of them. That was silly, I know, but I felt that with luck I might get on the Maserati team for 1957, if

I could just make some kind of a showing in Rome." Bonnier was 4th, 1st, and 6th in the 3 starts in a single day; he was signed by the Italians and, later that same year, also signed by BRM of England. He also continued to drive Alfas and Porsches and competed for Centro-Sud as well. Major successes still eluded him, although he did win the Finnish Grand Prix and scored a class victory for Porsche in the 12 Hours at Rheims. And, for the 2nd straight year, Bonnier won his class at Nurburgring.

The next season was a bad one, mainly because of difficulties with his factories. Still he managed a few triumphs, including his first in the United States at Watkins Glen in a Maserati when he beat Phil Hill and Dan Gurney. That year he also competed in hillclimbs for the first time in a Borgward that demonstrated his amazing versatility behind the wheel. He finished 2nd in the European title chase to Wolfgang von Trips. Jo was 5th in the Buenos Aires GP, 2nd at both Syracuse and Caen, and a casualty at Monaco. At Zandvoort he was 10th, in the European GP 9th, and in the French GP 9th. For the British, German, Portuguese, and Italian Grands Prix he had nothing to show but DNF. In the Moroccan GP he was 4th.

In 1959, Bonnier gave up his Maserati berth after the New Zealand GP and another car failure, devoting himself strictly to BRM drives. After his startling and rewarding victory at Zandvoort, Jo and his friend, Trips, shared a 3rd place at Sebring. Then Jo was 3rd at Rheims, and at Nassau he won his class. In the Glover Trophy in England he was 4th, in the German GP 5th, in the Italian 8th, and in the Tourist Trophy a class winner and 2nd overall. Not a great season but impressive nonetheless.

In 1960 Bonnier took to driving Porsches in Formula 2 and sports car events in addition to his F1 BRM ride. He and Hans Herrmann shared honors in a Targa Florio victory; Jo won the Modena GP, the German GP for F2 cars, and at Clermont-Ferrand. He was 2nd at the Aintree 200 and in the Nurburgring 1000, 3rd at Buenos Aires and at Solitude. And he was 2nd in his F2 Porsche in both the South African and Cape races. On April 2, 1960, he was married to a beautiful blonde kindergarten teacher from his native land, a girl named Marianne, and they had a child two years later.

Starting with victory in the Teretonga Park International Race in the Australasian Series (forerunner of today's Tasman Championship), driving a Cooper F1 car, Jo was determined to make 1961 his make-or-break campaign. He quit BRM and signed full-time with Porsche, joining Gurney as a factory entry, but their machines were underpowered and never reached full potential. Bonnier's finishes in championship racing were 11th in the Dutch GP, 7th in the Belgian and French races, 5th in the British and 6th in the United States. He retired in the Monaco, German, and Italian races, the latter when his Porsche was run down from behind by John Surtees's Lola. In other forms of competition, he was 2nd overall and 1st in class at Mosport in a sports car race; took a 2nd overall and won his class in the Targa Florio with Carlo Abate as a codriver, scored 2nds in the Solitude and Modena GPs and at Karlskoga.

Bonnier remained with Porsche for the 1962 GP season and had a dismal year as the marque was largely unsuccessful. In 7 races, Jo managed only 3 championship points for 13th place in the final driver standings. But in sports car racing he did share the winning car at Sebring and was 2nd in the Brussels and the Solitude races, 3rd in the Lombank Trophy, Targa Florio, Guards Trophy, and at Karlskoga. Porsche withdrew from F1 racing in 1963, freeing Bonnier for a good offer from England's Rob Walker to be his number one driver in a Cooper-Climax. But he continued with the German marque for other races, scoring a victory, for example, in the Targo Florio in a 2-litre Porsche co-driven by Carlo Abate, his 2nd outright win in the contest. Jo also was 5th in the Daytona 3-Hours in a Porsche. In the Cooper, Bonnier scored a 5th in the Belgian GP, a 6th in the German, 7th in the Monaco and Italian races, and 8th in the U.S. contest. He finished 2 others, retiring only from the British GP.

There was talk even then that Bonnier was getting too slow for big-time racing; that he was too much an old-fashioned driver. He was indeed a Renaissance man. The bearded Swede spoke fluent English, French, German, Italian, Spanish, Norwegian, and Finnish. He owned an art gallery and had a personal art collection of museum quality. He himself painted rather well, a favorite customer being Graham Hill. But the people who predicted that Jo would slow down were wrong. Racing was part of his life that he would relinquish only very reluctantly. He still had many more miles ahead of him.

The Cooper-Climax provided Bonnier's mount at the start of the 1964 GP season, and in it he was 5th at Monaco and 9th in Holland. The same car carried Jo to a 2nd in the Snetterton International, a non-championship round. The Cooper was swapped for a Brabham-BRM for the Belgian GP, but Bonnier retired from that race. France was skipped, but he appeared at the British and German races without success, both starts ending in mechanical problems. At the Austrian GP, he finally crossed the finish line again, 6th. Jo was 12th in the Italian GP, but mechanical problems again cropped up and retired the car from the U.S. and Mexican races —4 finishes out of 9 starts.

Porsche sports car rides were little better: Bonnier's best major efforts were in the Daytona Continental in which he shared a 6th and at the Nurburgring 1000 in which he shared a 5th. The season's brightest spot was the Paris 1000 in which Jo and Graham Hill codrove a Ferrari 330P and won outright. Sports cars were to provide the Swede's best finishes the next few seasons as well. In 1965, he shared a Porsche for 4th at the Targa Florio and codrove with Jochen Rindt to a 2nd at the Nurburgring 1000, a race he won outright in 1966 with Phil Hill in a 5.4-litre Chaparral-Chevrolet 2D entry.

Bonnier had no such luck in Grand Prix racing. In 1965, he started 9 championship races, retired in 4. Of his 5 finishes, 4 were in 7th place, the other in 8th. But he was still fast on occasion. In the non-title Race of Champions at Brands Hatch, he finished 3rd to Mike Spence and Jackie Stewart. The following year, non-championship racing again accounted for his best work, a 3rd in the May Silverstone International to Jack Brabham and Surtees and a 5th in the Syracuse GP. He had a new F1 mount, a Cooper-Maserati, but that didn't help much. He crashed it at Spa. In 9 starts he again finished 5 races, his best a 6th at Mexico. Along with that were a couple of 7ths, an 8th, and a 12th.

Bonnier was now on his own, running his own racing efforts with the Cooper-Maser and with varied sports cars. The latter, in fact, eventually were to dominate his activity, although he continued in 1967–68 to try to run full GP seasons. In the first of those 2 years, he finished 4 of 8 races started, with 6ths in Germany and at Watkins Glen his top placings. In 1968 Jo finished only 3 of 7 starts, again a 6th—this time in Italy—his best placing in his own car. But the season's high spot was the Mexican GP in which Jo was lent a factory Honda —his best F1 mount in many a year—in the Japanese maker's swan song to the European racing scene. Bonnier surprised all (and pleased them, too) with a 5th place finish for his highest ranking since the 1964 opener at Monaco.

In 1969 he started only 2 Grands Prix, the British race in a Lotus 63 4-wheel drive experimental car, the German in a regular Lotus 49B. In both he was retired. In 1970, now equipped with a McLaren-Ford M7C, he tried, but couldn't qualify for the Italian GP. He made the U.S. field but again was retired. In sports cars he was doing well, mostly on the European circuit, but also in international competition. He shared a 5th in the Spa 1000 in a Lola-Chevvy T70 and a second in the Austrian GP in 1969.

After another slow F1 season in 1971, Jo announced his retirement from that segment of the sport in February 1972, hanging his last GP car, a McLaren-BRM M5A, on the wall of his Swiss chateau. In his 15 F1 seasons, Bonnier ran in 184 Grands Prix, 109 of them championship races, winning that 1959 Dutch GP in the BRM. But Jo would still be driving, as leader of the Lola team in sports car racing.

Back in 1961, the Grand Prix Divers Association had been formed, with Stirling Moss as its president and Bonnier as first vice president. Upon Moss's retirement, Jo became the president. No man ever worked harder at a nonpaying job than he did at this one. Much of his year was spent in meetings, informal discussions, and

touring potential race courses with an eye for improving their safety or driver accommodations. It was common for Bonnier to show up a week before a race for a last-minute check of a course to make sure that all was well. Many drivers, of course, have walked courses for their own benefit; Bonnier walked, and sometimes crawled, over courses to make sure that every possible hazard was inspected. Controversy erupted in the GPDA at the end of the Sixties and the beginning of the Seventies, some younger drivers saying that older ones were making too much of safety. But no one attacked Bonnier. He had done a job with which no one could find fault. In 1972 he talked of relinquishing the job—and tried one more appearance at Le Mans. He was in a Lola T280 sports-racer, attempting to overtake a private Ferrari just before Indianapolis . His mount hit the Ferrari and literally exploded as it became airborne and crashed. Bonnier was thrown about 300 feet from the track. Ironically, Bonnier had been instrumental in having the Le Mans course altered for the 1972 race to make it less dangerous.

BACONIN BORZACCHINI

Baconin Mario Umberto Borzacchini was born in 1898 in Italy at Terni, 50 miles north of Rome. As a youth he raced motorcycles, then about 1925 or so switched over to Salmson cars and later, Maseratis. In 1930 Borzacchini joined Alfa-Romeo, then Italy's greatest racing team. His first really big year was 1926, however. He was 3rd in the Coppa Ciano, 2nd at Padua and in the Florence-Cascine, and won the Targa Florio voiturette section at 38.38 m.p.h. in a Salmson. In 1927 Baconin repeated his Targa victory, taking the voiturette section again at 40 m.p.h., and was 3rd in the Tripoli race. The highlights of the next season were his victories in the Etna Cup in a Maserati at 60.58 m.p.h. and in the Tripoli voiturette in a Salmson at 65.60. Gaston Brilli-Peri nosed out Borzacchini in the 1929 Tripoli race as he bid to repeat as champion.

Borzacchini won his first major Grand Prix in 1930, the Tripoli race, at 91.05 m.p.h. in a Maserati. That same year he was 3rd in the Acerbo Cup and 3rd, shared with Tazio Nuvolari, in the Masaryk Circuit. In 1931, aside from a victory in the Coppa Principe di Piemonte at Avilino at 55.15 m.p.h., he was 2nd in a long string of races: in the Targa to Nuvolari, in the Belgian GP with Nuvolari sharing the car, in the Italian GP with Ferdinando Minoia sharing the Alfa, in the Monza GP to Luigi Fagioli, in the RAC Tourist Trophy Race, in the Coppa della Consumo, and in the French GP at Montlhéry shared with Giuseppe Campari. There were 2nds in 1932, too—in the French GP again, this time at Rheims, in an Alfa shared with Nuvolari; in the Targa and in the Coppa Ciano, both times to Nuvolari—

but there was victory as well. Borzacchini shared a Mille Miglia laurel at 68.10 m.p.h. In the Italian and German Grands Prix he was 3rd. In 1933 he was part of Scuderia Ferrari, racing the year-old Alfas from the 1932 factory team. He won the Mont Cenis hillclimb at 51.50 m.p.h., was 2nd to Archille Varzi in a close one at the Monaco GP, and 2nd to Nuvolari in the Tunis GP. In the Targa Baconin was leading when he crashed.

Then came the Monza GP. In the 2nd heat of the high-speed contest Baconin became involved in a 4-car accident. The cars skidded on an improperly sanded oil patch and smashed into each other and into trees and a house at the side of the course. Borzacchini was killed and so was Guiseppe Campari. Two years later a monument was erected to Baconin at Terni.

PAUL BOST

A native of Matthews, N.C., Paul Bost promised his girl in 1932 that he would quit driving if she would marry him. She did. He did—with only one violation, the Indy 500 of 1933. Bost was good enough to make 4 Indy races and rode the board tracks, acquiring his speed yen at Charlotte. Later he became a car owner, campaigning the Bost-Miller with Billy Winn and Billy Devore as his best drivers. The gentleman was eligible for the Autolite Pacemakers Club because he led the first lap of the 500 in 1931 as a teammate of Wild Bill Cummings. In 1932 Bost wrecked the engine of his Empire State Special so completely the hood was blown off by a flying piece of crankshaft and other debris. In 1933 he drove a unique car combining a Miller 4 engine with Duesenberg transmission. It lasted 14 laps before oil trouble sidelined it.

JACK BOWSHER

Jack Bowsher may not have been the best known stock-car driver in the country, but he probably was the most successful in 1965. The Ford driver from Springfield, O., born October 2, 1930, made a shambles of competition on the Automobile Racing Club of America circuits that year in winning his 3rd straight ARCA late-model point championship. There were 37 late-model races on the ARCA circuit, and Bowsher won 25 of them. (He actually won 26 races but was disqualified after 1 winning effort.) "I think I held just about every track record on the circuit after that season," said Bowsher, who owned and maintained his own cars. "I set a few in 1964 but most of them were set that year."

Bowsher had a garage behind his house, completely equipped to prepare and maintain racing stock cars. Bowsher saw his first stock-car race at Dayton in 1950 and decided it was the sport for him. He struggled along

in jalopies for years before buying his first new car, a Ford, in 1957. In 1963 Bowsher took to fulltime racing, and he had to struggle right from the start to keep his racing projects from going under. "In 1962," he recalled, "I bought a brand new car and then completely demolished it the first time out."

For races Jack used to collect volunteer help to work his pit. However, he employed no mechanics and did whatever had to be done to the car himself. If the job was too big he recruited talent from local garages. Bowsher started his record 1965 season in a Ford powered by a low-profile 427 cu. in. engine. ARCA rules prohibited the latest engines from supertuning until mid-season, when rules were revised. Then Jack switched to the medium-rise 427, similar to those then used in NASCAR, and swept easily to the ARCA crown.

Bowsher's mechanical ability began to count for more and more as the Ford competition department assisted in establishing him as a USAC-oriented racing team. In 1969 he concentrated more on setting up a Torino for A. J. Foyt than on his own mount, No. 21, and the 2 cars amassed $56,900 in prize money. But by that time Jack had risen to 6th in the all-time USAC stock car standings as a driver. The Foyt-Bowsher relationship arose from mutual admiration fostered as driving competitors. Bowsher, a throttle-stomper himself, admired Foyt's driving and A. J. admired Bowsher's meticulously prepared car. There were 4 Bowsher boys, all too young to assist the Springfield Flash in 1970, but he has hopes for the future.

JOHNNY BOYD

Born August 19, 1926, Johnny Boyd had begun driving midgets in the post-World War II boom in 1946 and rode his first championship car 8 years later after winning the Bay Cities and Northern California midget crowns. In 1955 he qualified the Sumar Special at Indianapolis. During the race he flipped it and slid upside down for hundreds of feet into a 4-car crash. When it was over, a close friend from around Fresno, Bill Vukovich, was dead. When they told him in the hospital about Vuky, the look in his eyes told how much he had lost. Two years later after 6th- and 8th-place finishes in the season standings, the Bowes Seal Fast people had bought him a new dirt machine. It was a car built especially for Langhorne and Salem and all the other places where the track was still dirt. It was a necessity if one wanted to win the USAC national championship—and Johnny Boyd was very much in contention for that crown in 1958 after a 5th at Milwaukee and a 3rd at Indianapolis. Would this finally be the year the chunky man from the California wine country would reach the height of his talents? Boyd smiled in anticipation as he got into the car. Less than an hour later the ambulance was rushing Johnny Boyd to the hospital with serious hand burns.

It had been a strange fire. Alcohol fuel, which burns almost invisibly, had dripped onto the exhaust. People could not understand why Boyd was bringing his car to a halt. He leaped when the car was not quite stopped, hitting the rear wheels. The fire crews, expecting the tank to explode, shot their foam from afar to no avail. While running out, they switched to water, but by that time the magnesium skin of the car was burning and the oxygen in the water fed the fire.

Boyd returned late in the season to drive the Bowes midget to 4th place, winning the midget 100-lap classic at Gardena, Calif., while displaying the smooth style that had given him his reputation. But he was off the full Championship Trail forever. The next year, 1959, Johnny ran twice at Milwaukee and at Indianapolis in the Bowes car, getting a 6th at Indy, a 5th in the 200, and a 2nd in the 100. With 3 top 10 finishes in a row in the 500, Boyd and his Bowes Offy became one of the 1960 favorites. He qualified but sprang an oil leak on the 77th lap in that year's race. Switching to a Leader Card spare car the following year, Boyd lasted 105 laps before clutch trouble kayoed him.

Joining again with George Salih, Johnny qualified in 28th place but finished 10th in 1962 in the Metal Cal Special Offy. The following year he lasted only 12 laps, and in 1964 Johnny did nothing after riding the Vita Fresh Orange Juice car into a 13th starting position. In 1965 he had a ride in the BRM Indy car as Masten Gregory's teammate.

Another of the many Champion Spark Plug safety lecturers, Boyd's connection with racing was not over. But so far, despite all the promise, Johnny's best finish was that 2nd in the 1959 Milwaukee 100. He also had 3rd places 4 times on the Championship Trail—besides Indianapolis 1958, the Milwaukee and Phoenix 100-miler in 1957 and the Darlington 200 in 1956.

JOE BOYER

"Tell the blonde in Phillipsburg I can't see her tonight," he grinned, taking his last puff on the cigarette. Then he closed his eyes and died. Joe Boyer, son of a wealthy Detroit family, had crashed September 1, 1924, in the final laps of a board track race at Altoona, Pa. Only a few months before, driving relief for rookie L. L. Corum after his own Duesenberg had broken down, he had won the Indianapolis 500. The quote comes from Pete De-Paolo, a contemporary and a teammate of the Motor City Madman. Despite a right front tire that was shredded and obviously ready to let go, Boyer had insisted on charging after winner Jimmy Murphy. The tire blew, the car hit the rail, and Boyer was thrown to the bottom of an embankment outside the track. He bled profusely and, despite transfusions, died in an Altoona hospital.

Born in 1890, Joe Boyer loved life and he loved cars, too. He helped finance the Chevrolet boys when they were building their Frontenacs, won with one at Uniontown, Pa., on the boards, and qualified another in the 1916 Indianapolis 500. After serving in World War I as an ordinary private, Joe came back to the Fronty/Monroe forces in 1919, again winning at Uniontown and at

Cincinnati. In 1920 he led the first Beverly Hills, Calif., board track race until a tire blew. In 1921 Boyer switched to Duesenberg, including a ride with the American team in the first postwar French Grand Prix at Le Mans. He drove for Packard part of 1923, then came back to Duesy in 1924 when Packard quit racing. Indianapolis, 1924, was the year Fred Duesenberg decided that once and for all he was going to show Harry Miller who could build faster race cars. For the first time in the Twenties, a major team was going to use superchargers at Indianapolis. Fred had 4 supercharged cars plus a non-blown car assigned to Pete DePaolo. In one of the wine-colored blown racers was Joe Boyer.

Boyer was in hot pursuit of the Miller favorites Jimmy Murphy and Bennett Hill when, in the 2nd lap, the innards of his blower addled and he found himself an unwilling spectator. Duesenberg watched, hoping that another of his hero drivers would take the lead, but all he got were more candidates for the garage. Finally, after the 108th lap, he made a fateful decision. Corum came in and Boyer went out, fresh and eager to get in his licks at the Miller crew. Lying a distant 5th when he assumed control, Boyer gained quickly on Hill and Harry Hartz, passing them before another 100 miles had gone.

He then trailed 2nd-place Murphy by 33 seconds and leader Earl Cooper by 85. He took Murphy in less than 50 miles, the blower wailing, and set out after Cooper who had lost 41 seconds of his lead. Cooper was running one of his patented races, figuring what he considered a winning average speed, then sticking to it. This time he figured 98.32 m.p.h. would do it. He was wrong. Boyer pushed him, increasing his tire wear. Joe took the lead at 445 miles when Cooper pitted for new shoes. But Boyer wasn't home free; Cooper roared back, eating up the distance between them until at 470 miles he was nose-to-tail. But a split second later it was all over. Earl, trying to pass, slid and was forced to pit for more rubber. Boyer won.

LORD BRABAZON

Bastogne, a name etched in American minds in World War II, is a tiny village southeast of Brussels near the Luxemburg border. It has its place in auto racing history, too. On a warm July 1907 morning at the ungodly hour of 4 A.M., Bastogne was packed with people for the start of one of racing's earliest great conflicts, the Circuit des Ardennes, through the rough roads that ran around Bastogne itself. Each "lap" was 53.26 miles long, and 7 laps had to be run to complete this race for 25 entries from all over Europe. Minerva, the Belgian factory, had 4 cars, the largest single entry, but other European marques, Pipe, Benz, Adler and Gaggenau, each had 3-car teams, and there were 2 Aries and 7 other single factory and private entries. The Minervas were driven by a Dutchman and 3 Englishmen, including Lee Guinness

and Minerva's British agent, the Honorable J. T. C. Moore-Brabazon, later to become Lord Brabazon of Tara.

Another British Minerva driver, Warwick Wright, was waved away as the first starter of the race at the stroke of 4 A.M. on the village clock. Each car in the race would be waved away at 1 minute intervals. Wright led the 1st and 3rd laps, but was not leading lap 2 when a 7th place starter, Hautvast in a Pipe, had charged into the lead with the body of a dog impaled on the starting handle. He was aided by the fact that 7 of the 25 starters already had crashed or blown their engines in just those first 2 laps. But punctures dropped the Pipe back, and Wright led again as he pitted after the 3rd lap for a new supply of tires.

Guinness was doing well; in fact, he set the fastest lap of the race on the 3rd round, a second under 48 minutes for the 53-plus miles. By the time Wright rejoined the fray, he was 6th: behind Guinness, Wilhelm in a Metallurgique, Hautvast, Brabazon, and Camille Jenatzy in another Pipe. But the toll began even on these leaders, and the Pipes soon were gone. Even Brabazon, a giant of a man, as strong as he was handsome, began to feel the strain. He had already accomplished miracles, moving up steadily from 17th to 2nd in 6 laps. Only Guinness lay out there somewhere ahead in another Minerva. The remaining competitors had to stop continually to change tires on the course, then stop at the pits to replenish the car's tire supply for the road changes.

On the 7th and final lap Brabazon came upon Lee Guinness changing a tire in his Minerva. Brabazon knew then he was in the lead for sure; Guinness had started behind him. But Guinness had been faster; the best lap that Brabazon could muster that day was the 7th (when it became apparent that it was do or die) at 49.42, or almost 2 minutes slower than Guinness's best. As he pulled across the finish line the winner, the village clock was ringing 11:15 A.M., 7¼ hours of ceaseless racing to cover 372.8 miles.

Brabazon's winning speed (59.5 m.p.h.) under those conditions, with those roads and those machines and tires, was the wonder of Europe. Guinness was 3rd, Koolhoven 2nd; the trio made a clean sweep for Minerva. Sylvain de Jong, boss of the factory, bussed the startled young Englishman on both cheeks. (Wright also finished, 6th, a truly amazing feat for the 4-car team.) Moore-Brabazon was 2nd in the Coupe de Liederkerke to Porlier, his own mechanic, who was driving for the first time competitively. The gap was half a mile after 200 miles of racing over much the same course as before. The year before, Brabazon had finished 3rd in the same race.

He raced once more, in the 1908 French Grand Prix in an Austin, finishing 18th. He was to have driven a Napier, but when a dispute arose between S. F. Edge and the French authorities, the team did not run, and the Austin was the best car he could find at the 11th hour.

After 10 tire changes and many stops to clear water from the carburetor, he completed the 480 miles. Then he quit auto racing, moving on to the even more exotic airplane.

Lieutenant-Colonel the Right Honorable John Theodore Cuthbert Moore-Brabazon, PC, GBE, MC, first Lord Brabazon of Tara of Sandwich in the County of Kent, was born February 8, 1884, son of an Irish-born military father and a British mother. Educated at Harrow and at Trinity College, Cambridge, Brabazon was attracted to the new sport of motor racing at the age of 15 when he saw the Thousand Miles Trial of 1900. With his family's connections, he was "apprenticed" to Louis Wagner and Victor Hemery (two of the day's top drivers) aboard Darracqs. His actual racing career spanned only 3 years, from 1906 to 1908, and included a spell as mechanic to a friend named Charles Rolls (as in Rolls-Royce).

Flying became Brabazon's passion after 1908, and he was the first Englishman to cover 450 yards in the air (in an airplane of his own design) that very December. He made a real flight, later acknowledged as the initial airplane flight in Britain, on May 2, 1909. He was awarded the first pilot's license issued in the United Kingdom (and in later years always drove cars with the plate FLY-1 in commemoration of that distinction). In World War I Brabazon was with the Royal Flying Corps, and is acknowledged to have been Britain's pioneer in developing aerial photography. He served in Parliament, usually on aviation committees, and as president of the Royal Aeronautical Society, and continued to drive a wide selection of cars—more than 200 different marques in his life, it was claimed. Brabazon excelled in many sports, including golf and bobsleddng. In 1954 Brabazon celebrated his 70th birthday by taking a sled down the Cresta Run at St. Moritz and in 1963, at the age of 79, he celebrated by racing a Mercedes over Salisbury Plain at better than 115 m.p.h. Brabazon was raised to the Peerage in March 1942, after leaving Winston Churchill's cabinet. He died May 17, 1964, at his home in Chertsey.

JACK BRABHAM

Just what Australia's Jack Brabham will most be remembered for is still unclear. Will it be as 3-time World Driving Champion? Will it be as a World Champion Car Constructor? Will it be as a discoverer, developer, and booster of young driving talent? Or will it be as one of those who, like Juan Manuel Fangio, proved that auto racing isn't necessarily a young man's game?

Brabham will be remembered for many incidents in an incident-filled career, too. He pushed his car to the finish line after it quit on him—not once, but twice—in World Championship Grand Prix races. He learned to

fly so well that he could comfortably fly the Atlantic or from England to Australia without even giving these feats a second thought. He progressed from a sliding, slipstreaming dirt driver of midget racers to a polished handler of some of the most exotic machines constructed by man. He was able to tear a car down to the last nut and bolt, and put it back together again in better shape than it was originally.

John Arthur Brabham was born in Hurstville, Australia, April 2, 1926, the only son of a vegetable store man who loved cars and passed that along to his son. Jack learned to drive at a very early age and became an expert driver (in private) long before he was eligible for a license. By the time he was 16, he was also an expert mechanic, and he was deep into the motorcycle world Down Under (except for the racing end). In 1944 he joined the Royal Australian Air Force, putting his mechanical expertise to work on the flight line. Discharged in 1946, Brabham opened his own thriving engineering business.

In 1947 an American expatriate by the name of Johnny Schonberg, who had raced midget cars both in the United States and in Australia, persuaded Jack to go to a midget race, then another and another. Initially, he said later, it scared and repelled him. But Brabham was soon building a midget racer for Schonberg and had agreed to mechanic for him. John drove it in a couple of races before his wife made him quit (he was no youngster anymore). No use letting a good car go to waste, so Jack Brabham, hero-driver-to-be, took the wheel.

Within a year Brabham managed to master the car, the tracks, and just about everything and everybody else. He became the New South Wales champion, the South Australian champion, and the Australian champion in 1948 and 1949. He was also South Australian champion in 1950 and 1951. His dirt-track activities were curtailed somewhat in the latter two seasons because he had met a young lady who really didn't like dirt track driving (although she didn't mind auto racing in general). On May 12, 1951, Jack married Betty Beresford. Betty asked Jack to give up the dirt tracks, and he did, switching to hillclimbing for a time. He won 2 championship races, but was disqualified because they said his brakes weren't good enough (in fact they didn't even exist). Annoyed, Jack installed brakes on the same car, then won the Rob Roy Hillclimb (then Australia's toughest) without once setting foot to brake pedal.

Betty had no objections to road racing, even after the arrival of the 1st of their 3 children, and so Jack bought a Mark IV Cooper 500 chassis and put together his own engine from spare parts around the garage. It was a winning car, no matter how unconventional it might have seemed, and Jack took the Redex Championship. That company knew a crowd-pleaser when it saw one—Brabham's dirt-track style was something new for the road courses—and it sponsored him the following season, financing Jack's purchase of a new Cooper-Bristol. Jack's initial race outside of Australia was in 1953 in New Zealand, and he was 6th against some of the best drivers in the world. By the year's end, he was sports car champion of both Queensland and New South Wales. His engineering business was booming and in capable hands when he was away, so Brabham proposed that they go to England for some European experience, visit the auto factories, and generally prepare to expand his garage business.

The Brabham family arrived in mid-1955. Brabham had sold his Cooper-Bristol, so the first order of business was to buy a new car. It turned out to be a Cooper-Alta once owned by Peter Whitehead. At Goodwood, his initial European race, he was 4th, but the engine blew up the next time out, and Jack went to see John Cooper about a new car. Cooper invited him to build one of his own, using Cooper parts and factory space. Given this opportunity, Brabham, who had his eye on the British GP at Aintree, decided to modify a sports/racing Cooper to meet the Formula 1 specifications. Finished just before the July 16, 1955, race, the car lasted 34 laps before retiring with valve trouble.

Jack returned to Australia, taking his rear-engined car with him. In it he won the Australian GP, a non-title race. But the lure of international racing and those European circuits was too much for Jack, and he returned to England in 1956, buying an ex-Rubery Owen Maserati 250F. Although he had little luck with his car, John Cooper liked Brabham personally and liked his engineer's approach to auto racing. He invited the Australian to join the Cooper factory team in sports cars and Formula 2. Brabham still had many of the techniques of dirt-track racing to overcome, and the year was spent in perfecting his style while making life interesting for his fellow drivers and the spectators. His best showings, perhaps, were in the Aintree 200, where he was 3rd behind Stirling Moss and Tony Brooks, and at Imola, where he was 2nd to Eugenio Castellotti. Brabham also appeared briefly in his 2nd F1 race, the British GP that July, where his car quit in the 4th lap.

A turning point in the Brabham career came in 1957 when he was officially a Cooper factory driver for F2 with Roy Salvadori, but he actually took over a Rob Walker-sponsored, 2-litre version of the 1.5-litre Cooper for F1. In the Monaco opener, Jack was running 3rd when his car quit. He popped out and with a furious uphill struggle managed to push the car across the finish line into 6th place. In championship F1 races, the car retired at Rouen, Aintree and Nurburgring, but Jack managed a 7th at Pescara. In non-title races, he won twice at Brands Hatch, and at Oulton Park and in Montlhéry's Prix de Paris.

Brabham scored his initial World Championship points—3 of them, to be exact, for a tie for 14th place in the season standings—May 18, 1958, at Monte Carlo where he was 4th. The same year he had 6ths in the Belgian and British races, 7th at Oporto, and 8th in the Dutch GP. Overheating knocked him out of the Belgian GP, a 2nd-lap accident eliminated his Cooper from the German race, and a suspension failure ended Brabham's Italian GP. Away from F1, Jack won the New Zealand GP, shared a winning Aston Martin with Moss in the Nurburgring's 1000-kilometer race (but drove only 7 of the 45 laps because he was about 40 seconds a lap slower than Moss), won the Lavant Cup at Goodwood, and took the British F2 championship.

Up to this point, there had scarcely been a hint that this 33-year-old Australian might do rather well in GP racing. He was looked upon as a fair driver, more useful than most because he could spot a car's problems quickly and talk about them technically. He could, in fact, help repair those ills, as he was one of the most mechanically talented drivers in some time. All that started to change at Monaco, May 12, 1959. Brabham not only won—his 1st victory of many championship victories—but he drove the fastest lap. In the Dutch GP he was 2nd, in the French GP 3rd. When Brabham won the British GP, it became apparent that he might win the title, for it was more than chance that he led from start to finish. He was driving better than he ever had and as consistently as anyone.

Retirements in the German and Portuguese races were only momentary setbacks, the former with gearbox trouble, the latter in an end-over-end accident. At Monza he was 3rd and at Sebring—a race which his protégé, Bruce McLaren, won—he was 4th. A fuel line leak cost Brabham his final supply at Sebring and his car coasted to a stop about a quarter of a mile from the finish. It was 1957 all over again, with Jack pushing for all he was worth as McLaren took over the lead, hotly pursued by Maurice Trintignant and Tony Brooks. But Brabham managed to push his way across the line to the World Championship with 34 total points.

In 1960 after false starts (in the Argentine GP in which a faulty gearbox eliminated his car, and in the Monaco GP in which he was unclassified), he won 5 Grands Prix in a row. The Dutch and Belgian GP victories (and fastest lap at Spa) came in June, the French and British victories (and fastest lap at Rheims) in July, the Portugese victory in August. Brabham also set the fastest lap at Riverside, Calif., in the U.S. GP, but finished 4th. He amassed 43 points for his 2nd World Championship. That same season, in non-championship racing, he took the New Zealand GP again, the Lady Wigram Trophy, and the Brussels and Pau races. He again won the British F2 championship.

Brabham was not one to rest on his laurels. He felt the Cooper needed reworking for 1961, or it was sure to be outclassed. But John Cooper had his mind on another project outside the GP area, Indianapolis. It had been some time since Europeans had made any serious effort there. Fangio had tried it a few years before and didn't do particularly well in his testing. But Jack Brabham had. He visited Indy briefly with his regular GP mount, unmodified and without any special tires, and startled observers (including the Indy veteran Rodger Ward) with his grasp of the track and his consistency. From a standing start, he did a 128 m.p.h. lap, then raised his times to the 143 m.p.h. area and consistently held them there, finishing with a lap fast enough to have qualified on the front row in the 1960 race.

Cooper threw his effort behind an Indianapolis appearance, to the detriment of his GP season, some said. Brabham qualified 13th at Indy in 1961 and finished 9th in a car half the size and power of his competitors. But in the World Championship chase, he suffered 6 retirements in 8 starts, 5 of these due to engine problems. A 4th at Aintree earned him 4 points, a 6th at Zandvoort brought nothing in those days. He was tied for 11th in the final standings. In non-title racing, he again won the Lady Wigram, the Longford road race, the Brussels GP, the Aintree 200, and some others. That year an old Australian friend, Ron Tauranac, had come over to join Brabham, and work had started on the first Brabham car, the MRD Formula Junior prototype, in a small shed in Surbiton. As the work progressed, Brabham resigned from the Cooper team.

As soon as BT1, the FJ car, was finished, work started on BT3, an F1 car, Realizing it would take some time to design, build, test and perfect, he purchased a Lotus-Climax in which he raced the first 5 starts of 1962,

managing a 5th in the British GP, a 6th in the Belgian GP and an 8th in the Monaco GP. The Brabham GP car made its appearance at the German GP and the subsequent U.S. and South African races. At the Nurburgring the throttle linkage gave way on the 10th lap, but Brabham managed 4ths in the other races, bringing his season total to 9 points and a 9th place in the standings. The points in the U.S. GP were the 1st ever scored in modern F1 racing by a driver in a car of his own design and manufacture.

Brabham drove a wide variety of cars in the 1962 season. In a Cooper, he took victories in Formula Libre races at Levin, New Zealand, and Sandown Park, Australia; and 2nds in the Lady Wigram and Longford races. In the Lotus F1 car, he also was 1st at Roskilde, Denmark, and 2nd at Mallory Park. In his own Brabham-Climax F1 car, he was 2nd in the Mexican GP and at the Oulton Cup race. In a Holbay Lotus 23 sports car, he won his class at the Canadian GP at Mosport.

From 1962 through 1965, Brabham 2-litre F1 cars achieved some modest successes for Jack and for Dan Gurney, who partnered Brabham before leaving to set up his own All-American Eagle marque and racing team. Jack won no World Championship races in this period, but Gurney won the French and Mexican races in 1964 in a Brabham. Jack had many non-title victories in the car, and it was raced with some success by private teams such as Rob Walker's, Jo Siffert's, and Bob Anderson's. Brabham won 15 points for 7th in the 1963 standings, 11 for an 8th place tie in 1964 and 9 for a 10th in the 1965 standings.

In 1966 Jack Brabham was 40 years old, a GP driver who had not won a *grand épreuve* for himself since 1960, a constructor whose cars were outpowered and unreliable as far as their Climax engines went. Between seasons there had been talk of his quitting. But back in Australia, a then unknown firm called Repco (Replacement Parts Co.) was finishing up a simple s.o.h.c. V8 that was intended to provide a temporary engine for the new 3-litre formula. And as the players assembled for the year's initial non-title race, there was old Jack Brabham sitting in a "new" Brabham—actually one that had been designed for a never-raced new Climax engine—equipped with Repco power. Since it was the only full 3-litre on the grid, the car dominated the field until it succumbed to an unspecified mechanical ill. Brabham next slipped in a 2.5-litre engine and tried a couple of Tasman series appearances, but could do no better than 3rd. Back in Europe in 2 more pre-season F1 starts, the car failed at Syracuse, but then led from start to finish in the Silverstone International; and the critics, who had already written him and his car off, reached for their erasers.

Monte Carlo was the scene of the first championship race. Brabham had a troubled practice, and he actually was sick on the grid before the race started. A faulty gearbox put him out on the 18th lap, but he was far from disheartened. The Belgian GP at Spa was run on a treacherously wet course that year, and Jack held back as he continued to feel his car and engine out. He took 4th. But in the French GP, on the high-speed Rheims circuit, he charged up behind Lorenzo Bandini's faster and more powerful Ferrari, fell into Bandini's slipstream, and let it carry him well out in front of the rest of the field. Jack didn't have the power to pass the Italian, but he could harry him, and he did. In the end, the Ferrari's throttle linkage snapped, and Jack Brabham cruised home in his own car, the first driver in history to win a GP race in a car of his own design.

At Brands Hatch for the British GP, Brabham and Denis Hulme, who was his team partner, made it 1st and 2nd in practice, and repeated that order in the actual race. Brabham ran the day's fastest lap. The Dutch GP was tougher, especially when Brabham had to contend with Jim Clark at his best and had to drive on a course covered with spilled oil that nearly equalized the performance of the 2 cars. Brabham again pushed Clark until his Lotus faded; Jim finished 3rd. It was at Zandvoort that Brabham pulled his "old man" act in response to all the comments about his age. Just before the start of things, an old man hobbled out to the line, bearded and leaning heavily on a cane. It was Brabham, whose act broke up everyone who saw it. The old man went out and won his 3rd in a row immediately afterwards. His 4th and last GP victory of the year came next in the German race in which, once again, he had a challenger who was driving his very best, John Surtees. To win, Jack had to drive a perfect race, which is exactly what he did.

An oil leak knocked Brabham out of the Italian GP, but he found himself the World Champion when his closest pursuer failed to win and, therefore, to catch Brabham. At Watkins Glen in the U.S. GP, his car again failed, but he came out of the race with his World Constructors Championship, another item for the record book. The season ended at Mexico City with Brabham 2nd. He had amassed 45 points, his highest total ever, and 3 World Championships since the age of 33. Brabham himself found nothing unusual in this: "Fangio was 40 when he won his first world title," he said. "He won the championship 4 times more, the last time when he was 47. If you have the right approach to racing, and are reasonably fit, it doesn't matter what your age is. I don't think this applies to everybody, but I'm convinced age is not the specific thing that makes a difference. It all depends upon the physical and mental outlook of the person concerned. Some people my age can't do it, and some people can. This applies to a lot of sports, not just motor racing. I just don't feel that age has ever affected my driving."

In 1967 Brabham won the French GP at Le Mans and the Canadian GP at Mosport. He also piled up enough 2nds to amass 48 points, but finished 2nd in the final standings. The event was mitigated by the fact that Hulme had won, in a Brabham-Repco, for Team Brabham. Hulme left to join McLaren in 1968, and Jochen Rindt became Jack's number 2. Neither man won a race because the newest Brabham F1 car was beset by mechanical problems. Jack, in fact, finished only the German GP at Nurburgring in 5th place, while Rindt was 3rd in the same race. Brabham's 2 points tied him for 23rd in the standings. In 1969, Repco power was replaced by Ford, and Jackie Ickx joined up as number 2; but Jack could manage only 10th in the standings, with 2nd in the Canadian GP (a fastest lap shared with Ickx) his best showing. Ickx won the German and Canadian GPs and ran in the British and Mexican races for 37 points and 2nd place in the standings to Jackie Stewart's amazing 63 points.

Jack had a nasty accident in mid-season; he was trapped in his car with gasoline everywhere for 20 minutes while a crew struggled to free him. An ankle operation put him on the shelf for the longest time he had been away from racing for years. Some thought he might retire at that point, but back he came for his Mosport 2nd, a 4th in the U.S. GP and a 3rd at Mexico City. And this amazing man opened 1970, his last year of driving, with a victory in the South African GP, including the day's fastest lap, for his 1st championship F1 victory since 1967. Another of his former charges, Rindt, was to win the World Championship that season, and Rindt hadn't even been out of grammar school when Brabham first took the wheel of a Championship GP car in 1955.

In addition, Brabham cars had consistently dominated various aspects of racing below the GP level. In 1963, the winning FJ car was a Brabham. In late 1965 and in 1966, the dominant F2 car was a Brabham, including a string of 10 F2 victories for Jack himself, 2 for Hulme, and 2 of the remaining championship races on the card won by Rindt in a Winkelmann Racing Team Brabham. Rindt dominated F2 in 1967 with 9 victories in a Winkelmann-sponsored Brabham-Cosworth. Even when other marques moved to the front, Brabhams continued to be respectable competitors in all areas, regularly taking a race here and there. And while his auto racing efforts were so successful, Jack Brabham's giant Ford dealership on the outskirts of Sydney was mushrooming, his light aircraft facility nearby was growing, and his 350-acre farm in Victoria was showing a nice profit.

Brabham's final season as a driver, 1970, saw a couple of 2nds at Monaco and in the British GP, a 3rd in the French race. The other finishes were a 10th in the U.S. race, 11th in Holland, 13th in Austria. And there were 5 retirements with mechanical problems and a single accident, fortunately not serious, at Monza. It was the season in which McLaren, Rindt, and Piers Courage were killed. It was a season in which a fellow who had accomplished so much behind the wheel could remember his age and call it quits for that phase of his career.

GIOVANNI BRACCO

Karl Kling seemed sure to win the 1952 Mille Miglia. With only 20 kilometers left, his only serious challenger, Italy's Giovanni Bracco, was limping badly from worn tires; the white fabric, in fact, was showing through on Bracco's Ferrari rear wheels. At Pescara Giovanni was greeted with the news that they didn't have the right size for his car, and substitutes were used. All seemed lost, but Bracco set out with renewed determination in a driving rain. Fortified by chain-smoking and gulps of brandy proffered by a frightened navigator, he charged through the wet, caught Kling, and won the race at 79.90 m.p.h. Kling was 4 minutes behind at the flag.

A textile executive, Bracco lived at Biella where a famous Itallian hillclimb passed his very doorstep, so it was natural for the amateur to try his luck in this event, first with a 1,500-c.c. Fiat sports car, then with a 2.5 Alfa Romeo. After World War II came a special known as the Maserati-Fiat-Tinarelli Special. The car rarely lasted in a climb, but attracted attention not only to itself but to Bracco. In 1947 he bought an old Delage and won several climbs. On the courses he had less luck. At Pescara Bracco led, only to run out of gas; at Modena a car spun in front of him and he had either to crash into a tree or run down some spectators frozen in their tracks (he chose the tree).

In a new 2-litre Maserati, after leaving the hospital, he won the Dolomite Cup in 1948 over Luigi Villoresi. He won hillclimbs in a Ferrari at Parma, Catania, Bologna, and other places, but was not too successful on the track until switching to a Lancia in which he won his class in the 1951 Mille Miglia and was 2nd overall to Villoresi. At Le Mans he won his class, at Pescara he won the only 6-hour race held there at 75.8 m.p.h. That same year, in a borrowed Ferrari, he won the Villa Real sports car race in Portugal at 66.65 m.p.h.

GORDIE BRACKEN

Road racing around barrels was a form of the sport practiced in the South in the decades from 1925 to the outbreak of World War II. It was a version of dirt-track racing that was quite inexpensive for promoters, who indicated the course with surplus gasoline drums, beer casks, pickle or cracker barrels.

The King of the Canebrakes was Gordon W. Bracken, Jr. He won regularly at Camp Foster, near Jacksonville Beach, Fla., where the barrels were set up on the sand, and at Savannah, where the track was a bit more formal. One of his bitterest foes was Hugh Dixon, a turpentine manufacturer alleged to have spiked his fuel with his own product. Bracken's imaginative but anonymous publicity agent crowned him the Southern dirt track champ, and he campaigned under this title as late as 1937, mostly in IMCA but with some excursions into AAA ranks. He strayed from his native Bainbridge, Ga., as far as Hibbing, Minn.

Assessing Bracken's record is difficult because of the then-current practice of "hippodroming" race results, which were printed verbatim because the newspapers of that day had no reliable auto racing writers. Hippodroming took its name from an American theater at which the acts were extolled extravagantly to titillate the theatergoer and lure him in. Fact was merely the framework on which to build a net of fancy.

Bracken is remembered by one contemporary as a mild man who turned into a veritable Mr. Hyde after imbibing some sour mash whiskey. He had 3 fingers on one hand, reputedly bitten off by a surly alligator with which he had hand-to-hand combat. But when he changed his image, the fingers supposedly had been shot off by revenue agents in a raid on his illegal whiskey still.

CALEB BRAGG

A millionaire sportsman from Pasadena, Calif., Caleb Bragg won the 1912 Grand Prize road race in Milwaukee and was 2nd in the Santa Monica races that same year. He led at Indianapolis briefly as a member of the Mercer team of Spencer Wishart and Ralph DePalma in 1914, but due to his flamboyant driving style he broke the car (as he did frequently).

But he was driving for Fiat when he scored his 2nd at Santa Monica in the 303-mile free-for-all over an 8-plus mile course. It was the first AAA championship race of the season, May 4. Bragg took the early lead, snapping off a 5:38 for the lap, but had to pull in for a tire change on the 2nd lap, relinquishing to David Bruce-Brown with Teddy Tetzlaff 3rd. At the 3-lap mark Teddy was leading with Bragg 2nd and Barney Oldfield next. Caleb lost 2nd to Barney at the 65-mile mark but got it right back when Barney's suspension broke. Bruce-Brown in the Benz then took 2nd, with Caleb hot on his heels. Both were in sight of Terrible Teddy at the 200-mile mark, and when he realized it, Tetzlaff took off like a scared rabbit. He widened his lead sufficiently to finish 3 minutes ahead of Bragg, despite crashing after a tire blew on the last lap. Teddy rode in on the rim to the cheers of the crowd. Bruce-Brown was 3rd.

Bragg tangled with Tetzlaff again in the ACA-sanctioned Grand Prize in Milwaukee that year. The course was 7.88 miles of washboard and potholes. Bruce-Brown had met death on it only a few days before. Tetzlaff again led in the best Fiat, but the motor expired.

That left Bragg and Ralph DePalma dueling for 1st, a duel Caleb was winning as they sped into the final around. Trying to make up 30 seconds, DePalma floored the accelerator in his Mercedes and caught the Fiat driver far out in the boondocks. Bragg would not move over to let him pass, so Ralph began nudging him. He nudged too hard, for the Mercedes suddenly catapulted into the air, tossing DePalma into the middle of a cornfield, impaling him on the toughened stalks. Caleb took the checker, then organized a rescue party. He headed right back to the scene of the accident and helped bring back the gravely-injured DePalma, who was given little chance to survive the night. The fact that further loss of blood was halted at the accident scene probably made the difference. Bragg's prompt action helped save the life of the greatest of the American racing pioneers.

DON BRANSON

Age mellows wine and makes steaks tender. But with racing drivers the problem is that some who need aging lose their desire or their lives before experience can have its effect. Don Branson was very much an active driver at an age when others are reliving their glory days at the movie nights of fan clubs. Born in Rantoul, Ill., June 2, 1920, he was that hamlet's main claim to fame besides blue-ribbon livestock. He was a quiet man, not unfriendly, just taciturn, and did not look as if he had 3 grown sons while still driving American ovals.

Branson will always be known as one of the great qualifiers of American oval track history. With his exquisite sense of timing, it is too bad he never became interested in speed record runs, for he could always put his car as high in the starting lineup as it was capable of running. Don was 26 before he ever raced. He had come out of the service to the heyday of the midget race car, and his first experience came with independent clubs in the Midwest. He then ran IMCA, on the dirt-track circuits until he decided to try his luck with USAC at the age of 37. He tried sprint cars initially on the USAC's then-rugged Midwest loop, finishing 4th and 5th in 1956 and 1957, winning the title in 1959, and coming in 2nd in 1960 there and in the Eastern sprint wars as well.

Branson, driving for Bob Estes, finished 2nd in Championship Trail points in 1960, although his best finishes were 3rd places at Phoenix and Sacramento and a 4th at Indianapolis. In 1962 he set a world mark at the old Langhorne Speedway, winning that 100-mile championship, and also captured the Trenton Speedway feature. This led to an eventual association with the Leader Car team of A. J. Watson, Bob Wilke, and Rodger Ward. Don put the LC roadster in 3rd qualifying spot in 1963 at Indianapolis and eventually finished 5th despite an improperly-firing engine. In 1964 Don piloted the rear-engined Watson Offy in a race which he obviously felt was strictly for the experience. He expressed his opinions on the subject early in the season, telling how the man thought:

"I think auto racing is changing and anyone who can't change with it had better think about getting out," he said. "These rear-engined cars steer differently and the whole feeling when driving them is strange to anyone used to American machinery. You sit so low and there's nothing out in front of you so you better not hit anything. And it's so quiet after years of hearing that engine throbbing away. But you go faster, and that's how you win money. I like to race, but I like to do a lot of things. It's the money that keeps me active. When I can't win my share, I'll quit."

He waited too long. And it was the old, not the new, configuration that did him in. The softspoken grandfather, officially 46, died in a crash at Ascot, Gardena, Calif., Nov. 12, 1966. He was driving a midget and flipped in the first turn, going upside down. A promising young driver, Dick Atkins, 28, hit the wreck and was killed, too.

MANFRED von BRAUCHITSCH

A familiar figure behind the wheel of the dominant German racing cars of the Thirties was a handsome, young, eligible, and talented driver who wore a red cloth helmet. He frequently was unlucky, yet managed to compile a good record in Mercedes Benz racing cars,

from the dashing sports models to the monstrous brutes that contested the *grande épreuve* circuits.

Manfred von Brauchitsch was born in Hamburg, Germany, August 15, 1905, of a family with a strong military tradition. Thus he found himself in military school at the earliest possible moment, but he also found himself fascinated with speed. Cars were forbidden him, but he did manage to have a motorcycle. A street accident ended with Brauchitsch's suffering a cranial fracture, which washed him out of military school, but freed the young man for his real love.

Once he was in shape again, Brauchitsch set about getting a car, and he bought exactly what you would expect a young German to buy, a Mercedes. At first Manfred concentrated on hillclimbs, winning several. In 1931 he started entering formal races, retiring from the German Grand Prix with engine problems, but coming in 3rd in the Avusrennen and in the Eifelrennen. The following season Brauchitsch installed a special lightweight streamlined body on his SSKL car and proceeded to win the Avusrennen with Rudi Caracciola 2nd in an Alfa. He was 3rd in the Eifelrennen. In 1933 he won the Freiberg and Kesselberg hillclimbs and was 2nd to Tazio Nuvolari in the Eifelrennen.

All of these private ventures had the desired effect, for in 1934 when Mercedes returned to racing officially, Brauchitsch was offered a berth as a member of the Mercedes factory team. In the French GP Manfred retired in 11 laps with a sick supercharger, but in the Eifelrennen he won the factory's initial victory with a new 750-kilogram formula car at 76.12 m.p.h., fastest time for the 8-year-old race at the Nurburgring. But the ill luck that was to dog Manfred saw him crash at the German GP and finish his planned season early.

In 1935 Brauchitsch retired on the Monaco GP's initial lap with a faulty gearbox, but in the French GP at Montlhéry he finished 2nd to team leader Caracciola and shared 2nd with Luigi Fagioli in the Belgian GP. Manfred was 3rd in the Spanish GP and 5th in both the Avusrennen and in the German GP. That latter race was perhaps his best drive of the year. He pushed his 3.99-litre W.25 Mercedes to its limit and was leading by a good 8 kilometers when a rear tire blew. Controlling the spinning car, he limped home, but finished 5th, thoroughly frustrated by his racing luck once again. A short-wheelbase version of the W.25 was used in 1936, powered by a 4.74-litre engine, but the car was not competitive. Brauchitsch was 7th in the German GP with Hermann Lang, and at Monaco he crashed on the first lap of the rain-soaked race, caught in a chain-reaction melee with Louis Chiron and Nino Farina. The 1936 cars were so bad that Mercedes withdrew from racing later in the season while awaiting a new car.

Originally the 750-kilogram formula was to end in 1936, but it was extended for another year. Mercedes introduced its new car, the W.125, anyway, equipped with a 5.66-litre engine that made it the most powerful GP car ever raced. Brauchitsch was retired in the Tripoli GP opener and in the Belgian GP, although he was 3rd in the Eifelrennen between those starts. Then he was 2nd in the German GP and at Monaco, defeating even his team leader Caracciola, he won at 63.27 m.p.h. despite the fact that the streets of Monte Carlo hardly constituted conditions for which his car had been designed. Manfred had his first *grande épreuve* victory, but had to content himself with following Caracciola home the rest of the season as Rudi won 4 subsequent races.

Brauchitsch was 2nd in the German GP, 2nd in Pescara's Coppa Acerbo, and 3rd in the Swiss GP to Rudi and Lang. His W.125 retired in the Italian GP, but he finished 2nd again to Caracciola in the Masryk GP in Czechoslovakia and 2nd in the Donington Park GP in Britain.

The year 1938 found Brauchitsch in still another car, the W.154, and it was the year of more bad luck. Dick Seaman, the British ace, was on the Mercedes team and was breathing down Brauchitsch's neck in this race, although team orders dictated it was to be Manfred's race, a prize that he had fruitlessly sought so many times. He pitted on the 16th lap for fuel, his face taut with the pressure that Seaman was giving him. Alfred Neubauer, the Mercedes team manager, assured his driver that Seaman was not to pass him, and when the Briton pitted at the same time he told Seaman the same thing. Then Neubauer turned and saw, too late, that one of the Brauchitsch fuel tanks was overflowing while another mechanic was fitting in the electric starter and

Manfred was pressing his ignition button. The back of the car burst into flame. Brauchitsch yelled as his coveralls caught fire; he popped the removable steering wheel as Neubauer pulled him from the car. The fire was quickly extinguished, the damage found slight, and Manfred was no more than singed. To the cheers of the crowd, he jumped back into the car and roared away. But as he hit a bumpy part of the Nurburgring's tricky course, the steering wheel came off in Brauchitsch's hands, for someone had forgotten to tighten the safety screws. He hurled the steering wheel from the cockpit and tried to steer using only the column, but he was finished for the day. Seaman went on to win his initial race for Mercedes.

Manfred did win another GP that year, the French race at Rheims at 101.137 m.p.h., and he was 2nd to Lang in the Tripoli GP, 3rd in both the Swiss and Italian races, and 3rd in the German hillclimb championship races. At Leghorn, he crossed the line an apparent winner of the Ciano Cup, only to be disqualified for receiving illegal help in restarting on the course. Lang won that race.

In European racing's last prewar year Brauchitsch retired from the German GP once more, this time with a punctured fuel tank; and retired from the French race with engine troubles. But he was 2nd to Lang at Pau, 3rd in the Belgian and Swiss races and 4th in the Eifelrennen. He then tried to flee to a neutral country, but Neubauer practically grabbed him off the airplane to race in the only Yugoslavian GP in Belgrade, where he pushed his W.163 Mercedes to 2nd behind the winning Auto Union of Nuvolari. Then the war came, and Manfred barely made it out of Germany.

Brauchitsch raced just once more—at the age of 45 in 1950—when he ran the German GP a last time in an AFM. His bad racing luck held, his car retiring with engine problems. After that he went back to East Germany, then to Russia. Many people half expected to see an East German or Russian GP team suddenly appear one day with a grayed but still handsome team manager, perhaps, but it just didn't work out that way.

CLINT BRAWNER

Clint Brawner was a quiet little man, ill at ease when he had to go to parties like the one his car owner, Al Dean, gave late in 1965 to celebrate Mario Andretti's ascension to the USAC championship. He stood a little off to the side at the country club in Hollywood, smiling and uncertain as about the proper procedure for descending upon the hors d'oeuvres. This sort of thing was okay for the owner of Dean Van Lines, but as Brauner later admitted, he would rather have hoisted a few at the corner pub. He knew his business, this mechanic's mechanic, and that business was to win USAC races. He had started with Dean back in 1952, and the measure

of their relationship was Dean's name for the balding Arizonian—"head magician." His career spanned the era of the Kurtis frame jobs, the Salih tilt-Offies, the Watsons, the Epperly clan, and the rear-engine Fords.

"I'm not an engineer," Brawner said that night. "I don't design cars on paper. I learned mostly by experience, mine and that of others. I like to let others make the mistakes but sometimes everybody has to make his own. I knew how to work with the front-engined Offies and then they sprung these Ford funny cars on us. They keep on calling Mario's car a Brabham. It was one when we started, but we keep changing and improving. I don't think it's the same now. That's what a chief mechanic has to do—not design the car but change it and improve it and make it go for the driver."

Brawner had great drivers in the Dean Van Lines Specials—Jimmy Bryan, Eddie Sachs, and many others before Andretti. He won the D-A Lubricants Achievement Award, which is like earning the DSC to an Indy mechanic. He won the Pole Position Mechanic's Award 4 times, twice with Sachs and twice with Andretti. Clint comprehended the new riches of big-time racing intellectually but not emotionally. The dirt tracks and their grimy powersliding oil-fumed environs made him smile in reminiscence. Bryan, he said, was the greatest, if it was not A. J. Foyt.

"Mario is a case of a driver for his time. He'll drive anything well, and he won't back off for anybody. But he's as good as you can find in these little rear-engined cars. He just fits the kind of racing we do. Drivers are people," Brawner continued. "They each do things different, and the important thing is to help them get the job done. Sachs was a very finicky guy, very nervous because he learned how to drive the hard way—going through fences and landing on his head. But he was the most determined guy I ever saw, and he made himself into a polished driver. He was always looking for the shortest route. Mario uses more track than most but he stays on the gas longer, too. He looks scary, but he really controls the car. You set it up for the way he drives. Chassis set-up is becoming so important. You have to tune the chassis to the engine as well as the driver. This Ford engine is much more complicated than the Offy, but that gives a man more places where he can find an edge. When it gets expensive like it is now, it becomes a matter of ten-thousandths of an inch. You have to devote full time to it," Clint added. "And I figure just when we get to know this engine, somebody will come along with a turbine or something and blow us all back to the beginning."

That statement was made before the STP turbine car of 1967 became a reality and before its 4-wheel-drive performed so well. Asked what he would do if just this happened, Brawner grinned and said, "We'll get one, and I'll start figuring how to improve it." However, he helped lead the fight to ban the car.

In 1932, while working in a machine shop in his

home town of Phoenix, Clint began to build midget racers. He visited Indianapolis for the first time in 1938 and decided the role of chief mechanic was the life for him. But a war intervened, and he spent it with the U.S. Navy Seabees. When it was over he returned to building midgets. In 1951 he began work on Bobby Ball's championship car, becoming chief mechanic the following year. In 1953, with Bob Sweikert as his driver, Brawner began the association with Dean that was to last until Al's death. The year Mario Andretti ran for Dean as the Overseas National Airways Team almost ruptured that driver-mechanic duo. But Andy Granatelli's STP money made everything work again. And in 1969 it gave Clint his first Indianapolis victory in 16 tries.

The Brawner total success record was awesome. Though the 1969 season his drivers had won 51 times—Andretti 29, Jim Bryan 17, Sachs 3, Sweikert and Ball 1 each—for 6 national titles in USAC Championship racing; they had placed 2nd 36 times and 3rd 25 times for a total of 112 top-3 finishes, or 45 percent of 230 race starts. No other mechanic even came close to equalling that record.

For 1970 Brawner parted company with Andretti and STP, choosing Roger McCluskey, USAC stock car champ for 1969 and a veteran driver, for the cars he was to build for Jim Hayhoe. The Scorpion Ford got as high as 6th at the 150-mile mark at Indianapolis before retiring with a broken suspension. It was rebuilding and polishing time again for Clint.

CRAIG BREEDLOVE

Once he was the fastest man on earth. Once he was worth an estimated $250,000 and spent his off-hours lolling by a swimming pool in Palos Verdes, a hilly, expensive suburb of Los Angeles. Once he was as close-cropped as an astronaut, with his hair waved, his clothes semi-conservative, just right for the corporate-backed holder of the Land Speed Record. All of that was back in 1965. A few years later, Craig Breedlove regularly collected unemployment insurance checks and lived off a garage in the industrial section of Torrance. His hair had lengthened, his face had wearied, and his normal dress was jeans and turtleneck. A string of financial setbacks, including the loss of his Goodyear tire dealership, the flooding of his garage that ruined about $100,000 worth of irreplaceable parts and machinery, and other blows had dissolved his financial fortunes. He had gone through his second and third wives—the latter his wife for only a few days. Worst of all, he had lost his LSR to Gary Gabelich, and he didn't really see a way to get it back.

They've never made a movie about a man who held the LSR, but if they ever want to, Breedlove's is the one to make. It has all the elements Hollywood thrives on. When he was born March 23, 1937, Craig Norman

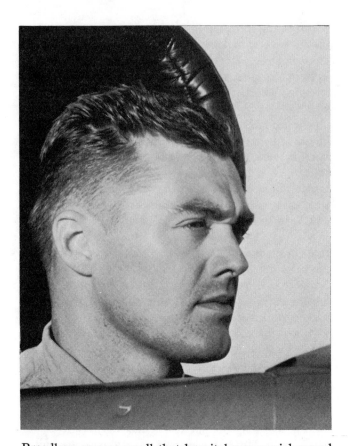

Breedlove was so small that hospital nurses nicknamed him "Streamline." His dad was a movie special effects man, his mother an ex-showgirl. Like most Southern California kids, he grew up with a mania for wheels. At the age of 12 he talked his parents into buying him a $75 jalopy, not for driving, but for "working on." Two years later, he had a working hot rod. At 16 Craig visited the Bonneville Salt Flats with a dragster and hit 154 m.p.h. At Venice High School, he spent all the time he could in shop and even took up drafting. No college for Breedlove. He got a job as a parts manager for a sports car dealership, switched to welding at a garage, then took a steady job as a fireman in Costa Mesa, Calif. By the time he was 20 Breedlove had married and fathered 3 children; by the time he was 22, he and his first wife had separated. It was around that time that Breedlove had a chance to buy a surplus J47 jet engine for $500. He jumped at it, quitting his job to devote full time to building a jet car, maybe with the idea of setting a Land Speed Record. He also met the future second Mrs. Breedlove, a carhop divorcée with 2 children of her own, who loved motorcycles and guys who went fast. Lee was her name, and she did more than just root for Craig. She kicked in with hard cash earned at her job while Craig concentrated on designing and building the car, and on seeking sponsors. Shell came first, then Goodyear, whose engineers were astounded that this high school graduate knew as much as he did about aerodynamics and the like.

In 1962 a new cycle of LSR-seekers had come to challenge the 1947 John Cobb mark of 394.196 m.p.h.

There was Mickey Thompson, the hot rod king; Art and Walter Arfons, the hot rod brothers who had gone their separate ways only to find themselves at the same destination, Bonneville; Donald Campbell, British, son of a one-time LSR-holder, Sir Malcolm Campbell; and now Breedlove, least-known of them all. In his first brush with fame, Craig fizzled, his 3-wheeled jet car not even approaching Cobb's mark. Back home, the Spirit of America, as his car was called, underwent many modifications, the most apparent of which was a big stabilizing tail (originally planned by Breedlove, but discarded when engineers claimed it wasn't necessary).

Breedlove was back at the Salts in late July 1963, and tests ate up the rest of that month and the opening days of the following one. On August 5 he was ready. With all of his tests, the Spirit had been run less than 200 miles, never at anything approaching its real potential. By 7:15 that morning the runs were over and the record was his. The 1st run, at 90 percent throttle, was 388.47 m.p.h., the 2nd run, at 95 percent throttle, was 428.37 m.p.h. The combined average of the 2 runs—the actual record—was 407.45 m.p.h. Cobb's 16-year-old record was smashed. Or was it? An argument raged. Was Breedlove's Spirit a car in the accepted sense? Should the Fédération Internationale de l'Automobile set up a category for these jet-powered vehicles, whether 3- or 4-wheeled? Would only the Fédération Internationale de la Motorcycle recognize Craig as holder of the LSR at that moment? Was it all for naught? Breedlove and his sponsors didn't think so. They talked as if they held the LSR, and in America, where his sponsors sold most of their products, he was accepted. No one could believe that a technicality would prevent the FIA from accepting, however grudgingly, the Spirit's run as a genuine LSR record.

Meanwhile, Donald Campbell, whom Craig had met and with whom a strange bond of friendship had grown, had nervously waited for floods and continuing rains to end at Lake Eyre, Australia, for his shot at the LSR. Campbell's car, unlike those of the Americans, was turbine powered, and because it had 4 wheels and was driven by them rather than by a jet stream, it was considered a "real" automobile, not a freak like the Spirit of America or Art Arfons's Green Monster. On July 17, 1964, Campbell roared over his Australian course the mandatory 2 times and raised the record to 403.164 m.p.h., eclipsing Cobb's 1967 mark but not matching Breedlove's. Yet some people still clung to the notion that Campbell's was the real LSR. It stood less than 16 months, until two American hot rodders, the Summers brothers, ran the axle-driven record up to 409.277 m.p.h. in the piston-engined Goldenrod.

The FIA by now had accepted the idea of jet-powered LSR cars. Campbell's mark (then Summers') was recognized for the axle-driven category, Breedlove's for the jet-powered. But the acceptance was shortlived. For in 1964, an extraordinary year in the continuing race to

see who was the fastest man on wheels, all kinds of cars were converging on Bonneville and its little timer's shack. Tom Green, the forgotten man of the LSR epic, shattered Craig's record October 2 in Walt Arfons's Wingfoot Express, traveling 413.20 m.p.h. Three days later brother Art Arfons, driving his own Green Monster, upped the record to 434.02. Breedlove loved competition, so he appeared on the course October 13 and raised the mark to 468.72 m.p.h. Art Arfons was a rather competitive fellow, too, and he reappeared in time to watch Breedlove race against his own mark October 15 just for the hell of it. . . . and for the idea of bettering 500 m.p.h.

Craig's first run was timed at 513.33 m.p.h. Anything near that and he was home in clover, although he knew Arfons would be out there to beat it in the time remaining before the salts deteriorated for another year. He pushed the car for all it was worth, and it responded with an incredible 539.89, the average for the 2 runs rising to 526.61 m.p.h. But stopping the car was something else again. One chute tore loose, then another. The brakes burned out, and still the Spirit rocketed on. It went off the course, skidded along the rough salts, snapped a telephone pole like a reed, sprayed through a quarter-mile of shallow water, hit an 8-foot-high earthen embankment, sprang into the air and plowed nose first into an 18-foot-deep reservoir. Breedlove walked—crawled at first—away mostly unhurt. "For my next act, I will set myself afire," he said unconvincingly. Arfons took his time and made his bid October 27, 1964. He took Craig's hard-won mark away from him with a 536.71 m.p.h. average. But Craig already was preparing to regain the LSR in 1965.

The first step was retiring the battered Spirit I. It went on permanent loan to the Chicago Museum of Science and Industry. A new Spirit, eventually named Sonic I, was being built almost at the same time. A more powerful, faster J-79 jet engine formed the heart of the new car. Everything that Craig and the engineers had learned from the first car went into the new one and, aerodynamically, it was as perfect a creation as could be conceived at that point in time. Where the first Spirit had cost about $100,000, exclusive of tire costs, this one cost $250,000.

Both Breedlove and Arfons were at Bonneville in November, 1965. As Arfons watched, Craig set a new record of 555.127 m.p.h. November 2 (after early runs had shown some unforseen quirks in the "perfect" Sonic I design and some more modifications had been built in). Then Arfons came out November 7 and upped it to 576.553. On November 15 Breedlove was ready again. The first run was timed at 593.178 m.p.h. "I can do 600," he said as they turned the car around. He did 608.201, with the average soaring to 600.601 m.p.h. Craig became the first man to do 400, 500 and 600, holder of the LSR the 5th time in 3 years. Arfons had damaged his car in his last run and was through for the year (perhaps forever). The record was to stand until October 23, 1970, when a California friend, Gary Gabelich, was to drive the Blue Flame (a car that Breedlove might have driven himself, but he couldn't agree on money nor engineering authority with its sponsors and lost the chance) to a 622.407 m.p.h. record.

Breedlove had hoped that a new challenger would bring an end to his doldrums, but it didn't work out that way. No one had the half-million dollars needed to build a new car and run the LSR attempt the way it had to be in the seventies, at least no one Craig Breedlove knew. He had the plans, and the desire, and the experience. But he didn't have the sponsor. He didn't have Lee either (they split in 1968), nor his 3rd wife. All he had were lots of memories, lots of dreams, and a niche in automotive history that should endure. But he intended to keep trying.

RICHARD BRICKHOUSE

It was to have been the high point of the career of Bill France, president of NASCAR and of the corporation that owns Daytona International Speedway. The new NASCAR jewel, Alabama International Speedway, 2.66 miles of tri-oval in the manner of Daytona but faster, was to open with the first Talladega 500. But at the last minute the members of Richard Petty's Professional Drivers Association announced that the track was unsafe and that they would not run. France claimed he would drive a car himself if necessary, then proceeded to put together a field of supposedly ineligible Grand American cars (then called GTs), with a smattering of factory machinery and independents. By such cataclysmic events is the circle of fame extended to bit players.

Richard Fleming Brickhouse, a truck driver from Rocky Point, N.C., had joined the PDA, possibly because this was his 2nd year in Grand National racing, and he was a part-timer trying to move up. He also had a farm to care for. However, he had showed flashes of brilliance with ordinary mounts. And he wanted to win big. So when he was offered the new Dodge Daytona that Charlie Glotzbach had placed on the pole at 199.446 m.p.h., he resigned from the PDA to race. His was one of 5 truly first-line machines in the 36-car field, and he made the most of it, surviving battles with Bobby Isaac, IMCA ace Ramo Stott, and Jim Vandiver to roll into Victory Lane. His average speed (with 10 pit stops to change tires) was 153.778 The average speed for the first Alabama 500 when all the PDA boys were back, and Brickhouse lasted 25 laps in a 1970 Ford was 152.321.

The blond farmer-trucker subsequently drove less often than he had the previous year. Perhaps the money won at Talladega was enough to satisfy him for the rest of his life.

GASTON BRILLI-PERI

The big Alfa whipped around a corner to find itself blocked by several slowly-moving cars. Behind the Alfa's wheel was a big man with a battered face, even more distorted by the wind, with a silver whistle hung around his neck. Quickly a continuing stream of shrill blasts let those ahead of the Alfa know that Count Gaston Brilli-Peri of Tuscany wished to get through, and the slower cars parted to let the speeding nobleman pass.

Brilli-Peri, born in 1893, didn't drive Alfas exclusively. His first major race was the 1922 Targa Florio in a Steyr, which crashed. In the same year he finished 2nd in a Fiat to Alfieri Maserati in the Mugello race. He was 2nd again in 1923, this time in a Steyr. The Count continued to run major Italian events, finishing 10th in the 1924 Coppa Florio, scoring his initial major victory the following year in the Perugia Cup when his Ballot averaged 66.20 m.p.h. The year 1925 saw Louis Wagner leave the Alfa Romeo team for Delage, creating a berth that the Italian company filled with Brilli-Peri. That the choice was a good one he demonstrated by winning the Italian Grand Prix in a 2-litre Alfa at 94.76 m.p.h., a good 19 minutes over Giuseppe Campari in 2nd place.

In 1926 the Count, driving an independent Alfa, was 2nd for the 1st of 3 times in the Rome GP, that year to another Count, Aymo Maggi, in a Bugatti. In 1928 and

1929 he would try a Bug himself and finish 2nd to Louis Chiron's Bugatti, then return to an Alfa and trail Archille Varzi. But 1929 was Brilli-Peri's greatest year in motor racing. After a 3rd in the Targa, the Count's bag included a host of victories: the Tripoli GP at 83.24 m.p.h. in a Talbot, the Tunis GP at 83.35 in an Alfa, the Mugello race at 44.46 in a Talbot, the 2-iltre heat at the Monza GP at 114.85 in an Alfa, and the Cremona race at 114.41 in an Alfa.

Like everyone else, the Count looked forward to 1930. But in practice for the season's opening race, the Tripoli GP, for which he was the favorite in a straight-8 Talbot, Brilli-Peri crashed and was killed. The silver whistle was forever stilled.

FRANK BRISKO

One of the more unusual drivers and engine designers of the Thirties in America was Frank Brisko, a Milwaukee native of German descent. Frank campaigned in IMCA before assaying the AAA circuits and Indianapolis. He competed 12 times at Indianapolis, his best finishes 2 9th places in 1934 and 1940. He lasted 138 laps in 1931; 81 laps in 1932; 47 laps in 1933; drove the Front Wheel Drive Special to 9th in 1934; lasted 79 laps in 1935; 179 laps in 1936; 105 laps in 1937; 39 laps in 1938, 38 laps in 1939; and drove the Elgin Piston Ring Special to 9th in 1940. His first Indy was in 1929, when he finished 11th, and his last was in 1941, when he lasted 70 laps.

Brisko drove Miller cars at Indy up until 1935, when he switched to a modified Studebaker, breaking its U-joint less than halfway through the race. In the Elgin Piston Ring Special of 1936, he had developed his own 4-cylinder engine, a version of the Offy with 2 valves per cylinder and capable of accepting a Ford transmission and clutch. He ran out of the gas allotment on lap 179. Frank next developed a new 6-cylinder engine for 1937 which was sidelined when it lost oil pressure. It was a 350-cu. in. o.h.c. design of about square bore-stroke ratio with 3 Winfield carburetors. The car used front-wheel drive and went fairly well. Brisko later modified the 6 to get down to 271 cu. in. by making a much smaller bore and keeping the stroke the same (4.375 inches). It went fast on gasoline when others were using alcohol. There were 2 of these cars in the race, the other driven by Emil Andres. Brisko broke an oil line, and Andres wrecked. One of the 2 Briskos in the 1939 race, that driven by Harry McQuinn, had a slightly smaller bore. The cars dropped out with ignition problems (McQuinn) and air pump failure (Brisko).

In 1940 Brisko made his car heavier by 43 pounds through bracing and a bigger gas tank and finished 9th using Good Gulf gasoline while winner Wilbur Shaw was letting his Maserati drink an alcohol blend. In 1941

the Brisko suffered a broken valve spring. After that Brisko retired to help sell a fuel pressure regulator, and his Brisko engine was not revived.

ERIC BROADLEY

Consider 2 men of about the same age and background. One has slightly more technical experience. He also has more drive, perhaps, certainly a greater flare for the dramatic, a gambler's instincts, and a rather large amount of luck in one way or the other. The other fellow is imaginative, industrious, associates himself with the right people, and does good quality work. Which one would you say would end up as one of England's richest private citizens and a household name in auto racing?

Eric Broadley wasn't the first man described. Colin Chapman was. Broadley and Chapman were contempories, but Colin was the one who charged his way to fame and fortune. Eric became a well-known man but not really famous. He became fairly well-to-do, but not one of England's richest men, as Chapman did. He got a taste of racing immortality, but never really had a chance to savor it. Part of the reason may be that Broadley was always a rather quiet, almost invisible fellow, certainly when compared to the extroverted Mr. Chapman.

Public information about Broadley is limited, for he has rarely been interviewed, and when he was, the subject was mainly his Lola cars. We do know that he was

born around 1929, and that the family was in the tailoring business. Tailoring didn't appeal to Eric, nor did his initial pursuit—architectural drafting. He was building houses and garages when he first got the urge to race. He designed his own car, then built it. The year was 1955, and the impetus was provided by the 750 Motor Club, which Broadley had just joined. His car was powered by a Ford 10 engine, and was called a Lola; who or what Lola was has not been divulged.

The first Lola won nearly every race Broadley cared to enter, and there were polite inquiries about whether he wanted to build any more. He didn't, but he was thinking about another car—a pure sports/racer suitable for international events, not just club meetings. This car materialized as the Lola Mk. 1, of which Eric was to build 35 between 1958 and 1962, plus one more for old time's sake in 1967. The Mark 1 was powered by a front-mounted 1100 c.c. Climax engine, and was extremely fast, but it took a year to sort out various bugs. Then the car started winning its class regularly, including a class victory in the Tourist Trophy (and 6th overall). Graham Broadley, Eric's brother, had been part of the Lola effort up until this point, but when Eric started building cars full-time, Graham went back to Bromley and the family tailoring business.

The race history of the car was interesting. Peter Ashdown, driving for Broadley, won at Silverstone, Aintree, and Goodwood, and was 2nd at Oulton Park. On the Continent, there was a victory over Porsche at Clermont-Ferrand, but at the Nurburgring 1000 the car crashed while running 1st in class and 11th overall, with Eric Broadley himself at the wheel. The Tourist Trophy victory capped a rather impressive year, then. Small wonder that ready-built and kit-form Lolas were in genuine demand.

The initial Lola Formula Junior car emerged from Broadley's shops in 1960. Twenty-nine of the front-engined Mk. 2 models were built, and 11 rear-engined of the Mark 3 models. The 1st was powered by a lightly modified Ford Anglia engine, but this proved unreliable. The other model featured a Superspeed modified Ford 105E power plant, which was better, but the Lola still was being outclassed by Chapman's Lotus FJ. Mk. 5 and 5A Lolas, built in 1962–3, featured 100-b.h.p. Cosworth or Ford Holbay engines, smaller frontal areas, and improved handling. But by this time Chapman was off on Formula 1 projects and not really interested in competing for FJ honors. Chapman always had a lot of irons in the fire at once, a trick Broadley didn't master until much later.

Broadley was initially involved in F1 around the same time, but not on his own initiative. Reg Parnell liked the chassis of the Lola FJ car, and he contracted with Eric to design and build 4 cars for the Bowmaker-Yeoman GP team he was managing. The delivered vehicles were loosely based on the FJ concept and powered by Coventry-Climax V-8s that yielded about 180 b.h.p.

One of the drivers was John Surtees. Surtees took 2nds in the British and German Grands Prix, and 3rd in the non-title Silverstone International Trophy. He also won a special 2,000 Guinea Race at Mallory Park. Thus began a long association between the quiet designer and the moody driver.

In 1963 Eric was charging off in another direction, one in which he was to do especially good work: the first Lola GT car. The Mk. 6 Lola was Ford-powered and looked like a winner. Unfortunately, in its 4 racing appearances that year—Silverstone, Nurburgring 1000, Le Mans, and Brands Hatch—it failed to finish any race, and at Le Mans David Hobbs totalled one of the 3 built when a gearbox failure caused the car to go out of control. But the Lola GT prototype led to an offer from Ford Motor Co. to Broadley to join in a new project it had under way.

Ford had decided it wanted to win Le Mans, and this meant a special effort and a special car. However, Le Mans became only part of the American company's desire. Eventually it aspired to a World Manufacturers Championship. British Ford would be part of the effort. but it was felt that someone else, with experience in European racing and car-building, should be part of it too. John Cooper was considered, but many at Ford rejected him because of his diminished innovation and receptiveness to new concepts. Colin Chapman was considered, but there were fears that he would be too independent. Into the hopper came Eric's name. His Lola GT had just been unveiled at the London Racing Car Show in January 1963, and it looked like the kind of thing Ford's own engineers had chalk-talked about in Dearborn and in London. They talked with Broadley, and in the end he was offered the job, with the proviso that he was to concentrate on the Ford project and let Lola lie dormant for the period of his contract. He agreed to that and was signed on.

There are 2 versions of the contract. Either (a) Broadley was given a one-year contract, which was extended 6 months, or (b) Broadley was signed and paid for 2 years, but let go after 18 months. Either way, he was associated with the Ford GT project for 18 months and produced a car—called the GT40—that looked just like the Lola GT, even down to the 40 inches that both cars stood off the track (whence the "40"). Lolas, in fact, were used right along by Ford as "mules" to test engines and other components. And it was admitted that Broadley was basically responsible for the chassis of the GT40 among other things.

In any case, Eric was back in the Lola business by mid-1964 in a new factory close to the Ford Advanced Vehicle Operations at Slough. His first project was rebuilding the Midland Racing Partnership's FJ cars; then he swung into designing and building 5 monocoques for Formulas 2 and 3, followed by 7 more advanced designs in this series in 1966. In the meantime, Eric was conceiving a new sports/racer that was to become the Lola

T70, one of his greatest designs. When the FIA finally conceived a special group for this type of car—first called Group 9; then Group 7, the CanAm group—Lola was ready with its Chevrolet-engined cars, thoroughly tested in British races by Surtees, still one of Broadley's biggest boosters.

Surtees had mixed luck with the car in Britain, but it was properly sorted out for later events, including the Players 200 in Mosport, Canada, and the Brands Hatch Guards Trophy race, both of which he won. He also raced the car in 1966 in the new CanAm series, winning at Mont Tremblant, Riverside, and Las Vegas and taking the initial Challenge Cup and more than $48,000 in prize money. Mark Donohue, who was 2nd in the series, was driving a Lola, too, as were Dan Gurney (7th), Graham Hill (9th), George Follmer (10th), and Paul Hawkins (14th). For 1967, a new version incorporating many of Surtees's own ideas was produced for CanAm racing, but that series was won by Team McLaren. Nevertheless, Surtees won Las Vegas again and Donohue was 2nd at Elkhart Lake. Surtees also inspired Broadley to build an Aston Martin-powered prototype sports/racer, but as fast and good-handling as the car was, it suffered a frustrating series of mechanical problems.

Broadley was cooking on every burner in this period. Every bit of the Slough works was occupied with projects: the T80, T90, and T150 Indianapolis cars; F2 and F1 cars; a BMW-powered Group 7 car designed specifically for hillclimbing; the T130 chassis for the Honda GP car of 1968; and the early SCCA Formula A/British Formula 5000 single-seaters.

The year 1966 was Lola's golden year, the season that Eric tasted the sweetest fruits of racing glory. (John) Mecom Racing Enterprises contracted for 3 T90 Indy cars, and George Bignotti, the chief mechanic, worked closely with Broadley to get the chassis ready for shipment to Los Angeles by the beginning of March. A 2.8-litre supercharged Offy was dropped into one car, and Rodger Ward drove it to 2nd place at Phoenix's USAC race. Ward won the next race at Trenton. Ford 4.2-litres were dropped into the other 2 chassis for the Memorial Day classic for Graham Hill and Jackie Stewart. All finished the 500-miler, Hill winning, Stewart 6th, and Ward 15th. Total prize money was almost $200,000. Later, Al Unser drove one of the cars, and he scored a trio of 2nds, a 3rd, and a 6th. At the season's end, an "extra" USAC race was held in Japan, at the Mount Fuji course, where a reprise of the Indy 500 was run on a near-replica of the Indiana Brickyard. Stewart and Hill diced their way around in Lolas until Graham's distributor failed, and Jackie won the big race. Hill was classified 5th.

That same year Denis Hulme was racing a private Lola T70 MK. 2. He won at Snetterton, the Tourist Trophy race at Oulton, the Grovewood Trophy at Mallory Park, Silverstone's Martini Trophy, as well as several smaller races. Surtees's races in the CanAm series already have been outlined. A Ford GT40 managed to win at Le Mans that season, too, and repeated that victory in 1967. If Eric Broadley's smile those days was a warm one, it was completely understandable. It is doubtful if any tailor or draftsman ever felt as he did that year.

PETE BROCK

Trust Carroll Shelby, the Cobra man, to pick up a General Motors reject, a youthful designer named Peter Elbert Brock, as his first Shelby-American employee. This must have made the Cobra's later domination of GM products twice as galling to the Detroit-based automotive giant. But Pete, a personable and handsome young man of the type that big companies like, never regretted his escape to the sunny shores of California, nor was Brock a stranger to the Golden State.

Born in New York City in 1937, raised and schooled in San Francisco, Pete graduated from the automotive styling department at the Los Angeles Art Center College of Design (after a year at Stanford) and was recruited by Detroit as a stylist. His talents were such that he eventually became involved in a project that ended up as the Corvette Sting Ray while carrying on his own design project on the side. This personal project was not moonlighting in any way, however, for Pete's GM superiors took an interest—albeit a skeptical one—in his ideas for a 67-inch wheelbase fastback that would sell for about $1,000. They even went so far in 1958 as to have him construct, on company time and with company facilities, a full-sized fiber glass prototype that lacked only an engine and other mechanical parts.

The Brock project, coded Cadet, eventually came to the attention of then board chairman Harlow Curtice who stopped by one day, looked at the economy sports car, and grandly announced that he didn't like "small" cars. It was the end of GM's interest in fastbacks—at least for then. The later Corvair, which was a small car by Detroit standards, contained distinct Brockian overtones, it is said.

Pete did not stay around for the Corvair era. Soon after Curtice's visit, Brock packed his personal 1100-c.c. ex-factory bobtailed Le Mans Cooper on its trailer and drove back to the West Coast. The British mount was raced only at Palm Springs before Pete was able to get a good price for it, so he sold the Cooper and bought a new Lotus 11. This lovely Colin Chapman design lasted halfway through Riverside, met a post, and ended up as a basket case. By now Brock had moved into an old house next to Riverside and continued to ply the track, but in other people's cars.

One of his hosts was a big, friendly Texan named Shelby who had just given up racing and was setting up the first of his enterprises, a driving school. Shelby gave Brock a job because he liked the way the youngster handled himself. Pete ran the school for 4 years, then, as Shelby-American was born to produce the hybrid AC chassis and Ford engine design that became the Cobra, Shelby brought Pete into that enterprise as well. Brock did just about everything for Carroll—letters, phone calls, making coffee, designing ads and insignia, sweeping—all except the one job he was most qualified for, designing automobiles. But Shelby already knew that he needed talent like Pete's, and his first designing job was not long in coming once the Cobra had gotten off the ground successfully.

An open Cobra sports/racer was one thing; what Carroll needed was an aerodynamically stable coupe for the big races likes those at Daytona, Sebring, and Le Mans. There were limitations, of course, like the existing chassis, seat heights and engine location, and the fact that Brock had never before designed a closed car for the fast speeds at which aerodynamic qualities become all-important. Brock did well. In its debut at Daytona, the new car was doing well enough to lead by a lap when it caught fire during a pit stop for gasoline and had to be scratched. Repaired, Brock's car went on to win the GT category at Sebring and set a lap record at Le Mans. Eventually, it won the World Manufacturers Championship, the first U.S. car to do so. With successes like these, Brock's new job as chief Cobra designer was assured. He also handled many of Shelby-American's outside commissions like the Lang-Cooper and the de Tomaso project.

In December, 1965, Brock took a big step, into a free-lance design and consulting business of his own. Never far from the Cobra's lair, he could always point in Shelby's direction whenever someone asked what he'd done lately. His design would be enough to guarantee him a chance at almost any auto task.

Nor did Brock leave racing. After some preliminary sedan racing on the coast, a rather lucrative association with Nissan Motors of Japan developed in 1969. By 1971, thanks to a rumored $400,000 annual racing budget, Datsuns were regularly winning "amateur" SCCA races and rallies, and the professional 2.5 Challenge—successor to the SCCA's under-2-Litre Trans-American sedan championship. All the winners were raced by BRE—Brock Racing Enterprises.

TONY BROOKS

If you were driving in Surrey, around Weybridge, England, stopped at a certain garage and were greeted by the owner, and if he were youngish-looking, with an engaging smile and tousled hair, you might be talking to Charles Anthony Standish Brooks. He was one of

auto racing's rare ones, a truly fine driver who retired at the peak of his prowess and stayed retired.

On October 23, 1955, Tony Brooks, a comparative newcomer to international racing, was offered his initial Formula 1 drive in the season's last race, the Syracuse Grand Prix in Sicily. Mercedes, still shaken by its Le Mans tragedy, was passing this race up, but Connaught, the British marque for which Brooks had been a Formula 2 driver, appeared to be outclassed even in this one, with Maserati fielding its entire F2 team, including Luigi Villoresi and Luigi Musso. Brooks's green Connaught was an old and tired mount, and he recalled that he had only gotten in a few practice laps with it because the Britons were afraid that prolonged practice might prevent the car from making the starting line in the actual race.

"Musso and I started out together," Tony said later, describing the race, "but he held the lead for awhile, before I could take it away. We diced quite a bit, then he fell behind. I wasn't really pushing or anything. My philosophy was, 'always go as quick as you feel like, but never force anything.' I was quite a bit ahead when the race was over." After 239 miles of circling the 3.4-mile triangular course, Brooks finished 51 seconds ahead of Musso and 2 laps ahead of the other Maseratis. "It was one of those storybook things," Tony laughed. "After all, it was my very first ride in a Formula 1 car, and it was the first time that a British car had won in a GP since (Sir Henry) Seagrave had turned the trick in the French GP in 1923—32 long years before. But it was one isolated race, and it didn't prove that much, really."

Tony Brooks was born on February 25, 1932, at Dukinfield, Cheshire, about 200 miles north of London. He was the son of a dental surgeon, and Tony qualified as one, although in later life he preferred to work in garages rather than mouths. He was very much an amateur, at first becoming interested in racing through his father, who had a real passion for the sport, although he had never raced. "I didn't have a burning desire to race," Brooks explained, "but I'd always enjoyed driving, and the only place to get the best out of a car and yourself was on the circuit, not the public road."

Starting at age 16 as a cautious motorcyclist, Tony was noted for the slow, careful way he drove his road car, in sharp contrast to his racing style. His initial race came in March 1952, in a Healey Silverstone. That same season he drove in 9 club races. "The Silverstone was a present from my father. It was a good car in which to learn, but it never had a chance for a victory. Then I met a chap who had a Frazer-Nash and wanted someone to drive it for him. I continued racing my Silverstone, his Frazer-Nash (in which I won my initial race), and even got a factory ride in the 1954 Tourist Trophy, but the car retired."

In 1955, Brooks was invited by Aston Martin, then a coming power in sports car racing, to join its team after he had starred in a drivers' trial the previous December. His first Aston ride was the ill-fated Le Mans race, sharing a car with John Riseley-Pritchard, a wealthy insurance broker who retired after the race, at his family's request, when the full effects of Pierre Levegh's Mercedes crash became known. Brooks's mate was to influence his career strongly, however, for Riseley-Pritchard had a Formula 2 Connaught, and he now needed a driver. Tony became that driver. Before his single-seater adventures started, however, Brooks was to establish himself as a rising addition to the Aston Martin team. He was 3rd at the Goodwood 9-hour race that season, but his Tourist Trophy car (shared with Peter Collins) retired.

In 1955, Brooks was a steady, speedy, but entirely unspectacular driver with Aston Martin and the F2 Connaught, participating only in British races in the latter. His driving had something about it that suggested that, with the proper mount, he would do well. Rodney Clarke, managing director of Connaught Cars, sensed it, and offered Tony a factory ride in a 1500 c.c. car for an Aintree meet. The youngster did not win, but was 2nd only to Colin Chapman's faster Lotus. Based on Tony's verve in that start, Clarke offered him the Syracuse ride that made the name of Brooks famous overnight.

BRM tabbed Tony for the 1956 GP season, along with Mike Hawthorn, while he continued in the sports car field for Aston. The car was still unperfected, how-

ever, and it almost killed Brooks in the British GP at Silverstone. "If you made the slightest mistake in the BRM in those days, you lost it," recalled Tony. "The car had absolutely no road-holding whatsoever. I was doing all right until the throttle started sticking. I went into the pits at once, and they started working on it. Right after the pits there is a bend that I'd been taking nearly flat out, but, of course, after I came out of the pits, I was going fairly slowly. I imagine that saved my life. The throttle stuck again, you see, and the car went 2 feet onto the grass. In a Ferrari or any other car, nothing would have happened, but the car threw me out, then burned itself out. I just broke a jaw."

Brooks's best finish that year in the unreliable BRM was a 2nd in the Aintree 200 to Stirling Moss. He also finished a 2nd in the Oulton Park Gold Cup that year, in an F2 Cooper, and shared a 5th at the Nurburgring 1000 with Collins, in an Aston Martin. Nurburgring was a race he was to win the following year for the British marque, along with 2 Spa races, one for sports cars and the other the GP of the Royal Automobile Club of Belgium. The German victory was especially sweet, for Tony was the 1st Briton to win there since Dick Seaman had before World War II. Brooks also was at Sebring in 1956, but his car retired.

The following season, his car retired at Le Mans, again with almost disastrous results for Tony. "It was about two or three in the morning," he later recalled. "I jumped into the car that Noel Cunningham-Reid had gotten up to 2nd place, despite a gearbox that was stuck in 4th. Two of our other cars already had experienced the same trouble and been scratched, but we were determined to have a go anyway. I thought I might be able to free the gear by accelerating hard and banging the lever into neutral in the overrun. I was looking down and pushing hard on the knob, when I glanced up and saw to my horror that I had passed the braking point for the Terte Rouge right-handed turn after the Esses. I braked hard, but the car ran wide on the exit, drifted across the road and climbed the sandbank. At the top it flipped, and ended up with its nose stuck in the sand and its tail sticking into the road. I was trapped underneath the car by my legs, couldn't see a thing in the darkness and was scared stiff that the fuel tank would catch fire—it had just been filled to the brim moments before.

"It seemed like ages, but it must have been about 10 seconds later that there was a crash, the car came off of me, and I felt a surge of fresh, cold air on my face. I was hurting all over, but I jumped up and over the sandbank like a scalded cat, and collapsed on the ground. People appeared from everywhere, it seemed, but the first face I recognized was that of Umberto Maglioli. It was his Porsche that had hit my car in the darkness, and spun across the road. It had been completely wrecked, but he was unscathed. He was really concerned for me, and looking back on it, I know why. There was a hole in my right thigh that was as big as my fist, my right shoulder and knee were deeply cut, and my left ankle was opened to the bone. I really felt bad, not only about the Aston, but about knocking Maglioli out of the race. But he was one of the real aristocrats of racing, and he insisted on going with me to the hospital in the ambulance, just to have someone near who knew me, and to see that I was properly looked after. I shall always remember his kindness."

Brooks was patched up, flown back to England in David Brown's private airplane, and set about building his strength. After 3 weeks he was sitting in a Vanwall at Aintree, waiting for the start of the British GP, his legs heavily padded and bandaged. It may sound like fiction, but Brooks drove 27 laps of that race, then turned his car over to Moss when the latter blew up his Vanwall, an arrangement that had been foreseen and settled before the race's start. With Brooks's placing, Moss went on to win the race, which also was that season's European GP, and the records give both drivers credit for the victory, Vanwall's 1st in a World Championship race. Tony also had a 2nd at Monaco in 1957. The following year, he came into his own in F1, winning 3 races for Vanwall. He took the Belgian (and European GP) race at 129.9 m.p.h., won the German GP at 90.4 m.p.h., and captured the Italian race at 121.2 m.p.h. Sharing an Aston Martin with Moss in sports car racing, Brooks retired at Sebring, but the pair won the Goodwood Tourist Trophy at 88.3 m.p.h.

In 1959 the Vanwall team was broken up by Tony Vandervell's failing health, and Brooks signed with Ferrari after a couple abortive attempts to run an ex-factory car for himself. He was 2nd to Jack Brabham (who would win his initial World Championship that year) at Monaco, then won the French GP—his 3rd straight European GP victory, by the way—at 127.5 m.p.h., and the German GP at 143.6 m.p.h. In sports car races, Brooks shared a 3rd place car at the Nurburgring 1000 and the Goodwood Tourist Trophy. His 5 1958–59 victories were recorded in just 14 months, and this feat caused Juan Fangio to tab him as a future World Champion, especially when he was 2nd to Brabham in the 1959 standings.

This was not to be, for several reasons. For one. Brooks had been married to a beautiful Italian girl, Pina Resegotti, in October 1958, and they had a child the following year. He began driving more cautiously, especially when the Ferrari found itself outclassed by the British Cooper. Collins's death in 1958, and Mike Hawthorn's in 1959, began weighing heavily on Brooks's mind. The following season he gratefully accepted a less powerful and, hence, less competitive car. His pride finally got the better of the still boyish-looking Briton, and in 1961, with another child on the way, he announced his retirement. Besides his garage interests, Brooks did both writing and broadcasting in the racing field. And there always was that DDS degree to fall back upon.

BOB BROWN

Competition sells motor cars. Ask Bob Brown, who started racing Chevrolet Corvettes in 1961 at the age of 21. Today Robert is a successful Chevvy dealer in Huntington, N. Y., but still a racer of no mean abilities in such major series as the Canadian-American Challenge Cup series where he demonstrated in 1971 that perseverence pays.

After the first race of the 1971 CanAm series, Denis Hulme sat happily in the cockpit of his bright orange McLaren, surrounded by "birds" and cameramen and the other hangers-on who always seem able to wrangle a pit pass at big automobile races. None of these people paid the slightest bit of attention to an exhausted Brown who climbed out of the seat of his battered McLaren M6B, reworked enough to be called a McLeagle. Brown hoisted himself over the pit wall and downed 2 milk bottles filled with ice water.

It should have been champagne, for Brown had driven the day's best race, better than Hulme, Jackie Stewart and 2 others who technically finished ahead of him. In a 4-year-old car, 300 or so pounds heavier than most of the others in the race, Brown had managed to win $5,050, which did not even cover his race expenses. And when a man is racing strictly on his own, without the big commercial deals of other serious CanAm com-

petitors, without the endorsements and appearance money and all the other "arrangements" that the Hulmes, Stewarts, and others are able to acquire in the course of a year's racing, covering expenses is an important factor.

But Bob always raced for enjoyment first. He started that way in 1961 with the Vettes, and then moved to Cobras. He had his own Chevvy-powered special called the Malibu in 1965 when he won the SCCA's C Modified title. He repeated the following season in a Lola T70.

Bob had a fling in single-seaters, too, driving in the SCCA's Formula A Continental series with a Chevvy-powered Eagle. The 1969 season started rather badly, when Brown was injured in a testing accident at Riverside, but he bounced back for a 4th at Laguna Seca, a 2nd at Sears Point, a 4th at Lime Rock, and 3rd at Mosport. He finished 5th in the final standings. In 1970 Brown concentrated on CanAm racing in the gutsy Group 7 cars, buying the McLeagle from Dan Gurney.

He did not finish in the Mosport opener, but was 4th at St. Jovite. At Watkins Glen Brown was 8th, and 4th again at Edmonton. Skipping Mid-Ohio, he finished 6th at Road America, then ran into bad luck for his next 3 starts and failed to finish at Road Atlanta, Donnybrooke, and Monterey. But in the Riverside finale, Bob returned to 6th place. His work for the season, worth $31,500 in Johnson Wax money, saw him 9th in the final standings.

In 1973, at age 33, Bob headed to Europe in a Formula 5000 team with Britain's Tony Dean, their objective to win some Rothman's cigarette money in the European F5000 series, and maybe some L&M money in America, too.

DAVID BROWN

The initials D.B. in the world of Aston Martin stood for the man who headed that marque, David Brown, a quiet, publicity-shy individual who until 1969 actively directed the fortunes of this $175 million complex of technology that became Britain's 2nd largest private business. It was not General Motors, of course, but, then, few British companies are. But David Brown showed that, if given the chance, he would have run GM about as well as anyone could.

Brown was born in 1904 at Huddersfield in Yorkshire, where a family business founded by his grandfather in 1860 was located. After Rossall School and Huddersfield Technical College, he joined the business as an apprentice at the age of 17 and rose to the top strictly according to ability rather than blood. He did this by broadening the original gear-making firm into the manufacture of machine tools, steel and bronze castings, tractors and farm machinery, cars, and other products. Yearly sales in 1969 were about 90 times those when he took control of the complex in 1932.

When the bespectacled Brown was 17, he built his first car. It was powered by the then-popular Sage engine, dropped into a Brown-designed chassis. Soon the young driver had graduated to Villiers Vauxhalls, and he was a familiar figure at hillclimbs and race meetings throughout Britain until the family called a halt to his participation. The business, they maintained, must come first. Brown agreed and for 20 years after that (1927 to 1947) he stayed away from cars pretty much, certainly as a competitor. He came close to resuming his old love in 1935, but stopped short and founded David Brown Tractors Limited against the advice of his father and company directors. Brown, in fact, had to rent the space in one of his company's own factories to set up a tractor production line, but he created a subsidiary of the parent company that later offered just about as wide a range of farm equipment as any company in the world. And it was to this personally-created company that David added an acquisition in 1947.

Reading the *Times* of London one morning he spotted a small, discreet advertisement on the front page, then fully covered with what Americans would call "classified" advertising. It offered an unidentified automobile manufacturing business for sale. The dormant flame of the 17-year-old flared up again and Brown made equally discreet inquiries. The company being offered turned out to be Aston Martin, a long-established, often financially-troubled concern that dated back to 1913.

Within months Aston Martin was his and, perhaps heeding an old law of acquirers that 2 of something are better than one, so was another equally long-established and troubled marque, Lagonda. These 2 firms gave Brown's new car interests tradition, designs, and hardware in both sporting and luxury classifications.

Brown's revived automotive interest soon moved to the head of the list of his interests, which included yachting, flying (he was an excellent pilot, but later let others do the piloting), horses (he was both a breeder of thoroughbreds and superlative rider and polo player), fox-hunting, and farming (150 acres in Buckinghamshire). All of which gave the slight, distinguished D.B. a real claim to the title of Renaissance Man. In 1968, the Queen added a real title, and he became Sir David. Shortly afterward he turned over direction of the company to his son. After a rapid succession of managements, and financial, labor, and political problems, the carbuilding end of the David Brown Companies began to lose money. In 1972 Aston Martin and Lagonda were sold to a Midlands investment firm.

DAVID BRUCE-BROWN

A handsome, wealthy Yale man, born in 1890, David Bruce-Brown campaigned as much in Europe as he did in his native land in the days before World War I. He was leading the 2-day, 950-mile 1912 French Grand

Prix, in a 14.1-litre Fiat, and with Ralph DePalma, was clearly setting the style in that event when he was disqualified for running out of gasoline and accepting a refill improperly. Even so, he finished out the race 3rd, though technically classified as a non-finisher.

Davey's most notable victories were in the 1910 and 1911 Savannah Grand Prize races, the top international events in the United States at the time. He was killed October, 1, 1912, in practice for the next renewal, which had been shifted to Milwaukee in combination with the Vanderbilt Cup. His death was exploited by a local attorney, who alleged that Teddy Tetzlaff had crowded him off the road. What actually happened was that Brown's Fiat blew a tire, careened off the narrow washboard road, and flipped him out, killing him instantly. Tetzlaff was able to prove he was yards away when the accident occurred.

Bruce-Brown's initial fling at driving fast came on March 23, 1908, when the 18-year-old blasted across the Daytona Beach sands at 109 m.p.h. in a 90-h.p. Fiat. "Apprenticed" to Cedrino, former chauffeur to the Queen of Spain, he proved to be a better handler of cars than a fixer. Following that, Bruce-Brown was kept in line by his worried parents until 1910 when Davey won one of the closest races in U.S. racing history, the 1910 Grand Prize in Savannah. His Benz came in just over a second ahead of Benz teammate Victor Hemery on handicap. In the 1910 Vanderbilt Cup race he was one of several cars flagged off when the winners crossed the line. And in 1911 he repeated his Savannah victory in a factory Fiat.

That year Bruce-Brown also entered his maroon Fiat at Indianapolis, led the initial 500 at one juncture by more than a lap, but, at the 200-mile mark, blew a tire and ran in on the rim, damaging it. Later ignition problems slowed him when he was pushing for the lead, and he finished 3rd. He was the favorite after Johnny Aitken convinced him to pilot one of the big blue Nationals in the 500 the next season, his initial ride in an American-made car. He cut the fast practice time of 88.15 m.p.h., then ran hub to hub with the leaders until piston troubles sidelined him. Davey's only other top finish was a 3rd at Santa Monica.

JOHNNY BRUNER

"A good auto race starter must have sound judgment, the ability to make a decision—and make it quick—and the ability to concentrate for hours. He must also know men, machines, conditions, the track, and a lot more. It's the best job at the track—and the hardest."

The speaker was Johnny Bruner, veteran NASCAR field manager and chief steward of the Grand National Division, who waved flags at race drivers for more than a quarter of a century in more than half of the 50 states.

Born in Birmingham, Ala., February 19, 1906, Bruner grew up in an orphan's home in Virginia and was just out of the Army after a 3-year hitch in the Coast Artillery in Panama when he came to Brooklyn, N.Y., in 1926. After trying his hand at a number of things, including window dressing, auto mechanics, and waiting on tables, Johnny's luck changed. In 1927 he got a job with the telegraph company that lasted until 1946, and met and married a Brooklyn girl who was to become his unofficial "assistant" at his racing avocation.

"It wasn't too long after my marriage that Mary and I became interested in racing," recalled Bruner. "We spent a lot of time around midget tracks—there wasn't any TV then, you know—and I did anything they wanted to me to do for nothing. I never got to drive a midget, though. It just never interested me. I always wanted to be a starter and nothing else."

In 1937 he earned his first money ($3) in the auto sport business serving as an assistant starter at a small New Jersey track. That got him a start as a more-or-less regular starter for the Penn-Jersey Racing Association. Bruner's big break came when he filled in for an ailing starter at the Thompson Speedway in northeastern Connecticut and did such a good job that 3 other midget promoters offered him regular jobs. But the biggest break of all was in 1949 when Bill France got John to help him with beach races at Daytona. "We struck it off right away," the veteran recalled, "and we shook hands then as a sort of contract."

Bruner moved to Atlanta in 1950 and took over the old Peach Bowl for France, and as Bill grew along with NASCAR, so did Johnny into his 2-title job. "The titles just add up to one thing," he said. "Get the job done!" Bruner had many thrills and many accidents, of course. Midgets bowled him over and ran over his toes. But the biggest incident that remained in his mind happened at Daytona on the beach in 1952. "I'll never come any closer to getting the real checkered flag myself than that day," John said. "I had just finished flagging down Marshall Teague's winning car when the 4th-place car, driven by Tommy Thompson, lost control. That big Chrysler headed toward me from about 200 yards out and I started backing away more as a reflex action than anything else.

"Well, I figured the car would drift away from me toward the dunes, and it was doing just that when the rear end hit a big pole that supported the finish-line banner. The Chrysler turned broadside and headed for me again, and I wasn't 15 feet away. I couldn't get away so I turned my back on it and jumped. Always jump when something is about to hit you—never get caught with your feet on the ground. The car hit me and threw me 30 or 40 feet into the air, but that was all. I got up with the flag still in my hand and still chewing on my cigar. Guess Gabriel wasn't quite ready to flag me off for good."

Looking back in 1963 after being given the Champion Spark Plug Company's Buddy Shuman Award for doing the most for stock-car racing in 1962, his 25th year in the field, Bruner summed up his career. "It's all as different as night and day since I got started in the game. Everything has changed—the men, the tracks, the equipment, the promotions, the planning—well, everything. I remember the days when we held up a race while we took whiskey bottles and beer cans away from the drivers in their cars. Now the drivers are 99 percent quiet, hard-working, sensible men.

"It's been fascinating to watch drivers change. As they move up in experience and class they quiet down, dress better, and acquire a dignity that goes with major racing today. There are still a few wild ones about, but not many—just enough to keep things lively. Very few are born great drivers. A few, yes, but most of them become great by hard work and application and an eagerness and willingness to learn. A great driver must be a bit of an egotist. He must believe he is the best and is going to win every race he starts. Racing is no place for shrinking violets."

Of starters, on which he was even more expert, John concluded: "There isn't any more important job on the track. The starter is the only bridge of communication between the drivers, officials, spectators, and the pits. He is the man who runs the whole race. Everyone is dependent upon his abilities and judgments."

The job was a big and rewarding one, and that was why Johnny was glad to see his son, John, Jr., out there with the various flags, carrying on the Bruner tradition, in his later days.

JIMMY BRYAN

How do you measure the greatest accomplishment in the career of a man like Jimmy Bryan? There were so many great races, so many dramatic accomplishments. He won the AAA-USAC national championship 3 times, 1954, 1956, 1957. He won the Indianapolis 500 in 1958. He won the Monza Race of Two Worlds in Italy.

James Ernest Bryan was born in Phoenix, Ariz., January 28, 1927, the son of a local fire chief. He was busting broncos at 15, and also crashing through the line for the high school football team. Bryan was an Air Force cadet during World War II, which probably saved him from becoming a college football or track hero.

When he returned to Phoenix, roadster—or hot-rod —racing was the accepted pastime. Bryan joined in enthusiastically and began learning his trade on the Arizona-New Mexico roadster circuit. It was in 1947 that Clint Brawner, the racing mechanic, convinced him that it was time to try something better—midget racing. He tried it on the West Coast for 2 seasons, then went East to the AAA midget-sprint wars.

Those were 2 tough years, both physically and financially. Many times he bummed a meal from a racing

buddy or a promoter. He never forgot the ones who helped him. But Jimmy was determined, and he learned. The kid with the rocking chair-style—he swayed back and forth in the cockpit as if on a rocker or on a bucking bronco—suddenly blossomed in 1951. He won his initial victory in the Ted Horn Memorial sprint at Williams Grove, Pa. It was a bullring of a dirt track where experience counted for almost everything, and a couple of Pennsylvania Dutchmen named Tommy Hinnershitz and Otis Stine had the most experience.

But Cowboy Jim had some experience by then, also. The 24-year-old formed the other half of a tandem with Stine and followed him past Hinnershitz. Stine tried all the tricks in the book to shake Jimmy, but he stayed with him. And suddenly, with the finish line nearing, Bryan used a bit of trickery himself. He feinted to the outside, then when Otis moved to block him, Bryan dove inside to win by the merest of margins. Cowboy Jim Bryan had arrived. He also passed his Indy rookie test in 1951, but then spun in a qualification attempt. In 1952, however, he finished 6th at Indianapolis in the Pete Schmidt Offenhauser. Then he went back to his sprint and midget commitments, finishing 3rd in the Eastern Sprint Championship and 5th in the Midwest midget standings.

Bryan spent 1953 on the Championship Trail. His car was Bessie Lee Paoli's Springfield Welding Offy and the mechanic was Clay Smith. It was still a time of learning for Jimmy, however. He was ill at ease on a smooth track—or so he said. Finally at Sacramento, track conditions were to his liking—rough and getting worse. He won the 1st of what were to be 19 championship victories in 5 years. Bryan had planned to drive a Bardahl car for Ed Walsh the following year, but Brawner re-entered his life. Clint told Bryan that Al Dean was building a new Dean Van Lines car for the following season, and that Dean would like him as driver. Bryan accepted.

The 1954 Indy 500 may have been Bryan's greatest, although he did win again in 1958. Jimmy pushed his white No. 9 into the lead twice during the early stages of the race, losing it both times when he had to pit for fuel and tires. But halfway through a front spring broke, overloading the shocks until the one in the right rear gave up, too. Every little bump jarred Bryan, every crevice rattled his teeth. An oil line gave way then, spraying his foot with hot oil until it was painfully burned. But Bryan hung on, running 2nd to Bill Vukovich, making fans wonder why he did not try for the lead. He held that position until the checker, then drove straight for the garage area. Brawner and the crew lifted him from the car grinning and vacant-eyed, unable to hear. They stretched him on the floor and when they examined him, they found bruises and welts from his shoulders down, where the car had pounded him; they found the seared leg. And he was grinning.

It seemed impossible that he could have finished the race in his condition, but he had. He skipped Milwaukee's 100-miler the following week because he couldn't sit, much less drive. But he was back for Langhorne, which he won despite burning his left leg again and seeking aid during a long pit stop. He finished 3rd in the Darlington 200, 12th at Springfield, got 3rds at the Milwaukee 200 and DuQuoin 100. He clinched his title September 11 with a 4th at Syracuse. It was then that Jimmy really got hot, finishing with 4 straight victories —in the Hoosier 100, Sacramento, Phoenix and Las Vegas. One had to hark back to Harry Hartz in 1926 to find a greater season point total than his 2,630. He had finished 9 of 12 races 3rd or better.

Jimmy led the 1955 Indy race only to have a fuel pump sideline him. Then the stogie (Bryan) and the straw hat (Brawner) hit the Championship Trail again. They won Langhorne, Williams Grove, and Springfield for 7 straight on dirt over a 2-year period. At Syracuse they conked out but popped right back for the checker in the Hoosier 100 at Sacramento, and at Phoenix. Bryan lost the national championship to Indianapolis winner Bob Sweikert by a few points. But 1956 seemed a worse year for Bryan. He spun at Indy, and suffered a clogged fuel line at Langhorne, which pushed him back to 6th. He failed to solve Darlington and finished 8th. He sat out Atlanta because the race car broke loose from its tow truck and was damaged. But, undaunted, Bryan won for the 2nd time at Williams Grove in another car. He won at Springfield and at the Milwaukee 250 in the Dean Van Lines car, then clinched his 2nd title by winning the Hoosier 100 for the 3rd time in a row.

After finishing 3rd at Indianapolis in 1957, Jimmy passed up Langhorne because he wanted Brawner to have his big car ready for its journey to Italy and the Race of Two Worlds. He used the alternate car at Milwaukee and crashed. But he came back to win at Detroit on the eve of his departure overseas with the USAC driving contingent. He won at Monza, and came back an exhausted hero. After losing at Atlanta—due to mechanical trouble for the first time in 4 years—Bryan took a long vacation with his family. But he failed to gain many points on leader Jim Rathmann in the next 5 races. People began to wonder if the Brawner-Bryan duo had lost its magic. He showed them in the last 2 races of the season.

First there was a 2nd place at Sacramento and then back to his home town—Phoenix—for the closer. He needed a top-3 finish to be certain of his 3rd season crown over Rathmann and George Amick. He got it. Staying up close, Jimmy took the lead for the first time on the 70th lap, but he almost lost everything on the 87th lap. The track was slick as Jimmy Hackson dropped the green. Pole-sitter Rodger Ward swung wide and lost 6 positions as Johnny Boyd in the Bowes Seal Fast roadster led Pat O'Connor, George Amick, Bryan, Johnny Toland, and Elmer George past. Boyd was running away at the 10-lap mark when Billy Carrett spun into the fence, showering the track with lumber, and eliminating Bob Veith who got some debris lodged inside his wheel mount. Five caution laps brought Boyd back to the pack as O'Connor charged at him. Meanwhile Bryan began to move on 3rd-place Amick.

Bryan inched up on George, dueling him wheel-to-wheel until Amick slid wide on a turn at 29 laps. Bryan took the opening and moved by. He had both point-contenders behind him now but was not satisfied. He wanted nothing less than victory. O'Connor, meanwhile, sneaked through on Boyd when Johnny slid trying to pass a slow car on lap 35. On the next lap Len Sutton removed some more fencing, causing another 4 caution laps. The green came on but not for long, for Elmer G. flipped after cleaning out about 75 feet of fence. The green flashed at 45 laps with the standings O'Connor, Boyd, Bryan, and Amick. That changed at the halfway mark when Pat skidded and Boyd dashed back ahead followed in the same lap by Jimmy. After another caution signal Bryan moved almost even with the fleeing Boyd. They duelled that way for several laps until, on the 70th mile, Jimmy won a game of chicken on a turn and moved in front. Soon after Boyd began to slow down, letting O'Connor and Amick by to chase the Cowboy.

Now Jud Larson began to move up through the pack, quickly taking 4th, so quickly that Brawner notified the Cowboy on the blackboard. The crowd focused on the Amick-Larson duel. George was not about to give up 3rd place and Jud was not about to be denied. They duelled wheel-to-wheel until their wheels actually touched on the 84th lap. They spun in opposite directions, Jud removing some more of the badly-battered wooden fence and putting the caution on again for 5 laps. When the green dropped, O'Connor's Sumar Special sounded sick and Bryan appeared an easy victor. But as he moved to lap Rathmann on lap 95, the Rathmann car skidded and pinched Bryan toward where the fence used to be. Jimmy actually went off the track but fought back on, pieces of debris in his cockpit. Had the whole fence been there, he would not have finished the race. O'Connor, however, roared by as the Cowboy took after him, tossing the lumber out of his cockpit as he rode. Jimmy drove as hard as he had ever driven in his life. Wood was lodged between his exhaust stack, wood was hampering the suspension, but Jimmy fought to close the gap. On the penultimate lap, he came even with O'Connor, drove daringly to the very apron of the track—and sneaked past as the home-town crowd screamed in exultation. The Cowboy had won in the style to which he had become accustomed.

There had been stock car victories in a Mercury-support car, too, enough to give him a 4–5 finish in

the 2 years. There remained only one unconquered peak for this man who in 5 years had scored more championship points than any other man in AAA-USAC history over a similar period. That was the Indianapolis 500. The 1958 Indianapolis 500 was wild and tragic. Dick Rathmann, the refugee from NASCAR, set a new qualification record of 145.97 m.p.h. to win the pole but Ed Elisian grabbed the lap record from him in another A. J. Watson creation with 146.508. Jimmy Reece filled out the front row in another Watson car. Bryan was in the 3rd row in the defending George Salih car.

The 500 was trying a new way of starting because of pit row changes. The cars were to exit from the pits in single file, then assume rows of 3 in rolling formation behind the pace car for their parade lap instead of lining up that way on the track. Rathmann and Elisian, however, passed the pace car and Reece caught up with them. Realizing the *faux pas*, the trio slowed to let the field catch up. But the pace car thought they would try to overtake the field and continued driving slowly. So the 3 cars crossed in perfect order half a lap ahead of the field. Chief Steward Harlan Fengler waved them to speed up while their pit crews displayed "SLO" signs. Completely confused, they held their position. On their next trip across, they finally got the message to overtake. But then the pace car swerved off and the rest of the field roared away. Fengler kept the caution flag out one lap, and the trio squeezed into position. Then the green came out.

Rathmann and Elisian were almost abreast through the first turn with Dick holding a slight edge on the 2nd turn. Ed pulled even on the inside going down the back straight and the twosome hurtled toward the 3rd turn at full throttle. It was a game of chicken again, and both held too long. Elisian's car started to spin, tail first, sideswiping Dick who was trying to go around him. Reece, close behind, applied his brakes and was rammed by Bob Veith, knocking him sideways into the path of Pat O'Connor. The O'Connor car ran up one of Jimmy's wheels and flipped upside down before rolling upright some distance away. Johnny Parsons, the other 2nd-row driver, could not avoid Veith.

Bryan and the rest of the 3rd row dived inside the wreckage. But A. J. Foyt, still in the racing groove, spun to avoid the stopped cars, starting a new series of crashes. When it was over, the Northeast turn looked like a junkyard. O'Connor was dead, 8 cars were debris and 9 others in urgent need of repair. Jimmy led the pack through 18 caution laps while the crews cleared the track. He lost the lead to Tony Bettenhausen as soon as the green flashed, with George Amick and Eddie Sachs charging too. The lead seesawed back and forth before the first pit stop. That's where Jimmy had the edge. After the first stop the nose-to-tail phase was over, for he led Tony by 6 seconds and George by 16. He led from lap 66 to 105, when Boyd took over after Bryan made his second trip in. Johnny tried to skip one stop, but he could not because Bryan challenged him for 20 laps.

The Salih car held up admirably and Bryan rode grimly into the Victory Lane. It took him time to muster up a smile for the photographers and when he did it was mechanical. Shortly after, he announced he would not try for his 4th national championship.

Bryan went to Monza for the 2nd of the Two World races and finished 2nd, winning the Two Worlds Cup for the highest finish in both the 500 and the Monza race. He competed in 3 stock-car races, winning 1 in Phoenix. But he was otherwise inactive competitively until Indianapolis 1959. The Cowboy returned to the Brickyard confident. But his Belond Muffler car was left at the post on the parade lap and retired after one racing lap with a broken cam housing. He competed in 6 races, his best showing being a 3rd place.

For 1960 Bryan again switched cars—to the Metal Cal Special. He qualified in 10th starting position at Indy, but was never really a factor as he retired at 152 laps with motor woes, despite the tender ministrations of George Salih. He skipped Milwaukee's paving and, partly as a favor to old friends Irv Fried and Al Gerber, Langhorne's promoters, decided to return to the dirt tracks where he once was king. The other part of the reason was that the Leader Card car was available because Rodger Ward would not drive dirt anymore.

It looked like the old Cowboy Jim Bryan when he qualified 2nd behind Don Branson in the Bob Estes Special on June 19, 1960. But he lasted less than a lap. Diving for the lead immediately after the starter's flag dropped, the Cowboy lost control and flipped. He was dead before they reached him, snuffed out at the age of 33. He had won $191 for making the starting field.

PETER BRYANT

Born in London, on April 3, 1937, Peter Bryant attended Regent Street Polytechnic Institute because, even at the age of 15, he already knew that he wanted a career in racing as a designer, not a driver. He became, in fact, the designer responsible for the Shadow, the Canadian-American Challenge Cup car of the Seventies. Even before that, he was the man responsible for the dramatic new Autocoast Ti22 CanAm car.

Peter's education continued at Paddington Technical College, and, when he was 20, he set out to conquer the racing world. As did so many British neophytes, he found his way to Colin Chapman's Lotus operation and became a development fabricator. After 2 years of such work, he left Lotus to start working for a variety of independent racing teams. In 1963 one of these independents, headed by none other than John Surtees, offered Peter a full-time job, and he jumped.

The new job brought Bryant to the United States for his initial visit. Surtees was competing in the precursor to the CanAm, the North American Road Racing series, and that put Peter in contact with a variety of American builder-racers. With Surtees's blessing, Bryant started preparing other people's cars, including Mickey Thompson's Indianapolis machines. Carroll Shelby was another satisfied customer. Both 1967 and 1968 were spent in preparing, and updating, a variety of CanAm cars, but Peter was developing the ideas for his own car. His ideas materialized as the Autocoast Ti22, which, in the hands of Jackie Oliver, showed promise late in 1969. The following year the Ti22 went from 3rd starting position into the lead, passing the 2 McLaren cars on 2 successive laps, something not seen in the series for better than 2 years. Oliver eventually had to yield the lead to Dan Gurney and settle for 2nd.

The future looked rosy, but then the Ti22 was destroyed in a freak accident on the 1st lap of the St. Jovite race that followed the Mosport Park inaugural. The season was over. Bryant was a plugger, however, and he had a car on the track at Laguna Seca, in the season's penultimate start. Again he had a contender, Oliver taking the 3rd starting spot, and moving immediately into 2nd, battling Denis Hulme in the lead McLaren all the way. Oliver and the Ti22 finished only 100 feet behind Hulme. The act was the same at the finale at Riverside, despite the car's braking problems. While Bryant was working out his Ti22, another car, the original Shadow, was debuting, and fizzling, in the CanAm. Its concept was advanced, but as they fiddled with it, the car became increasingly conventional. About the same time as the Autocoast Ti22 was retired due to loss of sponsor interest, the original Shadow was being padlocked for the same reason.

The Shadow's promoter, Don Nichols, got together with Bryant on a 1971 Shadow project, and acquired a sponsor, Universal Oil Products, which was in the petroleum-additive business. Bryant started from scratch, except for the general approach and created a new Shadow, ultra-low in profile, with 12-inch wheels, the smallest in major auto racing. The Shadow missed the opener, and retired at both St. Jovite and Road Atlanta. It finished 20th at Watkins Glen after spinning off course. Bryant tested 13-inch tires while the team passed up Mid-Ohio. Oliver was 12th at Road America, retired at Brainerd, but finished 3rd to Hulme and Jackie Stewart at Edmonton. Could the secret be at hand? No, for the car was retired again at Laguna Seca. Peter would have to head back to his drawing board.

The CanAm crowd wished him well, for in the socializing end of racing, Bryant ranked with the better singers, comics, and impersonators in the sports scene. Peter and his family, which included 2 children, were thoroughly Americanized, and were living in California. When the Shadow team entered GP racing in 1973, it wasn't Bryant who designed the car, but Tony Southgate. Maybe Peter didn't want to leave California.

BUCCIALI BROTHERS (ANGELO and PAUL-ALBERT)

Not many Bucs or Buccialis were built, and few survive today, but they were true sports cars—cars that take a sportsman to drive them. The marque was named after 2 wealthy brothers, Paul-Albert and Angelo, who started in the carbuilding field as early as 1917 when Paul-Albert was a pursuit pilot in the French Flying Corps. He was a flight commander with the 2d Régiment d'Aviation de Chasse, the Cigognes group that used the stork as its emblem. As ever, rank had its privileges, and these included the obtaining of automobile parts, the use of machining facilities at the airfield, and the sweat of a few flight mechanics.

Paul-Albert's first car, designated Buc 1, was finished before he was separated from the service. Low-slung as all future Buccialis were to be, it was powered by a 3-litre Ballot engine and featured front-wheel brakes and bucket seats. From 1919 to 1925 Paul-Albert and his older brother (who died in 1946)—known as Bucciali Frères—built other cars for themselves and raced them with limited success in the day's popular voiturette races.

In that same period they built a Tour de France entry that failed to finish, but it became their first production automobile. The prototype was designated AB 4 and was powered by a 2-cycle, 1,496-c.c. engine. The production car of 1925 used a 1,600-c.c. SCAP 4-cylinder o.h.c. engine instead, which developed about 40 h.p. It was capable, with fine tuning, of about 65 m.p.h., while offering 25 m.p.g. fuel consumption. The production car was called AB 4–5. A racing version of this model was called the Quatre Spéciale, and the final version had little resemblance to the street car. Powered by 1,484-c.c. SCAP o.h.c. engines with Cozette superchargers, 3 Spéciales were built with long, pointed tails, Bugatti-like bodies, and a single, silvery exhaust pipe down their right sides.

In 1926 Paul-Albert designed a new, lighter, 6-cylinder, dual carburetor engine that was designated the AB-6. With a top speed of 105 m.p.h., the car was raced extensively during 1926 and 1927, participating in the San Sebastian Grand Prix in 1927. But this was the Buccialis' final fling at regular competition. Thereafter the brothers concentrated on supplying the needs of the very rich with the kind of long, low cars that became the rage of the late Twenties and early Thirties.

They nearly relented in 1927 and went so far as to contruct 2 prototype racers at their Courbevoie factory with 4- and 8-cylinder SCAP engines respectively. But these were never to see a track, only city streets, as the 2 brothers adopted them for personal transportation. The pursuit pilot, Paul-Albert, took the heavier and more powerful car. Soon after, the Buccialis came to New York to raise capital by licensing their forward-looking French patents to some U.S. manufacturers, but the Depression ended any possibility of doing that, ending also some nearly-sealed deals with the Peerless and Ruxton marques. Their sample car, the TAV-30, was a sensation, but moral victories cannot be eaten and the brothers returned to France.

In the 1934 Paris Auto Salon, a single Bucciali—like its predecessors a breathtaker, whose picture would make an enthusiast drool even today—was shown. After that, the brothers concentrated on free-lance designing assignments, including Jeep-like military vehicles. Paul-Albert did produce a single, Volkswagen-like light car in 1947, but the Bucciali saga was over. Paul-Albert spent his final years with Cotal, the gearbox manufacturers.

RONNIE BUCKNUM

Michigan International Speedway was so new in 1968 that for the first race held on the 2-mile oval USAC veterans were predicting an average race speed approaching the lone visit of the championship cars to NASCAR's Daytona Speedway, back when that track was new in 1959. The race was 250 miles long but some said it would be over more quickly than some 100-milers.

Bobby Unser and Mario Andretti were locked in a struggle for the USAC season crown. No one paid much attention to Ronnie Bucknum in the Weinberger Homes Special because this was not even a road course race. But Bucknum paid attention. He studied the track in

practice and formed a plan based on experience in a kind of racing far removed from the USAC oval fold.

There had been amateur and professional sports car racing in his past, including a 3rd place at Le Mans in 1966, codriving with Dick Hutcherson. There had been long painful years spent with the unsuccessful Honda Formula 1 effort. And just that year there had been a TransAm victory at the Daytona 24-hour and a 3rd at Sebring.

Mario had won the pole a full second faster than Bucknum, who qualified 8th at 183.976 m.p.h. Unser qualified 2nd. "I was perfectly satisfied," Bucknum said later. "I figured that the idea in this race was to finish. I figured the real racing would come in the last 50 miles."

Bucknum came to the starting line with an engine geared down as if for an enduro. He started with as much fuel as the rear-engine turbocharged Offenhauser would carry. And when the 55,108 fans cheered and screamed as the cars took the starter's flag, he knew few of them were cheering for him. Bobby Unser jumped Andretti and widened his lead to a mile before pitting on lap 66. Mario stayed on the track to gain the lead briefly, only to run out of gas, barely making pit row and giving Bobby the lead back. This also was relatively shortlived because the Eagle Offy engine let go spectacularly on the front stretch. Mike Mosely then inherited the lead. However, Mosely was called in so that Unser could take his place and win some championship points.

Now Bucknum, who had not pitted, took over with Mel Kenyon in hot pursuit. And the Bucknum strategy paid off. Kenyon, who also had not refueled, was forced in to replenish his stock and the geared-down Bucknum rode blithely on, eventually winning by a full 2 laps over Andretti.

Ronnie Bucknum, born in California in 1936, was not always the thinking man's driver. Quite the contrary. In 1956 around Los Angeles he took a Porsche drag racing; in 1957 he began a long successful SCCA career driving the same Porsche, winning the West Coast E Production championship the following 2 years. In 1960 Ronnie moved up to D in a Bristol and won that class. He was a card-carrying member of the sports car set, which meant he drove fast and lived fast, too. During the 1961 season he joined the Hollywood Sports Car Racing Team, setting the stage for Michigan 1962, which placed him a notch above the gentlemen drivers. Bucknum drove an Austin-Healey 3000 to 24 victories in 24 races for a runaway D Production crown, and then came back in 1963 for a double; he won 20 of 24 in an MGB for the D title. He then went aboard Ol' Yaller III for the modified crown as well.

The crown (and impressive rides at Laguna Seca, and Chavez Ravine) brought him an offer to join Honda as the Japanese team was seeking to become a factor in F1 racing. He went over to Japan, bettered the existing

lap marks in the car, and signed a contract guaranteeing him 4 races in 1964 or the equivalent in money. He commuted to Japan 4 more times for further tests on the car. Bucknam began his formal Grand Prix career in August in the rain at Nurburgring. The steering broke 2½ laps from the end, and he crashed, demolishing the car but escaping virtually unscathed himself. At Monza, he had brake problems.

For a club driver to jump directly into GP racing, which is among the more demanding forms of driving extant, is unprecedented. Bucknum did it and showed flashes of brilliance. For instance, just before his brakes failed, Ron had passed Lorenzo Bandini, Jo Bonnier, Jack Brabham, and Richie Ginther, all in one lap. In 1965, certainly a frustrating year, Ginther joined the team as a driver and development problems continued. The vehicle that Bucknum called 95 percent perfect the first day he sat in it soon displayed an assortment of problems—overheating, ignition, trouble with the fuel injection, brakes, front suspension weakness. At Monaco, Ginther lasted one lap and Ronnie 32 before retiring. At the Belgium GP Ginther took 6th, but Ronnie lasted 10 laps before the ignition got him. Both failed to finish the French GP, and Honda only entered one car in the British race, which Ginther led before retiring after 20 laps. More changes in the car saw it gaining reliability apparently at the expense of speed. Ginther took 6th in the Dutch GP at Zandvoort, and at Watkins Glen Richie rode home 7th to Ronnie's 13th. At Mexico City the boys seemed to click as Ginther gave Honda its only victory with Ronnie a solid 5th. However, the formula changed for 1966 to 3 litres unsupercharged and 1.5 litres supercharged. The Japanese went back to the drawing board and did not reappear until late in the season. Ginther took 4th, and despite a spectacular fire in the cockpit of his car, Ronnie rode home 8th. That was about it for Honda in Grand Prix—at least for that year.

Speculation as to why Bucknum and Ginther were chosen as the drivers centered about the company's less-than-successful attempts to merchandise the Honda 600 mini-car in the United States. The marketing experts had expected the Southern California area to provide the main invasion point. Unfortunately 2 other Japanese cars, Datsun and Toyota, expected the same thing with products more suitable to the American psyche. Since there was no success, there was no justification for California-type drivers, or for racing overseas.

Bucknum did better as a combination test driver and team driver for the Ford-backed Carroll Shelby effort with the Cobra and the GT40. This brought a 3rd at Le Mans codriving with Hutcherson, a 3rd which could easily have been a 1st if the team manager so ordered. In 1967 he had a Ford J car to run at Le Mans and Daytona, and a whole new dimension—Indianapolis. Ron had passed his Indy driver's test in 1966, but the Vita-

Fresh rear-engined Ford mount was not fast enough to qualify or do anything much in USAC road course races. His best was a 3rd at St. Jovite. In 1968 he got the Weinberger Homes Offy and made a few waves besides his Irish Hills, Mich., victory, coming in 3rd again at St. Jovite and adding a 3rd at Mosport. At Indy, he lasted 76 laps in 1968 before a transmission gear gave out, and only 16 laps in 1969 when a piston burned. In 1970 he rammed the wall on the 172nd lap while avoiding Roger McCluskey's stalled car, and his MVS Special caught fire. He was credited with 15th position and sustained minor injuries and burns.

Bucknum, who married early and had 4 children, spent a year (1969) as number 2 driver to Mark Donohue in the TransAm series for Penske Racing. He was to have codriven a Lola sports car, too, but someone stole it.

IVOR BUEB

Ivor Leon Bueb was a cheerful, burly, almost monumental Briton who delighted in the role of hoaxer. The stories of his escapades in the Fifties are legion, as, for example, the time in Paris he donned a bushy beard and assumed the role of a Russian rallyist who "revealed" Soviet plans for dominating the world of auto sports. His revelations were about to be spread all over the world by several newsmen who were in the cafe in which Ivor pulled off this coup, when a friend who had seen Bueb in this role before walked into the room and broke up the act. Once in Stockholm he played cab driver for half a day with a Sunbeam team rally car. And there was the time that a mysterious trunk addressed to a high-ranking RAC official appeared on the sidewalk in front of the biggest hotel in Monte Carlo. The trunk defied the hotel staff's efforts to move it, and why not? Bueb had put it there, then filled the trunk to its brim with heavy concrete blocks.

The garage-owner from Cheltenham, born in 1923, was not a full-time Grand Prix driver, although he occasionally did drive GP cars. He was best known for his roles as long-distance driver and rallyist. Without doubt, Ivor's finest hours came at Le Mans, where he twice shared victories. In 1955 he and Mike Hawthorn prevailed at 107.7 m.p.h., and in 1957 he won at 113.85 with Ron Flockhart, both victories coming in D Jaguars. The Bueb-Hawthorn car was the one involved in the Pierre Levegh accident at Le Mans, Mike driving at the time. But Bueb drove anything in sight, including Connaughts, Sunbeams, the Lotus, Formula Cooper-Borgwards, Lister-Jags and Maserati GP cars. In 1955, his best single year, perhaps, he won at Silverstone and Castle Combe and took the Irish Championship in a 500-c.c. Formula 3 Cooper. He drove a Ferrari to a 3rd place in the 1956 Venezulan GP, took a 3rd with Hawthorn at Sebring in 1957, and finished 9th in the Monza Race of Two Worlds—best of the Jaguar finishers—in 1958. He was doing well the following year when his F2 car crashed during the Circuit of Auvergne at Clermont-Ferrand, France. His chest crushed, the 36-year-old Bueb died after 6 days.

ETTORE BUGATTI

Between 1911's Grand Prix du Mans, when Ernst Friderich won the small-cylinder class with a 1.4-litre Bugatti, and France's first post-World War II motor race, the Coupe des Prisonniers of September 1945, when Jean-Pierre Wimille took a 4.7-litre Bug to victory in the Bois de Boulogne, Ettore Bugatti's machines won something like 4,000 races. The exact number of victories is lost for all time, for the carefully assembled records of Europe were scattered and destroyed by the war, and most of the living testimonials to the Bug's supremacy over those 35 years have passed on. Even the exact number of cars that bore Bugatti's nameplate is no longer known, although a good estimate is a mere 9,500 cars—hardly the kind of production that would seem to rank Bugatti with Ford, Fiat, or even Ferrari.

But Ettore Bugatti will live forever in automobile history. And in racing, exact figures are not always necessary. It is sufficient to say that Bugattis were the most successful racing cars in the world prior to World War II. Any list of great racing machinery automatically includes the Type 35 Bugatti, whether the criterion is racing success, design ingenuity, or beauty. Ettore Bugatti designed beautiful cars, cars that caused sane men

101

to grow slightly insane in their desire to own one. Had he not built cars, Ettore probably would have been an artist like his father and several other members of his family. In our day, when machinery has reached the level of art, and when museums regularly hold exhibitions of utilitarian art that happens to have that special kind of beauty, Bugattis are regularly "hung" in the best museums in the world; appearance never fails to create a new host of admirers.

Ettore was born an Italian in Milan September 15, 1881, but always considered himself a Frenchman, a citizenship he only managed to attain just before his death in 1947. In his mid-teens, after declaring that his brother Rembrandt's skill at sculpture was superior to his own, he convinced his father to have him apprenticed to a short-lived local motorcycle builder, Prinetti e Stucchi. By 1898, he had taken the standard Stucchi cycle and converted it into his own racing machine for the Paris-Bourdeaux Race. It hit a dog and was retired. That same year Bugatti built a 4-cylinder car from the ground up, even to casting his own parts and assembling them himself. One design followed another, the third one winning a prize from the Automobile Club de France and a gold medal from a Milan international exhibition in 1901. The design also won him an offer as a designer with De Dietrich and a move to Alsace.

Over the next few years, Bugatti also participated in designing cars for Mathis, Deutz, Peugeot, and Isotta-Fraschini. While with Deutz, a Cologne-based firm, he designed a car of which he was especially fond, and when the company declined to build it Bugatti decided that he himself would go into business. With Ernst Friderich, a friend and associate of some 5 years, he located an abandoned dye factory in Molsheim and re-opened it as the Bugatti plant. That first year, 1909, 5 cars were built.

Friderich's 1911 race victory firmly established the Bugatti as a potent and beautiful automobile, and while the bulk of the Bugs sold to the not-so-general-public were touring cars and limousines, racing machinery always played an important role in production as well as in publicizing the Bugatti name. When Ettore set up shop at Molsheim, the Type 13 was the first model put into production. The Type 22 of 1913 had a slightly bigger engine, 65×100 millimeters, pressure oil feed instead of wick, and quarter-elliptic instead of semielliptic springs. It had a 7-foot 10½-inch wheelbase. With 6 inches more, it became the Type 23.

Meanwhile, in 1911–12, a single racing car was built using 2 of the 1.4-litre engines that had powered the little car Friderich had won with at Le Mans. The engines were attached with "rubberized leather," and the vehicle did 86 m.p.h. Another 1911–12 car was a Bugatti treatment of the chain-drive principle, a 5-litre overhead-camshaft-engine automobile that could do 100 m.p.h. A long-stroke, conventional-drive variant of this

5-litre was entered at Indianapolis in 1914, with Friderich driving; it dropped out with axle failure in the 134th lap, but was placed 15th at the finish.

The famous Brescia model, so called because it took the first 4 places at that circuit in 1921, had a 16-valve, 1496-c.c. engine. The Brescia Modifié was, as the name might suggest, less potent. The slab-side cars that ran at Tours in 1923 were of Type 30, and so were the GP cars of 1922 and the Indy cars of 1923, the best of which finished 9th. The Type 35 series included A, B, C, and T versions. The 35A was a 35 Modifié—sometimes referred to as an "imitation" car. It looked like a Type 35, but it ran on wire wheels and was about 10 m.p.h. slower. The 35C was supercharged, the 35T had 2.3-litre instead of 2-litre engines and the B was a blown T. Type 37 was 4-cylinder, 1500-c.c. GP car and 37A was supercharged. Type 39 was an 8-cylinder, 1500-c.c. GP car and again A marked the addition of a Roots blower. Type 45 had a 16-cylinder engine, similar to the King-Bugatti aircraft engine, in a GP chassis. A special version of the Type 50 engine, called the 50B and said to put out 500 horsepower, was used in several GP chassis, including the 4.7 single-seater, just before World War II.

When Bugatti went from single to d.o.h.c. engines in 1931, the car was known as Type 51, 2.3-litre. It was the familiar sharptailed GP design that Bugatti authority Ken Purdy often called "the most beautiful racing automobile, surely, of all time." The 51C was a blown 2-litre, and the 51A had a blower. Types 53 and 54 were 4.9-litre GP cars, but the 53 had 4-wheel drive.

A special 2.8-litre Type 51 was adapted to the 750-kilogram formula of 1933, and it finished 4th and 6th in the Spanish GP that season. It was bored out to 3.3 litres for subsequent years. This was the car that had the distinctive "piano-wire" wheels with almost invisible spokes. Type 59 won the Belgian, Algiers, and Picardy Grands Prix in 1934, and in 1937 Jean Pierre Wimille lapped Monthléry for 162 miles at 91.13, just a bit slower than the vaunted Mercedes-Benz record for a single lap. The 3.3 later was bored out to 3.8, and ultimately replaced by the 7-litre supercharged single-seater. A 4.7-litre supercharged car ran 2nd in the 1936 Vanderbilt Cup. Eventually there were 3.8-litre blown and 4.5-litre unblown GP cars. The 4.7 with which Wimille won the 1939 Coupe de Paris just before the war and the Coupe des Prisonniers in 1945 was probably the fastest Bugatti that ever ran.

In 1946, Bugatti designed a 4-cylinder, 220 h.p. supercharged GP car designated Type 73C, but none was built then, although 2 were later assembled from original parts. The Type 251 was a postwar GP car designed by Colombo. Its 2.5-litre straight-8 engine was mounted transversely in the rear. The last Bugatti racing car was the Type 252, a prototype sports car that never reached production.

In World War I, Bugatti had designed an aircraft engine for the French and their allies. A variant of it was built by Duesenberg, and a claim can be made that Harry Miller's little American creation, still with us today as the Offenhauser, thus was "influenced" by Bugatti's genius of almost 6 decades ago. Back in Molsheim after the war, Ettore created his own little empire of factory, chateau, stables, kennels, and rolling acres on which he could live out his life. The mighty and the rich came to him. Money did not particularly impress him, and he never worried about it. If he did not pay an occasional bill exactly on time, what of it? He was Bugatti, and he was a man of his word. The local power company didn't see it that way, and it pressed for payment. Bugatti paid their bill, but he also designed and had built his own generating plant, and in a little ceremony to which the head of the power company was invited (perhaps summoned would be a better word), switches were thrown at the Bugatti plant that cut off the power company's line and turned on the builder's own lines.

Such independence (and his nominal Axis citizenship) enabled Bugatti to operate on his own terms when France was overrun by the Nazis in 1940. The death of his son, Jean, already a brilliant designer in his own right, in 1939, had embittered Bugatti, and he would have nothing to do with the Vichy Government or its Axis overlords. Jean, incidentally, died in a freak auto accident, when he purposely swerved his car off the test track to avoid striking a drunken French mailman who had bicycled onto the course. At the war's end, Ettore finally became a French citizen, successfully fought an action to seize his factory as alien war booty, and made ready to design and build the automobiles, railway cars, aircraft, fishing boats and other items that he felt were needed to aid France's postwar recovery. Some of the car designs got off the ground, but all else died with Ettore Bugatti himself on August 21, 1947. Valiant attempts were made by his other son and daughters to keep the factory going, but without the man they called Le Patron, it was not really possible. What remained of Bugatti's life work was acquired by Hispano-Suiza in 1965.

BOB BURMAN

Who was the greatest American professional driver in the early days? Bob Burman had the greatest popular following in America, greater than Barney Oldfield, whom many people today think of first when the nation's pioneer auto days are recalled. Burman, in fact, beat Oldfield regularly, and even replaced the great Barney at the wheel of the Blitzen Benz when he was put under AAA Contest Board suspension.

Bob was born in Imlay City, Mich., on April 23, 1884. In his teens, he left the farm where he was born

and by 1901 was a test driver for the Jackson Automobile Shops. Two years later the Buick Company opened a factory at Jackson, Mich., and offered the local boy a testing job; it is often claimed Burman drove the first Buick ever made. But the Jackson forces did not give up easily and offered Bob a car to enter for his first race at Detroit in 1906, a 50-mile stock chassis contest, which he won. A 24-hour race at St. Louis on July 3–4, 1907, next took Burman's attention. Though he had a co-driver, Ernest Kelley, Bob drove more than 22 hours and won by 82 miles.

Buick was convinced that Bob was the man for them and signed him to its newly-formed racing stable. Burman won his first race under his "new" colors, the 187-mile Garden City Sweepstakes on Long Island. In November 1908 Burman led the Buick forces in their assault on the light car events run in conjunction with the Savannah Grand Prize races. In the 200-mile, 4-cylinder race the day before the big one, Burman went into the lead early, won the cheers of the crowd, then suffered a broken rear spring and had to pit for 8 minutes. From far back in the field, Burman battled his way back into 2nd place and held on to finish directly behind a Lancia. Thus encouraged, Buick entered a car for Burman in the main race but it soon expired against the heavier Fiats, Benzs, and other European machinery.

That race established Burman as one of the best drivers in the nation nonetheless, and he entered the Championship Trail circuit at Crown Point, Ind., in 1909. In February he carried away the 100-mile event with a record time of 1:42:39.4 at the Mardi Gras Festival in New Orleans. In July at Columbus, Ohio, Bob bettered the mark with a 1:41:00 clocking for the 100 miles. A 3-day Speed Carnival opened the new Indianapolis Speedway on August 19–21, 1909, with the opening day feature the 250-mile Prest-O-Lite Trophy dash. Burman won after a thrilling duel with Louis Chevrolet, and a crash that killed Bill Bourque and Harry Halcomb. Mechanical troubles ended Burman's chances in the final day's 300-miler. In his first full season in the AAA, then, Bob finished 4th with 1,100 championship points in a list of 70 drivers.

The following season's high spots included the Memorial Day Indianapolis meet—before the 500—in which Burman introduced Buick's semi-streamlined Bug Special and set a record 105.87 for the quarter mile. Two months later at the same course, he won the 100-mile Remy Grand Brassard. In that October's Vanderbilt Cup, he was leading the field when an accident disabled his mechanic on the 17th lap and he retired. On November 12 he saved American honor at the Savannah Grand Prix with his 588 cu. in. Marquette Buick by finishing 3rd behind the dominating Benzs of David Bruce-Brown and Victor Hemery. The year ended at Jacksonville, where Bob set 20- and 50-mile marks and a one-hour record of 81.65 miles.

Burman's Blitzen Benz feats followed in 1911 when E. A. Moross handed over the 200-b.h.p. monster to Bob on his 27th birthday; he drove the white car 10 m.p.h. faster than Oldfield ever had, 141.73. At the inaugural Indy 500, Bob was named "World's Speed King," with a $10,000 crown covered with jewels, after going around the circuit the day before in 35.25 seconds (102.127 m.p.h.) for the fastest lap up to that date. In the actual race his Benz 120 let him down, however. Later, on July 4, 1911, at Brighton Beach, N.Y., a track near Coney Island, a crowd of 15,000 watched Bob set a new world dirt-track record of 48.72 seconds.

Buick lent Burman to Marmon for the Vanderbilt and Savannah Grand Prize races late in the year after Joe Dawson, the top Marmon driver, was badly injured. Mechanical failures kept him out of the money in both contests. In the 1912 Indianapolis 500 Bob was running 2nd in a Cutting when his 2 rear tires blew simultaneously on the 157th lap; the car flipped, but both driver and mechanic emerged unhurt. In 1912 Benz delivered another Blitzen Benz for Burman's use, a 21.5-litre, 200-b.h.p. car that proved faster than the original Oldfield car and therefore was dubbed the 300 b.h.p. Benz. On Labor Day, Bob set a new dirt-track record of 47.85 seconds at Brighton Beach in this car, then took the Benz to San Diego the day before Christmas and ran the beach course there at 129 m.p.h. Then the car caught fire and he to drive into the surf to extinguish the blaze.

In 1912 Burman won 33 dirt track battles and was 2nd 8 times in the 43 races he entered, earning the Driver of the Year Award from a leading trade journal. The next season he was out of the money again in the 500 with a slope-hooded Keeton powered by a Wisconsin engine. Things continued in that vein for the year, possibly the poorest in Burman's blazing career.

In 1914 Bob started the Burman Special at Indy but it went out on the race's 47th lap with a broken connecting rod; the rest of the year on the dirt tracks he was back in top form. In August he won a consecutive pair of 50-milers at St. Louis. The following month Bob set 5- and 15-mile records at Peoria, Ill., and 5 days after that he grabbed 20- and 25-mile records at the Illinois State Fairgrounds in Springfield. At Ascot Park in Los Angeles, Burman in a blue Peugeot and Barney Oldfield in a borrowed Stutz met in a $5,000 match race on December 27. Even though Bob had to pit to replace a tire blown off by running over a nail, he caught and passed Oldfield almost at the wire, winning by 5 seconds after the wildest dash in Ascot history.

Barney bowed to Burman again on January 3, 1915, at Bakersfield, Calif., and Bob whipped both Earl Cooper and Louis Disbrow in other match races at Ascot before heading to Indy for another try at the 500. He finished 6th, his best effort at the Brickyard, and, as it turned out, his last. Board Speedways were being built,

all over the nation, and Burman and the other dirt greats moved into this new competition at such places as Sheepshead Bay in Brooklyn, N.Y., and at Chicago. It was at the Brooklyn track that Bob took his last ride in the Blitzen Benz No. 2 in November, bowing to Ralph DePalma.

Burman's last race after 7 years of championship competition came at Corona, Calif., on April 8, 1916. The city's 3-mile boulevard course had been called a semi-speedway and had lost its chances to host William K. Vanderbilt's Cup Race and the American Grand Prix as well. More than 100,000 turned out for this first speedway event at Corona with Burman in a blue Peugeot. He twice took the lead but lost it each time when pitting for tires. In the 97th lap, Bob had glued himself to the inside curb of the boulevard course and had floored the accelerator in a valiant effort to catch Eddie O'Donnell, the leader, when a tire blew. The car slammed into a telephone pole, hit a policeman and a parked car, broke a second pole and flipped, throwing Burman and his riding mechanic, Eric Schroeder, more than 50 feet through the air. Bob was still alive when his wife reached him, but he died in her arms. And because of the outcries of the thousands who had seen the accident, the boulevard race at Corona died with him.

GEORGE BUZANE

"When George Buzane drives in a speedway race," the gentleman who wrote the driver biographies for the 1917 Chicago Auto Derby wrote, "the whistles on peanut stands are silent, bootblack stands are closed and checkrooms of hotels and restaurants are closed, for the Greeks turn out en masse to see their fellow countryman in action. Buzane, who was born in Athens, is the only Greek driver in captivity."

The few contemporaries still around say that this soft-spoken man was one of the finest of his era, that it was a major racing tragedy that he met his death when hit by a truck after stepping off a streetcar in Toledo, Ohio. Buzane, so the account goes, learned the rudiments of gasoline engines by repairing the motors that put fizz in ice cream sodas, and then applied this knowledge as a taxicab chauffeur.

He began his racing career in 1911 as mechanic for the Grand Prize and Vanderbilt Cup events in Savannah. After 3 years as a garage mechanic in Chicago, George entered an ancient DeDietrich in the 1915 Elgin, Ill., races and in the Kalamazoo, Mich., dirt track race. He never finished in the money until Arthur Bernstein, a Chicago devotee of auto racing, supplied him with a Duesenberg for 1916. Buzane took 2nd in the Pikes Peak Hill Climb, 3rd at the Chicago Speedway Grand Prix in a 100-mile dirt track contest at Kansas City, and 4th in the Cincinnati Derby and the 100-miler at Indianapolis Fairgrounds.

Buzane had switched to a Detroit Special for 1917 but never got the chance to do much with it. The truck got him first.

RED BYRON

The full story of this phenomenal early hero of NASCAR stock-car racing can never be told because the freckle-faced redhead lived every minute of his 44 years to the fullest and had no time for memories. Robert Byron died in a Chicago hotel room November 7, 1960, an ironic death for a man who started racing when Atlanta was the hub of Dixie stock-car activity and the connection between drivers and whiskey-running was more than close. The amazing part about this Atlanta garage man was that he beat the rough whiskey boys and their high-tailed cars with his own creations, then went on to be a NASCAR founder, a Grand National season champ and a hero of the renaissance of road racing in the United States.

When he died, Byron was managing the Meister Brauser Scarab SCCA team. Earlier he had operated an imported car dealership in West Palm Beach, Fla., worked with Briggs Cunningham on the Cunningham racing car, and had been retained as the manager of the Corvette racing team when Ed Cole, then an engineering executive, had dreams of Le Mans and world sports-car domination.

Originally from Anniston, Ala., Red spent World War II as a tail gunner in the Pacific Theater. He walked with a limp, something that never bothered his driving, but which grew more pronounced with the approach of an attractive woman. He impressed a kid from Daytona Beach named Glenn Roberts so much the boy decided to stake out a career in racing, becoming an immortal in the process.

The 1948 NASCAR championship was contested in modified cars. It was a crucial year for the fledgling organization which had to prove its worth to promoters other than Bill France. Byron helped with a thrilling point duel with the Flock brothers, Fonty, Tim, and Bob. It was rough competition with such as Buck Baker, Curtis Turner, the fabulous Buddy Shuman, Marshal Teague, and veteran Bill Blair. Red bested Fonty for the title and became the organizations's main drawing card. There is a story that Red was privately dubious when France announced he was crowning a strictly stock-car champion, the Grand National division. But Byron honed up an Oldsmobile 88 and easily bested Lee Petty, Bob Flock, and Blair for the first Grand National crown. It was soon after that that he tapered off on racing because his health was not good, and there were now greener pastures.

One greener pasture was the Cunningham project in West Palm Beach. The idea was to produce a sort of American Ferrari out of as many American components as possible. Byron's job was to aid Phil Walters, another racing great, in developing the new marque to Le Mans-winning potency. They never quite made it, but Red became hooked on sports cars and, more especially, the posh sports car set of that pre-mass appeal era. He liked rubbing elbows with a Rubirosa, and he admired Porfirio's tastes more than his driving. And so he followed the races when he could—which was often. His mechanical skills were never under-estimated; he was a pro among rich amateurs who were willing to pay for his talent. When he died, he left a thousand uncheckable stories behind, and the world was a little bit drabber for his passing.

RAY CALDWELL

"Some day," Ray Caldwell was saying, "Marblehead will be known as the home of Autodynamics Corporation, world's largest builder of specialty and race cars exclusively. That day hasn't arrived, but we're working on it every year." Marblehead, Mass.? Why, that's posh yachting and fishing territory, far removed from the great racing venues of the United States. That's the place for a holiday, not a factory.

Raymond W. Caldwell, Jr., was far removed from the town of his birth, Toledo, O., and of his upbringing, Fond du Lac, Wisc. An engineering graduate of the University of Wisconsin, he came close to Marblehead when he elected to attend the Harvard Business School to earn a master's degree in business administration. Both Air Force service and a short tenure as one of the General Electric Corporation's bright young men convinced Caldwell that he was not an organization man—not if he was on the bottom looking up. With a fellow GE refugee, Fred Jackson, he founded Autodynamics in half of his 2-car garage in Marblehead, after he had driven his prototype Formula Vee to the 1964 National SCCA class crown and Rookie of the Year honors. "Prototype" is gilding the lily. He had merely had a vague desire to race and, as any Harvard MBA would do, he wished to do it as economically as possible. That the Formula Vee chassis he designed and constructed turned out to be so sound and desirable it drew unsolicited orders was a byproduct of Caldwell's racing. Six years later Autodynamics was America's largest racing car factory.

VW-based vehicles were Ray's stock in trade then—more than 1,000 Vees had been sold, and the Autodynamics Deserter was one of the most successful of the dune buggies. However, now there was also the Caldwell D-7 Canadian-American Challenge Cup sports car, a vehicle with solid axles fore and aft, the development costs for which were partially underwritten by Autodynamics' top driver, Sam Posey. The D-7 went fast in a straight line, but never quite made it against the McLarens, except at Mt. Fuji Speedway in Japan where it took a 2nd in 1968. A more successful Caldwell effort against the Europeans was his D-9 Formula Ford single-seater, which in 1969 (its 1st year in competition) won the American Road Race of Champions and dominated the class in America. The D-9, first American design in the class, had a much more rigid chassis than European FF versions, a higher-capacity cooling system because track temperatures go higher here than in Europe, and a totally adjustable suspension, not to mention more cockpit space for the larger American driver.

In 1970 Caldwell undertook to make the Dodge Challenger a factor in Trans-American sedan racing. The bright green car, again with Posey at the wheel, was not an immediate sensation as had been other Autodynamics efforts. It suffered from development problems and a constricted Dodge racing budget. It gave every promise of being a potent race car as the season drew to a close but the promise remained unfulfilled as Dodge withdrew its support.

Caldwell retired temporarily from driving to the role of administrator-designer, but he was not above testing his own machines. It might be said that he enjoyed his greatest success in racing in formula-type machinery. Besides the Vees and the Fords, there was a Caldwell-prepared Formula A Eagle in which Posey made a strong bid for the 1969 SCCA Continental series. That car, powered by a 500 h.p. Chevvy, was partially sponsored by entertainment personality Steve Allen and by Simoniz.

The Autodynamics factory in Marblehead was a strange building for a race and performance car builder. The brown, weathered shingles of its exterior blended with the New England resort scenery, and inside the most feverish activity went on in the offices. In the factory area—really 3 concrete block additions thrown up as the need for more and more space became pressing—the 35 or so employees seemed to work quite leisurely. They made race car frames, formed fiber glass polyester car bodies, and rebuilt engines and transmissions. It was a strange jumble of Vees, Super Vee D-10s, Deserters, and even the Hustler sports car, another VW-based effort. Occasionally the Challenger would appear in the shop, looking monstrous among the Formula cars. It reminded an old reporter of the original Carroll Shelby shops 3,000 miles away in California, before that ex-driver had outgrown himself into retirement as a millionaire.

It was unlikely that Caldwell could take that route because he was treading a more diversified path. As the world's largest builder of Vees and one of the largest in dune buggies, the potential rewards loomed much larger, but the risks greater. Besides, what major car company executive could justify acquiring a factory in Marblehead. The financial thinness of the operation was demonstrated at the end of 1970 when Posey quit Auto-

dynamics, taking a lot of Caldwell's financial backing with him. That, plus the American recession, forced Ray to become a Lola dealer as his car building operations wound down. But at least he had time to take up driving again, for the first time in many a year in a car he had not himself designed.

CALLOWAY BROTHERS

Foggy and Buddy Calloway, brothers from Macon, Ga., flourished in IMCA competition from about 1927 through 1938. The boys were known for their excellent voices, and for their car, powered by the 6-cylinder engine from a Curtiss airplane. They sang on national radio on a hillbilly program, and traveled the Central States Racing Association and IMCA circuits. Foggy also had a d.o.h.c. Offenhauser, which gave him something of an advantage in the circuits in which he competed.

Whenever one of the brothers won a race, he would break into song over the public address system. Foggy also played a guitar, but they could not figure out how to fit it into the car, so he sang *a capella*.

Buddy Calloway drove the Curtiss to track records at Memphis, Jackson, Topeka, Grand Rapids, Kalamazoo, and Atlanta. He was a huge man, well over 6 feet and almost as wide. Fitting him into his car was a routine part of the act, with help from his brother, pit men, and innocent bystanders. The Calloways eventually retired to Miami, where they may still be singing for all anyone knows.

GIUSEPPE CAMPARI

Guiseppe Campari, a short, stout, dark-complexioned man, nicknamed "Negher," or "Darkie," because of his coloring, was born in 1892 in Fanfulla, Italy, about 20 miles southeast of Milan. He began racing about 1912 with Fiat; by the outbreak of World War I he was well-established as a racing driver and tester. His greatest feat, perhaps, was in 1914 when he drove a 4.5-litre Grand Prix car to a 91.50 m.p.h. record over a flying kilometer course near Brescia; the GP car itself never raced in a formal contest, thanks to the war, and it was not until 1919 that Campari could resume his racing with a new ride from Alfa. His greatest prewar race success probably was a 4th in the 1914 Coppa Florio in an artillery-wheeled Fiat 20/30.

Campari's return was not met with instant success; he retired in the Targa Florio in 1919. But on June 13, 1920, at Mugello, Giuseppe won a 230-miler that marked the start of Alfa's rise in racing. He was 2nd at the Parma-Berceto meeting and 3rd in the Consuma Cup. At Gallante, near Milan, he ran a flying kilometer at 79 m.p.h. to win his 4.5-litre class. In 1921 Campari was 3rd at Parma and in the Targa, but won again at Mugello. He was 3rd in the Aosta-Grand St. Bernard hillclimb and ran the fastest lap at the Monza GP before a broken valve retired his car. A broken valve also took him out of the Brescia GP while he was far in the lead. Bad luck continued to plague Campari in 1923; while running 2nd in the Targa on the final lap, he ran out of fuel. But his luck changed in 1924.

August 3, 1924, was a warm, sunny day, a good day for an automobile race, and the European GP over the Lyons road course was one of the big ones of the year. For Alfa Romeo, then a comparatively young marque, it was a really big race, its initial major race outside of Italy, its first *grande épreuve,* its chance to make a good showing. In all, 3 Alfas were entered, for Antonio Ascari, Louis Wagner, and Giuseppe Campari, each in a brown uniform with "Alfa Romeo" lettered in white script across the chest, which led to their being called the Brown Men.

At the starter's flag, Henry Segrave grabbed the lead in his Sunbeam, Ascari's supercharged Alfa taking 2nd, close behind, and Albert Divo 3rd in a V-12 Delage. Before the lap was over Ascari was breathing even harder down Segrave's neck, but Lee Guinness, another Sunbeam driver, had roared into 3rd and Campari into 4th. Giuseppe yielded his slot to Pietro Bordino on lap 2 as the latter's Fiat moved steadily through the field toward 3rd, then 2nd on the following lap, then the lead when Segrave pitted to change misfiring spark plugs.

Bordino led for 6 laps, then yielded for a lap to Ascari, recaptured it, but had to pit to have work done on his brakes and Ascari again became the leader. Guinness was running 2nd at this point, Campari 3rd, but Lee took the lead when Ascari had to pit to change wheels. It was quick work in the pits that put Antonio back into the race, in 2nd, and able to retake the lead when Guinness again pitted following a puncture. Quick Sunbeam work sent Guinness back into 3rd behind Campari until a universal joint failed and ended Lee's chances.

By the 25th lap, Ascari and Campari were running 1st and 2nd, Divo 3rd, Robert Benoist 4th. But on lap 33 Ascari pitted once more, this time to change plugs, and his car died in the pit area, unable to restart, just 28 miles from victory. Campari led at last, but Divo was determined to win this race, and he charged faster than ever, only a mile back from the lead Alfa. But time and the experienced, determined Campari were to combine to end Divo's dream; he still trailed by 66 seconds (after 7 hours 5 and one-half minutes) when Giuseppe crossed the finish line for the last time, a 71 m.p.h. winner over the difficult course. Divo was 2nd, Benoist 3rd, Wagner in the second Alfa 4th after a steady race. Up to 1971 it was the only time in Grand Prix history that a manufacturer had won the initial *grande épreuve* it had ever entered.

Lyons was Campari's greatest victory, and certainly one of the great victories in Alfa's long and distinguished history. That season Giuseppe was 4th in the Targa, 3rd in the Coppa Florio, run concurrently with the Targa, and 3rd in the Italian GP. Campari came close to repeating his European GP victory in 1925, but was 2nd to Ascari at the flag. This was the famous race at Spa during which Alfa's Vittorio Jano, incensed by the incessant booing of the Belgian crowd because Alfa was making such a strong showing, called Ascari and Campari into the pits for a 5-minute cheese-and-wine break while the crowd—and the rest of Alfa's competitors—went wild. The Alfa drivers then re-entered the race and won going away. Campari was leading the French GP when Ascari crashed and was killed later that season; he and the other Alfas left the race out of respect to Alberto. In the other major race that season, the Italian GP, Campari was 2nd to Count Gaston Brilli-Peri.

When Alfa Romeo announced its retirement from the GP circuit at season's end, Giuseppe bought his P2 and went racing as an independent. In this car he won the 1927 Coppa Acerbo at Pescara at 64.76 m.p.h., then repeated the feat the following season at 68.25. In 1928 he sold the car to Achille Varzi, a new driver, but shared the car—and 2nd place—with Varzi in the Italian GP. One of the reasons Giuseppe sold the car was his determination to become an opera star. He had a fine voice. Perhaps no one really knew just how good it was until one evening on a dare he and a leading Italian female singer sang an impromptu duet in a Milan restaurant and brought down the house. He also established his own coachbuilding firm, Campari & Sorniotti.

Campari continued his driving while searching for the best way to break into opera, and while refining his singing. In 1929 he was 3rd in the Coppa Ciano, 2nd in the RAC Tourist Trophy at Ards, Northern Ireland. In 1930 he was 2nd in the Ciano race, 3rd in the Targa, and 3rd in the Irish GP standings, a compilation of the Saostat and Eirean Cups. He also was 2nd in the Tourist Trophy. In 1931 Campari tasted victory again, winning the Coppa Acerbo for the 3rd time, this season at 81.68 m.p.h. After a 2nd in the Mille Miglia, Giuseppe won the Italian GP at 96.17 m.p.h. with Tazio Nuvolari sharing honors. In the Irish GP he drove a Maserati and finished 2nd after suffering an eye injury when a flying stone shattered his goggles. Campari was 2nd in the French GP that season also, but retired from the Belgian 10-Hour Race, ending his chance to be the European Driving Champion—the equal of today's World Driving Championship—for the 1st time. But he was the Italian champion once again, having achieved that status initially in 1928.

Campari was driving less, but still turning out for races like the Ciano Cup in which he was 3rd in 1931 and 1932, the latter the year that Giuseppe became an official member of the Maserati team. It was in a Maserati that Campari ran the fastest lap and won the French GP over the full Montlhéry course at 81.52 m.p.h. in 1932; but in 1933 Giuseppe rejoined Alfa Romeo's Scuderia Ferrari operation. At the Monza GP he roared off on the first lap; a 4-car accident killed Campari and also Baconin Borzacchini on the south curve.

DONALD CAMPBELL

Donald Malcolm Campbell was the only son of Land Speed Record king Malcolm Campbell; he was also a less than likely successor to his father in land and water speed record breaking. Despite an early goal of following in his father's footsteps, Donald ran into a series of obstacles that seemed to have ended any ambitions in that direction. He was born March 23, 1921, and was 14 when his father made his last LSR attempt in 1935, captured the mark at 310.13 m.p.h. and retired from land competition to concentrate on the Water Speed Record. Young Donald was sent off to school at Uppingham, but contracted rheumatic fever, damaging his heart. Recovered, he finished school, joined an engineering apprentice program, and enlisted in the RAF pilot training program.

The RAF doctors decided that he was a bad risk as a fighter pilot because of his rheumatic troubles, and despite the need for fighter pilots at the outbreak of World War II, he was invalided out of the service in August 1940. "Nearly broke my heart," he recalled

later. "Battle of Britain, and all that. A terrible blow for a 19-year-old." He spent the war in machine tool work and continued at this business afterwards. His father, who had set the WSR in 1939 at 141.74 m.p.h., died in bed December 31, 1948. That started Donald thinking of speed again. An announcement from Henry J. Kaiser, the American industrialist, that he would support an assault on Malcolm Campbell's WSR decided Donald.

Donald made his first WSR attempt just 9 months after his father's death, using the same boat Sir Malcolm had used in 1939, and even the same mechanic, Leo Villa. Weather and engine trouble—prophetic of the kind of trouble that would always seem to follow Donald—prevented a real attempt. By the time Campbell returned to Coniston Water, England, in 1950, the Americans had taken away the record. His own run in the 11-year-old boat came within 0.6 m.p.h. of his dad's old mark, but failed to beat the new U.S. mark of 160 m.p.h. In 1951 he successfully competed on Lake Garda for the coveted Oltranza Cup, dedicated to Sir Henry Segrave, which had been won only once before in 20 years of attempts because of the difficult race conditions under which it was awarded.

Later in 1951 he made a 3rd attempt at Coniston for the WSR, but the Bluebird hit an underwater obstruction and crashed. Both Campbell and Villa were dunked, but rescued. The boat was a total loss. He set about building a new WSR boat, this one jet-powered, with a capability of reaching about 185 m.p.h. By the time he was ready to make his initial run in this boat, the Americans had raised the record to 178 m.p.h., thanks to Stanley Sayers. But in July 1955 Campbell made a 215-m.p.h. run, followed by a second run of 189, which gave him his first record—a WSR average of 202.32 m.p.h.

Donald came to Lake Mead, Nev., in late autumn and raised his own record to 216.2, than raised it again at Coniston the following September (1956) to 225.63 m.p.h. At Coniston once again in November 1957 Campbell raised his record to 239.07, and almost a year later raised it a 5th time to 248.62. In May 1959, not content with passing the 400-kilometer per hour mark he had set the year before, he raised the WSR to 260.35 m.p.h., well over the 250 barrier. On one run, he exceeded 275 m.p.h.

Meanwhile, Campbell and his advisers had evolved a scheme to retain the Land Speed Record for Britain. John Cobb's record of 394.20 m.p.h. set in 1947 at Bonneville Salt Flats still stood in 1955, but the LSR was in mortal danger from a group of ambitious Americans, including do-it-yourselfers like Mickey Thompson and jet-propulsion pioneers like Nathan Ostich, Art and Walt Arfons, and Craig Breedlove. And Britain had only Donald Campbell, who had driven only boats, not cars, at high speeds.

When he wanted to be charming, extroverted, and all

the rest, Donald could be, despite the fact that his normal character was introspective, moody, almost fatalistic. It took his charm, his name, and the deep roots of British patriotism to get the new Bluebird LSR car project off the ground. But he did get it off the ground, and eventually no less than 72 British companies joined in the effort, the bill for which totaled some $3 million by 1960. The latest Bluebird was completely unlike his father's cars. Turbine propulsion was only one difference. The new car was more of a rolling laboratory than a machine built simply for a fast tour down a measured course.

Kenneth and Lewis Norris, who had built Campbell's boat, designed the car. One of Sir Alfred Owen's companies built it. A 5,000 h.p. Proteus gas turbine provided power, fed by British Petroleum, Dunlop, at fabulous expense (they were not equipped as were America's Goodyear and Firestone for this kind of thing), provided the huge supplies of tires needed for testing and actual runs. The Bonneville Salt Flats were chosen as the site; Donald would have liked to keep this venture all British, but there was no place in Britain for this kind of thing. And anyway, what better place to accomplish the feat than in the "enemy's" own back yard?

The Campbell expedition reached the Salts in the fall of 1960. Americans were used to people coming out, and with a minimum of fuss making their attempts. It was get in, do your job, or at least try, and get out. But the British crew looked as if they intended to stay awhile. Each day a caravan of 26 vehicles would dash out to the Salts from a plush motel many miles away, and it seemed that a minimum of actual business was conducted. The Bluebird, supposedly a 500 m.p.h. car, was expected to get up quickly to the 400 m.p.h. area for early testing, then be readied for the real tries. But it was not happening. Tests were around 200 m.p.h., and Campbell seemed genuinely disturbed at Bonneville. It was true the Salts were not ideal, but so what?

The spectacle was even more disturbing when Mickey Thompson showed up with a piston-driven car, Challenger I—powered, in fact, by a stock Pontiac engine hot-rodded up—and proceeded to make a one-way run of 406.6 m.p.h. with an absolute minimum of fuss (his caravan consisted of 3 cars, one of them the Thompson family automobile). Four-hundred-plus m.p.h. No one had ever done that on wheels before. The fact that Mickey's car broke down on the return run and so the whole attempt was unofficial in the eyes of FIA did not matter much. The contrast between the home-built Challenger, built for peanuts, and the Bluebird, which rolled on millions of pounds sterling but could not get out of its own way, was obvious.

Campbell was incensed at the American press treatment. A week after Thompson's unsuccessful runs, he was out in Bluebird again, and let the car go, though supposedly only making medium-range test runs. Campbell's clockers had his speed at about 365 m.p.h. when

the big blue car was either deflected by the wind, or hit something, or its pilot lost control. At any rate, it swerved, bumped a few times, became airborne for some 235 yards, then crunched into the salts on its side and bounced upright. Donald came out of the spectacular thing with a hairline fracture and severe bruises and lacerations.

Everybody learned something from that crash. The driver learned to be more careful. The press learned to curb their quick-in, quick-out look on LSR attempts when talking about jet-powered and turbine-powered cars. Time was of the essence in preparation, and newsmen learned to curb their impatience; as they showed with future Arfons, Breedlove, and Gary Gabelich attempts, which took long windup periods but were not criticized the way Campbell was. The British builders learned that they had built a pretty strong craft. Bluebird needed only minor repairs, and a new stabilizing fin, but Donald had the craft torn down and put together again just to be on the safe side.

It was 1963 before Donald was ready for his next attempt. This one was to be at Lake Eyre, Australia, which reminded some old-timers that his dad had refused to run his Bluebird in New Zealand because it was "too far away" back in 1928. He had personally surveyed this site in October 1961 and his findings were seconded by many experts; this was a perfect site, certainly far better than Bonneville. One dissenting voice, an old-timer who operated a large sheep station in the area, warned that they were due for heavy rains again very soon. But no one paid attention.

They came, they saw, and they were conquered. The 20-mile course Campbell laid out had to be abandoned when too many soft spots were uncovered. A substitute shorter course was begun, but it started to rain, just as the old sheepman had predicted. Uplands became flooded, and the waters rushed into the salt beds. In April and May of 1963 Campbell and his crew tried valiantly to get their show on the road, but it ended in a washout as complete as any LSR attempt in history. He did not even have the satisfaction of some lesser records that his father salvaged out of his abortive African expedition in 1928 when he, too, was beaten by rain and terrain.

If the American press had learned patience, the Australian and British press had not. Some accused Campbell of being a hustler. Others suggested that perhaps the Utah crash had made him "chicken." Others said it was simply that he was an amateur who had no business being in a car, whatever his father's name might have been. British Petroleum withdrew all support, as did some of the other backers. Sir Alfred Owen made some remarks that led to a suit. On August 5, 1963, Craig Breedlove made his two runs at Bonneville—ironically the Salts there were the best they had been in many a year—and averaged 407.45 m.p.h. It did not matter that his Spirit of America was a 3-wheeler with a jet engine, not recognized by the FIA, only by the FIM, as a recordholder.

The British stiffened their upper lips. Owen and Campbell made up. If BP was out of it, Ampol, an Australian gasoline, was in, as was Wills cigarettes, another Australian brand. From that point on, Campbell was a chain smoker; he started in late April 1964. But the Campbell luck returned. Rain again; wind; minor malfunctions that kayoed Bluebird each day. Ruts in the salts that had to be repaired. And Fridays off; Donald had developed a fear of Fridays—the day he crashed in Utah, the day he sank in the original Bluebird boat, many evil things all happened on a Friday.

But it was on a Friday, July 17, 1964, that it happened at last. The wind was calm, the salt was as right as it ever would be, the car was finally ready. Only 50 people were on hand, in contrast to the several hundred that had started out as witnesses to his LSR attempt back in April. Campbell flew in by light plane, walked over to the car for a final cigarette, slipped off his shoes and vaulted into the cockpit, donning his suede slippers for a better feel of the pedals. The first run was absolutely perfect: 403.1 m.p.h. "Bloody awful," reported Campbell as he sat in the cockpit while the car was turned around. "I was all over the track."

But with 10 minutes to go before the mandatory hour for the record try was up, he was off again in the opposite direction. He was at 390, just passing the red marker of the official mile when vibration started. The car bounced about like a toy. The wheel was pulled out of Campbell's hands more than once. His foot slipped off the throttle, then on again. He smelled death, he said later, but on he went, on and on, until the second red marker that marked the end of the measured mile flashed by. Deceleration did not end the torment until the car was below 200 m.p.h.

It was a despondent Donald who rolled silently into the base camp and hoisted himself from the cockpit. "The vibration, the vibration. I couldn't read the instruments, but we didn't make it, I'm sure. We missed the record." The radio crackled out: "403.1 m.p.h." So what? That was the 1st run. Then it came again: "Official time for the 2nd run is the same: 403.1." He had done it. Two identical runs—a rare thing indeed in the LSR business—breaking Cobb's record for 4-wheeled, piston-driven cars. It had taken several years and an estimated $6 million to do it, but the job was done.

He turned once again to the WSR, although there was talk of another, 800 m.p.h. Bluebird in the style of the American jet-powered cars. He was in Australia again—they had sustained him in his hour of need and now he was prepared to give them all he could—in November of that same year to break his own record at Lake Bonney, South Australia. Bad luck dogged him again, but once more he perservered, and won. With less than 9 hours left in 1964, Campbell made a run of 286.3 m.p.h., turned about, and just beating a wind that would have prevented a run, notched a 269 m.p.h. run. The average was a new WSR of 267.33 m.p.h. He was the only man in history to win both LSR and WSR in the same year.

On January 4, 1967, Campbell was back in England, on familiar waters—Coniston, the scene of so many successful attempts. His goal was 300 m.p.h. He was there 9 weeks before the final try. The jet boat was roaring through the water at better than 300 m.p.h. when it became airborne. Campbell's last words, via radio, were: "It's going, it's going. I'm almost on my back . . ." His helmet, shoes and oxygen mask popped to the surface, but no other trace of man or boat rose from Coniston Water. Ironically, his LSR had fallen in November, 1965, when two youthful Americans, the Summers brothers, took their Chrysler-powered Goldenrod to Bonneville. Bob Summers averaged 409.277 m.p.h. for the highest speed ever for a "conventional" car. On June 30, 1967, Donald's hard-won WSR fell to another unknown American, Lee Taylor, Jr., a Downey, Calif., businessman who had one run of 299.181 m.p.h. and a 2-way average of 285.212 m.p.h. in a jet-powered boat called Hustler.

MALCOLM CAMPBELL

Back in 1928 a stocky, muscular man in his early forties became a familiar figure on the beaches of the world. His name was Malcolm Campbell, and he was already world-famous as a speed racer. Campbell had set his first Land Speed Record 4 years earlier. In the days when Campbell was challenged by other Britons like Henry Segrave and Parry Thomas and by Americans like Ray Keech and Frank Lockhart, he had defended his record regularly, regaining it 4 times. But the end was in sight for the LSR seeker's favorite course, the sands of Daytona Beach, Fla., where mere wheelspin could cost a record run some 10 or 15 m.p.h. Daytona might last a few more years, but with the kinds of cars Campbell had in mind for the future, a new site had to be found.

So off he went to look at possible new sites. Campbell was expert at this. He had raced on Yorkshire's Saltburn Sands soon after World War I. He had raced on the coast of Denmark at Fanoe. He had set his first internationally recognized LSR—a mere 146.16 m.p.h. —at Pendine Sands on the barren coast of Wales. And he had come as one of the earliest to Daytona. So Campbell took to the road to check out reports of various sites. One was at Rutba in the Syrian Desert, but it proved unsuitable. Another near Timbuktu also failed Campbell's inspection. He passed up a trip to Ninety Miles Beach in New Zealand; it was too far away in those pre-jet days. But Campbell did scour the northern

coast of Africa—walk it, in fact—from Oran to Cairo. None of the possibilities worked out upon actual inspection.

Then one day a newspaper clipping arrived from South Africa. Papers the world over had carried stories of Campbell's search for new race sites, and these stories reached the frontiers of 1928 civilization. One of these was Brandvlei, over 350 miles from Capetown, 30 miles from the nearest railroad. Here Dr. Israel Marin read of Campbell's search and took pen in hand to write the editor of the *Cape Times*. His letter told of a potential LSR course. Verneukpan, 50 miles beyond his village, was a dry lake bed 20 miles long and 10 miles wide, hard and smooth, and unpelted by rain for more than 20 years. The editor was interested enough to send a reporter and photographer, who duly returned and verified what Dr. Marin had written. The story was printed and posted to Campbell in Britain. He needed no coaxing. He replied almost at once that he would come.

Malcolm Campbell was the only son of a Scottish diamond merchant. He was born in 1885 in Chislehurst, Kent, England. At 15, his father sent him to the Continent to study and learn more about the diamond business. He became a bicycling enthusiast there, then a bike racer. Back in England in 1904, young Malcolm continued his education in the diamond business apprenticed to Lloyd's of London, but he also graduated from bikes to motorcycles. Almost on a dare, Malcolm won his first prize in 1906 when he competed in a

London-to-Edinburgh reliability race. To prove it was no fluke, Campbell repeated with victories the next 2 years as well.

Campbell owned a couple of cars around this time, flivvers that he called Flapper I and Flapper II. He also had an airplane, home-built, that had one flight and one crash, but he walked away from it. In 1910 Malcolm finally bought a real car, Louis Wagner's 1906 Darracq, which had won that year's Vanderbilt Cup. He called it Bluebird. Malcolm had picked up the name from a stage show in London that he had attended the day before his first Brooklands race. He was to use the name for almost every car that he raced from then on. Monday to Saturday Malcolm was a diamond merchant; Sundays he was an auto racer, principally at Brooklands, the banked bowl that was the center of all British auto sport in those days.

With the outbreak of World War I, Campbell became a motorcycle dispatch rider for a time, then switched to the RFC for pilot training. Campbell came out of the RFC a captain; he was Captain Campbell thereafter, until a knighthood made him Sir Malcolm. First, however, there came a lot more club racing at Brooklands, then the first speed car, a special 12-cylinder Sunbeam that Campbell again dubbed Bluebird. The car was purchased in 1921, but it was 1924 before Campbell ran his first official LSR at Pendine Sands, the 146.16 m.p.h. one. The following year he upped it to 150.87.

The Captain was off treasure hunting (literally) at Cocos Island in the Pacific when Segrave raised the mark to 152.33 in 1926—in those days the regulations were not what they are today and any increment was acceptable. Parry Thomas came up with Babs the following year and raised the LSR to 169.23 m.p.h., then 171.09. But Malcolm was back in Britain, and he had a new car, the first real Bluebird (with the name on the side), a Napier-Campbell powered by a Napier-Lion aircraft engine. In this car, Malcolm Campbell became the first man to try for 200 m.p.h., but he did not make it. He had a record of 174.88 set at Pendine February 4, 1927, but Segrave erased it on March 25 with a 203.79 clocking at Daytona.

Daytona obviously was the place to try to beat Segrave's mark, and Campbell and his Bluebird were there in January 1928. Testing in Florida, he had a crash on the beach when the car hit a soft spot. Damage was slight to man and car, and the following month he was again ready. February 18, 1928, Bluebird II—a revamped version of the original Napier-Campbell now powered by a 23.9-litre aircraft engine—roared to life. The 1st run was 214.70 m.p.h., including a frantic moment when Campbell almost crashed. He turned for the 2nd run, and a new record, 206.96 m.p.h. He was back in England when Keech made 207.55, and Malcolm resolved to find a new LSR site to improve his next effort.

So it was that Campbell came to South Africa in

February 1929. People marvelled at the convoy: Bluebird, packed away in a case. A small airplane. Fifty-six cases of timing equipment. Leo Villa, his head mechanic (who also was to serve Malcolm's son, Donald), and a crew of mechanics. Nine sets of special Dunlop tires. Eight hundred gallons of fuel. Five hundred spark plugs. Extra parts and tools galore. And a small tent city in which everyone was to live. Campbell flew to Verneukpan to inspect the course and was appalled to find that as smooth as it looked, lurking below the top salt was sharp-pointed shale. It would cut the Dunlops to ribbons in a few feet. What to do? Native labor provided the answer, the local highway department the work and direction. A "road" 50 feet wide and 20 miles long was constructed, using mud that the African sun baked to a brick-like hardness. A white line ran down its center.

All was ready. But for the first time in 20 years, a torrential rain belted the Pan, and everything was washed away: road, camp, the works. Malcolm Campbell was a stubborn man; he refused to leave. Rebuild was the order of the day. But it was 2 weeks before work could start, before the damage would dry. Campbell hitched a truck ride to Capetown to celebrate his 44th birthday. He was sitting in a restaurant when he picked up a newspaper and read the headline with fascinated horror: "Segrave Sets Speed Mark at Daytona." Segrave had upped the mark to 231.44 m.p.h. The challenge was greater than ever.

Back at the Pan, Campbell was ready to go on April 21. The 1st run read 230 m.p.h. on Malcolm's speedometer. Turnaround; the 2nd run was slower, for the "road" was deteriorating, unable to withstand the weight of the giant car. Campbell's meter read 220. The official clockings came in: 1st run, 222.5 m.p.h.; 2nd run, 212.5 m.p.h.; aggregate, 219 m.p.h. Malcolm had failed at the basic LSR. But there were 5-mile and 5-kilometer records that he might capture, and he went for those and bettered both.

A new Bluebird would be needed before his next attempt. The Air Ministry permitted him to build the car around a secret new aircraft engine. In 1931 the car was ready, and Campbell was at Daytona. Almost without trying he erased Segrave's record with a 246.09 clocking. Back in Britain, called to Buckingham Palace, Campbell became Sir Malcolm. In 1932, again in Florida, he upped it to 253.97, the 1st man to exceed 250 m.p.h. In 1933, with still another version of the original Bluebird, now powered by a Rolls-Royce airplane engine, he raised it again to 272.46, in 1935 to 276.82 at Daytona, and to 301.13—another barrier passed—at Bonneville Salt Flats in Utah. That September 3, 1935, run was Campbell's last LSR quest. After that he turned his attention to the Water Speed Record.

Sir Malcolm lived until December 31, 1948. He saw George Eyston crack his LSR mark in 1937 and raise it again the same year. He saw John Cobb raise it in 1938, Eyston recapture it, then Cobb take it again in 1939. He saw Cobb reach 394.20 m.p.h. in 1947, a record that was to stand 16 years. But Malcolm Campbell's name would live on as one of the great speed seekers of all time.

JOHN CANNON

The SCCA Continental Championship is a series for single-seater racers contested on road courses. It is highly competitive; there are two classes, which now race separately. The Formula B cars are powered by engines of 1,600 c.c., mostly Ford Cosworths. Formula A cars run on 5,000 c.c., production-based engines or all-out 3-litre power plants, so often they are faster than Formula 1 cars.

But almost every successful series needs stars to succeed. If drivers from some other already-established series cannot be attracted regularly, it must develop its own. So the question then becomes, are there enough top-calibre drivers to staff all the various series—and are enough fans interested? A wise automobile columnist once wrote that in the "scenery" at any given championship race there is at least one driver waiting for the right equipment to become a star. British-born, Canadian-resident John Cannon was part of the "scenery" at sports car venues for quite a while before he began to show the ability to pilot good machinery.

Cannon came to California before starting to race in SCCA club events in an Elva Courier in 1960. He was

112

23 at the time and he liked the life of a gentleman racer. He was good enough to hang on to good rides; John Mecom, the Texas oil heir, hired him in 1964 for the Group 7 effort of the Mecom Racing Team. The machinery ranged from Scarabs and Genies to Lolas, but Cannon proved that he was more consistent than inspired. In 1966 Dan Blocker, the late television star, and Nickey Chevrolet of Chicago combined to put the Englishman into something called the Vinegaroon Nickey Genie Chevrolet. John surprised himself by winning the initial race of the USRRC season. He was well behind Jerry Grant in the All-American Racers Lola Ford, when on lap 34 (of 60) over Stardust International Raceway in Las Vegas, Nev., Grant's gearbox packed it in. Cannon held off Chuck Parsons to win his 1st major race.

John shifted to Canada and continued to concentrate on USRRC, then Canadian-American Challenge Cup competition. But his mounts were generally older machinery with lesser power, and he did well to share each year in the generous Johnson's Wax point fund, except for the Monterey Grand Prix in 1968. It had come up rain on race day at the Laguna Seca road course within sight of the Pacific ocean. And when it rains there, it comes down in gray sheets. Cannon had qualified only 15th fastest on the dry pavement the previous day in his 3-year old McLaren. He was giving away not only 3 years of chassis development to the highly favored duo of Bruce McLaren and Denis Hulme, but also approximately 80 h.p.

The contest, for Cannon, was not against the other drivers but against himself. In 7 laps of racing he managed to lap the entire 29-car field. And while others were making pit stops to change befogged and mud-covered goggles, Cannon had cut slits into his so that they could not fog, though his eyes took a fearful beating. Still another factor aiding the Canadian independent's peace of mind. Jim Hall had not been able to start after the starter motor in his Chaparral broke on the grid. Cannon could not believe his eyes when he saw the Hall crew working for him and Jim directing strategy. But it was a one-of-a-kind race; John was not a factor in the CanAm again that year.

In 1969 Cannon finally found a series and a sponsor. The series was the SCCA Continental and the sponsor was Malcom Starr, a young Columbia University graduate who had decided to make racing his profession. The Starr Racing Eagle was a Formula 5000 car, and Cannon took to it as he had never taken to the big Group 7 CanAm machinery. In the series opener at Riverside, he broke both the absolute track record and Gurney's 45-lap mark set the previous November in a brilliant victory. At Sears Point, Calif., it was another flag-to-flag victory. But at the other stops, there were too many DNF's for him to rise above 4th place.

In 1970 fresh money brought Cannon a new Mc-

Laren single-seater, and the Starr Racing Team another victory at Riverside. Cannon scored no points at Edmonton, where young Ron Grable, a refugee from a Javelin TransAm ride, won, but he scored again at Kent. Grable took Laguna Seca, then Gus Hutchinson made it 3 drivers with 2 victories each by winning Sears Point and Dallas in succession. Now it was Road America time, with a field strengthened by the arrival of British Formula 5000 king David Hobbs. Cannon bested Hobbs at Road America to break the tie in victories, finished 2nd in the next 2 races (Mt. Tremblant and Donnybrooke, Minn.) and 3rd at Lime Rock, Conn., to take an apparently unbeatable lead. But Hobbs and Hutchinson had an outside chance if Cannon scored no points in the final 2 races.

That chance ended at Mid-Ohio. As Follmer barrelled his Lotus-Ford to a wire-to-wire victory, Cannon and Hobbs locked into a duel unusual for SCCA road racers. Cannon stole 2nd place on the 1st turn by daringly taking Hobbs on the inside. The outraged Briton then began 6 laps of probing, bumping, and putting the nose of his Surtees TS5A near the rear wheel of the determined Cannon. John refused to back off. On the 7th lap in the final turn into the straight, John went a bit wide and Hobbs darted through to take 2nd briefly. Cannon closed immediately, his right front wheel bumping Hobbs's left rear. The contact broke Hobbs's suspension member, forcing him out of the race.

Two laps later Ron Grable moved up to press Cannon for 2nd. The 2 went into a turn almost wheel-to-wheel, Grable barely out front. Again there was contact, this time Cannon's right front against Grable's left front, damaging Ron's tire and sending him to the pits. Cannon took 2nd comfortably over Mark Donohue, who had charged through the field from last place, and became the 1970 Continental Champion. He was not a factor in the anticlimactic season finale at Sebring, as Donohue scored another victory. But John Cannon had found his place in the racing sun, and the Continental series—with L&M cigarette money behind it to push purses ever higher—had found its stars in Cannon, Posey, Hobbs, Hutchinson, and even comedian Dickie Smothers.

In 1971 Cannon still was casting about for the big break. He drove an ex-Mario Andretti March 701 in the Questor Grand Prix at Ontario, Calif., and finished 12th. He bought a Formula 2 car and ran it both in Europe and in the U.S. at several races. He got a ride from Andy Granatelli for the Ontario 500 USAC race, but wrecked the car in practice. John wanted to run the Canadian GP, but could not get a ride. BRM had an extra car for the United States GP at Watkins Glen, and Cannon got his 1st official F1 drive, finishing 14th. He hadn't made the big time yet, but he was trying. In 1972's L&M series, Cannon had a fast March 725-Olds that suffered teething problems most of the season.

SHORTY CANTLON

Each era in racing has men whose talents were misplaced in history. Shorty Cantlon—pronounced "Catlin" —who began his career about 1925 on the dirt tracks of the Midwest, was born too soon for his talents. Small, meticulous around the garage, and absolutely fearless, William Cantlon's forte was not the dash for the lead, but the strategic pass, setting up the driver ahead until the exact moment came when the victim could do nothing but fume and let Cantlon by if he wished to stay in the race. Shorty drove the final years of the board era and was a redoubtable midget race car performer.

Sometimes, because of poor judgment or pique, the victim chose to contest the matter, and the result usually was a crash. Cantlon, who called the Fort Miami Speedway in Toledo, O., his home track, had a shocker at Winchester, Ind., when he and another pilot drove right off the high banks over the lip of the track; fortunately both emerged unscathed. Another time, at Roby Speedway in Chicago, his midget racer did a double somersault and pancaked; he received a fractured leg. And of course there was the crash that finally got him, in the 1947 Indianapolis 500. Cantlon never won the AAA Championship because he was too busy on the sprint circuit. However, his record lists a Championship Trail triumph at Syracuse, N.Y., in 1934.

Cantlon first entered Indy in 1928, but he did not make the race. His best finishes were 2nd in 1930 and 6th in 1935. In the 1930 race he had the 3rd fastest car, a Miller Marine 4—four m.p.h. slower than that of winner Billy Arnold. He held 2nd ahead of Lou Schneider and Lou Meyer, who had the 2nd fastest car but finished 4th. In 1931 Shorty broke a con rod on his Miller 16-cylinder and was out after 87 laps; he had run as high as 3rd place. Cantlon did not make the 1932 race and burned a rod on lap 49 in 1933 on his Miller 4; he lasted 6 laps after racing among the leaders.

In 1935 Cantlon put the Sullivan-O'Brien Special into 6th place after running as high as 2nd for 40 miles late in the race. Only the foulest of luck robbed Shorty of a 2nd straight top 10 finish the following year. He had a leaky gas cap on the car, and since there was a fuel maximum he had to stop and install a new gasket. He returned and advanced as high as 3rd place. But the leak had taken its toll, and Cantlon ran out of gas 15 miles from the finish line.

Shorty finished 14th in the Bowes team car in 1937, then drove his first blown Miller 183 the following year, retiring in 13 laps because the blower tore loose. In 1939 he switched to an Offy, and the main bearing burned out after 15 laps. In 1940 he qualified the Surber Offy, but Babe Stapp drove the race and retired after 64 laps. He was not a factor in 1941 either.

In 1947, after the war, Shorty's shock of gray hair was turning white, but he still thought he could win the 500. He qualified his car in the 2nd row on the initial day of qualifying, but stuck around to watch other drivers. He was a helpful sort and very loyal to friends. He worried more for them than for himself. He had a plan—let the Novis and the new cars burn themselves out, then come on to win. The opening of the race doomed this plan. Cantlon's car was left at the post. When he got it going, the field was already in the back stretch. But he raced hard, with the crowd cheering him on, and caught up. A balky motor on a pit stop dropped him back again, and he was trying to unlap himself when it happened. Bill Holland skidded onto the grass in the south turn, held control and veered back onto the track. Cantlon, coming up very fast, looked as if he had to hit the Blue Crown driver.

But he apparently made a split second choice, the implications of which he must have known. He turned right, driving head-on into a concrete wall. The car whipped around, banging the tail into the wall, then the nose again. Shorty remained in the car upright, his head sagged over. The ambulance took him away, but the announcement came shortly afterward. "Veteran driver Shorty Cantlon has met with a fatal accident."

RUDI CARACCIOLA

When talk gets around to the greatest Grand Prix drivers of all time, names like Fangio, Nuvolari, Moss, Clark, and Stewart are most often recalled. Strangely, the name Rudolph Caracciola is just as often omitted. Why this is so cannot be explained in any rational way; perhaps emotional resentment of the fact that the man was a German, driving German cars in a time when Nazism dominated that nation, would explain some of the omissions, but certainly not all. Besides, Rudi was an anti-Nazi who fled Hitler and became a Swiss citizen in his later years.

No, the answer must be that Caracciola did his job too well. In his glory years, driving the most powerful GP cars ever built, he never spun out, never lost control of his mount, and skidded but once in the recollection of those who saw him perform. This is not to say he never crashed, for he did, with bone-crushing results. (Characteristically, he overcame these injuries.) But he was not in GP cars when these unhappy occurrences marred his otherwise perfect record. Caracciola, then, was too perfect to attract the following of other great drivers. He was rarely far enough behind to make any thrilling dashes to the lead; he never had to leap from a flaming wreck; and he took no delight in wine, women, or song when he toured the GP circuits.

Small wonder, then, that little note was taken when the gray-haired, stocky man of 58 died of cancer in a Kassell, Germany, clinic in 1959. Only a few hundred people even bothered to attend a subsequent memorial service at the Stuttgart works of Mercedes Benz for

which Rudi had performed most of his driving miracles, but at least those there were reminded of Caracciola's more than 225 victories over 30 years and of his 3 titles as Champion of Europe—equal to the World Driver's Championship of our time.

Born January 30, 1901, in Remagen, which had a bridge that was to gain the town some measure of fame 44 years later, Caracciola was of German parentage on both sides (the family had some Sicilian origins that account for the Italian cast of his name). His father was a well-to-do hotel owner, and Rudi was expected to follow in his footsteps. But he was mechanically inclined, and even though he made a success of a teen-age try at hostelry, he soon found himself apprenticed to an automobile works, Fafnir, in Dresden. Young and personable, Caracciola became a sales agent for Fafnir, and to influence possible buyers (few and far between in postwar Germany), he started racing the company's lightweight product in 1922.

Speed gripped him, and the idea of becoming a professional racing driver appealed to the youngster, as it did to many Europeans in those days. The trick was to get a factory berth and so be assured of good cars, good backing in the pits and a steady income. Many tried; most failed. For a while it looked as if that was to be Caracciola's fate too. His initial victory, a year after he first took the wheel, was in April 1923, in a borrowed 4-cylinder EGO at the Berlin Stadium. And he had managed to gain a position with Mercedes Benz, then the greatest name in German automotive production and racing. But his pleas for a real chance at proving his

value to Mercedes as a racing driver were ignored, except for some minor starts.

This situation continued until July 1926, when Rudi caught his employers in a weak moment. The regular Mercedes drivers and cars were in Spain for an important race, and it looked as if Germany's greatest marque would not be raced at the German Gand Prix, a brand new and as yet unrecognized event. Caracciola convinced Mercedes that they could and should be represented—by a private entry driven by him. If he did well, the factory could take credit. If he failed or fared poorly, they could ignore his performance, and no one would think anything of this unknown. On that basis, the factory agreed to lend him a car, and Caracciola set off for Avus and the start of one of motor racing's most fabulous careers.

It rained on race day, and the track was incredibly slick according to those who were there. The inexperienced and nervous driver stalled his car when the flag fell and needed a push from his riding mechanic to get started. An inauspicious beginning, certainly. It seemed he never could catch the pack, but somehow he did, seemingly throwing caution to the winds; although it was later to become apparent that Rudi was a natural driver who could push himself and his machine to their absolute limit, but never go past it. As car after car slowed in the driving rain, the man who would be nicknamed "Der Regenmeister" (the rainmaster) picked up speed and distance on his rivals. Twenty laps later he splashed across the finish line, an unbelieving winner initially, then a happy and completely dedicated one. He then married the girl he had loved for some years, and opened a plush Berlin Mercedes showroom, which was left for someone else to manage while Caracciola himself competed in almost every important European race from then on, winning many. He was gaining the experience and the tempering that all truly great drivers need before their greatest days.

Disappointments were many, as in the 1930 Le Mans classic when Rudi and his codriver, Christian Werner, battled the famous 5-car Bentley team for 10 hours on even terms—only to be retired by a generator that failed. That same year the Depression caused Mercedes to suspend racing. Sales at his auto showroom had fallen off tremendously, and that, too, was closed. Rudi was out of a job. Still he refused to give up, and used his last major funds to purchase a 225 b.h.p. Mercedes SSK to race privately. He won the Irish GP in this car.

In the 1931 Mille Miglia, a 1,000-mile test of man and machine, Caracciola proved that he was ready for the preeminence that was to be his for many years. No foreigner ever had won Italy's great classic, yet Rudi felt that victory could be his despite opponents like Nuvolari, Campani and 150 others of varying skills and mounts. In the race he led at Bologna, but by Rome Nuvolari had taken over. A broken exhaust pipe on the white Mercedes had cost Rudi 10 precious minutes. But

115

he caught and passed the Flying Mantuan, only to fall back again when his throttle jammed and he pitted for repairs. He was 6th when he regained the course, and victory seemed unreachable.

Yet he passed 3 Alfas virtually abreast, in one thrilling outside sweep that brought even Italian partisans to their feet with a mighty roar almost equalling that of the Mercedes. The lead increased; but another obstacle was to be thrown in his path before Brescia and the finish were to be reached. A tire burst, and only a frantic change saved the remnants of his lead. Yet once more Caracciola drove off, with bleeding hands and heat-and-pressure-blistered feet, choked with fumes, covered with sweat and grime, his throat parched, his ears deafened. And he won. Rudi won the Avus, Eifel, and German Grands Prix, too.

Alfa Romeo was impressed. The following year the great Italian marque offered Caracciola a team berth if he could earn it. At the start of the 1932 season he was an independent, attached to but not part of the factory team. Only when Nuvolari, Campari and Borzacchini agreed to accept him as an equal would he become an official team member. That acceptance came when Rudi graciously let Nuvolari win the Monaco GP when he himself could easily have taken it after the Italian's engine began to falter near the finish. It was a gesture worthy of a team member, and for it he became one.

Caracciola could no longer be denied. That year he won 10 races, including the Grands Prix of Germany, Poland and Monza; placed 2nd at Avus and Pescara as well as Monaco; and was 3rd once. While Rudi was winning 10 races, Nuvolari, driving an identical machine on the same courses, won but 6. Those who have deprecated Caracciola's skill with the explanation that he won so often because he had the fastest machine should note that fact well.

That was Caracciola's only season with Alfa, for the Italian factory did not sponsor a team the following year, and he had to make other arrangements. He joined with an old friend, Louis Chiron, who had left Bugatti, to form Scuderia C.C. and field 2 Alfas purchased from the factory. Rudi's was white with a blue stripe, Louis's blue with a white stripe. But they were never to race together. In practice for the opening GP at Monaco, a moment's inattention on Rudi's part as he worried about Chiron sent his mount into a wall at 70 m.p.h. The result was a badly shattered thigh bone that put the unhappy German driver on the sidelines for the entire 1933 season. And disaster still plagued him. That winter his beloved wife, Charlotte, was killed in an avalanche while skiing. For a long while, Caracciola would see no one save Chiron, whose attentiveness, Rudi said later, helped him overcome his grief, even though the two men talked mostly in a mixture of French, German and sign language.

In 1934 Rudi drove an honor lap at Monaco, and the smells and sights and sounds of the circuit were too much for him. He put his grief behind him and accepted a Mercedes offer to join the newly reformed team, despite continuing pain from his still-healing leg. A new style of driving to compensate for his injuries had to be devised, but he shared an Italian GP victory with Fagioli, and by the start of the 1935 season he was again ready to demonstrate his mastery of the racing art.

The 1935 season will always live in racing history. Rudi dominated the GP scene as did Juan Fangio and Jim Clark in later days. He won at Tripoli, in France, Switzerland, Belgium and Spain. He became Champion of Europe for the 1st time. The epic battle between Germany's two automotive giants was getting under way —Mercedes against Auto Union (later merged, along with DKW). The latter dominated the circuit in 1936, Caracciola's underpowered Mercedes winning only at Monaco and Tunis. Young Bernd Rosemeyer of Auto Union took the coveted championship.

But 1937 was another story. Mercedes astounded the world with its newest car, a long, slim monster that put 646 b.h.p. at Rudi's command. Its supercharged 5.6-litre engine enabled him to reach 140 m.p.h. from a standing start in but 11 seconds. He won the German, Tripoli, Swiss, Italian and Czech Grands Prix and his 2nd championship, leaving an almost-as-powerful Auto Union and a frustrated Rosemeyer in his exhaust trails as often as not. It was a good year for Caracciola for still another reason—he courted and married a longtime friend, Alice Hoffman. Their honeymoon was spent in the United States, and while there Rudi competed in the revived Vanderbilt Cup Races at Roosevelt Field on Long Island. But Rosemeyer, by now a good friend despite their intense rivalry on the course, was destined to win there when Rudi's Mercedes came down with engine trouble.

The following year their friendship ended tragically. Both men drove not only races but speed record cars, usually along a closed-off section of the Autobahn. On January 28, 1938, Rudi set a new mark and Rosemeyer, despite warnings about a rising wind, set out immediately to better the still-wet record. The wind proved his undoing at 260 m.p.h. when his car lifted into the air and exploded on impact. Caracciola went on to win his 3rd championship with victories in the Swiss and German GPs and the Acerbo Cup, but something was gone from his driving. He retired the next year, soon after winning the German GP, when Hitler tried to "honor" him with a Nazi title and moved to Switzerland to escape the madmen who had taken over his nation. His retirement was briefly interrupted in 1946 when the Indianapolis Motor Speedway promoters, trying to assemble a card of great drivers, asked Caracciola to participate in that year's 500. Joel Thorne offered Rudi one of his 6-cylinder Thorne Specials, and he easily passed his rookie test—some "rookie." But in qualifying the car, disaster struck again. A flying rock stunned Caracciola as he was entering the Brickyard's south turn, and his car slammed into the wall, catapulting Caracciola onto the track head first. It was some time before he was fully recovered from this accident.

In the early fifties Rudi tested cars at high speed for Mercedes and competed in such events as the 1952 Monte Carlo Rally for his beloved factory. In that same year's Mille Miglia he was 4th. Even though he was now past 50, the old skills were there. At Berne for an important sports car race, Rudi drove competitively for the last time. On the 13th lap his reflexes may have failed; Caracciola missed a curve and hit a tree. He again smashed a leg and spent the next 8 months of 1952 in traction. In 1958, quite near the end, he drove a few exhibition laps at Le Mans in a 1930 Mercedes and gave the crowds—the older spectators certainly—the thrill of seeing the blunt-featured, almost puckish-faced driver behind the wheel once more. It was the same thrill that many U.S. servicemen stationed in Europe and North Africa experienced when Rudi, acting as a Mercedes sales representative, gave driving demonstrations in a company drive for export business in those same years.

He deserves to be remembered more than this.

BOB CAREY

To earn the accolade of "greatest driver of his time," young Bob Carey must have had considerable talent. Contemporaries said the young Hoosier had that combination of courage, cunning, and complete physical control of the car that bespeaks a natural driving great. Born in Anderson, Ind., September 24, 1905, Carey knew he wanted to be a race driver before he ever saw a race. He and his brother, Fred, 5 years his senior, used to play near the shop of the local automotive genius, Robert M. Roof. Roof designed special motor modifications and also complete motors for both racing and street use; his dream was to found an automotive dynasty by selling runabouts powered by a modified Chevvy 4 or Model T Ford engines. Roof never made, it but he started a national champion on his way.

The Carey brothers were fascinated by the noise and the excitement of the automobile and hung around the shop helping out when they could. It was a scene unimaginable in modern America, a scene made obsolete by the pace of life and the awesomeness of modern technology. The inventor and other mechanics took time to answer small boys' questions, even letting the children sit and watch and listen. Impossible now.

Even more impossible was Carey's initial race at the age of 17 on a Converse, Ind., dirt half-mile. It was also the 1st race the brothers had ever seen. Roof's driver failed to show; Bob begged to be allowed to warm up the car, which had a new engine, and suddenly he had talked himself into the competition. He won 3 heats,

finished 2nd in the main (or feature) race, and had himself a driving job.

Carey gave Roof and his engines whatever fame they achieved by winning consistently over the next 3 seasons. His brother Fred, who also wanted to drive, was persuaded by the family to be satisfied with watching from the pits. Fred Carey later had a 43-year career with General Motors' Delco division. Even then, Bob was a quiet stylist who preferred to run past competitors, not over them.

It was inevitable that car owners higher up the ladder should beckon. So Carey came to drive the John Vance sprint car for the Dayton, Ohio, sportsman. Vance had 2 cars: in one was Carey, in the other a young man named Mauri Rose. The combination made the Vance Racing Team automatic favorites in any Central States Racing Association meet. (In the twenties and for much of the next decade CSRA sanctioned many dirt-track races throughout the Midwest, and parts of the South and East. It was at least equal to the AAA except for Indy).

The Carey–Rose rivalry became so bitter that Mauri would complain of favoritism every time Bob won. Eventually it broke up the team. Carey moved on to the McLain Trucking team, driving a car powered by a Miller marine engine. Carey, on his own, won regularly and was always in contention. He set track records, like the one on Frank Funk's Winchester banking, that were to stand for years. In 1929 the stock market crashed; the purses dropped down steadily. In 1930 Carey went to southern California where a man still could make a living racing cars—not a good one, but enough for a 26-year-old to eat regularly.

Other Midwestern heroes like Bill Cummings, Gus Schrader, and Howdy Wilcox II had preceded Carey to join the gladiators at Legion Ascot Speedway every Wednesday night in Glendale. Some had done well but none gathered a following as quickly and convincingly as Bob Carey. Whether or not he won—and he usually did not—he gave an assortment of 2nd-echelon machinery fantastic rides. Carey spent 1931 as one of the favorites of the movie colony. He spent 1932 becoming AAA national champion.

Louis Meyer, the meticulous multiwinner of earlier days, gave Carey his Indy chance in 1932. Lou had elected to drive Alden Sampson's V-16 in the 1932 race; he turned over a 249 cu.in. Miller straight 8 with a chassis built by another driver, Myron Stevens. For a 2-man car it was light, only 1870 pounds.

Carey (and his riding mechanic Lawson [Useless] Harris) qualified 23rd fastest; but since, under the regulations that govern Indy it was on the first day, he sat in 14th position on the grid. That was strictly temporary, however, as he charged from the back to 4th place in less than 25 miles. At the 150-mile-mark he was leading, and by 200 miles he was beginning to open up a lead on the field. But then misfortune struck. Bob spun on some oil, kissed the wall, and damaged a wheel about 25 miles shy of the halfway point. He spent 10 minutes in the pits as the Meyer crew worked feverishly to repair the car. He came out charging; by the 275 mile mark he was 9th, moving to 7th at 400 and 5th at 450. In the final standings he moved to 4th behind Fred Frame. He had made up some 3 minutes on Frame, a fantastic ride.

The points from that 4th place finish made him a prime contender for the AAA national championship in those depression days when the Championship Trail was virtually a footpath. He had won the main at El Centro, Calif., won on the Oakland mile in the 100 there, setting record time, and picked up a few more points with a 5th at Ascot and a 4th at Oakland. After that showing he was determined to go for the title.

Carey won on June 6 at the Michigan State Fairgrounds (84 miles, then rain), won at Syracuse in another race shortened (to 81 miles) by rain, then picked up several more points in stops in Pennsylvania and the late California races. He became the 1932 AAA National Champion.

During the opening days of the 1933 season—a season that looked quite promising for Carey—he was practicing in a revised Jadson-Miller. He was alone on the track at the time and did not seem to be pushing too hard. But suddenly the car flipped. Bob Carey was dead when people at the track got to him. It had come as suddenly as his rise in AAA ranks, so suddenly that for years drivers and mechanics used to speculate on whether he would have become the greatest driver of all time. The car was repaired and raced for several years.

ERIK CARLSSON

In Sweden, where they raise some of the best rally drivers in the world, one of the best of the best was Erik Carlsson. A giant of a man (6 feet 4 inches, 250 pounds), he had many claims to fame: 5 Swedish ice and road racing championships, victory in the famous Monte Carlo Rally twice in succession, winner of Britain's RAC Rally 3 times in a row, and husband to Pat Moss Carlsson, sister of Stirling and an accomplished rallyist in her own right. The Carlssons resided near Canne on the French Riviera with a daughter, a swimming pool and a pony.

He was born March 5, 1929, at Trollhattan, Sweden, near where the Saab cars are built. Naturally he was an accomplished skier and slightly mad, at his own admission, about motorcycles long before he took any interest in 4-wheeled mounts. He started dirt-track cycle racing and cross-country dashes when he was about 17 on Norton and Royal Enfield machines. Late in 1950, Carlsson was inducted into the Army for mandatory service, and became Sweden's Soldier of the Year in 1951. Mustered out, he took up rallying Volvos. In 1954 he began his long association with Saab, initially as a prototype tester at the factory, then as a professional rallyist, last as a public relations representative after his 1968 "retirement." There was a very short defection to the Swedish VW team but Eric quickly returned to Saab.

Carlsson won his first Saab outing in western Sweden and quickly established himself as the man to beat in Scandinavian circles. In later years Erik established the same reputation internationally. Among his early major successes were a victory in the Swedish National Cup Trials in 1955 and 1st overall in the Finnish Rally of 1,000 Lakes in 1957 and 1958, as well as both ice racing and road racing championships at home.

In 1959 Carlsson came into his own, winning the European rally title. Along the way, he also repeated as both road racing and ice racing champion in Sweden, and took 1st overall in both the Rally to the Midnight Sun and the major German rally, and 2nd in the Adriatic Rally. The following season was relatively quiet. Erik won the Swedish racing title and took his initial RAC victory. In 1961 Carlsson repeated in the British rally, was 1st overall in the Acropolis Rally in Greece, and 4th overall in the Monte Carlo, which stretched from the northern part of Europe to the Mediterranean.

He won Monte Carlo outright in 1962, along with the 3rd successive RAC title. In the Geneva and Acropolis Rallys he was 2nd. In 1963 he met Pat Moss. She recalled this of their meeting: "There was this huge paw, knocking on the window as I was looking at a map. I rolled down the window, and it held out an orange. As

118

I took it, I saw Erik's face for the first time." Pat became his wife later that year. In cars, Erik scored his greatest triumph by winning his 2nd consecutive Monte Carlo. He was also 2nd in the Midnight Sun and in the Spa-Sophia-Liege Marathon de la Route. Only 20 of the 124 starters managed to finish. On an attempt to win the RAC again, he was 3rd.

In 1964 Carlsson won the Ralli di Fiori in Italy. Pat was 2nd. Ninety-four cars started the East African Safari that season. Only 21 finished on time. Erik was 2nd overall and a class winner. He was 2nd in the Coupe des Alpes, Pat was 3rd. He won his class and was 2nd overall in the Polish Rally. In the Spa-Sophia-Liege, he was 2nd and class victor, and Pat was 4th. They were 2 of the 20 survivors of 106 starters that season. Erik was 2nd in the Geneva Rally.

Erik started tapering off after that, and in 1968 he supposedly retired. But in 1969 he came back for a "last" challenge, the Baja 1000 Off-Road Race in Mexico. Despite a broken drive shaft that required 7 hours to fix, he finished 3rd in the production car class. The following year, he was stuck 6 hours in a bog. Pat got stuck there, too, but managed to get away to a 5th in class. Pat hadn't let the birth of their daughter, Susan Patricia, late in 1969 slow her down.

PAT MOSS CARLSSON

Pat's father was Alfred Moss, dentist and Indianapolis racer back before British and other European drivers were doing that sort of thing. Her mother was a hill-climber and rallyist both before and after marrying Alfred Moss. Her big brother was Stirling Moss. No surprise, then, that Pat Moss became interested in cars and what could be done with them. The surprise was that she took so long in getting around to it.

Born about 1935 in Thames Ditton, horses came first in her life. And she was good with them, being at one time a member of the British National Show Jumping team. Stirling had his cars in the barn near her horses, and she "hated the bloody mechanical things," she said later. But he thought it was amusing to teach her to drive, so she learned at age 11, but never got behind the wheel again until she was 16. She failed her 1st official driving test. "The idea was for me to be able to get around from horse show to show. I was horse mad. Cars didn't matter then."

In 1954 Stirling's manager, Ken Gregory, got her involved in a treasure hunt rally, and that sparked her interest. She was driving a Morris Minor at the time, and started in that car, then went up the line through Austin A40s, MGs, Rileys, Sprites, Austin Healeys, and Minis. She became a factory rallyist with BMC, Ford, then Saab, and did some rallies for people like Lancia. On July 9, 1963, she married Erik Carlsson, the premier Saab rallyist. Through 1967, she also kept

active as a horsewoman, but gave up that sport little by little until, in 1970, she sold off her last jumper.

In her career, she won 7 or 8 European Ladies Championships (depending upon who's counting), competing in more than 200 rallies with remarkable success. In the gruelling 1960 Spa-Sophia-Liège Rally Marathon de la Route, strong men wilted under the 5 days of constant driving, but Pat won her class, the Ladies Cup, and the rally outright, to the consternation of most people except those who knew how perserving she was. "Stirling always said women were only good against the clock, not against other people or the elements," she said later. "I think that rally changed his mind. Or he may have been saying that just to bedevil me. He knows I react to remarks like that by trying just a bit harder the next time out."

There has never been a real rivalry between the Moss children—but plenty of kidding around. Stirling once took the young Pat to Silverstone when he was testing a new Lotus sports car. He asked if she would like a ride around the circuit, and she said yes, if he wasn't going to go too fast. Oh, no, he assured her, then proceeded, unofficially, to break the lap record, passenger and all. "Never saw a thing," said Pat. "Had my eyes shut the whole time."

DUANE CARTER

Duane Carter was one of the very few drivers who ever raced at Indianapolis after passing the age of 50. But, then, this unique man had a career in racing that dated back to 1932, or perhaps that should be 3 careers.

First, there was the normal progression from California roadster and midgets before World War II to the AAA Championship Trail and Indianapolis afterwards. Born May 5, 1913, in Fresno, Calif., Carter was racing by the age of 18. He never won a Championship Trail race, finishing 2nd in the 1953 Phoenix 100. In sprint cars on the AAA circuit he was 1950 Midwest champion, finished 2nd in 1951, and was still a top contender in 1955. His best finish at Indianapolis came when he relieved Sam Hanks in 1953. He got the Bardahl Special up to 3rd place. For the full 200-lap distance, he finished 4th in 1952.

Carter's next career in racing was perhaps more important than his driving. The Californian preceded Henry Banks as USAC's Director of Competition. He had big ideas—which brought him into conflict with important USAC executives—and he found himself out in the cold early in 1958. The behind-the-scenes story has never been told, nor is it likely to be fully related soon. Under Carter, USAC expanded aggressively into road racing, tried to beef up its stock car racing activities and attempted to expand further with international racing. Besides The Race of Two Worlds, Duane attempted to negotiate the introduction of Indianapolis-type racing

into France and Germany. A contemporary report said he envisioned a 3-race series. He also wanted to open a New York office for USAC and eventually others around the country. The New York office was apparently primarily for expansion of the professional road racing program. It only lasted a week or so because the road course owners got cold feet.

Obviously Carter was doing things on a high, wide, and handsome scale. There was conjecture that it was too high, wide, and handsome for USAC's conservative money men. USAC road races were shy of experienced personnel, plagued by short fields, and, in most cases, lack of spectators. Carter was about 6 or 7 years ahead of his time. The European idea fizzled, too, in the aftermath of the Monza episode. This was not because of the refusal of the Grand Prix drivers' union to participate; it was the result of the refusal of the European negotiators to advance the money needed to assure racing sites in France and Germany. They got gun-shy when Monza lost money 2 years in a row. Carter was also an enthusiastic proponent of realigning the U.S. formula with that of the rest of the world—too enthusiastic for Indianapolis car owners.

After remaining out of important competition much of 1958, Carter restarted a driving career, teaming with ace Daytona Beach mechanic-builder Smokey Yunick to place Smokey's Reverse Torque Special 7th at Indianapolis in 1959, earning his year's salary or a good part of it. He raced also at Springfield. In 1960 he was a Mickey Thompson driver at Indy and finished 12th. There was a gap of 2 years, then in 1963 he qualified

the Mickey Thompson Harvey Aluminum Special and drove it 250 miles until the engine blew.

Now there is a Duane Carter Jr. coming up through USAC ranks so there may be another career for Duane Sr.—adviser and No. 1 fan.

LUCKY CASNER

Ex-airline pilot, one of racing's "characters," and a wheeler-dealer of the first order, Lloyd Casner's famed luck ran out April 10, 1965. "Who wants to be 40?" he used to say. He was 39 when death found him moving along the Mulsanne straight at Le Mans at 180 m.p.h.

Casner was nominally a Miamian, but in his later years he was more an international citizen than an American, although he never gave up his citizenship or his love of his native country. Lucky's Camoradi USA cars—he *was* Camoradi from 1959 to 1961—were emblazoned in America's blue-and-white racing colors. While Stirling Moss figured in Camoradi's best known victories, Lucky himself had at least one moment of glory, in 1961 when he and Masten Gregory won the Nurburgring 1000. That same year Lucky reinforced ownership of his nickname in the Pescara Grand Prix for sports cars when, driving a Maserati, his favorite mount, to an early lead over a swarm of factory-entered Ferraris, his car overturned as he swerved to avoid another racer. Casner was badly burned, but he was back in the driver's seat a year later, again at Le Mans, which was a favorite venue.

Many people liked the lean, happy-go-lucky American. Colonel John H. Simone, another U.S. expatriate, often lent him Maseratis like the one he was testing for the 1965 endurance race at Le Mans. "He was a sensible lad, a good friend, very happy and cheerful," said Simone later. "He loved driving and was delighted when I gave him the Maserati to drive here. Just before going out on the track, he said to me: 'I'll drive for 2 or 3 laps to get the feel of it, and then we'll see what the car can do.'"

The Maserati coupe could do 200 m.p.h. on the Le Mans straights. Lucky was just braking down from such a high speed when the car spun on some wet track, slammed backwards into an earthen bank, climbed into the air, and neatly clipped a row of trees before returning to earth in a heap. Casner was thrown clear of the final smash, but he suffered fatal injuries and succumbed shortly after reaching Delagenier Hospital.

EUGENIO CASTELOTTI

Eugenio Castelotti had a short, rewarding career. Improving each time out, the promise was great, even after his inauspicious debut in the 1951 Mille Miglia when he finished 50th overall and 6th in class in a 2-litre Ferrari. By 1955 Castelotti was as fast as Ascari at

Monaco, and slightly faster than Fangio in practice at Spa.

Castelotti was born in Milan October 10, 1930. He started young, but grew up fast. In the 1952 Mille Miglia he was running 2nd before being retired. In the Portuguese sports car race he won at 85.71 m.p.h., then was leading the Monaco Grand Prix for sports cars when he stopped for a Coke. Another driver was less thirsty and won, Eugenio coming in 2nd. At Bari he was 3rd. In 1953 Castelotti was the best of the privateers, 5th overall. At the Messina 10-hour sports car race, his Ferrari won at 68.47 m.p.h. Lancia offered him a team ride in the Pan-American Road Race and Castelotti was 3rd behind Fangio and Taruffi. That same year Eugenio won the first of 3 Italian Mountain Championships. In 1954 he was running 3rd in a wet Mille Miglia when he lost oil pressure; but at Oporto he was 2nd to Villoresi.

In 1955 he saw victory at the Messina night race for a 2nd time, shared with the veteran Maurice Trintignant at 74.71 m.p.h. Castelotti also had a 2nd to Gendebien in the Dolomite GP and a 3rd to Fangio and Moss in the Swedish GP. His car gave out in the Mille Miglia again, but he finished 3rd after leading Moss for a time. At Le Mans he stormed into the lead, holding off both Fangio and Hawthorn before blowing up his engine. In the Monaco GP he got his initial formula ride and was 2nd to Trintignant. Ferrari gave him a car for the Italian GP and he was 3rd again.

The following season he scored his greatest victory, winning the Mille Miglia at 85.40 m.p.h., ahead of Col-lins, Musso, and Fangio in a pouring rain, then won the Rome GP over Moss and Behra at 103.38 m.p.h. With Fangio that year he won the Sebring 12-hour at 84.07 m.p.h., was 2nd at Nurburgring and 3rd at the Supercortemaggiore GP. He was the Italian Champion for 1956. The next season started well with victory shared with Masten Gregory, Musso, and Perdisa in the Buenos Aires 1000 at 100.77 m.p.h., as well as 3rd in the same race—Ferrari liked to move his drivers around in his cars like pawns. But there came the fatal day at Modena when Eugenio was testing a newly modified model with Behra. As the Commendatore watched, Castelotti lost control of the car entering the chicane and crashed to his death. It was March 14, 1967. Eugenio was 26 years old.

SOAPY CASTLES

Neil Castles's thing was never winning a race. Between 1950 and April 1, 1972, Soapy made over 400 starts without winning; then he went out and spoiled everything. At Greenville, S. C., he outlasted the field in a 200-mile Grand National NASCAR Eastern Division race. It was no April Fool's joke. Driving a red and white 1971 Dodge, Castles won on the race's last lap in a battle with Elmo Langley, David Pearson and Lee Roy Yarbrough. He even held the lead several times before that, and his winning average was 70.456 m.p.h. "First time I won anything since back when I was a Soapbox Champion," said Neil, who didn't appear to

be frustrated about finally winning and ruining his hard-won reputation as a loser.

Soapy always found his victory-less condition understandable and explainable simply because he was an independent in a forest of factory drivers. "I am the class of my class," the Charlotte, N.C., native declared once. "If NASCAR had class racing, I would be the independent champion. My cars go just as quick in the turns as the factory jobs, but they outpull me on the straights because they can afford to risk a higher gear and the chance of engine damage. They race, I ride.

"I once was second at Spartanburg (S.C.) in 1967. I never even thought of being first. I was worrying about blowing my engine going that fast. G.C. Spencer and me—we even share the same pit crew to save money."

The Soapy Castles Benefit Racing series was really the NASCAR qualifying race on the last day of time trials for a Grand National championship. A check for $150, plus a higher spot in the starting lineup, go to the winner. Soapy said, "These things got to be a joke. In the past couple of seasons I won all but three or four. It was fun to see how long I could keep the streak going but the money counted. They paid part of the motel bills. Motel rates have gone out of sight, but a married man has to have some place to stay."

Born January 10, 1934, Castles became committed to cars by age 10, with Buddy Shuman's garage in Charlotte his main environment outside of home and school. He resolved to become a great race driver, and began his career by running errands for the heroes of the day, many of whom doubled as moonshine runners. He became "21" at about the age of 16 or 17 and rode in Modified races. He drove in the relatively short-lived NASCAR convertible circuit, but quit when NASCAR claimed his car was illegal. Then he ran a Modified series in Europe in 1954—stocks cars, not FIA racing. He came home, made his peace with NASCAR, and began his official Grand National career in 1957 with 5 races, an average finish of 31st (rather difficult since some of the races go off with 30-car fields) and total winnings of $475. His average finish in 1969 was 11th and his purse winnings $38,822, both career highs. There was a short stint as a contract driver for Ray Fox Dodge but it didn't work out.

The 6 foot 1 inch driver-mechanic had a short career as a stunt man too, for such forgettable cinematic gems as *Thunder In Carolina* starring Rory Calhoun and various NASCAR back-up automobiles. Since he had wrecked cars for a TV series best forgotten, Castles was engaged to be the guy who went through the fence at Darlington. This was very hard on the car, but easy on Soapy's pocketbook. Besides, it was something he was unlikely to do in a race, where discretion is the better part of having undented fenders. However, in another movie stint at Charlotte, for the picture *Speedway*, Castles and another driver were to spin their mounts at 110 m.p.h. in the 3rd turn. The drivers obeyed, but a wheel came off the other car and just missed coming down in Castles's lap. Neil declared that he didn't know whether to duck or to check out the tire to see if there was still enough racing rubber for him to use. For 1970 he bought 2 Bobby Allison Daytona Chargers, considered total wrecks, and rebuilt them. He also had a Charger 500 and a Super Bee. He maintained them all, trucking them to races. Maybe that's why Soapy never won much. He was just too tired to press down on the accelerator. In 1971 he earned $22,939 driving in 38 races, nine less than the previous year. He was in the Top Five only once. And then came '72 and the victory that changed Soapy's life. He went out and won the Grand National East title.

PIERRE DE CATERS

When they first appeared, cars were the playthings of the rich. As racing started, it usually was the rich, or those who worked for the rich, who raced these monstrous machines from city to city or over the country roads pressed into service as courses. One of these early pioneers was a bearded Belgian millionaire, the Baron Pierre de Caters, born in 1875, who was most often associated with Mercedes.

The 1st major race in which the Baron did well was the 1901 Nice-Salon-Nice run of 243 miles, in which his 24-h.p. Mors finished 3rd. The following year, Caters ran the first stage of the Circuit du Nord to test a new 60-h.p. car, already entered in the Paris-Vienna race. He was 18th in the latter among 80 finishers. Caters also set an early Land Speed Record of 75.10 m.p.h. on July 29, 1902. In 1903 came the great Paris-Madrid race, which turned into a horrendous "Race to Death," as it was dubbed by its critics. The run was stopped at Bordeaux after 315 miles, many accidents, and several deaths. Caters himself ran off the road in his 90 h.p. Mercedes, but repaired the car and placed 20th of 52 finishers. In the Gordon Bennett Cup at Athy, Ireland, the Baron ran well, but dropped out on the final lap.

In 1904 de Caters raised the LSR to 97.257 m.p.h., and in the Gordon Bennett Cup, transferred to Germany, Caters finished 4th. The following year, when the race was run in the Auvergne Mountains, he was 7th. That same season he was 6th in the Circuit des Ardennes. In 1906, in the first running of a rugged road race in Sicily, the Targa Florio, the Baron pushed his Itala to 5th. Driving the same car in the Italian Grand Prix, he lasted less than a lap when a wheel collapsed.

Finally, in 1907, once again in a Mercedes, Caters won a major race—the GP car class of the Circuit des Ardennes. Averaging 57.3 m.p.h., he nipped Lee Guinness's Darracq, then announced his retirement. It was a fitting way to end an active racing career. Starting in 1908 he concentrated on aviation, becoming Belgium's first aviator, then making the first flights in Germany, Greece, Poland, and Turkey. Caters died in 1944.

DAVE CAUSEY

The Canadian-American Challenge Cup series was the story of Bruce McLaren and Denis Hulme for many years. But there are also wonderful one-shots like Tony Dean and the "scenery" (as some people call the back of the field) like cattle rancher Dave Causey, grandson of Teddy Roosevelt's Vice President, Charles W. Fairbanks. In 1970 Causey was much more than scenery; he finished the CanAm series in 4th place, with 47 points and $58,430, even though he was operating on a shoestring.

Born about 1930, Dave began racing fairly late, around 1956, in SCCA circles with a Jaguar XK140. He had few major drives in his career before the Can-Am, although he did win the Road America 500 in 1960 in a Maserati Tipo 61, and he did make Sebring for the 12-hour race as early as 1961 in a Maser. His 1st CanAm drivers were in 1967, strictly as a weekend filler; but in 1969, in a McLaren-Chevvy Mk. 6B that Dave just happened to pick up one day at a good price, he got serious. At Michigan he was 9th, in Texas 7th; the result for a few hours work, 6 CanAm points and $5,100. Not bad for a guy who couldn't even find a sponsor for his car. For 1970 Dave decided that he would try the full 10-race CanAm card if he could find a competitive machine. The car turned out to be a year-old Lola T163, driven in 1969 by Peter Revson. The car was powered by a 427 Chevrolet engine; the availability of replacement parts for this engine was a plus since Causey and his crew were all weekend volunteers who got nothing for the work except a share in the season-end pot (if there was one).

With wife Barbara scoring, and a couple of Carmel, Ind., friends who traveled to the CanAm's when they could or worked on the car nights and other weekends when they weren't earning their regular livings, Causey set forth to do battle with the pros of the well-heeled, multistaffed shops of Team McLaren, et al. In the rather no right to expect too much in the way of winnings or even finishes, even if he really pushed hard. Of course, he could just motor around and keep his nose clean, making sure to finish, but that was not his style.

So Causey raced in 1970, and aided by some good luck, he did pretty well. Ten starts, 8 finishes, and even in one of the DNF's he was classified 9th. At Mosport he was 7th, at Mt. Tremblant he broke a valve spring but was classified 9th. At Watkins Glen he had his worst finish of the year, 13th. At Edmonton things brightened considerably with a 5th. "I myself failed, not the car, he said of Mid-Ohio when the Lola spun and Dave could not restart it. But at Road America he was 3rd, and at Road Atlanta—with the leaders burning each other out—he was 2nd. At Donnybrooke Causey was 8th, at Laguna Seca 9th, at Riverside in the finale 8th again. Even scenery can have some fun after all.

FRANÇOIS CEVERT

Albert François Cevert may well typify the young driver of the Seventies. A bachelor, living in a slick Paris apartment and driving about in a Mercedes, occasionally escorting Brigitte Bardot. Tall, lean, and a standout snow and water skier. Piercing eyes, framed by a pop singer's long hair. "Not the sort of driver to be caught with grease under his fingernails," one veteran reporter of the Grand Prix put it. He arrived at these exalted heights with a minimum of experience, a maximum of confidence, and enough ready cash to buy his chances. The money also seemed to be a necessary ingredient for a successful driver of the seventies.

Cevert, born February 25, 1944, was the son of a successful Paris manufacturing jeweller. Education was an essential in his father's eyes, so François was hustled off to various schools to learn several languages as well as economics and law. His transportation at school was a 50-c.c. motorcycle, which gave way to a more useful Vespa scooter, then a Panhard Junior. His father did not think much of auto racing and went so far as to prevent Cevert's participation in the Argosy Motor Club's racing program, for which François had been nominated by a friend of his dad.

Cevert's father relented after François came back from two years of Army service (partly in Germany) in 1966, and he permitted the young man to attend the Magny Cours race driving school. There the youngster won the Volant Shell contest—this meant that as the school's best pupil he won a Formula 3 car of his choice.

He picked a 1967 Alpine, but when it was not ready for the season's opener, Cevert agreed to take a 1966 model until the new car arrived. He never did get the new car, and with the old one it was one frustration after the other. In 22 starts, he finished only 6 times. In 1968 Alpine offered a new car to make amends for the lemon, but François would have none of it. Instead, he scraped together enough money to buy a Tecno, which he drove as a private entry to win the French F3 championship, clinching the title at Albi.

Tecno offered him a factory car for 1969, and in this machine Cevert was 5th at Tulln (Vienna), 3rd at Enna's Mediterranean GP and at Monza's Lottery GP, and 5th at Pau. In the combined F1/F2 German GP, he dropped out. But the season seemed worthwhile at Rheims, when Cevert pulled out of a group of 7 cars striving for the finish and won by a tenth of a second. Among those behind were Jackie Stewart, Pedro Rodriguez, and Piers Courage. That same year Jean-Pierre Beltoise—who recently had become Cevert's brother-in-law by marrying his younger sister Jacqueline—offered him a 3-litre Matra prototype for Le Mans. François turned it down because he wanted to be ready for a proposed Tecno sports car entry, which never materialized.

Cevert was with Tecno again in 1970, driving an FVA-powered 68/70 machine for them, also piloting occasional Elf-gasoline-supported Matra Groups 5 and 6 sports car entries and—following Johnny Servoz-Gavin's decision to retire and a recommendation from Elf—getting his feet wet in F1. François's Tecno drives included a victory at Sweden's Mantrop Park, 3rds at Tulln and Paul Ricard, and a 6th at Pau. The season also included crashes at Hockenheim and Crystal Palace, but he emerged reatively unscathed.

In F1 with Ken Tyrrell, Cevert got a March-Ford 701 to drive, starting with the June 20, 1970, Dutch GP, where he retired with engine problems on the 32nd lap. But in the French GP he finished 11th, and 7th in Britain and Germany. The engine kicked out on the March again on the initial lap of the Austrian GP, but François finished 6th and earned a championship point at Monza—his best F1 appearance of the year—and was 9th in Canada. But the rear hub kayoed the car on the 63rd lap at Watkins Glen, and the engine balked again on the 9th lap in Mexico. Small wonder that team leader Stewart had switched to the new Tyrrell car for those last 3 races. The Italian GP 6th gave Cevert a single World Championship point and tied him for 22nd in the standings.

The next season was a new and exciting chapter for Cevert in both in F1 and F2. In the latter François was with Tecno, and, after a 4th at Thruxton, he got going at Pau, running the race's fastest lap before retiring. Cevert won at the Eifelrennen. At Jarma he suffered an accident. At Vallelunga he won again, and again ran the fastest lap. Another accident followed at Rouen, but not before Cevert again was fastest that day, winning a

preliminary heat. Imola saw another retirement. Mantorp Park saw another heat victory, but retirement as well.

While this F2 racing was going on, François also had a full F1 season with which to contend, backing up Stewart with a Tyrrell. The F1 season started badly. Cevert retired after 47 laps at South Africa. He was 7th in Spain while Stewart was winning. François hit a barrier at Monaco; Nanni Galli crunched the Tyrrell at Holland. But in the French GP Stewart won again, and Cevert was 2nd, 30 seconds back. François won the day's fastest lap honors, however, at 116.07 m.p.h. After a 10th in the British GP, another 2nd to Stewart followed in Germany. Cevert retired in Austria, but took a 3rd in Italy, just 9/100ths of a second behind winner Peter Gethin. A 6th in Canada was followed by Watkins Glen and the U.S. GP. Stewart faltered early in the race, finishing 5th, but his young French teammate won at 115.092 m.p.h., collecting $50,000 American dollars in the process. The victory put Cevert into 3rd place in the final season standings to World Champion Stewart and Ronnie Peterson. The future looked bright indeed.

DAVID CHAMPEAU

Dave Champeau came to races dressed as if he were a customer's man in a brokerage house—white shirt and conservative tie, slacks pressed to a knife edge, and an immaculate driving coat. Running mainly in IMCA and CSRA circuits, this native of Washington registered out of Grand Forks, N.D. He came to race and, had he survived past World War II, Dapper Dave might have become a movie star or a race champion.

Champeau was a featured player in the host of auto racing movies that poured out of Hollywood in the Twenties. Such screen stars as Clark Gable, Spencer Tracy, and Pat O'Brien were cast in these, and the racing scenes were quite real, being filmed at places like Los Angeles's Legion Ascot Speedway. The scenes were so real that at least one driver of note, Frankie Lyons, lost his life in a crash that was not part of the script of *Ten Laps To Go*. Top IMCA people like Gus Schrader and Emery Collins did some of the driving, but Champeau was one cut above them in filmland. He got fairly long speaking roles, sometimes as a secondary villain who charmed the heroine away from the garage of her future husband.

Champeau had many close calls because he was a throttle stomper who relied on his reflexes to pull off gamble after gamble. One of his closest calls was at Lakewood Park in Atlanta in 1936, when his car burst into flames coming down the main straight, then looped over. Gus Schrader unsnapped the dazed Champeau's seat harness and saved his life by dragging him out. Champeau married the widow of Billy Winn, and the war made her a widow twice over.

COLIN CHAPMAN

The sign over his parking space read "ACB Chapman." That stood for Anthony Colin Bruce Chapman. Nobody in auto racing ever called him that; it was always simply Colin Chapman. ACB Chapman sounded a bit better, perhaps, for one of the richer men in England, a man whose personal worth in Group Lotus Car Companies, Ltd., in 1970 stood at something like $17 million. Considering that Chapman started out pretty close to poor, that wasn't bad for a fellow just past 40.

The biographical details of Chapman's life are few indeed, and he has apparently preferred it that way. He gave many interviews in his days as the head of Lotus —that is, *as* Lotus, for Chapman *was* Lotus. He was chief of design from 1948 (when the Mk. 1 Lotus was built) on. He was master of the factory from the time it was located in his back yard. He was head of the racing team since driving his revamped 1930 Austin 7 trials car when a college student. He has given many interviews, but they usually ended up in a long history of various Lotus models that totaled 72 different ones through 1970.

But Chapman the man stayed pretty much hidden. All that has leaked out was this kind of thing: Anthony Colin Bruce Chapman. Born May 19, 1928, in Richmond, a suburb of London. Built his first car at age 7 when he sawed a pram axle in half and equipped his soapbox racer with crude but effective independent front suspension. Entered the University of London's College of Engineering in 1945. Did not study automotive engineering, but civil engineering. Became a regular reader at the Institute of Mechanical Engineering's Library and read just about every book and technical paper on file there before building his first real car.

The first car, Chapman built, based on a 1930 Austin 7 saloon, and later dubbed Lotus Mk. 1, had a radiator front reminiscent of a Rolls-Royce. It was entered in 2 trials and won both, with Chapman driving. Chapman built the car strictly for his own enjoyment. He had some fun with it, then put it aside to finish up his studies. Then followed a short RAF stint. He came back to the drawing board and developed Mk. 2, another trials car, again based on Austin 7 components, but powered by a Ford 10 engine (a portent of the future) and featuring recessed headlamps that swiveled with the steering. About this time he joined the 750 Motor Club, and Mk. 3, a 750 racer, was the result. He took all the silverware in sight with this car in 1951, until the club changed their rules to make Chapman's car ineligible. He retaliated by announcing Mk. 5, a 100 m.p.h. 750 Formula car that kept them guessing for years, especially each time Chapman announced he was unveiling a new car. He never built a Mk. 5, nor apparently ever had any intention to; he just used the announcement as a way to get back at those who tried to legislate him out of competition.

The first car Chapman designed and built for someone else was the Mk. 4, which he sold to Mark Lawson, Lotus's first paying customer. The first real production car was the Mk. 6, which was a kit car; that is, one that the buyer put together himself, thus saving a lot of money in taxes and labor. Just over 100 were sold between 1952 and 1955. Power plants included 2-litre BMW's, 1,172-c.c. Fords, 1,100-c.c. Climaxes, and 1.5-litre MG engines, the latter the most successful. Chapman himself also was racing through these years, especially the Mk. 8, an aerodynamically finned sports car, powered by an MG engine. But Lotus still was very much a cottage industry for him. He held a full-time engineering job with British Aluminum, and continued to hold that job until 1955, when he finally quit to become a full-time car builder.

Chapman's first company was known as the Lotus Engineering Co., founded January 1, 1952, with his wife, whom he met in 1945, and Michael Allen as partners. Up until the time he married the former Hazel Williams (Lotuses were being built in a garage in back of her house), money was tight, and only the destruction of the first Mk. 6 prototype on its way to a race late in 1952 saved the company, as the car was transmuted into insurance money. It was reorganized as Lotus Engineering Co., Ltd., in February 1953. Mks. 9, 10, and 11 quickly followed Chapman's full-time attention to car matters. The breakthrough was accomplished in 1957, when Lotus made a big splash at the Earls Court Auto Show. Mk. 7, an improved version of Mk. 6, debuted at the show (nearly 3,000 of these were to be sold eventually), as did Mk. 14, more familiarly known as the Elite (although production did not start, for monetary reasons, until 1959).

Chapman himself already was recognized as a design genius. In 1957, for example, he advised BRM on suspension improvements and designed a new chassis for Vanwall. Perhaps it was the Vanwall work that finally sparked Chapman to enter the single-seater field. (He had that goal, of course, all along, as do most men who take up sporting design in Britain and on the Continent.) Anyway, before 1957 had ended, the Mk. 12, a front-engined Formula 2 car, powered by a 1,475-c.c. Coventry-Climax engine, was introduced by Lotus. Raced in F2 in 1957, the same basic car, now powered by 2- and 2.2-litre engines, made Formula 1 grids in 1958. But they were plagued by many different ills, were basically unreliable, and generally proved that even a genius can sometimes flub. The best F1 finish for Mk. 12 was Cliff Allison's 4th in the Belgian Grand Prix.

There is no point to detailing every car Chapman's fertile brain evolved. The majority proved successful enough for Lotus to grow into one of the richest "cottage" builders in Britain. The profitability of the company started rising at the rate of some 50 percent a year. On sales of $10.7 million in 1969, as a recent example, Chapman's profits were $1.7 million before taxes. Small wonder that while other builders of quality, small-production machinery were having problems—Ferrari, for example, had to bail himself out by tying himself to Fiat in 1969—Lotus just raked in money (and Chapman kept most of it; he had a well-deserved reputation for holding onto his money with both hands).

Chapman the designer/builder was fabulously successful. So, too, was Chapman the racing entrepreneur. After a second false GP start the Mk. 16, which again was unreliable in both Formulas 1 and 2, Chapman got on the racing beam with Mk. 18, which was his first rear-engined car, following the lead of John Cooper. There were early teething problems and some crashes. But in 1960–61 Lotus successes included victories in the Monaco GP (1960–61), U.S. GP (1960), and German GP (1961), all scored by Stirling Moss, driving a Rob Walker-entered Lotus.

As important as Moss was to Chapman, the most important driver of them all was Jim Clark. The Scotsman joined the factory as number 1 driver in 1960 and stayed with Chapman until his death in 1968 in an F2 Lotus. The Englishman and the Scot were alike in many ways in temperament, and Chapman was almost a second father to Clark. Jim won his first *grande épreuve* in 1962 (Belgium), then scored 24 more for the most victories in GP racing history. He also scored many times in F2 and sports cars, and in the 1965 Indianapolis 500 as well.

The major Chapman racing car designs were: the Mk. 21 (1961 GP car, in which Innes Ireland won the U.S. GP); the Mk. 25 (1962 GP car, the first modern monocoque racing car, and winner in 12 World Championship races in Clark's hands); the Mk. 29 (1963 Indy car in which Clark was 2nd); the Mk. 33 (1964 GP car, winner of 7 championship GPs, all by Clark); the Mk. 34 (1964 Indy car); and the Mk. 38 (Clark's 1965 Indy winner, also used in 1966, when Clark was 2nd again). Maurice Phillippe joined Lotus and worked with Chapman on the Mk. 42 (1966's original Indy car, but used in 1967 instead); the Mk. 43 (a stopgap GP car for 1966, which won only the U.S. GP); the Mk. 49 (1967–68 GP car, in which Stewart scored his final 5 championship victories, and in which Graham Hill won 4 GPs, Jo Rindt 3 and Jo Siffert one for Rob Walker); the Mk. 56 (1968 4-wheel-drive Indy car); the Mk. 63 (1969 4-wheel-drive GP cars); and the Mk. 72 (1970 GP car in which Rindt won 4 GPs and Emerson Fittipaldi one, and in which Fittipaldi dominated GP racing in 1972).

Between 1960 and 1972, Chapman's designs won 52 Grands Prix—every one held in modern times at least once, save for the Canadian GP. Clark was World Champion in 1963 and 1965, Hill in 1968, Rindt in 1970 (posthumously), and Fittipaldi in 1972. Chapman won the F1 Manufacturers Championship in each of those years, of course. He flew back and forth to the races in his own private aircraft (which became a passion, and possibly a new source of Chapman activity in the seventies). The garage behind Hazel's house gave way in 1952 to a small factory in Hornsey, then to a real plant in Chestnut in 1958, and finally to Hethel in 1966, where production soared to 4,500 vehicles.

No matter how large Lotus sports car production went, however, a small section of the factory and a large part of Chapman's own time were devoted to pure racing. It served him well, and did not cost all that much considering that Chapman always was able to get first class sponsorships such as Gold Leaf and John Player cigarettes for his F1 teams, and varied F2 sponsors. Also, many of his later drivers actually paid for their rides, either directly or by bringing sponsors with them; Rindt, for example, was alleged to have bought his ride in his championship year of 1970. And his racing activities actually were Lotus's main promotional effort; little was spent in advertising or publicity outside of these racing activities. Chapman had come a long way from his days as an impecunious student, but not too long a way when it came to watching where his pence and pounds went.

FERNAND CHARRON

Fernand Charron was born in France in 1866 and was a bicycle champion long before he ever saw a motor car. In all, Charron won 116 two-wheeler races, so it was only natural that he would try the new fangled four-wheelers. Besides, the girl he married was none other than Adolphe Clement's daughter.

Charron was 31 when he first raced a car, a Panhard, in the Marseilles-Paris-La Turbierace. He crashed. But in the Paris-Dieppe race, Charron was 3rd that same year, and the following season won 2 big ones—Marseilles-Hyers-Nice at 21.3 m.p.h. and the Paris-Amsterdam-Paris race of 889 miles at 26.9 m.p.h. Fernand also was 2nd to Rene De Knyff in the Paris-Bordeaux and retired from the Tour de France after his gearbox jammed and he had to drive 25 miles in reverse.

In 1899 Charron won the 351-mile Paris-Bordeaux race at 29.9 m.p.h., and the next season he took the initial (and longest) Gordon Bennett race at 38.6 m.p.h. He also was 3rd in the Nice-Marseilles. In 1901, after recording a 6th for Panhard in the Paris-Berlin, Charron left to become a partner in CGV—Charron, Giradot, Voight—and it was in this marque that he drove his last race, retiring from the 1902 Circuit des Ardennes. In later years Charron joined his father-in-law at Clement-Bayard and later founded Alda. He died in 1928.

BILL CHEESBOURG

Big Bill Cheesbourg came riding out of the great Southwest, tall in the driver's seat, so tall that he might have posed a streamlining problem in the modern low-slung Indianapolis-type car. He was 6 feet 2 inches and weighed a muscular 200 pounds with shoulders suited for a football tackle. That is why he began driving stock-car races as his part-time career progressed. When he decided to try for Indianapolis and tributary races, after a successful debut as Arizona midget sprint and roadster champion, the cars were mainly rugged, spacious Kurtis designs where a full-sized man, had room to stretch. In the rear-engined, low-slung cars running nowadays, there would just be no place to fit all that Cheesbourg.

Born June 12, 1927, in Tucson, where he lived with wife and 5 children, Bill passed his rookie Indianapolis driver test in 1956 after much urging from long-time friend Jimmy Bryan. There was no Cheesbourg ride, however, until the following year when he qualified a dog car, saw it bumped, got another ride in the Seal Line Special, and settled down to wait out the early trophy dash when a leaking fuel tank sidelined him. He enjoyed 26th-place money (which, after all, is more than 1st prize in many World Championship races). The next year he qualified a Novi at 142.546 m.p.h. and just made the field; he drove a steady race to finish 10th.

That made him a member of the Champion 100 m.p.h. club and virtually assured him of an annual ride in something or other for the Memorial Day classic. And, with the exception of the Dean Van Lines car that he had in 2nd place in the 1961 renewal (before becoming involved in the 5-car accident), the vehicles he drove

fit the "something-or-other" category. He drove mainly Fords in the USAC stock-car circuit with just enough success to make the tour worthwhile. It was inevitable that Big Bill would be at Indianapolis for some years to come, hoping to get that annual ride, and hoping that by some miracle his Clunker of the Year would outlast the really competitive cars. He was. But with the advent of the rear-engined jobs, Cheesbourg finally came only as a spectator.

There is a saying that it's all very nice to have anywhere from 2 to 10 hotshots in a given race, but the "scenery" is a must, too. Big Bill took up a great deal of scenery while he was competing.

CHEVROLET BROTHERS
(LOUIS, GASTON, and ARTHUR)

Joseph Felicien Chevrolet, a clock maker of La Chaux-de-Fonds, Switzerland, was the father of Louis Joseph Chevrolet, who was born on Christmas Day 1878. Gaston was born 5 years later when the family had moved to Beaune in Burgundy, France; and Arthur was born 3 years after him.

Louis learned about machinery early; he also learned about wine, spending the earliest part of his youth as a guide in local wine cellar. While still a boy, he invented a wine pump to ease the task of decanting the casks. Apprenticed to the local bicycle shop, he found there a 1.25-b.h.p. De Dion motorized tricycle. He taught himself to repair it and moved on to become a technician at the factories of Mors, Darracq, Hotchkiss, and De Dion Bouton—all early automobiles involved in the first French town-to-town races.

Inflamed by the stories—however inaccurate—of the rapid motorization of the New World, Louis came to Montreal in 1900 where he spent about 6 months as a chauffeur (then synonymous with master mechanic). He rejoined De Dion at its U.S. headquarters in Brooklyn, N.Y., moving in mid-1902 to the Fiat agency in Manhattan. In 1905 he married Suzanne Treyvoux and also began his official racing career.

Morris Park in the Bronx was "the countryside" in those days, and the Hippodrome there was the scene of many sporting events, including automobile racing. On May 20, Louis won a miler, then in the 3-mile feature he beat Barney Oldfield and Walter Christie for the gold medal and a watch. He drove his 90-h.p. Fiat a record average speed of 68 m.p.h.

That set Louis up for the 1906 Vanderbilt Cup on Long Island, 2nd of its kind and boasting an international field. A clipping of the day tells what happened: "Driving at high speed, he grazed a pole which deflected him into a fence, a large section of which he carried with him into a field, where his axle was broken by striking a projecting boulder. . . ." That time he was relatively unscathed, but he was to spend approximately

3 years between 1905 and 1920 recovering from serious racing accidents. He received a tremendous press for this reckless style, with one journalist tagging him as "the most audacious driver in the world."

That was good enough to make Louis part of a touring group organized by Carl Fisher (later to conceive the Indianapolis Motor Speedway and Miami Beach). They toured America's fairs and horse tracks giving exhibitions. Fisher, Oldfield, and Earl Kizer were other drivers in this endeavor, one of several touring groups that did much to popularize the motor car. Louis brought Gaston and Arthur over to join him when they were old enough.

In 1906 Louis left Fiat to join Christie in Philadelphia and help build a new front-drive passenger car as well as a Darracq-engined Land Speed Record machine. Chevrolet drove this monster at Ormond Beach, Fla., to a new record of 119 m.p.h. The record was soon broken in the same car by either Victor Hemery or his mechanic Victor Demogeot; one of them was the first man to go 2 miles a minute on land.

In 1907 Chevrolet went to work for William Durant, who had just bought out Buick. Brother Arthur also was hired. It is said that Durant invited the two Chevrolets to Flint, Mich., to get a personal glimpse of their abilities by holding a match race. Louis won easily, but Durant selected Arthur to be his personal chauffeur-mechanic, declaring he "would not take any chances with that crazy Louis." The famed Buick Bugs, which the Chevrolets and Wild Bob Burman drove to many victories, came in 1909. Louis and Bob acted as design consultants, with A. E. De Waters and E. C. Richards apparently executing the actual design work.

The 2,600-pound Bugs boasted a 622-cu. in. displacement from an over-square bore-stroke ratio of 6.0×5.5 inches. The 4-cylinder o.h.v. engine boasted 2 spark plugs per cylinder. Arthur, Louis, and Burman all performed feats of derring-do in these cars. Arthur won his class and set a world record in the first event ever held at the Indianapolis Speedway, in 1909. One of the cars is still owned by General Motors.

Meanwhile, the Chevrolet brothers were racing to vicorty in the hustings. Often, the reports of the day failed to differentiate between them, by omitting even the first initial, so it is difficult to know who won what. An educated guess is that Louis won 27 major events during his driving career, not to mention innumerable match races. That would leave 36 to be divided between Gaston and Arthur.

The significant action for Louis by 1911 was not in driving, but in the business and engineering world. Durant had lost control of GM in 1910 and was plotting to regain primacy in the automobile industry. He bought the use of the famous Chevrolet name at the same time that he contracted with Louis to design the car—with emphasis on the engine—to go with it. Louis's designs, with engineering detail by Étienne Planche, resulted in

a prototype in November 1911, by which time the Chevrolet Motor Company had been organized. Louis was a major stockholder. Almost 3,000 cars were sold in 1912. In 1913 Durant decided he wanted to challenge the Model T head-on, so he bought two other firms in Lansing, Mich., the Little Motor Car Company and Mason Motor Company, giving the Little's economical runabout the Chevrolet name. This did not sit well with Louis, who wanted his name and talents devoted only to the 6-cylinder luxury car. In 1914 they split, and Louis was so disgusted he disposed of his stock, thus losing the chance to become incredibly wealthy.

Even before his breakup with Durant, Chevrolet was involved with Albert Champion, also from France, who was to found 2 spark plug empires—Champion and AC. Here again he had the opportunity to amass a fortune. However, they argued over a personal matter—during which Chevrolet administered a terrible beating to Champion—and that was the end of that prospect. Some time later Bob Stranahan, Champion's racing representative, managed to get Champion's new spark plugs into an Indianapolis-winning Frontenac by working through Gaston and C. C. Van Ranst, who worked for Louis.

Louis had founded the Frontenac Motor Corporation in 1914. named after a French colonial governor of North America, with the eventual aim of producing a passenger car. With Planche assisting, he began to create the plans for such a car, including 4 racing versions. The Blood Brothers Machine Company of Allegan (near Kalamazoo), Mich., had been planning a runabout called the Cornelian for about 2 years. Louis was hired to collaborate in the design and construction of this revolutionary light passenger car and act as team captain for a racing team of modified Cornelians. He put his own Frontenac project in mothballs and enthusiastically joined in. The racing version won on the Kalamazoo dirt track, then Joe Boyer qualified it for the 1915 Indianapolis 500. It lasted exceptionally well, 75 laps, and was to be the prototype for a passenger car. It was at least 500 pounds lighter than any other car in the race, used a stressed aluminum skin, and it had no axles. Instead it had 3 transverse springs, one above and 2 below, attached to brackets which carried the rear wheels. Power was transmitted via 2 universal shafts from the frame-mounted final drive unit. The front wheels were attached via brackets to 2 transverse springs and were steered through chain and link rods. The car was revolutionary, but the Blood Brothers, just after beginning production, abandoned the project because they were selling all the steel U-joints that had been developed for the Cornelian to other manufacturers.

Undaunted, Louis revived the Frontenac for the 1916 Indy. By generous use of aluminum and close attention to weight saving, his cars weighed in 500 pounds lighter than the competition, while still boasting 300-cu.in. long-stroke o.h.c. engines. Remember that such use of aluminum was new, yet Louis made even such items as the cylinder block, pistons, crankcase, camshaft cover, intake manifold, transmission cover, water and oil pumps, rear-axle center section, pedal brackets, and starting crank of aluminum—as well as the body and underpan.

The Frontenac engine was quite ingenious. All 4 valve seats for a given cylinder were in a single iron casting, around which the cylinder head was cast. The head was integral with the block, which had open sides and ends covered by aluminum plating. The cast-iron cylinder sleeves were shrunk into the heated block. Pistons were "umbrella" form and were designed for minimum weight and bearing surface, combined with optimum cooling capability. The engine had dry sump lubrication; the oil reservoir (12 gallons) mounted in front of the firewall was finned with copper. The underpan was contoured to force air over these fins. The engine was mounted entirely apart from the transmission, which was carried a midships on its own 3-point mounting. The rear end was without a differential. Gasoline was carried in 2 narrow tanks toward the rear and below the frame, thus equalizing weight. Minor mechanical woes plagued the cars at the Brickyard, but on the board circuits they became the cars to beat.

The 3-year gap in racing caused by World War I found Chevrolet working on the American Beauty 6 and on airplane engines. It was then he met C. W. Van Ranst and learned about supercharging. An auto racing version of Van Ranst's gear-train-driven 300-cu.in. engine with d.o.h.c. and supercharger was supposed to be ready for the first postwar Indianapolis in 1919. It did not make it, but Louis refurbished the Fronty cars to be driven by himself, Gaston, Joe Boyer, and Ralph Mulford. Boyer and Mulford were casualties of mechanical trouble, but Gaston finished 9th and Louis staged a spectacular duel with Ralph DePalma for 6th. The 2 had been fighting for the lead until both had to repair parts outside the power train. The duel ended when Louis lost a wheel and roared down the straight on 3 wheels, the grinding wheel spindle snapping the timer's wire (and almost killing Elmer Shannon in the car behind).

For 1920, the Frontenacs were ready again. Louis had contracted to make a set of 4 cars to run under the name of Monroe Motor Company and had also entered his own 3 Frontenacs. He convinced Van Ranst to join him in the venture. The racing formula had dropped to 183 cu.in. Chevrolet used much of the o.h.c. Fronty design for his new power plant, but went to iron for the block and head casting and to a dual o.h.c. layout driven by spur gears. Louis also sought to solve steering component failure by going to heat-treated vanadium steel steering arms. Unfortunately the factory producing them forgot to heat treat them properly, and although all 7 cars qualified, 6 retired with broken steering arms. One lasted with Gaston Chevrolet at the wheel. He won the race—only to be killed in a Fronty crash with Eddie O'Donnell at a Beverly Hills, Calif., board

track on November 25, 1920. Meanwhile, Arthur had been severely hurt in a practice crash for the 1920 Indianapolis and never competed at the Brickyard again.

Louis quit driving when Gaston was killed, but he did not quit designing. He startled his competitors—Duesenberg and Ballot—by designing his own straight-8 engine for 1921. They had gone that route, but never expected Chevrolet to abandon his d.o.h.c. 4. Chevrolet's 8 copied Ernest Henry's Ballot crankshaft and integrated it into an 8-cylinder version of the d.o.h.c. design of the previous year. The cars ran perfectly up to 3,000 r.p.m., then began wiping con rod bearings. Tommy Milton qualified in a hastily patched Frontenac (Monroe) and went on to win, never exceeding 3,000 r.p.m. One of the 16 spark plugs gave up firing so Tommy, won on 7½ cylinders. Jules Ellingboe in a Fronty 4-cylinder finished third, and Mulford finished 9th. Chevrolet had designed 2 cars for Indy in successive years and had won with both.

But he was still a loser in the business world. This time Allan A. Ryan and the Stutz Motorcar Co. raised $1 million to back production of a Frontenac passenger car as part of the Stutz line. With Van Ranst's aid, the prototype had passed all tests, and Louis watched production begin in a giant new factory in Detroit. The joy was cut short by the depression of 1922. The Stutz empire collapsed, and because there was no differentiation between the bills of Louis's Frontenac Corp. of Michigan and Ryan's Frontenac Corp. of Delaware, Louis inherited all the debts.

Chevrolet still had the Fronty-Ford conversion head for the Model T going for him. This had been developed in 1920 at the urging of Van Ranst at the Chevrolet Bros. Manufacturing Co. of Indianapolis. They built 5 machines for dirt-track racing, and the Fronty-Fords were immediately successful. Two were entered by others in the 1922 Indianapolis race, proving reliable, if too slow for the competition. Louis's entries in 1922 were 4-cylinder cars, using the top end of the straight-8. Tom Alley brought a Frontenac-Monroe into 9th place. For 1923 he put rotary valves in one of the straight-8s, but the car never started. More important was the Barber-Warnock Special entered by an Indianapolis Ford dealer —a Fronty-Ford which finished 5th overall, humiliating the factory Mercedes and Bugattis. Arthur Chevrolet had prepared the car, making himself a hero with Model T owners everywhere.

Barber-Warnock entered 3 cars for 1924, but although all were running at the finish, they were blown off by the supercharged straight-8s of Deusenberg. Louis built a front-wheel-drive Fronty-Ford for 1926, its stock Ford block sleeved to make the 91-cu. in. limit (a special short-throw crank helped). Peak r.p.m. were 6,000 with a Roots supercharger gear driven off the nose of the crankshaft. This Hamlin Special was one of the most durable of race cars, still competing in 1932. Although it was successful on short tracks, something always went wrong at Indy. The Chevrolets produced all sorts of Frontenac heads, right up to 1928 when a s.o.h.c. version spelled the end of Model T racing development.

Louis, meanwhile, managed to suffer a few more business reverses. A fresh attempt to get into the passenger-car field flopped in 1924 when he was unable to complete financing in time to pick up his option on the Aryll engine, power plant for the new Frontenac venture. In 1926 Louis and Arthur evolved the design of an efficient aircraft engine, called the Chevrolair 333. The brothers split their lifelong partnership over it, Arthur getting the speed equipment business, and Louis joining Baltimore Ford dealer Glenn L. Martin in a new aircraft company. With the Depression in 1929, Louis ceded his interests to Martin, who eventually used the Martin 4-333 (née Chevrolair) as the base of an aircraft empire. There was even a Frontenac built in Canada. It was just another example of how a good lawyer could have helped Louis; Chevrolet had reserved the Frontenac name only for the United States, not for Canada.

Louis designed a 10-cylinder radial aircraft engine for which he received a patent in 1935, by which time he had turned the corner into true old age; he did not try hard to do anything with it. In 1934, his eldest son had died, and the home of his sister in New Jersey—where he had the memorabilia and documents and engineering drawings of a lifetime stored—burned down. Then Louis had a cerebral hemorrhage. He retired to Florida where he stayed until 1941, when he and his wife came back to Detroit for medical treatment. He died there on June 6. Brother Arthur, working as a boat mechanic at the time, hanged himself in Miami on April 16, 1946.

LUIGI CHINETTI

Ferraris are delicate automobiles? That's the impression you got when you visited any auto show in the Eastern United States at which the Italian marque was displayed. They inevitably were shown behind barricades, as if the merest touch of a finger might dent a fender, the merest breath might scratch the paint. The man responsible for such treatment of a car that should be able to hold its own even in the wildest American auto show crowd was Luigi Chinetti.

Born about 1906, Luigi Chinetti was a short, square man with a strange accent—Frenchmen thought it Italian, Italians French, Americans didn't really know. But he was Enzo Ferrari's personal representative from the Atlantic Coast to the Mississippi River. Anyone in charge of a territory that large for as valuable a commodity as Ferrari cars understandably might choose to run his business like a fiefdom. Chinetti did.

The word most often used to describe him is unpre-

possessing. Yet he knew cars as few other men do. Chinetti's knowledge came from the driver's seat, both with Alfa Romeo at the time Ferrari worked for that marque, and with Ferrari from its earliest days.

Of Chinetti's own earliest days, little is known because he not only refused to talk about himself but rarely obliged visitors seeking information, even about Ferrari cars. But record books show that by 1932—when he was 26—Chinetti was a member of Alfa's competition department. Between then and 1953 he drove in every Le Mans 24-Hour Race; since there were no races in 1936 and from 1940 to 1948, this adds up to 12 Le Mans appearances in a row.

The bespectacled Italian won no less than 3 times. In 1932 he and Raymond Sommer shared a 2.3-litre Alfa; Chinetti was not well and drove only 3 hours of the 24. Yet he shared the victory at 76.48 m.p.h. The following year Chinetti's car crossed the finish line just 10 seconds behind the immortal Tazio Nuvolari in Alfa's last year of competition until the late sixties. To salve his hurt feelings, Chinetti shared the same Alfa with Louis Chiron, and together they won the Belgian 24-Hour Race that year at 72.66 m.p.h.

In 1934 Chinetti was back at Le Mans with Philippe Etancelin. A stone punctured the Alfa's gas tank, and it limped into the pits leaking furiously. Chewing gum, mashed assiduously by the drivers and the pit crew for the rest of the race, saved the day. The gum held, and Chinetti crossed the line for his 2nd victory at an average of 74.74 m.p.h., 112 miles ahead of the 2nd place

130

car after crashes had cut the field. Following the race, Etancelin attempted to drive the car home—and the gum fell out.

It was 1947 before Chinetti was again to taste victory at Le Mans. In 1939 he fled to France to escape Mussolini's police; the following year he had to flee to Spain, Portugal, and, eventually, to the United States. Chinetti spent World War II using his mechanical skills to the fullest. When peace came, he joined forces with a fellow Italian mechanical magician, Alfred Momo, tuning Rolls-Royces in New York City.

In 1946 Chinetti returned to Italy for the first time in 7 years and visited his old Alfa friend, Ferrari. The story is told that it was Luigi's suggestion that Enzo—then a machine-tool maker—go into the carbuilding business. Enzo agreed if Chinetti would buy 5 cars a year to resell in America; with incredible optimism for that time, Luigi promised to order 20.

In 1948 Briggs Cunningham, then of Greens Farms, Conn., purchased the first Ferrari brought into the United States by Chinetti, a 2-litre car. Chinetti's first garage was on West 19th Street, a dark, completely unidentifiable location except for a prancing horse decal stuck in one window. Like the man with the better mousetrap, Chinetti let his customers grope their way to his door. In time newer, larger (but certainly not fancier) Ferrari premises were opened on West 54th Street near the docks on 11th Avenue. There he remained, although Ferrari sales in the United States, dominated by Chinetti, were larger than anywhere else in the world, including Italy.

Chinetti still was not through as a driver, however. In 1947—when he was 41—he brought a 2-litre to Montlhéry and won the 12-Hour Race at 72.96 m.p.h.; a feat he repeated in 1950 at 69.4 m.p.h. In between these high spots was an even higher one; in 1949 England's Lord Selsdon of Croydon purchased a Ferrari for Le Mans, and Chinetti agreed to act as his codriver. The owner drove all of 20 minutes; Chinetti piloted the car the rest of the 24 hours. The American Ferrari dealer had won his 3rd Le Mans at 82.27 m.p.h., the initial victory for the Ferrari marque there.

In 1951 Chinetti took a 4-litre Ferrari to Central America with Piero Taruffi and won the inaugural Pan American Road Race at 88.04 m.p.h. The following year —at age 46—he scored his last big placing, a 2nd in the same race. Small wonder that, when Chinetti gave out an opinion on a race, or a car, or a driving technique, men listened. With his driving days numbered, the maestro turned to aiding promising racing talent. Back in 1932 he had spotted Sommer; through the succeeding years, others he chose to bring under his mantle included Guy Moll, the Marquis de Portago, Eugenio Castelloti, Americans Richie Ginther, Dan Gurney, and Phil Hill, and the Rodriguez brothers from Mexico.

If you wanted a Ferrari to race and could prove you knew what you were doing behind its wheel, perhaps Chinetti would speak to you kindly on occasion. If you were one of those people who had money to spend to show off a Ferrari on the streets of New York or Washington or Atlanta, he would tolerate you, provided you were humble and awaited his pleasure. But if you were merely one of the curious, one of the fascinated, who found the Ferrari an irresistible draw when you entered an auto show, he would have none of you and your fingerprints on his car fenders. You had to stay behind that fence where you belonged.

LOUIS CHIRON

Louis Alexander Chiron was most unusual among racing drivers—he pursued his chosen profession until the age of 60, then retired from active competition to manage one of the world's great races, the Grand Prix of Monaco. Chiron was born in Monaco in August 1899 with dual Monegasque and French citizenship since his father was a Frenchman. He was only 13 when he passed the French driving test of the day. Three years later he volunteered as an artilleryman in the French Army after the outbreak of World War I, but because of his age and driving skills he was assigned as a chauffeur to Marshals Foch and Pétain.

Following the war, Chiron drifted for a time, building his savings, and by 1923 he had saved enough to buy the dream car of that day, a 1.5-litre Bugatti with which he entered amateur hillclimbing competition. Switching to a 2-litre Bug, Chiron became a professional the following year, competing in 6 hillclimbs and winning his first event.

In 1925 Louis moved into flat racing at Monza and Comminges and in the Grand Prix de la Côte d'Azur, in which he finished 2nd in a giant Delage behind Robert Benoist. The feat earned Louis an offer to join the Bugatti factory team, an offer he quickly snapped up. In the years remaining before war clouds began to darken the racing scene on the Continent, Chiron won 2 dozen major Grands Prix and the Spa 24-Hour Race, and was 2nd in another dozen major GPs and other races. His Bugatti victories included Italy (1928), Spain (1928–29), Germany (1929), Belgium (1930), Monaco (1931), France (1931), and Czechoslovakia (1931–32). In a Alfa Romeo he won Spain and Czechoslovakia a 3rd time in 1933 and France a 3rd time in 1934. He won the French GP in a 4.5-litre Talbot in 1937 and 1947.

For all of his victories, Chiron was most identified in that period with a race he never won, the Targa Florio. In his best finishes he was 2nd twice, and also 3rd and 4th. Louis himself said the Targa was an overblown, boring version of the hillclimb, but that did not prevent him from trying repeatedly to win this oldest road race in the world. In his initial Targa, in 1928, he had the unusual distinction of doing more than the required 5 laps because Vincenzo Florio failed to flag his finish, something the Targa organizer never failed to do again.

In 1930 Louis had probably his best Targa Florio performance; for a time it was thought he had won the race since he had crossed the finish line (properly flagged) 1st, but it turned out that Archille Varzi, who started after Chiron, was the winner in an independent Alfa Romeo. That race's finish was really exciting. On the last lap from Polizzi, some 3,000 feet in the Sicilian hills, Chiron's racing mechanic, a youth who never before had competed in such a race, fainted from the excitement and, possibly, from cockpit fumes. The boy rolled about helplessly in his seat, jostling Louis just enough to let the Bugatti slide along a patch of gravel and break its left front wheel. Chiron changed the wheel himself, leaving the remnants of the effort on the road as he tore off toward the finish line.

Varzi, meanwhile, was having his own troubles. A mechanic refueling his car accidentally poured gasoline on the hot exhaust, and the Alfa caught fire. Varzi and others beat out the flames, and he was off in pursuit of Chiron in a scorched but still serviceable car. Chiron was 1st across the line, but the tally sheets showed Varzi had a 2-minute advantage after nearly 7 hours of gruelling driving.

Chiron continued racing with Bugatti through 1932, when he joined Rudi Caracciola in the Scuderia CC with twin Alfas. Back in 1929 he had driven a 2-year-old Delage, a 1.5-litre supercharged GP car, at Indianapolis and finished 7th after spending better than 16 minutes in the pits for fueling and tire changes. But most of his fame was gained in the Bug.

A favorite race, especially in light of his later service as master of the same competition, was the Monaco GP, which was started in 1929. Chiron was there in a Bugatti in 1930. He set a lap record and finished 2nd, despite a broken throttle stop that gave him carburetion when he wanted none and stopped it when he needed it. Given a new twin-cam Bugatti in 1931, he won his only Monaco after a brilliant duel with Varzi.

After an unsuccessful stint with Mercedes-Benz in 1936, Chiron went into semi-retirement in 1937, appearing only once with a Talbot in the French sports car GP at Montlhéry, which he won, and in a couple of trial runs with an Auto Union before World War II broke out. Chrion served in the French army once more until the fall of France, then was demobilized and spent the rest of World War II smuggling Allied airmen out of Switzerland (which was his official wartime home) to Spain and England.

With the war's end, racing revived slowly in Europe. Chiron's old Talbot was at a distinct disadvantage, yet he won the 1st postwar French GP, copped a 2nd in the 1948 Monaco GP, and survived a flaming crash that wiped out the car in a Syracuse (Italy) meet. Chiron

drove in his last major GP at the age of 56 when he finished 6th in a factory Lancia at Monaco. Four years later, in his final year of active competition, he brought a Citroën DS19 to 2nd in its class in the last running of the Mille Miglia.

Prince Rainier had the happy inspiration of asking Chiron to run the Principality's 2 great events, the Monaco GP and the Monte Carlo Rally (which Louis had won in a Lancia Aurelia in 1954 in the best of his 11 starts in this gruelling test of man and car). A better choice could not have been made.

JOIE CHITWOOD

The Cherokee Indian nation's gift to the Indianapolis 500 and to the sport of auto racing was Joie Chitwood. He made his first appearance at the Brickyard in 1940 after he had been racing on dirt tracks for 10 years. He finished as high as 5th in both 1946 and 1949. He will be remembered longer, perhaps, for his thrill-show activity.

He started his own show after Luck Teeter died in action. He soon had 5 units on the road, leaping off ramps, crashing through fire, and doing wheelies. Chitwood drove Indianapolis each year after his success in the thrill business.

Joie and Ted Horn were close friends and used to rib each other unmercifully, but when Horn made a stab at promotion, Chitwood came out of semi-retirement to drive for him. Always a good salesman, Joie talked Ford Motor Company into a long-term contract to use their cars in his thrill show.

Later, Joie Jr. made an attempt to succeed in oval racing. There was one difference. The original did not have a millionaire for a father.

SARA CHRISTIAN

The motherly-looking woman in the Atlanta restaurant hardly looked like a forerunner of Women's Liberation. To imagine her as a driver of stock cars so talented and so nerveless that she rode over cars who blocked her way was a task that challenged the most imaginative. But Mrs. Sara Christian was all of that, and her driving career fell victim to equal parts of male chauvinism, commercial considerations, and growing disinterest.

Sara Christian came to racing after raising a family. Her husband Frank, a sometime driver in the early days of Southern stock-car racing, was a garage owner. But there was no doubt that Sara was the brains of the partnership, at least as far as business went. There was the garage, there had been restaurants in several Georgia cities, and there were investments in promotions like county fairs. Sara claimed she was smitten with love for the sport when, to help out a friendly promoter, she drove in a racing card in 1947. Some old-timers swear "Stock-Car Sara" was competing in around-the-barrels races at Florida beaches before World War II. The question became academic when, in his desire to build NASCAR racing as an attraction by every means possible, William H. G. France saw the promotional value of a few female drivers.

But Sara was an exercise in tokenism that turned out unexpectedly. With a crack mechanic like husband Frank to maintain her vehicle, and natural driving talent plus experience, Mrs. Christian began to mop up the male opposition. In 1949, her most active year, Sara won 6 of 17 races before suffering 2 fractured vertebrae in an accident at Lakewood Park in Atlanta.

Sara asked and gave no quarter on the dirt tracks of the South and East. "I set a certain course on each track and stick to it. The men drivers know where I am and what I will do. I am just one of the boys during a race," she said.

In an Atlanta 150-miler in 1948 she worked her way to 12th in a field of 40 when she was forced into the pits with a clogged radiator just before the 50-mile mark. Repairs took 17 minutes, and during all that time no one bothered to refuel the car. So Sara was soon back in the pits for a 4-minute gas and engine-check stop, dropping down to 20th, 11 laps behind the leader. In the remaining 60 miles, Mrs. Christian moved to 11th place and gained back 8 laps from the winner, the great Red Byron. It was embarassing for a field of men to be so handled.

By 1953, however, France had decided that female drivers should not be a part of NASCAR. Yet women— and Mrs. Christian—were never barred per se; the races were made longer, and it became increasingly difficult for a woman's car to pass inspection on the Grand National circuit. Mrs. Christian gently faded back into the kitchen and the task of bringing up a son and daughter; partly according to Red Vogt, because the men were treating her too much like one of the boys and the weekly repair bill on the car was eating up all the profits.

Occasionally she would invest in young racing hopefuls, and there was car sponsorship at local tracks, but it is significant that when Bill France invited old stock-car heroes to the opening of Daytona, he somehow forgot Sara.

BOB CHRISTIE

There is plenty of room in the Great Northwest, so Bob Christie, born April 4, 1924, near Grant's Pass, Ore., used some of that room to practice before his first venture onto the race track. He took his stock car out into an open field and learned there what cars do at speed when you turn them sharply, and how to control the machine when the back end begins to slide out.

In 1947 Christie entered a midget race at Salem, O.

In 1950 he was Oregon midget champ, repeating in 1951. Then there was the Pan American Road Race and Christie buzzed on down to begin a stock-car career that brought him a 3rd in the AAA 1953 stock car championships. But the Indy bug had bitten him, and Bob bought a car and came to the Speedway in 1954 to pass his rookie test. He did, and he also learned that it was much easier when someone else was paying the bills.

After sporadic forays into stock-car racing, he returned to Indy in 1955 and encountered the bad luck of wrecking during qualification. The Memorial Day debut of this 6-foot Oregon businessman finally came in 1956. He improved 12 positions to finish 13th in the Helse Special. The next year he barely qualified, but again finished 13th. The Federal Engineering car (in its 3rd year of Indy) got him to 10th place in 1960, although he had been closing on the leaders in 1958 on the 189th lap when he spun out.

Christie was known as a finisher, which meant he was relatively easy on machinery. This, of course, appealed to those cold-turkey car owners who do not want the machinery bashed up because they do not like the price of repairs.

JIM CLARK

James Clark Jr. was born March 4, 1936, in Kilmany, Scotland, the first and only son of a wealthy farmer (who had 4 older daughters). Writers liked to refer to Jim as a sheepherder. He liked sheep raising and farming in general, and when he had finished at the Loretto boarding school (that he had attended from age 10 to 16). Clark returned to tend his father's prize flocks of sheep. He started building his interest in automobiles at a young age. Jim learned to drive at age 10, and through the years he had managed to drive a bit every year. At 17, his dad gave him the family's old Sunbeam.

Properly tuned, it became Jim's first competition machine. In 1951 the racing bug had bitten him on a trip to Ireland when he watched Mike Hawthorn win the Ulster Trophy Race. It was 4 years later that Clark starting winning rallies in the Scottish border country. The following year he entered his 1st formal auto race in Aberdeen and finished last in a borrowed DKW. Undiscouraged, Jim kept driving the Sunbeam and a borrowed Porsche 1600 well enough over the next couple of years that his legion of local backers founded the Border Reivers Team and put him into a dark blue D Jaguar once raced by Archie Scott-Brown and Henry Taylor. Jim's 1st major victory came June 3, 1956, in the Sunbeam. In 1958 the Reivers purchased a Lotus Elite from Colin Chapman, who still was doing much of his own driving, and Clark competed against his future chief at Brands Hatch on December 26, 1955, Britain's Boxing Day.

Clark led for 8 of the 10 laps, was hit by another car, spun out, and lost the race to Chapman in the factory entry. Right then and there, Chapman later claimed, he knew Clark might be a future World Champion. He did not sign Jim at once, but started watching the boy's steady progress.

The Border Reivers next purchased a Lister-Jaguar that gave Jim 8 important local victories. They also arranged with Chapman for the loan of an Elite for the Le Mans 24-Hour Race that Jim and Sir John Whitmore raced to 10th overall, and 2nd in its 1,500-c.c. class. After the race, the Reivers bought the Elite, and Jim scored another dozen victories in this car at the same time his Lister-Jag string was growing. The Reivers and other people wanted Clark to turn full-time professional and assault big-time racing, he was reluctant at first, but in the end he relented.

On Boxing Day 1959, the future champion got his first ride in a single-seater, a Gemini Formula Junior car, but failed to finish the race, Early the next season, however, he was tested by Reg Parnell for the Aston Martin GP team and signed for a ride. He never drove for the team, however, and was released so that he could sign with Chapman in FJ and Formula 2 events. He won at Goodwood in an FJ Lotus 18 for his initial single-seater victory. On June 5, 1960, Clark drove his initial F1 race, the Dutch GP, also his 1st World Championship event; he retired in mid-race. The following Belgian GP saw him finish 5th and he repeated the feat at the French GP after finishing 3rd overall with Roy Salvadori in an Aston Martin at Le Mans. Clark also

was brillant in FJ racing, co-winning the 1960 championship with teammate Trevor Taylor. In 1961 he won the non-championship Pau GP. That season in title races, he was 10th at Monaco, 3rd at Holland, 12th in Belgium, 3rd again in France, retired in Britain, 4th in Germany, retired in Italy, and 7th in the U.S. GP.

But it was in 1962 that Clark emerged as a serious contender for the World Championship, battling tightly with Graham Hill. Clark always believed he was the better driver that year, winning more races in all forms of competition, although Graham had the edge in the F1 chase. Because only the points from a driver's top 5 races counted toward the title, however, Clark was in the thick of every race until the very last. He won his 1st GP at Belgium's Spa-Francorchamps on June 17, 1962, and won again in Britain and in the United States in title races, to go along with non-championship victories in the Lombank Trophy, Aintree 200, Oulton Gold Cup, Snetterton 3 Hours, and Mexican and Rand Grands Prix. Hill won the title when Clark's Lotus retired in the last race of the year, the South African GP, December 29, 1962.

The next season was Jim's without question. He started off with a 2nd in the Lombank Trophy Race, won 3 warmup races in a row (British Empire Trophy, Pau, and Imola Grands Prix), was 3rd in the Aintree 200, and won the International Trophy Race at Silverstone. At Monaco, the GP opener, he retired, then scored 2nd at Indianapolis.

Clark won the hearts of racing fans everywhere with that runner-up spot at Indy. Before Clark and Chapman brought their Ford-powered Lotus 29 to Indiana, the overwhelming majority of Indy cars were "dinosaurs"— big, heavy, front-engined monsters about as modern as a Central Park brougham. When the Indy version of a European Formula 1 racing car—low, light, rear-engined, and every inch a thoroughbred—rolled onto the track, the inhabitants of Gasoline Alley chuckled at the toy.

When Clark and his toy proved fast and threatening, the Indy Old Guard stopped laughing and started complaining. The car wasn't safe. Its 15-inch tires were unfair. Its "rookie" driver had to be tested a 2nd time. And so on. Clark, Chapman, and Dan Gurney, who originally suggested to Chapman that Lotus might drive Indianapolis, gritted their teeth and went through all the motions. On the tire problem, they were adamant, however, and with Firestone backing, they prevailed.

The race itself was almost anticlimactic. Clark qualified the Lotus in the middle of the 2nd row, but at the start Jim Hurtubise's Novi, just ahead of him on the grid, got stuck in gear and Clark almost climbed up Hurtubise's exhaust. By the time they had straightened out, Jim was back in the middle of the pack, but he soon moved up to the top 3, along with Gurney in another Lotus and Parnelli Jones in a Watson-Offy. Jones's car was fast, Parnelli was a top driver, and he already had been tabbed by the Lotus team as the man to beat. Chapman's stategy included limiting Clark and Gurney to one pit stop, while Jones would have to make 3. It almost worked that way, except that several yellow lights (at the right times) gave Parnelli the chance to make 2 of his 3 pit stops without serious loss of time.

For 170 laps Clark contented himself with playing bridesmaid to Jones, confident that he could pick up the necessary time in the final 50 miles or so. Later he was to demonstrate that he had the ability to do just that, picking up a second a lap on Parnelli and getting to just 4 seconds behind him before deliberately backing off because Parnelli's car had turned into an oil gusher. With 100 miles to go, Jones's Offy started smoking, occasionally at first, then more steadily. And it started leaking, then spurting oil in a thickening trail behind it. Twice Clark went sideways on oil patches from Jones's car, but fought his Lotus back into control without much loss of time. Eddie Sachs and Roger McCluskey were not so fortunate, losing control of their spinning cars and falling from positions in the first 5 to retirements (but placing 15th and 17th).

At the starting line, Chief Steward Harlan Fengler was under pressure. He could see the blackening tail of the Jones car and the trail of oil the machine was leaving as it went around in a cloud of smoke. Chapman had moved toward Fengler's position and quietly suggested he consider calling Jones off the course, Jones's owner, J. C. Agajanian, had also rushed to the steward to make sure that Fengler did not do that very thing, rule book or not. Fengler continued to toy with the flag, but he determined to "excise my prerogatives" and refused to black-flag the leader. The leakage eventually stopped, either because a low level had been reached in the tank or because the oil was all gone. Gone too, was Clark's chance of a rookie Indy victory.

But there were no recriminations from him. Though he was used to winning, he accepted 2nd. "Better not to win that way, with the man in front of you flagged off the course," he said quietly. "I could have beaten him if the situation hadn't arisen the way it did, and I'd rather have another chance to do it that way." Sachs did not take such a gentlemanly view, and he exchanged a few punches with Jones at the race's end. The reactions were characteristic of each man. No matter how deeply he may have felt at losing his potential victory, Clark would never show it. (And in 1965, he did what he said he would [after another frustration in 1964 when a piece of rubber from his tires mangled his suspension while he was in the lead]. Leading for 190 of the 200 laps, Clark won Indy in 1965 and beat 2nd-place finisher Jones—now fittingly in a Lotus-Ford—by more than a lap.)

He drove a couple of sports car races, then won 4 straight GPs to practically clinch the 1963 championship right then and there. In June Clark won the Belgian, Dutch, and French Grands Prix. In July the British

GP. In August Jim was 2nd in the German GP, won a Brands Hatch sedan race, the non-title Swedish GP, and the Milwaukee 200 USAC race. The next month saw him retired in the non-title Austrian GP, win his 5th championship F1 race in Italy, and secure his own title as well as the constructor's title for Lotus. He also scored a double at Oulton Park in the Gold Cup and in a sports car race on the same day. He retired in another USAC race at Trenton and won 2 races in the same day at Snetterton, one a 3-hour enduro, the other a sedan race in a Cortina.

Clark was 3rd in October's United States GP, won at Riverside, was retired at nearby Laguna Seca in the Monterey GP, but won the Mexican GP late that month and the South African GP in December to close out one of racing's most memorable seasons for any driver.

In 1964, he came very close to repeating for the Championship, winning the Dutch, Belgian, and British GPs. Going into the final race in Mexico a broken oil pipe ended his bid. Lotus reliability was not what it should have been that season, knocking Clark out of all the other Grands Prix, except Monaco where he was 4th.

Then came his 1965 World Championship year. Clark won the South African opener, dominated the non-championship Tasman series, and won a series of non-championship races that included the Sebring 3-Hour Race. He won at Indianapolis easily, only losing the pole position to A. J. Foyt, who went out after 115 laps of dicing with Clark. Jim set a new track record for a winner (broken 2 years later by Foyt). Back in Europe, he won 5 straight Grands Prix—the Belgian, French, British, Dutch, and German—to clinch the crown, despite later retirements in the Italian, U.S., and Mexican races.

Clark had troubles in 1966 and 1967. The Lotus had grown old, then the improved model had teething troubles. There were victories, but on the whole the seasons were disappointing especially 1966 when he managed to win only the U.S. GP after a series of retirements, and did no better than 3rd at in the Dutch GP. At Indianapolis, Clark managed a 2nd to Graham Hill's winning effort, after surviving the opening 11-car accident and spinning twice on the slippery track. The next season was somewhat better, Jim winning the Dutch, British, and U.S. Grands Prix, finishing 3rd in the standing behind Denis Hulme and Jack Brabham.

The first championship race of 1968 came on the year's first day at Kyalami, South Africa, far from Clark's usual haunts. He flashed his familiar Lotus 49 around the 2.55-mile circuit brilliantly, taking the lead in the 2nd lap and never relinquishing it for almost 2 hours. Jim's winning speed was a blistering 107.42 m.p.h. As 80,000 spectators roared their approval for this virtuoso performance, he lapped most of the field, which included (in the order of finish) Graham Hill, Jochen Rindt, Chris Amon, Hulme, and Jean-Pierre Beltoise, as well as Dan Gurney and Jack Brabham.

The race was Clark's 25th F1 championship victory, putting him one up on former all-time winner Juan Manuel Fangio. No one realized it was to be Clark's last championship GP race.

Jim's string included 5 British GPs, 4 Belgian and Dutch GPs, 3 South African and United States GPs, 2 French and Mexican GPs and one victory in each of the German and Italian GPs. Only Monaco had eluded Clark.

His South African victory was followed by 8 races in the Tasman series, winning the non-championship Australian GP. Next came as F2 race at Barcelona, from which Clark's Lotus 49 was retired. And then there was another insignificant F2 race, a race, true enough, that counted toward the European title, but one that he could have passed up, as he had intended to do for a British sports car race, until a date conflict arose.

April 7, 1968, found Clark—just past his 32nd birthday and probably at the height of his driving prowess—sitting in a flashy red-gold-and-white Gold Leaf Team Lotus as a light rain fell on the Hockenheim course, near Heidelberg, West Germany. He started back in the pack, an unfamiliar position for him and to teammate Graham Hill. By the 4th lap, the field was strung out somewhat, and Clark, running alone, was 8th and moving up toward 7th. There were 16 laps to go, and plenty of time for him to make his move. Perhaps that was what he was doing, still all alone in a secluded portion of the track, when the Lotus suddenly seemed to shudder and break toward the trees, just after he had accelerated into the straightaway at some 175 m.p.h.

The car smashed sideways into the trees, shattering to pieces. Jim still was strapped in; the doctors said he died instantly of a broken neck and multiple skull fractures. Exactly what happened still is not known, but the consensus seemed to rest on mechanical failure rather than driver error or the rain.

The consensus was unanimous in another area: that this apple-cheeked young man was one of auto racing's great drivers. He had won 25 World Championship Grands Prix (more than anyone else) for a total of 163 victories. Any list of all-time great drivers must carry the name of Jim Clark near the top.

MAYNARD CLARK

Maynard (Hungry) Clark was a thrill show motorcycle rider from Milan, Ill., who survived all other members of a group of dirt and midget drivers called the Tri-City Boys. He specialized in dirt track racing and, while not adverse to agitating the accelerator pedal, was better known for his showmanship.

Among the other Tri-City Boys, all killed in racing accidents, were Glenn Hyatt, Lou Penno, and Bryan Saulpaugh, who made one Indy 500 before his death. Later Maynard teamed on the fair circuit with Johnny Gerber as the Racing Rubes. That he still could race was evidenced when he took the 100-miler at Atlanta's Lakewood on Labor Day, 1935. Apparently, Hungry must have become well-fed for he disappeared from competition about 1940.

FRANK CLEMENT

One of the Bentley Boys, Francis C. Clement, usually called "the Governor" by his mechanics, was born in 1886 in England. After stints with Vauxhall, Napier and Star, Clement was with DFP in the 1914 Tourist Trophy Race when he met W. O. Bentley before the marque that would bear that gentleman's name was founded. First there was World War I, with Frank serving in the Royal Engineers, then becoming involved in the new aviation field on the technical side. It was 1920 before Clement and Bentley, who had struck it off well 6 years before, got together at the Bentley company, Frank signing on as a test driver. The following year he was promoted to head of the Experimental Department.

In 1922 Clement started racing, coming in 3rd in the Tourist Trophy in the rain. The race that Clement, and Bentley, of course, is most identified with was Le Mans. Starting in 1923 Clement was there every year through 1930. In 1923 he was 4th with John Duff, and the following year the pair won for W.O. at 53.78 m.p.h. Clement's car was leading again in 1927, had run the race's fastest lap, but then found himself without a car when his codriver crashed at White House. Fourth with Jean Chassagne in 1929, Clement came close to repeating his 1924 victory in 1930, but had to settle for 2nd.

There were other races. In the 1927 Essex 6 Hours, Clement was leading until mechanical trouble sidelined his car. He replaced Tim Birkin in another Bentley and finished 3rd. That same year he won the Grand Prix de Paris in a 4.5-litre car. In 1929 Frank won the Brooklands 500 with Jack Barclay, and the next season he won the Double 12 at Brooklands with Woolf Barnato. It was a case of the right man and the right car. Clement died in 1970.

JOHN COBB

John Cobb held the World's Land Speed Record longer than any other man—from 1939 until 1963 or 1964, according to whether you accept Craig Breedlove's 3-wheeled jet-powered mark in 1963 or Donald Campbell's 4-wheeled turbine mark in 1964 as the record-breaker. World War II helped Cobb to this distinction, of course, because it eliminated from competition challengers like Germany's Mercedes Benz, which had a 450-m.p.h. car ready to overcome Cobb when the war began. The war also froze automotive development. With the war's end, Cobb was able to dust off his old LSR

car, rename it, make a few modifications and add another 26 m.p.h. or so to his previous record set back in 1939, and it was this 1947 record that Breedlove, Donald Campbell, Mickey Thompson, Tom Green, and Art Arfons would be shooting for beginning in 1962.

John Rhodes Cobb was born in 1899. Little is known of his early life, for he was basically a shy, reticent man, though entirely approachable and friendly once he had gotten to know someone. From early childhood Cobb was interested in cars and racing. He was at Brooklands, possibly when it first opened in 1907, as a spectator. Unlike most youngsters, he was not after autographs or vicarious thrills. Cobb was remembered as a precocious youth, always asking suprisingly adult questions about racing and mechanics, the things that he would later put to use.

His initial Brooklands rides were exactly that. Rides. He was a racing mechanic, or ballast, in the 2-seaters of that day. His 1st drive came in 1925. By then, Cobb had firmly established himself in the London fur brokerage business that was to support him—and his automotive activities—for the rest of his life. The car was a 10-litre Fiat. He did not win that 1st race, nor too many others in those early years, but he learned the track well; some said he was the best, or certainly one of the best, men ever to compete at the big paved oval (which was not really oval in the Indianapolis or Monza sense).

By 1927 he was winning, now in a Vauxhall, and placing with regularity. Two years later Cobb purchased a brute of a car, a V-12 Delage, the one in which Rene Thomas had set a LSR of 143.31 m.p.h. at Arpajon,

France, in 1924, the only time between 1914 and 1963 that a non-Briton held the LSR. In this car Cobb ran the Brooklands outer lap record up to 132.11 m.p.h. to start the string of such marks that he would push to 143.44 m.p.h. before he was finished. In 1929, driving a Sunbeam, he finished 3rd in the first 500-miler held at Brooklands, despite a broken frame in his car through the latter stages of the race. In 1934 he won the Brooklands Championship at 131.53. The following season he won the 500-miler at 121.28 m.p.h.

So Cobb was used to speeds, albeit fairly moderate speeds compared to the LSR. In those Brooklands races in the Thirties he had a new car, a Napier-Railton, named after its engine and its designer, Reid Railton. The designer had promised Cobb a specific performance level in the car and had exceeded it. Railton and Cobb worked well together, and finally Cobb was convinced Railton was the man to build him another car, designed from scratch, to capture and defend the LSR. It took several years to conceive, design, and build the Railton. Cobb characteristically refused to name any of his cars after himself, but several times named them after Reid, whom he greatly admired.

The Railton that appeared at Bonneville Salt Flats, Utah, in 1938 was a special kind of machine. Railton had designed the body first, using an aircraft wind tunnel to get maximum performance before moving on to design the chassis. An angled pair of supercharged, 12-cylinder Napier Lion VIID airplane engines were used to power the beast, giving the car a potential of 2,500 b.h.p.

Cobb and Railton had a challenger, too. George Eyston's car, Thunderbolt, was bigger and heavier than Cobb's mount. And Eyston got away first in the LSR quest, visiting Bonneville in 1937 and raising the record to 312.00 m.p.h., with one run at 319.11. The following year, as Cobb watched, Eyston raised his own mark to 345.50 with an opening run of 347.49 m.p.h. Only Malcolm Campbell, who had retired from the LSR chase to worry about the WSR, had previously gotten over 300-m.p.h.

John Cobb became the 3rd member of the exclusive club. In the Railton, half the weight of Thunderbolt (3.15 tons as opposed to 6 tons) and with half the b.h.p. of Eyston's car, he started testing at Bonneville 3 days after Eyston's latest record and kept testing until, on September 12, 1938, after a test run of 342.5 m.p.h., he announced he was ready to make an official try in a day or two. As Eyston watched, the radiator-less Railton (which used circulating ice water to cool the engines) ripped down the course at 353.3, then returned within the required hour at a 347.2, for an LSR average of 350.20 m.p.h.

Eyston hopped into Thunderbolt the next day after slight overnight modifications (he had discarded his radiator for water cooling and dropped his stabilizing fin in an effort to improve his aerodynamics) and he dashed down the salts at 356.4 and 358.6, which averaged out to a recaptured record of 357.50 m.p.h. Cobb's LSR had lasted just 24 hours! The salts were deteriorating and his supply of special Dunlop tires was too low to try again that year. He and Railton were confident that their car could beat Eyston's record; why rush? They headed back to England and waited for next year.

Cobb's 1st official try at Bonneville on August 22, 1939, was not successful, probably due to the engines' needing some running time to become properly fit; they had not been stripped down over the winter and spring. Nor was the car extensively reworked, although the back axle now was restricted to vertical movement only. The next day, August 23, the beautiful aluminum body shell, removed each night to allow the mechanics to fiddle with the chassis and engines, was refitted over the car, hiding the Utah license plate that local law required Cobb to carry (he and members of his crew were issued local driving licenses, as well, although driver tests were waived).

Cobb, wearing the white cloth aviator's helmet and goggles as usual, watched all this in his usual calm manner. Then he stepped out on the plank laid across the car to prevent denting the soft aluminum shell, slipped into the cockpit, and, in a few moments, felt a gentle bump as an old Dodge truck with a metal probe push-started the Railton. He then put in a day's work: 368.86 m.p.h. for the mile (LSR); 369.70 for the kilometer; 307.2 for 5 miles; 326.7 for 5 kilometers; 270.4 for 10 miles; 283.0 for 10 kilometers. He was the 1st man to go faster than 6 miles a minute.

The speed became familiar to Cobb during World War II, except now he was in the cockpits of assorted British fighters, bombers, and other aicraft, as a ferry pilot in the Air Transport Auxiliary. Meanwhile, the Railton was carefully stored and protected. With the war's end, it was rolled out (always on "slave" wheels, not the wheels and tires used for LSR racing) and found to be fit enough for some more records.

Cobb made it back to Bonneville, thanks to the generous sponsorship of the Mobil Oil Company, in 1947. The car was about the same as it always had been, except it now was called the Railton Mobil Special, in deference to the sponsor. Cobb spent 7 weeks in preparation. American newsmen first were shocked, then dismayed at his complete lack of flamboyance. Standing in front of a newsreel camera, he was ill at ease, and in one famous "interview" grunted once or twice, and that was it. It was not that he was uncooperative; but it was against his nature to carry on about what he was doing.

On September 14, 1947, his renewed attempt at his own LSR was aborted when a crack appeared in the Railton's body shell. But the run he had made was electrifying enough—375.32 m.p.h. The repairs were made in 2 days, and despite a poor track and threatening rain, he was off again. Cobb's 1st run was faster

still—385.645—and his 2nd was officially clocked at 403.135, although he was still accelerating as he left the electronic traps and a clocker timed him at 415 m.p.h. before he shut down the power. The official LSR stood now at 394.196 m.p.h., and stayed there until 1963. The next day 6 inches of rain deluged the salts and that was it at Bonneville for 1947.

Cobb drove the Railton at least once more, in England, at a low-speed demonstration. But without a challenger, there did not seem any point in trying to up the LSR again. Eyston was still around, but more interested in record-setting in lower classification cars. Cobb turned his attention to the WSR after pocketing his 4th Gold Star Award from the BRDC (he previously had won Gold Stars in 1935, 1937, and 1938). It was in his quest of the 200 m.p.h. WSR that he met his death on Scotland's Loch Ness on September 29, 1952, when his Crusader boat hit something in the water and exploded.

OSCAR COLEMAN

Topsy Coleman of Dallas always wanted his son to be a racing driver, and that is what Oscar Lloyd, born in 1905, became. Topsy helped all the way as chief mechanic. Oscar won the Southwest dirt track title in 1932 and 1933. He piloted a Crager Ford in IMCA competition. Oscar soon realized that the easy way to go racing—easy on one's arms and legs, that is—was to turn to promoting. He ended up as both promoter and used car dealer.

COLLIER BROTHERS (MILES and SAM)

Born of well-to-do parents, Miles and Sam Collier never had to worry about where their next meal was to come from. That was fortunate, for it freed Sam—the dominant brother—to tinker with automobiles and eventually allowed him to become a leading light in the formation of the Automobile Racing Club of America, predecessor to the SCCA, and thus the savior of American road racing.

In the silent film era, Hollywood made a film based on the New York-to-San Francisco race. The hero, Wallace Reed, piloted a "Dent," apparently a disguise for a Model T Ford; the villain piloted a 1922 Cadillac, without the emblem, which was dubbed a "Lorraine." Collier, about 9 at the time, identified with the hero and hissed the villain, who did such dastardly things as reversing detour signs, setting booby traps, sprinkling nails on the road, and absconding with the heroine.

Several years later Sam and a friend built a tiny car, powered by a 4-cylinder Henderson motorcycle engine. It is said to have accelerated magnificently to 35 m.p.h., but seized from overheating at 40. The boys called the car "Look" and drove it perhaps 10,000 miles over the back roads of Westchester County where the well-to-do from New York City's business community lived. By 1933 Sam had a black 12-cylinder Auburn Speedster. As a student at Yale University, he used it for 24-hour non-stop trips to Florida. As his skill improved, Sam became more cautious, but he seems to have studied the dynamics of fast driving as assiduously as he pursued his college courses.

In the summer of 1933 Collier finished 3rd in class in the Coupe International des Alpes, a 5-day trial. In an MG he took 3 seconds out of 1934 ARCA events. He finished 3rd in the RAC's County Down trophy and won 1 heat in the Albigeoix Grand Prix during the summer of 1935. On May 13, 1936, he won the Memphis Cotton Carnival Road Race, and finished 5th, 2nd, and 1st in class in Mount Washington Hillclimbs in 1936, 1937, and 1938.

In 1934 Sam, George Rand of New York (later an ACCUS executive), and John Marshall of Boston formed ARCA to race over public roads temporarily closed to regular traffic with the approval of the authorities. ARCA held 15 major road races between 1934 and 1941 and tried to set a precedent of races without prize money for sports cars. Meanwhile, Collier graduated from Yale, served for a time in the family business, and, when he joined the Navy in 1942, was a vice president of the New York Subways Advertising Company. He had married, too, and set up housekeeping in Jacksonville and Puerto Rico. The Navy made him a navigator in the Naval Air Transport Service.

The business opportunities in Florida intrigued him, and after the war he involved himself in developing the Southwestern part of the state. Meanwhile, after an 8-year hiatus—his last race before the war was the World's Fair Road Race, October 6, 1940—Sam became one of the enthusiastic competitors at the Watkins Glen races of October 2, 1948. He finished 4th overall in an MG. His major post-war feat came at Le Mans in 1950 when he finished a stock Cadillac sedan 10th overall, covering 1,956.9 miles. The effort inspired Collier to approach the SCCA, in which he now was a leading light, about establishing an American enduro. Unfortunately, Sam died in a crash at Watkins Glen in September 1950 before he could see the start of the Sebring, Daytona and Watkins Glen events. Miles died of natural causes in 1954. The boys were credited with hastening the popularity of MG by importing them for friends.

EMORY COLLINS

The red and black No. 7 of Emory Collins was famous in Western Canada long before anyone knew that the forward of the Minneapolis hockey team was also a racing driver. In 1926 Emory threw off the cloak of anonymity; in 1927 he quit hockey to devote all of his time to racing cars. And in 1928 at about 26 years of age he joined IMCA's top ranks, swooping down the Canadian dirt tracks to challenge the great Sig Haugdahl.

But it was not Haugdahl whom Spunk Collins spent a career chasing; it was Gus Schrader, an independent little man who disagreed with the AAA Contest Board's idea that drivers ought to limit their earning capacity to the slim schedule approved by that body during the Depression. In 1933 Collins won 11 IMCA races, but Schrader won the title. This was to be the pattern of his career, for Schrader was one of the great finishers of auto racing history. While Collins went for broke, Schrader always finished high, though he was always willing to bump a foe out of his way.

The 1934 IMCA season was a 3-way battle among Haugdahl, Collins, and Schrader. All were mounted on Miller Specials, and all were ready by 1934 to win it in Schrader's style. The IMCA racing setup favored the 2 more experienced men. There were heats leading up to a short 15-mile feature. Collins won the heats, the others won the features.

In 1935 Collins and Schrader came to the final race tied in points. Schrader won easily for his 3rd IMCA title in a row. In 1936 the key race was the IMCA classic at the Minnesota State Fair; the judges decided that Schrader had beaten Emory by 1 yard. In 1937 it came down to the last race again, and again Schrader won. One might get the idea that Collins, now an Iowa resident, would be frustrated. Apparently he was, for he bought himself a new Offy dirt machine. But Schrader did, too.

September 5, 1938, was a gray Labor Day, but 45,-000 had jammed the Minnesota State Fairgrounds to see the IMCA championship program. It rained during the program, a drizzle at first, then heavier and heavier until the track was a quagmire. Officials could have called the program, but they would have had a riot on their hands—not only from the fans but from the drivers, especially Collins and Schrader who were again contending for the title. The officials did the next best thing; they cut the feature to 5 miles. Mud or no, Collins sprinted to the lead, with such stalwarts as Lynn Musick, Ben Shaw in his Curtiss-engined sprinter, and Buddy Callaway in another Offy churning up mud in an attempt to catch him. But it was Schrader who circled the pack on the final lap to draw even with Collins. The cars ran hub to hub into the last turn until suddenly Schrader lost it, spinning in the muck and spraying Collins with it. But Emory kept control of his car and rolled across the finish line a winner, his face and goggles covered with mud.

He ripped off his goggles in the heavy downpour as the crowd roared. Emory Collins had clinched his 1st IMCA title. It was the only one he was to win against Schrader, who regained the title in 1940, with Collins running 3rd to rookie Jimmy Wilburn. And Gus had clinched the 1941 crown before he was killed in a late-season race. Collins came back after World War II to duel annually with Wilburn, but Jimmy ran off with 3 straight titles. Collins retired after 1948 as one of the all-time greats of dirt track racing, remembering a fellow Iowan named Schrader who, except for one glorious year, made him eat the dust of tracks the length and breadth of the country.

PETER COLLINS

The death of Peter Collins on August 3, 1958, was a bitter blow to auto racing generally and to British racing particularly. The handsome Collins was a hero prototype right from the start, and his nickname, the Gay Cavalier, suggests the heroic way he handled himself off the track as well as on it. Patrick Collins, Peter's father, was a Kidderminster auto dealer, and Peter grew up around cars, so it was natural for him to go racing in 1949 soon after he had turned 17 (Collins was born November 8, 1931). His first mount was a Cooper-Norton in the 500-c.c. British class that was to become the 1st international Formula 3.

In 1950 Collins won the initial Goodwood International Trophy Race, later a traditional feature of the racing calendar, and he took the 1st 100-miler at Silverstone as well. For hillclimbs, Peter used a Cooper-JAP and scored many successes. In 1951 John Heath approached Collins about a better ride, namely the Formula 2 HWM. Peter joined with Stirling Moss and Lance Macklin to form what could have become a team of immor-

tals, had it not been for the tragic death of two of them. The Grand Prix experience Collins gained with HWM paid off with an offer from Reg Parnell, to drive not GP cars but sports racers that required talent equal to that demanded by the bigger cars. For 1952 Collins joined the Aston Martin team. Here Collins teamed with Pat Griffith to take the 9-Hour Race held at Goodwood, and in 1953 the same pair won the RAC Tourist Trophy race held that year on the Dundrod circuit in Northern Ireland. They were 2nd in the 1953 9 Hours and 3rd in the Eifelrennen.

Tony Vandervell signed Peter for Formula Libre, entrusting him with the famous Thinwall Special, a thinly disguised Ferrari, built to bedevil the BRM teams with which Vandervell was having a dispute. Collins took the Snetterton Trophy that year, won the Whitsun Trophy at Goodwood, and captured the Woodcote Cup and Silverstone sports car race. He was 2nd in Trophy races at Crystal Palace and Goodwood and 3rd in the Buenos Aires 1000, farthest he had travelled from home at that point. Even though it was a 7th-place finish, the Italian GP at Monza that year was a high spot for Peter, for his mount was the original (and still very experimental) Vanwall, fitted with a 2.2-litre engine. He had repeatedly bested the BRM, so Raymond Mays asked him to drive the Gold Cup meeting at Oulton Park for that marque. Collins led the formidable field—Moss, best-friend Mike Hawthorn, and Eugenio Castellotti, among others—for 10 laps, then retired with failing oil pressure.

In 1955 came the call from one of the world's best racing teams, Enzo Ferrari's Modena forces, with an agreement to let Peter continue his Aston Martin drives in the sports car field. That year Collins won at Aintree, took the Silverstone International Trophy once again, shared a Targa Florio victory (enough to snare praise from Mercedes Benz's Alfred Neubauer) and won the Chichester Cup. He shared an Aston Martin 2nd place in the Le Mans 24-hour race with Paul Frere and finished 3rd in the Goodwood 9 Hours and in the Oulton Park International. His Targa drive helped snare the constructors' championship for Mercedes. Peter took over from an exhausted Moss, picked up time, then handed back the 300SLR to the revived Stirling, who smashed Collins's record lap several times.

Juan Manuel Fangio was a teammate of Collins in 1956, and this changed Peter's haphazard outlook on racing to that of pure dedication. His Ferrari won the Belgian GP at Spa-Francorchamps, then the French GP at Rheims. He was still in contention, as was Fangio (for his 5th title) when the Italian GP took place at Monza, and Peter demonstrated for all time what sportsmanship really is. Fangio's Ferrari was out after 19 laps with faulty steering, and Luigi Musso refused to yield his car to his fellow driver as was the team arrangement. The pact did not include Collins's vehicle, but Peter, seeing Fangio's predicament after bringing in his own Ferrari for a tire check, immediately offered his car to the Argentinian, who needed only a good finish to clinch his title. Fangio drove his usual cool, calculated race, finished 2nd to Moss and, even splitting points with Collins, won the championship for the 5th time. Peter was 3rd in the standings. That same year he was 2nd at Le Mans again, this time with Moss in an Aston.

Hawthorn had been with BRM that season, and the dark green British cars had a terrible year, so Mike leaped at Ferrari's offer of a team slot for 1957. Thus 2 of the 3 potential greats of British racing (and the best of friends) found themselves delighted teammates. The Prancing Horse also could call upon the talents of Musso, Castellotti, the Marquis de Portago, Phil Hill, and Olivier Gendebien for a concentrated array of driving talent that rarely has been matched. Unfortunately the cars were not good that year, and, while Peter won non-championship races at Syracuse and Naples, Ferrari did not capture a single championship point. Collins also won the Caracas GP, was 2nd at the Nurburgring 1000 and in the Swedish GP, and 3rd in the French GP and the Buenos Aires 1000.

Castellotti was gone in 1958 (killed while testing an experimental Ferrari), so Collins shared his F1 berth with Hawthorn, Musso, and the newest Ferrari talent, Wolfgang von Trips. Portago was the reserve GP driver and a regular on the sports car team. Not one of the 5 is alive today. Ferrari had a shaky start, but the team soon settled down. Collins's greatest day, he said, came when he won the British GP at Silverstone. That same year he again won the International Trophy at the same course, the Buenos Aires 1000, and Sebring. He was 2nd in 3 other races and 3rd in the Monaco GP.

The end came in the German GP at Nurburgring. Collins had just finished his 10th lap and had lost his lead to Tony Brooks in a Vanwall. With Hawthorn close at hand, Peter tried to overtake Brooks at the Pflanzgarten Curve, a rising right-hand turn. He apparently decided the time was not right, started to pull back, then lost control of the Ferrari for some unexplained reason and swerved sideways into the earthen banking. The Germans were efficient as ever, and Collins was rushed by helicopter to the hospital, but to no avail. The Gay Cavalier's time had come.

Enzo Ferrari always remembered Peter Collins. He has had many great drivers, and he has had many killed in the eternal quest for speed and fame. When Collins's name was mentioned, Ferrari would murmur: "That was a really great one."

COOPER FAMILY (CHARLES and JOHN)

Charles Newton Cooper, founder of both the Cooper Car Co. and Cooper's Garage (at Surbiton), was the man who advanced the modern rear-engined racing car into Formula 1 racing and thereby revolutionized not

John Cooper

only the Grand Prix but single-seater racing the world over. In this formidable task he was aided by his son John, who built the first Cooper racing car—a 500-c.c. machine—with his own hands in 1946.

The Cooper family was long associated with the theatrical rather than automotive world, tracing itself well back into the 18th century and the Drury Lane theatres. But Charles, born in Paris on October 14, 1893, was apprenticed, at his own request, to Napier in 1908, where he worked on Selwyn Edge's car, among others. He was still with Napier when World War I broke out. Charles volunteered at once and spent almost 4 years in the cavalry; he was gassed in 1918. After the war Cooper found himself jobless, so he started his own operation reconditioning surplus Army motorcycles.

In 1920 Charles leased a small site on Ewell Road, Surbiton, that became the original Cooper's Garage. From pumping petrol and making repairs, the garage prospered into an automobile sales agency and a small factory just down the road. In 1922 Charles married, and John was born the following year. Charles competed regularly on Zenith motorcycles, and he and Elsie, his wife, teamed up for rallies and regularity runs in an AC. He also became a pilot, after 30 hours of instruction.

John, meanwhile, had taken the natural route; he was car crazy and he became a regular spectator at Brooklands from his earliest years. In 1938 he left school and started working in his father's operation while looking around for a suitable apprentice program, but World War II ended that scheme rather suddenly.

141

John Cooper spent 4 years in the Royal Navy and returned in 1945 with a burning desire to race and build cars. His father went along with the idea, and the pair settled on the new 500-c.c. class, then newly introduced in Britain. They missed the first postwar meeting of the new class at Prescott in May 1946, but were ready with a car for the next one, July 28 that same year. John had built most of the car, assisted by Eric Brandon. Charles concentrated on the power plant, a single-cylinder JAP dirt-track engine tuned up from a standard 38 b.h.p. to 45 b.h.p. Before the war, Charles had worked with Kaye Don on the Wolseley Viper, Don's Type 54 Bugatti, and the famed "Silver Bullet".

John had taken 2 Fiat front ends and welded them together to have independent suspension front and rear. The engine was mounted on leaf springs, to minimize vibration, and placed at the rear. A Triumph motorcycle gearbok was the other principal component. The car was fairly refined, but not as fast as some others at Prescott its first day. More work solved that, and a week later John won the 850-c.c. class at the Brighton Speed Trials. Brandon ordered a replica, which was delivered in 1947. More development work followed, and Cooper Cars was ready for the inaugural 500-c.c. race that July at Gransden Lodge airfield. Brandon won the race at 60.21 m.p.h. Next he was 2nd at the summer Prescott meeting, then won his class—and set a class record—at the Prescott hillclimb in August.

Real production started in 1948. Originally only 12 cars were planned, but 24 orders were received almost simultaneously, so the 2 dozen machines were gotten under way. That season every sprint and hillclimb for 500 c.c. cars, and all 3 British races for these machines, were won by Coopers, except for 2 speed trials taken by a Monaco. Over the next several years, almost 400 of these 500-c.c. models were built, and such men as Stirling Moss, George Abecassis, Raymond Sommer, and Peter Collins raced Coopers. Moss made his first Continental appearance and was 3rd in a Cooper at Lake Garda in 1949.

The 500-c.c. Coopers continued to dominate Formula 3, as the class became known in 1950, until it died around 1958, with John Cooper still occasionally taking the wheel. But new horizons had opened. In 1951 work had started on the new Cooper-Bristol Formula 2 car, and it debuted at the Easter Goodwood meeting the following season. It had a front-mounted engine and looked something like the Ferraris of the same vintage. Unlike the 180-b.h.p. Ferrari, however, the Cooper-Bristol developed an underpowered 127 b.h.p. In the hands of a skillful driver, though, the car could still perform well, as Mike Hawthorn proved that season. At Goodwood that first day, he won both the F2 and Formula Libre events, was 2nd in the F1 race. Hawthorn won at Boreham, was 2nd in the Ulster Trophy race, 4th in the European GP, 3rd in the British GP and 4th in the Dutch. These Cooper drives led to an invitation to Mike to join the Ferrari team and a World Championship in later years.

When a new F2 was announced for 1957, Cooper was ready with a rear-engined car and driver Roy Salvadori (later their race director) who ran away from the field at Silverstone in 1956 and beat a Lotus by half a minute. The Cooper chassis and new Coventry-Climax engine were well-suited to each other. The marque took 8 of the 10 international F2 races run that season (coming in 2nd in the other 2 to a Ferrari and a Porsche respectively). Jack Brabham had joined Salvadori on the Cooper team by this time. The following year in Rob Walker-entered Coopers, Moss won the F1 Argentine GP and Maurice Trintignant won the Monaco GP to get the year underway properly. Coopers won 10 of the 12 international F2 races that year. In 1959–60, concentrating on F1, 2.5-litre Cooper-Climax cars won the manufacturers' crown and Brabham the World Driver's Championship. It was the high spot of the factory's effort.

From this pinnacle, Cooper Cars slipped to the depths in the 1961–65 period. While Colin Chapman at Lotus, Ferrari, and even BRM were adopting the rear-engined approach pioneered by John Cooper and successfully perfecting such cars, Coopers seemed in a vacuum. Brabham left after the 1961 season to set up his own marque. John was seriously injured in a road accident just before the 1963 season. And in October 1964, Charles Cooper died at age 70. The short, pugnacious man would be sorely missed. There were some successes in racing, principally with Bruce McLaren at the wheel and, later in this period, Tony Maggs, Phil Hill and Jochen Rindt. But most of the victories and high placings were in non-title races; the only Championship race falling to Cooper was the 1962 Monaco GP.

In 1966 Cooper Cars left Surbiton and moved to Byfleet to a factory at which Brooklands cars had long been prepared (remnants of that banked oval were less than half a mile away) and John Cobb's Land Speed Record breakers were built. John Cooper had built his monocoque for the new 3-litre F1 and signed as drivers such men as Richie Ginther, Rindt, John Surtees and Pedro Rodriguez. In 1966 Surtees won the Mexican GP, in 1967 Rodriguez took the South African race, and there were good placings for all the others.

But the Maserati power plant of 1966–67 was clearly outclassed, and John switched the following season to BRM engines. These, too, soon proved uncompetitive, and Cooper's driving team was decimated by accidents —mostly in other people's cars. Brian Redman suffered the only injury in a Cooper, when his suspension failed at the Belgian GP, but Ludovico Scarfiotti was killed in a Porsche during a Continental hillclimb, and Robbin Widdows was injured in a Mirage sports car test. Vic Elford and Lucien Bianchi lasted out the year, but 3rds and 4ths were the best any of them could do.

After the 1968 season, Cooper gave up GP racing.

While the factory also had made and raced several sports cars as late as 1965, this effort had been abandoned in later years. For the first time since World War II, a Cooper was not a major part of the British racing scene.

EARL COOPER

Earl Cooper's greatness cannot be measured by any current standard. He was a member of the Auto Racing Hall of Fame, 3-time national champion, and one of the greats of automotive racing history. His career spanned 1908 to 1926 as an active driver and a decade more as a team manager. He won every kind of race in the United States except Indianapolis. He came in 2nd there though by 90 seconds when 2 tires blew. Cooper set precedents. He won his national championships when a man had to excel both in road racing and oval track racing. He won one crown despite a standing order by Harry Stutz that the cars must be geared to finish, not win. He was the original scientific race driver and one of the earliest to rely wholly upon his mechanic (Reeves Dutton) in preparation of the car.

A case in point was the Corona, Calif., championship of 1913. The city had paved a 3-mile horse track into a perfectly circular boulevard and received permission to run an auto race to open the road.

While others predicted fantastic speeds from the constant left turns, Cooper came months early to find out what it would take to win. First he tested many brands

of tires to find the most durable. Then he found out what would happen if he drove at various speeds, for he felt that the race would be won by the man who stayed out of the pits the most. Ninety m.p.h. was possible, but tire wear was excessive. He settled on 79 m.p.h. as the average speed needed to win. That is what he drove his Stutz at, though early in the race teammate Barney Oldfield lapped him in a torrid duel with a Fiat. But Barney wrecked, and the Fiat blew a tire. Cooper won—at 78 m.p.h.

Cooper began his racing career and lost his job as a Maxwell mechanic at the same time. In 1908 he convinced the owner of a new Maxwell, a lady of some age, to let him enter her car in a San Francisco race. His boss, the owner of the Maxwell agency, had refused him a company car because the boss was driving in the same race. Cooper beat the boss and became an ex-mechanic. The lady is supposed to have been so enthusiastic, however, that she never did learn to drive and let Cooper maintain the car for racing. When Earl joined the Stutz entourage, he was already a driver feared on the West Coast. However, he was running mostly what the AAA chose to call outlaw. The combination of the Stutz, Cooper, and Dutton was a natural. Earl dominated the 1912 Tacoma Montemarathon road races, winning the trophy of the same name, the Golden Potlach trophy race, and a 150-mile warmup.

In 1913 Cooper amassed 2,610 points for his first national title. Jules Goux, the Frenchman who won Indianapolis, had 1,000 for 2nd place. It was all Cooper and Stutz—with the exception of Indy—from the word go. Earl won 7 of the 8 major road races and finished 2nd in that one. Hurt in 1914, Earl returned to outscore Dario Resta in 1915, again despite fewer Indy points, 3,780 to 3,350. He was 5th in the 1916 point standings, won the abbreviated 1917 national crown, then quit. He came back in 1922 and drove during the latter half of the board track era, retiring for good as a driver with 13,530 championship points after 1926.

Perhaps the high-water mark of his career was the 1915 championship. Ill with an infection much of the California season, he returned for the April 29 Oklahoma City road race and wrecked. His first points were scored at Indianapolis where he drove his Stutz to a 4th behind Ralph DePalma, Resta, and teammate Gil Anderson. He was never really a contender for the lead. He took a 4th at the Maywood, Ill., 500-mile race on that board track's inaugural on June 26, then a pair of 2nds behind Mercer Raceabout drivers at Tacoma. In the 50-lap invitational on the Chicago board track, Cooper came in 2nd to Resta in a field of 4 on August 7. The 2-event Elgin, Ill., races were all Stutz. An 8.35-mile course had been laid out, and Anderson and Cooper were in no danger after the early part of both races, the Chicago AC Trophy and the Elgin National Trophy. They traded positions occasionally, but Cooper won the Chicago AC and Anderson the Elgin National.

The real competition came at the cement speedway at Fort Snelling, Minn., near Minneapolis. It was the third 500-mile race of the season and drew a rather slim crowd and slimmer field. Only 14 faced the starter's gun, and tire wear immediately became a factor on the 2-mile cement oval. Resta led on the 1st lap, only to be superseded by Bob Burman. Then Cooper edged in front on lap 9 and led until lap 31, when Resta sneaked into the lead. But Cooper hung Dario up in traffic and regained the lead 2 laps later, only to be caught himself in 4 miles when he pitted for tires. Stutz sent Anderson after Dario to keep up the pressure; that he did, and Gil sailed into the lead just shy of the 90-mile mark. The pressure was too much for the Peugeot, and Resta retired after 102 miles. Anderson had a 6-lap lead on Cooper with Mulford and DePalma fading fast.

Stutz, ever mindful of the publicity, allowed Cooper to come within 1 lap of Gil's car as they both rode casually around. Or so he thought. (Both men even had relief drivers, Tom Rooney and Johnny Aitken, but regained their mounts near the end.) The drivers asked the pit for a lap count as the cars were rolling easily side by side. Stutz checked with the scoring stand and found that the cars were on the same lap. He was in a dilemma, bound by race tradition to give them an accurate lap count, yet knowing that if he did he risked a trophy dash that might blow up both machines. He stalled the puzzled drivers until the last lap, then he held up a sign saying "Position?"

Both drivers must have read the blackboard simultaneously, but Cooper comprehended the situation a split second before Anderson. He shoved his foot down on his accelerator pedal, edging about a wheel-width in front. Anderson chased him, and they roared into the 1st turn almost hub to hub. The 2 Stutzes stayed that way, Cooper a bit in front all the way around the track. And they crossed the finish line with Earl a quarter of a second ahead. That fraction of time was worth $19,000 to Earl, and also gave him the points that, would give him the title over Dario Resta.

Stutz made it 1–2 again at Sheephead Bay, N.Y., on October 9 in a 350-mile race, but with Anderson and Rooney this time. Cooper went out after 23 laps, but it made no difference in the point race for Resta broke down 30 laps later. But Resta won an invitational on the same track a month later to send the point-scramble down to the wire, drawing to within 60 points of Cooper with 2 championships of the record 25 left. Harry Stutz had refused to let his aces enter the invitational. The Maricopa Auto Club set out a 5-mile road course for a 150-mile race in conjunction with the Arizona State Fair. This event was to take the place of the Los Angeles-Phoenix point-to-point race that had proved to contain little revenue possibilities. Cooper won, but the race was called by darkness at the end of 109 miles. The final "championship" was a 4-man match road race

over the 3.85-mile San Francisco course, with Cooper edging Oldfield's Delage by less than a second.

Cooper was champion in the newsman vote, and also by the point system that was not to become official until the following year. But Earl did not defend his title until late in the season because Stutz quit racing. It took the champ half the season to get Harry to sell the Stutz racer to him. By that time it was too late to cut in on the leaders, but Earl put on some good showings. He finished 2nd in the 3 final races of the season—the Vanderbilt and Grand Prize races on Santa Monica's 8.4-mile road course, and at Ascot. In the latter race his famed planning was a bit too close, for he coasted over the finish line out of gas. With victories at Ascot, Chicago, Minneapolis, and Tacoma, the Earl of Cooper won the 1917 crown, and then virtually retired until 1921 when the urge again hit him at a West Coast board track race.

The event was an October 200-miler at Fresno, Calif. Earl was offered the mount of Joe Thomas who had suffered a broken arm during practice. He became a new Cooper, not the precise, scientific man, but the charger. Despite an absence from competition of almost 3 seasons, Cooper won a photo finish from Jimmy Murphy. Sportsman driver and money-man Cliff Durant brought Earl back on a full-time basis in 1922 for his stable of Millers; and Earl did not disappoint him. In 1923 Cooper compiled a 5-victory streak on the boards, winning against the board heroes just as he had on the street and on dirt and cement.

In 1924 Cooper felt he finally had a car that would bring him the crowning glory, victory at Indianapolis. His Studebaker Special had, indeed, built up a 44-second lead by the 400-mile mark. But Joe Boyer's supercharged Duesenberg pushed him too hard, and the new Cooper abandoned the plan and drove deeper into the corners to shake him off. With only 60 miles to go a tire blew, and Cooper limped into the pits. With only 55 miles to go for Boyer, Cooper charged out, 11 seconds behind now. At the 470-mile mark he was on the tail of Boyer's car, trying to slip past. Then another tire blew, sending him into another slide. He pitted and finished 2nd, charging to the end. It was at this race the 37-year-old Cooper noticed in the stands a redhead who was to become his wife.

Cooper's Indianapolis record had been dotted by such occurances as the tire mishap. In 1913 he replaced Gil Anderson at the wheel of a Stutz that held a 10-second lead; he spun out, breaking the car. In 1914 his Stutz broke a wheel and blew 2 tires, departing after 135 laps. In 1915 a wheel again broke early in the race when he was crowded into the wall, but he saved 4th place. He did not run in 1916. At Indy in his only race of 1919 valve trouble hit his Stutz. In 1923 his Studebaker Special was in contention until the 178th lap when tire trouble doomed him. In 1925, he set fast lap of 110.728, then hit the wall late in the race. He won the pole in 1926 in a Miller, but lasted only 73 laps. He came back again in 1928 with the Marmon team, did nothing, and quit driving for good. Cooper, incidentally, was one of the charter members of an early Indianapolis group called the Automotive Drivers Protective Association. Its purpose was to institute added safety measures and obtain adequate driver insurance.

Cooper even had a fling at international racing. In a Cooper-Marmon—a car of his own design—he assayed the 1927 European Grand Prix at Monza. He and co-driver Pete Kreis finished 3rd. Years after he quit driving, his Specials were still contenders. He later acted as a steward for the Mobil Economy Run and spent 22 years as a consultant to Union Oil of California. In an earlier phase of his career, he helped devise pressure lubrication and hydraulic braking systems.

Cooper finally met his wife—in a car crash in September 1924 in Los Angeles. His car collided with the girl with the red hair. She was Jane Nickel Bailey of Troy, N.Y., and she had just come West. They were married 10 days later and were together until he died of a series of strokes at 79 on October 22, 1965, in Atwater, Clif.

GORDON COPPUCK

Indy, 1971. Mark Donohue in practice doing 180.977 m.p.h., 49.73 seconds around the 2.5-mile Indiana oval, breaking a mythical 50-second barrier. Peter Revson qualifying for the pole at 178.696 m.p.h. Denis Hulme, shy a bit by an earlier Indy practice spin, qualifying 4th at 174.910. Racing luck kayoed them all except Revson, who finished a strong 2nd. All of these drivers were in McLaren M16s, and a new name became familar overnight along Gasoline Alley: Gordon Coppuck.

Coppuck was born in December 1936 at Fleet in Hampshire, England. An early passion was the motorcycle. Coppuck left school at 15 and became an apprentice at the National Gas Turbine Establishment at Farnborough. That was the British jet propulsion operation that grew out of Frank Whittle's World War II jet experimentation.

Gordon spent 2 years in the British Army, then returned to Farnborough where he became an accomplished technical draftsman, working under a young Senior Scientific Officer named Robin Herd. Robin left to join Bruce McLaren's new operation—Herd was a driver as well as designer in those days—and soon asked his Farnborough buddy, Coppuck, to join him. After a 2-week test period for both sides, Gordon came aboard in December 1965.

He was pursuing his motorcycle passion in those days, too, preferring trials—that is, cross-country racing—to oval races. He competed in Scottish and international trials, and drove for several factories, including Tri-

umph, winning class races and several Gold Medals. But Coppuck's McLaren work took more and more time from his riding. At first he functioned as Herd's assistant, detailing Robin's ideas, then assuming greater responsibility when Herd left Team McLaren early in 1968.

Coppuck's first solo assignment was working on the suspension of the M7A, McLaren's first Ford-powered Formula 1 design. Jo Marquart joined Bruce's operation about this time from Lotus, and between them the 2 young men went to work on revamping the M6 Canadian-American Challenge Cup series car into what became the M8. Jo did the front, Gordon the rear. Eventually Marquart was given F1 responsibility and Coppuck had the rest of the field. That included CanAm (M12), Bruce's pet GP project (M6GT), and Formula A/5000 (M10). And there was that incredible M16 Indy car.

The first prototype M16 was built for Roger Penske's use, and it was this one that Donohue ran so fast at Indy (180.977 m.p.h. in a practice run in 1971). It was this one, too, that was destroyed as it was parked "safely" alongside the track after Mark's dropout at the Brickyard, but it was rebuilt in 3 days or so and managed to run at Pocono, Pa., in July 1971. The M16 did a bit more than win, in fact, taking Donohue to his first great USAC victory at the new speedway over an Indy-like field of potent machinery and top drivers.

Gordon's first Indy car was the M15 that won an Indiana Chapter Society of Automotive Engineers award.

It was designed and built in just 12 weeks, starting in September 1969, and rolled out in November. Coppuck characterized the M15 as a single-seater version of the CanAm car, powered by Offenhauser because it was as reliable as Ford and a bit lighter, which he felt was important at Indy. Chris Amon could not seem to adapt to Indy's special requirements for drivers, and Hulme was badly burned during testing. So the actual 1970 race was run by Revson and Carl Williams in the Team McLaren cars. Peter dropped out in the race, and Williams finished 9th.

Gordon considered it all a learning process. He proved in 1972 that he was a fast learner when Donohue won it all at Indianapolis.

FRANCO CORTESE

Born in Oggebio, near Turin, in 1903, it was inevitable, perhaps, that Franco Cortese would be connected with the Italian motor car industry. But every young man in Italy in the Twenties and thereafter wanted to be a racing driver; Cortese is one who made it, and made it big.

His career began with Italia in 1926, and the following 2 seasons his major successes were 3rds in the Leghorn Cup for sports cars. By 1930 Franco's reputation was big enough for Enzo Ferrari, then with Alfa, to offer him a spot. Fourth in that year's Mille Miglia, Cortese also was 2nd in the Belgian 24-Hour Touring Car Grand Prix. At Le Mans 2 years later, he and a codriver were 2nd to Raymond Sommer and Luigi Chinetti in another Alfa. In 1933 he was 2nd in the Mille Miglia behind the great Tazio Nuvolari.

A fantastic streak began in 1924 when Cortese won the Targa Abruzzo at Pescara at 64.26 m.p.h. He repeated the feat in 1935 at 66.73 m.p.h. then a 3rd time in 1937 at 67.66 m.p.h.—this race marked by a virtuoso solo drive—and still a 4th time in 1938 at 69.29 m.p.h. It was Cortese's style to drive just fast enough to win, never faster than he had to. There were other races and other cars in those years, too. In 1937, for example, Cortese was 2nd to Rene Dreyfus in the Tripoli voiturette race in a Maserati and scored 3rds in the Pescara and Milan voiturette races. In 1938 he won the Modena and Verese races, and was 2nd to Luigi Villoresi in the Lucca Circuit.

War erupted in 1939, but Italy raced on through 1940, and Cortese stayed with the sport. In 1939 he won the Grosvenor GP at Capetown at 76.80 m.p.h., scored 2nds in the South African GP to Villoresi, the Coppa Ciano at Leghorn to Nino Farina, and 3rds in the Naples GP and the Rome-Lido Trophy race. Before Italy went to war in 1940, Cortese managed a 2nd in the Targa Florio to Villoresi.

In 1946, he was back in action, winning Modena in a Lancia sports car at 46.43 m.p.h. and taking a 2nd in a Turin voiturette race in an old Maserati. In 1947 Franco, at age 44, went single-seater racing in the Cisitalia, the Porsche-designed car, and won the special race for this marque in Cairo, Egypt, at 61.88 m.p.h. Alberto Ascari was 2nd, Piero Taruffi 3rd.

That same season Cortese drove Ferrari's first cars, the V12, 1.5-litre Type 125, retiring at Piacenza. But he won the Rome GP at 54.99 m.p.h. and Varese at 60.37 m.p.h. Seconds were recorded in the Coppa Acerbo and in the Parma sports car race, the latter to Nuvolari. In 1948, Cortese didn't do much, his best drive a 2nd to Felice Bonetto in Cisitalias in the Nuvolari Cup at Mantua. When Franco still didn't win in 1949, registering only a 2nd to Alberto Ascari in the Bari GP and 3rds in the Rome and Czech Grands Prix, there was talk that he was over the hill.

Talk stopped in 1950 when he won the Naples GP in a Ferrari borrowed from Count Johnny Lurani at 65.45 m.p.h. In 1951 he did something even more startling, winning the Targa Florio in, of all things, a Frazer-Nash at 45.57 m.p.h. Cortese kept driving through 1956, but there were no more major victories, and he confined his work pretty much to Italy as he had through much of his long career, perhaps one reason that he is not remembered as well as some less talented drivers of his day.

MEO COSTANTINI

Born in Venice, Meo Costantini was best remembered as the manager of the Bugatti racing team, but he was a highly successful driver before assuming the leadership role in 1926. And his own great racing successes were crammed into 3 short seasons. He became a Bugatti factory driver in 1924 and was 2nd in the San Sebastian Grand Prix to none other than Henry Segrave in a Sunbeam. In 1925 Costantini won the Targa Florio for Bugatti at 44.50 m.p.h., a feat he was to repeat in 1926 at 45.68 m.p.h. as he led a 3-Bugatti sweep across the finish line.

Meo won other races in those 2 Targa victory seasons. In 1925 he was the 1.5-litre class winner in the French GP at 52.24 m.p.h., and was 3rd overall in the Italian GP, and won its voiturette section at 86.53 m.p.h. In 1926, perhaps his greatest season, Costantini won the Spanish GP at 76.88 m.p.h., scored 2nds in the Italian and French races, and a 3rd in the San Sebastian, or European, GP. He also won the Milan GP at 95.41 m.p.h. Why he quit racing at that point to concentrate on team management is a great mystery, unless he believed in that old axiom, "quit while you are ahead." Costantini continued in racing until 1935 when he left France to return to Italy. He died in 1940.

PIERS COURAGE

The 1967 Formula 2 racing season in Europe had just finished, and John Coombs, who was running a sort of second-string quasi-factory team consisting of a single McLaren that traveled in the same transporter as Bruce's car, sat down with his driver and had a heart-to-heart talk with the young man. The driver was Piers Courage. He was tall, handsome, intelligent, and, in Coombs's mind, foolish to stay in auto racing.

At 25, Courage had been racing 6 years without major accomplishment, argued Coombs. That past season he had wound up 4th in the non-graded drivers' F2 championship standings, thanks to a 2nd at Zandvoort, a 3rd at Hockenheim and 5ths at the Eifelrennen and at Crystal Palace. But he had crashed badly at Pau, again at Brands Hatch, and nearly a 3rd time at Enna. Coombs's advice to Courage was to retire then and there before he hurt himself. Truly competitive Formula 1 racing—the big apple that had been Piers's goal right along—seemed as far away as ever.

Piers Raymond Courage undoubtedly did a lot of soul searching in making up his mind. He had a lot to think about. Born May 27, 1942, at Colchester, England, eldest son of the chairman of the Courage group of breweries, Piers could remember sneaking away from Eton to attend Silverstone meets with some of his

friends and how the desire to drive became stronger and stronger until it overcame his charted business career. Upon leaving Eton, he had joined a firm of accountants while continuing his studies. But at the same time his weekends were spent putting together a Lotus 7 kit that his father had given him because he thought it would be good for Piers to have to put it together himself. In later years, Courage was fond of reminiscing about his technical ability on that project; he was so technical, he said, that when he took the car up to Chestnut for Lotus to check it over, it was jammed in 2nd gear and the wishbones were mounted upside down.

Courage's competition debut came in May 1962 in the corrected Lotus 7. He did not win that race, nor any of the other 2 dozen or so starts he made that initial season, but he did place twice. Piers claimed to have kept an accurate count of his spins, however, and he said that the total reached 27 by year's end. In 1963, at the suggestion of Jonathan Williams, a friend who was to become a teammate on the Charles Lucas Engineering Team, Courage purchased a Merlyn-Climax sports/racer Mark IV. But the need for cash, and approaching accountancy exams forced Piers to sell the machine before he accomplished anything with it.

Racing won out over accountancy the following season, when Piers purchased a Lotus 22 Formula 3 car identical to the one Jon Williams had bought. Together they formed the Anglo-Swiss Racing Team, but like many another private effort in F3 it was a hand-to-mouth existence, Piers and Jon living in the old Ford Zephyr they used as tow car.

At one point, Courage's Lotus chassis was so bent that it required straightening, which was accomplished by leaning it against the pit wall at Monza while the Zephyr was gently backed into it. Piers led his first race that year at Nurburgring, but retired. He was 3rd at Rheims behind Jackie Stewart and Lucien Bianchi, 5th at Caserta in his Lotus, and 2nd to Stewart in a borrowed Radio Caroline Brabham in the European Cup at Zandvoort. "From my point of view," Piers said, "the year was a great success. I learned more of what motor racing is all about than in all my previous years of driving." And the team just about broke even in paying its way.

Charles Lucas, a sometime roommate with Piers and Jon Williams (and Frank Williams, Charles Crichton-Stuart, Bubbles Horsley, and even Innes Ireland) on Pinner Road, Harrow, decided that 1965 was the year to attack F3 more seriously. He formed a 2-car team of Brabhams with Courage and Jon as drivers. Piers won at Goodwood, Rouen, Silverstone, and Caserta, finished 2nd at Monza and Rheims, and registered a brace of 3rds at Monza. At season's end, Courage was awarded the top Grovewood Award for British drivers.

Elated, Piers decided to visit the Argentine Temporada series, but the throttle of his Lotus 35 jammed during the opening race and he crashed, ending up with a concussion and foot injuries. On top of that, he caught typhoid in the Argentine hospital. That gave him a chance to think about other things that had happened during 1965; like a wheel coming off at Monza; or the time another driver's throttle stuck, and he rammed Courage from behind, driving both cars off the course; or the time he drove off the course to avoid hitting a car that had spun broadside in front of him (the fact that he was about to lap this particular car adding insult to injury).

Lotus introduced its new F3 car in 1966, and Colin Chapman asked Lucas to run the factory team, with Courage and Roy Pike as drivers. Although the Lotus 41 had its teething troubles, Piers won at Albi, Brands Hatch, Pau, and Rouen. He was 2nd at Brands, Crystal Palace, and Karlskoga, 3rd at Rheims. That same year he and Pike shared a Maranello Concessionaires GTB Ferrari at Le Mans and won the GT class while finishing 8th overall. And then came 1967, more crashes, and Coombs's advice to hang up his helmet. That was the same year that Courage got his 1st F1 rides in rather uncompetitive machinery. At South Africa he got Tim Parnell's old Lotus-BRM 2-litre, in a 3-litre race of course, and worked up to 5th place before spinning off and damaging the car. At Teretonga, in the Tasman series, Piers got a BRM and was 3rd when he spun off again, then broke a camshaft. At Lakeside he spun again. In his first real race at Monaco, he tried again but spun off into a barrier. That was the end of his 1967 F1 career.

Courage's reasoning was different from Coombs's. He had done well up to 1967, and while that season was a disaster, no question about that, he still had faith in his own abilities, faith enough at least to give the upcoming Tasman series a try to see if he could sort himself out. He offered to buy Coombs's F2 car for that purpose. Coombs agreed, and the Tasman opener found Courage pitting his year-old, 1600-c.c. McLaren against Graham Hill and Jim Clark in factory 2.5-litre Lotuses, Chris Amon in a factory Ferrari, and Jack Brabham in the factory BRM. Despite this handicap, Piers scored a 2nd, a trio of 3rds, a 4th and two 5ths in the 7 races. No spinoffs, no crashes in these F2 races. Then, in the series finale at Longford, Tasmania, racing in a pouring rain, he beat the lot of them, and Courage suddenly was a sought-after driver once again. Parnell wanted him for BRM, Chapman wanted him as Lotus number 2, after Clark's tragic death. Piers stayed with BRM, despite its uncompetitiveness, and he was 4th in the Italian GP and 6th in the French GP in 1968.

In F2 he had joined forces with Frank Williams—no longer his roommate since Piers's marriage in April 1966 to Lady Sally Curzon, daughter of Earl Howe—in a private team formed by Williams after his own retirement from active competition. Piers's BT23C Brabham was 2nd at Enna, 3rd at Rheims, Albi, and Hockenheim; and 4th at Barcelona. He also won his final race in that car, the final round of the Argentine Temporada at Buenos Aires. Based on these successes, Courage and Williams determined to go F1 racing together in 1969. To get things under way a Brabham BT24 with a Repco engine was acquired, but the car was converted to Cosworth power for the Tasman series, and in this machine Piers wound up 3rd in the series with a 1st, 2nd, 3rd, and 4th.

Meanwhile, Williams acquired a BT26 and had it readied for the European season. At the Brands Hatch Race of Champions, the new team, car, and driver debuted. It retired with gear linkage problems and a split fuel tank. But in its next outing, the Silverstone International Trophy race, Courage was 5th despite a gear failure. The opening Spanish GP was a muddle with a start failure on the grid and a mini-riot among police and mechanics when the latter tried to push-start the car. Later a cam broke to finalize Courage's frustration. But at Monaco Piers dueled with Jackie Ickx most of the way and grabbed 2nd to Monaco-master Graham Hill in a Lotus. In the British GP at Silverstone (Courage's favorite course) he was 5th after a 5-way battle for that, placing with Hill and Jo Siffert in Lotuses and Amon and Pedro Rodriguez in Ferraris. After a crash in the German GP, things did not go all that well, but Courage dueled Brabham wheel-to-wheel in the United States GP for some time before dropping back. A 10th in the Mexican GP, the season finale, gave him a total of 16 points and 8th place in the World Drivers Championship.

The new, more professional Piers Courage was becoming serious about sports car racing, too. At Le Mans in 1969 he started a factory Matra V-12 with Jean-Pierre Beltoise and finished 4th overall. John Wyer tried to sign Courage for his Gulf-Porsche effort in 1970, but Piers accepted an Alfa Romeo factory ride instead, since it was as team leader. In the Buenos Aires 200, he won. In the BOAC 1000 in Britain, he charged through the rain bravely, but his codriver, Adam de Adamich, crashed the car. In his 1st Targa Florio he was 4th fastest in practice behind the veterans like Siffert, Nino Vaccarella, and Vic Elford, but crashed in the race itself 2 laps from the end. In F2 racing in 1969 Courage won at Enna and was 3rd at Hockenheim, Pau, Jarama, Zolder, and Rheims in a BT30.

Things looked good for 1970, especially since Williams had set up a new F1 team with de Tomaso, the Italian carbuilder. A new car was designed, with proven Ford power, and it was constantly improved in its preseason starts, culminating in the Silverstone Express meet in which Piers captured 3rds in both heats behind Stewart and Amon. Courage still was sorting out the new car when the GP circus landed at Zandvoort for the Dutch race. He had crashed in practice for the Spanish GP, and he banged into the dunes again in Holland after skidding on an oil patch. But as the race got under way, Courage was in the 4th row, and he was off to a good start. Effectively, there were 2 races. The big boys —Jo Rindt, Stewart, Ickx—were in one race. Back a bit, Courage, Beltoise, Clay Regazzoni, and the others were battling for 4th.

Piers had worked loose of this fight when it happened. On the 23rd lap his De Tomaso slid once again—perhaps on more oil—just before the East Tunnel. The car climbed the embankment, knocked down three poles, hit another bank and rolled over, exploding. Firemen were immediately on the scene, but the blaze was so fierce that the surrounding woods immediately caught fire as well, and no one could get near the car. Its magnesium frame showered the track with blazing bits, and a thick black smoke cloud covered the scene of tragedy. Rindt went on to win the race, but there was no joy in that victory for the sport had lost another valuable asset. Sally Curzon Courage was a widow with 2 children.

CHRIS CRAFT

Christopher Adrian Craft, was a young gentleman who made the big switch from junior buyer in ladies' underwear to racing driver with relative ease. Born in 1940, Craft was the son of a retired bank official who became a volunteer missionary in Africa. One of his brothers was a respected British obstetrician and gynecologist. Another shared a bodywork and painting shop with Chris in Woodford Green, Essex, which he called home.

Chris made a late start in auto racing and confined his activities—more because of cost than desire—to saloon racing for a long time before entering single-seater and sports car ranks. He started driving his own Anglia—painted in a bright orange to hide its age and rather battered condition—and first made an impression in Britain in 1962. The following year he switched to John Young's Super-Speed Team, initially driving Anglias in Group 2 for a couple of years to prove himself, then driving in Group 5 in 1966.

He handled bigger machinery, too. In 1965, for example, he codrove an E Jaguar with Jackie Oliver to a class victory (3rd overall) in a race at Brands Hatch. At other times, Chris had been in a Mustang 2/2 and a Merlyn Formula 3 car, with which he was singularly unsuccessful because it was woefully underpowered. In 1964 he visited the United States for the Road America 500 at Elkhart Lake, Wis., and took a class with a Lotus-Cortina. He signed his initial single-seater team contract for 1967, a F3 BWA from Italy. Chris reminded some people of Mike Hawthorn, Peter Collins, and Harry Schell, in personality, and he may have had some of their driving traits as well.

In a day when racing drivers are much more like technicians, and very businesslike in demeanor on the course, Craft was very much a personality. Well-liked, he was not one to spend all of his time with racing people. Perhaps it was his own varied background; he had tried his hand at selling used cars and had worked as an assistant competition manager for Ford of England. His leisure time interests included legitimate theater, music, art, and boxing matches.

He put his long-time image as a saloon racer to bed for good in 1969 with outstanding performances in a Tech-Speed Lola-Chevrolet T70 and a Porsche 908. In 1970 Chris entered F5000 with a Ford-powered Leda challenger to Chevvy, switched to a McLaren-Ford, but failed to gain a point in 2 starts. Instead, he concentrated on sports car racing, winning the Swedish GP at Karlskoga in a McLaren-DFV M8C. But the year was frustrating enough for a talented racer to think about doing something else if his luck did not change soon. The frustrations continued in 1971, both with Chevron in sports and F2 racing and with a Brabham in Formula 1 at the United States Grand Prix, where he retired early, and 1972 was no better.

PETE CRAIG

Pete Craig is worth mentioning in the saga of automotive speed for 2 reasons. In 1930 he held the 100-mile mark at Daytona Beach, when the boys were racing around barrels. And he used to race cars as a pasttime! He was actually a newspaper reporter and later wrote fiction.

149

Craig started competing in 1923 and he was still driving in 1937, mostly in the South in dirt cars. While he raced a flathead Ford all over the Southeastern United States, Pete was particularly identified with Daytona where he is said to have competed for 17 years. Since he ended his career just prior to World War II, that means there were races straight through the Twenties, something to which no present Daytona authority will admit. Born in Gainesville, Ga., Craig eventually became an employee of the *Atlanta Journal*, but he continued to race. He had an edge on the other reporters at Lakewood Park. They saw the races, but he made them.

CURTIS CRIDER

Curtis Wade Crider of Charleston, S.C. never won a Grand National championship race. Born October 7, 1930, this near 6-foot father of 2 was one of the better racing mechanics; as a Grand National driver he had a perfect average—no victories in almost 200 starts. But in modified-sportsman meets, the Crawfish was a feared foe. The nickname came from one of his first races, on a very muddy track at Danville, Va., when Curtis slithered out of his car looking like a crawfish crawling out of the mud.

For a decade Crider was a faithful modified-sportsman competitor in the Piedmont area, winning the Greenwood, S.C., track championship in 1952 and 1953. His greatest thrill came when, at Columbia, S.C., he won the feature on the very last lap with a move around the leader worthy of a Lee Petty. During the decade of his modified success, Crawfish drove an occasional Grand National race, but he never had a Mercury ready to compete against the specialists in the field. In 1960, lured by the bigger money, he began to campaign in the late model stocks and, after 21st, 12th, and 17th place finishes the preceding 3 seasons, he moved up to 6th place in 1964.

While he never won a race, the payoff structure in NASCAR was such that he was able to earn more than many Grand Prix heroes in 1964, without ever finishing higher than 3rd. He earned $17,750 with 7 top-5 and 30 top-10 finishes. Crider's ambition was to own a small cattle ranch, and whenever he finished high, he stowed away the necessary gear—cowboy boots, britches, jacket, hat, lasso.

CHARLES CRIGHTON-STUART

Charles Crighton-Stuart, born in London on March 10, 1939, came from an old Scottish Catholic family, the Butes. His grandfather was the 5th Marquis of Bute, his father was Lord Patrick Crighton-Stuart; and Char-

lie himself was the Honorable Charles Crighton-Stuart, disguised in blue Dunlop racing coveralls and checkered crash helmet and crouched in a Formula 3 Brabham-Ford. At one point Stuart looked as if he might make the big jump from F3 to a higher classification, but it never happened.

Crighton-Stuart was educated at Ampleforth in Yorkshire, where he excelled at sports—swimming and playing rugby and cricket for his house, as well as boxing, shooting and running for his own enjoyment. He did well enough at the books to graduate satisfactorily, and immediately joined the RAF. In 5 years the youngster managed to crash 3 times, which led the authorities to suspect that there might be some physical cause. After much poking around, they discovered he had high-altitude deafness, and his flying career was over. The Transport Command did not appeal to Stuart, so he left the RAF.

It was around this time in 1961 that Charlie was dragged to a Brands Hatch meeting by his father, who had raced MGs in his younger days, including the Paris—Nice race. Charlie immediately was hooked. He acquired an ex-MRP Mark 2 Cooper-BMC and practiced several times a week at Brands. He took the plunge at Silverstone, coming in 6th, in July 1962. In all, Stuart entered 12 races that year, with his highest finish a 2nd. For the next season, he switched to a Mark 3A Cooper-Ford and continued concentrating on club meetings. He did take the car to Ireland once, however, and finished 6th at Kirkistown. In 1964 he kept the Cooper but swapped the Ford powerplant for a BMC one, which was not the most successful change of the year. Still, Charlie managed a 2nd at Montlhéry's May meet, 3rd at Magny-Cours, 4th at Montlhéry's September meet, 5th at Mallory Park, and 6ths at Oulton Park, La Châtre, Monza, and Nurburgring.

In 1965 Stuart bought Jo Rindt's Formula 2 Brabham chassis and equipped it for F3 with a Cosworth-Ford engine. He raced under Stirling Moss's colors and managed major wins in the East German Grand Prix at Sachsenring, and twice at Montlhéry in the Paris GP and in the Coupe du Salon. The latter really put the youngster in the public eye when he won after a race-long, wheel-to-wheel duel with Jean-Pierre Beltoise's Matra-Ford. It was especially sweet to Charlie because it was his first victory in about 3 months. His career was studded with dry spells, and no one was able to explain them satisfactorily. That year he was also 2nd at Goodwood and another Montlhéry meet; 3rd at Oulton Park; 4th at Silverstone, Magny-Cours, and Monte Carlo; and 5th at another Goodwood meet.

The drought hit Crighton-Stuart in 1966 after an auspicious start in the Argentine Temporada, a 4-race series at the year's start, which Charlie won at Mendosa and was 2nd at both Buenos Aires and Mar del Plata. These finishes accumulated enough points to give him the Temporada title. After that flurry, it was a long season. Crighton-Stuart had a 5th at Snetterton and a 6th at Barcelona, then went a long time before scoring later-season finishes at Monza (2nd) and Montlhéry (6th).

This kind of trial has made many a man quit. Stuart himself, while he admitted that it was discouraging, also added: "What really matters is that a driver give his best. It is this trying that really matters, not the end result. If this were not true, then you could hardly call this a sport. You must, however, have a good mill. Without that you might as well give up. After that, it is just a matter of practice and more practice until the faults—of the car and of the driver—are ironed out. For instance, I used to be bad on starts, but I soon realized it, and by a concentrated effort, I managed to rectify that fault." Racing luck plays a role, too, and Crighton-Stuart could have used some. With it, he might have gone all the way.

WILLIAM CUMMINGS

Wild Bill Cummings born in 1914, may or may not have been very wild, but he came from the west end of Indianapolis, and that was enough to give him the sobriquet. By 1930 he had established his reputation by smoking up the dirt tracks of the Midwest for qualifying record after quaifying record. He placed in the top 10 in 4 of his 9 Indianapolis appearances. And in 1933 Cummings set race records for several distances through 75 miles that survived for 4 years. This was in an era when car constructors had to worry about fuel consumption because of the fuel-allotment limit.

Cummings, who wore a tiny mustache, originally came to Indy because the money at the dirt tracks dropped appreciably after the 1929 stockmarket crash. He placed 5th in his 1930 debut. He sat on the pole in 1933 and led the first 75 miles, retiring eventually with a leaking radiator cap (that had him in the pits regularly after that first burst of speed). For 1934 Cummings and the Boyle Valve people were worried about how to go fast on 45 gallons of fuel. Their answer was partially in minor adjustments to the front-drive Miller Four. They used the 2-valves-per-cylinder version with a square bore-stroke of 4.125 and shaved the car's weight to 1,950 pounds. They used 20-inch wheels fore and aft instead of 18, and, there were special instructions to Wild Bill.

William was enjoined to forget the trophy dash for the front of the pack and move up only after the leaders had been sorted out. So he was 8th after 25 miles, afternated between 3rd and 4th for the first 250 miles, and led only afte. 290 miles had been run. Mauri Rose roared back into the lead in the rear-drive Duray Miller when Bill pitted, and Mauri held Wild Bill off until only 25 laps were left. At a signal from the pits, Cummings drove into the lead, as easily as if Rose were held back by some giant rubber band, and then held Mauri off for the closest Indy finish up until then, 27 seconds.

The victory earned enough points to give Bill the AAA 1934 season championship, for the Championship Trail was rather sparse during that era. That was the year that such traditional venues as Langhorne, Michigan State Fairgrounds at Detroit, and Milwaukee left the AAA circuit temporarily. On the Championship Trail, Wild Bill had gathered many fans. He had won at Syracuse, N.Y., in 1930 and 1933, at Langhorne in 1930, and at Detroit in 1933. There were few other stops until the postwar renaissance; that is why Indy was so dominant in American racing.

In 1935 Cummings took 3rd behind Kelley Petillo, never having the speed in his Boyle Valve Special to challenge Kelley or Wilbur Shaw. In 1936 Cummings was left at the starting line because the clutch blew in his Boyle Offy. He finished 6th the following year despite having one of the fastest cars on the track, an amazing job because he made 6 pit stops to winner Shaw's 2, runnerup Ralph Hepburn's 3, and 4 for the next 3 finishers ahead of him. Switching to the IBEW Special in 1938, he lasted 72 laps, withdrawing because of a leaking radiator. This was a Miller 8 and a team car to the Maserati of Mauri Rose and the Offy of Chet Miller. Cummings died in a 1940 highway accident when he skidded on wet pavement and hit a concrete abutment near Indianapolis.

BRIGGS CUNNINGHAM

No single man had a greater influence than Briggs Cunningham on the course of American road racing development after World War II, when very few men had the willingness or wherewithal to dream of an American car with American drivers that could win the Le Mans 24-hour race. It took a corporation to accomplish that years later, but Briggs's efforts with stock components against the sophisticated Italian, French, and English racing cars were fabulously successful, the 3rd-place finish in 1954 especially so.

Born to a meat packing fortune in Cincinnati, Briggs Swift Cunningham lost his father when he was a boy of 7. Shortly after that unhappy 1914 moment, his mother bought a huge Pierce-Arrow. Briggs wheedled the chauffeur into teaching him how to drive the car in less than a year. Eight years later, he owned his first car. A Yale engineering student, Cunningham spent much time in sports—boxing, track, tennis, sailing. He lasted 2 years in school before he married Lucie Bedford, daughter of a New York industrialist, an equally enthusiastic sailor. The young couple went to Europe on their honeymoon, bringing over a 6-metre yacht and buying an Alfa Romeo.

One day while waiting for his bride in the lobby of his hotel in St. Moritz, a casual acquaintance asked if he would care to go bobsledding. "Sure," said Cunningham, who had never seen a bobsled, "when?"

"Right now."

"Well," Cunningham said, "I'm waiting for my wife."

His acquaintance laughed, "You'll be right back. All you have to do is drag your leg as a brake if we go out of control."

Walking over to the bobsled run, Briggs discovered that the bobsledding he was about to do was in international competition. Lashed onto their sled, the 2 men were shoved on to the fearsome ice track. Less than a minute later they had completed the mile run. Cunningham shook his team-mate's hand and walked back to the hotel. Lucie met him in the lobby and asked where he had been.

"I was in a bobsled race," he told her, "and we were lousy. We finished 3rd."

Sailing and golf next attracted him. In golf he applied a basic Cunningham theory: all you have to do in order to become good at anything is practice enough. By playing golf every day for a year he improved to the point where he could beat par regularly. Then he took up flying. At the outbreak of the war, Cunningham, 34 by this time, and with children, attempted to enlist as a fighter pilot. He was turned down and spent World War II flying for the Civil Air Patrol, searching Atlantic coastal waters for German subs. Meanwhile, he repeatedly won sailing titles against the best yachtsmen in the world.

After the war Briggs began racing in MGs. Once he had solved their rather simple style, he looked around for something more complicated to labor over. A crack mechanic and an inveterate tinkerer, he began to move Buick engines into Mercedes bodies and produced a car that he called a Bu-Merc. This fitted in admirably with the ideas of 2 talented mechanics he met at Watkins Glen in 1949, Phil Walters and Bill Frick. They were in the forefront in the engine-swapping era of American motor sports, fitting Cadillac engines into Fords and Studebakers. They got to talking and B. S. Cunningham, Inc., was formed. A factory was established at Palm Beach.

Sam Collier, a close friend and one of Cunningham's mentors in sports-car racing, was killed in his Ferrari in the 1950 Glen race. After that, Briggs seemed to change, and he embraced and amplified Sam's dream of a preeminent U.S. sports car. He wanted to make it the fastest and the safest car in the world. The era of the Cunningham sports car lasted almost 5 years, and might have lasted longer if Detroit had shown any signs of real cooperation.

Meanwhile, Cunningham had become involved in another venture—the New York area distributorship for Jaguar in conjunction with Alfred Momo, his pit chief. He was still driving as he had throughout the years, when the cars of his own marque were helping keep sports-car racing alive at Strategic Air Command airport races. But now the racing cars were Lister-Jaguars, C Jags, D Jags, with an occasional outing in small-bore machinery. And the Cunningham appearances were relegated more and more to Sebring rather than shorter races. He began to turn back to sailing, too. Yet in the 1958 Sebring race, at the age of 51, Briggs pushed his Lister-Jaguar back to the pits, a walk of 2 miles, then climbed into it after repairs and finished 15th.

In 1959, while sailing in the America's Cup Challenge round, he still had part of his thoughts on his racing cars. Shortly after the start of the first race with the British boat Sceptre, his Columbia spurted into the lead, and Cunningham realized that the America's Cup was in no danger. But he nevertheless pushed the boat to the limit, not to humiliate the British, but to get back and find out how his cars had made out at Watkins Glen. As soon as he got ashore, he raced for the nearest telephone and called Momo. "How did we make out?" he asked. Momo told him they had finished 1st and 2nd. Breathing a sigh of relief, Cunningham hung up. A well-wisher who had seen his yachting victory pounced on Briggs and said, "Great race." Cunningham smiled genially.

"It must have been," he said. "Too bad I had to miss it."

In 1962, at the age of 55, he was still racing, co-driving an XK-E Jaguar to 4th place at Le Mans (he also ran 2 Maseratis), then competing at least 5 times during the SCCA season. His season was cut short by a visit to Newport to watch the America's Cup renewal. In 1963 Bruce McLaren and Walt Hansgen rode one of his Jaguars to an 8th overall at Sebring, but his Cooper-Maseratis failed to finish. But the end of his Jaguar campaigning—in fact all of his active campaigning—was drawing near. With the denigration of the SCCA national in favor of the U.S. Road Racing Series and his withdrawal from the business, Briggs tapered off from racing, eventually running only Sebring. In 1965 he entered a Porsche 904 and finished 20th, sharing the ride with John Fitch.

He moved from his long-time home at Greens Farms, Conn., across the country to Newport Beach in southern California, taking his magnificent collection of some 80 pedigreed cars with him and setting them up in a museum at Costa Mesa. He sold off the Jaguar distributorship and went into semi-retirement, coming back in sailing to help make an unsuccessful try for selection as the 1967 America's Cup defender.

Cunningham was associated with more great and near-great drivers than any other patron. The original group included Fitch, who later drove for Mercedes, Phil Walters, Bill Spear, Sherwood Johnston, and John Gordon Bennet, a Briton who made money in the States and then emigrated to the Caribbean. Later came Dick Thompson, Watt Hansgen, Dan Gurney, Roger Penske, Bruce McLaren, Archie Scott-Brown, Stirling Moss, Roy Salvadori, Bob Grossman, Lake Underwood, and others.

Briggs never was a playboy, never smoked or drank. He did have his strange moments, however. He admitted to the truth of stories about his grabbing a broom and sweeping the pits just to have something to do with his hands when not driving. "I like to keep my hands busy. I get nervous and irritable otherwise," he said. Cunningham was missing as a driver after 1965, having once again returned to sailing. But the dreams he dreamed were at least partially realized. American cars were competitive or supreme all over the international scene and so were American drivers.

STANISLAUS CZAYKOWSKI

Among the European nobles who populated racing in the years between the wars was a Polish Count who lived in Paris and was a highly successful Bugatti privateer, Stanislaus Czaykowski. He appeared on the racing scene in a prominent spot in 1929 when he was 4th in the Comminges Grand Prix. In 1930 he was 2nd in the same race's voiturette section.

The Count got going in 1931, winning the Casablanca GP at 85.08 m.p.h. and nabbing 2nds in the Lorraine, Dieppe and Comminges Grands Prix—the latter two to Pierre Etancelin. Czaykowski also was 3rd in the Marne GP that season. The following year was a successful voiturette season, the Count winning the Dieppe (72.10 m.p.h.), Nimes (80.06 m.p.h.) and Comminges (time unrecorded) races. He was 2nd in the Lorraine voiturette, 3rd in the GP race and 3rd in the Casablanca GP.

In 1933 Stanislaus put his name in the speed record books with a Type 54 Bugatti run around Avus at 132.87 m.p.h. That year he won the British Empire Trophy dash at Brooklands with a 123.58 m.p.h. clocking, won the Dieppe GP at 76.12 m.p.h., and was 2nd to Archille Varzi in the Avus GP. But at Monza Czaykowski's rising star exploded, his Type 54 spinning off the banking and literally exploding and killing the Polish nobleman who seemed destined for even greater heights behind the wheel.

JIMMY DAVIES

The lure of the 6-wheeled car once infected American track racing. It stands to reason, or so many have thought, that a car with 4 wheels in the rear would be more stable and less prone to spins than a car with 2. It also stands to reason, as many have forgotten, that the weight of 2 extra wheels, plus attachments, is a penalty no one can overcome—or has to date.

A gentleman named Pat Clancy brought a 6-wheeled car to Indianapolis in 1948 and remained convinced of its competitiveness even though it managed to do very little. He reasoned that if 6 wheels worked on his dump trucks, they should work on a race car. When he returned to California, he picked a new driver, a tough kid from the roadster circuit named Jimmy Davies. In

1949 Davies, a slender 6-footer born August 8, 1923, in Glendale Calif., drove the Pat Clancy Special as a 6-wheeler in a few dirt races before the owner converted it to a conventional 4-wheeler. He then won the Del Mar 100 in 1949 (held on the horse track) and the Phoenix 100 in 1950. His rookie year at Indy, he drove the same vehicle, qualifying 27th and being flagged in the rain in 17th, after completing 128 laps. In 1951 he drove the Parkes Special and led for 25 laps before breaking the car's rear end. He was in the Army in 1952, but returned from Korea in time to drive again for his first benefactor, Clancy, finishing 10th at Indianapolis.

The same car qualified as 2nd alternate in 1954 and Jimmy performed the unusual feat of driving 2 cars in the actual race. He substituted for Sam Hanks in Bardahl No. 1 for 36 laps, then relieved Art Cross in Bardahl No. 45 from the 174th lap to finish in 11th spot. Davies also gave Clancy victories at Springfield and in the Williams Grove, Pa., championship sprint feature. He came back to the Brickyard for what was to prove his finest hour there in the Clancy-owned Bardahl Special, starting 10th and finishing 3rd in 1955. He finished 6th on the season.

It was as if Davies, married and a father, had 2 careers, for we pick up the threads of his success again in 1959 when he began to terrorize the country as one of the finest midget—or as USAC preferred to call it, Offy 110—drivers around. In a side excursion into the Championship Trail, he finished 3rd at Trenton, but he made most of his reputation in the small cars. Second nationally in 1959, Jimmy won the championship in 1960, 61 and 62 before dropping to 4th in 1963 and 5th in 1964. A master of the quarter-mile dirt track, Davies in 1965 still held records at 16 tracks.

FLOYD DAVIS

Floyd Davis, who was born in southern Illinois, came to racing during the depths of the Depression when men hauled their equipment 500 miles on the promise of making $100. Active at first on the dirt tracks in the Illinois-Missouri area, Davis came East with the stable of Johnny Gerber in 1935. In Mineola, N.Y., he bested a large field of eastern hotshots, showed well at Woodbridge and Hohokus, N.J., and then toured the South.

Davis won at Langhorne in 1936 in a Joel Thorne car and campaigned for Thorne off and on for the rest of his racing career. He drove in 4 Indianapolis 500s, and by far the most important victory of his career came in the 1941 race when he codrove the winning car with Mauri Rose. In his previous 500 outings, he had crashed at the end of the 1937 race after the checkered flag had dropped, missed 1938, lasted 107 and 392 miles the next 2 years.

Davis was in the backup car in 1941, Thorne and Rose being the chargers. Thorne was involved in an early accident and Rose was sidelined by spark plug trouble after 60 laps, so Davis was called in after 180 miles to relinquish his mount to Rose. Davis was in 14th place at the time. After Mauri took over, Floyd sat and watched his share of the purse get bigger and bigger. Later that year Davis quit to become a successful businessman. He figured that winning half an Indy 500 was the best he ever could do.

JIMMY DAYWALT

It was the 1953 Indianapolis 500, and 29-year-old Jimmy Daywalt was "Rookie of the Year" for taking his Sumar Special from the 21st starting position to finish 6th. He did not know it then, but this was to be the zenith of a career that began in 1947 in the so-called minor leagues of big-car racing. Jimmy had passed his driver's test in 1949, but the Sumar car was his first good ride.

The 1954 race was the tragic turning point in a story that had started so well. Jimmy had qualified 2nd, but finished in the hospital. On lap 111 he hit the wall on the northwest turn, demolishing himself and the car; Bill Vukovich went on to win easily. It was the 1st of 4 serious accidents, 3 of them in the 500. In 1955 he pushed the Sumar from 17th to 9th place, but in 1956, in his last ride in the Sumar Special, Jimmy hit the wall on the southeast turn at the 134-lap mark, again landing in the hospital. In 1957 he collided with the northeast wall on the 53rd lap, and that ended that racing year.

Daywalt did not return until 1959, when he secured a ride in the Federal Engineering Special. It was the first time that he finished 200 laps without improving his position, dropping from 13th to 14th place. There were 2 other Indy appearances, 27 laps in 1961 before a brake line broke in the Schulz Fueling Equipment car, and 75 laps before transmission failure overtook his Albany, N.Y., Special in 1962. He died of cancer 3 years later, leaving two young children.

ANDREA DE ADAMICH

Alfa Romeo's Formula 1 effort in the early seventies consisted of Andrea de Adamich, an Italian driver for whom Alfa prepared engines on both the McLaren and March teams. He had personal sponsorship and arrangements that gave him his F1 ride in whatever car he chose, but only with Alfa power. He also drove Alfas in sports car/prototype racing.

De Adamich was one of Italy's top racers at the end of the Sixties, partially because so many of the older drivers had been killed or retired. But that was not the only reason; Andrea was experienced and talented beyond his years. Born October 3, 1941, in Trieste, he

was the son of a wealthy landowner. Not having to worry about money, Andrea was able to take up auto racing when he felt like it. At 19 he started racing a Triumph TR-3, tuning the car himself. He moved up rapidly in national racing, in both sports sedans and Formula Junior, and in 1966 de Adamich first became associated with Alfa Romeo's Autodelta team. Giving up law school for racing, he won that season's European Touring Car Championship, and won again in 1967.

Ferrari gave him a test drive in a F1 car at the end of 1967, and he joined the factory F1 squad in 1968; but his Grand Prix season was a short one. In the South African opener he was the fastest Ferrari driver in practice, he spun on oil in the race's 13th lap and crashed. While practicing in March for the non-title Race of Champions at Brands Hatch, de Adamich crashed much more seriously, and was not able to get back into a single-seater until October, when he ran 2nd in the Formula 2 Rome GP by less than 6 seconds.

In the winter leading into 1969, de Adamich won the F2 Argentine series for Ferrari, but there was no F1 berth available with the Commendatore's forces. Instead, Andrea concentrated on Alfa's T33/3 sports car, with some other drives that displayed a startling versatility. With Frank Gardner, the Australian veteran, he ran the Monza 1000 in a Lola-Chevrolet and finished 5th. Over in the United States for another race, he ran the Michigan Canadian-American Challenge Cup as a lark, finished 5th in a McLaren-Chevy Mk. 12, winning $5,200 and 8 championship points. In Formula 5000—the 5-litre, stock block, single-seater racing then brand new

in Britain—he ran 5 races, his best being the North Sea Trophy battle, where he raced the fastest lap, but finished only 4th because of mechanical troubles plaguing his Lola-Chevvy T55; he finished 12th in the final standings for the Guards European F5000 Trophy.

In 1970 de Adamich really got going. In F2 racing for the Jolly Club Milano, he had a good Brabham-FVA BT30. He squeezed in some races between other assignments, to get more single-seater experience, and was 4th at the Crystal Palace in his best appearance. In Alfa sports car racing he was 2nd with Henri Pescarolo in the Austrian 1000 and with Nanno Galli in the Imola 500, then won at Buenos Aires with Piers Courage and in the Nurburgring 6-hour Touring Car Challenge with Picci in an Alfa GTA. And the coveted F1 berth came, too, thanks to Alfa's sponsorship. With Team McLaren he started the season with an M7D that suffered teething troubles as British mechanics had to learn to deal with an Italian engine so different from their own. De Adamich did not qualify at either Spain or Monaco, managed a sputtering 15th in France, could not start in Britain, and failed to qualify again in Holland.

Switching the Alfa power to a new M14D McLaren did not help; in the German GP he again did not qualify. He finally entered a race in Austria where he finished 12th. In Italy he had his best F1 race of the year, a mere 8th. Retired in Canada, he failed to qualify again in the United States GP. In 1971 Andrea and his Alfa power moved over to the STP-March F1 team. The new combination did not do the bespectacled, dark driver any real good, but Alfa power, housed in a revised T33/3 did earn Andrea and his codriver, Ronnie Peterson, a spectacular, 2-lap victory over 5-litre Porsche 917s in the Watkins Glen 6-hour enduro, which, coupled with an earlier BOAC 1000 victory with Henri Pescarolo, made it perhaps, Andrea's biggest year.

Other 1971 enduros included a 4th in the Buenos Aires 1000, 3rds in the Sebring 12 Hours and the Spa and Monza 1000s, and a 4th at the Nurburgring 1000, all with Pescarolo; as well as a 2nd with Gijs van Lennep at the Targa Florio behind teammates Nino Vaccarella and Dickie Attwood. In F1 de Adamich suffered through a 13th in South Africa, retirements in Spain and France, an unclassified 14th in the British GP, retirements again in Germany and Italy, and an 11th in the United States GP. He drove a private Surtees in 1972, managed a 4th in the Spanish GP, and a tie for 16th in the standings. Ferrari drove the Alfas into the ground in sports car racing, and with them Andrea.

TONY DEAN

The impossible becomes the possible when a man is in the right place at the right time, and knows what to do when the door opens a crack. A. G. (Tony) Dean knew what to do in September 1970 at Gainesville, Ga., site of the Road Atlanta course, when he won the 7th run-

ning of the year's Canadian-American Challenge Cup series. Dean's winning the race, his 1st major race victory and the biggest payoff of his professional racing career, was one thing. The fact that he won a CanAm without being a member of Team McLaren was another.

The last time someone other than a McLaren driver had won a CanAm was October 13, 1968, and that was 20 races—and 3 CanAm championships—before. Dean and other assorted hangers-on had their day in the inaugural event at the $1.3 million facility 40 miles north of Atlanta. It was a day that saw 4 collisions and 12 spinouts, McLaren's Denis Hulme ram a slower car and eliminated himself, and Peter Revson spun and crashed into an embankment, followed by Bob Brown who had just inherited the lead. George Eaton, the Canadian department store heir, was to lead until his gearbox jammed and he rammed an embankment. Through it all, no one was hurt, except their pride.

Tony Dean, rather rotund, bald, driving a second-hand Porsche 908 that had no chance ever to win on its merits, was willing to take the victory any way he could get it. Born in 1932, he started racing in 1959 in go-karts. He switched to cars in 1964, with a Lotus 11 and a Formula 3 Cooper-Ford. In 1965 Tony put in a full British racing season with a Repco Brabham-Ford. He won only at Croft, but had lots of 3rds there and abroad and won the BRSCC 500 Club F3 title, as well as assorted other awards.

Dean was quick to concede he was a bit advanced in years to have any serious single-seater aspirations; although he still liked to get into such a cockpit occa-

sionally for a lark, and in 1967 he started concentrating on sports car competition. In both a Porsche Carerra 6 and in a Ferrari 206S Dino he did well on European courses. Both cars were used when he acquired them in one of his two-garage used-car businesses in Leeds, Yorkshire, England. He came to the United States in 1969 to drive in the Watkins Glen 6-Hour sports car race, then ran the next day's CanAm as part of the scenery. He finished 9th, but got as much money for that as for some of his much better European finishes.

Tony decided the garages could survive without him for a time, and he ran the rest of the 1969 CanAm season. He was 8th at Mid-Ohio, 5th at Elkhart Lake's Road America battle, 6th at Bridgehampton, 7th at Michigan, Monterey, and Riverside, and 8th at the Texas finale. Overall, Dean won $34,000 for an 8th-place finish in the standings, well ahead of people like John Surtees, Mario Andretti, Revson, Dan Gurney, and even Jack Brabham. Heady stuff for a garageman running an old Porsche 908.

There was talk of Tony moving up to a used Porsche 917—the World Manufacturers Championship car—in 1970, but the Yorkshireman kept his old 908. At Mosport he finished 4th, his best-ever running in the Can-Am, but at the Glen he was 16th, at Edmonton 11th, and at Mid-Ohio he failed to finish. This definitely was not part of the strategy; his idea was to finish, even down low, and pick up the Yankee dollars as the real contenders burned each other out. At Elkhart Lake the strategy worked for 5th place. Then came Road Atlanta, a $16,450 payoff. A lap back, 72 seconds, was Dave Causey, part of the scenery; it was that kind of a race. A 7th at Donnybrooke and a 9th at Riverside, were anti-climactic.

Dean finished 6th overall in the 1970 CanAm standings, with cash winnings of $48,850, and a niche carved out in the history of that exciting race series as the man who beat Team McLaren at long last. Anything that happened after that would be pure gravy.

ERNEST VON DELIUS

In an era of great German talent, Ernest von Delius went relatively unnoticed, although his career, short as it was, suggested genuine potential. Born in 1910, Delius tried everything in sight as soon as he was old enough to get behind the steering wheel, and his list included Dixi, Alfa Romeo, Zoller, Rohr, BMW and ERA before he arrived at one of Germany's pre-war greats, Auto Union.

Delius's Auto Union career started in 1936. Second in the Pescara Coppa Acerbo, he was 3rd in the Italian Grand Prix to teammates Bernd Rosemeyer and Tazio Nuvolari, 4th at Penya Rhin, 5th at Budapest and 6th in the German GP. In 1937 Delius won the Grosvenor GP at Capetown at 80.37 m.p.h., 2nd in the Avusrennen to Hermann Lang, 3rd in the Tripoli GP to Lang and Rosemeyer, and 4th in the United States Vanderbilt Cup. How far Delius might have gone from that point would never be known. In the German GP his Auto Union brushed with Dick Seaman's Mercedes at 170 m.p.h. Seaman came out of it all right, but Delius's car flew 400 yards through the air and crashed, killing the 27-year-old German.

FRANKIE DEL ROY

A respected USAC technical expert later in his career, former riding mechanic Frankie Del Roy was small in stature but a giant when it came to the development of racing talent and ideas. He was born Frank De Rosa in Philadelphia on November 7, 1911. According to family plans Frankie was destined to become a violin virtuoso, but he thought differently. On the way to school he had discovered Zeke Meyers's garage, which had a racing car. He cut school to listen to the stories of the drivers as they worked on their cars and decided that he was going to be a driver and a mechanic. Zeke let him wash engine parts. He cut violin lessons, too, which brought matters to a head, when his father, a builder, walked into the garage one day. Poppa De Rosa apparently was an unusual man, because when Frankie pleaded to be allowed to work in the garage, he agreed.

Frank Farmer and Jimmie Gleason also helped Del Roy (he took the name because he did not want anyone to know what he was doing until he proved himself as a racer). Meyers was running Nationals in the East—with people like Russ Snowberger, Ray Keech and Fred Winnai—and was an excellent teacher as well as a top wrench man. He taught Del Roy most of the basics about being a racing mechanic. When Frankie was 13, Zeke took him to see a race in Pottstown, Pa., and he let Frankie warm up the car in places like Atlantic City, Pitman and Pottstown. He is supposed to have dubbed Del Roy "Barney Youngfield."

But Frankie did not drive in his 1st race until 1930, when he bought an old Chevvy for $200. He rode his 1st race at Pitman, N.J., and won the 1st of 7 that year at Roanoke, Va. He met Norris Friel—long-time NASCAR chief eyeballer—at Salisbury, Md., whom Del Roy credited with making him into a full-time mechanic. Norris pointed out that the Chevvy went so well because of Del Roy's skill with the tool box, not his driving. After considering this, Frankie retired as a driver. But then 2-man race cars returned to vogue in America, and Frankie was in demand as a riding mechanic for his size and his skill. His first ride was on the Altoona boards with Jimmy Gleason. He switched to Zeke's car for Syracuse the day Gleason was killed, and in which accident the mechanic who replaced Frankie sustained a broken back.

Other rides came with Benny Hill, Rick Decker, Fred Frame, Wilbur Shaw, Floyd Roberts, and Wild Bill Cummings. He met Cotton Hennings, the man who influenced him as much as Clayton, in 1937. Cotton taught thoroughness, and he was a bug for cleanliness and painstaking preparation. Del Roy rode with Cummings in 1937 the day Wild Bill wrested the pole from Shaw. He rode with Cliff Bergere and Chet Miller before the two-man cars departed. Del Roy recalled that the garages that really had a chance at the Brickyard used a professional mechanic who took the pit signals and relayed them to the driver. Relay signals to the driver were fairly standard. One pat on the back meant a car was gaining. Two pats meant he was too fast and to move over. A tug on his uniform meant to pit. The mechanic watched the tires on his side; Frankie tested them for blisters with a paddle-shaped piece of wood.

Del Roy went to the Vanderbilt Cup revival in 1937 with Henning and Jimmy Snyder, acting as interpreter for the Alfa Romeo team, including Tazio Nuvolari who was nicknamed "Nervous Larry." His admiration of Tazio's driving skill extended to the accolade of saying he could hold his own on an American dirt track. Of course, Del Roy pumped the Italians for the information he needed to set up Rex Mays's private Alfa ride correctly. He told this story of Mercedes's Alfred Neubauer: the Mercedes c.c. measuring glass had broken in transit, and Neubauer was told that Frankie had one. Neubauer exploded that it was verboten to get help from a Jew. Told Frankie was not Jewish, but of Italian extraction, Neubauer approached him with: "Welcome Axis partner. Lend me your c.c. glass." But the Auto Union crew never mingled with the rest, Del Roy remembered.

Frankie left Henning to become chief mechanic on the Grandma Marks Specials for a little more than 2 years, with all sorts of bad luck thwarting the car and drivers George Connors and Tommy Hinnershitz whom Del Roy imported from the East. Frankie was so disgusted that he quit and went to work beside Rose at an aircraft plant. But in 1941 Lou Moore lured him back to Indy as a crew member, and Rose and Davis won.

It was Rose, a long-time friend, who introduced him at Milwaukee after World War II to Ted Horn, then a young California kid with a home-built car. Frankie agreed to make the car go right and fixed the racer with 50 cents' worth of gasket material and many hours of labor. Horn was Frankie's ideal driver, and they worked well through 3 AAA season championships. Meanwhile Frankie was also building midget race cars. The Wheeler midget team—Dutch Schaefer and Tony Bonadies—won 47 straight victories in a circuit that boasted almost every name American pilot of the era at one race or another. Frankie was at a Langhorne midget race one day when Dick Simonek asked Del Roy what to do with his famous sprint car "Baby," now that Horn had been killed. It was then that Del Roy suggested one-legged midget star Bill Schindler, whose story is recounted elsewhere in this book.

Del Roy opened a speed shop in Paterson, N.J., which was so successful at the time that he was reluctant to leave it for any kind of chief mechanic's job. But Detroit plastics manufacturer Jim Robbins offered him such excellent terms he had to accept. Frankie was to name the driver and would have complete charge of the operation. He picked Mike Nazaruk for the Robbins Special, and Nazaruk finished 2nd in the Indy 500 in a car Del Roy had rebuilt completely. This was the best Frankie ever did, and personal problems interfered to chop up efforts in later years. He left Jersey for a time, then opened a performance parts business in the southern part of the state. When USAC was formed, he became an eastern zone official, rising to technical chairman for sprint cars and a member of the national technical committee, taking other official jobs after that.

JOHN DePALMA

John DePalma did not particularly want to be remembered as Ralph's little brother; he wanted to be known as the father of the motor tune-up. Of course, people were tuning engines before John opened his garage in Tampa in 1931, but they didn't know it. John devised the idea of offering this service, named as such, to the general public. The idea of a garage doing such a job on a passenger-car engine was then unique.

DePalma, born in Pennsylvania, began competition on motorcycles. J. Alex Sloan took him West in 1926 to race against his fabled brother Ralph and Sig Haugdahl at that IMCA bastion, Ascot Park in Los Angeles. John usually lost. "Ralph was the big star, and I fought for what I got," John told a reporter years later. Nevertheless John campaigned on the IMCA circuit for 5 years. The probable reason that he went to Tampa was that he enjoyed some of his greatest successes there at Plant Field. He set track records in a Maxwell and a Duesenberg. He also crashed twice there, once getting hit with the front crossmember of another car, the other time splintering a fence and sharing the car with a beam that came up through the floorboards to pin him in his seat.

John's best year was 1927 when he finished 2nd to Fred Horey for the IMCA crown. That was the year he and Ralph Mulford averaged 83 m.p.h. for 1,000 miles on the Culver City, Calif., board track in a Chandler. Cliff Durant brought him to Indy as a car "tester," but like many others he found the bricks hard to get used to. He also worked on Haugdahl's Wisconsin Special, the first car to go 3 miles a minute, when it ran at Daytona Beach. John tried that scene, too, but said later, "I can't stand sand in my shoes."

Before World War II, DePalma was tapped by the government to help set up the National Youth Aviation Corps. When hostilities began, DePalma—and another

IMCA hero, Emory Collins—became instructors in aircraft maintenance. He returned to Tampa after the war to work in the automotive field and work up several voluminous scrapbooks.

Why didn't he ever make it big like brother Ralph? "There was too much traveling," he said. "You got little rest, and it was hard to keep the cars in good running shape and drive, too. I got to thinking one night in Atlanta that I might like to retire vertically instead of horizontally. So, since I liked Tampa, I went into business there. I figured at least I'd get some rest."

RALPH DePALMA

Ralph DePalma was so great that his brother John—there were also Frank and Tony—who apparently had very little talent for the endeavor, enjoyed a long career as a driver largely because of the relationship. Ralph De Palma was so great that in a 25-year career he won about 2,000 races, including the Vanderbilt Cup, the Savannah Grand Prize, the Elgin, Ill., Grand Prix and free-for-all, and the Indianapolis 500. He won races on dirt tracks, board speedways and road courses in many different cars.

The greatness of the man was exemplified by his most famous loss and by his most serious accident. The drama of DePalma and riding mechanic Rupert Jeffkins pushing the famed "Grey Ghost" Mercedes toward the finish (and disqualification) in the 1912 Indianapolis 500 as Joe Dawson whizzed by toward victory in his blue Na-

tional probably did more to establish the 500 as a premier race than if Ralph had won.

Part of his greatness was his sense of sportsmanship. After the 1913 Indy when, sidelined by mechanical ills after 13 laps in his Mercer, a *Motor Age* correspondent quoted him as saying (before it became a cliche), "It's the luck of the game." To condense the correspondent's report: "On the glorious afternoon of August 31, 1912, when Ralph DePalma won the Elgin National Trophy—in a car over which he had but partial control—the clutch plate of the Grey Ghost was cracked—E. C. Patterson, entrant of the Mercedes-Knight said, DePalma is a popular winner because he is a good loser. No doubt Patterson is thinking of last Memorial Day. No doubt he sees . . . DePalma pushing his disabled car, a vanquished challenger in a race conceded to him without question 10 miles from the finish . . . with face dripping perspiration, DePalma rolls his car over the wire, raises his handsome head and smiles at the cheering throng. DePalma is a man. He does not cry or curse his luck when beaten. DePalma is a sportsman. He is the first to grab the hand of Dawson."

There was an even more compelling example of this sense of fairplay—Ralph's most serious accident, which came near Milwaukee in the 1912 Grand Prize road race. He had won the Vanderbilt Cup over the same course a few days before. Attempting to overtake Caleb Bragg, DePalma crashed on the last lap. As he was carted out of the ambulance bleeding profusely and injured internally, DePalma told reporters, "Boys, don't forget that Caleb Bragg wasn't to blame. He gave me all the road." That and other incidents placed DePalma among the most popular drivers ever. No matter how much they tried to best him, foes honored him as a sportsman. DePalma competed in 10 Indy 500s, the last in 1925. He had strong feelings about the posture of a racing hero, saying he owed the crowd the best race he could give. In addition, he was punctillious about honoring appearances, and his entire racing operation was impeccable, serving as the model for others in those rough and ready days.

All of this didn't mean that DePalma wasn't a fearsome competitor. Born in 1883 in Italy and an 1893 arrival in the United States, he was recognized as dirt track king from 1908 through 1911, was the national champion in 1912 and 1914, and the Canadian champion in 1929 after he had forsaken places like Indianapolis for his first love, the dirt ovals. As late as 1936 he was still setting records in stock cars.

With a career like that, it would be presumptuous to pick out one race and call it Ralph's greatest. Ralph saved everyone the trouble. His greatest race, he said, was beating Barney Oldfield in the February 27, 1914, Vanderbilt Cup over the roads of Santa Monica. The Oldfield-DePalma rivalry was one of the greatest in sports history—and one of the most lucrative. Ralph did not let personal feelings stand in the way of an inter-

mittent series of match races that earned large amounts of money for all concerned. Yet the circumstances leading up to the 1914 Vanderbilt Cup would have made perfect strangers the bitterest of rivals.

Early in 1913 DePalma had accepted captaincy of the Mercer factory team, supervising development and construction of three 450 cu. in. racers. As in most cases, the 1st year turned out to be a year of correcting weaknesses, a year of hard work and much disappointment. With a relief drive from DePalma, one Mercer finished second at Indy, but it was a smaller 300 cu. in car. All the 450 cars broke down, as they did at Elgin and every stop except Brighton Beach, N.Y., where DePalma won a 100-mile race. Testing early in 1914, however, showed the 450's finally were ready—one ran 117 m.p.h. on a straight. But with about 30 days left before the Vanderbilt Cup, Mercer executives signed Oldfield on as a driver without even telling their team captain, DePalma. It meant that Spence Wishart or Eddie Pullen, who had worked to perfect the car with him, would be without a ride. It also meant that being Mercer captain meant nothing. The fact that Barney had wangled a princely deal rankled no end. Ralph resigned, swearing vengeance. A Los Angeles paper quoted him as saying, "I would rather beat Oldfield than eat 5 plates of spaghetti in a row." (In later life he did not remember the quote, noting he always preferred linguini to spaghetti.)

Unable to gain a ride on another factory team on such short notice, DePalma prevailed upon his old friend and sponsor, New Jersey lamp manufacturer E. J. Schroeder, to take the old Grey Ghost Mercedes out of retirement. More than willing, Schroeder financed complete overhaul and shipment to California. DePalma and the car arrived 5 days after practice had begun and, on his very first outing, burned a bearing. No suitable bearing metal could be found, and if it hadn't rained 3 days in a row, postponing the race, DePalma would have been through then and there. He appeared for practice on February 23 and again burned out a bearing. Oldfield said Ralph would never be near enough even to see him. DePalma was desperate, but, as if *deus ex machina*, a gentleman named Kelly appeared and said he would pay Ralph $200 if the Grey Ghost burned a single bearing made out of his "Kelly's metal." Ralph ordered a full set made and finally turned in a qualifying lap 40 seconds slower than Barney and his former teammates. He knew he couldn't compete with Oldfield on sheer speed, but had to win with strategy. Out of his knowledge of the Mercer, which he had built and driven, and his knowledge of Oldfield, he had to think of a way to capitalize on the weaknesses of car and driver.

Approximately 125,000 people waited, watched and cheered as the cars started single file a few seconds apart on the approximately 8-mile laps. Wishart in the Mercer led the first lap, with teammates Pullen and Oldfield 3rd and 4th respectively; DePalma was well back. On the 2nd lap Pullen led, Wishart was in the pits, finished, and Oldfield was 3rd; DePalma was still well back. On the 3rd go around, Pullen was preparing to lap cars, and Oldfield stayed in 3rd behind Stutz's Gil Anderson; DePalma was not a factor. The field began to string out as the laps piled up, but on the 7th, Oldfield gave the "coming in" signal. In the pits, Barney was the victim of organized confusion; one pit hand even handed him a fresh cigar when all he wanted was a spare wheel lashed to the car. He dropped to 4th, but regained 3rd two laps later with ease. Meanwhile, attrition had put DePalma in the top 5.

On the 13th lap Pullen, well out in front, crashed against a stand. Eddie had the race easily won had he eased the pressure on the accelerator pedal, but he couldn't or wouldn't and he was out now, leaving Oldfield alone of the Mercers. And Barney had to pit again for tires and oil. Anderson was leading but while Oldfield was pitted, the Grey Ghost passed him for 2nd, DePalma as relaxed as if he were on a pleasure jaunt. On the 18th lap Anderson was sidelined by a frozen propellor shaft, and now the battle was joined. Barney had roared back into the fray in 5th place; he gained 2 places in 3 laps and, with only 8 of 15 starters left after the Stutz departed, had only DePalma ahead of him. With a much faster car, he came closer and closer. On the back stretch of the 25th lap he finally passed the Grey Ghost, leading with 10 laps to go. But suddenly he could not pull away, DePalma slipstreaming him lap after lap on the straights, leading Barney slightly on the turns because he took the inside line. Ralph still hadn't made a pit stop.

DePalma knew he didn't have the speed to overtake Oldfield. He could see, however, that Barney's wild driving style had worn rubber like a grinding machine off the left front tire. Would Barney risk a pit stop with only 50 miles to go? It was unlikely; the daredevil knew he had the faster car and the tire just might last. Suddenly, as he led slightly coming off the turn into the main straight—when Oldfield could not help but see—Ralph slowed appreciably, signalling he was going to pit for oil. Oldfield roared ahead at top speed, soon losing sight of the Grey Ghost. Playing it safe, Barney pitted next time around for new rubber, confident he had won. But as he sat there in the pits, there went the Grey Ghost racing past into the lead. It never had stopped, and despite a desperate attempt to catch up, Oldfield couldn't close the gap.

DePalma's average was a record 75.5 m.p.h., but the most amazing thing about his feat was how closely he had figured the winning pace and the pace needed to force Barney to tire-grinding bursts of speed. Ralph's fastest lap was 6:20.2, while Barney got down to 6:10.8, but DePalma's superb sense of pace kept him within a second of that 6:20 all 35 laps. Ralph took the Elgin laurels away from Mercer in 1914, too, and then won Indy in the Grey Ghost. Ironically, Stutz hired Oldfield away from Mercer before the 1914 Indy race.

In later years DePalma acted as honorary referee for the 500, the final time in 1954. He died 2 years later.

PETER DePAOLO

"Keep your mouth shut and your eyes open, and you'll be a good driver some day." That was what Uncle Ralph DePalma told little Pete DePaolo of the Roseland, N.J., DePaolos. Uncle Ralph was right. Pete became one of the best of his era, later adding importance as the American S. C. H. Davis with his reminiscences, and topping matters off by managing Ford's entry into factory stock car racing in the 1950s. In 1969, he was named director of industrial rotations of the new Michigan International Speedway.

Pete idolized Uncle Ralph, and he got his big break as a riding mechanic for DePalma. In the 1920 Indy 500 he remembered being ordered to put out a fire in the engine of the Ballot while they were going full tilt. He climbed out over the fender to the front of the car, straddled the bumper facing DePalma, and, holding on to the radiator ornament as DePalma handed him the fire extinguisher, put out the fire and then climbed back in.

Pete rarely drove dirt, jumping into board racing in 1922, when he also competed in his first Indianapolis

160

race as a driver in the Frontenac which had won under Gaston Chevrolet the previous year. He led for 4 laps. He had a bad accident in Kansas City in September and spent the succeeding year campaigning vainly in Europe, but returned for a 6th place in a Duesenberg in the 1924 Indy. DePaolo's greatest year came in 1925 when he won both Indianapolis and the AAA championship. He won the AAA crown again in 1927. His 101.13-m.p.h. average speed in the Duesenberg Special was the 1st time the 500 was ever run at over a 100-m.p.h. pace. Norman Batten drove 34 minutes of relief for him at mid-race and lost the lead, but Pete took the lead back from Dave Lewis at the 435-mile mark and was never headed. In 1926 he finished 5th in a Duesenberg after starting next to last, and fouling on a restart after a rain squall. The 1926 Indy went only 400 miles because of rain, or he might have fought his way to victory in that one too, as he had the other one in 1925.

Switching to his own Perfect Circle Miller racing team in 1927—as a car owner—Pete qualified the front-drive car 2nd to Frank Lockhart, but broke its supercharger gears on the 31st lap. He took over a twin to his own car from Bob McDonough and led the race until he handed the car back. The car eventually finished 6th, but those relief driving points, along with victories at Altoona and Salem, gave DePaolo his 2nd national crown.

He almost ended his career trying for the pole in his Flying Cloud Special before the 1928 Indianapolis classic. He took the green flag late on a dark overcast day and wrecked the car before completing one lap. He was carted to the hospital in serious condition. Because it was faced with a short field, AAA told Arthur Chevrolet that if the car could be repaired, it would be allowed to qualify the morning of the race. Pete approved the arrangement only after getting permission to view the start of the 500. An ambulance arrived at the starting line just before the start, and out came DePaolo on a stretcher. He waved to the crowd and stole the headlines. Wilbur Shaw lasted 42 laps in the car. Pete made the field in 1929 and 1930, his Boyle Valve Special departing on the 25th lap in 1929 and wrecking in 1930. In that race De-Paolo gave up the car on lap 9 because he felt it was not handling well, and relief driver Red Roberts hit the wall on lap 20. He returned to Indy as a car owner and managed Kely Petillo's victory in 1935.

DePaolo was born in 1898 to comfortable circumstances, son of a builder. He claimed he missed an initial chance to see Uncle Ralph in action when in 1910 his father took him to the washroom just when DePalma was in the process of winning a bet from Harry Harkness by running his Fiat Cyclone around the Nutley, N.J., motorcycle board track. After serving during World War I as an airplane mechanic, he obtained a job in New York as a chauffer-mechanic, maintaining a Hudson Super 6 for Al Donovan. DePaolo, then 21, saw his 1st board track race that same year, 1919, in a match between DePalma in a Packard Twin 6, Barney Oldfield in the Golden Sub, and Louis Chevrolet in a Frontenac 6 at Sheepshead Bay. He remembered widespread betting on the race, which DePalma won easily, with Oldfield a poor 3rd. In January 1920, he became De-Palma's riding mechanic, replacing Jimmy Stakes who had returned to college. His 1st race was in the Beverly Hills Speedway inaugural in a 300 cu. in. Ballot that he had helped remodel. Suffering from tire troubles (the tread kept flying off), DePalma was not a factor after the 13th lap. They then went to Havana, Cuba, for the Oriental Park race promotion of Bill Pickens, where betting was recognized. DePalma won; then came Indy and the fire episode.

Pete started as a driver almost 2 years later, winning his 1st board race at Culver City (a heat) in a Duesenberg in April 20, 1924. He had wrecked 5 of his first 6 mounts, but convinced Fred Duesenberg to take him on as a team member in 1924. His initial big victory came April 30, 1924, in a 150-miler on the steeply banked one-mile Fresno, Calif., board track, by almost a lap over Harry Hartz.

Before the race he had his son Tommy's booties attached to the left and right front springs respectively. When he won he swore that 2-year-old Tommy would never in his life have to pay for shoes, a bargain he claimed he kept. This car became the "Banana Wagon" with which, in 1925, he won the AAA National Championship by one of the widest point margins in history. The victory at Indianapolis was joined by triumphs in 250-milers at Altoona, Pa., Laurel, Md., and Salem, N.H. This car won the only race ever run at Fulford-by-the-Sea in Florida, a 300-miler, in 1926. A hurricane swept that track and Carl Fisher's money away soon after.

DePaolo went on to win at Indy and on the boards. Right after that victory at Indy, Duesenberg used him as part of a deal to clear financial obligations, and DePaolo found himself working for Albert Champion, founder of the AC Spark Plug Company. The Altoona, Pa., board track race was the next stop. Pete had the same car, but he had to use AC plugs instead of Champions. He soon found out that, despite the ministrations of his newly hired mechanic, Cotton Henning, the car would only run at three-quarters throttle with ACs. To win a $1,000 top time prize offered by Altoona businessman Sam Cohen, DePaolo sneaked the Champions back in and beat Leon Duray. But for the race itself he installed the ACs and won over the dangerous track, even then disintegrating. He went on to amass 3,250 points, the most of any champion of his era.

DePaolo's driving days came to an end after a serious accident in a race in Spain in 1934. After 11 days in a coma, he somehow fought his way back to good health. He did his racing thereafter from the sidelines.

DEVORE FAMILY (EARL and BILLY)

Earl Devore and his son, Billy Devore, were among the most talented father-son combinations in the history of American racing. Earl began his racing career in 1909 in his native California, competing in road races and dirt tracks alike. By the time he found his way to Indianapolis, he had 16 years of experience and was considered a veteran star.

Devore, driving a Miller Special, planned a prescribed speed in his 1925 rookie year at the Brickyard as so many had, before and after, and chose too low a figure. He got up as high as 8th at 100 miles, but this was the year Pete DePaolo and the next 3 finishers broke the 1924 speed record; Earl finished out of the money. He was not in the 1926 race, but came back in 1927. Again he chose a speed too low for the initial year of the 91.5 cu. in. formula at Indy. He inherited 2nd place 2 laps from the end when Babe Stapp fell out with rear-axle trouble. Then he held off Tony Gulotta. Devore had 54 laps of relief in the middle of the race from Zeke Myers. He made 4 pit stops to winner George Souders's 2.

In the 1928 race, plagued in the middle by a light rain, Devore skidded on the north turn just after the red flag (which meant the same as the green does today), came out, but was no longer a factor in the race. Devore and Norman Batten left for winter racing in Brazil and Argentina on the ill-fated liner *Vestris*. When the ship began sinking, Devore placed his wife and baby son in a lifeboat and dived back into the water repeatedly to rescue others; a shark got him.

The son, Billy, started his big-time racing career in 1934 as riding mechanic to Doc McKenzie at Indy. The next year in his 1st race as a driver, the Cleveland 100, he finished 3rd, and moved to 2nd in the Labor Day 100 at Lakewood. In May 1935, he was injured seriously at Atlanta and had to wear a back brace for 6 months before resuming his career. In 1937 he took 7th in the 500, making 5 pit stops.

In 1938 he switched from Miller to a new Offy. The PRW Special did not do well, but in 1939 he switched to the Barbasol Special, a supercharged 4-cylinder created and owned by Leon Duray. The car was not very fast—12 m.p.h. slower than the leaders—but Billy sneaked it into 10th place. In the Holabird Special in 1940 he lasted 452 miles before mechanical difficulties got him. The next year Devore lasted until the 122nd lap, when the car broke an oil line and threw a con rod, stopping on the course.

Billy was still driving at Indy in 1946, qualifying a Schoof Special Offy. He crashed, but was still awarded 10th place because it was not until the 167th lap that a throttle stuck in the open position. He did not make the race in 1947, but in 1948 there was Billy piloting the 6-wheel Pat Clancy Special to 12th place. He was around as late as 1951 after failing to qualify the Joe Scopa Offy in 1950. Billy later became a used car sales-

man in Indianapolis and worked with Firestone on their Indy tire projects.

HUGH DIBLEY

The Nag's Head Pub was on the corner, but North Street, Clapham, London, S. W. 4, was a rather nondescript street in a non-tourist part of Britain's capital city. You went up a slight hill, past the pub bearing the legend "Take Courage," reminding you of Piers Courage who lost his life in 1970 in the Grand Prix wars, and went over a bump to find a series of little, one-story garages bearing the numbers from 59 to 65. This was the home of Palliser Racing Designs, Ltd.

Palliser was the middle name of Hugh Dibley. He was the man who caused it all, a tallish, good-looking version of David Frost, but without the perpetual grin or the continual energetic, outgoing manner of the Anglo-American TV personality. Dibley, in fact, could have been said to be a rather reticent man with a definite Colin Chapman quality about him. He was even more like Chapman in other ways—like building a racing car business out of nothing, integrating his car building with racing.

Hugh Palliser Kingsley Dibley was born in Hong Kong (where his father was serving in the Royal Navy) on April 29, 1937. At the earliest possible age he headed for the Royal Navy's Fleet Air Arm to complete his National Service. He got in his basic flight time there

162

and moved directly into a pilot training program with the British Overseas Airways Corporation—BOAC—when he left the Navy. He also moved into motor racing, the first race coming in 1959 in an AC Aceca-Bristol. Testing at Goodwood before the scheduled Silverstone race, Dibley recalled later that "the Duke of Richmond blackflagged me twice for rather wild driving, and he said I never should come back." But Dibley's driving, wild or not, got him a 4th in the Silverstone debut.

Formula Junior Lolas followed for the next 3 seasons, and Hugh holds the distinction of being the 1st racer to ever win with a rear-engined Lola—at Goodwood, where the Duke had relented. In 1963 he had a Lola GT on order, but it never materialized because Eric Broadley was involved in the Ford GT project. In 1964 Dibley became part of SMART—the Stirling Moss Automobile Racing Team—with a 2.5-litre Brabham BT8-Climax as his mount, the car in which he won the sports car opener to the British GP that season, beating such talents as Denis Hulme and Roy Salvadori. Hugh called that particular start "my best race," which is something considering he raced 100 or more times in his career.

The Brabham was interesting for two other reasons. First, it brought him to the States for racing the 1st time in the Riverside and Laguna Seca in the United States Road Racing Championship series. The Brabham also provided a fresh introduction to Len Wimhurst, who was working at the Brabham factory. Business contacts at Lola led to friendship; and when Dibley decided in 1966 that he wanted a car of his own to race, Wimhurst became his chief designer, builder, and partner. "Len came up to me at one point," Dibley later recalled," and asked me if I would be interested in racing a car—and providing the engine—if he produced a chassis. We shook hands and that was the start of it all."

The first unnamed-as-yet Palliser was produced by December 1966, and some months were needed to experiment with it before Dibley took the car into its 1st race in October 1967. The Twin-Cam Ford-powered machine was fastest in practice, but TBN, as it was called ("to be named," said Dibley with a laugh), retired of fuel starvation in the race. Hugh, meanwhile, had still been racing other people's cars: a Lola-Chevvy for SMART in 1965; a Lola T70 (alternately powered by a Ford and a Chevvy) for Tony Sargeant in 1966—in which he won the supporting sports car race to the British GP that season, beating off the likes of Chris Amon and Jacky Ickx; a David Piper Ferrari 250LM in 1967 —in which he scored a class victory in the BOAC 500, co-driving with Roy Pierpont; a Chevrolet Camaro in 1967 and 1968, run without much success; and the gas turbine Howmet TX in 1968, which he started at both Le Mans and Watkins Glen, but was retired at both courses.

The year 1968 saw Dibley's racing career start to wind down, while his BOAC career, as pilot, pilot-navigator, and pilot navigational instructor increased in tempo, especially in the monstrous new jet then on the way. Dibley became an instructor on the Boeing 747, working with pilots in simulators as well as in the cockpit. Another distraction was the newest company in race car building, Palliser Racing Design, founded in October. Wimhurst had built three more cars earlier that year, specifically designed for the SCCA Formula B championship in the U.S., and their sales had been taken over by the elder brother of Roy Winkelmann, the Winkelmann Racing sponsor of Jo Rindt and Alan Rees. Bob Winkelmann was an ex-BOACer, but met Dibley only after Winkelmann had left the airline. Dibley was so reticent, in fact, that he allowed Winkelmann to market the cars under his name as distributor rather than under the Palliser name.

Nearly 50 cars were built in 1969 for the U.S. market, the only one Dibley was exploiting at that moment; 40 of these were Formula Fords, making the Palliser WDF1, one of strongest and best designs to come off Wimhurst's drawing board, a familiar race car in the States long before British drivers got to know it. The other cars produced in 1969 were updated versions, the WDB2, for Formula B racing. A projected Formula 5000/Formula A car never got into production. In 1970 the story was much the same, the bulk of Palliser's production going to the U.S., including the WDF2, although a factory car was raced in England with good results by Peter Lamplough; and Vern Schuppan took over another factory car later that year and moved up to Formula Atlantic, the British equivalent of the SCCA's F/B, in 1971. Formula 2 and Formula 3 versions also were produced, a F5000 prototype raced in the Tasman series, a Super Vee WDV1 introduced for a big push in 1972, and the Daren sports car—a Group 6 racer—added to the line. In the States the WDF3 was raced successfully by up and coming young drivers like Jas Patterson of New York.

Dibley raced an F/B in October 1970, after a long layoff, and just equalled the lap record. But he had his problems because of the American recession; this just about ruined his sales effort and caused a retrenchment in the Palliser operation, which had been steadily growing up to that point. Dibley struggled on until the beginning of 1972, when he finally closed down his Palliser factory. Wimhurst would go out and start his own factory, and Schuppan, Patterson, and other drivers would have to find new mounts. Palliser had been a good thing while it lasted.

LARRY DICKSON

The question may not be what is a hero driver, but when? Consider Larry Dickson, all of 5 feet 9 inches, born September 6, 1938, a solid citizen of the town of

Marietta, Ohio. Dickson won more than 120 features in super modified racing, a facet of the sport that is fragmented into a myriad area sanctioning groups, each with its own set of rules. He switched to United Racing Club sprint cars in 1965, winning 5 features and the title. At Sacramento that year, Dickson made his USAC debut in a clunker of an automobile and did nothing.

He gained further experience at the Phoenix 200 as part of the "scenery." But that was good enough to win him a ride in the Michner Petroleum Special at Indianapolis in 1966. Visions of the frankfurters awarded to the year's best rookie no doubt dancing in his head, Larry made the field. He lasted zero laps because he had the misfortune to be involved in that year's incredible first-lap accident. Stoically purchasing his own hot dogs, Dickson turned to the USAC sprints and midgets on the kind of tracks germane to his supermod and URC days. He won 3 sprint races for a 5th overall in the standings and 2 of 66 features in the midgets. He traveled to Japan for the Mount Fuji 200 and finished a creditable 6th, Jackie Stewart winning the race. Several very respectful Japanese racing fans requested his autograph. Suddenly Larry Dickson was a star again, Nippon style.

In Indianapolis, in 1967, Dickson qualified the Vita Fresh Orange Juice Special. Life seemed sunny; he had a season-long ride on the Championship Trail and all the orange juice his kids could drink. Starting 21st, Larry moved up steadily. Then fate intervened again. He had to spin to avoid the final lap accident, and was credited with 15th place. There were 15 other championship races, but the best Dickson could do was a 4th. He added 2 sprint victories in 19 tries for 4th overall in that USAC division.

The big year was to be 1968. The great Mario Andretti had concurred with Clint Brawner that Dickson was just the driver to be number 2 on the Overseas National Airways team after Larry's original mount, the Dayton Steel Wheel, fizzled. Came Indianapolis, and there was Larry Dickson again in the starting field. By lap 16 Dickson was sitting on the pit wall, relieved by Andretti after Mario's own car broke. However, his ex-car broke several laps later anyway. But there were better times. At Springfield, Ohio, Dickson managed 2nd to Roger McCluskey, and at Sacramento he was 3rd to A. J. Foyt, duelling for the lead at one time, And in the USAC sprints there was stardom, a record 12 victories and the USAC sprint crown in his Smith Speed Shop Chevvy. Many of the tracks—like Heidelberg Raceway in Carnegie, Pa.—he knew from his supermod days. And many of the fans were cheering him on. It was nice to be Numero Uno again.

George R. Bryant, the heating and cooling man from Englewood, N.J., gave Dickson his 1969 shot at glory at the last minute. Starting 31st in the field at Indianapolis, Larry finished 9th in spite of an 11-minute pit stop to repair a leaking transaxle. However, that was it

on the Championship Trail; he did nothing in 7 tries. Meanwhile things were not going as well as expected on the USAC sprint circuit. A youngster named Gary Bettenhausen was making life less money-filled. Dickson was particularly upset when he found out that Gary had pasted a picture of him on the dash of his car; this was carrying things too far. Larry won 3 features, and finished 2nd to Bettenhausen for the title.

He did not make the field for the 1970 Indy classic, but Dickson had regained his winning touch in the sprints. Six quick victories in the new Ken Lay Chevrolet tied him with A. J. Foyt and put him within reach of the all-time record of 29 victories held by Don Branson. Almost a month later he passed Branson to became the all-time sprint big winner. Dickson had lined up rides for the Championship Trial dirt track stops in a Ken Brenn Offy, but decided to eschew the road courses and paved ovals. He finally explained matters to an inquiring reporter and, as some suspected, it was true he had been born some years too late. Dickson, it was reported, preferred the old spring-type front-end cars with their engines in the front and with rears that could be set up loose so that one could grind through the turns. Shades of Jimmy Thompson, Jim Bryan, and the old dirt track days! But can anyone gainsay the talent of a driver who in five years set an all-time victory total? Hot shoes come in various sizes.

DAREL DIERINGER

It is the fate of some people to be remembered for seeming inconsequentialities rather than for the talent and worth they put into their line of endeavor. Darel Eugene Dieringer could be one such person. A fine late-model stock-car driver, Yancy (a nickname picked up from a TV character) made his mark as the leader of the "used car division" in the 1965 NASCAR season. The UCD came about because Mercury management decided to retire from stock-car racing after 1964, before the competition with its sister car, Ford, became too intense, and because Bud Moore decided to campaign the 1964 Mercury yet another year. With the decision of Chrysler Corporation to sit out 1965 NASCAR competition, enterprising press men seized on the excellent times Mercury was compiling at Daytona Speed Weeks to create the UCD. Dieringer's hang-out-the-rear-and-devil-take-the-risk driving style had much to do with the car's early season success.

The "King of the Used Cars" actually had won only 2 major NASCAR races before his ascension to the title. These were the Golden State 400, a stock-car road race at Riverside on November 3, 1963, and a year later the Augusta, Ga., 150-miler, also in a Mercury. Running for points in 1965, he finished 4th in NASCAR standings, using at one time or another the famed

Mercury, a year-old Ford, and an ostensibly new 1965 Chevvy. He finished 3rd in the used Merc in the 1965 Southern 500 despite the loss of a rear end.

Born June 1, 1926, in Indianapolis of farming stock, Darel grew up in nearby North Vernon, a more rural atmosphere. He played basketball in high school. At 19 he competed in his first auto race on a quarter-mile track, and this led to convertible racing with NASCAR starting in 1955. He was, as the saying goes, gaining experience, if not riches. After 2 years of this, he virtually retired to less dangerous pursuits, including regular membership in the Firestone tire-changing crew that shows up at every NASCAR race. In 1958 he drove 3 USAC stock-car races and in 1959 another 3, gaining one 3rd-place finish.

It was not until 1962 that he returned to full-time driving. In between was an unsuccessful marriage, out of which came a son, Darel Jr. Then Miss Mamie Reynolds, a tobacco heiress who later married the son of the famed Luigi Chinetti, decided to sponsor a Ford in stock-car competition. Darel drove it to 33rd in national point standings, and moved himself to 7th the next year, most of which he spent in a factory Mercury. Racing less in 1964, he dropped to 11th.

Darel was a broad-shouldered man who affected a close crewcut and to a perpetual squint. He is also likely to be remembered as one of the pioneers of the racing safety tire first promoted by Goodyear. He smiled out of advertisements to inform the American public that he had blown a tire at 170 m.p.h. and still finished. The implication was that, should this occur while hurrying

to a cocktail party, one could be assured of still making the 1st round of martinis if one had a car equipped with the street version of the Goodyear racing safety tire.

The Golden State 400 of 1963, run over the 2.7-mile road course, will be remembered as the apex of a USAC-NASCAR feud. After Dan Gurney, classified as USAC because he preferred that license as a convenience to drive at Indianapolis, had won the pole position for Ford, the USAC officials decided to ban their licensees from the internationally approved NASCAR race. That meant that Jim Hurtubise, Parnelli Jones, Rodger Ward, and A. J. Foyt were taken out of the field. Paul Goldsmith elected to defy the ban, leading to the long battle with USAC. The action forced Marvin Panch into Gurney's car and SCCA ace Dave McDonald into Panch's.

Goldsmith, although he was the fastest qualifier, started 16th because he did not make his speed run on the first qualifying day. This is a procedure that makes sense at Indianapolis Speedway, but not in a road race of any sort. Sidelining Jones made Dieringer the hero driver for the Bill Stroppe Mercury team, and he did not disappoint anyone. Goldsmith was removed early by a collision with the Ford of Bob Bondurant, better known for Cobra and Ferrari exploits. Panch led only one lap, then Ford's Fred Lorenzen was 1st through the 21st tour of the circuit. The stock car boys were spinning merrily every now and then as they got used to the course, and the sports car set spun as they got used to the big stockers.

McDonald, a quick study, took the lead on the 22nd circuit and held it through the 30th when Dodge boy David Pearson led for one lap while Dave pitted for fuel on the Goldsmith wreck caution flag. Then David went in and McDonald took over again. He got the lead, thanks to an unusual miscue on the part of the pace car, which held back all the racers except McDonald while Dave was out front. It amounted to a free pit stop, even though he was later held back one lap to equalize matters. Dieringer showed up in the lead briefly on the 83rd lap, but McDonald, who had pitted, was back in front almost at once when Darel needed gas. But this race was won in the pits. With 18 seconds in hand over the Mercury driver, Dave pitted on lap 115. He came out in second and Dieringer swooped in immediately, coming back only 1.8 seconds behind Dave. The Stroppe crew had gained him more than 6 seconds.

Now Darel was charging hard. He led lap 117, Dave led lap 118, and Darel moved in front to stay on 119. Even the Hollywood starlets in the administration press setup looked around briefly to see what the excitement was about. Dieringer won by more than a lap with the Wood Brothers team of McDonald and Panch taking 2nd and 3rd. For this Darel received a garland of flowers around his neck, a relatively large amount of prize money, and an enthusiastic hug from the race queen. The hug was repeated several times for cameramen;

Darel didn't seem to object. Fittingly, his victory came the day before the 25th anniversary of the Mercury marque. Four of the top 10 were Mercs.

A Charlotte, N.C., resident, Darel had business interests there. He was capable of scoring against any NASCAR competition, but, as he grew more successful off-track, it was inevitable that Dieringer would retire. He did with 7 Grand National victories to his credit.

DUKE DINSMORE

J. Carlyle Dinsmore, born in Williamstown, W.Va., April 10, 1913, began racing in the Central States Racing Association back in 1932 when that organization was one of the major sanctioning groups. The Duke of Dinsmore looked deceptively young, even when he came to the Indianapolis Speedway at the age of 33 in 1946. Dinsmore was one of the great dirt-track drivers before the war, and had kept so busy on the sprint and midget car circuits that he never previously had the time to try the paved confines of the Brickyard.

It was the Duke's trademark to race sometimes with a pipe clenched between his teeth. If he had a runaway, he would lean back in his car and puff on the pipe as if he were back in his Morris chair. During World War II, Dinsmore became an aviation mechanic, but jumped at the chance to return to his beloved racing when the war ended. He went straight to Indy and in 5 races there managed only a 10th in 1947. The 5-foot, 10-inch Dinsmore had to stow his beloved pipe to run at the Brickyard, and he once said that this ruined his concentration.

In Milwaukee in 1948 he hit the wall and was thrown into the middle of the track. Rex Mays drove into the wall to avoid him. Earlier in his career he had set records in winning at Dayton Speedway; Sharon, Pa., Speedway; and in the races held at Rankin Airport in Portland, Ore. In the Brown Motor Company Special, he won at Sacramento in 1950, and was always among the leaders during his AAA racing career. In 37 AAA races he also had a 2nd, a 3rd, four 4th places, and three 5ths, or 10 of 37 in the top 5. He retired in 1951 to care for his wife and 5 children via more conventional occupations.

ALBERT DIVO

Albert Divo, a motorboat mechanic and World War I pilot, began racing seriously with Sunbeam in 1919 as a riding mechanic to famed French racer Rene Thomas, and when Thomas moved over to Talbot, Divo, a Parisian born about 1895, moved with him. It was with Talbot that Divo became a driver in 1922 when Thomas left for greener pastures.

Divo's first race in 1922 saw him place 2nd to Lee Guinness in the Isle of Man Tourist Trophy. The fol-

lowing year Albert was 2nd in the French Grand Prix to Henry Segrave's Sunbeam, then won the ultra-fast Spanish GP at Sitgas at a speedy 96.91 m.p.h. In an accompanying voiturette race, Divo also made a hat trick, but was 2nd to Dario Resta. That same year he won the Penya Rhin GP at 67.54 m.p.h.

Delage secured Divo's services, and in 1924 Albert almost won the European GP at Lyons, being nipped by Giuseppe Campari's Alfa Romeo, however. At San Sebastian, Divo was 4th, but the following season he won there at 76.40 m.p.h. Jumping back to Talbot in 1926, Divo suffered through a period of bad cars, then rejoined Delage. In 1927 Albert won the only "Free for All," or Formula Libre, race held by the Automobile Club de France, clocking 74.69 m.p.h.

In his eternal search for a better, faster car, Divo went to Bugatti in 1928, and after finishing 4th in the French GP, based on fuel consumption rather than regular racing standards, he won the Targa Florio at 45.65 m.p.h. The next year he repeated as Targa winner, this time at 46.21 m.p.h. In 1930 his main accomplishment was a 3rd in the Belgian GP at Spa, also called the European GP that season. He also was 3rd in the 1931 Italian GP, then announced his retirement.

But Divo's career wasn't over yet. When sports cars became popular in the mid-Thirties, he went to Delahaye and registered a 4th at Marseilles during the 1936 season. In 1937 he was particularly active, with a 2nd to Jean-Pierre Wimille in the Marne GP and 3rds in the Marseilles and Montlhéry races, all of these in Talbots, which he raced that one season. In 1939 Divo was at Le Mans in a Delahaye, but his car retired early. The war ended his career for good. He was in the truck business for a time, and in November, 1966, he died in his native city of Paris.

FREDDIE DIXON

They called him the Indestructible Freddie Dixon, and this Yorkshireman certainly gave the British press reason. But for all his Bunyanesque adventures on motorcycles and Dixonized Rileys, he was one of the most underrated automotive geniuses in the relatively short history of the motor car. Born in Yorkshire, England in 1892, Freddie did not fit the mold of the clean-cut race driver. His competitive career spanned 42 years, yet when he died on November 5, 1956, he had been banned from driving on public roads. He was still competing at an age and after accidents that would have retired lesser men.

Short of stature, Dixon was so wide and so strong he could lift the end of his Riley 7 inches from the ground and hold it there while mechanics worked on the underside. He apparently had an absolute contempt for officialdom of any sort, and, whether it was in engineering or carousing, he was always willing to strike out for new ground. Years before Daimler-Benz's epic Grand Prix cars, he was building his Rileys with restricted air flow to the radiator and had abandoned the universal hood louvres. He pioneered 1-carburetor-per-cylinder setups for European 6 cylinder engines and was a fanatic on low weight. His "Crab" car, with automatic tracking 4-wheel drive, transmission braking, and other technical flourishes, offered remarkable traction. Its relation to the more famous Ferguson 4-wheel system is still moot, for he settled a suit out of court for about 10,000 pounds sterling.

Several tries at the Land Speed Record were made by Dixon, but his most remarkable idea for an LSR car, the 3,000-pound, 10-litre Dart, never found backers. That car was designed in a prison to which he had been remanded for punching a policeman. Fred had earlier bought Kaye Don's Silver Bullet, a 1200 h.p. record car, but abandoned it because he felt the transmission was too liable to break. Dixon would work for days on a knotty technical problem or to get his car to the peak of perfection he desired, often not eating, and when this was done he would go on a monumental jag, drinking more booze and wrecking more hotels and restaurants than any man of his era. But he would always go back to pay for the damages, so restaurateurs from England to Italy ducked and shrugged—often he would pay more than the cost of what he wrecked.

Dixon came into auto racing after retiring from a long and illustrious career as a motorcycle star. He began when most drivers are already retired, at the age of 40. One motorcycle exploit worthy of note inaugurated the legend of his indestructibility. In 1921 Brooklands held a 500-mile race for cycles, the only one it was ever to hold, for the single rider per motorbike rule proved too tough on the men, if not the machines. Dixon was given a Harley-Davidson for the contest—set up for sidecar racing. This was discovered later, for Dixon only knew he was landing on his head regularly in practice. To thwart this tendency, he covered the seat with sandpaper and stuck that way until he felt a painful sensation. His sandpaper had rubbed clear through his horsehide breeches in less than 90 miles. Freddie removed the sandpaper before further abrasion to himself and, 30 laps later, went sailing over the handlebars as the front tire blew. Bystanders said it looked like a circus act—he cartwheeled through the air, rolled several times along the concrete track, walked back to the twisted bike and battered it into a semblance of normality, and rode into his pits without the tire. He eventually finished 2nd.

Dixon had 2 pair of auto racing tenets. First, there was no such thing as special tuning for hillclimbs as against road races, and second, a car should always be driven flat out. His auto racing debut, made partly because the family larder was growing bare as the British cycle industry now shunned him, came in the 1932

Tourist Trophy race, Britain's premier road racing event and much more important back then because the factory teams were numerous and stronger.

Dixon had bought a used Riley 3 months previously and proceeded to make it more Dixon than Riley. He altered everything, with the possible exception of the gearbox, working almost until race time to get the vehicle to his liking. With his little 1100-c.c. car, Freddie led the race for almost 4 hours until his pit crew hoisted out a confusing blackboard message. The weary Dixon took his eyes off the road to look again and found himself entering the next turn much too fast even for the escape road. At 80 m.p.h. he scooted over a shallow bank, split a young tree, flew into the air, over a stream, and landed right side up on the road beyond after a 40-foot flight. A photographer caught him in midflight in one of those pictures that legends are made of. Fred turned off the ignition while airborne, so there were no further iron-man feats that day. He also infuriated the tech men by stowing a deflated Austin Seven wheel as his spare to satisfy the letter of the rule.

The Riley company became interested in his services, but Fred, wary of even these innovators, accomplished what he did virtually by himself. In 1932 Dixon broke 5 class international records in his unsupercharged car in continuous rain, topping 111 m.p.h. and defeating a host of blown MGs. Two years later, after he codrove a 1.5 Riley at Le Mans with Cyril Paul, Dixon piloted a 2-litre Riley straight into a huge tree stump at some 110 m.p.h. Unconscious for 10 days, he took 7 months to recover and then decided to fly an airplane to get back his nerve. He hated airplanes and figured if he could pilot one he could race again. Dixon got the plane just high enough to demolish it completely when he crashed, the fuel tank braining the pilot and bathing him with gasoline. Yet he returned to win the 1935 Tourist Trophy and the 1936 Brooklands 500.

After his plane accident, Dixon suffered from an eye condition in which he had trouble focusing his eyes forward after looking right or left. Though he raced despite this merely by rarely looking right or left, the lifting of his driver's and competition license before World War II (after the highway accident where he bashed the bobby) probably saved his life. After his forced retirement, Fred spent the years until his death in 1956 living relatively quietly in Yorkshire and acting as an automotive consultant. The 4-wheel-drive Crab and the lawsuit against Ferguson came in this period.

Dixon was far ahead of his time in many engineering practices. He seems to have originated the sliding plate throttle and to have been among the pioneers in calculating carburetor airflow for optimum power with economy. He shunned supercharging though it was then in its heyday. Assuredly, he was one of a kind. It is unfortunate that such individualists are finding it harder and harder to break the mold of an ever more rigid technology.

CHARLES DODSON

Mario Andretti was the mighty mite of American auto racing in the Sixties and Seventies. Mario was all of 5 feet, 3 inches. Nobody has ever dared to call Mario "Tom Thumb" after the famous P. T. Barnum midget, to anyone's memory, but that was what they called the British driver, Charles J. P. Dodson, who happened to measure the same 63 inches, back in the Thirties. Nor should the Andretti-Dodson comparison stop there; like Andretti, Charlie Dodson was a verstaile driver. He won early fame in a tiny MG, and he was equally at home in the 23-litre Napier-Railton Land Speed Record car.

Born in 1902, youngest son of a Manchester barrister, Dodson was left fatherless at the age of 5. The family was not penniless, but there was enough of a money problem for Dodson to skip advanced schooling and go into an apprenticeship program as soon as he was 17. Motorcycles were a passion, so he worked at the old Royal Ruby cycle factory at Altrincham, England. His salary was a munificent 5 shillings a week, in those days about $1.25 American.

Dodson showed enough skill to be granted his request to build his own machine, and over 3-month period he constructed a 350 c.c. special that would do 75 m.p.h. without breathing hard—pretty fair for 1919. With this cycle he started his competition career, moved on to a Sunbeam, and became a 2-wheel Grand Prix star. Dodson was 32 before he switched to automobile racing, perhaps because he considered a four-wheeled mount an "old man's" form of competition. Anyway, that first season, 1934, he won the Ard, Ireland, version of the Tourist Trophy in an MG at 74.69 m.p.h., about what he used to do in a motorcycle.

After that, Dodson won with frequency, and in 1936 he repeated in the TT with a Riley, sharing victory with Fred Dixon at 78.01 m.p.h. It was quite a comedown from his 1935 activity—at Bonneville Salt Flats, Utah, where, with John Cobb as team leader and codriving with Cobb and Tim Rose-Richards, Dodson helped wrest the 24-hour record from the United States in the 8,000-pound, 23-litre Napier-Railton. The trio averaged 134 m.p.h. for the day-long run, temperatures reaching 110 degrees Fahrenheit in the shade during the daytime.

Dodson won races in all kinds of cars, á la Andretti. In 1938, for example, he took the 200-mile British Empire Trophy Race at Donington in a tiny 744 c.c. d.o.h.c. Austin 7 Special, nipping Prince Bira's ERA with the astonishing time of 69.62 m.p.h. At that juncture, Auto Union, then racing some of the most powerful racers in the world along with Mercedes Benz, offered Dodson a factory driver spot. He thought it out and turned it down; the Munich Crisis soon afterwards proved his decision the right one.

During World War II, Charlie became a lieutenant in the Royal Navy Volunteer Reserve and was part of the D-Day armada, with the dangerous assignment of bringing highly volatile fuel ashore for the invading troops. He lived through it all, and made one more racing appearance, at Silverstone in 1951, when he drove a Jaguar XK 120 in a production car race and won at 83 m.p.h.

MARK DONOHUE

The International Symposium on the Automobile was a prestigious engineering event held several years in New York City by the Society of Automotive Engineers at the time of the April International Automobile Show. Technical experts from the world over were among the speakers. So what was a racing driver doing there on the platform?

Mark Donohue Jr. was a special kind of racing driver. He was the son of a well-to-do lawyer from Summit, N.J., and a graduate engineer (Brown, 1959). The young-looking Donohue had taken a scientic approach to the sport from the time, when at the age of 22, he began ice racing a 1957 Corvette. 'That's when I found out I was allergic to the isophthalic polyester resins in fiber glass," Donohue recalled. "We were fitting a new fender on the Corvette when I broke into a rash." Mark won his first competition, a hillclimb in Rhode Island, in that car; then, taking a tip from Roger Penske, whom he knew casually, sold the car and got himself an Elva Courier for SCCA racing. It took a year of scientific analysis of the problem of road racing for Mark to figure

things out well enough to win a National Championship with the Elva.

Racing, however, was still an avocation, even in 1965 when Mark won an unprecedented double crown and the SCCA Kimberly Cup, driving a Mustang and a Lotus 20B. Born March 18, 1937, in Summit, N.J., the young engineer had only passing thoughts about driving professionally. He had codriven to 5th overall for the John Mecom team at Sebring in 1965, with Walt Hansgen whom he had met at meetings of the Road Racing Drivers Club. Living in neighboring towns, the two became quite friendly, Mark becoming known as Walt's protégé.

Donohue's big break came in Charlotte, N.C., in January 1966, in the office of John Holman. John was then handling a major portion of the Ford racing program. As Mark tells it:

"We came in and, after introductions, Walt told John he wanted me to codrive with him in the Ford at the Daytona Continental and at Sebring. John asked if I ever had driven this type of car before. Walt said no. Then John asked if I ever had driven at 200 m.p.h. before. Walt said no. Then John asked if I ever had driven on the high banks before. Walt said no. Holman was quiet a second, then he yelled, 'Then what in the hell is he doing here?'"

Hansgen finally threatened to quit if Donohue was not included. Holman capitulated, but he entered an extra car as insurance (6 instead of 5). Hansgen-Donohue finished 3rd overall at the Continental and 2nd at Sebring. The performances launched Mark on a professional career, and also got him the job of chief engineer of Griffith, a short-lived luxury GT. In June 1966 Donohue was signed on a race-to-race basis by the Penske Racing team for both the USRRC and the Can-Am series. The offer came as a surprise because Donohue still knew Penske only casually. The relationship developed into one of the most successful owner-driver combinations ever. In 1966 Mark drove the Sunoco Lola-Chevrolet to victories at Mosport, Nassau Speed Weeks, and Kent, Wash. and finished 2nd behind John Surtees in the CanAm standings. In 1967 he won 6 of the 8 races to sweep to the USRRC crown and finished 3rd—highest American—in the CanAm.

There have been few drivers who ever have had a year like Donohue's 1968 campaign. He won 5 of 8 in USRRC to repeat as champion; then, in a beautifully-prepared Camaro, broke Ford's stranglehold on the TransAm series, winning 10 of 13 races. Although he never expressed animosity toward the marque, he always seemed to be trouncing Ford entries. One wondered whether he got an extra kick out of winning because of Ford's lack of confidence in him.

Indianapolis is where virtually every American and most foreign racing stars eventually try their hand—despite deprecating noises about the boredom of it, the lack of challenge, and similar comments. The truth is that any stretch of road or prescribed path is a challenge, if there are 33 of the best drivers in the world and 33 of the most expensive and specialized cars in the world competing for a million dollars in prizes in a single 500-mile race. Drivers may prefer some other kind of racing, but they come away knowing they have faced a unique challenge because their business is racing and a million dollars is a lot of business.

Donohue never put down Indianapolis. He was surprised by the unscientific approach taken with so much money at stake. "You have to come here and see what the problems are and then go away and decide what you are going to do about them," he once said. "It's 4 left turns, and I figure the driver is working for 150 yards coming into each turn. Positioning on the entrance approach is where one driver is better than another. Then it's up to the car and the tuning of the chassis."

The first time out, Mark was Rookie of the Year for qualifying 4th and finishing 7th. In 1970, his next time out, he won some $86,500 for finishing 2nd, leading 4 laps in his Lola turbocharged Ford that apparently was a slower machine than that of winner Al Unser. He had 3rd place nailed, then moved up when the Coyote Turbo-Ford of A. J. Foyt dropped out. Donohue already knew how even the most minor mechanical woe can cost places, since the year before he had seemed likly to finish 4th, only to spend precious moments in the pits.

One might call this Indianapolis race a continuation of the rivalry that had grown up between Parnelli Jones and Donohue, because Al Unser was piloting a vehicle owned by Jones. The rivalry flourished most directly in Trans-American sedan racing; Jones always in a Ford Mustang and Donohue in a Camaro in 1968 and 1969 and in a Javelin in 1970. A more unlikely juxtaposition of competitors was hard to imagine, the Brown University college man versus the graduate of the rugged roadster circuit in southern California. Even the driving styles were different—Mark seemingly relaxed and sparse with his maneuvers, Jones preferring his rear suspension setup to be "twitchy." In 1968 Jones was an occasional TransAm competitor, but true hostilities began when he appeared in the seat of the factory team cars prepared by Bud Moore in 1969.

A scoring mixup inaugurated matters. At Michigan International Speedway, Jones was declared the winner 5 hours after the race ended, with Donohue apparently in 1st place, when embarrassed SCCA scorers found they had dropped a lap. The pair clashed again at Mid-Ohio, but neither figured in the victory, and Jones won at Donnybrooke Speedway in Brainerd, Minn. Donohue led by 30 seconds in that race with 5 of the 84 laps remaining when his engine blew. Parnelli and Horst Kwech in another Mustang had caused Mark to continue charging with their constant pressure. Kwech had wrecked seconds earlier.

It had started as all 1969 TransAms started, the 2

169

Mustang factory teams versus the Sunoco Camaros. There was as much rivalry between the Carroll Shelby Mustangs and the Moore Mustangs as between them and the Roger Penske Camaros. On the first turn, Kwech of the Shelby team passed 4 cars to lead. On lap 12 Parnelli moved from 5th to 2nd with a series of spectacular passes at close quarters in the esses. The picture was altered radically when a noncompetitive car moved the wrong way and triggered a crash that took George Follmer, Jones's teammate, out of the race and caused damage to the Jones car. In the confusion, Donohue moved up to challenge Kwech for the lead with Parnelli ending up 4 seconds behind, a deficit he quickly cut. The cars were so close for the next 30 laps that Jones was able to take the lead on lap 52, only to drop back to 3rd a lap later as both rivals shot past him when he took a turn a little wide. Parnelli seemed to have lost the race on a 21-second pit stop when he was forced to change his left side tires, but then the effect of different driving styles on the machinery took over. Completely out of brakes, Kwech lost control and disappeared into the trees. Two laps later, Mark's engine disintegrated. Jones and his tire-grinding dirt-track style had prevailed.

At Bryar Motor Park in Loudon, N.H., Parnelli set a blistering pace for 19 laps, then spun out, and it was a Donohue cakewalk. Jones lasted only 9 laps at St. Jovite, where an 8-car pileup several laps later wiped out both Mustang threats and caused an hour and a half of delay. Donohue won on the restart with little competition. Parnelli led the first 36 laps at Laguna Seca, then departed from contention as the leaky rear end of his mount caught fire; another Donohue victory. Trans-Am round 10 saw Ronnie Bucknum uphold Chevrolet's primacy as a faulty check valve and a flat tire foiled Parnelli in the pits of Seattle International Raceway in Kent. Mark was no factor, leaving with a blown engine after 32 laps.

Sears Point International Raceway in the sleepy wine town of Sonoma, Calif., was the scene of the climactic battle. Ford had to win to preserve even the slim hope of the TransAm crown, and the engineers at Dearborn were working overtime along with the Moore crew and the Shelby forces. When Parnelli scorched to the pole position in a record 85.734 m.p.h., the stage was set. The Penske Sunoco forces had heard rumors that all the Mustangs had large containers installed in the breather pipes allowing them to hold an extra 2 gallons of gasoline. This meant they expected to make only one pit stop instead of the usual 2 for the 80 laps. Jones held the lead until that stop in the 40th lap with his mate Follmer coming out in 2nd place after fuelling a lap later. The Shelby Mustangs already were sidelined.

Donohue, meanwhile, had pitted on lap 36 and refuelled in 5.5 seconds. Mark began to charge in midrace, overtaking Follmer who, in team strategy, had apparently been blocking back on him. Now it was again between Jones and Donohue—the Camaro closing the gap as Parnelli gambled that he could conserve his fuel all the way. Mark made his 2nd pit stop on schedule and was out in a lightning 3.5 seconds, preserving 2nd over Follmer. The question seemed to be whether Parnelli's fuel would last, when Jones suddenly slowed. The Indy champ was going to be forced into the pits to replace a front tire that had flat-spotted. First Jones and then Follmer pitted, with 10 laps to go, and Mark seemed an easy victor. But then he, too, was forced to come in for a left front tire. He reentered the race in front by 12 seconds with 6 laps left. Parnelli, with 2 new tires to Mark's 1, was smoking the circuit in a desperate effort to close the gap. He closed the gap by 10 of the 12 seconds, but Donohue preserved the victory and clinched for Camaro.

The Mission Bell 250 at Riverside on October 5 thus became a race for the sake of racing. The pattern was familiar—with an added bouquet. Parnelli won the pole and led the first 21 laps when Donohue, then Follmer, took over the lead. As Mark left the pits on lap 35 with a full load of fuel, he found Jones coming up on him fast. Mark braked sharply for turn 6, and Parnelli bashed him from behind, breaking his own radiator, but leaving Mark in the rear. Spinning on the radiator fluid in turn 7, Donohue caught the car and moved at less than full power around the course. It almost seemed that Jones was waiting for Mark to catch up. On turn 6 again the Camaro did catch up, and Parnelli rammed him up the little hill there, continuing around the course to pull out of the race. Afterwards Jones declared: "Mark shut the door on me, but I slowed him down a little." Donohue denied this, saying it was his practice to be extra cautious on turns during the first lap after refuelling. Mark won only because Follmer's car broke a wheel spindle.

The rivalry resumed in 1970 as the Penske boys attempted to develop the American Motors Javelin into a winning car. Jones won easily over Donohue in the season's opener at Laguna Seca, even though he was forced to use his 1969 car. He repeated his easy victory at Lime Rock, Conn., when Donohue broke his engine, and Parnelli watched his teammate in the orange Moore Mustang, Follmer, edge the Javelins at Bryar after Jones was disqualified when his hood blew off. Donohue broke the Mustang primacy with a victory in a rainstorm at Bridgehampton, N.Y., despite replacing a gearbox at the last minute and despite a generally sick engine. Follmer was 2nd and Jones, also in an ailing car, 3rd. Neither Parnelli nor Donohue was a factor at Donnybrook, where an independent Camaro driven by Milt Minter won over Follmer.

The battle was to continue all season, but not in 1971. That year Donohue dominated the TransAm in his Javelin AMX with fair opposition, despite the factory pullouts. He clinched the title for American Motors early enough to permit him to start his first Grand Prix, the Canadian race, in a McLaren M19 that he already had tested secretly in Britain. Mark finished a strong 3rd, and he looked forward to the U.S. race at Watkins

Glen where he knew the course like the back of his hand, except for the new addition. It was not to be; rain and other problems forced him into honoring a USAC commitment in the postponed Trenton 200, and David Hobbs, his sometime enduro companion in the Ferrari 512M that Penske ran with Kirk White, drove at the Glen.

USAC wasn't exactly a bed of roses for Donohue in 1971. His biggest victory came in the Pocono 500; his biggest gaff in the Ontario 500 when he ran out of gas on the 52nd lap, and taxed the engine so much it died later in the race (lap 123) while he was trying to recapture some of the 14 laps his fuel stop had cost him. This was pretty tough to take after Mark had qualified the car at 185.004 m.p.h. on the pole. They knew he was around all the time, though. He sat on the front row at Indy, leading the first 50 laps before retiring with gear-box troubled at 66 laps. In 1972 Donohue won the big one, the Indy 500; it finally was Mark's turn to win. In 1971 he had been the 1st to lap the Brickyard at 180 m.p.h. in practice and had the pole, but his gearbox packed it up. In 1972 his Indy luck was all good, even if others outqualified him, especially Bobby Unser at 195.940 m.p.h. Mark's 191.408 was only good enough for 3rd starting spot, but his 163.465 won the 500. Driving home, Mark's Porsche (he drove a Porsche-Audi in the CanAm until a crash sideline him much of 1972) ran out of gas on the Pennylvania Turnpike. Fate would have its little joke. And so would Mark—in the first race of the 1973 Winston Trail at Riverside, Donohue won his 1st major NASCAR race, beating Bobby Allison by a lap. He drove an American Motors Matador, first time that marque made victory lane.

DALE DRAKE

The Drake family had been involved in automobile racing way back when—but not son Dale. J. A. Drake & Sons opened a valve manufacturing shop in Reedley, Calif., in 1919. The Jadson valve, used in many of Harry Miller's racing designs, was the result—later to be merged into the Thompson Products empire, which in turn became the basis for the TRW conglomerate giant.

Dutch Drake, one of several older brothers, won the last race held on California public roads, at Visalia in 1917, in a specially modified Chevrolet Baby Grand. Lem Drake, another older brother, was considered one of the fine wrench men of the Golden Twenties of auto racing.

It was with this background that young Dale developed—as an airplane enthusiast. He became so adept at learning-by-doing that at 28 he taught aeronautics at the local high school. However, the family moved the business to Los Angeles in 1929 to be nearer their customers. Dale came along reluctantly. He had worked on

every aircraft in the area; he even barnstormed for a while around the fairgrounds circuit with a nephew who did wing walking.

He also piloted gliders. One of his feats was a world towed record, bringing a glider from Reedley to Long Beach. It was an eventful trip, Drake being slammed with a strong updraft which broke the thin towline—as programmed for such an eventuality. However, the glider seat had collapsed onto the control cables. Holding the seat off the cables with one hand, Dale flew the rest of the way to Long Beach, thinking the line had all been left with the tow plane. It was not, and as he started his landing approach, at about a 200-foot altitude it snagged and the nose snapped down. Drake pushed the control stick full forward, diving at the earth. At less than 50 feet, he yanked back. The glider pulled out of the dive, perked the rope free and landed safely.

In 1929 the fledgling American Civil Aeronautics Authority turned Drake's thoughts to racing, automobile style, by making pilots' licenses difficult for private citizens to obtain. The high point in his competitive automobile career came and went quickly. He was the riding mechanic to Louis Meyer in the 1932 Indianapolis 500. The car was the 16-cylinder Sampson Special, powered by two 8-cylinder, 91 cu. in. Miller engines, geared together at the front where the power take-off was. The clutch and transmission were at the rear of the engine. After 150 miles the power take-off gears failed and ended Dale's only Indianapolis ride.

However, it began the acquaintance that led eventually to the Meyer-Drake engines, which dominated a generation of Championship Trail (and therefore Indianapolis) racing. Drake became Meyer's mechanic or, as some call the position, crew chief. And so, at 30, was launched the real career of Dale Drake. Meyer won the 500 in 1933 and again in 1936, with Dale as the crew chief. The winter of 1933–34 can well be considered the direct beginnings of the engine that, as it evolved, was to dominate Indianapolis for decades.

The 4-cylinder design was one of the last of Leo Goosen's Miller era, and the patterns were rented from Richard Lyons, who had purchased them from Miller. Oil surge problems doomed it in 1934. In 1935 Dale could not get back to Indy; but in 1936, with still further changes, the car and engine returned to Indianapolis. As Drake told it later, he and his crew split 3 blocks before they realized that the nitrided cast-iron sleeves had an expansion rate greater than the untreated block. On May 28 a 4th block was flown in from California. The Drake crew fitted the valve gear, bolted on the bottom end and Meyer qualified the car.

"After qualifying, I climbed into the riding mechanic's seat and went out for a test," Drake recalled. "Coming up the back straight the engine went completely sour. The valves were hitting the pistons. At 1:30 p.m. we knew we'd have to tear the engine down, replace the valves and valve guides, and resurface the heads of the pistons to clear the valves. Lou told me he wouldn't dare tackle the job, and if I didn't want to, he'd run it until we had enough money to get home or the car quit. After Lou left the basement where we'd rented space to work, Lawson Harris, Frank Elliott, and I pulled the engine and got to work. After working all night, we finally got the engine back into the car the next morning. We didn't even have time to start the car; just time to put it on the trailer, get to the track and get it in line for technical inspection before they closed the gate. When they put the starter to the engine, I didn't have time to worry whether or not it would start. It fired off and we scrambled for the pit wall. Lou was in the next to last row." Meyer went on to win the race, his 3rd 500.

In 1937, Jadson valves were sold to Thompson, and Dale and brother Lem started their own machine shop. It was the heyday of the midget racer, and Fred Offenhauser's 4-cylinder job was supreme. Dale countered with 2-cylinder opposed engine similar to an aircraft design he had once conceived. A motorcycle champion named Sprouts Elders is said to have convinced Drake he should base the detailing on the bottom end of a Harley-Davidson motorcycle. Dale agreed for the sake of cost, but made new cylinders, pistons, crankshaft, and water-cooled the engine. The Drake gave away 9 cu. in. to the Offy, but had more torque and weighed less. Bill Vukovich won his first midget crown in a Drake-powered automobile.

World War II saw the Drakes switch their talents and facilities to subcontracts on defense work. It was after the war that Lem decided to retire, and Meyer and Drake formed a partnership in a new machine shop. Patterns for the Drake Midget engine had been sold to Fred Gearhart, so when Fred Offenhauser quit, the duo bought the Miller and Offy designs and patterns, and they began to fill the back orders. At one time their Offy midget production reach the rate of one a day.

Meanwhile, the championship engine was put back into production, acquiring attributes of the 1936 Indy winner as well as the Offenhauser versions of the Miller designs. The Meyer/Drake Offy, however, would have had few if any components that would be interchangeable with its predecessors. It was to rule USAC racing until 1963, when the Ford d.o.h.c. 8-cylinder made its presence felt, with Jim Clark's 2nd place on gasoline and Dan Gurney's 7th. In fact, it was soon after that that Lou Meyer split with Dale to assemble and distribute the Ford 4-cam engine.

Taking over complete control of the Offy operation in 1965, Drake carried on with development of the design, moving it into turbocharging and ultra-lightness, so that it still was competitive virtually anywhere on the single-seater U.S. circuit. The Drake Offy still retained such basic design factors as 4 valves per cylinder, d.o.h.c., barrel crankcase, dry sump, and pressure lubrication. The engine shed more than 100 pounds and well surpassed the 500 h.p. barrier. And Drake was still

cranking them out as the seventies arrived . . . in a 50-man factory. In 1972 it was one of Drake's Offys that powered Mark Donohue's winner at the Indy 500. Dale enjoyed that, but less than 6 weeks later, July 10, he was dead of a heart attack.

RENE DREYFUS

Louis Chiron, a Monaco-born veteran, was the favorite of the parimutuel bettors in the 1930 running of the Monaco Grand Prix around the streets of Monte Carlo. And Chiron was quick to reward his followers at the flag, taking a good lead over his Bugatti teammates, Phi-Phi Etancelin in a private one among them, 2 Maserati team cars, Hans Stuck in an Austro-Daimler, and a powerful Mercedes that had no business being on this twisty, 1.97-mile battleground. There were others, of course, including yet another private Bugatti, entered by a 25-year-old Parisian named Rene Dreyfus, at Chiron's own suggestion. But the early battle was taking place among those already cited.

Dreyfus was motoring along very well in the 2nd rank of racers, feeling out this street course once again—although by now he knew its every nuance—fiddling with the fuel mixtures, getting everything just right, all the while steering, shifting, doing the thousand and one mechanical driving actions that were involved in just one circuit around the Monte Carlo streets. Under his driving gloves, Dreyfus's hands already were becoming raw,

and they would be bleeding as if lashed before this race was over.

At first Dreyfus ran 5th or 6th, but as attrition took Stuck and the Mercedes, then the Maseratis, Dreyfus moved up, his pace never changing, just keeping up with Chiron, the master, up there ahead of Rene's Bugatti by 2 minutes or so. At the midpoint of the race, he stood second to Chiron, 2 minutes behind. By the time 25 laps or so were left, it seemed over, yet Dreyfus had a trick up his sleeve. It had been no real secret. Many people had noticed that the youngster had a reserve fuel tank added to his car in an area alongside his seat. Very interesting, but highly impractical, it seemed. Even Chiron, who was Dreyfus's friend, had smiled at the "trick" when he saw it for the first time a day or two before the race.

But the trick was about to pay off. Chiron pitted for fuel, a process that was done quickly for European GP racing of the thirties—44 seconds—but as he regained the course, he had only to look back through his mirror to see, for the first time, Dreyfus's Bugatti coming over a hill. As they motored along, at a pace Chiron thought still sufficient, he noted the Bugatti in the mirror seemed larger; Dreyfus had stepped up his pace, so he must, too. But no matter how fast Chiron went, Dreyfus went faster. Eleven laps from the end, Rene overtook Chiron and passed him. The private Bugatti had snatched away the factory's lead; unthinkable, and Chiron fought back more furiously than ever. He smashed his lap record each time around, but so did Dreyfus.

Dreyfus, in fact, was even faster, increasing his lead by a second a lap, then 2 seconds a lap. By the time he took the checker Rene had a 22-second lead over Chiron, and the groans of disappointed bettors were drowned out by the cheers of a crowd delighted to see David beat Goliath. The amateur became a professional that day, averaging 53.63 m.p.h. Betting on the GP (at least official betting) was dropped after that day until 1972, and the losers never did get a chance to regain their money on this new champion.

Dreyfus was born near Paris on May 6, 1905. A family story is that at the age of 6 he rode a pedal car into the Seine accompanied by a sister, brother Maurice (a year older) and another youngster; all survived. At 9 Dreyfus formally took the wheel of a real car, his father's Clement-Bayard. But his racing was confined for the next few years to bicycles, then motorcycles. The family had moved to Nice in southern France when Rene's father died in 1923, and he and Maurice took over the family fabrics business. In the course of going on the road to sell, Rene decided a car was needed, and if one could be found that could be raced as well as used for transportation, so much the better.

The result was a 6-horsepower, 750 c.c. Mathis, which —with certain parts stripped away and a long exhaust pipe added, among other things—could be made to look like a racer. In 1924 Dreyfus took the course for the 1st time in this car at Gattieres, near Nice, with Maurice in the seat alongside him. He scored a class victory, which was not hard, Rene confided later, since the Dreyfus Mathis was the only car in class. In 1925 the Mathis was swapped for a Hotchkiss, but the following year the car was finally purchased—a "really beautiful little 4-seater Brescia Bugatti," as Rene later described it.

Success followed with this car, and it led to something better, a 1,500 c.c. supercharged 4-cylinder Bugatti Type 37A on a GP chassis. For 2 seasons Dreyfus dominated auto racing in southern France, winning some 55 or 60 starts. He took a 3rd behind Chiron and "Williams" (Capt. William Grover) in the Antibes GP in 1928, which was Dreyfus's introduction to the top European racing of that day. Chiron persuaded Rene to enter the Targa Florio that same year, and Dreyfus finished a respectable 8th, but he preferred the out-and-out road race to the Targa's endurance race/rally quality.

Every Frenchman at this time had to give the government 6 months for military training. With the fabrics business under control, his racing credentials fully established, and other personal matters in hand, Rene decided this was the time. He spent his military hitch in Marseilles in the Transportation Corps, even bringing along his Bugatti and giving his fellow troopers demonstrations, until one day the car frightened too many military mounts, and he was ordered to mothball it. Fortunately his duty was up soon after that unhappy day. Back in Nice, he and Maurice agreed that the fabrics business could get along without Rene, so he accepted a job with a new Bugatti agency being opened by Ernst Friderich.

Dreyfus had a happy return to competition, bringing his 1,500 c.c. Bugatti in 5th in the first Monaco GP in 1929, then taking the winning 2.3 litre car from that race (driven there by Williams) and winning the Dieppe GP at 71.00 m.p.h. Friderich was instrumental in obtaining a year-old former factory car, a Type 35B supercharged, straight-8, single-cam GP car that the factory was abandoning for a Type 35C which had a more compact engine with shorter stroke and supposedly lower power and acceleration but greater reliability. Rene went to Molsheim, seat of all that was Bugatti, picked up the car, and motored leisurely home, stopping off to win the St. Raphael GP and the La Turbie hillclimb along the way. He won the Marne GP at 88.50 m.p.h. and was 3rd in an all-Bugatti sweep at the Algerian GP.

Next came that glorious Monte Carlo victory. Rene expected a Bugatti berth after his showing; instead Ettore Bugatti was furious that Dreyfus had beaten a factory car and driver, and sent the young man packing. A shocked Dreyfus returned to Nice to find an offer from Maserati awaiting him, and he signed with the Italian team, very much on the rebound from Bugatti. There were 2 unhappy years with Maserati. The Tunis GP, his 1st for Maserati, augered what was ahead, perhaps. Leading, Rene had to pit and lost his lead because of a minor oil pipe fracture. Spurred on by team orders, he drove all-out, very foreign to his personal style, cutting corners more sharply than usual while trying to shave tenths of a second here and there. Finally, a shave was too close, the car nicked a curb, spun and accordioned against a tree. Fortunately, Rene was able to walk away.

There were some finishes in 1931, including a 2nd in the Marne GP and a 3rd in the Rome race, but mechanical troubles, or ordinary breakdowns, plagued Dreyfus. At the Monte Carlo race he lost a wheel while in the lead, a pattern that followed for 2 years, culminating in the 1932 Avus GP when Dreyfus led, but repeated tire failures forced him to pit so many times that he finished dead last, though he set the race's fastest lap, at 130.4 m.p.h. On some days he raced borrowed Bugs; there was a bad time in one of those, too. While leading the Comminges GP, Rene hit a wet spot at around 100 m.p.h., spun 3 times, hit a bump, and flipped the 2.3-litre Type 35C he had borrowed from Chiron. But there were good times. He was 3rd in the Nice Formula Libre race, 2nd in both the Nimes GP and the Eifelrennen.

He asked for his release from Maserati, and the factory obliged sadly. That winter, at the Paris Automobile Show, a chance meeting with Ettore Bugatti revealed that Chiron was leaving the factory. Would Dreyfus be interested in replacing him? He would, and he was signed up on the spot. The team he was joining consisted of Tazio Nuvolari, Jean-Pierre Wimille, Antonio Brivio, Robert Benoist, Williams, and others.

In 1933 Dreyfus was 2nd to Marcel Lahoux in the Dieppe GP, 3rd at Monaco and Belgium. The following season he was 3rd at Monaco again, then won the Belgian GP at 86.91 m.p.h. But there was a missing ingredient in Dreyfus's makeup. Meo Constantini, a great driver himself in Bugatti's racing effort, said it best, Rene later recalled: " 'Aggressiveness was not one of my major characteristics,' he said. 'I would never be a Nuvolari.' " True enough, yet he was one of the best. In 1931 Dreyfus was invited to join Scuderia Ferrari, the Alfa Romeo factory team. In 13 starts that season he finished 12 times, winning the Dieppe GP at 82.89 m.p.h. and the Marne GP at 98.03, taking 2nds at Pau and Rome, and a 3rd at Nice. Dreyfus was running 2nd and rapidly closing on Stuck in the lead Mercedes when he was called in and his car turned over to Nuvolari, a native son.

Nuvolari broke the car, but still limped in 2nd. Afterwards, he joined with Dreyfus in saying that the arrangement was far from satisfactory; Rene should have kept the car, and probably would have won the race if allowed to do so. That was nice for the ego, but Dreyfus left Alfa nonetheless. He drove a few races for Tony Lago's Talbot team, then switched to Ecurie Bleue, the private team financed by Laurie and Lucy O'Reilly Schell, parents of later GP driver Harry Schell.

His first start for this Ecurie was not really a race,

however, but the unusual La Course du Million on August 27, 1937. It took place at Montlhéry, a race against the clock to see who could push the GP car average for 16 laps of the course (124 miles), to its highest, starting with 87 m.p.h. Dreyfus's mount was a Delahaye, a car he would compete in for the next several seasons. The preparations for this million-francs stakes (about $50,000 in U.S. funds) took 6 months; and 4 days before the August 31 deadline Dreyfus took the course to see what he could do against the time of the only contender left besides the Ecurie's Delahaye—Wimille's supercharged Bugatti—and he shaved about 5 seconds off Jean-Pierre's best time despite a strong crosswind.

Wimille took 4 days to get ready. He was going well enough on the final day to cause Dreyfus to go out again, at the same time, to shave some more from Wimille's time. But the Bug's engine was going sour, so Rene did not have to do much shaving; instead he happily motored around and stopped to receive the check for a million francs (for the Schells). Rene also kept his competition hand in with occasional free-lance drives, such as victories at Tripoli and Florence in a 1500 c.c. Maserati, and 2nds at the Turin and Picardy GP's. He also ran a small, 6-cylinder Delahaye to several minor victories.

In 1938 he won enough races to again win the title Champion of France, as well as other international races such as the Cork GP. The year's big victory—his last big one as it turned out—was at Pau when he faced an "invincible" German team of Mercedes-Benz. Dreyfus prevailed for France, at 54.64 m.p.h. France was mobilized the following year, of course, and Dreyfus was back in the Army, driving transport trucks the length and breadth of the nation. But he and Rene LeBegue, a youngster who was a promising driver, were given 45-day leaves during the "phony war" period in 1940 to race at Indianapolis where the Schells had sent two Maseratis. Luigi Chinetti went along as a relief driver and to act as liaison.

One car blew its engine in the rain, and misunderstandings about Indy's regulations under the yellow caution periods kept the other one back in 10th place. By now, however, the war in France was not phony any more, and an armistice was called, leading to the French surrender to Germany. The French ambassador told Dreyfus to stay in the U.S., then discharged him from the French Army. With a friend in the same fix (a discharged French naval officer also trapped here) Rene opened his first American restaurant in New Jersey, but after December 7, 1941, he was ready to fight again.

At first the American army would not accept a French citizen, but they relented. Rene learned fluent English in an Army school. He was offered a commission but turned it down, participating as a sergeant in the North African and Southern Italian invasions. At one point, he even ran an Army motor pool in Naples.

Back in his adopted home in 1945, Rene opened a new restaurant with his brother (who came over in 1940 with their sister). The enterprise was called Le Gourmet, and it lasted 7 years until a larger, more ambitious restaurant was opened—Le Chanteclair, on East 49th Street off Manhattan's Fifth Avenue. Rene remained a contented restaurateur thereafter, with only 2 lapses. In 1952 Dreyfus and a Parisian banker ran a 4.1-litre Ferrari at Le Mans and lasted 4 hours before a clutch broke. In 1953 (2 years after his wife's death) Rene captained a 3-car Arnolt-Bristol team that finished 1, 2, and 4 in their class at the Sebring 12-Hour race.

Dreyfus's logs showed 36 victories, 19 places, and 17 shows; 106 finishes out of 148 starts between 1924 and 1940. He was one of the best in an era of generally fine drivers in European racing. He also became one of the best in the French restaurant business in America.

KEITH DUCKWORTH

For many years, the engine that ruled the Grand Prix roost was the Cosworth-Ford, a true production racing engine—as opposed to the kind of GP engine with individual peculiarities and characteristics—in the days when there really was no such a thing as a production racing engine. The man most responsible for this chance is the "worth" part of Cosworth (Mike Costin supplied the "Cos"), Keith Duckworth.

Born in 1933 in Blackburn, England, David Keith

Duckworth had family motoring connections through a grandfather who took part before World War I. The young Duckworth took an early interest in model aircraft, making his 1st rubber-powered model at the age of 8, before moving on to more complicated radio-controlled designs for which he also made the electronic equipment. Keith had a motorcycle as soon as the law permitted, and in due course he became the owner of several rapid 2-wheelers, among them 3 water-cooled 2-stroke Scotts. Faced with National Service on leaving school in 1951, Duckworth chose the RAF, hoping for pilot training; he was accepted for aircrew training and did 140 hours (some of it in twin-engined Oxfords) but was switched to navigating. Duckworth's career took its direction when he left the RAF, for not only did he start a successful course in engineering at London's Imperial College, but he also became the owner of a Lotus 6. It had one of the first 1100 c.c. Coventry-Climax engines manufactured, making it pretty competitive; but after 3 events its disillusioned driver decided that he could not afford it. The Lotus was sold, but some valuable lessons about tuning Climax engines had been acquired.

Keith asked Colin Chapman for a job with the budding Lotus organisation, having worked there during college vacations, and was put to work on transmissions. There was a sudden parting of the ways after only 10 months, which resulted in Duckworth setting up Cosworth Engineering in October 1958, with Costin, a friend from Lotus. With Costin working out his contract at Lotus, Duckworth and his wife, Ursula, were left in charge of the new concern; their aims were to continue Coventry-Climax development and also to build a complete Cosworth car. The latter got as far as the chassis, but only in 1969 did an actual car carrying the firms's name get to a racing circuit. A 4-wheel drive machine, it was a class failure. It now resides in Tom Wheatcroft's Grand Prix collection in Britain. Cosworth power plants found a happier home in many famed racing cars, including those of every World Champion after 1967.

Before that, however, Duckworth-prepared Climax engines were giving private owners in Elvas an edge over factory Lotus drivers, so it was not long before Keith decided to convert a Fiat engine for the newly introduced Formula Junior. An early examination of the Fiat revealed that it was not going to prove an ideal base, so Keith decided to use the Ford 105E unit instead. Later, no one would contemplate any engine other than the small Ford in Formula 3 but in those days, this little unit was giving tuners some nasty headaches, mainly due to camshaft design problems. Duckworth redesigned cams that worked, and Cosworth became the pace-setters in this field. The Cosworth FJ engine made its first appearance at Brands Hatch on Boxing Day 1959 (where a sump plug fell out during practice, the resulting loss of oil ruining the engine), and it went on to power the majority of the winners in subsequent races.

The company had been faltering until that time, but now it outgrew its premises, first at Friern Barnet, then at Edmonton, later at Northampton. The 1st true racing engine from Cosworth was the one-litre Formula 2 SCA (Single Cam A series), introduced in time for the 1964 season. There was Ford support, so it was natural once again to use the Ford block. The SCA used a single overhead camshaft, while the rival BRM and Honda units both had 2, but it was not until the 3rd and last year of the formula (1966) that the Honda caught up and passed the Cosworth. Of his own engine, Duckworth said simply: "Its combustion was poor, the Honda's was good." Yet the SCA was still being used in 1970 in American club racing, and under those less arduous conditions continued to win races.

Ford's association with Cosworth became even closer in 1966, when a joint project was announced, not only for a new F2 but also for a Formula 1. The F2 engine soon was running in an old Brabham that Cosworth had purchased for Costin to drive in club races as a mobile test bed, and he had already won several as well as cracking some lap records by the time the first 40 customers took delivery of production FVA engines. In its 1st and 3rd years, the FVA won nearly every F2 race, the exceptions being 5 victories for the Ferrari Dina V6 towards the end of 1968. The FVA was an unqualified success, and was followed by the FVC (Four Valve C series, the B series having been an experimental 1500 c.c. version) which had a stroke dimension increased from 2.72 in. to 3.06 in. Power was only marginally more, but torque was greatly improved.

The F1 DFV engine was a joint effort with British Ford, an effort to restore British prestige in racing from what seemed to be a low ebb. As a Ford statement said at the time: "In November 1965, the future offered a lot of reasons for pessimism. British racing-car constructors had relied until then largely on engines for BRM and Coventry-Climax. At the end of 1965, Coventry-Climax said they would make no more Grand Prix engines. And Honda was coming in with more and more money. Ferrari was still fighting for supremacy, while in France de Gaulle himself was on the point of offering £500,000 for anyone who would develop a French Grand Prix engine." Ford wanted a V-8, essentially comprising 2 FVA cylinder heads mounted on a common block.

Duckworth took only 5 months to complete the design stages of the unit that Ford personnel had said would require 2 years. The engine won its 1st race—the famous 1967 Dutch GP—in the hands of Jim Clark, which must surely go down as one of the greatest motoring achievements of that decade. Duckworth's Cosworth V-8 shared with the BRM H16 the idea that the engine should increase the lightness of the car by being a stressed member of the chassis. This is one of the more significant advances to be seen under the 3-litre F1, at a time when GP racing did not undergo many annual technical changes. By dispensing with side members, it became possible to mount oil and water pumps on each side of the crankcase. The Cosworth sump itself was exceptionally shallow and actually carried the main bearings, which were thicker than those seen on any previous racing unit, an innovation pioneered by Duckworth. With no pumps cluttering up the front of the engine, and the electric componerts tucked away in a box between the vee of the engine, overall length was kept to a short 21.5 inches.

Of course, there were problems. One of the most difficult was getting the oil and air out of the engine separately. The timing gear layout was redesigned for 1969, when different camshafts and other minor alterations enabled the rev limit to be raised by 500 r.p.m. from the previous 9,000 mark. The engine, which had only been available to Lotus in 1967, then to McLaren and Matra in 1968, went on general sale in 1969.

Still a young man, Duckworth expected to contribute his engineering genius to GP racing for many years. He might even get a full-blown Cosworth car off the drawing board successfully one of these days. Meanwhile, his horizons expanded to include aviation products, as well as automotive, and other areas were explored. Keith never was a man to shun innovation. He would try anything once, almost: but not any different combination of his name with Mike Costin's. Who would ever take seriously an engineering company called Ducktin?

CAMILLE DU GAST

One of the earliest woman drivers in the world, Camille du Gast was the wife of a wealthy Paris merchant, but used her maiden name to avoid embarrassing her husband. Her career was a short one, as were so many of the pioneering automobilists. In 1901, attired in stiff corsets and dress more suited for a ballroom than a race course, du Gast participated in the Paris-Berlin race in a Panhard. She finished a creditable 33rd.

Though she didn't finish the bloody Paris-Madrid race 2 years later, her conduct was such that she set a pattern that has survived in motor racing down to this day. Du Gast was running a strong 6th in the No. 29 De Dietrich, a 5.7-litre car that had left the start line decorated with lilacs and roses from the lady's admirers. Then, down the road, a British driver named Stead brushed against another car and spun off the road, crashing badly, Lorraine atop him. As Camille came abreast of him, she saw the car being lifted off the unfortunate racer, but decided her services, which included some nursing training, might be needed. Du Gast pulled off the road and parked. She spent an hour with Stead, who called on her to race on, but gratefully accepted her help when she assured him that he was more important than any race. The gallant Parisian stayed with the Briton until a horse-drawn ambulance arrived and took him away to the hospital.

In 1904 Du Gast reached a height and was plunged to a depth. Based on her strong talents behind the wheel, the Benz team made the precedent-shattering move of offering Camille a team drive for that season, but several race organizers protested so vigorously that the offer reluctantly was withdrawn. Du Gast took it bravely, but also hard. She gave up motor racing soon after and turned to racing motorboats. She lived until 1942.

CLIFF DURANT

Cliff Durant, son of the great American auto tycoon W. C. Durant, was referred to, rather unkindly, as a Morris chair driver. For those too young to remember them, the Morris chair was one built for relaxation, and the implication was that R. C. never went very fast when he drove at Indianapolis or anywhere else. He competed in 6 Indy races, his best finish a 7th in 1923 when he brought a fantastic 5-car team to the Brickyard. That year Harry Hartz, Jimmy Murphy, and Eddie Hearne finished 2nd, 3rd, and 4th respectively in Durant cars, and Frank Elliott brought the other team car home 6th.

Cliff entered the Indianapolis scene with an old Stutz that he had renamed the Chevrolet Special, and took 2nd money in the 1919 race with Eddie Hearne piloting. Durant went out on the 55th lap with a broken steering gear. He did not do much in 1920 or 1921 or 1922 himself, but he sponsored such drivers as Tommy Milton. Durant lent Milton the chassis for the car with the 1st Miller engine specially commissioned, but the car was not finished in time for the 1921 race. Cliff bought the rest of the car from Milton for the 1922 race after the car had been suspended by AAA for a violation of its rules; Tommy's victories in the car had been advertised by a Durant Six dealer as having been scored in the passenger car field. Durant drove the car to 12th with conked out on the 44th lap. The 1923 classic found Cliff in the lead for laps before Milton passed him.

Cliff also bankrolled Jimmy Murphy for a 1925 Miller front-drive car that the Le Mans winner never piloted, since Murphy was killed at Syracuse the previous fall. Cliff was also in back of the 1927 Milton-designed Detroit Special, a vehicle that cost more than $100,000, but he lacked the ability to make it go at that late stage of his career. Five years later the front end assembly of this car was used in the 1932 winner, and subsequently it finished 2nd, 3rd, 4th and 8th under Harry Hartz ownership.

In 1924 Hartz and Fred Comer brought his cars home 4th and 7th respectively, while the other 3 cars broke down or were not in the top 10. Durant had cars driven by Harlan Fengler, Leon Duray, and Ira Vail, among others, in subsequent 500s. In the Thirties, he bankrolled some of his former drivers in car ownership, to what extent is not exactly clear.

But Indianapolis demonstrated only part of Cliff's impact on racing. Born in Flint, Mich., before W. C. made his first million, Cliff was old enough to appreciate what money could buy when papa's largesse began flowing his way. He turned to motor racing apparently about 1912, when W. C. installed him as head of the Chevrolet agency in Los Angeles. Partly for the thrill of it, partly to publicize the merits of the marque, Cliff assayed record runs between Los Angeles and cities such as Seattle and Oakland. He got an AAA license and entered some dirt track races also in a stripped-down Chevy. In 1914 he drove in the L.A.-to-Phoenix road race and finished in the money, despite snapping his front axle near the finish. He and his riding mechanic fastened the axle together, attached fence pickets to the front wheels so that they could go only straight ahead, and drove over the finish line this way.

Then came the 1st Chevrolet Special, actually a 1913–14 Stutz team car, altered by Al Nielsen (later a noted riding mechanic). Cliff was competitive but not a winner at the old Ascot mile, the San Francisco World's Fair Vanderbilt Cup and Grand Prize races, and a series of special exhibitions at various horse tracks, all in 1915. He then bought Barney Oldfield's old chain-drive Fiat and in 1916 toured the California dirt circuit.

The 2nd Chevrolet Special, also an altered Stutz with Fred Comer now the riding mechanic, was more successful. World War I may have taken some of the younger drivers out of the sport, but it did not take old Cliff, who proceeded to win at Ascot, Fresno, Santa Rosa, and Hanford (all dirt tracks) and, surprisingly, at the Liberty Sweepstakes on the Tacoma, board track on July 4, 1918. The latter was one of 2 major victories for Durant: he bested Earle Cooper, Roscoe Sarles, Eddie Hearn, Eddie Pullen, and even Ralph Mulford in the 25-mile, 75-mile, and 100-mile events. He then won a wire-to-wire victory in the 250-mile Santa Monica road race in March 1919.

After Santa Monica, Cliff called racing "recreation . . . like playing golf." At Elgin, Ill., in 1919 his car skidded through a barbed wire fence, sending Cliff and his riding mechanic to the hospital slashed up by the barbs. W. C. prevailed upon him to retire to the car business. He did—for about as long as it took him to recover completely. Meanwhile, in 1920 he bankrolled the famed Beverly Hills board track in Los Angeles, as well as providing the land. That land—at the juncture of Beverly, Wilshire, and Olympic Boulevards—is invaluable today. On Feburary 28, 1920, the Chevrolet Special rode again; Cliff and his mechanic lasted half the race until engine trouble intervened.

Many racing buffs of the era were apparently also interested in aviation, but Cliff had the wherewithal to do something about the interest. He opened Durant Field in Oakland and founded Durant Air Craft Corporation, a pioneer commercial aviation firm. His driving was very limited that year.

It really seemed as if his driving days were over, for the entire year of 1921 saw no Cliff Durant activities on the track. Off the track, he was having the Chevrolet Special rebuilt yet another time, installing a new Miller racing engine. He felt his aircraft interests needed more publicity than his car interests, so he renamed the car the Durant Special. Driven by Tommy Milton, it won the AAA Contest Board crown and incurred the wrath of the officials because the Durant dealer said his passenger cars had the same engine. Since it was named the Durant Special, they ruled Cliff had to drive—or change the name. Cliff returned to action for the 1922 Indy 500, finished 12th, and made the circuit on the West Coast, at least, competing in San Carlos, Tacoma, and Cotati. For Kansas City he turned the machine over to Roscoe Sarles. Sarles crashed and died in the flaming wreckage of the vehicle.

Durant's dream of a team of identical racing cars to dominate automobile racing began to take shape in August 1922. The dream became reality in the Thanksgiving Day race at Beverly Hills when 6 bright yellow 183 cu. in. Millers were in the top 10—Earl Cooper, Jimmy Murphy, Dario Resta, Eddie Hearne, Art Klein, and Durant. Murphy won, and led the team to victory at the 1923 Beverly Hills race and at Fresno. Cliff was also staging record runs—and battling the Los Angeles Motor Car Dealers Association, which revived the claim that his advertisements implied that people who bought his passenger cars were getting the same engines. Cliff beat this by pointing out that all he was doing was advertising his team's victories. In 1923, new Durant Specials with 122 cu. in. engines dominated Indianapolis's top 10 and won at Altoona, Kansas City, and Fresno. An overseas jaunt to the Italian Grand Prix by Durant and Murphy resulted in a 3rd.

This was the high point of the Durant racing fortune. In 1924 things began to go downhill as Cliff found that advancing years and lavish living were taking their toll. He had built a new all-aluminum car for Jimmy Murphy for the final race at the Beverly Hills board track in 1924—a single-seater whose most memorable feature was its headrest for the driver—but Murphy had died at Syracuse, N.Y. The car's best run was at Indy, where it lasted 199 of 200 laps. For the opening of the new Culver City board track, Durant took the wheel of a new front-wheel drive Miller he had also built for Murphy. Cliff never hit the "loud pedal," so the car's merits were never tested. He competed only intermittently after that, his final ride coming in the 1928 Indy 500 where he lasted 175 laps.

Durant retained his interest in the sport until his death in 1935. Was he a Morris chair driver? Not unless you consider speeding around at over 100 m.p.h. at almost the age of 50 to be sitting in a Morris chair.

W. C. DURANT

Horatio Alger, the arch-proponent of the theory that hard work and common sense could turn the local chimneysweep into Croesus himself, would have been pleased with William Crapo (Billy) Durant. Durant, the man who had more to do with the makeup of the American automobile industry—and, therefore, its racing activities—than any other single human being, was raised from the age of 7 by a stern grandfather, Henry Howland Crapo, in Flint, Mich. His father, a Boston bank clerk, had disappeared on a fishing trip, so his mother had taken the boy back to her family. This event might have seemed to assure W. C. an easy life, for Crapo, a former Michigan governor, had plenty of money. It did not; the grandfather was steeped in Algeresque notions and set the youngster of 15 to work as a stacker in his lumber yard for 12 hours a day, 6 days a week, on a $6 wage.

Billy responded with bitterness and determination to get out from under the grandfatherly thumb. He soon rose to foreman, on sheer merit, and began to work nights. By 21 he had his own insurance agency. Soon after that he realized the potential of a particular spring-suspended buggy and, with a friend named J. Dallas Dort, bought the company out for $2,000. Dort was a hardware clerk, but he, too, had been raised on the Alger dream. This company—with Durant as dreamer and salesman—made both men multimillionaires at 40. It was 1901 when Durant retired, taking his wife and 2 children to New York City, where he expected to dabble in the stock market. Instead he got into the car business, buying the Buick Motor Car Company in 1904 for approximately $10,000.

It happened this way: David Dunbar Buick, a young man who had Americanized his Polish name, had brought out a motor car in 1902—just like hundreds of others across the country who saw in the horseless carriage the possibility of great wealth. But Buick was different; he realized that the engine he had developed through years of tinkering needed improvement by a professional engineer. He hired Eugene C. Richard, a French emigré, to do the job, but did not have the capital to keep the company afloat. Then his main creditor, Briscoe Sheet Metal Company, capitalized Buick's company and left its founder with a token 3 per cent interest. Briscoe in turn sold out to E. B. Whiting of Flint, who went to Durant for aid. Billy was getting pretty bored with retirement, and though only 3 years earlier he had rebuked his son for riding in one of the contraptions, he now came home to Flint with great plans. It was he who thought up the slogan "When better cars are built, Buick will build them." It was he who made the decision to employ the Chevrolet brothers as drivers for his cars in races, endurance runs, exhibitions, and hillclimbs all over the country.

From 1905 on, Durant thought big. He realized that the motor car was a national rather than a regional product; he is credited with setting up the dealer franchise system of selling. His greatest coup was sparked in 1907 when one of the great economic panics hit the United States; other car makers suspended production. Durant doubled his output and stored the 2,295 cars he had made against the time when people could buy again. He was right, for when the panic ended and people looked for a car to buy, they found Buicks readily available. Durant was not satisfied, however. He wanted more control in the new industry, the products of which were still looked upon as toys or status symbols.

Durant unsuccessfully to combine Ford, Maxwell, and Reo. He lined up $500,000 of J. P. Morgan's money to buy them out and form the International Motor Company, but the deal was called off because W. C. imagined a Morgan representative had slighted his concept of the combine's potential. He changed "International" to "General" and founded GM as a paper entity on September 16, 1908, with $2,000 of his own money. He made it the parent company of Buick by transferring stock, failed in an attempt to raise the money to buy out Ford, but got Olds Motor Works instead and embarked on a program of car company and supplier company acquisitions that took GM to worldwide domination of the automobile business.

Cadillac, Oakland (Pontiac), and other less successful marques (Ewing, Welch, Cartercar, Rainier) came under the tent. Durant helped set up Albert Champion in AC Spark Plugs, from which Champion later defected to form Champion Spark Plugs. Walter Chrysler, Charles W. Nash, and Henry P. Leyland (Cadillac) all left him to set up their own successful marques. But in 1910 the empire collapsed and Durant had to surrender his direction of the company to Eastern bankers to save the value of the stock he retained.

At 49, Durant was far from through. With William D. Little, former general manager at Buick, he founded the Little Motor Car Company to compete with Ford in the $650 price class. He was not satisfied with the firm's modest success. Then somebody reminded him that Louis Chevrolet, the racing driver, had a name that was a household word. W. C. forthwith organized the Chevrolet Motor Company to put out a fine luxury automobile. The liaison did not last long. The apochryphal story is that Louis insisted on appearing before Durant with a cigarette between his lips; Durant had just given up cigars and was enforcing a "no smoking" policy. The real reason for the split was much more

basic; the men could not agree on what kind of car the Chevrolet was to be. W. C. won; he also retained the Chevrolet name. Louis lost, and made the mistake of selling off his stock. The company was worth $80 million by 1915; one factor was the magnificent dealer organization Durant built.

W. C. wanted GM back, however; he bought stock quietly through dummy operators. Then, when he was about to make his bid, he passed word to large investors that he would trade Chevrolet stock for GM in the ratio of 5 to 1. Many agreed. Then he sought and obtained the backing of the du Ponts, to take the huge corporation back at the stockholders meeting of 1918. Durant added the huge and profitable Chevrolet business, and the current GM marque lineup was complete.

In 1919 the corporation was capitalized at over $1 billion, and Durant was again making great coups and greater blunders. He acquired Fisher Body, virtually founded Frigidaire and bought Wright Airplane, but he lost his shirt competing with Ford and International Harvester in the farm machinery field. By 1920 he had lost control of GM again, having spent millions to support the stock in the market panic of that year. He came out of the attempt with some $2 million in stock and no control. It is said that other large shareholders felt that to save the company they had to engineer Durant's removal from authority, so they engineered the break in the price of GM stock.

Durant began anew, and the Durant Motor Company was born. It was his last fling in automobiles and seemed about to succeed until he went to Europe for a long rest. While he was away, the resident management tried to change the price category of the cars upwards, with disastrous effects. The Locomobile was one of the new models, a name borrowed from an extinct marque. Durant was virtually unscathed in the collapse. He made millions in the stock market in the twenties, and when the bubble was about to burst, he personally pleaded with President Herbert Hoover to ease credit restrictions to cushion the crash. Friends like Bernard Baruch pleaded with Durant to sell short, to get out, but while he agreed about the crash, Billy thought he had the resources to ride out the coming disaster. He bought instead, and lost untold millions. Seven years later, at the age of 75, he had to plead bankruptcy.

Durant foresaw the shopping center and bowling alley booms and began to recoup slowly. However, a stroke cut him down and, though he lived years longer, Billy was wheeling and dealing no longer. He died at 81, a relatively poor man considering the billions that had passed through his fingers. He had been a catalyst in industry and a man who saw in racing the quick way to popularize the automobile and sell it. Just as the Chevrolets and Bob Burman had driven his Buicks, it was W. C. who sanctioned his son's racing activities and, by indirection, supported them. Horatio Alger would have been proud.

ARTHUR DURAY

The thing about Arthur Duray, the foreign driver after whom America's "Leon Duray" was named, was that he was an American, too. Tall and fair, Duray was born in New York City of Belgian parentage and went back to Europe. He delighted in later years in bedeviling immigration authorities about his American citizenship, or was it Belgian?

Born in 1881, Duray had just turned 21 when he began his competition career with Gobron-Brillie, but their cars weren't that good. Arthur's greatest feat for the marque was a Land Speed Record run at Ostend—really a flying-start kilometer since there was no official LSR in those days—of 83.47 m.p.h. In the Paris-Madrid race that tested so many pioneer drivers, he was 35th.

In 1904 Duray switched to Darracq and immediately showed his talents by leading the Circuit des Ardennes, although slipping back to 6th by the race's end. In the Coppa Florio he was 4th. The next season saw a lucrative offer from De Dietrich, with whom he stayed several seasons. It was in one of their cars that Duray won the 1906 Circuit des Ardennes at 65.8 m.p.h. and was 3rd in that year's Vanderbilt Cupper. He started marque-jumping again about 1909, spending time with Excelsior and Delage, but his two notable feats of the period were in other cars. In a Peugeot in 1914 Duray registered a 2nd at Indianapolis in the 500 and in a 28.4-litre Fiat at Ostend, he made a run (one-way) of 132.37 m.p.h.

After World War I, Duray returned to racing, staying active as a driver through 1928 when he was 7th in the Boillot Cup. The last victory came the year before when Arthur won the Boulogne voiturette race in an Amilcar.

LEON DURAY

George Stewart was a veteran of World War I who might never have become nationally famous if the great promoter, Alex Sloan, had not decided that he needed a new imported hero to play the American fair circuit. So Stewart became Leon Duray, named after a racing hero from Belgium (Arthur Duray), and was represented as a flying ace. He was the subject of a bookshelf of war fiction and was told how to dress and how to act at the track.

Since he could not speak a word of French, "Leon" was kept far away from enterprising reporters who were told he could not speak English. By the time he reached the Mecca, Indianapolis, the fraud was generally known but completely forgiven. Stewart/Duray was a magnificent driver. He campaigned at the Ascot board track in California and others as an IMCA and AAA functionary, always among the leaders. He competed in 8

Indy 500 milers, his best a 6th place in 1925. But he was a charger. He retired on the 76th lap in 1922 with a broken axle after staying 5th or better to that point. He lasted 10 laps in 1923, his Miller Special retiring with a broken oil line.

Leon was not in the 1924 race, but came back for a 6th place in the Miller Special in 1925, sharing the ride with Fred Comer. He grabbed the pole position with a 113.19 m.p.h. run, but some experts still liked Bordino in the Fiat and Dave Lewis in the Junior 8 front-wheel-drive Miller. Duray never led in the race, slipping steadily down after holding 2nd for a while. Duray left the 1926 race with a gas leak after qualifying his Locomobile Junior in the front row. The car would not start, and he finally rolled out late, racing to get to his position on the preliminary go-around. He lasted 34 laps, then only 26 laps in 1927 as his Perfect Circle Miller caught fire after a gas tank broke. He relieved Eddie Hearne later in the race and, in turn, was relieved by Ira Vail. He also drove relief for Tommy Milton.

Old Leon was really charging in 1928 while setting records through 100 miles, including a lap at 4 m.p.h. faster than the previously standard, but he paid the penalty. Cliff Bergere relieved him after 2 pit stops. The end came on the 132nd lap when the engine cooked solid. Dirt in his carburetor on the 65th lap pit stop wrecked his 1929 try after Leon got as high as 3rd in the Miller front-wheel drive.

He skipped 1930 and came back in 1931 with a Boyle Valve Special that boasted an engine he had personally designed. Two were in the race, the other handled by Cliff Durant. They were 16-cylinder, 2-cycle power plants of 233 cu. in. displacement, Roots supercharged. There were 2 cylinder blocks, each containing 4 bores. Each pair of bores had 2 con rods linked to one crankpin, the pair of pistons moving up and down together. Above was a single combustion chamber. Thus he had 16 vertical cylinders but only 8 combustion chambers. Near the bottom of the stroke one piston uncovered the intake port and the other the exhaust port, and the Roots forced the fuel mixture in. The car went out in the 6th lap with cooling problems. It never returned because the money to develop the design was not forthcoming, and the rules changed also. Thus another interesting brainchild died early. According to one authority on 2-cycle engines, the design had much merit.

In 1933 Duray became a car owner of record, entering the Mallory Special with Wilbur Shaw as his pilot. Shaw finished 2nd for him. His Duray Special in 1934, also a Miller 4, was driven to 2nd place Mauri Rose. He continued to sponsor cars periodically until World War II.

J. FRANK DURYEA

There were three Duryea brothers—Charles, Frank, and Otho—the first two intimately involved in the birth and growth of the early American automobile. For years Charles was given the place of honor, but it turned out that James Frank Duryea was *the* brother. Consider the following: he designed and built almost single-handed the 1st practical American motor car (George Selden to the contrary). He did the same with the 1st American racing car. And he drove that car to victory in the 1st American race back in 1895. Then he went to England and drove the 1st car to finish the London to Brighton Emancipation Run.

Charles Duryea was born December 15, 1861, which made him nearly 8 when J. Frank came along in Washburn, Ill., on October 8, 1869 (Otho was much younger). Frank went to high school in Wyoming, Ill., but skipped college to charge after Charles, who had taken time to attend college and polish his debating talents (This was to lead to his almost stolen reputation as the inventive Duryea brother, until a lot of research was carried on in later years.) Charles worked on bicycles, and so did Frank. They moved around—Washington, D.C., New Jersey, and finally Springfield, Mass., where Frank joined the Ames Bicycle Co. as a tool and die maker.

Charles was in Illinois when Frank built the initial Duryea car; Charles did not see it until he got a test ride from Frank when he returned to Massachusetts. His sole contribution appears to have been the steering lever; everything else was from Frank's practical brain. Another car was built for a paying customer. Still another was under way as soon as the Chicago *Times-*

Herald announced a "motorcycle" race—a name the newspaper had coined for automobiles. (Car No. 2 by the way, is the one that found its way to the Smithsonian Institution.)

The car was entered under the auspices of the Duryea Motor Wagon Company of Springfield, Ill., organized in September, 1895. Originally, the race was to have been run July 4th of that year, but only the Duryeas and two others were ready by that time, so things were postponed until Thanksgiving Day, November 28. The prize was $5,000, $2,000 of which, plus a gold medal, would go to the winner.

A blizzard the night before almost made a disaster of the initial American auto race. The racers faced 8 inches of snow, with higher drifts. The Duryea had a secret weapon, however—pneumatic tires, the first ones that were ever used on an American automobile. Despite the cold, a thousand people cheered lustily as the race started. Most cars had trouble starting without help from some willing pushers, but not the Duryea, which was driven by Frank and followed by Charles in a horsedrawn sleigh. Through Jackson Park the Duryea plodded along, to 55th Street, then to Michigan Avenue, north to Evanston, then back again through the West Side parks to the starting point. Ten thousand people were counted along the way, an extraordinary number for the time and weather conditions.

The electrics gave out; then even the Duryea sputtered to a stop, allowing the Macy—entered by the department store—to take a momentary lead. But Frank, aided by Charles, got the car going again and, despite going 2 miles out of their way because of a misread sign, Frank got the lead again and crossed the finish line at about 6 m.p.h. some 9 hours after the race had started, or an average of slightly better than 5 m.p.h. for the 54-mile test.

While Frank slept, recovering from the ordeal, Charles handed the press a picture of the car with himself at the wheel, which led to the long-held idea that it was Charles who had run the race. It also contributed to a growing coolness between the brothers. Frank was an activisit, however, and he had other races in mind. The 2nd American race was held in New York City on Memorial Day, 1896, from the Cosmopolitan Club in Manhattan to Irvington-on-Hudson in Westchester and back. He won it.

In Britain a movement to legalize the motor car had succeeded, and a race between London and Brighton was run in 1904 to celebrate the end of a law that required an outrider, waving a red flag, to precede a car in motion, and limited speed to 4 m.p.h. Frank won that one, too. He had won the 3rd American race in Providence, R.I., and, in 1899, left the Duryea Wagon Co. to go to Stevens-Duryea Co. of Chicopee Falls, Mass.

It was only after Charles died in 1938 that investigations of the early Duyea activities revealed it was Frank who was the real racing brother. In 1941 the Automobile Old Timers started the controversy that raged for several years by handing Frank a citation attesting to his true role. The arguments added a lot of heat but little light to the controversy, but by 1945 the truth was pretty much accepted by everyone. Capt. Eddie Rickenbacker, acting for the AAA Contest Board, handed Frank a testimonial resolution attesting to his feats. In 1959 at the age of 89 he took part in an antique automobile run in New York City and charmed everyone in sight. On February 15, 1967, Frank Duryea died in Saybrook, Conn., leaving a second wife, a son, a sister, three grandchildren and a prominent place in auto racing history.

MAURICE F. EARGLE

The greatest safety hazard that confronts the men of racing is fire. It was Johnny Allen's fiery crash in the 1952 Southern 500 Race that put Maurice (Pop) Eargle to work. (Eargle, at 342 pounds, was probably the nation's biggest do-it-yourselfer.) Just after the accident a NASCAR official commented to Eargle that some sort of a valve was needed to keep the fuel from pouring out the breather hose of an overturned stocker.

Two days later Eargle sent him a working sample of his answer to the problem—a one-inch steel ball from a pinball machine enclosed in a metal-strap cage. It enabled air to pass through while the car was right side up, but closed the mouth of the breather hose when its normal equilibrum was upset.

By 1963 all late-model stock cars on the NASCAR circuit were equipped with Eargle's valve and, in the following year, all Modified and Sportsman cars competing on tracks more than a mile long were required to be equipped with the patented device. Soon most stock-car drivers owed a debt to the cigar-chewing racing mechanic, who worked out of the Cotton Owens Garage in Spartansburg S.C.

Eargle made a specialty of creating things, from tiny safety valves to the giant auto "rotisseries" which enable a car to be rotated completely to permit mechanics to work erect. While Pop prepared Dodges for men like Dave Pearson and Jim Paschal his devices were adopted as standard equipment by other racing mechanics and many were written into the rule books as mandatory equipment.

As a football tackle in high school, Pop weighed a mere 255 pounds, but he never stopped growing, either in size, knowledge or the number of friends he acquired. He started tuning motorboat engines and building micro-midget racing cars before becoming interested in stock cars in 1959. That year he helped Jack Smith set up his Chevrolet for many thrilling wins, and the following season was part of the reason Buck Baker, driving Smith's '60 Chevy, won the Southern 500 and why Smith himself won the Daytona Firecracker 250. Pop was also a mechanic for Joe Weatherly before moving over to the Owens Garage and Dodge.

It was on his first day with Owens that he devised the now famous rotisserie. He removed the car's bumpers and mounted it on 2 pedestals, which allowed the body to turn to any angle he desired, locking it securely in place. Pop started with an abandoned railroad lift hoist, then added about $12.50 worth of pipe, channel braces, and other pieces of iron. After 4 or 5 hours of work, he had the 1st of the widely copied auto rotisseries.

Eargle's slight-of-hand extended to fashioning heavy-duty spindles, racing hubs, fuel and oil tank baffles, special steering pieces, spring hangers, and the minor miracles that convert a stock car into a 160-m.p.h. plus racing machine. The sight of those cars out on tracks like Daytona gave Pop his reward for the long hours his trade demanded.

GEORGE EATON

The question asked about George Eaton, an heir to Canada's largest department store chain, was whether he was as good as he looked or looked good only because ran in the best of equipment. In the early Seventies the betting was that George had talent as well as money.

Born in Toronto on November 12, 1945, Eaton began racing a Sunbeam Alpine at age 19, and soon moved up to a Cobra and eventually a McLaren Mk. 3. After finishing 13th in the Mosport CanAm, Eaton

once more. He placed 11th in Austria, retired again in Italy, managed a 10th in the Canadian GP, but retired for a 5th time in the United States GP. Eaton received no points in the World Championship standings, and his CanAm earnings and points fell to $10,900 and 12 respectively. He was tied for 20th in the final standings, based on a retirement at Mosport in the initial appearance of his BRM P154 Group 7 car, a 3rd at Mont Tremblant, and then an unbroken washout for the rest of the year DNFs at the Glen, Edmonton, Road Atlanta, Donnybrooke and Laguna Seca.

Louis Stanley of BRM summed up Eaton early in 1972 when George had virtually retired—at least for awhile—from racing: "Eaton was an eager amateur, but he has never been a professional." An unkind cut that perhaps would spur the Canadian to return to the cockpit and prove Stanley's opinion wrong.

BERNIE ECCLESTONE

Perhaps the least known of all the Grand Prix entrepreneurs is the owner of Brabham, or more specifically, Motor Racing Developments, which manufactures, races and sells Brabham cars. Bernie Ecclestone shouldn't be unknown, however, for even though he is in his early forties (born 1931), Ecclestone has been around motor sport for some 2 decades.

He started out as a racer himself, in 2-wheelers, not cars, but soon was driving a Cooper-Norton and then a Cooper-Bristol that once was Mike Hawthorn's. Like

gained greater fame and experience when George Eaton Racing fielded an entry in the 1968 United States Road Racing Championship. He finished 3rd in the season standings behind Mark Donohue and Chuck Parsons. That same year he ran the Canadian-American Challenge Cup series in a McLaren-Ford, finishing in 11th position with 4 points. His record included a 10th at Edmonton, 8th at Road America, a retirement at Bridgehampton, a 3rd at Monterey (his best showing), a retirement at Riverside, and 27th at Las Vegas. His total earnings that year (considered only as a gauge of success by the independently wealthy Eaton) were $10,750.

His 1969 CanAm earnings ballooned to $51,300, based on 50 points and 5th place in standings with his McLaren-Chevrolet Mk. 12. After a 9th at Mosport and a 7th at St. Jovite, Eaton placed 4th at Watkins Glen, 3rd at Edmonton, and 6th at Mid-Ohio. He retired at Road American and again at Bridgehampton, was 8th at Michigan, but retired again at both Monterey and Riverside. His best finish that year was a 2nd in the Texas finale. That October George bought his first Formula 1 ride with Yardley-BRM. At Watkins Glen, running 76 of 108 laps in the United States Grand Prix, he retired with engine failure. In the Mexican GP he lasted 7 of 202 laps before his gearbox failed.

Eaton was back in both F1 and CanAm racing in 1970, which proved to be his most frustrating year. Eaton retired in the South African race in his year-old P139. Equipped with a 1970 Yardley-BRM he failed to qualify for Spain or Monaco, and retired in Holland. In the French GP he was 12th, but in Britain he retired

Ken Tyrrell, however, Bernie decided early that his talents were better directed at operating rather than driving for a racing team. He retired as a driver in 1956 at the "advanced" age of 25.

Ecclestone's initial team efforts were moderately successful, though tinged with sadness. One of his key drivers was a close friend, Stuart Lewis-Evans, who was killed while driving someone else's car (a Vanwall) at Casablanca in 1958. Lewis-Evans was about the best Ecclestone driver in the ex-factory Connaughts Bernie was operating. Ivor Bueb was another top Ecclestone driver. But after Stuart-Evans's death, despite having already arranged to run a team of ex-factory Cooper Grand Prix cars, Ecclestone retired from car racing, although he was involved lightly with Norton motorcycles for a time.

The retirement lasted some 8 years until Bernie met another driver who became a personal friend. Jochen Rindt, who was then driving in both Formula 1 and Formula 2. When Winklemann Racing decided to withdraw from F2, Ecclestone and Rindt formed a partnership.

Bernie also became a close friend of Graham Hill, looking after the World Champion's business matters. When Jack Brabham quit and Ron Tauranac took over MRD, Ecclestone eyed the company for a time and then made an offer to take over control. Although he was resisted for a time, Bernie wore Tauranac down, and in November 1971 he became the major shareholder of the Brabham racing car business. Soon afterwards Hill rejoined the team, despite previous personal differences with Tauranac, and eventually Ron moved out. Under Ecclestone, Brabham would continue as a F1 team, but not operate factory cars in F2 or F3, preferring to support customer efforts in these lower classifications of racing.

CHRIS ECONOMAKI

The Atlantic City board track has left only a few memories of its existence, but in 1927 it made a lasting impression of speed and noise on an excited 7-year-old boy. Chris Economaki was born in Brooklyn, N.Y., October 15, 1920, and moved to Ridgewood, N.J., his present home base, in 1926. It was, however, 2 years after his Atlantic City experience that he felt old enough to investigate similar noises that drifted over his home every Sunday. He walked to the adjoining town and discovered a half-mile dirt track called Ho-Ho-Kus Driving Park. Chris first peered through the knotholes in the fence to catch glimpses of the racing cars, but in less than a season, had found a way to beat the gate—by lying on the running boards of the cars as they passed the ticket taker.

Before long, Economaki was getting tossed out of the pit area regularly as he sought to increase his technical

knowledge, but not before he became an incurable racing fan. He soon discovered that the town barber was the father of Bob Sall, the local racing hero and a future NASCAR zone supervisor. Chris was invited to the races, and in 1931, as a member of the Sall entourage he visited Langhorne, Woodbridge, Altamont and New-market—all dirt tracks in Jersey and Pennsylvania within 100 miles of his home.

The making of an internationally known TV announcer and national auto racing weekly publisher took unusual forms. Economaki got his first taste of journalism in 1933 by selling the drivers pictures of themselves in their cars for 10 cents apiece. A year later Chris added to his lucrative business by selling the *National Auto Racing News*, later to become the *National Speed Sport News*, at trackside. His first byline in that paper came on a report of the Flemington Fair races in New Jersey; earning him a press card that enabled him to see the 1936 Vanderbilt Cup races at Roosevelt Raceway.

After carrying water and cleaning windshields for the Sall crew in 1937, Chris managed to convince the high school principal that it was important for him to go to the Indianapolis 500 in 1938. The visit—made in an old Model A Ford with several friends—convinced him that after graduation he should find a career in racing. That June, he went to Gasoline Alley in Paterson, N.J., to find a job. Duane Carter hired him at $10 a week to help maintain an outboard-engined midget. Economaki would disassemble the Model T rear end after every race, then Carter would reassemble the gears. Economaki worked 60 races that year, including his lone try at driving. That came at Ashley, Pa., on a track that was a used car lot most of the week, but was converted because it had lighting. There was no railing, and they raced around the light poles. Chris terrified himself in the one race so thoroughly he has been talking ever since. He went with the midget when it was sold in 1939 to Eddie Cox of Rochester, N.Y.

The saga of Peckville, Pa., had been a dark secret until Economaki revealed it recently. In March 1939, an old board-track racer named Sam Greco decided to promote an outlaw midget race in Peckville. The drivers competing that Friday and Saturday in a race inside Atlantic City's Convention Hall—one man crashed into the organ—said they wouldn't go. Economaki, however, was told by Cox to tow the midget to Peckville late that night to ensure secrecy.

Sunday morning found the greatest drivers of the day present—Bill Schindler, Ronnie Householder, and Harry Hart among them. A legitimate promoter would have swooned at the field.

The "track" was a baseball diamond with 18-inch high flags on sticks marking the beginning of the infield. The drivers used fake names (Householder, for example was "Harry Tupler") and the racing was great.

Whenever anyone wanted to pass the leader on the inside, he would mow down a row of flags, causing infield to grow increasingly smaller. What started as a quarter-mile track ended as about an eighth. Householder won, and when the promoter said he didn't know how to split the purse, Ronnie volunteered to help him. Householder and his 300-pound sidekick locked the office door and walked out some time later with 85 percent of the purse.

The other drivers protested but returned to race the next Sunday, staging a "strike" beforehand, however, to assure purse distribution. Hart won this time, but the vexation did not sit well with Greco and, besides, the baseball team wanted its diamond back. That was the end of Peckville racing. Had the ARDC and AAA known the details then, numerous careers might have been interrupted.

A truck salesman after the war, Economaki got his first chance to announce in 1947 at Selingsrove, Pa., for $35. It was a 370-mile round trip but he took the job, even paying the sound man $2 to make a record of him. "I was awful, screaming, with everybody in 3rd place," he recalled, "but they wanted me back." In 1949 he became a full-time worker for *NSSN*, and late that same year he asked impressario Sam Nunis for a job. Nunis hired him as a regular announcer after a tryout and he eventually traveled the whole circuit from Skowhegan, Me., to Greensboro, N.C., handling the publicity as well. He became editor of *NSSN* and ultimately began announcing such classics as the Daytona Beach Road Races and the Indianapolis 500.

In 1957 Economaki was one of the American party at the Race of Two Worlds at Monza, Italy, and in 1958 he announced at Rouen for the English-speaking audience. He called races in some 15 countries and 40 states. His affiliations included the American Broadcasting Company, Triangle TV Network, and MCA. He also participated in the closed-circuit telecast from Indianapolis.

SELWYN FRANCIS EDGE

To get a new idea like the motor car off the ground, men of both vision and practicality are required. The infant British automobile industry at the turn of the century had several such men; perhaps the most famous of these was Selwyn Francis Edge.

Edge was not born in Great Britain, but came from Sydney, Australia, with his parents soon after his birth in 1868. He became a keen bicyclist, when the 2-wheeler was king, and by the time he was in his late twenties, was famous as a bicycle racer and was employed as manager of the Dunlop Tire Company.

In Paris, during the winter of 1895, Edge was given his first ride in an automobile by a friendly French bicycle competitor named Fernand Charron, winner of the first Gordon Bennett Cup. Convinced of the future of the automobile, Edge bought a succession of cycle cars and light cars until, in 1896, he was able to buy his first true car, the 2nd-place finisher in the Paris-Marseilles race that year, a Panhard. It was in this car that he took part in Britain's initial "Emancipation" run from London to Brighton in 1898—motor cars were at last being permitted on British roads. Today this event is commemorated each year by a vintage car run over much the same route.

Eventually Edge wanted to improve his Panhard, and with an engineering genius by the name of Montague Napier, an aquaintance of his bicycle competition days, the changes were made. Late in 1899, Edge, Napier and their financial angel, Harvey Du Cros, formed the Motor Power Company—later the Motor Vehicle Company—to build and offer automobiles to the British public. This company eventually became the Napier marque.

Car companies were being born at a great rate, with a failure rate almost as high. What made the difference for Napier was the talent of S. F. Edge for attracting the attention of the public. In the Thousand-Mile Trial of 1900, a sort of demonstration run from London to Bristol to Edinburgh and then back to London, the Napier won a silver medal. In 1901, Edge won the Gaillon hillclimb and the Bexhill speed trial. However, his greatest public relations accomplishment—and greatest driving feat—came the following year in the Paris-Vienna race.

The Paris-Innsbruck section of the race was designated as the Gordon Bennett course, and the binding restrictions of the big race did not apply to cars in this concurrent competition. Edge was able to switch to Continental tires (when his Dunlops proved unsuitable to the demands of the race) without penalty. Rene de Knyff and his Panhard were favored, and it was this car that led most of the race until it was sidelined some 5 miles from the finish with irreparable mechanical ills. Behind Knyff, only Edge and his Napier were left, barely finishing as parts fell from the car during the last 3 miles. But finish Edge did, the only Gordon Bennett contestant to do so.

The win, at the then-startling speed of 31.9 m.p.h., made Napier and Edge famous, and even an 8th place finish in the 1903 Gordon Bennett competition (which was moved to Ards, Ireland, in commemoration of the British victory) could not detract from his original great British racing feat. Edge drove competitively only a few more times, and, in 1907, set a world 24-hour driving record at the then new Brooklands speedway a 65.9 m.p.h. In 1913 he severed his connections with Napier, and was not directly associated with the British auto motive industry again, except for some ties to AC in the twenties.

In 1922, at the age of 44, he came out of driving retirement to perform another 24-hour feat. Complaints about noise at Brooklands prevented night running, and so the feat was performed in two 12-hour daytime stints. Driving a Dutch Spyker, Edge averaged 72.27 m.p.h. The appearance must have whetted his appetite, for at Brooklands that same year, he drove a Lanchester for 400 miles at 81.1 m.p.h. for still another record. It was, however, the last hurrah for Edge. He lost most of his fortune in the AC effort and the Depression. When he died in 1940, he was a comparatively poor man and was relatively forgotten, until his reputation took an upswing after World War II.

RAY ELDER

The Elder family in Caruthers, Calif., owned and worked a large farm where they grew cotton and alfalfa. That was by day. By night they were the most successful team in NASCAR's Western Grand National Circuit, a division that covers a territory larger than Europe west of Poland and that includes the prestigious Riverside and Ontario 500s along with Oildale, Calif., Saugus, Calif., Roseburg Ore., and Langley, British Columbia. Not to mention the quarter-mile track in North Las Vegas, Nev.

There was Fred, the father, car owner of the No. 96 Dodge. There was Richard, chief mechanic, and there was Ray. He drove. He drove well enough to win $50,635 in the 1971 season—is more than most of the graded drivers in Formula 1 ever see. Farmer Ray Elder—the family showed up in overalls and floppy hats in a rare bit of showmanship recalling the days of J.

Alex Sloan—drove well enough to best NASCAR's own best, men like Richard Petty, Bobby Allison and anyone brave enough to come into his bailiwick. But Raymond Marvin Elder, born Aug. 19, 1942, and weighing a portly 225 pounds for a man an inch under six feet, never had any interest in pursuing a part-time avocation fulltime far away from home. The racing was fun, but the kids (Kendal and Peggy) and the family farm came first.

Western Grand National racing, Elder's fiefdom, needs some explanation because it is an atavism. Started in 1954 when Bill France planned to build regional equivalents of the NASCAR circuit in the Southeast, it never really grew away from its bull ring beginning. No one was building superspeedways suited to late model stock cars so it adapted itself. Riverside's 500 miler in January was a WGN race but WGN people played spear carrier to stars like Dan Gurney, A. J. Foyt, Richard Petty and the other NASCAR aces. They filled out the field on the difficult road course so alien to the rest of their circuit and they faded out the quickest, too. Until 1971 when the Racing Farmer suddenly found his 1970 Dodge competitive with a field of vehicles no longer nurtured by factory money.

He made the most of it in a race on one of the most grueling road circuits in the world. He lasted while David Pearson and Richard Petty were wearing out their cars—only 11 of 40 finished—and then on the 85th lap for the first time in WGN history a WGN regular led Riverside. It was the beginning of a duel with Bobby Allison that was to last the rest of the way with 1st one then the other leading, the lead changes usually coming when the other pitted for fuel. Elder won by 10.5 seconds over Allison as he crossed the finish line eased up. Bobby had been forced to pit for fuel 10 laps from the end.

Elder was only 7th at the Miller 500 in Ontario about a month later—he improved that to 5th in the 1972 race —but by that time the pros had re-established their superiority of equipment. Besides, that was an oval track not a road course. Elder went back to WGN after that compiling a fantastic record of finishing in the top 3 for 22 of 26 races including 9 victories. It was his 3rd straight WGN crown.

Ray Elder began racing in claimer racing, now rare, where anyone could put in a claim to buy any car before the race. That was in 1962. In 1965 he won the California Limited Sportsman crown. A year later he won Rookie of the Year honors in WGN for winning 2 races. He finished 2nd on the season twice to Scott Cain before beginning his string of championships. In 1972 he won the most money—besting the top NASCAR stars again in Riverside's Golden State 160—but Harschel McGriff, an Oregon lumber mill owner and a living legend out of NASCAR's early days, won the most races.

No matter, Elder still was racing for fun.

VIC ELFORD

"What had happened was that Mario Andretti had lost it two corners back. He shot all over the place, crashed into the banking, and ended up squarely in front of Vic, who ran into the remaining front wheel on Andretti's Lotus and became airborne. When we found the wreck, the car was simply frightful, upside down, and nearby were two trees it had knocked clean out of the ground.

"How in hell Vic wasn't killed nobody will ever know. But he came out of it with a broken wrist, a triple arm fracture and a shattered shoulder blade. It was Andretti's first Formula 1 race and Vic's last. Mario walked away without a scratch and he's still in the Grand Prix. I doubt if Vic will ever get another chance, and that's too bad both because he wanted it so much and because he could have been one of the good ones, I think."

The speaker was Colin Crabbe, a former Guards Officer in Her Majesty's Army, and sponsor of the Antique Automobiles Ltd. Racing Team. He was talking about Victor Henry Elford's 1969 accident at the German Grand Prix at Nurburgring.

A tall wiry man with great determination, ambition and sheer guts, Vic Elford drove F1 infrequently after Nurburgring, but still managed to operate at speed. He won, among other things, both the Nurburgring 1000 sports car race (in a Porsche 908 shared with Kurt Ahrens), and the Watkins Glen Trans-American sedan race—Chevrolet Camaro's 1st victory that year—in only his 2nd TransAm start. In 1970 he took the Sebring 12-hour classic at a record speed of 112.50 m.p.h. over 1,352 gruelling miles, and the Nurburgring 1000 in a Porsche 908/3 at 106.51 m.p.h. Both these 1971 wins were shared with Gerard Larrousse.

In his mid-thirties, then, Elford was one of the more underrated drivers on the international racing scene. Vic had always been underrated, right from the start of his racing career, which came late because he had first been sidetracked into rallying. "Rallying is bad enough as a racing start," Vic said, "but I started navigating first, which is about as far away from racing as you can go.

"Why navigating? Simply because I couldn't afford a car. This was back in 1956, and it was 1959 before I could even afford to buy a motor car. That's why young fellows who tell me how hard it is to get going in racing really annoy me. If you want to race, you will find a way, just as I did. Sure, if I had had my way I would have been starting racing in a saloon car, or a Formula 3 single-seater, or something. From there I'd have progressed up the scale of motor racing and reached F1, which always was my goal, at a proper age."

Elford was 33 before he got his first GP ride in 1968; he was 32, in fact, before he actually began racing sports cars internationally. Vic was born in South London June 10, 1935, which put him in that group of British youngsters who were evacuated during the height of the German Blitz. Elford found himself in Kent, and his earliest motoring experiences occurred there. One of these early experiences, in retrospect, was traumatic for a racing driver. Vic was used to hitching rides on the running board of a tiny Morris that his mother drove to the village. One day he was struck by the gatepost and knocked under the rear wheels. But the car was light and the ground soft, and Vic came out of the experience none the worse physically.

It was 3 years before he would get into a car again. At that point, though, he not only got into a car, but he learned to drive the local farmer's 3-ton truck. School was never very interesting to Vic, except for athletics, so at 16 he left and became an apprentice to the Southern Gas Board. If all went well after 5 years he would be a part of the outfit's staff as a civil engineer. Elford bought a 125-c.c. James motorbike, ran some trials, and then earned his driving license in the family saloon. Soon Vic was a member of the Sevenoakes Motor Club (whose badge decorated his F1 cars) and navigating for a friend in rallies. Even as a navigator Elford was a pretty dedicated sort—the characteristic most mentioned by those who know him—and after 4 years he had to choose between rallying and the Gas Board. Rallying won.

He joined a firm as a design engineer, then switched to become a sales engineer with a piling firm. However, rallying on the major scale on which Elford now was running—the RAC Rally, the Tulip, the Acropolis—demanded a lot of time for preparation as well as the actual running, so it came down to a choice again, and again Vic chose rallying. In order to eat, however, he became an insurance salesman.

In 1960 Elford had rallied for Triumph, then for the parent BMC team. In 1962 he drove for DKW in Formula Junior on an arrangement that gave him a factory car, but required the driver to pay for repairing any damage. Elford later laughed about this when he considered of what went on in international racing at places like Sebring and Daytona. "I'd have to work until I was 101 to pay for some of the things that happen to cars these days," he said.

Ford of England hired Vic as a leading rally driver in 1964, and midway through the next season he gave up the insurance business to devote himself to driving full-time, quite a decision for a 30-year-old man to make based on his credits as of that date. Before he quit the insurance business, however, it had paid off in one way for Elford. One of his prospective clients was a racing driver named Alan Rees (later a power at March Engineering). Rees had a Formula 2 that he offered Vic for a Monza race, which the insurance salesman accepted with alacrity. In the race Elford led the field for the best part of 20 laps before Derek Bell spun out in front of him and eliminated both cars, an incident previewing the Andretti accident in 1969. It was that ride, however, along with Elford's sports car racing experience, that led to offers to test BRM and Cooper F1 cars, and to Vic's signing on with the Cooper GP team in 1968.

"Up to that point, the F1 Cooper was the most precise machine I had ever driven" said Vic. "And F1 certainly came up to my expectations. It gave me complete satisfaction, the absolute pinnacle of delight in driving such a beautifully prepared piece of machinery." He admitted, however, that the Porsches he had driven in earlier years also qualified as rather good machines.

"Porsche has always been good for me, as a machine, as a team, as a way of getting really involved in racing. My first drive in a Porsche was in rallying, of course, in the 1966 Tour of Corsica, in which I was 3rd. After that, it was more rallying, but also racing. In 1967 I won the Group 3 rally title with a 911S, took the Tulip and Geneva and another one I can't remember outright, was 3rd in the Monte Carlo. It was in 1967 that the Porsche racing manager, Hanstein, asked me if I had ever raced, and I allowed as how I had. There had been the FJ thing in 1962, and just before that, races in my own Mini, purchased from BMC just so I could earn a full racing license by doing the necessary 6 club events. I had some interesting times with the Mini, including especially fine races at Brands Hatch and at Oulton Park. But that was the sum total of my racing when Hanstein offered me a ride in the Targa Florio in 1967, about the closest thing to a rally in sports car racing, I guess."

Elford shared a Porsche 910 with Jochen Neerpasch, later competition manager with several teams, and they finished 3rd. Hanstein paired them again for a real race, the Nurburgring 1000, and again they were 3rd. At Le Mans Elford shared a 906 with Ben Pon, finished 7th overall, and won his class. At Mugello he and Gijs van Lennep codrove a 911R and were 3rd. Engine failure kayoed a BOAC 500 race at Brands Hatch with Lucien Bianchi and ended Elford's 1967 racing. He really arrived as a racing star in 1968, at the age of 33. He won the Monte Carlo Rally to cap his rally career, and then in a week's time, his racing season started with victory at Daytona's 24-hour enduro. At Daytona Elford and Neerpasch shared a 907 that became everybody's car near the end of the race, so that Jo Siffert, Rolf Stommelen, and Hans Herrmann also were listed as codrivers of the winning car (106.69 m.p.h.), but it was clearly Vic's race.

Sebring in 1968 was Elford's race as well, although wheel bearing problems kept Vic and Neerpasch back enough to finish 2nd. They later placed 3rd in the BOAC 500. Elford then had a rather interesting month of May. With Umberto Maglioli, a giant Italian driver who forced Porsche to run an open-roofed 907 to accommodate him, Elford won the Targa Florio May 15, 1968, at 69.04 m.p.h. Two weeks later to the day, sharing a closed 908 with Siffert, Elford posted 95.04 to take the Nurburgring 1000 for the first time.

Winning tells you one thing about a driver like Elford. The way he wins tells you many other things. That Targa victory, for example, didn't exactly fall into his lap. On the first lap, the lock nut on the Porsche's right rear wheel became loose, and the wheel slid off the driving pins. Vic braked to a smooth stop, and tightened the nut with an enormous socket wrench carried along with the spare in the car's nose. Restarted, he stopped at the first "outpost" (or pit-away-from-home) and a completely new unit was put into place. But the new unit worked loose as well, out on a fast curve, and the loss of drive caused the car to hit a rock and blow a tire. Again Elford made the necessary repairs. He rode back to the pits at a fast clip, with the tools jangling on the passenger seat alongside him.

Siffert's car had reached the pits first, so Elford had to cool his heels for a time and was left trailing the leader by 18 minutes after just one lap. On the next lap he worked his way back to 7th and handed over to Maglioli. When Elford regained the cokpit on the 8th lap, the car trailed the leader by 2.5 minutes with only 3 laps left. But 2 Elford laps did it, both run almost precisely to the same hundredth of a second, and the Tipo 33 Alfa was passed with a lap to go.

The rest of 1968 wasn't all that happy, however. Neerpasch crashed their Spa 1000 car, and wheel bearings acted up again on the Elford-Siffert car at the Watkins Glen 6-hour race. At Zeltweg, in the so-called Austrian GP that year, a rod on the fuel metering unit and the throttle on Vic's 917 broke simultaneously, and he limped home 8th. At Le Mans, Hanstein took a chance replacing a faulty alternator, hoping officials wouldn't see the rules violation, but the change was spotted and Elford and Gerhard Mitter were disqualified. The sports/prototype season ended with some profit when Vic and Rudi Lins came in 2nd at the Paris 1000 at Montlhéry.

In Cooper F1 cars, during what turned out to be the British marque's last GP season, Elford made that impressive French GP debut in the rain, finishing 4th to Jacky Ickx, John Surtees, and Jackie Stewart. Vic was then retired by mechanical malfunctions or accidents in the British, German, and Italian Grands Prix. In Canada he was 5th, but retired in the U.S. race and was a no-points 8th in Mexico.

That rainy debut in F1 brought home the fact that Vic liked driving in the rain, not a commonplace feeling among drivers, GP or otherwise. "Yes, I like the rain very much. Maybe the reason is that other people don't like it, and that gives me an advantage. In rallying I was brought up in the rain, of course, and if rallying meant anything to my racing career, I guess that was it. I probably spent half my life rallying under bad conditions, so I had to come to terms with them early, and they haven't worried me at all. Generally speaking, motor racing is a summer sport, and most drivers don't have a lot of opportunity to practice in bad weather. Perhaps the most truthful answer is that I dislike the rain less than other drivers do."

Elford also felt that he owed a lot to an unidentified friend, in terms of his rain experience. "Many years ago I was motoring up to Sevenoaks in the rain when a tire blew, and I crashed. It was a pretty bad smashup, and bones in my back were broken and so forth. Anyway, I had to wear a steel belt, and I wasn't that comfortable about driving, especially when it started to rain again first time out of the box. My friend said he felt safer with me driving, steel belt and all, and off we went in the pouring rain all the way. Did me a lot of good. It was just the kind of treatment I needed at that time. No mollycoddling. After that I got to like the rain, or at least not to fear it."

In 1969 Elford didn't win any races. In Porsches he ran well, but not with luck. A broken camshaft drive ended his bid with Brian Redman at the Daytona 24-hour race, and at Sebring with Dickie Attwood he was 7th. With Attwood again, Elford finished 2nd at the BOAC 500, but they crashed at Monza. Teamed with Maglioli for a replay of the Targa Florio, Elford came close to winning again, but finished 2nd. With Kurt Ahrens he was 3rd at Nurburgring, and with Attwood 3rd at Spa. Vic and Attwood got their first 917 rides of the year at Le Mans, and they were leading with 3 hours to go when the transmission failed. Elford ran the race's fastest lap, however, at 145.42 m.p.h. At the Glen 6-Hour race, he was 2nd.

In GP racing Crabbe provided the McLaren when Cooper closed up shop on Elford. Vic ran one last race, Monaco's GP, in a Cooper-Maserati T86B, finishing 7th. In the McLaren M7B, he used the Dutch GP as a prolonged test session and finished 10th. Vic was 5th in the French GP, 6th in Britain, and then came the German crash. "I was about to go past Andretti's Lotus," he later recalled, "when it slewed across the road in front of me. It was probably only 10 feet or so away, and we were both doing 80 to 90 m.p.h., or something like 120 feet a second. There was probably only a 10th or 12th of a second between the moment I realized there was going to be an accident and that first bang when I hit Andretti's car.

"My car leaped into the air. It happens very quickly, you know. Suddenly you're in the air, and the next thing is that you're upside down, and you've got twigs and little pieces of dirt and leaves and all kinds of things trying to force their way up your nostrils and into your eyes as your head is scraped along the ground. Then it stops, and there is dead silence, comparatively speaking. I wasn't knocked out, I remember, and there was a definite pause. Then I thought, 'Well, I'm still alive.' Then I really started to think, 'O.K., I'm still alive, and I'm still awake. So how do I get out of this?' I'm afraid that one becomes completely practical in this situation.

"My mind first went to my right hand. Three or four switches are on the right side, and I wanted to switch them off. But then I found my right hand wasn't working, so I used my left hand. Cool, calm and practical. Having switched everything off I could, I was waiting patiently for the marshals or someone to get me out from under. Half a minute went by, and I said to myself, 'What the hell are they doing?' Frankly, I started to feel panic at the thought that the car still might explode. It was the worst moment of my life, because I was completely trapped. I couldn't move anything except my left hand. If the car had caught fire, I would have been burnt to a cinder underneath it. Nobody could have gotten me out, and the fire extinguishers could not deal with 40 gallons of fuel cascading everywhere."

Andretti, shaken but in command, arrived on the scene and took charge, just as Graham Hill had in a famous Jackie Stewart accident. The car was righted, Elford unstrapped and sent on his way to the hospital. Everyone said that he was through for the year, but he managed to appear for a few late sports car races, and although he didn't win, he showed the old drive and speed.

The 1970 season saw sports/prototype racing, but no GP ride. It saw another Nurburgring 1000 victory with Ahrens, another in the non-title Nurburgring 500, and a 2nd with Denis Hulme in the BOAC 1000. Vic placed 3rd at Spa with Ahrens, 4th with Attwood in the Austrian 1000 and with Hulme at the Glen 6-Hour. In August Elford, driving in only his 2nd TransAm in a

Jim Hall-entered Camaro, outduelled the U.S. champion, Mark Donohue, at Watkins Glen. Vic took the flag 10 seconds ahead of the Penske Sunoco Javelin. That September also saw Elford behind the wheel of Hall's controversial Chaparral 2J "sucker," or ground-effect, car. By the end of the season Vic had qualified for Riverside a full 2.2 seconds faster than Hulme in the CanAm title-winning M8D McLaren. "It was like being glued to the road," Elford recalls. "In traffic, it was especially good at holding the road, even when you had to go off line to go around slower cars." He believed the 2J was legal, but would not elaborate much beyond that. "I'm paid to drive them, not to dissect their technical attributes," Elford said simply.

"I enjoyed the CanAm racing, and that's why I came back in 1971 with what I thought was a competitive ride." Elford's 1971 rides illustrated the man's sheer versatility. A McLaren M8E for the Canadian-American Challenge Cup series, an 8-litre brute; a USAC open-cockpit Indy-type car (unfortunately not ready in time for running the 500, always an Elford dream) for Marlboro Championship Trail events; an American Motors Javelin for the TransAm; and, of course, the inevitable Porsche ride.

In 1971 Elford joined the Martini & Rossi Racing Team, successors to Porsche Konstruktionen KG of Salzburg, or Austrian Porsche, which ran as an alternate factory team to the Gulf-Porsches of JW Engineering in 1970. In U.S. racing, such as at Daytona and Sebring, the Martini team also raced with Porsche-Audi sponsorship.

Of the Group 5 World Championship races, Elford's best had to be Sebring, where he and Larrousse won at 112.50 m.p.h., a course record. Elford took the lead just past the halfway point of the 12-hour race, and let nothing get ahead of him after that, though momentarily slowed by a brush with a slower Lola. The winning margin of the silver Porsche 917 over the 2nd-place Alfa 33/3 was 3 laps, and Elford had added 12 laps to the 1970 race total of 248 before the 12 hours were up.

Vic's other 1971 Martini sports car rides, besides the Sebring and Nurburgring 1000 victories, included the longest string of retirements in his career: in the BOAC 1000 with Brian Redman, in the Monza 1000, in the Targa Florio and the Le Mans 24-hour race with Larrousse—all in Porsches—and in the Watkins Glen 6-hour race with Nanni Galli in an Alfa-Romeo T33/3, when he showed his style to the Italian firm in hopes of driving for it in 1972 (Porsche quit the Manufacturers Championship series when it was lowered to 3 litres).

Elford got another F1 chance that same year when BRM offered him a car for the German GP, with the understanding, at least as he understood it, of continuing for the rest of the season. A recurring ignition problem that had plagued BRM all season centered itself on Vic's car in Nurburgring practice. But he managed a start anyway on race day and lasted a couple of laps

before the car's power all but died. On the 11th lap it did a complete swoon, and Elford parked in disgust. Two BRM mechanics showed up with a coil—Siffert's car had problems similar to his and a new coil has solved it—which Elford himself had to change or be disqualified for outside help. It worked and he was back in race momentarily but retired later. No car for Austria, no car for Italy, no car, period.

"As long ago as the middle of 1970," Elford wrote a British motoring publication in a public attack on British F1 teams after this series of disappointments, "I was tentatively approached by March and later by Brabham regarding the following GP season. After fairly long discussions with both . . . the end situation became simply 'find a sponsor and you have a car.' I approached, amongst others, . . . Shell to be told that Shell, as a company, would be very interested if I only were Italian, French or Austrian . . . what a pity I was English! In other words, the Championship of the World for drivers is fought out amongst a number of drivers best able to provide sponsorship for the cars they drive. . . ."

Vic charged that the BRM ride was his only because he had won 4 of the last 5 races he had run at the Ring (and he went on right after his letter was written to win at Nurburgring in a Lola T212). The fact he had not won the German GP had ended his chances, apparently. He was bitter—perhaps all those Porsche retirements also had caused his private sense of frustration to become so publicly evident—but he was realistic, too. He expected the outspoken statement to end his GP chances forever, but, perhaps, it might help the other bypassed British drivers like David Hobbs and Brian Redman. In 1972, GP racing appeared to be over for Vic Elford.

QUINN EPPERLY

You would ask this transplanted Virginian about the 2 lost years in his life when he built a radical streamliner for the Indianapolis 500 only to have the project abandoned when it was near completion. Its about the only way you could upset Epperly—and sometimes even that did not work. That car never ran though it was supposed to be ready for the 1956 classic. But it was good practice, for despite being in the shadowy background of single-seater USAC racing for a long time, Quinn returned to build and rebuild many winning cars.

After World War II, Quinn Epperly, an unemployed aircraft sheet metal worker and welder, answered a blind help wanted advertisement and found himself working for Frank Kurtis, the racing car builder. Epperly helped build at least 300 of the 782 Kurtis midgets produced during the height of the postwar boom, and helped construct the original Novi front drive. It was an education with the best teacher in America, and the mark of

Kurtis—strength, simplicity and painstaking detail—influenced all Epperly creations.

Epperly worked for Kurtis, from 1946 to 1950, and then took traveling jobs, first maintaining the M. A. Walker car, then the Murrell Belanger racer. Dissatisfied with the work, Quinn jumped at the chance to return to California at the end of the 1950 season to build a new Belanger machine in partnership with Lujie Lesovsky. During the 2½-year partnership one dirt track car (for Lindsey Hopkins) and 2 championship cars were built from raw materials.

Quinn opened his own shop in Lawndale, Calif., after the 1953 Indianapolis. Most of his early work consisted of repair orders on wrecked racers until the Belond people asked him to streamline their Indianapolis entry in 1955. In 1956 he built a new roadster for Lindsey Hopkins and altered the body work, fuel and oil tanks of the George Salih-designed Belond vehicle. Sam Hanks won in the Belond car, and Jim Rathmann came in 2nd in Hopkins's Chiropractic Special. Using Salih's laydown engine principle, Epperly built two cars for the 1958 race. George Amick took 2nd in one, the Demler Special, and Tony Bettenhausen finished 4th in the Jones and Maley entry.

Two more laydown engined cars were ready for 1959. Amick crashed in one at Daytona, after setting a track lap record of 176.887 m.p.h. Johnny Boyd drove the rebuilt car to 6th at Indianapolis. The other car finished 4th with Tony Bettenhausen at the wheel. Epperly collaborated with George Salih in the Metal Cal car for 1960, using a shorter wheelbase for less weight and more control. The other car made no attempt to qualify until 1961, when Lloyd Ruby placed 8th with it. Epperly's Hoover Express car qualified in the middle of the front row that same year, but lasted only 2 laps before burning a piston. The same car finished 5th in 1962 with Bobby Marshman driving.

Epperly was among the traditionalists studying the problem of the rear-engined Indy car when Jim Clark's Lotus appeared. Reportedly inclined to seek a way to keep the laydown roadster competitive, he immediately engaged in a project to build a pusher Offy for Indy 1965. But the car never was finished to Quinn's satisfaction and the repair business was too good to try anew.

JACKIE EPSTEIN

Rolypoly Jackie Epstein, son of British sculptor Jacob Epstein, had been a racing driver, but was better known for his sponsorship and management of young British drivers. Among the drivers with whom he was associated are Paul Hawkins and Mike Hailwood.

Jackie, a founding member of the Surrey Sporting Motor Club, took part in his 1st race in 1953 at the age of 18, running part of a 6-hour relay race. After competing in several races in his MG Special, Epstein arranged with an Alta owner to prepare his car in return for alternate starts in it. His initial start in the Alta in April 1954 ended in a creditable 4th in a Goodwood handicap, which was followed by an offer from Alta builder Geoff Taylor to maintain the car at the factory itself.

Epstein was studying aircraft engine maintenance at the Chelsea College of Aeronautical Engineering when the National Service drafted him into the RAF. While in the service he was taught to maintain and repair Rolls Royce gas turbines. He managed to keep racing when he could, with as motley an assortment of mounts as could be imagined—a Frazer-Nash Le Mans Replica, Vernon-Crossley, an SS100, and a TR-2, "the first modern car I'd ever driven," according to Epstein. He was separated from the RAF in 1957, and spent the next 5 years working in a garage near Hyde Park Gate in central London.

In 1959, John Dashwood announced that he had a Frazer-Nash entered for Le Mans with Epstein and Bill Wilks down as codrivers. The sorting out of the car continued almost up until race time, then Wilks drove for in first 3 hours of the race. Dashwood hopped in, managing to lose one of his contact lenses in the process. He had foreseen this and had an extra pair taped to the dash, but when he popped the substitute in he discovered that he had 2 in the same eye and none in the other. The Frazer-Nash quickly ended up in the dirt. Once restarted and back on the course, Dashwood managed to do the same thing again, sticking the car fast in the sand. After 3 hours of digging, Dashwood gave up the ghost, and Epstein never did get into the contest. He did drive in the 6-hour relay as a consolation, but the Frazer-Nash was handicapped out of real contention.

Epstein's racing career ground to an abrupt halt after that, due partly to his serious involvement in his own garage early in 1960, and partly to his marriage. It was 1962 before he had the itch to go racing again. It started innocently enough when Jackie bought a used Copper-ERA, which was actually an old Formula 1 Cooper powered by a 2.5-litre Connaught-Alta engine. He raced in several Formula Libre races and found some success in hillclimbs. Shortly thereafter, he fitted a Buick engine to a lightweight Formula 2 chassis and ran the car for a friend. He took the Cooper Monaco chassis that came with the Buick powerplant, dropped in a 2-litre Climax engine, and prepared it for the 1963 Targa Florio. Epstein and Wilks codrove this car to a 3rd in class and 23rd overall.

In 1964 Epstein sold his interest in the garage and went racing full-time. In partnership with Mike Eyre he bought a F1 BRM, and managed to finish 6th at Snetterton, 9th at Syracuse, and 10th in the Mediteranean Grand Prix. While practicing for the 1964 Targa in a specially modified Brabham-Climax BT8, Jackie crashed and was burned badly enough to require a month of hospital care. He was still wrapped in bandages when he was lifted into a Formula Junior Cooper to run the Leinster Trophy chase. It was 9 months after the crash before Epstein was finally rid of the bandages and associated discomfort.

Epstein bought a Brabham BT14 for 1965, with alternate power plants for either F2 or F1. With the F2 engine he placed 8th in the Eifelrennen and 9th in the Pergusa Grand Prix. He sold the car after a long talk with Paul Hawkins and bought a Ferrari 250LM to codrive with him in the Springbok Series in Africa. They finished 3rd in the Kyalami 9-hour race, and Epstein alone took 2nd in the Pietermaritzburg. He did well in other races in the series. A short stop back in Britain and the car and drivers were headed for Daytona for the 24-hour race. Jackie and Paul were leading their class when, after 17½ hours, the crown wheel broke. They were leading their class in the Targa as well when tire problems dropped them back to 23rd in the final tally. At Spa the pair placed 7th, and then 5th in Australia.

Epstein acquired a brand new Lola T70 Mk. 2, and Hawkins raced it to a 5th at Brands Hatch the first time out. It was decided that Paul should race the car in the Canadian-American Challenge Cup series, and the pair headed for America. Hawkins was 5th at Mosport, 15th at Bridgehampton, 13th at Monterey, 7th at Riverside, and 8th at Las Vegas. In a pickup race at Pacific Raceways, Hawkins was 3rd. The CanAm engine was dropped into a new T70 coupe in 1970, and Hawkins finished a sensational 4th at Spa. At Rheims for the 12-hour battle, Hawkins set the fastest lap, but the gearbox broke while Epstein was driving. At Surfers Paradise in Australia, despite cracked heads and brake problems, the pair was 2nd in a 12-hour race, and Hawkins won 3 short sprints at Warwick Farm.

A T70 with a 5-litre Chevy engine was purchased for 1968. A fuel tank split in the BOAC 500, David Hobbs crashed at Silverstone, and at Le Mans the crown wheel and pinion broke in mid-race. When the Springbok series was equally disappointing, Epstein decided to quit as a driver and concentrate on getting a properly mated car and driver. Hawkins started an ambitious program in 1969 and Epstein was made manager for Hailwood and him in both sports car racing and the new Formula 5000. After Hawkins's death at Oulton, Epstein carried on at the request of Lola's Eric Broadley and Paul's partner, Nick Cuthbert. In 1971 he joined Trojan, manufacturer of McLaren customer cars, as its racing manager. The next season he left to run some private Surtees F5000 cars.

JOE PAUL EPTON

While his 5 brothers marched off to World War II, Joe Paul Epton worked as a construction foreman, helping to build America's first atomic installation at Oak Ridge, Tenn. Association with such a highly scientific program seems to have rubbed off, for in later years he became chief scorer for NASCAR. Born February 6, 1920, in Cherokee Springs, S.C., Joe Paul was 7th of the 8 children of building contractor Henry Epton. He began scoring races long before NASCAR was in existence, which was how he met Bill France, who employed him to work many of his promotions. Epton, whose carefully waved tresses could grace any hair tonic commercial, used to score these races himself, or with a single assistant. That's how he performed at the 1st Grand National on June 19, 1949. Later he built a crew of some 20 to 30 helpers at smaller tracks with as many as 120 double-checking the electronic equipment at the Daytona 500.

Epton was at his best when a NASCAR driver demanded a recheck. He had all the salesmanship learned as a drummer, all the quiet strength learned directing construction men, all the patience and tact learned in raising two families, on instant command. Always dressed immaculately, Epton would listen politely to the grime-stained contestant and his equally greasy crew. In a soft voice, he quickly admitted that he and his army of scorers could be wrong, his tone implying that the possibility of a scorer's error was as likely as Tazio Nuvolari returning from the grave to win the NASCAR championship. When Epton displayed the full panoply of his trade—the long sheets of paper, the little numbers running off into eternity, the punched tapes, the watches—only the most courageous protester could retain his hopes. Veterans of such encounters, like Ned Jarrett, insisted upon washing off race grime and combing their hair before coming to grips with Epton. Some even changed to clean driving suits.

Few can remember when Joe Paul had to reverse himself on a race at a half-mile track. On the superspeedways—Daytona, Charlotte, Atlanta, Darlington—the few reversals seemed never to involve 1st place. Even in the famous Petty-Beauchamp race at Daytona in 1959, Epton flashed the results provisionally—the only thing that counts for the money is the official standing.

Epton lived in Daytona Beach with his second wife, supervising the largest race scoring operation in the world—a man with a certain knack for mathematics and the interpersonal abilities of a UN Secretary-General. For a chief scorer that is almost a necessary combination.

PHILIPPE ETANCELIN

Philippe Etancelin was 33 when he began racing, and then raced—with an 8-year layoff during World War II—until he reached the age of 60. He won the French Grand Prix and Le Mans, as well as many other races,

ished with less than a litre of fuel, making victory all the more sweet.

He again won the Dauphine Circuit (72.72 m.p.h.) in 1931, this time in an Alfa Romeo. The Alfa was to be his mount for the next several seasons. He won again at Comminges (87.07 m.p.h.), and took the Dieppe GP (74.49 m.p.h.). Etancelin was 2nd in the Casablanca GP, the 1st of 3 unsuccessful attempts to repeat there, finishing 2nd each year in a different marque—Bugatti, Alfa, and Maserati. In 1932 he won the Picardy GP (77.76 m.p.h.), and was 3rd in the Tunis GP. The following season Etancelin won the Marne GP (90.07 m.p.h.) and the Picardy GP (85.06 m.p.h.), was 2nd to Campari in the French GP and to Nuvolari in the Nimes GP, and placed 3rd in the Pau GP.

Victory came again in the 1934 Dieppe GP (75.16 m.p.h.) with Etancelin in a Maser. At Le Mans he shared an Alfa with Luigi Chinetti (later to become more famous in America as Ferrari's right-hand man), and won after driving 1,793.94 miles at an average speed of 74.74 m.p.h. During that season Etancelin's Bugatti placed 2nd to Nuvolari's Bug in the Nice GP and to a Count Trossi Alfa in the Montreaux GP, ran 3rd in both the Vichy GP, and the Swiss GP.

Both 2nds and 3rds filled Etancelin's later years, with an occasional victory, such as the 1936 Pau GP (a mere 51 m.p.h.). The Maserati gave way occasionally to Talbots and Darracqs. The major victories seemed to elude him. At Monaco, for example, he was retired 4 straight years (1931–34), running 2nd near the end of the last one when a crash eliminated his Maser. In 1935 he finished 4th at Monaco. The other big races saw similar hard luck, although he did manage 4th in the 1939 French GP before World War II interrupted his racing activity.

Etancelin was 55 years old when he resumed his career in an old Talbot in 1948. For the most part, the big title races still eluded him, but when the car held up he did well. In 1949 he was 2nd to Alberto Ascari's Ferrari in the European GP at Monza, 2nd to Peter Whitehead's Ferrari in the Masaryk non-title race in Czechoslovakia, and won the Montlhéry-Paris GP at 93.12 m.p.h. That same year he placed 2nd to a new driver named Juan Manuel Fangio at the Marseilles GP, and 2nd to Ascari in the Italian GP.

Etancelin's carreer then began to fade. He placed 2nd in the Dutch GP of 1951, 3rd in the Acerbo Cup that same year, 3rd to the powerful Ferraris of Nino Farina and Mike Hawthorn in the 1953 Rouen GP, and shared a 3rd in the same season's 12-hour race at Casablanca with Pierre Levegh. Etancelin announced his retirement in 1953 after a 5th in the Ulster Trophy at Dunrod, but was lured out of retirement for the Rouen GP, which practically passed his own doorstep. Rouen was the last race of his career.

But you could still find him at many of the old, familiar haunts—Le Mans, Monaco, the French GP—re-

and placed well in many more, yet never once was he a factory driver. He raced as an independent against people like Nuvolari, Varzi, Dreyfus, Chiron, and Campari. Phi-Phi was the name that the racing fans of France gave the gritty, cap-wearing racer.

Etancelin was born in Rouen in 1893, not 1898 as is popularly believed. He was firmly established in the wool business before turning to automobile racing, which enabled him to bear the cost of an independent racing career. After some preliminaries, he made his first splash in the Coppa Florio of 1926, finishing 3rd. Still picking his spots, Philippe was a victor in the Marne GP at Rheims the following year, averaging 71.32 m.p.h. in a Bugatti, his choice for most of his early racing accomplishments. By 1929 he was winning with some frequency, taking the Comminges GP (81.31 m.p.h.), the La Baule GP (80.00 m.p.h.) and the Marne GP for the 2nd time (85.59 m.p.h.). That year he started running in such major events as the first Monaco GP, in which he finished 6th.

With his wool business in good hands, success encouraged Etancelin to race more often. In 1930 he won the Dauphine Circuit (73.88 m.p.h.), took the 3-hour Algerian GP, was 3rd in the Lyon GP, and was running well at Monaco when he retired with a broken fuel line after 60 laps. Etancelin's greatest success came that same year: victory in the French GP—to a man from Rouen, the greatest GP of them all. Etancelin won his 90.38 m.p.h. victory with Tim Birkin's Bentley breathing down his neck, waiting for a mistake that never came. Unable to afford the planned last pit stop, he fin-

splendent in a blue blazer with the Anciens Pilotes emblem on the pocket. Who had a better right to be a charter member of that noble organization?

GEORGE EYSTON

Captain George Edward Thomas Eyston was a tall, thin, bespectacled man, born June 20, 1897, in Oxfordshire; a racing driver of some note, and holder of the Land Speed Record on 3 occasions. Eyston, a mechanical engineer, was the 1st man since Henry Ford designed and built his 999 in 1903 (which unofficially held the LSR), to actually design the vehicle in which he captured that record.

Although born in the 19th century, Eyston was strictly a 20th century man. A Trinity college rower, Cambridge graduate, and a decorated British officer (Military Cross) in World War I, Eyston had a practical background in mechanics, serving as an apprentice during his youth to one of Britain's largest manufacturers of marine propellers and racing motorcycle under an assumed name. He had a sense of the poetic as well, and would recall accompanying his father on coaching rides around the 400-year-old ancestral seat of the Eystons at East Hendred, Berkshire. He was occasionally given the whip hand to spell his dad. Many of their wild rides ended up at the Red Lion Inn in a place called Abingdon, which was to be in later years the site of the MG factory with which Eyston was so closely associated. An early riser, he was often up at 3 a.m. to go off some-

where and watch the sun rise and listen to the birds calling.

Eyston's association with cars started at Le Mans in 1921 as a spectator fascinated with the spectacle, and enhanted by Ralph DePalma racing in the International Voiturette Cup that preceded the famous 24-hour race. Two years later Eyston was driving a Sunbeam himself at Brooklands, and was on his way. While record-breaking turned out to be his real automotive speciality, Eyston drove competitively on a fairly regular basis in these early years. He was winner of the 1926 Boulogne Light Car and Voiturette Grand Prix at 64.14 m.p.h. and of the 1927 La Baule GP at 74.48 m.p.h., both victories coming in Bugattis.

Notable as well were some of Eyston's less successful efforts—blackflagged at the 1927 French GP in an Aston Martin-based Halford Special, and retired at Le Mans in 1928–29 in an Aston and in a 5.3-litre Stutz, Eyston shared a 2nd with Boris Ivanowski, in the Belgian Touring Car GP of 24 hours in 1929 and a 3rd in a 2.3 Alfa Romeo in the 1933 French GP. He shared a 4th in the 1931 French GP with Tim Birkin. There was a class victory in an MG in the 1933 Mille Miglia.

Back home at Brooklands Eyston appeared to be jinxed, once placing 3rd only a fifth of a second behind the winner. In 1932 he dead-heated John Cobb in a stunning, 100-mile, wheel-to-wheel battle around the banked Outer Circle, and then had to wait several days before the sanctioning and governing bodies declared Cobb the victor.

But it was record-breaking that firmly fixed Eyston in the shrines of speed. His history between 1927 and 1954, when he was nearly 60 years of age, was greater than any other Briton in terms of the number of records set, broken, or recaptured. John Cobb, Malcolm Cambell, and Henry Segrave captured greater portions of the public fancy, but Eyston won the respect of the professionals and longer lines in the record books. His vehicles ranged from 750-c.c. MG Midgets to the 73-litre Thunderbolt LSR car. George had a few minor records under his belt when he first became associated with MG in 1929. The 750-c.c. (Class H) record fascinated him, and he had a goal of buying, adapting or building a machine that could go faster than anything in this class ever had.

After several false starts, Eyston connected with an old schoolmate, Jimmy Palmes, who was sleeving down an 850-c.c. MG Midget to 750. Eyston joined the project with an enthusiasm that was transmitted to MG's top man, Cecil Kimber, who opened the factory's technical and monetary resources to the hopeful record-smashers. Palmes's old car became the EX120, equipped with an Eyston-designed Powerplus blower. It became the first car of its displacement to exceed 100 m.p.h. (One-hour record, 1931). Then came EX127, also known as the Magic Midget. It was a built-from-scratch, streamlined, big-wheeled car in which he topped

2 miles a minute at Montlhéry in 1932. It was in this car, too, that Bert Denly made Montlhéry history by being the 1st man to win a 200-kilometers per hour badge in an under-2-litre car.

Denly was an integral part of the Eyston story. As short as Eyston was tall (Bert was a mere 5 feet), he was a motorcycle rider who had never raced a car at speed until Eyston needed a temporary driver after being called away from a Brooklands tire test. Bert did well enough that day for Eyston to give him other assignments when an alternate was needed. In 1931 Eyston (Bert liked to call him the Skipper) hired Denly permanently, and the pair were almost continually together thereafter. There was a wartime hiatus, but when Eyston became a director of Castrol Oil in 1946, he hired Denly for the oil company's engine-testing department as one of his first duties.

Today when cars are built for individual drivers, it is amusing to think of trying to find a happy medium for a pair like Eyston and Denly. In the thirties they had solved the problem by having a special uplift seat that Bert substituted for the Skipper's when taking over the wheel. The seat is gone, unfortunately, like most of Eyston's best known mounts; it is one of the ironies that, while most LSR cars are preserved—even Parry Thomas's Babs, originally buried in the sands, was eventually dug out and restored—Eyston's cars suffered a variety of mishaps that eliminated them from view. A German bomber got the Speed of the Wind during World War II. Thunderbolt perished in a Wellington, New Zealand, fire while on an exhibition tour. So while the cars of Campbell and Cobb turn up regularly at veteran car exhibitions, or sit resplendently in museums, Eyston gets no such publicity.

Eyston was, however, a genuine LSR holder—3 times in 2 years (1937–38)—in head-to-head duels with John Cobb. Sir Malcolm Campbell had made 301.13 m.p.h. in 1935, and this was the record that Eyston set out to break in the superheavy, eight-wheeled Thunderbolt, powered by 2 Rolls Royce airplane engines. Eyston and his team, including Denly, were at the Bonneville Salt Flats in Utah late in 1937, waiting out the drying of the course, which had been saturated by an unexpected rain. His initial attempt came on October 25, and on the first of 2 required runs Eyston achieved 309.6 m.p.h., but the Thunderbolt's clutch disintegrated in the process, preventing a return run and negating the first. After repairs, the clutch was to thwart the 2nd Eyston try on November 6, this time negating an opening run of 310.685 m.p.h. Eyston took the offending part back to Los Angeles where he not only redesigned it but supervised its recasting personally.

Eyston was back at Bonneville the 2nd week of November. On November 19 he was ready again, and clocked off a 305.59 m.p.h. opening run, enlivened by having his aircraft goggles nearly blown off (Thunderbolt still had an open cockpit that season). The return run was 319.11 m.p.h., giving George a new LSR of 312.00 m.p.h.

Cobb was watching the following year at Bonneville as Eyston set out to raise his own record. Thunderbolt now was even more streamlined, with its cockpit fully enclosed, and he ripped off a 347.16 m.p.h. opening run on August 24, 1938, but the gleam of the sun off the polished aluminum body failed to trigger the electric eyes on the return run (unofficially clocked at 354 m.p.h.), negating the attempt. He solved the problem with the directness so characteristic of Eyston; Thunderbolt was painted black. On August 27, with runs of 347.49 m.p.h. and 343.51 m.p.h., he raised his mark to 345.50 m.p.h., but Cobb roared back a week later to make the LSR 350.20 m.p.h.

Eyston's car weighed more than twice as much as Cobb's, with only 2½ times the potential power. He exerted every effort the following day, September 16, 1938, stripping away the car's radiator and fin to save weight, and recaptured the record with runs of 356.4 m.p.h. and 358.6 m.p.h. for a combined clocking of 357.50 m.p.h. Cobb would retake the LSR 11 months later, raise it again in 1947, and hold it until the assaults of the sixties. To compete, Eyston would have needed a new car, for Thunderbolt was very much at its performance edge at these speeds. Immediately following his 1938 record run, he had continued testing the car at Bonneville and had hit almost 400 m.p.h. in one run when a rear suspension wishbone broke. Eyston was almost 50 at this point, and he began to think that the LSR chase was a young man's game, although he found speeding for records in the lower classes was still intriguing.

After World War II service, including duty helping plan the Normandy invasion, Eyston slowed down. In the years 1953 and 1954 he did his last record-breaking as part of a British Motors Corporation team at Bonneville. In 1953 he was driving with Donald Healey and others when the group set 10 Class D records in an Austin-Healey 100. On August 17, 1954 he and Ken Miles took an MG streamliner—EX179 officially—to 7 records in Class F. Eyston was back at the Salts in 1959, but only to boss an effort that saw drivers like Tommy Wisdom capture 14 international records under his direction. After this he retired from racing, to live quietly in Winchester, with an Order of the British Empire, awarded in 1948, and a French *Legion d'Honneur* among other mementoes.

LUIGI FAGIOLI

There were so many great drivers in Grand Prix racing from the thirties to the fifties that many men of that period who would stand out in the modern driving scene have been forgotten. One such man was a short, swarthy Italian of independent attitude named Luigi Fagioli.

Born in Abruzzi in 1898, Fagioli began driving in 1926 and was a top pilot of some of the world's most potent machinery until 1952. Luigi's first mount was far from potent—an 1100 c.c. Salmson—and that first year the best the late-starting driver (he was 28) could record was a 3rd in the Circuit of Florence. But he persevered for years, gaining the experience he would need for GP racing. Though he often finished 2nd (1927 Voiturette Tourist Trophy, 1928 Circuit of Senigallia, 1929 Tripoli Voiturette Race, and Bologna Circuit of the Three Provinces, for example), in 1930 Luigi began winning races in a Maserati, and for the next 3 years he starred in the Orsi Brothers's creations. His first victory was the 1930 Coppa Principe di Piemonte, quickly followed that year by the Coppa Ciano and Coppa Castelli Romani. The following year Fagioli won the Monza GP, the Prix of Rome on the Littorio circuit, and came in 2nd at Monaco and Tunis.

The new P.3 Alfa Romeo was asserting itself then, so after the 1932 season, in which Luigi won only the Circuit of Senigallia, was 2nd in the Italian, Masaryk, Monza, and Rome Grands Prix, and 3rd at Monaco and in the Coppa Pincipe, he moved to the Alfa team, then run by Enzo Ferrari. His one season with Alfa made Fagioli Champion of Italy, with victories in the Grand Prix of Comminges, the Italian GP and Coppa Acerbo, and 2nds in the Spanish, Marseilles, and Masaryk Grands Prix. The year's work also brought an invitation to join the Mercedes Benz team for the new 1934 Formula chase. It was a temptation that Fagioli could not resist, though he knew that preference would go to his

less-talented German codrivers under Alfred Neubauer's strict orders. Heading the team was Rudi Caracciola, who had cracked up badly in 1933. The number 2 man was Manfred von Brauchitsch, experienced in sports cars but needing big-car seasoning. Fagioli, admittedly the most experienced of the trio and already an acknowledged GP driver, was the number 3 man. In Italian races, Luigi's independent nature was never restrained, but in other countries, and especially in Germany, he was supposed to follow team discipline.

Repeatedly he harried the other team members when they were in the lead, and passed them with relish when he could, enjoying grim satisfaction at the consternation these acts created in the Mercedes pits. Fagioli won the Coppa Acerbo that year, and the Spanish and Italian Grands Prix. He was 2nd in the Masaryk and German races, the latter because he chose to honor his agreement with Neubauer, at least for that race. In 1935 his disgust with the "Germans-first" arrangement boiled over at the Belgian GP, when he breathed down Caracciola's neck for the first half hour of the race, even though he might easily have passed. Then he pulled into the pits for the first scheduled pit stop, threw away his helmet and goggles, and stalked away in a rage. Brauchitsch, who had already been retired, was recalled from a siesta to take over the car, dutifully finishing 2nd to Caracciola. The points were shared with Fagioli. That year Luigi won the Avusrennen at 148 m.p.h., captured the Monaco and Penya Rhin races and the Coppa Acerbo for the 2nd time, placed in the Belgian and Swiss Grands Prix, and was 3rd in the Tripoli GP. The year 1936 saw a new mount—the short-chassis W.25—and a disastrous Mercedes season. Luigi's best finish was a 3rd at Tripoli; at Monaco he crashed. Relations between Fagioli and the Germans were more strained than ever, with the Italian now an active hater of Caracciola and Herman Lang—formerly his mechanic—who had joined the team as a full-fledged driver. Neubauer's patience was at an end, especially because he now felt that with Lang and Louis Chiron aboard he could dispense with Luigi's services. Luigi's contract was not renewed for 1937.

Fagioli immediately surprised everyone by signing with the other German team—Auto Union—to replace Achille Varzi, who had become involved with painkilling drugs and was no longer capable of handling the 520-b.h.p., rear-engined V-16 monsters. But neither was Fagioli, it turned out, because of his hatred of the Mercedes forces in general and Caracciola in particular. Matters exploded at the Tripoli GP which was then the fastest race on the circuit at 130 m.p.h. and more. Lang won the race, with Auto Unions second through 5th. The 5th-place finisher was Fagioli, who was blocked through the whole race by Caracciola until the final lap when he managed to hurl his car ahead of the German, leaving him 6th. Caracciola was back in the Mercedes pits when Luigi charged in, snatched up a wheel hammer and threw it at Rudi. Then he grabbed an open knife from the pit wall and threw himself at Caracciola. They were separated, but Fagioli's hatred grew rather than subsided. Before the year was out, he retired from racing.

A dozen years later, when Fagioli was 52 years old, he came back, joining Nino Farina and Juan Fangio on the Alfa Romeo team for GP racing, and Osca—run by his old employers, the Orsi Brothers—in distance races. For Alfa he finished 2nd in the 1950 Belgian, British, French, and Swiss Grands Prix and 3rd in the Italian GP. He was 7th in the Mille Miglia for Osca, and won the 1100-c.c. class for that marque in the same race the following year. Sharing a car with Fangio, he won the 1951 French GP. Lancia signed Luigi for 1952, and he promptly brought his car in 3rd in the Mille Miglia, taking care to finish ahead of his old nemesis, Caracciola, who was driving a Mercedes sports car. Fagioli's final ride came in the practice sessions for the Monte Carlo preliminary saloon race when his Lancia Aurelia glanced off a curve in the long, curving tunnel, bounced from curb to curb, and crashed. Three weeks later Fagioli was dead.

His style had been to drive to the limit, and then some. Yet he managed to escape crashes regularly, and blew up his cars infrequently. Fagioli recorded a fastest lap in GP racing only 3 times, and he won only one of those races (Monaco 1935, with Mercedes). Luigi won his place in racing history with equal amounts of steadiness and fire, of courage and independence. He didn't look especially like a racing driver—not by modern standards—until he sat behind the wheel of a car and took the starter's flag; then there could be no mistake.

JUAN MANUEL FANGIO

Nurburgring is probably the most demanding course over which the virtuosos of auto racing have a chance to display their skills. It is some 14 miles long, with more than 170 curves, hemmed in at most spots by trees, rocks, and ravines. To drive the Nurburgring at speed is a true test of a driver. To drive it and win— at record speeds—is something special.

In the German Grand Prix of August 4, 1957, this was done by Juan Manuel Fangio. His car was a Maserati, already obsolescent and much slower than the Ferraris of that day, especially when the latter were in the hands of such daring young men as Mike Hawthorn and Peter Collins. Fangio was from Argentina, though born of Italian parents. At 46 years of age he already had won the World Driver's Championship 4 times. Winning at the Ring this day would make it his 5th, a feat still unduplicated adecade and a half later.

That Fangio's Maserati had a weak rear suspension, and the full load of fuel—necessary for going all the way on Nurburgring—also meant a risk of snapping the

de Dion tube. Fangio decided the risk was too great, so he planned to build up a good lead in the 1st half of the race, and refuel without dropping a place to the Ferraris that would go all the way without refueling. His plan went according to schedule—up to the pit stop. Despite the mechanical superiority of the Ferraris, and the obvious skills of their British drivers, the old master whittled away at the course to build up an imposing 27.8-second lead.

But the Maserati mechanics performed in comic opera style, falling all over each other through a long-drawn refueling and tire change. In his car, Fangio sat impassively as the time was frittered away and Collins and Hawthorn swept into the lead. Finally his car moved back to the course, 28 seconds behind Collins. His hard-won lead had evaporated.

For any other driver, perhaps, the race would have been over, but the huge crowd sensed that Fangio was going to give them a fight. On the 14th lap, following his pit's orders to go all out, Collins circled the 14 miles in 9 minutes, 29.3 seconds, a record. Hawthorn moved along beside him almost at the same speed. Yet Fangio seemed to pick up ground. On the 17th lap, Fangio lowered the lap record for the first of 9 times that day, circling in 9:28.5, and he was 25 seconds behind. On the next lap, he did it in 9:25.3 and was only 20 seconds behind the speeding Collins. Lap 19 was still another record lap, and on 20, when Fangio registered 9:17.4, even the German announcer at the track was incredulous. Fangio now trailed the two Ferraris by only 150 yards. Hawthorn had taken over the lead, and if he

197

looked back in his rear-view mirror, he might have seen the grim Fangio overtake and pass Collins. But it was not the cool, calm and precise Fangio that was so familiar on the European circuit. It was an open-mouthed, arm-lashing, frenzied man who had not driven like this in 20 years, not since he was on the Argentine pampas.

In the final lap Fangio overtook Hawthorn passing the Ferrari easily on the north turn, and carved another 6 seconds off his own lap record. After 312 miles, the Maserati crossed the finish line a winner by 3.6 seconds. "A race of inspiration," a newspaperman was to say to Fangio. "Inspiration? No," he replied. "Necessity. I had to catch them." With his wife, Beba, at his side, with photographers clicking away, with thousands of well-wishers crowding him on every side, Fangio walked over to the Ferrari pits to talk with Collins and Hawthorn. He shook hands with the two men warmly and said simply: "You are both very fine and skillful and courageous drivers. It is a great honor for me to race against you."

Years later, Fangio revealed that the bolts holding his seat had broken, and he had kept himself in the car by bracing his knees against the sides of the cockpit. He also revealed a secret. "The circuit had a bridge, followed by a curve, and with the new tires after the pit stop, I found I could hold the curve using third gear instead of second, gaining seconds on each lap." Fangio also disclosed that he had said to his friends at the time, "I never want to drive like that again."

Juan Fangio was born on San Juan's Day, June 24, 1911, near Balcarce, a valley town in Argentina's table mountains. His father was an immigrant Italian plasterer and potato farmer. Juan went to work as an apprentice in a garage at about the age of 10. At 18 he nearly died of pneumonia, but was nursed back to health by his mother. Where he had been withdrawn and physically inactive before his illness, he became outgoing and a participant in everything from soccer to racing jalopies afterwards. Most of Fangio's early racing was done locally on open fields in cars that just barely deserved the name.

First he was a racing mechanic; then, at the age of 23, he drove his first race in a converted Ford taxi that disintegrated during the race. Success eluded Fangio for most of those early years, yet he still drove, still competed, still sweated away building his racers from scratch, working long hours as a mechanic to spend minutes as a driver. Just before World War II he moved up to regular stock-car racing with a Chevrolet, and in 1940 Juan won the Gran Premio Internacional del Norte, a race from Buenos Aires to Lima, Peru, and back, a distance of nearly 6,000 tortured miles. Fangio and his Chevy became famous overnight. In the next couple of years, he won practically every major endurance race in South America, until racing was interrupted by the war and Fangio took to driving a taxi.

In 1947 racing returned with a vengeance to Argentina. Juan Perón wanted to put his nation among the first-ranked in auto racing as well as in other sports activities. Fangio, now 36, was to be his instrument, despite objections that he was too old and unskilled in modern racing. Fangio had "retired" from racing at that point, following a harrowing crash in another Gran Premio that came near to killing Juan. But when he was offered a gleaming red Maserati by a group of Argentine businessmen, he came back to the sport.

Fangio continued to drive Chevvies for a year while he prepared himself and his car to race against the world's best in Europe in 1949. What the European drivers saw did not frighten them, surely, and in fact what they saw probably amused them. Juan was short, stocky, almost bandy-legged. As one writer put it, "Out of his driving suit, he looks like the man who sells peanuts alongside the track." On the track he was something else again. By the end of the year, Fangio had won the Albi, Monza Autodromo, Pau, and San Remo races, as well as the GP du Roussillon in his Maser; he also took the Marseilles GP in a Simsa. With 6 victories in 10 starts, he had earned his place as a national sports hero in Argentina.

What Juan also earned was an invitation to join the Alfa Romeo GP team for the 1950 season. Although driving year-round, and winning the Argentine 500 back home, he accepted. He proceeded to finish 2nd in the World Driver's Championship standings, with victories in the Belgian, French, and Monegasque Grands Prix. Fangio also won non-title races at Geneva (Grand Prix des Nations), Parana, Pau, Pescara and San Remo. He was 2nd at Bari and in the Silverstone International Trophy Race, and 3rd in the Mille Miglia.

Alfa was able to withdraw from GP racing on a victory note after the 1951 season when Fangio captured the 1st of his world titles with victories in the French, Spanish, and Swiss races and 2nds in the British and German championship races. He also won at Bari. The following year was a lost one for the 41-year-old wonder, after a crash at Monza in a Maserati team car broke vertebrae in his neck, fractured his skull, and incapacitated him for the whole year. But he was back in 1953 when, despite the Maserati's technical subservience to the Ferrari, Fangio again ranked 2nd among the world's drivers.

He won at Modena and at the Italian GP; was 2nd in the British, French, and German championship races, at Pau and Naples, and in the Woodcote Cup; and was 3rd at Bordeaux. Juan also demonstrated his endurance racing abilities with victory in the Pan-American Road Race, a 3rd in the Targa Florio, and with a 2nd place finish in the Mille Miglia. It was in this race that he startled everyone with his brilliant driving of an Alfa Romeo Disco Volante that suffered partial steering failures during the race, repeatedly leaving only one front wheel responsive to the driver's steering. With performances such as this, the Italian immigrant's son was as popular in Italy as he was in his native land.

That popularity was put to the test in 1954 when Fangio made a mid-season switch from Italy's Maserati to Germany's Mercedes Benz, introducing its new W.196 in the French GP. Juan had won the Argentine and Belgian races for Maserati; then in the silver German car he won the French, German, Italian, and Swiss GP's for Mercedes. Added together, these victories also brought Fangio his 2nd World Championship. In 1955 it was the same story, Juan winning his 3rd crown with victories in the Argentine, Belgian, Dutch, and Italian GP's, and a 2nd in the British GP. Fangio also drove to 2nd place finishes in the Mille Miglia, Targa Florio, and Tourist Trophy Races. In 1956, his 3rd title year, he returned to Italy to drive for Ferrari after Mercedes quit the GP circuit. The championship again was composed of victories in the Argentine, British, and German races, and 2nds in the Monaco and Italian races. Juan also won at Mendoza and Syracuse and in the Sebring 12-hour race. He was 2nd in the Nurburgring 1000 the Venezuelan GP, and 3rd in the Supercortemaggiore GP.

In 1957, at the age of 46, he won still another World Championship, his 5th and final one, with Maserati, to which he returned despite its acknowledged 2nd rank machinery. Superior cars did not faze Fangio. As Phil Hill once put it, "With most drivers, you figure 25 percent driver, 75 percent car. With the old man, you know it's 40 percent Fangio, 60 percent car, so he's already got us beat with that something extra inside him." The aging 250F Maserati was good enough for Juan to win the Argentine, French, German, and Monaco races and take 2nd in the Italian GP. In non-championship racing, it was good enough in Fangio's hands to win the Portuguese, Buenos Aires, Cuban, Interlagos and Rio Grands Prix and the Sebring 12-Hour race.

Fangio retired in 1958—after winning one more race, the Buenos Aires GP—with only a drive in the French GP to test the newest Maserati 250F at the factory's request. To the end there seemed no diminution of his driving skills, his split-second timing, his cool and sure handling of wheel and race strategy. Today, the controversy that raged during his active driving career still rages: who was better, Fangio or Britain's Stirling Moss? Juan had the edge in the Grand Prix area, Moss was slightly ahead in 2-seater racing. Moss himself always considered Fangio the greatest n the world, while Fangio's favorite was the Briton. In later years, after another Briton, Jim Clark of Scotland, won his 25th GP, erasing Fangio's 24 GP victory record, Clark's name joined the others in the controversy. Still later another Scot, Jackie Stewart, added another name to the game.

In total victories, Fangio is ahead. In percentages of races won to races started, Fangio is ahead. In versatility, there is a draw, all of them driving equally well a wide range of the machinery of their day. Whether the diminutive Clark and Stewart could have successfully wrestled the heavier GP cars of the forties and fifties as well as they did the slim, fast GP cars of the sixties and

seventies is a question that cannot be answered. Fangio drove only one "modern" racing car, a Formula Junior, in a test several years after he retired. "I didn't like it at first," he said, "but then I felt more comfortable. You could feel the road and the car in every muscle of your body. The slightest movement of your arms, and the car responded. Yes, these modern cars are good racing cars." But his favorite machine remained the Mercedes of 1954–55.

Fangio, Moss, Clark, Stewart, four premier road racers, each with his strong points, each with his own amazing story. Those who favor Juan Manuel Fangio, a man who didn't even look like a racing driver but who certainly performed as well as anyone in history, have nothing to prove. Fangio proved it all, out on the race courses of the world, for two decades.

NINO FARINA

Enzo Ferrari called the Italian lawyer-turned-racing driver, Dr. Giuseppe Farina, "a complete driver," a man capable of any performance demanded of him, a man of steel, inside and out, a man who was a racing champion in every sense of that word.

Farina was born in Turin October 30, 1908, of a father who was the older of the Farina brothers of the famed custom coachbuilding family. (Capital "F" Farina cars at one time were the product of Nino's father's factory; small "f" Farina cars those of his uncle, Pinin, who carried on the family name in coachbuilding after the

elder Farina's death.) He learned to drive at the age of 9, it is said, in a massive Temperino 2-cylinder car.

Farina, who was a brilliant student (earning a doctorate in political economy) and a crack athlete (skier, soccer player, rider, trackman, and cyclist), had a good future as an Italian cavalry officer, but left the Army because it interfered with his first love, motor racing. While still a student, Nino bought his first car, a second-hand 1.5-litre Alfa Romeo, and promptly smashed it in his first event, the Aosta-Grand St. Bernard hillclimb. His own injury in that crash (broken shoulder and face cuts) was the 1st of a string of hard finishes in his racing career. When he mended, the young Italian continued to drive his own and other private entries, mostly Maseratis and Alfas. His early years included few 1sts, for Farina's mounts usually were outclassed by the giant German machines of the day, but his skills were growing enough to attract even Tazio Nuvolari, who took Nino under his wing.

By 1939 Farina was Alfa Romeo's number one driver, having won the Italian championship the 2 previous years. He repeated the feat a 3rd time, winning such races as the Antwerp Grand Prix and the Prix de Berne outside his native Italy. In 1940 Nino won the Tripoli GP and was 2nd in the Mille Miglia. The war prevented competition until 1946, when Farina returned with victory in the GP des Nations at Geneva in a prewar Alfetta. His 1st real postwar mount was a Maserati in 1948, in which he won the Monaco GP, the Mar del Plata in the Argentine, the Circuit de Garda, and the GP des Nations again. He spent 1949 with both Maserati and Ferrari, then returned to Alfa Romeo after an absence of a decade, bringing it new glory in 1950 by winning the first World Driver's Championship as we know it today. His Alfa teammates in the Type 158/159 were the rising Juan Fangio and the veteran Luigi Fagioli.

Farina won the British, Italian, Swiss, and Bari Grands Prix and the Silverstone International Trophy race that season, and was well-placed in the other point-scoring events. He was 41 by then. The following year Nino failed to repeat his success, although he did win the Belgian and Paris races, the Ulster and Goodwood Trophy races, and the Woodcote Cup, which was also contested at Goodwood. Alfa gave up GP racing in 1952, and Farina joined Alberto Ascari and Emilio Villoresi on the Ferrari team. He won at Naples and in the Monza Autodroma GP, and came in 2nd at no less than 8 other major races, including those in Belgium, France, Germany and Holland. Whether his decline was the fault of the car or a veteran's fading reflexes was vigorously debated until 1953 when Farina won the German GP, the GP's at Naples, Rouen, and Buenos Aires, the Nurburgring 1000, and the Silverstone Formula 1 races. It was a brilliant season for a man of 44. The German victory was an especially thrilling one. Ascari was leading, followed by Fangio, Mike Hawthorn (who had joined Ferrari that year) and Farina. Suddenly Ascari dropped a wheel, and Fangio moved into the lead. Nino moved the pace up to the lap record and passed Hawthorn 1st, then Fangio, to win going away.

Nino was named Ferrari's number one driver in 1954, but it was an unlucky year. After eluding disaster (while capturing victory) at the Syracuse GP by driving through two flaming wrecks with inches to spare, Farina crashed a 5-litre Ferrari in the Mille Miglia. Ready to drive again in June, Nino took a car out for practice at Monza, but a joint broke, rupturing his gas tank and setting the car on fire. Farina was badly burned even though he dove out of the car as soon as it had slowed sufficiently. In 1955, pain-killing injections allowed him to start a few races, but even though took a 2nd in the Argentine GP and a 3rd in the Belgian GP, the end was at hand. Farina retired that year, except for a few half hearted appearances at Indianapolis in 1956–57. He became involved with the selling of Italian automobiles, notably Alfa Romeo, after a short stint as Jaguar's Italian representative. He also dallied with a driving school in Turin, but it was not a success. Eventually he concentrated on the Pininfarina coachbuilding business, and late in June, 1966, Nino died in an ordinary road accident near Chambéry, France, when his Lotus Cortina skidded on an icy road and plowed into a telegraph pole.

FARMAN BROTHERS (MAURICE and HENRY)

Of the 3 Farman brothers, only Maurice and Henry—or Henri as some perferred to call him—were involved with auto racing. Born in France, they actually were British, sons of a Paris-based British correspondent. A bicycle champion, Maurice started competing first, driving Panhards exclusively. Henry soon followed, although he drove other marques as well. Maurice was 9th in the 1899 Paris-Bordeaux race. The brothers competed together for the 1st time in 1901 in the Grand Prix du Pau, which Maurice won outright and in which Henry took the light car class in a Darracq.

Both brothers had 40-horsepower Panhards in the Paris-Bordeaux race of 1901, where Maurice was 2nd to Henri Fournier's Mors, and Henry was 6th. In the Paris-Berlin grind, Maurice dropped out, but Henry came in 5th. The following season Maurice won the Circuit du Nord and was 3rd in the Paris-Vienna race. Henry, meanwhile, took the light car, or voiturette, section in the Circuit du Nord and won the Paris-Vienna run outright. Both brothers were in the new 70 h.p. Panhards in that race.

In the fantastic Race to Death—the 1903 Paris–Madrid race, stopped by governmental intervention at Bordeaux—both brothers dropped out with mechanical troubles. Maurice's close friend, Marcel Renault, however, died in that race, causing Maurice to pretty much retire from auto racing for something less dangerous—flying. Henry kept driving and finished 3rd in the Gordon Bennett Cup at Athy, Ireland, in 1903. Although he kept on racing, he never again achieved the successes of his earlier years. Maurice prospered in aviation, founding the Farman Aeroplane Co., which produced civil and military aircraft throughout World War I.

After the war, the brothers collaborated in building a luxury car, but the project failed because of engineering difficulties and cost problems. Maurice eventually took up painting and lived on until 1964, when he died at the age of 96.

CARMEL FERNANDEZ

A California grandfather of 7 in his late 50s who tooled around a track every Saturday night—and still won occasionally (as recently as 1970)—was NASCAR's oldest active driver. Carmel (Pappy) Fernandez was born in Maui, Hawaii, in February 1908. He emigrated to the mainland and became interested in racing in the twenties but was 30 years old before he went into the sport seriously, building his 1st race car in 1938. More amazingly, Fernandez was all of 42 before he took up competitive driving. By that time he had joined the Warren Transportation Co. in Hayward, Calif., as a mechanic, a job he continued to fill while racing. What with his weekend racing and nighttime machine shop, in which he built and maintained not only his own cars but racers for other West Coast drivers, Pappy claimed he had little time to grow old. He kept racing even after his 60th birthday and outlasted even his son, Carmel, Jr., who had retired a few years previously.

Before Junior left the field to his father, Pappy and Junior used to be one of the hottest pairings in West Coast midget racing, at one point winning 17 features in a row between them. Their favorite tracks were San Jose Speedway—site of a "night" for Pappy in 1965—and San Francisco's Cow Palace. The 5-foot, 6-inch 125-pounder won Oakland Speedway's Hardtop Championship in 1954, but he rarely left "home" in San Jose after 1970.

ENZO FERRARI

Once there was a small boy in Italy who had 3 dreams. He wanted to be an opera singer, a sportswriter, and a racing driver. Only his first dream failed to come true, for his voice wasn't good enough. He became a sportswriter, of sorts, and he became a racing driver of more than ordinary accomplishment. He also became famous, rich, disillusioned, insular, probably rather bitter, and certainly very sad. No one remembered the last time Enzo Ferrari left Italy. He may never have done so, as his movements became as shrouded as those of Howard

Hughes. He became the foremost name in international auto racing, yet he never went to races.

Enzo was born in Modena, February 18, 1898, to a modest, middle-class family with a tradition of metalworking. His father owned a small ironworks that made corrugated sheds and parts for the Italian state railways. When he was 10, his father took Enzo and his slightly older brother to their first auto race at Boulogna, where Ferrari watched Felice Nazzaro take his giant Fiat around the track at nearly 74 m.p.h., speed enough to make a lasting impression on anyone in those days. In 1916, his father and brother both died, and the following year he himself fell ill while serving in the Italian mountain artillery. He was not expected to live, but pulled through on sheer willpower. Discharged, he determined to join Fiat, even then headed for a dominating position in the European automotive market. Fiat turned him down, so Ferrari's introduction to the auto business was with a scavenger operation that bought up old vans, stripping them to the chassis and reselling them to a bodymaker who put on a torpedo-shaped body and sold the car as new.

Part of Enzo's job was to drive the stripped chassis to Milan. In the big city he became friends with an Isotta-Fraschini test driver named Ugo Sivocci who got him a job with Isotta. Next came a job with CMN, Costruzioni Meccaniche Nazionali, the company which eventually became Vespa. Ferrari was 1st a test driver, than a racer for this company, starting with the 1919 Targa Florio in Sicily. A series of misadventures followed him in Hollywood fashion that year. Driving through a blizzard, Ferrari's car was attacked by wolves. Racing through a small town, he was stopped by the local police to allow the Italian President to cross the road. The President stopped in the road and gave a speech for almost 3 hours. By the time Ferrari and some other contestants reached the finish line, the officials had packed up and gone home, convinced all of the racers who were going to finish had done so.

Enzo was back in the Targa in 1920, this time with Alfa Romeo. He finished 2nd overall, ahead even of his famous teammate, Giuseppe Campari, the opera singer. He won at Mugello and took the Aosta-Grand St. Bernard hillclimb. In 1921, he trailed only Campari at Mugello. He won at Savio, and at Ravenne he averaged 57.81 m.p.h. to win a 166-miler. The following year Ferrari took the Gargano hillclimb, finished 1st at Savio with Tazio Nuvolari 3rd, and won at Polesine and Pozzo. In 1924, too, he won at Padua and in the Acerbo Cup race at Pescara at 64.95. m.p.h.

At the 1923 Savio event, Enzo acquired the insignia by which he is now identified. Francesco Baracca, one of Italy's aces in World War I, had been shot down late in the war and his prancing horse emblem had been sent home to his parents as a memorial. So affected was Baracca's father by the young Ferrari's performance in the race that he offered the emblem to Enzo as a tribute. Ferrari was overwhelmed, and gratefully accepting the insignia that day, he has used it ever since as his personal emblem. The prancing horse first rode only on one car, Enzo's own, which was seen with less and less frequency after 1924 because of Enzo's health and because his administrative skills were being called upon more and more by Alfa. But in 1929, after the Alfa Romeo was withdrawn as a factory entry from racing, the prancing horse appeared as the insignia of a new organization, Scuderia Ferrari. Initially, this consisted of Enzo and some friends, acting as Fiat distributors for several Italian provinces, and forming a central distribution and service center. A small part of that center was set aside for a racing team, partly subsidized by the factory, to keep the Alfa Romeo active in the lists.

Ferrari's Alfas did battle with Bugatti, Maserati, and then Mercedes, with startling success, thanks to its technical caliber and the driving skills of men like Nuvolari and Alberto Ascari. Enzo broadened the Scuderia's activities by fielding a team of Ridge motorcyclists, who dominated that form of racing as much as the Alfas did the 4-wheeled arena. He himself continued occasionally to appear behind the wheel until his only son, Dino, was born in 1932. The final victory came at a minor race, Bobbio-Pellice, with Enzo at the wheel of an Alfa 1750.

Six years later, Alfa Romeo was back in racing as a factory entry, but without Enzo Ferrari. An agreement was made such that no car bearing the Ferrari name would appear for 4 years from the date of the termination of his Alfa association. But a car simply numbered 815 did appear in 1940, with the device of a prancing horse on its hood, and everyone who knew anything knew Ferrari was producing his own cars. His first ones were extremely advanced for their time, 8-cylinder 1500 c.c. machines with graceful bodies produced by Touring. In the 1940 Gran Premio di Brescia, in which the 815 debuted, the 2 entries led the field until both expired as the 2 drivers diced for the lead. Obviously the iron control that would characterize Ferrari racing later was yet to be formed at that date.

During the war, Mussolini had awarded Ferrari the order of Commendatore of the Kingdom of Italy. After the war, he, along with others, was stripped of that title, although many still refer to him by it today. In 1946 Ferrari had no time to worry about lost titles. He was busy with his life's work again, building and racing cars. He had an immediate goal—to beat Alfa Romeo at the racing game. This was no mean accomplishment, for he was starting virtually from scratch, while Alfa still had some very potent machines. Beginning with 1500 c.c. Formula 2 cars, Ferrari charged into design and production of racing and high performance road cars. Replicas would be produced for those who desired—and could afford—them. His early cars were fast but unreliable. In 1950, he set off on a new tack, concentrating on Formula 1, which in those days allowed 4.5 litres, if unsupercharged. His Ferrari engine was built as a 3.3-litre powerplant, then developed to 4.1 litres, then to a full 4.5. By such staged development, its fullest potential was realized. In 1951, while a Ferrari did not beat an Alfa Romeo, the gap was closed enough that everyone knew it was only a matter of the right moment for the first great Ferrari victory.

That moment came not in Italy but at Britain's Silverstone race circuit. Jose Froilan Gonzalez practiced with a Ferrari that was a full second faster than Juan Manuel Fangio's Alfa. In the race, Fangio's skills kept the Ferrari at bay, until he finally had to pit for fuel (which the more efficient unsupercharged Ferrari did not have to do). So Gonzalez won, and back in Modena, when he heard the glorious news, Enzo remarked, "I have killed my mother." At Monza, seat of Italian racing, Ferrari won again, and the marque had arrived as the premier constructor of Italy. Though Alfa won its championship that year, it then withdrew, leaving the field to Ferrari's cars of the future.

In 1953 and 1954, Enzo's cars won the World Driver's Championship (had there been a constructors title then, he would have won that, too). And his street cars —finely tuned, handsome, expensive machines more like thoroughbred horses than mechanical products—came to replace Rolls Royce, Bentley and Mercedes Benz as the supreme road cars of the time. All was not without cost to Ferrari,, however. Between 1956 and 1961, he suffered a staggering number of personal losses. His son died of nephritis. Alfonso de Portago ran a Ferrari into the crowds at the Mille Miglia, and Ferrari was denounced by the Vatican newspaper as a Saturn—a devourer of his own children. Enzo and his wife went through a bitter separation. In 1961, though, Ferrari again provided the World Champion's mount (America's Phil Hill), but another Ferrari, driven by Wolfgang won Trips, cut a path of death through a crowd at the Monza course as it carried Trips to his death.

It is understandable that Ferrari withdrew even further from that world outside his factory gates at Maranello. But still they came, to buy cars, to pay homage to the man who so dominated auto racing. After a 6th World Championship was won in a Ferrari in 1964, his F1 star seemed to diminish under the British onslaught, but there were other titles to be won. Between 1960 and 1965, Ferraris won every Le Mans, and between 1958 and 1964 they won 6 of the 7 Sebring races. The British domination of the late sixties and early in seventies only seemed to make Ferrari, the man, more determined than ever to win, even though his factory now only was a division of the Fiat empire. He announced his withdrawal from the sport several times (the latest in 1972), but no one could believe he could stay away as long as he lived.

MARIA-TERESA DE FILIPPIS

It was the opinion of many veteran observers of motor sports that a woman would not be capable of competing in major racing, such as the Grand Prix. But there always was one exception because she already had shown that she could compete, if not win, in a single, short GP span back in 1958.

Miss Maria-Teresa de Filippis of Italy was what is known as a sportswoman in pre-Women's Liberation days. That meant she worked at several sports, and was successful at most. Motor racing is a demanding pastime, but Filippis managed a 10-year career in the sport, mostly in sports cars, and for that brief time in single-seaters. Her debut as a GP driver came on June 15, 1958, in the Belgian GP, also designated that year as the European GP, which was held at Spa-Francorchamps. Of the 19 cars qualified for the race, Maria-Teresa was last in her own Maserati. She drove a quiet, sensible race, and as 9 of the starters fell by the wayside, including such names as Stirling Moss, Peter Collins, Graham Hill, Jack Brabham and others, she kept gaining places. De Filippis finished 10th, two laps back of the winner, Tony Brooks.

What enabled the diminutive woman to make the switch from sports cars to single-seaters was expert instruction, first from Luigi Musso, a countryman, then Jean Behra. Less than a month after Maria-Teresa's GP debut, however, Musso was killed in the French GP, and it was a severe blow. A practice accident wiped out Filippis's Maserati, but a deal was made with Centro-Sud for some of the remaining Grands Prix. Maria-Teresa made the starting grids of both the Portuguese and Itaian races, although in both she again qualified last. She also retired from both races, her Maserati quitting on the 7th lap of the Oporto race and on the 58th lap of the Monza battle.

The plan for 1959 was to race a Porsche in some races that Behra could not make or for which he got a better car. But Behra was killed in practice at the Avus circuit in preparation for the German GP. After a short while, Filippis announced she was retiring from the sport.

CARL FISHER

The man who was the driving force behind the building of the Indianapolis Motor Speedway also made millions founding the city of Miami Beach. Then he lost almost as much money trying to develop Montauk Point on Long Island as a summer resort and died relatively impoverished. He was a man who fit his age, a brash one for an era in America that was bursting with opportunity for the promoter and the entrepreneur. Born in southern Indiana, Carl Fisher quit school in 1886 at the age of 12 to make his way in the world. At 17 Fisher was in the bicycle repair business and competing as professional cyclist with Barney Oldfield and Tom Cooper. Before he was 20 Carl was a major cycle dealer, having talked his way into his 1st inventory. In 1898 he was associated with the building and promotion of races at Newby Oval, a quarter-mile board track in Indianapolis. The following year Fisher owned the first horseless carriage in town, a 2.5-h.p. De Dion motor tricycle. In 1900 he owned a Mobile Steam Wagon,then founded the Fisher Auto Company to sell the curved-dash Oldsmobile.

In 1901 Fisher toured the fair circuit with a 1-cylinder Winton, racing against horses ($500 a performance, minimum distance of race, 200 yards). Each performance also included a record run and, at $10 a head, a drive in the Winton. He cleared $20,000 the 1st season; there was no 2nd season, for the car had become less of a novelty. Instead Fisher organized, with Oldfield, Cooper, Earl Kizer, and others, exhibition auto races at county fairs. The split was not as profitable though the races were a great success. Fisher withdrew in 1903, leaving the deal to Oldfield, who repaid him by setting a world mark of 60.4 m.p.h. at Indy Fairgrounds June 19, 1903. The car business boomed, but not as much as a $2,000 Fisher investment in carbide headlamps invented by P. C. Avery. Jim Allison, his partner in this and in the Speedway, shared in the $9 million Union Carbide paid for the resulting Prest-O-Lite Corporation in 1917.

Fisher, meanwhile, had hoped to enter a 923 cu. in. Premier in the 1904 Vanderbilt Cup, but found the car was overweight. He did win the 5-mile Diamond Cup event on Chicago's Harlem race track on October 1,

1904. He helped Herb Lytle prepare his Pope-Toledo for the Vanderbilt Cup and watched that race. In 1905 Carl went over to watch the Gordon Bennett Cup races on the Circuit de l'Auvergne, an 85.3-mile course in France. Two Pope-Toledos (Lytle and Bert Dingley) were entered, with Fisher a possible relief driver. Carl lost interest when he saw the dangerous mountain roads. However, he toured European auto factories and was so impressed that he returned to America to tell U.S. manufacturers they were falling farther and farther behind. His solution was factory competition on a new closed road course for he, along with many others, felt that road racing on public roads was doomed in America. Thus began the idea for the Indianapolis Motor Speedway.

Manufacturers around the city—Marmon, National, Premier, Marion and American—formed the Indianapolis Auto Racing Association. The first program excited interest throughout the entire Midwest (an area larger than Western Europe). Held November 4, 1905, in the Fairgrounds, were a 5-mile handicap race, which Fisher won in the Premier that he had hoped to race in the Vanderbilt Cup, and a 100-mile feature, which evolved into a battle between Charlie Merz and Jan Clemens in Nationals. Merz crashed and Clemens won by 43 minutes over McNamara in a Premier, setting what was called a world record for that distance on a dirt track of 52.93 m.p.h.

Fisher convinced the National officials to try for the 24-hour record, which Guy Vaughn held with 1,015 miles, in a Decauville car at Empire City dirt track in Yonkers, N.Y. The International Auto Racing Association supervised the new attempt, starting just before 3 P.M. November 16. Merz and Clemens were the drivers, starting in two cars, but Clemens crashed and became Merz's relief. A heavy frost during the night made driver changes every 30 minutes necessary and forced the pilots to abandon goggles, their only protection against the wind. They broke the record by driving 1,094 miles.

Shortly after this, an attempt was made by Fisher and his backers to locate a major oval at French Lick Springs, Ind., but the move failed because there was no suitable site. Carl became sidetracked into speedboating, and the panic of 1907 further delayed plans to construct a track. Fisher, however, continued to sell and promote automobiles with more imagination than many major firms exhibit today. One of his stunts was to float a Stoddard-Dayton over the city of Indianapolis underneath a huge balloon, settle to the ground, detach the balloon, and drive the car away. He advertised it as the first car to fly over the city, of course.

Soon after that a real estate agent named Lem Trotter located what was to became the site of the Indianapolis Motor Speedway, a 320-acre parcel called the Old Pressly Farm. This had trolley and railroad tracks right next to it and was about 5 miles from downtown. The site cost Fisher a mere $80,000. B. T. Andrews of New York actually designed the future Brickyard; Ernest Moross was the first public relations man and director of contests. Another critical decision was to allow the AAA to sanction the contests, rather than the ACA. Fisher had to convince his partners to sink an additional $200,000 into repaving the track with bricks after a disastrous July 4–5, 1909, crash that left three dead. Fisher was married while the paving job was being done, and the grand reopening was held in 9-degree weather on December 17 with about 500 in attendance. On December 18, Louis Strang set an American mark of 91.813 m.p.h. for 5 miles, and Fisher & Co. saw some hope of recouping their investment of three-quarters of a million dollars. The 3-day Memorial Day weekend program in 1910 set the Speedway on the road to success. The decision to switch to one major event was the idea of Jim Allison, one of Fisher's partners. Though manufacturers wanted a 24-hour race, Fisher and associates decided that few fans would stay that long, and picked 500 miles because they figured it would be about as long as they could run during daylight hours.

In 1913, Fisher invested $50,000 to buy part of a land reclamation project from John Collins; it was to become Miami Beach. That year he was also responsible for the formation of the Highway Association to build a coast-to-coast highway across America. The Lincoln Highway was completed in 1928, aided by both Federal and State money. Fisher was financially interested in the Sheepshead Bay Speedway in New York City and in Fulford-by-the-Sea, a board track south of Miami, which lasted one race before being blown away by a hurricane. He had less and less to do with Speedway management after World War I until, in 1924, he turned over the Indianapolis presidency to Allison and concentrated on Miami Beach and the Montauk Point project. On August 15, 1927, he and Allison sold the Speedway for about $700,000 to Eddie Rickenbacker and his Detroit backers. Allison died the following year, and his aircraft engine company became a division of General Motors. Fisher used much of his personal fortune unsuccessfully to try to save Montauk Point after the 1929 market crash. After that, he spent his remaining years in semi-retirement in Miami Beach, dying July 15, 1939, of complications resulting from sclerosis of the liver.

JOHN FITCH

Ten years in the life of an active man is not a very long time. In John Cooper Fitch's life, 10 years encompassed his career as an active driver. In that short span of time he established himself as one of America's best in his own day and one of the best of all time in road racing. The credentials Fitch then established as an expert in the automotive area were later to involve him in highway safety, course design and other endeavors..

He was born August 4, 1917, in the right town for a

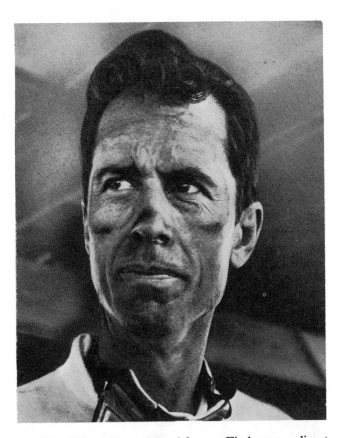

racer, Indianapolis. A lean 6-footer, Fitch was a direct descendent of the John Fitch who invented the steamboat (Robert Fulton being the popularizer rather than originator). Invention was even closer at hand; Fitch's father, Robert Vanderbilt Fitch, was a contractor and builder who, around the turn of the century, produced the first closed body for a horseless carriage. John Fitch was 6 when his parents were divorced, but his new stepfather, George Spindler, also had automotive connections, as head of the Stutz Automobile Company's Indiana sales division.

Spindler often ran Stutz cars on the Brickyard for record-setting publicity purposes, and John got his first rides at speed in some of those. He grew up to be an independent young man, used to being on his own. In the summer of 1938 Fitch bought a new motorcycle and broke it in by touring from Indy to New Orleans, a sort of "Easy Rider" trip 30 years ahead of its time. In the Crescent City he swapped the cycle to some sailors who, on the eve of departure, were happy to exchange a 500-c.c. Fiat Topolino for the more easily stowed motor cycle. That was Fitch's 1st car. The 2nd one was an MG Magnette, acquired in London in 1939; John had spent a year at Lehigh University, but felt that European travel could be more educational. In England he had a chance to visit Brooklands, the big, Indy-like oval that was the center of British racing before World War II and was impressed by Prince Bira in action in an ERA.

Fitch and a friend traveled around the Continent just before the outbreak of war, but were back in Britain before the final act that ended peace. Fitch immediately tried to enlist in the RAF, but at that time, contrary to later practice, the British were not keen on taking American nationals into their armed forces. John headed back to the United States, bought a boat and learned to be pretty fair navigator and sailor. The flying bug wasn't a momentary one, however, and when the United States entered the war, he was already in the Army Air Corps, getting his wings December 12, 1941. First an attack bomber pilot, he was among the early contingent flying out of Britain in borrowed planes, then went to the Mediterranean to participate in the Algerian invasion and other actions. Fitch later became a Mustang fighter pilot, specializing in ground attack.

It was while strafing a train on February 20, 1945, that he was shot down over Germany, captured and interned. It was no "Stalag 17" for Fitch. By the time he was rescued May 8, 1945, he had lost many pounds and was having trouble with his eyesight. But rest, good food, and fresh air back at his stepfather's new farm in Brewster, a bit north of New York City, helped him recover. Soon John was back in the pilot's seat again, this time in a Taylorcraft floatplane that he used to commute to the city, to fly out to Indy for the 500, and for other such civilian pleasures. Strangely, Fitch did not buy a sports car until the spring of 1948; then not only did he buy an MGTC, but also he became a dealer for the marque in White Plains. In the 1st year Fitch sold just 3 cars, but he slowly expanded the business and opened his own garage-salesroom.

The year 1949 saw John Fitch's initial race. It happened on an auspicious day, the one that his future wife, Elizabeth, accepted his proposal. The automobile race was at Bridgehampton, a sleepy summer resort on eastern Long Island, in the days before a road course existed; racing was held on the village's actual streets. Fitch finished 5th. In his next race, at Linden Airport in New Jersey, John was late and drove in just as the 12-hour race started; so he joined at the back of the pack—without technical inspection, physical, or anything. He finished (unofficially for even if regulations weren't all that stringent in those days there still were some) 4th overall and 3rd in class.

In September 1949 Fitch ran his initial race at Watkins Glen, the equally sleepy upstate New York town of those days, and managed a 2nd to Tom Cole's HRG. After more races at Linden Airport, Palm Beach Shores, Fla., and other places in 1950, the Fitch Model B, a Fiat 1100 chassis with Ford V60 engine and Crosley body, appeared at Bridgehampton in June. Fitch drove it to 3rd in class. At Westhampton Airport he was 2nd in class and at the Glen the same. In a borrowed Lagonda-Mercury he contested the Mount Equinox hillclimb, where he found himself holding a steering wheel that no longer was connected to anything.

Fitch won an SCCA national championship in 1951, coming in 1st or 2nd in 12 of 13 starts. More important, however, he had his initial big rides in international competition, winning his very 1st start overseas: the March 1951, Peron Grand Prix, a 40-lapper in Buenos Aires for sports cars. Cole furnished the mount, his Allard-Cadillac, and Fitch ran the race's fastest lap, as well as winning the race. Almost at once Briggs Cunningham called and offered a Le Mans car, which John immediately accepted. Before that, though, there were other assignments. Driving a 500 c.c. Effy-JAP, John was a class winner in the Giant's Despair Hillclimb, won the 500 c.c. race at Bridgehampton in another special, and was a class winner in a Jaguar Special shared with Coby Whitmore.

John's first son, John Huntley Fitch, was born July 7, 1951, and 4 days later the new father left for Le Mans. Sharing a Cunningham with Phil Walters, Briggs's team manager, Fitch was running 2nd overall at 18 hours when the engine started failing. Walters and Fitch nursed the car in, but far down the list. Cunningham was impressed, and Fitch obtained a steady ride with the Connecticut millionaire's stable. At Elkhart Lake, before a crowd of some 50,000, Fitch pushed a C2 to victory at 80.82 m.p.h. in a strong 38-car field. A month later at the Glen, Walters won and Fitch was 2nd in the meet's main race, after John had scored a 2nd in the preliminary Seneca Cup in a Ferrari and had won the Sportsman's Trophy. This latter came about because during the race John stopped to check into a crashed car, then resumed racing when he saw all was well, still managing to place in the race.

Fitch contested the fantastic Pan-American Road Race in a 6-litre Chrysler Saratoga that same November and was leading when his engine died after 340 miles. He finished 1951 with 2 important Palm Beach victories in an XK Jaguar and in a Ferrari. The following season saw a lot more European action, in addition to the regular Bridgehampton, Glen and other United States appearances. At Le Mans in June, John made it away 1st from the flag, suffered mechanical trouble, and pitted, to restart dead last. But he battled back to 3rd overall by the 4th hour when engine failure retired him, while le patron Cunningham finished 4th overall. In July, Fitch and Britain's Peter Collins shared a Sunbeam Talbot for the 2000-mile Alpine Rally, but a wheel bearing failure kayoed their car.

In August, 1952, Fitch was at the Nurburgring to race a Porsche in a preliminary to the German Grand Prix (in which he finished 4th). But the real test came before either race when Daimler Benz gave the American a test. It was a grudging one, to be sure. Probably the Germans were not certain an American sports car driver could handle the super Mercedes 300SL; the day was bad, the hour was late, and the car needed adjustments. Alfred Neubauer told Fitch to take it easy—strange orders indeed to someone being tested to see what he could do. Fitch disregarded the order and went all out, even though he had never driven the course be-

fore except in an ordinary ride around in a passenger car. His time clipped a few seconds off those of some Mercedes team drivers that same day. Neubauer suggested another turn after noting the car was none the worse for wear. A few more seconds fell, and a future Mercedes team driver was born.

Not right away. Neubauer said he'd call when Fitch was needed. Back in the States John came in 2nd to Walters at Thompson, Conn., then won Elkhart Lake with Phil 2nd and Briggs 3rd in C4s. At the Glen, Fitch won the Seneca in a C Jag, and at Turner Air Force Base he won in the C4 again in the Sowega (SOuth WEst GA.) races, with 60,000 fans cheering. Small wonder that Fitch, along with Cunningham and his other team members, were considered the men who reintroduced major league road racing to Americans after along hiatus.

Fitch's horizons were even broader in 1953. He was in a Sunbeam again for the Monte Carlo rally. He beat Phil Hill at Tampa, then 2 weeks later won Sebring's 12 hours with Walters at 74.96 m.p.h. Back to Europe for the Mille Miglia, where he failed to finish. At age 35 the Indianapolis native appeared for his Indy rookie test, passed it, but couldn't qualify the Brown Special (nor could anyone else, because the car just didn't have it). In June it was Le Mans again with Walters in a C5, and they took 3rd overall behind Duncan Hamilton/ Tony Rolt and Stirling Moss/Peter Walker, both teams in Jags. Fitch/Walters averaged 104.14 m.p.h. for the 2498 miles. At Rheims, for the 12 hours there, Fitch had just taken the lead when he crashed the Le Mans Cunningham and totalled it, going end over end. He walked away with relatively minor injuries, considering the condition of the car.

Fitch was in shape for the Alpine Rally later that month, again in a Sunbeam, with Peter Miller. They finished 20th overall, 6th in class, and Fitch was one of 25 drivers to win a Coupe des Alpes, or symbol of a perfect score without penalty. He was the first American to accomplish the trick. A few days later John got a single-seater ride for the 1st time, in a rather worn Formula 2 Cooper-Bristol for the 2-heat Aix-les-Bains Grand Prix. He finished 4th overall after a horrendous initial heat. He was back in a sports car for the German GP preliminary race, bringing a Porsche in 4th. A wheel fell off to end Fitch's Frazer Nash ride in the Dunrod Tourist Trophy race. He got a Maserati factory trial at Monza before the Italian GP, but drove an HWM in the race and retired.

Fitch's 2nd son came along in October 1953, the same day he took off for that season's Sowega races in which he finished 2nd to Bill Spear's Ferrari in the 50-mile feature. On November 8, 1953, more than 70,000 fans packed March Field in Riverside for the sports car races there, and they saw Fitch win, Cunningham take 2nd, Spear 3rd and Masten Gregory 4th. Dick Powell, the movie star, presented the trophy, and Powell's wife

June Allyson gave John a big kiss—several times for the photographers' benefit. The C4 averaged 88 m.p.h. in winning. From that high spot Fitch went to another low, once again failing to finish the Pan-American Road Race in a Chrysler.

The previous season he had learned in Europe from some movie people of a planned film to be based on the book *The Racers*. He expressed interest in it, and in January 1954, he was hired as technical advisor on the film that starred Kirk Douglas and Gilbert Roland. Fitch not only advised, but assembled the necessary cars and drivers, acted as liaison between the movie makers and European racing people, and did all of the spectacular stunt driving that finally ended up on the world's motion picture screens. But there still was time for racing, too. At Sebring in March 1954, he shared a Cunningham-entered Ferrari with Walters, but they retired. In Briggs's final appearance at Le Mans, John and Phil shared a modified 4.5 Ferrari, but suffered differential failure.

Moviemaking took up most of the year, however, although in December Fitch was summoned to Stuttgart and signed up as an official member of Mercedes's sports car racing team for 1955. In May Fitch won his GT class in the Mille Miglia, finishing the 300SL 5th overall. In June at Le Mans he shared a Mercedes with Pierre Levegh, the deadly No. 20 SLR Mercedes that crashed and killed not only Levegh but 81 spectators at that race. In the Mercedes hiatus that followed the disaster Fitch drove an ancient Maserati, on loan from Moss, to a 9th in the Italian GP; and his 3rd son was born. In September Mercedes was back for the Dunrod Tourist Trophy. Fitch was supposed to drive with Wolfgang von Trips, but was switched at the last moment to Moss's car. The Fitch/Moss combination won 1st overall and 2nd in the Index of Performance; Moss liked driving so he did all but half an hour, John getting the wheel only for that long to give Stirling the necessary break.

Moss and Collins won the Targa Florio that season, with Fitch and Desmond Titterington coming in 4th in the SLR. Soon after Mercedes retired from competition. John returned to the States and joined in the Chevrolet Corvette effort. At Daytona Beach in February, 1956, he ran a flying mile at 145 m.p.h. in a Corvette to set a new production car mark. In March he led the Corvette team at Sebring, also codriving a car with Walt Hansgen to 9th and a class victory. That fall Briggs Cunningham asked Fitch to run at Elkhart Lake in a D Jag with him, and the veterans finished 2nd. In races at Thompson he won one and took a trio of 2nds to Hansgen. At this point Fitch started tapering off, limiting himself to occasional SCCA races and to Sebring.

At Sebring 1957, he managed the Chevrolet Super Sport effort and drove with Piero Taruffi until they suffered a suspension failure at 23 laps. The following year he was back with Ed Hugus in a Ferrari, but retired after 86 laps with valve spring failure. In 1959 Fitch

and another European veteran, Edgar Barth, ran a Porsche RSK factory entry to 5th overall. It was a fitting last hurrah to John's serious driving, save for a Porsche entry (and 20th place finish) with Cunningham at Sebring 1965, for old times' sake. There were other interests by this time, including the design and operation of Lime Rock Park in Connecticut, both as a race course and as an eastern United States automotive testing center. There was the modifying of the Corvair and the Fire-bird into kinds of sporty cars. There were safety barriers for the ordinary highway that would minimize car damage and save lives. There were articles, speeches and advisory assignments. Some people wouldn't really call it retirement.

EMERSON FITTIPALDI

In Watkins Glen, N.Y., on October 4, 1970, 100,000 chilled, wet spectators were watching under leaden skies as 24 of the fastest cars and drivers in the world assembled for the United States Grand Prix, next to last of the year's championship races and, as it turned out, the one at which the World Driver's Championship would be decided. Jacky Ickx was on the pole, barely nabbing that honor from Jackie Stewart. Third fastest was a young Brazilian, Emerson Fittipaldi, driving in his 4th Formula 1 Grand Prix. Beside him on the 2nd row was Pedro Rodriguez; behind were Chris Amon and Clay Regazzoni, and all the rest of the circus. At the flag,

Stewart shot into the lead, a lead that he was to build steadily until he had lapped almost all the field, leading his closest pursuers, Ickx and Rodriguez, by better than half a minute. Fittipaldi, meanwhile, had gotten away slowly and was 8th after the first lap, but he popped up to 7th on the 5th lap, to 6th on the 15th, to 5th on the 38th. By lap 48 he had cut away another notch, and when Ickx pitted on 57, Fittipaldi made 3rd. And there he found himself on the 70th lap, when Stewart's Tyrrell-Ford started to smoke. The Scot held on to his lead, albeit slowed, until the 83rd lap when his engine finally gave out and Rodriguez was the new leader. Emerson Fittipaldi was now 2nd, and likely to stay there. Rodriguez was both a charger and an experienced driver who would not be passed if he didn't want to be.

But fate was to intervene after 18 laps, with Fittipaldi 17 seconds back and Reine Wisell about half a minute behind the Brazilian. Unexpectedly, Rodriguez's BRM pulled into the pits for fuel. Someone had miscalculated how much was needed for this 248.4-mile race, and as Rodriguez died a thousand deaths, his mechanics sloshed gas into the car and lifted the nose to drain it back into the collector tanks. In scant time—despite the eternity it seemed—he was roaring out of the pits, leaving black lines down the track and infuriating a marshal who had tried to hold the Mexican back a few seconds more while the official viewed the course for oncoming cars.

Wisell was coming, but Rodriguez stayed ahead of him. Fittipaldi now was uncatchable, though, and after leading 8 laps he took the checker, delighting the crowd, his new wife, and Colin Chapman, the Lotus man, who threw his cap into the air and ran wildly onto the course. In winning for Lotus, Fittipaldi also had won for his deceased teammate, Jochen Rindt, because now neither of the remaining contenders—Ickx or Regazzoni—could beat or tie Rindt's 45-point championship total, giving the Austro-German the first posthumous World Driver's Championship ever awarded.

Emerson Fittipaldi was a sharp-featured, intense young man from Brazil who would go on to become the 1972 World Champion. The family into which he was born in Sao Paulo, December 12, 1946, gave Emerson many precedents for his racing. His father, Wilson Sr., was a one-time motorcycle racer, a contemporary of Juan Manuel Fangio, who turned to the microphone and the typewriter in 1952 after a serious cycle accident ended his racing career. The first son, Wilson Jr., a couple of years older than Emerson, took to racing cycles and go-karts. Emerson began acting as his brother's mechanic and started cycling himself at 15, winning his 1st race aboard a 50-c.c. machine. The progression to 4 wheels followed very naturally, and so did Emerson's habit of winning. At 17—the minimum age—he got a kart of his own, won the local championship the following year, and earned a drive in a Brazilian-assembled Renault Dauphine 850, with Gordini competition

touches, in Group 2 racing. He won the G2 novices' championship, then moved on to an Alpine-Interlagos GT for a 500-kilometer race in which he drove to a creditable 5th overall and 1st in class.

An old stocker, suitably modified, came next, and Emerson placed himself 2nd in a Corvette-loaded race to attract both attention and better offers. His initial choice, an ex-Autodelta Alfa Zagato GTZ 1300, broke down in almost every race, giving Fittipaldi some early frustrations. By now, the brothers had opened their own speed shop, and they began producing their own karts, as well as components for resale. "I like karts very much," Fittipaldi was to say later. "It's good for the balance. And it is profitable in Brazil, where kart races pay you twice the cost of building the kart itself. Besides, often it is the only way to keep racing."

Another locally assembled car, an Auto Union/DKW-powered Malzoni, was offered Emerson for some long-distance racing. In this one he scored 2 class victories, with 2nd overall at Interlagos and 4th overall at Rio. In 1967 Emerson centered his efforts on a Volkswagen-powered Formula Vee of his own design. There were 7 FV championship races for the Brazilian title; Fittipaldi won 5 of them, and was 2nd in the other 2. He also raced a Porsche-engined Karmann Ghia, won 3 races and placed in 2. This was enough to give him 2nd in the Brazilian GT championship, in addition to his FV title and Brazilian Kart championship.

Emerson and his brother next constructed their own car, a Fittipaldi-Porsche GT, which had a space-frame chassis with Carrera-like body enclosing the various Porsche mechanical elements. In this car, they appeared at the opening long-distance Brazilian race and led the field by about 8 seconds until the gearbox broke. The same part was to plague Fittipaldi for 2 seasons in various GT attempts, but the high cost of importing a new gearbox kept the boys at work trying to repair the ones they had on hand. Meanwhile, Emerson kept his hand in by driving FV and saloon races in a VW. And there continued to be serious kart racing. The year 1968 ended on a triumphant note with the Fittipaldi brothers winning the year's final G2 long-distance race after 12 hours of dicing in the rain, their VW besting a field that included Carlos Pace in an Escort Ford.

With the money from that victory, plus the sale of his other cars, Fittipaldi headed for Europe to buy a Formula Ford. "I arrived in March 1969," Emerson said in recollection. "The only person I knew there back then was Frank Williams, but he didn't have a Titan to sell me, so I went to Merlyn. I bought a Mark 11A, and got an engine for the car from Denis Rowland." Fittipaldi tested the new car for half an hour, then headed for Zandvoort, Holland, for his initial FF race. Such was the confidence of youth. In practice he was 2nd fastest to Tony Trimmer (later on Lotus's Formula 3 team when Emerson was as the F1 team), then blew his engine in his heat. But victory at Snetterton followed, and

Fittipaldi was on his way. After 8 FF races, with 3 victories (never finishing lower than 4th in the others), he was signed in July by Jim Russell of the driver's school to run a Formula 3 Lotus 59. Then followed an almost incedible streak of luck.

At Mallory Park he was 5th, having had gearbox problems, but at Brands Hatch he tied for fastest lap and finished 2nd. Back at Mallory, he again tied for fastest lap and won his race over Roy Pike, the experienced expatriate American F3 driver. The feat was repeated at Brands Hatch, which rapidly became his favorite course, for the following week he won a Brands International heat after setting fastest time in practice, but spun on oil in the final to finish 3rd. On successive days he won at Crystal Palace and Brands again, followed by his initial Continental victory at Montlhéry. Another Mallory victory, a shunt that totalled the car but left Fittipaldi unscarred, was followed by the British F3 championship clincher at Brands in the rain. Emerson closed out the season with another victory at Thruxton.

Colin Chapman immediately signed Fittipaldi for F2 and F3 racing in 1970–71 with Lotus Components, the factory team that Russell ran for Chapman. Brother Wilson also was signed for F3 at the same time. Emerson, meanwhile, started testing various Lotus cars, including the Model 70 Formula 5000 mount, and he raved about their power. But he was content to stay with F2 and F3 for a while, he said. "It is always good to test cars. Luck will have much to do with what happens to me. A driver can go very quickly to the top—and come down just as quickly, you know."

Fittipaldi's drives early in 1970 were good enough for Chapman to elevate the Brazilian to the F1 team by the time the British GP rolled around. He was given a Lotus 49, a hand-me-down from Rindt, but the car in which the Lotus number 1 driver had won the Monaco GP and started his run toward the 1970 World Driver's Championship. Fittipaldi qualified 20th in the British race, lost 4th gear during the race, but finished a creditable 8th. The German GP was next, run at Hockenheim instead of at the Nurburgring for the first time in years. Fittipaldi tied with Jack Brabham in qualifying, the old master taking 12th place, Emerson 13th. It was a far from unlucky placing, because Emerson finished 4th, and European writers started finding out who he was.

In the Austrian GP he started 16th, was among the top 7 and going well when he was forced to stop for fuel unexpectedly and dropped back to finish 15th. For the Italian GP, Emerson was handed a competitive car for the first time, a Lotus 72 like Rindt's. He was qualified when Rindt's crash and death occured, but Chapman withdrew the Lotus team, and he also skipped the Canadian GP. For monetary reasons, as well as to prevent Ickx or Regazzoni from taking away the dead Rindt's championship lead, Team Lotus cars appeared for the U. S. GP and Fittipaldi got his chance. At Mexi-co, the year's finale, however, the Fittipaldi luck ran out. Three engine changes in practice and qualifying got Emerson ready for the race, but a 4th engine blew on its very first lap. In his first F1 season, then, he won 12 points and finished in 10th position in the driver standings. And it happened just 2 years after he was racing in a go-kart.

There was no victory in F1 the following season, although Fittipaldi moved up in points and placing in the final standings. His Lotus retired in South Africa and Spain, and in Monaco he was 5th. Hurt badly in an ordinary road accident, he passed up Holland, but came back for a 3rd in the French and British Grand Prix. After another retirement, this time in Germany, Emerson's best race of the season came in the Austrian GP, where Jo Siffert hung on for BRM to win by just over 4 seconds. After that things didn't go all that well with an 8th in Italy, 7th in Canada, and an inglorious 19th in a pitstopping U. S. GP. It added up to 16 points and 6th place in the standings. There were F2 victories, however, at Jarama and Albi.

Technically, there were no more Lotuses in 1972. The cars, painted a startling black with gold trim, were called John Player Specials after a cigarette brand that was a sponsor. There was a new sponsorship from Texaco petroleum, too. But the driver was the same, and Fittipaldi's year started in an old familiar way with a retirement in the Argentine GP after a rear suspension failure on lap 61. But in the South African GP Emerson ran a quick 2nd to Denis Hulme and 2 weeks later in the nontitle Race of Champions at Brands Hatch, Emerson ran the fastest lap and won at 112.22 m.p.h. Retired at Interlagos back home in Brazil in another nontitle start, Fittipaldi won the Silverstone International by a mere 1.8 seconds over Jean-Pierre Beltoise, then the following weekend won his 2nd official GP in Spain, beating Ickx by almost 19 seconds. His 92.35 m.p.h. was a record race speed, and Fittipaldi led all 90 laps at Jarama.

At Monaco in the traditional race round the houses, though the course now was changed, Fittipaldi was 3rd, a lap behind Beltoise in a rain-soaked race. Hulme won the nontitle Oulton Park Gold Cup with Emerson 2nd, but in Belgium when it all counted again, Fittipaldi won by 26.6 seconds over Francois Cevert, leading the last 77 laps at Nivelles and averaging 113.35 m.p.h. Still another nontitle F1 victory was recorded at Vallelunga, Italy, despite a damaged rear wing. In the French GP, Stewart, out with bleeding ulcers for a month, returned to win with Emerson 2nd. In Britain it was Fittipaldi again, 4.1 seconds over Stewart at Brands Hatch. In winning, Emerson averaged a convincing 112.06 m.p.h. over the bumpy course. In the German GP later that same month, both men retired, but in Austria at the Osterreichring, it was Fittipaldi again, nipping Hulme by 1.18 seconds at 133.32 m.p.h. Two weeks later, Emerson walked away with Europe's richest race, the

Rothmans 50,000 Formula Libre race, at Brands with a 109.8 m.p.h. clocking in his F1 Lotus and with Henri Pescarolo 2nd. Stewart and most other GPers passed up the contest to get ready for Italy.

They might as well have come. For in the Italian GP at Monza, Fittipaldi proved the master of the situation once again. Stewart dropped out on the 1st lap with mechanical trouble, and he watched from the sidelines as Emerson let others battle away for the lead until 9 laps from the end, when the Lotus took over for good, winning at 151.33 m.p.h., with Mike Hailwood 2nd a lap back. The victory cinched the 1972 World Championships for the Brazilian and for Lotus as F1 constructor. The Canadian and United States Grand Prix were left, plus a non-title race at Brands, but these all would be anti-climactic exhibitions of motor racing's youngest-ever World Champion at 25 years of age.

The year 1973 would be an interesting one, with Stewart already announced as setting out to recapture his crown with a vengeance and with Ronnie Peterson signed to be an "equal number 1" on the Lotus team. Emerson won Argentina and Brazil to get the season started right, however, and he would battle Stewart in every race.

PAT FLAHERTY

For one glorious afternoon out of a glorious month, George Francis Patrick Flaherty, tavern owner, was the king of American automobile racing. He won the 1956 Indianapolis 500, an accident-ridden marathon which featured fast and bitter competition interspersed with more than 86 minutes of running under the caution lights.

A red-headed Irishman born January 6, 1926 at Glendale, Calif., Pat was always associated with Chicago, although he began racing at the age of 20 in Bakersfield, Calif., against the likes of Troy Ruttman, the Rathmanns and Manny Ayulo. Maybe his best years were not in Indianapolis cars at all. Maybe they were in 1950 and 1951 in Chicago's Soldiers Field when Andy Granatelli was packing in weekly crowds of 40,000 to see the likes of Flaherty wheel their roadsters in slam-bang fender-bending action. Pat was good at that; he got involved in his work, fighting like Erin Go Bragh for victory. In 1949 Flaherty passed his rookie tests for Indianapolis. In 1950, in a brand new Andy Granatelli Kurtis Kraft built to look like the BRM of the day, Pat lay 10th and was preparing to make his move when rain ended the race. He had no ride the next 2 years before Peter Schmidt took him on; Pat steadily improved his position until on lap 115 he hit the wall.

Flaherty got married then and the rods became a thing of the past. He raced less often but still as much as he could in the big cars. For 1954 Pat relieved Jim Rathmann in the Bardahl car at Indy and lasted 15 more laps before he was involved in a main straight collision. But in 1955 Flaherty finally finished the full 200

laps, coming in 10th in the Dunn Engineering Special. He scored his 1st Championship Trail victory at the prestigious Milwaukee 250 after finishing 3rd in the earlier Milwaukee 100.

That kind of racing was enough to convince A. J. Watson and his car owner, John Zink, that Flaherty was their man for a new Watson Offy for the 1956 race. The redheaded Irishman with the shamrock on his helmet put the Zink Trackburner on the pole with a record lap of 146.056 m.p.h. and a record 10-mile average of 145.594 m.p.h. Jim Rathmann and Pat O'Connor, the favorites of the insiders, qualified 2 and 3.

The 1956 classic was competition from the start. The first 3 cars took the green flag together, and Rathmann in the Lindsey Hopkins Special grabbed for the lead while Pat Flaherty took the low groove, leaving O'Connor (in the Ansted-Rotary car) on the outside. Pressed all the way, the Hopkins car completely demolished first-lap records, going 7 m.p.h. faster than the previous year. The trophy dash continued with Tony Bettenhausen coming up to join the fun; on the 3rd lap O'Connor swooped down into the lead and held as Flaherty dropped to 4th. Meanwhile the eerie whine of the Novi could be heard coming through the pack to charge at the leaders. Flaherty had taken 3rd back, but now Paul Russo in the Novi passed him, turning laps of better than 144 m.p.h. and planning to interrupt the O'Connor-Rathmann duel. On the 9th lap Russo moved inside on the main straight and screamed past both Rathmann and O'Connor. The 10-lap average was 141.916 m.p.h. and still the pace increased. At 20 laps Russo was averaging 142.255 m.p.h. but on the end of the straight on the 21st lap, the Novi had had it for another year. Russo's right rear tire exploded, slamming the vehicle into a retaining wall. The car spun and seemed in danger of catching fire. The minute it came to rest, Russo scampered out and off the track unhurt.

Flaherty now lay 2nd as the caution light showed behind O'Connor with Rathmann, Troy Ruttman in the second Zink car and Sam Hanks following. The yellow had not gone off when Hanks and Keith Andrews went into separate spins in front of pit row. To avoid them, Ruttman had to swerve into the infield. Andrews was stalled, but Hanks kept the motor running and rejoined the fray. Meanwhile, Johnny Thomson came on this sudden excitement. To avoid contact, he also spun—right into the pits, knocking down a mechanic. The Dunn Engineering crew got Andrews restarted, so the casualties, ironically, were the 2 cars who strove to avoid the accident. It took over 15 minutes to straighten matters out and that was that for record average speeds. The green finally was given with O'Connor having completed 30 laps and the average down to about 118 m.p.h. At the go signal Flaherty resumed the trophy dash, pressing O'Connor at every corner, often pulling abreast. At 40 laps O'Connor still led and the speed was back to 123 m.p.h. Johnny Parsons had moved into 3rd, with Rathmann and Bettenhausen waging their own war behind Johnny. The duel of the Irish continued at a 141 m.p.h. pace with neither giving ground. It ended temporarily when Ray Crawford totally demolished his car though climbing out unhurt. It took 8 minutes to clear the debris. Pit stop time saw Parsons hold the lead until his own pit stop on the 71st lap when he gave over to Don Freeland, who had moved from a 26th place start. Flaherty was gaining when Al Herman brought on still another caution with a skid on the main straight. Al's car played pinball with the wall, shedding bits and pieces as it spun. Freeland dashed in for his pit stop but he needn't have rushed. Patrick Flaherty was in the lead for good. Other cars seemed to have tire trouble, but not Pat's. Sam Hanks closed to 14 seconds and seemed to have a bead on the Chicagoan, but caution lights and Hanks's own wheel troubles kept the Californian at bay. On the 131st lap, when Bob Sweikert brought on the yellow for the 7th time, Flaherty dashed into the pits, took on fuel and a tire, and got back out without losing the lead. Hanks was still 19 seconds behind.

More caution lights, then more speed brought the race average up and down, but Flaherty sailed serenely on into Victory Lane, fame and the arms of actress Virginia Mayo, his wife, fans, and photographers. On his victory lap the throttle arm on his Zink car broke. Had it happened a few minutes earlier, Pat Flaherty would not have gotten a share of that $282,000. Flaherty won the Milwaukee 100 that directly followed the Indy race, but never saw the top 3 again, that season or ever. He faded out as quickly as he had gained his fame, partly due to a serious crash at Springfield, Ill., August 18. He spent 18 months recovering, but returned in 1958 to win a 200-mile USAC stock-car race at Milwaukee. He was set at Indy in 1959 and running 4th when he kissed the wall on the 163rd lap. Flaherty kept trying until 1961, when he retired to open another Chicago tavern. But for a month and a day out of that month, George Francis Patrick Flaherty had been king, and the luck of the Irish was his alone.

FONTY FLOCK

"I went into that little old race in North Carolina in this car that was so stock I couldn't have made her go 80 if I had to catch the promoter running away with the prize money." Truman Fontell (Fonty) Flock was talking about the 1st NASCAR Strictly Stock race at the Charlotte Fairgrounds in 1949, won by Bill Roper from Great Bend, Kans., in a Lincoln. "I got there late, too late to qualify, so they started me something like 30th. All I did was ride around playing the radio and waving at the girls in the stands," the moustached driver recalled. "I wasn't pushing, but suddenly I get a signal I'm 19th, then 11th, then 6th. The other cars were trying so hard they were blowing up. I crossed the finish line 3rd, and when they disqualified Glenn Dunnaway for spreading his springs, I wound up with 2nd money. And I never passed anybody the whole way. That was the most enjoyable money I ever got from racing."

Fonty Flock, next to the youngest of the racing Flock brothers, was born in Fort Payne, Ala., March 21, 1921, but stayed there only 7 years. His father, who had been a bicycle racer, died then, and Mrs. Flock followed Carl, her oldest son, who was 27 years old, to Atlanta near where Carl and an uncle were gainfully employed as moonshiners. The inalienable right of free men to make the world seem rosy through the use of alcoholic beverages was then at its point of greatest issue in the United States. Nowhere did the resistance to Prohibition reach more sophisticated proportions than in the Southland. Flock later admitted learning to drive at the age of 12, while acting as lookout in the family car or truck while senior members of the family served customers. "I used to back the car up and move it forward, making believe I was driving," he said. Concurrently he recalled having to bicycle back and forth to school, keeping one eye out for hijackers. One of his duties was to deliver a stray gallon or two to steady customers en route—the contraband taped to the cycle's handles.

It was bootlegging that gave Fonty—not Tim—the practice for later competition. He used to make 2 trips a day to Dawsonville, Ga., for the liquor. "I used to deliberately seek out the sheriff and get him to chase me," Fonty said. "It was fun, and, besides, we could send to California to get special parts to modify our cars, and the sheriff couldn't afford to do that." But the thrill of it was only part of what sent the Flock boys into racing. "My hero was Ted Horn. I wanted to be a race driver like him," Fonty recalled. "Whenever he came to Atlanta, he used to visit and have breakfast at our house. We got to know him because sometimes at Atlanta's Lakewood Park they would have boat races and car races the same day. Horn, Gus Schrader, and Emory Collins all raced there then."

Fonty earned some local fame in 1934 when he loaded his Soap Box Derby car with bricks and broke a policeman's leg. "My brother Carl was a boat racer—he went to the New York World's Fair in 1939 or '40—and he brought Ted home from a Lakewood program. My sister Reo used to parachute jump for $50 a jump. Coretta, another sister, was a barber."

Flock's own start in racing came officially at Lakewood Park, because Atlanta, center of the moonshine industry, was also the center for the modified cars used. At first the bootleggers used to have private races on the weekend out in the country, but then, Fonty recalled, "a boy was killed, and the police made us cut it out. It was after that we moved to Lakewood and, eventually, to other tracks around." The competitors would drive mostly for the fun of it with purses minimal. It was only as World War II approached that the sports began to pay enough to attract even part-time pros. Fonty rolled in his 1st race, but came back to win the 100-miler in 1940.

He served 4 years during the war with the Army Air Force. After the war came an immediate attempt to put the sport on an organized basis, and Fonty considered himself the 1947 modified champ. He probably won more races than any other NASCAR member. There were, for example, the beach-road classics at Daytona before 1941. This was the winter mecca of every hot rod and modified car in the South.

Fonty was hurt seriously at one of these races. "It was in 1941," he recalled. "That was a rough bunch of boys and the beach road course was different, too, with an S turn on the paved part. I was leading the lap 1 when someone tapped me while I was taking that S. My car went out of control and took down 10 mail boxes. Luckily I was thrown out because when it quit tumbling, the car was about desk height. We never wore shoulder harnesses; the only belts most people had were the ones to hold up their pants. I ended up with a broken pelvis and was on my back for 6 months. The doctors thought I wouldn't be able to walk for a year." He came back to win the Labor Day feature in Atlanta.

Fonty raced mainly dirt tracks until 1947, when fledgling NASCAR went up to Providence, R.I., for its initial race in the north. Flock could recall winning with Buddy Schuman and Red Byron in the van. He was in a car owned by Ray Parks, a fellow Atlantan who had come to town during the Depression with $40 and determination and had parlayed that into a fortune. "He had the best cars; cars even then were 90 percent of the game—they're 98 percent now—so we did OK driving for him. We never had to worry about drafting in the early days. We were too busy dodging. They used to start up to 80 cars on the big tracks."

After winning the 1947 title in Bob Osiecki's E & S Special 4-carb Ford, Flock switched in the latter part of 1948 to the modified Ford of Joe Wolf of Reading, Pa., in an unsuccessful attempt to beat out Byron for the crown. However, they swept to the 1949 modified crown. He won 11 features, starting with the 100-miler at Broward Speedway (a 2-mile paved circle at Fort Lauderdale) and winding up with the final modified race on clay just before the 5/8-mile banked North Wilkesboro, N.C., plant was paved. That same year Fonty went to Indianapolis looking for a ride, but he didn't find one. He came back to Dixie, hoping to try again sometime in the future. "Bill France and I flew to Indianapolis," he recalled, "Bill offered to buy the tires for any car they would lend me to take my rookie test, but there were no takers. So I flew to practice for the Mexican road race, where Bob and I had a car entered." In 1950, when Wolf retired as a car owner, Fonty began to drive more and more Grand National races. For 1950–52, Fonty was driving for Frank and Sara Christian. It was in the Christians' Olds that Fonty led the entire beach-road race, only to have Bill Blair win when Flock ran out of gas on the final lap.

Though the character of stock-car racing changed, he still considered Darlington his favorite track. "There is only one groove at Darlington and you have to follow it until you can pass in the straight," he said. "When they start 75 cars, like they used to, you can very well get trapped behind a slow car. But that track is a driver's track; it separates the men from the boys." "I was born 20 years too soon," he added. "The boys nowadays have such good equipment, and all that money is lying around for prizes. But I had fun. I wish the boys today would go up and sit in the stands with the fans; I used to do that after I qualified. I once stopped a race until they played MY national anthem—Dixie. I was on the pole, and the other cars couldn't go around me. And the day I won the Darlington 500 in 1952, I drove the distance wearing fancy short pants in an Olds 88. The next year I was driving a Hornet when I won the Raleigh 300. I set fastest qualifying for the Southern 500 of 117.40, a record for strictly stock cars then and still a record for cars with front-seat upholstery left in." He had started his Hudson dead last because he hadn't qualified and moved through the field to win.

Fonty finished 5th in the 1953 Grand National standings and 2nd at Darlington to Buck Baker. He drove the first 5 races of 1954 with NASCAR, then jumped to MARC, and had to post a $1,000 bond when he came back in 1955 for the beach-road race at Daytona. Fonty spent that season and part of 1956 on the Keikhafer racing team. "We really worked as a team," he said. "Carl wanted Tim to win the races, so I would set the car on the pole, and Tim would win the race. I respected old man Kiekhafer. He ran the team just like a school. We had to be in bed by a certain time, and the married boys were only allowed to visit their wives by permission. We lined up and marched to breakfast together, and we had to keep our uniforms clean. But he was a winner. I quit to drive a V8 Chevrolet for Frank Christian and won the 1st race for a V8 Chevvy in 1956 down in Columbia, S.C."

In 1957 Fonty was spending more and more time on his insurance business around Nashville, but came to the beach to finish 3rd in a Mercury. He hadn't expected to run at Darlington, and didn't even bring his racing helmet. But when the noise and excitement in the pit area got to him, he asked Herb Thomas—who had been recovering from injuries—how he was feeling. Thomas told him he could help drive the car. "I didn't know Herb had wrecked this car during practice and had just barely gotten it together," Fonty recalled, "so I thought it was starting 26th because Herb couldn't make it go. I started the race, expecting to be relieved. I got her to 6th when I blew a tire, spun backward and stalled, almost facing traffic. I couldn't get out, and maybe they couldn't see me. There was no yellow. Bob Meyers came around the turn and hit me, and Paul Goldsmith also plowed into me. The whole thing got me so disgusted I quit driving right there."

But Fonty still couldn't stay away from racing completely. After a serious illness, he came back in 1964 to work on a fan club program for NASCAR. All he had to do was tell stories, like when he bounced off another car in Orlando and went through the fence into a lake. Air inside the car made it skim along the surface a few feet before sinking. A moment later Fonty bobbed up and let out a moan. Some fans rescued him. When the ambulance official asked him if he was OK, Fonty burbled: "I feel fine but, before I drive this track again, there's one thing I gotta do. I gotta learn to swim."

On July 15, 1972, the Crackup King died in Atlanta after a long illness. He was 51 and left not only his wife, but 2 sons and 3 daughters back home in Decatur, Ga., where he had returned from Nashville.

TIM FLOCK

"I never shaved nor wore green nor let anyone with peanuts around my car on race days. Once was enough. I'll never forget one day when a guy who didn't know any better strolled into our pit and threw peanut hulls all over the place. That was the day four of us crashed." The speaker was Julius Timothy Flock, a slender 6-footer who quit stock car racing, NASCAR version, when he was way ahead of the game financially. Like an old college football hero, memories of his past have become blurred like a view through aging cut glass. All

that filters through is pleasant and heroic. But there's one wreck he remembered—that bad one at North Carolina's old Charlotte Speedway around 1950 that followed the peanut-hull incident. The cars were modifieds, and the young Atlantan was duelling with the great Red Byron when he lost control on the 2nd turn of the three-quarter mile dirt track. His car piled into the back stretch, which was dusty after the modifieds had churned it up, and slammed into three other cars including Byron. Along with the others, Tim was loaded into an ambulance unconcious. "When I woke up and found myself in that ambulance, it was a bigger scare than the accident itself," he recalled. "I thought I was dying. It was worse than the time a couple of years later at West Palm Beach when my car broke a spindle and took a curlicue course through the fence."

Flock was the youngest of 4 brothers. The eldest, Carl, never drove in automobile races, but raced boats while doing well in the construction business in Miami. The others were Bob and Fonty (whose career is detailed elsewhere). A sister, Reo who was named after the car, was a sport parachute pioneer. The father of this brood was a bicycle racer of some repute and owned the 1st car in Fort Payne, Ala.

Born May 11, 1924, Tim remembered seeing his 1st race in early 1937 when he was 13, and the bug bit deep. He started pestering his big brothers about becoming a racer, but they tried to discourage him. At 19 Flock decided it was time to get some driving experience, choosing an unusual route for it—driving a taxicab in Atlanta. Jobs as a fireman, bellhop, and parking lot at-

213

tendant followed until after a faltering start in 1947 his sister, Ethel, married to restaurateur Charlie Mobley, put him into serious racing. In 1948 she and Charlie deserted the restaurant business and began hauling a race car around the Southland with Tim as driver. He won his 1st big race, a 35-lap feature, at the 5/8-mile North Wilkesboro, N.C., track, and he and big sister were on the way to a good year. As with his brothers, Tim always regarded racing as an occupation. There was none of the *pour le sport* attitude, and he stood ready to grind his own kin into the railing if that was what it took to win. In fact, when the mother of the Flock clan, Mrs. G. W. Knight, affectionately known in the business as Big Mama, found the 3 sons in the same race she is said to have crossed fingers on her right hand for Bob, on her left hand for Fonty and her arms for Tim. Eventually the Mobleys went back to the restaurant business, and Julius Timothy decided to try his luck in late-model stocks. His car owner was a man named Ted Chester, his mechanic B. B. Blackburn, who, until Chester prevailed upon him to maintain the Tim Flock stable, had had no interest in racing.

In 1951 Flock drove a Lincoln and managed to lose the Daytona late-model beach race because his pit crew hadn't seen a signal that he was coming in for gas. He lost the modified race the following year on a protest by Jack Smith that the Flock Ford didn't have a proper roll bar. But 1952 was a year Tim remembered happily —he won the NASCAR Grand National Championship that season for the Hudson Motor Car Company, taking 8 victories in 34 races. And in 1955, Flock set a NASCAR record, 17 Grand National victories in a single season, driving a Chrysler 300.

RON FLOCKHART

To drive a Le Mans winner once is a good thing for any driver. To win twice in the gruelling 24-hour race is a great thing. To win 2 years in a row is somewhat fantastic. Ron Flockhart did it a few years ago, competing against Stirling Moss, Juan Manuel Fangio, Peter Collins, Mike Hawthorn, and the Le Mans regulars like Oliver Gendebien, Maurice Trintignant and Jo Bonnier. Flockhart was the original Flying Scot, an engineer-driver in days when such a combination was less familiar, and a skilled aviator as well as a skilled driver. Furthermore, he did it in a private entry, not a factory car.

William Ronald Flockhart was born June 16, 1923, in Scotland's big city, Edinburgh, and he always claimed his initial racing experiences were recorded starting at age 4 in soap-box cars on that capital city's long hills. At 14 he was tooling about (illegally) on a motorcycle, and 2 years later when he could get a license, he started hillclimbing on the cycle. With the war approaching, Flockhart joined the Scottish Home Guard and was made a dispatch rider on his own Enfield Bullet. He matriculated at Edinburgh University, and even though the war had started, he was ordered to finish his education by the Technical Manpower Board, despite Flockhart's enthusiasm for the RAF. Graduated in 1943, he found himself in the Royal Electrical Engineers and into another school for 6 months of training, then on a boat to Italy for the war's final stages. After a tour in Egypt where he organized cycle races for the troops in his spare time, Ron was discharged from the Army as a Captain in 1947. While working as an electrical engineer, he took up cycle competition seriously and won the Scottish Open Trials Championship in 1948 on a bike of his own design. He gave up cycling soon after, however, to take up gliding and, as he put it fooling around, with an MG TC. Over the next 2 years, he rallied, competed in trials, and raced on the Scottish sands at St. Andrews.

There was more of the same in 1951 with a Cooper-based JP Special. Flockhart's initial road race came in the Ulster Trophy, where he shared the day's honors with Mike Hawthorn; the former winning the main race, and Ron winning the Under 1300 c.c. honors. Much of Ron's pay went into a 1.5-litre ERA that he raced on long weekends taken out of his annual vacations from a local textile mill. The big annual race was the Ulster Trophy, of course, and in 1952 Flockhart had the thrill of passing Fangio (in a stricken ERA), only to run out gas because he was so excited. He next purchased a 2-litre ERA from Raymond Mays, and scored 7 victories out of 17 starts, setting 6 lap records along the way at such places as Charterhall, Goodwood and Silverstone.

In 1954 BRM offered him a factory slot, and Flockhart promptly quit the textile business. It was a learning year; the next season Flockhart spent much of his time helping develop the 2.5-litre model. That and his mother's death kept Ron from too much racing during that period, but he bounced back, first with the Scottish Ecurie Ecosse and D Jaguars. Victories at Goodwood and Snetterton were followed in July by his next trip to the rain-lashed Le Mans course (the 1st was in a Lotus in 1955, but Ron did not finish that year). Only 24 of the 49 starters finished, and Flockhart, along with Ninian Sanderson, led the parade home. Moss and Collins in an Aston Martin actually had the lead for a time, but the Scots regained it and finished about 10 miles ahead of the other Britons. That season BRM had an unreliable car, and Ron didn't finish a single Grand Prix in that marque, although at Monza he scored a 3rd in a last-minute ride in a Connaught. Because he was so tall, the seat cushion and slim foam padding were removed, leaving Ron sitting on the bare metal. "Couldn't sit down for a week after that," he said later.

The next Le Mans victory was shared with Ivor Bueb. The Ecurie Ecosse Jag plugged away as the big fellows blew each other apart. No forgetting how much gas he had that time, nor overrevving the engine or anything else that could have knocked the dark blue car from the race. The year 1957 also saw 5 of 6 sports car starts won by Flockhart in a 1.5-litre Lotus. The BRM still was erratic, and despite qualifying at Monaco, Flockhart couldn't do much about crankshaft failures. At Rouen, in July, he had a very serious crash, but Ron came back in September at Silverstone for a full card of races. He tooled a 3.4-litre Jag to a 3rd, won with the Lotus and pushed his BRM to another 3rd.

In the beginning of 1958 at Rouen again, officials failed to warn cars on the track about an ambulance that had strayed onto the course, and Flockhart went into a wall trying to avoid it. Fighting his way back once more, this time from 6 broken ribs, a fractured spine, and a punctured lung, he rejoined competition at Charterhall and won in a D Jag. He continued his racing career with BRM, but being 35 years old, he began also devoting more and more time to engineering and aviation. There were plenty of races though, in Britain, on the Continent and even in the revitalized Tasman series in Australia and New Zealand, where BRMs were regularly tested in the winter seasons. He tried again at Le Mans as well, but without success. It was in Australia April 11, 1962, that Ron Flockhart, who was as much a contributor to the renaissance of British auto racing as any man, was accidentally killed in an aircraft accident while preparing for a new adventure, the London-to-Sydney air record attempt.

JOCKO FLOCKO

Grease monkeys are an integral part of stock-car racing, but Jocko Flocko was the only *true* simian known to have participated in the sport. He was from North Carolina, but the Tarheel State never mentions this in its promotional brochures, probably because of Jocko's tragic end. The tensions of competition and his natural curiosity finally proved Jocko's undoing, and he retired after 11 races so nervous he couldn't eat. His name is the tip-off. The great Tim Flock was his owner, and in that climactic race of Jocko's career, Tim became the only driver ever to ride with a real monkey on his back.

It was in 1952, when the strictly stocks were running full front seats. Flock, a young man with a wry sense of humor, installed Jocko in a special roll bar cage set in a perch on the other half of the front seat. He got Jocko a little cloth racing cap and a specially-sewn nylon shoulder harness. The monkey would sit in his seat and watch the fans go by with seeming great interest; on pit stops he would chatter away at the pit crew, not caring that they didn't understand him, probably because he spoke with a Northern accent. Jocko became a great favorite at tracks throughout the Southeast. There was some talk among the press that he was being primed to run a companion car in the Flock Equipe, but this was patently false. Jocko's mount couldn't have met the wheelbase regulations.

Flock often recalled with some sadness Jocko's last race. It was before the home folks in Charlotte, and Tim was riding 3rd behind brother Fonty and another car when Jocko somehow slipped his shoulder harness off. The monkey had been strangely silent in the pits before the race, watching with baleful eye as he was inserted in his place. Now the reason became apparent; he had resolved to explore this monstrous conveyance. First he scrambled around the back of the car; then, seeing the small hole cut in the floorboards to allow Tim to check the condition of his right front tire, Jocko scuttled down to look through. "The tire must have grazed his head for he screamed and scrambled up onto the back of my neck, hanging on," Tim recalled. "I reached up and plucked him off. The time it took cost me about $750, for I dropped from 3rd to 6th. I left him home with the kids after that, but he wouldn't eat. We took him to a vet who said that Jocko just wasn't meant for this climate." The best monkey specialists in North Carolina confirmed this diagnosis, and Jocko eventually died. But he left behind him a heritage for all monkeys who want to become race drivers—and a warning: use your head when you race, but not to check tire wear.

VINCENZO FLORIO

Vincenzo Florio's brother once locked him away on a remote island to prevent the then 20-year-old youth from racing in an early town-to-town race, the famed 1903 "Race of Death" from Paris to Madrid (stopped at Bordeaux because of all the accidents and injuries that occured in its first leg). Little did big brother realize that this would only whet the young man's appetite. When he proved not quite as fast as he had envisioned behind the wheel, he went on to become one of the earliest and most important patrons of auto racing. This is not to say that Vincenzo, born of a wealthy Sicilian family in 1883, was without his own driving accomplishments. The 2nd son of Ignazio Florio, he came late in life; his brother was already 15 when Vincenzo was born. Their father died in 1891 and Vincenzo thus became the responsibility of Ignazio Jr. Like a doting father, the brother fed the young man's curiosity about the new motor cars. At 15 Vincenzo was handed his 1st auto, a De Dion Bouton. He later owned (before he was 21) a Peugeot, a Benz, and a Fiat, delivered by none other than Felice Nazzaro, who stayed around to teach Vincenzo racing and, incidentally, be sponsored in his own racing activities.

Still under age, Florio was kept away from the Race of Death, but upon reaching his majority in 1904, he took actively to the road. In the Coppa Florio, which he conceived and donated 1st in 1900, Vincenzo was 3rd in the 231-mile race around Brescia. The Targa

Florio was created in 1906 and Vincenzo was to be 2nd in the 1909 running of that one, his best race ever. But for all his youth and daring, he saw that he was over his head and that the role of patron was as important—perhaps more so in some ways—than that of mere driver. No one could question his courage nor his interest even at that early stage of racing. At any rate, Florio retired from the wheel and devoted himself to furnishing the money that made the wheels go around. He took an active interest in the construction and promotion of the Monza Autodroma, Italy's big, banked bowl and road course, opened in 1922, and several of the circuits there were named for Vincenzo.

GEORGE FOLLMER

George Follmer did not have to race for a living. Personable, outgoing, a graduate of Pasadena City College in California, he could have gotten his pleasures in any of a myriad ways open to upper-middle-class Americans. He chose racing. Born January 27, 1934, in Phoenix, Follmer bought a Volkswagen when he was 23. It was good cheap transportation and well accepted in his peer group. George wanted several things out of life: fun, girls, and a good supply of money. Then some friends invited him to see some SCCA racing at nearby Santa Barbara, and the 1st seeds were planted.

The entry was amazingly gradual, starting with local rallies and gymkhanas in 1959, and membership in SCCA, which then as now is equally social and sporting. His idea was to try his hand at some "real" racing in a

Porsche Speedster. In 1960 Follmer discovered that he had some talent for driving cars competitively, winning 15 races in his class. He was the California Sports Car Club's E Production title-holder and its rookie of the year. Then, in 1961, he moved up to a 550RS Porsche Spyder, finishing 3rd in divisional points and winning $600 in the Los Angeles Times Grand Prix at Riverside. Running RS Spyders is not what most young insurance salesmen can afford to do, and George had to sit out 1962 working to build his insurance business. He had no great commitment to automobile racing yet.

In July 1963 Follmer took possession of an engineless Lotus. Finally his "addiction" was ensured. Follmer spent the winter of 1963 sleeving down a Corvair engine to 2 litres and fitting it into the British chassis. His first time out in 1964, George finished far back at the Phoenix sports car races, and at Riverside he was retired. That ended a winter's work and the Corvair experiment. Follmer went to an expert, Bruce Burness, and the 2 of them found an angel, a Pasadena import car dealer who donated a Porsche 904 engine. The car was barely ready for the 1964 Times Grand Prix, finishing 11th overall. A few more sorting-out races, and Follmer and mount were ready to try the United States Road Racing Championship. Starting with Pensacola, Follmer became the surprise USRRC champion in the under-2-litre class, winning 6 of 9 races.

This brought him a factory ride at Sebring in 1966 for Huschke von Hanstein, the merry majordomo of Porsche competition. George finished 7th overall and 1st under-2-litre. And the Sebring feat brought him a trip across the ocean to Le Mans and the 24-Hour race, highly esteemed by all who have never had to survive 24 straight hours of racing even as a spectator. Follmer's Dino Ferrari mount wasn't going to keep at it for that period of time and retired early. But George got to drive briefly for Texan John Mecom during the latter's auto racing period—Mecom later became owner of the New Orleans Saints professional football team, clipping oil coupons on the side. The Mecom Lola was his initial over-2-litre ride, and he finished a CanAm in 10th place.

In 1967 Follmer still thought he could be a car owner and driver. In his own Lola-Chevrolet he led all 5 of the USRRC races in which he competed but broke down in all. He also got some driving assignments in the Roger Penske Lola for the CanAm series. Somehow, so gradually it was like osmosis, George Follmer, insurance broker and part-time driver, had become George Follmer, pro driver and part-time insurance broker. There was the 1st USAC race at Indianapolis Raceway Park, the Trenton 200 and a 6th at USAC's Riverside race.

The switch became complete in 1968 when George stepped into an early model stock car at Riverside and took 2nd. He found it so much fun, he went on to Nevada and won the Las Vegas 100. He had determined to press his Championship Trail exposure because the biggest purse in racing remained the Indianapolis 500.

He drove at Hanford, Las Vegas and Phoenix, was bumped by a faster car in his rookie year at the Speedway, drove Mosport, and then finished 8th in the Riverside 300. Besides this, George had a season-long ride for Javelin in the SCCA TransAm Sedan series, with little success. But he managed a 2nd in the final CanAm Cup race at Stardust Park, Las Vegas.

Then something special happened. It was at the Phoenix International Raceway, and the USAC clan had gathered for the inaugural of the 1969 Championship Trail. Promoter J. C. Agajanian was happy because the racing fans filled the stands of this mile track, and a few had even bought standing room. The Unser brothers were happy because they regard Phoenix as their home track. Mario Andretti, A. J. Foyt, and a score of other drivers were happy because it meant "real" racing time again. George Follmer was happy, too, with his very own car, a rear-engined Chevvy V-8 Gilbert Cheetah, and the beast had purred in practice for the Jimmy Bryan 150. The initial race of any year is special. Some of the cars are last year's, used because the newest of the new usually go to Indianapolis first. Others feel this is the place to test the Indy cars and still others decide whether or not to go to Indy by how their cars perform. The track surfaces are blown and washed clean of rubber by the winter's wind and rain, and consequently are rough on tires as they fill the asphalt anew with rubber.

Al Unser made the home fans happy by getting Parnelli Jones's car, a turbo-Ford Lola, up to record speed to win the pole. He took the lead in the race, with Follmer holding easily in the top 5. On the 11th round Andretti snatched the lead. On lap 14, Al pitted, effectively out of it with a dropped valve. Then it was Bobby Unser charging, with young Wally Dallenbach moving, too. The Follmer Chevvy was running around 4th or 5th.

Action came in the 3rd turn when Roger McClusky and Gordon Johncock both looped. The caution lights flashed briefly as the two made it back to the pits, their tires flat-spotted. On lap 28 Andretti pitted, a loose halfshaft removing his chances. It was Bobby Unser and his Turbo-Offy who held the lead with Dallenbach dogging him. Cars were leaving, one by one, as the full spectrum of woes afflicted them. And soon it was Bobby's turn, on the 122nd mile, when his engine let go. Who was that in 2nd place? George Follmer and his Chevvy stock block.

Follmer ran away to win by 3 laps, earning some $8,400 and his 1st USAC Trail victory. The 35-year-old thought he had started something. He hadn't. In 11 races he managed enough points to finish 16th overall. At Indianapolis he started and finished 27th, out on lap 27 with exhaust woes. But there was a new TransAm assignment as number 2 driver to Parnelli Jones on the Bud Moore Mustang team. George won the Bridgehampton TransAm. In 1970 Follmer added another Trans-Am victory at Bryar Park, N.H., and he lasted 18 laps at Indy in the STP Hawk Ford before the engine failed for a 31st-place finish. It was to be his year for victory

in the CanAm series, for he had a ride in the AVS Shadow. However, the Shadow faded quickly. Follmer didn't make a single starting grid.

Two years later, however, soon after George had clinched the 1972 TransAm title for Javelin, Mark Donohue was injured in the new L&M Porsche-Audi 917K CanAm car, and Penske called upon Follmer to replace Mark in the series. In his initial outing at Road Atlanta, all George did was win the race after two short practice sessions in the turbocharged 1000 h.p. racer. He went on to become CanAm champion and to sign for Formula 1 in 1973 with the new American UOP Shadow team—at age 39, scoring a World Championship point in his initial start.

Follmer may have started a new trend in racing when he went to court in California to make the USAC powers show cause why they should not be enjoined from suspending him. At stake was a ride in the Ontario 500. George had been handed an indefinite suspension by USAC for competing in a Continental championship, sanctioned by SCCA, when he might have been tooling along in a USAC race. His lawyers cited the California right-to-work law—perhaps the strangest switch ever since the law was put on the books to beat union closed shops—and USAC quickly suspended the suspension.

HENRY FORD

Henry Ford's contribution to racing was threefold. As a driver he held the world Land Speed Record briefly; as a car owner he evolved a sponsorship of Barney Old-

field that helped the sport in its American infancy; and as a manufacturer he was one of the earliest to appreciate the public relations value of auto racing.

"John and William are all right, but Henry worries me," said his father, William Ford, who ran a farm in Springwells Township, Mich., where Henry was born July 30, 1863. "I don't know what will become of him." What became of him is a classic among stories of unexpected success. He never learned to spell correctly, or read and express himself well in writing. He just understood machinery and instinctively realized that its development was something he had to pursue.

He became chief engineer of the Edison Illuminating Company in Detroit, but he was regarded with great suspicion when—a married man—he chucked that job to experiment with a 2-cylinder, 4-cycle engine to power a low-cost automobile. He kept home and hearth solvent by repairing steam engines and mending watches. He had married in 1888, and his first working engine and Edsel, his only son, both arrived at 58 Bagley Avenue in 1893. The engine sputtered to life on the sink; the child chose the more conventional locale for stork visits —the bedroom.

Thomas Alva Edison, Ford's idol, gave Ford verbal encouragement then for his concept of a high-horsepower, lightweight, self-contained engine. Three years later, in 1896, the 1st working Ford car was finished. Henry was the precursor of a whole host of auto creators who literally had to knock down walls to get their brainchilds out in the open—W. O. Bentley and Paul Russo (Basement Bessie) come to mind immediately. Ford knocked down a brick wall to get his out.

The Ford Motor Company may be said to have been founded on a racing reputation. Ford's initial corporate effort, the 1899 Detroit Auto Company, failed after 18 months. He built racers and attracted backers with his success in racing specials, which he then put into production. In June 1903, Ford and 11 backers founded with $28,000 capital what was to become the industrial giant of today. He sold a car in July. On January 12, 1904, Henry went out on the ice of Lake St. Clair in his "999" and hung up a 39.4-second mile, a world record that lasted about a month. Nevertheless, it was magnificent publicity, and it was exploited fully. Barney Oldfield began to drive "999" all over the country for Henry soon after that—thus aiding both Ford and auto racing. The cigar-chomping Barney had met Henry when they were opponents and had quickly had agreed to drive "999" because it was the fastest car he could lay his hands on at that time. The association lasted several years, until Barney went on to new cars.

Ford also seized upon cross-country races to prove his vehicle's worth. The most successful was the 1909 New York-Seattle race, sponsored by the Alaska-Yukon-Pacific Exposition, for the M. Robert Guggenheim Trophy ($3,500 worth of silverware). There were absolutely no restrictions on car design, schedule, or engine power.

The idea was to get from New York to Seattle, no easy job with roads the way they were in those days. The Manufacturer's Contest Association disapproved of the contest on the grounds that it encouraged violation of the speed laws and gave too many opportunities for rebuilding cars along the way. The rules were changed to provide a daily schedule to St. Louis, and to eliminate the possibility of rebuilding.

Under ACA sanction, 6 cars—2 Fords (1200-pound, 20 h.p. Model Tours), a Stearns (4600 pounds, 46 h.p.), an Acme Six (3500 pounds, 48 h.p.), a Shawmut (4500 pounds, 45 h.p.) and an Itala (4000 pounds, 60 h.p.)— started with 30 cities between them and the Seattle finish line. A Ford Model K (6-cylinder, 40 h.p.) was the pacemaker to St. Louis, which only the Stearns failed to make. One Ford T survived "bone-headed pilots," quicksand, fire, a fall off a rise, mud, and snow to beat the Shawmut. The other finished 3rd. Then the winners made the return trip by a different route. Henry at that time was offering 6 models for sale, starting at $900. The Shawmut, in comparison, cost $4,500.

The Model T, introduced in 1908, became such a huge success thanks to nationwide publicity from racing activities and its low price that Ford evolved assembly-line production. Henry announced a $5 minimum for an 8-hour day (twice the going pay rate); it might be said that racing helped the labor movement. Ford was one of the early backers of the Indianapolis Speedway and remained interested in the Indianapolis 500 even into the late thirties. Several times during the long history of that race, entries affiliated either directly or indirectly with FoMoCo were around the Brickyard, although no Ford-engined vehicle ever won until Jim Clark did it in the sixties. Model T cars, not all of them in proper tune, were climbing Pikes Peak and competing in every kind of race imaginable even before World War I. And it was the Ford identification with racing that led to the first massive effort in stock-car racing under the aegis of Peter DePaolo, the old race driver. By that time Henry Ford had long since passed on. Ford had used racing, but he also had supported it. There was a complete power blackout in Detroit the night he died, April 7, 1947.

HENRI FOURNIER

A big, blond native of Le Mans, born in 1871, Henri Fournier was a champion cyclist who naturally became an auto racer. Cycle makers went into the auto business very early, and Henri's mechanical skills attracted racers, so he became a riding mechanic. Fournier's career may be said to have begun and ended in the United States. In 1896, he took a De Dion Bouton cycle to Chicago for a series of trick rides and demonstrations. Within a few years, he was a full-fledged riding mechanic, his most memorable race probably the inaugural of the

Gordon Bennett Cup in a car driven by Fernand Charron. With about 10 miles to go in the 354-mile Paris-Lyons contest, the Panhard ran over a St. Bernard dog, which became wedged in the car's steering year. The car crashed and the water pump became dislodged. Fournier lay down the side of the car and held the pump in place for the rest of the race. Charron won.

Promoted to driver, Fournier joined the rival Mors firm in 1901 and proceeded to become the sensation of France with 2 startling victories over the favored Panhards. In the Paris-Berlin race, 687 miles and 16 hours of driving, his Mors averaged 44.1 m.p.h. to win over 2 Panhards; in the Paris-Bordeaux race, the result was the same with a 53 m.p.h. average. After these victories, Henri's career began to decline, although in the 1903 Paris-Madrid race, shortened to Bordeaux because of the frequent accidents and deaths in the first section, he finished 8th of the 50 cars that reached the city.

Fournier allied himself with the Hotchkiss Company of Britain in 1904 after a dispute with Mors, but his race appearances were fewer and fewer. In 1908 he made 2 Itala appearances, finishing 20th in the French Grand Prix and dropping out of the Savannah Grand Prize race. Fournier died in Paris on December 18, 1919.

RAY FOX

Ray Fox's drivers read like a who's who of NASCAR racing. There were Buck Baker, Fireball Roberts, Dave Pearson, Junior Johnson, Marvin Panch, Lee Roy Yarbrough, Buddy Baker, and Bobby Allison. Fox was known as the master mechanic, not for a new years or even a decade, but for nearly a generation. A Ray Fox-prepared car was done meticulously, in the manner of the legendary German mechanics. Success was up to the driver and the luck of racing.

Fox was around so long that his pit crew included his sons, David and Ray Jr. And for a time there was the son of another mechanical whiz, Smokey Yunick Jr. But every time a race car was torn down and reassembled, it was Ray who personally approved each step. Along with his reputation as a master mechanic there was another reputation; Fox was willing to give young driving talent a chance.

He put Roberts into a winning modified and showcased Fireball's talent for all to see. Then there was Pearson, who won 3 superspeedway victories in his rookie year in the Ray Fox Pontiac. And then there was Robert (Junior) Johnson, a fat country boy who looked about as unlikely a major league hot shoe as could be imagined. In February 1960, Junior came down from the hills of North Carolina, took over a year-old Fox-prepared Chevrolet, and proceeded to drive it to victory in the Daytona 500. In that same automobile Junior set 9 qualifying marks at tracks ranging from quarter-milers

to Daytona itself. Even after he moved on to Fords, Junior credited Fox for the quality of the automobiles he had provided.

It was in 1956 that Ray, who had come south from Massachusetts to Daytona Beach a decade earlier, got seriously involved in NASCAR racing. He was 39 and had a reputation already as an engine builder of modifieds. But if you asked him about stock cars, Fox would credit 3 men as his mentors above all others: Herb Thomas, 2-time National Champion when drivers worked to set up their own machines; Red Vogt, who had spent 20 years as an Indianapolis mechanic and had helped Floyd Roberts to the 1946 victory; and Red Byron, a magician with an engine, who ran the gamut of American racing—Indianapolis, NASCAR, SCCA and international.

Born May 28, 1917, in Pelham, N.H., Ray was the oldest of 3 boys. He quit school at 13 when his father, a carpenter, died. At 15 he was already helping support the family. Ray worked as a café counterman and held other odd jobs briefly before he found his true vocation. He became an inspector in the shop of a Ford dealer, checking out cars after the mechanics had worked on them. At 18 Fox opened a general repair shop at Lawrence, Mass.

For 3 years Ray also raced in small homemade cars which were called midgets then. They were powered by 4-cylinder Star and Whippet engines, motorcycle engines —anything that would enable the little cars to scoot around the tracks. The boys would get cinders from nearby mills for surfacing their tracks and, even though they covered everything but their eyes with handkerchiefs, they nearly always finished a race with cut faces. Ray ran on such tracks at Keene, N.H., and at Groveland and Haverhill, Mass.

Soon after Pearl Harbor, Fox enlisted in Army Ordnance as a private and was assigned, strangely, to truck maintenance at Massachusetts's Fort Devens. He was so good at the job they kept him at Fort Devens for the duration, and when he was discharged in 1945, Fox was a lieutenant with 40 men under his supervision. On money he saved in service Ray headed south for a Florida vacation. He found Daytona Beach residents to friendly and hospitable he decided to stay a while. He stayed in Daytona some 22 years, until he got the chance to acquire Holman-Moody's old Charlotte Airport shop. Then the Foxes moved to North Carolina.

Fox taught mechanics under the GI training bill for several years, then spent 8 years with the Fish Carburetor Company, a Daytona firm. Robert Fish, the inventor of the carburetor and head of the firm, kept two Modified race cars—M-1 and M-2 Fords—to demonstrate its efficiency, and Ray drove them on tracks in Florida and south Georgia.

When Fish died in 1958, Ray took over his big shop on the Halifax River near downtown Daytona. It was well-equipped and staffed with 6 top men for general mechanical work as well as race-car engineering. It was here that Fox prepared Lee Roy Yarbrough's Dodge which upped the Daytona closed-course mark past 180. Fox had started in NASCAR's Grand National circuit, first as mechanic on Buck Baker's Chrysler, then Herb Thomas's Chevrolet. Thomas, the Olivia, N.C., sawmill operator, had won the Grand National Championship in 1951 and 1953 and was headed for a 3rd title when he was badly injured in a wreck at North Carolina's Shelby Fairgrounds on October 23, 1956. With the season about over, Baker moved ahead of the inactive Thomas, and won the championship by a slim point margin. Yet Ray was honored as NASCAR's Mechanic of the Year 1956, after nomination by Baker. Usually the award goes to the champion's mechanic, but Buck knew Fox deserved it.

Fox did some mechanical work on race cars in 1957 but for the next 3 years he stuck to his general repair business. Then, in February 1960, just 7 days before the 2nd annual Daytona 500, the Daytona Kennel Club handed Ray a 1959 Chevvy and asked him to set it up for racing. Junior Johnson drove it to victory in the 500, outracing the 1960 models, and Ray went back to his shop. It was Fox's only effort that year.

In 1961 Fox set up a new Pontiac for Jim Paschal and Marvin Panch at Daytona and Atlanta. Panch put it on the pole at Atlanta and was leading the race when an axle broke. Fox took the car to Charlotte's World 600 without a driver, not knowing whether he could get one. Norris Friel, NASCAR's technical director, and Joe Littlejohn, veteran Spartanburg, S.C., race promoter, urged Fox to try promising rookie Dave Pearson.

Pearson did nothing less than win in the World 600, then captured another major victory in the Daytona Firecracker 250, and took Atlanta's Dixie 400 in September. Rookie Pearson and the Fox car set a new NASCAR record for money won on the Grand National circuit in a single season, $49,580.

Junior Johnson and Fox got together again in 1962, starting 23 races and finishing 18 times in the top 10 Johnson won the National 400 at Charlotte and had several other major races nearly won when tire or mechanical troubles knocked him out in late laps, in a run of ill luck fans remembered long afterwards. Winnings totaled $33,940. They teamed again in 1963, this time in a Fox Chevrolet. Johnson started 33 races, won 7 and finished in the top five 13 times. He won the National 400 again, becoming the 1st victor to repeat on the Charlotte Motor Speedway. The car's winnings for the year came to $65,710. Then Fox threw in his hat with Chrysler. The Fox Dodge won only $23,180 in 1964 because it was plagued with driver switches, but after that there were many good years until Fox threw in the sponge in 1970 as far as major racing went. In all, Ray had built 12 superspeedway-winning cars, a record to shoot at for all NASCAR designers.

Fox and his wife, Virgie, had 4 sons and a daughter—Raymond, Jr., David, Danny, Sandra, and Donald, his youngest. Raymond made Ray, Sr. a grandfather long before he was ready to retire to the spectator seats.

A. J. FOYT

When you looked on the ground at the 2 cracked rear brake discs that mechanic George Bignotti had removed from Anthony Joseph Foyt's front-engined roadster after qualifying for the 1965 Trenton 200-mile race, you would not have given a red cent for the Texas hero's chances of winning an unprecedented 6th straight USAC title race. He had qualified only 4th fastest, doing the mile Trenton Speedway track in 32.60 seconds—behind 2 rear-engined Fords and the rear-engined Offy Trackburner, chassis courtesy of former World Driving Champion Jack Brabham—for Oklahoman John Zink. And A. J. had broken his brakes to do it.

The sun was beating down on the track with tropic intensity, and the humidity of the Jersey air made a man sweat through his racing coveralls even if he stood perfectly still. A fantastic crowd of more than 27,000 was packed into the New Jersey Fairgrounds oval and had exhausted the soft drink concessionaires twice before the start of the race; now numerous programs were being used as fans to stir the oppressive air. When the starter's flag fluttered down, Foyt and his front-engined roadster were rolling, a poor 4th, with brake discs that had been hastily borrowed and installed. Young Bobby Marshman in the Lotus-Ford set the pace, after grabbing the lead from pole-sitter Jim McElreath in the

Brabham Trackburner, with Rodger Ward in 3rd. The sun was merciless and the hot exhausts of the cars raised the temperatures a notch more for the racers. Marshman retired with a broken radius rod, and Ward took over for 81 miles, setting record after record. Suddenly, Troy Ruttman, a huge 6-footer who had once been the *enfant terrible* of the Indianapolis set, swerved into the pits and, a second after he brought the car to a halt, collapsed. He was carried off on a stretcher, a heat prostration victim.

Then Ward, the leader, pointed to himself as he rolled past his pit, signalling for a relief driver. Rodger swooped into his pit coughing, unable to lift himself from the low car without aid. Marshman took over for him, but the lead was lost to the burly McElreath. Jim had what looked like an unsurpassable 25-second lead over Foyt, with less than half the race to go. Still the sun beat down, track temperatures reaching 143 degrees, and soon McElreath wavered down the front straight, shaking his head as if trying to clear the effects of a blow, and slowing. Texas Jim drove into the pits on the 127th mile, his fullback's shoulders slumped forward like a man who had been shot. Foyt in his front-engined "antique" had inherited the lead and the victory.

"It was hot," A. J. said afterward, "but I was too worried about my brakes to notice. I lost the rears again at about 55 miles, and I was having trouble in traffic. But I decided to go a little farther because I was holding 4th easily. I was lucky, but I guess the antique has got something on the new cars—reliability."

In the background, mechanic Bignotti snickered and said, "The guy won because a blowtorch couldn't melt him and because he's the biggest worrier on the Championship Trail. He needs something to worry about, and if he doesn't have it, like today, he'll make up something. But he's smart. Let others pay to work out the bugs in the pusher cars. We'll come in next year." George, who later left A. J., had revealed a little-known side of the man who was to win his 4th USAC crown that year and prove his credentials among the immortals at such widely separated venues as Daytona Speedway and Le Mans, in American late model stocks and in the Ford road racing prototypes. A. J. Foyt of the beaming Victory Lane smile, was—to put it euphemistically—a nitpicker.

Perhaps in American oval racing that was the way to win, because Foyt, who took his 5th USAC championship in 1967, was perhaps the all-time great in this phase of the sport and in its tributary, sprint racing. He won the title in 1960, 1961, 1963, and 1964; won more major single-seater championship races than anyone ever; and proved his versatility in occasional jaunts into late model stock cars and sports car road racing. His codrive to victory at Le Mans in 1967, for Ford Motor Company, merely displayed to the world a fact that Americans had known for some time—Foyt was a natural talent honed by great confidence and an even greater drive for success. These qualities made him a candidate for top driver of all time.

It is Trenton Speedway again, September 24, 1967, a warm Indian summer day. A. J. now owns all his own cars, rear-engined designs modified by his own experience: Ford-powered, Sheraton-Thompson sponsored Coyotes, low, with chassis-suspension setups capable of switching from oval racing to road racing. Foyt qualifies in the front row, next to Mario Andretti in the Dean Hawk. There are 200 miles to go, and the lead in the hottest USAC Championship Trail points battle in years is at stake. Andretti takes the lead, and Lloyd Ruby in a Turbo-Offy passes A. J. for 2nd and sets out after Mario. At only the 5th mile, Ruby goes underneath Andretti on the notorious far turn. Mario drops down to cut his chance of getting past, but Lloyd never lifts his foot, and the two cars spin as they make contact. A. J., following, has no choice; he spins his car masterfully to avoid making it a threesome. When the green flag slashes down again, Andretti and Ruby are finished, and Foyt is last, behind Al Unser.

Immediately he sets out to redress this situation, but the green refuses to stay out. Another spin in the back stretch involves three others, including former USRRC champion George Follmer. By the 39th mile Foyt is running 10th, despite another spin right in front of him. Follmer hits the wall on the 55th mile, starting another 3-car fracas, but escaping his flaming car. Foyt steers through, moving into 8th place. Up in the front of the pack, Bobby Unser is now challenging his brother successfully for the lead as Roger McCluskey, the former sprint champion, moves toward both. The first half of the race is becoming history as Foyt works his way to

6th; at the same time McCluskey passes Bobby Unser for the lead.

On the 102nd lap, A. J. moves to 5th, then 4th. Suddenly McCluskey rolls into the pits with a broken oil line that is to sideline him, and Foyt is 3rd, behind the 2 Unsers, who are staging a family donnybrook. Seventeen miles later, Anthony Joseph butts in, relegating Bobby to 3rd and closing on Al. It seems inevitable that A. J. will catch Al, but will it be in time? Unser's car breaks the suspense and a magneto with 37 miles to go. Foyt has come from last to 1st, and now the question is whether he has enough fuel to outlast Unser. He has and as Bobby must make a gas stop, A. J. takes the checker. Gordon Johncock is 2nd. Only 10 of 26 cars finish, and A. J. the master nitpicker, has mopped up.

Two years earlier at Riverside, January 25, 1965, the nature of the man had perhaps been revealed. He lay in a small California hospital; where the bandages didn't cover him, the bruises showed. His eyes were wide, and it seemed they had only returned to the sockets reluctantly. Yet he managed to smile. Foyt's charmed life almost had ended because he would not chance taking someone with him to the land beyond the Pearly Gates. His Ford stock car had flipped and rolled when he deliberately turned off course to avoid Marvin Panch and Junior Johnson. Had he gone straight he most assuredly would have hit either or both. It was late in the 500-mile late model race, and he was charging, trying to overtake leader Dan Gurney, trying to pull off another storybook finish as he had in rival NASCAR's Firecracker 400 the previous July 4 at Daytona.

But this was 1965, not 1964, which had been the year of his pride, his talent and his daring. His Riverside decision must have been instantaneous. What else had there been left for him to prove? In 1964 he had played Don Quixote, tilting his antique Offenhauser front-engined car against the Ford d.o.h.c. windmill, and he had knocked down the windmill time after time. He had become the first 4-time champion in the history of AAA-USAC. He had won 3 USAC stock car races and one international event; he had won 5 sprint events; he had even dazzled the road racing crowd at Nassau Speed Weeks, in the Mecom Zerex Scarab-Chevrolet, by beating all comers.

Born January 16, 1935, in Houston, son of a race driver, Foyt owned 27 Championship Trail 1sts by the time he was 30. His point total was 2nd among active drivers, and he was the 1st race driver in history to approach the $250,000 mark in annual purse winnings more than once. In 1964 in the Sheraton-Thompson Special, his Offy antique, Foyt won 7 championship races in a row, including the Indy 500. On August 23, for the Milwaukee 200, he accepted a ride in a Lotus-Ford and couldn't get it out of low gear, finishing last. Back to the antique for DuQuoin and the Indy Fairgrounds victories, and then A. J. went into the Trenton 200 to battle Parnelli Jones in the Lotus Ford. He tried, but he broke the car trying, and Jones became the only man to beat him twice on the 1964 Championship Trail.

Where do you begin with a phenomenon? You begin in Houston where A. J. Senior ran a garage and competed with some success in midgets, and where A. J. Junior ran roadsters, motorcycles, and finally midgets by the time he was 18. You begin when he tried his luck on the IMCA circuit and won at a fair in Nebraska and somewhere in the Dakotas. You begin when he switched at age 22 into USAC, determined to make money and beat the world to its knees. He competed in Midwest sprints, midgets, and 5 championship races. His smooth driving style, plus a desire to win so intense that it radiated from him, attracted car owners. He talked a good race, too.

In 1958 he came to Indianapolis in the Dean Van Lines car and passed his rookie test, then qualified on the 1st day out with a speed of 143.130 m.p.h. A spin took him from the running in the 148th lap. At the Race of Two Worlds in Monza that year there was praise for many of the Americans, but for A. J. there was the offer, made in all seriousness, of a place in the Grand Prix sun. (According to one source it was made by Alfa Romeo, which entertained passing hopes of returning to GP competition at that juncture.) He won his 1st championship at Sacramento Fairgrounds that year. In 1959 he finished 10th at Indianapolis and joined the Champion 100-Mile-an-Hour club.

In 1960's Indy he began 3 years with the Bowes Seal Fast team in which he won 12 Championship Trail stops, including his 1st victory in the Indianapolis 500 at an average speed of 139.130 just before the car's clutch failed. In 1962 he lasted 70 laps, crashed, and returned to drive Elmer George's Sarks Tarzian Special for 20 laps before that car was sidelined by starter failure.

For the 1963 season Foyt switched sponsors. He joined the Sheraton-Thompson racing equipe of William B. Ansted and S. D. Murphy. His 1964 Indianapolis victory at 147.350 m.p.h. average speed was one of the Offy engine's most glorious moments and the Ford forces' darkest. When Foyt joined Sheraton-Thompson he acquired Bignotti as a chief mechanic. In 1965, after the Riverside mishap, A. J. began to lose. Yes, he was not strong yet, and he was still in pain when he returned to competition for Phoenix and Trenton. But his 1st Indianapolis ride in a so-called funny car—the term passed out of oval racing once everyone had one—was a losing one, and that was unforgivable. The rupture became official at Langhorne's 100-miler, and A. J. acquired Parnelli Jones's chief wrench man, John Poulsen, who also later left. So he became a car owner and constructor as well as builder, and the hair on his head rapidly disappeared. There was no question of Foyt's place in American racing. He was the among the greatest drivers —until someone better comes along.

One would think a record 42 championship victories

222

and 5 national championships, 26 sprint car victories, 19 midget car victories, and 22 in stock by 1970 would be the basis for enough immortality for one human being. But there was another side of Foyt—the businessman. That impelled him to take over the distribution of Ford d.o.h.c. racing engines (at $27,000 the copy) when Louis Meyer passed out of the picture. That also impelled him to design his own funny car, the Coyote. He became a nitpicker here, too—testing and improving the fuel jets, figuring out ways of reducing the cost of the engines. Foyt got the chance when Ford, slowly disengaging from a monstrous commitment to racing, told Louis Meyer, Inc., that it could have $800,000 worth of engines and parts for $40,000. Not having won Indianapolis in quite a while, the Meyers had to pass. Foyt Engine Corp. stepped in and took over. Luckily—for his engine business—he managed to finish 10th at Indianapolis in 1970. The finish seemed to lend credence to his claim that he assembled every engine the same way, and he did not have a special design for himself. At Springfield, Ill., in 1971 he was in the back of the pack with less than half the race left and passed everyone for the victory.

Back home there were an A. J. Foyt III, a daughter, and Jerry Foyt. As they grew up they did not see much of their father. Foyt realized this and still he went on racing—stocks, midgets, championship cars—despite 5 USAC championships. Some said he would never retire but Bignotti disagreed. "A. J. will quit on the spot when he knows that he, not his car, lost a race he should have won."

Obviously that time wasn't at hand. By scoring his 43rd Trail victory at Phoenix, A. J. finished 2nd on the '71 season. And both in 1971 and in 1972, Foyt terrorized the NASCAR boys. In '71, before vacating the Wood Bros. Mercury, he won the Miller 500 at Ontario and the Atlanta 500. In '72 he won the Daytona 500, repeated his Miller 500 triumph and finished only a car length behind Bobby Allison in the Atlanta 500. But even though an injury shelved him for most of the 1972 season A. J. managed one national title, the USAC dirt crown.

FRED FRAME

Born in Exeter, N.H., in 1895, Fabulous Fred Frame moved to the California sunshine to become a part-time gardener and motorcycle expert. The gardening led to a contact with the horseless carriage and a chauffeur's job for a wealthy Los Angeles family. As the holder of this exalted position, Frame was expected to keep the car running. That was no small task before World War I but the youngster managed rather well.

There always is a first race, usually one which the hero driver would rather forget. Fred's came at the old

Ascot Speedway in Los Angeles on Christmas Day 1915, in a stripped-down Model T Ford. He fouled a plug and in the process of trying to clear it set a new record for oil and smoke coming from a 4-cylinder engine going nowhere. He and mechanic Ed Winfield had installed a 3-gallon oil tank for a 10-mile race and the poor T engine had no recourse but to spew out oil and smoke like a child protesting an overdose of cod liver oil.

Frame began racing at Ascot with increasing regularity and lost his chauffeur's job, some say because he practiced broadslides with the mistress of the house on board, but it was probably because he didn't want to be tied down so many days a week. Although Fred enjoyed racing, money was the important thing to him. He is one of the few drivers on record to have passed up Indy (1930) to drive in a half-mile sprint car race.

Frame's Model T in which he resumed racing in 1919 was a marvel, maybe the ultimate Model T conversion. He slapped a Craig-Hunt head on the T block. This head incorporated a single o.h.c. design with 16 valves, 4 per cylinder. Mounted on a Model T frame lowered as much as possible, this engine had its debut at an AAA-sanctioned race some 200 miles north of Los Angeles at a place called Santa Maria. It was a half-mile oval, and Frame started in the middle of the front row. He took the lead on the 2nd turn because both his competitors went straight through the fence on the 1st, and he never was headed for the entire 25 miles. He won $529 and this decided him—he was going to be a pro driver. By the early twenties, Frame was an established dirt track ace and usually tried to play every angle to wring more money from each appearance. One of his ploys was to have someone else drive the car he owned, while Fred hired out as a chauffeur for someone else. This gave Fred 2 shots at the money.

Frame believed his No. 99 Hooker T was the most potent Model T Ford ever built. What the engine was in reality was a Miller d.o.h.c. superimposed on a Model T block, with 4 carburetors. This 1923 wonder had one defect; it snapped crankshafts with amazing consistency —one every 7 laps or less. Frame had to have special shafts made out of German steel for about $600. These endured, and the Hooker T (named after car owner Harry Hooker) was virtually unbeatable, even besting Miller championship race cars. Fabulous Fred ran the boards at California's Culver City and the dirt at Ascot, but made his reputation on converted horse tracks in tank towns from there to the shores of the Atlantic. He got appearance money and a share of the purse when he won, which was usually. He survived his first bad spill trying to guess his way through a cloud of Abilene dust. In 1926 he won the 100-miler at Kalamazoo, Mich., grand daddy of the championship circuit's dirt stops, for his first major AAA victory.

But to old-timers in the Eastern part of the U.S. at least, Frame is equated with the old board track at Woodbridge, N.J., where the great rivalry between

Frame and doughty Lou Moore waxed strong through the life of the high-banked half-miler. The track opened in 1929, and in the next two years Fred won 16 of 18 features, receiving appearance money and the maximum $775 share of the purse. Moore gave Fred his stiffest competition and finally challenged him to a series of track record attempts. The track owner imported a timer from New York with a clock accurate to one hundredth of a second for the event. Frame broke his own record, going 20.60 seconds around the half-mile. Moore turned 20.40. Frame came back and went 20.03. Moore spun on his final lap and crossed the finish line backwards. The New York timer's equipment chose that moment to break down, but a couple of hand watches caught Lou under the 20 seconds that was announced. The AAA observer disallowed this, offering Lou another lap. Moore was still green from his backward excursion and he refused.

Fred consistently passed up championship races in order to take part in the AAA fair circuit that extended from Maine to Illinois and Pennsylvania. He did so because he got $400 appearance cash per race, and could win another $500. He could do this twice a week all season. That's why Frame passed up the 1930 Indy race for an event at his beloved Woodbridge. Freddie's Indy record is deceptive. He drove relief for 2 cars in 1927, which finished 10th and 11th. In 1928 he relieved Bill White and finished 8th. In 1929 he was running 2nd in an Earl Cooper-owned, supercharged 91 cu. in. Miller when the blowers cut out. In 1931 Harry Hartz enlisted him for his Duesenberg Special, a d.o.h.c. 8 of 150.3 cu. in. Fred finished 2nd, just 44 seconds behind Lou Schneider.

Then came the 1932 race, run before rows of half-empty seats. Fred was in Hartz's 181-cu. in. Miller front-wheel-drive 8. Lou Moore set fast time of 117.363 m.p.h.; Fred was almost 4-m.p.h. slower. Moore led the 1st lap; then Billy Arnold led until he crashed in the 147th mile. Freddie was running as fast as the leaders when he was running. He was practically commuting to the pits because the radiator had sprung a leak. Ira Hall, Bob Carey, Howdy Wilcox, Ernie Triplett all forged into the lead for brief moments of glory. Wilbur Shaw led, and even Frame—until the water temperature gauge sent him pitward once more.

Shaw led comfortably at 300 miles with Frame 2nd thanks to 6 pit stops, riding 8-m.p.h. faster. Some 2½ miles later Wilbur was on the sidelines with an addled axle. Frame inherited the lead and gave his riding mechanic orders to watch for "overtaking cars." Meanwhile he slowed down sufficiently to keep the engine reasonably cool despite the leak. He won ($32,500) with Wilcox, Cliff Bergere's Studebaker, and Carey following in that order. His 104.144 average set a record.

Frame led in the same car in 1933, but a broken valve eventually sidelined him. He did make Henry Ford happy that year by winning the stock-car part of the

revival of the 203-mile Elgin, Ill., road races, in a Ford roadster. He praised the transmission highly because it enabled him to negotiate a sharp left after a downhill straight by dropping into 2nd gear and shuddering around the corner. Of course, the reason he did this, he added, was because the Ford's brakes were so bad.

After failing to qualify at Indianapolis in 1934, Frame drove the Hartz car to 7th overall in 1935, but lasted only 4 laps in 1936. He drove relief for Billy Devore, helping him to a 7th-place finish. The next year saw Frame at the Brickyard with his own Duesenberg racer, but rain during the qualifying period kept him on the sidelines. Shortly after that he switched to IMCA allegiance because the AAA fair circuit had lost most of its best dates.

Competing with mixed success against Emory Collins and Gus Schrader, Frame retired at the end of the 1938 season. He came back in 1939 to drive a Hudson stock car in practice at Oakland Speedway in California and crashed, sustaining injuries that hospitalized him for months. That convinced Fred, and permanent retirement stuck after that. He lost his son, Bob, in an IMCA sprint-car crash at the Owatona Fair, Minn., in 1947, and seldom came to see auto racing after that. He died in 1962.

WILLIAM C. FRANCE

William C. France was known as Bill France, Jr., and like his father was a NASCAR delegate to ACCUS-FIA, president of NASCAR, and an executive of the Speedway Corporation that controls Daytona and Talladega International. There had never been any doubt where his place in life was or what he was going to do. Younger brother Jim had some options, but decided to come back to the family business eventually. Billy would be around to take over when that phenomenon called William Henry Getty France moved into reluctant retirement.

Billy was not quite as tall and prepossessing as his father; he was a baby when the Frances moved from Washington, D.C., to the Daytona Beach area, but he was old enough to remember when the family wasn't wealthy. He grew up with stock-car racing, helping out in the days when France was promoting at dirt tracks by tacking up signs and maybe selling programs. He favored his mother in looks and size and even personality—a quiet little boy who knew from the beginning that his father was special to others besides himself. He grew into a quiet man who accepted the ever-increasing number of tasks WHGF imposed upon him, and did them as well as he could. He learned by repetition, and his mistakes were minimized because there was WHGF in the background, moving in like *deus ex machina* to set things right.

It was inevitable that he would try driving race cars. WHGF, a former driver himself, was not exactly over-

joyed at the prospect, but in 1954 Billy was racing—in a Rambler. There were about 6 starts, mostly on dirt and at tracks where 50 m.p.h. was daredevil speeding. Buck Baker and Jimmy Lewallen sandwiched him once, and he tapped the wall. Another time he played hare to the regular drivers' hounds and wound up 3rd. Quickly he realized that collecting tickets, parking cars, flagging, scoring—anything—was what racing was all about for him, as long as he was not driving. He had a natural-born talent as a spectator.

When he was made a NASCAR vice-president, he rubbed silences with the greats of Detroit, for WHGF was doing the talking, but even that gave him confidence and polish. Finally he was put in charge of the Daytona 500 and the other superspeedway races. He was the man who flipped caution lights, stopped races, acted on information that specialists like the chief steward fed to him. He sat high in the control tower and did his job while WHGF revealed himself to VIPs and fleetingly to the press and TV.

Billy France, Jr., married a beauty queen—he was a good catch by then—and sired a son and a daughter. He learned how to fly; it was a real release. He professed to enjoy auto racing, but he loved flying, and earned a multi-engine rating. It is difficult for the sons of self-made fathers if they remain in the same profession—difficult but not necessarily unpleasant. Problems are different when one starts from the top, and no one ever knows how proficient a son is until the father is no longer a factor. Meanwhile, Billy France did his job as best he could, and in 1971 he became top-dog at Day-

tona when his father handed over the reins and concentrated on NASCAR and politics.

At times before he took over, Billy France had his silly moment. Moments like the time he precipitously banned Shell Oil from Daytona about half an hour before the 24-hour race. Well and good, except Ferrari and several other teams ran on Shell, and they needed the fuel. An emergency shuttle had to be set up to bring drums of gas inside the Daytona compound as the Shell trucks stood outside.

Or the time Billy decided he didn't like a certain soft drink company's sign because "we're committed to Pepsi." He tore the sign down. But this company was sponsoring a car and had cleared the sign—on the side of their race team's trailer headquarters—with Pepsi and Bill France, Sr. It was tempest-in-the-teapot time. This kind of thing seemed over by 1971, however, and maybe that's why William H. G. France now was willing to let his son assume a more significant role in the father's personal fiefdom, American stock-car racing. He succeeded Big Bill as president of NASCAR in 1972.

WILLIAM H. G. FRANCE

The big man was smooth and polished, well-barbered and thickening slightly at the waist, all trophies of good living. His clothes were well cut and he spoke easily to generals and congressmen and would-be presidents, just as he did to corporation presidents. But he was angry now and the polish seemed in danger of dropping away

225

like a costume to reveal the real man underneath. William Henry Getty France was confronting the unpleasant prospect of rain on his parade and he did not like it. This was Alabama International Speedway, faster than Daytona, newer than Daytona, potentially more profitable than Daytona, and the drivers were spoiling its debut. Corporation presidents could not help. George Wallace could not help. Mendel Rivers could not help. Mere drivers had rained on his parade. They wouldn't race.

Well, if Richard Petty, Lee Roy Yarbrough, Cale Yarborough, David Pearson and the rest of the reigning stars of NASCAR thought the track was unsafe for the 200 m.p.h. stock cars, France was prepared at the age of 60 with a bad leg to prove them wrong. There would be a Talladega 500 in 1969 if he had to drive his personal car. No Professional Drivers Association, no group of men who were mere drivers, were bigger than NASCAR. And Bill France *was* NASCAR.

Fonty Flock and Tim Flock and Curtis Turner had been stars who thought they were bigger than NASCAR. They had learned. Back in the beginning Glenn Dunnaway had fought NASCAR and where was he? Just a footnote in some histories to the effect that he had been disqualified for spreading his springs.

Bill France had fought his way to his position. Remember the beach races at Daytona back in 1936? He and Annie and Billy, Jr., had run out of money there en route to Miami from Pikeville, Md. He was 25 then and a driver himself with a Model T dirt track car into which he shoehorned his 6-foot, 5-inch frame. He got a gas station job and finished 5th in the race, but promoting the beach races seemed like a better idea. It still was a long way from Horse Pasture, Va., where he had been born or Washington, D.C., where he had been schooled.

He had worked and driven his way up to the founding of NASCAR in 1948, establishing himself as president. There were races around the barrels on Jax Beach, Fernandina Beach, and elsewhere, where he had ensured a payoff by promoting and competing and keeping protection handy. There had been the long hauls into moonshine country where he and colleagues literally scratched a track out of a cow pasture, held their race and hauled on to the next stop. His rise had been steady because he stayed around to pay off the prize money, and he made sure none of the good old boys taking a busman's holiday from running illegal whisky had any unfair mechanical advantage. Bill France was physically big enough to do that.

During World War II he had helped build sub chasers at Daytona because the money in that was better than anything around. After VJ Day it was time to promote again. There was the 1945 race at Raleigh, N.C., which he hoped would turn into a classic. It didn't. There was the revival of beach racing at Daytona in 1946 and there was the hope that AAA Contest Board would sanction a stock-car division. He went to Washington to present the proposal of a stock car division for himself and a group of promoters based mainly in the south. Jim Lamb laughed at him. France remembered that, and NASCAR was the answer, although Red Vogt, Ray Parks, and a bunch of Atlanta guys actually chartered an organization of that name in Georgia. The real organizational meeting came in Daytona Beach at the Streamline Hotel. Lou Ossinsky, a lawyer, and Ed Otto, a promoter from up north, and about 37 or 38 other men were in at the beginning, but William Henry Getty France was the president. Twenty-two years later he still was.

Speed Weeks was his idea. The beach-road course—4.1 miles of pure excitement and low comedy—was his idea. And finally, when he felt Speed Weeks was important enough to the winter economy of Daytona Beach and Volusia County, the Daytona Racing and Beach Recreational Facilities District was his idea—although the dog interests and the horse interests and the motel operators all thought the idea was theirs. He was talking about a superspeedway as early as 1955. His last driving feat, the 1950 Pan American Road Race with Curtis Turner, was long behind him, and through trial and error and the magnificent tech inspections of Norris Friel—a boyhood acquaintance—NASCAR was a fairly solid and respected sanctioning group. The first corporation money was already finding its way into NASCAR coffers, and while several NASCAR projects—the motel recommendation service in competition with AAA, the product performance bureau, and the record run department in competition with AAA—were doomed to disappointment, racing was becoming the number one Southern American pastime.

Daytona International Speedway was a stepping stone to millionaire status. The polish had been applied—or rather, Bill France had learned that at play, away from home, the biggest tycoon was just a good old boy in a $250 suit who drank scotch or martinis instead of corn whiskey and whose drunken babblings likely had a northern accent. He found his backing, some from tycoons who played hard and some from tycoons for whom he conjured up the same visions of golden plums that he dreamed himself.

Now they were raining on his parade at Talladega, on his Alabama International Speedway, at the track which had the perfect location for crowds of 100,000, at the track that was all that Daytona was and a little faster, a little better built, a little more the property of France. Richard Petty, the president of the PDA, had called a press conference and said that he and the other members of the PDA thought Talladega was unsafe at the speeds Grand Nationals would go. The track surface was wavy and no tires could stand up to it. Goodyear had said so. Firestone had withdrawn.

France remembered that 1959 Daytona inaugural. It had been a photo finish between an Iowan named Johnny Beauchamp and Lee Petty. He remembered how it took him until late in the evening to discover evidence that Lee Petty had won. He remembered the awful day when Lee Petty and Beauchamp had gone over the wall at the last embankment before the stretch. Both lived, but Lee Petty hovered near death for awhile, and France had wondered out loud if any activity was worth a friend's life. Richard Petty had won more NASCAR Grand Nationals than any living man. With the victory totals of the other boycotters, there was little left out of the NASCAR record book. But they had rained on his parade.

There would be a Talladega 500. He called Johnny Marcum of ARCA to see who was available to drive. He called Ford and Chrysler to see if the cars—the swift Ford Talladegas and the Dodge Daytonas—were to be made available. He started a search for defectors and inquired what defection from PDA might cost. The drivers had announced the boycott Saturday; the race was Sunday. There would be a Talladega 500.

There was. Old Ramo Stott came down from IMCA country, and Jungle Jim Hurtubise came down from Tonowanda, N.Y. Bobby Isaac had decided to run: he wanted a superspeedway victory so much he could taste the kiss of the Union 76 Racestopper girl. A handsome kid named Richard Brickhouse had quit PDA for the chance to drive the pole-winning Daytona droopnose. The rest of the field was mostly from the GT class—Mustangs, Javelins, Camaros, Darts. Maybe 5 cars out of the field of 36 could run at the speeds to which the PDA objected. Coo Coo Marlin and some of his modified boys were also around for scenery.

It was a good race, such as it was, and Richard Brickhouse got the kiss and the money and went back to his Carolina farm. William Henry Getty France smiling, urbane, polished, barbered, congratulated the winner and said the fans could have a free ticket to the next attraction because the advertised drivers were not there. And he said the PDA boycotters would have to post bond guaranteeing their appearance at Martinsville, Va., before NASCAR could allow them to race because they had disappointed fans who now could not trust them.

Lee Roy Yarbrough got into his Continental and drove away looking dark looks. And Richard Petty and father Lee and brother Maurice went home to Randleman, N.C. And Pearson, Yarborough, and the rest went away too. They had rained on Bill France, and he had won the victory—his parade had gone on.

But France knew this was another turning point, another step down a road which seemingly had become the superhighway to wealth and glory. Would he beat the PDA as he had beaten Curtis Turner's union? Could he ultimately find a way to end the threat to his sovereignty in NASCAR with compromise, as he had adjudicated among the car companies each time the engine formula was changed? It seemed the same, yet it felt different. The jury was still out, and the PDA still solidifying as the 1970 season began and progressed.

Mendel Rivers, successor to Harley J. Earl of General Motors who succeeded Cannonball Baker as high commissioner of NASCAR, could not help from his post as chairman of the House Armed Services Committee. Only Bill France—whose commissioners seemed to reflect the stages of his life—could help NASCAR. But would he?

He had to, and he did, but it took time, a few months to find the right way to woo the drivers back. He figured out how to make the drivers feel safe again. The change came in plenty of time to be tested before the 2nd Talladega 500—mainly a metal plate in the carburetor to limit speed and match the cars more evenly. France was still NASCAR. He could still keep his legends intact as the saviour of the man behind the wheel.

"The big day for me came in 1930, when I was living in Washington, D.C.," he would say. "I took the sprint car I had built to a race in Pikeville, Md. When the promoter announced the size of the purse to the crowd, I was ready for some big money. But when I finished 4th in the main event, what I got was $10. I was pretty angry. I asked the promoter where all the money from that big purse went. He laughed and told me that was just to impress the fans.

"In 1934 when I ran out of funds in Daytona, I took a job as a house painter to feed Billy, Jr., and to get back on the racing trail. When I started to race at Atlanta, Savannah, and all over Florida, I became more and more disturbed about how the promoter could tell a driver anything and get away with it—we weren't accountants and we couldn't have seen the gate money anyway. That's what eventually started NASCAR. Whatever purse is announced, the drivers get every penny."

France bore the scars of many battles as he presided over the growth of a giant combination of business and sport. In 1954 at Daytona Beach on the old beach-road course, thousands left the resort thinking Tim Flock had won. Newspapers from coast to coast printed the results. Much later NASCAR announced Tim had used an illegal carburetor and was thus disqualified, giving the victory to Lee Petty. The protest threatened to destroy the credibility of NASCAR; Tim Flock quit racing and took the case to court; newspapers threatened never to print NASCAR results. France solved that one by indirection—a new NASCAR classic on a regulation track to be built especially for the purpose, the Darlington Southern 500. Time did the rest.

The next 3 years—of unbridled Detroit interest in promoting car sales through horsepower and racing—France was on a 24-hour-a-day treadmill, trying to be instant judge and jury and keep NASCAR rules fair. He did it well enough that, when the factories all left in 1957, NASCAR survived as a major league. Unions, factories, even the establishment of an improbable but successful international road race in an area of stock car fans, he accomplished them all. NASCAR was Bill France's own parade, rain or shine, and as long as he drew breath the rain wouldn't fall for long.

He stepped down officially from the presidency of NASCAR after 1971 after installing Billy, his son, in the job. He also had finally convinced Jimmy, his other son, to come back to race administration and he had insured their future by installing an enormously competent backup team headed by Lin Kuchler, Russ Moyer and Linn Hendershot. Kuchler he had lured from the American Motorcycle Association, Moyer was a NASCAR veteran executive and Hendershot came from USAC.

And then Bill France, now merely president of the corporation controlling Daytona and Talladega, had gone off to make Gov. George Wallace of Alabama the President of the United States. They won in Florida and in Michigan and they were very strong elsewhere. But a would-be assassin's bullet crippled Gov. Wallace and ended that effort . . . at least for 1972. So Talladega and Daytona again became Bill France's parade. The larger one had passed by with a different grand marshal at its head.

LARRY FRANK

Larry S. Frank grinned and joked with the reporters at Riverside for the 1965 NASCAR road race, for his Ford—as in past NASCAR contests—had movie cameras attached to it. Howard Hawks was making a movie about Grand National stock car racing and there was to be film footage of actual competition. The prematurely graying father of 5 obviously enjoyed the attention. "Heck," he said, "wouldn't it be funny if I were to go out and win, too. That front movie camera wouldn't get much, only the back one." He knew it was next to impossible, for he had to pit frequently to reload cameras, but the urge of competition was still burning. Frank had summed himself up after his 1962 victory in the Southern 500 in a Ratus Walters Ford, his only major victory in 15 years of racing. "Once you get competition in your blood, it's there to stay," he said. "There's nothing you can do about it but go out and race as well as you can and as often as you can."

Born April 29, 1931, in Mountain City, Tenn., son of a farmer who moved to Ohio, Larry was a Marine at 14 in the latter stages of World War II when he lied about his age to join up. He saw service on the Pacific Islands and in China, played fullback on the Pacific all-service football team. He was tattooed and became a sailor before coming home. In 1947 Frank became a regional Golden Gloves boxing champ in the light-heavyweight division. That was the same year he began to race, first on motorcycles, then in midgets at Culver City, Calif., in September. His goal originally was Indianapolis and he moved there while competing in midgets, sprints, convertibles and stocks. But, as in boxing, he somehow learned this goal was wrong for him and switched to

NASCAR ragtops moving South. He finished 2nd in the convertible division in 1958 and 1959, front-charging all the way, but never winning a race. Hard on equipment because he did not like to be in the pack, Frank was hard on himself, too, crashing frequently. In the Bob Osiecki Mad Dog car that was trying for the Daytona Speedway purse of $10,000 for the 1st runs over 180 m.p.h., Frank travelled 200 briefly and spun out.

A Thunderbird once disintegrated under Larry, dunking him in the lake at Daytona, and he slid on the roofs of stockers so often he is nonchalant at the thought. But there was always that 1 big victory to be remembered for the self-styled "hardest-luck guy in auto racing." Frank was far from a favorite as the Labor Day stock-car classic held its 13th renewal in 1962. Fireball Roberts had won the pole for the 4th consecutive year, wrecking all qualifying marks in his Banjo Matthews Pontiac—130.256 for 4 laps and 130.503 for one. Roberts elected to sit on the outside because that is the fastest way to the "groove" at Darlington. Next to him sat Junior Johnson in a Pontiac, and behind them were Fred Lorenzen in an air-conditioned Ford and Bobby Johns in still another Pontiac. There were 3 Petty Plymouths, too, driven by young Richard, Bunkie Blackburn and Jim Pascal, while Nelson Stacy in the other Holman-Moody Ford also rode in air-conditioned comfort.

All were considered better risks than Frank, far back in the pack, in a Ford sponsored by a Washington restauranteur. When the green flag dropped, Fireball made the groove quickest and stayed in front for 58 laps before Bobby Johns passed him. Trying to regain the lead, Fireball blew a tire and was wrecked against the guard rail on lap 74. The caution flag was just what the Petty Plymouths needed. On lap 76 Petty moved to the front before turning over to Pascal for laps 77–85. But Johns was not through yet. He snaked his car in front on lap 86 and held on through the 125th lap, aided by a caution from lap 111, when Ralph Earnhardt wrecked Jack Smith's Pontiac.

Meanwhile, Frank was improving his position slowly, but there were hotter boys to be heard from now. The factory-sponsored Ford-Pontiac-Plymouth battle was far from over. Lorenzen took over for Holman-Moody for 31 laps only to lose to Richard for 4, then to Junior Johnson for 19. Petty charged ahead again on the strength of a faster pit stop, and this time held on for 106 turns around the one and $\frac{3}{8}$-mile track. He ran much of the Pontiac and factory Ford threat into the ground, but he didn't shake Frank now pushing him in 2nd place. On the 295th lap, Larry finally led as fans and old stock car hands blinked and shouted in amazement. He led until the 341st of 364 laps.

Then the familiar Petty blue was ahead again and the Pontiacs were charging. It was a temporary situation; Frank had decided this was it—go for broke until you're broken or win it all. On lap 346 he charged ahead of

Petty and stayed there. As the laps ticked by, he could hear the crowd screaming as Johnson and Pearson in Pontiacs and Marvin Panch in a Ford closed the gap. Could he last? The redoubtable Junior was drawing closer and closer. Finally the white flag flashed, then the checker. Larry had won, just 5 seconds ahead of Johnson.

Frank started around the track for his insurance lap and he gave the crowd something else to roar about—he blew a tire and spun off. The hard luck had been about a half lap late, a delay worth $21,730 to Frank and his car owner. For 1963 Frank didn't even have a ride to defend his crown. In the first 3 races after Darlington, Larry lost a wheel at Lincoln Speedway in Nebraska, broke a rear end at Richmond and an axle at Moyock, N.C. Some time later the kart track operator caught on as a teammate to Ned Jarrett in the Bondy Long cars, mostly for the camera work. He finished 3rd in the 1965 Daytona 250 modified classic after leading the race earlier. After that he faded into the sportsman ranks because he found Grand National life as an independent too unprofitable.

ARCHIE FRAZER-NASH

Archibald Frazer-Nash took out his 1st driving license for a motorcycle in 1904 and used it when switching to a De Dion Bouton even though he was technically under age. In his teens he was an apprentice to a predecessor company of English Electric, then entered City & Guilds College, from which he graduated with an engineering degree and an acquaintence with H. R. (Bill) Godfrey.

Frazer-Nash's first post-college project was to build himself a car, a simple, wooden-framed 4-wheeler powered by a 7-h.p. Peugeot motorcycle engine. With characteristic humor the "car" was dubbed the Creepabout. Bill Godfrey checked into the stable that was behind's Archie's home, and in 1910 this became the place in which GN, one of the great cyclecar manufacturers, was born. The stable showed Archie's humor as well, for it was renamed the Elms Works. The first car the pair actually produced, in 1910–11, was temporarily dubbed the Duocar, but as soon as a formal production car was introduced in 1911—a JAP-powered 2-cylinder car—the GN name superceded Duocar.

Archie was competition-minded, and in 1913 he took out a Cyclecar Grand Prix entry in a 2-seater, but in the race an overhead crankpin came adrift. Things turned round rather quickly after that, though. In the Amiens Voiturette GP, Archie ran the race's fastest lap before retiring. Then he built a special, nicknamed Kim, that was highly successful both before and after World War I; so successful, in fact, that it was rightly billed as the fastest cyclecar in the world.

Frazer-Nash came back from the war and the Royal Flying Corps as a Captain and quickly got back into the cockpit, both of Kim and of Akela, another GN-based racing special. Sprints, hillclimbs and Brooklands races all were contested and won. The high spot, perhaps, was Archie's victory in the 1,100-c.c. class at the first 200-miler at Brooklands in 1921 at 71.56 m.p.h. In 1922 Godfrey left GN, but Archie carried on until 1928 when he, too, left, selling out to the Aldington brothers. He became a consulting engineer in several fields, continuing nearly until to his death in 1965, as capable and humorous as ever.

PAUL FRERE

The year 1960 was Paul Frere's year. With fellow Belgian Olivier Gendebien he won the Le Mans 24-Hour race in a Ferrari at 109.19 m.p.h. Alone, he won the Spa Grand Prix for sports cars in a Porsche at 97.45 m.p.h. and in a Cooper single-seater he won the South African GP, not a World Championship event to be sure, but a major Formula Libre battle, at 84.88 m.p.h., edging none other than Stirling Moss. The most interesting thing about Frere was that, although he raced for some 15 years, he really was a automobile writer who enjoyed total involvement in the sport he was covering.

Frere was born at Le Havre, January 30, 1917, and saw his first race at the age of 9, a 24-hour race at Spa, which might explain his long-standing later involvement with that enduro. Paul first competed in 1935 in a borrowed Amilcar in which he won an Austrian gymkhana. He didn't compete again until 1946, although he bought

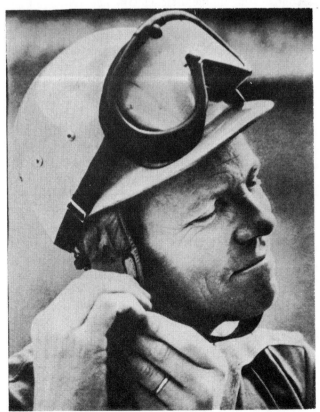

a bent Imperia in 1939 with the intention of trying his luck, only to have the war intervene. The car was sold in 1946 and the profits partially used to buy a 125-c.c. DKW motorcycle. Paul raced and won his class his 1st time out on this machine, but, he always pointed out, his was the only machine in its class. In 1948 he joined Jacques Swaters's 12-year-old MG PB Special for the Spa 24-hour race, and they finished 4th in class. The following year the record books say Frere shared an Aston Martin with St. John Horsfell, the Briton, at Spa and finished 2nd in class and 4th overall, but Frere said he never once drove in the race, Tim Horsfell going all the way alone.

Starting in 1950, Frere drove in the Spa 24-hour production car race in both sedan and sports car categories and consistently won, no matter what kind of car he piloted. In 1950 and 1951 he won in Dyna Panhards, in 1952 in an American Oldsmobile, in 1953–54 in a big Chrysler, in 1954–55 in an Alfa, in 1955 in an Aston Martin, and in 1956 in a Jaguar and a Ferrari. But starting in 1952, he also was racing in single-seaters and in major endurance races for sports car prototype machinery. Britain's John Heath would provide the formula car opportunities with his HWM Formula 2 cars when F2 was the major formula in international racing. That first year in F2, Paul won the Frontières GP at 90.15 m.p.h., but was 5th in his initial major *grande épreuve*, the Belgian GP, which was also the European GP that season. In the German GP he retired.

The next season Frere was 2nd in the Eifelrennen to Baron Tulo de Graffenreid's Maserati by a mere 1.7 seconds, 10th in the Belgian GP, and retired in the Swiss. But in other racing he did a bit better. With a Chrysler he won his class in the Mille Miglia, and at Le Mans, sharing a Porsche with another racing journalist, Richard von Frankenberg, he scored still another class victory. With George Abecassis in an HWM sports car at the Rheims 12-hour, Frere retired. In 1954 Paul became associated with Aston Martin, being run by John Wyer, and shared a car with Carroll Shelby at Le Mans, but they retired (originally he was to ride a Mercedes with another American, John Fitch, but the car was not ready for the 24 hours). In a Gordini, Frere retired once again in the Belgian GP, and his fate was the same in the Supercortemaggiore GP at Monza in a Gordini shared with Jean Behra. He retired, too, in the French and German GPs (in the latter losing a wheel at speed though able to stop safely).

In 1955, the year Paul was crowned Belgian Champion, he signed on with Ferrari as a reserve driver, 1st appearing as a few-lap relief to Piero Taruffi at Monaco, then coming in 4th in the Belgian GP. In the Swedish GP he crashed and broke a leg. But in sports car racing the year was a success, Frere winning the Spa GP in the Aston at 107.80 m.p.h. and sharing a 2nd with former HWM teammate Peter Collins at Le Mans and a class victory. The year 1956 saw a Le Mans retirement in

a D Jaguar, a 3rd in the Rome GP for sports cars in a Ferrari, and 3rds in the Belgian and Spa Grands Prix, both in Ferraris. In the Rheims 12 hours Frere was 2nd with Mike Hawthorne in a D Jag. And, despite a flip that almost wrecked his Renault completely, he won his class in the Mille Miglia. That year, too, was enlived by Frere's giving his monarch, the King of the Belgians, a demonstration Aston Martin ride at some 125 m.p.h. along the highway at royal command, then getting a royal chauffeuring back to the palace at a similar speed.

Frere and Gendebien shared Grand Touring victories in the 1957–58 Rheims 12-Hour races with runs of 104.02 m.p.h. and 106.05 m.p.h. in Ferraris. In that latter year Paul's Aston Martin was 2nd only to Masten Gregory's Lister-Jaguar in the Spa GP; in 1959 he shared 2nd with Maurice Trintignant in an Aston at Le Mans as the tail end of an Aston 1, 2 finish led by Roy Salvadori and Shelby. After the fantastic 1960 season, when Frere was 43 years old, he was about to quit racing, although there were still a few rides and a startling 2nd in a Fiat with Lucien Bianchi in the 1963 production car Nurburgring 12-hour race. In these later years there were books and articles to write for the American as well as European markets, and 45 was getting old for a racing driver to battle against the likes of the Jim Clark or Graham Hill.

NORRIS FRIEL

Born in 1906 in the Washington, D.C., area, Norris Friel brought to his job, as chief of NASCAR's technical men, 20 years of experience as a service manager in a car agency and 16 as an area representative for the AAA Contest Board. He met and became friendly with Bill France in the Washington area in the early thirties, when France was tooling motorbikes and Norris was running a sprint car with no great success at the old Arlington Fairgrounds (present site of the Pentagon). When AAA suddenly quit racing, France, who had had to contend with some embarrassing rhubarbs like Tim Flock's and Fireball Roberts's disqualifications after apparently winning major races, needed Friel. Long considered one of the finest AAA racing officials, Norris, a stern-faced, portly man, did an exceptional job for NASCAR in keeping some of the sharpest engineering brains and mechanical whiz-bangs in line with the organization's rules. In fact, his recommendations often helped fashion the rules.

Friel traveled the Dixie superspeedway circuit to ride herd on the boys. Most of his staff were part timers who did not need to rely on the inspection job for their incomes. Friel and his men were dedicated to their task of making sure no one got an illegal advantage. If a crew worked late, there was a NASCAR inspector present to keep things honest. At the big NASCAR races, the top 3 finishers were impounded in case of protest.

Before each race, NASCAR inspected and sealed each car. If the seals had not been tampered with, NASCAR assumed everything was all right. In case of tampering —very rare—or in case of protest, a complete engine teardown and car inspection took place.

Friel and his boys were concerned mainly with the motor, the transmission, the ignition and fuel systems and the manifolding. With the cars so evenly matched, weight had to conform to a prescribed minimum. For safety's sake certain changes were mandatory. A roll cage had to be installed, doors had to be practically welded shut, and hood and trunk lids had to have extra locks. Competitors had to run special heavy duty wheels and were allowed to strengthen the chassis, suspension and steering components. Each car was disassembled completely by its own crew before an inspector, at the car owner's expenses. The inspector measured more than 140 different parts with a micrometer against the manufacturer's inspection book. Internal engine changes that did not alter bore and stroke were legal and absolved him of the necessity of checking pistons and so on. The cars were sealed by drilling head bolts, universal bolts, and most other available fasteners and running a safety wire through them. Then a lead seal was attached. If, after practice, a part needed changing, the procedure started over. Cars had to remain within a guarded impound area after initial inspection except for practice. All work had to be done in front of inspectors.

Altered carburetors and manifolding were the usual ways of trying to beat the game, Friel said. But with the advent of factory racing, the experts tried doctoring transmissions and other parts of the power train. Friel and his crew checked all pit stops, for only a certain number of men could work on a car, only a certain amount of gas could be available there, and safety regulations had to prevail. There was a NASCAR inspector at every race. Norris also had to tell the top mechanics just what was legal. He had the final say on rules interpretations that could mean victory or defeat.

If anyone wanted to know how American stock-car engines could stand the punishment, the answer was that were they not "showroom stock." Friel was the first to admit this: "These engines were hand rebuilt copies of the showroom version, and they were remade within manufacturers' generous tolerances for optimum performance." The tendency of the firms in factory racing to make these tolerances so generous as to defeat the old NASCAR rules led to a Friel-inspired setup with its overall car weight minimum and its bore-stroke rule.

FRANK FUNK

As he grew older and richer, Frank Funk's tales of his beginnings began to sound more and more like that of a country bumpkin version of Horatio Alger with a bit of Dick Whittington tossed in for good measure. Funk was one of the finest sprint track promoters in the history of American auto racing. His Winchester, Ind., Speedway, which opened in 1916 as little more than a half-mile dirt oval out through the family cornfield, grew and changed until it could boast that it was the world's fastest half-mile oval. As Frank told it, he built a skating rink on the shores of a spring-fed lake owned by his father, Henry Funk, because a man from the big city (Muncie) suggested it. He did pretty well with this enterprise so, when another stranger suggested that he build a race track, he went to the bank and got the money to do the job. The two men were incidental to the story, but their names were Bill Saucer and Earl Hinkle, and they promoted the 1st race. It attracted 1,500 fans but was marred by large clouds of dust and a serious accident when two blinded drivers collided. The 2nd and 3rd shows drew few fans (they remembered the dust), and Saucer-Hinkle gave up. Frankie didn't. He became his own promoter, but couldn't get a field for a Labor Day 1916 race. Instead, he presented motorcycles; these were successful, mainly because they raised less dust.

By 1917, however, Funk learned tracks could be oiled, and he was on his way to great success. He usually plowed the profits right back into the track, gradually raising the banking in order to get faster and faster times. C. W. Belt of Indianapolis, Ford Moyer and Wilbur Shaw were among early record holders. Funk gave $500 for a new lap record, which could be more money than a high finish in the feature would draw. Belt's record was 38 seconds; Ted Horn—Funk's all-time favorite—got it under 20 for the first time, and Chuck Rodee got it down to 18.66 in 1964, making it the fastest half-miler on the USAC circuit.

The track was paved in 1932 when the banks had grown 25 feet high, and the stands held 6,000 easily (from an original 500), and from 12,000 to 14,000 could crowd into the place. Funk at one time had an interest in 6 other Midwestern sprint car venues, and managed to attract most of the finest American pilots because he ran one race around Indy time. Besides Shaw and Horn, Howdy Wilcox, Ralph DePalma, Rex Mays, Bill Cummings and a host of others competed for him. Funk retired because of ill health in 1951 and died soon after that.

GARY GABELICH

How does it feel to be the fastest man ever on 4 wheels? "I'm looking through a tiny window like 5 miles ahead, and it looks like I can see the curvature of the earth, except they tell me it's a mirage. I don't really care because I'm in a world of my own and, even though I'm trying hard to remain calm, the adrenalin has started pumping and I'm self-hypnotized. I push the throttle to the floor, and my head is forced back. At that point I'm no longer just a guy sitting in a machine, but I'm part of the machine itself. It's strange, but I can see the markers go by, even though in 22 seconds I've gone from standing still to better than 650 m.p.h.

"At about 600 my hearing goes completely and though my oxygen mask is tightly fastened, I swear I can smell

the heat of the engine and the heat of the wires. At the measured mile I see 630 on the indicator, and I'm more confident than ever that I'm going to break Craig Breedlove's mark. At halfway, it's 650 and I'm out of fuel, which is exactly as we calculated. I'm pulling something like 7 Gs, and the blood seems to be rushing to the top of my head like an express train.

"I release the chute and begin to brake at about 150 m.p.h., and almost immediately I pitch forward from the dropoff to 4 Gs or so. The harness is tearing at my shoulders and gut. As we're stopping, I turn off the cameras, the tape recorder, everything. It's unreal, it's fantastic, it's victory, that's what it is."

That was how it was to Gary Gabelich October 23, 1970—55 days after his 30th birthday—when the California bachelor set a World Land Speed Record of 622.407 m.p.h. in the rocket-powered Blue Flame, eclipsing Breedlove's 5-year-old mark of 600.601. How he made it to that point in time is a story of perserverence and of the good fortune of being in the right place at the right time.

Originally Craig Breedlove had been sought by Reaction Dynamics, Inc., builders of the Blue Flame LSR car, to attack that record in late 1969, but when he couldn't come to terms, a driver named Chuck Suba was signed. Suba was killed in a drag racing accident at Rockford, Ill., soon after, and the hunt was on for a replacement. Gabelich was then a test astronaut—a stand-in for real astronauts—at North American Rockwell, which was participating as a supplier in the Apollo space program. In those days, Gabelich was short-haired and conservatively dressed, the very model of the American astronaut. He had worked his way up from NAR's mail room where he had started at $1.29 an hour, and had been a statistician and a planning engineer before becoming an astronaut. But Gabelich had something else lurking in his background. He was racing hot rods even before he graduated from Long Beach Polytechnic High School. He 1st raced when he was 19 at Bonneville Salt Flats, Utah, where he was eventually to become the fastest man on 4 wheels. In a jet car called Valkyrie, Gabelich traveled a mere 356 m.p.h., which probably made him the fastest teenager around at that time. He revisited Bonneville in later years in another jet car called the Untouchable I but without great success.

As a test astronaut, he spent days on end sealed in space vehicle-like capsules, trying out environmental systems, dropping out of airplanes in special high-altitude chutes to record photographically the action of new-design parachutes for the reentry of space vehicles and the like. He played the astronaut role to the hilt, running up to 6 miles every other day, swimming, playing handball and tennis, scuba diving and waterskiing, all the things that condition and fine-tune potential spacemen. Then program cutbacks put Gabelich on the beach. He was offered a desk job at NAR, but preferred to strike out on his own with about $6,000 personal savings and severance pay. Finding a sponsor who matched his nest egg, he bought a "funny car."

Gabelich took up racing seriously and managed to keep his head above water until his car blew a piston during a race, and his suit caught fire. He had to jump and roll along the ground to put out the flames. He spent only a night in the hospital, but Gabelich had scars on his arms and legs several years later to attest to the nearness of the thing. He went back to racing almost at once, both on land—including a Lotus-Traco and go-karts—and on the water where he set a National Drag Boat Association record of 200.44 m.p.h. in a hydro boat in 1969, following a 1968 American Power Boat Association fuel hydro championship.

But cars were Gabelich's real passion, and the challenge of the Blue Flame was one he couldn't ignore. The giant car—6,500 pounds, more than 38 feet long, over 8 feet high—was sponsored by the natural gas industry. It took two years to build and cost more than $500,000 before it ever set tread on a track. Power for the car was supplied by the type of engine used to propel space vehicles, and Gary's technical background came in handy. The 22,000-pound thrust engine was powered by LNG, liquid natural gas chilled to minus 258 degrees Fahrenheit.

The scheduled September 1969, LSR run of the Blue Flame didn't come off because of technical problems, but Gabelich continued to plug away at his conditioning program and to contribute his technical knowledge as static tests and low-speed runs were extended over another year. In July 1970, the car was finally declared ready for the Salts, but it was September 15 before it had arrived, been readied, and the first runs started. Things went badly for the next 5 weeks. The weather at Bonneville was poor much of the time. When the weather was acceptable, parts broke in one subsystem after the other. By September 22, the Blue Flame had reached only 426 m.p.h. and Breedlove's 1965 record hardly seemed in danger.

Gabelich, now modishly long-haired, seemed mired at 440 when it was discovered that he was getting only 6,000 pounds of thrust instead of the 16,000 pounds anticipated. More changes, more tests, more record attempts. On October 15th, Gary made an opening run of 609 m.p.h., but before he could make the mandatory return run, a small fire broke out when a hydrogen peroxide fuel line was cracked as the car was being turned around. The Blue Flame had to be torn apart and put together again. While that was going on, an inventory showed the supply of LNG was growing short with no prospect for immediately adding to the supply. On October 28th, Gary made a one-way run of 621 m.p.h., but again a minor mechanical problem—an O-ring which helped control the flow of fuel had given way—negated the 2nd run.

As Gabelich sat in the Blue Flame's cockpit, September 23, 1970, he knew that there was enough fuel left for no more than 10 more runs down the salt. Then the year would be over because the area's weather was closing in fast, which would mean a break-up of the salt course. There were rain clouds in the sky that day, and the winds seemed on the verge of freshening, which might abort his try, since the rules governing the world record would not allow clockings in winds of 6 m.p.h. or better. But the breeze and the rain held off, and Gabelich got a green light to go.

With a high-pitched whoosh, the big car started rolling along on its nearly 3-foot-high tires with paper-thin treads. Tested to withstand speeds up to a theoretical 1,000 m.p.h., the Goodyears were inflated not with air but with nitrogen to 285 p.s.i. The first run was over just before noon, and Gabelich knew it was a good one even before the dockers announced 617.602 m.p.h. The car was carefully turned, painstakingly refueled and off he went in the opposite direction. At 12:12 P.M. Gabelich crossed the final marker at an average of 627.287, and he had the title. A few minutes later, the winds rose steadily to 8 m.p.h., but they were too late.

"Really far out," Gabelich said. "Really a far-out ride, one that sets you back in the seat. It's plenty boss." Thus he became the 11th LSR-holder to capture that diadem at Bonneville since John Cobb first did it back in 1947 at 394.200 m.p.h. in a "real" automobile. "I think we can go a lot faster in this car," added Gabelich. "Who knows how fast? Maybe 750. I'd sure like to try."

In April 1972, however, driving a "funny car"—a 4-wheel drive station wagon modified for dragging—Gabelich hit a guard rail and flipped, sustaining a fractured right arm and left leg, a crushed left heel and severed right hand. Doctors sewed the hand back on and a series of operations followed. Whether the fastest man would get a shot at 750 was now a genuine question.

NANNI GALLI

Giovanni Giuseppe Gilberto Galli, son of a wealthy Italian textile family, wanted to go racing, but he knew his parents would object. So he chose the simple solution, of racing under a pseudonym, Nanni. Later, when he used his own name, the pseudonym stuck. Galli never seemed a first-rank single-seat racer, but he could handle a sports car rather well.

Born in Bologna October 2, 1940, Galli went racing in go-karts at age 18, but he didn't get going in real cars until 1964 when he bought a Mini-Cooper. In 1965, he won his class in the Italian Touring Car Championship by winning all 10 races he entered. In 1966 he switched to an Alfa Romeo GTA and started racing outside of Italy. The initial significant victory came at Austria's Danube Cup race. One thing led to another, and Galli found himself with an offer to drive a factory Autodelta car. 1967's high spot was a class victory at

the Nurburgring 1000; 1968's an overall 2nd in the Targa Florio with Ignazio Giunti.

The next season Tecno offered a Formula 2 ride, and Nanni left Alfa for a time, but he was back in 1970 and placed 2nd in the Imola 500. He was a reserve at the Italian Grand Prix but did not start. Galli's 1971 sports car season was his best, with a 3rd in the Buenos Aires 1000, a 2nd at Sebring, a 4th in the Monza 1000 and a 3rd in Austria—all with Rolf Stommelen—and a retirement at the Watkins Glen 6-Hour Race with Vic Elford. He got some regular F1 starts, his best finish a 5th in the non-title Jochen Rindt race at Hockenheim in an STP March-Alfa 711. Galli had a shunt with former F2 teammate François Cevert in the Dutch GP, practiced but didn't start in France, was 11th in Britain, 12th in Germany and Austria, and retired in Italy. After a 16th in Canada, he retired in the U.S. race. In 1972 Tecno brought forth its F1 car, and Galli was the driver, but it did nothing in championship racing, and he moved on to Frank Williams's Politoys GP team for 1973. In sports cars, Galli shared a 2nd in the 1972 Targa Florio with Helmut Marko.

HOWDEN GANLEY

New Zealand, that tiny island off the Australian continent, has produced more than its share of Formula 1 racing drivers in recent years—fellows like Bruce McLaren, Denis Hulme, Chris Amon, and lately, James Howden Ganley, who popped into the F1 prospective-drivers book in 1971.

Ganley was no johnny-come-lately. Born December 24, 1941, in Hamilton, he had come to Britain in 1962 to race, and it took quite a bit of heartache and hard work to get onto the international grids consistently. "I mucked about in boats and even used to race yachts as a boy back home," he recalled, "until I was about 13 or so and went to see the 1955 New Zealand Grand Prix. Jack Brabham was there, of course, and an old-timer named Prince Bira in a 250F Maserati. Well, up to then I had wanted to be an admiral or something, but now I was really keen on auto racing."

Howden's father liked to race, and he had just imported the first MG TF to reach New Zealand. Howden and his brother became their father's enthusiastic pit crew from that point on—at least that's what they claimed, in order to get as close to the cars as they could. With a 2-h.p. engine, the teen-aged Ganley constructed his own racer which unfortunately lacked brakes. He ended up stopping against an iron fence but without injury to himself. Racing was still on his mind when he finished high school and took a job as a newspaper reporter. He also sought out and became the New Zealand correspondent for a British sports car magazine, bought a more-than-used Ford Anglia and ran it in the Hoirara hillclimb. Howden's first regular race in 1959 was at a local airport in his mother's Morris Minor; 3 bent pushrods ended the borrowing program.

In 1960, at age 18, he managed to buy the remains of a Lotus 11, patch it together in one week, and race the following weekend at Ardmore. There were no victories in this kind of machine, but he was racing, at least until he made a mess out of the Climax engine toward

234

the season's end. The obvious thing to do was to go to Britain and really learn to race. Selling the car would enable him to do it; unfortunately, he wrecked it and the rebuild cost wiped out any profit. He set sail anyway, and arrived with less than $50 in his pocket. He saw an ad for a job as a racing school team mechanic, got it, and hoped for some rides. He got just one, then switched to Max Moseley's stable as a mechanic. An early task was building a GT car for Falcon, working strictly from a basic design, but without any detail drawings. Next came a light-weight version, and early in 1963 the racing Ganley was ready again.

At Silverstone he lost an oil line, but the next day at Brands Hatch he was 4th, and later at Snetterton Ganley found himself duelling Jackie Oliver's Marcos before brake fading put him back into 5th. But at Aintree the Falcon's power plant blew, and Howden's season was finished. Next came a Formula Junior opportunity, 1st as a mechanic, rebuilding 2 Gemini wrecks, in one of which Roy Pike won. Later Ganley had one at Goodwood, then Nurburgring, finally Brands Hatch, but without great success. It was about 18 months since he had come to Britain to race, but not too much had happened. So Howden took a job working on the street construction gang for the Fulham Council. That job only lasted 2 weeks, however, because a job as a "go-for"—go for this, go for this, go for that—opened up with McLaren's operation. Howden stayed 2 years, helping to build the prototype McLaren sports/racer and the 7-litre Ford GTX on which he became crew chief for Amon.

Ganley came to America with the car and stayed after Amon headed home, working on the Ford transmission with the factory for 3 months, then started assisting on chopping the 4.2-litre Ford Indy-car V-8s down to 3 litres for McLaren out in California. He also was building parts of what he hoped would be his own racing car. In 1966 he was at Monaco and decided enough was enough. He had became a mechanic, not a driver doing some mechanical work in the interim, and to change that he quit McLaren, joining Lola to finish his own car. But America's Skip Scott came along with what Howden called "about a million dollars" to crew for Skip and Peter Revson in the Canadian-American Challenge Cup series. He made enough to forget about completing his piecemeal racer and to order a factory-fresh Brabham BT21 Formula 3 car for 1967.

In March 1967 Howden Ganley, race driver, was back on the grid. He was 25, with as fine an engineering background as anyone sitting around him. He thought he had to develop a driver's approach once again, however, for he felt too cautious. Still, he couldn't divorce himself completely from the mechanical side, because this brought in good money. He assisted Hewland in repairing gearboxes after a shunt had necessitated rebuilding the Brabham. He improved steadily through 1968, and the next season Ganley switched to a Chevron B15. He had good runs at Monaco and Crystal Palace heats, making the final in each case, yet at Rouen

some said he should quit, that he just wasn't fast enough. Howden decided there was something wrong with the engine. Indeed there was. A valve had dropped off. At Karlskoga in August 1969 he came in 3rd behind Ron Peterson and Tim Schenken, the fair-haired boys in F3. At Crystal Palace he beat out Emerson Fittipaldi—just a year away from F1 glory—in his heat, at Caldwell he was 2nd to Schenken, and at the Hatch he had a 100-m.p.h. lap driving through traffic after getting away badly. His skills were such that McLaren hired Howden to test-drive the M8A CanAm car at Goodwood on a regular basis. This was OK for a past-time, but he wanted to race, not test. The year 1970 gave him his chance at last. In Formula 2 Ganley had rides both in a Brabham-FVA BT30 and with Malcolm Guthrie Racing's March-FVA 702. It was good for experience, but there mostly were retirements and a crash at Zolder. But in Formula 5000 the results were far different.

Howden won a 1970 F5000 race at Oulton Park, and collected 5 seconds, 6 thirds and 3 fourths among 16 finishes. There were only 2 retirements for his McLaren-Chevvy M10B, and Ganley finished 2nd in the European F5000 Championship standings to Peter Gethin. In 1971 it was F5000 again, and in March a F1 debut at last in BRM, starting from last and retiring when ill. Two weeks later, at Brands Hatch for the non-title Race of Champions, Ganley started 10th, finished a strong 5th. He very nearly was 4th, but former World Champion John Surtees nipped Howden right before the checker. The man who had been told to retire 2 years before had arrived. In 1971, too, Ganley garnered 5 championship points and was tied for 14th place in the GP standings. Ill in the BRM, he retired from the South African GP, was 10th in Spain, passed up Monaco, was 7th in Holland, 10th again in France, 8th in Britain. There were retirements in Germany and Austria, a 5th in Italy, a practice crash in Canada, and a career high spot for Ganley at the U.S. GP when he finished 4th behind François Cevert, Jo Siffert, and Ronnie Peterson. In other non-title racing, Howden was 4th in the Oulton Spring Cup and 2nd to Surtees in the Oulton Gold Cup.

In 1972 Ganley added the Interserie—Europe's version of the CanAm—to his regular driving beat. In April he won a wet opener in an Alcan-BRM P176. The previous fall he had returned to Riverside, where he had been a mechanic 5 years before, and raced the BRM CanAm car, finishing 3rd to Denis Hulme and Revson. Small wonder Ganley is one of those drivers who believe anything is possible if you try hard enough.

DEREK GARDNER

It can't really be much effort to design a Grand Prix car, especially one that wins the World Constructor's Championship in its first full season of racing. An outrageous statement, you say? What about the British designer Derek Gardner and his Tyrrell-Ford, introduced

late in 1970, freshened up for 1971 and winner of the Formula 1 championships both for driver and constructor that year? It took just 2 years from the day Derek sat down in his Leamington Spa bedroom and first put a drawing pencil to a fresh sheet of white paper to the time when the Tyrrell won its world title. And you really couldn't say that Gardner had prepared for that feat in a very special way.

He was born and educated in Warwick. In 1947, while still in his late teens, he decided the aircraft industry was for him, a natural decision in the days after the Battle of Britain, the conquest of Fortress Europa by airpower as well as manpower, and the introduction of the jet airplane. While working within the industry, he also started college, first signing up for aeronautical engineering, but changing his course to mechanical engineering along the way. After school he left aviation and joined a firm of local consulting engineers. It was here that Gardner got his first automotive assignment. Nothing spectacular; merely designing the hood framing for the Healey Silverstone sports car. It was his only automotive task in several years. Service with the RAF followed, and upon his separation, Gardner again found his way into the auto industry by accident. He joined Hobbs Transmission, the automatic transmission company founded by the man whose son was to be David Hobbs, racing driver. But Derek wasn't interested in racing at all, and he had no contact with it at that time.

In 1960 he left Hobbs and joined Harry Ferguson Research. Ferguson's speciality was 4-wheel drive, of course, and Gardner had a brush with the firm's main

project of that moment, the P99 4-wheel drive race car, but he wasn't especially interested. His first real racing involvement was set in motion by the P99, however. The car was raced and demonstrated to Andy Granatelli, who was impressed enough to commission Ferguson to build a Novi-Ferguson 4-wheel drive car for the 1964 Indianapolis 500 race. Gardner was assigned to design the transmission. Bobby Unser was 5th fastest qualifier in the experimental design, but the car went out of the race on the tragic initial lap that killed Eddie Sachs and Dave MacDonald.

Derek next was assigned to work with BRM on a feasibility study for a 4-wheel drive version of the H16 BRM F1 car. Nothing much came of that. Gardner was then assigned to design, draw, test, build, and deliver about half a dozen transmissions in 3 months to outfit the Lotus 56 Indy turbine cars. In mid-project, he was off to Indy to deliver the units and "supervise Ferguson interests" in Gasoline Alley. He spent 6 weeks working shoulder-to-shoulder with the mechanics on the Lotuses, and this was where the racing bug finally infected Derek Gardner. Matra gave him his next shot at racing when the French builder commissioned Ferguson to develop a 4-wheel drive F1 car for 1968. While flying to France for a conference one day, Derek met the man who would really change his life and involve him in racing.

"I think we met at London Airport and flew across together," he later recalled of that first meeting with Ken Tyrrell. They worked together rather well, but Gardner was double and triple-timing in those days on Ferguson projects, and even when the car was debuting at Zandvoort, he was up to his eyebrows in projects for Granatelli and for Bob McKee's Canadian-American Challenge Cup car. "In my honest opinion, that Matra became the most competitive of any 4-wheel drive car up to that point, although it unfortunately posed more questions than it answered." It did answer one question for Gardner himself, however; he was now determined to go into motor racing full time, and he envisioned doing it in the States. But when Tyrrell heard Derek was leaving Ferguson, he picked up the phone and arranged a secret meeting in a pub along the Thames at Henley.

The time was February 1970, and Ken's proposition was nothing less than that Derek should design a Tyrrell GP car from scratch. "Actually, I was only commissioned to build a prototype car—one car—for Ken, and if it didn't work out—or if it wasn't ready by the Oulton Park Gold Cup—too bad. I had burned my boats, but the project would be scrapped. It was really a case of having faith in myself."

Tyrrell's recollections back up Gardner's: "I only looked upon the new design as an insurance policy in case we were left without a car in 1971, largely because I didn't feel that Derek could come up with a successful car at his first attempt at F1. I insisted on only a few things. The car had to be conventional because we were not going to have a lot of spare time to develop a radi-

236

cal new design. I also insisted that the unsprung weight be kept low and that as much weight as possible be placed in the center of the car because we discovered that had worked on the Matra. This dictated to a certain extent bulbous center section as on the MS80, but there the similarity ended. We had a fair amount of antidive and antisquat; the Matra had very little. We used different drive shafts, we mounted our wheels differently, and, in fact, the majority of the details were very different."

Gardner cleared out the spare bedroom in his home and converted it into a design office. He sold his Bentley to free the garage downstairs for building a wooden mockup. And he faced that awful moment when he first put pencil to blank paper. Many drawings and weeks later he had a wooden mockup ready, finished off with bits of sheet aluminum, cardboard and some blue paint that happened to be handy. In great secrecy (and he could be secret when he wanted to be), Jackie Stewart flew to Coventry and motored to the Gardner garage. He sat in the "cockpit" and pronounced himself pleased. Work started on transferring the ideas into reality. Derek recalled the moment of great relief when that phase of the project started: "I had never been concerned with chassis or suspension, I had never been involved with cockpit design, I had never been really that deeply involved with racing. Literally I started with a completely clean sheet of paper."

The Tyrrell March was raced for the last time at Monza, and the Tyrrell-Ford was unveiled at the Canadian GP. It led for 31 laps until a front stub axle broke. Gardner flew back to England and completely redesigned the front uprights. He felt there was no time to investigate why the original design had failed. The parts were fabricated, and he flew with them as his luggage to Watkins Glen. Again Stewart and the Tyrrell led for 83 laps until an oil pipe retaining clip was snapped by vibration and the pipe rested on a hot exhaust, burned through and leaked out all the oil. In Mexico a steering column not worked loose and the Tyrrell hit a stray dog on the course.

The year 1971 started with testing in South Africa, then the GP there. Stewart was 2nd to Mario Andretti in a Ferrari, but François Cevert crashed the other Tyrrell when sweat blinded him at the wrong moment. In the Spanish GP the Tyrrell F1 car finally won its first race. "It looked ragged," said Gardner, the worry-wart. The car won again at Monaco and at France and at Britain and at Germany. How ragged can a car be? The day he clinched the two championships, Stewart broke a stub axle and shed a wheel at the Austrian GP. Stewart won again in Canada, and Cevert in the United States GP for his 1st F1 victory ever. Gardner was seen to smile at last, In 1972. Stewart won 4 Grands Prix, despite Emerson Fittipaldi's domination and championships. But a new car was needed, and it was ready for the nontitle Silverstone International in April 1973.

Gardner got to smile again, for Stewart won 1st crack out of the box.

FRANK GARDNER

It sounds like the outline for a movie. There's this tall, muscular Australian kid who is 14 years old. His father, who is a trawler captain, dies, and he is left to go it alone. He starts earning money as a professional boxer, then he becomes a virtuoso motorcycle racer and makes a pile at that. He is so good a swimmer that he represents Australia internationally, and he's a crack surfer, too. He opens up a garage business and becomes proficient at building cars, then emigrates to Britain. He builds a successful car for a big-name racing driver/constructor and races it himself right on up to Grand Prix racing. He drives in Britain, on the Continent and back home in Australia. He drives real racing cars and stock cars—saloons, the British call them—and wins championships. He plays golf with Jackie Stewart and skindives with Jack Brabham, and he beats them both. The guy has a golden tongue and a fantastic sense of humor. He turns down Formula 1 rides because he's content with winning stock-car titles, but maybe someday he'll give it a real crack and then watch out. All of this and he's under 40. Maybe one could get Michael Caine for the part, with Julie Christie for the love interest. How's it end? Don't know yet, because Frank Gardner hasn't yet lived the rest of it.

Gardner was born October 1, 1932, in Sydney, Australia, and death taxes took his dad's trawler and almost everything else. "I was left with my backside sticking out of my pants," Gardner said. At that moment he spied a sign advertising for someone to fight at a country fair, winner to take some $600 in prize money. Frank fought and won, there and at 7 other fairs. "None of the lot lasted longer than 4 rounds, but I was determined not to go longer," he said. "Stay in there fighting too long and your brains will get scrambled for sure, not to say what it does to your looks."

He opened a garage and started attending Sydney Technical College on the side. He surfed and swam well enough to represent his state and country in competition. In the meantime, he picked up 7 years of engineering training and a degree, changed his garage into a light engineering business, and decided to have a go at auto racing in Europe. He started motorcycle racing at 16 in 1949—"I bought a bike, skidded around in the mud for a day or two to get the hang of it, then entered a race and fell off while I was leading by a mile," he said in a way that still showed resentment at that turn of events. In 1954 he bought his initial car, an XK 120 Jaguar, and was soon racing it. Six straight victories got him off on the right foot in Australian sports car circles. The following year he bought a C Jaguar that someone had crashed into a ravine on its initial go.

Driving the rebuilt Jag, Gardner won 23 of the 24 races he started in Australia; in 1956 and 1957 he wrapped up the New South Wales sports car title with a new D Jaguar that replaced it. With this kind of success, he decided to launch a European driving career. He tried other machines, up to a Maserati 250, to ready himself. But when he landed in England in 1958, no one was interested in an Australian flash, and pretty soon Frank "moved backwards rather rapidly" by taking a racing mechanic's job with Aston Martin under John Wyer. Like Graham Hill, he quickly found out that it was a long way from working on a car to driving it, and besides, Aston Martin quit racing. "I didn't quite see myself in a research department, making tea at four and all the rest. So I took a job straightening bent fenders and bumpers at Jimmy Russell's driving school," Gardner recalled, "Pretty soon someone realized that I could drive these cars, too, and I was given a ride in a Formula Junior race." He won it, and 7 more.

Right about then, Frank heard that Brabham was starting his own marque, and he went over to work for his fellow Aussie, joining Ron Tauranac and Peter Wilkins in building the 1st MRD Brabham FJ car. He was paid a fat $30 a week, but got to drive the car when it was ready, which was what he really wanted. The sports car was next, and Frank got to build and drive that one, too. He started getting to be known as a pretty fair driver, and Colin Chapman arranged a copilot's seat for Gardner in a Lotus Elite for Le Mans in 1962 with David Hobbs. They finished 8th overall and captured

the Index of Thermal Efficiency. Frank took Brabham's FJ car back home and swept a series, causing Brabham to offer him the regular number one team spot, but he turned it down because he already had accepted an Ian Walker offer to race FJ cars. Denis Hulme got the Brabham FJ seat and proceeded up the ladder to an F1 World Championship a few years later.

In 1964 Gardner switched to Willment to drive F2 and start his saloon racing career with Cortinas and Cobras, maintaining and driving his own cars. His performances were such that, in 1965, Frank was given a Brabham-BRM for GP starts. In a non-title tune-up, the Brands Hatch Race of Champions, he was 3rd. At South Africa he was 12th, at Monaco his engine mounts broke in the 29th lap, and at Belgium distributor damage stopped him. Passing up the French race, Gardner worked feverishly to get the car ready for the British GP, in which Frank made it to 8th. In Holland he was 11th, but in Germany one of the gears snapped, and in Italy a flywheel let go. "We had tried to improvise on that car, but it was hopeless," Frank said matter-of-factly. "I was just making a fool of myself out there, but I was determined to carry on as long as I could. I had my crack at the GP cherry and failed." An interesting statement, but not exactly the whole story, as we shall see.

In the winter Tasman series, while driving a Brabham-Climax against world champion Jim Clark, Graham Hill, Stewart, and the like, Gardner showed what he could do with a properly prepared, competitive car. At Levin he set the fastest lap time before mechanical trouble, in the Teretonga he was 2nd to Stewart, in the Warwick Farm race 3rd to Clark and Hill. He was 2nd in the Australian GP to Hill and ahead of Clark. Midland Racing Partnership came up with a Lola F2 ride in 1966–67, which was good for smoothing Frank's ego, but his more important bid came from Alan Mann, who produced a Falcon for Gardner to drive in the British saloon series in 1967. Perhaps Gardner's 2nd place with Sir John Whitmore in a Ford GT Mk. II at the Spa 1000 influenced Mann's choice. It worked out well for both sponsor and driver.

In 1967 there were 10 races counting toward the British title, and Gardner's Falcon copped the prize for cars over 2000 c.c. in 7 of them, with two 2nds and a 4th. The following year, he piloted a Cortina in the 1301-c.c.–2000 c.c. class for several races, then switched to a newly homologated Escort Twin-Cam. A victory and two 2nds in the Cortina, then eight consecutive 1sts in the new Escort gave Gardner his 2nd consecutive saloon championship. Since he likes driving all kinds of cars, Frank also accepted rides in F2 Brabhams and T70 Lola-Chevrolets. For Brabham, he finished 2nd to Jacky Ickx in the European F2 championship series. And the call for F1 came again, not once but twice, from John Cooper and from Brabham, but the Aussie turned them down. "I'm enjoying myself immensely in the saloons and with these other machines," he said. "Oh, maybe I'll give it a go once or twice more if the right opportunity presents itself."

In 1969 Gardner had a bad racing year since the turbocharged Ford Escort he was to have driven in the over 2000 c.c. class in saloon racing failed to live up to expectations and was scratched from competition after several poor starts. The Ford prototype was a dismal failure, and Mann's Canadian-American Challenge Cup effort failed to catch fire also. But the year was not completely lost to Gardner. He set up his own company, Motor Racing Research, Ltd., in Woking, Surrey, and with the retirement of Mann from racing at year's end, he took over much of the latter's business at Chobham. Under wraps, MRR worked on secret projects for both Ford and Brabham, and it shared its quarters with designer Len Bailey, who was nominally independent of Gardner's efforts. The year was successful in another way as well—Frank married.

He raced a Formula 5000 Lola-Chevvy T190 and a former TransAm Boss Mustang 302 provided by Ford. The latter was a KarKraft special job, but Gardner's MRR boys had to modify it extensively to meet European Group 2 rules. With this mount, Gardner's 1970 racing made up for 1969, his Mustang setting new lap records and winning almost every start, including races at Snetterton, Brands Hatch, Thruxton, Silverstone, and Crystal Palace. In F5000 he came in 3rd to Peter Gethin and Howden Ganley in the European series, winning 2 races. Gardner showed he still had it in single-seaters as late as 1971 when he won the British F5000 championship, and in 1972 when he won the New Zealand GP and finished 2nd in the Australian in his factory Lola T300. But that was to be Frank's last open-wheeled race, he announced, adding, "I'm getting too cautious, and you can't afford to in these projectiles. You look back on the miles you've raced and suddenly you find it's time to let go of the tiger's tail." He remained as Lola's chief development driver and faced the British saloon series with renewed zest.

GOLDIE GARDNER

The 1st driver to pass 150 m.p.h. on engines of 500- and 750-c.c. capacities, and the 1st to reach 200 m.p.h. in the 1100- and 1500-c.c. classes was tall, partially crippled, and possessed of about as untechnical a mind as any one who ever participated in record breaking. His name was Arthur Thomas Goldie Gardner.

Goldie was born in 1889, which made him just the right age for World War I, after work in Ceylon and Burma. With his aristocratic background and his education, of course, he was an officer, in the Royal Artillery. He served successfully in France for several years, then was wounded in August 1917. Two years of hospitalization and some 20 operations followed. In 1921

he was discharged from the service, and he was still limping when he first drove competitively at Brooklands in 1924 in an Austin 7 variety known as the Gordon England Special.

He continued racing—"unobtrusively active," as he himself once put it—for many years thereafter in Salmsons, Amilcars and MGs. None of these was a very large car, and why Gardner, who was tall for his time (6 feet, 3 inches) kept to these smaller machines is a puzzle. The marque he was longest associated with, of course, was MG, starting in 1931. It was in a Montlhéry Midget MG that he almost ended his racing career, and very nearly his life, in the 1932 Tourist Trophy race at Ars, Ireland. Crowded onto the grass apron while trying to get around a slower car, Gardner's MG hit a drainage ditch and flipped a couple of times. During its flight the car landed atop Goldie, smashing his weakened right leg and further damaging his hip.

Amputation seemed inevitable, but the doctors fought to save the leg at Gardner's insistence. Four months later he went home, both legs still there, although the right one was a shell of what it should have been. From then on, every time he sat in a car Goldie Gardner would be fighting sensations that ranged from discomfort to outright pain. A walking stick became part of his indispensable equipment for moving about. Connected with his limp, it gave the impression that Goldie was missing a leg, which newspaper headline writers kept alive as "truth" for years. But the leg was still there; the pain was enough to remind Gardner of that.

Goldie accepted without comment the fact that he couldn't race any more, but that he would take up record-setting more seriously than ever to compensate for that loss seemed completely natural to him, too. Between 1936 and 1952, when his last speed exploits were recorded, Gardner smashed nearly 100 international records. With 6 years lost to World War II (during which Goldie talked his way back into the Royal Artillery and came out a Lieutenant Colonel with an MC, to which was added an OBE later) that meant an average of something like 9 records a year for 11 years. At one time or another, Gardner held the fastest-ever mark in something like 60 percent of the recognized international classes, and about the only thing he never really went for was the Land Speed Record, which was in British hands for that whole period.

It was George Eyston's EX135 that went on to its great glory in Gardner's hands. Gardner had accompanied Malcolm Campbell to Daytona in 1935 and was infected with the record-setting bug. That same year MG announced it was quitting record-setting, and Eyston sold the EX135. Gardner conceived the idea of reviving the whole thing a couple of years later and set off to the Frankfurt-Dessau Autobahn with a K3 Magnette-powered special to successfully capture all the Class G (750–1100 c.c.) records—a 142.6 m.p.h. mile and a 142.3 kilometer, for example. At Montlhéry he racked up 5- and 10-mile and kilometer marks, then back at the Autobahn upped his mile record to 148.7 and the kilometer to 148.8. MG was convinced anew of the worth of these efforts, so help was forthcoming when EX135 was acquired by Gardner in 1938 from the man who had bought it as a curiosity from Eyston.

Beginning in November 1938, the EX135 served as a bed for a variety of engines. It was bored and sleeved to increase and decrease the cubic capacities for various international record categories. This was to be Gardner's car right through his last record runs in 1952, and it would have been his mount for a planned assault at the Bonneville Salt Flats in Utah in 1953 that was cancelled because of Goldie's finally failing health.

The 1st records, set November 9, 1938, were Class G marks again: 187.62 m.p.h. for the mile, 186.567 for the kilometer. The following year, with only minor changes, the Class G mark was raised still further to 203.2 for the mile and 203.5 for the kilo. This happened on May 31, 1939; then, 2 days later after reboring was done on the spot (again the Dessau Autobahn), Class F (1100 to 1500 c.c.) records were smashed —203.85 and 204.28 for the mile and the kilometer respectively. Gardner's next objective was Class H (500 to 750 c.c.). Work started to modify the engine, but the war interrupted things until 1946.

After some preliminary testing on the Brescia-Bergano road in Italy, the 1946 work was performed at the so-called Jabbeke Highway, or Ostend-Brussels Highway, in Belgium. That September-October Gardner took over a Class H mark of 159.15 for the mile and a Class I (350–500 c.c.) record of 118.0 m.p.h. Jaguar Cars lent Goldie a 2-litre XK 100 engine in 1948 for an assault on the Class E (1500 to 2000 c.c.) records, and he rewarded them with a 173.7 mile and a 176.6 kilometer. It wasn't as easy as it all sounds; during that flying kilo run, one of EX135's tires disintegrated at better than 170 m.p.h., and providing a few anxious moments until the Colonel could bring the car to a halt. On another of the runs, he almost struck a farmer and his donkey cart (a similar incident many years before had killed at least one racer not too far away) on the supposedly closed road.

Class J (below 350 c.c.) marks fell July 24, 1950, in Belgium when Goldie became the 1st man to go 2 miles a minute (121.048 for a mile) on so few cubic centimeters. On August 20, 1951, Gardner held was at Bonneville and, while he missed what he wanted most— beating his own 13-year-old Class F marks—he captured all kinds of American records for that c.c. class. In 1952 he tried again with similar results—remarkable activity for a 62-year-old man whose shattered leg now was tearing him apart each day. He planned on a 1953 expedition to get those Class F records properly raised, but his health intervened for the first time in his life. Goldie died in 1958.

DON GARLITS

Drag racing is deceptively simple. Two cars race from a standing start for a quarter of a mile. The loser is eliminated, and the winner is matched against other winners in successive sprints until only one car remains. That is the basic form, but in 20 years drag racing has evolved into a complex competition for some 80 classes, based on the weight of the car, its body style, the kind of fuel it uses, its modifications, and many other factors.

There is no doubt about what kinds of cars are the fastest. They are called AA fuel dragsters, weird monsters with three-quarters of their weight on the rear wheels and a long tapering, needle-thin body ending in spidery little bicycle-like front wheels. They are the royalty of the American and National Hot Rod Associations because they go down the strip quicker and more spectacularly than anything else in the sport—over 230 m.p.h. in a quarter mile from a standing start, with a fuel consumption rate of one gallon every 330 feet. And their drivers wear the "spaceman" fire suits to protect them against the violent flames which can erupt if an engine flames up, or if the fuel, a highly volatile secret mixture, explodes.

There has been one king of fuel dragster racing for almost 2 decades, a man who soon after high school graduation in Tampa, Fla., walked into the office where he was a clerk, looked around as if to say, "What am I doing here?" and walked out, never to return to a 9-to-5 job. Donald Glenn Garlits, the scrawny son of a

240

dairy farmer who had died when Donald was 10, went back to his first love, auto mechanics, and blossomed into an all-time great in his specialty. He became a man capable of making more than $70,000 annually, building the fastest straight-line racers of all time.

Don Garlits wanted to be a chief mechanic on a winning car at Indianapolis. He became instead a midnight drag racer and part-time racing mechanic, collecting speeding tickets as the Florida State Police—among the most fearless drivers in the law enforcement field—nailed him continually. Drag racing was a means of testing the engines he built. It became his profession only after he discovered that he was the best in the business. His machines were the best—1st in the Tampa area, then throughout Florida, then in the East and, finally, nationally. By 1956 he was also a national officer of AHRA, and eventually its president (until one of his serious mishaps forced him to relinquish the post in 1960).

Before that, however, Garlits had taken his sparsely decorated "Swamp Rat" AA rail to Southern California where the sport had received its greatest impetus. In the sunshine of Southern California hot rodders got emotional about their cars, building gleaming chromed showcases with 10 coats of paint. When the California boys saw Don's car, they derisively nicknamed him Don Garbage. Garlits, who had been the 1st to go 170 m.p.h. and 180 m.p.h., finally ground their derision into the pavement of their fancy drag strips, beating the best cars the NHRA could muster, and becoming a national drawing card. He began asking travel expenses and appearance money when a Texas promoter wanted him to haul from Tampa to the Lone Star State. He developed this into nationwide tours grossing him $70,000 to $80,000 annually.

Although Garlits scorned the exotic jargon of the California rodders, he learned from them, too—in chassis construction and weight distribution, and in the construction of the sparse cockpits. His Swamp Rats and Wynn's Jammers became prettier, but not much. He also scorned the libertine life style affected by some in drag racing in those early days, preferring to perfect his engines rather than play, to raise a family instead of hell. His awesome success helped drive the hellions either completely out of what has become a family participant sport or into the same kind of relatively conventional life style—as conventional as continual touring allows.

But it wasn't all triumph and greenbacks. In 1960 the supercharger on the Mopar engine exploded, and Don swallowed some of the fire. Burned inside and out, he spent some 2 months in the hospital with third-degree exterior burns and in extreme pain. He was injected with morphine to kill the pain and became addicted. He caught pneumonia, but recovered. Finally he was sent home, where he fought his addiction until he beat it. It was a year before he was back driving and building and

mixing his secret fuel brew. Another time he was burned when hot oil spurted from the engine onto his face mask, sidelining him for 6 months. Still another time the Swamp Rat flipped, cracking 3 of his vertebrae. But he would never again allow medical teams to give him morphine no matter how great the pain.

Garlits's lists of drag racing 1sts and feats were a fantastic compendium of success in his chosen field. Three times he won the NHRA Nationals. He developed the 1st dragster to attain a 170 m.p.h. trap speed (other than the jet exhibition cars of Arthur Arfons), then was the first to hit 180. In 1964 he broke a sports barrier as formidable as the 4-minute mile in running.

It happened fittingly 1st at Detroit. Garlits cranked out the first 200 m.p.h. trap speed. But this was not an official record run although the automatic lights and the timing equipment were of record caliber. The official run for a record would come 500 miles east a few days later at Great Meadows in western New Jersey. The place is not easy to find. It is built in farm country and, if you miss the sign on Highway 46, you motor blithely on into Pennsylvania. But it is one of the most successful drag tracks on the East Coast.

Big Daddy and his crew wanted that record. They had the 392 cu. in. engine tuned to dispense all 1,350 h.p. the minute Garlits hit the loud pedal. Don had mixed his witches' brew fuel to go for every drop of power. As usual, the ring of people watching his final preparations and his final checks was large and generally quiet. A mere decade earlier he had been a hero for going 147.05 m.p.h.; now he was testing *the* barrier. The fueler had changed in those 10 years; it was much longer and lighter and had evolved from the semblance of a passenger automobile into a 92-pound skeleton with the driver wedged like a silkworm in the half-cocoon of the tiny cockpit directly behind the engine.

The crew pushed the car to the staging area, wiping the huge treadless rear tires free of every speck of dirt. Garlits could hear the nonstop prattle of the announcer and the awed hushing of the audience. The column of lights that signal the start seemed to flash slowly down toward the green when really it was only a matter of a second or two. On the green a cloud of white smoke enveloped him, and when he crossed the finish line he had set a new elapsed-time world record of 7.78 seconds and had broken the magic 200 with 201.34 m.p.h.! The feat was followed by the NHRA Summernationals crown, the championship of England in the first British Drag Festival, and a match race with Bobby Langley, AHRA top fuel eliminator, at Houston, where Big Daddy won easily.

In 1965 at Bakersfield Garlits performed another feat of derring-do. It was the U.S. fuel and gas championships and most of the top fuel machines were present. Garlits in his Wynn's Jammer swept into the finals the 1st day, then switched to the Garlits Chassis Special (usually driven by Marvin Schwartz, his associate), and mopped up the best in the world once again. So in the finals Don had to race himself for Top Fuel Eliminator (TFE). Schwartz took back the Chassis Special for the final but Daddy mopped him, too, with a 205 m.p.h. run. In 1966 he went to the AHRA Nationals and won easily, eliminating on the way his friend Art Malone, 1965 TFE, and Chuck Hepler, 1964 TFE. His speed was 219.55 m.p.h., and his record low elapsed time (e.t.) was 7.77 seconds. This was a title he hadn't held since 1958 when he won it at Great Bend, Kans. Thus he held 2 association top speed marks, because he went 213.76 m.p.h. earlier for the NASCAR record when that organization had such a division.

Garlits also set a fantastic record in special match racing that year, winning 45 quarter-mile rounds to his foes' 10. He held the edge on every competitor, beating Don Prudhomme (then a double champion) 7-4, and Connie Kalitta 5-4. The other 2 losses were to Pete Robinson, and Don beat Pete 5-2. Don moved to Detroit then and the success stopped.

Some 18 months later, safely back in Tampa, Fla., Don came back for another unequalled feat. He won the Summernationals of NHRA in 1967 and 1968 to become the only 3-time winner. Meanwhile he was developing a business back in Tampa against the day he wouldn't be travelling 70,000 miles a year.

In 1969 misfortune struck when he broke his ankle in a motorcycle accident and then, in 1970, a transmission exploded, severely injuring his feet. But that didn't stop Garlits; it challenged him. Concerned with the increasing difficulty of keeping the fuelers safe, Don designed himself a rear-engined dragster and once again revolutionized the sport. The driver sat ahead of the engine and was thus protected from it. The idea of a rear-engined car had been tried before but had been unsuccessful. Garlits made it work by proper weight distribution and an airfoil which kept it straight on course, and began to reel off times in the 6.50's. The gleam came back into his eye and thoughts of retirement receded. He won the 1970 Winternationals, then followed that with a victory in the 1971 Springnationals, clocking 6.44 seconds and 227.27 m.p.h.

Then, at his home track at Gainsville, Fla., Don blasted out a record 6.26 e.t. and qualified for the $200,-000 World Championship Finals, one of the few events in which he had never competed. He had seemed ready to set low time en route to what looked like an unprecedented 4th NHRA Nationals victory when he had reeled off a practice 6.211 e.t., but in the finals he unaccountably dropped to a 6.652. He had already won the AHRA World Finals at Fremont, Calif. To annex the NHRA version would have made him the undisputed champion of all drag racing, something no one had ever accomplished. But he failed in the finals.

Garlits was the prime mover in formation of the Professional Racers Assn., a driver & owner group dedicated to larger purses for pro dragsters. That fight had not reached the crucial stage but it might be Garlits longest.

OLIVIER GENDEBIEN

He was an aristocrat, but as a racing driver, he was a thorough-going professional. He won races like Le Mans (4 times), the Targa Florio (3 times), the Mille Miglia (the last ever run), the Tour de France (3 times), Sebring (3 times), Rheims (twice), and Nurburgring, yet his name can draw a blank from all but the most rabid auto racing fan. He stayed with Ferrari 7 years—a long time for a non-Italian—then walked away from major league racing at the end of 1962 without so much as a backward glance. "Racing didn't amuse me so much any more," he said. "It was fun to win the 24-hour race at Le Mans the first time—and don't think I'm being conceited—it's not that. Winning it four times in five years was thrilling too, because I was the only one to do that. But as for winning again? You reach a point at which there seem only two alternatives—you lose or you get killed. But there is a third, and that is the one I chose."

One of Gendebien's forbears, Alexandre Gendebien, helped organize the Kingdom of Belgium in 1830. Olivier was born January 12, 1924, and seemed headed for a family business when World War II changed all that. He was 16 and an engineering student, but he would neither try to remain in school nor flee immediately to England. Rather, he joined the underground, used his

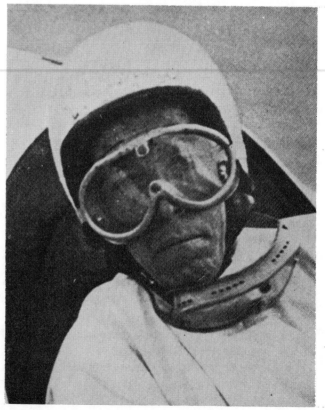

fluency in English to act as liaison with British agents parachuted into his area, helped them sabotage installations that would have aided the enemy, fought with them, and was taken out with them when the job was done. He then joined a Belgian paratrooper unit in the British Army.

After the war, Gendebien switched from engineering to agriculture in order to finish school in half the regulation time (due to a government edict that was designed to restore Belgian farm production quickly). But Olivier had other ideas; he wanted to be a gaucho, he admitted later without the slightest trace of humor, and planned to emigrate to Argentina and buy a ranch there with his income from the family fortune. As part of his plan, he went to Spain, intending to become entirely proficient in Spanish in 6 months (he became proficient not only in that tongue but half a dozen others besides his Belgian dialects). Instead, almost on a whim, he accepted a 6-month job in the Belgian Congo clearing virgin forest for what was to be the new residential quarter of Stanleyville. It was early in 1949, and if you think Africa was a detour from the auto racing world of Europe, you are wrong.

One night in the Congo, several years later (the 6 months turned into 4 years), a friend of Gendebien's named Fraikin was lamenting the fact that he would miss the many new and revived European rallies because his former codriver had retired from competition. Olivier immediately offered his services, and the pair returned to Europe for the 1952 Liège-Rome-Liège rally. Gendebien had invested his money in the Congo and was reaping a good profit, having pretty much abandoned the life of the gaucho for the rather unappealing life of a businessman. The pair had a Mark VII Jaguar, a superb touring car, but not ideal for this rally. Nonetheless, they finished 22nd—among 132 starters and just 23 finishers.

Fraikin and Gendebien continued rallying and occasional cross-country racing for several years, mostly in Jaguars, and in a stretch they came in 2nd 7 straight times. Olivier did not find this as funny as many sportswriters did (who called the pair the "eternal bridesmaids"). He parted with Fraikin in 1955 and bought himself a Mercedes 300SL. He first hit the headlines that same year when he won the Dolomite Gold Cup at Belluna, Italy, a 189-mile sports car test, which he took at 55.75 m.p.h. He was still an amateur, but not for long. The night after the victory dinner, Enzo Ferrari called Gendebien to Modena and pushed a contract in front of him. The Belgian had not yet mastered Italian, and he couldn't discuss the pact with the Commendatore, much less read it. His business-minded ancestors must have winced as Olivier grabbed a pen and signed on the dotted line, making him a professional and starting one of long-distance racing's most successful partnerships. He was one of 5 Ferrari factory drivers at the age of 35.

In 1956 Gendebien was 2nd both in the last Dolomite Cup race and in the Buenos Aires 1000, sharing a car in the latter with Phil Hill, with whom he was to score some of his greatest successes. At the Nurburgring 1000 he shared a Ferrari with Hill and Alfonso de Portago, and the trio came in 3rd. At Le Mans Gendebien and Maurice Trintignant were in a 2.5-litre car that also finished 3rd. His transitional period over, the Belgian got down to serious business in 1957. He won the Circuit of Sicily outright at 66.5 m.p.h. and codrove with Paul Frere to his initial 12-hour victory at Rheims. Their winning speed was 104.02 m.p.h. The pair won the same race in 1958 at 106.05, and Gendebien also shared a winning car at Le Mans with Hill (106.1 m.p.h.) and at the Targa Florio with Luigi Musso (58.9 m.p.h.). Olivier also shared cars with Taffy von Trips at Nurburgring, where they were 3rd, and at Buenos Aires, codriven by Musso, where the trio was 2nd. Musso was his mate at Sebring for another 2nd place.

The year 1959 saw victory at Sebring for the Ferrari forces, the car being shared by Gendebien, Hill, Dan Gurney and Chuck Daigh, with an average of 80.26 m.p.h. The Belgian, also was 2nd at Nurburgring with Hill and 3rd at the Goodwood version of the Tourist Trophy with Hill, Tony Brooks and Cliff Allison. In 1960 Olivier and Frere won for Ferrari at Le Mans at 109.19 m.p.h., and he and Hans Hermann won Sebring for Porsche at 84.93 m.p.h. Gendebien had a Formula 1 ride that season, coming in 3rd in the Belgian Grand Prix in a Cooper, and his Formula 2 performances included 3rds at Pau (Porsche) and at Syracuse (Cooper). He and Hermann shared a Porsche for the Targa Florio and were 3rd; he and Jo Bonnier shared a Ferrari for Nurburgring and were 2nd.

Sebring, Le Mans, and the Targa all fell before Gendebien in 1961. Hill shared the U.S. and French race victories at 90.70 and 115.00 m.p.h. respectively, Trips the Targa at 64.27 m.p.h. Trips and Richie Ginther codrove with Olivier at Nurburgring and were 3rd, all of these with Ferrari. With Porsche, the Belgian was 3rd at Mosport Park. In what was to be his final season (mainly because of opposition by his wife), he and Hill won Le Mans again—the 4th win in 5 years for Olivier —at 115.24 m.p.h. The pair also won at Nurburgring at 82.38 m.p.h. Willy Mairesse and Ricardo Rodriguez shared the Ferrari with defending champion Gendebien for the Targa, and the trio won at 63.47 m.p.h.

At the height of his career as a long-distance racer, he stepped down, except for an occasional drive for old time's sake. "The race I am proudest of," he said, "was the 1957 Mille Miglia, in a Ferrari 250GT, when we made the best time on the fastest section of the course although the car was a good 25 m.p.h. slower than the pure racing cars taking part. That same year, I won another race, to the altar."

There were 2 bad accidents in his career, both with Ferrari and both resulting in brain concussions, but generally he was skilled enough to avoid trouble. "Only 10 percent or so of auto racing accidents are caused by mechanical failure. The rest can be put down to human failure. Race driving calls for intense concentration— you let up for a thousandth of a second, and there's your accident. Both of my accidents were due to split-second lapses, not mechanical failures." He once noted to a close friend that 24 men against whom he had raced in his career from 1955 through 1962 had died at the wheel. By 1962 Olivier was the father of 3 children and he did not want them to become orphans.

BOB GERARD

Latter-day motor racing enthusiasts know Bob Gerard as a Formula 2 sponsor with Merlyn factory assistance. But Frederick Robert Gerard, born in 1914, had a long and distinguished career behind the wheel, starting in 1933 when he appeared competitively for the initial time in the Land's End Trial. His car was a Riley 9, a marque with which his family had been associated, and the precursor of the ERA racing car with which Gerard was to make much of his reputation.

After club experience at Brooklands and Donington, Gerard made a big splash in 1937 with a Riley Sprite, sharing a 3rd in the only 12-hour sports car race ever run at Donington Park. But it was after World War II and in the ERA that Bob made his real impact on British racing. In 1946 Gerard scored a 3rd in the Ulster Trophy at Ballyclare, Ireland, behind the veteran Prince

Bira in an ERA and Reg Parnell in a Maserati. The next year was highlighted by victories in the same race at 71.48 m.p.h. and in the Formula 1 Isle of Man British Empire Trophy Race at 68.02 m.p.h. Gerard also shared a 3rd in the last Marne Grand Prix at Rheims and scored a solo 4th in the European GP at Spa.

In 1948 Gerard was 3rd in the 1st British GP ever, held at Silverstone. Only Luigi Villoresi and Alberto Ascari, both in Maseratis, topped him. Second to Reg Parnell in the Goodwood Trophy, Gerard won the Jersey International road race at St. Helier at 87.3 m.p.h. that same year. In 1949 he won the British Empire Trophy on the Isle of Man for the 2nd time at 71.06 m.p.h., won the Jersey road race the 2nd straight time at 77.10. Driving his ERA, Gerard was 2nd to Switzerland's Baron de Graffenreid in a Maser in the British GP. This was the initial time a British car and driver had finished in a *grande épreuve* in the top 3 in a single-seater.

The British Empire Trophy fell to Gerard for the 3rd time in 1950 at 70.05 m.p.h., and he was 2nd in the Ulster Trophy and 3rd in the Dunrod version of the Tourist Trophy, the latter in a Frazer-Nash sports car. Young Stirling Moss broke Gerard's British Empire Trophy string of victories in 1951, Moss edging Bob, and in the TT race, Moss and Peter Walker (both in Jaguars) preceded the Frazer-Nash driver.

In 1952 Bob won a Goodwood Formula 3 race at 77.98 m.p.h. and a Charterhall Formula Libre battle at 82.4 in his 15-year-old ERA when the BRM team of Reg Parnell and Ken Wharton retired. In the Sussex Trophy at Goodwood, Gerard was 2nd to Mike Hawthorne. Hawthorne, a future World Champion, and Gerard both soon were driving Cooper-Bristols, the most successful of the generally unsuccessful British F2 cars in the fifties. Gerard won the 1953 Castle Combe Fry Memorial, was 2nd to Ken Wharton in the Aintree Formula Libre race in his old ERA. With a new Cooper Grand Prix car, Bob tried some Continental racing, but his best placings were 8ths in the Rouen and French Grands Prix. The following year he won Crystal Palace's London Trophy at 72.16 m.p.h., was 3rd to Moss and Parnell in the Oulton Gold Cup for Formula 1 cars. He won the Hastings Trophy at Castle Combe for Formula Libre cars and Oulton's FL meet, too.

The year 1955 saw victories at Charterhall in the F1 International in a rare Maserati ride, and at Brands Hatch in the Rochester Cup and Farningham Trophy races, both in the Cooper-Bristol. There was a 2nd to Peter Collins in the Crystal Palace London Trophy race, 3rds at Castle Combe in the Avon Trophy F1 and Empire News Trophy FL meetings. Gerard was beginning to wind down his driving in 1956, although he did win at Mallory Park in an FL start and was 2nd in the Aintree 100. In the Goodwood Richmond Trophy he piloted a Connaught to 4th, and he also made some Turner sports car starts. Gerard's last major placing was a 3rd in the Mallory FL race in 1958.

EIGHTY YEARS AMONG THE SPEED PEOPLE

The early racers, besides being competitors, often were men who pioneered the rise of the automobile, men such as Marcel Renault (1) at the wheel of the car that won its class in the 1902 Paris-Vienna cross country race at 38.9 m.p.h. Selwyn Edge (2) watches Charles Jarrott prepare to race in the 1903 Paris-Madrid in a De Dietrich car. Louis Chevrolet and his mechanic in a 1904 Darracq (3). Winning the Targa Florio in 1907, Felice Nazzaro is all business while his mechanic waves (4) from the F.I.A.T. that averaged 33.50 m.p.h. Racing in America started in 1895 (a year after Europe) with Frank Duryea (5) at the steering bar in the car that won the Thanksgiving Day Chicago race.

5

2

3

4

1

6   7

American racing mostly was on tracks, even in the early days. Barney Oldfield gave 1910 exhibition runs in his Lightning Benz (6), and became a bigger hero than the first American Grand Prix driver, David Bruce-Brown of Yale (right), masked much like a modern GP driver and ready for the French GP at Dieppe in 1912 (7). There were road races, like those in Elgin, Ill. (8), before World War I—the number 2 National on the right eventually winning—but the emphasis on tracks led to the rise of races like the Indianapolis 500, which started in 1911 with Ray Harroun winning at 71.59 m.p.h. (9) and introducing the rear-view mirror.

8

9

10

Foreign drivers and cars began running Indianapolis in 1913. Jules Goux in a Peugeot started in the second row that year, but won at 75.933 m.p.h. (10, 11). But the winning car in most big races was the Mercedes, and it was a favorite of drivers like Louis Wagner (left)—he and his racing mechanic ready their car for the French GP in 1914 (12), the last great race in Europe before the outbreak of World War I. Another Mercedes (13), driven by Christian Lautenschlager won that famed classic.

11

12   13

14 15

Mercedes won in America, too. Here the Schroeder Mercedes (14) is whipped to victory by the great Ralph DePalma in the Vanderbilt Cup race at Santa Monica in 1914 at 75.50 m.p.h. The big American cars were Stutz and Mercer (15), with Earl Cooper on the right dueling with Eddie Pullen in another Santa Monica race. Dario Resta (16) won the 1916 Indianapolis 500 for Peugeot, passing Dave Lewis's Crawford along the way (17). Racing in Europe ended in 1914, in America in 1916, with the world plunged into a global war.

16

17

18   19

20

21

After World War I, racing returned, and with it, new faces and names that would become famous. In 1919 Fiat's Antonio Ascari would be a great name (18) and would sire a still greater driver, who would follow in his father's footsteps. Another famed racing name of that day and later was Alfred Neubauer, here at the wheel of an Austro-Daimler Sascha (19) in 1921. That was the year America's Jimmy Murphy won the French GP (20) in the white Duesenberg to the right of the starter, with Henry Segrave in a Sunbeam alongside. Major endurance races were back in vogue, too, like Italy's famed Targa Florio, contested in 1924 by Mercedes and Christian Werner (21).

22

23

Board tracks were unique in America in the twenties. Harry Hartz (22) won the 300-miler at Atlantic City in 1926 at 134.091 m.p.h., fastest race ever held up to that time. On the other coast, dirt track racing (23) at Ascot, Calif., was popular, with Millers dueling with Model T cars, usually with inverted starts, or the fastest cars being placed at the rear of the field.

24

25

The thirties found more magnificent cars in action, like this Type 35C Bugatti (24) in the hands of Count Czaykowski, leading the French GP, with Tim Birkin's Bentley close at hand. A typical Indy car of the day was Louie Schneider's Bowes Seal Fast Special (25) in which he won the 1931 race at 96.692 m.p.h.

26

27

Arch rivals in the thirties, and well ahead of their time in terms of streamlining and power, were the German cars that dominated European road racing. The rear-engined Auto Union (26) was designed by Dr. Ferdinand Porsche, but it met its match in the three-litre front-engined Mercedes (27), here in the hands of one of the era's great drivers, Hermann Lang.

28

There are always drivers who dominate an era. For this period, in Europe, it was Tazio Nuvolari (28), still considered one of the all-time greats, here visiting the United States for the revival of the Vanderbilt Cup. A great American driver was Wilbur Shaw (29), who won his third Indy 500 in 1940 (others in 1937 and 1939). France had several fine drivers in those days, including Rene Dreyfus and Raymond Sommer (30), the latter in a 308 Alfa Romeo in the Pau GP. A second world war again ended most auto racing in the U.S. and Europe in 1941.

29

30

Postwar racing blossomed in Europe mostly with old equipment at first, but including some new designs like the first Ferrari (31), introduced in May, 1947, at Piacenza, Italy, with Franco Cortese driving. Ferraris evolved rapidly, like the 375 driven by Fro Gonzalez (32) in the 1951 French GP and the Formula 2 car driven to a World Championship by Alberto Ascari (Antonio's son) in the 1953 Dutch GP (33). In America, however, road racing was slow getting started, with slightly less esoteric equipment like Briggs Cunningham's Bu-Merc (34, left) with Briggs tying his shoe before the start of the 1948 Watkins Glen, N.Y., Grand Prix. Watching is Mike Vaughn in a Lagonda. In England, racing was reviving, too, with a nonchalant young Stirling Moss showing how to drive a Formula 500 Keift (35) one-handed in 1951. Indianapolis was reborn in 1946 after a four-year suspension due to the war. Three-time winner Wilbur Shaw showed off the Borg-Warner Trophy (36) to his wife and son, Billy, who became in the seventies a road-racing driver and instructor. The typical Indy car continued to be a front-engined special like 1952 winner Troy Ruttman's Agajanian (37), which won at 128.922 m.p.h. A decade later and more, the Indy car was pretty much the same, as shown by Parnelli Jones's 1963 winning Agajanian car (38, 39), which registered 143.137 m.p.h.

36

37

Troy Ruttman
Indianapolis Motor Speedway
1952

38

39

40

41

Things were changing in Europe. Once again Americans were casting their eyes toward winning there, too. A pioneer in the fifties was Briggs Cunningham, second from left, in this group of Cunningham team drivers (40) discussing the 1953 LeMans race. Others included are John Fitch, Sherwood Johnston, a sleepy Phil Hill. The car was the Cunningham C5R (41), here in less formidable street form. Fitch and Phil Walters finished 3rd, Cunningham himself 7th, which was cause for celebration (42), though even better days were ahead. Two of racing's greatest drivers were contemporaries. Juan Manuel Fangio (43) won five World Championships in four different cars, including this 1955 Mercedes (44). Stirling Moss (45) never won the big crown even once, but was acknowledged as Fangio's only serious rival, and Moss excelled even Fangio in sports-car and endurance races. In 1955 he was Fangio's Mercedes teammate, driving cars like this streamlined W.196 (46) on the Monza banking in GP races. Fangio's last victory was in the 1957 German GP at Nurburgring where he trailed Ferrari's Mike Hawthorn and Vanwall's Tony Brooks temporarily (47), but won a thriller. Fangio's last race, July 6, 1958, the Rheims GP, saw the Maserati-based Juan dueling with Moss in a Vanwall (48).

42

43

44

45

46

47

48

49

50

51

52

53

American Indianapolis car drivers gained a false sense of security from the 1957 Monza 500 or Race of Two Worlds, which saw Jimmy Bryan win a contest suited to the bigger, more powerful U.S. machinery on the banked Monza autodrome at 160.067 m.p.h. (49). But the rear-engine, road-racing revolution was near at hand. Peter Collins (50), a Briton driving for Ferrari, was typical of the new stars that were emerging in Europe, and so was Bruce McLaren of New Zealand (51), who won the 1959 United States GP at Sebring, Fla., only time it was held there, in a Cooper-Climax. Another star emerging was Australia's Jack Brabham (52), here trailing Jean Behra and Stirling Moss at Monaco in 1959. Americans still were trying in Europe, men like Lance Reventlow (53), who started in his own Scarab car in its first championship race at Spa in 1960, and Masten Gregory (54), racing a Camoradi team car at LeMans that same year and a Lotus-Climax (55) at Aintree in 1962, trailing Innes Ireland's similar car. Britons were the real stars, like Stirling Moss, (56), taking the Monaco GP in a Rob Walker Lotus, that marque's first major success, and Tony Brooks (57) winning the German GP on the Avus banking in a Ferrari.

54

57

55

56

58

Another fine British driver was mustachioed Graham Hill (58), World Champion in the 1962 BRM. Fields were international and included the less professional and skilled like Count Carel de Beaufort of Holland (59) in his "Old Fatty Porsche" at Pau in 1963. Back in America, they were catching up, with cars like Roger Penske's Telar and Zerex Specials, based on European designs. Here Penske (60), who soon would retire as a driver to become a major racing entrepreneur, grins after winning the 1962 Riverside GP.

59

60

Another all-time great, Jim Clark of Scotland (61), who should have won the Indianapolis 500 in 1963 and did win in 1965, was a two-time GP champion and sports-car ace as well. Clark and Lotus were inseparable, such as this Lotus-Climax (62) in which he leads Graham Hill's BRM while winning the 1964 British GP. Clark's 1963 rear-engined Lotus helped change the American oval track racing, and clinched the trend when Jim won Indianapolis in 1965 (63) in his Lotus 38, powered by Ford. Old-line veterans (64) like Parnelli Jones, left, went so far as to adopt the Lotus, while others developed their own rear-engine cars like Rodger Ward's Watson-Offy, right.

61

62

63

64

65

66

67

Americans had their special forms of racing, including the stock car that battled on paved tracks and, later, superspeedways. Here, Bobby Isaac in a Hemi-Charger Dodge (65) leads a race in 1964. American sports cars often were hybrids that sometimes worked out very well, like this Cooper-Olds (66) bought by Bruce McLaren in 1964 and both raced and studied for Bruce's own later designs. A home-grown British sports car was the Tojeiro-Ford, raced that same year at Silverstone by a short-haired Scot named Jackie Stewart (67) under Ecurie Ecosse sponsorship. Stewart was a wonder, who soon found himself (68) in GP racing and at LeMans with the likes of Graham Hill in a Rover-BRM.

68

69

70

71

72

73

In 1965 Jim Clark won six Grands Prix in a row, a record. Here (69) he charges off to a typical Clark start—in front—at the South African GP. With stars like Clark, it was easy to overlook all the little fellows who were trying to win and who made up a third of any starting field. Privateer Bob Anderson (70) used old equipment, but beautifully prepared like this Brabham-Climax BT 11. America's Richie Ginther had a team ride with Honda (71) and won his only GP in the Mexican race in 1965, beating Dan Gurney's Brabham by under 3 seconds. Another American, Bob Bondurant (72), had a private BRM when he raced at Monaco and in some other races in 1966. Another British star was John Surtees (73), who won in a Ferrari Tipo 312 in the Belgian GP, his last race for the Italian factory.

74

75

As with many of the greats, America's Dan Gurney
(74) was a versatile racer, at home in Grand Prix or
Indy cars, sports/prototypes, or even stock cars like
Bud Moore's 1967 Mercury (75) which Dan raced at
Riverside, a race he figuratively owned. Retired as a
driver, Jim Hall still had racing ideas like his various
Chaparral cars, this one (76) a Chap 65 with a high
"spoiler" for Canadian-American Challenge Cup rac-
ing in 1966. Ford had better ideas, too, in 1966 when
the impetus that Briggs Cunningham had launched at
LeMans brought a three-fold dividened (77) with
Ford II-A sports/prototypes winning all.

76

77

*An all-time great of a specialized racing area was Richard Petty (78),
king of the stock-car set. The fastest pit stops of all came in American
stock-car racing, with crews like Ray Fox's picking up valuable time
for Buddy Baker in a Charger (79). But Petty, though he had a great
crew, did most of the time-gaining himself (80), maneuvering inside
when necessary in fender-to-fender dicing at 150 m.p.h. and more.*

82

One of the greats except in longevity was Jochen Rindt (81), racing's only posthumous World Champion. Always a charger no matter the conditions, Rindt was running GP races at an early age in 1966 when he had a Cooper-Maserati at Spa (82). But it was in the Lotus cars that Rindt made his greatest mark. His Lotus-Ford 49B had a high aerofoil early in the 1969 season (83), but it was later banned. The 1970 Lotus 49C saw Rindt a GP winner (84), here at Monaco in May 1970, his World Championship year, when he also raced the new 72. The man Rindt beat was World Champion in 1969 and 1971, Jackie Stewart (85), the world's highest paid athlete and a dollar millionaire by 1972. Stewart won his first title in a French Matra-Ford, but the next one came in the 1971 Tyrrell-Ford (86), introduced late the year before.

83

81

84

85

86

87

88

89

Probably the closest Grand Prix finish ever came in the Italian GP on Sept. 5, 1971, at Monza. Peter Gethin's BRM P.160 (87, his hand raised) won the race; only 61/100ths of a second covered the first five finishers. Less close was Porsche's domination of the sports/prototype racing scene. The 917K won many races each year, including Sebring in 1971 when Vic Elford codrove a Martini & Rossi car (88) that beat even the factory Gulf-Porsches. In America, Indiana-polis now featured many European-designed cars as well as American. Peter Revson, another versatile American racer, won the pole in the 1971 (89) quali-fying in a McLaren M16, which showed how much alike GP and Indy cars now looked, on the surface at least. A familiar scene in 1971 was a McLaren driven by Denny Hulme of New Zealand winning another CanAm race (90), with Jackie Stewart's L&M Lola trailing. McLarens dominated the Canadian-American Challenge Cup racing series almost from the start (91), except for the Lolas and the UOP Shadow, driven by England's Jackie Oliver. In 1972, however, a new car appeared, and it won the CanAm title and everything else in sight. The L&M Porsche-Audi 917K (92), an outgrowth of the endurance racing champion car, put the McLarens in the background at last.

90

91

92

93

94

95

Still another top American driver was Mark Donohue (93) who excelled in nearly everything he drove, all the while managing the mechanical end of Roger Penske Racing. After frustrations in USAC racing, Mark won at Indianapolis in his Sunoco McLaren (94) in 1972. He already had many sports-car and endurance-race victories in the bag by then and was a familiar figure at places like Daytona with Penske (95) in the pits. Donohue also drove CanAm and even sedans in the Trans-American series that he won in 1971 (96), from fields that included Parnelli Jones, Dan Gurney, and others. Do we have the next great GP driver? Time will tell for Emerson Fittipaldi of Brazil, already a World Champion in 1972, his fourth year of international racing. Fittipaldi won the United States GP (97) in a Lotus-Ford 72C in 1970 in just his fourth Formula 1 start. It was a happy Emerson who won five Grands Prix in 1972, here in Austria (98), in the latest version of the basic 72 model, now called the John Player Special after its British cigarette sponsor (99).

96

97

98

99

Consistency made Joe Leonard a two-in-a-row United States Auto Club champion in 1971–72 in his Maurice Phillippe-designed Samsonite Special (100). It was Phillippe who also designed the 1970–72 World Championship Lotus in GP racing. The car's rear wing, side radiators and low-slung profile (101) made a sharp contrast to the racing stock cars of its day —here a 1970 NASCAR (National Association for Stock Car Automobile Racing) race at Charlotte, N. C., with the Southern stars (top to bottom) Bobby Isaac, Bobby Allison, and James Hylton driving.

100

101

Another versatile American (though Italian born) was Mario Andretti (102), who won at Indianapolis, in Grand Prix racing and in sports/prototype endurance races . . . and also in such esoteric cars as this STP hillclimb version of a championship car (103). A more specialized star in a very much more specialized car was Don Garlits in a fuel dragster (104), a form of motor sport that has made only minimal impact outside North America. Many American-inspired racing classes have crossed the seas, however, including Can-Am into the Interserie, Formula B SCCA cars into Formula Atlantic, and the Formula A SCCA cars, like those of Bob Brown and Tony Adamowicz here (105), into Formula 5000.

103

102

104

105

106

110

107

111

LAND SPEED RECORD

Most specialized motor sport of all, perhaps, is the Land Speed Record quest. It started before the turn of the century, with even electric streamliners like Camille Jenatzy's Le Jamais Contente (106) at 65.79 m.p.h. An early American LSR was Henry Ford's 91.4 m.p.h. on a frozen Michigan Lake (107), in place of driver Barney Oldfield. Through the early years others included Parry Thomas's Babs (108) in 1926, Malcolm Campbell's Bluebird (109) in 1928, Henry Segrave's Golden Arrow (110) in 1929, and George Eyston's Thunderbolt (111) in 1934. John Cobb became the modern speed king with a variety of cars, including this Napier-Lion-engined car with its innards exposed (112) before his 350.20 m.p.h. run in 1938. Cobb kept at it until he owned the 394.19 m.p.h. record of 1947.

108

109

112

Donald Campbell's Bluebird (113) ran 403.164 m.p.h. in 1964 on a gas turbine engine. It was a mad year for LSR cars and drivers. Tom Green, driving Walt Arfons's Wingfoot Express (114), did 413.2 m.p.h. Walt's brother Art, who did his own driving in the Green Monster (115), held the record several times, including a 544.13 m.p.h. mark in 1964. Craig Breedlove's Spirit of America (116) and Sonic I raised the LSR to 600.6 m.p.h. in 1965. That record was broken by Gary Gabelich in the Blue Flame (117), which averaged 622.407 m.p.h. in 1970.

113

114

115

116

117

118

OTHER CARS AND COMPETITION

Formula 5000, an outgrowth of America's SCCA Formula A, flourished in England with drivers like Frank Gardner in a Lola (118) and made the series a new hit in the United States. Formula 2 attracted rising young drivers and established Grand Prix stars like Emerson Fittipaldi (119) in a Moonraker Lotus. Formula 3 was for still maturing young men like England's Tony Trimmer (120), here in a 1972 John Player Special. Rallying was world-wide, with the U.S. rapidly catching up to established European fixtures such as the Monte Carlo, which attracts such stars as Timo Makinen in a Mini Cooper S (121) and Erik Carlsson in a SAAB (122). Almost on a par with Formula 3 was a Cortina-engined Formula Ford, popular everywhere, but especially in Britain, where even Americans like Jas Patterson (123) sought that elusive first rung to big time motor racing in Europe or the States, in cars like this Wimhurst Mk. 4 with body by Bert Ray.

119

123

120

121

122

PETER GETHIN

Bruce McLaren was dead. Dan Gurney, his immediate replacement in the rich Canadian-American Challenge Cup series, had a contract problem that pulled him from the McLaren team after 3 races. And thus the hand of fate reached out and brought Peter (Texas) Gethin, as British as they come despite the American nickname, to the seat of a McLaren M8D for the 4th CanAm of the 1970 series. Peter finished 2nd to his team leader, Denis Hulme, at Edmonton, Canada. He could have won for his McLaren had a more powerful engine than Hulme's, and once or twice he pulled out from Denis's slipstream and looked as if he might pass to the lead. But each time, he dropped back in deference to Hulme.

They finished that way, Hulme winning, Gethin 2nd, at Edmonton. Two races later, at Elkhart Lake in the Road America CanAm, Gethin tried to be a good team man again, but to no avail. Hulme became involved with "helpful" track workers who gave him a push after a spin while he was attempting to restart his car, a technical rule violation. Gethin was in the lead, but slowed to let Denis regain it (both cars having lapped the entire field, they could do pretty much as they wanted), and dutifully Peter crossed the line as the trailer to Hulme's tractor. But he suddenly found himself the winner when Denis's car was penalized enough seconds to make him 15th rather than 1st. An embarrassed Gethin was handed the cup, the laurels, and the kiss, for a victory he had really earned, despite his seeming reluctance to beat the boss. In a sense it was poetic justice to see a a good thing happen to Gethin, who has had his share of bad moments.

His 1st year in big-time auto racing was, in Gethin's own words, "an utter failure." Yet his name immediately became prominent in the lists of drivers to watch in the future, and his promise after that 1st big year, 1965, was enhanced rather than diminished. Racing and the name Gethin seem to go together in England. Peter Kenneth Gethin, who was born in Ewell, Surrey, on February 21, 1940, was the son of a famous English jockey, Ken Gethin. Peter was educated at Badington College in Leatherhead, which, he later claimed, about described his intellectual prowess in school. He tried horse riding, gave up jockeying at age 11 because he thought it too dangerous.

Gethin left school as quickly as he could (age 17) and signed on with Ford of England as an apprentice mechanic. After 4 years, he was ready to set himself up in the garage business when the motor racing bug infected the 22-year-old. In the middle of 1962 he purchased a 997 c.c. Lotus-Ford 7 and immediately entered the 1st available race, which happened to be a big meeting at Britain's famed Brands Hatch. There were some raised eyebrows when the novice qualified for the pole position, but Peter quickly reverted to form when, while leading the pack after a lap or so, he spun and was out of it.

Gethin won 2 races and picked up several 2nds the rest of 1962, then traded the old car for a Lotus-Ford 23 of 1100 c.c. (the deal suitably sweetened by a liberal dose of cash borrowed from father, friends and anyone else Peter could hit for a few pounds). His next year was a fairly unproductive one, however, although it was more the car's fault than Gethin's. Tony Hegbourne, who was having considerably more success with his Lotus-Ford 23, took pity on Peter and helped him work out the bugs in the latter's car late in the season. Peter's best showing of the year came the day after Christmas, known as Boxing Day in Britain, when he won his 1200-c.c. class and was 2nd overall to a 2-litre Attila-Climax at Brands Hatch.

The year 1964 was a glorious year for Gethin when he won race after race in his now well-functioning car, 21 races in all, with the most important victory coming in the Guards Trophy Race. Charles Lucas, proprietor of C. Lucas (Engineering) Limited was setting up a racing team in 1965 and, based on Peter's 1964 performance, asked him to join the new scuderia, piloting an old but seemingly still competitive Lotus-Ford 22 Formula 3 car that had been handled formerly by Roy Pike and others. The first thing the Lucas-Gethin combination did was bring the car up to current Lotus-Ford 31 specifications.

The revitalization was not successful. Gethin had a miserable season, as indicated, although there were enough bright spots to indicate that the future could be better if he had competitive machinery. At Silverstone he led until the car started to die on him, but still managed 2nd. At Croft he held off several challengers to win a national meeting. Adding to his woes were several drives Gethin made in the old Formula 2 Graham Hill car, which Lucas himself had driven earlier in the year in F3 racing, but had given up after a complete lack of success. In Gethin's hands the car performed somewhat better, although still without much vigor. It quit more often than not, although Peter was able to wring out of it 2nds at Goodwood on Easter Monday and at Brands Hatch during the August Bank Holiday meeting.

Gethin and Lucas parted company at the end of the year as friends; Lucas and his race manager, Ken Tyrrell, originally had planned to race 2 cars, but had tried to give it a go with 3. "To be successful with 3 cars in any kind of real racing is virtually impossible for a small team," said Tyrrell in explaining the retreat. "Someone has to suffer, even in the best of teams, and I feel a 2-car setup is ideal." For 1966 Gethin was not without a ride, however. Rodney Bloor, another wealthy patron like Lucas, had a F3 Brabham-Ford that he wanted driven by a good man. That "good man" turned out to be Peter Gethin.

Gethin spent 2 years driving the F3 for Bloor, and although he won some races, the time was spent mainly in frustrating mechanical breakdowns. He and Bloor parted company amicably in 1969, and Peter drove a Chevron B10 in F2 for Frank Lythgoe for a time, then switched to a Repco-Brabham BT23C. The season was not his brightest, but he did manage a 2nd at Albi and a 3rd—to 2 very fast Ferraris—at Vallelunga. September 2, 1968, at Brands Hatch, he broke into the victory column, and the crowd applause was both warm and genuine. Gethin's performance, in the wet, against good opposition, in his heat and in the final, showed that he still had the potential to win if he had the proper mount.

In 1969 Gethin at last found a proper mount, a McLaren M10A for the new Formula 5000 series in England. Here was Grand Prix racing, but with 5-litre engines. Peter won the first 4 races in the series, then took a holiday by bringing his McLaren to the States to drive in the comparable Formula A series of the SCCA. He returned that fall in time to wrap up the Guards European F5000 championship. Over in the U.S. Gethin won the Lime Rock, Conn., F/A race and convinced himself that he wanted to go racing there—the States—as a steady proposition when possible.

The chance for regular work in America came in 1970 in several areas. Even though Gethin was successfully defending his F5000 title, with 8 victories in 13 starts, plus a trio of 2nds and 2 retirements, he also signed up for a more extensive F/A series in the SCCA ranks. Fate intervened with McLaren's death and the offer to join the reshuffled Team McLaren, both for the CanAm and for Formula 1 in the McLaren-Ford M7A. Gethin jumped at the chance with the happy CanAm results already outlined. In F1, victory would prove more elusive.

Peter's 1st real F1 drive came in the Race of Champions when he brought an old McLaren M7C into 6th place, and after Hulme injured his hands in an accident, he carried the McLaren colors to Zandvoort alone. Gethin proved faster in practice than Jack Brabham, John Surtees, Jo Siffert, and Gurney. He was running 7th in the actual race when he spun off and crashed. There was little question that Gethin belonged, however, and that championship points were in the offing in GP racing for him as they were in CanAm, F5000 and other areas.

The points came in 1971, but only after a series of frustrations in championship racing and success in non-title starts. Eighth in the Questor GP, Gethin was 2nd in the Oulton Spring Race and tied Pedro Rodriguez for the day's fastest lap, was 2nd in the Silverstone International, retired in the Rindt Memorial. So much for glory without points. In championship racing he retired in South Africa, was 8th in Spain, retired at Monaco, was 15th in Holland, 9th in France, retired in Britain and Germany. He switched from McLaren to BRM at this point, amicably however. In a BRM he was 10th in Austria. A poor season? The whole series was outweighed by the Italian GP. It was the closest GP in years. Five cars were covered by a single second, and the winner was Peter Gethin by a hundredth of a second —3 feet—over Ronnie Peterson at 151.634 m.p.h. Those 9 points tied Peter with Rodriguez, Chris Amon, Reine Wisell and Hulme. Despite a 14th in Canada and a 9th in the U.S. GP, the future boded well. But Peter's future seemed to be once again in F5000. Besides running in Europe, he signed on for the L&M Championship in the States with a new Chevron in 1973. To prove he was a man to watch, Gethin warmed up by winning a F5000 and combined F1-F5000 races in one weekend at the Brands Hatch Race of Champions.

RICHIE GINTHER

On October 24, 1965, the sky over Mexico City was a shimmering blue, the air warm and clear, and Richie Ginther, a small, freckled man sat in a white and red Honda in the 2nd 2-car row. The redhead had never won an international Grand Prix, despite 15 years of racing, and time was growing short, for he was 35 years old. His Japanese car had never won either; Honda was new to GP racing.

When the flag came down the Honda's ignition failed to catch properly, and for an instant, Richie sat battling the switch and pedal while cars flashed past him.

Then the Honda caught hold, and Ginther pushed down on the accelerator. "I put it down, man, and I was gone," he recalled later. "I was all by myself at the 1st corner, and at the end of the 1st lap, I looked back in the mirror, and I couldn't see anyone behind me. I thought for an instant that they must all have spun out." The chase was on. Lorenzo Bandini's Ferrari ended up off the course and Jim Clark (the polesitter), Jack Brabham, Jackie Stewart, Bruce McLaren, and Jo Rindt,

American Road Race in a 4.1-litre Ferrari. A bad start put the Hill-Ginther team in 10th place after the initial day, and on the 2nd leg of the treacherous race, the pair met disaster somewhere between Puebla and Mexico City. The Ferrari was going flat out when it topped a steep rise to find an unmarked, sharp, right-handed downhill turn. The car plunged off the road's edge tail first and landed among some boulders 50 feet below. Both men were shaken but relatively unhurt.

Climbing back to the edge, they spied a road sign that would have warned of the turn; it had been removed by a hidden group of Mexican spectators who had wanted to enliven their vantage point. When the 2 drivers ran over the hill to warn other competitors, the spectators, who included some soldiers, tried to stop them. Undaunted by mutterings, shaken fists, and even a few bayonet jabs, Hill and Ginther remained at the crest of the hill to warn oncoming cars to slow down. Seventeen hours later, the last—14th—car appeared and the pair hitched a ride in it to Mexico City.

Despite that experience, they were together again in 1954 in Mexico, and this time their effort in Alan Guiberson's white 4.5-litre Ferrari earned a 2nd place behind Umberto Maglioli's factory Ferrari (only 20 seconds apart after 1,909 miles of racing). Ginther, meanwhile, was gaining valuable experience in Aston Martins and Austin-Healeys, and in 1955 he went with Hill as Phil's mechanic to that ill-fated Le Mans race as part of Guiberson's team. John von Neumann, who helped many an American racer's career, lent him a Porsche Spyder and other Ferraris to drive, then gave Richie a job managing a Ferrari agency, one of California's biggest. This led to trips to Modena and exposure to the factory people. Luigi Chinetti, a 3-time Le Mans winner himself and Ferrari's biggest importer in the United States, sponsored some of Richie's drives, including his initial one at Le Mans in 1957 where Ginther's Testa Rossa was running 2nd in class when it quit.

That same year Richie won the GT class at Sebring and took races at Lime Rock, Conn., and at Riverside and Torry Pines. At Sebring the following year, Ginther and Von Neumann were running 3rd overall when their Testa Rossa broke its rear axle. In 1959 Ginther finally won the GT class at Sebring, and that season he was the best Ferrari driver in North America. In January 1960 the freckled 29-year-old codrove a factory car with Wolfgang von Trips and took 2nd in the Argentine 1000. Back in the United States, he quit his distributorship job with the intention of quitting the whole business. But an overseas phone call from Italy changed all that. It offered Richie a 4-race factory Ferrari contract.

Ginther's debut was in the Targa Florio, in which he crashed. In the Monaco GP, his debut in a Formula 1 car, Richie drove a rear-engined prototype Ferrari into 6th place. At Zandvoort and at Monza he was 6th, then 2nd. The Commendatore was impressed. Richie accepted his offer of the job of chief test driver in addition to his race team berth, and his contracts were renewed for

among others, broke down in the effort to overtake the inspired Ginther. Only Dan Gurney, Richie's old friend who was driving his last GP race in a Brabham-Climax before moving into his own Eagle marque, had a chance near the end. Dan put on the pressure, and in the last 15 laps over the 3.2-mile circuit, Gurney cut Richie's lead from 7 seconds to less than 3. But Ginther refused to panic or break his car, and he flashed over the line at the end of the 65th lap with a winning speed of 94.262 m.p.h., Gurney just 2.89 seconds behind him.

Paul Richard Ginther was born August 5, 1930, in Hollywood, youngest of 3 children. The family moved to Dayton just after his birth, but returned to Santa Monica in 1935. In 1946 Richie, who already was driving a 1932 Chevrolet, met a fraternity brother of his older brother, a guy named Phil Hill, who channeled his general enthusiasm for cars in a proper direction. Ginther ignored academic subjects and concentrated on shop and mechanical drawing in high school, and upon his graduation in 1948 he joined Douglas Aircraft's jig and tool division, where his father worked. A year and a half later, he left to join Hill as his mechanic at International Motors, then took a better-paying job as Bill Cramer's mechanic and occasional driver. Ginther made his competition debut in Cramer's Ford-powered MG TC early in 1951 and finished 5th. On his 21st birthday he entered the U.S. Army and spent the next 2 years repairing helicopters stateside and in Korea.

In 1953 Richie was discharged and went to work as the manager of a foreign car shop. His friendship with Hill having been renewed, Ginther took time off that year to act as copilot to Phil in the 4th Mexican Pan-

1961. One of the most memorable of his drives came with Ferrari that year at the Monaco GP. Stirling Moss had qualified his Lotus for the pole position, and Ginther was right next to him. They were to remain that way through most of the race, their wheel-to-wheel duel menaced only briefly by Phil Hill before mechanical trouble claimed him.

By the 85th lap, the difference between Moss's green car and Richie's red one was a mere 4 seconds; in the final go-around it dropped to less than that, as Ginther pressed closer and closer. But he ran out of road, Moss taking the flag just barely ahead of Ginther. Richie finished 5th in the World Championship standings with 16 points, then mysteriously was dropped by Ferrari to be replaced by Willy Mairesse. However, Ginther's reputation was such that he was signed immediately by BRM for 1962. Some crashes and many retirements marred the next two seasons while the BRM got sorted out, but Ginther managed to improve his standing in the point tables from 8th to 2nd, in a tie with teammate Graham Hill. That year he also drove the Rover-BRM turbine car in its Le Mans demonstration run.

By this time Ginther's skill with cars was so good that he finished every GP he started in 1964, coming in 4th in the tables, and was asked regularly to participate in the development programs of new cars such as the Ford GT that he drove at both Le Mans and Rheims that season. He had a serious crash in a BRM at Aintree when his car flipped and ended up on top of him. Except for a few cracked ribs, he was okay. The Californian later summed up his racing philosophy in these years rather matter-of-factly. "I wasn't much of a charger. I used to lie back and pace myself, picking off the front runners as they faltered, one by one. You can gain a lot of places that way, but I guess you can't win too many. Maybe I knew too much about the cars I was driving— I had worked on them and on their engines too much. If I thought I heard something, I'd be inclined to drop back or even drop out.

"I know I got the most you could out of a car. I used to nurse them. I know I finished races that other drivers would not have—and this isn't any knock at them. If anything it's a knock at myself. I wasn't one of those 'win or else' guys and I guess I outsmarted myself out of plenty of victories. I know damn well I lost races I should have won, races others would have won. Summing up, I guess I wanted to finish more than I wanted to win."

Ginther's philosophy was ideal for a new marque, like Honda, which was trying to mate chassis and engine, theory and practice, crew and car. Ginther switched from BRM to Honda in 1965, then moved on to Gurney's Eagle in 1967. If he had an unrealized dream after that victory at Mexico in 1965—he long ago had given up the idea of becoming a World Champion, he admitted later—it was to win at Indianapolis, a race in which a thinking driver, a driver who nurses his car

properly, has a good chance to win when the fastest, flashier cars and drivers have fallen by the wayside. But it was not to be. Gurney gave Ginther his first try in 1967, and things looked good. Richie practiced smoothly and was tabbed a "rookie" to beat (all initial-time Indy drivers are "rookies," even World Champions like Jim Clark or Graham Hill). But in the official qualifying runs, he just couldn't seem to reach a fast enough speed. Finally he turned the Eagle over to Jerry Grant, who qualified it 1st crack out of the box. That seemed to crystalize something in Ginther's mind. He went away and thought for a long while, then startled the racing world with the announcement of his retirement as a competitive driver. He would remain—at least for a little while—as a tester and development man.

Richie had given a lot to racing—including his marriage—and his name, if not in the first rank, would be remembered at least. It was he who drove both the last front-engined Ferrari and the initial rear-engined one. He drove the Rover-BRM turbine. He drove the Honda to its initial victory. That kind of knowledge was put to good use by Ginther on the team management side in the late Sixties and early Seventies.

IGNAZIO GIUNTI

The first championship status race in Argentina in a decade, the opening round of the World Manufacturers' Championship for Group 5 sports/racing cars was held in Buenos Aires on January 10, 1971. Five-time world champion Juan Manuel Fangio, serving as Grand Marshal for his native country's great day, smiled broadly as he brought the 22 cars around the turn and toward the starter's flag of the 1000-kilometer race. When that flag dropped, the big Porsches and Ferraris leaped ahead, a new 312P Ferrari taking the early lead. It was driven by Ignazio Giunti, a veteran driver, but a relatively new name on the big-time scene. He was to shave the lead of this important race for 39 laps, and writers already were burrowing for some background on this new name and face.

Giunti was born August 30, 1941, in Rome, of a well-to-do family. He was still in his teens when his racing career started in 1961 with an Alfa Romeo Giulietta that he used in club races and hillclimbs. Over the next 2 seasons Ignazio progressed to a Giulia, then a Giulia Super. In 1965 he received a factory ride from Abarth, then one from Autodelta the following season. This group was preparing a program that would lead to the T33 Alfa. The ride started with hillclimbing and some stock-car races, then progressed in 1967 to GTA, and Ignazio won the Touring Car section of the European Hillclimb Championship with class victories at Mont Ventoux, Ollon-Villars and Gaisberg. In his first T33 ride, Giunti finished 2nd in the Trophy Bettoja.

In 1968 Giunti and Nanni Galli led the Targa Florio for a good part of the race and almost won, finishing 2nd to Vic Elford. At Le Mans they again teamed for a creditable 4th, even though Ignazio still was suffering from arm injuries he received at Daytona. He won Italy's Silver Helmet Award as the best national driver for the second time that season (having first taken it in 1966). Autodelta retained Giunti for 1969, of course, but their cars were suffering from all kinds of problems, including a complete failure at Sebring and a fatal crash at Le Mans for Lucien Bianchi, which caused a temporary racing halt. Still, Giunti had some bright moments, including a victory at Imola over Jacky Ickx in a Mirage and another in the Ronde Cevenole hillclimb in France. He also won at Belgrade and Jarama in European stock-car races.

In 1970, Giunti went to Ferrari, following an impressive test ride in a 5-litre sports car. He immediately captured a victory, sharing a 512S at Sebring with Mario Andretti and Nino Vaccarella. At Monza he and Nino were 2nd and at Watkins Glen 3rd in the 6-hour race. He was 3rd in the Targa Florio and 4th at Spa. The year also saw Giunti's F1 debut, his initial ride giving the Roman his best finish. In the Belgian Grand Prix, Ignazio drove a steady, unspectacular race and captured 4th behind Pedro Rodriguez, Chris Amon, and Jean-Pierre Beltoise. In the French GP, Giunti was 14th, in the Austrian 7th (he lost several places because of a tire puncture that forced a pit stop). In the Italian GP he retired in the 15th lap with engine problems. Overall, for his half-season's work, Giunti collected 3 points in

the World Driver's Championship standings and tied for 17th place.

The Buenos Aires 1000, then, was his 1st race of 1971, a season that held out rich promise for the Italian in both sports/racing and GP competition. Giunti lost his early lead to the more powerful Gulf-Porsches of Rodriguez and Jo Siffert, then replaced Siffert when the Belgian pitted, but dropped to 3rd again when Vic Elford pushed his Porsche ahead, passing even Rodriguez until hit by a fuel problem on the 31st lap. Four laps later, Pedro pitted for fuel and Giunti regained the lead, setting up a chain of events that was to take his life.

Back in the pack, Beltoise, driving a Matra 660, missed a scheduled pit stop and ran out of fuel while negotiating the Autodrome's hairpin turn. He managed to get out of the groove the other cars were taking before the car rolled to a halt, then jumped out and started pushing it toward the pits. The racers passed him with some margin for safety on the right, and officials, noting this, failed to display the yellow caution flags that might have prevented what happened next.

As Beltoise pushed the Matra, he moved it slightly to right, eliminating the safety margin of a moment before. An Ecurie Filipinetti Ferrari 512 codriven by Jo Bonnier and Mike Parkes came roaring out of the hairpin, closely followed by Giunti, who was intent on lapping them and was screened from Beltoise and the Matra until too late. The Filipinetti car swerved to the left to avoid the obstacle, but Giunti was unable to do so, and he ran straight into the rear of the Matra at speed.

Beltoise jumped for his life, and he saved it, but Ignazio was unlucky. On ramming the Matra, his Ferrari flipped into the air, simultaneously bursting into flame, somersaulted some 200 yards down the course, and came to rest in front of the grandstand. A red flag was quickly displayed, but only a few cars stopped at once, others roaring at speed through the smoke that obscured the flag. It was 5 minutes before they could pull Giunti's body from the burning wreckage—his teammate, Arturo Merzario leading the way into the flames.

Giunti was alive, but burned over some 70 percent of his body. He had multiple concussions and his heart stopped twice on the way to the hospital. Two hours later he was dead.

CHARLIE GLOTZBACH

It was almost as if Someone were trying to tell them something that September of 1968. There had been the way Charlie Glotzbach had slid into the wall at Martinsville, Va., while leading the race and had escaped as the orange Dodge Charger burst into flames. There had been another freak wreck at North Wilkesboro and now, here at Charlotte International Speedway in North Carolina, the race had been postponed a week by a torrential

downpour after Glotzbach had smoked his way into the pole position. The Cotton Owens Dodge forces were wondering what they had to do to get a break or an affirmative nod from Fate.

The National 500 at Charlotte paid $19,380 to the winner. For an ex-driver turned car owner and an ex-peach farmer turned charger that would help refurbish the larder nicely. It was an important race to others, too. For instance, Cale Yarborough was looking for an impressive 5th superspeedway victory while Buddy Baker in the Ray Fox Dodge sought his 3rd straight Charlotte triumph. In addition, David Pearson and Bobby Issac were waging a close battle for the NASCAR championship.

A crowd estimated at 40,000 turned out for the confrontation. And, although Glotzbach sat on the pole, other names were on everyone's lips in speculation about the winner. A Cotton Owens car hadn't won a major NASCAR event since Owens himself was driving. Glotzbach had run 6 NASCAR races back in 1960 and 1961 and done nothing; he had been campaigning since 1966 without a victory or anything close to it. The Edwardsville, Ind., driver qualified fast but something always happened to preclude that ride into Victory Lane. When the starter's flag dropped, Charlie charged into the lead of a 45-car field that circled the 1.5-mile speedway like a pack of oversized hornets. The crowd stood up and hardly ever got the chance to sit down. Glotzbach kept the lead for 2 laps only to be boxed by a tail-ender, letting Pearson in for 3 laps. Then Charlie nosed in front only to be passed by Dodge star Buddy Baker for 9 laps.

Charlie came back—and suddenly the caution flashed on. Baker had hit the wall after a tire had been cut by debris.

Cars began diving into the pits for gas and tires: the early pace had taken a quick toll of rubber in some cases. When the green flashed on, Butch Hartman was leading—but not for long. Pearson took over and began a duel for the lead with the Allison brothers, Bobby in a Dodge and Donnie driving relief in A. J. Foyt's Ford. Then two other northerners, young Pete Hamilton of Massachusetts and Paul Goldsmith of Indiana, inserted themselves into the lead-swapping sweepstakes. All this time Glotzbach was never out of the top 10, usually in the top 5, his pit crew working impeccably, his ability to stay with the leader unimpaired.

It was not until the 245th lap—when more cars were out of the race than in it—that Glotzbach moved in front of Pearson, who had made one less pit stop than he. The lead changed hands 5 more times before Charlie took over for good. It was his first and greatest victory.

Glotzbach, father of 4 and owner of an earth-moving equipment business in Edwardsville, earned the nickname Charging Charlie with his 1st ride at a superspeedway. It was at Daytona in 1967. Harry Hyde, head mechanic for the K & K Insurance Dodge racing team, asked him to try the team's 2-year-old back-up car. Although he had never driven a race car over 120 m.p.h. he proceeded to qualify the vehicle at 175 m.p.h. Driving the same car, he amazed everyone by finishing 4th at the Atlanta 500 a few weeks later. In 9 races, 3 times Charlie made the top 5 in 1967. As number one driver for Cotton Owens, Glotzbach took the pole in 3 out of 10 superspeedway starts and rode in 22 races overall. In 1969 he lost on the last mile at the Daytona 500 to Lee Roy Yarborough after a 95 mile side-by-side duel that left 100,000 fans limp. In 12 superspeedway appearances, Glotzbach finished 5 times in the top 5. He had qualified on the pole for the inaugural Talledega 500, but relinquished the ride when the Professional Drivers Association boycotted the race.

Glotzbach ran only the superspeedways in major competition, but back in 1959 when he was 21 (he was born June 19, 1938), Charlie began driving professionally at the quarter-mile Sportsdrome in Jeffersonville, Ind. He was a born hot shoe; he talked friends and relatives into helping him with the short-lived NASCAR excursion in 1960 and 1961, then confined himself to local competition until his excursion south to fame. For 1970 Glotzbach shifted to the K&K Insurance Dodge with Paul Goldsmith as crew chief and Ray Nichels Engineering Company, Inc., of Highland, Ind., as home base. A mix-up in the pits cost him a lap at the 1970 Daytona 500 where he finished 4th. While he was leading at a 400-miler at Michigan International, his engine exploded late in the race, and the car went up in flames. Charlie was unscathed thanks to a full fireproof suit. He came back, however, in 1970 to win the Michigan 400 with a steady ride. In 1971 Charlie won the Volunteer 500 in 19 starts but, more importantly, he was picked to campaign the Junior Johnson Chevrolet in the return of that marque to regular competition. For 1972, Charlie was virtually retired from NASCAR without a good ride.

GWENDA GLUBB
(JANSON STEWART HAWKES)

The name of Glubb is an honored one in England. There was a Major General Sir Frederick Manley Glubb, promoted in the field during World War I, and the famed Glubb Pasha who created the Arab Legion and commanded it for so many years after World War II. Glubb Pasha was the son of the major general and there was also a daughter, Gwenda, decorated in the field as an ambulance assistant during World War I in Russia.

Gwenda Glubb was an unusual woman, slightly built and small in stature, apparently not unattractive in her youth. Married 3 times, she spent her life seeking excitement. But she was tough, a pioneer woman when all the decent pioneering had been done already. Gwenda spent several years of her youth in Canada, touring the northern wilds by dogsled, often alone. She wore her hair in a mannish cut and submerged her femininity most of the time. She was a fair shot with small arms and a superb motorcyclist, both at Brooklands and Montlhéry, in the Twenties (as Janson). At one time she held the world's 3-wheeler record for 24 hours of racing and the speed record at 118 m.p.h. (as Stewart). And another time, though in great pain, she averaged 102 m.p.h. in the snow, driving a 3-wheeler Morgan. She had to be lifted out of the car after that feat.

Honored with the BRDC Gold Star for her feats in the record-setting business, in a Derby-Miller front-drive 91-cu. in. car, she set absolute world records in the class (1501–2000-c.c. engined cars) for the flying start to 10 miles, and standing start to 100 and 200 kilometers in the Thirties (as Hawkes). According to S. C. H. Davis, who codrove with her, she may have been the greatest woman speedway driver of all time, holding ladies' lap records of 135 at Brooklands and 149 at Montlhéry. But advancing age and other interests interfered, and she turned her attention to boats, fading from the motor scene by World War II.

PAUL GOLDSMITH

It is easy for armchair experts to sit back on the soft leather and in the comfort of a cool drink compare one driver against another. The truth is that there is truly no way to compare one driver against another even under the most favorable circumstances because the in-

gedients are as imprecise as the human psyche and its interaction with lifeless machinery. It is better to look at records and compare lap times and victories on the premise that talent will out and therefore command the better machinery.

Yet how great was Paul Goldsmith? Given the sponsorship of the ruler of his country as Juan Fangio was, would he have been as incomparable a Grand Prix driver? He was not motivated in this direction, yet he was of championship caliber in every facet of motor racing he attempted. Born in Parkersburg, W. Va., October 2, 1927, Goldsmith's family moved north to Michigan and the automobile industry. But Paul chose motorcycles; at 19 he assayed his first competition because the local motorcycle dealer encouraged him. After a stint in the Merchant Marine, it seemed like a good way to make a living. Goldsmith won the American Motorcycle Association crown 3 years in a row—1952–54—before he tapered off into automobile racing. In 1953 he and a friend prepared a Ford for a 250-mile race in Detroit, and Paul won. He raced once at Milwaukee in 1954 and returned to the Detroit Fairgrounds less successfully in 1955.

Goldsmith really was interested in a USAC Championship Trail ride, but Smokey Yunick got there first. Waving Chevrolet money, Yunick enlisted Paul in that marque's factory effort in NASCAR for 1956. Goldsmith ran 10 events, won the Langhorne 300, and was a top 10 finisher 7 times. In 1957 he won 4 races, finishing among the leaders 15 times.

He was accepted quickly by his Dixie rivals because,

in his first NASCAR race at the old Charlotte, N.C., Fairgrounds, he flipped the car, landed on his wheels, and still finished 2nd to Curtis Turner. Goldsmith's biggest early victory was the final race on Daytona's 4.1-mile beach-road course.

The year 1958 was without factory support in NASCAR, and Yunick and Goldsmith saw greener pastures at Indianapolis. The venture was a partnership; Goldsmith and Yunick found a used Indy car just outside St. Louis, Mo., which they paid for with borrowed money. They carted the bits and pieces back to Daytona Beach, and the City of Daytona Beach Special was born. Goldsmith passed the requisite Indy rookie tests and started 14th. It was too good a start. He became involved in the pace lap snafu of 1958 where the first 3 cars on the grid somehow got half a lap ahead of the field before the starter's green flag dropped, and was out of it immediately. (But he felt lucky because Pat O'Connor, a former 500 winner, was killed in the crash that followed the mixup.)

The association with Yunick ended amicably after this race when Paul decided to try his luck in USAC circles fulltime. The decision brought him together on a business basis with Ray Nichels, a Highland, Ind., enterpreneur-garage owner. The pair were to become close friends as well as partners. Paul had real estate interests and a part interest in a timber mill at this juncture and was selling a kind of brake shoe on the side, too. He remained a shrewd businessman and eventually, with Nichels, owned a flying service and a small airport in Indiana along with his management role at Ray Nichels Engineering.

The year 1959 at the Speedway saw him in the Demler Special with Nichels as chief mechanic. He started 19th and finished 5th. For 1960 he returned in the Demler and took 3rd place, his highest finish ever at the Brickyard. He was to run the Racing Associates Special to 14th in 1961, sidelined by an oil leak. In 1962 he drove the American Rubber and Plastics Special (a 1958 Quinn Epperly-design which had once held the lap record at Daytona Speedway courtesy of George Amick who was killed there) to 26th place, sidelined by magneto trouble after 26 laps.

Goldsmith had competed intermittently on the Championship Trail, freelancing as a driver, and had followed the USAC stockcar circuit—a Nichels-prepared Pontiac was his mount—finishing 2nd in 1960 was winning the stock-car championship in 1961 and 1962. He won 10 races on that circuit for his 1st title and 8 for his 2nd. (That was a USAC 2-year victory record.)

Meanwhile he came south for the FIA-NASCAR races in 1962 and managed a 6th in the Dixie 400 and a 2nd in 1 of the 2 preliminary Daytona 100-milers. Nichels was acting during this period as the back door to Pontiac's parts bin, that division ostensibly being out of motor racing competition along with all others at General Motors.

The door was shut at the end of 1962, and Nichels

and Goldsmith switched allegiance to Plymouth for the 1963 season. There was another unsuccessful Indy 500 appearance in 1963, bearing failure ending the effort this time, and Paul concentrated on stock cars.

In November 1963 Goldsmith became embroiled in one of motor racing's bitterest battles. The big blowup came at the Golden State 400 at Riverside. Goldsmith, A. J. Foyt, Dan Gurney, and Parnelli Jones were among the USAC stars scheduled to run in this internationally listed NASCAR event. The USAC aces had their mounts at the track when USAC unexpectedly banned their participation. Foyt, Gurney, and Jones complained bitterly but obeyed. Goldsmith said USAC was acting illegally because it had previously approved the event's international status. He added that he had a binding contract to drive his car, and he ran the race. USAC promptly suspended him.

Paul retaliated by switching his legal residence to Mexico City, switching his allegiance to the SCCA, and competing in some of the 14 Grand Nationals of NASCAR which for 1964 were on the FIA calendar. His best finishes in the Ray Nichels Plymouth were 3rds —at the Daytona 500, the Bristol 250, and at Atlanta's Dixie 400. Since the Indianapolis 500 was an international race, too, Goldsmith filed an entry under the ACCUS-FIA agreement. The entry was rejected on the grounds that USAC had suspended him, USAC chose to ignore his SCCA license and his foreign residence. Paul promptly filed suit to force Indy and USAC to let him compete. He lost preliminary legal skirmishing and did not compete, but appealed. He had become a *cause célèbre* in the maneuverings between USAC, SCCA, and NASCAR who, with the National Hot Rod Association, form the uneasy alliance that rules major segments of American racing as joint CSI representative.

The price of peace for USAC was a compromise that included elements not even remotely related to Goldsmith. Originally the U.S. Grand Prix was supposed to move around the country to various racing venues. Indianapolis Raceway Park in Clermont, Ind., working through USAC, had exercised the right to bid for the race. Since the GP at Watkins Glen was the brightest jewel in the SCCA schedule, SCCA did not want to see it moved. After assaying true costs, the enthusiasm of the IRP promoters cooled measurably, and they indicated privately to their backers at USAC that they would not mind relinquishing the date. SCCA had taken up the Goldsmith cause even though he had never competed in an SCCA race because he was listed as a member of their organization. NASCAR's Bill France, meanwhile, was swinging behind SCCA in this squabble, thus threatening to isolate USAC and force it either to honor FIA-listed dates or resign from the ruling body.

The compromise lifted the GP from IRP and reinstated it at the Glen, limited international listings of U.S. races for the future severely, reinstated Goldsmith as a USAC member, and got USAC's promise to honor driver interchanges henceforth and forevermore. Everyone saved face, and the court battle was ended quietly.

Paul finished 2nd in the 1965 USAC stock car championship, then switched allegiance to NASCAR for 1966. Still in the Nichels Plymouth, he smoked to victory in a Daytona 100-miler. Then, in the initial running of the Peach Blossom 500 at Rockingham, N.C., he won his initial superspeedway victory. It was a grueling race lasting 5 seconds short of 5 hours. Goldsmith's 426-cu. in. hemi-engined Plymouth made 10 pit stops, 8 during the 69 laps of caution. The first 350 laps were one long thriller with as many as 5 cars bunched and contending for the lead. But then the many small mishaps and spins took their toll and near the end it was Paul versus Ford's Cale Yarborough. Goldsmith took the lead for good 48 miles from the end. Third-place Bobby Allison was 12 laps behind. Paul added a victory in the Volunteer 500 at Bristol, Tenn., to a year in which he finished 11 times in the top 5 out of 21 races. In 1967 there were no victories but 7 top-5 finishes in 21 starts, and in 1968 only 2 top-5 finishes in 15 starts. In 1969 Paul further restricted racing activity, finishing in the top 5 four times in 11 races. Since all this activity was on superspeedways, the money was excellent for part-time work, $130,000 in 4 years. In 1970 Goldsmith became the car owner of record on Charlie Glotzbach's Ray Nichels Dodge and refrained from driving to shepherd that mount. After much mechanical trouble, he took the wheel and won the Yankee 400 at Michigan International and followed with a 3rd place in the Talladega 500. For 1971 the Goldsmith-Nichels crew had the parts to campaign a Dodge even though their arrangement with Chrysler Corporation had ended. But Paul was through as a driver and remained only as a team manager occasionally. In 1972 he was involved in the Nichels episode with Chris Vallo, the alleged millionaire mystery Greek who ordered a Pontiac prepared for David Pearson. That effort ended in a court case and Goldsmith turned to non-racing interests.

JOSÉ FROILAN GONZALEZ

One of the high spots of Ferrari racing history was in 1951 at the British Grand Prix at Silverstone when, for the first time, a Ferrari was able to beat Alfa Romeo, Enzo Ferrari's former employer. The driver of that Ferrari was an Argentinian named José Froilan Gonzalez; the driver of the Alfa, Juan Manuel Fangio, a countryman and one of history's greatest drivers. It was a poetic victory, too, for Gonzalez was a protégé of Fangio's, in Europe only because he came as a companion to Juan.

He was born in Arrecifes, (about 3 hours from Buenos Aires) in 1922 the son of a local Chevrolet dealer. Fro was a chubby baby and grew into a chubby youth and a chubby man. How he stayed chubby was a mystery, for Gonzalez was a crack swimmer, a standout soccer player, a cyclist, and a stock-car racer like Fan-

gio. His father had set up Fro in the trucking business, and in 1949 he was self-sufficient enough to jump at the chance to accompany Juan to Europe when the Perón government sent Fangio over to see what he could do against European competition.

Gonzalez was just supposed to be a companion, but Fangio arranged a few rides for him at Maserati that season. He took a 5th at Palermo. The following season he was in a Maserati again, with mixed results: at the Monaco GP Fro crashed on the 1st lap, part of a 10-car crash; at Rheims he lasted 4 laps before his engine blew Gonzalez out of the French GP. But in the Albi GP, Fro wheeled his 4CLT Maser to a 2nd behind Louis Rosier. People started to take him seriously.

The year 1951 showed that Gonzalez had to be taken seriously. In an Alfa he was 3rd to Alberto Ascari and Fangio. In a Ferrari he was running 2nd when Ascari took over his car on team orders, making Gonzalez more determined than ever to excel. He had a lot of 2nds that season—to Fangio in the Bari and Spanish Grands Prix, to Ascari in the Modena and Italian races. But he won the Acerbo Cup at Pescara at 85.50 m.p.h., both heats of the Perón Cup races back in Argentina over a strong Mercedes team, and that British GP over Fangio and Luigi Villoresi at 96.11 m.p.h.

Gonzalez drove a Maserati in 1952 in major races and a BRM in some British races. He even drove a Ferrari again back in South America. There were victories at Goodwood twice and in the Rio Formula Libre race. There were 2nds at the Italian and Modena Grands Prix. There was a 3rd at São Paulo. But there was a crash at Monza that pretty much closed out Fro's European racing. In 1953 he alternated among several marques again, finishing 2nd to Rosier in the Albi GP, 3rd in the Argentine, Dutch, and French races, all in Masers.

He returned to Ferrari in 1954 and recaptured that old magic at the British GP, winning over teammate Mike Hawthorn in a spirited battle at 89.69 m.p.h. He also won the Bordeaux GP, was 2nd in the Swiss GP, and 3rd in the Argentine and Italian Grands Prix. After 2 fruitless years, he won at Le Mans in the 24-hour race, sharing a 4.9 Ferrari with Maurice Trintignant, at 105.09 m.p.h. over the 2,521.97-mile race. Frenchmen noted that Gonzalez' ample waistline made him look like a walking advertisement for Michelin tires. They and other European fans expected to see more of this warm, friendly man, but it was not to be. In practice for a Tourist Trophy race, Gonzalez crashed and was badly injured.

He never raced in Europe again, although he did in South America. With Trintignant he shared a 3rd in the Buenos Aires GP and a 2nd with Trint and Nino Farina in the Argentine GP in 1955. The next season he shared a 3rd with Jean Behra in the Buenos Aires 1000. There were other races of lesser magnitude in those and other years, but Fro's health, never robust despite his earlier athletic prowess and his burly appearance, didn't permit him to return to big-time auto racing.

AMÈDÉE GORDINI

Amèdée Gordini was a designer, builder, rallyist, racer, team manager, development engineer, and member of the *Légion d'Honneur* of France, although born in Italy and a Fiat apprentice at the age of 10. He was long associated with Simca which was then almost a one-man band of French racing, bringing along such drivers as Jean Behra, Robert Manzon, Maurice Trintignant, and even Juan Manuel Fangio (before Gordini gave up the competitive ghost to join Renault as a designer.)

Gordini was born June 23, 1899, in Bazzano, a village not too far from Bologna. Apprenticed to a Fiat agency there, he learned enough by 1918 to design and build his first car out of spare parts after getting out of the army. Next Gordini went to Isotta-Fraschini where he came under the influence of Alfieri Maserati—one of the 6 great brothers who came to dominate Italian racing. But Amèdée's fortunes lay in France, not Italy. He went to France on a vacation, but spent all of his money and couldn't get back to Italy until he earned some more.

Gordini settled in France in 1922, met and married a French girl, and earned enough to set himself up in business with a Fiat-tuning garage. Eventually he applied for citizenship papers and became a French national. He also became an auto racer. Initially (in 1929) it was rallying, then (in 1935) racing, always in specially modified and tuned Fiats. In 1936 Amèdée scored a 3rd in

the Montlhéry Silver Cup and followed that with a victory in the Bol d'Or race at St. Germain (driving 24 straight hours without relief). He won the 1100-c.c. contest at 56.41 m.p.h. Two years later, with the Bol upped to 1500 c.c., he won again at Montlhéry in another 24-hours-straight performance at 63.40 m.p.h.

Simca, which was Fiat's French licensee, offered factory help for the racer and formed Equipe Gordini for him. But World War II intervened, and it was 1946 before the operation could start. Even though he was in his forties, Gordini still liked driving fast himself, and he won the 1945 Paris Cup race in the Bois de Boulogne at 58.54 m.p.h., then the 1946 Nantes voiturette race at 63.50. But Gordini's work lay more in designing and building cars during this period. For 1947 Formula B, or Formula 2 as it became known soon after, was imminent, and for this kind of racing Amèdée (retired as a driver) produced a car powered by a finely tuned 1100 c.c. Fiat-Simca engine. By 1950 Simca-Gordinis were racing both Formula 1 and F2, swapping engines in the same chassis, adding a supercharger for the F1 races. There never was enough money, nor enough time for development, yet Simca officials thought it was big-time racing. They were shocked when their house of cards collapsed at Le Mans; Gordini had told them not to race the 24-hour contest; when he was overruled he instructed his drivers to go all-out, convinced that even if the cars were nursed, none would survive. Going all-out, they indeed expired early.

The die was cast for a parting of the ways between Gordini and Simca, and even successes later that year like Trintignant's victories at the Albi GP (won at a fastest-ever time of 101.30 m.p.h.), and Cadous (where he led a 1-2-3 Gordini-Simca sweep at 65.98 m.p.h.), or like Manzon's similar feat at Mettet, Belgium (at 92.49 for the second year in a row), nor André Simon's 63.59 m.p.h. victory in Les Sables d'Olonne could change the Simca management's minds. Amèdée was satisfied with the break, and these late successes enabled him to get backing for his own small factory to produce the 2-litre F2 engine needed for what was now Europe's principal form of racing.

Although it practiced at Pau for the Easter GP there, the first Gordini racing car officially debuted at the Marseilles GP with Manzon driving but retired when the transmission broke. At the Silverstone International in England he won his heat, but retired in the final. Gordini had arrived, however. The reputation of the Gordini team was further enhanced by the Swiss GP. Manzon arrived in good order with one car, but Behra was back at the factory anxiously awaiting completion of a 2nd car. He painted on the numbers there and hopped in to head for the course. Passing through the border, he got a friendly push restart from the guards on both sides, arriving practically at the race's start.

Behra lost his exhaust pipe midway in the race, and his cockpit became superheated. Gordini poured cold water over Jean and sent him back into the fray. Behra finished 3rd in slightly parboiled condition. Manzon, curiously battling the other extreme, a water leak, finished far down. At the Paris and Albi races, Behra suffered rear axle failures, but at Monaco he won the 2000-c.c. race in his 1500-c.c. Gordini, and was leading the unlimited GP when he crashed. Manzon and Behra were leading at Le Mans in the 24 Hours when they suffered brake failure. "If there were better drivers available," they told the reporters later, "Gordini would have won. The car is wonderful."

The wonderful car still suffered from the lack of necessary financial backing. Yet Manzon finished 3rd at the Belgian GP, while Behra cracked up. At Rheims a week later, in the midst of a terrific heat wave, Prince Bira, that old prewar ERA warhorse, joined the team along with Trintignant again, and Behra roared off to a thrilling 105.33 m.p.h. victory (while toying in the early part of the race with Alberto Ascari's Ferrari). Bira was 4th. At Rouen, Manzon (still suffering from arm burns from a sports car crash) managed a 4th while Behra was 7th after spinning out. At Les Sables d'Olonne GP Bira was 4th, Manzon 5th. In the British GP despite a bad arm Behra was 5th, at Comminges 3rd, and at Zandvoort 5th again.

Gordini's efforts to keep the team's head above water were successful, though barely, throughout 1953–54, although they were slipping closer and closer to mediocrity. Some of the bright spots were Trintignant's victories at Cadous and in the Grand Prix des Frontières in 1953, Harry Schell's 3rd at Pau, and Fangio's 3rd in the Bordeaux GP that year. In sports car racing Gordinis were impressive. Trint and Schell finished 6th overall at Le Mans and won the 3-litre class at 102.45 m.p.h., a feat the team repeated in 1954. Trintignant won the Nîmes sports car race and Franco Bordoni the Coupe de Vitesse at Montlhéry. The Italian was also 2nd in the Tuscany Cup and Trullo d'Oro, and the 3-litre won 8 of 9 speed contests in the 1953 Tour de France Rally.

In 1954 Behra won Pau when the Lancia-Ferraris dropped out and was 2nd in Silverstone's International, with André Simon 3rd. Jean was 3rd at both Bari and Caen, won the Coupe du Salon at Montlhéry over Masten Gregory in a Ferrari, and won at Cadours with Simon 2nd. But these were comparatively minor races; in the real battles, lack of finances and the general sloppiness of the Gordini team would not permit any real contest. The year 1955 was worse. A 2.5-litre GP car was ready for Monza, but did nothing. The design was good, but the execution lacked polish. Manzon won the Naples GP with this car in 1956, but after the same GP in 1957 Amèdée announced the end of the Gordini firm and team.

He joined Renault almost at once, working as a special consultant on the development of rally cars and the like. In 1958 a Renault Gordini model was introduced. It ran up a lot of rally successes and was introduced to the U.S. market in 1961, along with a visit by Amèdée himself. He was a success as a personality, but the car failed to stir the American imagination.

JULES GOUX

The year 1913 saw a full-scale European invasion of the Indianapolis Motor Speedway for the annual 500-mile race. Sunbeam of England was there, Mercedes of Germany, Isotta of Italy, and from France came 2 Peugeots to battle America's Stutz, Case, Mason, and Mercer factories, plus a host of other independent American entries. The French drivers were Paul Zuccarelli and Jules Goux—2 members of the Charlatans Racing Team, the first independent factory racing team in history.

The Peugeots were fast. Goux had demonstrated it a month or so before when he ran 100 miles nonstop on England's Brooklands course at a record-shattering speed of 106 m.p.h. Zuccarelli proved it again when, in the coming race, he set a lap record of 93.5 m.p.h. But stamina, not sheer speed, won Indy, and it was Goux, not Zuccarelli, who took the honors (Paul's car dropped out on the 18th lap of the race when its main bearings failed).

Goux started off well. In the initial turn he was 6th and by about the 5th lap after shredded tires knocked out some of the earliest leaders, he was in the lead. He built it to about a quarter of a mile, then eased off a little bit. But the pace still was 80-plus m.p.h., and his tires started going. On the 15th lap, Goux headed for

the pits with a shredded right rear tire. Two tires were changed and an order was placed by Jules for some chilled wine. (Thanks to members of the French Alliance, who had gathered from several points to root for the Peugeot team, wine—properly chilled—was on hand the next time Jules pitted.)

The pit stop had dropped Goux from 1st to 12th, 2 minutes 15 seconds behind Bob Burman. His urge was to charge, but he curbed it. Attrition was cutting down those in front of him, and steady driving would eat up the space between the lead and his blue car. By the 32nd lap—80 miles into the 500—he was 5th. When 2 cars pitted, and he passed Ralph Mulford, he found himself 2nd to Burman. The leader pitted for tires, but his crew was fast enough to get him ready to go out again before Goux could get ahead. Then Lady Luck smiled on France. Burman's engine would not start, and his mechanics discovered the carburetor needed replacement. Burman had to watch Goux sweep into the lead.

When Jules pitted for new rubber a while later (and 2 bottles of champagne) he kept his lead. At 200 miles he still was the leader, but an unexpected tire change dropped him back to 3rd. At the same time he topped off the car's fuel tank, and drank another bottle of champagne. He quickly passed a car, then the other pitted and he was ahead of the field once more. At 300 miles, he was the leader (there were trophies for the leading car at all the early 100-mile marks). Ten miles later, he pitted for the last time. Another tire change, another bottle of wine. Gil Anderson had sneaked past Goux's car during that stop, and Jules quickly set out after the Stutz. Averaging nearly 90 m.p.h. over the next 10 laps, he swept up to the leading car and passed it on the 136th lap.

When Anderson pitted for his last tires and fuel, Goux's lead increased to 4 minutes. He slowed down considerably, but the Stutz dropped out in vain pursuit with a broken camshaft. The next car was 13 minutes behind the Peugeot, and all Goux had to do was coast home for a sweet 75.93 m.p.h. Indy victory. And he won more than that race on his American visit, meeting, wooing, and wedding an American girl by the name of Ruth.

Jules was born in 1878 and grew up around another youngster, the French automobile industry. His father, in fact, was superintendent of the Peugeot factory and got Jules his initial job with that firm. By 1903 he had become the chief tester for the firm's Lion-Peugeot cycle car division. That same year he won the Ballon d'Alsace hillclimb, his 1st notable victory. But Goux was approaching 30 before his racing career really blossomed. In 1907 he was 3rd in the Coupe de l'Auto, a finish he repeated the following season. In 1908, too, he was 3rd in the GP des Voiturettes at Dieppe. The following season Goux won the Sicilian and Catalan Cups, was 2nd in the Coupe de l'Auto. In 1910 he won the Catalan Cup again, was 3rd in the Sicilian race and 2nd in the

Coupe de l'Auto to Paul Zuccarelli in a Hispano-Suiza. Out of this race grew a friendship between these 2 men and Jean Chassagne that led to their racing team, the Charlatans. It took a year to get the Peugeots ready for serious racing, but in 1912 they were at work. Goux won the Coupe de la Sarthe. He covered 403 miles at Le Mans at 73.01 m.p.h. At Brooklands he set that 100-mile nonstop record of 106 m.p.h. And at Indy the following year, he tasted lots of champagne and victory.

A slow-speaking, slender man, rather clean-cut save for a short mustache, Goux was a dandy throughout his life. How he managed to charm and marry Ruth was no mystery to those who knew him. If she thought he was near retirement, she couldn't have been more wrong. The year they were wed, Jules was 2nd to Georges Boillot in both the French GP and the Coupe de l'Auto, and in 1914 he was back at Indy, finishing 4th, the same placing he achieved in the French GP. During World War I Goux, like many racing drivers, took to the air.

He was in his forties when the war ended and racing resumed, but that didn't stop Goux. At Indianapolis in 1919, he placed 3rd in a prewar Peugeot at 85.93 m.p.h. Jules returned to seek another 500 victory in 1920, 1922, and 1923, but without success. In 1921 Goux had switched to Ballot cars, bringing in a 3rd in the French GP at Le Mans, the race that Jimmy Murphy won for the United States in a Duesenberg. Goux also was driving Schmids, but it was a Ballot that brought him his next great victory, the 1st Italian GP at Brescia in 1921. Chassagne was 2nd, with Louis Wagner 3rd to Goux's winning 89.94-m.p.h. average. The following season he almost won the Targa Florio in Sicily, but finished 2nd. A crash in the 1922 French GP slowed Jules down, but it didn't stop him.

Some final moments of glory came in 1926 when Goux was near his 48th birthday. In the French GP at Miramas, a boycott cut the starting field to a mere 3 cars. Only 1 finished the full 100 laps (311 miles), a Bugatti driven by Goux. His average speed was 68.16 m.p.h., with the day's fastest lap also his at 79.4 m.p.h. That same year, in the Spanish GP, he again ran the fastest lap—81.5 m.p.h.—and won in a Bugatti at 70.4 m.p.h. Goux lived until April, 1965, honored to the end as one of racing's early greats.

EMANUEL DE GRAFFENRIED

A real, live Swiss baron, Emanuel de Graffenried appeared on the motor racing scene in the middle of the Thirties. His first real success came in 1936 when Graffenried won the 1.5-litre class at the Prix de Berne in a private Alfa Romeo. The following season the Baron switched to a Maserati Type 6C, and it was with this marque that he scored his greatest successes.

Perhaps the greatest race Graffenried ever drove was the British Grand Prix at Silverstone on May 14, 1949, the first actual race in this series, although the previous year a "starter" had been held that set the pattern for the future World Championship race. The Swiss driver had a 4CLT/48 San Remo Maserati for Silverstone, and the field was filled with equally potent or better cars.

As the Union Jack dropped to start the battle, Prince Bira and Luigi Villoresi jumped ahead in their Masers and duelled for the lead. It was the 3rd lap before Villoresi got it and some breathing room. Bob Gerard and Louis Chiron were further back, awaiting the retirement of either the Siamese prince or Villoresi, and it was Luigi who went out first with failing oil pressure. A few more minutes went by, and Bira ran into an oil drum loaded with sand that was being used as a safety barrier. The front-end damage that resulted from that shunt ended the prince's day.

As the long race droned on—it was to last 3 hours, 52 minutes, 50 seconds, or twice as long as the comparable modern day Gp—one car after the other would lead, then fall back with problems or be retired. Reg Parnell led for a few laps, bringing hope to British hearts that a home driver might win, but he fell by the courseside, too. And the man who took over was Graffenried, followed by Louis Rosier's Talbot. This leader became the winner at 77.31 m.p.h.

The baron was no surprise victor. Between his 1936 class victory and the GP, he had scored several other class victories at the Prix de Berne before the war, then reappeared at the end of World War II, again with a Maserati in Ecurie Autosport colors. In the first GP des Nations at Geneva in 1946, Graffenried was 5th, and he won the Maloja hillclimb that same season. The following year the baron won the Circuit of Erlen before it gained major status and was 3rd in the Laussane GP behind Villoresi and Jean-Pierre Wimille. In 1948, Graffenried was 2nd in the Geneva race to Nino Farina and 3rd in the Monaco GP to Farina and Chiron.

The same season he won the British GP, Graffenried again won at Erlen and recorded 2nds to Juan Manuel Fangio at Pau, Bira in the Swedish Summer GP, Gerard in the Jersey Road Race, and Villoresi in the Zandvoort GP. He also recorded 3rds in the San Remo and Laussanne Grands Prix. In 1950 Graffenried had no major victories, but a 2nd to Fangio at the GP des Nations driving an Alfa and 3rds in the BRDC Empire Trophy race at Douglas, Isle of Man, and in the Jersey Road Race at St. Helier, Channel Islands. That was the season of the birth of the modern World Driver's Championship, and in these starts, Graffenried did not do well. Halfway through the British GP he retired, at Monaco he crashed, in Switzerland he was 6th, and, after missing both the Belgian and French races, he finished 6th in the Italian GP.

There were no 6th-place points in those days, so the baron was shut out in the standings, but in 1951 he managed 2 points and 12th place in the standings, earned for a 5th place in the Swiss GP. In the French race,

Graffenried retired on the initial lap with transmission trouble, in the German GP on the 2nd lap with engine trouble. Switching from his Maserati to an Alfa, the baron retired in the Italian GP after 2 laps with supercharger problems, finished 6th in Spain, as well as the Swiss 5th.

The next season the formula changed, and in a Maserati-Plate, Graffenried was 6th in Switzerland, retired from the French GP, was 19th in the British GP. In non-title racing he scored 3rds in races at Silverstone, Aix-les-Bains and Cadours. The 1953 season saw Graffenried's best World Championship season despite a lack of a victory. In Holland he was 5th, Belgium 4th, France 7th, Germany 5th again, but retired in both the Swiss and Italian Grands Prix. Away from the points races, Graffenried won the Syracuse GP at 92.07 m.p.h., Goodwood's Lavant Cup at 87.63 m.p.h. and Chichester Cup at 79.48 m.p.h., the Eifelrennen at 70.40 m.p.h., and the Freiburg and Ollon-Villars hillclimbs.

The baron also was moving back more into sports car racing, recording victories in a 2-litre Maserati in the Rio de Janeiro and São Paolo races at 47.30 m.p.h. and 65.60 m.p.h. respectively. Beginning in 1964 the non-sports car starts were few and far between, that season, for example, Graffenried finishing 8th in the Argentine GP and retiring from Spain. In 1956 he was 7th in the Italian GP, his last World Championship appearance. Meanwhile, he was 2nd to Masten Gregory in the 1955 Lisbon GP for sports cars and 3rd in the Venezuelan GP to Fangio and the Marquis de Portago in similar machines. Over 20 seasons, Graffenried had a good, solid, but unspectacular career that earned the respect of the best drivers of his day, including Stirling Moss and Fangio.

ANDY GRANATELLI

The little round man in the rumpled raincoat walking down the Indianapolis Motor Speedway in the television commercial for STP oil additive was a merchandising classic, as was the STP sticker craze that swept the world. The little round man himself was a classic, a one-off model that somehow combined business acumen and salesmanship with a lasagna version of the Horatio Alger story. It was all a true story that somehow seemed unbelievable, a new Tom Swift series—Andy Granatelli and his Windy City Hot Rod; Andy Granatelli and his Indianapolis Ford; Andy Granatelli and his Money Oil; Andy Granatelli Meets Novi; Andy Granatelli and his Racing Turbine. The list could go on and on, each a little gem of a story.

A millionaire many times over, Granatelli (and brothers Vince and Joe) once begged chicken heads and feet in Texas (he was born there in 1923) so they could make soup to eat. The family moved first to California and finally settled in Chicago, already car-oriented, al-

ready imbued with the notion that it is a good idea to eat regularly and live comfortably even if it means some hard work. The sales ability of Andy (born March 18, 1929) seemed to have surfaced early, manifesting itself in a successful gasoline station and carwash operation, Andy's Super Service. Granatelli's first real contact with automotive competition came extra-legally. He and his older brother Joe were among the pioneer midnight drag racers in Chicago.

There is the story of the battle of George McHenry, a story that pleads for fuller treatment in operatic form. McHenry's fenderless yellow 1934 Ford roadster was the king of the Chicago hot rodders; it had a much-modified Mercury engine and oversize tires on the rear. McHenry even employed a driver named Willie Sternquist to fend off the competition. The car embarrassed an early Granatelli hot-rod effort and he was determined to do something about it.

So Andy built a 1934 Ford convertible, with a 1939 stroked Mercury engine, plus assorted equipment salvaged from junkyards and lovingly adapted to the task at hand. When he was ready the challenge was thrown and the match made—a 5-mile stretch of Highway 83 at 3 in the morning. From nowhere, a crowd of 300 materialized as the cars rolled side by side toward the approximate starting line. A beep of the lookout's horn declared that no police were in sight, and the race was on. It was no contest. Granatelli won easily, out-thinking McHenry by using a high-winding 4:1 gear ratio to McHenry's 3:1. Thieves wiped out Andy's Super Service, however, and it took the brothers some time to

build another nest egg for a new business. They called it Grancor (for Granatelli Corporation) and it was to be the foundation of the collective fortunes. A fire wiped them out temporarily but this time the Granatelli reputation was large enough to float a bank loan to replace it.

Grancor specialized in performance equipment. It was a pioneer Midwest speed shop, then a mail order house, then a distributor of speed equipment and a franchiser. Grancor came up with the Grancor Ford engine, made the most money from the Fordillac (a Ford with a Cadillac engine), and sired the most successful portion of Andy Granatelli's driving career.

This chapter of the Andy Granatelli serial is called Antonio Granatelli and his Firebug Rocket Car. Grancor had converted the Don Hulbert Special, a 1934 Indianapolis entry of singular ineptness, into the Firebug Rocket Car with money from Al Sweeney, promoter for many IMCA contests. Sweeney wanted a co-attraction for his races and even supplied the rockets, Navy JATO types. Andy toured the hustings with considerable success, learning dirt track technique, but more importantly learning the promotion. The Firebug made its final appearance, however, on Highway 83 against another McHenry creation. Granatelli won and to top it off, at the end of the 5-mile straight he punched the JATO system. Great clouds of white smoke filled the air, and the rocket flames glared orange and awesome against the dark 4 A.M. sky. In their light Granatelli could see the hundreds of hot rodders diving backwards, more terrified than any farmer in Hutchinson, Kans., or Webster, Ia. He retired the Firebug to his showroom the next day.

After an abortive attempt to break into Class A midset racing—Grancor Fords were dominating Class B—Granatelli and other Chicago rodders formed the Hurricane Racing Association in July 1947 to put on hot rod races. With Andy finally a promoter, the HRA programs drew as many as 89,000 to Soldier Field—racing twice a week. In 1948 HRA paid more prize money than Indianapolis and the Championship Trail combined. It spawned such drivers as Pat Flaherty, Jim Rathmann, Jack McGrath, and Jimmy Reed. A circuit grew up—Soldier Field, Rockford, and Springfield, Ill.; Milwaukee; Cincinnati; St. Louis; Kokomo and Crown Point, Ind.; and Indianapolis, of course. The circuit disappeared almost as quickly as it had come as the hot rod fad gave way to stock cars, then to drag racing. But the Granatellis made money. They opened a drag strip at Half Day, Ill., expecting 5,000 but getting 26,000. They of course lost control of the crowd, the concessions and the racing. They didn't try that again until they had adequate facilities.

In 1946 the Granatelli clan invaded Indianapolis with a modified flat-head Ford engine that made the old pros laugh. This was before the business and promotional success, so all of them had driven to Indy in the car they were to enter in the race. They only had enough money for one hotel room, so they all slept crosswise on the bed—crew members slept on the floor. But, with Danny Kladis driving, the car made the race, 1st of 9 consecutive attempts to win the classic. Kladis started 33rd and finished 21st when he couldn't seem to remember to keep his fuel flow switch in the on position.

Andy tried driving in 1948, cut some 130 m.p.h. practice laps, then lost control on his qualifying attempt. He was injured so badly—fractured skull, broken arms, broken ribs—doctors feared for his life. An automobile accident some months later in which Andy, a passenger, was thrown through the rear window (refracturing his skull and rebreaking an arm) contributed to the demise of a promising driving career.

In all the years through 1954, the best Grancor finish was in 1952 when Jim Rathmann finished 2nd. In 1953 Granatelli claimed Fred Agabashian had finished 2nd, but was wrongly placed 4th in a scoring mistake that "Wilbur Shaw himself admitted." In 1954 the stewards failed to see Rathmann's raised arm signifying the start of his qualifying run, and a new car was ruined. Furious, Granatelli quit the place, vowing never to return. He did, of course, when he could use the track for possibly the greatest promotion of all time, use it as it had never been used before.

In 1957, at the age of 34, Andy Granatelli was a millionaire; he had a new wife named Dolly, and he was prepared to retire to Southern California, selling out of Half Day Speedway, Grancor, California Muffler, Racing Enterprises, and Chicago Auto Racing. He located in Escondido, stayed retired just long enough to buy Paxton Products from McCulloch Corporation, then turned what had been a loss leader into a profitable corporation in one year. He also became friends with Sherwood Egbert, then a vice-president of McCulloch, who was tapped to revive Studebaker Corporation soon after. He embroidered on old acquaintances at Chrysler to become part of their Plymouth ad campaign. And he managed to get into the record run business with Paxton and Chrysler both at Bonneville Salt Flats in Utah and in the final NASCAR-sponsored record run on the sands of Daytona Beach. In that Andy drove a supercharged Chrysler 300F to a 2-way average speed of 172.166 m.p.h. on February 18, 1961. Although possible tie-ins with Chrysler and Ford were in the works, Granatelli threw in his hat with Studebaker when Egbert beckoned.

Studebaker was to buy Paxton and install Andy as president of the company. Granatelli responded by setting a whole series of records in Studebakers of various sorts, the most startling in a special Avanti some two years later. That actually was after he had given up his Paxton presidency to Joe and assumed the presidency of Studebaker's STP division. He went into the record business with a vengeance, even employing Bill Carroll, then West Coast editor of Automotive News, to act as

major domo of a new trans-U.S. nonstop record. On that run were 2 women drivers, Paula Murphy and Barbara Nieland. Granatelli employed both to set records on the Salt Flats, Paula's fastest in an Avanti being 162.70, her official clocking 161.29.

But STP was Granatelli's greatest triumph. Called "mouse milk" by some petroleum companies, who claimed it added no special quality to oil, the additive was just the kind of thing for which Andy could utilize his sales and marketing talents. There were other additives on the market—Wynn's Friction Proofing for instance—but Andy resolved to dominate the market. The first thing he did was get rid of the wizard emblem on the STP can, the second thing was ban any denigration of competitive products. "All oil additives are good. Ours is just better," he told field men. Then he added exposure in competition to give the product credibility. And that led him right back to the place he had vowed he would never revisit—Indianapolis Motor Speedway.

Never let it be said that Granatelli couldn't recognize an undervalued marketing ploy. Here was the Novi race car languishing in semi-oblivion, the monstrous, nostalgic distinctive Novi. It evoked fierce partisanship in those old enough to remember how its screaming supercharger helped to accelerate the vehicle so quickly down the straights that even the infield blanket sitters and picnickers knew it was coming. Granatelli bought the whole Novi dream in 1961 for $111,000. It was a dream that had killed drivers like Ralph Hepburn and had broken men like Lew Welch, a 4-OHC V-8, 550 h.p. dream that in later years had 167 cu. in. of displacement. Dick Rathmann, Paul Russo, and Russ Congden all took laps in the car in 1961, but Andy withdrew it when he couldn't sign a qualified driver. In 1962 the car failed to make the field when builder Frank Kurtiss and Andy got their signals crossed on mating the chassis to the engine. But Jim Hurtubise winged the car along at 146.8 —after qualifying—in a special gesture.

In 1963 Andy qualified 3 cars—Hurtubise, Bobby Unser, and Art Malone—but none finished (the Hurtubise car being blackflagged for oil by mistake, according to Andy). Also according to Andy, the Novi engine was putting out 837 b.h.p. when he rolled 3 cars into the fateful 1964 field that included the Ferguson-Novi, a 4-wheel drive car. Unser was in the Ferguson and McElreath and Malone in others. The Ferguson was wiped out in the 1st lap fire, McElreath's swallowed a valve in the slow restart, and Malone, in the oldest, finished 11th. Pre-race crashes wiped out any real chance for 1965 and 1966, and by then the Novi had done its job, getting STP hooked into the racing image. Who could ever forget an entire pit crew dressed in uniforms made of a cloth entirely covered with STP emblems? Besides, Granatelli had latched onto the turbine.

Granatelli's No. 40 Turbocar was bad for racing because it was too quiet but it was the most important vehicle technologically ever to appear at the Brickyard.

There had been other turbines—John Zink's Trackburner, for instance. But this No. 40 car had money behind it, and it came at a time when the piston engine was coming under siege as a major polluter of the air. To have such a car win the Indianapolis 500 and eventually spawn a turbine engine revolution in racing would have been disastrous for the U.S. automobile industry. The public—which is not interested in what's under the hood ordinarily—would have asked rightfully why turbines could work in racing cars and not in passenger cars. Besides, a generation of turbine racers might have advanced the technology of the engine far faster than it was moving. A generation of turbine racers—burning cheap fuels like kerosene—could have triggered an unpleasant revolution in the automotive industrial complex. Not only car makers, but petroleum companies were terrified at the prospect. It is interesting to note that when the turbine was rendered uncompetitive by reducing its annulus area, the experts who made the alleged equalizing conversion came from places like Ford Motor Company.

In 1966 Granatelli and STP were all over the Indy 500. They were sponsoring Jim Clark and builder Colin Chapman, as well as Al Unser. Clark, of course, finished 2nd although Granatelli claims he was robbed of a lap when it was mistakenly announced he had crashed (Unser crashed). The turbine came to race in 1967 after a false start the previous year. Parnelli Jones led 197 of the 200 laps in it until a gear bearing failed. The No. 40 Turbocar, which Jones called Clyde, was obviously the fastest car on the track, and USAC had to face the possibility that about $30 million worth of racing machinery was being rendered obsolete before the eyes of the public. It should be noted that USAC was not the only racing association to effectively ban the turbine. The SCCA also took that position, even though the turbine would have been less useful in road racing despite its 4-wheel drive.

Granatelli fought for the turbine *and* 4-wheel drive. It is interesting to look at USAC actions in making the turbine uncompetitive. In January 1967 the rules committee voted for an annulus area (air intake area is a key factor in a rotating engine) of 29.9 square inches; the directors cut this to 23.9. Granatelli opted for a turbine with annulus of 21.9, and the board promptly passed a rule requiring an internal protective shield around the "hot section" of the engine, supposedly in case the engine blew up at high turbine speeds. Granatelli had a titanium shield built, which added only 40 pounds to engine weight instead of the expected 200–300 pounds, and ran the engine that way in 1967.

On June 25 the annulus area was cut to 15.999 despite the announcement of USAC's own turbine board that the engine, dubbed ST-6, had produced the equivalent of 550 b.h.p. (to Ford's 650 b.h.p.) with a 21.9 annulus. USAC also banned side-by-side construction (the turbine engine was next to the driver); air brakes

(they were the best way to slow the turbine car); and in January 1968 they restricted tire size on the 4-wheel drive car. Yet Granatelli, with Chapman's aid, came up with Turbine No. 60, the STP Wedge car (3 of them in fact). He also sued USAC January 18, asking that No. 40 be permitted to race equipped as it was in 1967. However, he may have ruined his own case by proving he was not barred by the rules changes. He had modified both turbine No. 40 and the new 60 to fit the new rules. On April 17 the judge declared that Granatelli must be permitted to race his new cars, and restored his USAC membership, but let the rules changes stand.

Mike Spence was killed practicing one of the wedge turbines; Chapman packed up but stayed as a spectator, Joe Leonard crashed No. 40; but Granatelli was a determined man. Graham Hill, Leonard, and Art Pollard were installed in new cars. Leonard got the pole at 171.559, Hill sat beside him at 171.208, and Pollard was in the race, too. Hill crashed; on the 190th lap with Leonard leading, both Joe and Pollard went out simultaneously. They had just finished running under caution at slow speeds and that, in combination with the hotter air being sucked in, heated the air, expanded the fuel mixture and finally snapped the fuel pump drive shafts. USAC's directors again went to work on the turbine in the June rules meeting, slashing annulus area another 25 percent and banning them altogether after 1969 unless they were "automotive" types (there was no such animal outside Detroit and none was likely to be let loose from the labs).

Granatelli determined that he had brought the turbine as far as it could go. For 1969 STP (now a corporation in its own right, independent of Studebaker-Worthington) that teamed up with Mario Andretti and a nice conventional 4-cam Ford car. Presto, Granatelli finally had an Indianapolis winner. He made sure the whole world knew it. The national championship was an added tasty tidbit as sales of STP soared. The combination continued in 1970 with less success, and by mid year Granatelli was exploring the possibility of a 1971 STP Grand Prix effort. After all, there were all those consumers in England and Europe who had not had the real impetus to get STP, the "Racer's Edge." The tieup came with Britain's March marque, and it was not crowned with success. Nor was USAC racing, with Andretti. The season ended with Mario and Andy calling it quits. Whether there would be a great GP future—or even a great USAC season—was still problematical.

In 1972, never one to pass up a sure thing, Andy affiliated STP with Petty Enterprises, and for the first time the great Richard Petty was driving a bright red Plymouth instead of his familiar Petty blue. Richard, of course, won frequently. The Granatelli promotion budget also covered USAC racing, Formula 2 in Europe, and Graham McRae's successful F5000 effort. Needless to say, the sales of STP Oil Treatment and other Granatelli products continued to grow.

HARRY GRANT

The Vanderbilt Cup, 1909. One of the first major stock-car races in the world. The chaos that had surrounded the previous year's race, won by George Robertson in Old 16, the famous Locomobile, had forced the race sponsors to alter the rules to provide for more equal racing. The answer was to require all chassis, engines, and running gear to be stock items, although bodies could be stripped for racing. Twenty-seven stock cars, more or less, met the starter's flag that day. The favorite was Lewis Strang in a huge Fiat. He already had victories at Briarcliff, N.Y., and Savannah, Ga., to his credit. Strang, like most of those watching, fully expected to add the Vanderbilt Cup to his string. Also starting were fellows like Louis Chevrolet aboard a Marquette-Buick, Joe Seymour on an Isotta, Spencer Wishart and Eddie Hearne aboard Mercedes cars, and Billy Knipper in a Chalmers. There was also a rank outsider, Harry Grant—a giant of a man physically, but rather quiet in his way, compared to some of the flambuoyant men he faced. Grant was a dealer in Boston for the car he drove, Alco. These were unusual machines, built by the American Locomotive Company. Back in 1905, Alco had taken a license to build French Berliets. The Berliet license was dropped 2 years later, and Alco had gone its own way, producing 3 basic models with a wide variety of coachwork.

Grant's mount was the Model 60, the big car of the Alco line. The "60" came from 60 b.h.p. It was a huge car on a 126-inch wheelbase. The 6-cylinder engine was small for its day, but finely made. The Alco block was cast of vanadium alloy, and crankshaft, connecting rods and cams were machined from solid vanadium billets. The car's valves were made of a secret corrosion resistant locomotive alloy. The same alloy was used in the transmission; main components in the suspension were vanadium. Many people thought it was an advertising gimmick. It was much more. It was the secret of the Alco's durability and strength. No single part of an Alco car made of this material was known ever to fail.

Handling this deceptive giant was a 5-foot 11-inch man who weighed a hefty 230 pounds, so well-distributed that he didn't look fat, just massive. Strength meant a lot in racing in those days, and Grant had it. He was clean-shaven, and his face, framed by an old-fashioned aviator's helmet, was impassive as he waited for the start of the race around a treacherous 12.5-mile course. If he was still virtually unknown to many people in the crowd, his fellow racers knew Harry Grant pretty well.

He had, in his 2-year-old racing career, beaten Robertson, last year's Cup winner, twice at the Lowell, Mass., road races. Both years he had set the day's fastest time. In New England, Grant had entered some 20 hillclimbs and won all of them. He had taken a midwestern trip and won several major events there. At the Readville, Pa., road races, he had surprised the field by whipping Robertson, Chevrolet, and a Benz team composed of Barney Oldfield, Bob Burman, and Ralph DePalma. But being a rather quiet man, he had not gotten a lot of press recognition.

Grant's Alco was exactly the same car he had used in every other race. Reportedly he had not even bothered once in 2 years to strip it down. He just hopped in when the urge to race caught up with him, drove the car to wherever the races were, made a few minor adjustments, and was ready to go. Unbelievable. This October 30, 1909, was a bitter cold day, with a hard northeast wind blowing. Grant felt comfortable, though, in his warm, high-collared jacket—a lot more comfortable, in fact, than some 200,000 fans who lined the Vanderbilt Motor Parkway and the other roads which would be used for the race. There were 5.15 miles of paved parkway and 7.4 miles of dirt-covered country road to the lap.

Strang and his Fiat took the lead at the wave of the starter's flag, but his bid ended 6 miles away with a hole in the radiator. Chevrolet roared into the lead at that point, averaging something like 76 m.p.h. But the pace was too much for his basically frail machine a snapped crankshaft sidelining Louis. Billy Knipper inherited the lead, with Grant a minute behind. Knipper increased his pace, but on the next go-round, lap 17, Grant was alone. Somewhere behind him, Knipper's Chalmers had snapped a connecting rod in a vain effort to stay ahead of the charging locomotive.

With 12 miles to go and nobody even close, Grant eased off to an easy victory in his initial Vanderbilt Cup race at an average speed of 62.82 m.p.h. for the 278 miles. It was below Robertson's speed the year before, but Harry was no record-seeker. It didn't matter to him whether he won by a second or an hour, as long as he won.

In 1910, 30 cars showed up for the Vanderbilt Cup, Grant among them. Some 350,000 fans were watching along much the same course, except that it had deteriorated a bit from the year before.

Chevrolet roared away into the lead as Fred Wagner waved the starting flag. Louis made the 1st lap at a startling 75 m.p.h., then completed the next at 80 m.p.h. The others were almost as fast. He led at lap 5, with Burman 2nd, Grant back in 6th battling with Hearne. His pit crew had told Harry he was running 2nd. At the start of the 9th lap, Chevrolet crashed, killing his mechanic. Burman took the lead, and Dawson moved up to challenge him. But Dawson had a challenger of his own, Harry Grant. By lap 17, Grant was only 10 seconds behind Dawson. Burman's Marquette-Buick quit, and he turned to watch Dawson pass him. But Harry Grant had the lead and held it until near the end of the race. Then, on the last lap, a tire blew, sending Grant spinning. He fought the car for control, pulled it to the side of the road, and hopped out to repair the tire or replace it. One tire was substituted, but collapsed immediately, then another was produced and slid on. All the while, Dawson's car was gaining somewhere back in the rear. Just as Grant got rolling again, Dawson's car appeared at the end of the straight. In 5 seconds Grant's Alco was away, but Dawson was on top of him.

Grant usually didn't dice very much, for he had a superior car, and he could wait for a mechanical failure in his competitors. This time he had to dice, and dice he did. Tooth and nail. Dirt road or paved, the rougher the better. The Alco came through, widening the gap to 25 seconds as they crossed the finish line. A new record average of 65.2 m.p.h. was set.

Alco never won another great race, and by 1913 the marque was discontinued. It was expensive to make and expensive to sell, and the Alco had no place in the auto revolution brought on by Henry Ford. How good was Harry Grant as a driver? The record says pretty darn good. Why he never raced again is a good question. He was, after all, not a racing driver like Oldfield or De-Palma. He was a businessman, who saw in racing a way to make a buck. Nothing more, nothing less. And he'd never get as good a mount as the Alco again.

JERRY GRANT

It takes one to know one, says the old cliché. It refers to thieves, liars, and, apparently, racing car drivers. Otherwise why would the talented Dan Gurney have tapped the unlikely Jerry Grant for his All-American Racing effort? Grant's reputation had been always that of a charger, and often he had been called a car-breaker.

Grant and Gurney claimed these descriptions—certainly the latter—were inaccurate. "A race driver is out there to drive to win, to drive the hell out of the car," said Jerry. "If that's being a charger, I'm guilty. But as for being a car-breaker, I plead not guilty. A car-breaker does two things—he blows his engine by abusing it, or he chews up his gears. When you have wheels fall off, tie rods break and spindles snap, you don't have a car-breaker. It is in the mechanical preparation, not in the cockpit."

Born in 1936, Grant, started racing when he was only 16. His first car was a hopped-up 1940 Ford coupe. "The officials didn't want us to run at first," he recalled of that first race at Shelton Airport, southeast of Seattle. "But I think we impressed everybody—the running boards were scraping on every turn and we were leading overall in the big modified race until the brakes gave out." After that Grant graduated to a Model A roadster beneath which lurked a Corvette engine and gearbox. The performances of the huge pilot (6 feet 3 inches and better than 220 pounds) were good enough to earn him a bid to drive a Yakima, Wash., enthusiast's Kurtis-Chrysler. After several successful years in that machine, Grant was handed 2 successive Ferrari 3-litre machines. The combination of Modena design and Washington State driver proved virtually unbeatable on the West Coast circuit. Kent's Pacific Raceway became Grant's happy hunting ground as he ate his SCCA opposition alive.

Grant purchased his own machine about this time, a used Lotus 19, one of the first in the country, into which he first stuck a Buick engine, then switched to a Chevvy mill that eventually became a powerful Traco-Chevvy. A local Chevrolet dealership bought the car from Grant and kept him behind the wheel. The Bardahl people also came forward with money as Jerry turned pro. His troubles in the pro ranks prior to the All-American berth were too numerous to list. Suffice it to say that Grant failed to win a single pro race, even those at his favorite course, Kent. Yet he never lost his zest for racing, nor his friendly grin.

A bear of a man compared to most drivers, Grant had only 2 rides in the open-wheeler Indy-type cars prior to joining Gurney's group. One of his rides was not even a race; he started to qualify a car in 1964, then withdrew because the car's handling was unsatisfactory. It was a surprise, then, in 1972 when Grant appeared at the Speedway in the 11th hour and without much practice proceeded to qualify what was called Gurney's "Mystery Eagle" (because it had no formal sponsor). In the race, marred by the usual USAC official snafu, Jerry finished 2nd unofficially behind Mark Donohue after pitting because of a wheel problem while in the lead. The pit stop was costly, however, because Grant's car was given fuel from teammate Bobby Unser's supply, and USAC dropped Jerry from second to 12th in the official standings, a $72,000 loss, not to mention the vexation, for the burly sports car racer. It was not the last vexation. At Pocono's Schaeffer 500 he was not in the starting field and at Ontario, Calif., Jerry sat on the pole but blew the engine in the very first lap of the race. It was enough to make a man flip his hairpiece.

PETER GREGG

The automobile dealer who races is a European, if not an American, tradition. But there are some Americans who do it. Roger Penske was one, of course, although he retired early to continue his financial empire-building, while employing Mark Donohue as driver. Peter Holden Gregg was another, and he continued racing long after he became financially successful with bank directorships and the other establishment trimmings.

Born May 4, 1940, in New York City, Gregg was the son of a mechanical engineer who was involved in the manufacture of marine incinerators. Peter lost his mother when he was 6, which made him an independent sort quite early. Graduating from Deerfield Academy in 1957, he moved on to Harvard University and a degree in English, a career as a film maker before it really was fashionable among the young, a stint as a serious squash player, and motor racing.

Gregg started with gymkhanas and ice races after an initial appearance in 1958 at Laconia, N. H., in a hill-climb. His car at that time was an Alfa Romeo Giulietta, and his sanctioning organization the Harvard Motor Sports Club. After graduating from college in 1961, Peter moved to Europe and attended the Centro-Sud Driver's School, operated by Italian great Piero Taruffi. Gregg entered the U.S. Navy and eventually became an Air Intelligence officer, ending up at Jacksonville, Fla. This was a turning point in his life.

He married in March, 1962, and resumed his motor sports career, now as an SCCA racer. In April 1963, at Osceola in a completely stock A Production Corvette, Gregg won. By the time he was discharged from the Navy in October, 1965, racing and Jacksonville were in Gregg's blood.

Casting about for a new career, he took over a local Porsche agency from a recently deceased owner's family. By 1968 he had prospered enough to acquire another local foreign car dealership, this one for Mercedes Benz, and by 1970 he had a 3rd one, created by Gregg himself. SportAuto offered Fiats and MGs. Meanwhile, Gregg's racing career was prospering also. He became a serious Porsche racer in 1964 with a 904, then moved on to a Carerra 6, 911, 911S, 914/6 and so forth. In 1967 Peter was the SCCA's Southeastern Division champion in 2 classes, and he had scored class victories at Daytona and Sebring in the major enduros there.

Gregg also was running the Under-2-Litre section of the SCCA's professional Trans-American championship, taking 2 races. In 1968 he ran a similar NASCAR series for GT cars and became the 2-litre titlist. The following season Gregg won 6 TransAms and the title, and he also took the SCCA's B sedan national championship. In 1970, racing for Porsche-Audi, his cars placed 1–2 in the Southeastern division. Gregg also tried out a Lola T165 in 3 Canadian-American Challenge Cup races and managed to finish all 3.

The major TransAm races of 1971 saw Gregg finish 3rd behind Donohue and George Follmer, Peter driving a Bud Moore-entered Mustang. Because of his IMSA championship with codriver Hurley Haywood, Gregg was honored by Porsche as the best American driver of the marque's cars. His face became familiar on U.S. television screens in several commercials, and boating enthusiasts knew a different Peter Gregg, a fellow who raced a "cigarette" ocean-going speedboat out of the exclusive Ponte Verde Yacht Club. He was also a director of the Jacksonville National Bank, a club tennis star, and the proud father of 2 sons.

And 1973 saw Gregg score his greatest victory, taking the Daytona 24-hour race in a Porsche Carrera, co-driven by Haywood. He impetuously announced his retirement, later retracted it. Winning makes a man thirst for more, as Peter showed by taking the opening TransAm at Road Atlanta soon after.

MASTEN GREGORY

"I won't do it forever because I can't," Masten Gregory said, "but I love it. I love the life. Motor racing can be very pleasant, you know, if you don't have too much fear, if you can enjoy what you are doing. Frankly, if I couldn't go motor racing I'd have to do something else

involving hazard because it is the moment of risk that makes the rest of life bearable, valuable, or delightful. It helps to be a bit strange, though."

Gregory started racing in November, 1952, and 20 years later he was still at it, if on a vastly reduced schedule. Being a bit strange helped, of course. So did the fact that Masten started before he had turned 21 and had enough money to blow $75,000 in two years while he learned to race competently. And so did incredible luck. Luck, fate, good fortune, how should it be described? For Masten Gregory survived not just a single crash, not even a handful, but 7 serious crashes, the kinds of crash that killed Portago, Trips, Clark, and others. "When I was about 32 or 33 years old, it came to me," continued Gregory, "that up until that point in my life I had never believed I would live to be 30. I hadn't made any plans because it didn't seem worthwhile. Stirling Moss told me flatly that I was going to kill myself soon after I got to Europe. Everybody thought I'd kill myself, and looking back I'm surprised that I didn't. I was driving mainly on reflexes. I really didn't know anything about racing. I just had quite a lot of natural ability, I guess."

Gregory was born in Kansas City, Mo., February 29, 1932, of parents who were both deeply involved in the insurance business. Without the family funds Masten might have been labeled a juvenile delinquent. At 15 he started borrowing one of the family cars at night and drag racing it in Kansas City streets. At 17 he married and set up housekeeping in Mission Hills, Kans. (He had four children but eventually got divorced.) That same year he acquired his own car, a dual exhaust Ford, that he hot-rodded. A brother-in-law named Dale Duncan drove a midget and thought of Masten as a pit man, but the youngster got so interested he bought an XK 120 Jaguar. This was his show car, not for racing. For that there was a J2X Allarad.

Duncan had introduced Gregory to this car as well as to racing. When Masten's father died—he had been the founder of the Postal Life and Casualty Insurance Co.—and his mother sold out the family's stock holdings, the son received a share of the proceeds. This provided all the capital he needed for racing, and then some. His debut, in a Mercury-powered Allard at Caddo Mills, Tex., in an SCCA 50-miler, was not very successful. Masten blew a head gasket after 5 laps of sliding sideways but keeping up with the leaders in a driving rainstorm. He swapped engines, a Clay Smith-prepared 325 b.h.p. Chrysler for the Merc, and headed for Sebring in 1953.

The Allard went out after an hour with rear suspension failure. But Gregory came back from the trip with still another car, a white C Jag, which he bought "because it was so pretty." At Stillwater, Okla., he won his first race, with Duncan 2nd in the Jaguar. Masten was in the Jag at Bergstrom AFB in April after scrambling the Allard's gearbox in practice for the 200-miler, and

he finished 3rd behind Jim Kimberly and Phil Hill. Then followed a string of good finishes at similar SCCA airport races: Golden Gate in San Francisco and Offut AFB were victories, Lockbourne AFB and Janesville, Wisc., were 2nds. But at Floyd Bennett Field, Gregory suffered his initial crash, totalling the car as it exploded and burned in a preliminary race. Unleashing his checkbook again, he bought another C Jag on the spot and finished 3rd the same day in the feature behind Phil Walters and Bill Spear. A few more races convinced Gregory that he was ready to conquer Europe.

What Europe beheld was a somewhat scrawny, diminutive young man wearing horn-rimmed glasses and equipped with a startling basso voice that came out in a Kansas City cowboy drawl. He was ready to race in a potent 4.5 Ferrari purchased from the factory immediately after the Argentine 1000 in which this car had won (driven by Umberto Maglioli and Nino Farina) while Gregory was being retired with overheating problems. He had wrapped the Ferrari around a tree at Pebble Beach, Calif., soon after buying it, the tree shearing the car in half directly behind Gregory's seat, but it was repaired and ready to go for the Rheims 12-hour race. With Clemente Biondetti, Gregory finished 4th and at Lisbon for the Portuguese GP for sports cars he was 3rd. Meanwhile he was learning life in Europe was for real. After a poor start in the Lisbon race Masten had managed to edge up to 3rd, saw Mike Hawthorn put Froilan Gonzalez down an escape road ahead of him, and was congratulating himself on 2nd when Fro reappeared. Before the race was over both Hawthorn and Gonzalez had lapped Masten, but he did finish 3rd. At the Tourist Trophy with another American, Bob Said, as codriver, Gregory finished 9th overall, but 2nd in class. At the Prescott hillclimb he went off the top of the hill into a hedge, but was 2nd to Hawthorn at Goodwood and won at Aintree. At Montlhéry Jean Behra's Gordini beat him. Back home he raced at Nassau in the annual Speed Weeks, lost to Alfonso de Portago in a preliminary race, but won the main event at 89.10 m.p.h. with Portago 2nd.

The year 1955 saw a 3-litre Ferrari and victory in the Lisbon GP at 82.88 m.p.h., 3rds at Bari and in the Eifelrennen, and a class victory with Carroll Shelby codriving a Porsche Spyder in the Tourist Trophy. The following season he was with Temple Buell of Denver, won Nassau's 2-litre class in his best showing toward the end of the year, then started 1957 off by winning (with Eugenio Castellotti, Luigi Musso, and Cesare Perdisa) the Argentine 1000. "I also got my first crack at Formula 1 a week later," Gregory fondly recalled. "Peter Collins had a ride with Lancia, and when he nearly blacked out from alcohol fumes leaking into the cockpit, I got a chance to take the car out for the next heat.

"Through some good fortune I was 3rd after 1 lap with Fangio breathing down my neck. We were coming into a corner, and I decided to make myself useful to the team by blocking Fangio at this corner, so I got the Lancia broadside, front wheels touching one curb, back wheels the other, and figured I'd foxed him. All Fangio did was drive past me on the sidewalk. Never felt so foolish in my life."

Centro-Sud's Signor Dei was impressed, however, and he offered Gregory an F1 ride for the rest of the season in the 3-year old Maseratis that formed the private team. Masten accepted and found F1 racing both interesting and rewarding. It was interesting sliding between some trees and a brick wall at 150 m.p.h. out of control at Pau, nearly flipping off and plunging 4,000 feet into Naples Harbor with locked brakes, nearly ramming a power pole at Pescara after sliding on some oil, and so on. But it was rewarding because despite these incidents he finished every event, scored a 3rd in the Monaco GP and a 4th at Monza, and finished up tied for 6th with Harry Schell in the World Championship standings. In Buell's sports cars, Gregory was 2nd to Fangio in Portugal and nearly killed himself in the Caracas GP when he flipped his car.

Next came a Lister-Jaguar with Ecurie Ecosse, then a factory ride in 1959 with Cooper as number 3 to Jack Brabham and Bruce McLaren, and his best GP finishes, a 3rd in Holland and a 2nd in Portugal. After a row with Cooper's management, he went back to Centro-Sud, then moved to Camoradi. He was restricted by outmoded machinery and wasn't about to spend huge amounts assembling his own team, although he was tempted to several times. His best victory in these years came in 1961 when Gregory and Lucky Casner shared one at the Nurburgring 1000 in a Camoradi Tipo 61 Maserati. Masten went to UDT/Laystall for F1 late that year, stayed in 1962, but had a dismal year in the pale green Lotuses, earning a single championship point for the year's work. In non-title racing his luck was better, with victories at Karlskoga and Mosport. Beginning in 1963 Gregory's drives were less frequent in F1 and in sports car racing. He started 4 Grands Prix in 1963, for example, retiring in 3 and finishing 11th in the other.

The year 1965 was Masten's last major F1 year, with 2 retirements in 4 starts and an 8th and 12th to show for his efforts. But he had a moment of glory that season, too, winning Le Mans in a NART Ferrari 275LM with Jochen Rindt, a young man on his way up. Gregory looked much the same as he had a dozen years before. He certainly had a young man's adventuresome spirit, abandoning Paris, where he now lived permanently, in 1966 to try his hand at Canadian-American Challenge Cup racing. A 5th was the best Masten could manage in 5 starts. So it was back to Europe where he could drive when he felt like it without his every move being dissected. The only time his native land saw him was at Daytona's 24-hour race and at Sebring's 12-hour. Happily the crashes also were less frequent, and not just because he was racing less frequently. Gregory's crash log showed a demolished D Jag at Nurburgring

in June, 1958; Lister-Jags at Silverstone in July, 1958, and May, 1959; a Tojeiro-Jag at Goodwood in September, 1959; a Cooper at Nurburgring in July, 1960; and finally a tapering off to 1962 and 1968. That last one was spectacular; doing 180 m.p.h. in a Ferrari at Daytona, he hit the brakes when a car materialized out of the gloom in front of him. Hitting some oil, he spun, was belted by a Porsche, and flipped. Rolling down the course, Gregory undid has seat belt, but held on to the ends as the flipping continued. It was right side up and going 20 m.p.h. or so when he let go of the belts, rolled out the front window space (it had ejected, of course, as it should) onto the hood, calmly stepped off and walked into the infield.

That same year, 1969, Gregory tried for an Indianapolis 500 ride, but things did not work out. In Europe, though, his racing continued apace in Porsches and Alfas, at Salzburg and Hockenheim, winning occasionally such races as the 1969 Osterreichring sports car race in a Porsche 908. Motor racing was still pleasant 20 years after he had started; the life still offered everything Masten Gregory desired, even though he had found a prospective new wife, and had learned to live as the Old World thought an international man should, even one without a high school diploma.

BOBBY GRIM

Jungle Park, Ind., was a small dirt track that is now more valuable as real estate than it ever was as a site

for competition. But the competition was rugged stuff, and men who survived this sort of bull ring sometimes went on to greater things.

Born September 4, 1924, at Coal City, Ind., Robert Grim never had any doubt about what he was going to do. As a teen-ager he ran jalopy races. He and 2 friends built a Studebaker-powered sprint car and hauled it to nearby Salem, Ind., where Frank Funk was staging an IMCA program. Al Sweeney, then Funk's publicity man, convinced Funk to let him enter. Grim didn't win, but he showed enough natural talent to become Sweeney's protégé. In 1947 he started racing sprint cars at Jungle Park, and he went on to become one of the all-time greats of IMCA, racing the Offenhauser prepared and owned by Hector Honore of Pana Ill.

When he departed IMCA for more lucrative fields with USAC, Bobby had averaged about $40,000 per year and earned 14,380 IMCA points by winning 183 features in 15 years, enough to assure himself of staying among the top 3 in that circuit's annals for many years to come. He was IMCA big-car champ for 1955 through 1958 and, as late as 1964, held the mile dirt track record for the 3-mile distance (set August 28, 1954, at Sedalia, Mo.) the 4-mile record (set September 26, 1953, at Nashville, Tenn.) the 20-mile record (set September 25, 1955, at Nashville) and the 100-mile record (set August 27, 1955 at Sedalia). He also held 3 half-mile dirt track records and a half-mile banked track mark that had withstood 17 years of assault by 1964.

Grim's list of track marks was equally impressive. At one time Grim held speed marks at 22 IMCA county and state fair stops. Six years after his switch to USAC, records of his were still in existence at Cedar Rapids, Eldon and Spencer, Ia.; Topeka, Kans.; Sedalia; and Tampa. Even granting the fact that the Honore cars were always among the best in IMCA, Grim was obviously a special talent, especially on dirt tracks. The Travelon Trailer Special became his first USAC ride in the fall of 1958. It was the next to the last race of the season at Sacramento, a dirt mile. Bobby qualified 3rd and finished 10th in a vehicle that was tired from campaigns and crashes. At the old Phoenix dirt track he finished 12th.

But the lure of USAC is the lure of one race, the Indianapolis 500. That's what brought Grim into the fold. Grim, a quiet, spare, almost cadaverous man just shy of 6 feet tall, passed his driver's test in the Sumar Special in 1959. He went right out and placed himself in the middle of the second row with a then-exceptional 144.225 m.p.h. qualifying attempt. A freak accident finished that first Indy for him. Running with the leaders during the first 5th of the race, Bobby raised his arm to signal his pits on the 85th lap. A gust of wind dislocated his shoulder. Even so, Grim won the Stark & Wetzel Rookie Award. After the shoulder was reset, Grim became a regular competitor on the Championship Trail, winning 11 events. He placed 12th in the

season standings, a 35-year-old "rookie" trying to adapt to vastly different racing conditions.

In 1960 Grim seemed to be adapting. He qualified the Bill Forbes Special 21st at Indy and his strategy was to move up in the later stages of the race when, hopefully, the field would be diminished by mechanical ills. Bobby never got the chance because of a faulty magneto that forced him to go slow. He finished 16th, completing 194 laps. But Grim made the money lists 6 times on the Trail, gaining his initial championship victory September 10, 1960, at the Syracuse Fairgrounds. He led from the 35th lap on. Bobby began dividing his time between USAC midgets and the big cars after that turning up regularly at the Brickyard also.

In the next three 500 miles, he failed to last half a race—a burned piston in the Thompson Industries car sidelined him after 26 laps in 1961; in the Morcroft car in 1962 the transmission oil leaked away after 97 laps; and in 1963 the same car suffered a broken oil tank after 79 laps. In the Konstant Hot Special in 1964 he finished 10th. He did not get a ride in 1965 at the Brickyard, but scored 500 points, mostly on dirt, to finish 18th in the season standings.

One question always will remain about Grim. What would have happened if he had switched to USAC sooner, when he was younger and dirt-track racing was much more important and Indy was the realm of the Offy roadster? He will always be an IMCA great, but no one will ever know how well he might have done if—say in 1957—he had come to the land of Indy.

BOB GROSSMAN

Bob Grossman was retiring—again. He said so as he wearily pulled off his helmut at Sebring in 1970 after codriving with Don Yenko to a 17th place finish. "There were so many guys out there so much faster than I was," the man remarked. His curly gray hair and clean forehead contrasted with the grime on his tanned cheeks. He had been running a GT Camaro, not the Maseratis or Ferraris of an earlier time in his career as a gentleman driver, not the factory-prepared Ford GT40 that he had shared at Le Mans with Fireball Roberts.

Bob Grossman was 47, still a handsome bachelor, still the successful Volkswagen dealer who also held national distributor rights in the U.S. for Maserati. He would still be around racing renues because of his business, which had made him wealthy, but he claimed it was over. "I kept thinking about how great it would be if I were in the pits," Grossman said wistfully.

In 1953 in Brooklyn, Alec Ulmann of Sebring fame was promoting another race at Floyd Bennet Field, a Navy airport. Bob Grossman was 30 then and rather old to begin even as an amateur driver. He had joined the New York chapter of the SCCA as one of its first Jewish members. Bob did not concern himself with so-

ciological aberrations; he had joined because it would be good business and because he found he enjoyed racing. SCCA evolved quickly from the private club concept, and Grossman, by competing as often as possible, evolved into one of the recognized amateur heroes of early road racing. He won at Watkins Glen on the original course through the village, and he won at most of the traditional road courses—Road America, Bridgehampton, Thompson, Lime Rock, Marlboro, Danville.

But his specialty became the long-distance race—10 starts at Le Mans with 6 top-10 finishes, the first man ever to finish that classic in a Corvette, 12 times at Sebring, several times in the Daytona enduro. Urbane, polished, he turned into a competitor on the track as fearsome as in business. If the likes of Curtis Turner had their "baby dolls" and their fender-banging fights, Grossman had legions of women who wanted to marry him or at least share the life of the gentleman driver who seemingly had everything. He had his moments on the track, too, and not just in North American Racing Team Ferraris.

On one of NASCAR's northern tours at Bridgehampton road course, Grossman was given a Ford, both to appeal to the SCCA fans and to fill out the field. The Ford was in virtually showroom condition. He let his Maserati mechanics loose on the car to do what they could to make it handle—there was nothing they could do in such a short time to the engine—and he went out to race knowing he could not win.

There is an awesome blind downhill turn at the end of Bridgehampton's straightaway that has to be taken on memory, faith, and guts. Richard Petty, Billy Wade, and Ned Jarrett learned to respect the turn by motoring off into the sand during practice. But they learned—or thought they did. At mid-race Grossman was far back in the standings because his showroom Ford could not compete on the straightaway. By the simple process of being lapped he found himself slightly ahead of Petty and Wade, thundering toward the 1st turn. He moved to the inside ostensibly to let the Plymouth and Mercury pass, and the fans at the corner started to clap and cheer. But as the 2 leaders made their move, they suddenly found they had a race on their hands. They had been outmaneuvered. Grossman had taken the inside of the groove, leaving only a little of the outside for the 2 NASCAR stars.

It was wheel-to-wheel through the turn with about 4 centimeters of air space separating the Ford and the Mercury, while the Plymouth, blocked, fought to hold any part of the pavement. Grossman disappeared into Echo Valley with a 4-car-length advantage over Billy and somehow lengthened that, so that when the 2 came around on the next lap Wade could not make up the distance on the straightaway. It loked like a rerun into the 1st turn but this time, to the delight of the crowd, Wade backed off rather than tangle anew. Grossman was eventually passed again, and the Ford finally broke, but when he climbed out of the Ford he was grinning broadly. The gentleman driver had had his fun. And he had some fun with the 1970 "retirement," too. Bob Grossman was back driving in 1971 and planning for 1972, too.

GUINNESS BROTHERS
(ALGERNON and KENELM)

There were 2 Guinnesses, Algernon Lee (Algy) the older, the seat-of-the-pants driver just after the turn of the century, and Kenelm Lee (Bill), the younger, more scientific driver who continued on into the Twenties. They were of the Irish Guinness family, landed gentry who operated the famous stout business. Algy inherited the title; he was the leader in more ways than one. At a tender age, when cars of any kind still were hard to come by, Algy obtained and quickly mastered a 200 h.p. Darracq (with Bill along as riding mechanic). His initial major competition appearance was in 1904 in the Gordon Bennett Trials, but his major placing came at the 1906 Tourist Trophy race on the Isle of Man, where Guinness finished 3rd. The following season he qualified for the Circuit des Ardennes by finishing 3rd in a Minerva, then finished 2nd in the major race to Baron de Caters's Mercedes in a Darracq. In 1908 he tricked the opposition into thinking his Darracq was much faster than it was by cutting across country instead of running the full Isle of Man Tourist Trophy circuit in practice; that way he insured losing several potentially faster opponents who dropped their gear ratios in a vain attempt to "catch up" with the seemingly faster Darracq. He drove into the lead with abandon, then dueled another Briton (driving a Napier-Hutton) on the last lap, being nipped at the line for the victory.

That same year, 1908, Algy set a 121.02 m.p.h. mile record at Saltburn Sands, then pretty much backed off racing. There was a 1914 Tourist Trophy race in which he drove well, but victory went to his younger brother. He didn't race again—due partially to the war in which he served in the RNVR—until 1922, when a 1500 c.c. race was run with the annual Tourist Trophy race over the Isle of Man course. A Talbot-Darracq was forthcoming for the veteran Darracq racer, who was "amusing" to his younger fellow drivers until he proceeded to run away with the race at 53.30 m.p.h. in a pouring rainstorm.

Bill Guinness, meanwhile, was racing, too. His 1st big placing was a 3rd in the 1913 Coupe de l'Auto in a Sunbeam. Then he won the 600-mile 1914 TT in another Sunbeam at 56.44 m.p.h., for once overshadowing his brother. The war slowed up this Guinness, too, but he came back strong. In 1921, for example, he was 2nd to René Thomas, a Talbot-Darracq teammate, in the Le Mans Voiturette Cup, and to Henry Segrave, another teammate, in the Brooklands 200-miler. In 1922, his greatest year for victories, he won the Le Mans Voiturette at 72.10 m.p.h., the Brooklands race at 88.06 m.p.h. and the Penya Rhin Grand Prix at 65.31 m.p.h. In 1923, he didn't win the French GP, but finished 4th with a dead car when Segrave won Britain's initial major GP. In that race Guinness set the early pace, wore out the Fiat opposition, and did his part in bringing home that 1st *grande épreuve*.

The year 1924 saw more victories, including the Swiss Voiturette GP at Geneva, taken at 70 m.p.h. with Dario Resta 2nd, and the 200-miler at Brooklands at 102.27 m.p.h. But that was the year his racing ended, too, when a crash resulted in head injuries that sidelined Bill Guinness for good as a racer. In the lists of great British drivers, lists that usually start with Edge and Jarrott, the Guinness brothers fit between these pioneers and the first of the moderns, people like Segrave and the Bentleys. Bill died in 1937 and Algy in 1954.

DAN GURNEY

Daniel Sexton Gurney came to Riverside, Calif., from Manhasset, N.Y., when his father moved west after retiring from opera singing. Dan himself couldn't sing at all—he let his engines do that. He built a Mercury flathead (so called because the top of the engine was flat compared with the V-8 shape) and ran it at 138 m.p.h. at the Bonneville Salt Flats in Utah in 1950, becoming an early drag racing hero.

That move to Riverside, site of a junior college in which Gurney enrolled, became the most important move of his early life because there he discovered something more challenging to him than Bonneville. He discovered sports cars. "I had thought about racing when I was young and saw the stock-car races at Freeport," Gurney recalled, "but this time it hit me stronger. Road racing is real driving—I mean it's related to driving on a regular road in a regular car. I liked dragging and record runs, but there was something that I missed in those that road racing seemed to offer."

If Dan had any idea of a driving career, the Korean War put it out of his head. Just the right age for military service (born April 13, 1931, at Port Jefferson, N.Y.), Gurney entered the Army in 1952, going to Korea with an anti-aircraft division. When he came back to Riverside he was a family man with wife and toddler to support. One of the good things about his Riverside home in those days was that it was out in the country. There were yellow dirt roads that wound into the nearby mountains. And they were quiet deserted roads, because the Freeway from Los Angeles hadn't extended its tentacles quite that far yet.

"Skip Hudson, a friend from college days, and I learned how to drive on those back roads," Gurney said. Dan had bought a Porsche on the installment plan, using an old TR-2 (in which he first competed at Torrey Pines, Calif., in 1955) as down payment. With it he won his class at Pomona and Santa Maria, Calif., in 1956. These small victories had a special importance for him. "I learned that racing even as an amateur costs a great deal of money if you want to win, but I learned also that it was great fun. The answer was to get to drive someone else's car," Dan said.

In 1957 a road course (optimistically called Riverside International Raceway) came into being. It was a 2.7-mile circuit laid out on the rolling foothills of the mountains. It was a driver's course, meaning there were enough challenging turns to make the way the driver handled his car important. From the very beginning Dan owned it. Cal Bailey gave him a Corvette to drive in the September race, and Gurney beat a horde of $14,000 Mercedes-Benz 300SL sports cars by 29 seconds. Then he drove to 6th overall against the stronger modified cars. This led to his 1st real ride in powerful machinery—a 4.9 Ferrari owned by Frank Arciero. "I found out something in that Ferrari," Dan said. "I found that the better you can concentrate while driving, the better lap times you have.

"It was also a different sensation. All the cars I had raced before this were tame and quiet. This Ferrari felt as if I had to hang on for dear life to control it. I couldn't take my attention away from it for a second." He broke a lap record at Willow Springs in northern California almost the first time he was in the car, then came back to Riverside in November where he fought Carroll Shelby, Masten Gregory, and Walt Hansgen on even terms. Phil Hill recommended him for a chance with Ferrari, and suddenly he was on his way to Le Mans as a member of the North American Racing Team (NART) run by Luigi Chinetti. Gurney came back to Riverside several times after that, each time a step higher on the ladder in his racing career. He remembered one evening in 1958 when he had just returned home from the Nurburgring in Germany where he had piloted a weary little Osca to 7th overall. "The phone rang," Gurney recalled, "I was dead tired, and I hadn't even had a chance to get reacquainted with my children. Chinetti was on the other end. He said that Enzo Ferrari himself had asked me to make a personal test and asked if I could leave at once for Modena, Italy. The plane ticket was ready and waiting for me. I whooped and yelled. My wife must have thought I had gone crazy. It was a fantastic break."

He then got a factory ride in a sports car for Sebring. "I learned something there, too. I was exhausted at the end of my initial turn at the wheel. I hadn't made any effort to see if the seating was comfortable for me. I was a little longer than Chuck Daigh, my codriver in that race, and before the car was turned over to Phil Hill I was aching." When Gurney came back to Riverside in January, 1963, he was a full-fledged pro and an international driving star. He had driven on the Ferrari Formula 1 team and was one of the very few Americans in history to have won a Grand Prix race overseas. He had left Ferrari because Enzo didn't like his drivers taking other assignments, and Dan had too many good offers. He had been to Indianapolis and had a Lotus-Ford

ride for 1963—a ride that was to give him 7th place in the 500.

But this Riverside race was different. *Motor Trend* and NASCAR were going to run American stock cars for 500 miles on the Riverside circuit, chopping off one severe hairpin to make it an 8-turn test. Gurney had a ride in a 1963 Ford sponsored by Ford Motor Company. NASCAR had tried its stock cars on road courses before, but never under very favorable conditions. Now the conditions were favorable. By using international rules, NASCAR would have USAC aces like Gurney, A. J. Foyt, and Troy Ruttman, as well as its own hero drivers like Fireball Roberts, Joe Weatherly, and Bobby Johns.

"I was amazed when I first got into the Ford," Gurney said. "There wasn't much difference in the way it handled compared to sports cars. The biggest difference was in the braking. These big cars were harder to stop." Of course, it was different from driving a sports car. There's a lot more car in front of you, and NASCAR's big roll cage around you. The doors were bolted shut and you have to crawl through the side window. I felt different, not more confident, but maybe safer."

Before any race on any course—be it Indianapolis, Goodwood in England, or even Riverside, which he knew like his own fingers—Gurney seemed to wear his nerves directly under his coveralls. It was not that he got nasty. He merely directed his whole attention, his whole being, as it were, to the job at hand. He was painstaking and methodical. All systems on a Gurney car had to be in perfect order by race time, including the driver himself.

"A race track isn't always the same even if they don't change anything. The condition of the road changes all the time," Gurney remarked. "The only way to find out about it is to go out and see and make a note of it. Even so, you miss things that driving over it bring out."

Gurney's reputation as ruler of Riverside was communicated early to the Buck Bakers, Ned Jarretts, Parnelli Joneses and Ruttmans, but if they expected to pick up tips on the quick way through any of the corners during practice, they were off base. He seemed to take a different route through each turn every time he went through. When asked about it, he grinned and said; "Maybe I'm practicing." But some of the routes were so out of line that even a casual observer could see that they had to be the slow way.

Under NASCAR's qualifying system for Riverside that year, the cars that qualified the first 3 days could not be bumped or forced out of the big race even by faster cars. As many as 10 could make the race the first day, and the fastest of these was to sit on the pole. Five Pontiacs took all the top spots, led by Paul Goldsmith and Foyt. Fireball Roberts was 3rd, Len Sutton 4th, and Joe Weatherly 5th. The fastest was Goldsmith's 1:39.10. Gurney just sat, watched and grinned.

On the 2nd day of qualifying Dan indicated he was

ready to try his skill. Work in other pits gradually stopped. Dixie mechanics as well as the drivers from all over the country stood along pit row trying to look nonchalant. The stop watches were in many hands as Gurney crawled into his car. They were poised as he took a warmup lap, poised to click when he crossed the electric eye's beam for his timed laps. The tone of the engine rising and falling told a story of Gurney working the transmission, braking, and steering. He smoked around in a 1:37.67 almost 2 seconds faster than Goldsmith, who was on the pole, and as much as 8 seconds faster than some of the other qualifiers. That he would start 11th was academic; Dan and his No. 28 Ford were the combination to watch.

On January 20, 1963, more than 52,000 fans packed Riverside International Raceway. The 44-car field stood parked along the main straight waiting for the pace car to head toward a flying start. Only one car of note had an automatic transmission, Richard Petty's Plymouth. The rest packed heavy-duty, standard-shift units, just as all of them had fitted extra stabilizer bars and reinforced wheels. Some tense accidents in practice had convinced the boys from the southeast that the handling had better be as strong and as steady as possible.

The Riverside stock-car course looks like a pointing hand. The short pit straight is on the bottom of the index finger, then the cars run toward the sleeve and down the fist, up a short straight where the edge of a cuff might be and then down the long back straight along the top of the finger. It is a fast course with the only places where the cars have to slow way down at Turn 8 at the top of the back straight and Turn 9 at the tip of the finger. Turns 2, 3, 4 and 5 are part of the "S" undulation and there is a wall and a grandstand at Turn 6, a rounded right angle. There is no Turn 7 on the stock-car course, just as for the sports cars, Turn 8 isn't used. "Sitting waiting for a start, I don't think of anything much," Dan explained. "I'm keyed up, and I'm waiting to put my racing plan into practice. I'm not scared, and I'm not concentrating so hard that I can't hear anything but race sounds. Any race is a thrill and waiting for it to start is part of that." At the start of the race, Gurney was content to hold his position as the cars sorted themselves out. His strategy proved effective, for Weatherly came into the pits with a broken gearbox as early as lap 2, and Goldsmith, the USAC stock-car champ, took the lead from Foyt on lap 3. But Paul was out of the race permanently by the 59th lap with a stewed engine. The painted tires implanted in the ground at curves as a safety barrier were taking a beating as drivers with little experience in handling a car through both right and left turns skidded and spun around the course. For them, the long back straight was the most likely passing zone. It witnessed some of the most exciting drag races fans had ever seen, as Gurney and the other hot cars tromped on the gas pedal to pass—always with the knowledge that they must get around the slow Turn 9. Gurney had gradually started to work up in the standings, using the backstretch drag to whistle past the others and even making some thrilling passes in the esses. Meanwhile, Jones had taken the lead, lost it to Lorenzen, who lost it himself eventually to Gurney, who, in turn, pitted and gave it back to Jones. Petty and his automatic transmission were out by now, and NASCAR's main hope was the only other driver in the race who had had experience in a road-course enduro, Fireball Roberts.

Sure enough, Roberts, pacing himself beautifully, edged his monster Pontiac into the lead after 87 laps. But even he couldn't hold off Gurney, and Dan went in front on lap 101.

It was an easy Gurney victory. Only 21 of 44 cars finished, amazing even Dan. "It was an easy race," he said, "I was told to keep the engine under 5,800 r.p.m., and I did easily."

In 1964 the weather at Riverside for the MT 500 was as sour as some of the backstage maneuvering between rival NASCAR and USAC officials. But all this was partly smoothed over by the presence of USAC aces Foyt, Jones, and Ruttman. Gurney's factory Ford this year was No. 121 and had been prepared by the Wood Brothers. He had a teammate in Marvin Panch and much more competition. "More than half of any race is the car and the way they prepare it," Gurney said, while waiting for a chance to practice. "Preparation—setting the car up—is not easy at a road course, especially on a stock car."

But the NASCAR boys had learned a great deal. Rear axles were strapped more securely and there were oil coolers to make sure the heat of competition wouldn't fry the gears. The brakes, always drilled to assist cooling, had air scoops to channel even more air through. And the suspensions were set up better . . . especially No. 121. "Leonard and Glenn Wood are known for their ability to set up a stock car chassis," Dan explained. Most important, the oval track drivers were getting used to this road racing business. The cars started in the order in which they had arrived at technical inspection because no full qualifying could be held in the rain. The track was still damp so the first 7 laps were run under caution to try to dry the surface. This also had the effect of eliminating a couple of non-contenders that would only have cluttered up the competition.

When the green flag finally went out, Petty and his new Hemi Plymouth led, followed by Lorenzen and David Pearson, in a Ford and Dodge respectively, then Gurney. "These boys are not afraid to tap you if they think they can get past," Gurney said. "It adds a new element. You have to watch out for anyone close to you."

The green flag was furled almost at once when an also-ran went head over heels. All the cars scooted for the pits to change tires, and Gurney had the fastest men in NASCAR for that—the Wood boys. In the pit shuffle Gurney emerged the leader and held on until Parnelli Jones began snapping at his heels. Dan held him off until Jones's Mercury snapped its axle.

Then Petty, in the most talked-about car at the race, snaked past and held the lead. The Hemi was fantastically fast and the Petty family—father Lee and sons Richard and Maurice—was gambling on making it even faster with a high rear-axle ratio. But the gamble didn't work out. With only about 30 percent of the race finished, Richard limped in for repairs too serious to handle at trackside. The fatal accident to Weatherly (whose restraining harness was loose when he whacked into a steel wall) cast a pall over Gurney's victory. This had been the only such mishap in NASCAR in 7 years and it re-emphasized the risk attached to the profession despite the safety precautions. Gurney and teammate Panch were 1st and 2nd, followed by Roberts in a 3rd Ford, then Darel Dieringer in a Mercury.

In 1965 he returned at the wheel of a Ford, once more with the Wood brothers in his pits and Panch as his teammate. The Chrysler products were absent because of a feud over the 1965 racing formula, so everyone who was anyone was piloting a Ford. This was a unique challenge, a true driver's race. Only Parnelli Jones in an old Mercury provided a competitive product and he left early. That it was a driver's battle became apparent on the first day of qualifying. Gurney and Foyt both blew engines, thereby relinquishing any chance to gain the pole position. Junior Johnson got that, edging Jones and posting a new lap record of 102.846 m.p.h. The top 4 cars on the opening day of qualifying were within a mile an hour of one another. The next day Gurney and Foyt qualified. Dan broke Johnson's short-lived record by 1.1 m.p.h. and A. J. became next fastest with the only other car to top 103 m.p.h.

More than 61,000 fans were present to see how Gurney did it. It was just as easy this time. Dan and A. J. took over the top spots when Parnelli parked. A fire in Ned Jarrett's car while it was pitted enlivened matters. On the 117th lap, A. J. led while Dan refuelled. When A. J. had to pit, Dan opened a big lead. Foyt departed the race the hard way when he drove off the Turn 9 embankment and had to be hospitalized. From there it was a case of merely finishing. Gurney did, then came back to win the MT 500 for the 4th year in a row in 1966 before Jones broke the string in 1967 thanks to an extra wide rearview mirror and the Wood Brothers. Gurney got the Wood Brothers back in 1968 and made it 5 for 6.

There have been many other triumphs in many kinds of cars all over the world for Daniel. But the greatest tribute to him is that no one in modern history ever dominated an event so basically foreign to his main line of racing endeavor as Gurney did the Motor Trend 500. Stock-car racing was literally a single race a year proposition to him for most of his career.

Despite his height (6 feet 2 inches) he was primarily a single-seater driver, whether USAC or Grand Prix with Ferrari BRM, Porsche, Brabham and his own marque. His dream—to build an American GP car that could pilot an American to the world title—burned on even after he retired at the end of the 1970 season at the age of 39. He had come in 2nd at Indianapolis twice in cars of his own design (1968–69); he had won his initial USAC championship race, the Rex Mays 300—appropriately at Riverside in 1967—in his own All-American Racers Eagle. And he won the 1967 Belgian GP in his own Formula 1 Eagle, adding it to earlier international victories at Le Mans (1967), codriving with Foyt, and 3 other Grands Prix. He also won the initial Daytona Continental ever held, Sebring, and races at the Nassau Speedweeks. Overseas he had shown his versatility by driving for Porsche and Brabham in world sports car events, and he reinforced it in North America by winning the first 2 CanAm Cup races of 1970 after Bruce McLaren was killed.

Although he never won the World Driver's Championship, Gurney probably was the best American GP driver ever. Better than Phil Hill, America's only World Champion, better than Mario Andretti, Richie Ginther, or any of the others. As with all of his racing, he made it look so easy despite wretched racing luck. Consider, if you will, that when he first drove a F1 car for Ferrari in 1959, he was just 4 years away from his 1st motor race and a junior member of what was one of the mightiest teams in racing history. The debut came in the French GP on July 3, 1959, and Dan lasted 19 laps until a stone holed his radiator while he was running sixth. He didn't start the British GP, but in the German race at Avus all Gurney did in his 2nd GP start was finish 2nd to Tony Brooks in a race run in 2 heats that were added together for aggregate placings. Gurney was 2nd in the opening heat, 3rd in the next. In the Portuguese GP Dan was 3rd, in the Italian 4th. Strangely there was no car for Gurney in his own United States GP, so his initial season saw a 7th-place standing in the championship tables.

In 1960 Gurney was with BRM. At Monaco his suspension gave him problems. In Holland he crashed when his brakes failed, killing 2 spectators as he left the track at 130 m.p.h. In Belgium it was the engine, the same story at Rheims for the French GP. Dan finally finished a race in the British GP, 3 laps back in 10th place. The engine kayoed Gurney from the Portuguese GP. British teams boycotted Monza's Italian GP, and the finale at the U.S. GP saw another retirement, this time with a water system failure. One race finished, no points. Gurney went over to Porsche, and things improved immeasurably. In the Monaco opener, Dan was 5th, in Holland 10th, in Belgium 6th. In the French GP at Rheims, a single tenth of a second separated Gurney from Giancarlo Baghetti, who had slip streamed Dan's Porsche until just the right moment, slingshotting ahead for the victory. In the British GP Dan was 7th, in the

German the same, in the Italian 2nd again by 31.2 seconds to Phil Hill, who cinched his World Championship in that race. In the U.S. GP, Dan was 2nd once more, this time to Innes Ireland by 4.3 seconds. The points gave him a 3rd-place tie with Stirling Moss in the championship tables.

Still with Porsche in 1962, Gurney had problems. In the Dutch opener, his gearbox gave away, at Monaco he crashed on the 1st lap with Ginther and Maurice Trintignant. Porsche skipped Belgium, but they were there at Rouen for the French GP, and Gurney awarded their effort with its initial GP victory, besting Tony Maggs by a full lap. But in Britain, Dan was 9th, and in Italy he retired with transmission trouble. In between those races, he finished a strong 3rd in the German GP at Nurburgring, 4.4 seconds back of winner Graham Hill. In the U.S. GP Gurney was 5th, and Porsche passed up South Africa. Dan closed the year 5th in the GP standings. Going to Brabham in 1963, he retired with transmission trouble in the Monaco opener, finished 3rd a lap back in Belgium. In the Dutch GP he again was 2nd, this time to Jim Clark by a lap, in the French race he was 5th. Engine problems eliminated Dan from the British GP, gearbox ills hit him in the German. Sitting on the sideline, Gurney was classified 14th in the Italian GP, but in his native GP he retired with fuel troubles. Mexico saw a 6th, South Africa a 2nd to Clark by about a minute. Gurney was 5th in the standings.

In 1964 Dan retired from Monaco with gearbox troubles, from Holland with steering ills. In Belgium he was 6th. Then came another victory, at Rouen in the French GP, when he gave Brabham its first-ever championship victory, matching his feat for Porsche. Graham Hill was 2nd, Jack Brabham himself 3rd. In Britain Dan was 13th, in Germany 10th, in Austria retired with chassis problems. A 10th in Italy and a retirement in the U.S. GP was followed by a 2nd championship victory in the Mexican race. Gurney was 6th in the final season standings. The next year started with a retirement in South Africa, and Dan passed up Monaco for the Indy 500. Back in the Brabham for Belgium, he was 10th. A British GP 6th followed a French GP retirement. Then Dan went on a tear, finishing 3rd in the Dutch, German and Italian races, and 2nd in the U.S. GP to Graham Hill by less than 10 seconds and in the Mexican GP to Ginther by less than 2 seconds. The late-season rush made him 4th in the standings.

Gurney left Brabham to form his Eagle team that winter, and by the 1966 Belgian GP he was ready to take the grid in his own car. The debut saw him unclassified, 5 laps back of the winner. In the French GP he was 5th, in the British he retired with engine failure, the same thing that got him in the Dutch race. It was to plague Gurney in these opening Eagle races. After a 7th in Germany, his Eagle again retired with engine woes in Italy, and with a distributor failure in the U.S. GP. In Mexico Gurney finished 5th. His personal standing at the year's end was a tie for 12th with 4 points. But 1967 was a far better year, despite chassis failure in the South African opener and metering unit failures at Monaco and in Holland. June 18, 1967, was the day the Eagle spread its wings with a convincing minute-plus victory in the Belgian GP. In the French race, a fuel line failed, and in Britain it was the fuel feed and clutch going together. In Germany it was the engine again, but in Canada Dan was 3rd. He retired in the final 3 Grands Prix and finished with an 8th-place standing.

In 1968 reliability was elusive. It was the German GP before Dan managed to finish a race, that one in 9th. His next finish came in the U.S. GP where he was 4th in a borrowed McLaren-Ford, the same car in which he retired in the Canadian race, and was to retire in the Mexican. Dan's 3 points gave him a tie for 21st place in the standings. There were no F1 starts in 1969, and it was mid-season, 1970, before he again made a GP grid, this time in a McLaren. Retired in Holland, Dan was 6th in France, retired again in Britain. One point and a tie for 22nd in the final standings. Dan decided it was time for his retirement as a driver, even though that very season he had won 2 CanAms in McLarens and finished 9th in another. But his niche was already secure, no matter what else he might do as constructor or team entrant. Who else had given 3 different marques their first F1 victory? And in the years ahead he showed that he would excel in both in USAC and other areas.

JANET GUTHRIE

When they talk of modern American drivers who happened to be women instead of men, they mention Denise McCluggage or Donna Mae Mims or Paula Murphy or Lee Breedlove because these gals had pretty good publicity mills going for them. But there's another one, perhaps the best of them all, who let her driving predominate, not her newspaper column, or pink car, or trick record runs. And so she is forgotten until the name is mentioned, and then the reaction is, oh, yes, she was one of the best.

That name is Janet Guthrie. She only got to drive a few races each year—races like Sebring and Daytona and the Watkins Glen 6-hour—but she consistently finished cars meant only to fill out the fields. Going into 1971 Guthrie had a string of 9 straight enduro finishes going that was snapped when right on the starting line she was bumped from a competitive car to a last-minute entry on the same team. So Janet's lucky driving gloves, left behind in what was to have been her car, finished their 10th in a row, but their owner had her streak snapped by a balky engine.

Janet was born in Iowa City on March 7, 1938, the first child of a local airport operator named William

Lain Guthrie who later became an Eastern Airlines Captain and gained some attention in 1970 by making the airlines change their operating procedures to prevent unnecessary pollution of the air. Janet inherited a lot of Lain Guthrie's best characteristics: a professional approach, willingness to do the hard work to fine-tune acquired skills, and determination, among others. Raised in Miami, Janet became fascinated with flying at the age of 13, soloed 3 years later when of legal age, and 3 years after that earned her commercial rating. By 1971 she had more than 400 hours in better than 20 different types of aircraft, and after 7 years in engineering research and development in America's aerospace industry (when not racing), she had become a technical editor. After graduation from the University of Michigan with a degree in physics, Guthrie had been one of a handful of girls who tried for a scientist-astronaut's berth, and she actually got past round 1 before the National Academy of Sciences counted her out.

Janet got her start in racing in 1962 when she bought a Jaguar XK 120 coupe. For all of her flying background, cars were something new. "I had to ask my 10-year-old brother how the clutch worked, but I learned fairly quickly," she recalled. In a characteristic quest for proficiency, Guthrie went to Lime Rock to a touring school, and Gordon McKenzie spotted something in the way she handled a car and encouraged her to try racing. An SCCA drivers' school at Marlboro, Md., followed in 1963. Janet had moved up to an XK 140, which she tore down completely, disassembling the engine in the back of an old station wagon, then reassem-

bling it again in a 3-month project. That 1st season, once the Jag was working again, Guthrie raced at Vineland, N.J., the Glen and elsewhere, 13 races in all. One of the best was the 1964 Glen 6-hour race, in which she drove her 8-year-old XK 140 to a class 2nd and 5th overall against strong opposition.

Women drivers are unusual enough—talented women drivers, that is—that Macmillan Ring-Free Oil, a company that sponsored a girls' team as part of its year-long racing promotion, spotted Janet early and came up with an offer for her to drive at Daytona.

Macmillan's talent scouts were pretty sure-eyed. Through 1970 the team's all-girl entry had never failed to finish a race. After Daytona more Ring-Free offers came Janet's way. Aside from her paid drives, Janet also continued SCCA action in regionals and divisionals, and in 1967 she went to the American Road Race of Champions, the SCCA's World Series at Daytona, but blew her only engine in practice.

Her trophy case ballooned with Ring-Free race trophies, as well as the SCCA silverware. At the Glen she was in the top 3 in 1964–65, at Sebring in 1967 and 1970, at Daytona for the 24 hours in 1966–67. In SCCA racing, high spots came along fairly regularly. Typical of these perhaps, was the 1969 Bridgehampton Enduro in which, despite a 45-minute pit stop, Guthrie and her talented codriver, Jas Patterson, brought a bright orange Austin-Healey 3000 to a 2nd in class. All kinds of cars fell under the Guthrie mastery, from Mustangs to mid-engined Matras and Chevrons.

It was a Chevron that, in the 1971 Sebring 12-hour, provided one of Janet's most frustrating experiences in racing. She and 2 Ring-Free codrivers were scheduled for a "super" B16 Chevron-Cosworth FVC, but got bumped at the starting line into a Chevron-BMW that was a late arrival. The team lacked a car because a Spyder hadn't arrived, and so everyone got bumped down a peg. The BMW-powered Chevron lasted about a lap, then died. Janet jumped out, sprinted across the infield for tools and, accompanied by a consulting mechanic (who couldn't touch the car or he'd disqualify it), sprinted back.

For 45 minutes she worked on the engine, got it going several times, only to see it die each time. She gave up after an hour and a half. For the time being it was back to piloting a typewriter and editor's blue pencil and to turning young men's heads when she swept by. In 1972, however, chafing at prolonged racing inactivity, she bought a Toyota Celica and was off to the races once more.

ALBERT GUYOT

A ruddy-faced Frenchman from Orleans, Albert Guyot raced some 20 years in Europe and America without ever winning a major race, yet was consistently well-placed in rich contests like the Indianapolis 500, and even directed an Indy victory in 1914. Guyot's initial success came as early as 1908 when he won the ACF's Voiturette Grand Prix at Dieppe in a Canzan-powered Delage—the marque's first victory in racing—at a mere 49.80 m.p.h. He first appeared at the Indiana Brickyard 5 years later, driving a Sunbeam, and finished 4th. Albert's luck had much to do with his never winning a major race, the 1913 French GP at Amiens being a case in point. While leading in a Delage, Guyot suffered a tire blowout which spun the car off the road, threw out his riding mechanic, and injured him, costing Albert 15 minutes. He finished the race in 5th place.

It was 1914 that he came closest to winning at Indianapolis. Leading a 2-Delage team for himself and René Thomas (like Guyot an experienced racing driver and aviator) Albert finished 3rd behind Thomas and Arthur Duray in a Peugeot. During the war Guyot flew for France, but he was back at Indy in 1919 and finished 4th in a Ballot. His was the only one of the 4-cylinder French cars that finished in the prize money; teammates Thomas, Louis Wagner, and Paul Bablot all dropping out of contention.

Guyot was back in Indiana in a Duesenberg 8, described as being painted "Confederate Gray," in 1921. He finished 6th. Two years later he was there again, this time in a Rolland-Pilain, but the entry was withdrawn before race time. In 1925 Albert tried once more, this time entering a car of his own design, the Guyot Special which used the 1923 Rolland chassis, but failures to finish either the Spanish or Italian GPs that year indicated that the design needed sorting out. He did not race at Indy that season either. But in 1926 he was there and raced. There were actually 3 Guyot-designed cars in that year's race, but 2 raced under the Schmidt marque name. None of the 3 finished the race; Guyot's own car suffered a broken steering knuckle on the 8th lap and was the first car to drop out of the race.

Once his own building activities were over, both with Rolland-Pilain and with Schmid, Guyot joined Citroen in 1929 as a consultant to the engineering staff. At first Albert's racing approach stimulated the engineers, but then he came to think more their way than they his. By the time he died in 1933, the last vestige of the veteran racing driver had been thoroughly stamped out of Guyot.

MIKE HAILWOOD

Motorcycle champions sometimes make good racing drivers. It's a matter of balance, coordination, timing, and guts. John Surtees made the jump fairly easily. It took Stanley Michael Bailey Hailwood, holder of 9 different bike championships between 1961 and 1967, a bit longer to make the transition. Originally tabbed as a Grand Prix prospect, Hailwood didn't succeed as a 4-wheeler until the advent of Formula 5000, the bigger, heavier, faster, more rugged form of GP racing 8 years after he first tried cars.

Hailwood was born near Oxford, April 2, 1940. His father had the biggest motorcycle business in Britain, King's of Oxford, but his early ambition was to "be an admiral or something." Mike spent three years (1954–56) in a prep school called Pangbourne Nautical College before deciding the life of the seaman wasn't for him. He enjoyed music and won 13 of 14 boxing bouts at school before leaving to work for his father, then switching to an apprenticeship in the Triumph motorcycle factory.

Starting April 27, 1957, at Oulton Park, he raced the 2 wheelers. During the next 10 years, Hailwood won nearly 300 races, had about 80 or so 2nds, and set about 220 race or lap records aboard such machines as Triumph, MV, and Honda. He had started driving cars at the age of 14, the first one being his mother's XK 120 Jaguar, but nothing happened in 4-wheeled competition until 1961 when he got a UDT-Laystall Lotus 18/21 Formula 1 car at Silverstone. He crashed. He next drove in 1963 when Brabham sold Hailwood a BTG Formula Junior. In 1964 Reg Parnell signed Hailwood for the British GP but he handed him an obsolete Lotus Climax, beginning a succession of BRM-powered Lotus and Lola mounts in which he didn't really have a chance to do very much. After the 1965 Monaco GP, Hailwood chucked in the 4-wheelers for what he thought was going to be for good. He was used to winning: he won his 1st bike World Championship in 1961 aboard a 250-c.c. Honda, took 500-c.c. title in 1962–65 with the Italian

MVs then won the 250 and 350-c.c. titles in 1966 and 1967 with Honda again.

In 1968, Honda left cycle racing to go F1 racing, but not with Mike. But Hailwood headed back to the car-racing business again, both in single-seaters and in endurance races (with JW Automotive, among others, in GT40's 2nd Mirages through 1969). The stocky, balding Mike got going on the right track in F5000 once the car was adapted to his rather unique style. Paul Hawkins gave him his 1969 shot at the series, superseded by Nick Cuthbert and Jackie Epstein, Hawkins's partners, after Paul's fatal accident that year at Oulton Park. It took a while to get the T142 Lola-Chevvy sorted out, especially the Camaro Z28 engine, but it was finally done. After a slow start, Hailwood finished 2nd at Mondello Park, 3rd at Zandvoort in Holland, 2nd at Snetterton, 2nd at Hockenheim in Germany, and then finally won a race, at Brands Hatch, in the Guards European F5000 championship series. Added up, he was 3rd in points (though 4th in money earned) after Peter Gethin and Trevor Taylor. In 1970 the T190 Lola-Chevvy was not as fast as its competitors, and Mike had several accidents; yet he finished 4th in the standings to Gethin, Howden Ganley and Frank Gardner. Hailwood had 2 outright victories at Silverstone and Salzburgring, the latter in a thrilling slipstreaming duel with Gethin. There were also 3 seconds and a couple of thirds, including one at Zolder where he smashed the lap record outright in the wet to show he had guts and skill in abundance.

The blue-eyed Michael Hailwood, MBE, was a remarkably fit fellow for his age, so he looked forward to continued racing in 1971, troubled only by the possibility that he could not advance beyond F5000. He seemed unsuited to other forms of 4-wheeled competition and there were few berths for a fellow in his 30s, who still occasionally used only 2 wheels at a time. But he was wrong, for at the Italian GP, Hailwood started and finished 4th in a photoflash finish that saw the top 5 covered by a mere second. He also ran a Surtees TS9 in the U.S. GP and finished 15th. For 1972 he continued with Surtees, John's retirement making the season even more enticing. In F2, Hailwood became European champion, and things seemed to be looking up in F1 too.

TED HALIBRAND

Ted Halibrand, a mild, bald man running slightly to fat, had a succession of dreams, and they all contributed mightily to the advancement of American and international auto racing. Halibrand was an implacable foe of weight on cars. He was always trying to make things lighter, an effort that brought him from a position as war surplus service representative at Douglas Aircraft Corporation to virtual monopoly on the wheels and some other parts of the Indianapolis cars. The wheels are important. They represent the greatest single saving of weight in Indy history. They are cast magnesium nowadays, lighter than aluminum alloys or special steels and stronger, too, for the job they must do. But magnesium is porous and so tubed tires had to be used. Ted intended to mount tubeless tires—after he found a way to end the air leakage—and make a further saving in unsprung weight.

Halibrand disc brakes also became almost universal. They were so good at stopping a car that even Detroit considered them seriously. But like many quality items, they also were so expensive that they were not suitable for low-priced passenger cars. Halibrands were spot discs utilizing 2 small discs that clamped down on a drum. Halibrand Engineering also made quick-change rear ends, drive lines, torsion bars and any suspension part other than the shock absorber, and a complete race car (except for the engine) called the Shrike, suitable for an engine behind the driver. It was another of his ideas to lighten the load, financial in this case, on the car owner.

Ted was a restless man in spite of his mild manner. He seemed to be conducting a personal race against time—time to do all of the things he wanted to do. For several years he owned a personal plane in which he could fly needed parts to and from his Los Angeles factory and also save time getting himself around the country. The Halibrand business was built on that ability to deliver mechanical parts to custom specifications quickly. Ted also did engineering design work for the aircraft, marine, and auto industries. When he came to a race, Halibrand tried to view proceedings from the grandstands like any other spectator. He wouldn't say for whom he was rooting because they were all his customers. Watching him, it seemed he was rooting for racing itself.

Halibrand began as a man-of-all-jobs for Fred Lecklider, a West Coast driver of the early thirties. He graduated into his own midget that he ran at old Gilmore Stadium in Los Angeles. He did well enough and was a good enough businessman to enlarge his stable to 3 midgets and one Indianapolis-type car. Then he quit driving to maintain the *équipe* which at times boasted Duke Nalon and Bill Schindler in the cockpit. At Douglas Aircraft during World War II he assisted in aircraft maintenance with the military, gaining him a great deal of knowledge of light metals. The official story is that Halibrand Engineering began accidentally. Ted had experienced difficulty with Rudge-type wire wheels on his own race cars. They were heavy, expensive, and a different set was needed for virtually every track. Also, they wouldn't corner as hard as he wished.

Ted credited Rex Mays with popularizing the magnesium wheel. Ted was successfully using an experimental set on his own midget, but there was a rumor that under extreme stress the wheels would shatter. Mays, however, watched the wheels under racing conditions, was impressed, and began using them. More and more requests for complete sets of wheels came, and the Halibrand company was founded formally in 1947. The following year the Halibrand wheel came to Indianapolis as part of the 6-wheeled Pat Clancy Special. The wheels were successful even though the car placed only 12th. Later Ted branched into production of other parts of the car suitable for light metal casting. There is evidence that Halibrand's magnesium wheels were not the first in racing. That honor apparently belongs to someone in the Midwest, who equipped some midgets with them in 1946. But the firm seemed to have abandoned the idea to concentrate on more lucrative pursuits.

JIM HALL

The cover neatly zipped over the part of the transmission that showed under the Chaparral was pure showmanship, as was the thin-lipped mechanic in the Texas 10-gallon hat who unsmilingly guarded the car in the pits at Bridgehampton on the sand dunes of Long Island. It was 1965, and that was the year Chaparral won 16 races out of 21 starts. Jim Hall stood near by, arms folded over the steel pit guardrail, an amused look in his eyes. "Everybody thinks five thousand General Motors engineers are working only on making up goodies so we can win," he grinned. "I only wish that were one per cent true."

Jim Hall was never going to have to worry about where his next meal was coming from. He had inherited $15 million when, a month before he entered presti-

gious California Institute of Technology, his parents and sister were killed in the crash of a private plane. An older brother, Richard, and a younger brother, Charles, survived. along with Jim. Hall stayed at school as a geology major. Born in Abilene, Texas, in 1935, he was already married (at 17) and the father of two. Commuting to New Mexico and Texas via plane didn't help his grades, and after his sophomore year, Hall switched to mechanical engineering even though it meant making up courses. The switch worked out for him because Hall, who already had begun driving in SCCA races during his summer vacation, was vitally interested in sports cars. He began in 1954 with an Austin-Healey and backed a sports car dealership with Carroll Shelby, then the resident sports car hero of Texas.

Hall credited Shelby with two things: teaching him how to drive better and spending a great deal of money in an unprofitable enterprise. Hall's older brother, Richard, was very much involved at this time. In fact, it was he who had gotten Shelby and Jim together. The Hall-Shelby enterprise for a time was one of two importers of Maseratis. Should one attempt to trace Hall's development as an engineer and car builder and driver as one would trace the periods in the life of a great painter, this period would be notable for one other development. Shelby talked British builder Brian Lister into making over a Lister-Jaguar chassis so a Chevrolet Corvette engine could be installed. The Lister Corvette was an unsuccessful car, but it did get Hall started on engineering his own mounts. The Dallas sports car dealership ended in 1958, and Hall spent 3 years as a parttime SCCA racer, part-time oil man. He eventually moved to the middle of the oil country, Midland, Tex.

In 1961 he became reacquainted with Hap Sharp, one of the few excellent customers the Dallas sports car dealership had had. Six sports car enthusiasts in the Lubbock-Midland area soon banded together to build their own private sports car track. Hall and Sharp became neighbors in the garage area of Rattlesnake Raceway. In 1961, primarily in order to be competitive, Hall began the Chaparral project. Dick Troutman and Tom Barnes, temporarily at liberty, built the first Chaparral from their own designs and sold 2 to Hall and 2 to Harry Heuer, a Milwaukee beer baron, while one went to England and one was retained by T-B for Skip Hudson to race. Hall won only 2 races in this car, the Elkhart 500 in 1962 and the June Sprints, at Road America that year.

In 1962 Hall and Sharp finally got together to form Chaparral Cars, Inc. Hap had gotten tired of being the dumping grounds for John Cooper's old cars and agreed with Jim that the only way to have the latest machinery was to build it yourself. By the time Jim, still hoping to become an international driver, accepted number 2 spot on the BRP Formula 1 team and went off to Europe in 1963 the Chaparral project was well under way. Hall and Sharp freely admitted that they were influenced by both the Lotus 19 and the Cooper Monaco in working out Chaparral 2. The man who actually designed and bulit the semi-monocockque fiber glass chassis-body was an aerospace man named Andy Green. The man who screwed the pieces together was Gary Knutson, who later worked for Bruce McLaren before returning to the Hall enterprise. The "pieces" included at various times, both the Olds aluminum V-8 engine and the Corvette engine, a Cooper 5-speed gearbox, Cooper steering, Lotus wheels and hubs, and a Colotti gearbox.

Hall's European sojourn in 1963 earned him 13th place in the standings on a 5th at the Nurburgring and a 6th at Silverstone, and convinced him that he did not want to make the sacrifices necessary to get into the top echelon. For one thing, after Texas, Europe was a cold, damp place to be living most of the year. For another, it wasn't as much fun as building your own cars and racing in the U.S.A. Chaparral 2's debut in the Times Grand Prix at Riverside in October, 1963, was quite auspicious—this version had the Corvette-Colotti tandem—until an electrical fire burned up its chances. Nassau Speed Week was a total disaster: Hall's steering collapsed and Hap Sharp's Olds V-8 Cooper broke an axle.

Now Hall was up to his ears in design work, work that he found as interesting as driving. The 1964 Chaparral 2 had a whole new front end and, by May, an automatic transmission. Hall admitted that Sharp first thought of the idea of utilizing an automatic, then both worked on it. Hall drove the car to victory in its debut as an automatic at Laguna Seca, yet none of the West Coast automotive press even noticed the presence of the unique transmission. It was 2 races later before anyone—even competitors—noticed it. Then the campaign was on. Out came the zippered cover and the secrecy that continued through the 1970 season and beyond. The Chaparral had arrived as a car, and Hall won the 1964 U.S. Road Racing Championship with it. But it was in 1965 that the shovel-nosed, fiber glass creation really dominated American road racing—16 victories out of 21 starts. Hall, Sharp and a spare car, all were prepared to sweep the opposition before them.

When Sharp won at Nassau Speed Week that year, he was satisfied and quit regular competition, but not Chaparral Cars. Meanwhile Hall had plunged the company into a project for a new, more aerodynamically advanced car. This one was to be aluminum. The test version was designated 2B and the first racing version 2C, making its debut at Kent, Wash., late in 1965. The 2D was a version with front and rear spoilers for downthrust, and then came the 2E, Hall's next tour de force, a car with a full wing to exert downthrust directly on the suspension.

This was the car that set the 1966–67 trend which eventually led to the CSI's ban on wings. It was not immediately successful; Chaparral decided to campaign the old 2C in European and U.S. enduros leading to the championship of manufacturers, thus diluting the team effort needed to develop a new racing car. The European excursion was saved from total disaster only by victory in the Nurburgring 1000. The winged 2E made its debut at the Bridgehampton CanAm with Phil Hill joining the Chaparral effort. Hill finished 4th, and Hall DNF because of wing problems. But Phil took a 2nd at Mosport and won Laguna Seca; and Hall added 2nds at Laguna and Riverside. For 1967 there was the dual effort again and a winged coupe called the 2F. More drivers were signed on a race-to-race basis—Mike Spence, Bruce Jennings—and Hall found himself involved in projects like trying to develop the Chevrolet 427 into a strong and reliable engine. It took Hall until the last of the European races to get the 427 mated durably with his automatic transmission. Chaparral won the Brands Hatch 500, easily. Meanwhile, for the CanAm, the E model had been redesigned into the G model. More trouble came when engines broke in these sprints as if they were papier-mâché, not aluminium. Hall never got the car running perfectly for a whole race.

But for the 1968 CanAm series, the 2G was competitive with the McLarens. It took Hall 13 laps at Bridgehampton to seat the brake pads because he didn't have a chance to in practice; then he was able finally to slip past Dan Gurney. The car was superior to its opposition—which included the best Group 7 vehicle that Ford Motor Company could develop—and won easily (despite the fact that only 7 cylinders were actually in operation). The car did not win again, though, because of a succession of tiny breakdowns.

Las Vegas, 1968, was the last stop of that year's CanAm series, at a place called Stardust International Raceway which was to disappear after a short unsuccessful life among the slot machines. Hall was in contention when a serious accident put him in the hospital. Coming around a blind curve, he collided with Lothar Motschenbacher. Hall's car was demolished, and Jim, who had never had a serious accident in 14 years of competition, found himself with teams of doctors watching over various broken and damaged areas of his body. It was 9 weeks before he was permitted to leave the hospital, and 1969 was virtually written off as a racing season.

In 1969 there was the 2H, which was never very successful. The car, like many of its predecessors, was fast, but it had a lot of problems still unsolved when Hall moved on to another of his revolutionary ideas for downthrust—the so-called "vacuum cleaner." Utilizing the principle of the hydrofoil, Hall employed an auxiliary engine-fan arrangement to create artificial downthrust. Enter the 2J, a shocking shape from Rattlesnake Raceway to startle the eye of racing fans accustomed to the smooth, sinuous lines of European race cars. The vehicle had a vertical rear end, and it hugged the road as intended during practice at the Watkins Glen CanAm. With Jackie Stewart in the driver's seat, the 2J set fast lap in the race before it had to retire with boiling brakes. Stewart claimed Hall's reverse ground effect of 2 turbine fans, powered by a transaxle-mounted 2-cycle engine, worked well, but was 2 years away from development. CSI banned the car before 1970 was finished.

That year Hall fielded a team of Camaros in the TransAm. Jim drove some of the early races, but retired in favor of Vic Elford. The Camaros just did not have it, and represented perhaps the greatest failure in Hall's long association with racing. The TransAm experience indicated that Hall's driving days were over. When he entered the L&M championship with Carl Haas in 1973, it was strictly a sideline involvement.

DUNCAN HAMILTON

The scene was Le Mans, France. The time was summer, 1953. The car was an improved C Jaguar, with better cooling and disc brakes for the 1st time. Co-drivers J. Duncan Hamilton, a giant Anglo-Irishman, and an Englishman named A. P. (Tony) Rolt had been friends and seekers of a victory at Le Mans since 1950. They were gentleman drivers; that is, they usually raced their own cars, although on occasions there were factory drives, and this Le Mans was one of them. Hamilton was a surprisingly good sports car driver. In practice that year he was lapping a full second faster than Alberto Ascari's big 4.5-litre Ferrari, and prospects for a Hamilton/Rolt victory at long last looked pretty good. But there was a protest by Ferrari—the Commendatore was good at that—about the use of a practice car, and the organizers had ruled that Duncan and Tony were ineligible. This ruling came at midday Friday, the day before the race itself. The 2 friends were disconsolate, and headed for the nearest bar. They started lubricating their sorrows around 3 P.M. and were still at it when the proprietor finally closed up 12 hours later. A bottle or two went along with them to their rooms, and dawn had passed before either one stopped for breath. Sir William Lyons of Jaguar found the two of them sitting outside their hotel at 10 A.M. Saturday morning. Six hours away was the start of the Le Mans race, and, having paid their fine for them (a stratagem cooked up to satisfy both Ferrari and Jaguar), Sir William wanted them to start. Hamilton looked at Rolt, Rolt looked at Hamilton, and the par staggered toward cold showers, hot baths, chilled brandy, and buckets of hot coffee.

At the proper hour, they were on the line. At the signal the Hamilton/Rolt Jaguar started, and almost 2,000 miles and a full day later they crossed the finish line winners of the 1953 Le Mans race with an average speed of 105.85 m.p.h., the initial time the 100 m.p.h. barrier had been crossed in this most grueling of all endurance races.

While Tony Rolt was left celebrating the victory, Hamilton headed west with his wife Angela to run in

the Oporto Grand Prix in his own C Jaguar. Early in the race, Duncan was ripping along at 125 m.p.h. when a Ferrari spun into him, sending the Jag off course, where it crashed into an electric power pole and ejected Hamilton into a tree. He fell from the tree, was hit by another Ferarri, bounced into an iron fence and was impaled by a spike. When they reached him his face was terribly battered and he had (by later count) 9 broken ribs, a broken collarbone, and a broken neck. They announced over the public address system that J. D. Hamilton was dead, and the race went on. Someone carried the body to a hospital where a doctor who wasn't a racing enthusiast discovered that he was breathing still and started to patch him together without anesthetic (since the anesthetist was a racing fan and couldn't be found). His wife and a friend, who refused to believe he was dead until they saw the body, finally tracked Hamilton to the obscure hospital, got him transferred to a British hospital, and the patch job continued. Would you believe he was back racing within 3 weeks? Well, he was.

J. Duncan Hamilton was born in Cork, in what later became Eire, April 30, 1920. He lived there with his wealthy parents until the age of 6, then came to England. At 13 he was in Brighton College, and without any previous training in the sport proceeded to win all kinds of shooting trophies just so he didn't have to go out for cricket, which he loathed. Next came Chelsea in London and the Aeronautical Engineering College.

Around this time Hamilton started experimenting with an Austin 7 engine in his attic, which eventually crashed through the ceiling into the bathroom. Then it

278

was out to the stable, into the car, and a crash into a garden wall on the rebuilt car's first trial run. It seems Duncan forgot to connect the brakes. The engineering classes moved on to Brooklands—as much an aeronautical establishment as an automotive one—and fate had set Hamilton on the right road at last.

He learned to fly at Brooklands and, despite a few accidents in a Wolseley and in an Austin Nippy, to race fairly well too. Joining the Auxiliary Air Force in 1939, Hamilton never got off the ground with the RAF; his solo flight consisted of running down the runway straight into an officer's mess. The aircraft (and the pilot prospect) was written off. The Royal Navy was less choosy, considering Hamilton's aeronautical engineering background worth a commission. He was in the Fleet Air Arm and posted to Norway. On the way over, 2 ships were sunk from under him but he made the fjords on the 3rd one.

The Nazis captured Hamilton and others engaged in espionage work with him and sentenced them to death by firing squad. Hamilton never told how he escaped, but he and one other fellow did manage to get away, although he was wounded in both legs. Duncan spent the rest of the war spying, getting into and out of occupied Europe regularly. He also did a fair amount of flight testing of experimental aircraft. Over the Orkneys in a bomber late in the war, he picked up the wrong rubber tube in answer to a call of nature and managed to urinate on an admiral through a speaking tube.

Despite all this, Hamilton was a full commander at 24. He met and married a Wren officer named Angela Sanderson, then nearly died from a kidney infection. With the war's end, Hamilton was offered a test pilot's job by a major U.S. aviation company, but bowing to Angela's wishes, he passed it up. His replacement was killed 3 weeks later. But Angela didn't know what she was agreeing to when she okayed motor racing as a substitute. The initial racer was an MG, purchased from Mike Hawthorn's father, Hillclimbs came initially, with the MG and a Bugatti that he saw at a Shelsley Walsh climb. Next came a Maserati 6C and the British Empire Trophy race on the Isle of Man. Duncan crashed. But he kept racing, with a 3rd and 4th at the new Dutch Zandvoort course and a 5th at the new Goodwood course in England. In 1950, while recuperating from still another accident, Hamilton and Rolt cooked up their attack on Le Mans. Donald Healey was a co-conspirator, producing a 3.4-litre Nash-engined Healey. They finished 4th overall at just under 88 m.p.h. while the winners averaged 89.73.

That same year Hamilton took another 4th overall in a Healey Silverstone in another Le Mans race—for production cars—and won the Wakefield Trophy in his own Maserati back in Britain. In 1951 he bought an ex-Prince Bira ERA B-type. Bira won the Richmond Trophy at Goodwood in another car while Duncan came in 3rd in the old one. Lago Talbot gave Hamilton a fac-

tory ride at the International Trophy; he was 2nd behind Reg Parnell's Thinwall Special. At Le Mans, Duncan and Tony Rolt shaved a closed-in Healey-Nash and grabbed 6th overall. He kept racing the Talbot and added an HWM—brainchild of George Abecassis and John Heath—for Formula 2 starts (F2 being the principal formula in those days).

The 1953 adventures of Hamilton and Rolt at Le Mans and the terrible events at Oporto followed. Starting in 1954, he raced his own and the factory's Jaguars almost exclusively. He won the Paris GP at 93.30 m.p.h. and was 3rd in the Coupe du Salon at Montlhéry. At Le Mans and at the Rheims 12-hour race, Hamilton finished 2nd. In 1955 he and Rolt were 2nd again at Le Mans, 2nd in the Paris Cup, 3rd in the Portugese GP, and 3rd in the Dakar race in Africa. The following season he was 2nd in the Coupe du Salon and in the Frontiers GP, and won the Paris Cup at 97.47 m.p.h.

The year 1956 saw Hamilton and Jaguar come to a parting of the ways at the Rheims 12-hour race. He was leading by more than 100 miles when pit signals indicated the factory wanted the Hawthorn/Paul Frere car to win. Hamilton ignored the signals and ripped across the line (with Ivor Bueb) at 109.94 m.p.h. He was fired on the spot. Two hours later he was hired by Enzo Ferrari, his old nemisis from Le Mans. In his initial Ferrari race, the Swedish GP, he shared a 3rd with Hawthorn and Alfonso de Portago. In 1957 he raced Le Mans with Masten Gregory in his own Jaguar; they finished 6th overall despite a fire and other assorted adventures. That was about the extent of Duncan's racing for that season.

Hamilton opened 1958 with good placings at Goodwood and Oulton Park. But at Le Mans a crash pulled all the ligaments from both legs. Though still on crutches, Hamilton shared a 6th in the Tourist Trophy. It was to be his last season. Duncan and Hawthorn were talking about merging their firms, but Hawthorn died in an ordinary road accident on the afternoon they had planned to meet and cement it. Duncan had to identify Mike's body on a mortury slab. Hamilton retired that afternoon to concentrate on his business interests.

PETE HAMILTON

Peter Goodwill Hamilton used to look as if he should have the Good Housekeeping Seal of Approval right in the middle of his forehead. He spoke impeccable English, as the son of a Harvard Ph. D. should, and his nails were clean. Yet Richard Petty, the living legend of stock-car racing, picked him as number 2 driver for Petty Enterprises in 1970 because he was willing to work on the automobiles and learn how to drive in the Petty manner.

Born July 20, 1942, Pete came to the attention of NASCAR owners in 1967 when, racing mostly around his native New England, he won the national Late Model

had to hold the car in 2nd. But the fortunes of racing change quickly. Lund pitted on lap 23, removing him as a contender; then Paschal had to stop the following lap. That put Pete into the lead, and he held it until Jim caught him four laps later. Hamilton kept the pressure on the Javelin driver, pressure that finally paid off when Paschal rolled into the pits on the 36th lap. Miraculously the gear trouble cleared up, and Hamilton actually cut his fastest laps of the race then, as he won easily over Lund and his Mercury Cougar.

This, then, was Peter Hamilton, the soft-spoken blond youngster with a career all planned out. In 1968 he had a Ford ride, but switched to A. J. King's Tennessee Dodge because it was a better Grand National car. At the end of the 1968 season NASCAR ruled that a driver could not compete in both the pony cars and the Grand Nationals. King had sold his Dodge operation, and White had offered the Camaro berth. After looking over the mixture of veterans and bright newcomers in Grand American, Pete chose the Camaro. He told one reporter, "Race drivers probably practice less than any other pro athlete. That's because its too expensive to practice so they have to get their experience in the actual races. At this point I need experience."

Yet Hamilton received special permission to run the Banjo Matthews car in the 1969 Atlanta 500 when Donnie Allison became ill. He rode the car to impressive 5th place. Then it was back to the Camaro, including a race in TransAm competition at Bridgehampton, Pete's opener on a road course against a field of road racing specialists. He flipped the car and landed upside down in a sand dune before the midway point .

When 1969 was over Hamilton was king of the pony cars, NASCAR version, and looking for the next step forward. Richard, Lee, and Maurice Petty provided that with a SuperBird ride for 1970. Hamilton worked on the car he drove, practiced in the car he worked on, and in between got lessons in Grand National driving from the Petty family. He was an excellent investment for them, the kind that paid off quickly. The 1970 Daytona 500 had all the factories and all the best independents. Richard Petty, a 2-time winner, was one of the favorites. His protégé, Hamilton, was considered a long shot despite the fabulous Petty backing. There were too many other good experienced drivers in hot cars around. Almost 104,000 fans packed the huge speedway for the biggest of the NASCAR classics, lured by the field and the fact that Cale Yarborough had set a new qualifying mark of 194.015 m.p.h. The pressure was on every driver who thought he had a chance to win, and Pete thought he had that chance.

The Petty fortunes seemed under a cloud, however, when the engine of Richard's No. 43 blew on the 7th lap. But Richard piled out of his car and took over the direction of Hamilton's pit. Hamilton stayed off the pace, but close enough to strike. He was able to lead 3 laps just past the quarter mark primarily because the

Sportsman crown. The next year he came South in a shortened attempt to run Grand National and finished 6 times among the top 10 in 16 races, becoming NASCAR's Rookie of the Year. That earned him a ride in a Camaro in what is now called Grand American racing, fielded by the redoubtable Firestone-backed Gene White organization of Atlanta. Hamilton won 12 out of 26 starts, including the Paul Revere 250.

The Paul Revere 250-mile race begins at a minute after midnight on July 4, American Independence Day, and could be held only at a well-lighted superspeedway like Daytona International; and only the rabid stock-car fans of the southern United States would crowd in to see 250 miles of racing on the twisting 3.81-mile road course at that hour of the night. But the Paul Revere provided the kind of racing that would have been exciting even in broad daylight. As the flag dropped, young Joe Chitwood—son of the famed thrill show rider—jumped pole-sitter Jim Paschal and his Javelin to assume an early lead. Bob Tullius, the SCCA stalwart in another Javelin, held 3rd position. Paschal used the high banks to move up on Chitwood; he passed on the 5th lap, and Joe was soon out of the running with a broken transmission. But Tullius also was waiting and passed Paschal. Then the battle was between Paschal and Tullius with Hamilton running his own race behind them. It was a short battle; Bob blew a head gasket on lap 17 leaving the lead to Jim.

Now Cougar's Tiny Lund was moving up to challenge him, and it seemed that this night Pete Hamilton would be thwarted. He had apparently lost 1st gear, and he

leaders were pitting. Soon Yarborough, A. J. Foyt, and Donnie Allison had joined Petty on the sidelines. Bobby Isaac, Charlie Glotzbach, and David Pearson were battling over the lead. It wasn't until lap 139, when others pitted, that Hamilton could lead again briefly. Bobby Allison in his Dodge joined the battle for first. It was Pearson in his Holman-Moody Ford (a Ford that seemed faster whenever it wanted to lead) against an assortment of MoPar machinery. Then Richard Brooks, NASCAR's Rookie of the Year, spun and the caution blinked on. That meant the field closed up behind the leader. Both Hamilton and Pearson took advantage of the yellow and pitted, Hamilton to get right-side tires and Pearson to change left-side tires. Hamilton returned to the pits a lap later to get his left-side tires changed. The green came out on the 190th lap, and Hamilton was right behind Pearson, close enough to execute the famous slingshot maneuver. Pearson let Pete into the lead so that it would be his Ford Talladega that pulled any last-turn heroics. But suddenly he found that Hamilton, with new tires all around, had better traction and was running easily ahead of him.

David made his move on the 198th lap. He dipped low off the bank; Hamilton dipped down to block him. But the slingshot was working and Pearson pulled alongside the blue SuperBird. Suddenly, however, the Ford lost traction, and Pearson found himself using all his skill (which was considerable) to keep the 625 h.p. Ford from looping. He held it, but it took him a lap to move up behind Hamilton again as they sped into the final lap of the race. This time David did not wait; he tried passing on the first turn; the youngster blocked him. He tried passing on the back straight; the youngster forced him over into a line that would have taken away any advantage from that final turn. And he tried to come up for one more try at the slingshot; but Hamilton foiled that and sped across the line, his initial Grand National victory worth $46,00 in prize money alone.

At the Alabama 500 in Talladega in April, Hamilton paid off again as teacher Richard finished 7th. This time he conserved his tires in the early going and didn't take the lead until the 140th of 188 laps. Hamilton gave it right back to Buddy Baker and let him have it for 30 more laps. Then on lap 170, he passed the Dodge pilot and won easily.

When Baker was forced to evacuate his mount in a hurry as it burst into flames. Pete was not through with his heroics. In the Motor State 400 he won the pole, then battled wheel-to-wheel with Cale Yarborough, officially losing by only a few car lengths. (The Petty forces protested vainly that Yarborough had been credited with one lap too many.) There was also a 3rd, two 5ths and an 8th as he learned from Petty how to pace himself in a distance race. Back at Talladega for the 500 it was Pete's turn to play rabbit, however. Although there were 10 lead changes before he led a lap, he led 153 of the 188 in the race as his SuperBird seemed to be measur-

ably faster even than Richard's car. Richard finished 7th, 5 laps off the pace. In 16 starts under the Petty banner, Pete won $131,406, 2nd only to Richard's $131,965 for 40 starts. He was in the top 5 in 10 of the 16 races.

Yet when MoPar announced a cutback in factory support to a single Plymouth and a single Dodge, both under the Petty banner, Pete was unemployed for 1971 while Buddy Baker was tapped for the Dodge ride. Hamilton acquired his own Plymouth ride for 1971, and the question arose as to whether he would win without the Petty back-up. The former University of Maine drummer would find out quickly. He was top five in 11 of 22 starts, winning one of the 125-mile qualifiers at Daytona Speed weeks, but without sponsor money, he had problems in 1972, suffering 4 engine failures in the 5 races he managed to start that year. It was comeback time in 1973 with Hamilton again trying to go his own way. It was as if there were a conspiracy to shut Pete out from the big money. Or was it that in stock-car racing, the car is that much more important than the driver?

RALPH HANKINSON

The father of auto polo could also be called one of the saviours of AAA Contest Board racing. Born August 1, 1879, in Russell, Kans., Ralph A. Hankinson was a born promoter. His auto polo show toured the world. The cars were divided into 2 teams and were expected to bash a huge ball through a goal. Rules were few, the vehicles about equally agile, and the whole promotion made hordes of money.

From this it was a quick step into auto race promotion. Hankinson presented Bob Burman and his Blitzen Benz, and other lesser attractions, and transported his entourage by rail in as much luxury as the great Alex Sloan provided for his men. Ralph promoted under the IMCA banner until 1926, when the old techniques of promoting racing failed to support him. Nearly bankrupt, he decided to try the less pretentious AAA Contest Board method of permitting the drivers and car owners to run for prize money, making deals only with such stars as an Indianapolis champion.

Ralph felt the most money was to be gained by owning, leasing or managing speedways. As a division of the vast George Hamid booking enterprise, Hankinson's organization confined its main efforts to the East Coast. In fact, he rescued this area for AAA from IMCA. In 1932 he bought Langhorne, a one-mile white elephant, and managed to make it pay even in the depths of the Depression. He drew crowds of 60,000 into Philadelphia's huge Kennedy Stadium for midget auto racing at night in 1936, one of the first instances of night outdoor auto racing in the United States. He was the last promoter at the Altoona, Pa., and Woodbridge, N.J., board tracks. Hankinson was probably the most successful promoter of "still dates" in history. A still date in American racing parlance used to be an event held without benefit of a state, district, or county fair to gather a crowd. Now it is any event held on other than the scheduled day of the race because of rain.

Hankinson, who died in the forties, trained many others in his methods. Essentially he was of the old school, regarding auto racing as a form of show business, but he was shrewd enough to realize that honest competition open to all was the best product he could sell the public.

SAM HANKS

It was 1957. The man sitting in Victory Lane at Indianapolis had flowers around his neck, and he grinned a tired grin when photographers asked him to, shook hands with people he didn't seem to see. When the crowd gave him some respite, he was asked the traditional question, "Will you be back next year?"

He grinned and, as if he had been saving it inside for minutes, hours, years, said, "Certainly I'll be back—as a spectator."

With a little luck, Samuel Dwight Hanks would never have become a race driver. He would have been an airplane mechanic or a pilot or even an aeronautical engineer. Born July 13, 1914, in Columbus, O., Sam came to California in 1920 when his father, a contractor and builder, moved the family there. The Hanks clan lived across the street from an airport, and Sam had his first

plane ride when 10, soloed when he was 14. He washed planes to earn money for flying lessons and was working on the engines by the time he was 15. He took shop courses in high school at Alhambra, Calif., and mainly because his teen contemporaries did so, he built his own roadsters. There was a Model T and then a Model A Ford with a Riley head, which he ran during the early Thirties on Muroc Dry Lake, later a hot-rod center.

Hanks worked as a machinist after high school, then became a truck driver for a Los Angeles Brewery in 1935. One of his fellow drivers was Ted Horn, but it wasn't Ted who steered Sam toward auto racing. An acquaintance named Slim Ruhland, took him to Gilmore Stadium in Los Angeles as a pit crew member. The next day he let Sam drive his car on the deserted track. Hanks thought he had done horribly, but Ruhland was ecstatic and convinced Sam he should drive in the next Gilmore feature.

"I began racing halfway through 1936," Hanks recalled later, "mainly because it seemed an easy way to make more money. Before the season was over, I had one of the better West Coast midgets. In 1937 I began to drive Danny Hogan's Offy and won the Pacific Coast Championship. But if I was to make any real money out of this I knew I had to own my own car, so for 1938 I bought the black Offy which I drove and did all the mechanical work on until 1948."

Hanks campaigned the car on the Coast in 1938; then, seeking more fields to conquer, raced in the East and Midwest. It was a rugged life—tow to the race, prepare the car, race, tow to the next race. He did no Championship car racing, yet in 1940 Leon Duray picked him to drive at Indianapolis. "I really felt honored," Sam said, "and for the first time I realized I really enjoyed racing and had all along. Here one of the greatest and toughest drivers of his era had picked me. We qualified about 125 m.p.h. and were in contention until the gas tank broke. We finished about 14th."

Hanks went right back to midgets, drove relief at Indy in 1941 for Joe Chitwood and finished 5th, then returned to midgets. When World War II came, he joined the Army Air Force where he became a first lieutenant assigned to engine flight testing at Wright Field in Ohio. There he met and married Alice Hanks. Only the decline of the thunderbugs after the war changed Hanks from a once-a-year Indianapolis visitor into a full-time championship circuit competitor. His Indy record between 1940 and 1952 shows 9 starts, nothing better than a 5th and no full 500-mile trips until 1952.

That was the year Hanks joined the Bardahl Racing Team owned by Ed Walsh with Harry Stephens as chief mechanic. Sam finished 3rd in a dirt track machine that had a Kurtis 400 chassis (only partly because Walsh was a heavy backer of Frank Kurtis). He campaigned the same car all of 1953 and shared a 3rd-place with Duane Carter in that hotbox Indy. In 1956 he finished 2nd and time seemed to be running out on the man who was admired for his seemingly effortless driving style. Back in 1941 and again in 1949, Sam had won the AAA national midget title. In 1953 he had won the AAA National Championship for the big cars. Now there was only one prize in auto racing he considered important—an Indianapolis victory. By this time shrewd off-track investments had removed the financial necessity for him to race. The lean crew-cut 6-footer with the ready smile and soft voice now dressed in custom-tailored suits and hobnobbed with business executives. But Hanks went to Indy to fulfill a dream.

In 1957, mechanic George Salih finally realized a dream of his own—to build a car according to his theories of chassis development—he got Hanks to run it. Salih's car had several innovations: the Meyer-Drake Offy was modified to run on its side only 18 degrees from horizontal, for example, and the top of the hood was only 21 inches from the ground, affording a lower center of gravity than even the conventional roadsters.

The formula changed for 1957, being reduced to 256.284 inches unsupercharged and 170.856 supercharged. Because of this, the Meyer-Drake people had multiple problems and spins were common as drivers sought to equal last year's speeds with the smaller engines. Hanks refused to push the Salih car, known as the Belond Exhaust Special. He was still getting the car just right as the first 9 starting positions were filled, including polesitter Pat O'Connor. Sam qualified the next week at 142.812, just comfortably fast enough to assure him of a position toward the front. He was there to run 500 miles, not just a trophy dash.

It was a magnificent day for the race, sunny but cool enough so that even the gentlemen in the new Tower Terrace could keep on their jackets in comfort. And Sam Hanks was running just as cool a race. He brought his machine up to within hailing distance of the leaders and stayed there as Pat O'Connor and Troy Ruttman traded the lead for the first 11 laps, only to lose it to Paul Russo in a Novi. Hanks closed in on Paul but made no attempt to pass him. For 20 laps he seemed to be studying how the Novi accelerated out of each turn. Then Hanks burst off turn number 2 at full throttle on lap 36 to take a 2-car-length lead over Russo. He knew that although the Novi was more powerful, its torque curve rose more gradually and he could keep Russo in check by going through the turns more quickly. Only sloppy pit crew work during his tire stop on lap 50 lost him the lead, to Johnny Thompson, and he took it back on lap 54. He stopped on lap 111 again, and the pit crew lost him 11 seconds to new challenger Jim Rathmann. Sam made the time back the hard way, shaving about 0.9 seconds off Rathmann's lead on each of the 4 turns. The smaller Belond car was handling better, and Sam took the lead back on lap 135, widening it to a 5-second margin when Rathmann pitted on lap 151. When he in turn pitted 4 laps later, he lost only 3 seconds to the Rathmann entourage, and kept his hard-won lead.

Hanks won the race by 21.5 seconds and his dream was fulfilled.

Soon after that, Hanks became an official of the Speedway for each 500-mile race. He also published a periodical called "Racing Pictorial" and lived very comfortably in Southern California. "If I had it to do over again, I'd still go racing again," he said.

WALTER HANSGEN

Westfield, N.J., is a town out of a Booth Tarkington novel, the place where the archetypical American Boy grows up in a white clapboard house standing on a wide street lined with towering elms, maples and oak trees. Downtown has no tall buildings; it doesn't need any for the population is too small and too close to New York City. F. K. Hansgen & Son was a coach repair shop that turned into an auto body repair shop. There Walt Hansgen—born October 28, 1919—grew up, tinkering with automobiles the way other boys play with kites. When he returned from service after World War II, he went back into the family business because there was plenty of work and because he had a wife to support.

Westfield is important because environment shapes and alters a man, acting upon him and turning his life in directions which would have seemed impossible or undesirable in a different setting. Westfield is a rich town, even by American standards, and F. K. Hansgen prospered in the period when U.S. cars were hard to get and had to be kept running. The young Hansgen had

been a race buff before—the local track racing. He began to learn about another kind of car and another kind of racing from customers who brought their MGs, Jaguars and Singers in for repairs.

He drove the cars, and about 1951 came the chance happening that started him on his career. He was able to buy a wrecked XK 120 Jaguar. He fixed it up and raced at Bridgehampton, added an aluminium lightweight body to the stock chassis and engine that winter, and took third in this version's debut. In 1952 and 1953, with help from restaurateur Vincent Sardi, the Jaguar Special and Hansgen became kings of East Coast amateur racing. He won the Cumberland Cup in Maryland and Watkins Glen. In 1954 a new C Jaguar managed to beat even the cars of Briggs Cunningham, so Walter was hired by Briggs as a contract driver and Jaguar dealer for Westfield. In this dual capacity, Hansgen began to win SCCA titles and to travel to Europe, mainly for Le Mans and British races.

Hansgen, now in his late thirties and prematurely gray, was SCCA C-Modified champion for the period 1956 through 1959, winning the title twice in the D-type and twice in a Lister-Jaguar. Quiet and friendly off the track, he became president of an organization of the best American road course drivers called the Road Racing Drivers Club. The club was dedicated to improving the caliber of U.S. road course driving, and Hansgen was an unpaid teacher for many amateurs.

Meanwhile, Hansgen finally made it to Sebring's Grand Prix d'Endurance in 1959. He codriving a factory Corvette with John Fitch. He returned regularly with the Cunningham équipe after that, never lasting, a circumstance that didn't seem to bother him one whit. He liked the shorter races better and carried the Cunningham colors through a wide assortment of machinery—Maseratis, Cooper-Buicks, ever Formula Juniors—with great success in 1961 and 1962. But when Briggs dissolved his racing effort, Hansgen was not unemployed long. John Mecom, Jr., the Texas oil heir, hired him as a driver and racing manager. In 1964 and 1965 when most drivers his age were already retired, Walter initially drove at Indianapolis (in the Kjell Qvale MG Liquid Suspension Offy). He finished 14th twice.

At the age of 45 Hansgen just seemed to be getting better and better. He scored Lola's initial major victory in the U.S., winning the 1965 Monterey Grand Prix USRRC stop. In 1966 although still officially team manager for Mecom, he was heavily involved in the Holman-Moody Ford factory sports car effort in a Ford GT40 Mk. 2. For Ford he took 3rd in the Daytona Continental and 2nd at Sebring with Mark Donahue his partner in each case.

Now the Ford effort shifted to Le Mans, and, after Sebring, Hansgen flew over to participate in April practice in the Ford GT. His protégé Donohue was to join him later. This was to be Walt's 10th appearance at the famed endurance classic. It was a rainy Saturday morn-

ing in Le Mans but rain does not bother a road racer. Hansgen ducked into the 7-litre monster and accelerated onto the wet roadway. Soon (Shelby-American timekeepers noted with pleasure) he was clocking the fastest times in the practice.

His accident occurred with startling suddeness. Just before the old 1st turn, the car lost traction on the water-covered road and spun into the escape road. It hit a dirt barrier and flipped end-over-end, landing finally on another embankment. Extricated from the crushed car, Hansgen was rushed by helicopter to a nearby American military hospital. He had suffered multiple skull fractures, a broken pelvis, and broken arms and legs. He lingered long enough for his wife and children to visit him, then died of brain injuries.

Hansgen had had no intention of retiring as a driver. He was already under contract to drive a Mecom car at Indianapolis, and the Ford factory effort wanted him for the World Manufacturers Championship. He had told a reporter, "Why stop doing something you enjoy if you still can do it well just because you reach a certain chronological age?" Hansgen had never stopped.

HUSCHKE von HANSTEIN

First Hanstein drove, and drove well. His greatest triumph perhaps, came in the 1940 Mille Miglia with its 102-mile laps, in which he and Walter Baumer co-piloted a 2-litre BMW coupe to victory at 105.43 m.p.h. Then he directed, and directed well, the fortunes of one of the great teams of auto racing: Porsche of Germany. Fritz Huschke von Hanstein was a team manager for the silver cars and normally could be found operating in a cheery but dignified way without the physical or verbal performances that were standard with some managers. Invariably he more a checkered English cap and had stopwatches, lap charts, and cameras on the alert. He spoke perfect English with an Oxford accent, picked up at school in England long before World War II (he was born in Halle in eastern Germany, January 3, 1911). At college he started racing motorcycles, then graduated to cars in 1933. By 1936, Hanstein's talents were such that he was offered an Auto Union contract. However, a rally accident crippled his right arm and ended his GP career before it began. But he still could drive smaller cars, and Hanstein's racing career, mostly in Germany with Hanomag, Adler, and BMW, with occasional forays elsewhere, spanned both prewar and postwar European history. He joined Porsche in 1950. If the 1940 Mille Miglia was the high spot of his first period, surely Hanstein's codrive of a Porsche with Umberto Maglioli to victory in the 1956 Targa Florio was the high spot of the future manager's middle racing period.

Porsches rarely raced with more than a couple of litres under their bonnets, so that the overall victories

went to other marques with their 3, 4 or 5 litres. But class victory after class victory, indices of performances, and class records by the score fell to the German entires. Hanstein himself won 12 of 15 GT races in 1956. Often, as late as 1965, a silver-headed, silver-mustachioed Hanstein would be piloting one of the victorious Porsches in races like the Targa or the Eifelrennen, at Montlhéry or Hockenheim. As good a driver as Huschke was, he was an even better selector of driving talent, from Stirling Moss and Jo Bonnier to Vic Elford and Paul Hawkins. And always there were good German drivers, including Trips, Hermann and Mitter. Porsche not only contested the distances, but hillclimbs and rallies as well, and for each form of competition, Hanstein was ready. In 1969 he retired from Porsche, but remained in racing as Germany's FIA and CSI representative.

FRED HARB

Fareed Joseph Harb, Jr., later a garage owner in High Point, N.C., deserves a footnote in racing history for several feats. A jump master in the American paratroopers just after World War II, Harb tried jalopy or old car racing on the dirt ovals of Dixie, and is said to have once managed to run his vehicle up a guide wire on a pole with such precision that the car remained balanced there.

In his first race he used an Army pistol belt as a safety belt and drove his 1934 Ford convertible from the street to 5th place. Then in 1958, after a moderately successful career in NASCAR, Fred made his notch in the record books. Forsaking the race in Atlanta's Lakewood Park, he blocked the track with his own car to protect driver Bill Morton, pinned unconscious in an overturned racer. This act won him the John Naughton Sportsmanship Award for that year. Fred bowled a lot and raced very little thereafter.

HARRY HARKNESS

When Harry Harkness got to feeling a bit dicey, he would go to his suite in the Waldorf-Astoria (or maybe one in some posh Park Avenue apartment building) and chop up a piano. Now, chopping up a piano—especially a baby grand—is reputed to give special satisfaction, especially if it is done correctly. The piano's keys fly into the air spectacularly before falling like oversized snowflakes onto the carpet. The strings twang, ping, and bang in many tones. The hammers thud and slide uselessly floorward—true experts can make them also leap ceiling-ward. And if the legs are severed gradually, the bulk of it sinks slowly to the floor like a Wagnerian tenor in his death agonies.

For all that, Harry Harkness was a pioneer of auto racing. He was infatuated with cars and able to treat them as playthings because of his great wealth. On July 20, 1904, he set a mark for the Mount Washington Hillclimb in New Hampshire. In 1905 he held the speed record between Boston and New York. He used to drive his own Mercedes at Daytona and elsewhere. He seems to have quit competition when the motor car caught on with the general public, but his love of expensive cars did not diminish. At any given time, Harkness had 4 or 5 vehicles at his disposal. A dapper man with a mustache waxed to twin razor points, Harry's main contribution and eventual downfall was the Sheepshead Bay, N. Y., Speedway, opened October 9, 1915. Built of steel and concrete with a board track over the concrete, it was the most durable of the stops on the fabulous board circuit. Yet like the others, it failed eventually and Harry didn't do well with it.

In character with his piano chopping and his enjoyment of the good life, Harkness threw himself wholeheartedly into this project despite warnings that his choice of a site was unwise. It was too far from Manhattan and Long Island centers to attract big crowds. He sought help and got some financial backing from Carl G. Fisher, resident genius of the Indianapolis Speedway, but alienated him when he insisted upon parity with Fisher's Brickyard. Fisher, in fact, had accepted the presidency of the Sheepshead Bay Corporation, but resigned in a huff over track policy. The board speedway era was one of racing's golden moments, and Sheepshead Bay had its fleeting share of glory. Unfortunately Harkness was encouraged to further financial expenditures, even to forming his own "house" racing team of three Delages. But Sheepshead Bay was destined to remain a neglected hulk for years before the highways that would have made it a success forced its demolition.

RON HARRIS

Ron Harris was one of England's best-known motorcyclists before World War II and has since become known among motion picture enthusiasts as the best source for 16 m.m. film in the British Isles. In automobile competition circles, however, the bespectacled Mr. Harris gained his reputation as the man who after warming up with Lola and Lotus Formula Junior cars, ran the Team Lotus Formula 2 stable for Colin Chapman.

Harris started racing cycles in high school, even going so far as to try the 200-milers at Brooklands with underpowered Nortons. Ron did well elsewhere, including such remembered victories as the 250 c.c. Manx Grand Prix on the Isle of Man in 1933 and in 1935; and the Senior Mountain Championship in 1933 and 1938. The war stopped his racing, but as late as 1947 he was out on the 2-wheelers rounding corners at speeds of up to 100 m.p.h. on the twisty, 38-mile Isle of Man course. Retired from active competition, he turned to sponsoring and managing with an MV Agusta cycle team in 1955.

But in 1960 Harris gave up motorcycles for automobiles, starting out with 2 Lotus 20 FJ cars. Searching about for drivers, he chose John Gee-Turner and Mike Ledbrook, neither of whom had any FJ experience but were willing to try. The 1961 season ended badly when Ledbrook collided with a Lotus 18 driven by John Fenning at Snetterton. In 1962 Gee-Turner and Fenning, whom Ron had admired from afar, became Ron Harris Team drivers. Then Gee-Turner suffered a serious injury at Oulton Park that ended his season just as it was starting. Fenning did well, however, beating Denis Hulme his first time out in Harris Team colors. A few weeks later John finished 2nd behind Peter Arundell in the big Snetterton International.

Soon the bearded Fenning and the immaculately-prepared red and white Harris Team cars were the rage of the FJ circuits, and John went from victory to victory, including a memorable weekend when he won both the Silverstone and Snetterton nationals. In July 1962 Eric Broadley of Lola approached Ron and asked him to take over his official factory team under his own name. Lola driver John Hine joined Fenning, and the Ron Harris Racing Division went hunting. It did well at home but not too well in its first Continental outing at the Albi GP that September, when Fenning had a mechanical failure and Hine left the road. The year was a good one, nonetheless, especially for Fenning who won 9 races and scored 4 each in 2nd and 3rd, and 4 "places" in 28 starts.

In 1963 Harris was expected to continue with Lola but instead moved back to an association with the Lotus organization. It happened after Colin Chapman asked Ron to run Lotus's FJ cars, and Harris consulted Broadley, who wasn't a man to stand in the way of anyone. With Lotus in the fold, Ron had Arundell as his number one driver, backed by Mike Spence and Fenning. Red and white were junked—"Colin said I could have any color as long as it was green," Ron quipped— and the yellow-wheeled green cars were lettered "Ron Harris-Team Lotus."

The Lotus 27 monocoque won its initial outing at Oulton Park, then troubles set in with the new model. They were not alleviated until the aluminum and fiber glass chassis and body were replaced by all-aluminum ones and the suspension adjusted to the new factors. It was July before Arundell won again at Silverstone, but then he reeled off 5 more in a row at Solitude, Goodwood, Zolder, Albi, and Brands Hatch. The year ended on a solemn note when Harris's favorite, Fenning, was injured in a road accident on the way to Albi and was retired temporarily.

In 1964 the team moved up to Formula 2 with Mike Spence and Peter Procter the leading full-time drivers, headed by Jim Clark and Arundell when they were free from Formula 1 commitments with the main Lotus team. Arundell, in fact, was in a Harris FJ car when he crashed at Rheims and was injured seriously enough to miss the rest of the season. Spence won the British FJ championship, and Procter showed steady improvment, even though the Lotuses were a bit outclassed on the F2 trail by the Repco-Brabhams. In 1965 Brian Hart was added to the Team Lotus forces for F2, with Clark again racing whenever possible. Clark made it a successful season, but 1966 was a bad one, with the Lotuses outpaced by Brabham-Honda's. Harris and Chapman severed connections.

RAY HARROUN

Whether or not Ray Harroun really won the Indianapolis 500 in 1911—a result still in dispute today—this brilliant engineer should be remembered for more than a single race, undertaken only to prove out the soundness of his engineering thinking after he had retired officially from racing.

Born in Spartansburg, Pa., January 12, 1879, Harroun was trained to be a dental technician. However, he attended school to become a sailor during the Spanish-American War, and when he came back he was quickly drawn into the fledgling motor car industry. Working as a riding mechanic with the Buick team of Bob Burman, Louis Chevrolet, and Louis Strang, Harroun got his 1st chance to drive in 1906 at Lowell, Mass. He finished 2nd to Chevrolet. After that he competed more— enough to win the 1910 designation of the AAA as National Champion—but retired to become chief engineer for Marmon. Ray was pursuaded to try one more race in 1911—the new 500-mile event—because it was important as a promotion for the Indianapolis-based company. In return, Harroun was allowed to design his own car. After reading the rules carefully, Harroun designed a lightweight single-seater, reasoning that such a car would be easier on tires. He installed in it a rearview mirror, one of his inventions, and pointed the tail of the car, adding a small stabilizer. Harroun's victory easily proved the capability of the car, which was unfortunately then banned for 1912.

Harroun also invented a carburetor in which the fuel mixture was heated by exhaust gas, and he produced pressed steel wheels when others clung to wood. He designed a racing Maxwell for 1914 that ran on kerosene and finally produced a $500 passenger car under his own name in 1918. But when World War I came the government asked him to utilize his 200-a-day production line (one of the first) to produce war equipment. He later designed a monoplane and a low-slung bomb cart which was in use until recently. Harroun spent some years as chief engineer at Maxwell and the kerosene-burning Maxwell racer he made was competing until the late Twenties.

Ray worked for Chrysler, among other companies, in a long career in the automobile industry, returning regularly to the Speedway. He finally retired to a mobile home near Anderson, Ind., where he lived until his death, January 19, 1968. As late as 1934, he envisioned an automobile that contained a transverse engine, á la Issigonis, in a front-wheel drive layout. Harroun, honorary chairman of the 500 Old-Timers Club at the time of his demise, was perhaps the most talented engineer of all the pre-World War I American drivers.

HARRY HARTZ

Harry Hartz may have been the fastest car salesman that ever lived. Hartz also may have been one of the most underrated heroes of American automobile racing. Certainly his Indianapolis record was remarkable, unsurpassed for a 5-year stretch even though he did not win. And his record at Indianapolis as a car owner and mechanical innovator also made him one of the heroes.

It was just after World War I that Harry Hartz signed on with the Duesenberg brothers as a mechanic, sweeper-upper, and riding partner for Eddie Hearne. He wanted to be a driver and he let people know it. But despite his outspokenness, he seemed to have the makings of a fine mechanic. He moved into the driver's seat when Hearne and others sought more money elsewhere. The Duesenbergs were not free with their money, so eager young men who wanted to drive so much that money was secondary always got a fair hearing. Hartz was eager.

He got his chance before the 1922 Indianapolis 500, and he rewarded Duesenberg with a 2nd-place finish, behind Jimmy Murphy. By 1923 Hartz had learned about money and he was driving for Cliff Durant in a Miller-designed Durant Special. He finished 2nd to Tommy Milton after leading at the 300 mile point. In 1924 he qualified 2nd fastest but an extra pit stop dropped him to 4th place. For 1925 his Miller Special qualified 6th and the methodical Hartz drove it to 4th place.

And then there was 1926, the high point of the Hartz driving career. Harry was a consummate driver in a Miller, but even though he won the National Championship and several board-track stops, he remained 2nd in the Indy 500, 3 laps down to Frank Lockart at 400 miles, when rain stopped the race. Thus, in a 5-year span he had never been out of the top 4, with 3 finishes in 2nd place.

It was inevitable that the National Champion should be a favorite for the 1927 race, especially since he had a tie-in with the Erskine Motor Car Company. But in the 38th lap, the car retired with a broken camshaft key. Some months later on the Salem, N. H., boards, Hartz's active driving career (and almost his life) came to an abrupt end in a crash. Hospitalized for months, Harry was able to accept the forced retirement only because he had decided that he could stay in racing as a car owner. In 1930, he was the listed driver for a revised Miller 8 although Ralph Hepburn had first call on his car. Hepburn demanded too many changes, finally took another ride, and after Harry tried a few practice laps himself, the car was given to Billy Arnold. Billy won easily in the front-wheel drive vehicle, Hartz had improved the front suspension and had made other minor changes in the chassis.

In 1931 Hartz entered Indianapolis with a Duesenberg 8; Fred Frame was the driver. Harry and Fred finished 2nd. For 1932 Hartz had Billy Arnold and himself lined up as drivers. He put Arnold in the slightly revised car which won in 1930; for himself he collaborated with Harry Miller in one of the quickest car design and construction jobs ever. Hartz approached Miller in March, barely 2 months before the race. Miller was impressed by one thing: Hartz's ability to pay for the effort. A combination of Hartz ideas and Miller ideas was translated into drawings by Leo Goossen and into reality by Fred Offenhauser and chief mechanic Jean Marcenac. The car shared some parts with earlier vehicles; most notable was the front drive unit from the Detroit Special. However for the Hartz-Miller Special the gear train was moved to the front of the 181.8 cu. in. o.h.v. 8 and larger constant-velocity U-joints made the front end much more durable.

The car was shipped to Indy still unfinished and arrived May 14. The qualifying arrangements in those days left some time to make the field since one could qualify on any day between qualifying weekend and the race (as long as there was a place on the grid). It took them most of those 2 weeks to get the engine sorted out. Meanwhile Fred Frame showed up without a mount. So great was his confidence in Fred that Hartz relinquished the driver's seat to him. The Hartz-Miller car finally qualified at 113.856 m.p.h., good for 27th place. The crew, which had worked virtually without sleep for at least a month, was satisfied. The car was as good as it was going to be.

Frame was probably the calmest man on the track. He waited relaxed back in the 9th row, after handing Houck (his riding mechanic) the package of chewing gum he needed during the race when his mouth went dry. The starter's flag fell and the Hartz-Miller car methodically worked its way from 27th to 3rd in the first 100 miles. Then the car began to lose water and Frame rolled into the pits steaming like Fulton's Folly. The overflow tube had broken inside the radiator. Quickly it was crimped off and pinched together, the filler cap gasket was removed to relieve the pressure, and more water was taken on. Each time Frame accelerated a fountain of water would rise from the filler cap. Slowly Frame dropped back to keep the vehicle running; 2 more stops for water helped drop him to 10th at the 200-mile mark. On the next water stop, Hartz put a rag under the cap to reduce the leakage and Frame fought back to 7th at 250 miles. The obvious speed of the car (when it was running) had not been lost on the crowd. But his chances of victory seemed slim until Houck had a brainstorm. He began chewing the package of gum and when they pitted again for water, Houck applied the gum as a sealant around the filler cap. It was their last stop for water and Frame began to work his way back up. At the 300-mile mark, he was 2nd. At about 400 miles he had taken over the lead. Then the transmission began to slip so Frame slapped it into top gear indicated that Houck was to hold it there, and ran the final 5th of the race to Victory Lane flat out, eclipsing Peter DePaolo's 1925 average winning speed of 101.30 with his 104.44 clocking. (This in spite of almost 15 minutes in the pits.) Billy Arnold, who had led most of the first 125 miles, wrecked on the 59th lap, suffering a broken shoulder.

In 1933 Hartz went with Hartz-Miller and Frame-Houck and saw his Special in the lead briefly before retiring with a broken valve. In 1934 Pete Kreis was his driver. Unaccountably the car left the track during practice and split into 2 pieces against a tree outside the wall. Both Kreis and his mechanc, Art Hahn, were killed. That year the Hartz-Miller 8 spawned its most distinguished offspring when the Offy midget engine, a 4-cylinder with striking design similarities (even to the same stroke, valve size and con rod offset) made its debut at Los Angeles' Gilmore Stadium.

Hartz was set back by the lack of any prize money from the 1934 race but he still managed to rebuild his Special to a 101-inch wheelbase, putting updraft Win-

field carburetors on instead of the original 4 Miller downdrafts. Fred Frame finished 11th in the car, probably worried about exceeding the 42.5 gallon fuel limit. Harry had begun to sell passenger cars between 500-miles and dabbled in several other businesses. But for 1936, he dusted off the veteran car again, acquired Ted Horn as his driver and devised a stratagem to combat the 37.5 gallon fuel limit. They carefully calculated the maximum speed which the car could go without running out of gasoline. They were hoping this was enough to win; it wasn't, but Horn moved the car into 2nd place by the midway point and stayed there, optimistic to the end. The same driver and the Special, equipped now with a supercharger, finished third in 1937.

In 1938 the Hartz-Miller underwent still another change, being rebuilt as a single-seater. Horn finished 4th but Hartz realized the car no longer was among the avant-garde at the Speedway and he had ideas for a newer vehicle, but not the kind of money to rebuild from scratch. So back came the Special with Herb Ardinger qualifying it at 124.125 m.p.h., some 10 m.p.h. faster than at its first appearance 7 years before. Ardinger lasted 140 laps. The final Indy appearance for the car before it was sold was in 1940 with Mel Hansen at the wheel. Hansen upped the qualifying speed another. 0.62 m.p.h. and finished 8th. The car is now in the Indy Speedway Museum. Hartz eventually joined the AAA Contest Board's technical staff, settling in Indianapolis, and when USAC was formed he became an official for that organization. He died in 1972, still a car salesman, still dreaming.

WALLY HASSAN

Back in 1920, there was a 15-year-old boy who didn't do very well in a job interview at Sunbeam. But as he left the big factory he noticed a smaller one down the road with the legend "Bentley Motors" on it. He went in for a spontaneous interview, was hired, and became the 14th employe of a firm that would one day be as big as Sunbeam in reputation.

Walter Hassan was born in Holloway, London, in 1905 and educated at Hackney Technical Institute of Engineering. Hassan had no family tradition of engineering, let alone automotive engineering. His grandfather made furniture, his father sold shirts and socks. But Wally's first job was working with W. O. Bentley and Frank Clement. Soon, too, he found himself riding alongside Clement, Woolf Barnato, Tim Birkin, and other Bentley Boys in such races as the Brooklands Double 12 hours, the Phoenix Park races in Dublin, the Brooklands 6 hours, Le Mans, and others, including the 1928 German Grand Prix.

Hassan remained with Bentley until 1930 when the Rolls-Royce takeover was accomplished. Then he went to work directly for Barnato, the South African diamond millionaire. In a Belgrave Mews "factory," Wally designed and built a variety of special cars for Woolf, including a short-wheelbase Bentley 8-litre and the famed Barnato-Hassan Special. The latter started as a regular 6.5-litre Bentley, but Wally converted it into an offset single-seater with pointy tail. It lapped at 115 m.p.h. at Brooklands in 1934, then blew its engine. This was replaced with an 8-litre model, tuned to run on alcohol. It won several records, including the Brooklands mark of 142.60 m.p.h. In 1936 the car was further modified, and it raced for another 2 years before being retired. By that time Wally had left Barnato—with Woolf's blessing —for an offer at ERA, where he stayed only 6 months before moving again. He went to work with Reid Railton at Thomson and Taylor helping Reid on the John Cobb Land Speed Record car that became known as the Railton-Mobil Special. But he moved again in 1938 when the chance to run his own operation came his way.

Tommy Wisdom had told Wally that William Lyons's SS company, forerunner of Jaguar, was looking for a man to head its experimental department. Hassan got the job and stayed with Jaguar until the fifties (save for a 1942–44 wartime stint with Bristol Aero Engine Co.). He left Jaguar after the pioneering work had been done on the XK series that was to make Jag famous, only because a greater opportunity opened up for him. This was the position of chief engineer at Coventry-Climax, then a relatively unknown concern. When Wally Hassan was through, Coventy-Climax was a household word throughout the racing world.

The company built all kinds of engines, but racing engines became a major project with Hassan aboard. In 1954 he started designing his first Formula 1 power plant, a V-8 alloy engine. A sports car engine for Kieft came out first, and on the strength of this design, orders came in from such companies as Lotus and Cooper for Climax engines. The first one was rather successful: in 98 starts Coventry-Climax engines scored 69 victories. Before the Hassan designs had run their course, Climax engines had powered British racing cars to 4 World Championships. Jaguar took over Climax in the Sixties, and Hassan found himself working on the new V-12 power plant introduced in 1971. Wally Hassan's career had come full circle.

PAUL HAWKINS

Graham Hill won the Monaco Grand Prix of 1965—his 3rd time in a row. That is the race in which a Lotus 33 went sailing off the course and into the Monte Carlo harbor during the 80th lap (later immortalized in the American movie *Grand Prix*). The trip was strictly unplanned and could have resulted in disaster, but the driver, Paul Hawkins, swam away from the submerging Lotus in his best Australian crawl.

Son of a former builder-contractor and sportsman

who had become a Protestant minister, Robert Paul Hawkins was born in Melbourne on October 12, 1937. His father, William Hawkins, had raced motorcycles and was Victoria high-driving champion before turning to the cloth. His mother was a leading amateur gymnast and coach. Paul was 8 when she died, but he assumed many of the home responsibilities for his baby brother and sister. At 10 he found himself in Brisbane and much later the family moved to Tasmania. Hawkins had won himself a scholarship to Queensland University and was studying electrical and mechanical engineering when the urge to become a racing driver hit him. He quit school and apprenticed himself as an electrician and motor mechanic, racing cycles at the same time.

After an incident in which he partially wrecked the family Holden while practicing for a hillclimb, Hawkins decided to go out on his own. First he repaired the car, saved up a few pounds, then made his farewells and flew off to Melbourne to a mechanic's job. But the Australian Army draft caught up with him there, and he spent that time as a driving instructor on heavy trucks at an Armoured Corps base north of Melbourne.

Out of the service, he returned to a garage, raced a MG TC informally, then made his real competition debut in March 1958 an Austin-Healey 100S on the Philip Island road circuit outside Melbourne. Even though he spun off on the last lap, he finished 1st in class. A 5th overall in the Albert Park race the following weekend convinced Hawkins that he had the makings of a good driver, and he concentrated on racing though it proved to be an expensive hobby. Paul decided if he was going to go broke, he might as well do it in Europe, and he set sail for Southampton, arriving in February 1960.

John Sprinzel, the rallyist, who was starting a development project on the Sebring Sprite, advertised for a mechanic in a London paper. He hired Hawkins as soon as the Australian presented himself and described his background. Sprinzel went even further. He handed Paul a car and told him to go racing when not working on the project or preparing customer cars. Hawkins's debut in the big time came in April at the Aintree course, where he won the 1100 c.c. class the first time out.

Victory (in class) at the Nurburgring in a 500-kilometer race followed, as did good showings in the Nurburgring 1000, at Rouen, and in the Goodwood Tourist Trophy and similar races. Paul's technical skills were good enough that Sprinzel arranged for him to become a junior partner in the speed equipment division of Austin-Healey. In March 1961 he came to the United States codriving a Sprite with Pat Moss and finishing 5th overall and 3rd in class. At Le Mans, he shared a factory Austin-Healey with America's John Colgate. They went out around midnight with piston trouble. He had another factory car with Ian Walker at Nurburgring in his 2nd 500 and finished 7th overall. The season closed with victory, codriving with Sprinzel and Walker in the Silverstone 6-hour race.

When Walker retired as a driver and formed his own racing team, he offered Hawkins the job of chief mechanic and team driver, using a Lotus 23 sports car, a Lotus-Ford Formula Junior and a Ford Zodiac. In 15 races, Hawkins made fastest lap 8 times, won 2 races, was second 3 times, and scored class victories in 2 other races. In 1963, he partnered with Frank Gardner, another Aussie, in FJ Brabhams under Walker's bright yellow colors. There were several spectacular accidents in this car, notably at Aintree, Montlhéry, and Crystal Palace, but he also won some races outright and scored other class victories. Late in the season he switched over to the Willment Team when Walker decided that he needed some name drivers.

In 1964 Hawkins won the Rhodesian GP in a Willment 1.5-litre FJ Brabham-Ford, then won the same event's saloon race in a Ford Galaxie. He was 2nd to Graham Hill in the Rand GP, winning the saloon section of that meeting. In January 1965 he won the Cape GP in the Brabham, impressing among the spectators a one-time Porsche racer named Dick Stoop, who offered to bankroll a Formula 1 car for Hawkins. Though Paul wanted a Brabham, Stoop was a Lotus fancier, so Lotus it was—a former factory car with 1.5-litre Coventry-Climax power. It was in this car that he took his Monaco swim.

Salvaged and dried out, the car went to Silverstone next where a mechanic ran the car into a bank and wrecked it for good. Hawkins, meanwhile, was busy on other tracks in assorted machinery: Healeys, Galaxies, Porsches, Ferraris, factory Ford GTs, Lolas, anything

with 4 wheels that seemed competitive. When the "big-banger" Group 7 cars—like those in America's Canadian-American Challenge Cup series—were legislated out of Britain, Hawkns traded in his Lola-Chevvy for a Group 4 Ford GT40.

That was in 1967, and it was a notable year for Hawkins because, driving a factory Porsche, he won the Targa Florio, then came within a whisker of also winning the Nurburgring 1000 for Porsche. In 1968 he drove for JW Automotive, helping Ford win the World Manufacturers Championship in a GT40. But on May 26, 1969, Hawkins found himself at Oulton Park in a Lola T70, seeking a Tourist Trophy victory after winning at Snetterton on Good Friday. The car was fully gassed and just pulling out of the pits when it swerved and smashed into a tree at trackside. It exploded and burned, and Paul Hawkins was dead.

MIKE HAWTHORN

John Michael Hawthorn was a professional, good enough to win the World Driver's Championship, but the handsome blond with the omnipresent bow tie never lost his amateur enthusiasm for the sport. Hawthorn was born April 10, 1929, at Mexborough, Yorkshire, but grew up in Surrey where his father operated the TT Garage at Farnham. He had been a motorcycle racer at Brooklands, which was his reason for moving so close to the giant British course. Later he moved on to 4 wheels and a Riley. In 1950, when Mike was 21 his

290

father bought an 1100-c.c. Riley Ulster Imp and a 1.5-litre Riley Sprite to start a family racing team. In their initial try (at the Brighton Speed Trials) his father was 2nd in the 1.5-litre race, and Mike won the 1100 c.c. class.

The following year, an injured back kept the elder Hawthorn out of racing, so his son raced both cars around the British circuit. His Sprite victories included the Ulster Trophy at Ballyclare and the Leinster Trophy in Eire. He also won the Brooklands Memorial Trophy for his consistently good performances at BARC meetings at Goodwood. Mike's big break from promising club driver to potential professional came at Goodwood on Easter Monday, 1952, when he was racing a 2-litre Cooper-Bristol owned by family friend Bob Chase. Hawthorn took the lead on the intial lap to the roar of some 50,000 spectators and stayed there for the entire 6 laps of the Formula 2 race. Then he did it again in the Formula Libre 6-lapper.

The performance, in a car he had never driven before, in a class of racing (single-seater) new to him, astounded everyone and made Hawthorn the favorite for the day's main 12-lapper for the Richmond Trophy. He came in 2nd to the veteran Froilan Gonzalez's 4.4-litre Ferrari Thinwall Special. The next month he won the initial heat of the Silverstone meeting, but his car retired with a broken gear lever in the final. In June he went to the Continent and finished 4th (the best-placed British car and driver) in the Belgian GP.

Mike was 3rd in the British GP at Silverstone that same year, and in the Boreham International run for Formula 1 and F2 cars he came in 3rd again. Hawthorn led that race in the pelting rain for many laps, passing the 4.5-litre Ferraris and Lago-Talbots and the giant BRM with ease, until the rain stopped and the big Ferraris zipped past the Cooper-Bristol, now suffering from a flapping flywheel. That same year he competed on the factory team for Sunbeam in the Alpine Rally and won the Coupe des Alpes. As with all new, bold drivers, he was given chances to test many new machines, including a V-16 BRM and the 4.5-litre Thinwall.

In 1953 he reluctantly joined the Ferrari team—Hawthorn wanted to drive for Britain, not Italy—and acquitted himself nobly. Mike won the French GP (his 1st), as well as the Spa 24-Hour Race, the Pescara GP, the Ulster and Goodwood Trophies, the Woodcote Cup, and the Silverstone International Trophy. He was 2nd at Pau and Rouen, 3rd in the German and Swiss Grands Prix and at Buenos Aires. The French GP attracted the greatest notice, for he duelled the supreme Juan Manuel Fangio wheel-to-wheel for that one, winning on the final lap's last corner.

The tall, towheaded driver (he was 6 feet 2 inches) certainly had been a Golden Boy of racing. In 1954 things went bad, however. He crashed in flames at Syracuse, Italy. Badly burned in the legs, Mike wore ban-dages and suffered severe pain throughout the rest of the season, but he won the Spanish and Supercortemaggiore sports car races, and was 2nd at the British, German, Italian, and Portuguese races and in the Tourist Trophy and in the Aintree Trophy races. His personal problems mounted though, concerning his draft status (he had a bad kidney and was unfit in Army doctors' eyes, but he looked healthy enough, especially behind the wheel) and his father''s death. One dark night, Mr. Hawthorn had rolled his Lancia in an accident from which he never regained consciousness.

The year 1955 wasn't much better for Mike. He left Ferrari so he could spend more time in England to look after the family garage business, and he signed with Tony Vandervell's new Vanwall team. The car was not really ready, however, and after several frustrating starts, Mike reverted to Ferrari for the rest of the year. He won the Crystal Palace International Trophy, Sebring, and Le Mans, the 2 latter races for Jaguar, shared with Phill Hill and Ivor Bueb respectively. At Le Mans he was involved in the Pierre Levegh disaster in which 81 spectators were killed, and many people tried to put the blame for the deadly chain reaction upon the Briton. An impartial board of inquiry exonerated Hawthorn after many months of study, including detailed analysis of films and weeks of testimony, but the stigma hung on for many months.

In 1956 he left Ferrari once more and signed with BRM, which had a new, 2.5-litre car that was probably the fastest car that season, although not yet perfected. Mike also signed with Jaguar for sports car racing. It was a bad year, and in 1957 he was back for a 3rd time with Ferrari. He drove steadily though not spectacularly throughout the year, as if readying for the next season, which was to be his best. From no World Championship points in 1955, he advanced to 4 points in 1956 and 4th place in the standings in 1957.

But in 1958 Hawthorn won the French GP and scored 2nds in the Belgian, British, Italian, Portugese, and Moroccan Grands Prix. He was 3rd in the Argentine GP, 5th in the Dutch race, and he recorded the fastest laps in 5 starts. When the points were totalled, Mike was the World Champion (Britain's 1st), while Stirling Moss—who had won 4 championship races—was 2nd by a single point. Hawthorn also had won the Goodwood Glover Trophy and was 3rd in the Targa Florio and the Race of Two Worlds at Monza. But his best friend, Peter Collins, had been killed in a team Ferrari at the German GP that year, as was teammate Luigi Musso. Mike was a sad young man when he startled the racing world with the news of his retirement. He intended to keep his hand in at veteran race car meetings, he said; and he would serve as an official and in other non-driving capacities. But his driving was to be confined to the ordinary road.

It was on an ordinary road, near Guildford, that Hawthorn met his death January 22, 1959. He was going very fast, as he always did, in a Jaguar 3.8 saloon when he hit a slippery patch and slid into an oil truck that knocked the car against a tree. He was killed instantly.

CHARLIE HAYES

Charlie Hayes was a dedicated man; he once pared about 40 pounds off his frame to fit better inside a single-seat racing car. Taking off that many pounds is never easy, and when you are not overweight to begin with, it is even harder. But Hayes had twin goals in auto racing: nothing less than Indianapolis, mecca of most serious American racing drivers, and Formula 1 Grand Prix racing.

Charlie was a gentleman driver. Born December 14, 1936, of a moderately wealthy family from Chevy Chase, Md., he started as an SCCA amateur. In 1958 he visited SCCA races at Cumberland, Md. as a lark and became convinced he could do as well or better than those he was watching. He bought an XK 140 Jaguar and entered a June race at nearby Marlboro. The initial time out he spun out; the next 3 times he won over all comers to begin an outstanding career as a club competitor. By 1961 Hayes owned a Ferrari 250 GT Berlinetta and won the SCCA's Class A Production crown with this machine. The next year he continued competing with his own Ferrari and drove a GTO for Bill McKelvy in other races. Then he switched to Formula Junior with an Elva for 1963, finishing 2nd in that competition nationally. (Charlie's wife, Evey, said it was at this point that he started losing weight and turning his thoughts to bigger things.) Hayes turned professional in 1964, taking over Ollie Schmidt's Elva-Porsche for the USRRC series and finishing 3rd, with class victories at Augusta, Ga., Laguna Seca, and Watkins Glen.

Cooper-Chevrolets and McLaren-Elvas were Hayes's cars in 1965, the latter especially powerful, though often plagued by teething troubles. But Charlie's cars and his improving skills provided competition at West Coast venues like Kent, Riverside, and Laguna Seca against the domination of Jim Hall's Chaparrals. Hayes's reputation was that of a steady, smooth driver who got the most out of his machinery. He was fast and smart on tactics, but he never made it to the GP wars or Indy.

DONALD HEALEY

Donald Mitchell Healey was a Cornishman, born in Perranporth in July 1898 and educated at Newquay College. Donald hoped to make aviation with Sopwith Aircraft Company his life's work. But the war, a crash while a member of the Royal Flying Corps, and an invalided discharge changed all that. He headed back home, looked about, and decided to go into another relatively new field: automobiles. Healey opened a garage and was soon running trials in an ABC powered by a 2-cylinder air-cooled engine. From trials he moved to Brooklands, as did all pre-World War II British racers, driving such machines as Triumphs, Rileys, and Invictas.

When the RAC put on its 1st major rally in 1928, Healey won it outright. That was all the encouragement he needed to tackle Europe's most challenging rally, the Monte Carlo. Between 1929 and 1939 he ran it enough times to amass the best record of any Briton in the competition: an outright victory (in 1931), a 2nd, a 3rd, and a class victory in the light-car category. He also managed to stall on a railroad track in 1935 and his car was sawed neatly in half by a train—without injury to Healey himself. He also managed in those years to win such events as the Alpine Trials in both Austria and Hungary for Invicta—9 times.

Joining Riley in 1933, Healey moved to Triumph the following year. By 1937 he was that marque's technical director. World War II found Donald back in the cockpit commanding the regional wing of the Air Training Command and working with several government departments. It was at this time that he started thinking about building his own cars. In this he was assisted by an old Georges Roesch protégé, Achilles Sampietro, and what emerged from their combined work was a 2.4-litre, Riley-powered Healey prototype just 3 months after the war's end. Small-scale production started in 1946 and exporting in earnest commenced in 1950 when the Nash-Healey was born. Donald was always pro-American, so an American deal had been almost inevitable. So was

Donald's appearance, along with son Geoffrey, in the 1948 Mille Miglia, heading a 3-car Healey team; he finished 9th, while Count Johnny Lurani in a Healey sedan won his class.

It was Healey's cars that started Briggs Cunningham racing; in fact, Briggs' personal debut was in a Silverstone Healey powered by a Cadillac V-8 in place of the production Riley. The Nash-Healey would have been the Cadillac-Healey but GM was dubious. Nash-Kelvinator rang up 1,200 American sales as a result. Donald's next idea was to use an Austin A90 engine in a new Healey chassis. It debuted at the Earls Court Auto Show in 1952, and right up there on the stand acquired the Austin-Healey prefix when the head of Austin got a look at the finished product. The big company's production and distribution facilities were the lure. That partnership resulted in 14,000 American sales.

In 1956, on America's Bonneville Salt Flats, Donald ripped off a 203.06 m.p.h. kilometer, and that dramatic run at age 57 introduced the 100-6 model to America. The Sprite followed, but so did absorption by BMC (later BLMC) and the virtual disappearance of the Austin-Healey marque, although the car was still being raced (and not just in vintage car races by any means) long after production ceased. In 1968 Donald and Geoffrey built a 2-litre Le Mans special, powered by a Coventry-Climax Grand Prix engine. It ran with the same power plant in 1969, then was fitted with a 3-litre Repco-Brabham for 1970. That was the year Donald joined Jensen Motors as chairman and Geoffrey joined the builder's board. Two years later the Jensen-Healey appeared on the scene, a handsome and fast sports/luxury car. Donald had not lost his touch, more than 50 years after entering the automobile business. Healey had 2 other sons, one of whom went into another of his interests, small sports boats, and the other into a completely different business. He would have been a hard man to follow, this holder of the number 11 card in the 200-m.p.h. club.

GEORGE HEATH

When the green flag fell on the Vanderbilt Cup race on Long Island October 8, 1904, George Heath was at the back of the pack, but on the first lap Heath clawed his way to 4th place as 2 cars dropped out, one in an accident that killed its riding mechanic, and the rest of the field fought not only each other but the rough course. By the 4th lap he was in the lead; by the race's midpoint, he led by 35.5 minutes. Then Heath's Panhard & Levassor suffered a blowout, and he had to fight hard to keep the big car under control and bring it safely to a stop. A pre-race arrangement stipulated that if the car needed a tire replaced, the Panhard crew would rush with one from the pits to wherever on the course Heath was parked and change it; he was not to attempt to change it himself. So George sat there, first waiting patiently—then with growing impatience—for his pit crew to appear and get to work. He watched the other cars go by once, then twice; 15 precious minutes were gone from his lead and no one was in sight. Finally, he decided to change it himself, orders or not. It took him 2 minutes to change the tire; then he was back into the race. Heath motored more cautiously now, for he couldn't afford another blowout, nor any avoidable calamity that might shave his lead some more. The Clement-Bayard, driven by Albert Clement himself, zipped by. No sweat. Clement trailed him by several minutes according to the last information George's pits had given him. But as he came around, he saw to his horror that the original information had not only changed, it had reversed. Clement was leading, Heath was 2nd.

No time for niceties. Flat out from now on, tires or no. George's foot slammed down hard on the pedal, and he gripped the wheel tighter than ever. It was a race after all. Round they went a couple of times until Heath could regain a slight lead. Clement fought back, but the Panhard responded to George's insistence, and he stayed in that precarious lead. The last lap was the fastest: 67.9 m.p.h. He flashed across the line with at 52.2 m.p.h. average for the entire race.

Heath was thought of in the States as a Frenchman, but he was really from Long Island, N.Y. It became fashionable after World War I to talk of American expatriates in Paris; George was ahead of his time, drawn to Europe by the growing interest in automobiles and racing over there that predated the American infatuation. He had gotten a factory job early and a factory ride, too. By 1898 he already was wheeling along in Panhards in major races; that year he was 13th in the Paris-Amsterdam-Pau race, 889 miles of endurance racing, which to finish was actually to win, no matter in what position. Heath was in all the early major town-to-town races: 4th in the 1899 Paris-St. Malo, 11th in the 1901 Paris-Berlin, and 6th in the 1902 Circuit des Ardennes, for example.

The year of his notable Vanderbilt victory, he also won the Circuit des Ardennes (a 367 miler) at 56.4 m.p.h. But the following season he was 2nd (to Victor Hemery) in the Vanderbilt Cup race, just beating out Joe Tracy in a Locomobile, and 5th in the Ardennes battle. Faster cars, driven by younger men, were proliferating. In 1906 he finished the Vanderbilt race, no mean feat in itself, but was so far back that he was unclassified. He was 6th in the French GP at Le Mans that year, DNF in 1907, but 9th in 1908. Heath's racing was about spent when World War I put a finale to racing in Europe itself. But his spot was an honored one, and his 1904 Vanderbilt victory a milestone in American as well as world auto racing.

TONY HEGBOURNE

Like John Surtees and many others, Anthony V. Hegbourne came out of Britain's motorcycling ranks to become a top-rank racing car driver. How far he might have gone no one will ever know because the popular teammate of Mike Beckwith for Normand Racing died July 1, 1965, a few weeks short of his 34th birthday, after lingering for more than a month in the hospital following a crash in the Spa Grand Prix.

Born July 24, 1931, Hegbourne first attracted attention in 1955 aboard 350 and 500 c.c. Norton cycles, and he won the Hartley Award the following year as Britain's best amateur rider. Tony first drove in automotive competition in 1958, winning his first race in an 1100 c.c. Cooper-Climax at Brands Hatch. In 1959 he switched to a Tojeiro 1100, then "retired for 2 seasons" to devote himself to business. He returned to competition in 1962, winning the Brooklands Memorial Trophy in a Lola-Climax sports car.

In 1963 Hegbourne took over a Lotus 23BX and scored 2nd at Montlhéry, a class 3rd at Rheims and a class victory at Clermont Ferrand in the 3-hour race, where he was 2nd overall. Among his other impressive performances that season were a 2nd in the Brands Hatch Guards Trophy Race and a 3rd—2nd in class— in Oulton Park's Gold Cup.

The Normand Racing Team signed the handsome driver, now married, for 1964 and assigned him a Formula 2 Cooper. He won the Berlin GP and was 2nd in the Rome GP in this car. In saloon racing that same

year, Tony shared a Lotus Cortina with Sir John Whitmore. They were 2nd in the Nurburgring 6-hour race and the Marlboro 12-hour race. Their car retired in the Spa 24-hour race. Hegbourne also was forced to retire in the Nurburgring 1000 while driving a Lotus Elan for Ian Walker that season.

Big things in both single-seater and sports-car racing were expected of Hegbourne in 1965, and he was offered a wide variety of cars. At Spa, Tony was driving an Alfa Romeo when his fatal crash occurred.

COTTON HENNING

Few mechanics have had better records at the Indianapolis Speedway than did Harry Charles (Cotton) Henning, a jovial, tobacco-chewing Missourian whose cars scored 4 victories at the Indiana oval and 4 3rds, 4 4ths, 2 5ths, 2 6ths, and 1 7th-place prize. Henning also is remembered as one of the far-sighted men who anticipated today's U.S.-European Indianapolis complexion as early as 1937 when he brought a Maserati to the Brickyard for Wilbur Shaw.

Born in Alma, Mo., in 1896, Cotton started working on cars when he was about 17, right at the start of the growth of the American automobile industry. His desire always had been to make the cars run, not to run them himself, although in later years he tried the other side of the coin as a riding mechanic in 2-man cars. During World War I, Henning was an aviation mechanic, then went to work for Cadillac for a couple of years before switching over to the competitive side of the automobile world exclusively.

He went into racing full-time in 1921, starting out at Indianapolis as a riding mechanic with Louis Fontaine. On the 34th lap Fontaine's brakes froze as he was rounding the grandstand turn, and the Junior Special overturned, then bounced back into an upright position straddling the concrete retaining wall. Henning and his driver were not seriously hurt in that spectacular accident. The following year Cotton rode alongside rookie Pete DePaolo and Frank Elliott in a Frontenac, but that car, too, went out (on the 111th lap) when it hit the wall at the race's midpoint after leading for a few minutes. Then the one-man cars took over, and Cotton did not return to riding even during the 2-man cars' brief return between 1930 and 1937.

Henning's mechanical acumen increased greatly through the years as did calls upon his services. He initially became associated with Wilbur Shaw in the late twenties and they became lifelong friends (Cotton even became a baby-sitter for Shaw's infant son nearly 20 years later). Shaw's first ride in a completely Henning-prepared car was in 1930 when Cotton rebuilt the crashed Flying Cloud Special in Louis Chevrolet's shops, and Wilbur finished the 500 in 8th place. In 1937 Shaw and his sponsor, Michael J. Boyle, the Chicago Electrical union official, sent Henning to Italy to purchase a Maserati road racing machine for use at Indianapolis. The first of the famous Boyle Specials, that racer was too small in c.c. displacement to win at Indy, and Shaw passed it up for a standard Brickyard machine.

In 1939 Henning went to Italy once more and this time returned with a machine much more to Shaw's liking, a 3-litre Maserati, in which Wilbur won that year and the next (after a last-minute replacement of the cracked cylinder block, which the Italians forgot to drain before its wintertime trip across the Atlantic). In 1940 Shaw accidentally ran over Henning's foot getting away after his first pit stop, which no doubt left an indelible impression on Cotton's memory of the 2-in-a-row victory. In 1941 Shaw's bid for an unprecedented 4th Indianapolis win—and 3rd in a row—went awry when a pre-race fire broke out in Gasoline Alley and water from the fire hoses supposedly washed off a warning chalk mark on a discarded wheel. At least that was Shaw's story when the Maser's right rear wheel suddenly collapsed on the 152nd lap with Wilbur a good 80 seconds in the lead. The car turned about and smashed into the wall tail first with such tremendous force that its fuel tank was ruptured. Fortunately for Shaw, who was temporarily paralyzed in the crash, it didn't burn.

World War II ended Indy racing until 1946, when Henning (who stayed with the Maserati) and Boyle prepared the car, now slightly modified in the tail, for Ted Horn. A faulty magneto that had to be replaced in mid-race took so much time that Horn finished 3rd. The Henning-Horn combination was 3rd again in 1947, when Cotton entered the car himself after buying it from Boyle for about the same $15,000 price that had been paid for it in 1939 in Italy. The Bennett Brothers, the Texas oilmen, sponsored the entry. In the next year's race the combination was 4th. That was Cotton's last before his death, of natural causes, in Indianapolis at the age of 53.

Cotton is remembered as a deliberate, methodical man who always managed to keep his head no matter what the crisis. It was the ideal Indy mechanic's temperament, considering the confusion and color that is associated with America's most famous and richest race. "Anything done well," Cotton once said, "is seldom done in a hurry." The moon-faced, sandy-haired mechanic's observation still is followed by the world's best race car preparers.

HANS HERRMANN

Versatility can be a blessing to a driver, and a curse as well. Perhaps Hans Herrmann is a case in point. He drove sports cars. He drove hillclimbs, which in Europe is a major form of racing. He drove single-seaters right on up to Formula 1 with Mercedes Benz. But because he moved from category to category, because he was

moderately successful in almost all of the categories without ever emerging as a dominant figure in any one, Herrmann is not as well-remembered (nor was he as highly regarded) as he might have been if he had put all of his energy into one category.

Hermann was born in Stuttgart, Germany, February 23, 1928. He was 23 before he went racing, perfectly understandable in postwar Germany. His competition debut in 1951 was in a Porsche 1100 c.c. car, and it was in this kind of machine that he raced locally for 2 years. Hans's first big victory came in 1953 in the Rhineland Cup sports car race at Nurburgring in which he averaged 75.81 m.p.h. He was to win the Cup again in 1954 and still a 3rd time in 1956, always in a Porsche, which he favored for sports car racing. In this car he was retired at Le Mans, but took 3rd in the Pan American Road Race and won the 1500 c.c. class at 97.6 m.p.h. But by 1954 Hans had another car, the silver Mercedes W.196 with which the marque returned to Grand Prix racing in 1954.

Herrmann's luck that first year was not good; the car needed a full season of shaking down. At the French GP, Herrmann raced the fastest lap before retiring with mechanical ills. There were retirements in the Spanish and European (German) GPs, too, but a 3rd in the Swiss GP, a 3rd in the Berlin GP or Avusrennen, and a 4th in the Italian GP. Herrmann expected 1955 to be a good season for Mercedes and for himself. It was a good one for the marque, but Hans's worst, for in practice for the Monaco GP, the Mercedes's brakes failed at speed, and he crashed. He was in the hospital for months and

had to convalesce at home for some time after that, writing off completely that racing season.

In 1956 Hermann was back behind the sports car wheel but not in F1. For Porsche he was 2nd to Wolfgang von Trips in the Berlin GP, won the 3rd Rhineland Cup at 81.09, won the Solitude GP (nipping Trips) at 92.02, was 6th with Trips at Sebring and 6th with Richard von Frankenberg in the Nurburgring 1000. Sharing a Ferrari with Olivier Gendebien, Herrmann was 3rd in the Targa Florio. Borgward had some grandiose plans starting in 1957, and the German marque signed Hans as its number 1 driver. The only one of its many planned assaults on the race world that got off the ground that year was the European Mountain Championship. Herrmann was 3rd overall at Freidbourg and captured the sports car class. He won his class and was 2nd overall at the Gaisburg climb, then repeated the feat at the Swiss Mountain GP. At Aosta he was 3rd, and at Mont Parnes near Athens, 2nd.

In 1958 Herrmann continued Borgward's mountain climbing, contested by such other luminaries as Trips and Jo Bonnier. Hans was 2nd in Greece, 4th at Mont Ventoux, 2nd in Italy, 3rd at Freibourg and Gaisburg, and 8th at Ollon-Villars. But Borgward's other racing wasn't nearly as successful. At the Nurburgring 1000, for example, Hans and Bonnier were retired. In a Porsche start at Le Mans with Jean Behra, Herrmann was 3rd. Porsche provided his only bright spots for several years, such as the Formula 2 Coupe de Vitesse at Rheims in 1959 when only Stirling Moss at his best could edge Hans in a Porsche F2. Moss nipped him again in 1960 in the Zeltweg F2 race, but Hans beat Trips in the Innsbruck F2 battle, winning at 67.31 m.p.h. In major racing after some fruitless BRM F1 starts in 1959, he was 2nd to Trips's Ferrari in the Solitude GP in 1960, and 6th in his F2 Porsche in the F1 Italian GP. Porsche provided cars that won, too, for the Targa (with Bonnier) at 59.24 m.p.h. and for Sebring's 12-hour race (with Gendebien) at 84.93 m.p.h.

These early Sixties were frustrating years as well as sweet ones. In 1961 Herrman's only good placing was a 3rd with Edgar Barth in the Targa. In an F1 Porsche he was 9th at Monaco, 15th in the Dutch GP, and 13th in the German GP, earning no World Championship points at all. Retired at Sebring in a car shared with Barth, Herrmann and Edgar were 7th at Le Mans. In 1962 he moved over to Abarth without noticeable improvement in his fortunes. That season his best placing was a 2nd in the Innsbruck sports car races. But in 1963 he shared winning Fiat-Abarth rides at the Nurburgring 500 GT race at 77.75 m.p.h. and at the Sebring 3-hour GT race at 80.42 m.p.h. Abarth was interested in hillclimbing, so Herrmann took to that again, and was still at it in 1965, winning Mont Ventoux that season in Abarth 2000 GT among other excellent placings.

In 1966 he went back to Porsche. At Daytona he shared at Carrerra 6 and 6th place. At Sebring, with America's Joe Buzzetta, he shared 4th place. In 1967 Herrmann and Jo Siffert were 4th at Daytona in a Porsche 910, 4th at Sebring, 5th in the Monza 1000 and at Le Mans (in a 907), 6th in the Targa Florio, and 2nd in the Spa 1000. In the BOAC 500 at Brands Hatch, Hans and young Jochen Neerpasch were 4th. In 1968 he shared victory with 4 others at Daytona's 24-hour race at 106.69 m.p.h.; strangely, Herrmann and Siffert also, technically brought home the 2nd-place car. The Herrmann-Siffert team won Sebring all by themselves at 102.512 m p.h., and Hans and Neerpasch in a 907 took 2nd to Siffert and Vic Elford (in a 908) at the Nurburgring 1000. At Spa, teamed with Rolf Stommelen, Hans was 3rd; in the Austrian GP, with Kurt Ahrens, he was 2nd to Siffert, both in a 908.

He got similar high placings, in 1969 but no victories. At Nurburgring with Stommelen, Le Mans with Gerard Larrousse, and Monza with Ahrens, Herrmann tasted 2nds. In the Targo he and Stommelen were 3rd, in the Spa 1000 4th, in the BOAC 500 6th. The following season saw fewer finishes, but a crowning victory to Herrmann's long career. After a 3rd in the BOAC 1000 with Dickie Attwood, a 6th with Attwood at Spa and a 2nd with him at Nurburgring—all in a Porsche 917K entered by the Austrian, or 2nd, Porsche team—Hans and Attwood won Le Mans at 119.29 m.p.h. At that point, for the first time Hans distinctly heard his wife's pleas for him to retire. Bruce McLaren's death also played a part in making him decide to quit.

HARRY HEUER

The Meister Brauser team, sponsored by Peter Hand Brewery, was an important element in the development of American road racing toward the exalted status it now has achieved. Drivers like Carroll Shelby, Lance Reventlow, Chuck Daigh and Dick Rathmann wore the Meister Brauser colors, but there was really only 1 key man, the son of the owner of the Peter Hand Brewery. Harry Heuer was nine when he first took the controls of an airplane. Born in 1936, he was 23 before he decided to drive a sports car. By that time his self-professed idol, the Marquis Alfonso de Portago, was dead. "De Portago once said he'd rather be a dead lion than a live mouse. That about sums it up," Heuer declared. "I race because I like it. Nobody can help you as far as driving goes. The crew builds you a tremendous car but its up to you to be slow or fast, good or bad; you are alone."

That doesn't really sum it up when one can assemble an *équipe* that factory racing efforts envy. The custom-built Meister Brauser "Duster" trailer was a mobile repair shop that could practically rebuild 2 cars. And Heuer, a pleasant, handsome young man with as much driving skill as many of his contemporaries, was a walk-

ing Marshall Plan for aspiring carbuilders. The first aid recipient was a Denver mixed breed called the Bo-Car, a tubular frame job with a fiber glass body and a modified Corvette engine. Not all the beer money in the world could make it handle or stay together in 1959. However, when Lance Reventlow put his Scarabs up for sale, both landed in Chicago—one at Nickey Chevrolet, the other in Heuer's hands. Harry hired Augie Pabst to help him continue the Reventlow dream of world domination by an American car. Pabst won the 1959 USAC road-racing crown in the Scarab, and young Harry drove the Bo-Car, getting tips from Augie. In November of that year, Heuer bought the other Scarab, powered by a 339 cu. in. fuel-injected Corvette. The car weighed 1,900 pounds, despite extensive use of aluminum. Jim Jeffords, not Nickey, was the owner of record and as part of the sale, he signed on for a race or two.

So the 2 Scarabs, the Bo-Car, Jeffords, Pabst, and Harry set off for Nassau Speed Week. Only one Scarab made it; the other was demaged when a trailer came unhitched in Georgia. Thus Heuer had nothing to do in Nassau except what 99 percent of the Speed Week crowd was doing—drinking, partying and showing up occasionally at the track. Jeffords and Pabst did not set Oakes Field afire with their driving either. It was a matter of priorities, drinking or driving, and they chose the only sensible course at this casual race meeting. But Heuer had met his 1st real pro. He turned on the money spigot and lo, the great Robert (Red) Byron, former NASGAR champion, was team manager for Meister Brauser. It was no wonder that 1960 was a banner sea-

son. That year under Byron's tutelage polished Heuer as a driver and turned the Meister Brauser into an impressive, well-run show. Pabst and Harry often had 2-man races in the B-Modified SCCA class in the Scarabs, the best series then available in the United States. Augie won the championship. The team also had acquired 2 Formula Juniors, which were run assiduously.

In 1961 Harry was the star, and he won B-Modified as Augie left for other endeavors. But he lost Byron, who succumbed to a heart attack at Daytona Beach. Byron's 2nd in command, Willie Weis, originally hired away from Andy Granatelli, moved up. In 1962 a Scarab was retired, and the Marshall Plan swept into Texas oil country to relieve Jim Hall of the aluminum-bodied Chaparral, with engine built by Troutman and Barnes. This swept to the C-Modified championship as various guest pilots had a shot at the remaining Scarab—which was getting long in the gear teeth. Heuer's father was beginning to grumble a bit, but Harry kept the cash cascading by winning where it would do the brewery the most good—at Meadowdale Raceway near Chicago—no less than 3 times in 1962. Heuer won the 1963 C-Modified title for the 3rd time in a row, but he was less successful in the new USRRC series. Competing in 5 of the 7 events, he led 2, but failed to finish any. Now the aluminum Chaparral, too, was shedding half-shafts, but in that car, now renamed the Meister Brauser, Harry had what was probably one of his most virtuoso rides October 29, 1963, when he came in 5th overall in the Monterey Grand Prix. Dave McDonald had outduelled A. J. Foyt for the victory, and Lloyd Ruby, Jim Clark and Graham Hill were behind Heuer.

The Meister Brauser was de-fuel-injected for 1964, and Heuer appeared with Weber carburetion for the Augusta, Ga., USRRC. He earned 3 points by sheer driving talent, stealing 4th place by out-maneuvering a rookie pilot. But it was evident that the old Meister Brauser, née Chaparral, was obsolete. And, besides, the tab was too high to refurbish the team with new machinery. So the big Meister Brauser équipe stayed home, the promotional effort at an end. Harry Heuer's personal Marshall Plan had ended, on balance a success.

GRAHAM HILL

The 1966 running of the Indianapolis 500 was a fiasco for many Americans. Only 6 cars were running at the end out of 33 starters. There was an 11-car crash on the opening lap that eliminated a third of the field in one swoop. And the race was won by one of those "outsiders"—in this case an Englishman—with a Scotsman in 2nd, and save for a last-minute bad break, it might have been 1-2-3 for the tiny little Grand Prix contingent that thought of Indy as just another race.

Jim Clark, who won in 1965 at Indy, Graham Hill,

pletely surrounded to escape. Besides the 11 cars eliminated, 5 more were bent but repairable, so 22 cars answered the second call to start 1 hour and 23 minutes later.

At 5 laps another car was gone, by the 30th lap 5 others had pitted for good. The lead changed hands frequently, thanks to pit stops, Clark's unaccountable spins (2 of them, yet he finished 2nd), and other factors. Clark led in laps 17–64, Lloyd Ruby 65–75, Clark again 76–86, Ruby once more 87–132, Clark still again 133–139, and Ruby again 140–150. Jackie Stewart, meanwhile, had worked his way from 9th at 25 miles, to 6th at 75, to 3rd at 250. When Ruby was black-flagged at the 150th lap for losing oil, Stewart took the lead and held it until lap 191 when he lost oil and shut down. His steady drive and 6th-place classification were to earn the Scot Indy's Rookie of the Year honors.

And Graham Hill, meanwhile, was Graham Hill. Almost a last-minute replacement on the Mecom Team for Walter Hansgen, and a 2nd choice after Denis Hulme had refused an offer of this car, Hill had motored in his usual way, bringing the Red Ball Special Lola-Ford to 8th at 100 miles, then steadily passing sick and dying cars until he took the lead at the 191st lap and won handily, despite a short-lived claim by Clark's pits because of scoring confusion that Clark had won.

Norman Graham Hill, born in London's Hampstead suburb, February 15, 1929, elder son of a stockbroker, has always taken things calmly. Part of that reaction may have been his traditional English temperament, part of it certainly is that he has always been one to take his time in sizing up a situation, deciding what he should do, and then doing it. Finishing secondary school in 1942, he was sent to Hendon Technical College for 3 years, then apprenticed for 5 years with a technical firm that immediately decided he needed further schooling and packed him off for more of it. While in college he took up cycling, both as transportation and as a sport. One weekend he had a road accident and badly smashed his left thigh, making his left leg half an inch shorter than his right. Later auto crashes have made the limp more noticeable.

The leg didn't stop Britain from drafting Graham into the Navy in 1950. He served 2 years, rising to Petty Officer; then back to his job he went, working on combustion heating. But his ambitions were changing, and in 1953 he purchased a car, a 1934 Morris 8. Graham went round to collect it, drove the seller around the block to test the car, then drove off in it. It was assumed that he knew how to drive, but this was the only time he had driven a car in his life up to then. Two weeks later he passed his official driving test. That same year he stepped into his 1st racing car after paying 5 guineas to join the Universal Motor Racing Club and an added pound to drive 4 laps at Brands Hatch.

Hill introduced himself to the club proprietor, described his technical background—possibly fudging a

and Jackie Stewart were big names in Europe, but just intruders into the tight little world of Indianapolis racing. A. J. Foyt even tried to blame the 11-car crash on Hill, claiming his foot had come off the pedal to start the trouble. Foyt was unavailable for comment several hours later when Hill flashed across the finish line the winner, Clark 2nd, and Stewart, whose engine ran out of oil and pitted him 10 laps from the finish, classified 6th.

Hill was always the forgotten man. He was twice World Champion, runner-up 3 times, 5-time victor in the Monaco GP and 3-time victor in the United States GP. Quiet, professional, steady on course, and a gentleman (if addicted to some fun) off course. Hill probably did take his foot off the pedal, or else he might have been a 12th victim of that incredible Indy foul-up. What really happened was that an overloaded American pace car had gone so slowly that the 33 cars were fiercely bunched, so bunched that disaster was inevitable.

When the pace car waddled off the Brickyard, the racing cars charged ahead. Chuck Hulse zipped away; Johnny Boyd and Billy Foster both dove for his opening. Foster swerved as Boyd reached it first, and in so doing ran over the front wheel of Gordon Johncock's car. Into the wall went Foster, and that started the chain reaction. Graham Hill was behind Foster and alongside Boyd. He could see what was coming, and his reactions were swift . . . and correct. Behind Hill was Foyt, he of the step-on-the-gas-and-charge school, blindly piling into the mélée. Clark was ahead of the action, but Hill and Stewart, both in the midst of it, managed to elude the crash. Dan Gurney, another GP hand, was too com-

bit on his vast automotive experience—and proceeded to become the unpaid but free-to-drive-the-racer mechanic for the club. This venture folded soon after, but Graham had determined that auto racing was for him. He resigned from his paying job, went on the dole and made another arrangement in which he swapped mechanical services for track time with another shoestring auto racing club. In April, 1954, Hill answered his 1st starting flag as a driver. The car was a Formula 3 Cooper. He was 2nd in his heat, 4th in the final. Soon afterwards he left the club and started looking for a paying job in racing, preferably driving.

Broke but game, Hill bumped into Colin Chapman at the Brands Hatch August Bank Holiday meeting, fast-talked his way into a ride back to town in the Team Lotus truck and into a free meal with the great man himself. Over dinner he then talked Chapman into hiring Hill as a mechanic, as well as letting him free-lance on the side. In 1955, one of his private clients, Dick Margulies, who owned a C Jaguar, went racing at Spa, Bari, Nurburgring, Sardinia, and Sicily, and Graham went along. At Messina he codrove, then immediately hopped a train and headed home to marry, on August 13, 1955, Bette, a rower he had met at the Auriol Rowing Club. (Hill was a keen oarsman in his preracing days, good enough to stroke the first 8 to victory at the Henley Grand Challenge Cup races.)

Late in the year Chapman let Hill test-drive the newest Lotus on its introduction day after all the well-known drivers had had their go. To everyone's amazement, except his own, Graham set the 2nd fastest time of the day, and Chapman delighted in publicizing this feat. In 1956 Colin went further and let Hill drive a factory car at Brands Hatch in place of Cliff Allison. Graham won the 1st race, was 2nd in another. He got some other rides in 1957 from Chapman, but the idea that he was really a mechanic was still there.

In August, 1957, Hill quit Lotus, then joined Speedwell Conversions, where he became a director and later chairman. Distance lent enchantment, apparently, for Chapman offered Graham a factory drive in his Formula 1 Lotus for Monaco, 1958. Hill was motoring in 4th place when he retired. He stayed with Chapman 2 seasons, but the Lotus was going through one of its bad periods, and Graham failed to earn a single championship point. He switched over to BRM, and suffered through 2 more bad seasons as the car was properly sorted out and modified, although he did earn 3 points in 1961.

Than came 1962. Hill won his 1st *grande épreuve*, the Dutch GP, the year's championship opener. At Monaco he was classified 6th after his engine quit while he was in the lead 7 laps from the finish. At the Belgian GP Hill was 2nd to Clark, at the French race he finished 9th after fuel injection troubles had knocked him out of the lead late in the race. Graham did set the race's fastest pace, a lap record of 106.92 m.p.h., be-

fore his engine acted up. He was 4th in the British GP, then won in Germany after surviving a crash in practice that demolished his first BRM. A camera had fallen off a car in Hill's path at some 140 m.p.h., cut the car's oil lines, and sent it careening off the course. In the German race, run in terrible rains, Graham gave one of his finest performances, taking the lead from Gurney in the 6th lap, then grimly holding off John Surtees for the remaining 9 laps. Surtees never left Hill's rear-view mirror, and the final margin between the 2 cars was a mere 2.5 seconds. Hill also set the fastest lap.

Italy was next, and once more the BRM handled by Hill was to win as well as set the day's fastest single lap pace. In the United States GP, Clark won, with Graham just over 9 seconds behind the Lotus, although Clark actually was coasting home after having built nearly a 20-second lead near the end. The South African GP closed out the year, and here Hill once more won rather easily to annex his initial World Championship, as well as earn BRM the constructor's title.

From 1963 through 1965 came Hill's bridesmaid period. All 3 seasons he finished 2nd in the championship race, in 1963 and 1965 to Clark, in 1964 to Surtees. The latter was particularly bitter to swallow, for Graham had entered the year's finale, the Mexican GP, with a good chance to win his 2nd championship. All he had needed was a 3rd or better. But Lorenzo Bandini pushed Hill into a guard rail, partially crippling his car. Later, Bandini eased off and let Surtees pass him at the finish to nip Hill.

Yet these years were not without their high points. In each of them, for example, Graham won the Monaco GP, also setting the fastest lap times in 1964–65. He also won the United States GP in each of the 3 seasons, with the fastest lap mark in 1965. There were 2nds to Gurney, Clark and Surtees in 1964 in the French, British, and German races. There were 2nds in 1965 to Clark and Stewart—his 1st GP victory—in the German, British, and Italian races. In the latter, Stewart's time over Hill was 3.3 seconds, in the British race Clark's was 3.2 seconds.

In these years, too, Hill was driving other types of cars. He was 3rd in the 1963 Sebring 12-hour race in a 4-litre Ferrari shared with Pedro Rodriguez, and he won the Tourist Trophy in a Ferrari GTO. In 1964 he shared 2nd at Le Mans with Jo Bonnier, won the Tourist Trophy alone, and shared the Paris 1000 victory with Bonnier, all in a Ferrari 330P. That year was memorable, too, for a spectacular crash at Snetterton in the March International from which he walked away without a scratch. In 1965 he won the New Zealand GP for the first time as part of the year's Tasman series.

The pattern changed in 1966–67 when Hill slipped to 5th and 7th in the championship standings. In 1966 he was still with BRM, in 1967 he had returned to Lotus and Chapman. In championship racing, he failed to notch a single victory in these 2 years, but again there were 2nds—to Jack Brabham, 1966's champion, in the Dutch GP; to Denis Hulme, 1967's champion, at Monaco; to Clark, also in 1967, in the United States GP by 6.3 seconds, although Hill set the day's fastest lap time. Away from the championship, he won the 1966 New Zealand GP and raced well in other Tasman contests.

Graham's 2nd crown came in 1968. It started at South Africa, where Hill trailed Clark. Then 2 victories in a row, at the Spanish GP and at Monaco for the 4th time, where he edged Dickie Attwood by 2.2 seconds. Retired at Belgium, classified 9th at Holland, retired in the French and British races, Graham rebounded with a 2nd to Stewart in Germany. His last retirement came in Italy; he came in 4th in Canada, trailed Stewart in the United States GP, then won in Mexico to clinch his crown.

At 40 years of age, Graham Hill could hardly be considered a serious contender in 1969, even after his 1968 feats, especially since his Lotus was not as competitive as some of his opponents' mounts. Yet he started off well, coming in 2nd in South Africa to the eventual champion, Stewart. After retiring in the Spanish GP, he won at Monaco for the 5th time. After that, things did not go well. He was 7th at the Dutch GP, 6th in France, 7th again in the British race, 4th in Germany, and 9th in Italy. His car was retired in the Canadian race and ailed its way through the United States GP until a spin and resulting crash threw Graham out of the cockpit. With 2 broken legs, it was a bitter way to end the year.

Months of pain and a 4½-hour operation back in London followed. They doubted he would ever drive again, let alone race. They smiled when he said he would race at the South African GP March 7, 1970. By December he was in a wheelchair, by January he was on crutches. Soon he was flying his own plane again, then cycling. Just before South Africa, he discarded his canes. And on March 7th, he was sitting in Rob Walker's blue Lotus-Ford (having left Lotus, though Chapman said his spot was ready for him) to answer the starter's flag. It would be nice to say he won, but he finished 6th. Considering that he moved with great discomfort, if not pain, Hill deserved the ovation that he received as he crossed the line. He finished out the season with Walker, his best effort a 4th at the Spanish GP, and garnered 7 points for 13th in the standings.

With a Brabham, Hill won only 2 points in 1971 GP racing with a 5th in the Austrian GP, which tied him for 21st position in the standings at season's end. He was 7th in the U.S. GP, 9th in both South Africa and Germany, and 10th in Holland. There were shunts in Spain, at Monaco, in the British and Canadian races, retirements in France and the non-title Brands Hatch Race of Champions. In the Italian GP he was classified 11th, though not running at the race's end. Graham did considerably better in F2, in which he was a gate draw, winning at Thruxton, placing at Hockenheim and Brands Hatch, generally making a good showing. Wherever he went, he brought an air of distinction, and was an outstanding spokesman for the sport of motor racing. In 1972 he rejoined Brabham, moved over to a private Shadow in 1973, hoping to better his Italian GP 5th of 1972. In sports cars, Hill shared a Le Mans victory with Gijs van Lennep in 1972. "There's life in the old fellow, yet," he said.

PHIL HILL

The year 1958 was not just another ordinary year in Grand Prix racing; it was an unusual time. Consider if you will this scene: 7 GP drivers gathered in front of a Rheims hotel, picking up a tiny Vespa 400 and carrying it upstars to "park" the automobile outside the door of its owner, driver Harry Schell, while he slept in anticipation of the next day's French GP. Juan Fangio, 5 times World Champion and not one of the pranksters, offered to drive the car down, but the consensus was that vases, telephone booths, assorted furniture, cats, and the like were "road hazards" too great even for Juan Manuel. So the drivers had to take the car back to the street.

One of the 7 pranksters was literally a GP rookie, Philip Toll Hill. Then 31, Hill had been a professional driver of note, a champion in sports cars, in fact, for 8 years, but this French GP was to be his initial *grande épreuve,* his initial try for points in the World Championship series. The fact that this was his initial Formula 1 outing must have explained how Hill, normally an introspective man, could have brought himself to participate in such a prank. It is true that he knew most of them —Moss, Musso, Gurney, Gregory, and the others—and that they readily accepted Hill even though he was yet unproved in the F1 cars of the day. But Hill was always a loner, not a joiner.

He was also a fine driver. He was the 1st American to win the 24-hour race at Le Mans. He was the 1st to win the Sebring 12-hour race 3 times. He was the 1st to win a modern GP. He was the 1st to win a Grand Touring race in Europe in an American car. And, of course, he would be the 1st, and to date, only American to win a World Championship. His GP career was amazingly brief, all of 8 seasons, but his entire driving career covered 18 seasons.

Hill was born in Miami, but raised in Santa Monica. He had an unhappy childhood despite the best efforts of an aunt after the death of both of his parents while he was quite young. That aunt, in fact, bought Phil his first car when he was 12—an old Model T Ford that he raced around on a dirt oval back in the Santa Monica hills. But no great dream of becoming a champion driver burned in Hill at this time, nor in high school, nor in college (University of Southern California) where he studied business administration for a time although his interests lay more in things mechanical.

Finally Phil quit college, spent most of his time work-

ing on Offenhauser-powered midgets, and even drove them occasionally. He also became interested in old cars, starting a lifelong passion, and purchased an MG TC. It was in this automobile that Hill started on the road to racing fame. In his initial race at Carrell Speedway in Los Angeles, Hill won, and other races followed. But in 1949, he went to Great Britain in study maintenance at the Jaguar factory in Coventry as part of a new job with a local dealership.

Hill returned with an XK 120 and proceeded to run it at Santa Ana, Calif. in an airport race in which he was 2nd. In 1950, the initial real road race in the United States was held at Pebble Beach, and Phil won it. Things started happening, and Hill raced—and won—in his own car and in the cars of others who were eager to sponsor this really good American driver. The MG gave way to an Alfa Romeo, which yielded to the West Coast's 1st Ferrari, sold Hill rather cheaply by Luigi Chinetti, who already had tabbed him as a serious professional driver.

Phil drove someone else's car in the 1952 Mexican Road Race, in which he finished 6th against drivers like Karl Kling, Hermann Lang, Chinetti, and Luigi Villoresi. He was to race the following 2 years in this spectacular enduro, each year with a youngster who one day would be also a GP driver—Richie Ginther—as his passenger. In 1953 their car went off a cliff, but both walked away with minor bruises. That year, too, Hill drove at Sebring, Le Mans and Rheims, and retired from each race. Whereupon he "retired" to work on his old cars. But he was back, with Ginther, in the 1954 Mexican race, and

this time they finished 2nd in the Ferrari. On the strength of this feat, Hill was invited to drive a factory car at the 1955 Le Mans, but the Pierre Levegh accident, close on the heels of Bill Vukovich's Indianapolis crash and death, again gave the American pause, and he once again "retired." At the Nassau Speed Week that December, Hill came back once again. His victory there led to another factory drive, this time in the Argentine 1000 in Buernos Aires with Oliver Gendebien. They finished 2nd, and Hill was invited to sign a full-season factory contract for sports car racing.

In 1956 Hill won the Swedish GP and the Messina, Sicily, race. The following year's bag included the Caracas, Venezuela, race and Nassau. In 1958 he won the Argentine 1000 (with Peter Collins), Sebring (again with Collins) and Le Mans (with Gendebien). But no GP offer for F1 was forthcoming from Enzo Ferrari. So Hill jumped at an offer by Jo Bonnier to drive the Swedish driver's 2-year-old Maserati in the French GP. Ferrari was horrified, but Phil was adamant and drove to a creditable 7th after the Schell hotel incident. In that same race, Fangio finished 5th in the very latest Maser, his last F1 race.

In the season's non-title "Race of Two Worlds"— American Indianapolis cars against the tricked-up GP cars on Monza's Indy-like banked oval—Hill finished 3rd with Mike Hawthorn and Luigi Musso sharing honors. No F1 car was available for the German GP, but Hill was given an F2 mount in which he finished 9th. That race cost Collins his life, however, and created an opening on the F1 team, so Phil had his initial factory F1 ride at the Italian GP September 7, 1958.

Hill charged off into the lead at the flag, led for 4 laps, spun out and had to pit for a wheel change. Returning 9th, he fought his way back into the lead on the 36th lap, setting a fastest lap on the way, then led to 40. Then Hill eased off to let Hawthorn, fighting for the World Championship, get those extra points by taking 2nd. Tony Brooks won the race. At Casablanca a few weeks later, Hill was to do the very same thing—yield to Mike so he could clinch his title—while Stirling Moss won. At season's end, Hawthorn was Champion, and Hill was tied for 7th with Jean Behra and Wolfgang von Trips with 9 points each.

In 1959 Hill rose to 6th in the standings, thanks to a 4th at Monaco, 6th in Holland and a 2nd (to Tony Brooks) in the French GP. A strike cancelled Ferrari's British GP entry, but Hill was 3rd, behind Brooks and Dan Gurney, in the German GP. Retirements at Portugal and Sebring (U.S. GP) were rapped around a 2nd to Moss in the Italian GP. In 1960, Ferrari was concentrating on readying his 1961 cars, and Phil was 5th with 16 points, his best finish a 3rd behind Moss and Bruce McLaren in the Monaco race. He retired 3 times in 8 starts in F1, and drove an F2 car only in the Italian GP, boycotted by British drivers, but won there.

A new formula came on the scene in 1961, and with

it the Ferrari came into its own. All season Hill and his teammate, Trips, battled it out for the World Championship, an interesting time for everyone at Ferrari. At Monaco Hill was 3rd, behind Moss and Ginther, with Trips 4th. Trips won the Dutch GP, with Hill on his heels. Phil won the Belgian race, with Trips 2nd. After a 9th in the French GP, Hill again battled Trips to the line of the British GP, but finished 2nd. Moss won the German race. Trips was 2nd, Hill 3rd. At Monza Trips was killed, taking 14 spectators with him. Hill went on, though shaken, to win the race, and with it, the World Championship by a single point, 34–33. Trips's death caused Ferrari to skip the United States GP robbing Hill of the recognition that he might have received otherwise in his native land.

Phil slipped to 6th in 1962 with 14 points. One of his most electrifying drives came that season, however, in the Monaco GP, when Hill was 17 seconds behind Bruce McLaren on the 90th lap, then started making up 2 seconds a lap and almost caught the New Zealander at the wire. McLaren won by 1.3 seconds. Thirds in Holland and Belgium wrapped around this race gave Hill a shot at a repeat title (he was trailing Graham Hill then by 2 points). But strikes in Italy cost Hill 3 appearances; he retired in 2 of his 3 remaining starts and finished 11th in the Italian race. Even though he won Le Mans once again, Nurburgring's 1000, and was 2nd at Daytona with Gendebien, Hill was released by Ferrari.

ATS was a new marque in 1963. It lasted a single year, a painful year for Phil Hill. The car was late for its initial start, finally making a grid in the Belgian GP, but Hill retired after 13 laps with a bad gearbox. In the Dutch GP, his ATS lost a wheel and crashed on the 15th lap. For the French race, Hill switched to a Lotus-BRM because his ATS was not ready. Though running at race's end, he was unclassified. Back in an ATS, he was 11th in the Italian GP, then retired in the U.S. race at Watkins Glen. Hill's misfortunes continued in sports car racing: his codrive with Ken Miles ended 11th in an AC Cobra at Sebring, his Solitude GP and Le Mans starts ended in retirements, and his Nurburgring 1000 drive resulted in another crash.

Phil's last F1 season was 1964 (he was number 2 at Cooper's). The car never was competitive, a 6th at the British GP the best it could do. He took 7th in France, 8th in Holland, 9ths at Monaco and Mexico, retired at 3 races, and passed 2 others up. But his interests were building again in the sports car area. He and Pedro Rodriguez won the Daytona Continental in a Ferrari GTO in 1964. With Ford's factory team, he was one of those who established the GT40 as a competitive car in 1964–65, although Phil never won a race in a GT40. By the time they were capable of winning, 1966, he had switched to Chaparral. In Jim Hall's creation Phil won the Nurburgring 1000 (with Bonnier as codriver) and the BOAC 500 (with Mike Spence) in 1967.

And then America's only GP champion retired to California and his many hobbies, from old cars to player pianos. He was all of 39.

TOMMY HINNERSHITZ

The Flying Farmer became competition director at Reading, Pa., Fairgrounds after he quit racing. It was a logical position for a man who had built one of the most loyal followings ever in auto racing. Tommy Hinnershitz was Pennsylvania Dutch, a member of that unique group of people who, 3 centuries after leaving Germany and the Low Countries, have retained their special way of life in the rolling hills of northeastern Pennsylvania. Hinnershitz didn't speak fluently; he preferred to do things, which is how he got to be known as one of the greats of dirt track racing and one of the kings of the sprint car.

In October 1956, the Checkered Flag Fan Club gave him a new passenger car as part of a program in appreciation of his racing accomplishments at Reading Fairgrounds. Tommy grew more incoherent with each new gift, as each city and county official praised him. The stocky 5 foot 7 inch Hinnershitz tried to show his appreciation the only way he knew how—behind the wheel of a race car. Tommy was disappointed when he lost the feature to Eddie Sachs but, if there was ever a time when fans were relieved to see their hero lose, that was it. After running roughshod over the opposition on the rain-rutted course for 20 laps, Tommy's shocks collapsed. He tried twice as hard, sliding, raising the wheels off the ground, and seeking the smallest opening. One driver left the track muttering, "That crazy Dutchman is so happy today, he'll kill himself and take someone with him. Not me, though."

Hinnershitz drove on pavement, but he never liked it. He once finished 9th at Indianapolis (1948) and could have had the experimental independent front suspension Kurtis again the following year, but he said, "If they make Indy a dirt track, I'll run." The same design won the national title (Johnny Parsons) and the Indianapolis 500.

It all started April 6, 1912, in Alsace Township, a tiny community just outside Reading. Ralph DePalma and Barney Oldfield were among the heroes Tommy had seen race on the Uniontown, Pa., board track. At 18 he drove his first race—at Reading Fairgrounds, naturally—in a stripped Model T. Two years later, he won his first race (at Reading) and cherished the old trophy ever after. He suffered his first crash in 1934—again at Reading. "I kept my feet on the gas too long and I went straight through the fence all the way to the horse barns," Tommy recalled. "I dragged myself out of that Model T and jumped into the hay. All I could think of was that more cars would be coming through."

But it was at Reading and at dirt tracks, mostly half-milers from Maine to Georgia, that he developed the incomparable style that at one time gave him track records at no less than 14 racing plants. Yet while he was a determined and spectacular competitor, Tommy did not usually take chances. He waited to pass for as much as 3 or 4 laps so he could go by and make it stick. Hinnershitz studied his competition very carefully and it was a measure of respect when he dared race wheel to wheel with a driver.

"Eager rookies I stay clear of," he said. "They usually have too much car for themselves and they can scare the seat off of your pants. I steer mostly with my foot on most dirt tracks. Lighten the foot pressure on the gas and the car is cocked for the turn. Feed the gas back correctly and you stay in the powerslide through the turn and are ready for the straights." The most treasured memory of many an enthusiast, according to the USAC yearbook, is the sight of Hinnershitz driving to the outside, pitching his car into a seemingly wild slide and, amid a shower of dirt, passing another car. The Flying Dutchman won the Eastern sprint title no less than 7 times, (1949–52, 1955–56 and the last one in 1959 when he was 47). He not only drove that year but maintained his car, the Pfrommer Special, in addition to a championship car for Jim Packard. He also finished 7th in the Midwest sprints and was 6th in the 1946 Championship Trail, but didn't like being away from his wife, his farm, and his two daughters that long. He passed his rookie test in 1939 at Indianapolis; in 1940 he hit the wall and luckily escaped with a broken wrist. On dirt Tommy bested the best—Eddie Sachs, A.J. Foyt early in A. J.'s career, and just about any one else who dared come into his half-mile stamping grounds. In 1959 Hinnershitz scored his 100th feature victory and the next year competed in few races to "sort of retire" from driving. He came back occasionally, however, "just for the fun of it," during the next decade.

CHICK HIRASHIMA

What is bravery really? In the case of Takeo (Chick) Hirashima, it was storming the beaches of Anzio, Italy, in World War II and before that, serving as riding mechanic to such drivers as Kelly Petillo, Jimmy Snyder, and Rex Mays in the final days of the 2-man cars. Hirashima became a member of the all-Nisei (Japanese-American) 442nd Combat Team after his country had interned him and hs relatives. The 442nd saw perhaps the heaviest fighting in southern Europe.

Hirashima became a riding mechanic because Art Sparks, who helped turn this grocery clerk into one of the most respected of American engine builders, felt that this small man was less ballast and less wind resistant. Chick had to use lead weights to make the 122-pound AAA minimum. A quick-thinking, intelligent man born in Glendale, Calif., May 4, 1912, Hirashima never went to college, but he found his university in Mr. Sparks, the carbuilding genius. Chick was an apt and willing student of engine building. He advanced so well that, as a chief mechanic, he had 2 Indinapolis 500 winners and was a consultant to the many-degreed Ford technical people who developed the 4-cam Ford Indy engine. When he retired as chief wrench for Len Sutton on the Leader Card team in 1962, he noted that the chief mechanic was becoming a chief scientist because the race cars were becoming so complicated. He estimated that it took 700 man-hours to put a car into condition for a USAC Championship Trail race.

Hirashima came to racing in the depths of the Depression in 1932. His first job was sweeping out the race-car building premises owned in Glendale by Sparks and a partner. Chick was fascinated by the creation and assembly of some of the fastest racing cars of the era. And Sparks taught him, apparently because of his potential as a riding mechanic. Riding mechanics earned 3 per cent of a driver's purse for their efforts. They were an anachronism, but Chick waited patiently for his big chance in a Sparks car. It arrived late in November 1934 at a rutted mile dirt track called Mines Field in Los Angeles. It was only because the stands were filled with paying customers that the race went on, because Mines Field was a quagmire from heavy rains the previous week. Hirashima had no idea he was to ride with Kelly Petillo that day. Paul Weirick, Sparks's partner, told him just minutes before the race. It was a wild ride as Petillo steamed through the field into the lead after 10 miles, then kept going full ahead even when the fog rolled in. Takeo remembered that the race eventually was stopped because of that fog, but Petillo went 2 extra laps because he couldn't see the red flag. Chick rode with him in the final races of the season.

In 1935 and 1936 the Sparks driver was Rex Mays, and Hirashima went to Indianapolis. Although both times the car was among the fastest, mechanical failures ended those attempts to win the 500. In 1935 the Gilmore Special suffered a broken spring shackle on lap 123, and in 1936, after setting pole speed, Mays was hampered by a throttle rod pin. Sparks had put his fortune into a new supercharged 6-cylinder car for 1937, a 337-cu. in. single-carburetor design with a centrifugal supercharger mounted on its rear. Snyder set a record for 50 miles; then the transmission failed. The Sparks effort to stay in racing was in jeopardy, and Hirashima chose to stick with him for 1938 when Sparks signed with Joel Thorne, the 6-foot 6-inch millionaire who wanted an Indy win more than anything.

Chick finally quit the grocery business to work full-time on the 2 new Thorne cars designed by Sparks. The 179 cu. in. engines were supercharged, and the 6 cylinders were driven by an o.h.c. The body was placed off center so the driver could sit low, next to the crankshaft, and the entire vehicle was cross-sprung. Both Ronnie Householder and Snyder, the drivers, left late in the race while in contention because their blower hoses split. In 1939 Snyder finished 2nd in a 182 cu. in. improvement of this car, again winning the pole. Later that year he was killed in a race. By 1940 Sparks and Thorne hardly spoke without arguing, yet Hirashima remembered working on some wildly exotic engines, including one that had 6 cylinders and 6 carburetors. The Sparks-Thorne rupture came in 1941, and soon after came Pearl Harbor and internment for Hirashima. Hirashima seldom mentioned his subsequent war exploits because he hated the life of a soldier.

Discharged in time to think about the 1946 Indy 500 revival, Chick returned to the old Thorne shop and put together 2 cars from the bits and pieces. Rudi Caracciola demolished the best one in practice. That left Chick's backup car with George Robson in the cockpit, and it was overheating under racing pressure, so the orders were to go slow. Robson did and won. That was Hirashima's first Indy winner, and a reminder to the men who were in the pits that he had not lost his touch. He worked on several crews in the succeeding years as the engine expert. Rodger Ward, Len Sutton, Sam Hanks, Walt Faukner, and Cecil Greene all benefited from it. Eventually he joined Meyer-Drake, building and experimenting with the Offenhauser engine. He is said to have been the father of the short-stroke Meyer-Drake. In 1955 and 1956 the Hirashima touch was on the engines in the A. J. Watson cars in which Bob Sweikert and Pat Flaherty won at Indianapolis. And in 1959 the Rodger Ward car had an engine by Chick.

In 1960 Hirashima came back to racing full-time on the Ken-Paul Special. He accepted the job on hearing that Jim Rathmann would drive and Smokey Yunick would also work on the car. A. J. Watson, for whom he had built all those engines, told him of the opportunity. In exchange for a Watson chassis identical to that of Rodger Ward, Chick built identical Offy engines for both the Ken-Paul (his) and Leader-Card (Watson's) machines. The historic duel of 1960 ensued, Rathmann winning only because he waited a tiny bit longer than Ward before slowing down to conserve a badly worn tire. In 1961 Hirashima became chief mechanic on an experimental Leader Card car that didn't qualify; in 1962 Len Sutton brought his car in 2nd.

He retired from the chief mechanic's duties at that point and began to sell Autolite spark plugs as Ford attempted to infiltrate the single-seater fraternity, then was utilized as a consultant on the 4-cam Ford engine. The immediate racing success of the 4-cammer was credited to his genius. Hirashima continued his keen interest in racing until he retired from his job with Autolite.

MIKE HISS

In 1972 Mike His went out and bought himself a March 722 to race in SCCA Formula B regionals. Nothing un-

usual about that, perhaps? But Mike Hiss was the Indianapolis Rookie of the Year in 1972, a regular on the Championship Trail, and the highest finishing rookie of all time in USAC point standings. Hiss, in other words, was a complete professional.

"The Formula B thing is just for fun. I just really like to race, no matter what the car or the series," he said. "I can't race it in the professional races, of course, but I'll run it in regionals and it will be strictly for fun, something like my wife's running her Austin Healey Sprite Mk. 1. You know, she's been racing longer than I have, but I don't tell too many people that." Hiss's wife, Arlene, used Mike as her "chief mechanic, go-for, grease wiper-offer and just about everything else on the car," Mike laughed.

Mike himself had a young, dedicated crew on the Eagle-Offy, originally Swede Savage's Dan Gurney team car, purchased by Mary and Tom Page, a Southern California couple, for Mike in November 1971. "We could have waited for a new car, but we wanted to get started right away with practice and readying the car. We didn't realize how much faster the new cars would be."

Hiss didn't do badly at all in his opening year in USAC, however. At the Phoenix 150 he was 10th, in the Trenton 200, 7th. At Indy in the 500, Hiss surprised everyone, and especially Sam Posey, by walking away with rookie honors (worth $1,000) and another 7th. Thirteenth in the Milwaukee 150, 24th in the Michigan 200 when he spun out to avoid hitting the crippled Merle Bettenhausen, Mike returned among the top finishers at Pocono with a 6th. Pocono was especially interesting. Two weeks before, Hiss had a motorcycle accident and broke his leg. Instead of a cast, he agreed to a new surgical process that involved a steel band around the broken bone, with a screw right through the latter to secure the support. Hiss was up and walking in 10 days, and in 2 weeks he was proving to USAC and Pocono officials he could race there. Passing up the Milwaukee 200, Mike made his best showing of 1972 with a 2nd in the rainy, unpredictable Ontario 500 in California, Roger McCluskey taking the top prize. Mike's car was Roger Penske's Sunoco-McLaren that time as he filled in for Mark Donohue.

Hiss was born on July 7, 1941, in Norwalk, Conn. Two years later, the family moved to the Bahamas for a year, then came back to Connecticut again. Later, after his parents were divorced, Hiss grew up in California and Florida. He got in some time at Stetson University, studying electrical engineering, "but like so many kids these days, I guess I was somewhat confused," he recalled. "Anyway, I enlisted in the Navy for 4 years and came out an Electronics Specialist 2nd Class.

"I was discharged in Norfolk, and decided to stay around there. A friend and I went partners in an old TR3, but pretty soon he sold his share to me. I had all of $500 in that car, but it was pretty expensive to own in those days." Hiss was working then at the Johns Hopkins Applied Physics Laboratory as an electronics technican.

This was 1965, and Hiss had become a member of the Old Dominion Region of the SCCA, later moving over to the Washington Region. The 1st race was at Marlboro, Md. "By the time Arlene and I got married in 1967, I had pretty much decided that I wanted to give auto racing a real try. I bought a Brabham BT15 F/B car and really settled down to single-seaters." That year he finished 2nd to Gus Hutchinson in the Continental. Two years later he won the F/B title. In 1970 Mike moved to California as manager of Charlie Hayes's Racing Equipment operation, a Lola distributorship, and raced a Lola Formula Ford in the SCCA, all the way to the American Road Race of Champions, placing 5th. The operation closed down, and Hiss was on his own.

"Most people think the transition from road racing to the ovals involves getting used to a larger amount of power and the handling of the race car," Hiss said. "But the difference between a F/A or F/B car and a Championship car isn't that great. The real thing you have to learn is to race with these USAC drivers on their own terms . . . their type of racing. In road racing, for example, you usually can have some particular advantage over another driver, and you usually can count on passing him in the corners, outbraking him or something like that. But in oval racing, the techniques are much more subtle, although I still enjoy courses with some variety rather than the more simple ones. Pocono is a special favorite of mine, and I like Trenton and Phoenix, too. A variety of turns and conditions."

Hiss, a collar-ad type with an outgoing personality and willingness to listen, attracted in 1972 a good deal of volunteer help that every rookie needs. Bobby Unser gave him his grounding at Indianapolis by taking Mike round the Brickyard innumerable times in a pace car. At Ontario, Hiss's teacher was Donohue, at Phoenix, McCluskey. All heady stuff, yet Mike Hiss still harbored a dream. "Formula 1 is my fondest dream," he said. "The challenge there is so much greater there than anywhere else, Indianapolis included. I'd give my eye teeth to get a shot at it."

DAVID HOBBS

The adjectives applied to David Wishart Hobbs varied according to whether the person speaking was friend or foe. He was opinionated or confident, loudmouthed or outspoken, spoiled or dedicated, opportunistic or disloyal, realistic or flighty, but always talented. There could never be disagreement about that quality. In single-seaters, stock cars, sports cars; sprints or enduros; Europe or America, David Hobbs demonstrated that auto racing was the right choice of professions.

Hobbs was born June 9, 1939, at Leamington Spa, England. He grew to be fairly tall for a driver (6 feet 1 inch) and lean, with wavy hair and (to Americans at least) a sort of Bugs Bunny look about him. Perhaps it was because Hobbs always seemed, like Bugs, to be a bit of a sharp fellow, watching out for the angles, ready to beat you any way he could. And Hobbs could really talk your ear off. Bored with school early, at 17 Hobbs had left the books to join a Daimler apprentice program. In 1959 David started racing in a Morris Oxford sedan equipped with his father's own Hobbs Mecha-matic automatic transmission. This was club racing, as was the racing in 1960 when David graduated to an XK 140 provided by the senior Hobbs. He had some hairy moments, like rolling at Oulton Park, but managed to win 4 races that season. In 1961 Hobbs married and simultaneously got serious about his amateur racing, starting 22 times in an automatic-transmissioned Lotus Elite, winning 14 races, including the 1600 c.c. class in the Nurburgring 1000.

Outside sponsorship followed in 1962, with the Peter Berry Racing Team. Berry, a wealthy chicken farmer, found eggs profitable enough to hand Hobbs an XKE Jaguar and a 3.8 Jaguar sedan. David visited America for the first time, but DNF at the Daytona 3-hour Continental. For laughs, he tried an American stock car (Holman and Moody Ford Galaxie) and averaged about 155 m.p.h. around the Daytona banking, compared to Fireball Roberts's pole-winning speed of 159 m.p.h. The Berry cars back home were not very successful, however, so neither was Hobbs.

In a Team Elite Lotus Elite shared with Australian Frank Gardner, Hobbs did manage to win the Index of Thermal Efficiency at Le Mans. He had his initial single-seater race in a Formula Junior at Oulton Park and won it. He also became a development engineer with his father's Hobbs Transmission firm, so the year certainly wasn't lost.

More FJ followed with the Midland Racing Partnership. Hobbs finished 3rd in the British series in 1963 and set a lap record at Silverstone. In his initial Le Mans (with Richard Attwood in a Lola-Ford GT), he crashed. Even so, after Hobbs Transmissions closed down that November, David decided to turn professional driver. In 1964 he got a berth with the Merlyn factory team in Formula 2, driving for the Lotus factory team as well in a Lotus Cortina for races like Roskilde, Denmark (which he won), Marlboro, Md., and Elkhart Lake. At Le Mans, David and Rob Slotemaker—the skid-king—shared a Triumph Spitfire and finished 21st overall.

Harold Young Limited provided a Lotus 23 sports car in 1964; then Hobbs switched the following year to a Lola T70, the 1st owned by a private entrant, with which Hobbs won at Mallory Park, Croft, Snetterton, and finished 2nd in the Tourist Trophy. He had a pair of 2nds and a 3rd in this car as well. The Mallory victory was especially sweet because David defeated Graham Hill in a McLaren in a close battle. His other rides that year included an extended visit to North America, where Hobbs was 3rd at St. Jovite but retired at Mosport, Kent, and Riverside, each time while well placed. Tim Parnell came up with a Formula 2 Lotus-BRM, but nothing spectacular happened.

In 1966 Hobbs joined John Surtees's operation for the first time, an arrangement that was to last 5 seasons. The mount again was a T70. A favorite opponent was Denis Hulme, whom David led twice, only to succumb to mechanical failure. Much of his later confidence came from his continuing good showings against Hulme, a World Champion: "I've raced against him for years," David explained, "and I've never been slower, always as fast, maybe faster. That shows that with the right car I should be a winner."

That same season Hobbs recorded his first Formula 1 ride, again with Tim Parnell. He finished 3rd at the Syracuse Grand Prix behind Surtees and Lorenzo Bandini. There were Ferrari sports car drives, too, including a Maranello Concessionaires Dino Ferrari 206S at Le Mans and a David Piper Ferrari 250LM. Bernard White came up with a GT40 ride. But none of these attracted any great attention.

And 1967 was the same story. Hobbs partnered Surtees in the World Sports Car Championship series in a Lola T70, powered by an Aston Martin engine. Their cars failed to finish a race, although later in the season Hobbs drove a Chevrolet-powered car to victory at Croft, toppling Hulme, who was driving a similar car. Spice was added to the run because Hobbs started dead last after missing a qualifying heat. In F1, Bernard White prepared an antiquated BRM 2-litre car for a couple of starts, and David was part of the "scenery" in the British and Canadian GPs despite giving away some 100 b.h.p. to the other starters. In a Lola-BMW F2 car, he had some good drives, including a 3rd in the German F2 GP.

An F1 factory drive—with Japan's Honda, backing up Surtees—came for a single race in 1968, the Italian GP. He retired while running 5th. More importantly, John Wyer's JW Automotive came forward with a GT40 drive partnering Paul Hawkins. The pair led Sebring, Daytona, and Le Mans before being retired in each race with mechanical ills. But they won the Monza 1000 and finished 2nd to teammates (although they could have won) at the Watkins Glen 6-hour race. In the BOAC 500, Hobbs/Hawkins was 4th; ditto at the Spa 1000. In November, codriving with Jacky Ickx, David won the Kyalami 9-hour race, then came in 2nd (with Mike Hailwood) at the Capetown 3-hour race. He also piloted a Ford Falcon in the British Saloon Car Championship, winning once, finishing 2nd 3 times, and copping a 3rd.

After that season Hobbs took stock of his career: "I think I'll have to forget F1. It's too frustrating to drive an uncompetitive car—that year with Bernard White's BRM in 1968 was really disheartening. The only good F1 drive I've had was the 2nd Honda at Monza last season. I enjoyed that immensely—it was a well-organized team, the car handled well, went well and stopped well. I made reasonable time in practice, went reasonably well in the race and was 5th or 6th when it packed up with a dropped valve."

He decided to settle for long-distance driving and trying to do more in America. "The money over there is much better," he said. "The average American drivers are not as good as average Europeans. They are rather flamboyant and don't seem to realize half the time exactly what they're doing. They're inclined to let their emotions get the better of them." Not exactly the kind of thing to endear Hobbs to American drivers or press, but off to the New World he headed late in 1969.

Before that trip, however, David ran Surtees's TS5 in the Guards European Formula 5000 series—bigger, heavier, faster single-seaters than the traditional F1 car —and was 2nd in the standings (a victory, a 2nd, a couple of lap records, on the pole twice, next to the pole twice in 4 starts). He was late in joining the comparable SCCA Formula A series in the States, but charged in with 8 of 13 races left. Hobbs won 4 of them—more than any other driver in the 1969 series—and finished 2nd and 3rd in 2 others. He set 4 lap records. For the half-season's work, Hobbs was 2nd overall to Tony Adamowicz, beating Sam Posey. In the Guards chase, despite missing the 2nd half of that season, he was 8th overall.

For JW Automotive, still in the Ford GT40, Hobbs shared a car with Hailwood and led Daytona, only to retire. The story was the same at Sebring, but in the BOAC 500 the pair was 5th, at Spa they were 7th, and the year's best showing was at Le Mans in the 24-hour race, when they finished 3rd. Ickx and Jackie Oliver won in another GT40 with Hans Herrmann and Guy Larrousse 2nd in a Porsche 908.

Hobbs's 1970 F/A season cinched his determination to "go American." He joined the 13-race card at Dallas, and was leading the 7th race for most of the 40 laps when his Castrol Surtees TS5A developed incurable engine trouble. At Elkhart Lake he looked like a winner again until John Cannon (eventual series champion) snatched away the top spot at the flag and David finished 2nd. At St. Jovite he was gaining a second a lap on the leader, George Follmer, when the car developed suspension problems, and he had to pit. Back in the race, Hobbs was 7th at the checker. But at Donnybrooke and Lime Rock came back-to-back victories. "I may win all the rest of the season's races," David confidently told newsmen. He didn't. At Mosport he was 3rd, at Sebring in the finale of the series he was 2nd. But it added up to a 3rd-place finish in the final standings and also many American dollars.

Hobbs spent the winter discussing various deals, although everyone assumed he would be with Surtees again, for John was talking also of concentrating much of his attention on the richer American races. But in January 1971 came a dramatic announcement: David was joining the Roger Penske team, a sort of number 2 to Mark Donohue, not only for long-distance enduros like Daytona and Sebring, but for USAC 500-milers at Ontario and Pocono as well as Indianapolis.

There were 8 Continental dates in 1971. Most races ran in 2 heats with the final standings determined by a combination of both finishes. In the Riverside opener, after capturing the pole in his Hogan-sponsored McLaren-Chevvy, Hobbs did not start the initial heat, finished 26th in the next. Hardly an auspicious beginning. Laguna Seca was a bit better; Hobbs captured his 2nd pole and 1st place in both heats. At Kent he repeated the feat—pole and both heats. At Mid-Ohio he had an off day, qualifying 4th, winning the initial heat, taking 2nd in the other and allowing Sam Posey to take the overall honors because he was 0.2 seconds behind David in the opener. Posey and Hobbs were becoming a bit of a news item away from the course, too, putting on a kind of Bob Hope and Bing Crosby act of gentle needling that made good newspaper copy. Posey was good; he captured the pole at Road America, but victory was shared by Jerry Hansen and Hobbs, with David taking overall honors. Posey won the Edmonton pole, then the 1st heat, with Hobbs 2nd. But David took the 2nd heat and overall. He took the Donnybrooke pole; won the initial heat but wasn't running after 7 laps of the next, dropping him to 7 overall. Hobbs was human after all. Lime Rock was run as a single race, and it was all David's with a pole and an outright victory.

Hobbs's Continental domination was such that he won a total of $53,050, or a fifth of the total L&M cigarette and other sponsor funds involved. His 5 outright season victories were a record. He scored points toward his championship in all races but 1, also a record. In all-time Continental Formula A/5000 records, Hobbs dominated every department: most points, most victories, most pole qualifications, fastest laps (7 of them in the 8 1971 races).

He also ran a varied card of races with Mark Donohue for Roger Penske/Kirk White Racing; including USAC races starting with the Indianapolis 500 where he was running 12th when an oil line broke and his McLaren was hit by another car, CanAm enduros like Daytona and Le Mans, and—in November, 1971—his first F1 start in 3 years, the 4th of his career and his 2nd in a fairly competitive car. He started 22nd in Mark Donohue's McLaren, finished 10th. There were fewer detractors after 1971, and there were many more boosters. But in 1972 the L&M Continental competition was much more fierce and Hobbs failed to retain his title. CanAm was even less successful. But with Brett Lunger as a teammate on the Carl Hogan Lola team, Hobbs now was a major racing figure, earning TV commercial money on the side Hobbs had found his proper niche—the golden U.S.A. pro circuits.

BOB HOLBERT

Robert McCormick Holbert retired at the top of his form but not before he left a lasting imprint on road racing, American style. Previously associated with Porsche, the Warrington, Pa., automobile dealer had been making a new name for himself as a Ford Cobra driver when an accident at Kent, Wash., put Holbert on the shelf and set him to thinking about his racing career. "I think I have reached the end of the line as a part-time race driver," he wrote Carroll Shelby early in 1964, "and think it best to retire while I'm ahead. I've been at it going on 12 years now and have won about all there is to win. I've gotten a lot of enjoyment and satisfaction out of racing but I'm not getting any younger."

Born in Warrington in 1923, Bob was raised in the Philadelphia suburb. In the late forties he started his first automobile business, a general purpose garage, across the street from his later, more famous Holbert's Garage headquarters building. In 1951 he started specializing in foreign and sports cars almost exclusively and, about the same time, was bitten by the competition bug. His first car, Holbert said, was an MG TD with a supercharger. "My first race was and wasn't at Thompson, Connecticut," he recalled. "I drove up to Thompson, but never quite made the race because during practice I blew the engine. As a matter of fact, I never even saw the race because I spent the whole day working on the car so I could drive it home."

Discarding the supercharger, Bob moved into stock MG competition, winning his initial race, again at Thompson, in 1953. Over the next few years he averaged about 6 big meetings a year, driving a variety of cars including MGs, Lister-Chevvys and Cheetahs. "It was at Cumberland in May 1956 that I was convinced a Porsche was the car for me. Jack McAfee and a 550 Porsche made quite an impression. In the 5th race that day, McAfee ran away from 2 Ferraris and in the feature he came up from 9th to 2nd place just behind Walter Hansgen's D Jaguar, passing men like John Fitch, Sherwood Johnston, and John Bennett. The sight of him working the corners by just blipping the throttle made me decide I had to try a Porsche."

Holbert's long racing association with the German marque started a year later when his RS-550 appeared at Cumberland, Md. He didn't win that race but lost few after it, at least in his class. At the end of 1957, Holbert's 1st full season in a Porsche he was tied for 2nd place in the Class F sports division with the veteran Lake Underwood .The following year he was the overall winner in Class F Modified with a new RSK. He and a long-time nemesis, Charley Wallace, codrove to a 2nd in class (25th overall) at Sebring. Holbert's overall record in Porsches included 4 SCCA national championships in his class (runner-up the other seasons), 3 Driver-of-the-Year awards from *The New York Times,* and a similar nomination from *Sports Illustrated.*

His performance in the 1961 Le Mans 24-hour race —a 5th-place finish overall and a 3rd in the Index of Performance in an RS-61 codriven by Masten Gregory —attracted Shelby, who, by now, had fast-talked the Ford Motor Company and AC Cars Limited into contributing the engine and the chassis that together form the Cobra. Holbert became a Cobra team driver in

1963 and won 37 Points and the first USRRC crown. His 3 1st places and a 3rd in 5 starts played a big part in Shelby American's winning of the U.S. manufacturers championship that same year. Holbert and Dave Mac-Donald, a codriver at locales such as Sebring (where the Holbert-MacDonald entry was 4th overall and 1st in the Grand Touring class in 1964), were good friends, and Dave's death at Indianapolis had much to do with Bob's decision to call it quits.

Always a spare, medium-built man who wore glasses off the race courses, Holbert scarcely looked his 40-odd years when he quit. Nor did he look like the father of two sons, one of whom, Al, made a promising debut in a Porsche in 1971. "The best way to drive a race?" he repeated the question. "That's easy. Use plain common sense—drive at your own speed, not the car's. Get experience. A competition driving school is a good way to learn the fundamentals under controlled conditions, but experience in actual competition is the only true instructor."

HOLMAN-MOODY
(JOHN HOLMAN and RALPH MOODY)

It was 1957, and Ford Motor Company was honoring the automobile manufacturers' agreement to withdraw from automobile racing. That left a 30-year-old former truck driver and his partner, a race driver who also was an excellent mechanic, high and dry in Charlotte, N.C.,

308

ex-employes of the Pete DePaolo factory Ford operation.

John Holman, the trucker, and Ralph Moody, the racer, gulped once, floated a bank loan and bought the factory operation lock, stock, and barrel. There were some squeaky moments, but they never looked back on their road to millionaire status. And when Ford, after returning to racing in the biggest possible way, again announced it was withdrawing all factory support for 1971, Holman-Moody gulped again and, like any executives of a multimillion dollar business, realigned their sales goals.

There was the marine division, which converted Ford engines for marine use; there was the line of high-performance parts; and there were engineering and research departments on engine development—with government grants, no less. And, despite the withdrawal, it was likely that Holman-Moody would field so-called independent cars. The former DePaolo operation had moved twice and now inhabited quarters more fitting for a multimillion dollar company. But, after the 1971 season, the twosome split and the taciturn Moody revealed the off-duty coolness that had existed through some of their most successful seasons. Holman and Moody were an unlikely pair to last as partners. Holman was a stocky man who talked easily and smiled easily; he seemed to be an oasis in the frenetic activity of the pre-race Holman-Moody operations. Moody was so close-mouthed with strangers and so edgy he seemed to want to fade into the wall. He made himself scarce when he came to races, which was not very often.

Ralph Moody

John Clarence Holman was born in Nashville, Tenn., November 9, 1917, but grew up in California. At 15 the death of his father forced John to work to help support the family. What he apparently remembered most vividly about that period was that he took piano lessons after work to get the credits for a high-school diploma. He wanted to go to college, but there was neither money nor any chance at the kind of scholarship that would make that possible.

Lack of schooling did not dull Holman's ambition to attain the good life—and he attained it, a fantastic brick and wood mansion on the banks of the Catawba River, a private airplane, and other accoutrements of wealth. He had used his native intelligence to build on his experience.

Salvage bought cheap in Texas brought premium prices in California, and Holman made a comfortable, if difficult, living this way for part of the thirties. Checks cashed in Texas took 3 days at least to clear in California because they were transported by train. Holman paid by check, loaded his truck with salvage, then raced the train bearing his check over the 1,700-mile route. He always covered his checks because disposing of the salvage was virtually automatic. After spending World War II as a tool and die maker and shipyard worker, Holman went trucking again. He once assembled a Mack Truck in the front yard of his home, to the consternation of the neighbors and the delight of his daughter.

In 1952 Clay Smith and Bill Stroppe needed a man who could drive the parts truck in their assault on the Carerra Panamericana in a Lincoln. Holman got the

John Holman

309

job. This was Holman's first exposure to auto racing. He was not impressed; he had to stay ahead of the Lincoln and, after racing trains to California, that was easy.

However. following the 1952 race in which Lincoln won its class, Holman went to work fulltime for Stroppe and Smith as a parts man and mechanic in the Long Beach shop. He helped bring Lincoln its 1953 and 1954 victories, then continued as Stroppe aligned himself with Mercury's stock-car racing effort. He continued to work for Stroppe for two years after Smith lost his life in a freak accident at DuQuoin, rising to an administrative post.

Then in 1956, partly with the blessing of Ford Motor Company, Holman moved to Charlotte and the DePaolo stock car operation. Nine years later Holman-Moody bought out Stroppe as a West Coast base—only to sell it back to Bill later when Ford began to cut back on competition. By that time Holman had found other ways of making money—like government projects concerning air pollution. John permitted himself a supreme luxury. He had the wood from giant redwoods transported crosscountry to help construct his palace on the Catawba River.

Ralph Moody, Jr., was as different as can be imagined from the expansive Holman. He was one year younger than Holman, born and raised in Massachusetts. Shortly after finishing high school, Ralph began competing in midgets on New England tracks. Before World War II he was one of the superstars of midget and sprint racing in that area and, in addition, operated 2 speed shops. After the war, determined to find a better climate, he moved his speed shop to Fort Lauderdale and almost immediately became involved in NASCAR as well as independent racing. In 1952 he was 55th in NASCAR modified standings, and in 1954 he rose to 34th. In 1956, his best year in Grand Nationals, he finished 8th. He was certainly never a superstar, with only 5 Grand National victories to his driving career credit. However, he spent 1957 driving USAC stocks before returning southward.

But Moody was one of the most respected of the early NASCAR drivers because his peers seemed to sense that if he could have spent more time driving and less on the mechanical end, he would have been a greater threat. He stopped driving in 1961, by which time Holman-Moody was on its way to huge success. Moody was credited with developing and improving the drivers who raced under the H-M banner. His most famous protégé was Fred Lorenzen, but he is credited with teaching Dan Gurney how to handle a stock car.

Holman-Moody drivers read like a catalog of racing stars, from Fireball Roberts to Cale Yarborough and David Pearson. And of course, H-M was the fountainhead for Ford equipment for many other Ford-supported teams, not only in stock cars, but also with the successful Ford effort to win the Le Mans 24-hour race and the much less successful effort to become competitive in

the Canadian-American Challenge Cup. At one time Holman had hoped to produce his own line of sports cars (powered by Ford, of course), but that was one idea that went glimmering. Holman-Moody boats have been quite successful in marine racing.

PADDY HOPKIRK

Irishmen must have endurance, as well as talent and skills, beyond those of ordinary men. Ask any Irishman, and he'll tell you about it. A case in point is Paddy Hopkirk, who certainly must be one of the great modern rallyists. Rallying—at least the European style—requires talent and skill and more than ordinary endurance. Hopkirk has all of these. Born in Belfast, April 14, 1933, Paddy made his living running automobile accessory and driving school businesses. But he also turned a fast quid behind the wheel of BMC automobiles, principally in rallies, although he participated in long-distance races and even in single-seater racing from time to time.

He started as a rallyist while studying engineering at Trinity College, Dublin, in 1950, raced for the 1st time 4 years later in a TR-2 in a Wicklow club race. In a TR-3 he won the Circuit of Ireland Rally in 1958, the 1st of 3 outright victories in that attention-getter. His other victories were back-to-back in 1961–62, both scored in a Rapier, the same car in which he was 3rd in the rugged French Alpine Rally in 1959 and 1961. The following year he was 2nd overall in the RAC's British Rally and

3rd in the Monte Carlo. As a result, he was signed by BMC at the end of 1962, and it was with the big Abingdon-on-Thames carbuilder that he scored his greatest successes.

Paddy, a jazz pianist, pushed the Mini-Cooper and Mini-Cooper S to its greatest heights in such rallies as the Monte Carlo (2nd in class, 1963; outright winner, 1964; 1st in class, 1965) and the Tour de France (outright touring category, 3rd scratch, 1st handicap, 1963), and in such races as Le Mans (1st in class, 1963) and Spa/Francorchamps' 24-hour race (1st in class, 1964). He also drove such other BMC products as the MGB (highest-placed British car, 1964, Le Mans) and the Austin-Healey 3000 (1st in class, 6th overall, 1963 Liège-Sofia-Liège Rally). Hopkirk raced in or rallied in Australia, Africa, and even North America (both Riverside and Sebring, his best finish at the latter being 2nd in class in 1965 with an Austin-Healey Sprite). In 1964 the BRDC awarded the likeable Orangeman the John Cobb Memorial Trophy for his successes in British cars that season. The single-seater racing? In 1962 when Paddy was 29, and possibly more venturesome, he drove a Lotus 18 Formula Junior car to a creditable 3rd in the Dunboyne Trophy Race. He probably didn't like being alone in a car that much, though. Irishmen like to talk a bit, and he probably missed a navigator's patient ear.

TED HORN

In the infrequent occasions when Eylard Theodore Horn came to the low row of garages in Paterson, N. J., called Gasoline Alley, he drew an admiring crowd of the adult citizens of that Eastern mecca of race preparation, as well as gangling pre-teens, to whom he was a demigod. Posty and Doc Greene and other nearly-forgotten garage proprietors would talk to the great man, who, maybe, just maybe, would let some awe-struck child of middle-class America get some water or bring him a tool he had left a few yards away. Unfailingly he would thank the favored youngster, thus striking a blow for good manners that no parent or teacher could. He would even tell the story of his latest race, not directly to the youngsters, but including all details that a seasoned mechanic would have known anyway. It was a learning experience under the best of teaching conditions. Ted Horn was an extraordinary person as well as a superb driver.

In 1947 at old Lakewood Park, a suicidal dirt track in Atlanta, Horn was en route to winning the 2nd of his 3 straight AAA crowns. As always, he was immaculately attired, and his car was equally immaculate, repolished after the dirt of every practice. He tried valiantly, but he did not win that day, just as he was never to win at Indianapolis Speedway where his Maserati entries often were the favorites. Yet always, Horn remained unfailingly courteous, almost unflappable.

Horn was a rebel as a youth, so committed to auto-mobile racing that he risked estrangement from his family for the sport—he always spoke of it that way even when he earned a comfortable living from it. Born in Cincinnati, February 27, 1910, Horn was supposed to be a musician like his father. Sent to an expensive private school, he studied music, art, and poetry, demonstrating some early talent in those fields. All his life he liked to read poetry and, if pressed at some private gathering, he could be persuaded to play the piano.

The Horn family moved to California to be closer to burgeoning Hollywood. Music to Ted was not the sound of piano or violin; he was tuned to the noise of racing cars. At 15 he earned $12 picking peaches, and he spent it on a jalopy. A year later, unknown to his parents, Ted began racing. His first ride in a Rajo-engined midget ended abruptly when he locked wheels with another car and plunged through the fence at the Banning, Calif., track.

At 18 he finally got the nod to appear for a tryout in a car at Ascot Speedway. His parents had looked with disapproval at this hobby, but Horn had told them there was no real danger. The tryout was a disaster. He locked up, slid and demolished 100 feet of guard rail. At this point his father laid down the law, pointing out as an aside that Ted had failed on the stepping stone to the major leagues. Horn sadly became a photoengraver and stayed in that job for 4 years. But in 1931 he got himself another ride at Ascot. He lasted 2 laps, crashed, and was hospitalized with a crushed foot and back burns. Horn was absolutely adamant about racing. When he recovered, he bought the old Rajo of his origi-

nal Ascot trial, entering himself in an Oakland race. He finished—last. The following month he set a record at Ascot—the slowest lap of the meeting.

He was a laughing-stock to most of the drivers and some of the fans, but Chet Gardner, another of the gentleman school of drivers, took him aside and began to instruct him on how to drive Ascot. Ted listened and improved his lap times by 3 full seconds. Yet for the 1931 season he was 83rd and last among AAA Contest Board drivers. In 1932 he was 20th. In 1933, Horn had earned 2nd in Class B racing, mostly at Ascot. Class B was for Ford-engined vehicles. Horn also had established the kind of rivalry that makes for newspaper headlines and partisan fans. Rookie Rex Mays provided the opposition, and their wheel-to-wheel duels made the show during those depression years.

Horn campaigned sprints and midgets in 1934 and received his first Indianapolis chance from Harry Miller, the engine designer who had created a front-wheel drive Ford V-8 special for the 1935 edition of the 500. Ted lasted until lap 145, when he retired with steering trouble. His performance, however, earned him a ride in the Harry Hartz entry on the AAA Trail. At Lewiston, Pa., a section of splintered railing crushed his shoulder and collar bone, threatening the usefulness of his right arm. He spent the year regaining its use, but he was ready for Indy in 1936. His drive in the 1936 race to 2nd behind Lou Meyer established Horn as a major-leaguer. This was in the days of 2-man cars and a limitation on fuel consumption. Ted averaged over 14 m.p.g., made an extra pit stop, yet still held 2nd.

He entered the Vanderbilt Cup race at Roosevelt Raceway, N.Y., but "Baby," the Miller front-wheel drive converted for road racing, failed in the early laps. There were so few events on the AAA trail that, although he didn't race the rest of the season, Horn finished 3rd for the AAA crown. In 1937, the last with 2-man cars, Horn took 3rd at Indianapolis despite an extra pit stop because Baby chewed up tires. The Vanderbilt Cup also was a rerun, Baby failing with engine trouble. But Horn barnstormed the nation until September when a crash at Nashville Fairgrounds hospitalized him. Horn rebuilt the car and set fast-mile for any AAA track up to that time—38.14 seconds—on the dirt at El Centro, Calif. That was virtually Baby's last fling, since Horn was to purchase another Miller Special for the dirt track season.

In 1938 and 1939 at Indianapolis, he had 4th-place finishes and, sponsored by a piston ring company, won 6 mains and 12 of 18 heats on the dirt with his Miller the latter year. Horn had changed; he was thinking about the future and about what he wanted from automobile racing. He founded Ted Horn Engineering, with a machine shop to rebuild or repair his own and other race cars. He became a stickler on physical conditioning and eschewed smoking and drinking. He wanted to be national champion. Meanwhile, there was the Ted Horn

Racing Team—Tommy Hennershitz, Rex Records, and Bob Sall—campaigning Ted's cars on Eastern and Midwest tracks.

In 1940 at Indy he set 20 track records yet, when the race was flagged after Wilbur Shaw took the checker, had another 4th. The question of whether Shaw would have won that race is problematic since the caution flag went out because of rain at 150 laps when Shaw's opposition was forming for the final 50 laps and positions didn't change thereafter.

There was another 3rd place in 1941 when Horn switched to a mount owned by millionaire Joel Thorne and prepared by Art Sparks. Then came Pearl Harbor and the 31-year-old Horn tried desperately to enlist in the Armed Forces. Old racing injuries made him unacceptable. He spent the war years at Ted Horn Engineering doing subcontract machine shop work, but made no real effort to build the business as others did in this period. His business was racing and he wanted that national championship. When AAA racing resumed in 1945 at Essex Junction, Vt., Ted Horn was there. He took the pole, his heat, and the main en route to 7 victories in 7 tries. If AAA had crowned a champion, it would have been Horn.

In 1946 the long Mays-Horn rivalry resumed at Indy. Rex had won the AAA title in 1940 and 1941 and wanted to become that organization's first triple titlist. Ted had other ideas. He was in a Maserati 8CTF, the 1940 Indy winner under Shaw, and he was considered one of the favorites. Mays lasted 25 laps, and Horn spent 12 minutes in the pits plagued by a faulty magneto (Italian GiGi Villoresi, also in a Maserati, suffered from the same problem). Yet he battled back to finish 3rd. The points were very important because they helped him to his goals, the national title and that big number one on his machine. In 1947 he put the Maser on Indy's pole; then, because of magneto trouble again that necessitated 4 pit stops to winner Mauri Rose's one, he finished 3rd. He beat off the challenge of Bill Holland for his 2nd national title.

In 1948 Horn's dirt-track car, Beauty, swept the 38-year-old into Indianapolis on a string of victories. Now it was time for Cotton Henning and the new version of Baby, the reworked Maserati. Horn took the lead early, was 2nd at 300 miles and preparing to challenge Rose when, at the next pit stop, he was told that the engine had sounded as if his bearings were going. Horn had no choice but to slow bceause he wanted that unprecedented 3rd straight national crown and he needed as many points from Indianapolis as possible. He finished 4th, his 10th straight time at 4th or better. But when he clinched that unprecedented 3rd crown with a 3rd place at DuQuoin, Ill., in September, Horn went with his family to Florida for a week. He had a few more contracts to fill and then he would take a long rest. One of these was back at DuQuoin, a full mile of dirt with the most modern steel guard rail.

Horn arrived from Florida, and as was his custom, began methodically checking the car. He asked about the suspension, then the wheel spindles. He asked whether the spindles had been magnafluxed to check for invisible cracks. The mechanic declared that they had not, but that he thought they could easily last another 2 or 3 races. Horn had the choice of withdrawing or racing on the used spindles. He raced. On the 2nd lap a spindle snapped, sending Horn and Beauty careening into the steel guard rail. Ted Horn died 20 minutes after his arrival at the hospital.

RONNIE HOUSEHOLDER

In every major car firm—even the ones that profess to be disinterested in competition—there is a man detailed to keep abreast of the racing scene. The gentlemen working for the "non-competitors" stay very much in the background, keep their eyes and ears wide open, and their mouths shut. The gentlemen working for the firms openly involved in the sport have a much more difficult job, for they must produce winners at the lowest cost and according to public relations guidelines laid down by corporate policy.

For instance, Chrysler Corporation, for whom Ronnie Householder worked, undoubtedly had the engineering skills and the wherewithal to build and test a race car that would be competitive at Indianapolis. But the firm's stated policy had been that racing must be based on the actual product—hence its interest in stock-car racing and in drag racing.

Meanwhile, there was Householder, a man with a gray bristly mustache, a shock of graying hair and a perpetual cigar. He was not the boss of the racing effort; he was the man who made it go. He was one of the shrewdest, most experienced in his business—a rare combination of engineering know-how and driving renown. He had retired the unchallenged king of the outboard-powered midget race car. A native of Southern California, Householder's first car was a 1925 Model T Ford which he worked over and drove in match races on the open road. Loyola Stadium in Los Angeles (no longer in existence) is the track where Householder first saw the midgets race circa 1932. The entire midget race car movement has been a homegrown phenomenon. What Householder saw were tiny single-seaters powered by all sorts of engines. One employed the 2-cycle motor of a washing machine, another cut an airplane engine in half, still others used 2-cycle engines from motorcycles and outboard motors from boats. Householder chose the latter route, installing an Elto 2-cycle outboard in a specially built chassis. When the original driver—whose father built the chassis—wrecked the car several times, Ronnie decided to become a driver.

He won his initial feature at Santa Ana, Calif., because he was started last. Almost every other car in the race was involved in a gigantic pile-up. Officials routed him through the infield, allowing him to build up a 2-lap lead. Such is the serendipity that launches successful careers. Householder drove midgets—outboards and Offenhausers mostly—while studying mechanical engineering at the University of Southern California and while working for an Arizona power company. But he had decided that auto racing could get him the most money quickly if organized on a businesslike basis.

First he built a car of his own chassis design. Second, he came to the Midwest as the "invader," hence the villain, in midget racing. He raced regularly at the Chicago Stock Yards amphitheater, and even toured the East Coast. Then, he made a compact with the Elto outboard people to utilize their engines. At the height of the midget racing boom, around 1936, Householder toured with a team, even employing contract drivers. He owned a huge truck with sleeping accommodations so he could race every night of the week in season and weekend afternoons. Each week he traveled the distance between New York and Salt Lake City, Utah, equal to that between Paris and Moscow. And he won because of better equipment and driving know-how.

Even though it went very fast, the Elto 2-cycle engine was not exactly the easiest engine to maintain for competition. After every race it had to be disassembled, decarboned, and reassembled. Householder beat the problem in several ways. When in the Midwest, he exchanged 8 or 9 Eltos with factory representatives who then did the rebuilding. When in the East, he utilized specialists in tearing down and cleaning the engine as well as young idol-worshipping boys who used to hang around Gasoline Alley in Paterson, N.J., waiting to see Householder, Ted Horn, and other heroes. The boys jumped at the chance to work on a real race car.

Householder was one of the few who realized that racing design can never stand still. He used to start every year with a new set of machines incorporating the experience and the ideas of the previous season. And, like many another midget hero, he shunned Indianapolis for much of his driving career because it just didn't pay to waste that much time at the Brickyard then. He made 3 Indy attempts, finishing 11th in 1937 and winning the pole position the following year in the Sparks-Thorne supercharged 6, but he failed to last. His final attempt came in a vehicle called the Barbasol Shaving Cream Special, one of the first to essay 16-inch wheels in front and 18 inchers aft. Unfortunately the car was designed for 15 inches all around, and the crew didn't have the know-how to compensate in chassis set-up. Ronnie flipped, ending upside down in the creek, and almost drowned. He retired from Indianapolis at once.

Householder raced until World War II, served overseas, and emerged a lieutenant colonel. He came back to racing as a midget car builder, but found himself competing successfully in 1947. He retired as a driver in 1948 to manage his own radio station, but returned to competition in 1955 when he was employed by Chrysler Corporation to monitor a stock-car program and put some pizzazz in the company image. Ronnie was development engineer on several projects including the Plymouth Fury.

When Chrysler moved wholeheartedly back to competition about 8 years later, Ronnie was the man in operational charge—the one who figured out how to make the cars more race-worthy, the one who talked with the Petty forces and their counterparts in other associations to find out their experience, the one who attended the little-publicized meetings with various associations to try to make sure the rules didn't hurt his employer. When Chrysler withdrew from active participation in racing in 1971, he became assistant manager of vehicle performance planning. Retirement loomed ahead in 1973, but he didn't make it. On November 11, 1972, Householder succumbed to cancer in Detroit.

EARL HOWE

Edward Richard Assheton, later to be known as Viscount Curzon, was 44 years old before he started auto racing in 1928. He raced for 11 seasons, became chairman of the BRDC and of the RAC's Competitions Committee, fathered Sally Curzon who became Mrs. Piers Courage, and helped modernize the FIA. The Brabhams and Gurneys of later days should have been ashamed of themselves for retiring before they even reached Earl Howe's beginning age (he was elevated to an earldom soon after taking up racing).

Born in 1884, Howe began racing because he felt an RAC chairman should know some of the problems of the driver to operate effectively. Most of his early racing on the British club level was in a Type 43 Bugatti. The first race was the Essex 6-hour battle at Brooklands in May 1928. The following year he was in the JCC Double-12 at the big British oval. Later he swapped the original Bug for a 2.3-litre Grand Prix car and acquired 2 GP Delages. In a Delage he won the Dieppe 4-hour race at 73.23 m.p.h. and was 3rd in the Dieppe GP in 1931. That same season, Howe and Tim Birkin shared a winning Alfa Romeo at Le Mans at 78.13 m.p.h. There were 4 big starts in 1932. Howe shared an Alfa with Birkin again for the Belgian Touring Car GP and was 3rd. He was also 3rd to John Cobb and George Eyston —the LSR kings—in the Brooklands running of the British Empire Trophy race. In a Delage again the Earl was 2nd in the Dieppe 4-hour voiturette race, and he won the Avusrennen voiturette race in his Delage at 110.00 m.p.h. There also was a momentous crash at Monza when his Delage met a tree.

In 1933 Howe won both the Donington Park Trophy race in his Bug at 60.88 m.p.h. and the Eifelrennen voiturette race in his Delage at 64.40 m.p.h. He was 2nd in the Dieppe 3-hour voiturette, 3rd in the Avusrennen,

both in Delages. The next year Howe had a flock of 3rds, including the Dieppe GP, Donington Park, and South Africa's Grosvenor GP, the latter in an ERA. In 1935 there were no victories, but Howe kept plugging away: 2nd to Robert Benoist in the Picardy GP and 3rd in the Albi GP, Prix de Berne, and BRDC 500-miler with Brian Lewis, and the Tourist Trophy at Ards, Ireland.

Howe's placings continued high in his selected starts for several seasons after that, although victory eluded him. There were 3rds in the 1936 Picardy race, in the BRDC 500 again with Lewis, and a 2nd to Richard Seaman's Delage in the JCC 200-miler. The next season he was 2nd in the Rand GP, was 3rd to two powerful Auto Unions in the Grosvenor GP, but narrowly missed death when the ERA somersaulted in a Brooklands start. He was back on the grid in 1938, was 3rd in the Donington GP and in the 200-miler. Then, at Capetown, Earl Howe, age 54, won the Grosvenor GP at 74.50 m.p.h. It was his last race, the final victory. He lived on to the age of 80, dying with a PC and CBE, and the affection of his countrymen, in July, 1964.

TONY HULMAN, JR.

The president and owner of the Indianapolis Speedway, Anton (Tony) Hulman, Jr., was an unusual Yale man. He helped save America's classic race and America's classic race track, yet he himself was a star in football and track with pole vaulting and hurdling his specialties. Hulman, of Terre Haute, Ind., certainly hurdled a great many problems after Wilbur Shaw convinced him to buy the decrepit, neglected Speedway in 1945. He installed Shaw as president and general manager and with Shaw built up both the race and the physical plant. The Indy purse is now the greatest for a single-day sporting event, and the race—watched by 200,000 plus in person and millions on TV—must be the most profitable attraction in sports. He has paid $1 million purses for years now, and has spent at least $5 million improving the facility.

Hulman assumed the presidency of the Speedway in 1954 when Shaw was killed in a private plane mishap, and installed Sam Hanks as director of racing. Off the track, Tony also managed the fortune and investments first acquired by his grandfather, the late Herman Hulman. Tony helped organize USAC, issuing the call for the Indianapolis meeting that set up the world's most democratic major racing organization. His influence in its policy could not be calculated for obviously the organization would not have survived its gestation period without Indianapolis.

At 9 A.M. Memorial Day, 1946, he nervously headed for the track. Despite the optimism of Shaw, Tony was worried that the big prewar crowds wouldn't show up, and the closer he got the more worried he became. "I was halfway down Kessler Boulevard, riding with a friend of mine, and there wasn't a soul," he recalled. "My heart sank. It was a beautiful morning too. Then we hit one of the cross highways, and it was so mobbed we could not get across. I never saw anything like it. Those cars were stacked up for miles and the radios were blaring and the people just sitting around eating and drinking and playing cards. I remember there was a 2-headed cow being shown. We tried another way around and ran into the same thing. Finally we went through a field and tried shooting up the shoulders of a road about 2 miles away from the track. 'Where the hell d'you think you're going?' someone shouted, and then they were all on us. 'To the races, we got tickets,' we said. 'Well, ain't that just too bad, so have we,' they roared back. I started breaking out in perspiration because it was close to starting time, and then a policeman came over. I finally had to tell him I had an interest in the track, so he let us go ahead. I guess it was the first time there were really as many people there as was claimed. We've never had less. Not even in 1956 when it rained so hard for 2 days before the race we thought we'd have to quit."

Hulman was a deceptive man. He didn't look or act shrewd even though he was. During an astonishing financial and sporting career, Hulman increased a tidy family fortune 20-fold by always demonstrating "a genius for knowing what people want," as one writer put it. Though the nucleus of the business was the 100-year-old general wholesale firm, Hulman and Company, which sold everything from baking powder to catcher's mitts, he owned many other properties, from midwestern gas companies and breweries to refineries and real estate. He bought Indy partly because of Indiana chauvinism, partly because it brought back his youth and partly because it was an excellent business investment. But business was not the most vital consideration because Hulman refused to buy Churchill Downs, site of the Kentucky Derby, at an equally attractive price.

His athletic career off the track was equally astonishing. Virtually a one-man team in prep school, he was a pole vaulter, broad jumper, high jumper, shot-putter, and hurdler, and there were afternoons when he won a score of points in 3 or 4 events. In 1919 he soared above 12 feet in the pole vault, put the shot around 40 feet, broad-jumped 22, ran the 120-yard high hurdles in 16 seconds and the 220 lows in 27. That year he was named to the All-America Scholastic Team of the Amateur Athletic Union. At Lawrenceville he played intramural baseball and basketball, and in his senior year at Worcester, varsity football. He was one of the early Yalemen to win 7 letters. In his freshman year he brought home 10 medals for pole vaulting and hurdling, and the following season he was a member of the mixed Harvard-Yale team that defeated Oxford and Cambridge in a special track meet in Boston, a victory that was reversed 2 years later in Wembley, England, though Hulman won his event, the high hurdles.

His emergence as a football star did not come until his junior year, when he was named on the all-Big Three team. In his last year, despite being eclipsed by men like Century Milstead, he was known for his downfield speed and his defensive play. This 1923 team, under Tad Jones, was undefeated in 8 games. Hulman also was a recognized virtuoso as a deep sea fisherman. For 5 years, starting in 1948, he became a member (once captain) of the 7-man United States team that participated in the International Tuna Cup matches on Soldier's Rip, 10 miles off Wedgeport, Nova Scotia. During a morning practice off Nova Scotia in 1949, Hulman brought in 2,000 pounds of tuna (3 fish) which earned him the nickname of "One Ton Tony." In the competition that year, he landed a 580-and a 525-pounder, which helped the United States take 1st place from Brazil, 7,591 to 5,920 in total pounds caught. In 1956, as a token of his own years of fishing off Wedgeport, he donated the Hulman Cup to the annual winner of an intercollegiate fishing competition there, and, fittingly enough, Yale won the first event.

Hulman married a hometown girl, the former Mary Fendrich. They had one daughter, Mari, who for a while owned race cars, and married Elmer George, a race driver.

DENIS HULME

Versatility in a racing driver is highly prized. If you can say anything about New Zealand's rough-and-ready Denis Hulme, it is that he was among the more versatile drivers in the world. Consider his credentials: a World Championship in Formula 1 Grand Prix racing, 2 titles in the fast and furious Canadian-American Challenge Cup series for Group 7 cars (as fast as the GP machines), Indianapolis Rookie of the Year, a consistent sports car winner when he drove them, and a winner in just about any kind of 4-wheeled vehicle you could name. Hulme didn't do just one thing at a time. In May and June of 1967, for example, Hulme won the Monaco GP, his first *grande épreuve* victory ever on May 1st; the rest of the month he zipped back and forth between Europe and America, testing and qualifying for the Indianapolis 500, which he drove Memorial Day weekend and finished 4th and Rookie of the Year. And then came Le Mans, one of the most demanding races in the world, in which he shared a Ford GT Mk. 4 during the 24-hour race. Denis set a fastest-lap-ever mark of 147.894 m.p.h. (tied by Mario Andretti in another GT Ford), before the car quit the race.

But Hulme had one fault, and it was a big one. He was content to be the perfect team man. If the team leader said to finish 2nd, he finished 2nd. He partnered Jack Brabham for years in the GP series, and Hulme was perfectly content to let the boss win a lot of races he might have taken. He partnered Bruce McLaren in the CanAm, and the story was again the same, except that McLaren had a policy of alternating wins just to keep spectator interest up. On his own, without a partner to worry about, Hulme proved a fast driver.

Denis Clive Hulme claimed to have started driving one step out of the cradle, in his case at the age of 8 when he borrowed the family Chevrolet for some unofficial practice. Born in the town of Nelson on New Zealand's South Island, June 18, 1936, Denis was raised in the town of Te Puke on the North Island, the son of a World War II Victoria Cross winner and trucking contractor, Clive Hulme. The chunky future GP driver was brought up in an atmosphere dominated by trucks and cars, so it was natural that the obtained an official driver's license as soon as eligible at 16. He started hillclimbing when he was 19.

Denny raced an MG TF 1500 twice in 1957 and won his first race at Ardmore, then switched to an MGA before moving into a single-seat racing car, a 2-litre Cooper-Climax, early in 1959. He gained immediate notice by driving at Levin in his bare feet, claiming this gave him a better "feel" for the unfamiliar car. That winter the Cooper was thoroughly rebuilt, and early in 1960 Denny and George Lawton, another Kiwi driver, diced back and forth for a year's sponsorship in Europe by the New Zealand International GP Association. In the end, both boys were sent to England to drive twin black and silver 1.5-litre Coopers in 1960 Formula 2 competition. Hulme's skills also were tapped in Formula Junior with the New Zealand Racing Team's new Cooper-BMC car, with his best race in this underpowered vehicle an outright win at the Pescara FJ Grand Prix. He had to wear shoes by then.

Towards the end of the 1960 season, Ken Gregory's Yeoman Credit Team signed the two New Zealanders for some Formula 1 racing. Lawton, being more experienced by several years, was given the primary assignment, but before he could try out the 2.5-litre machine he was killed in a Danish F2 race, and the assignment passed to Hulme. Though shaken by his friend's death just a week earlier, Denny made his F1 debut at Snetterton and finished 5th. Reg Parnell lent him one of the Yeoman 2.5-litre cars that winter for use in New Zealand, and he proceeded to win his own national title with 4 victories in 5 races.

Boak in Europe in 1961, Hulme was faced with a problem. F2 was finished, and FJ was uninviting. Still, he had to keep racing, both to perfect his skills and to keep his name before those who could give him a better ride. Rebuilding a FJ Cooper, Denis fitted a Ford Martin engine, but this car never was a real contender (Denis's best finish was a 2nd at Messina), so the 1961 European season was wasted. At Le Mans, Hulme and Angus Hyslop brought at Abarth 850 home 14th overall and 1st in its class, despite driving 12 of the 24 hours without a clutch. However, Jack Brabham of Australia

asked Hulme to join his Chessington shop as a mechanic and part-time driver. In addition to paying the bills, the job gave Hulme a chance to rebuild his Cooper, bringing it up to current specifications. Hulme spent 1962 racing this car and an underpowered Ken Tyrrell Cooper-BMC FJ. He also entered a Brabham-Ford FJ car that year at the Crystal Palace meeting, proving himself fastest in practice, but finishing 4th in the race itself.

Brabham was impressed enough, however, to give Hulme another ride at Brands Hatch near the year's end, and here Denis lapped at unofficial record speed in practice, then won with an official lap record clocking. It was the initial Brabham FJ car victory ever, and Hulme was signed to drive the Brabham Junior throughout 1963. He won 6 of 14 races, came in 2nd to Peter Arundell on 4 other occasions, and set 5 different FJ course lap records. Brabham took Hulme to the new Tasman Series in a 2.5-litre F1 car that winter, and Denis immediately served notice that he was a comer by defeating favored Bruce McLaren in the Levin season's opener. Hulme was 2nd at Pukekohe and Brisbane, and 3rd at Wigram and Christchurch. He also married a Te Puke girl with the enchanting name of Greeta.

Back in England again with Brabham's Racing Department, Denis built up his own F2 car and promptly won his initial major victory in these machines at Clermont-Ferrand. He finished as runner-up to Brabham himself in the French-sponsored F2 series. The lack of such competition in the previous 3 seasons certainly slowed Hulme's development. In 1964 Hulme got to only 15 events, but he was kept busy caring not only for his own car but his boss's, too, whenever Jack felt like taking a F2 ride. Cooper Cars attempted to lure him away from Brabham, but Denis loyally held on.

In 1965 Denny really got going in the Repco Brabham-Climax BT8 and never was beaten in his class with this car. He won the Tourist Trophy and notched several lap records. At Monaco he had his World Championship F1 introduction (in a Brabham-Climax, of course) and finished 8th. In the French GP Denny advanced to 4th, but a broken alternator knocked him out of the British GP. At Zandvoort Hulme finished 5th, but at Nurburgring a split fuel tank retired Denny's car, and at Monza a broken front suspension kayoed him. Hulme accumulated 5 points for a 10th-place tie in the World Championship standings that season and advanced to 4th in the 1966 season with 18 points. He was 2nd in the British GP and 3rd in the French, Italian, and Mexican races. Denny also won his 2nd straight Tourist Trophy in a Lola T70, was 2nd with Ken Miles at Le Mans (on team orders, for they could have won) and just about unbeatable in the Lola-Chevrolet. In F2, he shared honors with Brabham, taking 2nd behind Jack, or winning when Jack wasn't there at the end with the Brabham-Honda.

Next came 1967, and with it, a World Championship. Driving a BT24 Repco-Brabham, Denis led the South African GP opener until three-quarters of the race was over and brake trouble hit his car. Still, he finished 4th, and he had the day's fastest lap. At Monaco, he won his 1st championship race. In the Dutch GP, he battled Chris Amon and won 3rd. Retired on the 14th lap of the Belgian race, Hulme came back with 2nds in the French and British Grands Prix. In that French race, the gearshift knob came off in the 2nd lap, but Denny pressed on. At race's end, his hand was cut and bleeding, but he shrugged it off, as he often did hurts and injuries that would affect less rugged drivers. Brabham won that race, Jim Clark the British GP.

Denis came back to win the German GP, with Brabham 2nd. Retired in the Italian race, he clinched his title with 3rds at the U.S. and Mexican races, Clark and Graham Hill finishing before him at Watkins Glen, Clark and Brabham at Mexico City. Hulme had amassed 51 points, with Brabham 2nd in the championship tables with 46. For once, Denny hadn't stepped aside. Away from F1, he trailed Bruce in the CanAm series, McLaren taking the title in an M6A identical to Hulme's. It was the year of the 4th place finish at Indy and that fastest-ever lap and retirement at Le Mans, but nothing could surpass the championship.

In 1968 Denis was 3rd in F1 to Graham Hill and Jackie Stewart. He had left Brabham at last, moving over to partner McLaren in GP racing as well as the CanAm. For South Africa Hulme had a McLaren-BRM, in which he finished 5th, and for the rest of the series, he drove a McLaren-Ford M7A. Graham Hill nipped Hulme in the Spanish GP, and Denny was 5th at Monaco. After retirements in the Belgian and Dutch races, he was 5th in the French GP, 4th in the British, and 7th in the German races. Victories followed back-to-back in the Italian and Canadian Grands Prix. In the Monza battle (one of Hulme's toughest) only 6 cars finished out of 20 starters. The Canadian victory tied Hulme with Hill for the world title, leaving everything up to the final races in the United States and Mexico.

A whole series of mechanical troubles hit Hulme at Watkins Glen, and finally he crashed the car. Hill, meanwhile, finished 2nd, and it was all over early in Mexico when the McLaren again crashed and Hulme watched as Hill won the race and the championship. Away from the GP wars, Hulme won the non-title Silverstone F1 race and was 3rd in the Race of Champions. In the CanAm, in which he drove the powerful McLaren M8A, powered by a Chevrolet engine, Denis won the Brainerd, Minn., and Edmonton, Canada, openers—with Bruce McLaren 2nd in both; then he was 2nd himself to John Cannon at Laguna Seca, Calif. McLaren won Riverside, Calif., Hulme was 5th. And the finale in Las Vegas, Nev., went to Denny. Hulme was CanAm champion.

If anything, the CanAm assumed even greater importance in the Kiwi's driving career beginning in 1969, when he finished 2nd to McLaren again. In GP racing, his car was not as competitive as it might have been. In 1969–70, Hulme won only one race, the Mexican GP of 1969, beating Jacky Ickx by 2.56 seconds. In an improved McLaren M14A, he had a 2nd to Brabham in the 1970 opener, the South African GP, but these were his top finishes those 2 GP seasons. There were 11 starts in 1969, Hulme finished 7 of them. There were 9 starts in 1970—Denny missing 2 GP's with serious hand burns acquired while practicing for Indy (the fire also wiping out that race for him)—and Hulme finished 6 of these.

But in CanAm racing, his M8B won 5 races in 1969, was 2nd in 5 others. The following year, McLaren was dead, and Denis won 6 races in the M8D—in 2 strings of 3 victories each—to amass 132 points (highest ever in the series) and win by a long margin. Hulme was team leader, partnered with Peter Gethin, who was 3rd in the final standings.

In 1971 Hulme was partnered by a new CanAm racer, Peter Revson, who proceeded to dominate the series, although Denis won twice. He didn't win any events in the GP world, his best finish being a 4th in Canada, where he captured fastest lap honors in a rain-shortened contest. There were 4 other low finishes, 5 other retirements. Hulme had 9 points, tying 4 others for 9th place in the standings. In 1972, though, Hulme returned to his winning GP form, in fact leading the series after capturing the South African race when Stewart's Tyrrell-Ford died in mid-race. Jackie was supposedly a rival on the F1 courses, but a teammate in the CanAm, the Scotsman replacing Revson on Team Mc-

Laren, but ulcers laid Stewart low and Revson was lured back. McLaren was sorely challenged by Porsche Can-Am cars, and Hulme ended tied for 2nd with Milt Minter after victories at Mosport and Watkins Glen.

In 1973, Denis won his 1st pole in the latest McLaren in the South African GP, but pitting to change a damaged wheel, he finished only 5th, but with high hopes and no sign of quitting the racing wars.

JIM HURTUBISE

James Hurtubise, born December 5, 1932, at North Tonowanda, N.Y., weaned on modified stock cars, was 1960 Indianapolis Rookie of the year, winner at Sacramento in 1959, at Langhorne in 1960, and at Springfield in 1961 and 1962. This was the man who was one of the first to go 150 m.p.h. at Indy—Hurtling Herky, the epitome of the "charger." A terrible crash and fire came at Milwaukee in a stock-car race in August 1964. Herky was flown to the Army Burn Center in Texas to save his life. He recovered but the doctors doubted if he would drive even a passenger car again. Hercules, all 69 inches of him, disagreed. Jim Hurtubise was fighting a battle like no other in his life; he was trying to return to the sport he loved, the business he knew; he was trying to prove himself. His hands were raw, red and bony. He wore gloves most of the time and it must have been painful just to grip the steering wheel. Race cars are hard to steer but Hercules Hurtubise said simply, "I can get the job done." At Trenton Fairgrounds, a mile paved oval in New Jersey, in early 1965, Hurtubise was driving a championship car and he helped make the race, challenging for the lead, until his car let him down. When it was over, the little man was too exhausted to keep the pain from his face. His hands hung limp at his sides; he could not straighten the fingers. "They're hurting less all the time," he mumbled as if he were trying to convince himself.

He came all the way back. Only 14th in Championship Trail points for the year, Jim won the Milwaukee 250 stock car race, leading from the 64th mile on in a Norm Nelson Plymouth. He held up a gloved hand at the end, flexing the fingers slightly as if to say, "See, the hands are coming back, too. I'll be in top shape again soon." Others had faith, too. The Tombstone Life Insurance people gave him his 2nd ride in a row at Indianapolis. Herky demolished a new Halibrand in a spectacular crash during the first weekend of qualifying, then was given a Granatelli Novi that lasted one lap in the race before the transmission failed.

Except for qualifying, Indy was not kind to the upstate New Yorker. He finished but one race, in 1962, driving the Jim Robbins Special to 13th place. In every other race the car did not stand up for him. In 1960 a

con rod cracked, in 1961 it was a burned piston, in 1963 an oil leak and in 1964 the oil pressure left mysteriously. Hurtling Herky came back to Indianapolis again and again with no success. In 1965 it was a broken transmission on lap 1, then overheating in 1966, and a burnt piston in 1968. The string continued at Ontario and Pocono with an accident and a blown engine in 1970 and 1971 respectively. There was only one thing certain; as long as he raced, Hurtling Herky went as fast as he could as long as he could.

DICK HUTCHERSON

The man in David Pearson's pit looked lean and hard and except for the fact that he happened to have a torque wrench in his hand, might have been another driver. Actually he was another driver, a man who retired voluntarily to become the chief mechanic on the Holman-Moody Ford of David Pearson. But this was no ordinary driver; this was a man who had had enough talent to win the 1967 Dixie 500 at Atlanta International Raceway; this was a man who was good enough to be tapped by the moguls at Ford Motor Company as a team driver in NASCAR when money was no object.

Why did Dick Hutcherson retire to the role of chief mechanic? Part of it was that very same motor car company's realignment of its racing policy, but a man determined to be a driver would have made do with lesser equipment until he could find a sponsor again. Although he never said so publicly, part of it must have been that driving a race car was just another job to Richard Leon Hutcherson, and when a different job came along, a respected and well paid job without the risks of driving, Dick Hutcherson took it. Successful off-track activities also can color a man's thinking. While he was driving, however, Hutcherson was a contender, a man who could run with the best that NASCAR had to offer, maybe a mite cautiously, but a contender nevertheless.

Keokuk is a prosperous Iowa farm town that for some reason has produced a remarkable number of fine racing drivers. Most of these compete in IMCA, and that is where Hutcherson matured as a competitor. There is a dirt track at Keokuk that conducts some of the finest modified stock car racing in the Midwest. It was there that Richard Leon Hutcherson, born November 30, 1931, began racing in 1956. After a year as runner-up in 1957, he became track champ the following year, then began to campaign in IMCA in a Pontiac. As a rookie he placed 2nd in the season point standings, dropped to 3rd in 1960, moved up to 2nd in 1961 and 1962 with Fords, then won 2 straight season championships, garnering 60 victories en route with the Dearborn cars.

NASCAR however, pays much better even for its smaller races, and Richard, a rather handsome blond fellow, came South to seek his fortune at the behest of Ford Motor Company in a Holman-Moody car. A cautious man, he made trial runs of 4 early-season races in 1964. He set a qualifying record at Greenville, S.C., in his first start, but was sidelined with a minor mechanical failure. He finished 2nd at Hillsboro for his best effort. In 1965 Hutcherson came down South full-time and immediately served notice that he was to be reckoned with. He waged a battle for the Grand National season crown with Ned Jarrett that lasted into September. The 1965 Southern 500 proved the turning point, when Jarrett won and Hutcherson finished 19th because of vapor lock.

"Ned's been a big help to me, especially in getting the hang of drafting," said Hutcherson, speaking of the tow a driver can get by moving into the slipstream of the car ahead of him. "He went out on the track when I was practicing and really worked with me. It's a strange sensation when you find yourself drafting another car at high speed for the first time. I like to drive on the big tracks. It's mostly a matter of gaining experience. That first NASCAR year, I know I felt a lot more confident for the Firecracker 400 in July than I did at the Daytona 500 in February. The main differences between IMCA and NASCAR as far as I can see is the major tracks and the variety of plants we have to run. We go from 2.5-mile asphalt to quarter-mile dirt. It requires a lot of work getting set up and running all

the races. It is hard to get all the little refinements completed.

"In running IMCA, most of the tracks were half-mile dirt and once you had your car set up there wasn't much to do if the car wasn't torn up," Hutch continued. "NASCAR offers more money. I won $30,000 in 1964 as an IMCA driver, including point money. In 1965 I won more than $40,000 by October and there was more than $200,000 in prize money up for grabs during the rest of the season." Hutcherson credited what success he had to Ralph Moody. "He has helped me more than anyone else by explaining all the special tricks of each track we have run. He has been more help than I could say."

In 1967 Hutcherson threw his lot in with Bondy Long and his Bowani racing team. It was a strange year, marked by wild enthusiasm and spasms of alienation between Hutcherson and Long. It was a frustrating year, too, as Hutcherson spent most of his time finishing 2nd to Richard Petty. It looked as if the Dixie 500 at Atlanta International Raceway in Georgia was to be another one of those days. Buddy Baker, Charlie Glotzbach, Cale Yarborough, and Darel Dieringer fought for the lead in the early part of the race, with Hutcherson a factor only after the 2nd round of pits stops began. By that time only 27 of the 44 starters were left and after Baker, who had grabbed the lead back on lap 142, wrecked when a tire blew on the 175th lap there were only 24. It was a race on 2 levels. With both Firestone and Goodyear cutting back on racing commitments because of labor trouble, each qualifier had received only one set of new racing tires tailored to the difficult 1.5-mile Atlanta track. The rest of the tires had to be scrounged from leftovers and other sources. So tire durability was a big factor. Hutcherson, the steady pacer, figured to benefit if he could stay out of trouble. He led briefly; then Richard Petty, looking for an unprecedented 18th Grand National victory, took over.

Dick led again when Petty pitted on the 253rd lap but when, on the 260th lap, Petty caught a draft from fellow Plymouth driver Paul Goldsmith and shot past Paul and Lee Roy Yarbrough, the outcome seemed certain. Richard took Hutcherson on the 4th turn in the next lap as expected. What was not expected was that Richard headed for the pits, his engine blown. From there it was a matter of conserving tires. Only Goldsmith was within striking distance on the same lap as Dick motored home 3 laps ahead of Lee Roy in 3rd place.

Four months later, Hutcherson and Long parted company, dissatisfied with their relationship. And very soon after, Hutcherson became operations manager for Holman-Moody, with special responsibility for Pearson. He assembled a nicely balanced crew and proceeded to give Holman-Moody its first Grand National season champion. And the crew repeated in 1969 to make Pearson only the 2nd 3-time winner of the season crown in

NASCAR history. Lee Petty, Richard's father, had been the first. There were 3 not-so-little Hutchersons and a comfortable home and a chance occasionally to do some carpentering for fun—Hutcherson was a member of the carpenters union—so why not go racing as a chief wrench? After all, a top mechanic can last forever. Hutcherson signed on as manager of the Penske NASCAR Matador, but the agreement broke down in mid-1972.

JAMES HYLTON

For James Harvey Hylton, the ultimate change came on an August day in 1972. That was the day he won his first superspeedway race on the high banks of Talladega International Speedway in Alabama. It came 7 years after he first turned driver and the $24,865 1st prize for some 4 hours driving was more than he could earn from 40 races on the small tracks that spawned him.

In NASCAR racing there are the chargers and hot dogs like Bobby Allison and Richard Petty, and there are the men who run for points, conserving their equipment and finishing as high as racing luck will permit. Hylton had been the king of the conservatives, finishing 2nd in the season standings 1966, 1967, and 1971, and finishing 3rd in 1969 and 1970. And now here at Talladega Hylton had made a decision the day before the Talladega 500. His Pop-Kola Mercury would either last or it would break but he, James Hylton, was going for broke. The points man was going for broke.

Hylton started 22nd in that race but on the 22nd lap polesitter Bobby Isaac was eliminated in a multicar crash. And one by one the hot dogs encountered either engine trouble or tire trouble, so Hylton, the new charger, found himself leading the race time and again until in the final laps it was between himself and IMCA hero Ramo Stott in a Ford. He fought off Stott for 70 laps of the 2.66 mile speedway with the crowd cheering him on. Only 16 of 50 cars were still running at the finish but James Hylton was 30 laps ahead of some of them.

"It makes me feel good to win at Talladega," he said, "because earlier in the season I had suffered a lot of abuse for almost winning the 1st rung of the Winston Cup without a single victory. I guess people know I'm here to race from now on."

James Harvey Hylton, born August 26, 1935, emerged from under Ned Jarrett's Ford in the garage area of Daytona International Speedway to make his debut as a NASCAR driver. He was the chief wrench man on the Bondy Long Ford team and an acknowledged master mechanic. That meant that as long as there was NASCAR auto racing, Jim Hylton could always get a job. But in 1964, more as a lark than seriously, Hylton took the spare car out in 3 Grand National races. He drove a total of 72 miles and won himself $350. He also found out that the old urge that got him into racing in the first place, the urge to drive, had not dulled.

The urge grew all during 1965 when he was chief mechanic on the Dick Hutcherson Ford and, with the aid of a close friend who had retired to Tampa, Bud Hartje, Hylton decided to give up the $12,000 a year mechanic's job and try his luck in 1966 as a NASCAR independent.

Hartje and Hylton pooled their savings and Hartje agreed to become owner and mechanic. Cotton Owens agreed to sell Jim a year-old Dodge on the installment plan, gave him tips on setting the car up, and helped him with high-performance parts. David Pearson, then Cotton's driver, gave him driving tips. So Jim competed in 41 races, getting into the top five 20 times and earning almost $30,000. It was not really enough to support 2 families, but it was a promising beginning—2nd for the NASCAR championships and Rookie of the Year. In fact, he had forced Pearson to ride conservatively the last 3 races of the season to preserve his point crown. In 1967, Hartje found the grueling NASCAR trail too taxing. With the help of fellow citizens in his home town of Inman, S.C., Hylton bought Bud out. He was making a little money, a 3rd at Daytona and 26 out of 46 in the top 5. He even seemed likely to realize his dream of a factory contract as a driver.

Rockingham, N.C., is the smallest of the NASCAR superspeedways, a steep-banked mile track that leaves little margin for error. The American 500 is very nearly the last important superspeedway event of the season, and Hylton, running 2nd to Richard Petty in the point race, was hoping for a very strong race to cinch the factory support. The 5-foot, 9-inch Hylton's immaculately prepared 1965 Dodge had qualified toward the front of the pack, and he had every reason to be confident because the engine had sounded very strong.

Hylton seldom charged at the leaders early in a race. Independents can't afford to overstress and blow engines. He usually was content to stay in contention, hoping for the inevitable dropouts of the factory drivers and of less lucky independants, conserving tires as much as possible, preparing to charge late in the race, if there were a real chance at victory. It was no different at Rockingham. He was coming out of turn 2 in the 55th lap still in contention, setting up to pass Bobby Isaac on the inside, when the Isaac's car blew its engine. Hylton cut to the outside, hoping to avoid the cripple, but he was hit in the rear by Jim Pascal. He just nicked Isaac's car, but it was enough to send his own car sliding toward the outer wall where it bounced, careened down the track, slammed the inside wall, and ricocheted into the line of traffic where a horrified G. C. Spencer slammed into the driver's side. It was a tribute to NASCAR regulations that Hylton survived at all. He was hospitalized with a skull fracture, torn muscles, and possible internal injury.

He recovered. Even the double vision he had when he was released from the hospital subsequently cleared. He told everyone he was going to continue in racing, but when he saw the damaged car he really thought of quitting. It would be like starting over. Then friends again came to his aid. They put up the money to stake him. And the parts subsidy from Dodge came through to further lighten the burden of financing. Jim was back in business—if he could get out on the track and be competitive. There was one way to find out. He loaded his racer onto a truck and drove it across country 3,000 miles to the awesome Riverside road course for the first major event of 1968, the Motor Trend 500. It was at Riverside that Joe Weatherly died, crushed against a boiler-plate retaining wall. It was at Riverside that A. J. Foyt had suffered his most severe accident.

Hylton got his answer quickly. He took several laps at slow speed to familiarize himself with the car and the course, then stomped on it—through the Esses, around past the boiler-plate outside wall into the back end of the course, down the back straight and into the sweeping turns that set up for the front straight or into the pits. Hylton finally rolled in, smiling. He knew his lap time was poor because his reflexes were still dull from the 3-month layoff, but he also knew he could come back. In 1968 there were 41 starts, 28 top-10 finishes and 15 of these in the top 5. There were 52 races in 1969, 39 top-10 finishes and 28 of these in the top 5.

And, finally, in 1970 there was even victory—after 208 Grand National races and 16 finishes in 2nd place. Hylton drove his "last year's" Holman-Moody built Ford to victory lane in the Richmond 500. It was his initial ride in a Ford and came after another victory in the Grand American Citrus 250 at Daytona the previous month. Hylton took the lead on the 341st lap when Bobby Isaac's Dodge pitted to repair an oil leak. He held off a fast-closing Richard Petty, the pole-sitter, who had led much of the race until a battery and a distributor change forced him out of the lead. It was a classic battle of independent and factory driver, with Petty gaining at the rate of a second a lap as the race wore down to its finale. At the checkered flag, Hylton was only half a lap ahead of Petty.

Hylton, Isaac, Petty, and Bobby Allison were then locked in a battle for the 1970 point crown, Isaac finally winning on the last major race of the season at Rockingham with Hylton a very close 3rd.

Hylton said he never expected to leave the sport of automobile racing because, when his driving days were over, there was always the possibility of being a chief mechanic again. The Virginia kid who built chassis for Rex White, who left a top job with Dick Hutcherson to drive, had made his first move in that direction by hiring Cale Yarborough to drive one Pop-Kola car for the latter part of '72. Maybe charging really wasn't Hylton's cup of tea.

JACKY ICKX

Jacky Ickx, a Belgian, and Chris Amon, a New Zealander, formed the driving team for Ferrari cars in 1968. Amon was older, more experienced, the man next expected to win a *grande épreuve,* for he had come close so many times it wasn't funny. But as the cars took the grid for the French Grand Prix, Amon was in the 2nd row and Ickx sat in front of him, 3rd fastest of the qualifiers, next to Jackie Stewart and Jochen Rindt who was on the pole this strange July day.

It was strange because nobody could tell what the weather would be. Ferrari was hedging its bets, as usual; Amon had dry tires, Ickx wets. As it turned out, the choices were the right ones. Amon loathed the rain, and it rained. Ickx did not mind a little rain, and he raced for all he was worth, which was considerable. Troubled as much by his balky Ferrari as anything else, Amon finished 10th, Jacky Ickx, however, came in 1st with World Champion John Surtees and World Champion-to-be Jackie Stewart in his wake. And he did it rather easily, leading for 59 of the 60 laps at Rouen, easing off to 100.44 m.p.h. once the chargers like Pedro Rodriguez (111.82 m.p.h.—fastest lap) eliminated themselves.

Jacques Ickx had been one of Belgium's, if not Europe's, great racing writers and technical experts. On New Year's Day, 1945, he had a son, christened Jacques-Bernard, in Brussels. At the age of 12 Jacky, as the younger Ickx was known, saw his initial automobile race, the revived Belgian GP, which turned into an Alfa Romeo romp led by Jean-Pierre Wimille. He was bored stiff, and begged his father to take him home.

School bored Jacky, too, and he intended to quit as soon as possible until a gentle subterfuge induced him to stay —and also started his competition career. His father bought him a 50 c.c. Zundapp motorcycle, quite natural since Ickx, Sr., once was Belgium's scramble champion, and older son Pascal was already running 2-wheeled time trials.

Winning 8 of 13 starts, Jacky took the European 50 c.c. championship. This should have led to a factory ride with Zundapp, but Ickx was still 2 years under age for Grand Prix cycle racing, so he turned his attention to 4 wheels. The Belgian Zundapp importer was also an agent for Germany's BMW, so a car was forthcoming for hillclimbs and slaloms. In his first event Ickx rolled, hich was not altogether bad since the spectacle was shown over national TV and gained him added prominence (in the way that Sam Posey's accident continually shown on TV when he was an upcoming driver pushed his career). By 1963 Jacky was regularly winning climbs, slaloms, and even an occasional circuit race. In his last climb that year, Ford of Belgium lent Jacky a Lotus Cortina with which he smashed a great many course records, winning a handsome offer from Ford for the 1964 season. Alan Mann put Ickx in 3 rounds of the European Touring Car Challenge series and while in the Budapest GP, Jacky caught the eye of Ken Tyrrell.

Ken was to provide Ickx's first single-seater test ride, but not before 15 months of military service learning to drive tanks intervened. Leaves came regularly to enable Jacky to race Cortinas and Mustangs, his best service-time finish being a 2nd in the Marathon de la Route in a Mustang. The last leave was extended so he could fly over to England for his Tyrrell tryout in a Formula 2 Cooper-BMW at Goodwood. A 3-year contract followed. In 1966 he was racing F2 and F3 simultaneously, taking 2nds in F3 races at Silverstone and Zandvoort, and a 4th at Albi in F2. In the Marathon de la Route, he won again, this time in a Cortina. In a Brands Hatch Group 7 race he won his first time out in a McLaren-Oldsmobile. There was also a Le Mans ride in a GT40 for JW Automotive, shared with Skip Scott.

F2 and enduros took precedence in 1967, with the Matra (now fully sorted out) again his mount in the former and the Mirage in the latter, although Ickx's first Formula 1 drive was that season as well. Driving a Cooper-Maserati at Monza in place of injured Pedro Rodriguez, he finished 6th to earn a single championship point in the season GP standings. In Jacky's only other F1 start in the United States GP, he retired with piston failure. In F2 Jacky won at Zandvoort, Crystal Palace, and Vallelunga, was the 3rd in Eifelrennen and at Enna. He was crowned Europe's F2 champion. In Mirages for John Wyer's successful World Championship effort for Gulf, Ickx shared a Spa 1000 victory with Dick Thompson, also won at Karlskoga and Paris (with Paul Hawkins), and at Kyalami in the South African 9-hour race with Brian Redman.

Tyrrell intended to go into F1 with Matras in 1968 and followed through on that, although the deal did not include the car he had intended for Ickx. Ferrari had been wanting to sign the youthful Belgian, however, and contacted him at the 11th hour, as it were. On New Year's Day, 1968, his 23rd birthday, he sat in a Ferrari on the grid of the South African GP. He worked his way up from 9th to 4th before retiring with a broken oil pipe. Another retirement with ignition failure in Spain was followed by a 3rd in the Belgian GP in a car always seemingly ready to die on him. But only Bruce McLaren and Pedro Rodriguez finished ahead of the youngster. A 4th in Holland was followed by that French GP victory.

In the British GP Ickx was 3rd again behind Jo Siffert, winning one for Rob Walker, and Amon. In Germany Jacky was 4th, in Italy 3rd to Denis Hulme and Johnny Servoz-Gavin. But a practice crash at St. Jovite while readying for the Canadian GP ended any hopes he might have had for the title then, although he stood 2nd in points. He ended up 4th in the standings with 27 points. In sports/prototype racing for Wyer's JW Automotive, Ickx joined with Redman for victories at the BOAC 500 and the Spa 1000, and with Lucien Bianchi for a victory at the Watkins Glen 6-hour race. With Paul Hawkins he was 3rd in the Nurburgring 1000.

Jackie Stewart ran away with the World Championship in 1969. So it did not matter that Ickx had switched from Ferrari to Brabham in F1 because he wished to stay with Wyer in the enduros rather than run Ferraris. Even though the Brabhams left a lot to be desired,

Jacky had a good year; he added 2 more *grande épreuves* to his bag. There were retirements at South Africa, Monaco, and in the United States GP, a 10th is Italy, a 6th in Spain, and 5th in Holland. But there also were a 3rd to Stewart and Jean-Pierre Beltoise in France, and 2nds to Stewart in Britain and to Denis Hulme in Mexico (by a mere 2.6 seconds). Ickx ran 3 fastest laps—at Mexico, Germany, and Canada; in both of the latter he also won the pole and the race. Jacky had 37 points, but Stewart had 63 and the championship.

In a non-title F1 race, the August International at Oulton Park, Ickx beat out Jo Rindt. In enduros he shared a winning GT40 ride with Jack Oliver at both Sebring and Le Mans. Ferrari finally got Jacky for this kind of racing in 1970, and, sharing a car with Mario Andretti—a future F1 teammate—he was 3rd at Daytona. He was 2nd with John Surtees in the Spa 1000, and 5th with Peter Schetty at the Glen 6-hour race.

Ferrari got something more important from Ickx in 1970—their first GP victories since he left them in 1968. Things started slowly with the Ferrari 312B, with retirements in South Africa, Spain, and Monaco, and an 8th in Holland, although Jacky recorded the fastest lap. Two more retirements in France and Britain were frustrating also. Then came another fastest lap in Germany and a 2nd to Rindt. In Austria he won easily, again recording the race's fastest lap; then, after an Italian GP retirement, another victory in Canada. He took the fastest lap again at Watkins Glen, but finished 4th. His 3rd victory in Mexico was accompanied by the fastest lap that day. Rindt, who was dead by then, had accumulated 45 points, but Ickx was 2nd with 40.

Ickx was an odds-on favorite to win his initial World Championship in 1971. After all, he had what seemed to be the car for that season, the Ferrari V-12. But the oddsmakers had not figured on Stewart, nor Stewart's Tyrrell. Ickx was 8th in South Africa as teammate Mario Andretti won. In the Spanish GP he ran the race's fastest lap but finished 3.4 seconds behind Stewart. At Monaco he was 3rd. Victory came in the Jochen Rindt Memorial at Hockenheim, only this was a non-title race. But Holland did count, and Ickx won with a fastest lap and a 94.06 m.p.h. clocking. He was on his way, it seemed. But there were retirements in France (engine), Britain (engine), Germany (suspension), Austria (ignition), and Italy (engine); all in a row. Ickx was 8th in Canada, then the alternator failed in the U. S. GP, although he again ran the day's fastest lap at 117.495 m.p.h. Nineteen points tied him with Siffert for 4th place in the season standings.

Once again in 1972 Ickx was considered a pre-season favorite to contend for the World Championship, and once again he was more or less let down by equipment and by the battle among Stewart, Hulme, and Emerson Fittipaldi. Ferraris retired too many times to create a good chance for a tie. When the car held together, Jacky was still as fast as ever, as witness his victory in the German GP, 2nds back-to-back in Spain and Monaco— as two different races as was possible to plan in 1972— 20 some seconds behind Fittipaldi in the former, 38 seconds or so behind Jean-Pierre Beltoise in the rain-soaked Monte Carlo race. There was a 3rd in Argentina, too, but most of the rest of the starts were disappointments.

Not so in sports car racing, in which Ickx shared victory at the Daytona 6-Hour race with Mario Andretti, then repeated with the American at Sebring, in the BOAC 1000 and at Watkins Glen, and won the Monza 1000 with Clay Regazzoni and the Austrian 1000 with Brian Redman. There was a 2nd at Spa, too, in those all-conquering Ferrari sports cars. Small wonder that even after the first shock announcement that Ferrari would not race in 1973, the initial driver signing disclosed was that of Jacky Ickx, and others followed as it became evident that they all would be back for another try at the big prize, the World Championship.

INNES IRELAND

Robert McGregor Innes Ireland was, of course, a Scotsman who drove English racing cars. Born in Kirkcudbright on June 12, 1930, Ireland grew up with his year-older brother Alan in a happy home; his mother an accomplished singer, his father a veterinary surgeon. A stocky, strong boy, Innes starred at rugby and other sports, but a kindly old lady diverted much of his ener-

gies to automobile competition by giving him a copy of Tim Birken's book *Full Throttle*. At 15 he purchased a 17-year-old motorcycle. He and Alan rode it around the British countryside until Innes acquired an Ariel 500 at the cost of a favorite .22 rifle. By this time his father, who had hoped Innes would be a vet like himself, had acknowledged that mechanics, not medicine, was his younger son's main interest.

In 1948 Ireland's father arranged Innes's apprenticeship to the Aero Division of Rolls-Royce Limited at Glasgow. Later he was moved to the Car Division at London where he lived a Bohemian life aboard a former MTB torpedo boat anchored in Chelsea Reach. His first motor race was in 1952, in the Tim Birkin Memorial Trophy at Boreham where he drove a 4.5-litre Bentley to 4th place. Early the next year he entered the Army, eventually was commissioned and became a paratrooper, serving in Egypt for 18 months. Home again, he married and returned to Rolls-Royce for a time before going into the garage business with a friend, John Mason.

Ireland's competitive urge got him started in local races in 1955. The following year his brother Alan brought along a friend of his, Major Rupert Robinson, who helped inspire and finance a move to big-time racing with a Lotus 11. The first time out in Colin Chapman's little creation he cracked up, but by the end of 1957 Innes had become expert enough to be offered an unofficial berth on Team Lotus for the Swedish Grand Prix. Sharing a car with Cliff Allison, he finished 9th. He won the Brooklands Memorial Trophy for his club racing with a Riley that year.

Early in 1958 David Murray's Ecurie Ecosse gave Innes a D Jaguar at Silverstone, and Ireland was on his way to international ranking. The following season he officially joined Team Lotus, debuting at the Dutch GP at Zandvoort where he finished 4th in a front-engined car. When Graham Hill left the team at the season's end, Innes remained and became the number 1 driver of the new rear-engined cars—while adding Grand Touring competition to his schedule by driving John Ogier's Aston Martins.

After crashing in the tunnel at the 1961 Monaco GP, Innes startled doctors by returning to the racing wars only 5 weeks later. His engine blew up in the Belgian GP return, but he was 4th in the French GP, and followed that with victories in the Austrian and Solitude Grands Prix, the latter his favorite circuit, he later said. These were not championship races, but that fall's United States GP at Watkins Glen was, and Ireland won it convincingly. Despite this and the fact that he had scored Lotus's first GP victory and its first Formula 2 victory as well, Innes was not rehired by Chapman in 1961, the number 1 spot going to Jim Clark who made the most of it. Instead Ireland joined UDT-Laystall, which also raced Lotus Formula 1 cars, although they were inferior to those of the factory team, of course. They fell by the wayside with disheartening regularity in

1961 and 1962. In sports car racing the Scotsman did much better, however, winning the top British races and others at Nassau and Riverside.

It is, perhaps, indicative of his unusual approach to life and auto racing that he was born left-handed. He wore his hair long before it was fashionable, dressed well, and sported a deer-stalker in the pits, a checkered crash helmet, and a Churchillian victory sign, all of which added up to instant recognition by world racing fans when Ireland was around. Despite his lack of top machines—in 1963 he moved to the British Racing Partnership, racing first with Jim Hall, then with Trevor Taylor, until BRP called it quits, then raced a Parnell Lotus-BRM in 1965—he gave it his all, and that was considerable. Ireland's last GP was in Mexico in 1966 in Bernie White's BRM. Innes was one of those rare men on the modern GP circuit, a genuine wit, who made his forays to the racing scenes from a manor house in Wales, often flying his own plane.

CHRIS IRWIN

Baby-faced Chris Irwin was every inch a true professional, with a professional's point of view: "I personally have concentrated on F3," he said at the end of the 1965 season, "because I had a very good chance of winning there. If I were not successful, I would lose interest in motor racing altogether and try to be successful in some other profitable sport or profession. I have started driving Formula 2, and I think I will be successful there, too. I have been learning from the experienced graded drivers around me in that formula, and I will concentrate on it when I am really ready to do so. The same will be said for F1 when the time comes." If Irwin seemed conceited, it was merely that he knew what he wanted to do with his life. Those who knew him saw that beneath this highly professional exterior still beat the heart of a young man who got his thrills out of racing as much as any enthusiastic week-ender.

Christopher Frank Stuart Irwin, born in 1943, kept that zest through a serious crash at Zandvoort in 1964, when a car spun directly into his path. He emerged with nothing more than a few facial scratches while the car was demolished. In 1968, in practice at the Nurburgring, he suffered serious head injuries in another crash, leading to delicate brain surgery and an unfortunate end to a promising career that saw the young man compared favorably with Jackie Stewart.

"Before learning to drive a car in 1959, I also was quite interested in motorcycles," he reminisced. "We had one hidden away at school [the King's School, Canterbury], which I would sometimes take out in the evening, although one had to be extremely careful for fear of being expelled if found out." After Canterbury, Irwin attended the London College of Printing, and, while there, he stepped up his attendance at race meetings. On

October 8, 1961, Chris got his initial competitive ride at Snetterton in Jim Russell's Lotus 18. Other rides with Russell followed without too much success, although he did flash his ability occasionally.

A fellow student at the printing college, Sherry Thynne, lent Chris his Austin-Healey Sprite in 1962 to go racing. The car was strictly stock and it took a while to sort out its engine sufficiently to make it even somewhat competitive. About all Irwin accomplished in 1962 was to gain his FIA international competition license. The following year he purchased a Merlyn 1100-c.c. racer in which he won 4 races and placed quite a few times. He was ready for the big push in 1964.

Chris switched to a Merlyn-Ford F3, driving for the Checquered Flag team. It took a little while to get used to the new vehicle and to get it into the proper tune, but by July he was properly mated to his machine. At the Aintree meeting that month, he set a new lap record and won easily. That was followed by a 2nd at the Warwick Banks in the August Bank Holiday races. In all, Chris won 7 times, finished 2nd 6 times, and took 3rds 3 times, finishing 16 of his 22 starts. In 1965 mechanical troubles and incidents caused by other drivers hit Irwin's racing; he finished only 8 of his 12 F3 races, winning 4, and scoring a pair of 2nds and a pair of 3rds. But 1966 got off well when Chris won the opening race at the Buenos Aires Autodrome in Argentina driving a Brabham-Ford in the Temporada Series.

"F3 has been excellent for me," Irwin maintained. "It enables a driver to demonstrate his ability, and not merely that of his engine. This is especially true because the engine manufacturers have been meting out extremely unbiased treatment to all entrants. If I have any complaint, it is the largeness of the F3 fields, especially at international meetings, so that a good portion of the field is largely inexperienced. Some of these men are lapped two or three times in a race, a dangerous procedure at best."

Dangerous as it was, Irwin kept winning—at Goodwood, twice at Crystal Palace, at Roskilde, Karlskoga, Zandvoort, Zolder, and Brands Hatch. And there were 2nds at Mendosa in Argentina, twice at Silverstone, at Monaco (the most prestigious of F3 races), and Brands Hatch. Monza and Le Mans saw 3rds. Twenty races in all, 9 outright victories, 7 more races in the top 3. In F2 he only started twice, dropped out at Brands, but came in 3rd in the Albi GP, both times in a Brabham-Honda.

On July 16, 1966, Chris got his first Formula 1 start, albeit in a rather decrepit 2.5-litre Brabham-Climax that Brabham kept as a spare to his newer Repco-Brabhams. Irwin finished a creditable 7th in that British GP, directly behind Bruce McLaren. Based on this showing, as well as his highly successful F3 season, Chris was signed for regular F1 rides in 1967. Before the year was out he had also married Charlotte Lucas, sister of Charles, and had set up housekeeping in a Victorian house off Brompton Road in London.

The year 1967 saw a 7th in the Dutch GP, and a retirement in the Belgian GP on the first lap due to a broken camshaft in the Lotus-BRM. Then Irwin got a H16 BRM and was 5th in France, 7th in Britain, and 9th in Germany. Retirements followed in the Canadian GP (fouled throttle slides), Italian GP (ignition failure after 17 laps), U.S. GP (engine failure after 41 laps), and Mexican GP (loss of oil pressure). His bag for a year's work in World Championship racing was 2 points and a tie for 16th spot in the standings. This from the young man who was Stewart's equal in F3 and who had beaten out Piers Courage for the BRM job by a polished Tasman series the previous winter. Yet the talent was there, and John Surtees signed Irwin for Honda's F1 effort in 1968.

The 1967 season had seen some good F2 appearances also, such as a 2nd to Frank Gardner at Hockenheim in a Lola-FVA BT23, a 3rd at Madrid in a Lola-FVA T100 and a 2nd—to upcoming Jacky Ickx—at Zandvoort in the same car. Also, Chris had managed a 4th in the Syracuse GP and a 6th in the Brands Hatch Race of Champions in non-title F1 racing. He was looking forward to a more competitive 1968. And perhaps he had a right to do so, for he won his initial F2 start that year, the Eifelrennen at 101.78 m.p.h., and he was 3rd in the Limbourg GP. But at Nurburgring, practicing an Alan Mann Ford P68, Chris crashed, and his racing career was suddenly over.

BOBBY ISAAC

Robert Vance Isaac was born August 1, 1934. Professional stock car driver, advocate of speed and competition, he was defiant and proud of what he was. Somewhere along the way, sometime during those years, the Catawba, N.C., driver acquired the one ingredient of any successful athlete—an overwhelming competitive spirit. "I never have liked to do anything but drive race cars. I remember one year that I drove a rich guy around in Newton, N.C., just so I could make spending money to get me to the race tracks."

Some people choose to call a man shiftless if he likes to shoot pool, or hunt, or fish, or drive a race car for a living. But any man who has ever talked with Isaac would disagree. His life was stock-car racing and his goal was to become the best there is in a sport where men prove themselves with great amounts of skill and unlimited supplies of raw courage. Bobby received a well-deserved break in 1964 when veteran mechanic Ray Nichels chose him to drive a Dodge on the NASCAR Grand National circuit. It was really the beginning of life for him, although he had been South Carolina sportsman champion in 1958.

Isaac grew out of a large family and at the age of 12 went to work in a sawmill. "I saved my money working at the sawmill until I had enough to buy me a pair of shoes. I was on my own and it was cold in the winter and I didn't have any shoes. We used to go barefoot all the time anyway because it made your feet tough. I got tired of working at the sawmill and that's when I decided I wanted to make a living driving race cars. I used to sit up on top of a hill there in Catawba and watch the guys tow their race cars down the road on the way to Hickory and the races. I quit my job one day and hitched a ride over there with one of the racers.

"A fella let me drive his car and I turned it over and the promoter said I couldn't drive no more because I was too young. I guess I was about 15 at the time. Another fella built me a hobby car a year or so later and I went racing. After that, another fella, Ralph Hefner, let me drive his limited sportsman car. It was a 1939 Ford and I won a lotta races with it."

Isaacs grimaced. He was well-do-do now and it was like Buckingham Palace compared to the sawmill days: "I wasn't gonna do anything but race for a living and I was hoping that someday I'd get a good ride on the Grand National circuit. I had a bad temper and fought a lot when fellas would deliberately knock me into a fence or something. I guess that hurt me because I was all the time getting suspended and reinstated in NASCAR."

By the summer of 1962, Isaac had become a legendary figure on the short tracks of the Carolinas. A young race enthusiast, Bondy Long of Camden, S.C., offered Isaac a ride in a new Ford for the 1963 season. The car was as first-rate as money could make it but Long's crew left something to be desired. Isaac and the chief

mechanic on the car had words and Bobby lost his first chance at GN racing. Smokey Yunick, builder of cars driven by Paul Goldsmith and Fireball Roberts, offered Isaac a ride in his Chevrolet for the National 400 in Charlotte that October. Bobby gave it a real ride and was running with the leaders when a tire blew. Yunick said of Isaac afterwards, "He's a race driver. I know that."

So Nichels, an excellent businessman with a flair for picking stock-car driving talent, offered Isaac his Dodge for the 1964 season. The young driver did not take long to respond. He won a 100-mile qualifying race at Daytona in his initial outing, and was running well up at the front of the pack in the 500-miler when paper and debris clogged his radiator and forced him to make unscheduled pit stops. Later he said, "The car was the strongest I've ever driven. I guess you'd have to say getting the ride in the Nichels Dodge was my biggest thrill in stock-car racing."

Isaac was a leader in every major race he entered in 1964. He was outrunning everyone at the Atlanta 500 when tire problems ruined his chances for victory and he finished 2nd to Fred Lorenzen. "The other 2nd-place finish was probably the biggest disappointment I ever suffered," said Isaac, while sitting out the 1965 season when Chrysler's hemi engines were banned from NASCAR competition. "I had run all the way in the Firecracker 400 at Daytona. We had planned the race for the distance and everything had come off as scheduled. The car was running perfect.

"The crew gave me the sign for 10 more laps and I looked in the rear view mirror to see who was behind me. A. J. Foyt and I had been passing each other back and forth for about 20 laps and he had made a pit stop last. I thought maybe I had shook him from my draft a few laps before but there he was—right on my bumper. Daytona is a tricky track when you start passing somebody. I couldn't figure out whether to try and be leading on the last lap or not. I finally figured, on the last lap, that I'd let Foyt lead me into the third turn, then slingshot him coming off the fourth turn.

"He passed me in the 3rd turn," Isaac continued, "and when I started to pass him down the straightaway, he forced me low. The draft won't take effect that way and I finished 2nd. I guess it was the worst feeling anybody ever had for finishing 2nd. I tried not to act hurt or mad about it afterwards but I really was. I was mad at myself and hurt because I had let Foyt do it. Some writer asked me if I thought A. J. could go pretty good on the banks, and I told him: 'Yeah, he'll probably be pretty good in a couple more years after he gets a little experience.' Foyt taught me something that day I always thought I knew. You have to be completely competitive or not competitive at all."

Isaac made money in the succeeding years except for a futile foray into USAC. He drove for Dodge, switched back to Ford, then returned to Dodge. In 1968 he decided to abandon the chase for that first superspeedway victory. He would run instead for the season point championship. That meant finishing as well as possible at the superspeedways—which he did when his car held together—and winning on the short tracks. He led David Pearson until the Southern 500 when a 7-car crash put him out of the race and out of the point competition.

The year 1969 would have been another year of spinning his wheels except for NASCAR's initial visit to the new Texas International Speedway in Bryan. It was the final race of the year, and Isaac's droop-nosed Dodge went well in practice. But early in the Texas 500 proper a tire blew, sending Bobby in for an unscheduled pit stop. He returned to the track hopping mad and a lap behind. Slowly he began to regain ground, passing car after car—Richard Petty, Donnie Allison, Lee Roy Yarbrough, the whole Ford contingent. Only Buddy Baker in a winged Dodge, like his own, was ahead of Isaac now, too far ahead. Baker, however, hit a car he was lapping and left the race with a broken radiator; Isaac led with 18 laps left. Donnie Allison passed him in a kamikaze effort to win for Ford, but could not hold on because a tire was worn so thin the cord was showing.

So, after 31,828 miles of NASCAR competition, Isaac won his initial superspeedway victory. Afterwards he said he was happy but—now that it was accomplished—it felt just like the other 16 wins he had amassed during the season.

Running for the points crown is an expensive and grueling undertaking. It means having at least 2, possibly 3, cars set up for the various kinds of tracks Grand National championships are run on. It means running some 50 races, often 2 or 3 a week, during the season. It also means discipline, because the key to one's racing strategy is to finish high in every race. Harry Hyde, Isaac's chief mechanic on the K&K Insurance Dodge, was a quiet dedicated man when he was working. The decision to try anew for the NASCAR championship in 1970 was made without fanfare once sponsor Nord Krauskopf, who *is* K&K Insurance, okayed the money expenditure. And it would not be a bad investment—if the title could be won—for now $100,000 went with the point championship.

The K&K Dodge driver again showed his virtuosity on the smaller tracks—Beltsville, Langley Field, even the new high-banked 5/8-mile Nashville track which drew criticism from virtually everyone. Isaac merely "cooled it," let most of the hot dogs eliminate themselves, and romped home. When it came down to Rockingham's American 500, postponed into November, he had fought off point challenges from Jim Hylton, Richard Petty, and Bobby Allison, and needed only a 28th-place finish to win the crown. He motored around "trying to stay out of everyone's way," eventually finishing 7th and NASCAR point champion.

To cap the season, the K&K team went to Talladega, Ala., to try for a new world closed-course mark. It was a raw blustery day, with the temperatures near freezing, when Isaac made the try. The wind was blowing in the 10- to 18-m.p.h. range as the orange Dodge Daytona picked up speed and rose higher and higher on the banking of the 2.66-mile course. He circled the empty track 24 times, 4 of them faster than Buddy Baker's old speed mark of 200.447 m.p.h.; his fastest was the 22nd lap at 201.104 m.p.h.

Isaac was exhilarated when he climbed from the car. "This is the pinnacle of my career," he said. "Winning the championship and now this. What more can a man ask for?" Isaac answered his own question a few weeks later when he said, "We'll try for back-to-back championships in 1971. That really would be something to tell your kids."

But Bobby did not make it; stomach trouble caught up with him and Dave Marcis drove as his substitute in the K&K Dodge in several big races. He did have 4 victories and $106,000 to show for his year. In 1972, mechanical troubles dropped him off the championship pace, except for a victory in the Carolina 500 at Rockingham, N.C., his 37th career GN victory. That year he won 4 of 6 GN East starts, but with 3 months to go, Issac suddenly quit K&K which promptly hired Buddy Baker. Robert Vance Isaac was at another crossroad.

ALEC ISSIGONIS

Sir Alexander Arnold Constantino Issigonis, CBE, quite a mouthful for the lean, talented automobile designer who created, among other things, the Morris Minor, the BMC Mini, and even a single-seater named the Lightweight Special. He preferred Alec Issigonis, model trains, Benny Goodman records, vintage airplanes, hot-air balloon racing, and other esoteric pastimes to knighthood, Commander of the British Empire, and that kind of thing.

Issigonis's background was remarkably diverse. He came from Smyrna, Turkey—now Izmir—in 1906, of a Greek father who was a naturalized Briton and a Bavarian mother. The Turkish town was the Alsace-Lorraine of the Middle East; it was invaded successively by the Turks, the Germans, the Greeks, then the Turks again. In 1922, the last invasion, the Issigonis family was evacuated to Malta with other British nationals, the family engineering business being left behind. The following year 17-year-old Alec was in London's Battesea Polytechnic Institute.

To celebrate his graduation, mother Issigonis gave Alec a 10 h.p. Sunbeam that he proceeded to drive some 80,000 miles, touring the Continent. He swapped for an Austin 7 when he returned to Britain, and started to work with an engineering office at No. 66 Victoria Street, London—his initial project being a sort of semi-automatic transmission for passenger cars. In 1933 he went to Humber, working on suspensions, and also bought a supercharged version of the Austin called the Ulster, with which he ran hillclimbs at places like Shelsley Walsh, and sprints like those at the Lewes Speed Trials. Work started that year, too, in the Issigonis garage, on the Lightweight Special, a stiff monocoque beauty that was to take 6 years to complete and weigh all of 587 pounds.

Alec meanwhile had gone over to Morris in 1936. A dozen years later his great design, the Minor, was to appear after 4 years of work that actually began soon after D-Day. Eleven years after that the Mini—this one took 8 years from idea to introduction—appeared in 1959. The 1100 came in 1962 and the 1800 in 1964, the year Issigonis got his CBE. The Maxi came in 1969, the year he was knighted by the Queen. He retired from BLMC in 1972.

PETER JACKSON

Britain's Peter Jackson was trained as an upholsterer, but he was sidetracked by the notion that plastics would take over the world right after World War II, and he moved into a plastics partnership to mold motorcycle sidecar bodies. The company went broke, primarily because motorcycle sidecars were going the way of buggy whips, even in England. Next he formed his own company, W&J Plastics, whose big project was turning out a plastic-bodied child's pedal car based on a Formula

1 Vanwall racing car. It's a rare item today, but that didn't do Jackson any good. W&J folded when Jackson's partner walked out in disgust.

Peter's brother, David, had been trained as a cabinet-maker, so what was more natural than to bring him into plastics and start still another company. This one specialized in molding sculptures, murals, and the like for fairly well-known artists. The craftsmanship was of high quality, which may have been what attracted Eric Broadley.

Broadley was and is Lola Cars. At the time that Peter was telling David that a market existed for full-size car bodies made of plastics to cut weight and make them more attractive looking, Eric was telling himself the same thing. The result was a contract for the Jacksons to build a fiber glass body for Broadley's Lola-Climax 1100 sports car. Contract in hand, Peter Jackson started still another company, and this one prospered. Specialised Mouldings, Ltd., was born in 1959. The physical premises were a large shed in the Crystal Palace race course, and the initial Lola product was recreated about 41 times that first year.

In 1960 Broadley introduced the Jackson-molded Lola Formula Junior, and as other racing car manufacturers got a look at his craftsmanship, orders came in from names like Cooper, Lotus, and Brabham. Pretty soon SML was not one shed but a whole collection of sheds at Crystal Palace, and still it needed more room. In January 1967 the big move came, to Huntingdon, just off the Great North Road that links London and Scotland. It is 60 miles away from central London, but still conveniently close, and closer still to Coventry-Birmingham, the hub of the British car industry.

Jackson's work in the intervening years included bodies for the Ford GT and the McLaren in their varied forms, Brabham, Marches, Chevrons, and all the rest. Now, if British racing car builders needed a body, they picked up the phone and called Huntingdon. By 1971 the SML work force was over 50, and there was a spacious new factory in the new Huntingdon Industrial Estate, including a rather sumptuous executive suite for the man who failed at so many starts until he hit the right line. There were many nice little touches to the modern operation, including the first fully independent commercial wind tunnel to be opened in Britain. It was built mainly of fiber glass, of course.

DICK JACOBS

When Jacobs retired in 1964, the names of Dick Jacobs and MG had become almost interchangeable on the British motoring scene. Jacobs, whose own racing career in the marque began right after World War II, had been managing team cars since 1956, the year following his 40th birthday. Jacobs had begun with MG-powered specials and graduated to the factory team in 1950, racing the TC and TD for MG, and the YB and ZA saloons under his own name. Dick was driving an MGA prototype when he crashed at White House (just prior to Pierre Levegh's gruesome accident) seriously enough to put him out of action for 6 months. Even though he was declared fit for racing again, Jacobs decided to take up the managing end of the sport in 1956 and took over the MG Magnette team that won that season's 6-hour relay race. The following year Jacobs managed the Alan Foster-John Waller Magnette team and repeated the chore in 1958.

Jacobs founded Mill Garage, an MG dealership with branches in East London and West Essex, about this time. He began racing his own cars, starting with a Twin-Cam MGA which he entered in the Tourist Trophy, with driving shared by Foster and Tommy Bridger. The car, standard throughout, finished 3rd. Thus encouraged, Jacobs added more vehicles to his Twin-Cam stable and his pale green cars became familiar sights. In 1962 he added MG Midget Specials which were highly successful Grand Touring competitors in the 1000 and 1150 c.c. classes for 3 seasons. They also served as prototypes for a 1300 c.c. GT version, winning 1st and 2nd in class at the 1964 Nurburgring 1000.

VITTORIO JANO

The Alfa Romeo P2, the Alfa 8C, the PS Monoposto, cars for Fiat and Lancia, and cars for Ferrari are all among the claims to fame of a trim Italian draftsman, engineer, designer, and racing team organizer and leader, a man named Vittorio Jano.

Jano was born April 22, 1891, and died—by his own hand—March 12, 1965, just short of his 75th birthday. He believed his antecedents were Hungarian and that the family name originally was Janos; but Jano had been a familiar name around Turin since the middle of the 18th century. Raised in San Giorgio Canavese, Vittorio started work at the Rapid factory there. Soon ready for better things, Jano headed his Minerva motorcycle for the nearby Fiat plant and was hired.

At Fiat, Jano was quickly adopted by Carlo Cavalli, famed head of the company's design department. Vittorio rose from intermediate draftsman to head of a design group in 10 years. During his years at Fiat, Vittorio participated in the development of such famous machines as the Type 501 tourer and the 805. Fiat was satisfied, and so was Jano, until his doorbell rang and another soon-to-be famous Italian automotive figure named Enzo Ferrari stood there waiting to enter.

Ferrari, then a slim 25 year old, represented a new company called Alfa Romeo. Alfa needed an imaginative designer to replace an unsuccessful one just released by Senator Romeo, head of the new factory. It took a lot of persuasion—prestige, money, opportunity, unlimited design freedom—to get Jano to move from Turin to Milan, but in the end, he did, in September 1923. It changed Italian automotive history.

It took Jano just 8 months, working from scratch, to design one of racing's most successful cars, the P2 Alfa Romeo, a Roots-supercharged, 2-litre, 1987-c.c. car. After a few short test runs, the first P2 entered the Circuit of Cremona Race on June 9, 1924. Antonio Ascari and Luigi Bazzi won easily at better than 123 m.p.h. To cement its amazing debut, a 4-car Alfa team was readied for the 800-kilometer Grand Prix d'Europe at Lyon, France, August 3, 1924, led by Giuseppe Campari; the P2 won once again, and Fiat announced its retirement from racing.

Alfas won so easily from the opposition that hot-blooded European crowds sometimes booed and heckled the team on the course and even in the victory ceremony. Jano showed his contempt for this kind of thing in one of auto racing's great moments, during the 1925 Belgian GP at Spa. Ascari and Campari held a large lead over the rest of the field, and the Belgian crowd was reacting noisily; Vittorio waved in his two leaders for a routine fuel stop, and while his mechanics polished the machines, leisurely ate some bread, cheese, and wine with the two drivers in the pits for a full 5 minutes while the other competitors raced desparately to take advantage of this defiance. The Alfas won the GP easily.

In 1925 Jano also produced the first of his exquisite touring cars, the 1500 Alfetta, powered by a s.o.h.c. 6. A 1500 SS, a supercharged d.o.h.c. version, quickly followed, along with blown and unblown 1750-c.c. versions that quickly made Alfa a world leader in the sports

car field. In 1931 Jano produced a new racing car that rivaled the P2 for performance and beauty. Called the 8C, this was an enlarged version of the 1750, powered by a straight-8 of 2336 c.c. Among other things, it won the Targa Florio, the Italian GP—which gave the car its Monza name—and 4 successive Le Mans 24-hour races.

Another Jano classic was the P3 Monoposto, created in 1932, which was to dominate European road racing for 2 years until a new formula and the rise of Germany's Mercedes Benz and Auto Union designs of the later thirties. The all-aluminum P3 made its debut in the Italian GP June 5, 1932, with the immortal Tazio Nuvolari at the wheel and repeated the P2's feat of winning its first race, a 5-hour Grand Prix.

Alfa, however, suffered a racing decline with the advent of mass production techniques and an inability to compete with the state-supported German teams. Jano grew restive working almost exclusively on ordinary designs, and although he did turn out some racing machinery (some for Enzo Ferrari to race under the Alfa colors, but without factory sponsorship), he accepted the first interesting offer that came along.

In October 1937 he left Alfa Romeo and several months later, after a vacation, Jano took over at the late Vincenzo Lancia's Turin automobile concern as chief development engineer. He was to become its chief engineer during World War II. After the war, which once again had seen Jano designs in the truck and aviation engine fields prove eminently successful, Lancia brought out Jano's first personal designs, including the Appia and the Aurelia series. The latter, introduced in 1950, was the first successful V-6 in history. It also used a transaxle and inboard rear brakes; many commentators today call the Aurelia the first modern Gran Turismo car. The basic 1.9-litre car was expanded to 3.1 litres for competition.

In these same years Jano designed the Lancia D50 Formula 1 racing car in which Alberto Ascari led the Spanish GP in October 1954, until a crankshaft counterweight separated and retired the machine. In the Argentine GP, in Buenos Aires, the V-8 powered, 3.48-litre car again was leading when mechanical troubles of a production rather than a design nature struck. The design's 3rd race was the Circuit of Valentino in Turin itself; the Lancia won handily from top Ferrari and Maserati competition. Jano resigned as a member of Lancia's staff that night, but agreed to serve as a racing consultant.

But racing at Lancia was soon to be over; on May 22 Ascari sailed into Monaco Harbor on the 91st lap of the Grand Prix, and 5 days later, after a crash while testing a Ferrari at Monza he was dead. Partly because of this and partly because of financial difficulties, Lancia turned over its racers, its entire competition department, and Jano's services to Ferrari 2 months later. The partnership first paid off when the Lancia-Ferrari V-8s, with

Jano's assistance, won the 1956 F1 championship. Jano's Ferrari-Fiat Dino appeared in April 1965, at Monza. The association continued until Vittorio's death.

NED JARRETT

It was at Islip Speedway, a 1/5-mile paved oval in central Long Island, on one of NASCAR's summer northern tours. The big Grand National cars filled the track to bursting and created an ear-shattering din, a whining, rumbling cacophony, as the competitors accelerated for short spurts, then had to back off on the low banks. But the home of the demolition derby, 1/8-mile drag racing, and the figure eight race drew people, and some 12,000 were packed into the stands on the hot July evening sweating, cheering, drinking soda pop, and eating ice cream and hot dogs.

This was the night Ned Jarrett lost his temper. Gentleman Ned Jarrett was the only man who looked cool, clean, calm, and collected at the barbecue for the favored press and honored guests before the paying customers began to arrive. Every strand of his luxuriant wavy black hair was in place. His open-necked white shirt was starched and spotless, his car likewise. He was Mr. Clean among the Philistines.

The race was a close, fender-nicking affair with competition all over the small track, and it is doubtful if more than 10 percent of the fans knew who were runing in the top 3 at any given time. Bob Sall, the area superviser for NASCAR, was presumed to know, and so was scorer Johnny Bruner. When the checkered flag dropped, Billy Wade's 1964 Mercury had been declared the winner with Jarrett placed second by the announcer. Jarrett did not even wait for the fans to exit. He parked his car in the winner's circle next to Wade's and strode quickly across the track to Sall. The perennial smile was missing. From the press box it was apparent that Jarrett was disputing the victory vigorously, but he was talking quietly to Sall, so quietly that even though the fans knew what was happening they filed out. It seemed too gentlemanly to generate much heat.

Jarrett argued doggedly. An intelligent man, he reiterated his position as they moved slowly up toward the press box and scorers' booth, Sall retreating row by row like a battalion fighting a rearguard action. Wade, Jarrett declared in many different ways, had not repassed him to unlap himself so how could he have won? Even the announcer had been surprised when he was notified that Wade, not Ned, had been leading. Finally the lap charts and timing tapes were checked and found to disagree. Ned smiled. But Sall never lost his equanimity as he adamantly stood behind the decision of the scorer. The rest of the cars had loaded up, most of the press had written and phoned in their stories, but the two urbane men argued on. Finally Bruner stepped in. He had

NED   CAR N). 11

had it. In short Anglo-Saxon expletives, he told Jarrett his finish stood and what Jarrett could do.

The words were like a key turning in a lock. Jarrett started for Bruner his handsome face suffused with red under the tan, his arms raised. He opened his mouth but bit off the words. Bruner looked shocked. Sall saved the night. He interposed himself between the men, taking Jarrett's forward motion on his chest. "Now Ned," he said. Jarrett stood nose to nose with the bespectacled Sall for what seemed an eternity, the color leaving his face. Wordlessly he turned and marched down off the stands. Bruner's breath of relief shattered the silence. The dispute was settled in Daytona Beach in Wade's favor.

Ned Miller Jarrett was born on a farm near Newton, N.C., Columbus Day, 1932, one of 4 children. He was fascinated by automobiles early; his father let him drive the family car to church when he was 9. He saw some of the early dirt-track races and even went to Raleigh to see the likes of Fonty Flock, Joe Eubanks, and Herb Thomas. At 17 he quit high school to join a brother and his father in a lumber business, but he was already planning to race. In May 1952, at Hickory, N. C., Ned ran his first official race in a Ford sportsman in which he had a part interest. He finished 10th and incurred parental wrath.

A compromise was made to the effect that Ned was allowed to work on the car, but not drive it. One night the driver hired was unable to drive because of illness; he suggested Ned drive and use his name. Ned did, and

finished 2nd. He had won several sportsman events under the assumed name before his father found out. This time the senior Jarrett bowed to the inevitable and gave Ned his blessing. Ned did well enough on the sportsman circuit to enter the 1953 Southern 500. His Oldsmobile lasted 8 laps and he finished dead last.

Discouraged, Ned returned to sportsman racing, slowly extending his fame and his area of competition. In 1956 Jarrett finished 2nd in NASCAR's national sportsman title race, and he won the crown the ensuing 2 years. Jarrett quit the sportsman wars in 1959, trying to make up his mind whether to try Grand National racing. Finally, he decided to buy an ex-Junior Johnson Ford one Friday in 1959. Knowing there were 2 races that weekend, he wrote a check for $2,000 despite the fact that he had far less than that in his bank account. In the best derring-do tradition, he won both races and covered the check Monday morning. But the rest of the season on the Grand National Trail convinced him that to really compete where the money was—on the super-speedways— he needed much better equipment.

In 1960 Jarrett gambled that he could attract a sponsor. With the help of a friend, J. W. Abernathy, he bought a new Ford, prepared it and went to seek his fortune. He was running 2nd in the World 600 at Charlotte 8 laps from the end—unheard of for an independent— when a tire blew and sent him into the wall. He won 5 races, however, and managed to keep his operating loss to only $2,000. But he succeeded in attracting Bee Gee Holloway of Daytona Beach as an angel for 1961.

Holloway gave him a Chevrolet and told him to make all the races. Ned Jarrett didn't know it, but he was running for the Grand National season championship. He won only at Birmingham, Ala., but he placed in the top 5 in 22 races and was out of the top 10 only 12 times in 46 races. Ned squeaked into the title ahead of defending champ Rex White, and some thought it was a fluke. But in 1962 he finished 3rd, winning 6 races; in 1963, switching to the Burton and Robinson Construction Company Ford, he won 8 races and finished 4th. That was the year Jarrett led the Daytona 500 with only 3 laps to go when he ran out of gasoline, dropping to 3rd.

In 1964 the protective green mantle of Ford Motor Company was wrapped around Ned as he joined forces with Bondy Long to form Bowani, Inc. He won 15 Grand National stops and still lost the championship to Richard Petty. But he finally won his initial superspeedway race.

There are certain tracks where the racing just naturally seems to turn rough, and the 1.5-mile Atlanta Speedway in Hampton, south of the city of Atlanta, is one of those tracks. It is hard on tires, its turns are calculated to defeat the unwary or the weary, and its race dates have never been in ideal weather. The Dixie 400 for 1964 was held in June when temperatures on the track can reach 150 degrees and tires seem to melt away. The 1964 race was one of the roughest of competitions on tires and engines. Jarrett was not among the favorites. He had had a poor week of practice, and his old car had burned at the World 600 in the accident that took the life of Fireball Roberts. He had pulled Roberts out of the car, but Roberts had burns over 65 percent of his body. Ned had been a hero, but now it was time to race on a speedway much more dangerous than Charlotte, and his new Ford was not performing well. But when the race began, the hot shoes like Lorenzen, Marvin Panch, and Junior Johnson dropped out early. Ned was Ford's victory hope against Mercury and the Chrysler forces. As he wheeled in for his first pit stop, Jarrett saw a remarkable sight. Herb Nab, Lorenzen's chief wrench, was working his pits and had brought along all of Freddie's tires. Ned grabbed the lead for the first time on the 193rd lap, lost it to Rex White and his Mercury 40 laps later, then pressed White until the Merc driver's engine overheated in the pits and stalled. Ned then fought off Richard Petty and finished on Lorenzen's tires, a rival brand. "We found out quickly our brand was not going to hold up, and we wanted to switch like many others did, but, if Freddie's had not been available, I probably would not have won," Jarrett commented after the race.

The race typified what had to happen for Jarrett to win on a superspeedway. Ned preferred to run off the pace and let the flat-out chargers burn each other out, then make his move late in the race. But usually a Lorenzen or Petty or some other charger lasted and Ned had to settle for 3rd or 4th. On short tracks where the driver counted for more, Ned was a master at getting through traffic and keeping his mount in one piece. His 50 Grand National career victories testified to that. All but 2 were on shorter tracks.

In 1965 Jarrett convinced the doubters that he was a virtuoso. He won 13 races and the Grand National title for the 2nd time, placing in the top five 42 out of 54 races. He also won what NASCAR drivers in their hearts considered the big race back then, the Southern 500.

Ned's Bondy Long Ford stayed back in the pack, not taking the lead until the 233rd lap. By that time there had been enough thrills and chills for a season of racing. Sam McQuagg and Cale Yarborough had collided; neither was injured, miraculously. The wrecks had started in the 2nd lap, and the cars of the flat-out boys began failing soon after as Darlington took its toll. Only 21 cars were running when Ned led his initial 6 laps before Darel Dieringer passed him. The battle seemed to be between Dieringer and Lorenzen, but on the 319th lap Lorenzen left, victim of an oil fire in a rear wheel. But Ned wrested the lead from Darel on lap 326. When Darel departed with rear-end problems 19 laps later, Jarrett seemed to have the race won. Then his own engine started to overheat. He slowed a bit and rolled over the line 14 laps ahead of Buddy Baker in a Plymouth.

In 1966, he was running 4th in the point standings when Ford withdrew from NASCAR racing, stranding Jarrett and other factory stars. Announcing his retirement soon after, Ned just never came back in 1967. He had real estate and business interests in his adopted town of Camden, S.C., formed Jarrett & Pike, management consultants, and in 1970 promoted races at the Greenville, S. C., Speedway, the kind of track he used to dominate, later shifting to Hickory, N.C. In 1972 he was inducted into the stock car Hall of Fame at Darlington.

"I love auto racing. I think it's a true test of what makes a man, and it has been good to me," Ned told an acquaintance in 1970. "That's why I used to try to make one appearance a week during my active career. But big money racing is for younger men who have nothing to lose. I'm not a Curtis Turner who still loves to compete. I want to get to know my children before it's too late." Gentleman Ned Jarrett was now a gentleman 24 hours a day.

CHARLES JARROTT

Two names stand out at the beginning of British racing history. One is S. F. Edge, the handlebar-mustachioed Napier hero who established many racing traditions in Britain. The other is Charles Jarrott, like Edge a bicycle and motorcycle racer who graduated to auto racing.

Edge had about 5 major race appearances to his credit, plus some record-setting work. Born in 1872 Jarrott made only 7 auto racing appearances between 1901 and 1907, the years of his activity.

Unlike S. F., Jarrott drove whatever he could, and the only British car he raced was a Wolseley in the 1904 Gordon Bennett Cup at Taunus. He was 12th. Charlie's successes came in Continental machines, starting with the French Panhard. Harvey Du Cros, the financial angel behind Edge's association with Montague Napier, also was involved with Jarrott. It was Du Cros who helped Charlie get a Panhard discard for the 1901 Paris–Berlin race, and it was Du Cros who went along as Jarrott's riding mechanic on that harrowing 687-mile battle.

Jarrott's main concern was finishing. No mad dashes for him, no dropping out because things were so bad you would be last. He saw the automobile as a machine to be conquered. If you dropped out, the machine had won. If you finished, no matter how far back, you had persevered. He proved that, with Du Cros's help, in the Paris–Berlin when he brought the old Panhard home 8th in a clatter of falling parts.

Panhard was impressed enough with that effort to provide Jarrott a factory-prepared car in major races the following year. In the 537-mile Circuit du Nord, Jarrott's car was 2nd to the great driver-aviator Maurice Farman in another Panhard. He finished far down in the Paris–Vienna race, then won the 318-mile Circuit des Ardennes, centered around Bastogne, at an average speed of 54 m.p.h. A pair of Mors, one driven by William K. Vanderbilt, trailed behind.

Charlie switched to the De Dietrich marque after that, and in 1903 he pushed on to a heavier car for a 3rd in the Paris–Madrid grind of 342 miles. It was a De Dietrich that he drove in the 1904 Gordon Bennett eliminating round in the Ardennes, before switching to the Wolseley. And it was a De Dietrich in which he scored his last great victory, the 1907 Byfleet Plate race at Brooklands that he won in a dead heat. He later became a salesman for De Dietrich and for Crossley in London, and a familar host to groups of young drivers who found in Jarrott an enthralled listener to stories of racing success and failure. He died in 1944.

CHARLES JEANTAUD

Charles Jeantaud of Paris built his initial car in 1881. But it was not until 1893 that he went into the automobile business on a serious basis. Jeantauds were electrics and lasted only until fast-improving gasoline-driven cars destroyed the early leads of the electrics and steamers.

It is strange that Jeantaud's cars are little remembered today, for it was a Jeantaud driven by the Comte de Chasseloup-Laubat that held the world's first Land Speed Record. The Marquis, founder of the Automobile Club de France, had modified his Jeantaud considerably when it took to the road December 18, 1898, driven by the younger Count. The Jeantaud looked like most cars of the day, patterned after carriages, high off the ground and rolling on big wheels topped by hard-rubber rims. It was somewhat different, however, in that the Count steered the square-shaped vehicle by manipulating a vertical handle that was attached to the first recorded steering wheel, instead of using a tiller like every other known car.

The Marquis's Jeantaud was strictly a sprint car that day; everything was planned to see how fast it would go along a deserted stretch of road in Achères, between the villages of St. Germain and Constans, near Paris. That site became world-famous as the place where 6 Land Speed Records were set in the next 4 months. When the deed and the Jeantaud's batteries were done, Chasseloup-Laubat had travelled at the incredible speed of 39.24 m.p.h. over a measured kilometer.

The record stood until January 17, 1899, when Belgium's Camille Jenatzy pushed his own electric car along the same road at 41.42 m.p.h. Then Jenatzy, huddled in the fur coat that was to become his trademark, watched Chasseloup-Laubat regain his title with a run of 43.69 m.p.h. Three gasoline cars also challenged the new record, but they could not even tie it. When racing for the electrics was over that day (both cars had exhausted their batteries), each resolved to continue the battle. Jenatzy's car was shaped like a torpedo; Chasseloup-Laubat decided that he, too, would have to streamline his boxy car if he were to hold his crown as well as beat off the gasoline-powered upstarts.

The Count rebuilt the car almost completely and installed even more powerful batteries. Jenatzy, meanwhile, was not idle and, after improving his own battery system, he raced down the Achères road once again to a record 49.92 m.p.h. on January 27. The Count's rebuilt Jeantaud, now sporting a boat-shaped body from prow to stern, regained the record on March 4 with a run of 57.60. It was the last time a Jeantaud would hold the mark. Jenatzy reappeared at Achères April 29, 1899, and astounded the motoring world by registering an official 65.79 m.p.h., more than a mile a minute for the first time in history. Experts had said a motor car would not hold together at such speeds, and some had even said that drivers would lose control of their minds and, perhaps, be killed or, at the very least, rendered unconscious by the pace.

Jenatzy's record stood for almost 3 years until Leon Serpollet's Special, a steam car, pushed the record to 75.06 m.p.h. On the strength of its earlier record performances, though, Jeantauds continued to sell until 1906. Whatever its fame then, it is all but forgotten today, even among electric enthusiasts who remember its erstwhile foe, *La Jamais Contente*, and Camille

Jenatzy, but forget the first world Land Speed Record holder, the Jeantaud, and the Count de Chasseloup-Laubat.

CAMILLE JENATZY

Jenatzy's name may not be as familiar as it should be. It was this redheaded and red-bearded Belgian who built the first specialized car for breaking speed records; but his feats were packed into a few short years before World War I. The Jenatzys had been Hungarians, but they had lived in Belgium for nearly 110 years before Camille was born in Brussels on November 4, 1868. His father had founded the nation's first rubber factory and was a lover of horses. Camille, on the other hand, liked mechanical mounts; starting with bicycles, then graduating to automobiles soon after gaining his civil engineering degree. At first Jenatzy concentrated on their manufacture, his activities at the General Transport Company centering around electric carriages.

On November 28, 1898, a French newspaper announced a climb up Chanteloup Hill, and Jenatzy, on the spur of the moment, entered his latest electric. He won handily over the short distance, averaging 16 m.p.h., and prepared for the newspaper's next race—a straightaway on the central avenue running through the Parc Agricole d'Achères—2 kilometers, against the clock, from a standing start. The race was held December 18, 1898, and Jenatzy lost to the handlebar-mustachioed Count Gaston de Chasseloup-Laubat at the

then startling speed of 39.24 m.p.h. in his own electric. Jenatzy's car dropped out because of mechanical troubles. He immediately issued a challenge to the winner. On January 17, 1899, they met. Camille started in his torpedo-shaped car, and he broke the Count's record at 41.42 m.p.h. But the Frenchman regained it immediately with a 43.69 clocking. Back to their workshops, and on January 27, the Belgian raised the speed record to 49.22 m.p.h. Laubat had been busy, too, and he and his brother had rebuilt his car with a primitively streamlined body. On March 4, the Frenchman was the first man to go 50 m.p.h. in an automobile, clocking 57.60. Jenatzy was not to be outdone. On April 29 he was ready at Achères with his sleek car, now named *La Jamais Contente* (the never content) and became the pioneer in averaging better than a mile a minute. The feat astounded Europe and made Jenatzy more renowned than ever. He was clocked at 65.79 m.p.h.; and it was just about the last moment of racing glory for the electrics. Laubat retired from the contest. Three years later a steam car briefly took the prize before the onslaught of the gasoline-powered cars, the aero-engined cars and, eventually, the turbines.

The speed bug had bitten Jenatzy deeply. He realized that an electric was fine for short sprints, but that it could never compete in a true race with the piston-engined cars, so he purchased a 16-h.p. Mors. It was a new world, and in his initial race, the Tour de France, Jenatzy finished last after a series of mishaps. In the Paris-San Malo race he was 7th; in the Paris-Ostend 5th. Camille's other performances were lackluster, and he retired the Mors while readying a design of his own that was being built at the FN (Fabrique Nationale d'Armes de Guerre) works. It was ready by July 31, 1902, for the Circuit des Ardennes, but Camille crashed in the pine woods. When he emerged unharmed, the legend was born of the Red Devil, the man with the red hair and red beard, who couldn't be hurt by any automobile.

Jenatzy had decided to give up racing his own machines and invest his manufacturing energies in the family tire business. But the Mercedes factory offered him a car for the Paris-Madrid race and for future contests. One of these was the 3rd Gordon Bennett Cup, contested in Ireland. It was a race for gentlemen, and Jenatzy was one of Mercedes's choices. He did not let the marque down. Even when a fire destroyed its specially prepared cars and lighter vehicles had to be substituted, Camille was not to be denied; he took the lead and never relinquished it, even when his tires were worn almost to the point of breaking, and there were no replacements. In 1904, in the same race, he was 2nd.

From that point on, however, things began to deteriorate badly and quickly for the Belgian. In 1905 he retired from the Gordon Bennett, and failures followed in the Vanderbilt Cup and the Circuit des Ardennes. In the initial Grand Prix de l'Automobile Club de France

the next season, Jenatzy was next to last when he dropped out. He was 10th in the Ardennes, 5th in the Vanderbilt Cup. In 1907 he was 14th in the Kaiserpreis, then dropped out of the GP de l'ACF and the Ardennes.

Mercedes had carried the Belgian for many years, but a new management changed all that. Mors, his old, pre-Mercedes mount, came to the rescue with a car for the 1908 GP, and he finished 6th. It was his last race. On October 7, 1913, Jenatzy was gravely wounded in an accidental shooting during a wild boar hunt. He died in his own Mercedes as friends were speeding the former champion to a hospital.

AB JENKINS

In the Land Speed Record story there is a man who never even tried for speed's highest prize—yet had a great deal to do with its popularization and with the success of LSR holders from Sir Malcolm Campbell to our own day. This man was D. Absalom Jenkins, a tough, bespectacled, teetotaling Mormon, who was a successful contractor for 20 years and a onetime mayor of Salt Lake City.

Jenkins (born in 1883) became interested in cars in the late twenties, not so much in terms of track or road racing as in the endurance record area. Ab's first big try was a race, however, not against cars, but against a crack Denver & Rio Grande excursion train. In 1925 he raced the train from Salt Lake City to Wendover, Utah, for a $250 bet, a Studebaker dealer providing the car and a secretary to take notes on Jenkins's comments as he raced. A cop came along as a chaperone. Ab won.

Two years later Jenkins drove from New York City to San Francisco in 76 hours. In 1928 he set a 24-hour record on the Atlantic City Speedway, a board track, with an 82.5 m.p.h. clocking. Later, he toured the nation for Studebaker, breaking every existing hillclimb record of any prominence. His first great feat occurred September 18-19, 1932, when Jenkins ran a 12-cylinder Pierce-Arrow for 24 consecutive hours at the Bonneville Salt Lake in Utah at an average speed of 112.935 m.p.h. But the 2,710-mile record try was not officially sanctioned by the AAA and Ab's license was lifted for a short while. He served out his time, then reappeared at the Salts in the V-12 Pierce-Arrow on August 7, 1933, and, with proper AAA observers, ran another 24 hours, this time at 117.77 m.p.h. It was the first of some 60 records that Jenkins shattered in his speed career.

The locale of the record was even more interesting than the record itself. For some time the great speed kings—the LSR men like Britain's Campbell—had been looking for a better place to run their giant cars. The Welsh sands, the other beach courses, including Daytona Beach and the vaunted African and Australian salts, were all restrictive to the kind of speeds that these men had now reached. A new, long, flat, safe course

had to be found, and after Jenkins's success, and his own efforts in publicizing it, Sir Malcolm and others were attracted to Bonneville to begin Utah's preeminence in this specialized area of motor sport.

Ab learned from the LSR men, too. In 1934 he returned to the Salts with his own Curtiss-aircraft-engined special, the Mormon Meteor I, which he ran for 24 hours at 127.23 m.p.h. With a Duesenberg he ran it up to 135.58 m.p.h. With Babe Stapp as copilot in 1936, a reworked 700-h.p. Mormon Meteor II took a host of new marks, the principal ones being 171 m.p.h. for one hour, 153.77 for 24 hours, and 148.63 for 48 hours. Lou Meyer joined Jenkins in 1937 for more runs in the same car and they shared a 157.3 m.p.h. record for 24 hours. There was still a 3rd version of the Meteor—later enshrined in the Utah State House—that cost $40,000 to construct. Unveiled in 1940, Ab wanted to reuse this car after World War II only to have the state refuse to return it because it liked it as an exhibit.

So Ab built a new record car, a $65,000 Mobil Special, in which he hoped to raise his 1940 mark of 161.2 m.p.h. for 24 hours. On July 20, 1951, at age 68, he set several 24-hour records up to and including 196.69 m.p.h. for a flying 25 miles. Unlike many of his contemporaries—Campbell, John Cobb, Reid Railton, others—Jenkins was an early proponent of jet power for record cars. As early as 1947 he predicted that jet propulsion was the future as far as high speed was concerned. As president of the American Racing Society he pushed for the kind of experimentation that saw people like Art Arfons, Mickey Thompson, and Craig Breedlove eventually succeed.

There are some footnotes to the Ab Jenkins story. About 1928 he became Auburn's chief tester. Even during the glory days of the Mormon Meteors, Ab ran Auburns at Bonneville for various records, typified by 1935's 12-hour mark 102.9 m.p.h. in a supercharged production Speedster. He also regularly ran Pierce-Arrows at the Salts, once taking a stock 12-cylinder roadster for a straight 24 hours at 112 m.p.h. In 1929 Ab appeared at Indianapolis for the 500-mile race in a Miller Special, but he failed to qualify. As late as 1956, the year in which he died, Ab drove a stock Pontiac for 24 hours (2,841 miles) at an average speed of 118.375 m.p.h. Pretty good for 73!

GORDON JOHNCOCK

Automobile racing was not an obsession to Gordon Johncock; it was a measure of his ability to compete on equal terms in a world where most people were physically larger than he. There seemed to be that extra competitive drive that many small men have—that need to excel. Johncock, who may have weighed 150 pounds dripping wet, excelled.

There was the 150-mile USAC championship at Lang-

horne's D-shaped mile track in June 1968, for instance. In his Gilmore Broadcasting Gerhardt turbocharged Offenhauser, he had come from behind on St. Patrick's Day to win the 200-miler at Hanford, Calif. But that was partly because Roger McCluskey made an unscheduled pit stop and Bobby Unser took Art Pollard with him when he crashed. This time the Gerhardt Offy was performing perfectly, and Johncock had set a new lap record to earn the pole.

But it was a brutally hot day, the kind of day when the soft-compound rubber tires wear themselves to uselessness, the kind of day when the heated air seems to be visible as it rises from the track surface. It was also the kind of day when qualifying speeds were bound to rise. Six others besides Gordon broke the track record.

Only 8 of the 23 qualifiers were to finish, the brutal race taking the toll of Al Unser, Mario Andretti, McCluskey and many others. But Johncock, who assumed the lead at the start, held on doggedly as caution periods closed the field and dissipated hard-earned leads. The competition came from Indy champ Bobby Unser starting on the 31st lap. The New Mexico veteran qualified his Rislone Eagle Ford 4th and the attrition moved him up so that when the caution lights went off for lap 31 Unser lay right behind Johncock. Sensing that this was his chance, Unser challenged Johncock, running nose to tail, probing left and feinting right, harrying the little Michigan driver lap after lap. Finally in front of the grandstand 11 laps later, Unser found his opening. He swept into the lead. But now it was Johncock's turn to harry and probe. Gordon dogged the Ford driver for 12

laps before he swooped daringly down on the loop of the course to recapture first.

The heroics were not over. Unser dropped several car lengths back, preferring to "rest" awhile. But Sammy Sessions wrecked and the caution brought him back up behind Johncock the easy way. Three laps after the green, Bobby was leading again. But Johncock was not to be denied on this day; on the 104th mile of the 150 miler he recaptured 1st place. Unser made another charge, but fans in the stands could see his head bobbing suddenly as he began to slow a bit: a special tether he wore to counteract the effects of an old neck injury, running from his left shoulder to the left side of his helmet, had broken. So he drove with his right hand holding up his head, those with field glasses saw! It was a matter of who was the wearier, Gordon or Bobby. Third-place Gary Bettenhausen was 4 laps behind. Johncock won but had to be assisted from the car. He weighed 136 pounds after the race; he quipped later, "I thought I was going to melt away."

Born August 25, 1936, on a farm in Hastings, Mich., where he still lived many years later, Johncock drove his first stock-car race there at age 19. He became a hero of the midwestern modified circles, winning the Galesburg 500 in 1958, the Louisville 500 in 1959 and 1960, and 100-lappers at places like Jackson, Lansing, Pinecrest, Ottawa, Cana, Kalamazoo, and Eldora, Ohio. This in itself was a tribute to the man's determination. In 1959 he had run a circle saw through his upper left arm in a milling accident. The doctors declared that he would never drive a logging truck again, and that he could never again develop the precison needed to drive a race car. Gordon exercised the badly damaged muscles relentlessly. He missed hardly a beat in his racing career —perhaps his determination was intensified because of it—and in 1964, after a highly successful career in the modifieds, he started running the USAC sprints in the Fette Aluminum car. His performance was good enough to get the Weinberger Homes ride both in sprints and on the Championship Trail. Although he did nothing in 4 Trail races starting with Springfield, Johncock was learning and getting used to the competition.

He qualified 14th as a rookie in the 1965 running of Indianapolis and worked his way up to 5th. Then he rode the Trail in earnest—15 races culminating in Milwaukee on a bright September day. Sid Weinberger, the Hastings neighbor who gave Gordon the Trail ride, had bought a rear-engined Offenhauser a few days previously from Fred Gerhardt. He put Johncock in it, and Gordon didn't disappoint.

Milwaukee 1965 was the kind of competition that showed USAC at its best. A. J. Foyt won the pole and the early lead, only to be overtaken quickly by Dan Gurney who, in turn, was overtaken by Mario Andretti. Andretti blew his engine on the 130th mile, giving the lead back to Gurney who sustained engine trouble only 2 miles later. That put Foyt back on top, hounded by

Joe Leonard and Johncock. A. J. watched Leonard pass him on the straightaway 56 miles from pay dirt, followed soon by Gordon who in turn caught Leonard. Leonard broke his engine trying to hold off the Michigan flyer, and Gordon fought off a brief flurry by Foyt to waltz home with his 1st major championship victory. He finished 5th on the season, improving that to 3rd in 1966 and dropping to 4th in 1967. His best ride in these 2 years, other than victories at Hanford and Milwaukee, was in the 1966 Indianapolis 500. His Gerhardt Ford damaged its nose in a first-lap accident. The crew pulled him in, made repairs, and sent Johncock back out 2 minutes and 41 seconds to the rear. The bantam bomber made most of that up to finish 4th.

In Indy 1967, Johncock qualiled in the front row but spun, eventually finishing 12th. In 1968—the year he finished 5th on the season—he started 9th but broke down on the 37th lap. In 1969 a broken piston put Johncock 19th. In 1970 he lasted 45 laps, blowing the engine. In 1971 he was involved in a crash with Mel Kenyon, finishing 29th for his 11 laps, and in 1972 his Gulf McLaren popped a valve after 113 laps for a 20th place. In the Ontario and Pocono 500s through 1972, Johncock's 4th in the 1970 California race was his best finish.

Johncock Forestry Products and 5 children were the reason Gordon Johncock didn't feel that race driving was the be-all of his existence. But that didn't detract from the deep respect others had for his approach to the sport. A quiet little man not given to the extroverted antics of some, Johncock analyzed each race as he drove it, made his decisions based on long experience against these fields, and executed them precisely. Yet he always drove the car to the limit of its capacity, sometimes breaking because of this, more often not. In 1973, Johncock joined the exclusive 200 m.p.h. club with a 208.695 speed at the Texas World Speedway in a record-shattering practice week in his George Bignotti prepared USAC car.

That he didn't win the National Championship was more a matter of the cars he got to drive than his skill. At Donnybrooke road course in Minnesota, Gurney shook his head in wonder and said, "I never saw anyone as quick through turns as Gordie." When he got a competitive car—an STP Eagle Offy prepared by George Bignotti—and the breaks—a race stopped by rain at 332.5 miles—Gordy won the 1973 Indy 500. Only Bill Vukovich was on the same lap.

BOBBY JOHNS

Robert Johns lived by, for, and with cars. So did his father, Socrates (Shorty) Johns, a peppery little man who reminded one most pungently of the fabled stage mothers who push junior-grade Shirley Temples into careers. Shorty had an abiding and enormous faith in

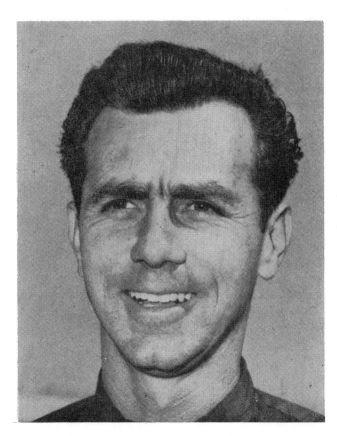

the driving ability of his son, and the son reciprocated by demanding that Shorty be included in any outside rides he was offered. This may have retarded Bobby's driving career, but that is a moot point. The fact is that the younger Johns was a member of the stomp-on-the-gas-pedal school of driving, which is very thrilling but also very wearing on the equipment. When the equipment held up, as his superbly prepared Pontiac did at the 1960 Atlanta 500, Johns won. It often didn't hold up.

Besides, Johns was not wedded to stock cars. He tried Indianapolis several times and was the driver of one of the most unusual cars ever to reach the Speedway, Smokey Yunick's Hurst Sidecar Special. This vehicle, which failed to qualify for the 1964 event, carried the driver virtually as a passenger in a motorcycle sidecar. The main chassis of the vehicle housed the engine, gasoline, and suspension components. The driver's seat stuck out on the left side.

Socrates Johns was an old midget driver. It was inevitable that when a son came along on May 22, 1934, he was filled with the stories of the excitement of motor racing. Bobby studied business administration briefly at the University of Miami, knowledge he put to use in Johns' Automotive, an auto repair business in Miami. But his forte was racing, which he began in 1951 at Palm Beach, becoming state sportsman champion 3 straight years. The move to Grand National came in 1956 after he was mustered out of the Army at Fort Jackson in South Carolina. It was evident, then, that Johns got his kicks out of racing cars. His face lit up when he spoke of particular cars he owned in the past.

His best NASCAR year was 1960 when he finished 3rd in the season standings, losing the Daytona 500 to Junior Johnson only by the worst of racing luck.

In 1965 Johns deserted his beloved Pontiac to do battle in a Holman-Moody Ford. His best finish of the year at a superspeedway was 2nd to Marvin Panch in the Atlanta 500. He wrecked in the 400-mile race there on June 13 as Panch won again. He quit Holman-Moody dissatisfied with their preparation of his cars.

Johns believed that the only way to get into big-time auto racing was to be absolutely fit. He swam and maintained a strict exercise routine, went to bed reasonably early, and generally made Jack Armstrong look like a rouser. As might be expected, he was an expert mechanic and described with great clarity what he wanted done to cars he drove—a clarity quite refreshing to pit personnel. But Socrates's son was the kind of man who makes racing interesting.

BOB JOHNSON

When Carroll Shelby's Cobra was brand new and still untested, Bob Johnson of Columbus, Ohio, decided that he would just have to have one. Now Johnson was no kid; he was 35 and vice president of an industrial catering firm that later bore his name. But hitching his star to this marque was the smartest racing move that he ever made. He mastered the mighty speedster and became a 2-time national amateur champion. In the process he helped establish Cobra's reputation.

Bob had already turned 30 when he bought his first sports car back in 1958. "It was a Corvette," he recalled. "Why? Simply because a Corvette was the only 'sports car' I knew anything about at all. I knew very little about competition back then, even that first day I rolled out to the grid in my shiny new Corvette, but I wasn't afraid to ask questions. And keep asking."

Johnson asked the right questions and got lots of right answers. In 1960 he won his first national championship in SCCA competition, the B Production crown. He kept on driving Corvettes until 1963 when he spied his first Cobra. "I decided the Cobra would beat the Corvette, so I set my mind on acquiring one," said Bob. That was easier said than done in those days. Shelby was too busy wheeling and dealing to bother with anything but serious inquiries. Bob Johnson was serious enough to show up at Sebring with check in hand, and one of the actual race cars was his soon after the checkered flag fell.

Johnson and his mechanic, Tom Greatorex, whom Bob gave a great share of the credit for his racing successes, stripped the race-worn vehicle to the frame and put it together again with tender loving care. Driving this car, the caterer from Columbus swept the SCCA's A Production ranks in 1963 and 1964. Even more startling was his continuing success in the professional ranks as part of the USRRC circus. East Coast enthusiasts still talk about his epic performance in the 1963 Watkins Glen race, where he took on the full might of Shelby-American in the persons of Bob Holbert, Ken Miles, and Dave MacDonald. The trio took turns in trying to overcome the surprising leader for 66 long laps around the 2.3-mile Glen course. One after the other Bob eliminated their challenges and walked away with the trophy, points, and cash that the boss of Shelby-American already had mentally banked.

Never a man to let a good thing get away from him, the Texan invited Johnson to become an occasional member of the Cobra factory team, including 1965 drives at Sebring, where he codrove a Cobra coupe to 7th overall and 2nd among the GT cars, and at Daytona, where Johnson took 1st in the GT class and 2nd overall. With this kind of schedule he had to abandon his SCCA driving and concentrate on the pro ranks. His fellow Midwestern amateurs were not sorry to see the gray-templed driver-executive leave their ranks; it was time somebody else got a crack at the silverware.

EDDIE JOHNSON

Eddie Johnson was born below the Mason-Dixon line in stock-car territory, February 10, 1919, at Richmond, Va. But he came before the glory days of the stock cars. Besides, he emigrated to California where at the age of 22 he began a career with midget racing.

Johnson never set any tracks afire, never won any rookie awards, never won on the Championship Trail; his best showing was a 3rd in the 1959 Trenton 100. Rather, he was known as a steady driver, a finisher, a man who would get the car into the money. This is not to say that he could not go fast enough to win, but that he was racing long after his contemporaries were rehashing old memories. He was good enough to finish 7th at Indianapolis in the Valvoline Offy at the age of 47, the 15th consecutive Indy in which he had driven, tying Mauri Rose for this endurance feat.

Johnson was a veritable yardstick of racing progress. His first car, the 1952 Central Excavating Special, qualified at the 500 just under 134 m.p.h.; his fastest, the Valvoline car, was 25 m.p.h. faster. He was running when the checked flag came out 9 of 15 times (another mark), and finished 5 times in the top 10, his best a 6th in 1960 in the Jim Robbins Specials. In 1953 and 1954, the 2 years his own car did not make the race, he was last to be bumped and thus first alternate. Both times he drove relief—for Jim Rathmann and Dodger Ward respectively. A resident of Cuyahoga Falls, Ohio, Johnson ventured forth for an occasional midget race until the age of 50. He has been competing in these cars and the sprints for 2 decades and more, winning enough to make it worthwhile—and keeping in shape for the Big One.

JUNIOR JOHNSON

Junior Johnson had on an old checked shirt and a pair of dirty work pants when he appeared before the nation's press to be interviewed after winning the 2nd running of the Daytona 500 in a year old Chevrolet at a disappointing average speed of only 124.470 m.p.h. There was some doubt as to who was more ill at ease, the Speedway and NASCAR public relations people, the assorted press who had heard that this rotund man with the close-cropped hair had served time for moonshining, or Johnson himself. Besides, there was the pall cast over the race when Lee Petty, defending champion, and Johnny Beauchamp had hurtled over the top of the huge track, their cars locked in what looked like a deathly embrace.

The fact that Johnson had run a cagey, canny race, conserving his car when necessary and charging like an enraged rhino when it counted most, had been lost on most of the press. But his fellow NASCAR drivers already knew the caliber of the chunky man from Ronda, N.C. He eventually won 50 Grand National victories, amassed fortunes in the chicken farming business and road construction equipment leasing, and quit while he was apparently at the top of his driving talents only to return as a car owner.

His name appeared initially on NASCAR's record books in 1954, but he had been competing several years before that. He retired as a driver in 1966, although several times afterwards he threatened to come back and teach the youngsters what it was all about. He was glamorized as a folk hero by several American collectors of offbeat human chefs d'oeuvre, but he never let it go to his head. Junior knew why he was in racing, and it was not to play the Carolina farm boy. It was to win money and get a little enjoyment out of doing what seemed to come naturally to him—driving fast.

He was a quiet, methodical man, setting goals for himself and working hard to achieve them. To recount his early victory totals is to talk about something that does not exist any more in major competition. The NASCAR Grand National drivers do not see dirt tracks any more; they have a different set of competitive standards now. Johnson was one of many who bridged the two eras; he was one of the few who had outstanding success in both. When he won the Daytona 500, he already had a following from at least 12 other victories to his credit.

But because he had hardly ever run the full Grand National circuit, he seldom ranked in the top 10 of NASCAR. In 1955 he finished 6th; in 1958, 9th; 1960, 7th; 1961, 6th; and after that he was mostly a superspeedway man. He was a charger, and when he held together, which was reasonably often, he won or came close. He won at Atlanta, the 1963 Dixie 400, in a Chevrolet. He won back-to-back National 400s at Charlotte in a Pontiac and a Chevrolet. He thought he

had won the 1962 Southern 500 at Darlington until a scoring recheck took the race from him and gave it to Larry Frank.

In 1965 he made up for it in the Rebel 300. The day had not started auspiciously. Junior met the only guard in South Carolina who did not know him on sight and had to show an ID card to gain admittance to Darlington. Herb Nab, the mechanic assigned him in the Ford factory operation, then told him that the engine was not churning out peak horsepower when he qualified 3rd. Junior took the information under advisement. When the green flag descended, he let pole-sitter Fred Lorenzen lead just a lap as he busied himself getting past Marvin Panch, the 2nd place qualifier. Then he swept in front, a position he held through lap 42 and through 2 caution flags.

It was a typical Darlington race. No sooner had Junior made his pass than newcomer Wayne Smith's Chevvy stalled. Since Smith was about to be lapped and the car was right in the middle of the high-speed groove, the competitors scattered every which way. Johnson's yellow Ford slipped under, and Lorenzen followed, almost losing it as he dipped toward the infield. Earl Balmer, leading the 2nd echelon of cars, hit an oil slick about the time he saw the stalled car and could not help plowing into the Chevrolet. Both cars were totaled, but both men walked away.

On the 41st lap, independent Larry Frank was forced into the wall by Bobby Johns trying to pass underneath him on the banking. Frank was still spinning when young Larry Hess slammed into him. Two more out and Junior had a chance to pit, one of 5 he made under the caution flag, which flew 7 times. As the race wound down it was obvious that only Darel Dieringer had a chance to catch the flying Johnson. Then Junior ducked in again, and the Nab crew from Holly Farms Poultry replaced the brake drum on the right front wheel with awesome precision and speed. The car would not start and the crew was apparently pushing it past the Johnson pits, in violation of NASCAR rules.

Junior roared back and when the checker sent him into victory lane, Bud Moore, owner of Dieringer's 2nd-place vehicle was already filing his $100 protest. The 1963 Darlington race seemed about to be run again, even though Nab filed a protest that Darel had improved his position under the caution light. The decision came the next day. Both protests were disallowed. NASCAR ruled Johnson had not violated the intent of the rule because he had not blocked off another pit crew—the next-door pit had been vacant—and Darel had transgressed but got back into place before the green had waved again. It was a typical Darlington race.

In 1965 Junior found a new reason to leave a major race. It was at Daytona in the Firecracker 400. Junior was one of the early leaders, but flying in for a pit stop he nudged into the next pit. The stewards waved him around again. This time when he whistled in, Dick Hutcherson's vehicle was blocking his way and he dinged it. The usually impassive Johnson was fuming. He shook his fist at the stewards as he sped back onto the track. Several laps later, for no apparent reason, he pulled into the pits, got out of the car and jumped across the wall. When asked why he stopped, Junior said one word, "Disgust," then stomped away.

He returned for his 9th and 10th victories in 1965 on the NASCAR northern tour. He did not win again until 2 months later in Winston-Salem, N. C. He lasted one lap in the Southern 500 when his distributor broke, but at Martinsville, Va., he scored victory number 12, and at North Wilkesboro, his "home" track, he made it 13. Soon after this victory, he announced his retirement to the position of car owner at the age of 34. He had amassed exactly 50 official Grand National victories.

The team of Johnson and Nab persisted through a succession of drivers—among them Bobby Isaac and Dieringer—then Johnson continued until Ford support money was no longer available. In 1971 Richard Howard made him an offer to build a Chevvy and drive it in the World 600 at Charlotte. He built it, but he did not drive it. Charley Glotzbach did, and led the race for awhile. And that put Johnson back in business building Chevvies—Chevvies that brought General Motors back to NASCAR competition as a major factor. In 1972 Johnson was inducted into the Stock Car Hall of Fame at Darlington. It was a good time, with Bobby Allison driving his Coca-Cola Chevvy, old Junior had a shot at being the leading car owner.

PARNELLI JONES

There is a part of America that even some Americans don't understand. It is not land or possessions, it is people and attitude. Horatio Alger lives, but he may be crew cut and have muscles and acquire polish only under the grinding wheel of life and experience. A tough kid who was born in the Dust Bowl in the Depression can become a millionaire owner of many business enterprises because he can outcompete everyone in a highly specialized niche of society, if he believes with absolute certainty that it is important and that it can be done and will be done. Such dedication to self-interest and self-gratification baffles people in other milieus. Some understand the goal, but do not understand the American approach to it.

Rufus Parnell Jones, co-operator of Ontario Motor Speedway, owner of the Colt Ford with which Al Unser swept the Championship Trail for 10 victories, explained when he said that Unser's 1970 Indianapolis triumph was as exciting to him as his own 1963 victory. Parnelli Jones, racing driver, said it when he said that winning a TransAm race for Ford in a Mustang SCCA was as exhiliarating at that moment as any other victory. The name of the game is competition, the reason for competition is to win, and in a society that is frankly and gloriously competitive, it is normal to expect human beings who glory in competing on every level and in every nuance of living.

To name a male child Rufus Parnell in such a society is to insure combat from the beginning of his age of understanding. An aunt helped Jones, nicknaming him Parnellie; he liked it better than Rufus and later dropped the "e." Born August 12, 1933, in Texarkana, Ark., Jones was transported at a very early age to Torrance, Calif., where he grew up. He was running hot rods at 17, and before that he used the fields near his modest home to learn to drive, even intentionally rolling cars as he had seen an auto thrill show stunt man do.

Official competition for Jones began in the jalopy ranks and progressed to the California and Western Racing Associations. He learned by doing, by spinning, crashing, somehow surviving until the driving style that caught the eye of J. C. Agajanian had evolved. It was Agajanian who brought Jones into the big time late in 1960 after Parnelli had clinched the Midwest sprint car crown. Parnelli finished 2nd for Agajanian in the Phoenix 100.

Still the dirt track ace, in 1961 he added two 2nds and a victory on the Trail and Rookie of the Year honors at Indianapolis for his 5th-place qualification and 12th-place finish. Winning the Phoenix 100 that year was notice that a virtuoso had arrived. Even though he was to win the Sprint Championship in 1961 and 1962, this virtuoso's style was not suited to the USAC championship or any single-seater cars. Considering his activity on the Trail, he seldom won—in 1962 there was

the Indy Fairgrounds 100-miler, in 1963 his Indianapolis 500 victory, and in 1964 there were 200-milers at Trenton Fairgrounds and Milwaukee, and in 1965 the Milwaukee 100. By 1966 he was eliminating most of the Trail from his schedule.

His forte seemed to be stock cars. In every venue, whether USAC, NASCAR or SCCA, Jones proved himself. Parnelli and Mercury were inseparable when that marque was competing. In 1964 he won 7 races outright and shared in an 8th victory with teammate Rodger Ward, sweeping to the USAC stock-car crown. He also took on Pikes Peak in 1963. It was a classic confrontation. The Pikes Peak course rises 4,707 feet in its twisting, 12.42-mile length. It has a maximum grade of 10.5 percent and offers the double challenge of poor road surface and ever-thinning atmosphere. There are no guard rails and the scenery straight down from the side of the road is specatcular—if one is standing still.

The road is never the same. Winter storms may erode the mountainside here and add rocks and dirt there. Even during a run, it takes on different characteristics as the weather changes from haze to sunshine to sleet or snow. Road crews repair the road only if it presents an undue hazard. Parnelli had come as a favor to Agajanian, who had undertaken promotion of the event. He set about learning the course and promptly fell in love with it. He pounded his Bill Stroppe prepared Mercury up the mountain day after day, learning the course as well as it could be learned, and when the actual climb came, he shattered Curtis Turner's record by more than 30 seconds. The next year he shaved that time

to repeat as stock-car champ. After that the challenge seems to have faded. There were so many other challenges around. The 1964 USAC stock-car crown was his, and he dabbled in sports cars and even tried his luck in NASCAR country, claiming, however, that the inspectors leaned unfairly on the way his car was set up.

But Jones was finding challenges off the course, too. He had saved his money and invested in real estate; he had an interest in an airplane service, owned mostly by his chief mechanic, Johnny Pouelsen. And with Vel Miletich, an early sponsor and long-time friend, there was the interest in Vel's Ford. Most important was the Firestone racing tire distributorship for west of the Mississippi and a Firestone store in Torrance, both highly profitable. Then there was a boat and a new house and a wife, and Jones began to eliminate racing venues. One of the hardest to leave was Indianapolis, the symbol of American racing success, for many years the only place in the world where for an afternoon's competition a driver could set himself up financially for life.

The very thought kept Jones returning to Indy even after he had known great success and great danger there. Jones passed his driver test in 1961, the year he was to finish 12th. That was his first race in a car called Ol' Calhoun, built by A. J. Watson, prepared by Pouelsen and worried over by Mobil Oil engineers, who personally prepared the witches' brew that served as fuel. Ol' Calhoun, now in the Speedway Museum, won the pole twice out of 4 starts, won a 500, led another, and ended its career in a fire which Jones escaped only because he happened to be in the pits when it started. One of those pole runs was the first time anyone had surpassed 150 m.p.h. in qualifying—1962—and the Agajanian Willard Battery Special, Ol' Calhoun's square name, was the toast of track racing.

Parnelli had had offers earlier of a ride at the Brickyard; he rejected them to study the race 3 years in a row before driving there. Agajanian and Ol' Calhoun were the right combination, especially with Pouelsen as crew chief. Parnelli led that race for 75 miles, but Calhoun sucked up some track debris that hit Parnelli over the eye, nearly blinding him with blood from the wound. Distracted, he adjusted his fuel mixture improperly and finished on 7 cylinders. Yet he shared Rookie of the Year honors with Bobby Marshman, who finished 7th.

In 1962 Jones smoked Ol' Calhoun to the pole and led 123 of the first 125 laps. Then an exhaust header broke, slipped enough to rub in the brake line, and allowed the fluid to drain. Without brakes, Parnelli slowed only enough to finish 7th. Even the 1963 victory, starting from the pole, was not without its shadow. Parnelli was 23 seconds ahead and less than 100 miles from the finish when his oil tank developed a horizontal crack, releasing a fine spray of oil onto his right rear tire and thence to the track. Thinking the strange behaviour of the tire was an air leak Jones slowed, allowing Jim Clark's Lotus to slash the 23-second lead. When he guessed what the problem was, Jones accelerated again.

However, by this time the drama in the race was taking place around chief steward Harlan Fengler. Lotus builder Colin Chapman was demanding that Jones be flagged in for inspection, and J. C. Agajanian was fighting a masterful case against such action. Allowed to continue, the oil spray from Jones's car stopped when the level of the oil dropped below the crack, and Jones sped to victory. The controversy that attended this race helped make Clark and Chapman better known in America, led Jones to punch Eddie Sachs's prominent jaw at a luncheon, and refurbished Parnelli's reputation for being rugged and rough-hewn.

In 1964 with a Grand Prix style chassis, Jones gave Ol' Calhoun one last chance even though a rear-engined car was available. He was leading when a fire broke out at the end of a pit stop. Parnelli suffered 2nd degree burns. But he returned in 1965 to earn 2nd place in a pusher car. The 1966 race with its terrifying 1st lap pileup was Jones's weakest Indy appearance. He finished 14th after a wheel bearing failed at the 217-mile mark. He had just begun to make his move. The experience disheartened Jones, and he retired from the Championship Trail completely for 1967—or meant to, until Andy Granatelli offered him the turbine-engined car.

Parnelli tried it, allowed himself to be persuaded to return to Indy once again, and almost pulled it off. A harbinger of what was to happen in the race came during qualifying. Like most new machines, the turbine still had minor bugs to be ironed out. Jones was plagued by gearbox trouble. The tremendous torque of the engine twisted off the transfer gear shaft at the gear's hub face every time the turbocar was pushed much beyond 166 m.p.h. So Jones qualified 6th at 166.075 m.p.h., well behind pole-sitter Mario Andretti's 168.982 m.p.h. But everyone knew Parnelli qualified on kerosene, the same fuel he would use in the race, while others used what the racers call popped fuel, a mixture including nitromethane.

Race day was overcast and the forecast was rain in Indianapolis. But somehow the clouds held back as the band played "Back Home Again in Indiana" and the perennial "Gentlemen Start Your Engines" brought the roar of 33 racing machines and the pulse-quickening anticipation of another 500 race. Jones and the turbocar, which ran so silently it was equipped with a horn, pulled from 6th to 1st on the 1st lap and assumed a 13-second advantage over Dan Gurney. The cold east wind finally blew the rain in on the 16th lap, rain that got harder and harder until the program was halted on lap 18. By then Jones had set 3 records and thoroughly terrorized both the racing and auto industry. Here was a working turbine-engined car that seemed a shoo-in to win the most prestigious race in the world. Racing might really improve the passenger car breed dramatically.

When the race was resumed the next day, Jones returned to his record-setting pace and led 171 laps. He had a 52-second lead over A. J. Foyt in the 197th lap when the bearings froze in the gearbox and his race was over. Foyt went on to win. Needless to say, USAC and the car makers cooperated to make the turbocar far less competitive the following year by attacking most of the technical advances it embodied, such as 4 wheel drive, the turbine engine, and the very construction of the vehicle. Studebaker Corporation's offer to build 20 more of the cars at $70,000 a copy to equalize competition obviously fell on deaf ears. (A conventional Indy car cost that or more.)

Jones was offered the 1968 version of the STP turbine, but refused the ride. His Indy career had ended—at least as a driver. Now he concentrated on his efforts as a car owner, producing winners in 1970, '71, '72. There was still competition in person—off-road racing, the SCCA TransAm series—but Rufus Parnell Jones was a businessman first, a race driver second. Letting go of the tail of a tiger like race driving is a slow process for someone who has ridden that tiger a long way. On a given day in a given car, responding to a given challenge, Parnelli remained as good a driver as there ever is likely to be. But as the bankroll got bigger, such challenges became fewer, save for off-road racing which Jones adopted as a safety valve. The owner of the Vel's-Parnelli racing show was a success with USAC champions like Joe Leonard, Al Unser, and Mario Andretti working for him.

ELIZABETTA JUNEK

On the same day as the 1969 LeMans race, the Bugatti Owners' Club of Britain held its 40th anniversary in connection with the Prescott Hillclimb; and the following weekend the British Vintage Sports Car Club held its annual Seaman Trophies Races meeting. At each, the center of attention was a handsome woman who spoke English with a Continental accent, Mrs. Ladeslav Khasova—formerly Mrs. Vinzenz Junek, a Mercedes and Bugatti driver of considerable repute, as her first husband had been until his death in 1928.

Born in 1900, Elizabetta Junek began driving in 1921 in order to know her new husband better. Vinzenz was a Prague banker and auto enthusiast, and he had the means to hand his wife anything she wanted. She learned to drive in a Laurin & Klement. In 1922 Vinzenz purchased a 100-h.p. boat-tailed Mercedes, which his wife quickly mastered. The Bugatti era for the Juneks began the following year. Initially, she codrove in competition with her husband, then went out on her own, her initial success coming in a Pilsen hillclimb in 1924. The next season, she won 6 climbs outright and scored 10 class victories in all.

In 1952 Bugatti's 2-litre supercharged model made its appearance, and one quickly found its way to Prague. Elizabetta swept all competition before her in Czechoslovakia, including all the men except her husband, and she and Vinzenz did well in other European races. What really made the Juneks' reputation was their showing in the Swiss Grand Prix, including Elizabetta's 2nd place overall (and ladies' championship), in 1926. The following year the Juneks bought a 2.3-litre Bugatti and prepared to enter the Targa Florio. Elizabetta went to Sicily first and immediately began test drives. From the start it was obvious she knew what she was doing, and expectations began to rise for this first woman to enter the famous Italian endurance test.

But it was not to be. When Vinzenz arrived and started driving, there was a slight accident and the car's steering was affected. They tried anyway, and she was 4th despite sluggish steering when the task became impossible. The Italian Racing Club awarded Elizabetta a special gold medal, and she was invited back the following year. That same season, Elizabetta won part of the German GP, the Coupe des Dames at Monthlhéry, and the Grand Prix du Salon Automobile.

The Targa in 1928 attracted a stellar field, and once again Elizabetta seemed very much in the thick of things. Her yellow and black car got the starting flag 2 minutes after a blue-team Bugatti driven by Albert Divo, yet within a lap she had passed him. By the 3rd lap, she was 2nd, behind Campari in an Alfa Romeo, and the possibility of her winning grew. But once again

it was not to be. Hot steam started to blow in Elizabetta's face, and her mechanic quickly pointed to a loss of power. A quick stop revealed the trouble to be a leaking water pump; with quick repairs and some warm spring water, they were on their way again, but other cars had passed. By the time the Junek car crossed the finish line, Divo had won. Campari's car had had mechanical troubles but held to the finish, and Conelli and Louis Chiron had edged past. Elizabetta was 5th, but behind her were such famous names as Fagioli, Dreyfus, and Maserati.

The German GP came next for the Juneks. Because he could not appear at the Targa (for he was a banker 1st and a driver next), Vinzenz took the car for this race. It was his last. Leading his category, he was killed when the car skidded from the road, but his mechanic was spared. Without Vinzenz, Elizabetta did not want to race again. She sold the cars and quit the grid forever. It was 1947 before she married again, to a Czech writer. But there was one more "race" for Elizabetta. It was at that Seaman Trophies meeting in 1969, and her mount was a Bugatti Type 35B, the type of car in which she did so well in the Targa Florio. Those who were there said that the nearly 70-year-old woman drove faster than anyone expected (in the opinion of one veteran motoring editor, "much too fast"). But that was Elizabetta Junek's way, surprising all men who looked and saw a pretty young girl and not a serious racing opponent. Successful racing drivers rarely change.

KAS KASTNER

Three out of four Triumph sports cars competing regularly in United States racing programs owe much of their success to a cigar-smoking sportsman by the name of Robert W. Kastner, formerly Triumph's U.S. competition director, then a full-time businessman in his own right. The marque is one of America's most successful in amateur sports car racing (10 SCCA divisional championships out of 18 possible in 1964, for example).

Kas was a working "director" and a familiar sight at top races with his cigar and his tool box, while helping out a name driver or an unknown with equal facility. Triumph's racing program was different from those of other marques; it owned no cars of its own, but used the entries of individual owners to develop its products and then shared the knowledge with every other competing TR driver who answered one of its familiar advertisements in the sports car papers. Kastner used cars like a TR-4, owned and driven by Californian Charlie Gates, or the Spitfire of another West Coaster, Ed Barker, as test beds. Triumph maintained both cars, including metal work, painting, and roll bars in addition to their mechanical ends.

"We're committed to aiding and advising the private

owners of our cars, not competing against them," said Kastner. "We do appear at some international races like Le Mans and Sebring, of course, but these are special cases. Parts and advice are available to anyone, whether he's Bob Tullius or not. We assume that if a man's interested enough to go racing, he's worth helping all we can."

This owner-driver orientation may come from the fact that Kas himself was an SCCA stalwart for many years. Born in 1929, Kas's earliest interests in sports cars came about as a result of moving to a small Colorado town with his new wife and new job. With "nothing else to do there" he became interested in foreign cars, ran his first race in an MG TD in 1952, and won his 2nd time out at Midvale, Utah. Since Kastner was an excellent mechanic, he took this engine and built an MG Special, which he raced until he saw his first TR-2 in 1955. From that point on, he said, it was Triumph all the way. He moved to the West Coast and joined a Triumph distributor, Cal Sales, which was absorbed by the parent company in 1960. An active competitor with SCCA (a cofounder of its Utah region) around Los Angeles, Kas had also become a power in the California Sports Car Club as a governor and contest board member by the time he joined the parent group's senior staff —a move that meant no more racing.

Kastner retired as a driver but remained active as an official and a "moonlighting" carbuilder and maintainer in the evenings after his daytime factory service supervisor's job. He must have been doing a pretty good job because another marque offered him a spot as its competition director. Kas accepted but never saw the inside of his new office; Triumph counter-offered with a similar position and there he stayed, when not tinkering with an owner's car on some U.S. track.

Finally, in 1971, he left Triumph to set up his own racing enterprise with Los Angeles businessman Tom Brophy. It was announced that Kastner-Brophy, Inc., would race 3 Triumphs in SCCA competition: a Formula A car, and a Formula 5000 car. Office-sitting can get to a man, after all.

HIROSHI KAZATO

Japan has been interested in motor racing for many years, but it has also been as insular as the United States once was. In the middle of the 20th century it is hard to stay cut off from the mainstream in any area if you are a civilized, technology-oriented nation, and Japan fits that description. So it is that Japanese racing is attracting overseas drivers and Japanese drivers are starting to appear at international races.

One of the better bets for stardom if he perserveres appears to be Hiroshi Kazato, 1970's Japanese sports car champion at the age of 19 (born 1951). Son of a well-to-do family, Hiroshi began racing in 1967, finishing 2nd in his first race, a junior championship event, in a Honda 800. After a moderately successful club career in 1968, Kazato won 3 races and was 2nd once in 6 starts in a Brabham single-seater, a Porsche 910, and a Honda in 1969. This earned him a start in the Nippon CanAm race, in which he finished 8th in his underpowered Porsche against American, European, and Japanese factory entries.

Kazato was aiming for the CanAm back in the United States, but first put in a season at home, driving 6 different cars in 9 starts. He began with the old Porsche and won twice in 3 appearances. Switching to a newer Porsche, he won the Suzuka 500, and the season continued apace in a Mazda rotary car and a Porsche 908, among others. He won 5, was 2nd twice and 3rd once, taking the championship easily.

In 1971 Kazato ran the full Canadian-American Challenge Cup series in a new Lola T222, operating out of Carl Haas's Highland Park, Ill., Lola dealership, as was Jackie Stewart in the radical T260. The season was as tough for the young Japanese driver as for the Flying Scot. Hiroshi's best finish was a 5th at Road America. Undaunted, he quickly announced plans for 1972—a Formula 2 March 722, sponsored by a number of Japanese firms. Over the winter he ran the local Japanese Grand Prix, finishing 6th overall in a Brabham-Mitsubishi BT30.

FOXHALL KEENE

Foxhall Parker Keene was a moneyed American who spent his life and fortune in the pursuit of sport. Boxing, horse racing, the hunt, all remember him in their annals, for he was a dedicated sort whose urge to excel would have brought him success in more mundane pursuits had it been necessary. Born into baronial surroundings in 1870, he became the most noted gentleman jockey and polo player of his time. He saw the sporting possibilities of the automobile in 1895, and first practiced driving his 3-wheeler in a huge attic. Later that year he managed 30 m.p.h. outdoors, and his first crash.

By 1901 Keene was driving a $14,000 Mors in the Paris–Berlin race. He planned to make up for his lack of technique by pouring on the power, and achieved 2nd place as the racers stormed through Bastien. He hoped to catch Henri Fournier, also in a Mors, who was leading. Bouncing across a culvert, Keene flipped. He and his mechanic were thrown clear and landed in a potato patch. It took them 2 hours to get the car going again, so as they went roaring through Aix-la-Chapelle, Keene was 16th. Between Hanover and Frankfurt, however, the car broke down completely.

This taste of road racing impelled Keene to practice for hours, as was his custom with any sport. He bought a Mercedes and practiced so assiduously that Stuttgart invited him to join its team for the 1903 Gordon Bennett Cup in Ireland. Living in England at the time, Keene kept the car at Dieppe and frequently crossed the Channel for a day or two of training over French roads. It is difficult now to imagine the wide-ranging freedom of motoring before the days of heavy traffic. Under those conditions, Keene once shot across Europe in time which would be hard to match today.

Entered in the Paris–Madrid race, he found that his car was in Stuttgart when it should have been in Paris for the weighing-in. Keene stepped off the night train in Stuttgart at 6 in the morning, picked up the car, and started back to Paris, 500 miles away, over roads still largely unpaved. He drove into the Tuileries at 7 that night, half an hour before the weigh-in deadline.

Keene was abroad when American road racing had its major start with the race to which William K. Vanderbilt gave his name and the winner's award in 1904. But Foxhall had high hopes that he could win its 2nd running in 1905. Germany entered 4 cars, and 4 teams of 5 cars each represented France, Italy, and the United States. Alden Hatch later described how Keene's Mercedes came from beyond the curve of the narrow road with a tremendous roar, tearing the early-morning mists apart as orange flame shot from its flanks and smoke swirled in its wake. He saw "in the midst of that streak of fire and smoke a slim calm figure . . . plainly master of the occasion." And he could not resist yelling at the top of his voice, "Yea-a-ay Foxie!"—as did thousands of others who hoped an American driver, even if in a German car, would win the day. But he did not. Keene was among the leaders, but lost his position almost at the price of his neck. The Albertson turn was to end the hopes of Louis Chevrolet, and here Keene also came to grief. He went into it in good style, though perhaps a little too fast to be absolutely sure of coming out right side up at the other end. In the middle of the turn his heavy car left the course and slammed into a telegraph pole. Keene and his racing companion were dazed but not seriously hurt. As a further piece of luck, there was a course observer's station nearby with a field telephone through which Foxhall was able to tell his worried mother that he had not been killed.

Foxhall again tried the Vanderbilt Cup 3 years later. This time his car caught fire, and he singed his mustache and eyebrows while coolly fighting the flames. Such exploits led a contemporary journalist to conclude, "Mr. Keene has two kinds of luck—the bad luck that brings on the accidents, and the good luck that somehow in the face of sinister possibilities manages to bring him off pretty well."

For all of his dash, Keene never did develop the skill that might have won him the top rank in motor racing. Thus his main attention was still devoted to horses, his first and lasting love. The family fortune was based in the blue-grass country of Kentucky where they raised and bred the finest thoroughbred horses. Foxie owned Sysonby, one of the great horses of all time, and many

others. However, his predilection for music-hall belles, bourbon, and bacchanals finally dissipated his part of the magnificent fortune, and he ended his days in a small cottage on the estate of his sister, reminiscing. He died in 1941 at the age of 71, a very old and full 71.

MEL KENYON

Born on April 15, 1933, in De Kalb, Ill., Mel Kenyon began competition in 1955, driving modified stock cars at Freeport and at Rockford, Ill. He and his brother Don had always shared a passion for racing; they operated a speed shop in the off season. The Kenyon Brothers 1940 Ford coupe still evokes memories in that downstate area because the boys rigged it so that a tail of flame shot from the exhaust pipe. Two years later the Kenyons switched to midgets. The first Kenyon midget had a Ford tractor engine in a Kurtis frame; with it Mel won the Blue Island, Ill., track championship, the Chicago United Racing Association title, and in 1962, NASCAR's Florida midget crown.

He switched allegiance to USAC in mid-1962, finishing 5th in the midget standings, moving up to 2nd in 1963 and the championship in 1964. He had qualified at Trenton in a championship car in 1963, but his appearances prior to Langhorne were sporadic on the Trail. He had hoped to make the switch in 1965 when the accident occurred.

On the 27th lap of the newly paved Langhorne Speedway that June 20, 1965, the engine had blown on Kenyon's Kemerly Special Offenhauser and the car had spun, setting off a chain reaction. Ralph Ligouri bumped Joe Leonard and caromed off into the rear of Kenyon's crippled car. The gas tank on Kenyon's car ruptured, bursting into flames; he had no chance to escape. When Mel awoke he was in the hospital, wracked with pain and burns over 30 percent of his body. The heat had baked his left arm and the left side of his head. But as he lay there he vowed never to quit automobile racing. He mumbled, "I'll go back, I'll go back" over and over again.

Flown to Brooke Army Medical Center in San Antonio, Tex., Kenyon was left with a stump for a left hand. He walked out of the famed burn center in 3 months, half the estimated recovery time, still determined to return to racing. In March 1966 in Tucson, Ariz., he carefully fitted himself behind the wheel of the Offy midget he and his brother had prepared, a special glove on his left hand giving him some leverage on the wheel. He had been USAC midget champion in 1964 and he was coming back—all the way.

In 1966 Kenyon placed 2nd in national midget standings, came back to Indianapolis for his initial ride in the race proper (he had not made the field the year previous) and worked himself up from 17th to 5th by the end of the race. It was about then that the railbirds

345

started calling him Miraculous Mel Kenyon. Mel freely admitted, "I haven't got the pulling power in my left hand to get the necessary speeds to win over long distances. I must drive a steady race and hope that some day this will be enough to win on the Championship Trail."

Kenyon was magnificent in 1966, winning 3 of 50 midget starts and finishing in the top five 27 times. In 1967 he was fantastic in the little cars, winning 17 of 49 midget features despite a hospital stay for plastic surgery. He wrecked in 1967 at Indy, but came back to finish 3rd in 1968 while winning the midget crown again. He picked his spots in his big car, the City of Lebanon Indiana Special, also finishing 4th at Michigan International's 250-miler. He had a 4th at Indy in 1969. His best finish in 1970 was a third in Milwaukee's Tony Bettenhausen 200. At Indy in 1971 he hit the wall after 10 laps, and in 1972 lasted 126 laps for 18th place before engine woes sidelined him.

Popular and outspoken, 5-foot 9-inch Kenyon served as the midget car division representative on the USAC Board of Directors. It was a foregone conclusion that he was in racing to stay. "I imagine that when I no longer can drive—and I feel pretty strong now—I'll be a car owner, or I might take a flyer at promoting," he remarked in 1971. "I count myself as the luckiest man alive. When I was in that hospital bed after Langhorne, I would have been happy to have come back as a member of the pit crew. That's why every race is so much fun as well as being good business." Kenyon drove one of the green Sprite Specials for Lindsey Hopkins in

1971, crashed on the 10th lap. He lasted 126 laps the next year before the injector failed on the Gilmore racing car, after he qualified at 181.388 m.p.h. He was classified 18th.

LEO KINNUNEN

Born August 5, 1943, in Tampere, Finland, Leo Juhani Kinnunen did not start serious auto racing until 1968, after fooling around with rallying and ice-racing. He bought himself a second-hand Titan Formula 3 car early that season and showed promise, although the Titan scarcely was competitive with the newer machinery around, even in Scandinavia. In the end, he returned to more conventional mounts, like the ones he had raced locally prior to 1968.

Leo's 1969 mount was a Porsche 908, with which he competed in the Nordic Cup series throughout Scandinavia and emerged as series champion despite serious international competition. At Anderstorp, Kinnunen won the finale over Brian Redman, Jo Bonnier, and Dick Attwood. In October 1969 Kinnunen was invited to a Porsche factory session at Austria's Osterreichring and saw the 917 for the first time. He not only had a chance to look at the beast, but drive it, and Kinnunen astonished the factory people by lapping the Ring only half a second slower than the veteran Redman, a JW regular, after only a few laps.

This kind of performance led to offers to test other exotic machinery such as the Lotus 69 Formula 2 car,

for example, and led to Kinnunen's contract with Wyer to help Porsche make a run at the World Championship for Manufacturers in 1970. Teamed with Pedro Rodriguez, he shared victories at long-distance enduros like the Daytona 24-Hour Race, the BOAC 1000, Monza's 1000, and the Watkins Glen 6-Hour Race, plus a 2nd in the Targa Florio and a 4th at Sebring's 12-Hour Race. Then he was fired.

Led's crime, apparently, was being the partner to one of the more talented—and temperamental—drivers of racing in the sixties and seventies. Rodriguez complained that he had to do most of the team's driving—such as some 20 of the 24 hours at Daytona—apparently not realizing that no matter who was his substitute, the result would have been the same. Rodriguez was never one to watch and wait very patiently, and the sight of the small, rather silent (since few people in JW Automotive, if any, spoke Finnish, and Leo's English lessons were progressing slowly), round-faced driver in the Rodriguez Porsche was enough to get the highstrung Pedro's adrenalin flowing even more rapidly. So Leo found himself out after an incredibly successful season. But such were the ways of big-time auto racing in the seventies. However, in 1971 Leo got a Porsche 917 for the European Interserie, their version of the Group 7 Canadian-American Challenge Cup. Kinnunen won the whole ball game, with Peter Gethin 2nd far back, and he repeated as Interserie champion in 1972 as well. Steady work makes perfect.

RENE DE KNYFF

Racing in Europe began in 1894, a year before the first American contest, and between then and 1906, when the first Grand Prix was run in France, racing was confined mainly to private estates or, occasionally, to public roads cleared for that purpose. A familiar figure of the period was a big man with a bushy black beard. As the years wore on, the beard grayed, but the man remained as erect as ever, until, at the age of 90 in 1955, Rene de Knyff, a Belgian but a Chevalier of France, died.

Born in 1864, de Knyff was a director of Panhard & Levassor, a pioneering French car builder, but his interest in cars far outdistanced that. The Chevalier, in fact, became chairman of the Automobile Club de France, which organized the early races in that country. No one, in the 40 years of his association with that sporting body, ever suggested that de Knyff's actions or decisions were governed by his Panhard association.

As a racer, he amassed an impressive record in the primitive early cars and in the bigger, almost brutish machines that succeeded them. In 1897 the Belgian was 5th in the 106-mile Paris-Dieppe race and 4th in the Paris-Trouville battle. In the 149-mile Marseilles-Nice-La Turbie race, de Knyff was 4th. The following season,

his Panhard was as active as ever, finishing 3rd in the 147-mile Marseilles-Nice race and 4th in the 889-mile Paris-Amsterdam-Paris run. Then he won the 357-mile Paris-Bordeaux race at 22.1 m.p.h., leading a Panhard sweep. There followed a triumphal tour to England, where the Chevalier gave the Prince of Wales, the future Edward VII, his first automobile ride.

In 1899, de Knyff did well in the Paris-Bordeaux race, finishing 2nd to Fernand Charron in a spirited battle, their averages 29.6 to 29.9 m.p.h. Charron was also aboard a Panhard, which perhaps mitigated the Chevalier's disappointment. In the first Tour de France, later converted to a bicycle race, he won the 1,350-mile grind at an average speed of 30.2 m.p.h. The feat was all the greater when you consider the almost nonexistent roads, the short life of an 1899 tire, and the lack of parts, tools, or even people who knew anything about cars. The racer and his riding mechanic had to be self-sufficient. They had to carry parts, or make them from something else. They could carry only so many spare tires, so patchwork was mandatory. In the face of all this, the 30-plus m.p.h. average was incredibly high.

Conditions were improving, however. In 1900, de Knyff won the Circuit du Sud Ouest, a 209.5-mile road tour centered around Pau, at 43.8 m.p.h. He then took the Nice-Marseilles race at 36.3 m.p.h. That same year he led the French team in the first Gordon Bennett Cup race, finishing 3rd. There had been some controversy about a Belgian representing France, but de Knyff ignored that and stilled his critics with his fine showing. His big memory of that race in later years was not the controversy but the fact that the racers were met by exactly 12 people as they reached a finish line in Lyon.

In 1901, the Chevalier scored a 3rd in the Paris-Berlin race, the following season a 7th in the Circuit du Nord. In the Paris-Vienna race, the first part of which—Paris-Innsbruck—was run for the Bennett Cup, de Knyff ran 3rd. He was leading in the race to Vienna when a sheared pinion put him beside the road. In 1903, in the ill-fated Paris-Madrid race, ended by the government at Bordeaux because of the many accidents and deaths in that first section, de Knyff was among the leaders when blown tires and a broken camshaft ended his bid. In the 4th running of the Gordon Bennett Cup, he battled Camille Jenatzy for most of the race and finished 2nd. At season's end the Chevalier hung up his goggles.

At the instigation of de Knyff the 1906 Grand Prix, the first GP, was organized. Whenever one is run today, it is a tribute to this great pioneer.

DAVE KOETZLA

His origins are shrouded on the circuits of the Midwest where he was a mechanic, car owner, and driver. David J. Koetzla managed Gilmore Stadium in Hollywood and must be called the father of the Offy midget. Koetzla, a show biz *Variety* type, broached the idea of creating a midget version of the Offenhauser Indy and sprint engine to Fred Offenhauser early in 1934. To be truthful, the Offy engine business for Indy or any place else was not very lucrative. Few sponsors had the money and there were plenty of other engines deemed more suitable to this era of semi-stocks at Indianapolis. So Fred created the first Offenhauser Special, a 98-cu. in. engine in a chassis that was conventionally engineered, but lightened. Curley Mills, the Ozark Mountain throttle stomper, took the midget for its first ride in October 1934. "We didn't even know if it would run," Koetzla was quoted later. "Fred and I pushed it and pushed it until the engine suddenly began to roar." Mills stomped on the throttle, and the lap times ensured Koetzla's place in history.

The car was so much better than most of its contemporaries that it soon dominated the sport. It looked fast and professional and—showcased with Gilmore—it contributed to midget racing's rapid rise before World War II. Koetzla faded from the auto scene along with Gilmore, but his idea lived on.

FRANK KURTIS

"I guess my first love affair was Indy," Frank Kurtis recalled later. "It was 1920 when I was 12 years old, and we'd just moved out to California where racing was a way of life. Two years later I built my first car, an old Model T, assembled from junkyard parts." He had the help of 2 younger brothers, Andy and Bill, to finish it in 3 months. The name was Kurtic in those days, a heritage, like his natural flair for mechanics, from his Czech father.

A year before, Frank had quit school and gone to work for Don Lee, a Los Angeles Cadillac distributor and enthusiastic racing buff. Studying mechanical drawing at night school for 4 years, he built his first out-and-out racing car in 1930, the Atlas Chrome Special, a roadster that, he said, enjoyed the same eminence in the thirties that sports cars enjoy today. His car became a contender at once and in 1933 Frank opened his own shop in Los Angeles. From it came more than 800 midget cars and many Indianapolis machines, in addition to other products, automotive and otherwise.

Kurtis brought intelligence and a native talent to the U.S. carbuilding scene. His cars were aerodynamically correct and good looking as well. One early milestone in his career was the Rex Mays Car Series, which displayed original ideas that shocked West Coast midget people, but won, again and again. The frame, for example, was of chrome steel alloy tubing, much lighter but stronger than anything in use then. The suspension gave a comparatively soft ride because the car was better balanced than competing designs.

Kurtis's Indianapolis designs were equally well thought out and rugged. His first chance at building a full-size Indy racer came in 1939 and he almost flubbed it. A week before the big race, Ronnie Householder piled the car into a wall in practice, and it looked like a washout. But Kurtis went to work with a will and had the car running in top form for a qualifying spin with Billy Devore at the wheel. In the race itself, the car performed perfectly and finished 10th, a standout performance for a rookie builder. After the war, Frank built the chassis for the 1st front-wheel drive Novi to Bud Winfield's plans and in later years built 3 more, as well as transplanting two of their engines to a conventional chassis.

When Johnny Parsons qualified the prototype Kurtis-Kraft 3000 rear-wheel drive for the 1949 Indianapolis race, at a then record 132.9 m.p.h. for unsupercharged cars, he set the stage for what was to become the Frank Kurtis era at the Brickyard. This car finished 2nd in 1949, then won the rain-shortened 300-mile race of 1950. The 3000 chassis featured a light tubular space frame, independent front suspension, and the reintroduction of torsion bar suspension. The resulting design, light, with a low center of gravity and less unsprung weight, had softer suspension than its predecessors, went faster in the turns and had better bite accelerating out of them, and was less tiring to drive at high speeds than previous machines. Kurtis was the first to admit that cars like this were not revolutionary when compared with European Grand Prix machines, but certainly were different when compared with other American racing cars.

Kurtis's designs were not greeted with enthusiasm. Opposition from the old-line builders and drivers—much the same opposition that has faced every change at Indianapolis through the years—kept many of his ideas from ever catching on. In 1950, for example, Frank rebuilt a rear-engined car owned by Nat Rounds and introduced a soft suspension system designed to keep driver fatigue down and safety up, as he put it. A top Indy driver took the Rounds Rocket out for only a lap, then came in and said he couldn't "get the feel" of the new car; that finished it because no other driver there would dispute the front-row man's opinion.

"Only during my biggest years," said Kurtis, referring to those glory years like 1953 when 24 of the 33 Indianapolis starters were in Kurtis-Kraft cars, "was I able to include some of my new ideas—the least radical ones—in my cars. Eventually, many of these ideas became accepted, but what was discouraging was that it never got any easier to introduce new ideas. It was just as hard in 1959 as it was in 1939 to get some of those people to see any benefit in a change."

He cites another case: in 1954 he had a rear-engined turbine-powered car design in which a buyer showed real interest but wanted some assurance that Indianapolis officialdom would permit it to qualify, if it could, for the big race. "My buyer was hot, but Indy was cool," recalled Kurtis. "We sent in the specs for approval, and when the response came—a sort of 'Dear John' letter, you might say—the buyer took one look at it and said he was sorry, but he couldn't take a chance. And I couldn't blame him; not many people can afford to gamble $50,000 or so on a car if there's even an outside chance of an official snag later on."

It was his reluctance to build "the same old car" year after year that led to Kurtis's gradual disappearance from the dominant place he had held at Indianapolis—that and his widening business interests in other areas. Through the years, in addition to his cars—Indianapolis, midget, and even sports car prototypes like the famous Old Yellow—Frank had manufactured streamlined house trailers, jeep-like vehicles (during World War II a big moneymaker), jet aircraft servicing vehicles, and even a 2,000 m.p.h.-plus land rocket sled for aeronautical and space research. Kurtis, who was married to the same girl for more than 40 years and blessed with 2 children, always hoped to go back to the Indianapolis grind once more. "I still love Indy, and I guess I'd like to keep building cars for it until the day I die," he said. "But I'm not going to keep building the same car, year after year. I'll go into full production only if they let me progress technically." And that attitude is why Kurtis disappeared from racing.

EDDIE KUZMA

Before the advent of the rear-engined car, there were only 5 important active Indianapolis car builders. One of them maintained a small shop at 12727 South Budlong Avenue in Los Angeles. He was a former midget car driver named Eddie Kuzma and was considered one of the best body men in the United States. Kuzma did as much car rebuilding—perhaps more—as creating. But in the hard competitive world of American racing, men do not become successful because they can fashion beautiful automobile bodies. There has to be solid achievement based on one standard—the car's victories.

Some of the most successful cars in United States single-seat racing came from the Kuzma shop. Before he enlisted in the Navy after Pearl Harbor, Eddie had built up a reputation as the owner-mechanic-driver of of the most beautiful midgets in the Northwest. He finished high because the cars were good, not because he was much of a pilot. So there was a ready market for his talents after the war. His first famous car was the Agajanian No. 98, built in 1948 for J. C. Agajanian. This was the first tubular-frame American sprint car— a pet idea of Kuzma's before sports cars of this construction appeared in American competition. Driven by Duane Carter and Troy Ruttman, No. 98 swept to 2 Midwest championships.

Ruttman's winning vehicle in the 1952 Indianapolis 500 was a Kuzma creation—for dirt competition. And in 1953 Ed's Dean Van Lines Special won the inaugural Hoosier Hundred and finished 2nd in the 1954 Indy race for Jimmy Bryan. It became one of the winningest vehicles of all time in oval racing, eventually winning 20 national championship races. Undoubtedly Kuzma could have had much more business than he accepted after this, but he has always preferred quality to quantity. Unless he could do much of the work himself, or be close at hand to lend a wrench, Kuzma was liable to refuse jobs. The Budlong Avenue shop did not grow as much as some others did.

Yet in the Frank Kurtis era at the Speedway, his vehicles still managed to excel. The 1957 Race of Two Worlds winner at Monza, Italy, was his creation, and the same car finished 3rd in the 500. His production was limited to a couple of cars a year, and in later years he preferred to use frames built elsewhere. His production, year by year, included an Agajanian Special roadster in 1958, Pete Schmidt and Dean Van Lines roadsters in 1959, the Bowes Seal Fast in 1961 (over a proprietary frame), and a new roadster for Gordon Van Lines in 1963. The following year's Dean Van Lines car was new from Kuzma. The rest of the time he spent rebuilding or modifying other cars. Sheraton-Thompson, Lindsey Hopkins, H. A. Chapman, and many others gave him cars to which he added the Kuzma touch. Eddie, incidentally, rarely went to any race except Indianapolis. He kept busy in the shop—except for the month of May and perhaps the Sacramento race.

JIM LAMB

James Hensley Lamb was born on April 2, 1909, the son of a rural mail carrier in Elkton, Va. He was destined to be the hero or the villain of American automobile racing administration, depending upon one's viewpoint. His influence on the development of the sport after World War II was as great as that of any single man.

Secretary of the AAA Contest Board from 1945 until its abrupt demise a decade later, Lamb served an apprenticeship that began in July, 1935. He had been a traffic manager for a shoe manufacturer when Ted Allen, an old friend, and his predecessor in the secretaryship, invited him to join the Contest Board staff. He had written Allen after seeing Ted's picture in the paper in conjunction with the Malcom Campbell Daytona Beach runs—not to ask for a job, but merely to renew an old acquaintanceship. Allen met him, and that led to the offer—at a propitious time, for the shoe company was financially ill. Lamb, who had previously had absolutely no interest in the sport, began his duties as the chief steward at a race in Richmond, Va. The chief steward, of course, is supposed to be the final authority at any racing event. It is to Lamb's credit that, when he ascended to the secretaryship after the war, his chief steward appointees at least had a connection with the sport and many times were retired race drivers.

Lamb had learned by doing, from 1935 to 1941. During the war he worked as an executive for the Ward LaFrance Truck Corporation. Allen resigned from the AAA for a job in business in 1945, urging Lamb to accept the powerful secretary's post. The secretary of the AAA Contest Board was the chief working officer, since the Board itself was of a consultant nature. As such, he wielded great power in setting policy, and in granting sanctions and licenses.

Lamb was a natural-born bureaucrat, in the finest sense of the word. He realized that if he were to be important, the domain over which he ruled must be expanded. Therefore, he set out to aggrandize auto racing. However, in 1946, he was one of the main dissenting figures in an historic meeting at the Hotel Stevens in Chicago—a meeting called in the hopes of uniting all auto racing in America under one authority. The meeting was foredoomed because, while AAA Contest Board policy at this time was to welcome wayward sons back into the fold, Lamb was not ready to share authority with IMCA or any other "outlaw" group. He failed to see the golden opportunity in uniting, nor was he Machiavellian enough to turn the meeting to his own benefit. But then, there are very few men who could have. (Bill France was not involved.)

Lamb was, however, a good administrator. He reorganized the AAA brand of racing and record runs after the war, and, through accommodations like that with J. C. Agajanian of the Western Racing Association, expanded it. He made blunders, such as failing to get started in stock-car racing until NASCAR was a thriving organization; but like a Calvinist of the old school, he propagated the doctrine that the AAA Contest Board is the only true racing faith for so long and so hard that vestiges of this type of thinking continue to this day.

Lamb helped to clear big-time auto racing of shady promoters and improved the sport's image by insisting on enforcement of safety rules plus non-involvement with such, "nefarious," things as the liquor industry. After a 4-year moratorium on suspensions, he shocked the drivers back into line by setting down Indianapolis winner Bill Holland for an outlaw stock-car appearance. But it is moot whether or not auto racing would have expanded just as fast and just as healthily without him. The cream has a way of rising to the top. What Lamb did was to help scour the pot that holds the cream.

FERRUCCIO LAMBORGHINI

Ferruccio Lamborghini—short, powerful, thick-set—was born over 50 years ago in the flat, grey-green farming country that surrounds the Northern Italian indus-

trial complex of Modena, Bologna, and Centro. His father's tiny 20-acre farm was within 20 miles of the places where Ferrari and Orsi, heads of the Ferrari and Maserati marques, were born. Lamborghini was not truly a contemporary of the famous pair (he was 20 years their junior), yet he was their contemporary— many say their equal—in the design and production of fine automotive machinery.

Lamborghini was always fascinated by machines, beginning with a motorcycle which he acquired around the time he started at the Bologna Technical School. After a stint as a garage mechanic, he opened his own repair shop near Centro, while racing Gileras and Nortons. "I was awful," he related later. "I crashed the Norton four times." He worked on the island of Rhodes during the war, repairing Army vehicles, but returned to his small business. In 1946, he branched out into the field of engine tuning, heating up Fiats. Two years later he tried his 1st and only auto race, the Mille Miglia, and managed to crash his Fiat 500 Topolino. "It went straight into a bar," he said, "car and all. That was enough racing for me. I stayed and ordered a glass of vino."

His wife died that same year, soon after his son Toniono's birth, and from that point on he drove himself to be a success in business, so that he and his son could enjoy life, and so that his name would mean something after he was gone. He started with 50 British Army surplus Morris 6-cylinder engines, fashioning several tractors for friendly farmers. One order led to another, and soon Lamborghini was known as a tractor maker. By 1952 he was manufacturing his own engines and gearboxes, and he had established a name for reliability with the yellow-colored machines that bore a bull insignia. Lamborghini adopted the insignia from Taurus, the May bull, since it was his birth sign.

Lamborghini branched out into heaters and air conditioners, and later into experimental helicopters for the Italian Air Force. All of Lamborghini's enterprises were his own, without shareholders and a board of directors to prevent him from doing exactly what he wanted. Thus it was that the energetic Italian was able, when the time came, simply to say, "I will build my own car."

The spark that resulted in the Lamborghini automotive marque was ignited late in 1961. "I was driving a Ferrari 330 GTC," Ferruccio recalled, "I was having a lot of trouble with the car, mainly the differential. So I went to see Enzo Ferrari in Modena to ask him to get the thing fixed according to some ideas I had. He said he would be damned if he would alter a Ferrari differential for a lousy tractor manufacturer. So I said, 'Okay, if that's the way things are, I'll build my own GT, a Lamborghini GT,' Ferrari laughed. 'Un trattore Gran Turismo,' he cried. But he isn't laughing now, he's crying." Lamborghini swore the story was true, and Ferrari has never been known to deny the incident, if not the exact words. Ferruccio did not rush out and start giving orders, however; he was much too good a businessman for that. He straightened up several affairs that needed his immediate attention, thought out the kind of car he wanted, eyed the kind of people he would need for the project, picked a plant site, checked his financial resources, and only then did he act.

It began in January 1963. In 2 weeks Lamborghini hired the complete design and development team, all young men on the way up. "They were all working for Ferrari, for Maserati, for Abarth and for others, but when I want, I get," he said. Higher salaries, freedom of research and development, and his reputation for never backing a loser attracted these men to the Bull banner. Cian-Paulo Dall'ara, not yet 30, headed the team. He had been merely a member of Ferrari's competition department, but with Lamborghini he became technical director and chief engineer. "He gave us the specification for his new car that same month," said Dall'ara. "He said he wanted a Ferrari class car, only more comfortable, with better acceleration, higher speed and tighter roadholding—that was all. Beyond that, he didn't elaborate, and he wasn't interested in details, only success."

Work began in the tractor plant initially, then moved to the new factory that October, in time for the first 350 GT prototype car to be ready for its Turin Auto Show debut. The 9-man research team got the car back from Turin and redesigned it from scratch. By March, 1964, a finalized car, complete with a 3.5-litre Lamborghini engine, was ready for the Geneva Auto Show. Orders started pouring in, and while the car lost money because of the lavishness with which it was produced and the cost of the plant in which it was built, it could easily have made money if Ferruccio had wished, by increasing production from the 20 or so a month normally produced. But Lamborghini wasn't really interested in making money on his car. "It's a hobby," he said simply, "and you don't really expect to make money from a hobby. The best I would hope for is to break even, but even that really isn't necessary as long as we are turning out a quality product that will bring honor to the Lamborghini name. I want to be like Rolls of Rolls-Royce; I want my name to stand for something in many fields."

The basic car was produced in 3 versions, the 350 GT, 400 GT and 400 GT2/2. There was also a Bertone-bodied, transverse-engined, advanced Lamborghini called the P.400 Miura, with a squat look (it was 3 feet high) and a 350 h.p. engine that pushed it to 180 m.p.h., at 7,500 r.p.m. Lamborghini initiated this project in July 1965. His instructions were that he wanted a "very fast touring car, with modern racing lines and a rear engine, mounted on a new chassis," recalled Dall'ara. All this was to be done in time for the Turin Show that year, only 3 months away, with a complete car ready for the Geneva Show. The Miura was a fighting bull, and the name be fitted the resulting product, which was not meant for racing, but just plain old Grand Touring— driving very fast, very far. A racing version was produced for the design staff to play with, and it clocked better than 200 m.p.h.

Where would Lamborghini go from there? Dall'ara had hoped it would be into racing; he and his staff already had a racer drawn to the last detail. But Lamborghini himself said he would not race until Ferrari had given up the sport. "I can wait," he said. "We have Ferrari. One in Italy is enough. When Ferrari goes, we might start, but not before. I have one immediate ambition for motor racing, however. I am going to build an autodroma, then play the gentleman and spend what I've got. It will be 3.5 kilometers, and I'll build near this factory if I can get the land. We'll do everything in it, and it'll be bigger than Monza."

In 1971, the Lamborghini factory passed into Swiss hands, industrialist Georges-Henri Rosseti buying 51 percent of the operation. Ferruccio had his mind on other things, at least for the moment.

TONY LANFRANCHI

Tony Lanfranchi was a throw-back to the older days

of motor racing. A big, burly, smoking and drinking, party-goer, Tony seemed noisy and boisterous to many people. He was, in short, a character in the tradition of Mike Hawthorn, Harry Schell, and Wolfgang von Trips. He was certainly not a Jim Clark or a Graham Hill. He was just the "King" of Brands Hatch, a driver who had probably won more races at that Kentish course than anyone else in its history.

Lanfranchi was born on July 25, 1935, and was educated in Britain until his teens, when he emigrated to Switzerland to serve as an apprentice to his father in the baking-catering field. He was brought back to Britain to serve out his 2-year National Service. In a rare moment of sanity the Army made him part of its Catering Corps, and Lanfranchi rose to the rank of Captain while feeding whole regiments of troops.

It was in the Army that he started his racing career, running a Healey Silverstone, at Brands Hatch on Boxing Day 1957. He won, of course, and more races in a variety of sports cars followed: Frazer-Nashes, a Healey 100S, and an Elva Courier. In 1962 he went big-time with a Mark 6 Elva, and did well enough to get factory drives in the Mark 7 and the 8 over the next 3 seasons. He spent most of 1966 racing not in races, but for John Frankenheimer's motion picture *Grand Prix,* which led to other motion-picture assignments.

But Tony regained the race course for legitimate reasons in 1967 with Motor Racing Stables furnishing a Formula 3 Brabham BT21. Later Essex builder Ken Bass provided a factory-backed Merlyn. This successful partnership continued in 1968, as did Lanfranchi's association with Alan Fraser's Imps and Mark Konig's Group 6 Nomad. In the latter Tony and Mark shared a victory in class at the Paris 1000 in 1967 and were the only British entry to last out the 1968 Daytona 24-hour race.

In 1968 Tony obtained a Formula 1 ride at Oulton Park in an old BRM P261 and showed well early in the race, but was forced to retire as the tired old car died on him. This, however, may have earned Lanfranchi his shot at Formula 5000. The Chevrolet-powered single-seater racing class was in its infancy when Tony got into his first F5000 cockpit (a Lola T142) in January 1969 for a test drive at Brands. He blasted Sid Taylor's car around in record time and seemed to have earned a ride for the full season, with Fraser as sponsor. The ride did not materialize, however, and all the F5000 racing Tony got in was a single ride in a 4.5-litre Hepworth-Oldsmobile 4-wheel-drive car that he pushed to 6th at Brands. In 1970 he finally got a Lola—a T190—for 3 races late in the season at Thruxton, Silverstone, and Oulton, and finished 7th and 6th in the first 2 starts, and failed to start the last one.

Lanfranchi talked of quitting after these 2 disheartening seasons, but he also talked of coming back in 1971 with a Surtees TS5A, lent to Lanfranchi and Hepworth

by John Surtees himself. However, with all that raw, young, semi-experienced talent begging for mounts in Britain those days, it was getting harder and harder for the old fellows like Lanfranchi to find a ride of any sort, let alone a competitive one. As chief instructor at the Motor Racing Stables, he should have known all about those hungry, new faces—he taught many of them.

HERMANN LANG

In the years prior to World War II, few mechanics who were good enough to serve a Grand Prix team could— or would—switch to drive racing cars as a full-time vocation. Hermann Lang did so with dramatic effect, establishing himself in only 2 seasons as an outstanding driver of the silver monsters of prewar German racing. Lang, who was born April 6, 1909, at Bad Cannstatt, a Stuttgart suburb, was the youngest of 4 brothers. Two of the family's sons were to die in automobile accidents, and Hermann's family was opposed to his early predilection for speed. He persisted, however, and his career started, as so many Europeans' did, on a motorcycle, soon after he was apprenticed to a cycle factory. Lang's 1st victory was at the Solitude circuit, on a Norton shared with one of his brothers. Hermann was good, and his skills earned him a factory berth with Standard and a promising career as a hillclimb specialist.

352

In the inflation-ridden Germany of the early Thirties, however, Lang's factory berth disappeared, and he was glad to get odd jobs as a stonemason and a diesel locomotive engineer. His locomotive experience led him one day to the Daimler Benz factory a chance to be a mechanic in the Mercedes-Benz test department, where an engine was being developed for the new 1934 GP formula. Alfred Neubauer found the young man's talents satisfactory on one job or another, and he had Lang transferred to his racing department to serve as a mechanic for the fiery Luigi Fagioli. Neubauer also knew of Lang's motorcycling prowess and intended to take advantage of this if the opportunity presented itself. That opportunity came in the German Reliability Trial, a 2,000-kilometer "race" that Lang won easily. He was promptly appointed "driver under training" after successfully passing a driving test in nothing less than a W.25 racing car.

His first race in 1935 was the Eifelrennen, in which he was only expected to gain experience. Despite running off the road in both practice and the race itself, Lang finished 5th. He gained a mistrust of wet circuits, however, which proved to be somewhat of a weakness in Lang's otherwise creditable early seasons. The following year, he officially became the reserve driver, the number 4 man behind Rudi Caracciola, Manfred von Brauschitsch, and Fagioli, whom he no longer served as chief mechanic. Again he was 5th in the Eifelrennen, and then led the German GP at Nurburg-

ring until he broke a finger and had to turn the car over to Caracciola. Patched up, he took over Brauschitsch's car and finished 7th.

When Fagioli and Mercedes parted company, Hermann became a full-fledged team member. In 1937 Lang won his races, the very fast Avusrennen and the Tripoli GP, the latter at 134.25m.p.h. when he outlasted his teammates, and Fagioli and Bernd Rosemeyer in Auto Unions. At Avus his winning time in a fully streamlined W.125 was a mere 162.61 m.p.h. In the Italian and Swiss Grands Prix, he followed Caracciola across the finish line by a split second or two, and he was 3rd in the Belgian GP. In the Masaryk GP his car rolled into a group of spectators, but none were killed.

The year 1938 brought a new 3-litre formula, for which Lang's tigerish instincts were ideally suited. Not only did he equal team leader Caracciola, but surpassed him, many say. He won at Tripoli and in the Coppa Ciano, was 2nd in the German, Pau and Donington races, and finished 3rd in the French GP. At Tripoli he lapped the entire field and won at 127.45 m.p.h. in a machine with just half the capacity of his previous winning mount there. In 1939, a season shortened by the outbreak of World War II, Lang still managed to win the European Championship and the hillclimb championship as well. He took the Pau GP, then the Tripoli race in a 1.5-litre W.165 at 122.9 m.p.h., despite backing off toward the end so as not to lap teammate Caracciola. Racing the new W.163 the rest of the year, Lang won the Eifelrennen and the Belgian and Swiss races. At Nurburgring for the initial race, he set a lap record that stood until 1956, and he set the fastest lap at Spa, too, despite his sorrow at Seaman's crash and death. In both the French and German races his car retired. Then, at his peak, the war reduced Lang to the status of an aircraft parts inspector. He returned to competition in 1946 in a 2-litre BMW, winning a hillclimb. He continued to dabble in selected races until 1950, when he joined in the Veritas Formula 2 effort. Lang's only top placing was a 2nd at Solitude.

In 1951 Mercedes swung into racing action again, and Lang was a factory driver once more. The old W.163 were shipped to Argentina; Hermann placed in the Peron Cup and showed in the Eva Peron Cup 97-miler, despite evidence of age such as an expanded waist-line and a bald head. The following year Mercedes reentered international sports car racing, especially Le Mans, the scene of its last official entry in 1930. Lang rose to the occasion even though his only other long-distance race was earlier in the year in the Mille Miglia, where he drove only 60 miles. At the 1952 Le Mans he drove a careful, controlled race—and won. He repeated the victory at Nurburgring and moved on to the demanding Pan American Road Race. This 8-day grind tested not only the cars but the steel of the drivers in them. He hung on, driving a controlled race once more, and

finished 2nd despite his 44 years.

When Mercedes returned to GP racing in 1954, Hermann was too old to make the full schedule. He did drive once, taking the reserve car, the number 4 mount, in the German GP for old times sake. For a quarter of the race, he ran 2nd, looking like the Lang of old, despite a lackluster practice session. His lap times were but a second off Juan Fangio's. At mid-race, however, Hermann's Mercedes spun, and he was unable to restart. For the old warrior, the race was over, and so was his competition career. He returned to Bad Cannstatt and took up duties as a service inspector on Mercedes production cars. When on occasion a W.163 was run out to impress some newsmen, the driver was invariably Hermann Lang.

GERARD LARROUSSE

Gerard Larrousse won the 12-hour race at Sebring (1971), and won the fast Nurburgring 1000 and the Tour de France rally, as well, that same year. Like England's Vic Elford, his codriver at Sebring and the Ring, Larrousse was not that well-known outside Europe, despite his successes. He was a fast, reliable, highly competitive driver, who generally was forgotten by his fellow Frenchmen when they enthused over single-seat-driving countrymen like François Cevert, Jean-Pierre Beltoise, or Johnny Servoz-Gavin.

The parallel with Elford might be extended. Like Vic, Gerard started as a rallyist, and he also excelled in it. Born May 23, 1940, in Lyon, Larrousse started rallying in 1966 and began attracting notice in Europe in 1968, when he won the Neige et Glace and Rallye Lorraine in an Alpine. In 1969 he was signed by Porsche, a true mark of distinction, and won his 1st Tour de France and the Tour de Corsa that season. In the famed Monte Carlo Rally he placed 2nd, a feat he repeated in 1970. Like Elford, Larrousse was fast in enduro races. At Le Mans in 1969 he shared a Porsche 908 with Hans Herrmann and finished 2nd. He was 2nd again at that same 24-hour race the following year, in a 917 shared with Willi Kauhsen. In 1971 the string broke, and Larrousse was retired at Le Mans.

His other racing successes have included a 5th in the 1969 Austrian 1000 with Rudi Lins followed by a list of 1970 runs: 6th with Gerhard Koch at the BOAC 1000, 5th with Helmut Marko at the Nurburgring 1000, 3-litre class winner with Rudi Lins in the Spa 1000, winner at Montlhéry, and 4th with Lins in the Imola 500—all in the Porsche 908.

In 1971 Larrousse placed 9th with Gijs van Lennep at the BOAC 1000, but this was his only World Championship finish aside from the Sebring and Nurburgring victories—there were retirements at Monza's 1000, the Targa, and Le Mans in the Martini & Rossi Porsches.

That was the end of the Porsche association for the Martini team, although Larrousse probably would find some drives in the German car just as he had in other cars through the years. Meanwhile, he joined the Ford of Cologne team for the European Touring Car Championship series by 1972, he was in a Matra-Simca 670 with Henri Pescarolo when they won the Dijon sports-car race over Ferrari, then won everything in sight including the Watkins Glen Six-hour race to give Matra a championship.

JUD LARSON

Although Jud Larson was one of the greatest contestants in the tough IMCA sprint circuit, he was never a champion. He might have been one of the greatest anywhere, but for a heart that gave out just as he seemed ready to reach for the stars, and a love of racing so great that it hampered his career.

A tough Texan, Jud got a ride at the Sacramento Championship Trail stop October 21, 1956, and proceeded to show the USAC hot dogs that there were some pretty good frankfurters elsewhere in American racing. He led from the 12th lap to the checker, beating Don Freeland by a third of a mile and national USAC king Jim Bryan by 100 yards more. He was only 7 seconds off the track record, set when the Fairgrounds dirt was in much better condition. On September 23, 1956, Larson had been just as sensational, but it had been 3,000 miles away at the Reading, Pa., Fairgrounds.

It was there, in the Pfrommer sprint machines, that he set a new one-lap record of 23.95 seconds, something that farmer Tommy Hinnershitz, acknowledged king of Eastern sprints, had not been able to do in 3 years of trying.

Born in Grand Prairie, Tex., on January 21, 1923, Larson was competing in Ford roadster races at the age of 15. He spent World War II with the Marines, and returned to the jalopies for the 1945–1946 season. But Jud's car owner switched to a midget with a Ford V-8, 60 engine, and the Larson star began to rise. Jud won the Texas-New Mexico crown in 1947 in an "outlaw" group—in 1948 he joined AAA and dusted off their version of the same title. The M. A. Walker midget team for 1949 and 1950 included Larson, Cecil Green, and Johnny Mantz, but it did not include Jud for long. There just was not enough AAA competition in his area to suit him, so the big, easy-going Marine took to running non-AAA stocks and midgets. The AAA suspended him for this.

Larson moved to Kansas City and began an illustrious IMCA career as well as campaigning with independent tracks. (IMCA really does not care where its drivers compete, as long as they appear for IMCA races.) He toured a flat half-mile dirt track, Lakeside Stadium in Kansas City, in 21.89 seconds in a sprint Offy, and made himself a fair living running late-model stocks, as well as sprints and midgets. Larson never concentrated on the full IMCA sprint circuit, and so he never won the title. Late in 1952 he was reinstated by AAA, but after he failed to qualify for Indy in 1953, he stayed in IMCA.

In September 1955, Jud's passion for racing almost finished him forever. "I had just won the IMCA big-car main in the afternoon at Topeka, Kansas," he drawled, "and I felt so good I went to the Kansas City Midget Auto Racing Association 100 at Olympic Stadium that night. I was second, chasing Bill Chennault, when a rod went through the side of the engine and the car started to burn. I spent eight and a half weeks in the hospital for grafts and nine months for healing. The hospital was good to me, but I just hate hospitals—you don't see anything."

Larson returned to AAA competition on September 15, 1956, at the Hoosier Hundred (courtesy of John Zink of Oklahoma, who had long admired his hell-for-leather driving style). Jud didn't disappoint his sponsor, setting a track record and leading the best USAC drivers for 70 of the 100 miles until he hit a pothole and broke his rear suspension. Larson fought the car for the final 30 miles to salvage 4th. After the race his mount looked like a clown's car—on every wheel revolution it lifted its left rear. At Reading he set his record and figured in one of history's great finishes, when Hinnenshitz wedged past both Larson and Van Johnson to pull out the victory. At Trenton, Larson finished 4th. Then came the Sacramento victory.

In his initial full year on the Championship Trail (1957), with A.J. Watson as his chief mechanic, Larson finished 5th without running Indianapolis. Jud won at DuQuoin, Ill., and at the Hoosier Hundred. He took 2nd in the Atlanta 100 and the Springfield, 100, and 3rd at Sacramento. The following season he won at Atlanta and Phoenix, and drove the John Zink car from 19th starting place to 8th at the 500. Larson finished 2nd at Sacramento and 3rd at Langhorne for 4th place for the season. He was still driving midgets and sprints but he had moved to Tampa for the sake of his wife, Valerie, and 2 daughters.

The Bowes Seal Fast people finally broke into the Zink-Larson combination for the 1959 season—Watson left for the Leader Card cars, too—but the new car seemed to be a jinx to Jud. He never got going at Daytona Beach, wrecked after 45 laps of the 500, took a 4th at Milwaukee, and, after winning the pole, only finished 2nd at Langhorne.

Larson's heart trouble began at Springfield during the 1959 season. He had just qualified the Bowes car on the pole and driven back to his pit when he seemed to faint. A doctor was called and soon the ambulance was screaming toward the hospital. Larson had suffered a heart attack. When his recovery was sufficient to allow him to work, he toured for about a year as a public relations man for Bowes.

It was late in 1963 before Larson finally got into a race car again, back in the IMCA ranks. It was a short warmup for his 3rd return to the Championship Trail. He did not make Indy, but he drove many races for Leader Card and Watson, one of his many old friends.

Jud increasingly turned toward his first love as tracks became paved, and he competed in sprint cars when he competed at all. In 1965, for instance, driving the Watson sprint car, Larson won 7 of 26 starts, including 4 of the first 6 races of the season. He slacked off after that to finish 4th in the season standings. He had finished 2nd to Don Branson the year previous with 6 victories in 19 starts.

The Reading Fairground was one of his favorite tracks. He won the season opener there in 1965 and again in 1966. At Reading again, on a warm June night, the 43-year-old Larson came into the race leading for the championship. It was all over on the 2nd lap when, between the 1st and 2nd turns, Larson's car tapped that of William (Red) Reigel, 34, pride of the Hatfield Speedway. It was like a bad racing film—the gasp from the crowed, the buzzing silence that enshrouded the packed stands as both cars flipped over the 3-foot concrete retaining wall, rolling 7 or 8 times on the high bank, then sailing back over the wall. Larson's car landed on its wheels and Riegel's turned upside down. Riegel was dead on arrival at Reading Hospital. Larson, with his winpdipe and jugular vein both cut, was dead on arrival as well, at Community Hospital. He left behind a wife and 3 daughters.

NIKI LAUDA

To go from a Volkswagen to a Formula 1 March is a big jump, but was negotiated by at least one driver, Nicholas von Lauda, a young Austrian who had visions of becoming another Jo Rindt. Born in Vienna February 22, 1949, Lauda and the family's 1st VW were acquired about the same time. By the time he was old enough to see over the wheel, the VW had been given to the Lauda children to play with on family property (Niki's father being a successful paper processing executive).

Driving fork-lift trucks in family factories and then, at age 15, factory trucks in rural Austria kept Lauda happy until he saw the 1966 German Grand Prix. After that he wanted to trade in his Mini-Cooper S for a racing car right away. He spotted a race-ready Mini in an advertisement and approached the owner, a local hero named Fritz Baumgarten. Niki offered to trade his Mini for the racing version and pay the difference when he sold the car. To deceive his father, the car kept its Baumgarten markings, and Niki indicated he was merely storing the car for Fritz.

When they went hillclimbing together early in 1968, Niki told the family he was just going along to help Fritz. Unfortunately, Lauda was 2nd to Baumgarten in class and made the local papers. Relations at home were strained for a while, even though Niki won 4 climbs in a row and graduated to a Porsche 911S that he arranged for in the same way as the Mini. Climbing gave way to circuit racing in 1969, Lauda acquiring a factory ride

with Austro-Kaimann in a Formula Vee. At Hockenheim in his first FVee start, the youngster led much of the race until he spun out on the last lap. The next day at Aspern airfield, Lauda cartwheeled the FVee in practice and wrote off the car.

An understanding factory provided another car, and Niki set a lap record at the Ring, although Helmut Marko won the race. Enter Francis McNamara, the American expatriate, who was trying to become another major racing factory. He offered Niki a Formula 3 car, but this proved unrewarding and Lauda went off on his own, buying a Porsche 908. He had success with this car in Continental races and in his own British appearance at Thruxton where he won a race-long dice with a strong Lola T210.

At this point Lauda seemed to have realized that the only way to move up fast was to "rent" better rides, much as Rindt had done. Obtaining backing from an Austrian bank—partially a sponsorship, the rest of the fund a loan that his family guaranteed—Lauda bought a March Formula 2 ride for 1971. Ronnie Peterson, his March teammate, dominated F2, of course, but Lauda showed enough talent to keep near him and on one occasion, at Rouen, for he actually managed to lead Peterson for a time. The year was memorable primarily, perhaps, for Lauda's F1 debut, when he bought a ride in the Austrian GP in a March 711 with STP sponsorship, but handling difficulties made his performance hard to judge.

Still another Austrian bank was willing to arrange a sponsorship-loan deal, however, and in 1972 Lauda secured $100,000 worth of funding to go GP racing with STP-March, about 85 per cent of it repayable to the bank in 3 years. Such was the economic state of F1 racing in the seventies. Lauda was 11th in the Argentine GP opener, 7th in South Africa, retired in Spain. It was going to be a long year, but it was a year in which to learn, and Niki's 3-year plan had a way to go. That he was learning well was demonstrated in F2 where Lauda had a March and scored a good 2nd in the Mallory Park opener, 3rd at Thruxton, and victory (in a torrential downpour) at Oulton Park. At Hockenheim, he led both heats comfortably before retiring, but he was still the early leader for the European championship. Unlike Rindt, however, he was not a dominant driver, but that could come in time.

CHRISTIAN LAUTENSCHLAGER

Mercedes Benz has had many champion drivers; one of the earliest and best of these was Christian Lautenschlager, who drove their brutish cars in the years before World War I. It was he who won what many men continue to call the greatest Grand Prix.

Christian was born in Magstadt, about 14 miles from Stuttgart, on April 13, 1877. At 14 he was sent to the

Lautenschlager remained the factory's principal driver after the war, and turned up in such scattered places as Sicily for the 1922 Targa Florio (10th overall, 2nd in class) and Indianapolis (did not finish) in 1923. The 1924 Targa was his last competitive effort; he again finished 10th. Lautenschlager had reached 47 years of age, but continued as head of a Mercedes department until his retirement. In the spring of 1954, at the age of 77, Lautenschlager died in his sleep, in a tiny cottage on Daimler Benz property given to him by the company.

DAVE LAYCOCK

Heaven to a racing mechanic is time to finish one racing car so that it is perfect for the driver and perfect for the track upon which the race is to be run. And there is never enough time, because even the greatest racing mechanic can think of things he might have done, or wonder whether the agglomeration of compromises that a race car is will prove the winning combination.

It is the lot of the chief mechanics in this world to work under pressure. They are the brigadier generals of racing, the men who must perform if the commanders-in-chief—the drivers—are to be heroes instead of losers. But their epaulettes tear off easily; there are too many colonels in the wings waiting to try the role on for size and for success.

There is pressure even when building or modifying the racing car in the ever-shorter off season because that is when decisions are made which affect an entire season. Dave Laycock knew about pressure. It existed even on his 12.5-acre farm in the Indiana countryside amid the quacking of a flock of ducks and the occasional bark of a collie chasing a fleeing rabbit. It was a farm bought and paid for by mechanical skill with race cars, a farm that had a garage where cars were hand-built for Indianapolis, hopefully tailored to the driver's preferences in suspension and feel. Because each race car is as much a hand-wrought creation as it is a machine, Laycock could not be certain he had even approached his goal until Lloyd Ruby drove it. Only then could the hundreds of decisions—how strong to make this, how heavy to make that—begin to be checked out. Five painsaking months of labor were judged in a 3-minute ride.

Ruby, a square-shouldered Texan who had driven every kind of racing car for years and years, was Laycock's driver for several years. Ruby was a contender, a man not afraid to push the loud pedal for more speed; he was one of the 10 best in USAC, yet he never quite caught the brass ring. For Indianapolis he was as good as there is. It was up to Laycock to tailor the car to Ruby's taste so that the big Texan could concentrate on race strategy, not the car.

Ruby liked cars with a live front end that grabbed the corners so he could steer through and set up his next move precisely; the car had to ride with little

city to become a locksmith's apprentice, and over 3 years later he went out as a journeyman locksmith. It was 4 years before Lautenschlager returned, after stays in Switzerland and Saxony where he worked in a bicycle factory. Back in Stuttgart in 1899, Christian took a job as a mechanic at the Daimler factory. He attracted the eye of both Gottlieb Daimler himself and Daimler's successor, Wilhelm Maybach. He quickly rose to foreman of the driving department—which meant road testing customers' cars.

In 1906 the wide-mustachioed Lautenschlager had his 1st taste of racing, serving as a codriver in one of 3 Mercedes entries; the car finished 9th. Two years later he was given a car of his own for the Grand Prix de l'ACF, held on July 7, 1908, along a 48-mile triangular course that started outside Dieppe. There were to be 10 laps, and after taking the lead during the 5th lap, Lautenschlager won by almost 9 minutes at an average speed of 69 m.p.h. He then retired to the factory until 1913 and the French GP, in which he finished 6th.

On July 4, 1914—the day after Archduke Ferdinand's assassination, an event that would plunge most of the world into war—300,000 spectators were drawn to the Circuit de Lyon for one of the great races in motoring history. Otto Sailer led early, but was replaced by the crowd favorite, George Boillot of France. Lautenschlager, however, was not to be denied. Aided by trouble in Boillot's Peugeot, Christian took the lead on the 18th lap of the 23-mile road circuit. Lautenschlager led Leon Wagner and Otto Slazer home in a 1-2-3 Mercedes finish.

bounce, and the back end had to be tight, slipping and sliding little in the turns. This kind of setup was suited to the new tires that were as wide as 16 inches, with footprints that made drivers who liked their rear ends loose uneasy, if not unhappy.

With Gene White, the Atlanta Firestone distributor, paying the bills for the race car, Laycock knew he would have the best tires available. There would be 2 race cars as Indianapolis month approached: No. 4, a conventional turbocharged Offenhauser, and No. 25, Laycock's interpretation of the latest racing developments. Both were Mongoose Specials, the name Laycock gave cars created by him, but No. 4 had a conventional steel frame and was little different from the car Ruby drove in 1968. Moreover, with that design, Ruby had taken the early Championship Trail lead with a 3rd at Phoenix and a 2nd at Hanford, Calif.

No. 25 was a radical wedge like the turbine cars of the previous year. It had a unitized aluminum alloy frame, a unique rear suspension, and bugs. The rear end had turned out to be loose, the suspension bouncy, and, worst of all, it was unaccountably slow. Laycock had very little time to remedy all the bugs and wean Ruby away from No. 4. It would be impossible unless the wedge could be made to go faster.

To win Indianapolis by age 30 had been Laycock's dream, and he was 30 now. No. 25 was to have been his personal breakthrough, and it wasn't working. He had a decision to make and he made it. No. 25 had until qualifying time to be made ready, but meanwhile No. 4 would get attention, too. No. 25 would not run unless it could run well over the 160 m.p.h. speeds it had made so far. The day of decision came quietly like all other days. The great speedway lay basking under the Indiana sun, and the garages in Gasoline Alley emitted occasional belches of sound as activity picked up. Laycock had not announced to the world or even to his own men that this was the day of decision for No. 25, and maybe he would not then even admit it to himself. But the crew rolled the wedge out, and Ruby prepared himself for the practice run, inscrutable as ever.

Lloyd talked easily only when he was completely relaxed; he was quiet, and that meant he was tense. Laycock made small talk with Ruby, hoping the Texan's dislike of the car would not affect him, hoping that enough of the bugs had been worked out that the car would indicate its potential. But when the lap times came through, Laycock knew that it had been a lost cause and that for Indianapolis 1969, it was No. 4 which Ruby would drive.

Ruby qualified 20th, in the middle of the 7th row, at 166.428, some 4 m.p.h. slower than pole-sitter A. J. Foyt, but that didn't bother Laycock, for Lloyd was not known as a top qualifier. It did bother him when Chief Steward Harlan Fengler made him remove an oil cooler he put on after qualifying. But then Mario Andretti's head wrench, Clint Brawner, was moaning be-

cause he had had to switch back to the radiator used in qualifying. Between qualifying and race day there was time to around watching other cars try to make the field —Bobby Johns in No. 97 Mongoose just made it—and check and recheck the car so that some 50-cent part wouldn't cost the big money. And practice pit stops. Laycock's crews were consistently 2 to 4 seconds faster.

Indianapolis before the 500 is like New Year's Eve in May. There are midget races. Outside the Speedway, 16th Street is jammed with people determined to be the early.birds into the infield. There is a carnival, and the bars are filled. There are noises and pretty girls and girls who, if not pretty, are at least young, and some neither pretty nor young. There are beer and excitement and occasionally some small child fast asleep in the back seat of a station wagon. Laycock was not a part of it. He came to the garage area very early the next morning, the excitement high within him as it had been for weeks. There were a thousand little details to look after.

Soon the stands were filled—and the pits, too—and the band was playing "Back Home Again In Indiana," and the cars were on the track. Then Ruby climbed into the car and Tony Hulman was intoning over that magnificent loudspeaker system, "Gentlemen, start your engines." The shriek of the self-starting machines and the growl of 33 engines cut into the rising noise of the crowd. The race was on.

Ruby started fast, working his way up through the pack. By the 30th lap he had gained 15 places and was 5th. He had the lead briefly when Foyt and Andretti pitted on the 50th lap, was in and out of the pits himself in excellent time, but was still 4th at 60 laps. Laycock was too busy to be excited. Ruby passed Andretti for 2nd. No. 4 sounded strong and fast, and Ruby challenged Foyt, rolling into the lead on the 79th lap with Mario right on his heels. Mario slipped past on the 83rd lap, but Ruby dogged him until Mario pitted on lap 102 and Lloyd again took the lead as the back half of the race began.

Laycock felt the pressure mount. Winning the Big One would mean a payday for the team of over $200,-000. With really quick pit stops to help Lloyd along, it was possible, very possible. He had Lloyd brought in on lap 107. The men broke their necks to finish their tasks quickly—screw on the gas nozzle, check the tires, wipe the windshield, hear a few shouted words from Ruby. Then, in a split second, it was all over—a shrieking, grinding, fuel-spewing second that tore the side of the car out. The crew had failed to uncouple the left gasoline hose, and as Ruby pulled away it was all over. Embarrassingly, maddeningly over—a Keystone comedy accident.

If 10 years of upward mobility in the garage flashed past his eyes, Laycock never said; 10 years that had begun washing parts and bringing coffee, progressively better jobs until this. He was too busy swearing and thinking dark thoughts. For Laycock there was always a next year. In 1970 Ruby charged into the lead for 2 laps before an axle case broke and the resultant fire demolished the car on the track. There was also Ontario when Ruby in a Mongoose No. 25 took pole honors only to have the car swallow a valve at 42 laps. Sic transit California 500. For 1971 and 1972 there were 3 of the 500s and still no brass ring. Well, maybe winning a big one by age 40 should be goal enough.

FRANÇOIS LECOT

There are 500-mile races, 24-hour races, and rallies that cover thousands of miles and several countries. There are even marathon runs, like New York to Paris in the old days, and London to Sydney today. None of them can compare, however, with the feat of François Lecot, a 57-year-old grandfather, who, in 370 days of driving, covered 250,000 miles. It was not done on closed roads, but on the busy open highway between Paris and Monte Carlo.

André Citroën came up with the idea to promote the new front-wheel drive car that would remain in production for a quarter of a century. Critics questioned the durability of the radically different 1934 Citroën, and Andre needed something dramatic to demonstrate that his new car was as good as any they had ever seen. The man he approached was a hotel keeper and sometime endurance driver who had gained some reputation for being able to deal with unusual situations. Lecot was immediately attracted to the challenge, and even after Citroën died unexpectedly, he plowed ahead on the project.

Very little factory support was left after Citroën's death. His successors felt the feat was impossible, and to fail would do more harm than good. Lecot sunk his own life savings into the project, and with small amounts from other sources, he got the endurance run under way.

The Citroën used was a stock model, save for some minor changes like removing the windshield since Lecot would drive in both rain and fog. A special horn was installed and distinctive lights, since much would depend on the cooperation of the police, truckers, and plain citizens. François's home was near Lyon, so each day he would leave home to drive either to Paris or Monte Carlo, then return by night to sleep at home again. Each day's driving would be 700 miles, with no days off for any reason.

Two mechanics were hired to work on the car while Lecot slept, and the French Automobile Club appointed a panel of 8 observers, one of whom would always be in the car with Lecot. The route either way was incredibly complex and usually heavily trafficked, not only with cars, but with livestock, bicyclists, and pedestrians. One stretch included 185 hairpin curves over 22 miles. It seemed optimistic indeed, especially when an arbitrary

speed limit of 56 m.p.h. was established by the Auto Club. Despite all this, Lecot was confident, and at 3:30 A.M. on July 22, 1935 the endurance run got underway. By noon, François reached the Auto Club's Paris headquarters, at which he would have to register every other day. After 30 minutes' rest, he was on his way back toward Lyon. At 9:00 P.M. he reached home, and after a hot dinner, exercise, and a shower, he was in bed. At 3:30 A.M. the routine would begin again, except that his destination would be Monte Carlo's Sporting Club, his alternate registration point.

Each day, each week, each month, pride in Lecot's achievement grew in those along the way. The driver's own personality had much to do with this. He was courteous to all on the road, and often carried passengers or packages to Paris or Monte Carlo. Often he would bring fresh fish or flowers back from the south to distribute to those along his way and at home. His driving schedule was so precise that police along the way could anticipate his arrival within a few minutes and so clear the way. Road workers were always made sure that the one-way traffic around torn-up portions was travelling Lecot's way when he was due to arrive. Priests offered prayers with their congregations for his safety, and aid from the factory and suppliers became more generous as he plowed on.

There were the inevitable accidents. Once a truck passed too close and tipped Lecot's car. He and his inspector simply got out and tipped it upright to continue the journey. The most serious accident came in the closing days of the run, however, when a truck came unexpectedly out of a side road, and the Citroën slammed into it. The front end was smashed, but Lecot called his mechanics, who raced to the accident and worked on the car for 72 hours straight—most of them aided by François himself—until the Citroën was back on the road. The Auto Club sent word that extra days would be added to the year's deadline to allow for the repair period.

He needed only 363 days, as it turned out, to cover the required 250,000 miles (400,000 kilometers). The run ended on July 26, 1936, with the 7 days additional time allowed by the sanctioning body as a comfortable margin that eased François's final stints at the wheel. There were no great prizes, no trophies, no medals for Lecot, only the warm congratulations and recognition of his fellow Frenchmen. Because of the rush of events in Europe, his feat did not receive the acclaim that it might have in calmer days.

Lecot went back to his hotel, which he sold in 1943 to form a retirement fund. But inflation dissipated that meager fund quickly, and at the age of 70 he took on a new job—driving a milk bicycle. Later he worked in a factory, until cripled by a stroke. Nearly blind, he ended life in a charity hospital, his days brightened only by recollections of a feat that everyone said was impossible, but that he had accomplished. On his night table lay the little book that all Frenchmen must carry from earliest manhood to the grave, their military papers. On Lecot's was a notation that never failed to startle anyone who knew of his feat—it read, "unfit to drive an automobile."

JOE LEONARD

It was 1968 and the height of the Turbine Era at Indianapolis Motor Speedway. Andy Granatelli and Colin Chapman, as unlikely a pair as could be found in racing, had collaborated on the STP Turbocar that was shaking the Indianapolis establishment to its foundations. The ebullient and rotund Granatelli had wanted Parnelli Jones as his driver, but Parnelli, after his 1967 experience, decided to forego the ride.

Parnelli suggested Joseph Paul Leonard, the 6 foot 2 inch ex-motorcycle champion, and the deal was arranged. By qualifying day, Leonard was a comparative veteran of the turbine-engined racer. He had compressed a lot of experience into something under 100 laps of practice, experience that included demolishing a car against the wall and a staggering unofficial lap of 173 m.p.h.

When Leonard raised his hand to indicate that he was prepared to take his 4 official qualifying laps, the 150,-000 fans in attendance quieted even as the almost silent turbine's whine rose in pitch. Though he was alone on the track, it was evident that Leonard was going around the old Brickyard faster than anyone ever had before. He turned in an average of 171.559 m.p.h., and Granatelli and the STP crew danced in joy as the Turbocar came back to its pit and a grinning Leonard pulled himself out.

Leonard did not win in the Turbocar in 1968, although he led it most of the way. The turbine engine quit, and then USAC attacked every part of the Turbocar that represented engineering progress—the turbine, the 4-wheel drive, the very layout of the vehicle. Leonard spent a frustrating year with the Turbocar, for like many new bits of machinery it never quite made it, even in shorter races.

Joe Leonard's racing career had started because he wanted to race so badly that he ran away from his San Diego home at age 16. Leonard, born Aug. 4, 1934, had an old suitcase full of clothes, $21; and he was looking for someone who believed in him enough to let him have a motorcycle ride. He found that ride in San Jose, his home ever since. He was good, so good that he won the U.S. amateur crown in 1951, his first year on the 2-wheelers.

That was the beginning of a career that stamped him as an all-time American motorcycle great—professional champion in 1953, 1954, 1956, and 1957, runnerup in 1955, 1958, 1959. "The fun was going out of it for me by 1957. There was nothing really left to win," Joe said.

"I started thinking of trying for a 4-wheel ride in 1959, and 2 years later I decided to take the gamble and quit motorcycles. I had been going to auto races for a long time, and I figured at 31 it was then or never."

A. J. Foyt, who was to be one of Leonard's boosters and one of the men who gave him a car to race, said this about Leonard: "Joe studies things. He studies the tracks and the way the other drivers run them. He's going to be very good at this racing business. The reason is he wants to win, only to win."

Leonard's 1st rides were in the difficult West Coast modified stock-car circuit. Then in 1964 another ex-bike rider, Paul Goldsmith, got him on the Dodge stock car team in USAC, and he responded by becoming USAC stock-car Rookie of the Year and finishing 5th overall. He won his inaugural title race at DuQuoin, Ill., on September 6, 1964, a weekend which began his pursuit of Championship Trail honors. He competed in 5 races (in 4 different cars), his best finish a 5th at the Phoenix 200-miler.

In 1965 the learning process went further, and Leonard drove Indy for the 1st time as a member of Dan Gurney's All-American Racers team. He finished 29th after starting 27th, the victim of a broken clutch plate. He also won his 1st Championship Trail race, the Milwaukee 150, and finished 6th in the season standings by virtue of his 2nds at the Milwaukee 100 and the Trenton 200. He made only 4 stock-car starts, winning none.

Leonard joined the Gurney Eagle Team and qualified 20th for the 1966 Indianapolis 500. He finished 9th in that crash-marred renewal when his engine quit at the

425-mile mark. In his Yamaha-sponsored Eagle, Joe was a factor early in the year on the paved circuit stops, but he then parted company with that car and was trying to qualify some of the worst racers around. At last he joined A. J. Foyt as number 2 driver for the final race of the season. His 5th-place finish at Phoenix was enough to assure him a 4th in the season standings.

The move to Foyt's Sheraton-Thompson colors paid off quickly when Joe finished 3rd to his teammate's victory in the 1967 Indy 500. He was tremendously impressed, however, with the potential of the turbine with which Parnelli Jones had scorched the field. After a good early season start, however, Joe did nothing on the Trail, and by season's end he was again free-lancing. He finished 9th in the standings.

The competitive urge still burned fiercely with the 36-year-old Leonard, despite family and business responsibilities. Joe considered himself a race driver 1st and a businessman 2nd. In 1970 he was number 2 on the Johnny Lightning team of Indy winner Al Unser, a team owned by the Parnelli Jones interests, and slated to dominate the next USAC season as it hadn't been dominated since Clint Brawner and Mario Andretti had worked for Al Dean.

First, however, in 1970 came the Rex Mays 150 at Milwaukee in the old State Fair Park. The race, bolstered by television money, was the richest of the 21 in this series, with a purse of some $78,350. Unser had swept past pole-sitter Andretti early in the 1st lap and controlled the contest until the 60th mile when Roger McCluskey gunned past him. McCluskey held on lap after lap through 5 caution flags and 140 miles. Then Leonard made his move. As the pair entered the northeast turn, Roger took the middle line, a mistake. Leonard slipped past on the outside, swooped into the stretch turn clearly in the lead and pulled away. Leonard kept the desperate Roger at bay for 9 miles to take the victory. Unser finished 3rd.

That race was only the beginning for Leonard. Al Unser had begun 1971 as if he would be unbeatable, but after mid-June misfortune seemed to dog him. Meanwhile Leonard was finishing well up in the standings in every race after Indianapolis, when turbocharger troubles held him to 19th. He never won, but was always in the top 5 finishers—2nd in the Schaefer 500 at Pocono, for instance. Suddenly, just before the Ontario 500, people woke up to the fact that Leonard was the favorite to win the Marlboro Championship Trail and thus the USAC championship. Leonard didn't disappoint them. After the chargers like the Unsers, Donohue, and Foyt were sidelined, Joe rolled into the lead of the 500 on lap 161 and won the race easily. That put the wraps on his first 4-wheel national crown.

Champion at age 37, Leonard looked toward 1972 with total aplomb. "It's a business with me now," he said. "It's a business but it's still fun. That makes it pleasant to continue but I don't need many more years like this to establish myself solid outside racing. I figure life begins at 40—life outside racing, that is." He repeated as National Champion, and his retirement planning seemed right on schedule. Because his Samsonite Special seemed to be the member of the Vel's-Parnelli team that was always the one to last the course, he won the Michigan 200, was declared winner of the Schaefer 500 at Pocono. Then he followed up with the Milwaukee 200 which, with a 3rd at Indianapolis, gave him an insurmountable lead and much money.

PIERRE LEVEGH

There was a Pierre Levegh who drove a Mors in the pioneering days of motor racing, but he had no sons to carry on what he conceived to be the Levegh destiny until his sister, a Madame Bouillion, had a son, Pierre, about the time of the first Levegh's retirement in 1905. Young Pierre grew up with stories of automobile racing and with the certain knowledge that one day he must carry on the tradition. As if to cement this idea firmly in the youth's mind, a family convention decided that Pierre Bouillion would have his name changed legally to his uncle's. This was the way the other Pierre Levegh was born; the man who, in the words of one motoring journalist, "inherited death."

The new Levegh started his automotive career at the lowest possible level, as an apprentice, pushing a broom in a small garage. By 1923 he was a mechanic, and that year was among the 100,000 spectators who trooped to the provincial town of Le Mans to see the 24-hour race. He was impressed, so impressed that he determined that this was the race he would win to uphold the Levegh tradition.

Each year after that, Pierre was to be found somewhere on the course—watching, studying, and waiting for his chance to drive a car in the 24 Hours of Le Mans. Between 1924 and 1935, when a Bugatti turned the trick, no French car had won, adding to Levegh's determination. Although accepted as one of better mechanics and car testers in France, he could not persuade anyone to provide him with a car for Le Mans. They did provide cars for lesser rallies and races, and Levegh surprised other drivers with his verve and daring. He turned to selling cars in an effort to gain recognition at the factories, and succeeded with the Talbot people.

Talbot's chief designer, Antonio Lago, met and liked the tall, knowledgeable, sharp-featured Levegh and, in 1938, offered him a ride for Le Mans. To be sure, it was no great offer, for all Lago wanted was a relief driver for Jean Thevoux, an old Le Mans hand who would pilot the 5th of 6 Talbot entries. But Levegh was not proud when it came to Le Mans, and readily accepted. However, Pierre never got to drive in the actual race; the car broke down before his turn came. He applied for a relief driving position in 1939, but none was available.

World War II closed down the sport, and Le Mans itself became a fighter air base, 1st for the Royal Air Force, and then for the Luftwaffe. British bombers and German bulldozers levelled most of the historic course establishments, and it was 1949 before racing returned to the site.

The Bishop, as the solemn Levegh was called, was now rather old to be seeking his 1st real ride in one of the world's major automobile races, but this did not deter him. At 1st he failed, but in 1951 he was again assigned to the 5th car in Lago's 6-car Talbot team, this time as the main driver. His 4.5-litre car was inferior to most on the course, even to 4 vehicles of his own team, but he finished 4th overall, behind a Jaguar, another Talbot, and an Aston Martin. René Marchand codrove the car.

Levegh, the master mechanic, had not been allowed to tinker with his Talbot—only factory mechanics could do that—even though he could see ways to better its performance. In 1952 he determined to enter his own car, a Talbot that he could prepare properly. It cost Pierre a good deal of money, about $10,000, and he spent half that much again in modifying the car to the specifications he felt were needed to win at Le Mans. The gasoline tank was enlarged, a 2nd complete electrical system was installed, a substitute, lightweight aluminum body was built to make up for the added weight of the modifications. In all, Pierre and his friends put 5,000 man-hours into preparing the car for the race.

Ferrari and Jaguar were more powerful than Levegh's Talbot, but he in turn outclassed the factory Talbots and even the Mercedes entries that year. He got off that June day with a fine start, and held back to let the more powerful Italian and British cars battle it out. Attrition worked on Levegh's side, and the dead car park soon held 17 vehicles, including most of the Jags and Ferraris. The Mercedes entries were still there, but Pierre did not worry about them. A Gordini led, but Levegh's No. 8 Talbot was 2nd, and he felt it was his day. At his 3rd fuel stop, Marchand stood ready to take over but Levegh waved him away. He wanted to take that lead away from the Italians and put some distance between himself and the Germans. At 3 A.M., as the headlights cut through the night, the Gordini's ignition gave out, and Levegh swept into the lead. He had driven 11 consecutive hours without relief and seemed as fresh as ever. As the massive crowds awoke that morning, they learned that a Frenchman in a French car was leading and a hero's name was borne aloft on more than 200,-000 French throats: "Levegh, Levegh."

Half way through in the 24-hour test, Pierre had a 4-lap lead on the nearest Mercedes. He again turned away Marchand at a fueling stop; he seemed obsessed. Again and again he stopped for fuel and resisted all efforts to make him yield the wheel for even a few hours of rest. With 4 hours to go, he was like a robot—he recognized no one in the pits, even his wife, he grimly held the wheel and would not yield, his head sagged, his color was frighteningly like that of a dead man.

With 23 hours gone, Levegh still sat—or rather slumped—in the Talbot's seat, but the machine hummed on at a steady 100-m.p.h. clip. His lead was better than 25 miles over the 2nd-place Mercedes, and a 60-m.p.h. average in that final hour would win the prize easily, but Levegh ignored—or was too tired to read—a pit signal to slow down. On he went, shifting, turning the wheel, finding the groove mechanically, not reasonably, until it happened. Pierre shoved his gear lever toward 1st instead of 3rd as he moved from 4th gear. The strain was too much for the crankshaft, and it split. The Talbot, which had led so long, faltered, then died at the roadside between Arnage and White House.

Levegh was in disgrace with his own countrymen for a time. His stubbornness had allowed the Germans to win at Le Mans once more, costing France a sweet victory that was within her grasp. Forgotten was the anguish that the loss must have meant for Pierre, sick not only in spirit but in body for weeks after the race. In 1953 he raced again, finishing 15th, best of the French entrants, but certainly no great feat even for a man of his age. In 1954 Talbot invested another car in his dream, and he was in the top 10 for several hours until it crashed at almost the same spot as his car had died in 1952.

There were no more French rides for Pierre Levegh, but there was a German one. Alfred Neubauer of Mercedes was left with a car and no driver when Paul Frere had to refuse at the last moment. Neubauer remembered 1952 and the Frenchman who had almost beat the Mercedes team single-handed. He offered the car to Levegh, and Pierre accepted, joining a team headed by 5-time World Champion Juan Manuel Fangio, who was to stage an epic duel with Britain's Mike Hawthorn.

At 6:10 P.M. on the evening of June 11, 1955, Hawthorn was in the lead, about 300 yards ahead of Fangio, with the two masters threading their way through lapped cars. Down the snaking road from the White House toward the pit area came an Austin Healey driven by Lance Macklin, a young British driver. His car was far to the right, trailed by the red-helmeted Levegh, whose own machine was almost scraping the thick earthen wall that protected spectators. Overtaking Hawthorn, who was preparing to go into his pit for the night's 1st refueling stop, Macklin swerved to the left to pass.

Levegh's Mercedes was on him at that moment and was catapulted into the air by the Healey's streamlined rear end. Levegh hit the wall and his car exploded. The engine cut an 8-foot-swath through the shoulder-to-shoulder crowd, killing 81 of the watching men, women and children. It is believed that Levegh died instantly. His funeral in Paris 3 days later was a macabre climax to a frustrating career—the funeral service took 2nd place to a wild scramble by onlookers to see, cheer, and try to get autographs from the world's leading figures in motor racing, there to bid Pierre farewell.

Much later John Fitch, scheduled to be Levegh's co-driver in the fatal car, revealed that Pierre had entered the race with misgivings. "This course is too narrow for these fast cars," Fitch quoted Levegh, "Each time I go by the pits, I feel hemmed in." He also said, "I do not like sitting on the left in a racing car. It is difficult enough to see pit signals in the pit, as narrow as it is. A driver needs to feel comfortable to do his best, and I do not feel comfortable in this car." Le Mans was revamped after that fatal day, the pits rebuilt, the approaches and the entire area around them widened, and the spectators pushed farther back from the course itself. But it was too late to help Levegh and the 81 people that his car killed.

GUY LIGIER

Star rugby player, French motorcycle champion, contractor, sports car and Grand Prix driver, car designer and builder—that in a nutshell is the life of Guy Ligier. He came from Vichy (born about 1930) and grew up to be one of the major contractors in that area. He later opened a garage in Paris and became a Ford importer, leading the GT drives on occasion. Always a fit fellow, thanks to his interests in rugby and motorcycling (the latter leading to a French title in the 500 c.c. class), Ligier was almost 36 by the time he decided to go into GP racing, yet managed top pull it off successfully.

Ligier started competition driving late in life, it was 1963 before he seriously started rallying, hillclimbing and entering occasional circuit races in GTs and Formula 2 single-seaters. In 1966 he decided to try his hand at Formula 1; it was a good time, for F1 had just changed to 3 litres, and it takes a year or so for things really to shake down, time enough for the independent to make his reputation.

Ligier always went 1st class, and his GP debut was that, if nothing else. He had a Cooper-Maserati ready for that 1st race, the 1966 Monaco GP, and drove a safe, conservative race, finishing 5th. He was far enough behind, however, not to classify(meaning no points). The story was the same at Spa for the Belgian GP—6th, and not classified. Ligier finished 9th in the French GP, 10th in the British GP and 9th again in the Dutch GP. He skipped the rest of the major Grands Prix, but notched a 6th in the non-title Syracuse GP. In sports/prototype racing, he shared a 4.7-litre Ford GT40 at the Nurburgring with Jo Schlesser and finished 5th.

The Cooper-Maserati was clearly not competitive, but Guy started the 1967 season with the same car, although he had his eye on something a bit better. He was 10th in the Belgian GP and 7th in France. Then his new

machine arrived—nothing less than the Denis Hulme factory Repco-Brabham in which the New Zealander had taken Monaco. Ligier's luck did not change radically, however, as he had hoped it might. He was 10th in the British GP and 8th in Germany. A dropped valve ended his race in Italy, and an oil leak combined with an engine bearing failure ruined his sole appearance in the United States GP. In Mexico he placed 11th. After that, he decided he really was not all that competitive, despite the mount, and ended his GP racing career.

Ligier was a good sports car designer and competitor. In 1967 he shared a 6th with Schlesser, a close friend, at the Monza 1000. Their mount was a GT40. In 1966 he had come within a few kilometers of winning his class in the gruelling Targa Florio, only to have a rear stub axle on his GT40 snap. Schlesser and Ligier shared a Rheims 12-hour victory in 1967. At Le Mans in 1970, he qualified a 1.8-litre car 30th of 51 qualifiers. The car was the fastest thing in its class, in fact, dusting off a 3-litre Porsche 908, every other car with a similar Cosworth engine, and even both of the two 7-litre Porsches that were there that year. Perhaps the most satisfying thing for Guy Ligier was that his Le Mans mount was a Ligier JS1 prototype, his own marque and partially his own design. The fact that the engine quit after 65 laps with a sheared distributor drive didn't detract from his feat at all. The car, JS a quiet recalling of Jo Schlesser who died in a flaming Honda in the 1968 French GP, was introduced at the 1969 Paris Salon as a sort of dream conception. Michel Tetu, a young man formerly with Deutsch Bonnet, and assisted by Ligier himself, came up with a practical design to make the dream a reality. Frua, second-guessed by Ligier, designed the body shell, which underwent wind tunnel tests.

Every last component was chosen by Ligier himself —much the way he designed and chose components for his award-winning headquarters building and home in Vichy—with suggestions from Jean Bernardet, a leading technical writer in French automotive circles. The car they created was very much a lightweight Lotus Europa, nicely styled but with real competition guts underneath the beauty. In addition to its closed-course tests, Ligier took a JS1 to victory in the 1970 Montlhéry sports car race in April, trailed by a couple of 5-litre cars—a GT40 and a Lola-Chevrolet. It must have been almost as satisfying as winning a Grand Prix.

FRANK LOCKHART

The life of Frank Lockhart would have made an ideal Hollywood plot for the movies of the thirties. The poor, illiterate, but honest boy, with a natural aptitude for mathematics and things mechanical, grows up to build and drive fast cars with verve and daring. He becomes king of the dirt tracks and the idol of the nation. He visits Indianapolis and, taking over the car of an ill driver, wins the big race. He designs, builds and races a new car toward a Land Speed Record, but dies in the attempt, his lifeless body hurled from the car and landing at the feet of his wife. This story has been told through the years by his white-haired mother.

An incredible story, but true in every detail. Frank Lockhart did all of this, and more, in just 25 years of life. Strangely, his story is not as familiar as you might think, even on his own old stomping grounds, the West Coast. In 1909, when Frank was 6 years old, he was brought to California by his mother after the death of his father in Dayton, Ohio. At 8 Frank had his first car, a soapbox coaster built of scraps of wood and tar paper. Later they said he won every time he raced; perhaps a slight exaggeration, but a forgiveable one.

Lockhart was a rebellious student, but somehow managed to get a high school diploma even though he spelled phonetically and cared for little but math and shop. He continued his education at a technical night school and even tried an entrance test for the famed California Institute of Technology, in which he is supposed to have scored higher than any previous applicant. Without money he could not enter, however, even if he had been willing to spend that much time in school.

Frank got his first real car at 16, an old, rusted Model T chassis given to him by a vegetable peddler named Mr. Gentle. He and his brother Bob carried it home, piece by piece, over a period of several weeks (home was 12 miles away). Ray McDowell, later a well-known builder of engines and racing components, gave him an ancient Ford engine (people were always giving Lockhart things as we shall continue to see) and he rebuilt it on his mother's kitchen table, adding a 16-valve Riley head among other things. A year later the car was finished and Lockhart entered a July 4th race at San Luis Obispo. The Hollywood plot slips a bit in this case; he did not win this 1st race, but dropped out when an exhaust manifold melted.

McDowell let Lockhart use his shop to rebuild the car, making it lighter in the chassis and installing a Frontenac engine. Ascot was next, and the story is that he was never passed at the California track. His 1st big win was Ascot's "Targa Florio," which ran from the track itself into Beverly Hills and back. Lockhart's borrowed Duesenberg staged a hot duel with no less a name than Cannon Ball Baker, who was waved in the winner. Frank protested and it was discovered that Baker was actually a lap behind. Lockhart's star had begun to rise at just the right time; Ralph DePalma, who had dominated the dirt tracks, gave it up for big-time racing once more, and Lockhart quickly replaced him in success and in the affection of West Coast fans. At 21 he married the only girl who had ever attracted him, Ella, and tried his hand at the then popular board speedways, finding them not to his liking.

The West Coast was one thing, and Indianapolis was another. When Lockhart visited the Midwest in 1926, no one rushed to meet him with open arms. A few veterans had heard of him as the guy who had replaced DePalma on the dirt tracks, but in their eyes that hardly qualified him for America's biggest race. Frank met a friend, mechanic Ernie Olson, who was preparing Bennett Hill's Miller, and Ernie arranged a test ride on Indy's historic bricks for Lockhart. The 23-year-old took to the bricks exactly the way he had taken to the dirt, wild yet controlled, spectacular yet sure and safe. Back in the pits, Frank found Hill, Olson, and the other fortunates who were in the park that day bug-eyed. He was told that he had been named Hill's relief driver.

Fate intervened once more, however, and another Miller driver, Pete Kreis, became ill during the time trials. Lockhart was offered his No. 15 car, and so he started on that cloudy May morning in the 7th row of a 28-car Indy field. At the flag, Earl Cooper and Harry Hartz in Millers and Leon Duray in a Locomobile held their front positions, but Frank started his move and made 5th place by the 3rd lap, 4th on the next one and 2nd at the 50-mile mark. The race was interrupted around noon—for the 1st time in its history—for 70 minutes by a sudden rainstorm, leaving the bricks slippery. Most of the cars slowed when they resumed the race, but not Frank. At the 150-mile mark he took over the lead, losing it to Hartz for 5 laps after a pit stop at the 225-mile mark. After that is was Lockhart all the way to the early checkered flag at the end of 400 miles because of another downpour. Frank's winning speed was 95.904 m.p.h. in spite of the conditions.

After that thrilling and unexpected victory, Lockhart could write his own ticket and pretty much did. Victories at Detroit, Fresno, Altoona, and Charlotte gave him almost enough points to win the AAA national crown, but Hartz eventually won it with Frank 2nd. Lockhart's car was now a factory Miller that he ended up buying with his race winnings when its builder objected to some changes Frank wanted to make to the car. The principal one was a supercharger intercooler, which is sometimes falsely credited to Lockhart as his own invention.

The intercooler was actually the brainchild of Zenas Weisel, the brother of one of Frank's growing staff of experts. Zenas was a recent mechanical engineering graduate whose thesis had been on that very subject. He built one for the Miller, and Lockhart took it out on the Culver City, Calif., board track March 6, 1927. He found it to his liking so much so that he set a track record of 144.2 m.p.h. that same day. With this edge, Lockhart dominated races for the rest of the season and set innumerable other records along the way. At Cleveland, for example, he set an incredible 101 records for the North Randall dirt track on one September day. At Roberts Dry Lake, in the Mojave Desert, he pushed the accelerator down enough to make a 171.02 m.p.h. record, 2nd only to the speeds of the larger Daytona monsters of Malcolm Campbell and Henry Segrave.

The 1927 Indianapolis race was another story, however. It looked as if Lockhart might become the 2nd repeat winner in history (Tommy Milton had done it in 1921 and 1923) and the first 2-in-a-row victor, but a connecting rod broke as he neared the 300-mile mark, and Frank finished the race munching on a hot dog and watching George Souders take the flag. His lap winnings totalled more than $11,000, however, and he invested this in his next big project, the Stutz Black Hawk. He won his season finale at Salem, N.H., in a race that saw the crash of his nemesis, Hartz, in a desperate effort to catch the high-flying Lockhart. Harry was 2 years in the hospital and never really raced again.

The Stutz Black Hawk has been called "the Stutz that wasn't" by the clever Griffith Borgeson. It was an apt description, for the car was a special, dubbed a Stutz merely to pick up $15,000 in financing and the use of some Stutz plant basement facilities in Indianapolis. Lockhart, the Weisel Brothers, and Olson, who had become Frank's right-hand man, lengthened a standard Miller chassis by a foot, coupled two 91.5 cu. in. Miller engines side by side with the two geared crankshafts turning in a single crankcase, and set about streamlining the package right down to its underside and engine spaces. In addition, a new type of aluminum intercooler was designed and brought the temperature of the fuel mixture from 280 degrees down to 110 degrees Fahrenheit, adding considerably to its actual horsepower.

Lockhart tried one slow (80 m.p.h.) test of the Black Hawk at Indianapolis—since the suspension was designed for soft sand, the unyielding Indy bricks made high speeds inadvisable—for the benefit of his principal outside backer, Fred E. Moskovics, the Hungarian-born mechanical engineer who had graduated from managing the first Vanderbilt Cup Mercedes team to the presidency of Stutz. The conclusions drawn in the Curtis Airplane Company's wind tunnel—Black Hawk was probably the 1st car to be so tested—seemed to prove out the design, and the party headed for Daytona.

Frank made 2 different attempts at Daytona and both were bad. The 1st came in February 1928, on Washington's Birthday. In less than ideal conditions, the little white car was doing about 225 m.p.h. as it hit some soft sand, flipped over twice and went into the surf, nearly drowning Lockhart and cutting a couple of tendons in his right hand. The car, which looked a total wreck, was actually not too badly battered, and 2 months of intensive work at the Stutz plant by Jean Marcenac, DePalma's old mechanic, made it right. Frank visited the plant around this time to conduct a tire test on a brand which he was switching to in order to pick up some extra financing. The test consisted of firing a loaded shotgun at the tire as it was doing 225 m.p.h. on a test wheel; the tire exploded and tore a big Miller engine from its concrete bed. "Well, I'm done if a tire blows," he summed up grimly.

A tire did go, weakened, perhaps, by an earlier skid, when Frank returned to Daytona on April 25, 1928. He was killed instantly as his car crashed on the 4th run of the day. The white car ended up as a pitiful ball of junk, but no more pitiful than Lockhart, whose body was flung through the air to land at his wife's feet. As a postscript, the car he had readied for that year's Indianapolis race did not start in 1928, but it won the following year in the hands of Ray Keech—a final victory for the improbable Frank Lockhart.

LARRY LOPATIN

Lawrence (Larry) LoPatin, a dark, pudgy, and bespectacled man, believed that "motor racing is the sport of the seventies," and that it would yield untold riches to the man who could package, market and manage it correctly. Larry was that man.

Larry LoPatin (pronounced Lo-Pay-Tin, accent on the 2nd part, rhyming with "Go Skatin'," as one writer put it) was 43 in 1969 and was sitting on top of automobile racing in the United States. He owned a corporation that owned, in its turn, Michigan International Speedway (a $5 million facility combining road courses, drag strips, and other facilities, that, after taxes earned $100,-000 in its first race), half of Riverside International Raceway, and a piece of Atlanta International Raceway (with options to buy most of the rest) and Texas International Speedway (a $6 million superspeedway outside Houston). In addition, LoPatin had announced a $5 million superspeedway for New Jersey; was openly negotiating for another venerable track, Hanford Speedway, in California; and was reportedly after a handful of others, including Road America, the famed Elkhart Lake race course. He had a contract with Bill France's NASCAR to promote a large number of races. He had put the fear of God—or something—into the oldline promoters. They moaned that nobody made money in racing, they merely ran it for the sake of the sport, sounding much like Kentucky horsebreeders of yesteryear.

The LoPatin bubble burst, however, within a year of that high spot. Texas became his downfall. The multi-million dollar promoter from Detroit—who had made his money by rehabilitating rundown buildings and producing mobile homes—had overextended himself, and by 1971 was out of racing for all intents and purposes.

LoPatin's father had deserted his family when Larry was only a small child. He grew up in poverty but persevered, finally reaching law school. After spending 5 years in the Navy, he came out with a nest egg and began dabbling in real estate. The Detroit real estate included entire square blocks of buildings, in rundown sections of town, that he systematically rehabilitated. It included Florida land where he developed an amusement park-recreational area complex. His investments also included mobile homes, a big business the America of the sixties and growing bigger in the seventies.

Larry, at 40 found himself on the boards of several companies, hobnobbing with the Fords, the Romneys, and the other planners, the doers and directors of American life. One day he picked up a chart that showed that auto racing had jumped into 2nd place among spectator sports in the U.S. and he decided it was a valuable part of leisure-time America, a favorite interest of his. He attacked racing as a marketing man would, and he horrified those with power in racing because he talked of it merely as a businessman and not as an enthusiast. People like Tony Hulman had grown rich from racing, but they still pretended (or believed) they were in it merely for the sport.

LoPatin had no illusions for himself and offered none to others. He saw racing as a way to make more money, perhaps with a little fun along the way, but certainly as a marketing-merchandising opportunity. That it was, but it also was part of American life that faltered in the economic realities of the late sixties and early seventies. As it faltered, so did LoPatin's vast holdings. Potential moneymakers all, they also were potential sinkholes for pouring down capital if they were not attracting customers. And that's what happened, combined with tight money-lending policies at the banks, tight recreational dollars with the individual customers, tight advertising and promotional budgets at those companies that could reasonably be expected to participate in the Lo-Patin empire.

A certain amount of naiveté also was involved, on both sides. LoPatin was not a respecter of old racing feuds, and he saw nothing wrong with playing footside with USAC today, SCCA tomorrow and NASCAR the day after that. Even though they were united in things like ACCUS, the old rivalries still existed, especially between USAC and NASCAR, and especially between people like Henry Banks and Bill France. USAC was fully in the LoPatin camp, but then he made his multi-race deal—20 firm dates over several years—with NASCAR, and Banks was furious, so furious that USAC pulled out on LoPatin.

Finally it was this kind of opposition, seemingly easy to overcome, that contributed to Larry's downfall. Whenever a man is on top, or on his way there, there are plenty of people to say that he is up to no good. The spectre of this outsider "controlling" racing was advanced in more than one board room and over move than one lunch table. LoPatin's virtues became vices. His industriousness became ruthlessness, his marketing approach was characterized as blue-skied. As he stepped out on the tight money rocks, the detractors swooped in for a kill, and they succeeded pretty much. In 1971 Larry LoPatin was no "controller" of racing; he was instead very much an outsider again, very far outside. The question was, would he drive his way back inside . . . or would he even bother?

FRED LORENZEN

With all his money, Fred Lorenzen never moved far from Elmhurst, Ill., where he was born on December 30, 1934. Elmhurst is a middle-class suburb of Chicago, and Fred Lorenzen, Jr., was one of 6 children in a family where no one ever went shoeless, but no one ever had a silver spoon in his porridge either. When he was about 13 he improvised a small car from junk parts and an old washing machine motor. The police took it away from him because it went too fast. He managed to finish high school, though not an exceptional student, before he began competing in races. There was, however, a demolition derby at Chicago's Soldiers Field before that. He entered in a junk heap and dodged skillfully enough to win a 1st prize of $100. It didn't take Freddie long to figure out that he had made a net profit of $83 for about 10 minutes of fun, while on construction work he was making $80 a week.

So Lorenzen began racing modified stock cars at NASCAR-sanctioned Soldiers Field and other nearby tracks, at night, while continuing work as a union carpenter by day. In 1957 he decided that the real money lay in racing late-model stock-cars, so he took a Chevrolet and moved into USAC competition. He finished 10th in each of 4 races. Undaunted, he bought a Ford, prepared it, and tried again. This time, in 7 races he won 5 and finished 3rd once for $16,939 in prize money. He won both Milwaukee races, Trenton, DuQuoin and

race, with Freddie starting from the pole. Lorenzen and his mechanic, Herb Nab, understood Atlanta—the hot dogs did not. Jones skidded on the 17th lap, taking Junior Johnson and Darel Dieringer out of contention as well. Paul Goldsmith led the first 77 laps, then blew a tire and flipped his Plymouth onto its roof, forcing Foyt into the infield. David Pearson took the lead, challenged by Hurtubise and Panch. Gurney and Johnson dropped out, followed by Panch and Hurtbise. At 150 miles Lorenzen assumed the lead without ever increasing his pace. Pearson took Roberts with him when his tire blew, and Rex White removed Jim Paschal. Petty was never in contention.

Just when Freddie thought he could cakewalk, Bobby Isaac charged past him. Lorenzen's own chassis setting had somehow gone sour, but he kept up the pressure, and Bobby soon pitted for tires, while Freddie rolled merrily back into the lead. He kept his date with history, the 1st driver ever to win the same superspeedway race in 3 successive years. He beat Isaac by 2 laps, with only 10 cars still running. He set a record pace of 132.959 m.p.h.

Fred followed that with victories in 250-mile races at North Wilkesboro, N.C., and at Martinsville, Va., for a string of 4 triumphs in races of 250 miles or more. Then he invaded USAC territory for the Yankee 300, an international race billed as the battle between NASCAR and USAC. The battle site was Indianapolis Raceway Park, a road course in the suburbs of Indianapolis. Fred was the NASCAR threat, and all the USAC stars were there. After the first 150 miles only 2 cars on the track were really in contention, pole-winning Parnelli Jones and his No. 15 Stroppe Mercury and the No. 28 Ford with Lorenzen aboard. Fred tried to pass Jones for the lead, but was chopped unceremoniously and had to spin to avoid an accident. He resumed the chase, tried again and got the same treatment, but his dogged pursuit wouldn't allow Parnelli to let up. The pace took its toll, and Jones lost 4th gear. Lorenzen passed him 22 laps from the finish.

Freddie was fighting his own troubles, too. His 3rd gear had slipped, and he was forced to hold the shift lever in that gear by brute strength. Then 10 laps from the end, he had to hold the car in 4th to conserve fuel. His right hand was blistered so badly it had to be dressed and bandaged, but he had won 5 straight. He added the Rebel 300 to his string easily, for his 6th triumph. A fortnight later a tie rod on the Charlotte track that hurt Fred's car and a careless crewman placed him 4th and ended his victory skein. In 1965 Lorenzen won a rain-shortened Daytona 500 and the National 500 at Charlotte for a 2nd consecutive year and at some 15 m.p.h. slower speed. When Rockingham opened late that year with a Curtis Turner victory, Lorenzen remedied that in 1966 with an American 500 victory. Then in 1967 he suddenly retired, with 26 Grand Nationals on his victory list.

Meadowdale, Ill. In that last road course race, he beat the likes of Jimmy Bryan, Chuck Daigh, Les Snow and Marshall Teague. In 1959 he won 6 of 13 starts, and had 3 other top 5 finishes to repeat as champion. The victories this time were at Langhorne, Milwaukee, Atlanta, Clovis, and Las Vegas.

Impressed by his victories, Fearless Freddie took his Ford and moved up to the big time of stock-car racing, NASCAR, in 1960. He quickly learned it was no fun to be an independent matched against the factory teams, but ran well enough to impress Ralph Moody. As a result, in 1961 he became a factory driver and won 3 races, including his initial superspeedway victory, the Rebel 300 at Darlington. In 1962 he won at Atlanta. In 1963 all the pieces fell together, and Lorenzen with his golden red hair and his rugged profile won everything not nailed down.

He won the Atlanta 500 again, added the Charlotte World 600 to his list, and took enough smaller races and high-place superspeedway finishes to earn a record $113,570. What did he do for an encore? Freddie won at Bristol, Tenn., and then it was time for Atlanta and the history books.

April 5, 1964, was a damp chilly day, but 60,000 spectators were in the huge speedway south of Atlanta. No wonder; not only were Fearless Freddie and Fireball Roberts there, but Richard Petty, Ned Jarrett, Marvin Panch, A. J. Foyt, Parnelli Jones, Dan Gurney, and Jungle Jim Hurtubise from rival USAC were there as well. It was a typical tire-chewed, wreck-strewn Atlanta

He remained in retirement for almost 3 years, but suddenly decided, while running his daily mile and a half, to come back to stock-car racing if he could get a decent car to drive. He began to make inquiries to see if anyone wanted a wealthy 37-year-old driver with 12 superspeedway victories to his credit. Even the news of his inquiries provoked interest and controversy among Dixie racing fans. Fearless Freddie was one of the old idols, stepping off his pedestal and into new machines, faster than those he had driven when he called it quits. Could he come back?

It was May 26, 1970, at Charlotte International Raceway and Freddie was running in traffic for the 1st time in 3 years. "It used to take me a long time to relax when I was racing all the time, and now I was back with 40 cars with a lot of strange faces in them. I found myself worrying about the first turn, hoping I'd get around it without spinning and taking 10 cars with me," he said afterward. "I stopped worrying quick because I found I could still drive, but it took me 200 miles to move up front. Soon I was going 175 m.p.h. with my left arm resting on the door like it was a Sunday drive." The fans cheered when Lorenzen took the lead, and that's where he was when the engine of his Dodge blew on the 253rd lap.

A highway accident late in 1970 seriously injured Fred Lorenzen, Sr., and inflicted minor hurts on Fearless Freddie. The final withdrawal of Ford from all kinds of racing left him with an interest in a Chicago area Ford dealership and an even greater desire to race in 1971. When the announcement came that he would do so, his sponsor was such a natural that all the rumor mongers wondered why they hadn't thought of it. Lorenzen would be racing in 1971 in a flame-red STP Plymouth built at Ray Nichels Engineering in nearby Highland, Ind., with Nichels's general manager, Paul Goldsmith, as crew chief. Fred had begun when Andy Granatelli of STP was promoting Soldiers Field racing. Stomach ulcer, blue-chip stocks and all, Lorenzen was back in harness. He raced 15 times, made the top 5 in 7 of them for $45,100. And he split with STP, eventually getting himself a ride in a new Ford for 1972. When that didn't work his car hopping propelled him into a Chevvy with which he finished 4th in the Southern 500. He won $19,255 in 8 starts and accomplished something off the track, too—he got married.

JOHN LOVE

When Pedro Rodriguez lost the United States Grand Prix in 1970 through the lack of enough fuel to make it across the finish line, forcing him to pit and yield a lead he couldn't regain, he might have thought back to 1967 and the South African GP when he won just that way from a local "boy" who almost made racing history

with an outclassed 2.7-litre Tasman Cooper-Climax. That fellow was 42 years old, a Rhodesian, and a big fish in a small pond. His name was John Love.

Love was born in 1924 and drove an Army tank in the Italian campaign in World War II. While in Italy, he pieced together a car and did some experimental laps on the temporarily occupied Monza speedway, before returning to his home in Rhodesia. He started actual racing around 1950, first in a Formula 3 Cooper-JAP that was reputedly raced by Stirling Moss. The 500 c.c. car soon was swapped for a more competitive Cooper-Norton, and then that went in a deal for a Riley Special that had won the South African Championship 3 times in the hands of Bill Jennings. In 1959 Love graduated to the big time, with a D Jaguar that had raced at Le Mans 5 years before. His initial time out in this car, he won the Angola GP.

In 1960 John Love sailed for Britain, a rather elderly rookie for big-time racing, but Ken Tyrrell, ever a spotter of good driving talent, had an open spot on his Formula Junior team, and there were some Lola rides available on the Fitzwilliam Team as well. It was a learning year, but in 1961, teamed with a countryman several years his junior, Tony Maggs, Love concentrated on the Tyrrell Cooper rides and was 2nd to Maggs in the FJ Championship. It was FJ again and success the following year, but the biggest Love story was in BMC Mini-Coopers, in which John captured the British Saloon Car title. A crash in an FJ race at Albi was only a temporary setback. John took a 1.5-litre Cooper-Climax back to South Africa to drive the Springbok Series with Maggs.

Love had to stay in South Africa in 1963 to build up his garage business, but he was active on local race courses, seeking that country's national championship, and the honor of being the first Rhodesian to turn the trick, but he had only one 2nd and two 3rds. The next year he was offered one European drive, the Italian GP, but the sick Cooper never made the grid. At home Love won the championship for the 1st time; the next year he won 10 of 12 starts and repeated as South African champion. In 1966–67 the story was the same. During these same years Love also was winning other kinds of races, in Porsches, Ferraris, an Austin Healey 3000, a GT40, and Lola-Chevrolets.

After the South African GP in 1967, people watched Love there each season to see what he might do next. He never did as well, but he had his moments. In 1968 he was 9th in a Repco-Brabham, retiring the next season in a Lotus-Ford 49. In 1970 he was in the same car and finished 8th, but in 1971 he retired despite a new March-Ford. Even after a serious crash later that year, Love gave no sign quitting; big fish like small ponds, and his sports car racing was as good as ever, as witness his 1971 Springbok series victory in a Team Gunston Lola T212.

TINY LUND

There are some people who succeed financially, but never find contentment in life. DeWayne Louis (Tiny) Lund hadn't done too badly in the money department, and he had also found the kind of life he wanted, operating a fishing camp on Lake Moultrie, S.C. Amid dogs, cats, ducks, chickens, a monkey, and an occasional possum, the 270-pound Lund lived with his wife, Ruth, and his stepson. It is not generally known that he held the world record for fresh water striped bass (55 pounds), a fish caught near his camp, located at a place called Cross because someone put a cross on the map to locate it.

Lund towered nearly 6 feet 5 inches in height, and looked like one of the amiable giants that occasionally come out of the back woods to buttress the defensive line of a Dixie football power. He was a Southerner by choice, however, having been born on November 14, 1929, in Harlan, Iowa. He played football and basketball at Harlan High School, but, like many another auto racing hero, preferred the smell of gasoline to that of sweaty shoulder pads. He was only 15 when he began racing motorcycles and had not reached his majority when he was the champion modified driver in the Iowa-Nebraska area. He tried sprints and midgets briefly, but had problems because of his size.

Lund was like an iceberg, the placid exterior hiding talents and attributes one would never expect of the man. He spent 4 years as a flight engineer in the Air Force, specializing in jets. He will be as long remembered for his heroism in the rescue of Marvin Panch from a wildly burning Maserati-Ford at Daytona in 1963, as for his considerable racing exploits. Tiny received a Carnegie Medal for that, which led to the ride that turned into his greatest victory, the 1963 Daytona 500. The injured Panch recommended him to car owner Glen Wood, but before that there had been 8 years of part-time racing, both in IMCA and NASCAR, in stock cars of one sort or another. In 1955, his 1st year out of the service, he finished 7th in IMCA stocks, and in 1958 he broadslid to a Grand National victory on the old Charlotte Fairgrounds dirt. He raced NASCAR convertibles with limited success and did little better over the years in limited sportsman racing, a very competitive sport in the Carolinas.

Tiny came to Daytona in 1963 without a driving assignment, expecting to work on someone's pit crew if nothing else. He had resigned himself to this fate when Wood agreed to let him drive the Ford that Panch was supposed to have driven. He started 12th on that wet and rainy February 24th. The largest crowd in the history of stock-car racing to that date had endured a drenching rain and 50 m.p.h. winds to see the race. Only a man with the determination of a Bill France would have insisted on trying to get the race run. It started so late there was some chance of its being called by dark-

ness. In fact, the first 10 laps were run at 97 m.p.h., under the caution flag, to help dry the track. But once it was dry, the Fords flew, and their main contenders —Pontiacs and Chevrolets—blew engines. The lead changed 30 times among 11 drivers in the early parts of the race. Tiny stayed close as Fireball Roberts, Jim Pardue, A. J. Foyt, Paul Goldsmith, Junior Johnson, and Jim Hurtubise retired with broken Pontiacs, Chevies and Plymouths.

The strategy of the Wood boys for Lund seemed doomed by the breakneck pace—no one could make it on 4 pit stops. Tiny ran out of gas, making the pits on the momentum of his car for his 3rd stop, then drafted and made Jarrett push him as the race came down to its final laps. He waited until the 395th mile to move ahead of Lorenzen, with Jarrett also in the drafting trio. Fred pitted first, 44 laps from the end, then Tiny went in on the 40th and Ned 7 laps later.

The battle was too much for the Lorenzen car; he had to make his 5th pit stop with 8 laps to go, and 3 laps from the finish Jarrett did the same. Lund gambled and barely made it. His car ran out of fuel on the final turn, and he coasted across 24 seconds ahead of Lorenzen, with Jarrett 6 seconds back. He had beaten Fred Lorenzen, Ned Jarrett, Nelson Stacy and Dan Gurney, in that order; all were driving 1963 Fords. In victory lane, after kissing his wife, Tiny did what any Iowa boy would do under the circumstances—he let out a hog call. His share of the winnings was spent on buying land near his fishing camp.

That year, 1963, he stayed in the Wood car for 22 races, not winning again, but placing in the top 10 a dozen times. It was a good enough record to assure him further work. He finished 10th in points, with a 2nd at the Martinsville Spring 250-miler, a 3rd at North Walkesboro, a 4th in the Rebel 300 at Darlington, and a 5th in the Atlanta 500—all in the space of 3 months.

It took the establishment of a new kind of NASCAR racing, the Grand Touring Championship for American sporty cars, to turn Tiny into a champion. He took to the Cougar-Camaro-Mustang circuit like a Lake Moultrie bass takes a fly, becoming the 1st title-holder in 1968, with 9 victories in 18 starts. He finished 5th in 1969, and in 1970, switching from Cougar to Camaro, Tiny ran off 10 victories in a row and 19 victories in 35 starts for the Grand American Challenge Cup crown (the new name for the Grand Touring series). Tiny took time off to compete in Japan, finishing 2nd in a strange car, then flew to Germany in the fall for NASCAR's first European race. Driving an Opel, he finished 2nd in class and 8th overall.

In 1971, the fishing camp business was pretty good but the Grand American was better as Tiny won his 3rd championship in this series, edging old Buck Baker. Tiny had 6 victories and 6 other top 5 finishes in his Pepsi Camaro.

In 1972 the Grand American series was downgraded drastically and Tiny followed the Grand National East circuit, too. He did very little in either and car hopped all season to try to change matters. Tiny did not run that much but told everyone he wasn't retiring, just looking for a ride. He earned $11,800 in 15 starts, winning only the 'Bama 200. But how can you leave a paradise like Cross, S.C., when the fish are biting?

BRETT LUNGER

"I'm sort of the black sheep of my peer group," said Brett Lunger, who looked anything but sheepish, despite his shaggy haircut. "Most of my friends are now doctors and lawyers and other things that are supposed to be normal. I suppose my family and my friends thought the auto racing bit would pass, especially after I spent 4 years in the Marines, but it was during that Marine hitch, especially in Vietnam, that I decided that when I got out I was going to concentrate on becoming a professional racing driver."

Robert Brett Lunger's peer group was that of a well-to-do industrial family, in his case E.I. du Pont de Nemours of Wilmington, Del. The thin, tall driver was born November 14, 1945, and raised in Wilmington, and he called the du Pont capital his home (except for 3 years at Princeton University) until moving to California to pursue his racing more seriously in 1970.

Brett started as a sports car driver. The initial race,

at Bridgehampton, was in a Corvette late in 1965; then he started mixing the Vette and a Lotus 23B single-seater in SCCA regionals all over the Northeast. He earned his senior SCCA license over a span of but 3 months, or as fast as it was possible for anyone to do it. Lunger's initial national race was at Cumberland, Md., and he won it. That fall found him in the prestigious USRRC and Canadian-American Challenge Cup series for the big, hairy Group 7 cars.

"All very exciting and very press-worthy, I'm sure," Lunger said several years later, "but I really didn't know how to race, just drive quickly. I was in there over my head, unable to really mix with the serious racers."

After a last fling at the annual Nassau Speedweek, in which Brett finished 8th in the Tourist Trophy and 2nd in the Governor's Trophy, he enlisted in the Marine Corps. After boot camp and officer's school. Lunger was able to race on occasion while on pass. He teamed with another blueblooded driver, Sam Posey, on the Autodynamics Team, running a McLaren M3, Lola T160, and Caldwell D7. That racing, mostly in CanAms for laughs, came to an end in November 1968, when Lunger shipped out for Vietnam. He spent 13 months leading a reconnaissance platoon before returning to finish off his 4-year Marine career in California.

Part-time racing gave way to full-time involvement after Brett's discharge; and after tasting the new L&M cigarette-sponsored Formula 5000 Continental in the fall of 1970, Lunger signed up for a hitch in the full 1971 series. The Posey-David Hobbs battle of words made most of the Continental copy in 1971, but Lunger ran his races and finished 3rd overall to Hobbs, who was to become his 1972 Continental teammate, and Posey.

At 3 of the F5000 battles, Lunger qualified fastest in his Lola T192M. He was 3rd twice, 4th once, 6th, 7th, 11th, and 15th, and he won a race outright. That was at Donnybrooke, Minn., and it was all the more auspicious because Lunger was racing despite the fact that he was under medication for mononucleosis. Driving in 90-degree heat, back-markers forced Brett into a spin in the initial heat, putting him far back before the race even was well under way, but he fought back to finish 3rd. Then in the next heat, despite another spin, he won in a dice with Canadian champion Eppie Wietzes by 6 seconds.

"It was about then that I knew I had made an intelligent decision to become a pro," Lunger said later. "If you don't feel like racing, but force yourself to go on to win, that's a sign that you're serious about the whole thing. The Continental was the greatest thing that could happen to me. The CanAm taught me a lot, but it just didn't give me the polish I needed so desperately. I needed the experience of competing against other drivers—better drivers—instead of just driving fast. The mono thing is funny now when you look back at it, but it wasn't funny then. I needed 3 shots a day of penicillin

and Vitamin B12 just to keep me from falling flat on my face. The doctor wanted me to go to bed for a month, but I told him that a racing car's seat is somewhat reclining, almost like a bed, and he just laughed and said okay."

The year 1972 saw Lunger in the L&M Continental 5000 again, but also in Europe in the challenging Formula 2 series that still drew top Formula 1 veterans like Graham Hill and up-and-coming youngsters like Ronnie Peterson. His F2 mount was a March 722, which gave him engine problems, but he was learning all kinds of new tricks. "At Oulton Park in England, for example," he recalled, "we literally were driving blind in a terrific downpour. I learned to drive by ear, listening for when the car just ahead of me backed off, then backing off myself." At Hockenheim, he applied the theory of slipstreaming, which he had known for a long time, to a race situation for the 1st time and found out it worked.

Even though he already had salted away his 1st Continental victory the year before, Lunger looked at his teaming with Hobbs on the Carl Hogan team for the 1972 series as another major learning opportunity. "Getting really first-rate in this business takes time," he said. Lunger was still saying the same thing toward the end of 1972, despite two straight victories in the L&M F5000 series at Road Atlanta and Lime Rock, Conn., with the surprising possibility left that Brett could win the Continental championship title if he won at Riverside in the season finale. Even though that was not to be, his late-season driving showed that he had been paying attention to his chosen teachers in road racing, and more might be expected of Brett Lunger than originally might have been of a little rich boy gone racing.

DAVE MacDONALD

Dave MacDonald was a natural-born race driver. In the space of 4 years, starting as just another 23-year-old weekend sports-car enthusiast, he became one of the better-known young drivers on the international scene, both in professional sports car and Indianapolis circles. He also precipitated one of the most gruesome accidents at the Indiana oval in many years, one that cost him his life.

A quiet, almost shy individual until he got behind the wheel of a racing car, MacDonald was one of those Southern California kids who have become such a dominant force in American racing since 1960. Born in 1936, it was not until 1959 that he became a serious racing competitor in amateur ranks, after a few years at dragging. In his first year Dave finished 2nd in the SCCA's B production class with a Corvette. MacDonald was not particularly pleased with that performance, however, and went faster than ever the next 2 seasons, taking the Class B crown both years. His style, highly personal and unorthodox, won him a following and the attention of Jim Simpson, who provided a car for bigger and more demanding modified event competition.

Some say that under the table help from Detroit also financed the venture, but wherever the money came from, it bought Dave a car with a Max Balchowsky chassis, powered by a Chevrolet engine and enclosed in a Corvette-like fiber glass body. The car looked fine, but under Dave's rough handling tires blew, treads parted in hugh chunks, suspensions collapsed, and engines overheated. Still, MacDonald showed promise, even if he had a rather frightening knack for going sideways in the turns and never using the same line twice. General Motors seemed ready to come out from under the table and talk of a Corvette Sting-Ray racing program gave promise of an interesting mount for Dave. But nothing came of it.

Fortunately for the young California, however, Bill Krause, the number one driver and tester for Carroll Shelby's mushrooming Shelby American venture—Cobra —yielded to the lure of an Indianapolis ride for Mickey Thompson; and Shelby offered the vacated Cobra spot to MacDonald. Dave showed his appreciation by giving Shelby everything he had, which was considerable. Winning 2 big, tough, and rich road races back to back at Riverside and Laguna Seca, MacDonald catapulted himself and the Cobra into national prominence. At Riverside he managed to lap the entire field, no mean feat. In the winter he teamed up with Bob Holbert to bring another Cobra home a victor in the GT class at Sebring.

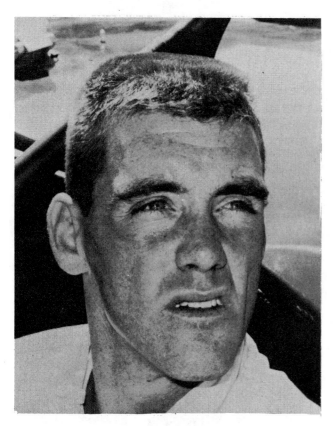

In 1964 he signed with Thompson for Indianapolis and with the Bill Stroppe Mercury crew, and also continued his lucrative and prominent position with Shelby. Not bad for an El Monte, Calif., suburbanite with 2 children. But Indianapolis proved his undoing. Dave passed his rookie test easily and qualified Thompson's Sears Special at 151.835 m.p.h. But he managed only a lap before disaster struck; his car swerved into the wall and exploded in a sheet of flame. He was killed instantly.

DOC MacKENZIE

The people of Bucks County in Pennsylvania are like the land they live on; open, friendly, tolerant, but with a clannishness and a pride in local residents that far surpasses anything the inhabitants of other places would demonstrate for their natives. Although he was not a great artist or author or scientist, as many in Bucks are, Doc MacKenzie was a local hero. Called Doc because his family had produced many doctors for generations, there has grown a legend that in the many retellings has mellowed and merged fact with hero worship.

Doc was a tall, bearded man whom some in Bucks said had been touched by the devil. He categorically refused to learn medicine; instead, he sought adventure. He prospected for gold in northern Canada; he was a construction worker on the Empire State Building's skeleton and on the Golden Gate Bridge 3,000 miles

away in San Francisco. He drove as if to taunt death. And Bucks County loved him for it.

It is fitting that his greatest race should have come at Langhorne in Bucks, where his neighbors could see. It was 1935—Sunday, August 8, to be exact—and the stands at the old dirt circular mile were packed. Doc had been having his greatest year. He had won at Milwaukee and at Dayton, and he was leading the race for the Eastern AAA title with 8 sprint victories. Bob Sall, later a respected NASCAR zone supervisor, was his closest rival; Sall was the pride of neighboring New Jersey, Champion of the East in 1933 and the son of the town barber in Ridgewood. Once MacKenzie had quipped that if Sall could beat him, he would let Sall's father clip his beard. It was an idle jest, but Bob is supposed to have made a scissors motion with his fingers every time the 2 were in a race after that.

MacKenzie could clinch the Eastern crown if he won one of the heats and the 50-mile feature; Sall could take the point lead if he won one of the heats. A young man from Paterson, N. J., named Ken Fowler threatened to make the duel inconclusive by winning the pole and the initial 10-mile heat, with Doc 2nd in the orange Cresco Special. Then the 25,000 fans saw Sall, driving his black and white car, come back to win the next heat. Now the feature became all-important, and the crowd buzzed with excitement as the cars lined up. There were other fine drivers on the grid—Walter Brown who later raced in NASCAR, Vern Orenduff, Frank Reynolds—but all eyes were on Doc and Sall. There was that scissors motion from the Jerseyan, and Bucks

fans could imagine their favorite with a nude chin for the first time since his youth.

The starter's flag dropped and Fowler took the lead, broadsliding expertly around the treacherous mile dirt circle with Doc and Sall close behind. On the 19th mile Fowler faltered ever so little and the crowd cheered wildly. Doc was leading—but only for 2 laps before a tire blew. MacKenzie pitted. Even a mere 11-second tire change was enough to drop him to 7th, however, far behind Sall. Doc attacked the track like a man possessed; he unwound lap after lap at qualifying speeds to pass one car after another.

He closed on Sall until, with but 11 miles to go, Sall pitted with a broken fuel line. But that was only half the problem: Doc had to win. He lengthened his lead over Walter Brown in the next lap or so, then suddenly the orange car slowed appreciably. Another tire had gone flat. For 5 miles Doc rode around the circle, feeling every revolution of the flatted tire, seeing his lead slip away, then finally pitted. The crew changed the tire as quickly as possible, but the motor stalled. A groan arose from the stands as the desperate pit crew began pushing the car, waved on by a frantic MacKenzie—it seemed an eternity, for Brown had taken the lead, followed by Reynolds. Walt was almost a lap up on Doc, and Frank almost a half lap, when the engine suddenly roared into life. There were only 5 miles left to do the impossible.

If MacKenzie sped before, now he semeed to skim over the reddish Bucks clay hunched over like a demon on the Devil's work. Some said he was turning the mile in 36 seconds but no one believed them; nobody could keep a stopwatch accurate in that howling mob in the stands. In 3 miles—3 turns around Langhorne—he overtook Reynolds and set out after Brown who was at least a third of a race track in front, with only 2 miles left to close the gap. Close the gap he did—to 600 feet with a lap left, to 400 as they disappeared into the dust in the back of the track on the final mile. When they emerged, MacKenzie was a car length behind with only a third of a mile to make it up.

The orange car seemed to drive straight for the outer fence as Doc gambled for better traction. He was gambling his life, for if the tires did not catch, he would crash into the steel with terrifying force. But they did, and McKenzie cut back into the groove, winning by a hair. He leaped out of his car, stroked his beard and waved at the cheering crowd. "No Jersey barber is going to touch this beard," fans swear he said.

There are some who credit his victory to Bucks County itself. MacKenzie's final maneuver was patently impossible, they say. Somehow the Bucks dirt knew him and responded with the traction necessary to save its native son and give him victory. MacKenzie was finally killed in a racing crash, but his feat at Langhorne will be remembered long after they chop up the old track for a housing tract.

TONY MAGGS

Anthony Francis O'Connell Maggs was one of those people who always seemed about to break through into the top driver ranks, he never quite made it. Born in Pretoria, South Africa, February 9, 1927, the towheaded Maggs was the son of a well-to-do businessman-farmer. After the usual infatuation with motorcycles, Tony turned his attention to cars in 1957 and made his racing debut at Capetown on New Year's Day 1958, in an Austin-Healey. Two more races followed that year, then he moved to Europe to gain continental experience with the idea of returning to South Africa that much ahead of his fellow drivers.

Maggs drove a Lotus 11 in European club meetings in 1959, won 2 races, was 2nd twice and 3rd once. Then he purchased a Tojeiro-Jaguar from Ecurie Ecosse and made a debut with it at Goodwood in September with 2 fastest-lap marks in as many races. Back in South Africa, he won 6 races and took 2nd in another. Maggs retired from both the South African and the Cape Grands Prix while still well placed behind such men as Stirling Moss and Paul Frere.

His South African season gave the youngster enough courage to scale the European heights once more, and enough of a reputation to secure a ride with John Ogier's Essex Racing Team. Driving a Formula 2 Cooper, he scored a 2nd, 3rd and 4th in 5 appearances, and he also broke the lap record at Snetterton. The Chequered Flag team gave him Geminis to drive in Formula Junior in which he again was a winner. Aston Martin came across

373

with a ride also, shared with Jim Clark in the Montlhéry 1000, from which the DB4GT retired while 4th.

In 1961 Maggs joined Ken Tyrrell's racing team to drive a Cooper-Austin to 8 FJ victories that season at places like Goodwood, Magny-Cours, Rouen, Monza, Karlskoga, Zandvoort, Oulton Park, and Montlhéry where he and John Love finished in a dead heat in the Coupe du Salon. He also had five 2nds and a trio of 3rds and ended up sharing the European FJ championship with Jo Siffert. On July 15, 1961, Maggs made his Formula 1 debut in the British GP at Aintree in extremely bad weather. He finished 13th, 6 laps behind the winning Wolfgang von Trips, in a year-old 4-cylinder Lotus entered by Mrs. Louise Bryden-Brown, an American expatriate. In the same car he started from 16th place in the German GP and finished 11th. The Essex Racing Team used Tony's services in the Monza 3-hour GT race, where he was 2nd, and at the Paris 1000 and Le Mans. In the latter, his Aston Martin, codriven by Roy Salvadori, was forced out with a ruptured gas tank while running 5th.

After a successful South African winter season in Tyrrell Cooper-Austins and Mini-Coopers, Maggs joined the Cooper F1 factory team in 1962 as number 2 driver to Bruce McLaren for 9 World Championship races. Maggs was 5th in the Dutch GP and retired at Monaco and Spa. In the French GP he was 2nd, however, 6th in the British GP, and 9th at Nurburgring in a borrowed machine after a spectacular accident in practice had written off his regular mount. Tony was running 3rd in the Italian GP when a fuel stop dropped him back to 7th. He finished 7th in the United States GP. In the final race of the season in his native South Africa, Maggs was 3rd, a car-length behind the winning McLaren, and his season's point total was 13, good enough for 7th in the standings. That same year he drove again for Tyrrell in FJ, winning a couple of races in a Cooper-BMC and placing 6 times. Driving for the Essex Racing Team, he shared a 4th with McLaren as codriver in the Nurburgring 1000.

Scheduled to join Bowmaker in 1963, Tony returned instead to Cooper when Bowmaker discontinued racing because of the costs. He started off well in the Tasman Series, then moved to Goodwood for 3rd the Easter Monday F1 Glover Trophy Race. He came in 2nd to Clark in the French GP and scored a 5th at Monaco, which was that season's European GP. Maggs was 6th in the Italian GP, 7th in the Belgian race, 9th in the British GP after his car failed at the starting line and he had to pit for repairs. He dropped out at Zandvoort while running 4th.

The following year Tony moved over to BRM, but his 4th in the Austrian GP and 6th at the Nurburgring race left him tied for 12th in the F1 championship standings. In F2, driving a Lola-Cosworth, he was 2nd in the Aintree 200 and 3rd at Pergusa and at Snetterton's Vanwall Trophy Race. In GT and sports prototype racing

with Ferrari, Tony shared a victory in the Rand 9-hour race with David Piper and a 4th in the Montlhéry 1000 with the same driver. He and Innes Ireland shared a 6th at Le Mans in a GTO, and Maggs alone was 3rd in class at Nurburgring.

Though only 28, Maggs seemed tired of it all, but he was back in 1965 for F2 races in a Lola-Cosworth in which he finished 4th in the Oulton Park Gold Cup, and in a Lola-BRM T60 in which he was 2nd at Rome and 4th at Pau. Tony and Piper shared a 3rd at Sebring in the 12-hour race in a 275LM Ferrari GT. That September Maggs surprised some—but not his wife Gaile, whom he married in South Africa on November 17, 1962—by announcing his retirement after his car hit and killed a boy standing in a restricted runoff area at Pietermaritzburg.

UMBERTO MAGLIOLI

The 5th edition of the Pan American Road Race in 1954 started in the jungle town of Tuxtla Gutierrez in southern Mexico and headed north toward Juarez, 5 days away. There were 149 cars on hand for the staged start beginning at 6 A.M. late in November. A squat red Ferrari driven by Jack McAfee and Ford Robinson was away 1st, followed in succession by the others. About 217 miles from that start was an advance base, and a few miles ahead of that were radio-equipped scouts to alert the base. Exactly 2 hours after the flag had dropped, the radio signalled the approach of McAfee in the lead. But

a few minutes later the first car that appeared was not red, but a white Ferrari with a blue stripe, closely followed by another red Ferrari. McAfee and Robinson had broadsided a curve, rolled twice down a 30-foot drop and ended their race. McAfee was shaken but alive, Robinson was dead of a broken neck.

The white Ferrari with the blue stripe was driven by Phil Hill, who had started far down among the large sports cars. In the red Ferrari was Umberto Maglioli (pronounced Moll-yo-lee) at 26 already accepted as one of the world's best road racers, especially in this kind of race. He, too, had started late in the field and followed Hill's rush to the lead. At this point he trailed by a scant 3 seconds. Hill was able to push his lighter, more nimble Ferrari to as much as a 4-minute, 9-second lead in the first few days, but then the story changed.

Maglioli was still 2nd when racing stopped for nightfall at Oaxaca, 329.40 miles from the start. Already 22 cars had been eliminated. On the 2nd day's run to Mexico City, another 15 cars fell, including that of Indianapolis 500 winner Bill Vukovich who plunged over a 150-foot ravine, somersaulted 5 times, yet lived. Hill had trouble getting through the crowded streets of Atlixco, and Maglioli zipped through to cut Phil's lead to 69 seconds. Just outside of Mexico City, going all out to catch Hill, Maglioli's Ferrari blew a tire. It swerved, started to slide, but Umberto fought it back into control and limped into the city still 2nd.

The 3rd day, 590.43 miles farther north to Durango, brought the race out of the mountains. Maglioli could have waited to start making up time, as his Ferrari was expected to outrun not only Hill but most of his serious opponents. But he did not wait. Startled to see the red Ferrari in his mirror and realizing he had lost his advantage here in the mountains, Hill moved aside and let Umberto through, preferring a safe 2nd to a possible crash. Maglioli led for the 1st time, and he would lead the rest of the way.

Only 95 cars made the 4th day's run from Durango to Chihuahua, 437 more treacherous miles. Maglioli had a 6-minute lead over Hill, yet drove as if Phil were breathing down his neck. On one stretch, on which he held the lap record from the previous year, he broke his mark at 112 m.p.h., then on an even faster stretch —including 160 m.p.h. straightaways—he turned 130 m.p.h. By the end of the day's run, Maglioli led by a commanding 25 miuntes.

The run to Juarez was almost perfunctory. Umberto played it safe and averaged only 134 m.p.h. He covered the 1,908 miles at an average speed of 107.9 m.p.h., 30 minutes faster than World Champion Juan Manuel Fangio's 1953 time. He had won over 87 finishers in one of history's most demanding races, a race that cost 6 lives —4 of them drivers, the other 2 spectators—plus numerous injuries. Asked about Maglioli by a newsman, an Italian friend said simply, "He is something different. He is not wild. He does not eat much, he drinks less

than he eats. He is not crazy over women, the head rules him. For a young Italian it is all very odd. For an Italian race driver it is nearly impossible."

Umberto Maglioli was born June 5, 1928, in Biella, Italy, of a doctor father who had hopes his son would follow in his footsteps. As he grew up, Umberto dressed like a doctor and behaved like a doctor, but his ambition was racing. He began early locally and by 1952 was beginning to make an international reputation for himself. That season he finished 4th in the Pan American Road Race behind the experienced Mercedes Benz team of Karl Kling and Hermann Lang, and Luigi Chinetti of Ferrari. In 1953 he was 6th in the Pan American, 3rd at Belluna in the Dolomite Gold Cup, and drove the fastest Ferrari laps at Monza in the Grand Prix there, although he did not finish.

The young driver's 1st great victory came in 1954 when he won the Targa Florio for Lancia in a D.20 sports/racing coupe at 50.1 m.p.h. In the Pescara 12-hour race that same year he won again, this time in a Porsche shared with Hans Herrmann, at 79.6 m.p.h. The following year, besides a Pan American Road Race victory, Maglioli won the Imola GP in a Ferrari at 87.05 m.p.h. and the Senigella Circuit at 102.32. Umberto shared victory in the Supercortemaggiore GP with Mike Hawthorn at 100.62 m.p.h. that same year, and 3rd in the Italian GP with Fro Gonzales. In the Argentine 1000 he shared a 4.5-litre Ferrari and victory with Nino Farina at 93.4 m.p.h.

In 1955 Hawthorn and Maglioli were 2nd in the Supercortemaggiore. Umberto shared a car with the veteran Piero Taruffi for the Tour of Sicily, and they finished 2nd. In the Argentine GP, under superheated conditions, he codrove with Farina and Maurice Trintignant to finish 3rd. It was in 1955, also, that Umberto was 2nd in the Imola GP, and 3rd—to Stirling Moss and Juan Fangio—in the Mille Miglia. He retired from the Pan American Road Race in 1956, was 5th in the Rhineland sports car race and 4th in the Nurburgring 1000 with Wolfgang von Trips in a Porsche RS (winning their class, however). Maglioli had another major victory for his efforts in the Targa, winning a 2nd time, with Huschke von Hanstein in a Porsche RS at 56.37 m.p.h. There was a 5th in the Mille Miglia in 1957, and a 4th in the Nurburgring 1000 with Edgar Barth, their car winning its class. In the German GP, Maglioli started in the Formula 2 section, but retired on the 17th lap. He crashed at Le Mans.

It was 1959 before he was back in action, retiring with Hans Herrmann at the Targa when their engine failed, and again at Le Mans. With Barth, Maglioli was 12th in the Goodwood version of the Tourist Trophy. He was 4th with Herrmann at Nurburgring, winning their class. The next year he did not drive in major races, and after 1962 he drove very infrequently. A favorite start was the Targa; in 1962 he retired with gearbox trouble, in 1963 he was 7th, in 1964 6th, in

1965 3rd—that same season also driving in the Nurburgring 1000 and finishing 5th. Umberto did not run the 1966 race and crashed in 1967.

He was in the cockpit once more in 1968, sharing a Porsche 910 with Vic Elford. It was Maglioli's 3rd Targa victory, at 69.04 m.p.h. Porsche prevailed on Umberto for one more time to try to repeat their Targa victory. They came close, finishing 2nd in a 908 Spyder, the 2nd car in a 4-car Porsche sweep. Not bad for a 41-year-old parttime driver.

WILLY MAIRESSE

They called Wolfgang von Trips "Count von Crash" in his heyday. A latter holder of that unenviable title might have been Willy Mairesse, a fast but unlucky Belgian driver who crashed more times than you could count, but managed to die in bed. Born in Momignies, a town near the French border, October 1, 1928, Mairesse made his competition debut in 1953 in the Liège-Rome-Liège rally codriving a Porsche 1500 with a doctor friend. They failed to finish. The following year the pair tried the Alpine Rally with the same unrewarding result.

Although his family was against his racing, Mairesse's father relented sufficiently to let him borrow a Peugeot 203 from his factory. Willy worked on this car carefully, fitted a blower, and managed to finish 26th overall in the Liège rally in 1954. The following year, in the same contest, he pushed the Peugeot to 8th overall, 1st

in class; then he won the Huy 12-hour race outright. Mairesse next acquired an old Mercedes 300SL with which he entered innumerable rallies and local races, winning his share of both. He also scored a class 3rd in his initial race at the Nurburgring, then startled everyone by winning the Liège-Rome-Liège, besting the 1955 victor, Olivier Gendebien, and setting up a longstanding rivalry. Mairesse followed this victory with a repeat of his Huy victory.

If 1957 looked like a big year at the start, it looked a lot different by its end. Mairesse wrecked a borrowed Mercedes 300SL at Huy, overturned in 2-litre Ferrari at Chimay, crashed a 3-litre Testa Rossa Ferrari at Le Mans, and did the same thing with the repaired car at Silverstone. He ended the frustrating year by crashing his own Mercedes into the side of a tunnel during the Liège rally.

Jacques Swaters, Ferrari's Belgian distributor (and himself a former driver), came to Mairesse's aid in 1958 when it looked as if he were through. With Swaters's help, Willy bought a Ferrari Berlinetta and proceeded to score welcome 2nds in the Rheims 12-hour race and at Clermont-Ferrand. Then he crashed again in the Tour de France. In 1959 in the Tour de France, he won several of the timed hillclimbs, causing Gendebien to sweat harder than he cared to on the way to his 3rd successive Tour victory. Gendebien was even more annoyed when Enzo Ferrari offered Mairesse a Targa Florio "test drive." Willy came in 4th (with Lodovico Scarfiotti) and was offered a factory berth.

Mairesse was 3rd (with Cliff Allison) in the Nurburgring 1000 and 2nd in the Paris 12-hour race. He made his Formula 1 debut in the Belgian GP, a crash-marred race in which 2 British drivers were killed, and in which Willy was retired with mechanical troubles. The story was pretty much the same for several other GP starts, save for the Monza-based Italian GP in which Mairesse finished 3rd behind Phil Hill and Richie Ginther, his Ferrari teammates.

The rivalry between teammates Gendebien and Mairesse reached a fever pitch in the 1960 Tour de France, which Willy was determined to win at last. Gendebien soon found himself clearly outclassed by Mairesse, yet in an outstanding display of sportsmanship—albeit an unhappy one for Olivier—he helped Mairesse to his victory one night on a mountain road.

Sweeping around a turn, Gendebien saw Mairesse's Ferrari off the road in a ditch. He stopped, and with Lucien Bianchi's help, the Ferrari was manhandled back onto the road. A Mairesse wheel was bent, and Gendebien opened his trunk and produced his spare wheel for Willy. Then he hopped back into his own car and sped off. Not a word had been spoken by either man. Willy went on to win, while Gendebien finished far down the list.

In 1961 Mairesse and Giancarlo Baghetti took 2nd overall at Sebring, then won the Spa GP. He was 6th overall (again with Baghetti) at the Nurburgring 1000, 2nd in the Rouen 4-hour race, and 2nd at Le Mans with Mike Parkes. Mairesse won at Clermont-Ferrand, but crashed in the rain-soaked German GP. For the 2nd year in a row he won the Tour de France, but then crashed once more, this time in the Pescara 6-hour race. He and Bianchi codrove to a 2nd in the Paris 1000 to finish the year. At that point he succeeded Richie Ginther as Ferrari's chief tester.

The following year he had a major accident at Spa that curtailed much of his racing work, yet won the Brussels GP and the Targa Florio (with Ricardo Rodriguez and Gendebien). After a victory in the nontitle Naples GP, Willy and Parkes shared a 2nd at Nurburgring. In F1, he went well for 90 laps at Monaco before going out, then crashed when he and Trevor Taylor bumped at 120 m.p.h. at Spa during the Belgian GP. Taylor walked away with scratches, but Mairesse suffered 2nd degree burns. It was not until October and the Italian GP that he returned. He finished 4th behind Graham Hill, Ginther, and Bruce McLaren who nipped Willy by 0.4 of a second for 3rd place.

In 1963, joined by John Surtees and Parkes, he charged ahead. He started with a 2nd at Sebring (with Nino Vaccarella) in a 250 P and a 2nd in the Targa Florio (with Bandini and Scarfiotti) in a 2-litre car. He wrecked an F1 Ferrari at Silverstone in May, but won the Spa GP for GT cars the very next day. With Surtees, Mairesse won the Nurburgring 1000. After retirements in the Monaco and Belgian Grands Prix, Willy was again badly burned at Le Mans when the car he had just taken over from Surtees caught fire. It was 2 months before he was back for the German GP, where he again was badly injured in a crash.

Mairesse's appearances started falling off at this point, but he was still capable of good performances. In 1965, for example, he won the Spa 500 in a Ferrari 275LM. That same year he shared 3rds at Rheims and Le Mans. In 1966 he again won the Targa Florio, this time in a Porsche Carerra; in 1967 he shared a 3rd there in a Ferrari. Yet the repeated crashes and burnings had taken their toll, and Mairesse lived in pain much of the time. On September 4, 1969, he may have had enough, or the pain might have been too great, or he may have erred. At any rate, Willy Mairesse was found dead of an overdose of sleeping pills.

TIMO MAKINEN

A few years ago, Timo Makinen of Finland estimated that he had already driven more than a million miles. Not all of them were as an international rallyist, the role in which most people know him in recent years. Born in the Helsinki area on March 18, 1938, Timo piled up many of those miles as a truck driver, working in the family's long-range trucking business, delivering freight and newspapers to the outer reaches of Finland. He used to enjoy "breathing on" the engines of his trucks to make them go faster, and Makinen was a bit of a hot shoe in those days. Reportedly he collected 32 speeding tickets in 5 years in his trucking career, which is no mean accomplishment in a country where speed laws are not that rigid outside the major population centers. Timo also lost his license on at least 5 occasions for periods of up to 4 months.

None of that sounds like good preparation for a team effort like rallying, yet Makinen became one of the world's best rally drivers with such marques as British Motors Corporation and Ford. Timo demonstrated just how good a rally driver he was in 1965 when he won the demanding Monte Carlo Rally outright without a single penalty point. The next year he also finished 1st in the Monte, but the car was disqualified over its lights —preparation, not performance, then, and out of Timo's hands. Most drivers would have been openly upset and critical of this turn of events. Makinen may have had some dark thoughts, but he did not show them publicly.

Makinen started big-time rallying in 1962 when he joined the BMC team and appeared in the RAC Rally. He was in a BMC Mini-Cooper S when he won the Monte in 1965, the only one of the 237 starters to finish without a penalty point. In the 1966 Monte he drove from Copenhagen to Monte Carlo—a distance of 1,175 miles over 4 frontiers—in just over 14 hours. BMC mounts also provided Timo with back-to-back class victories in the RAC Rally in 1962, 1963, and 1964; in the latter year he also took the Grand Touring class and

a 2nd overall. He had an especially good year in 1964, winning in class in the Nurburgring Touring Car Grand Prix, the Finnish Ice Racing Championship, and the Finnish Rally of 1,000 Lakes (and 4th overall). He also won the Tulip Rally and placed 4th overall in the Monte Carlo to help BMC take the team title.

In 1966 his luck changed. After the Monte disqualification, he ran as a conservative for the Finnish Parliament; he was narrowly edged by a left-wing candidate, despite "victory" reports circulated in many newspapers and auto magazines misled by early reports.

As a Finn, he skied of course, and he was almost as skilled in power boat racing as he was in rallying. In 1969 Timo won the Round-Britain Power Boat Race, although he discounted his skill in boats. You just put the boat on full throttle and hang on, he claimed. Perhaps that was why he never really tried closed-course racing. He liked the challenges of the open road rather than the track. In 1970, he started talking about retiring on the grounds that he had seen most of the roads and crossed most of the frontiers that are involved in big-time rallying, including many behind the Iron Curtain. Even so, driving with Ford that season (he had switched to Lancia in 1969 after BMC quit big-time rallying, then moved over to British Ford), Makinen was 2nd in the 1000 Lakes and 5th in the World Cup.

JEAN MARCENAC

Like Alexander Woollcott's Man Who Came to Dinner, French-born Jean Marcenac (1895) came to Indianapolis for one day and stayed for the rest of his life. It was the 1920 Indianapolis 500 that brought him there to install new brakes on Ralph DePalma's Ballot entry. Something about Indy struck a responsive chord in the young Frenchman's heart, because he stayed to become a riding mechanic and a pit mechanic for some of the nation's best drivers.

Marcenac had 4 winners at the Brickyard, all while acting as Harry Hartz's chief crewman. In 1927 it was George Souders, 2 years later Ray Keech, the following season Billy Arnold, and in 1932 Fred Frame. In 1931 the Marcenac-prepared Hartz car, driven by Arnold, was leading after 162 laps at an average of 109 m.p.h. when its rear axle snaped and it wrecked. The winning time that year was 96.629 m.p.h., the last under-100 average ever to win the 500.

In later years Marcenac's name was linked most closely with the fortunes of the Novi cars. The front-drive racers caught the public's fancy and the admiration of many veteran Indianapolis men, but could never seem to lick their myriad problems. Jean was 1st a mechanic under Bud Winfield, co-designer of the power plant that was used in the Novis starting in 1946. Then, after Bud's death in 1950, he became chief mechanic for the new Novi Racing Company. In 1955 Marcenac and the pre-

mier Indy builder of the day, Frank Kurtis, worked out a new Novi chassis design for 1956 in a vain attempt to better the marque's position. Jean was in his Van Nuys, Calif., home when he died on February 14, 1965, of a heart attack.

MARCHESE BROTHERS

In 1902 Luigi Marchese, a Sicilian, came to the United States because there seemed at least a chance for him to make a living for his family. He worked as a railroad section hand in Milwaukee and finally saved enough to send for his wife and 4 children—Joe, Tony, Tom, and Anna. He settled in a tenement on the lower east side of Milwaukee where Carl was born in 1905 and Tudy in 1907.

Like many other immigrant families, the brothers were very close: they had to be to survive. This closeness inevitably brought them together in their work. Tony had learned to be an auto mechanic, so in 1917, at the age of 18, Tom took a job with the Holmes Motor Co., leaving a promising career in candy making. Soon Carl and Tudy joined him. On the side, the brothers constructed a pioneer midget racing car using a Henderson cycle engine on a platform wooden body. This car, which took to the streets of Milwaukee in the early hours of the morning, was the beginning of a life-long involvement with the sport.

In 1922 the brothers took the next step with a Rajo head Model T dirt car. Carl was the driver although he was only 17; Luigi signed the papers enabling him to race. This was an important year for the Marcheses because they decided to go into business for themselves.

Joe and Tony set up a trucking business, which eventually was to blossom into a building contracting concern, and took in Tom as the head of the service department. As a sideline, the brothers sold an assortment of car marques—none of which survived very long. Meanwhile they fostered the driving careers of Carl and then Tudy, finally amassing enough money to purchase a Miller-engined racer for Carl in 1927. They campaigned dirt tracks in Wisconsin and Illinois with moderate success, primarily because the 122-cu. in. Miller engine was kept meticulously by Tom. In 1929, a lighter 122-cu. in. Miller was purchased. Carl took the new car and Tudy inherited the older.

The Marcheses had Indianapolis in mind when they bought that 2nd Miller. They sleeved it down to 91 cu. in. and departed for Indianapolis for practice. The weather was not as fair as usual at Indianapolis in May of 1929. It rained a great deal and practice time was limited; Carl hit a wall in practice after a rain squall, damaging the car badly. Their dream seemed dim as he called Tom in Milwaukee to bring down all the spare parts they had for the car. They eventually qualified at 108.440 m.p.h., (some 8 miles slower than veteran Ralph

Hepburn) in a vehicle that should not have been allowed near the track because it had reworked suspension members, some still a little bent.

Carl took the ill-handling vehicle and moved it steadily through the pack from 24th at the end of lap 10 to 4th three-quarters of the way through. But that was the best he could do because Ray Keech, Louis Meyer, and Jimmy Gleason all had much faster machines. He still won $4,350 and became a Wisconsin hero.

But Carl's driving career was destined to be short. Later in 1927 he was involved in a 4-car crash at Springfield, Ill., in which one of the cars catapulted into the crowd, killing 2 fans. Carl was seriously injured and never drove in competition again.

Meanwhile, the Marchese connection with racing took a new turn. The mile track at the State Fairgrounds in Milwaukee was one of the oldest and most consistently successful tracks in the United States. Its promoter, J. Alex Sloan, had been there for years; but there had been a steady deterioration in the relationship between Sloan and Ralph E. Ammon, manager of State Fair Park. This deterioration came to a head soon after Carl's showing at Indy. The official version is that Sloan recommended Tom Marchese as his successor. Another version said that Ammon and Sloan had words, and J. Alex said sarcastically, "Why don't you get that head bricklayer Tom Marchese to take my place?" Realizing that he was out one promoter either way and that Carl and the Marcheses were big heroes, Ammon approached Tom.

Thus began the career of one of the world's most successful auto racing promoters. Tom looked upon promoting as a chance to make quick dollar with the cars he loved. When the Depression hit, it was also a reliable a way of making a living. Carl finished 2nd behind Gus Schrader in the 50-mile feature at Tom's 1st program, July 21, 1929. Tom was not the exclusive promoter, however, until 1946.

All during the thirties the Marcheses stayed deeply involved in racing. Tudy continued in big cars for several years after Carl's accident, then switched to midgets for one great season because that was where the money was, what little there was of it. He retired from driving in 1935 as one of the leading midget pilots in the Midwest. But he and Carl continued to own midgets until late in the fifties.

In 1939 the State Fair Board awarded its spectacularly unsuccessful midget promotion to Tom and his associates. They quickly built it up to the point where crowds of 12,000 were coming in regularly. But it was after World War II, when he became the sole promoter, that Marchese's promotional talents really blossomed. In 1948 Marchese introduced stock-car racing under the AAA aegis and found he had an immediate success on his hands. Paul Bjork, later killed in a plane crash, drove a '47 Kaiser to victory. And 1948 was the year Tom first insisted that AAA award him a 200-mile race in addition to the 100 miler. Meanwhile he ran weekly

modified and jalopy races, helped organize the short-lived National Midget Auto Racing Circuit (which had failed elsewhere before Milwaukee). And it was also in 1948 that Tom sold his interest in the family contracting business to Joe and Tony and concentrated on his Wisconsin Auto Racing, Inc. Carl and Tudy founded a machine shop.

Tom was instrumental in having Milwaukee paved in 1954, heralding the beginning of the end of the dirt tracks. One by one the other mile tracks fell in line. Finally in 1971, with talk of a new State Fair Grounds site, the fabulous Marchese era seemed likely to be at an end. It was only a matter of time, and by that time Wisconsin Auto Racing, Inc., had promoted over 400 races, at least half of them for National Championship points. And that in itself must be something of a record.

ONOFRE MARIMON

In the early fifties Juan Manuel Fangio proved to be such a pleasant surprise that there was a sudden surge of South American drivers, people like Fro Gonzales, Roberto Mieres, and Onofre Marimon. If Marimon's name is not all that familiar, it is understandable, for his international driving career lasted only one year. But that was long enough to suggest that he might have been one of the better ones.

Onofre Augustin Marimon was born in a suburb of Buenos Aires on December 19, 1932. Two men greatly influenced his life. One was his father Domingo who was a racing driver in Argentina until 1947, driving modified American stock cars and specials of his own design. The other influence was Fangio, a close friend of Domingo's, who loaned Onofre a Chevrolet Special single-seater that had proven lucky for him. The luck rubbed off on Onofre; he won his 1st big race at age 18 at Cordoba in 1951.

In a few weeks Onofre found himself in Europe thanks to Fangio's recommendation to the Argentine authorities, who wanted to put their nation on the auto racing map and place their drivers in the top ranks of driving. At Le Mans Marimon joined Gonzales in a 4.5-litre Talbot, but engine trouble knocked them out of the race. At Rheims he was handed a Maserati Milano (not the most successful of the Maseratis) and lasted 2 laps before his engine blew up. At Modena, Ferrari gave Marimon a test drive in a 2-litre car, and then the European jaunt was over. It was not until June 23, 1953, that Marimon would again drive in Europe.

Fangio and Gonzales brought Marimon over with them for the Belgian Grand Prix, which he entered in a Maserati. He finished this race 3rd behind Alberto Ascari and Luigi Villoresi, 2 experienced, top-rank drivers. At Bern, Marimon dueled World Champion Mike Hawthorn on equal terms for a good portion of the race before dropping back. At Monza he alternated in the lead with Ascari, Fangio, and Nino Farina in a virtuoso display of talent.

In 1954, when Gonzales went to Ferrari (and Fangio went to Mercedes Benz), Marimon found himself elevated to lead driver at Maserati. He was an instantaneous success in this role, running the fastest lap at Syracuse and winning the Rome GP at 102.96 m.p.h. At Silverstone, the Maserati clearly being outclassed, Onofre nevertheless finished ahead of his mentor, Fangio, though trailing Gonzales and Hawthorn. The German GP came next, but Marimon never made the grid. In the last practice period his wheels locked at the entrance to the Wehrseifen Bridge, the Maserati skidded and sailed off the bridge, and Onofre Marimon met his death 60 feet below in a cornfield. He was 21 years old.

HELMUT MARKO

Dr. Helmut Marko was a lawyer, but he also knew fast automobiles, like his close friend Jochen Rindt. Europe knew that before the 1971 Le Mans; the rest of the world knew it after the race. Marko, a tallish, quite blond and handsome young man, and his smaller blond codriver, Gijs van Lennep of Holland, won the 24-hour race over a record distance of 3,314 miles at an average speed of 137.9 m.p.h. By the race's end, Marko could not clench his fists because of the blisters his manhandling of the Martini Porsche 917 wheel had raised.

The son of an electrical dealer, Marko was born in Graz, Austria, April 27, 1943. He was 14 when he met Rindt, and they proceeded to become fast friends, race motorcycles together and against each other, and share a Volkswagen. "When one of us made a mistake, the other would take over the wheel," Marko recalled, "and that made us more conscious of being better drivers." When Rindt went racing, Marko came along to help. Marko was determined to finish school, so it was 1967 before he started competing in automobiles. His first rally was in a Karmann Ghia VW. The following year he drove an Austro-Vee or Formula Vee single-seater. Also in 1968 Marko drove his initial international race at Nurburgring before the German Grand Prix. He did not win, but he was good at FVee, and Francis McNamara, the American ex-Army officer who had started a carbuilding business in the Black Forest, signed Marko on as a sort of factory driver.

Helmut raced Vees and a Formula 3 McNamara, then a McNamara-prepared Camaro. In the Austrian 1000 he codrove a Porsche 910 and won that class. A local BMW dealer came up with a couple of rides. Marko developed quickly and by 1970 he was signed by McNamara. He left that deal when a car was not forthcoming and signed with the Martini Racing Team

for a Porsche 908/2. Eleventh in his Porsche debut at Spa with Hans Dieter Dechant, he then shared a car with the experienced Gerard Larrousse at the Nurburgring 1000 and was 5th.

Marko shared a Le Mans car and was 3rd, earning a class victory, the Index of Thermal Efficiency prize, and a better car for 1971. At Watkins Glen with Rudi Lins he was 7th, but again won his class. Marko also shared a 3rd in the Nurburgring 1000. In nontitle sports car racing he was 2nd at Karlskoga and 3rd at Imola and Thruxton. Besides his Martini racing in 1971, Marko stood out in a Lola T212 in the European 2-litre sports car series, winning at places like Hockenheim and Auvergne and Clermont-Ferrand, and in a 2.9 Ford Capri in some European touring races. His eyes were firmly fixed on the same single-seaters that had provided Rindt with a World Championship. He did not get a good start, either with a rather uncompetitive Lola T240 Formula 2 car, or with a Formula 1 BRM P153 car. In the latter, he entered the Grand Prix series at Austria and was 11th. He then retired in the Italian GP, was 12th in Canada, and 13th in the U.S. race.

In 1972 Marko suffered an incredible freak accident in the French GP that left his career in doubt. A stone, kicked up by his own car from the pebble-stream course, shattered the visor or his helmet, cut a piece of his cheek away, and split the driver's right eyeball. At first it seemed he would lose the sight of the eye, but modern medicine later appeared to have saved Marko's eyesight, if not, perhaps, his career.

BOBBY MARSHMAN

Bobby Marshman was born into automobile racing and lived that life to the fullest until his death after a racing accident on December 3, 1964, shortly after his 28th birthday. The son of a former Eastern midget champion and owner of the Hatfield, Pa., Speedway, Bob was about 4 months old when he first went to the track, according to a family story. The sights and smells must have made a lasting impression because by the time he was 11 he was negotiating the dirt circuits—unofficially. Three years later, Marshman bought a midget car for $50 and acted as its mechanic while older men raced it for him.

After graduating from Collegeville-Trappe High School in 1955, Bob went to work temporarily as a maintenance crewman at his father's former Saratoga Speedway, near Pottstown, Pa., but that autumn he took to the circuits at nearby Reading. The following season he was voted the most improved driver on the URC program, and in 1957, at age 20, he was 2nd in the URC sprint car point standings. Concentrating on the midget circuit in 1958, Marshman finished 3rd in the ARDC standings, continued apace in both types of competition the next 2 years, and came to national attention for the 1st time in 1960 when he won a 300-mile midget race at Trenton, averaging 95.514 m.p.h. in blistering 110-degree heat.

Marshman was offered his 1st big-time ride on the USAC circuit by Henry Meyers in 1961 at that same Trenton track. During the race Bob's Iddings Special

locked its brakes and flipped, but he escaped uninjured. Later in the year Meyers offered Bob his 1st Indianapolis ride in the Hoover Motor Express car with its "laydown" engine (it was laid on its side). Marshman had been to the Brickyard as a spectator and pit visitor in 1959. He had tried to get a ride at the track itself earlier in the year but had returned home empty-handed until Meyers's phone call.

In the traditional rookie test he was awarded a rare perfect score by the jury of veteran drivers appraising the newcomers that year, and qualified the car in the final spot for the starting field. He finished 7th and shared Rookie-of-the-Year honors with future Indy winner Parnelli Jones. On the Championship Trail Bob took rookie honors, too, with a performance that included a 2nd at the Hoosier 100 and an 8th-place overall point standing at the year's end. The following season he was at Indy once more, qualified the Bryant Heating Special 3rd in the starting field behind Roger Ward and Parnelli, and finished 5th in the 500. Bob also won his only Championship Trail victory at the dirt oval on the Arizona State Fairgrounds in Phoenix that year.

Marshman qualified the Econo-Car Special for the 3rd row at Indy at 149.458 m.p.h. in 1963. He was running 5th with 10 miles to go when broken rear-end gears forced him out; he was placed 16th. Similar mechanical woes sent him falling to 15th in the final USAC point totals, despite a rich Terre Haute victory and a 3rd at Salem, N.H., on the wide banks there. In 1964 he lowered himself into a rear-engined Lotus-Ford owned by Lindsey Hopkins and fell in love with the car. At Indy he qualified at 157.876 m.p.h. for the 2nd starting berth, passed a factory Lotus-Ford driven by Jim Clark on the 7th lap to take the lead, and went on to set Indy's fastest competition lap up to that time, 157.646 m.p.h., before ripping out the bottom of his car (when he dove too low on a corner). He lost water and oil and was forced out after only 97 miles. He finished the season 7th in USAC standings for the National Championship and for stock cars as well.

Like many U.S. drivers, Marshman picked up extra money by testing cars and tires for leading companies. He was testing a reworked Lotus-Ford for the Dearborn firm at Phoenix International Speedway when his number came up. On the 18th lap of a 30-lap test on the mile-long asphalt-covered track, the car veered into the outside rail, ground along the retainer for several hundred feet and burst into flame. Pinned in the car, Bob was burned over 90 percent of his body before asbestos-clad firefighters could reach the car, cover him with foam and extricate the driver from the wreck. Six days later Marshman was dead. Surviving were his wife, Janet Fairlie Marshman, a son, Robbie, 6, his parents and 2 sisters.

The car in which Marshman crashed, a total loss, was the same one in which he had set an unofficial one-lap

Indianapolis record of 162 m.p.h. Just before his fatal crash at Phoenix, Bob had recorded another unofficial mark, eclipsing Parnelli Jones's 30.41-second lap with a 30.40 clocking. To the end he was a front runner with a promise of something bigger to come.

LIONEL MARTIN

Sports cars, racing cars, Grand Touring cars and Aston Martin. The classes and the name became virtually interchangeable, which is something that the founder of this famous marque—long since departed from the company that still bears his name—never dreamed of when he set out to make his first car in 1913.

Lionel Martin was a big, ruddy-faced man who had opened a repair shop and Singer sales outlet in partnership with a friend, Robert Bamford, in Kensington in 1908. Martin liked to drive cars as well as repair and sell them, and he soon achieved fame as a Singer driver in rallies, races, and even hillclimbs. Martin's Singer was radically different from those in the showroom, and other would-be racers soon were beseiging the premises for B&M-modified Singers.

Sensing that a new car would be welcome, Martin determined to build one. For a prototype he purchased a 1908 Isotta-Fraschini voiturette chassis and a 4-cylinder 1390-c.c. Coventry-Simplex engine. The car and company acquired their names after Martin drove this "new" racer to victory at Aston Clinton Hill near Aylesbury, and he decided to couple the site's name with his own to commemorate the feat.

World War I ended development of the new marque, but work was resumed soon after the Armistice by Martin alone, since Bamford was leaving the firm. The original engine went into a 2nd model in 1919, then was reworked for a 3rd prototype in 1921. By this time, however, Martin was convinced that he needed a s.o.h.c. engine to replace the side valve plant, and he commissioned a 16-valve design of 1486 c.c. that went into a track car that Count Louis Zborowski (of Chitty-Chitty-Bang-Bang fame) used to set 2 standing-start class records at Brooklands.

Martin cashed in on the records by offering his first cars to the general public, using the side-valve engine. Zborowski and others continued to pile up impressive press clippings for Aston Martin at Penya Rhin in Spain, Brooklands, and in a series of hillclimbs including the Aston Clinton. Few production cars were sold, however, despite such inducements as wire wheels and 4-wheel brakes. Only 60 side-valvers were ever made.

An interesting one-of-a-kind of the period was the 1923 "Razor Blade," so called because of its thin appearance. The chassis and body were as narrow as possible to reduce frontal area, a mere 36 inches in track and 18.5 inches at the widest point of the body. Sammy

Davis lapped Brooklands at 104 m.p.h. in this 1500-c.c. car but the record attempt failed because of tire trouble. Later the same car gained many successes in sprint events, but its initial failure detracted from sales, causing Zborowski to withdraw his financial support and forcing Martin to pass controlling interest in 1924 to the Charnwood family, although the founder remained as a director. A year later the company was reorganized again, given the new name of Aston Martin Cars, Ltd., and moved to Feltham.

A. C. (Bert) Bertelli joined the new company at this time, with W. S. Renwick, who had been associated with him in a 1.5-litre car project that was to be known as the R&B marque. Aston Martin's firmly established competition image influenced the new directors to retain the name, even though Lionel Martin's main connection with the company had now ended.

MASERATI BROTHERS

Carlo was the first-born of a Voghera railroad engineer, who also fathered Bindo, Alfieri, Mario, Ettore, and Ernestro. Carlo set quite a pace for his brothers. In 1898 he built his own steam engine and successfully ran a bicycle with it, then built his own single-cylinder 4-cycle gasoline engine to run another bike, all by 1899.

The oldest Maserati son raced bicycles for about 3 years, became head of Fiat's testing department at age 20, then was lured away after 2 years to become Bianchi's chief test driver. Carlo ran the major races in the generally outclassed marque, moving from 23rd to 9th in the Florio Cup, and finishing 16th in the Kaiserpreis in 1907. Isotta Fraschini hired Carlo, who moved over to the now defunct Junior marque to become its managing director at 26. At 30 he was dead.

Bindo was at Isotta for a brief time as chief tester, but the successful driving brother was Alfieri, who won the Dieppe race for Bianchi before moving to Isotta himself in 1910. Alfieri and Ettore, also an Isotta employee, were off to Argentina in 1912 to build and service racing cars there for the factory, and it was 1914 before they were back to create Officine Alfieri Maserati. It was a bad year to start a business (with the outbreak of World War I), and it was not until after Ernestro returned from wartime service in the Italian Air Corps that the Maserati brothers got into serious car-building—all but Mario, who had no interest in cars.

At first Isotta hired the Maseratis to build and race its racing machines. The first year of racing saw some successes with Alfieri at the wheel and Ernestro as his riding mechanic. But in 1922 their machines started to dominate the Italian racing scene, the pair winning at Mugello and in other important starts. Diatto recognized the Maserati genius in 1923 by turning over its racing program to the brothers, and typical of the results was

Alfieri Maserati

Alfieri's 2nd to Antonio Ascari in the inaugural Cremona race.

In 1926 the 1st car bearing the Maserati name was born, a straight-8 s.o.h.c. supercharged car called the Tipo 26. On April 25 it won its class and was 9th overall in the Targa Florio among 33 finishers. Alfieri was at the wheel, of course. On June 13 he won the Bologna Speed Trials at 103.9 m.p.h. The Tipo 26 kept winning for several seasons, from the Tripoli GP of 1927 with Ernestro driving to minor starts in the hands of far less experienced drivers. But there were many new designs coming out of the brothers' minds, including the 8C-2500, 8C-1100, and V-4, all in 1929. The middle car has an interesting footnote; in its 2nd appearance at the Cremona race on September 28, 1929, the car was so fast that it also established a 10-kilometer world speed record during the race, 152.6 m.p.h.

Still the new designs came and the old ones kept winning races, like Ernestro's Rome GP victory in 1931, the V-4's last race, and nearly his last, also. In 1932 Ernestro had to assume the presidency of the Maserati operation upon Alfieri's death, Bindo joining the firm the same year. Carlo died in 1937 and Ettore retired, leaving Ernestro and Bindo to sell out the operation to the Orsi brothers. They remained as consultants, however, until 1947, when a misunderstanding severed the connection at last. But the Maseratis were not through; they went into their own business again, Officine Specializzate Construzion Automobile, better known by its initials, OSCA.

JOCHEN MASS

"You might say that I was drafted into motor racing," said Jochen Mass, thinking back to 1968. "I had just left a job at a bank, and I had to find another job and sign an apprentice contract or be drafted. A local Alfa Romeo dealer offered me a job as a mechanic—why, I can't really say, because I knew very little about it—and I signed on to find that I was expected to drive one of his cars in small hillclimbs and circuit races."

Munich-born (in 1947), Mass thought more about becoming a flier than a racing driver when he was a youth. He left school at 17, an accomplished sailor and swimmer, and drifted into the German merchant marine as a trainee officer. He got tired of scrubbing decks and tried out a bank career. The deal was 3 months as a trainee, then 3 years—with contract—as a junior executive. On the last day of his trainee status, Mass was invited to sign on for the 3-year program, but he resigned instead.

Without a job and career commitment, he was eligible for the Germany Army's draft. And so to the Alfa dealer. Before long Mass found himself behind the wheel of a Giulia Sprint, climbing hills and racing on club circuits. Jochen won his initial appearances in both endeavors, so in 1969 his Alfa boss got serious about his budding Jo Rindt. Mass did well enough against factory Fords to be invited by Jochen Neerpasch, then Cologne Ford's competition head, to a test session at Zandvoort along with Tim Schenken and Helmut Marko, among others.

383

"I had raced a bicycle as a youth," Mass recalled, "and I had driven fast in my mother's car since I had been 16, but the Alfa driving was the only real competition experience I had ever had." Despite that, Mass found himself with offers from McNamara Racing and from Ford. He ended up with the latter after flirting with the former. In the European Hillclimb Championship he finished 2nd in class in a 2.4-litre Capri and also raced a BMW 2002 on stock-car circuits in Europe.

By 1971 Jochen was a factory driver for Ford, and he won the German stock-car title that year. Branching out, he raced a Capri at Monza, was leading until a flat, and the time lost to change, it cost Mass the top 3 spots. At Jarma he won outright, at Spa he was retired with piston trouble. At Brno he was leading until a backmarker cut him off and forced the car into the curb, damaging its suspension.

But 1971 was more significant for Mass in trying his skills in single-seaters. A friend suggested the young German try a Kaimann Formula Super Vee, and in his 1st race Jochen finished 2nd overall, with a victory in the 1st heat and a 4th in the final. He won the German FSV race, then mechanical problems retired his car in Holland and Sweden. All told, Mass started 6 FSV races and won 2. Toward year's end, and with German Ford's backing, Jochen tried his hand at Formula 3 in a Brabham BT35 and finished 2nd in his 1st start. He won his 4th start, this one in Britain, his only victory in 6 races.

For all of his limited background, Mass found himself signed on in both F3 and F2 in 1972. His mounts in both cases were Marches, the latter Ronnie Peterson's factory team car when Super Swede was tied up with Ferrari sports car races half a dozen times. Perhaps Mass's Springbok Series performances between seasons was a factor in getting him these opportunities. Jochen won the manufacturer's title for Ford and finished 2nd overall in the stock-car section of the South African series—five 3-hour races that Mass drove single-handed.

STEVE MATCHETT

You had be a real racing enthusiast to know the name Steve Matchett. His name didn't make headlines, and it rarely got into the top-3 finishers list that make the daily newspapers. He didn't drive the glamorous Grand Prix circuit or Indianapolis. Steve Matchett was just a guy trying to get a big break in motor racing. With 9 racing seasons behind him in 1972, he had just come off the Canadian-American Challenge Cup series as part of the scenery, an honorable if unrewarding part of the racing picture, in a Tony Dean 908 Porsche.

The scenery is that part of the starting grid that really doesn't have much of a chance of finishing up high, let alone winning. Matchett was scenery and, as such, may have pertinence as a type. Why race with little chance of winning? "I did the CanAm to get exposure,"

said Matchett, a compact, young-looking man with a ready smile and a kind of Mid-Atlantic accent, "I spent a lot of years learning my trade in small cars and getting relatively well-known in Europe, and I felt it was time to try and get some attention again in the States."

Matchett was an American, born in West Palm Beach, Fla., in 1942 and raised in Okinawa, where his father had a Coca-Cola franchise. He was educated in California and Massachusetts (Williams College), and spent much of his time in Europe, mostly in England. "My dad and mother started the Okinawa Sports Car Club," Steve recalled. "My mom was the hot shoe with a TR-3. I started my 'racing' career with a Fiat 500, if you can visualize that one. The speed limit on the island was a mere 30 m.p.h., so the Fiat could be considered a hot car, I guess."

Steve started dreaming of being a racing driver at age 11, but he didn't start actual racing until he was in high school in California. "I started with cycles, but in a race I fell, broke my leg and was run over, so that was that. Next I went to go-karts, finally to cars in 1963 in the SCCA. I was in a Lotus 11 in my first race at Pomona after three lessons, and I shunted the car when Ken Miles appeared in my mirrors and I started watching him. He was my idol."

Back in action, Matchett scored a class victory at Santa Barbara, rode out several more races in the Coast, and decided England was the place to learn. He landed in Britain in 1964, intending to stay a few months. But it was 1971 before he was again to spend more than a few days a year in the States. A Lotus 22 was Steve's

1964 mount in Formula 3. "F3 is terribly competitive and dangerous, I guess," he said. "You simply have to win or you're nobody, so everyone just goes all out and hopes for the best. It calls for total concentration and complete consistency. If you have just one bad lap, you're out of it; that's how evenly matched the cars and the drivers are."

In 1965 Steve had a Cooper-BMC, started 7 races, won 1, DNF'd 3 races. In 1966 and 1967 with a Brabham, bought as a wreck and rebuilt by Matchett himself, he had 8 starts, a single victory and 7 DNFs, and then 15 starts, 2 victories and 4 DNFs respectively. "I didn't race at all in 1968," he recalled. "I simply ran out of money and had to work. It was with Dan Gurney's Anglo-American Racers operation in Britain, and I learned a lot." Matchett spent two years with Gurney's AAR operation, responsible for parts on the Eagle engines.

In the latter year Matchett also raced, this time in Formula Vee, using an Austro, starting 22 times, winning 8 races, finishing every start, and winning the British FV crown and finishing 2nd in the Western Europe FV series. "I saved my money, too, and that, coupled with a small sponsorship, got me back into F3," he said. Steve was standing 3rd in 2 of the 3 British F3 championships in mid-1970 when the money gave out, the racing stopped, and his Chevron B15 was parked for good.

The lifestyle Matchett followed in his decade of racing between 1960 and 1970 could be said to be exciting, but also lonely, hectic, and rather primitive. For 3 years he lived in a tent, and Steve knew hunger pains more than once. "In a way," he admitted, "I guess some people might say I was a racing bum the same way there are tennis or golf bums." But he had that urge to race, and in 1971, when Tony Dean offered him the uncompetitive Porsche 908 for CanAm racing, Matchett still jumped at the chance. His season started well with a 2nd in a British warm-up race, but in the CanAm itself it was frustration.

At Mosport Matchett was hit by another car and DNF'd, ditto at St. Jovite, at Watkins Glen engine trouble, at Mid-Ohio he was 9th, at Elkhart 8th, at Donnybrooke and at Edmonton 11th, at Laguna Seca 13th. Dean drove the car to 14th at Riverside, later admitting it was a dog. What Matchett might have done in better machinery is problematical.

FRANK MATICH

The two best Australian racing drivers of the fifties and sixties were Jack Brabham and Frank Matich. Everyone knows the Brabham story, but Matich, who like Black Jack became a constructor, is less well-known except in motor racing's inner circles. Perhaps that was because, unlike so many Australian and New Zealand drivers,

Matich stayed pretty much Down Under, with only occasional races elsewhere in the world.

Back at home, Matich and motor racing were synonomous. In all he won better than 20 sports car championships in his 20 years of racing, including 5 Australian crowns (1964, 1966, 1967, 1968, and 1969), and those of Victoria, Queensland and New South Wales, among others. His bag included the Australian Grand Touring title, its Formula Junior crown, and just about anything that was loose in the Southwest Pacific area except the Tasman championship, which started in 1964.

Born in 1935 in the Sydney area, Frank 1st drove in trials about 1952 in a 1934 Ford B4, a car known locally as the Red Devil. Two years later Matich started road racing in an MG TC, later switching to an Austin-Healey 100/4. His club career was good enough for Leaton Motors Racing Team, a Total Oil-backed outfit, to offer Matich a berth in 1960. Using an ex-Frank Gardner C Jaguar, then a D Jaguar, Frank showed that he could race with the best of them, winning 7 GT races in the latter, for example, and thereby taking that championship.

Frank's real single-seater career started with a Lotus 15-Climax in 1960, Matich winning 22 of 24 starts, and his career continued apace but it was in Lotus 19s and 19Bs that Matich really got going. When Leaton retired from racing after the 1961 season, Total Oil founded a new team around Matich and equipped him with the latest Lotuses. The 1st season Frank won 37 of 40 starts in Australia, the following season 42 of 44. This period also saw Matich's most serious accident when a throttle

385

jammed in a race at Lakeside Raceway near Brisbane and his Lotus smashed into a bank and exploded. The resulting fire scarred Matich and sidelined him for a long period, but he came back as if it had never happened.

Matich raced Elfin factory cars with BP sponsorship, 2.5-litre Brabham-Climaxes, Ford GT40's, and many other cars, but his favorite mount in the late sixties had to be the first Matich-inspired sports car prototypes developed in conjunction with Elfin. Traco-Olds powered, they proved a big winner in Frank's hands, then continued its record of successes with a 2nd owner, Neil Allen. When Elfin went off in another direction, Matich went into the carbuilding business with SR3 and SR4 designs in Group 7 prototype racing.

In the seventies, Matich continued pursuing his goal of winning the Tasman, coming closest in 1970–71 when he drove a McLaren M10B to a 2nd in the final standings, winning the Australian and New Zealand Grands Prix and the Lady Wigram Trophy. In the same car he came to the United States at the start of 1971 for the emerging L&M Formula 5000 Continental Championship. At Riverside in the opener, Matich won, at Laguna Seca he was 2nd to eventual champion David Hobbs of England. With just these 2 appearances Frank earned 6th place in the final standing and some $14,000. It gave Frank ideas for 1972.

The 1972 ideas included a new car, a built-from-scratch F5000 design that became known as the Repco Matich A50. In its debut November 21, 1971, the new single-seater won the Australian GP, Matich driving to that victory for the 2nd consecutive year. Another idea was to come to the newly enriched L&M F5000 Continental with the new car, but business commitments prevented Matich from doing that. He would wait for those winter days when everyone came to Australia's sunny climes. Then he could pick off the unwary visitors once again.

BANJO MATTHEWS

The blond boy with glasses so thick and strong his eyes looked like twin banjos was driving in a jalopy race at Pompano Beach, Fla., when he was only 15. It seemed unlikely that the youngster, Edwin K. Matthews, could drive at all, let alone on a race track. It seemed even more unlikely that he could ever win, but he did. Banjo Matthews, born in Akron, Ohio, on February 14, 1932, won that 1st race and many others in the modified division of NASCAR. One year (1954) Matthews won 50 races on the modified circuit, but he never won a Grand National race. An operation later improved his eyesight enough to permit thinner glasses, but although he won the pole position at virtually every NASCAR track, Matthews often was not around for the finish. He left that for teammates like Fireball Roberts.

Matthews was as good a chief mechanic as he was a driver. He always prepared his own modifieds and when he tried GN's it was the same story. The Roberts-Matthews team was not permanent, although in 1958 the two shared a car at Ashville-Weaverville Speedway, in North Carolina, near where Banjo and his family settled down. In 1962, when Banjo decided to become a car owner, he prepared 2 Pontiacs for the Firecracker 250 at Daytona, one for himself and one for Fireball. It was the closest he ever came to winning a Grand National—and at a superspeedway at that. Banjo won the pole and led the race for more than 200 miles before the transmission failed. Roberts won in Matthews's other car. Then in 1963 Fireball defected to Ford and Banjo competed only through the Charlotte World 600, retiring from driving at the age of 31. Nelson Stacy campaigned for him for the remainder of the season and then retired, too.

Ford's Total Performance effort got to Banjo in earnest in 1964 when the retired driver built a Ford for A. J. Foyt's NASCAR raids. Foyt managed to lead the Daytona 500 that year, the only Ford to do so in a Petty Plymouth romp. Junior Johnson then took over the Matthews car and won several Grand Nationals, but went into business for himself in 1965.

So Banjo got veteran Bobby Johns, who finished 3rd at the Daytona 500. Johns accomplished little and they split up by midseason; Cale Yarborough got the ride. He did not do badly—a 2nd at Rockingham and then, in 1966, 2nds at Daytona, Rockingham, and N. Wilkesboro. Banjo parked when NASCAR and Ford argued over the rules. Ned Jarrett's 3rd at Rockingham late

that year was his final appearance as a driver. When Ford cut down, Banjo switched to Dodge.

At the "ancient" age of 43, Banjo could look back on a career that made him a NASCAR great. Three times he had won the modified race at Daytona, twice (1955 and 1958) on the old beach-road course and once on the big new Speedway (1959). The latter car was a 1956 Ford stuffed with a big Lincoln power plant.

By 1971 there was another Matthews in NASCAR style racing, Jody, his son, worked the pit crews and hoped to be like his father. But with better eyesight.

TEDDY MAYER

Edward Everett Mayer, was the brother of Tim Mayer. He was also team manager and part owner of Team McLaren and other enterprises of Bruce McLaren. Born in 1937, Ted was 2½ years older than Tim. He came into auto racing through Tim, who got Ted to invest in an Austin-Healey 100-6 with him. The decision to go racing followed very quickly, but Ted had a commitment in Chile that took him away for a while (learning how to ski), and by the time he was back, Tim was tearing up the sports-car courses with the car.

Law school was looming for Ted—a modern European history major in college, he was in for a lot of extra work for his chosen specialty of tax law—so he decided not to race but to assist Tim by managing the team. The Healey was eventually dropped and a 3-car team of Formula Junior Coopers was formed. Tim's codrivers were Peter Revson and Bill Smith. By 1962 there were as many as 16 races a year to manage, and the team record in that stretch was 15 victories, 14 2nds, and 14 3rds; the kind of dominance that Ted was later to find at Team McLaren. Ken Tyrrell in England was also running FJ Coopers, and he invited Tim to try out for a team berth with his private effort. Both brothers came over in the spring of 1963.

The brothers were 23 and 26 at that time. "I had no specific job with the Tyrrell thing except to try to further Timmy's career," said Ted later. "I also looked on the thing as a bit of a holiday, and a chance to try and straighten out in my own mind what I wanted to do." Tyrrell signed Tim believing he had signed a potential World Champion. But it was not to be. Tim had a good season, despite the underpowered Coopers, and so did McLaren, who was Tyrrell's other driver. For 1964 Tyrrell envisioned both men in Formula 1 Coopers, and toward that end he encouraged their trip to the Tasman series between European seasons.

McLaren and Mayer were provided with 2 slim-line 2.5-litre Coopers, based on Bruce's own thinking about what was needed for the Australian and New Zealand racing scene. McLaren won the Tasman title in his car, but Tim was killed when his Cooper became airborne over a hump in the Longford course and slammed into

a roadside tree. Teddy brought Tim's body back to the States for burial. "When I got back," he recalled, "I was very upset, of course, and I didn't know what I wanted to do or where I wanted to do it. I wasn't married, and I had no particular ambition in any direction.

"About that time, Bruce decided to buy the Zerex Special from Roger Penske, and I guess he thought of me to become involved in the thing to help me forget. He commissioned me to buy the car and arrange various other details. When that was done, he reminded me that Tim and I had discussed running cars together in Europe, and he proposed that I do it with him. It became a choice of working in a law office or doing that, and the choice wasn't difficult in those terms. We started in an area that Cooper was ignoring, and the thing just grew."

The thing became the McLaren marque, in Formula 1, Canadian-American Challenge Cup racing (Group 7), and other areas. And Teddy Mayer was an integral part of it. "In fact, Bruce and I became equal shareholders in the company. It took 3 years to start making a profit, but in recent years the gross income has doubled each year. We started with 5 people and now are past 45 with new people working there every time I come back from a race."

The Mayers had come from a wealthy family. Their father was a stockbroker, their uncle Pennsylvania Governor William Scranton. Hence it was no problem for Ted to come up with his share, but Bruce had to strain for it. In the end, they were in business. The

Zerex Special was torn apart and became the first McLaren, and this was followed by the McLaren sports car, F1 in 1966, and Indianapolis. But the CanAm cars were the most famous, of course. With Bruce's death in 1970, there was a question about what would happen to the McLaren marque and Team McLaren. In the end, Teddy sorted everything out, and both names went on. Ted himself was married and lived with his 2 children and wife in Surrey. Racing gave him just the right amount of travel, and Sally never had to worry about whether he would come home in one piece.

TIM MAYER

Tousle-haired Tim Mayer looked even younger than his 26 years, right to the day he died, February 29, 1964, while practicing at the Longford Course for the Tasman Cup in Australia. He had been in serious auto racing less than 5 years, but made an impression upon all who had seen him at the wheel of sports and racing cars of all kinds.

A native of Pennsylvania—a nephew, in fact, of that state's Governor William Scranton—Mayer made London his home in anticipation of filling a place on Britain's Cooper factory team. Tim started racing at the age of 21 in a 1959 SCCA race at Marlboro, Md. His first mount was an Austin-Healey. That season he finished 4th in Class D Production points, after starting a winning streak with his 3rd race of the year. The next season Tim acquired one of the 1st Lotus 18 Formula Junior cars to reach this country, which he crashed later in 1960. At the same time he met Frank Falkner, Cooper's American representative.

Even while serving as an Army enlisted man in Puerto Rico after his graduation from Yale with an English literature degree, Mayer (by then married) managed to become a familiar figure at important race meetings. He came in his own Cooper-Monaco sports racing car that was purchased from fellow Pennsylvanian Roger Penske. He also continued to race in FJ competition, winning the SCCA's national title in the class along with the organization's James H. Kimberly Cup as the SCCA's "most improved driver."

In 1962 Mayer got his first Formula 1 ride in a 4-cylinder Cooper-Climax at Watkins Glen. Tim's career as an international driver took a definite upswing upon his discharge from service in 1963 when he headed to Europe and secured a berth on Ken Tyrrell's Cooper FJ team. Tim also brought his Monaco to England and raced it at courses like Brands Hatch, then returned to the States later that year to race a new Lotus 23B at Riverside and Lagunda Seca. Teaming up his Tyrrell teammate, New Zealand's Bruce McLaren, Mayer headed for the winter's Australia–New Zealand circuits with a view to gaining added experience for his full-fledged entry into the GP field.

He had just turned the 2nd fastest lap of the day—behind Australia's World Champion Jack Brabham—when the fatal accident came on the bumpy Tasmanian course. Observers estimated Mayer's speed at 130 m.p.h. when his 2.5-litre Cooper-Climax became airborne and sailed 60 feet into a tree. Car and tree disintegrated and Tim was catapulted another 120 feet through the air, breaking his neck on impact.

He was still alive when the ambulance reached him, but died on the way to Launceston Hospital. His wife, Garrill, and elder brother Teddy, watching from the pits, reached the ambulance too late to be with him.

RAYMOND MAYS

Raymond Mays got his first taste of competition as a 9-year-old boy watching his father's Napiers and Vauxhalls in local hillclimbs and trials in 1909. He was in the Grenadier Guards in World War I. Commissioned in May 1918, he missed most of the horrors of that war and returned to attend Cambridge. Raymond's father, a wool merchant, gave him a 1.5-litre Hillman Speed Model that he souped up sufficiently to attain 80 m.p.h. (it was rated at about 55 m.p.h.). A close friend, Amherst Villiers, helped in those early years, highlighted by the best time of day in the Inter-Varsity hillclimb at Aston Clinton. At the end of 1922 Mays' name first appeared on a Brooklands pit wall as he ran his initial handicap races, won one, and finished 2nd in another.

The post-World War I slump hit the family business, and Raymond left Cambridge to apprentice himself to a friend of his father's at Glastonbury. But there was enough money, combined with the sale of the Hillman, to buy a Brescia Bugatti. And Mays's reputation by this time was good enough to wrest some support from commercial sponsors. In 1923 he ran the fastest time at the Shelsley Walsh hillclimb. Ettore Bugatti himself was sufficiently impressed by this feat to call Raymond to the factory where not only was the original Bug completely rebuilt, but Mays was given a 1.5-litre racing model as well.

Cordon Bleu and Cordon Rouge, as Mays called the 2 cars, were raced for the entire 1924 season, but in 1925 he became sufficiently dissatisfied to sell them. Selwyn Edge offered him an AC ride, which Mays accepted, but this did not work out either. Just as Raymond was bemoaning his fate, he won $5,000 in the sweeps, and met a young RAF cadet named Peter Berthon. May's good luck continued, Mercedes Benz offering him a 2-litre Targa model for British racing. Later he started driving a Vauxhall Villiers and an Invicta sports car, dubbed the White Invicta.

In 1933 Mays started racing the White Riley, using that car to regain the Shelsley record wrested away by Hans Stuck the year before. The Riley engine formed the guts of a new car the following year. ERA, or English Racing Automobiles, Ltd., was formed with Humphrey Cook as managing director and Berthon and Mays as directors. The "factory" was an old barn on his father's land at Bourne (the elder Mays now was

so ill that Berthon worked in the family wool business as well as in the car world). After an abortive practice in the Isle of Man Tourist Trophy week, the first ERA team raced at Brooklands and won its class. That same year, 1934, Mays ran the initial true road race held in England, the Nuffield Trophy at Donington, and won at 61.51 m.p.h. In the Brooklands Mountain Championship, his ERA was 2nd. In an attempt to beat Hans Ruesch's 88.87 m.p.h. world standing start kilometer record, Mays went 89.73 m.p.h. in his ERA.

Raymond started his first Continental races in 1935, beating Richard Seaman at the Nurburgring while running the race's fastest lap. In the 1500-c.c. section of the Eifelrennen, Mays won at 68.90 m.p.h. leading an ERA parade with Ruesch, Tim Rose-Richards, and Seaman in the 2nd, 3rd and 4th cars. The 1st competitive years of modern European racing came a bit too late for Raymond, but he continued to drive ERA's and other cars. The ERA operation ended in 1939, and Mays unveiled his own marque. Shelsley Motors was formed to market the Raymond Mays car, but only 5 were built before the outbreak of World War II. He got in his first planning for a British Grand Prix car, too, before Hitler ended all thoughts of such things for 6 years.

Peace brought Mays back to the track for a last fling in his old ERA, and also brought him out as a salesman for his GP car idea. Lucas and Rubery Owen were among those convinced by Mays, and a thousand more followed, big and small, to finance what became BRM in 1947. On May 13, 1950, Raymond made his final appearance as a driver, demonstrating the BRM at Silverstone before the crowd attending the British GP. After that came the frustrating years of making BRM competitive—and finally—winning the World Manufacturers Championship for Britain in 1962. The subseqent successes of Lotus, McLaren, Lola, Brabham, and other British racing marques always stood as a monument to Mays, who led the way.

REX MAYS

The racing career of Rex Mays spanned 18 years, but 4 of these were spent as a ferry pilot during World War II. During those 18 years, the handsome, 6-foot Californian never won at Indianapolis, and the records show his main claim to fame is a pair of AAA National Championships. But contemporaries stamp him with greatness, particularly on dirt tracks. Tazio Nuvolari of Italy, who saw Mays race only once, declared that if the American had had something more suitable for a road race than a reworked sprint car, the Vanderbilt Cup race of 1936 at Roosevelt Raceway might have turned out very differently. Rex and Bob Swanson, another master of the dirt, impressed one and all with their driving ability.

Born in 1913, Rex Mays picked a difficult venue for his racing debut, Legion Ascot Speedway in Los Angeles, when Babe Stapp, Bob Carey, Bill Cummings, and Floyd Roberts were racing there. Few made their mark as quickly as Mays, whose star began to rise in 1931. He defeated these men and terrorized West Coast midget racing before embarking upon a big-car career that earned him the national titles of 1940 and 1941.

Mays had one problem that was particularly significant in the long 500-mile race at Indianapolis. He could not find many cars capable of standing his punishing style for 100 miles, let alone 500 miles on pavement. Mays's best finishes in a dozen Indy 500-miles were a pair of 2nds (1940 and 1941), yet he had won the pole position 4 times.

Mays had first raced at Indy in 1934, finishing 9th. He led for the first 90 laps in 1935, leaving with a broken spring shackle on lap 123. In 1936, when the cars were limited to 37½ gallons of fuel, Rex ran out of gas 2 laps from the finish. He had been on the pole with his Gilmore Special and proceeded to hotlap until throttle problems forced him to pit short of 20 laps, and his attempts to catch up cost him precious fuel.

In 1937 Rex ran an Alfa Romeo supercharged 8, which lasted 24 laps before overheating. (He had been enthusiastic about the car's performance in the Vanderbilt Cup at Roosevelt Raceway on Long Island.) In the 1938 race the supercharger failed after 45 laps on a new Alfa. That was enough Alfa for Rex, and he drove a Sparks Six for Joel Thorne in 1939, leaving the race in the 145th lap because of stuck rings. Ironically, Babe Stapp drove his old Alfa to 5th place. His 1940 2nd place came in a supercharged 8 designed and built for the Bowes Seal Fast people.

In the 1940 race, won by Wilbur Shaw, the final 125 miles were driven under caution because of rain on the eastern part of the track. Mays was nearly a lap behind Wilbur at the time positions were frozen, but the final 100 miles is traditionally where the supreme effort to improve position is made. In the 1941 race Mays qualified at 7 m.p.h. faster than the winning Floyd Davis-Mauri Rose car. He finished 2nd because he made 3 pits stops to their one (the one in which Rose took over from Davis).

Mays was known as a spokesman for the drivers in the turbulent postwar period when several efforts were made to organize them by the Teamsters Union and by independent groups. It is little known how far apart the AAA pilots and influential promoters like Tony Hulman of the Indianapolis Speedway grew during this period; Mays helped keep the fuse from the powderkeg more than once.

A month before his death in a race at Del Mar, Calif., in the late fall of 1949, Mays averted what might have been a major riot at the Syracuse, N.Y., State Fairgrounds. A dispute over prize money delayed the start of the championship 100-miler for more than an hour and the fans were becoming more and more ugly. Finally, without a word, Rex got into his car and started circling the track. One by one the other drivers followed. He led the race until a flat sidelined him.

There is a plaque on the crash barrier at Wisconsin's Milwaukee Fairgrounds dedicated to Rex. In a 1947 race—he ended 5th that season—Mays was challenging for the lead when Duke Dinsmore crashed directly in front of him and was thrown onto the track. Rex deliberately crashed into the wall to avoid Dinsmore. He left a son and a daughter. He had no intention of retiring at the time, and foresaw the new golden era of auto racing of the late fifties and sixties.

DENISE McCLUGGAGE

Born on January 20, 1927, in El Dorado, Kans., the 2nd of 3 sisters, this lady driver was always a tomboy. She was also remarkably intelligent and had great determination. Denise finished high school in Topeka and went to California's Mills College, an incubator for young geniuses, on a scholarship. Graduated from that institution with a Phi Beta Kappa key at the age of 20, with a background of philosophy, economics, and politics, she decided to work on the nearby *San Francisco Chronicle* as a writer rather than pursue any of her childhood ambitions to be an archeologist, architect, or lawyer. So began a fascination with cars and speed.

Assigned to do a story on a school of midget race car pilots, McCluggage talked the owners into giving her complimentary lessons in her own MG TC. Her

first teachers, Eddie Bennett and Jim Massa, even let her practice with their cars after their races to use up the gas in the tanks. Other drivers did too, and she had "a tremendous thrill driving on a dirt track, broadsliding through the turns all crossed up, keeping the nose on the pole." Later came "Powder-Puff" jalopy races, a few of which she won. Dennise abandoned them as "ridiculous."

Besides, she had determined that it was time to come to New York to work for the *Herald-Tribune*. Denise started on the paper as a fashion writer, but managed to get a ski column and, finally, transferred to the sports section where she began to cover motor sports. By now she owned an XK 140MC Jaguar that, in August 1956, she entered at the Montgomery, N.Y., airport races, and where she won the ladies' event and did fairly well in one hitherto all-male sprint. The SCCA's New York Region had witnessed the birth of a road racing career.

In December she went to Nassau Speed Week to drive Bill Lloyd's Maserati 2-litre, but blew the clutch in practice. She borrowed a Porsche Spyder and won the initial heat of the ladies' race. She had to borrow different car for the next heat because the Spyder owner felt he did not have enough clutch for both of them. Jim Kimberley, then president of the SCCA, lent her an OSCA 1500. She spun so many times she must have felt like a child's top. Kimberley was impressed enough, however, to invite her to codrive with him at Sebring in 1957. Unfortunately he wrecked the car before the event. In a Little Sebring 3-hour race held that year the day after the Grand Prix, Hushke von Hanstein of the Porsche factory lent her a GT Carrera, with which

she finished 3rd overall. Then Denise bought Lake Underwood's RS Porsche after she won the ladies' race at Cumberland, Md.

The next year Denise departed for Europe. She did well enough and had great fun in the races, she said, and returned to Europe several times, driving in rallies for various European manufacturers. McCluggage left the *Herald-Tribune* and did magazine work for *Town & Country* and other publications, while preparing the Great American Novel. Not retired from driving, Denise just felt herself beyond anything but international competition. She became a consultant to several large corporations, one of them Fuller Brush. After racing an auto racing weekly called *Competition Press* into maturity she was able to sell profitably. She retired from big-city journalism to Vermont where she bought a weekly newspaper.

ROGER McCLUSKEY

The 1972 Ontario 500 will go down in history as the first race ever to be delayed by rabbits. That it also was delayed by a two hour rain was secondary to the sight of USAC personnel chasing jackrabbits off the track as the race cars slowed for fear of clobbering the hares. But when it was over Roger McCluskey, 42 and graying at the temples after 22 years of driving all kinds of race cars, was the happiest man in all of California. Driving a McLaren Offy for Lindsey Hopkins, Roger McCluskey finally had won a 500 and his biggest payday ever, $127,609.

It was somehow fitting that Hopkins was the car owner because the Florida banker, who was also part owner of the Atlanta Falcons football team, also had waited 22 years for that moment when Roger, a lap ahead of young Mike Hiss, rolled into Victory Lane. Only 10 cars were running of the original 33. It was only McCluskey's 3rd Trail victory, although down through the years he led more races than anyone but A.J. Foyt. In between the victories there were long dry spells when frustration grew until Roger relieved it by running sprints or stocks. There he could do well enough to garner two Sprint titles and two USAC stock car crowns.

Frustration 1st ended for Roger F. McCluskey on a hot August Sunday afternoon in 1966 at Langhorne, Pa., Speedway, then newly made into a D-shaped track. That was where he had begun his major league career in 1960, a race he had led briefly until the rough dirt that was the track then had worked his hood straps loose. It was 62 championship races later that he won in a Gurney Eagle Ford, 1st man to bring that car into the winner's circle. The victory had come so easily; he led all but eight laps. The next was to come four years later in a dirt track race and then there was the big one at Ontario only two years after that. The victories were coming gradually closer together.

Born August 24, 1930, Roger McCluskey was part of the great Southwest invasion of USAC's top ranks that shifted the balance of driver power away from California by 1970. He began racing in 1948 when he and Hank Arnold, who subsequently became a business partner, built up a jalopy to race at South Mountain Speedway in Phoenix and at the Rodeo Grounds in Tucson. The pair soon advanced to full-house jalopies (later called supermodifieds); then, in 1952, Roger decided to go as far as he could with auto racing. He teamed with a promising young driver named Art Bisch, later killed, and campaigned midgets with the United Racing Association in California.

He did not set the West Coast on fire, and in 1956 he and Arnold formed a race car construction business. Roger continued to compete, however, moving also into California Racing Association, sprint cars. He might have remained there if CRA had not competed in an invitational USAC show at Meyer Speedway in Houston. It was late 1959 and McCluskey impressed Elmer George, a USAC racer who had had the good sense to marry the daughter of Indianapolis Speedway owner Tony Hulman. George offered him a ride in the HOW Special in which he himself won the 1957 Midwest sprint title. McCluskey accepted.

When he quit sprint car racing 9 years later, Roger had 23 victories to his credit and had been national sprint car champion in 1963 and 1966. He won the Langhorne 150 in August 1966, his first victory on the Championship Trail in a Gurney-Eagle rear-engined Ford, leading all but 8 laps. Indianapolis was even less successful for him: in 1961 he passed his rookie test

and wrecked in the race after 29 laps. He spun out the next 2 years; in 1963 he was 2 laps from the end while in 3rd place. For the next 6 years mechanical defects got to him, although he always had a competitive car.

McCluskey found his forte relatively late in his career —late-model stock cars. Roger had tried his hand in a few NASCAR driver interchange races with indifferent success, and he did not run his first USAC stock-car division race until 1968 when Norm Nelson, the Wisconsin whiz, offered him a Plymouth ride. He finished 2nd that year, then won the championship twice in a row for the Nelson Plymouth forces. Interestingly, Nelson had been the last to win back-to-back stock-car crowns in USAC, 1965-66. The cars he gave to Roger won 4 times, finished second 7 times, and third 3 times in 15 starts, and Norm won 3 races himself, finishing 2nd in the standings.

USAC stock-car racing was a little like NASCAR was in the days before the superspeedways. The tracks were of all sorts—little dirt ovals, the Milwaukee Fairgrounds paved mile, the Sears Point, Calif., road course. But Milwaukee was where most of the points and most of the money was. In the 4 Milwaukee races McCluskey won one, finished 2nd twice and 3rd once.

But whether or not stock cars were the vehicle of his greatest success, McCluskey still considered himself a Championship Trail driver first. When Clint Brawner finally split with Mario Andretti, he and Roger headed into a team sponsored by an energy drink company. It was called the QuicKick Racing Team. The best the pair could do for 1970 was a pair of 2nds, both at Milwaukee. Roger had scored his 2nd victory of a long career in 1968 in the G. C. Murphy dirt car. August 17 was a blistering hot day in Springfield, Ill., and Roger had qualified only 4th fastest. But the favorites, Al Unser, A. J. Foyt, and Mario Andretti, were all parked when he won the dirt track race.

In 1971 McCloskey made $103,000 all in USAC although he didn't win a single Trail Championship race. The same $100,000 mark had seemed within his grasp for '72 even before his Ontario victory. He had lasted 92 laps at July before a broken valve sidelined him. And at Pocono, he won the stock car Pennsylvania 500, then finished 11th in the championship 500-miler despite turborcharger failure. As he drove into 1973, Roger had won 50 races in all sorts of USAC competition and was still going strong.

JIMMY McELREATH

There it was, glistening in the hot California sun, Ontario Motor Speedway, the Indianapolis of the West. It was a magnificent layout, virtually an exact replica of the famed old Brickyard in the oval track layout, but brand new in facilities, spectator vantage points and a twisty road course. Jim McElreath, the square-set Texas veteran, might have wondered a bit when he first set eyes on this monument to mechanical speed. His 1st race in 1945 had been on a hot dusty little dirt track down near Dallas, and his 1st car had been refugee from the scrap pile in which beat the biggest modified passenger car engine that he could stuff in.

Ontario was also going to be different from his initial Indianapolis when Jim, a hot shot in IMCA competition, first came there in 1962 a rookie again. That had been like jumping from a medium-sized pond where he was the big fish to an ocean full of whales. This was like moving from the old and honored grand hotel to the flashy new luxury inn . . . but there was something the same, too . . . the money was plentiful and waiting for anyone capable of grabbing some.

The 1st annual Ontario 500-mile race really would not be the same as winning Indy but it would be a historic moment nevertheless, he thought.

Jimmy McElreath, born February 18, 1928, in Arlington, a suburb of Dallas, Tex., never daydreamed for long. "I do the best I can with what I have," he once said after he had broken down in a dog of a dirt car at Langhorne. "I like to race and I like to win, but somebody always loses, too." That was the Mc-Elreath image on the USAC Trail—an even-tempered guy who drove anything consistently; the image of competency, not brilliance.

McElreath began racing stock cars around his home town when he was 17. He was a big, solid kid who married early, drove modifieds at night, and worked as a bricklayer in the daytime. He was physically strong and courageous and his tastes—for 15 years at least—were simple—a lot of good plain food, a good family, a little racing, and steady work.

He won regularly because he could physically overpower an automobile and ride it like a bronco that needed taming. Many people advised him to get out of the modifieds into something better, like IMCA or even the USAC sprints. But he was happy until late 1959 when, at the age of 31, he sensed he had to move on. "I don't know," he explained later, "I just felt I'd like to see how I could do in a different league." It was as if the IMCA sprint cars had been created especially for him. He could control them even more effortlessly than he could the modifieds, and he finished 7th in points and was billed as Southwest Champion on the fair circuit. In 1961 McElreath moved up to 6th and drew the notice of car owners in USAC. On September 16, 1961, he drove the Hopkins Special at the Indianapolis State Fairgrounds and finished a solid 3rd behind A. J. Foyt and Bob Marshman. He soon got another ride, this time in the Bardahl Special at Sacramento, Calif., and finished 10th despite a broken shock. He rounded out the season with a 4th on the Phoenix dirt track.

Despite his impressive rookie performance, no USAC owner moved to engage McElreath for 1962, so he finally signed a contingency deal to drive the Schultz Fueling Equipment Special at Indianapolis. This was a 7-year-old car which had had little success in the past. McElreath proved it was not what the Indy crowd called a "sled". He passed his rookie tests easily. He was the fastest rookie at the track (even though Dan Gurney was also making his debut that year).

McElreath's high old red roadster macerated the field of USAC's finest, moving to take 2nd at the end of 20 laps behind Parnelli Jones. With even a reasonably efficient pit crew he might have won. But that was something he did not have. The Schulz crew got so excited at having a car in contention that they once dropped the car off the jacks before they had refastened the wheels, and later one of the crew fell over the tire he was carrying. The time lost in the pits put Jim back to 6th, but he was named Rookie of the Year. This time the USAC owners got the message, and McElreath moved into equipment and teams that were appreciably more professional. Yet the victories were few and far between.

The 1st victory came in 1965, well after Jim had joined the Zink-Urschel Trackburner team. Some had already written him off as a casualty of the trend to rear-engined racing cars. After all, in 1964, Jim McElreath was 36 and had seen his Indy hopes dashed by mechanical failure at 77 laps. He had quit driving sprint cars the year before when, at Hatfield, Pa., he had flipped into a fence, injuring a shoulder. But Oklahoman John Zink gave him the nod for a chance at a 1965 rear-engined ride because Zink felt McElreath was one of the few men capable of beating the king of USAC, A. J. Foyt. The quickness with which McElreath adapted amazed his competitors. At Phoenix's

393

150-miler he finished 2nd to Don Branson. Then, across the country at Trenton, he flashed to his initial victory ever on the Trail, over Mario Andretti. It was a rainy overcast day, yet McElreath handled the rear-engined Offy as if it were riding on rails.

A 66-lap ride at Indy was ended by rear-end failure, but Jim was back in stride afterwards. He finished 3rd at Milwaukee, and then came his 1st race on the new D-shaped pavement at Langhorne. Virtually the entire field had trouble adapting to the strange track configuration, but not McElreath. He won both the 100- and 125-mile races there and eventually finished 3rd in the national standings despite a sour last half of the season.

In 1966 at Indianapolis there was another chance to win. McElreath was in contention when his engine stalled in the pits. He lost a full minute, yet roared out and cut into the distance between himself and Graham Hill, the eventual winner, unlapping himself on a daring inside pass late in the race. At the end he was 50 seconds behind Hill and gaining on both Hill and 2nd-place Jimmy Clark. McElreath drove for Zink for more than 4 seasons before he switched to A. J. Foyt's team and a Coyote Ford mount. He continued to be the perfect number 2 driver, giving the cars steady rides.

At Ontario in 1970 he was 42 and with gray hairs. Lloyd Ruby, another veteran, had won the pole. Jimmy, 5 m.p.h. slower, was back in the 6th row in his Sheraton Thompson ITT Special. That was all right. Foyt, the boss, was 3 rows ahead in a position to make a more immediate run at the leaders if he chose.

September 6 was a picture book day, as pretty as the starlets from Hollywood. The movie stars and the politicians moved in the stands and in the Speedway's plush carpeted clubs. McElreath had donned his spotless white driving suit and had listened more than he talked as the Foyt pit personnel joked and jabbered to rid themselves of the pre-race tension that seems to rise whether it is in the suburbs of Los Angeles or the local dirt track.

The race began with Ruby out in front, sorely pressed by Gurney, Al Unser, and Johnny Rutherford. Then Jim Hurtubise in the only front-engined car in the race skidded into the wall. Roger McCluskey had already retired. As the caution waved, the cars bunched into a jagged string of beads. Rutherford also retired, with a blown engine, and Mark Donohue was in obvious trouble. At the drop of the green, Al Unser moved easily ahead of Ruby into first place. As the race progressed, Al's Johnny Lightning Special lapped car after car. McElreath was moving up cautiously, maybe too cautiously, for on the 37th lap Unser lapped him, although he was running 10th.

The racing was not over yet, though. Gurney, Mike Mosely, and Peter Revson were close enough so that Unser's 19-second pit stop on lap 47 dropped him temporarily to 4th place. But Al poured on speed that seemed unlimited, retook the lead on the 50th lap, and

by lap 63 lapped 3rd place Mosely. But the yellow flag waved enough to keep the New Mexican hero wary—and meanwhile McElreath continued plodding onward and upward in the standings, helped as each hot shoe broke his car or spun out. At the halfway point Unser led over Revson, Mosely, and Andretti. He gave up the lead briefly to Revson on his 2nd pit stop, but by lap 157 of 200 he had lapped even Revson. With 62 miles of racing left, Al enjoyed a 2-lap lead over NASCAR's Lee Roy Yarbrough, and James McElreath had worked his way into the top 6. Revson was in the pits replacing a coil, and the competition seemed over. It wasn't.

Unser suddenly signalled that he was pitting. He stayed 15 seconds and roared back out onto the track on the 182nd lap. A lap later his rear-engined turbo-charged Ford slowed to a stop. Now Yarbrough was the leader, and the field was automatically a lap closer to the lead. But with 25 miles to go, Yarbrough's engine led go in a cloud of smoke. Art Pollard in the QuicKick Special (who qualified 32nd out of 33) was leading, and McElreath was right behind him. A lap later the yellow lights flashed as Foyt hit the wall on the 4th turn. If they stayed on, Pollard would win. Comprehending the situation immediately, Foyt helped the wrecker cart his car away. When the green came on Pollard, the oldest driver in the race, made the oldest mistake in automobile racing. Thinking he was a lap up, Pollard let McElreath pass him, then suddenly realized what he had done and chased Jim down on the backstretch, retaking the lead for an instant. But the effort was costly for Pollard. The QuicKick driver steamed into the 3rd turn too fast, slid off the groove attempting to control the car, and McElreath passed again on the final lap. The cars looked glued together as they raced for the check, but McElreath was the winner by 2 seconds.

It had been a $73,000 mistake for Pollard, who earned almost exactly half of McElreath's $146,850 first-place money. The McElreath-Foyt financial arrangement was private and race by race, but when his teammate won, old A. J. seemed as happy as if he himself had rolled into Victory Lane to be overwhelmed by photographers and press pepole. Only 5 of the 33 starters went the full 500 miles. Of the 8 still running, the last 3 were red-flagged 5 minutes after McElreath had taken the checker. Asked if he would retire, McElreath, now 42, seemed genuinely amazed at the question. "What for? They're gonna have 3 of these 500-milers next year." But in 1972 he was not in the field of any of the Triple Crown events. And a new McElreath, Jim Jr., was fighting his way up the same ladder Jim had climbed.

JACK McGRATH

John James (Smiling Jack) McGrath was born October 8, 1919, in Los Angeles, the son of a meat packer. Six feet tall and slender, McGrath seemed destined to become an all-time great until he was cut down in 1955 in a crash at Phoenix, at a time when his second wife, Lois, had almost convinced him he could stay near the sport as road racer or master mechanic—which he was; and his father—who had not spoken to him for years—was almost reconciled to the fact that Jack would never go into the family business.

McGrath worked during high school vacations at his father's plant, and bought a Model T Ford in 1933 for $15 at the age of 13. For 2 years he played with it, repairing it and driving around the plant grounds. At 15 came a 1929 Ford Model A that McGrath souped up. In the early part of the next year, he was one of the pioneer hot-rodders who drove at California's Muroc Dry Lake. He got up to 96 m.p.h. and that ended the meat business. Despite his father's disapproval, McGrath ran with the hot-rod crowd and opened a speed shop in 1942, about the least likely time to do such a thing since the war was in progress.

When hostilities increased, he was barely making a living, desptie occasional free meat. Promoter Bill White, casting about for young men with more guts than brains to pad his local programs, offered McGrath a ride. Jack had never seen an oval-track race, or a road race for that matter. Jack took to this phase of the sport and was soon minus one speed shop and plus one driving career. His idol and friend was Rex Mays, whose death in a crash at Del Mar, Calif., in 1949 saddened him, but did not dissuade him from his career. He copied Rex in not drinking or smoking and trying never to use worldly language. He was reputed to have preferred malted milks to any other beverage.

McGrath's racing career progressed apace; he campaigned in roadsters, midgets, and late model stock cars as well as sprint cars and Indianapolis machinery. The 1st time Jack tried his rookie test at Indianapolis (1947), he was rejected for lack of experience. The next year, however, he qualified the Sheffler Offy Special, placing 21st after his car stalled on lap 70. In 1949 his City of Tacoma Special broke an oil pump on lap 39, and he was placed 26th. In 1950 Jack joined forces with oil millionaire Jack Hinkle, and began a steady rise to the 1st echelons of the American sport.

McGrath was an unusual driver. He acted as his own chief mechanic, supervising every bit of work on the Hinkle cars. Contemporaries respected him for his mechanical knowledge, and he often said that when he got too old for racing, he would like to work in research engineering for an auto company. The 1st Hinkle at Indy slammed into the wall on the 131st lap during a caution period, revealing perhaps the weakness in the McGrath armor. A study of his career seems to indicate a lack of physical stamina; Jack was much better at shorter distances and was one of the best qualifiers ever.

In 1951 Manny Ayulo relieved him halfway through Indy, placing 3rd in the 500. He finished the 200 laps

in 1952, but wound up 11th. McGrath finished 5th in 1953 after fading from the leaders. And in 1954 he pushed the Hinkle into the pole position with a qualifying mark of 141.033 m.p.h., topping Chet Miller's 1952 Novi mark of 139.034 m.p.h. It was his best performance there. Jack set records at 10 miles, 25 miles, and at 50 miles had broken the Bill Vukovich mark (set the previous year) by more than 6 m.p.h. In 30 laps (75 miles) Jack had lapped 25 of the opposing 32 cars. He still led at the 100-mile mark but was beginning to fade. At the 125- and 150-mile marks he was no longer in the top 5 after a sloppy pit stop. But he worked his way back into 3rd at 175, 2nd at 200 and was leading again at 225. Jack could not hold off Vukovich, though, and lay 2nd at halfway. He eventually finished 3rd, taking over that position for good 75 miles from the end. And he had the fastest lap in the race, 140.537 m.p.h.

He finished 5th and 4th in 1951 and 1952. In the tragic 1955 Indy race, McGrath set another new qualifying mark of 142.580 m.p.h. and fought ill-fated Bill Vukovich for the lead for 100 miles. He was sidelined with magneto trouble after the Vuky fatality. In 1953 he finished 2nd in the AAA National Championship and won Milwaukee's 100-miler on June 7. He finished in the top 10 in 6 of the other 9 Championship Trail races in which he entered. McGrath's driving style in that season's 500 was a calculated risk that partially failed. He said he was counting on sliding through the turns at higher speeds by braking later, hitting the turns at 170 m.p.h. and sliding through at 130. He wore out an extra set of tires and himself with this strategy. The year 1954 was a good one for McGrath. His yellow Hinkle No. 2 had 7 top-10 finishes in 8 races, finishing 3rd in the point standings and failing only at the Pee-Dee 200 at Darlington July 5.

McGrath drove Hudsons in AAA stocks and set records at Richmond and Williams Grove, Pa., at Iliana on the border of Illinois and Indiana, and at Pomona. He competed for Lincoln in the 1953 Pan American Road race, finishing 3rd behind Chuck Stevenson and Walt Faulkner in the big stock class. McGrath died in the final race of the 1955 Championship Trail, the last one under AAA Contest Board jurisdiction, at Phoenix, November 6. There was an erroneous report that he had planned to retire, possibly brought on by word that Hinkle expected to sell his dirt-track racer. Actually Jack had tired of the oval tracks and had made some inquiries about a Grand Prix ride for 1956. He had made several friends during the Mexican road race, including the redoubtable Piero Taruffi and several Lancia people who promised to aid him in his search.

It happened on the 86th lap of the 100-lap race when the axle apparently broke, sending the car into a series of flips. McGrath died instantly of head injuries (even as late as 1955 roll bars were not required on AAA cars). Only Bob Sweikert, the 1955 champion, had added one of his own volition. Jack was running 3rd at the time, after having led during the early stages of the race.

BRUCE McLAREN

Sebring definitely was not the place to hold the United States Grand Prix, and it was doubtful if the cream of the European Formula 1 crowd would have made the flat, converted airport "course" a stop in their quest for a World Champion Driver in 1959 if a 3-way tie for the title had not developed among Tony Brooks of Ferrari, and Stirling Moss and Jack Brabham of Cooper. But the dogfight had developed, and here they were, all 3 of them, along with Phil and Graham Hill, Wolfgang von Trips, Innes Ireland, Roy Salvadori, Maurice Trintignant, even Rodger Ward of the United States, who ran a midget car in the GP just to "show these guys."

The field was filled out by other names, too. Harry Blanchard, Cliff Allison, Alejandro de Tomaso, George Constantine, Harry Schell, Bob Said, and Bruce McLaren. McLaren's job was to follow Brabham's every move through the race, just in case any trouble developed. He was 3rd man on the Cooper GP team, behind Brabham and Masten Gregory, the American expatriate who had banged himself up (as usual) in a Tourist Trophy race and, therefore, yielded his car to this 22-year-old substitute from New Zealand. The car that McLaren was driving was experimental. Brabham had the reliable machine, and his shot at the World Championship could not be wasted on an untried car. If McLaren managed to finish the race, fine, they might learn something from the engine when they took it apart.

Moss went out early after leading for 5 laps. His transmission simply gave up, and he walked back to the pits with a rueful smile on his face. Brooks was still there, but his chances had been dealt a terrible blow when Trips, his own teammate, had rammed him on the 1st lap. Precious minutes were spent in inspecting and straightening the car in the Ferrari pits, and Tony never was able to make up the lost time. That left Brabham, who found unexpectedly heavy opposition from Trintignant, who steadily increased his lap speeds until, on the 41st lap (of 42) he ran fastest lap of the day, for which he earned a championship point, the last driver to do so since the rules were changed that winter.

Brabham however, also found trouble. The Cooper fuel system malfunctioned, and instead of giving him the last dregs of fuel needed to finish the race, it dumped it unceremoniously on the course, causing the car to sputter to a stop. Jack leaped from the cockpit and started pushing, much as Tazio Nuvolari, Ralph DePalma and others had once done. On and on he pushed, more than a quarter of a mile, while cars flashed by, Trintignant in 2nd place, Brooks in 3rd. The crowd was on the course, but parted as Brabham approached the finish line, gave one mighty heave, got the checkered flag and fell alongside his burden exhausted but 4th in the race

and with enough points to be crowned World Champion for 1959.

Crowd, press, practically everyone closed in on the new champion. When everyone caught their breath, they suddenly remembered someone else. Bruce Leslie McLaren had won the race, stopped his car, accepted his trophy and disappeared back into the anonymity which had been his since appearing at the Cooper factory in March 1958, with a few bob, his own mechanic and a letter of introduction.

At 22, Bruce McLaren had won his 1st GP championship race, youngest man ever to accomplish the trick up to that point. He would rarely be overlooked by people in the racing world ever again, despite his quiet, schoolboy appearance and demeanor. McLaren did not become World Champion as some thought he might, he became a designer and manufacturer of racing machinery, a champion driver in the sports/racing field, and a legend that will probably outlive many of those who actually manage to win a World Championship crown.

He was born in Auckland, New Zealand, August 30, 1937, the son of a garage owner and one-time motorcycle competitor. When he was 9, Bruce contracted Perthe's disease—a deformation of the hip joint—that left his left leg a couple of inches shorter than the right one, and this gave him a noticeable limp when he was tired. He spent almost 3 years in hospitals, 2 of them in traction, and he had to use crutches, then canes, for several years after that. At 14 his father bought him a car, an old Austin 7, which he promptly started rehabilitating. After limiting his early driving to the family property, Bruce tried his first competitive driving event, a local hillclimb in December 1952; he won a class 2nd. Up to that time he had competed strictly as a navigator with his father, and Bruce later said he was a bit scared in that 1st event.

After that, father and son often ran against one another. And in 1954 Bruce, now a student at Seddon Memorial Technical College, took part in his 1st real race, finishing out of the money, but finishing. The faithful old Austin was traded in for a Ford 10, then that went in trade for an Austin-Healey 100, reputedly the 1st one to reach New Zealand. A 1500-c.c. Cooper sports car once owned by Brabham was bought next, then a Formula 2 Cooper-Climax. It was in this car that McLaren was runner up in the New Zealand championship series in 1957–58, and this feat won him a ticket to Britain courtesy of the local GP Association.

Brabham smoothed the way with John Cooper, and Bruce and his buddy-mechanic who came with him both had jobs with the factory. It was a relationship that was to last 7½ years, through good days and bad for the Cooper marque. A month after he walked in the door McLaren found himself in an F2 car at the Aintree 200. Within 2 months, Bruce was at Brands Hatch, where he won both ends of an F2 doubleheader against strong opposition. McLaren really served notice that he had arrived in that season's German GP, in which F1 and F2 cars were run together. Brooks and Vanwall won the big prize that day, but Bruce's Cooper was the first F2 car home (5th overall), and he found himself on the victory dias beside Brooks. Brabham described the day. "Two Arabs come over with three spanners and a spare wheel just to fill up the entry list, and then they win the bloody race." Bruce finished the season as runner-up to Brabham in F2. Home for the winter, he won enough races to take the New Zealand Championship.

McLaren became an official Cooper F1 team member the next season. At Monaco and in the French race he was 5th. He battled Moss all the way in the British GP at Aintree, sharing the lap recrod with Stirling and finishing 3rd. After the U.S. GP victory that December, Bruce found himself with 16½ points and 3rd place in the point standings in his first F1 season. In 1960 Gregory was gone and Bruce was officially number 2 to Brabham. He won the Argentine GP opener. He was 2nd at Monaco and Spa, 3rd at Rheims, and the point leader in midseason. His 2nd in Portugal, 4th at Silverstone, and 3rd at Riverside ensured McLaren 2nd place behind Black Jack in the point standings as the Australian took his 2nd World Championship in a row. The Coopers were outclassed in 1961, and the best Bruce could manage was a 3rd at Monza, but the year was a happy one nonetheless because that December he married a gal from home, Patricia Broad, who shared Bruce's love of auto racing.

Brabham left Cooper in 1962, and Bruce became team leader. He won at Monaco; was 2nd in South Africa; 3rd at Aintree, Monza, and Watkins Glen; 4th at Rouen; and 5th at the Nurburgring. He was 3rd in the final championship standings. McLaren also stepped up his sports/racing activities, winning the 3-hour race at Sebring in an Abarth, finishing 5th in the 12-hour race in a birdcage Maserati, and taking 4th in the Nurburgring 1000 with his number 2, Tony Maggs, as his codriver.

In 1963 came the founding of Bruce McLaren Motor Racing Ltd., which eventually became his carbuilding organization as well. But he stayed with Cooper's F1 effort that season and through 1965, although after the change from a 2.5-litre formula to a 1.5, Cooper was never really a contender. Perhaps Bruce's growing interest in sports/racing cars enabled him to reconcile himself to the situation, and he did feel he owed much to John Cooper. Two lightweight Cooper-based sports racers were built, one for Bruce, the other for an American driver he admired, Tim Mayer (subsequently killed in a Tasman start). Tim's brother, Teddy, became associated with Bruce at the same time as Tim, and he stayed with Bruce until the end. The year had a note of triumph for McLaren, for he finally won the New Zealand GP in his 8th try at that race.

At the start of 1964 McLaren purchased Roger Penske's Cooper-based Zerex Special, and after driving it unaltered for a few British races, he and his crew tore the car apart and rebuilt it, chassis and all, using a 3.8-litre Oldsmobile engine for power. The result was the 1st true McLaren car, and it won its 1st time out at Mosport on June 6, 1964. It was the start of an era. McLaren also continued to drive other people's cars, perhaps to help his own ideas along. He had helped develop the Ford GT effort, and now he drove the result at Le Mans and Nurburgring. The following season he was 3rd at the Monza 1000, 2nd at Sebring and was leading Le Mans when his GT40 gearbox broke. In a Ford Mark IIA, he and Chris Amon won Le Mans in 1966, and he and Mario Andretti won Sebring's 12-hour race in 1967.

His best F1 ride in 1965 was a 3rd in the Belgian GP, and that winter Bruce finally severed connections with Cooper and announced his own GP racing team. It took a couple of seasons to sort out these cars, but McLaren won his 1st GP since 1962 in a McLaren at Spa on June 9, 1968. That same season, Bruce's number 2, Denis Hulme, won the Italian and Canadian Grands Prix in the McLaren-Ford.

But it was in sports/racing, in Group 7 cars, where Bruce was to make perhaps his greatest contributions to auto racing, certainly those by which he is best remembered. It started modestly enough in 1966, when the new Canadian-American Challenge Cup series—road races created to fill some gaps in the international calendar and sited at various American and Canadian tracks for top dollar prizes—began and started to grow and grow. In 1966 McLaren's team finished 2nd twice and 3rd twice in 6 races. Then they started to win. In 1967 McLarens took 5 of 6; in 1968, 4 of 6; in 1969, 11 out of 11. McLaren won some, teammate Dennis

Hulme won the others. Once they entered a 3rd car, a spare, and let Dan Gurney drive it. The McLarens finished 1-2-3, Dan a respectful few seconds behind Bruce and Denny, who raced as if they were joined by an invisible cord most of the time. McLaren won the CanAm individual championship in both 1967 and 1969.

In 1970 F1 efforts, Bruce was 2nd in the Spanish GP. At Monaco he clipped a chicane and retired; it was his 100th championship appearance in GP racing, and it was also his last. On the afternoon of June 2, 1970, Bruce was at Goodwood with the track to himself, testing his latest CanAm challenger, the M8D, which he and Hulme planned to use in an attempt to dominate the rich series once again. Suddenly the rear section of the car broke away from the front end as he was at maximum speed—180 m.p.h. or more—on the Levant Straight. The car turned into a missile, uncontrollable and deadly. It rammed an earthen bank and exploded. Bruce was alive as he was pulled out, but died within minutes.

HOLLINGSWORTH McMILLION

Hollingsworth McMillion was a police investigator with the Virginia Alcoholic Beverage Control Board. He ran his 1st race in 1950 at Royal Speedway in Richmond. He recalled that it was a night race and his mount, a much modified Chevrolet, had not been handling well. In any case, Worth ran into a light pole, demolished the car and put the entire speedway in the dark.

Born October 8, 1926, Worth McMillion raced modifieds and sportsmen mostly as a hobby. He was a quiet man who seemed genuinely happy when he met a stranger—as if his life had been enriched by the contact. He began to take racing more seriously on June 23, 1962, at South Boston, Va., where he made his Grand National debut in a Pontiac. He finished 72nd in the 1962 standings, moved up to 34th the next year and to 30th in 1964. Campaigning the same Pontiac, he made 30th, with 6 top 10 finishes.

Racing was always secondary to the ABC job, but aside from the National Sheriffs' Association and some hunting, that was what occupied his spare time. He was an absolutely fearless competitor and preferred the driving challenge of the smaller NASCAR tracks. He finally quit when he was promoted by ABC.

FRANCIS McNAMARA

Can a Midwestern-born career Army officer find hapiness in the Black Forest of Germany building racing cars for Andy Granatelli? The answer probably was yes, if we were to accept the life of Francis McNamara, head of McNamara Racing KG of Lenggries, Germany, whose creations ran not only in Europe but at Indiana-

polis under STP colors beginning in 1970.

McNamara was born August 17, 1938, in Galesburg, Ill., but was raised by grandparents in Bloomington, Ind. They both died while Frank was in his early teens. A self-taught welder and car repairman, McNamara managed to evade do-gooders and finish high school while supporting himself. In 1954 he enlisted in the Army and found a new home. McNamara served in Okinawa, Thailand, and Vietnam (2 tours). He advanced through the ranks to become a Green Beret lieutenant in 1966. While touring as a Stateside member of a Green Beret demonstration team, he met a part-time circus performer named Bonnie Kiplinger of Washington, D.C., and married her. Soon after, the lieutenant and his new wife honeymooned in Germany, courtesy of a new Beret assignment there.

In Germany McNamara had time for some sport, including learning to drive competitively in an overage Formula Vee single-seater. Frustrated at finding a car built to his liking, Frank conceived the idea of setting up his own design and construction business for racing cars. He and Bonnie had enough money to get themselves going if they stayed in Europe, so in May 1968 he resigned his commission and settled permanently in the tiny German Alpine village of Lenggries, where the skiing was good. FVee Formula Ford, Formula 3 and Formula 2 designs flowed from the McNamara shops.

McNamara attracted a lot of other talented people who liked life in Lenggries better than what they had been doing; from Lola came Austria's Josef Karasek, a designer; from England, Peter Arundell; from Roger Penske's operation, America's Peter Reinhardt; from Brabham, Edward Marley, a stylist; and from Specialized Mouldings, England's Edward Watermann. The team's success in designing saleable racing machinery was capped in 1970 when Andy Granatelli's STP Corporation tabbed McNamara to design and build an Indianapolis mount for Mario Andretti. The basic design was like that of a Lola T153, but the car incorporated many Karasek touches by the time of its May debut. Andretti finished 6th, thanks to a seized shock absorber late in the race that caused handling problems.

The McNamara-Ford's 1970 performance was good enough for Granatelli and Andretti to renew their contracts with a 1971 McNamara, however. There were other big 500-milers at Ontario Motor Speedway in California and Pocono in Pennsylvania that the McNamaras would face. Frank McNamara returned to the United States to take charge of testing the 1971 cars in March. Even the boss had to leave Lenggries occasionally. But that did not help the cars do well, and McNamara was beset by personal tragedy. His wife, Bonnie, died suddenly, and McNamara's association with Granatelli ended in a lawsuit in which the builder claimed nonpayment for the STP cars that had been contracted. McNamara and Karasek closed the German operation, and the suit was dismissed. It was a cruel world.

SAM McQUAGG

The trouble with Samuel David McQuagg, born November 11, 1937, was that he neither looked like a race driver nor sounded like one. Born and raised in the vicinity of Columbus, Ga., on the extreme western edge of the state, Sam was doing carpentry by the age of 14 and the hot Georgia sun weathered his face, making him look much older. He married while still in high school, a marriage which quickly ended in divorce. He married again at the age of 20.

The McQuaggs were poor but proud and father McQuagg took his 7-year-old son across the state border to Phenix City, Ala., to the Idle Hour Park Speedway to watch midget racing. The event must have been the biggest in young McQuagg's life because then and there he determined to be a race driver. He became one at age 20 in sportsman racing when he bought half interest in a Ford. In 1962 he managed one Grand National championship race, finishing 12th. In 1964 he drove 5 GNs and his average NASCAR finish was 19th. Yet he had a fabulous sportsman record, once winning 35 of 37 starts.

In 1965, he came to Daytona, took one look at the huge 2.5-mile asphalt speedway, and is reported to have said, "They could have built a road to Birmingham with all that asphalt." He finished 48th in the 500 after a 12th in one of the 100-mile qualifying races. McQuagg quickly built up a "personality." Asked by one reporter why he never raced on Friday nights, McQuagg looked at him amazed, "That's the night I have to take my wife out." Asked why he didn't attend a racing dinner one Sunday night, McQuagg noted "My favorite TV program, *Bonanza,* is on then; I wouldn't miss it for the world." He managed 5 top-10 finishes in 15 races; Sam was named NASCAR 1965 Rookie of the Year.

For Sam McQuagg, there was only a single race in which he put it all together, the 1966 Firecracker 400. Chrysler decided that Sam was who they wanted in one of their Dodge Chargers. He was put in a Ray Nichels Dodge after that 1965 season in which Mrs. Betty Lilly, a NASCAR enthusiast, had purchased a 1965 Ford and given Sam the ride. He had finished 3rd in a 250-miler at Bristol, Tenn., but gained much more fame in the Southern 500 of that year when, in protecting the lead, he locked fenders with Cale Yarborough rather than let him pass.

McQuagg gave his factory a mild success by finishing 5th in the Daytona 500. Asked how he felt going 175 m.p.h. at the big supertrack, McQuagg replied, "It's less dangerous than carpentering. Heck, if the scaffolding breaks when you're on it, you could really hurt yourself." All sorts of mechanical ills plagued Sam that year with the Nichels team, but everyone now knew what McQuagg had always known—Samuel David McQuagg was a very quick race driver. Yet, although Sam had qualified 4th fastest he was a dark horse; his feat had

been eclipsed by the other Charger pilot, Lee Roy Yarbrough, who won the pole. Nichels had made one change to Sam's car for the Firecracker; he had fitted a spoiler, a low strip of metal across the trunk lid which broke up the air flow and forced the rear of the car down.

Sam was not eclipsed once the flag fell. He charged into the lead on the first lap, held it until the 9th when Lee Roy got in front of him, then took it right back. Yarbrough slipped ahead for laps 19–26, then Sam slingshot him. Jim Paschal in the alternate Petty Plymouth made it a 3-way battle for the lead for the next 40 laps until Yarbrough dropped out of the running with tire blowouts. But this was McQuagg's race; he fought off Paschal, Buddy Baker, Jim Hurtubise, and even Curtis Turner before assuming the lead for 30 laps from the end. Only Darel Dieringer in a Bud Moore Mercury was on the same lap with him at the finish. His time was a new track record of 153.818 m.p.h. McQuagg felt that the $13,000 he won entitled him to splurge a bit. He took his wife to a posh Daytona restaurant for a steak dinner before heading home that night for Columbus, Ga. The next day he was out delivering newspapers for a neighbor boy who had fallen ill, the fact that the headlines read "McQUAGG WINS AT DAYTONA" did not escape him. "It was great for my garage business," he said.

Subsequent races that season were only at the classics and Sam managed 2 other top-5 finishes. In 1967 he made 14 appearances, managed only 3 in the top 5. For 1968 the purse strings were tightening at the factories and Sam was doing well in the garage business so he drove only 5 times. In 1969 he only raced 3 times, then quit. The speeds at the superspeedways were just too much. Still running modifieds in 1973, Sam called it a career as far as major league racing went. He had averaged $4 a mile in his major league effort—59 championship races—and he had become comfortably well-to-do thanks to the fame. Not too bad for a man who still had to take his wife out every Friday night.

GRAHAM McRAE

Globe-trotting, race driving, car building Graham Peter McRae of Wellington, N.Z., and points east and west, was a latter-day version of another famed Kiwi named Bruce McLaren. Like Bruce, Cassius McRae, as he often was known because of his "lean and hungry look," came to Britain to seek his racing fortune and ended up as a builder as well as driver, tapping the Yankee goldmines in L&M Continental 5000 races the way McLaren did the Canadian-American Challenge Cup.

McRae was born March 5, 1940, in Wellington, son of an engineer. Still in his teens, he fell in love with racing when he attended a local race meeting dominated by some Australian-driven Aston Martin DB3S cars. "I originally wanted to be a fighter pilot, of course," he

recalled later, "then a civil aircraft pilot, but that race settled me on motor racing." The best way to go, he reasoned, was to build your own car. At age 17 he began the project as part of a five-year engineering apprenticeship program. Four years later, the Masarri, which was a crossbred Maserati and Ferrari of that day (hence the exotic name), took to the race course with McRae behind the wooden steering wheel; he had built the wheel, and just about everything on the car except its Austin A70 engine, himself.

The Masarri blew its engine 1st time out, but that was replaced by a Humber 80 powerplant, and with this kind of steady pull, McRae was able to race until his money ran out in 1963. Meanwhile, he had added to his bag of tricks, and to his notoriety as a quick, but wild man behind the wheel, by doing sprints and hillclimbs with a Humber, assorted MG models and an E Jaguar. "I went into business making exhaust manifolds, widening wheels and doing some general engineering work trying to earn enough money to resume racing," Graham said. "At the end of 1967 I bought an old Brabham BT6 Formula Junior, and I started working on it."

Both McRae and the car got faster, the more he worked with it, and soon he was of a mind to build his own car again. Using the Brabham spaceframe design principle, Brabham front and rear uprights, and Brabham wheels, Graham built a race-ready car in 9 weeks. Early testing suggested a further improvement, and in its 3rd race, in November 1968, the McRae car became the 1st one in New Zealand to race with an aerofoil. In this car Graham won the 1968–69 National Formula

McRae didn't exactly set the British race scene on fire in 1969. Arriving there with a well-worn ex-Piers Courage Brabham-FVA BT23C Formula 2 car, Cassius ended up against the Armco barrier in his initial race, and his best effort in major starts was a 4th at Zolder, Holland. He also won a few minor club races, but the money was gone. Sale of the car paid McRae's way back home. Admiring a McLaren M10A at an Auckland industrial show, Cassius must have really been wearing his best lean and hungry look. A chance conversation led to an introduction to veteran Kiwi racer Tom Clark, who bankrolled purchase of the car for McRae to race. The 1st time out with the Formula 5000 M10A, McRae won, and he was on his way to a 5th-place finish in the Tasman series, including victories at Invercargill and Surfers Paradise.

Graham never was too happy without his own homebuilt car either, so he constructed a smaller and lighter 1.5-litre single-seater and proceeded to finish 2nd in the National Formula Championship and to win the Gold Star 1969–70 Championship outright. Cassius's return to Britain in 1970 was on slightly better terms than before; this time he was there to put together his own McLaren M10B F5000 car at the Trojan factory at which all customer McLarens were fabricated.

Powered by a Bartz-prepared Chevrolet engine, this car had some early-season electrical problems, but McRae quickly showed himself fast and competitive. In his 3rd start, this at Zandvoort three weeks after initially taking to a grid, Graham dueled Frank Gardner for a whole heat and took 3rd, then trailed Peter Gethin closely in the Briton's all-conquering Sid Taylor M10B across the 2nd heat finish line to cop an aggregate 2nd. Two races later at Brands Hatch, he again took 2nd overall, despite spinning on his own oil a couple of times. But then a succession of parts-failures, accidents and blown engines, not to mention some wild rides off course and spins, gained McRae a reputation as a crasher.

McRae's year in Britain ended well, though, when he took both heats at a Brands Hatch finale and won overall honors. The car was shipped off to Levin, N. Z., for the Tasman opener, and all McRae did was make fastest time in practice, set a class record in the race and win rather easily. In the New Zealand Grand Prix, using a borrowed engine, he was 3rd, but in the Lady Wigram Trophy, Cassius won. In Australia, he had some problems, but won again at Sandown Park as Frank Matich sputtered out of fuel on the last lap. A 3rd at Surfers Paradise, and the Tasman title was McRae's. Faced with the choice of America's Continental or Europe's F5000 series, he accepted an offer to lead Team Trojan in the latter. But a practice accident wrote off McRae's car and put an end to that project, although Trojan paid to bring Cassius's old McLaren over to Britain so he could go racing in it. In his 1st start in the M10B, Graham won the race in fine fashion. After some misadventures, he won again at Thruxton, has a spell of problems, then won a 3rd race at Snetterton, mainly because Gardner and Brian Redman collided and eliminated themselves. At Hockenheim, McRae had a terrific shunt when a tire peeled off a rim. His car was wiped out, and Cassius suffered burns on the hands.

Even as he lay on his hospital bed, McRae announced a new project. He had joined forces with Leda cars to produce his own F5000 racer, which turned out to resemble the BRM P160 Formula 1 car in some ways. Finished, and sponsored by Andy Granatelli's STP Racing Team, the new Leda won the Tasman championship for the 2nd year in a row, cinching the crown at Sandown Park in Australia with his 4th victory. Two months later McRae picked up exactly where he had left off, winning 3 European races at Brands Hatch, Nivelles, Belgium, and Silverstone.

The Europeans weren't sorry to see McRae fly off to the United States for the L&M Continental 5000, and Cassius's American debut became an artistic and financial success when he won both heats and top overall at Laguna Seca. The rest of 1972 was a McRae walk-away in the Continental, and back in Europe, after buying out the Leda project and renaming the product the McRae car. During the crowded British GP weekend meeting Graham started at Brands Hatch from the back of the grid—his McRae GM 1 had missed practice—and won going away. The rest of the seventies looked golden, indeed, for Bruce McLaren's successor. He won the 1972–73 Tasman title again and Indianapolis, 1973, was in the wings.

JOHN MECOM

In 1966 when John Mecom, Jr., acquired a professional football franchise for New Orleans, La., he dropped automobile racing like a man letting go of the wrong end of a branding iron. He had spent about 5 years in the sport, losing money every year, although not on the grandiose scale of Lance Reventlow (about $1 million a year) or Briggs Cunningham (about $10 million give or take a few hundred thousand). He dropped out at about the time his Mecom Racing Team ceased to become a legal tax loss. By then he was interested in saving African wildlife by breeding them in his native Texas or in Louisiana, rare guns, off-shore powerboat racing and, most important of all, making more money.

Since the Mecom family fortune at that time was estimated in the neighborhood of $250 million, it was very obvious that making more money was as much a sport as auto racing, a sport John had been involved with around the world from the age of 15, when he was a courier for his father.

He was a linebacker-sized young man who had been educated both in Oklahoma and Texas, and had originally envisioned himself as a race driver. He did creditably in one amateur race and then his father pointed out that he was the sole male heir to the Mecom oil millions and therefore not driver material.

John, a soft-spoken and obedient son, sublimated by acquiring an Alfa-powered DeTomaso formula car plus driver Bob Schroeder in mid-1962. He expected—like many others—that Formula Intercontinental would catch on as a major pro road racing series. It did not. He got a 3rd to Dan Gurney from his team in the Pipeline 200 at Hilltop Raceway in Louisiana. For the Mexican Grand Prix, Mecom rented a Formula 1 Rob Walker Lotus; Schroeder drove it to 6th overall. Bob was around for some early 1963 races in which the Mecom Racing Team did rather well. But late in 1962 John had found a new hero driver, Roger Penske, who had stood sports car racing in the states on its ear with his Zerex Special. Mecom wanted Roger for Nassau Speed Week and he lured him with the Ferrari GTO in which Pedro Rodriguez had won at Montlhéry. However, somebody at Modena, Italy erred and a factory team car was delivered.

It is axiomatic that rich Americans who buy Ferraris are supposed to get last year's car. Shocked by this turn of events, Ferrari officials first tried to get their car back (the night before the race), saying the check had not cleared for its purchase. But Mecom knew better and Penske went out in the factory car and creamed the opposition at Speed Week. The GTO subsequently won several SCCA Nationals before it was sold in mid-1963. It took 2nd overall at the Daytona Continental, won the GT class and was 4th overall at Sebring. Penske then took his famed Zerex Special, now owned by Mecom, and polished off Brands Hatch.

Mecom continued to strengthen his operation all during 1963 buying a Reventlow Scarab, signing on Augie Pabst to drive, Walt Hansgen as driver and manager, John Cannon, and a host of administrative and mechanical talent. And, of course, he gave A. J. Foyt his initial good sports car rides. In the fall West Coast races, Penske managed 2nd in the Riverside GP with his Zerex, and Foyt took the rear-engined Scarab to a 2nd at Laguna Seca after the gearbox locked solid on him. Nassau in 1963 was a Mecom team picnic. Pabst in a Lola GT won the Tourist Trophy opener; Foyt in the Scarab won the Governor's Trophy and then came back to put the crusher on Jim Hall with a victory in the 250-mile Nassau Cup.

In 1964 A. J. beat Dan Gurney in the Daytona American Challenge Cup 250-miler but the team did poorly at Sebring. They did not burn up the tracks on either side of the Atlantic. Actually, Mecom became very disenchanted with Chevrolet, from whom he was buying engines and cars; he felt that others (such as Jim Hall) were getting more cooperation free of charge. He responded to feelers from Ford but a tactless Ford executive made some nasty remarks about him while he was within earshot. After that had been smoothed over, someone sent him a bill for the first shipment of engines he was supposed to be getting "for development purposes." Mecom severed the relationship.

The following year, Mecom got Chrysler Corporation to provide the power for a sports car of his own called the Hussein (after the King of Jordan where the Mecoms had an oil interest). The car was ineffective, and for that matter, the Mecoms made no money out of their Jordan holdings either, it is reported. Mecom was talking now about making the MRT pay for itself and so he took on the distributorship for Lola for North America and Mexico plus an assortment of other specialty racing parts. However, there was a single successful effort remaining for the Mecom Racing Team, the 1966 Indianapolis 500. John signed Rodger Ward, Hansgen, and, for a while at least, he even had Parnelli Jones. The car was a Lola T80 with Ford power or Offy power depending upon who was driving; George Bignotti was the supervising mechanic for the entire effort with Eric Broadley supervising design of the chassis.

Hansgen was killed at Le Mans practice; Jones sought other pastures, and the formidable MRT Lola team came up with Graham Hill, Jackie Stewart, and Ward. All qualified, Ward in the Lola-Offy.

Miraculously, all avoided the famous 1st-lap accident and suddenly John Mecom found himself with better than a 4-to-1 chance to win. His drivers improved position considerably as the race went on. Although Ward fell out with suspension failure at 185 miles, Jackie Stewart and Graham Hill were driving a well-planned race. Always among the contenders, the two moved up as much by attrition as by passing people, and just after the 300-mile mark Stewart assumed the lead when Lloyd Ruby began to have engine trouble. Then Hill moved up steadily until the 2 Mecom cars were running 1st and 2nd. The Indy establishment must have been shocked then—a rookie car owner with 2 foreign "rookie" drivers apparently on their way to a 1–2 finish.

But they were saved that ultimate embarrassment. Stewart stalled with 10 laps to go and Hill motored on to victory, having led for only the final 10 laps. Hill won $156,297, the 1st "rookie" to win since George Souders in 1927. Stewart was named Rookie of the Year despite Hill's victory. Rodger Ward, incidentally, retired after the race.

So, for all intents and purposes, did Mecom. The football team and the oil business took precedence. However, in 1971 he began talking about a 1973 re-entry into auto racing. Although the family had lost $100 million or so in business reverses, Mecom still had enough to mount a respectable effort.

MAJOR MELTON

When a grasshopper flew into his Dodge at the 1963 Southern 500, Major Melton left him perched there on the roll bar. The father of 4 from Laurinberg, N.C., thought it was good luck because it gave him the "feeling I wasn't riding alone." He wrecked on the 253rd lap, finishing 15th and, as NASCAR media man Abe Upchurch noted: "There is no record of where the grasshopper finished, or if he did."

Born January 25, 1930, Melton made his living driving for a motor freight line. He raced sportsmen and Grand Nationals between assignments, limiting his schedule, but not his ability behind the wheel. Why did a truck driver relax by driving racing stock cars? Because, after horsing those big trailer rigs over the road, handling the wheel of a racer was sheer ecstacy, he said. Melton firmly believed that there were many truck drivers who, if so inclined, could pilot racers better than some of the so-called stars of this era. Perhaps some day the match could be made—on a road course to keep things even.

ARTURO MERZARIO

Small and skinny—5 feet 8 inches and some 125 pounds—Arturo Merzario shared the clinching of the 1972 World Manufacturers Championship in a Ferrari 312P at the Spa 1000. Perhaps it was his small stature, perhaps it was his lack of color, perhaps it was his pairing with a more fiery codriver (in the case of Spa, Brian Redman) but Merzario got little recognition for his part. One paper, in fact, went so far as to say, "It would be rather unkind to say (Redman) won despite Merzario's assistance, though that's how it looked. . . ."

Son of a fairly well-to-do building contractor, Merzario was born March 11, 1943, at Como in the colorful Italian lake district. From his earliest years, Arturo wanted to be a racing driver, and he was 20 when his father provided an Alfa Romeo Spyder in which the son made his competitive debut in the Sardinian Rally. He won his class. A few months later Arturo appeared at Monza for his 1st circuit race; he finished 8th. In 1964 the youngster acquired a 10-litre Abarth Mille and entered the Italian stock-car championship, taking 2nd place.

Merzario's racing career was interrupted by a 2-year stint in the Army, in which the draftee learned to drive tanks. Back in civilian life in 1967, Merzario was offered a factory drive by Carlo Abarth, and he raced a Mille to another 2nd place in his division of the European Touring Car championship. The year 1968 was spent mostly in a 1-litre prototype, although Arturo made some 2-litre starts, winning at Vienna. The following season he concentrated on the European Hillclimb series, but it was being dominated by another marque, Ferrari. Merzario did manage a significant victory at Mugello with a 2-litre car, despite an unscheduled stop to grab a cola from a friend. Later Arturo won a 3-litre climb at Innsbruck.

In 1970 Merzario went over to Ferrari, which always

appreciates such sports/prototype versatility. Paired with Mario Andretti, Arturo shared a 3rd at Daytona, then was leading at Sebring by 21 laps when the Ferrari's gearbox broke and retired the seemingly safe entry. Paired with Chris Amon, Merzario was 4th at Brands Hatch and Monza. Teamed with Ignazio Giunti, he had still another 4th. At Mugello again, he drove an Abarth in the finale of that long climb series, winning his 2nd straight. He also won at Sestriere in the same car. In 1971, Merzario was down for a full-season Ferrari ride with Ignazio Giunti until the latter was killed at Buenos Aires. After that, Ferrari farmed Arturo out to favored customers (as a factory test driver, Merzario had a good reputation with customers who were able to see him perform in their cars). The year's frustrations were relieved somewhat by a special factory ride in the final Interserie race of the year at Imola. The Interserie is the European version of the Canadian-American Challenge Cup series, and Merzario was impressive in winning.

The year also saw a series of 2-litre drives in underpowered Abarths, but he managed some good placings and won Abarth's only race of the year in his class at Vallelunga, where he nipped Helmut Marko at the line. Arturo also got his 1st single-seater ride in the Iris Tecno Formula 2 car, a 2-year-old chassis redone for the first preliminary steps of what it was hoped would be Formula 1 power in a couple of years. Merzario also got in a few laps in a Frank Williams March in Brazil. But the slim Italian's forte seemed the sports/prototype, not the single-seater, as he showed again with his victory at Spa 1972, and never mind the occasional criticisms.

In mid-1972, however, Merzario threw the so-called experts who had downgraded his single-seater skills into a tizzy. At Brands Hatch for the British Grand Prix, Arturo was handed a Ferrari 312B and proceeded to set the track buzzing by qualifying 9th in what essentially was his 1st truly competitive F1 car. Not only that, but in the race itself, despite a ragged start, he was respectable and dependable, and when the checker fell, Arturo was 6th. That earned him a point in the World Championship standings on his 1st try. Only Ferrari's changing racing plans would seem to deprive Merzario of a real chance to show what he could do in an extended GP season in 1973.

LOUIS MEYER

The Meyer-Drake Offenhauser engine is an everlasting tribute to Louis Meyer, the 1st man to win the Indianapolis 500 mile classic 3 times, and a 3-time AAA national champion who got into racing because he wanted to prove something to his brother. It was at Ascot Speedway at Los Angeles in 1924 and the means of proof on this occasion was Eddie Meyer Jr.'s Model T Special.

Louis, then about 20, climbed into his brother's car with outward calm and inward trepidation. When the starter's flag waved down he hit the accelerator pedal hard. He lasted just 3 laps, spinning right in front of the bulk of the competition. Cars scattered every which way to avoid the whirling T but Meyer somehow emerged unscathed. Brother Eddie signalled him into the pits, said a few choice words and took over the driving chores himself. The racing Meyer family was now certain that Louis's forte was mechanics.

Edward Meyer, Sr., was winning bicycle races before the turn of the century. When the automobile became the major instrument of wheeled competition, the senior Meyer turned to it—after he had moved his family from New York City to Los Angeles. But it was his son, Eddie Jr. (11 years older than Louis), who was to build and race cars in the hothouse competition climate of Southern California. Louis, born in 1904, grew to manhood in an environment filled with the memories of the greats of an era only shortly passed. He saw his brother make a reasonable living as a driver and as a good racing mechanic. It was, therefore, really no surprise that by the time he was 18 Louis was already an established competition mechanic. And by the time he was 22 he had built himself a reputation as one of the area's best.

When that reputation caused Frank Elliott to sign him to maintain a Miller on the board track circuit in 1926, Louis jumped at the chance. However, he had not given up on his desire to drive. He used to take the Miller out to test it, and even though this was not at full speed in competition, it helped him learn the characteristics of the premier racing cars of the day. And it helped him get his 1st drive in major-league competition on a board track at Charlotte, N.C. The car broke early, but it whetted his desire to become a driver still more.

He went to Indianapolis in 1927, hoping to convince someone that he was good enough to drive. There were no rookie tests in those days; one either had a car or did not. Meyer stayed around the pits of the Jynx Special where another rookie, Wilbur Shaw, had the ride. When the car needed a new gas tank strap and a relief driver, Meyer got the nod. He maintained his position for 41 laps before turning the car back. That was his official baptism at Indianapolis and his acceptance into the fraternity-like atmosphere of those who had driven on the Brickyard.

Married now and obliged to make a living, Louie reasoned that Indy was the only place where reputations and money could be made overnight. He worked as a mechanic that season, doing some local racing, too. And he lined up a ride for the 1928 edition of the 500. He practiced in the car, a Duesenberg Special, for almost a month before he suddenly learned that the car was to be sold by the Duesenbergs for Ira Hall to drive. Angry and disgusted, Meyer made his plight known. Alden Sampson, a man who was to entertain a fascination with Indianapolis that extended even to designing a technically interesting but unsuccessful automobile, came to the rescue. Meyer had helped him in previous years, and he had great respect for Louis's mechanical ability. Meyer had cut some fast laps in the Duesy so Sampson had respect for his driving ability, also.

Sampson bought the Miller 91 that Tony Gulotta had placed 3rd the previous year from AC Spark Plug and Phil Shafer. Then he and Meyer agreed on financial terms—not only for the race but for the 1928 AAA circuit. This in itself was amazing because to that time Meyer had never finished a major-league race. But Sampson knew his drivers—and he was lucky, too, because he had to unseat Shaw who had been scheduled to drive the car before Shafer's AC Spark Plug sponsorship deal fell through and forced him to sell at a bargain. Shaw got into the race by special permission to qualify in a rebuilt Pete DePaolo car, but was never a factor.

Race day was gray and depressing with rain clouds hovering in the sky as if waiting to pick the best time to drop their notice of cancellation. Construction of a golf course had been started that year, and only its green fairways relieved the sombreness of the setting. There were many favorites—Leon Duray, defender George Souders, Gulotta—but Meyer was not one of them. When the starter's flag dropped and the cars accelerated to racing speed, Meyer stayed off the pace. He let Duray set a blistering average of better than 106 m.p.h. for the first 150 miles before fading out of contention with cooling problems. Then, although he stayed close, he made no effort to chase when Gleason and Souders, dogged

by Babe Stapp and Gulotta, battled for the lead. He was more worried about Lou Moore who also was holding back, saving his engine.

Gleason led at the 300-mile mark, but Gulotta was in the lead, apparently to stay, at the 400-mile mark when a light drizzle began. Meyer lay 3rd, followed closely by Moore. Track officials displayed the caution flag, which was then merely advisory, as they considered calling the race. But the drizzle ended quickly, and the racing flag came back out. The complexion of the competition changed as suddenly as the rain had stopped. Gleason's Duesy developed magneto trouble, and with only 18 laps to go, Gulotta's Stutz Special suffered a clogged fuel line. Meyer's rear-drive Miller rolled into the lead, followed by Moore, and that was how they finished.

Meyer went on to the AAA season championship rather handily, including an amazing 4 victories at the Altoona Board track. In 1929 at Indianapolis he assumed the lead and seemed to have the race well in hand just after the 250-mile mark, but his 3rd and last pit stop turned into a 6-minute disaster as the crew fought to start an engine stalled by an accumulation of fuel in the supercharger. He salvaged 2nd behind Ray Keech only because Moore suffered a broken con rod with 2 laps to go. Keech was to die in a Land Speed Record attempt at Daytona Beach. In the race-shy 1929 season, Meyer won enough to defend his AAA season crown successfully.

Eddie Rickenbacker's Junk Formula arrived in 1930, and with it came riding mechanics and a new mount for Meyer, the 16-cylinder Sampson, essentially 2 Miller V-8 engines side by side, each with its own carburetor and water pump, but connected at their front to a central drive shaft. Even the radiator core was in 2 sections. The car was set up so that if one engine's auxiliary equipment failed, the other engine would be able to continue in operation. Meyer led the first 2 laps, but faded to 4th because of handling problems and minor mechanical woes.

The major change in the Sampson for 1931 was to take advantage of the rules—the double V-8 had 8 carburetors, all Winfield downdrafts, and must have presented a fantastic problem in synchronization. Louis also entered a Miller 8 of his own with Myron Stevens assigned to drive. The Sampson broke an oil line on the 7th lap, and on the 72nd Meyer relieved Stevens in the Miller, in 20th place. Meyer finished the car 4th although the spot was credited to Stevens as the driver of record. The Sampson came back in 1932 and again went to the sidelines early when Meyer skidded on the 51st lap, breaking both crankshafts.

That was the end of the Sampson as far as Meyer was concerned. For 1933 there was a new sponsor, Tydol, and Meyer—who may have been the only race driver in history to carry his own doctor (Lawson Harris, his riding mechanic) with him during a race—returned to a

258 cu. in. Miller 8. He won easily, almost 4 laps better than 2nd place Shaw and his Mallory Special, a Miller 4. Chet Gardiner finished the Sampson in 4th place, and the only change of note in that car had been a reduction from 8 to 4 carburetors. Meyer also won his 2nd AAA crown.

Off the track he was now part owner of a garage and an expert in making close-tolerance parts for racing engines. Harry Miller had sold his engine plant to Fred Offenhauser in 1933, and Meyer and Offenhauser did business. In 1934 Louie switched mounts again, this time to a Miller 4 tied into a Ford. It was called the Ring-Free Oil Special; it departed on the 92nd lap. Meyer's Ring-Free car was very fast, however, in 1935. That may not have been much of an advantage since each car was limited to 42.5 gallons of fuel. He was as high as 3rd on the 150th lap, then dropped back steadily to finish 12th on the fumes in the fuel lines.

In 1936 Meyer returned again in the Ring-Free Special. The engine had been further refined, and Meyer had built his own clutch, transmission, and front axle. Fuel allotment had been cut to 37.5 gallons, and with his experience of the previous year and an attack of minor mechanical problems, Lou was not sanguine about his chances. His pessimism proved incorrect. The Special worked like a charm, averaging 14.46 m.p.g. despite the fact that Lou set a new race record of 109.069 m.p.h. Lou took charge of the race before the halfway point and, despite heroics by Ted Horn and Wilbur Shaw among others, won easily. He was part of immortality, a 3-time winner of the Indianapolis 500.

In 1937 Meyer sold his own car at a good price a few days before the race; he knew he could get another ride on the Boyle Products team. The Boyle car was powered by a revised Miller 8, and Lou drove it to 4th place. In 1938 Lou was in a Miller 8 with the Bowes Seal Fast name on the side. He rose as high as 4th before an oil pump failed on the 149th lap. For 1939 Lou went all out after that 4th Speedway victory. He had an engine that he had built himself, different enough so that it could be called a Bowes, after his sponsors, supercharged 8. He blew the engine in the final practice laps and flew in a new engine block from Los Angeles, working all night on the car. He was so tired that shortly before the race he had to take a nap in the garage area.

Awakened by his crew, Meyer climbed into the car and, unlike his usual style, jumped right into the lead, setting a torrid pace which apparently only Wilbur Shaw in the Boyle Maserati could maintain. For about 400 miles of the race he was the leader and then Shaw began to creep up. Louis could not seem to shake the Maserati as fatigue crept in to cut his efficiency. With 17 laps to go, Shaw made his move on the No. 1 turn after winning the drag race down the main straight. No more than a few feet behind, Meyer swung outside to dive down off the banking and force Wilbur out of the groove. But the car spun, making a shambles of his right front

tire. Meyer had to pit and before he could get back Wilbur had a lap on him. But then racing luck swung the other way; Shaw was forced in for fuel. Meyer was unable to make up the entire deficit before the Maserati regained speed, yet he still had an outside chance to win. He was only 200 yards behind Jimmy Snyder's Thorne Engineering car and then there was Shaw. He took Snyder and, driving as recklessly as he ever had in his life, barrelled after Shaw.

But in his exhaustion he had forgotten about an oil slick on the groove in the back end of the No. 2 turn. The car spun wildly up toward the outer wall, hit some wood bracing beams and flipped. Lou was thrown clear on the 1st flip. He was taken to the first aid building where it was quickly established that he was virtually unscathed. But the experience had shaken him. When his brother rushed in to find him, he was sitting on the edge of the cot. "Eddie," he said, "That was it. I'll never drive a race car again." When he quit he had driven 5,249 miles of competition on the Indianapolis Speedway in 13 races.

Meyer spent World War II rebuilding Ford engines and parts, and in 1946, when Fred Offenhauser decided to sell, Meyer combined with Dale Drake, another fine L. A. wrench man, to buy the Offy business. Meyer was content to allow the engine to evolve, both in the midget version and in the sprint and championship versions. Fuel injection, greatly improved materials, better cooling, all came under the Meyer-Drake banner and, since the formula never changed enough to matter, the engine came to dominate USAC racing for more than a decade. Meyer eventually sold out to Drake and assumed responsibility for FoMoCo's 4-cam Indy engine. The Meyer-Drake personal relationship had been remarkable for its placidity, because if the men disagreed they never did so before a customer. Lou Meyer was one of those very few who reached greatness in motor sport on the track and in the garage.

ROBERTO MIERES

Five years on the international scene, Roberto Mieres was one of those Argentinian drivers who invaded Europe in the early fifties. Born at Mar del Plata on December 3, 1924, Mieres was a college graduate with a keen interest in sports. He was a rower, a rugby player until a broken leg slowed him down, a yachtsman, a champion tennis player. And he was an auto racer.

It started with an MG, and Mieres won several events. In 1948 he bought an SSK Mercedes, then a 2.3-litre supercharged Alfa Romeo. His big break came after he won the Rosario sports car races and was invited to go to Europe with Juan Fangio and Fro Gonzales. His 1st European race was at Geneva in a Formula 2 Ferrari, and Mieres finished a creditable 4th. Back in Argentina

he won the sports car championship in 1949–50 with a 2.3-litre Bugatti that previously had been driven by Achille Varzi, a particular favorite in South America because he had so often competed there.

In 1952 Mieres returned to Europe and was signed by Amedée Gordini for his F2 team. At Albi he ran the fastest F2 lap and was invited to drive in the Formula 1 race. Instead of remaining part of the scenery, Roberto finished 4th behind Louis Rosier, Gonzales, and Maurice Trintignant, all in F1s. Mieres's association with Gordini continued in 1953; then the following season, after taking 2nd in a Maserati at Buenos Aires behind Trintignant's Ferrari, he continued with his own, uncompetitive Maserati. At Silverstone he was 6th, at Bern 4th. The Maserati team offered him a competitive factory car, and Mieres immediately showed that the choice was a good one. He was 3rd in the Supercortermaggiore Grand Prix, 2nd to Alberto Ascari in the Valentino F1 race, 3rd at Pau and Bordeaux, both of the latter won on team orders by Jean Behra. At Zandvoort Roberto ran the fastest lap. But he felt he was not getting anywhere and officially retired at season's end to take up yachting again back in South America.

How good was Mieres? Let's answer it this way. He un-retired twice with some interesting results. In 1957 he drove an Ecurie Ecosse D Jaguar in the Buenos Aires 1000 with Ninian Sanderson; their game plan was to drive at a steady speed and finish where they might. It was 4th. In 1959 Mieres shared a Porsche with a relative unknown at the only running of the Daytona Beach 1000. They won at 93.35 m.p.h. Not bad for a Sunday afternoon racing driver who spent much of his time at sea.

JOHN MILES

Being number two to a Grand Prix driver like Jochen Rindt for Gold Leaf Team Lotus suggests a certain amount of ability in a young man. That was the status of John Miles, a bespectacled young man (born in 1944) from Islington, England, in 1970. By year's end, what might have been a golden dream had tarnished completely, and the son of British actor Bernard Miles was looking for a new spot.

His first car was an Austin Nippy, purchased while Miles was a student at University College School in Hamstead. This unpretentious mount was used for rallies, hillclimbs, and even a few races; meanwhile, John collected a series of racing Austin 7s (or at least bits and pieces of them), and eventually an Ulster. This car gave way to an Omega-Jaguar that was raced once, Miles winning a Debden club race after a fearsome spin.

By then he had left school and gone to work at the Mermaid Theatre, painting scenery, taking still photographs for outside displays and publicity, and serving behind the bar that is standard at intermission time in the British theatre. He sold all his bits and pieces, his Omega, practically everything he had that was loose, and bought a Diva GT in kit form. The year was 1964. Powered by a 1650-c.c. pushrod Ford engine, the car provided Miles with his 1st racing successes and led toward the GP world. John started 15 times and amassed 11 overall or class victories. One of these was in the Nurburgring 1000, where he and Peter Jackson shared a class victory with the Diva powered by a substitute 1000-c.c. engine.

In 1965 Miles went with Willment. He was provided with an engine, worked on it and other engines, and was free to race as much as he wanted. In 18 starts he had 16 class or overall victories in club racing. John was awarded the Redex GT championship and the 3rd Grovewood Motor Racing Award that season. The Diva was sold the next year, and a Willment-powered Lotus Elan was the Miles mount in 1966. He never lost a race to another Elan all year, winning his initial 9 national and international races, then meeting his match in the superior Chevron GT. The year was also notable for Miles because he had his 1st test drive in a single-seater, a Formula 3 Lotus, in which he and Jackie Oliver both tried their hands. Oliver was a second faster and got a factory berth.

Miles also went with Lotus, driving some 45 races in the development Europa and in an F3 Lotus 41. Teamed with Oliver, he won the BOAC 500 in his class in an Elan, a feat he repeated in 1968 and 1969. In 1968

John worked on the Lotus 41X—a version of the F3 car with a lengthened body and some other modifications. He raced it independently at first, but by mid-year Gold Leaf became his sponsor, and in this car Miles won 4 of 6 international F3 races he entered.

In 1969 Miles planned on driving in Formula 2 and in Group 6 with a Lotus 62. The sports car part of his planning went well, but he managed only two F2 races, and these were beset by mechanical problems. Colin Chapman, the Lotus man, called one day and asked John to test-drive the radical new 4-wheel-drive Formula 1 Lotus 63 in a demonstration before the car was shipped off to the Dutch GP. Miles handled the car well enough to be offered a championship drive at the French GP. He leaped at the opportunity, of course, and even the failure of a fuel pump belt on the opening lap of the race failed to dampen his rosy glow. Chapman kept him on the team for another 4 races, but the car still had to be sorted out. At the British GP it became stuck in 3rd gear, but John hung on to finish 10th. The engine went at the Italian GP on the 4th lap. The gearbox seized on the 40th lap of the Canadian GP. The fuel pump did Miles in again at the Mexican race on the 3rd lap.

"It was a fascinating experience," said Miles later. "A 4-wheel drive car is a curious one to drive. Whatever you do, you are much more committed. You can't fling a 63 around as you would a traditional car. It is very quick out of a corner, once you have pointed toward the apex, but it is not very quick when you have reduced power and are trying to brake. At first we were slower than the Matra, but we got it to go quicker later in the season. But you are always in an understeering situation. And, frankly, there is far less effect when you turn the wheel than there is in an ordinary car."

In 1970 Miles became, in effect, number 2 to Rindt. Occasionally he would have to yield his car to Mario Andretti, it was said, but as it turned out, Andretti, did not show up very often. Miles made 10 GP starts, finished all but 3 races, and gained only 2 championship points. In an old Lotus 49C, he was 5th at South Africa. Then his troubles with the Lotus 72 started. He failed to qualify at either Spain or Monaco, retired from the Belgian GP, and finally finished 7th in Holland and 8th in France. A string of retirements followed in the British, German, and Austrian Grands Prix, and he did not start the Italian race, of course, when the team withdrew after Rindt's death.

John put himself on the beach when Lotus returned after sitting out the Canadian GP. He was replaced by an F3 hot-shot from Sweden, Reine Wisell, who had the good fortune—and skill—to take 3rd place in the United States GP, while Emerson Fittipaldi, another Lotus addition, won that race. Wisell also made 10th at the Mexican finale. For 1971 Lotus decided on a Fittipaldi-Wisell pairing, which left John Miles exactly nowhere in F1. But he helped DART win the RAC sports car championship and the British round of the 2-litre European series, and the next season Miles was named DART team leader once again.

KEN MILES

Perhaps the highest development of the racing driver is reached in the man who can tell what is wrong with a particular car, then suggest what might be done to make it right. These men are never plentiful, and they are fantastically valuable for the firms that employ them. Ken Miles was one of those men, meeting death, in fact, while testing what was eventually to become Ford's Le Mans winner in 1967.

Miles was one of the best. Both America and Britain can claim him, and he had enough accomplishments to accommodate all. Ken was responsible, even more than Carroll Shelby, for turning the Cobra into a race-worthy machine, and he had a major part in the development of the Ford GT and its Mk. II successor as well as that of the Mustang GT350. Though the victories in 1965 and 1966 at the Daytona Continental, the 1966 Sebring 12-hour race (the latter 2 with Lloyd Ruby codriving), and the 1966 Daytona 24-hour race were his most resplendent internationally, Miles had not been a stranger to the winner's circle ever since he raced the Flying Shingle MG TC derivative when he first came to California in 1952.

The Hawk (as he was known) was outspoken, and his

407

British accent, emanating from the side of his mouth, made some of his comments seem even more abrasive. It could be forgiven, however, since before the liaison with Shelby he had helped create the Porsche legend in the States, campaigning with fantastic success from 1956 up to 1962. Porsche, of course, had fine engineering going for it, but Miles's skill as a driver and mechanic contributed to one record spree of 49 finishes in 49 starts. One of his tours de force in this marque was dusting off the big iron to win the 1960 Laguna Seca Grand Prix.

Shelby latched on to Miles in September 1963 with a development contract. Miles kept his sports car business in Hollywood at first, but later gave it up as he became more involved with the Cobra. Ken helped campaign the Cobra in the USRRC series, then deserted it for the most part in its World Championship year to concentrate on the GT. He was a deceptively calm man in the cockpit and might be remembered in the land of his birth for the introduction of American V-8 power on the tight British courses.

Miles competed in motorcycles before World War II, then became a tank sergeant in the British Army. Born November 1, 1918, in Sutton Coldfield, England, near Birmingham, he was past 30 before he switched to auto racing in an old Ford V-8 powered Frazer-Nash which saw action at Silverstone, Brands Hatch, and other venues before Ken packed off to California to seek his fortune early in 1952. In England he had dabbled in old car racing with the Vintage Sports Car Club, then passed through Bugatti, Alfa Romeo, and Alvis enroute to the Frazer-Nash. When he came to the States, his 1st race was in a stock MG TD at Pebble Beach. He was disqualified for reckless driving when his brakes faded without slowing his lap times.

In 1953 came the tube-frame MG Special with which he racked up 14 straight victories, starting with Pebble Beach. Ken sold it in 1954 to campaign a TF while building the famed Flying Shingle. He also tried a Triumph TR-3 in 1955 during the Shingle era. In 1956 he tried a Porsche Spyder, and in 1957 the Pooper, a Cooper-Porsche combination that beat the factory Porsche at Nassau. He had been working with John von Neumann, the Porsche dealer, who according to one source, was ordered to get the Pooper off the competition trail or lose his franchise.

Miles ran an RSK Porsche for Otto Zipper, another dealer, in 1958. He bought the RSK out of his prize money, which included a Mexican triumph over the Rodriguez boys. His next mount was a Maserati in 1961, nothing sensational. That was the year he started test work for Rootes on the Alpine and helped develop the Dolphin Formula Junior. That brought Miles to the threshold of the Shelby era, which started with a Sebring ride and developed to where he held various titles including competition manager. He later returned to Zip-

per part-time in 1965 to campaign a Carrera successfully in the United States Road Racing Championship.

The end came swiftly and suddenly at Riverside International Raceway in California on August 17, 1966. It was a routine test run of the J-car at speed, a strange vehicle that was later developed into the Ford that swept Le Mans. Miles had run tests many times before. You take the car out on the deserted track and push her a little more than is safe—just to see what happens. Usually the car will spin or fishtail or remain reasonably under control. But this was the 10,000-to-1 shot. The J-car suddenly looped, flipped and crashed. Mollie Miles was a widow.

HARRY MILLER

The number of self-taught talents in the field of automobile engineering and designing is not small. The number who influence an era can be counted on the fingers of one hand. Certainly Harry Armenius Miller was one of these. He created wonderfully delicate and complex power plants for racing, although he was a self-taught native of rural Wisconsin who once ran a steam shovel for a living

When he was in his teens the wonderful creativity that was to mark his association with automobile racing had already blossomed into a spark plug of his own invention, and then came the invention that brought him to Indianapolis, then one of the centers of the automobile industry in the U.S. Miller came to Indianapolis to manufacture his Master Carburetor about 1911, the year of the initial Indianapolis 500. He made and sold enough of the carburetors to survive the first few years—after he moved to Los Angeles—and then Bob Burman changed his life.

Miller built his first racing engine in 1914, when Burman, realizing there would be no parts replacement from France, gave Harry a Peugeot engine that had broken apart when its connecting rod had split. Bob wanted Miller and his colleague Fred Offenhauser to duplicate the engine. Harry did the job and several years later built a similar engine for Barney Oldfield's Golden Egg. During World War I he was too busy building aircraft components to do much in racing, but he came into contact with another engine which was to influence his own future designs—the Bugatti d.o.h.c. 16-cylinder. This unsuccessful aircraft design had an influence in Italy on the Maserati brothers, in France on Ernest Henri, and in the United States on both Miller and the Duesenbergs. The Duesenberg brothers (in Elizabeth, N. J.) had a government contract to produce this design for the Army Air Corps. Miller spent much time testing the engine so he could build the carburetors and fuel pumps. Out of the association with the Peugeot and Bugatti designs came the Miller straight-8, with Peugeot's multiple inclined valves and hemispherical combustion chamber and the Bugatti d.o.h.c. layout and valve relationship. Thus, unwittingly, Ernest, Henri and Ettore Bugatti sparked the genius of a young American designer.

The Miller straight-8 was a direct response to the 1920 change in the AAA Contest Board formula from 300 cu. in. to 183. When the formula was cut again in 1923, it was still possible to drop the displacement to 122 cu.in. When Harry decided to capitalize on racing after war business left his shops expanded, he found himself in direct competition with the Duesenbergs. It was a rivalry that dominated the decade.

Some sources say that the Miller straight-8 came right out of the Duesenberg. In the summer of 1920, after the Elgin Ill., road races of that year, Cliff Durant, the General Motors scion and Los Angeles car dealer, bought a straight-8 engine from Duesenberg that, because Duesenberg production techniques were far from precise, did not work out well. The Duesey-powered car was slow, so slow that after Tommy Milton had driven it unsuccessfully on the Beverly Hills board track, Milton pointed out the deficiency to Fred Duesenberg. Milton threatened to build a better one himself if the Jersey man would not replace it with a good engine. Fred agreed to do so, but let his wife talk him out of the idea on the trip back home. Incensed, Milton took the engine to Miller's engine shop along with Durant's backing for a team of race cars.

That the Millers profited from other Duesenberg developments seems incontrovertible. For instance, both engines suffered valve spring breakage. Since the Duesy did not have the meticulous exactness of the Miller operation, the problem was more acute with them. Hall-Scott Motors of Berkley, Calif., was engaged to solve the problem for Duesenberg and came up with a new cam contour that transformed the engine into a top racing contender, giving it at least 10 m.p.h. more top speed. Milton, who had worked with Duesenberg for several years, used his old contacts to acquire a set of drawings of the new cam. Leo Goossen, as important to the Miller operation as Harry himself, converted the design and improved it enough to regain the initiative. But the car did not make the 1921 race because Tommy accepted a ride in a Frontenac from the Chevrolet brothers. He used his Durant Special, however, to nail down the AAA championship.

Miller created a duplicate engine in 1922 for Jimmy Murphy, who proceeded to take the Duesy engine out of his French GP winner and install his new Miller. Milton, in a Leach Special for that race (he had been forced to sell his interest in the Durant car) lasted only 44 laps as Murphy ran away with the 1922 Indy classic. This was a doubly bitter pill for the Duesenberg forces who finished 2nd. Miller completely dominated the 1923 race with 10 Miller-engined cars in the field, 8

from Durant, 1 a Stutz-sponsored vehicle for Milton, and 1 for Howdy Wilcox, sponsored by Miller himself. Milton won, and the next 3 finishers were Miller-engined cars. The only thing Duesenberg got out of the race was the privilege of driving a Duesenberg pace car in recognition of the relocation of his car plant to Indianapolis.

But Fred and Augie were not sleeping. There were 14 Millers in the 1924 field and 4 Duesenberg, 3 with the 1st centrifugal superchargers ever seen except for a 1920 entry by Fred which had a tiny 5-inch impeller. In 1923 Fred and Augie recognized the superiority of the Miller engine layout and copied the d.o.h.c. with its 4 valves per cylinder and cup-type cam followers. The spark plug also was moved to the center of the cylinder, and finally Duesenberg adopted a spur gear train. Thus, the real major difference between the rivals was the supercharger. That was quite a difference, though, because Joe Boyer and L. L. Corum won in a Duesenberg in 1924 and forced Harry to become a supercharger expert, which he did in a matter of months.

Now it was Miller's turn, this time with an assist from Murphy who reasoned that, with the engine formula soon dropping to only 91 cu. in., speed through the turns would be crucial. He concluded that front-wheel drive, with the engine pulling the car rather than pushing it, could minimize skidding and tire wear, and allow higher lap times. Unfortunately, he was not around to see his theories proved. He crashed at Syracuse, N.Y., September 15, 1924. But with Durant putting up the money, Miller completed the trend-setting race car. The 100-inch vehicle had the driver sitting between the frame rails, thus lowering both height and center of gravity, and it had a 122 cu. in. supercharged engine.

Harry got so excited about the car that he built 2 more, the 3rd being the famous Junior 8 that boasted a transmission and differential combined into a single compact unit. It was the only one of the 3 that made the 1925 Indy race, and it lost only because Dave Lewis, its original driver, overshot his pit when coming in for a relief driver on the 173rd lap, and was forced to make another circuit of the track. Bennett Hill, who had refused originally to drive the car, took over and not only unlapped himself, but made up a half lap in the final 50 miles.

For the 1926 season the 91-cu. in. formula was in effect. Rather than redesign completely, Miller changed the stroke on his 122's to 2.6 inches. Later, however, he moved to a 2.18/3-inch stroke/bore ratio. The supercharger was moved off the camshafts to be spur-gear driven off the crank, and the engines were reversed to place the supercharger directly behind the radiator. Miller was getting 1.7 h.p. per cu. in. at 7,000 r.p.m.'s. He also adopted a 3-section front axle for easier and quicker servicing. He priced the front-drive car at $15,000 and a rear-drive car with the same engine at $10,000.

The 1926 Indianapolis 500 was a runaway, with Frank Lockhart in a rear-drive Miller winning and 8 other Millers in the top 10. For 1927 George Souders in a Duesy won as the Millers faded early. Improved intercoolers and higher pressure superchargers were allowing the engines to turn 8,300 r.p.m. But in 1928 Lou Meyer and Lou Miller finished 1–2 in Miller 91s; and in 1929, the last year of the formula, it was Ray Keech and Lou Meyer in another Miller 1–2 finish.

Meanwhile, the Miller 91 had been driven to 50-kilometer and 50-mile records in 1926 by E.A.D. Eldridge at Montlhéry, France. And Lockhart set a flying mile record of 164.009 m.p.h. on Muroc Dry Lake in California in 1928. At one time the 91 held every U.S. speed record to 400 miles. That was the high point of the Miller saga, although he was to continue building racing cars virtually until his death. The Offenhauser engine, it may be argued, was developed by halving the 91 and incorporating some of the features of a marine engine the Miller shops had built.

But Harry Miller was not through with racing. In 1932 he built two 4-wheel drive cars, which were never fully developed technically; and in 1937–38, when he was working for Gulf Oil Company, he resurrected one of his few passenger car efforts to make another racing car.

In 1928 Harry was commissioned to build the ultimate road car by Philip Chancellor of Santa Barbara. He approached the project with great excitement since $30,000 was mentioned as the price. He settled upon a 303-cu. in. V-8 of d.o.h.c. configuration with a front-wheel drive unit designed by Goossen and C. W. Van Ranst who had just designed the Cord FWD. The V-8 was very compact for its day and was located almost over the front axle. The transmission and drive unit was forward of the front axle. The car was just 58 inches from the ground to the convertible roof that disappeared into a lidded compartment. This compartment had to be locked before the car would start. Unfortunately, someone in the shop interchanged the wheel hubs, and when Chancellor drove the car a wheel rolled off at great speed. Chancellor, undamaged, sold the vehicle quickly.

Miller had lost interest in this project when the chassis was two-thirds complete and sold his shop. Goossen and Offenhauser, however, completed the project. In 1932 the team was reunited for racing purposes when Miller found an Easterner who also wanted the ultimate car. He walked out on this one, too, because he could not successfully produce what he had promised, a boat-tailed FWD speedster with De Dion suspension all around and a 303-cu. in. blown V-16 engine. The Easterner came West to personally supervise completion of the vehicle, which was a dismal failure. Miller bought the car back in 1937 for $400, stripped off the body, and made a race car with the engine. The car never raced.

Harry had one other fling at designing and this, too,

never got off the drawing board because he died in 1943 before the project was completed. He designed a sports car for volume production with automatic transmission and a 6-cylinder d.o.h.c. engine sitting transversely, á la Issagonis, but tilted back at 45° in the frame ahead of the front axle. Only the shafts to the hubs were unsprung.

TOMMY MILTON

Eddie Rickenbacker, besides helping to found the American airline industry, taught Tommy Milton to be a *race* driver. It happened in 1916 when Milton had already gotten himself a berth on the Duesenberg racing team. He had been a star in J. Alex Sloan's IMCA circus on the dusty fair circuit, but only as what in vaudeville they call a 3rd banana. On the last day of the 1915 season, he decided to see if he could be top banana by beating Eddie Hearne and Louie Disbrow. He did—badly—and Sloan promptly fired him.

This allegedly was part of a Machiavellian scheme Sloan had to make Milton his new star of stars. J. Alex knew that the young Milton was anxious over being slated to lose most of the IMCA exhibitions; he also knew that Duesenberg had a record car and had persuaded Fred and Augie to use Milton as the driver. Then, according to the Sloan scheme, Tommy would return as the world speed king and become his number one gate attraction.

It did not happen that way because the record car

410

project was delayed some 4 years. But Milton had his ride with Duesenberg. He finished 4th, 3rd, and 2nd out of his first 4 races, but incurred the displeasure of the redoubtable Fred Wagner, who threatened to ban him from AAA racing as a menace to the other drivers. Wagner may have had suspicions that Milton was going to return to Sloan after mopping up AAA. However, Milton sought out Rickenbacker and told him his problem. Eddie took him out on the track and taught him the rules of the road in AAA, smoothing out his technique in the bargain. Tommy went on to win 23 out of 104 championship races and finish in the top 3 an incredible 82 times in what is considered one of the golden eras of U.S. professional motor sport.

Born in 1893 to a wealthy family in the dairy business in St. Paul, Minn., Tommy was fascinated by motor cars. Blind in one eye from birth—a fact not discovered by the racing world until long after he had won the Indianapolis 500 twice—he decided he wanted a Mercer Raceabout to use as a race car. After some strong language, he got it, and in 1913 traveled to Sioux City to compete against the likes of Ralph Mulford. The first race program was a shambles for him because the automobile's engine was not set up for racing. With a motor nearly ruined, Milton wired the Mercer factory for new parts. He got them on credit and promptly looked around for lesser worlds to conquer. J. Alex Sloan solved his problem quickly after seeing him in a minor-league race at the Minnesota State Fair. Milton and his Mercer had lost, but J. Alex saw a potential drawing card. Tommy signed on with the Sloan troupe at $50 a week, plus a cut of the gate. It turned out to be a very small and uncertain cut.

Traveling on the circuit meant "racing" as much as 8 times a day. It meant learning control of the automobile at speed, because even if the race had a predetermined winner, the race could not look predetermined. The circuit meant practice for the day he turned to AAA, which at that time was becoming the major automobile racing group in the nation. For 1916, his 1st season, Milton finished 7th.

In 1917 he won his 1st major victory, a thriller at Providence, R. I., from an illustrious field including Louis Chevrolet, Barney Oldfield, Eddie Hearne, Ralph Mulford, and Joe Boyer, but the ultimate battle was against Ira Vail. Vail had set fast qualifying time and won his initial heat. In the semifinal Milton had beaten Vail by inches. In the 100-mile feature, Vail and Milton stayed within a car length of one another for 80 miles. Then Milton went high on the outside rail to make his pass. His wheels scraped the railing but he pulled it off and won the race.

Although he finished well in most of the races in the next 2 seasons, Milton did not win his 1st national championship until 1920. Out of 9 championship races in 1919, however, Milton won 5. At the Uniontown board track, where he never finished lower than 2nd

place, he beat Louis Chevrolet by outfoxing him. He dropped back into the pack for the early part of the race as if the Duesenberg was performing balkily. Chevrolet had the faster car, but he was running nowhere near the groove, thus incurring excessive tire wear. Tommy let him grind his tires down and then, late in the race, moved up to press him to even greater speed. Soon Louis had to pit for tires, and Tommy won easily.

In his rookie year at the Indianapolis 500, Milton lasted 49 laps before the car threw a rod. Then he shipped to Sheepshead Bay in Brooklyn, N.Y., where Jimmy Johnston, the boxing promoter at Madison Square Garden, was organizing a police benefit race. The piece de resistance was to be a match race between Tommy and Ralph DePalma. The 2 disliked each other at first sight, and Ralph helped the matter along—and the gate receipts—by refusing disdainfully to match his Packard against what he called the American Can. (The reference was to the fact that the American Can Company was a sponsor of the Duesenberg racing effort.) Milton came to the program, won his heat easily, then set fast time for the track.

Milton, who had never even seen a road race, much less driven in one, relinquished his seat in the lead Duesy to Ralph Mulford for the 1919 Elgin road races. Instead of a new 300-cu. in. 8-cylinder car, he elected to run his board track car. He must have known something, because he won by 25 minutes over Roscoe Sarles in the 301-mile race.

It was at Uniontown on Labor Day that tragedy struck down Tommy. On the 190th lap, while in the lead, his car burst into flames, and Milton was carted off to the local hospital badly burned and in danger of losing his left leg. He refused to permit doctors to amputate and several months later hobbled out of the hospital directly into a special record car. At Sheepshead Bay he set records from one to 300 miles, then went across the continent to the Beverly Hills Speedway where he opened the 1920 season with a victory.

There was another record car which the Duesenbergs and Milton had built, one that was to go for Ralph DePalma's world Land Speed Record. Milton had also partially financed this car and, after a trip to Havana to earn additional money, he expected to return to Daytona and make the runs. But the Duesenberg brothers and Jimmy Murphy changed all that. Anxious to make sure that the vehicle ran well, Fred and Augie asked Murphy to run the car on the sands. The AAA timer just happened to be checking out his instruments—or so he later claimed—and Murphy shattered the LSR easily. Milton was met by this bitter news; the young riding mechanic whom he had befriended and whom he had insisted should be given his driving certificate had, to his mind, treated him perfidiously. He tried at once to break Murphy's mark but the car was tired and needed a complete overhauling. Tommy failed miserably and thus the treachery seemed doubly serious. After overhauling the machine, however, Milton added 5 m.p.h. to the mile LSR, but he received little mention after he was forced to drive the car into the ocean to douse an engine fire.

Tommy won his national crown in 1920 with 4 victories out of 10 title races, one 2nd and three 3rds. He severed his connection with Duesenberg as soon as he legally could, and tried a Cliff Durant Chevrolet, which proved too slow. Then, soliciting funds even from Barney Oldfield, he built his own Miller-engined car that was called the Durant because Cliff owned the chassis. With it he never finished lower than 2nd, but he knew it was basically slow. So for Indianapolis in 1921 he accepted a Frontenac ride in a car that was known to throw rods over 3,500 r.p.m. Soon after the beginning of the race, the main bearing began to leak oil. Milton solved this by slipping the clutch before each turn, thus burning the oil off by friction. Then a plug fouled, leaving him 7 cylinders. This was really a blessing because now the Frontenac could not rev to 3,500. Milton was driving a paced race, well behind Ralph DePalma who held the lead in his Ballot.

At 250 miles he was in 2nd place, 2 laps behind Ralph and trying to fight off Roscoe Sarles in a Duesenberg. Five miles later he took the lead; DePalma was finished with bearing failure. The final pit stop was accomplished without losing the lead, but Sarles obviously had the faster car. So Tommy resorted to psychology. He reduced his speed slightly—some claim they saw him pat the tail of his car—and moved over enough to give Roscoe an opening to get through on the inside of the No. 3 turn. Sarles took the bait, and Milton chopped him off unceremoniously. Despite urgent signals from his pits Sarles would not make another attempt at the lead, believing Tommy to be unfatigued. Milton won at an average speed of 89.62 m.p.h. On July 4 Milton won the Tacoma 250 and went on to the 1921 championship.

For 1922 Milton was so confident of an Indy victory he entered his new Miller-engined Durant on December 28, 1921. When several months later the Durant passenger automobile arrived, and a dealer said Milton had won races in it, the AAA Contest Board suspended the car. Milton had acquired the blueprints of the Duesenberg racing camshaft by stealth, and had Harry Miller create a duplicate for his Durant. Now all was lost. He was forced to sell the engine to Cliff Durant and start fresh just 10 weeks from the big race. His Leach Special lasted just 44 laps, Cliff led the 500 in his Durant, and his foe Murphy won it using a car with a Miller engine duplicating his original.

Tommy had no choice but to wait for 1923 when single-seaters would be eligible. Again he was certain he could create a car that would win the race, and Harry C. Stutz was happy to back his belief to the tune of $10,000. Milton won the pole position in record time in the Miller-engined HCS Special and got himself a uniform all in white—kid gloves instead of the usual cotton, white surgical tape around the steering wheel instead of the usual black friction tape, and new white shoes. All was fine until the kid gloves shrank from perspiration, the adhesive on the surgical tape oozed out in the heat, and the shoes began to pinch his toes.

With a lead of 5 miles halfway through the race, Tommy pitted and gave the mount to Howdy Wilcox while he got his hands taped and put on his comfortable old shoes. When he returned some 5 minutes later, Wilcox was trailing Harry Hartz, and the HCS Special was running with an orange pierced with copper tubing as a filler cap. Milton removed the filler cap from Wilcox's car (which was riveted on since both cars were using a pressure system), signalled Howdy in, and had the filler cap installed in 60 seconds. Meanwhile, Hartz had pitted and Milton took the lead to win as he pleased. He was the first 2-time winner in the history of the 500.

Tommy did not get any car going again like that HCS until that fall at the Syracuse Fairgrounds. Harry Hartz, best of the Durant drivers that day, took a wide early lead. He was a straightaway ahead after only 10 miles. For some reason, however, he slowed, possibly figuring that maybe the rest of the field was conserving tires. Milton passed him, and everyone else soon after, and got going so strongly that he finished the 100 miles more than 2 laps ahead of the nearest rival and nearly 15 minutes under the accepted dirt-track record for the distance. Then, at the behest of Governor Al Smith of New York, Tommy went out and broke the lap record, too. It was a year later at this track that Murphy died after he oversteered into the inner guard rail. Milton made the same mistake at the same spot later in that race, but there was no longer a guard rail into which to crash. He took charge of Murphy's funeral arrangements.

It was at a pre-race medical examination in Minneapolis that Milton's blind eye was discovered. He had been passing the eye test all these years by memorizing the eye chart so completely he could picture it in his mind. This time the doctor threw him a curve by holding up a page from a magazine. But the other drivers signed a waiver so Milton could drive.

In 1925, Milton's last competitive year, he was running a 3-car team. Because he had teammates, he scored his final victory. It was at the Charlotte, N. C., board track. Milton's most promising protégé was Bob McDonogh, a moody youngster who could run with anybody when the spirit moved him. Milton had taken a substantial lead when his supercharger broke. Milton wagged for McDonogh to give him a tow; in other words, Bob was to let Tommy slipstream him. The chance to tow the boss woke McDonogh from his daze, and the youngster proceeded to give Milton a tow the likes of which shook the older man to his teeth, dragging him through every oil slick and over every loose board in the track. But Milton held on to win. Tommy's son saw his father drive competitively to victory for the only time in that race. On the eve of the Fulford-By-the-Sea (Florida) board track race, Tommy's retirement was announced for him by Carl Fisher who offered to sell Indianapolis Speedway to him. Milton refused and put his money instead into Fisher's unsuccessful Montauk, L. I., land development. Milton worked for many years for Packard before becoming a businessman and engineering consultant with his brother Homer.

In 1949 Wilbur Shaw persuaded Milton to become chief steward of the Indianapolis 500 in order to save the race from anarchy. Milton accepted, beginning the tradition of using ex-drivers as high officials, and instituted an open-door policy on decisions concerning the race. He relinquished the post to Harry McQuinn who relinquished to Harlan Fengler. Milton was still coming to the race in 1959, even when serving as president of the Hercules Drop Forge Company. He died in 1962.

DONNA MAE MIMS

"I love my enemy, and I hate to fight, to argue," said Donna Mae Mims, by her own definition a "yummy blonde, devoted to myself and competitive with men," who was also the 1st woman ever to win an SCCA National Championship. "If I argue I get all emotionally shook up, all upset, and I don't want that. When people doublecross me, or do something shady, something treacherous, I don't let it stay uppermost in my mind. Of course," Donna Mae added with a smile, "I never forget either. I just say to myself, someday I'll kill him, maybe 19 years from now I'll kill him, and won't *he* be surprised?"

Born in 1930, Donna Mae was the only child of a Chicago restaurant manager. She was born in Pittsburgh and lived there and in its immediate environs most of her life. She was married and divorced twice before going into racing. "When I first began driving in 1958 I was still married," she said. "We had a Corvette, and I drove it faster than he did, which was part of our trouble, I'm afraid. It was black, and I hated its color, so I painted 'Think Pink' on its side because he wouldn't let me change it. When we parted, I kept his name—I was tired of changing names—and the Corvette, too."

Donna Mae sold the Corvette, and later acquired a 5th-hand 1959 vintage Austin-Healey Sprite (one of the former owners was Dr. Jonas Salk) for $600. The "Think Pink" legend was immediately added and, clad in self-tailored, size 8 pink coveralls and a pink crash helmet, she invaded SCCA competition. More than 300 men were contenders for the Class H Production title which she won in 1963. In 1964 she sold the Sprite for $2,000 and took possession of a pink-hued MGB in which she tried D Production competition. This proved too much. In addition, Mrs. Mims wrote for a number of racing publications, hoping to become a full-time writer.

Sitting in her pink apartment in Pittsburgh and play-

ing with her constant companion, a long-haired Mexican Chihuahua called Pedro-Gonzales-Gonzales-the-Mexican-Road-Rat, born white but dyed pink, Donna Mae was frank about her successes and shortcomings: "The front end of a car is a mystery to me. A good driver should be able to come in and tell the mechanic 'the number 2 cylinder is acting up; or some such. All I can tell Bill Hartley, my regular mechanic, is 'something's pinging.' I think its marvelous that you can put some evil-smelling liquid into the car and wind up with the back wheels turning, and that will give some some idea of how much *I* know about it."

Is her pink kick for real? "People always ask me if all this pink talk is a gag or a publicity stunt," Mrs. Mims replied. "Absolutely not. I just happen to like pink—I *feel* pink. It's a girl color and I am a girl." Donna Mae went so far as to dye her normally black hair a pink-blonde shade and had a full pink wig to pull over her tousled locks after she pulled off her crash helmet following a race. "Maybe it's because I'm competing in a sport that is so completely dominated by males that it makes me want to feel feminine. What I do know is that I feel pink, and I want to be as pink as I can get."

The 5-foot 3-inch, 120-pound hazel-eyed former secretary to a Pittsburgh steel-fabricating company president said her idea of luxury, even after she has gained national attention, was "a hot bath and a lot of cheese dip and potato chips to munch on." After that it's bed-die bye. "I sleep with all the lights on," she confided, "so that no one can get to me. I leave my living-room lights on, too, because I like feeling secure. I also like high-necked, long-sleeved, belted dresses for the same reason."

Does this longing for security follow her onto the sports car courses? "I never think about getting hurt," said Donna Mae. "I don't avoid thinking about getting hurt, and it's not a natural thought I have either. We all know we can be hurt, of course. And some people think it might be worse for me because I am a woman, a 'pretty woman' some say. I like the compliment but it still doesn't worry me, the racing I mean."

She was known to bump cars out of her way and even to tell little white lies to opponents to throw them off guard. In fact, once she was cited by another SCCA driver for "ungentlemanly conduct." It must have been a dark day—not at all pink. Eventually, however, the pink of Donna Mae's competitive urge faded, but not before she had competed at Daytona and Sebring. She turned to rallying, American style, and when you do that, you are a candidate for a book on computer analysis But in 1973 she (and other female enthusiasts) entered the Cannonball Baker race across the U.S. in a Cadillac and a see-through blouse. The vehicle did not make it, but Donna Mae had proved she was still Thinking Pink.

GERHARD MITTER

Gerhard Karl Mitter was European Hillclimb Champion 3 years in a row (1966, 1967, and 1968), a winner of the Targa Florio, a frequent visitor to Sebring and other American courses. Yet the quiet, unassuming Mitter was virtually unknown on this side of the Atlantic. A West German and one of the Porsche factory's best drivers, Mitter was born in the Sudetenland in 1936 and started out competitively as a motorcyclist in his teens. After finishing school, he became a successful tuner and driver of DKW cars. It was natural for him to progress to the favorite German sport of hillclimbing, and eventually to Formula Junior with a Lotus 18, powered by a 2-stroke DKW engine. In 1963 Carel de Beaufort lent him an old Formula 1 Porsche for the German Grand Prix, and he finished 4th.

Gerhard joined the Porsche factory team in 1964; the following season he was runner-up to Ludovico Scarfiotti (Ferrari) in the European Championship. That same season, because he was a Lotus customer who had done something with his car, he was offered and accepted a spare Formula 1 Lotus in the German GP. In 1966 Gerhard started his championship string of Porsche hillclimb victories. The factory also gave Mitter various sports car assignments, and despite a practice accident at Spa in which he suffered a broken leg, he shared an Austrian GP victory with Hans Herrmann in a Carrera 6. In the Monza 1000 Mitter was 4th overall and won his class.

His sports car racing in 1967 included a victory at

Mugello, a 3rd overall and a class victory at Monza shared with the rising star of Jochen Rindt, a repeat of that placing at Sebring with Scooter Patrick, and a 4th overall at Nurburgring with Lucien Bianchi. All this in addition to winning 4 climbs, 3 seconds, and a 3rd for his 2nd consecutive title in that area. In that year he also started racing his own Brabham-FVA BT23 in Formula 2.

The following season saw a stupendous crash of his Porsche at the very beginning, the car cartwheeling several times while Mitter was doing 170 m.p.h. at Daytona, but he walked away from it. A tire had blown. That season Gerhard won every championship hillclimb he started, and he started every one except for a rainout. He and Jo Schlesser teamed up for a 2nd to a GT40 at Spa, and he and Scarfiotti, his old hillclimb adversary, found themselves together in a car for the BOAC 500 that they brought home 2nd. In 1969 he won the Targa in a Porsche 908 with Udo Schultz codriving, was 5th at Sebring and 3rd in the BOAC 500. Entered in the F2 section of the German GP in one of the new Dornier-built BMWs, he was killed in practice when a wheel fell off during a high-speed run at Nurburgring.

GUY MOLL

As the flag dropped on the 1934 Monaco Grand Prix—that fast, slow, fast race through the streets and the tunnels of Monte Carlo—Louis Chiron roared into the lead with Rene Dreyfus close behind, Pierre Etancelin 3rd and Achille Varzi 4th. This was one of auto racing's golden ages, when competition was fierce, especially in a race like Monaco where skill and daring played a greater role than sheer speed or horsepower.

At 20 laps Chiron still led, Dreyfus hanging on 4 seconds behind, with Phi-Phi Etancelin still 3rd. But a new name had taken over 4th, Guy Moll, a 24-year-old driver who had been racing only a couple of seasons but who had already showed enough for Scuderia Ferrari to give him an Alfa Romeo car for major races. At 50 laps, the halfway point of the GP, Chiron led by 46 seconds, and the placings were the same until Etancelin hit a bump in the road outside the Hotel de Paris and spun into the sandbags to retire with broken steering. Moll was 3rd.

At 80 laps Dreyfus had to pit for a short time to work on a slipping clutch, and Moll became the 2nd-place car, 90 seconds behind Chiron. Louis was nearly a full lap ahead of Guy with 2 laps left when he misjudged the Station Hairpin and ran full speed into the sandbags. The seconds became minutes as he feverishly worked on freeing his car and restarting. Three minutes, in fact, and before he could regain the course, Moll flashed past, driving the same steady, fast pace he had maintained throughout the race.

Moll crossed the finish with a minute to spare over Chiron, with Dreyfus 3rd, Marcel Lehoux 4th, Tazio Nuvolari 5th and Varzi 6th. It was a remarkable victory and seemed to point the finger of good frotune at the young man. But the finger was to turn away that same season in a tragic way.

Moll was a French Algerian, born in 1910. His racing career started in that then North African colony of France in a Lorraine-Dietrich; then he moved to a Bugatti owned by Lehoux, using the Bug for his 1st European appearance in 1932, the Marseilles GP, in which he finished 3rd behind Raymond Sommer and Nuvolari. He was keeping fast company, so in 1933 he bought his own Alfa, initially running it in the Nîmes GP and again finishing 3rd behind Nuvolari and Etancelin. In the French GP Guy was 5th, in the Marne GP he again finished 3rd, but was disqualified for receiving outside help.

Moll was 3rd still again in the Nice GP, 2nd in the Monza GP initial heat, running the day's fastest time at 122 m.p.h., then 2nd in the final heat as well. In the Comminges GP, Guy was 3rd, and 3rd once more in his Marseilles GP to future Alfa teammate Chiron and Luigi Fagioli. In 1934 the invitation came to join the new Scuderia Ferrari, running Alfas. Moll shared 3rd in the French GP, relieving Count Felice Trossi on the blistering hot day that saw only Chiron and Varzi finish ahead of him. He was 2nd to Chiron in the Marne GP, 2nd to Varzi in the Coppa Ciano, 2nd in the Tripoli GP.

But then came 2 sweet victories, the Avusrennen at 127.57 m.p.h. and the Monaco victory at 55.86 m.p.h., contrasting speeds that illustrated Moll's driving skill. But then came, too, the Coppa Acerbo, another fast race, and Moll was at his best, ripping off 160-m.p.h. sprints on the straights. On the 17th lap the back of his Alfa swung sideways for some unexplained reason, uprooted some trees, and ended in a crumped mass against the wall of a house. Moll was alive as they pulled him from the wreckage, but he died within minutes. He was buried in Maison-Carrée Cemetary in Algiers.

ALFRED MOMO

When Alfred Momo was a boy at the start of the 20th century, he began hanging around the Fiat factory in his native Turin. At the age of 12 he was apprenticed to the factory for the sum of 20 cents a week. A few years later he became a racing mechanic for the marque when it went into road racing. That meant Momo shared the thrills and dangers of the open road with the car's driver and had to make repairs to the car even as it was speeding along the twisty, rutted Italian roads of that day.

During World War I he joined the Italian Air Corps, putting his mechanical skills to work to keep Fiat-powered airplanes flying. A few years before that, he had been bitten by the flying bug. In a Rome-to-Tokyo endurance flight he had been pressed into service by Fiat as a flight mechanic, which, like his daring auto exploits, brought him to the point of making in-flight repairs while hanging out on the cowling of the slow-flying Caproni. Momo learned to fly soon after returning to Italy.

Flying took a back seat to automobiles after the war, however. Fiat sent him to America in 1920 to study the way they mass-produced their products. He liked his

visit and 3 years later he was back to stay, settling near New York City as shop superintendent at the Rolls-Royce–Brewster Automobile Plant in Long Island City. Momo continued with Rolls until 1936, when it closed its Long Island City operation, then moved over to Manhattan as chief engineer at J. S. Inskip, the car importer.

At Inskip he met Briggs Cunningham, the Green Farms, Conn., squire who spearheaded post-World War II America's return to international competition with the Le Mans cars that bore his own name, and with assorted other machinery. The 2 men, different in background but similar in dedication to automobile racing, hit it off well, and Briggs decided Alfred was the man to watch over his stable of racing machinery.

Cunningham set Momo up in business in Woodside, Queens, as the Momo Corporation. Eventually the firm was to grow into a complete precision tool works, supplying local aviation firms as well as motoring customers, at the head of which list stood Cunningham and his next-door Jaguar distributorship, another hobby. After Briggs's courageous but abortive attempts at Le Mans glory, a succession of Jags, Lister-Jags, Lotus and Brabham Formula Junior cars, Stanguellinis, Abarths, and Maseratis were prepared by Momo and raced with great success by Cunningham and his stable of top-flight drivers. They parted in 1963 when Briggs sold his interest in the Jaguar distributorship and retired from major sports car effort.

Momo stayed in New York, although Briggs lured him out of the Woodside lair once or twice for some

SCCA Eastern races to prepare his cars. Alfred would have gone more often, but only if Mama, Mrs. Momo, let him. She was remembered by many as the heart of Alfred's pit operation for she handled the stopwatches that told how fast the boys were going. Without her, it wouldn't have been the same. In the 1970s there was a luxury car called the Momo offered by Alfred. It never replaced the Lamborghini.

BOB MONTGOMERY

It took American practitioners to raise the business of announcing auto races to the status of an art form. A North Carolina boy named Bob Montgomery was one of those elite few who could play upon the crowd as if it were a musical instrument, eliciting excitement with so many nuances that to the detached observer it was like hearing a Kreutzer sonata played by a virtuoso. "Chris Economaki and I sometimes play a game, seeing how often we can get the people up on their feet," the softspoken Montgomery said. "We use different techniques, but we get the same effect."

Montgomery had a playroom full of awards for his broadcasting prowess although he concentrated on NASCAR racing almost exclusively. A many-time president of the Southern Motorsports Press Association, Bob was Associated Press Sportscaster of the Year in 1961, and his jobs at Georgia's Atlanta Speedway and Florida's Daytona, among others, earned national praise. But the proudest moment of his career came in 1954 when, after a grandstand collapsed at Greensboro, N.C., "I talked 3,200 people out of there without having them panic, and I was credited with averting a disaster," he recalled.

The Montgomery announcing career began when he was 15, in November 1941. It continued in the Air Force with the radio program "On The Beam" and turned toward racing when Bob was staff disc jockey for WGBG in Greensboro. "Houston Lawing was then in charge of one of Bill France's earliest promotions, the modified races at Bowman-Gray Stadium in 1951. He called me and told me he wanted me to be the public address announcer. 'You're kidding. I've never done anything like that,' I said. But he insisted and that started me. Among the tracks at which I handled the mike are Hickory, North Wilkesboro, Hillsboro, and Charlotte Motor Speedway, in North Carolina; Bristol, Tennessee; Martinsville, Virginia; and Atlanta and Daytona.

"I became the anchor man of the Universal Racing Network, which broadcast the Riverside 500 in all but 5 states, and in addition I had 150 radio stations who used the 6,000 or so tapes I made with drivers. I also conducted a weekly racing program called "Southern Motor Racing Review." Much of this activity continued despite a heart attack in 1961. But the most interesting part of the Montgomery story was his technique as a public address announcer. His premise was "The people paid to see a good race, and it's my job to point out to them what's good in the race."

That meant he would switch back into the pack to describe a battle for 4th place if the top 3 were staging a parade. "They're racing all the way down the line, and sometimes it's a greater accomplishment for some independent driver to take 4th in the equipment he must use than for a factory car to win," Bob noted. Montgomery, therefore, tried to make the least of the drivers more important to the crowd by telling his background and his racing history. With this kind of careful preparation, a battle for 4th place became exciting because fans could identify with each driver.

Later Montgomery ventured into a part of motor sports where the announcer was even more important —drag racing. "This is the toughest job in announcing," he said. "You have 5 minutes buildup, then 15 seconds of actual race description. You must talk almost incessantly, and the only thing that helps you in explaining this very technical sport are some of the colorful auto names like Color Me Gone."

BUD MOORE

In 1947, when Bud Moore and Joe Eubanks decided to seek their fortune with a modified 1937 Ford flathead V-8, NASCAR and SCCA were infant organizations and it is unlikely that Moore had ever heard of the latter. Bud fancied himself a driver but learned differently

from the crinkled bumpers of Dixie racing. So Eubanks drove and Moore became the mechanic. The team won 13 races in succession that year and through 1950 were terrors of the modified circuit. In 1951, 1952, 1953, Walter Moore (born May 26, 1926, on a farm outside Spartanburg, S. C.) and Eubanks made the top 10 of the Grand National circuit during which time Joe scored the lone Grand National victory of his career. The Moore-Eubanks team continued through 1956, when Buck Baker took over a Moore-prepared car, driving it to the 1957 championship. Speedy Thompson won the Southern 500 in another Moore-prepared car.

Bud Moore had established himself as one of the premier chief mechanics in NASCAR and he did nothing to tarnish that reputation in subsequent years. In 1958 Jack Smith won 12 races for him and the amazing carbuilder won successive Grand National championships with Joe Weatherly in 1962 and 1963. In 1964 it was Billy Wade who won 4 straight, and in 1965 the Moore Mercury set some kind of record for frustration with 5 2nd places in major races with Darel Dieringer at the wheel. In 1965 Darel won the Southern 500.

Lincoln-Mercury division of Ford had designated Bud Moore Engineering as their racing outlet and that meant building cars for the new SCCA TransAm. Road course racing, though new to him, called forth all the knowhow of 2 decades of carbuilding. With drivers like Dan Gurney, Peter Revson, and Parnelli Jones on his side, the Moore Mercury Cougars finished in the top 3 in 9 of 12 races, winning 4 and losing the title to Mustang by a mere 2 points. In 1968 Moore dominated NASCAR's GT division (Grand American). Tiny Lund won 9, finishing in the top five 13 times for the crown. Moore's Cougar won the manufacturers crown. In 1969 Bud was all over the place—GT, TransAm, Grand National. Most successful was the TransAm where Jones held forth in a Moore Mustang. Parnelli was so good in the Moore cars that rival Mustang team Carroll Shelby was knocked out of the box. In 1970 Jones-Moore won for Ford. In 1971 Jones and Moore, running without the substantial factory support of earlier days, curtailed their schedule. After that Parnelli went back to USAC racing and Bud back to his NASCAR racing garage. Neither was starving at last look.

LOU MOORE

There is virtually no chance for a relatively poor man to parley his knowledge of racing and meticulous hard work into a victory in the Indianapolis 500 these days. All the mechanics are meticulous, all work hard, and the entry fee in equipment to the fraternity of 500 owners runs in excess of $100,000. Lou Moore, therefore, may have been the last and greatest of the Horatio Alger breed of car owner. His Blue Crown Specials won 3 Indy 500 milers and left him a comfortably endowed old age because of it. During those years, starting in 1949, Moore worked full-time and partly in secret on his cars. There also were a 2nd and a pair of 3rds as a driver in the 500.

Lou was born in Hinton, Okla., September 12, 1904, next to the youngest of 8 children. His mother, the former Ella Jefferson of Huntington, W.Va., claimed to be a 5th cousin of Thomas Jefferson. His father, William Moore, a building contractor, decided he wanted to pick his oranges off his own trees and moved the family to Pomona, Calif., when Lou was 7. The first winter a freeze broke him, and the family moved to El Monte.

At 16, Lou went to work as a machinist's helper. After 3 years, he fancied himself another DePalma and went up to San Luis Obispo in a hopped-up Model T Ford which he had bought with his earnings, to enter a 50-mile dirt race. A few minutes before the starting flag, another driver turned over in a practice run and was killed. The experience shook Moore, and he ran dead last until his engine quit. Regaining some of his nerve, he barnstormed up and down California, racing at San Jose, the old Tanforan track, Fresno, Stockton, Banning, and the Ascot Speedway at Los Angeles.

He won his 1st race at Tanforan and almost was killed there, when he ran out of control under a low fence, losing the car's superstructure. Spectators thought his head had gone with it, but when first-aid men got to the scene, they found him knocked senseless. At Tanforan he met Roscoe Ford who seemed to have the answer to winning races and staying alive. Roscoe won by the simple expedient of getting out in front, where there was no traffic congestion. He gave Lou a ride, and Moore won 18 out of 22 starts. Ford, who worked Moore's pit every year at Indianapolis, believed Moore would have written the books with those performances if the old-timers had bothered to keep records. He also believed Moore was the 1st man to win crossing the finish line backwards. In 1931 on a half-time speedway at Woodbridge, N.J., Moore's car hit a bump in the home stretch and skidded across the wire tail first to set a one-lap record of 19 and 2/5 seconds.

In 1928 Lou got his first chance to drive at Indianapolis. "In those days, it was even tougher to get a car," he recalled. "There weren't many cars, and those available were driven by a tight little clique of racers who tried to keep outsiders on the outside." A fellow Angeleno, Charley Hasse, was bucking the same insiders with a Miller racer. Impressed by Moore's California record, Hasse entrusted the car to him. The rookie finished 2nd behind 3-time winner Louis Meyer. In 1929, Moore again was running 2nd when his engine flew apart in the 198th lap. The following year the Indianapolis rules were changed to permit racing of bigger cars—up to 366 cu. in., and Coleman Motors of Denver entered 2 cars. Moore drove one of them for 23 laps until he came around a turn onto a 5-car pile-up. "Cars were standing on end and tires were flying everywhere," he said. "I

tried to head in the opposite direction, went into a spin, knocked a chunk out of the concrete wall and climbed it. The car ended up balanced neatly on top of the wall with me in it. I wasn't hurt, but I felt plenty foolish."

In 1931 Coleman had a new car for him. It was the first 4-wheel drive racer seen on the track and had 2 engines working at cross purposes with the wheels. Whenever Moore took his foot off the gas in practice runs, the car would pull to the right and go into slides and broadsides for no apparent reason. Watching all this was Moore's old friend, Pete DePaolo. DePaolo was getting old and had decided not to drive his own car. Moore wanted to get old, too. He refused to drive the Coleman, as did everyone else. He got DePaolo's car, and piloted it for 103 laps until the clutch failed. The following year Lou won the pole and would have won the race, he later said, except for a broken gear housing. In 1933 he finished 3rd in a Miller-Duesenberg, and in 1934 he arrived at Indianapolis from Tripoli, North Africa, after driving night and day from New York, only 3 days before the race. He finished 3rd again. Moore bought the car from its owner, Frank Scully, and drove it in 1935 until forced out by engine trouble. In 1936 when cars were limited to 42½ gallons of gas, a pinhole leak in his tank caused him to run out of fuel after 465 miles.

Then 32 years old, Moore wanted to start building cars that not only would run fast enough but long enough, and he reworked the old car and entered it in 1937 with Mauri Rose driving. It broke down, and he junked it in disgust. He then built a car from scratch to his own specifications, and Floyd Roberts won in 1938 at a record-breaking speed of 117.2 m.p.h. in it. The next year, Roberts was killed when he ploughed into a broadsiding machine driven by Bob Swanson. Moore's first 3-man team was Cliff Bergere, Rose, and Floyd Davis in 1941. Rose's car broke down and Davis was lagging in 14th position. Suddenly Moore flagged Davis and put Rose in the car. Rose came from behind to win the race, Bergere finishing 5th. "Davis was tickled to get out of it," Moore said. "He was white as a sheet. I knew nothing was wrong with the car, and Rose proved it. After the race, Davis acted like he was sore."

In August 1946 the Blue Crown Spark Plug Company advanced Moore some money to help pay for cars. Lou mortgaged his home for the rest, hired draftsmen who knew nothing about automobiles because he could not afford experts, and built 2 front-drive cars. "Now I'm glad I couldn't get automobile draftsmen, because they'd know what I got in the cars," he said. "Those other birds wouldn't know a wrist pin from a wrist watch, so I don't have to worry about them telling." At that time he tried to sell a half interest in the Blue Crown, but no one was interested—until after he won. Then *he* wasn't interested, even though 2 front-drives cost him $62,500 to build—3 times what competing cars cost in those days.

Moore's competitors laid his success to a combination of things. Frank Kurtis, then an Indy chassis maker, said, "Lou put his cars together like a watch and apparently found a winning combination of gear and compression ratios. He rehearsed his pit crews in speedy fueling and tire changing during workouts, and it paid off in the race." Moore personally could change a tire in as little as 10 seconds; he also personally checked the Indianapolis weather bureau for the humidity at the track in order to adjust his carburetors for exactly the right mixture of fuel and air. He thought of everything because he thought of almost nothing else all year.

Moore insisted on complete obedience from his drivers—which was why he split with Mauri Rose, a 2-time winner, after the 1949 race. Rose violated orders, disabling his machine by "driving like mad when he had nothing to gain." Teammate Bill Holland was a mile ahead of Rose with only 25 more to go and Rose, in turn, was 5 miles ahead of Kurtis's Johnny Parsons. "Rose couldn't have caught Holland, and he had nothing to fear from Parsons," Moore said. Moore claimed he signaled Rose to slow down, but the driver poured it on instead, losing a sure 2nd place by breaking down 18 miles from the finish. At the end of the race Moore and Rose decided to end the association that had made Rose a winner in 1947 and 1948.

After Rose left, Moore lost his winning touch, and much more quickly then he had gained it. To be fair about it, Mauri did not do much without Lou. The last Moore-built car, for Jim Rathmann, about 1952, failed to make the field. Moore, however, was fairly well-to-

do, and he spent his time travelling to races as a spectator. He died of a heart attack in Atlanta after watching an especially thrilling NASCAR Grand National.

SILVIO MOSER

Silvio Moser came from Ticino, the only one of the 13 Swiss cantons that is almost completely Italian, and therefore his personal racing colors were not the red and white Switzerland but blue and red, the colors of Ticino. Silvio at one time expected to make those colors familiar on GP winning cars, an ambition he never achieved although he kept trying while pursuing a varied driving career. Born in 1941, Moser was 20 when he first drove a competitive car, but it was far from an international race, only a local snow slalom, with a 5th-place finish driving a Volvo 122S. With the same car he won his class in the Mont Ventoux hillclimb and followed this with another class victory and 2nd overall in the Coupe de Paris at Montlhéry. Switching to a more powerful Jaguar XK 120, he won in class once and took a pair of 2nds that same season.

In 1962, his racing started in earnest with a Lotus 20 Formula Junior car. As befitting a beginner, Moser concentrated on Swiss and northern Italian events, both hillclimbs and circuit racing. For the season the Lotus won once, finished 2nd twice and notched a 4th. In 1963 Silvio again sallied forth in the FJ Lotus; winning in class twice (and a 3rd time in a borrowed Brabham

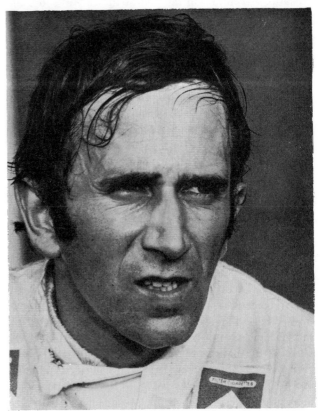

419

Junior) and scoring a 3rd and two 4ths in hillclimbs, and taking a 5th at Montlhéry in his best circuit appearance. He must have liked the Brabham, because for 1964 the young Lugano garageman purchased one of the Australian cars and headed for the Temporada Argentina series in February and March.

Moser won all 4 races in the Brabham and was rewarded by the Brabham factory upon his return to Europe by having the car converted to the new Formula 3 specifications to race for the remainder of the season. The first time out, at Garda, the F3 Brabham was pushed home in the lead by Silvio, after a 9th-place finish in his preliminary heat. At Monaco, the day before the major Grand Prix, Moser won his F3 heat, then finished 2nd in the final to the winner of the initial heat. Two weeks later Silvio started his 1st Formula 2 race at Avusrunnen in Berlin; his de Sanctis-Ford was 6th behind the more powerful Cosworth-engined Lotuses, Coopers, and Brabhams.

In 1964 Moser won F3 races at Clermont-Ferrand (International Cup), Zolder (Grand Prix), and Monza (City of Bergamo Trophy Race), and took 5 hillclimbs with international ranking. At the wheel of an Alfa Romeo Tubolare TZ, he also took the 3-hour Inter-Europe Cup Race, held prior to the Italian GP in September, and his class at Montlhéry's 1000, among others. The following season was his initial North American appearance at Sebring; he smashed up an Iso Grifo after a brake failure at a critical turn. In 1965 he again drove the F3 Brabham and a new Cosworth-engined F2 Brabham. It was in the latter machine that Moser won at Rosario, Argentina, in the 2nd of the early 1966 Temporada Series, his best showing that season.

In 1967 Moser got his 1st competitive ride in a Formula 1 car at the British GP in a Cooper-ATS, but failing oil pressure retired him on the 30th of 80 laps. He got another GP shot the following season in an ex-Piers Courage Brabham-Repco BT24 and was 5th in the Dutch GP, but unclassified in the British. In the same car in 1969, a snapped drive shaft universal joint kayoed Moser at the Monaco GP. At the Dutch race, he crashed in practice, but managed to start the next day at the rear of the pack and lasted well past the halfway mark until the steering failed. In the French GP he was 7th, through running mostly on fumes the last 3 laps.

At Monza in the Italian GP, Moser's engine deserted him 9 laps into the race. At Mosport in the Canadian GP, local boy Al Pease's elderly Eagle-Climax—the original Dan Gurney car—bumped Silvio on the opening lap and knocked him (literally) out of the race. Pease later repeated the feat with Jean-Pierre Beltoise and one or 2 others and was black-flagged off the course, although that did not make Moser feel any better. In the U.S. GP at Watkins Glen Moser had his best GP race ever, despite blowing a water hose off when, with a minute to go and all engines going, a 20-minute postponement was called. Patched up, Moser started from last place in a field of 18 and finished 6th. At Mexico, the

patched-up car lasted only 60 of the 65 laps, but was classified 11th although it did not finish the race. He was running around 6th for most of the action up to the time his car quit.

There was some cause for hope, then, that Silvio could do better with a competitive car. In 1970 he formed his own 1-car team and, working with Bellasi, a small Italian manufacturer, a Formula 1 car was constructed. Moser tried to qualify this car in various European Grands Prix 6 times. He made a single race, Austria, but was retired early. In the other 5, the car would not just go fast enough even to make the field. Bellasi slunk back to sports-car production and an occasional F3 mount in 1971, realizing that it just did not have the resources to make Moser's own valiant attempt to go GP racing a success.

MIKE MOSLEY

A. J. Watson had not had a Championship Trail victory in 6 years, ever since the Triple W combination of Watson, car owner Bob Wilke, and driver Rodger Ward had formed the Leader Card team. Johnny Rutherford gave him that 1965 victory at Atlanta. Now A. J.'s crew cut was gray verging on white. The youngster he had chosen to win for Ralph Wilke, the current car owner, was progressing quite well. Mike Mosley was his name and all agreed that this young man was a star of the future. But that did not bring the brass ring today.

Watson had picked Mike in 1968, when he was 24, because Watson liked kids who could go fast in sprint races and still look smooth; Mosley had progressed steadily upward. Before that Mosley had been given a ride in a backup car to Bobby Unser in the initial race held at Michigan International Speedway. Mike was leading the race by a lap when he was called in and his car was turned over to Unser. Mike did not get close to the winner's circle in the years that followed.

Mosley was a strange race driver. Born in California, December 13, 1944, he grew up around LaPuente. He was shy and introverted, spoke very few words in a voice hardly audible. But when he got near a race car, it was as if he released his emotions in the way he drove. Not especially tall, he had curly hair and the kind of open face that one associates with choir boys. And although the compulsion to drive race cars struck early in life, there was a strange lack of real confidence in his own abilities. In the face of the fact that he had moved up to 9th place on the Championship Trail in 1969 and to 4th in 1970 with 2 third-place finishes—at Langhorne and at Trenton, his best showings of the season—he would never say he was going to win.

Now Watson and Mosley and the G. C. Murphy Watson Offy were at Trenton, N.J., for the $76,000 Trentonian 200 that would be viewed by a live television audience. It was 1971, April, and he was practicing as fast, and more steadily, than the likes of Unser, An-

420

dretti, and Ruby. But he still had no confidence even after becoming one of 4 to break Bobby Unser's old track qualifying record. "There was no way I thought I could win," he said. "Once the race starts Bobby and Al and Mario just shoot out and you have to fight to stay close. It's better to drive a steady race and finish."

The Trenton race track, which is really in neighboring Hamilton Township on the Jersey State Fairgrounds, is a mile track with a half-mile loop in its back end to make it 1.5 miles. It is particularly hard on USAC machinery and it is a difficult track for the drivers, too. It poses problems in suspension setup, in finding the correct line, and in staying close to that "groove." The April race, when cars are still being shaken down for the Indy 500, is particularly trying.

The 1971 race was no different. Bobby Unser sprinted to the lead from the pole position but brother Al passed him early in the 2nd lap. Andretti was a close 3rd then but on the 9th lap he pushed his McNamara Ford into the lead. Mario stayed in front all the way through the 6 laps of caution after Roger McCluskey spun into the wall. Then cars began to drop out faster—Al Unser, Mark Donohue, and then on the 35th lap Andretti suddenly slowed and coasted into the pits, followed almost immediately by Bobby Unser. Mike Mosley was leading, a lead that had stretched to 2 laps over Lloyd Ruby after the 1st refueling stop. But on the 107th lap Ruby tangled with young Don Brown and both were out. Steve Krisiloff was 2nd 3 laps back. Watson had been signalling Mosley the "E-Z" sign, but the youngster had not slowed much since his car was handling so well. In anticipation of the green flag he accelerated a bit early and spun. Krisiloff, bunched up for

the caution laps, had nowhere to go but over Mosley's right front wheel and into the fence. Mike fought his car straight and sped into the pits for inspection. He had been lucky. The Watsonized Eagle chassis had suffered no damage. Mike rolled back out on the track to an easy victory. The brass ring at last!

When the Watson team came to Indianapolis in 1971, Mosley was still quiet but he was driving with much confidence—maybe too much, the railbirds snickered, because during practice he brushed the wall several times and in qualifying he crashed 2 cars inside of 30 minutes, walking away from both without injury. Then he got into the Watsonized Eagle and qualified easily. It seemed to be the steady Mosley of before moving up through the ranks as attrition and mechanical ills of competitors allowed. Then on the 165th lap, entering the 4th turn, Mike's No. 4 G. C. Murphy Special went out of control hitting both inside and outside walls and finally dive-bombing a group of abandoned race cars. Mosley struggled to get out as firemen—on the spot immediately—sprayed his wreck to prevent fire from consuming him. It took a pair of wreckers pulling in opposite directions to allow rescue workers to lift him out. Again he was lucky—lucky to be alive with a broken arm, a broken leg, and minor burns on his face and hands. He had not seen his friend Gary Bettenhausen halt his car during the accident and fall down in his haste to get to Mike's wreck. He seemed grateful when told about it, but it could be seen there was nothing on his mind but getting back into a race car. "A tire blew," he said of the accident. "I must have run over some debris. That can happen any time, I guess."

Mosley was at Pocono in a wheelchair to see the new superspeedway in 1971 and watch where the groove was. There was a hunger in his eyes in unguarded moments, the hunger of a man who knew what victory tasted like now and wanted more. A. J. Watson grinned when asked about it. "That kid's going to be something before he's through, "and I think I'll enjoy watching." But for Mosley it was obvious that he would only count himself lucky when he was sitting in Victory Lane.

Mosley returned with a great hunger to the 1972 Trail. But his determination was often more than his car could take. He crashed on the 56th lap at Indianapolis, then missed Pocono. But at Ontario Mike led 26 laps in his Eagle Offy and was battling eventual winner Roger McCluskey for the lead when on the 195th lap his engine began to smoke. He backed off and finished the McLaren Offy 5th.

STIRLING MOSS

When a man has driven in 466 major auto races and won 194 of them, is it possible to single out one race as his greatest? Probably not. But everyone is entitled to his opinion, and Stirling Moss, the driver in question,

usually points to the Monaco Grand Prix of May 14, 1961. That was the year that America's Phil Hill won the World Championship with only 2 victories in Grands Prix; Moss won 2 races also, but he didn't even make it to 2nd in the standings.

Moss liked driving British; that is, British cars rather than Continental marques. He didn't always feel that way, but in 1961 he did. So Monaco found Stirling in a year-old 4-cylinder Lotus-Climax owned by Rob Walker. The car had been stripped and rebuilt, but it still produced only 152 h.p., while Hill, Wolfgang von Trips and Richie Ginther, the Ferrari team drivers, had 180 to 190 h.p. derived from 8 cylinders. They were the pre-race favorites. That race covered the streets of Monte Carlo, of course, which negated some Ferrari power; but Hill and the others were experienced GP drivers, and over the 100 laps that made up the race Moss would have to contend with each of them, as well as the rest of the field.

In the early going it was Ginther who took the lead, Moss only gaining the upper hand on lap 14, with Jo Bonnier surprisingly close behind in a Porsche. Ginther fell back, presumably on team orders, to give Hill and von Trips a chance. On lap 32 he got the signal to go ahead, and easily repassed Wolfgang. On lap 41 he passed Bonnier. On lap 75 he passed Hill and was now in contention with Moss once more. By lap 81 Ginther's powerful Ferrari was trailing Moss by a mere 4 seconds; that he should pass seemed inevitable at this rate, but it was never to happen. Stirling Moss, shy almost 40 h.p. to Ginther, found power somewhere—perhaps it was

sheer will power. Ginther ran a 73.480 lap, but Moss tied it on the 85th. When the checker fell, Stirling had beaten the powerful Ferrari team single-handed, Ginther trailing by 3.6 seconds.

Stirling Craufurd Moss was born September 17, 1929, the first child of a champion horsewoman and a London dentist-racing driver who even made it to Indianapolis (16th in 1924, 13th in 1925). At 6 Moss could steer a car, and by 14 he was an expert driver in his own Morgan 3-wheeler. School bored him, although his potential brillance was apparent. He also was, suprisingly, sickly as a lad, suffering not only the usual ailments but such things as scarlet fever, nephritis and appendicitis. When school ended he joined a hotel management apprentice program, but left it, joined a farmer apprentice program, but left that one, too. Moss the hotel man? Moss the farmer? Wise decisions to quit those.

But what then? He was an expert horseman; he and his sister Pat used to shut out all other contestants at horse shows, winning every event between themselves. However, there was no real career in that. Perhaps auto racing? He could drive rather well, but he'd never competed in a single race because 18 was the age at which it was legal to start. Moss's parents didn't like the idea and said so. It was no career, they said; it was too hard to make a living at it. A perfectly sane and completely accurate statement of fact in 1946–47. A battle raged at the Moss homestead when Stirling's decision was made. But he stuck to it.

"I firmly believe," he said later, "that a man can do whatever he really sets his mind to doing. I believe that if I wanted to run a 4-minute mile hard enough, I would be able to do it. It would take complete dedication, complete shutting out of everything else in my life, but I could do it. Frankly," he laughed, "I'm so rabid on this idea that I can say to you with an absolutely straight face that I believe that if a man believed hard enough, and excluded everything else from his life, he could walk on water. I mean it. I'm not kidding."

Moss didn't walk on water, but he did become a racing driver at first chance. The cars he'd owned had been fairly ordinary: an Austin 7, the Morgan (technically a motorcycle under British taxing law), an MG and a BMW 328. The BMW was sold one day in 1948, and Stirling announced that the proceeds—exactly £1000 —were going to be spent for a Cooper Formula 3. After one last attempt to dissuade him, his parents capitulated, and he was on his way to the kitchen-sized garage that was the Cooper factory in those days. He hovered over the Coopers like a mother hawk guarding her young; each piece that went into the building of his racing car was examined, and some were discarded or machined down at Moss's insistence. Even then, a rather fresh 18-year-old, he knew that weight meant as much in winning races as power.

When the car was almost ready, Stirling mailed an entry form to the sanctioning body for the famed Shelsley Walsh hillclimb: "S. Moss, Cooper 500." The application was returned with a polite note of apology; all the berths were taken, so Shelsley lost a moment of fame. The Bugatti Owners' Club was holding a climb at Prescott May 9, 1948, and Moss's application was accepted. He didn't win that initial time out, but he did finish 4th and was fastest in his class. On June 5 he ran his 2nd event, the Stanmer Park hillclimb, sponsored by the Brighton & Hove Motor Club, and won the day. July 4 was a day to remember for Moss because he won his initial official circuit race at Brough at 48.90 m.p.h. —significantly, in the rain. Stirling also won a couple of speed trials and 3 more hillclimbs that 1st season of competition, including Shelsley Walsh in the fall.

The family was solidly behind him from the 1st start, of course, initial reluctance not withstanding. Their old Rolls-Royce became the tow car, and a horse van was converted into a trailer. His father supplied technical and management services, his mother the catering during race trips, while Pat, still a young girl, filled the number one fan role inspite of the usual brother-sister arguments and jealousies. Stirling's winnings that 1st year were £13 and a pint presentation tankard. A career that has been equalled by few men before or since was under way.

For 1949 a new 2-cylinder Cooper was purchased. All the previous season's races had been close to home, but now Stirling branched out. He won the Goodwood Easter Handicap, running the fastest lap. He won the British Grand Prix 500-c.c. race, again with the fastest lap. He won a hillclimb and was 2nd in 2 more. An invitation arrived, and was quickly accepted, for Moss to run in a race at Garda in Brescia, Italy. His expenses were defrayed; the Italians thought it would be good for a laugh to see this English boy wonder, pink-cheeked, curly-haired, with his little car. But Moss was 3rd in his heat—3rd overall, against people like Luigi Villoresi. Tazio Nuvolari was watching from the sidelines and pronounced him a future great. Moss was back on the Continent in July at Zandvoort, Holland, to win the 500-c.c. race. The Silverstone International, in which he took 2nd, was followed by still another Continental race, the Prix du Leman Formula B battle, in which Stirling retired but was awarded a gold cup for the most meritorious performance. He rounded off 1949 with 3 victories in hillclimbs and at Goodwood back in Britain.

As early as 1950 Moss demonstrated the versatility that set him apart from most other drivers. Where a Fangio might be king in the Grand Prix cars (and Moss himself always considered Fangio the best) Juan won relatively few sports car races; while someone like Olivier Gendebien might be a standout in sports cars but never that fast in the GP series. Moss was fast, and a winner, in whatever form of racing he undertook. Next to Fangio, if you will, he was the greatest GP driver of his era and one of the greatest of all time. He was also one of the all-time great sports car racers, winning every

important race you could mention except Le Mans, and this was true from the earliest days of his career.

In 1950 Moss drove 6 different cars. For example, he drove an 1100 c.c. Cooper to 2nd place at Goodwood's Easter meeting, then switched to an HWM 2-litre that same day for the 1st time and was 6th. In his 500-c.c. Cooper he had problems the 1st couple of times out, then won his heat at the Silverstone International. At Mons in the HWM he was 7th; at Monte Carlo he won both his heat and the final in the Cooper. The HWM continued to plague him, but with the Cooper he won twice at Brands Hatch, then twice again that same day in another set of starts. The Cooper was 6th at Rheims, but he got the HWM up to 3rd in another race the same day. At Bari the HWM was 3rd, and at Naples it finally won a race. The Cooper won at Brands Hatch, the HWM ran a record lap but retired at Bremgarten. On the same day at Silverstone the HWM was 6th, the Cooper 1st. At Mettet Moss was 2nd with the HWM; the next weekend he stepped into a competition Jaguar for the 1st time and won the RAC Tourist Trophy at Dunrod. The following day his Cooper 500 won at Brands Hatch. The HWM was 3rd at Perigeaux, 7th at Goodwood, but on the same day his Cooper came in 2nd. At Castle Combe Moss won 3 straight in the Cooper and a 2-litre Frazer-Nash. He retired from a Garda race in the HWM; and a week later set a new 24-hour record at Montlhéry in the 3.5-litre Jaguar at 107.46 m.p.h. To close out 1950 he ran a rally, finishing without penalty.

In 1951 Moss drove such varied machines as a Morris Minor (in a night trial), an HWM, a Jaguar, a Kieft F3 racer, a Frazer-Nash, and a Formula 2 Ferrari—his 1st ride in a non-British car, which he retired with bad brakes. His victories that year included the Lavant Cup at Goodwood, the Silverstone International, the Goodwood International, Aix-les-Bains, the Empire Trophy race on the Isle of Man, the 500-c.c. race preceding the British GP at Silverstone, the Zandvoort 500-c.c. race, the Freiburg hillclimb, the Wakefield and O'Brien Trophy races in Dublin, the Tourist Trophy, 3 Goodwood sports car races on the same day, Winfield, and 3 Brands Hatch 500-c.c. races on the same day. That same season Stirling set a lap record at Le Mans, but retired with engine failure, and crashed in the Mille Miglia.

As the fifties rolled by, his versatility and his won-lost record continued to startle those who followed racing. His bag included such varied things as a 2nd in the 1952 Monte Carlo Rally in a Sunbeam Talbot, a class victory in the Alpine Rally that same year, victory in the Rheims 12-hour race in 1953 in an XK 120C Jaguar, another Tourist Trophy victory that same year, victory in the Sebring 12-hour race in an OSCA (of all things) in 1954, and an epic 1955 Mille Miglia victory with Denis Jenkinson, the racing writer, in a Mercedes Benz 300SLR at 97.80 m.p.h.

The years continued with a British GP victory with

Mercedes in 1955; still another Tourist Trophy victory, shared with John Fitch, that same year in a 300SLR; a Targa Florio victory as well, shared with Peter Collins; a New Zealand GP victory in 1956 in a Maserati 250F with a Porsche Spyder victory that same day in the sports car race at the same circuit; a Buenos Aires 1000 victory; his initial Monaco GP victory in a Maserati in 1956; a Nurburgring 1000 victory, an Italian GP victory, and victories in the Venezuelan sports car GP and the Australian F1 GP in 1956; a Vanwall victory in the 1957 British GP and another in the Italian race. In 1958 there were an Argentine GP victory for Cooper; 1st place in the sports car Cuban GP that year; victory in both the Dutch GP for Vanwall and the Nurburgring 1000 for Aston Martin within the same week in 1958; winning the Goodwood version of the Tourist Trophy for Aston; winning the Moroccan GP for Vanwall; and winning the Melbourne GP for Cooper. In 1959 he captured the Nurburgring race still again for Aston Martin, the Goodwood Tourist Trophy, the Italian GP in a Cooper-Climax, and the modern U.S. GP precursor—the Watkins Glen GP—in the Cooper in 1959.

Moss was usually a favorite each year to capture the World Championship, created in 1950. But there was the short, squat Argentinian named Juan Manuel Fangio, with whom Stirling established a strange friendship that was a rivalry at the same time. Moss was great on the GP circuit, but Fangio was always just a bit better. His edge was attributed to many things, including Moss's rather poor choice of cars, especially his decision to go British whenever possible. This was partly due to an early, albeit unwitting, snub by Enzo Ferrari, and partly because Moss rather enjoyed the role of underdog. "Better to lose honorably in a British car than win in a foreign one," he once said. Whether he ever really regretted that decision he never said. It was probably just something that sounded good at that moment; and anyway, Moss won more than anyone else, thanks to his versatility.

He often said things that sounded good and psyched his opponents. After he retired from racing, Stirling admitted that he wasn't all that keen about racing in the rain, but, when he smacked his lips and rubbed his hands together in glee at the prospect of racing in a downpour, many of his opponents were unsettled. Before a race, most drivers betray some signs of nervousness, even if it is only a desire to be left completely alone. Moss never did. Rather, he was a picture of absolute calm—smiling, chatting (but never too much). He used to chuckle at the way Mercedes handled the psychological aspects of racing. "They used to enter 3 cars," Moss recalled, "then go around asking people who they thought would be 4th!"

Moss was a great individualist, but drove for teams. In 1950 he joined HWM, which wasn't really very competitive, but because it was a British team he stayed until the end of 1951 and even drove a few 1952 races while his new team, ERA, made the finishing touches to his new car. ERA was a complete failure, and Moss switched to Cooper-Alta, again without success. He drove a factory Connaught on occasion in 1952–53, then bought his own Maserati 250F in 1954. Meanwhile, he was a member of the Jaguar sports car team in 1951–54. While his private Maser wasn't much, he did well enough to be offered a Maserati team berth, and he accepted since there was no British car available worth his talents. In 1955 he accepted a Mercedes team berth to serve as 2nd to Fangio. Fangio won the world title, of course, with Moss 2nd. The important thing, though, was the polish that Fangio brought to his natural talents, and the great respect that grew up between the two greatest drivers of their day. When Mercedes quit racing after the Le Mans tragedy, Maserati was glad to welcome Moss back. He was 2nd again in the season's standings. For 1957 a British car appeared for him, Vanwell, developed by Tony Vandervell's group after his frustrations with Ferrari-based Thinwall Specials. Moss was 2nd again in the standings, both that season and the next (in 1958 by a single point) with Vanwall. Meanwhile, he was racing Aston Martin team sports cars, continuing with this marque through 1959, the same year he joined Rob Walker.

Walker's private GP entries were Lotuses and Coopers; the individual effort against the teams appealed to the cavalier in Moss, and though he occasionally drove other top machines—BRM furnished him some cars in 1959 through BRP—between 1959 and 1962 he acted as an independent affiliated with Walker. In 1959 Moss was 3rd in the championship tables; later he admitted that about 1958 or 1959 he had accepted the fact that he probably would never win the World Championship. "I would have liked to win," he said. "But what would it actually have proven? If I won it 2 to 3 times, or even 6 times, would it have proven I was the better driver than Fangio in F1? I think not. He was the best at that kind of racing, and I was almost as good. I think I was best, then, and perhaps for all time, in sports cars. I just wish that races like the Canadian-American Challenge Cup series and the present long-distance enduros were run while I was active. I would have liked that, and I think I would have won my share of them."

In 1960 Moss suffered his first really serious crash, at Spa, the track against which the GP drivers finally revolted in 1971. (They were led then by Jackie Stewart, acknowledged as the best of his day as Fangio and Moss were in theirs.) Moss broke both his legs, but the youth who had been sickly was now a medical marvel. Belgian doctors said that he was through for that season, that he would have to remain within a plaster body cast for up to 6 months. Back in Britain, the doctors said it was so if he was to heal with a minimum of pain; but he had the option of getting out of the cast within a month, and rebuilding himself, but with great pain.

He chose the quick and dirty route, was bicycling to build his strength within a few weeks, and was back in the cockpit in time to win that season's U.S. GP. Not to mention the Rand and South African Grands Prix at year's end, and sports and GT races in Europe, Nassau, and America.

If 1961 was the year of that finest race—the Monaco GP—Moss at 31 undoubtedly was just entering his peak period, with good expectations for another 5 to 10 seasons. Consider that 1961 season carefully. In the Tasman series Moss won the New Zealand GP's initial heat, retired with a broken half-shaft in the final. He was 2nd in the Lady Wigram, won the Warwick Farm International. At Sebring he was 4th in the 4-hour preliminary, then ran the fastest lap before retiring in the 12-hour race. On the same April day he won the Lavant Cup and Sussex Trophy, was 3rd in the Fordwater Trophy, 4th in the Glover Trophy in 4 different cars. In 3 heats of the Brussels GP he ran 14th, 8th and 2nd, running the fastest lap in the last heat as he got used to his Lotus mount. He won the Vienna GP, then captured the Aintree sports car race in a different Lotus. Magneto trouble held Moss to an 8th at Syracuse; his Targa Florio ended when his Porsche broke its differential (he was in the lead at the time, 8 laps from overall victory).

Moss won the Silverstone International and a sports car race on the same May day. The Monaco GP victory came next, then a 4th in the Dutch GP, an 8th (but class victory) in the Nurburgring 1000. He won at Brands Hatch, retired at Le Mans with a broken water pipe when the fan blade flew off his GP Ferrari. Moss was 8th in the Belgian GP, won both heats of the Players 200 at Mosport Park in Canada, was knocked out of the French GP when Phil Hill ran into him in the pit area. In July he won both the Empire Trophy and a Silverstone sports car race on the same day, but retired from the British GP and the Solitude GP. He then won the European GP at Nurburgring, won at Brands Hatch, took the Tourist Trophy at Goodwood, the Karlskoga sports car race, and the 3 heats of the Danish GP.

He won the Modena GP, was retired in the Italian GP, and won the Oulton Gold Cup. At the Canadian GP he was 3rd, despite running the fastest lap; retired from the U.S. GP; was leading at Riverside in a sports car GP until his brakes gave out, but managed to coast in 16th. That same day, sharing a tiny Alpine with Jack Brabham, he was 1st in class in the Riverside 3-hour race. He won both heats of the Pacific GP at Laguna Seca, the Nassau Tourist Trophy, and was 2nd in the Natal and South African Grands Prix.

He began 1962 with a victory in the New Zealand GP, turning the fastest lap. At Levin, Moss was 2nd to Brabham by 100 yards when the race was called unexpectedly because of rain, after 9 of 28 scheduled laps. Stirling won the Lady Wigram, was 2nd at Teretonga,

won at Warwick Farm in the Tasman series. Moss was 4th overall and 1st in the Touring class at Daytona in the 3-hour Continental. He flew back to Australia to finish 3rd at Sandown Park, came back to Florida for another 3rd in the 3-hour at Sebring, ran the fastest lap there in the 12-hour but was disqualified in a dispute over the rules regarding refueling. In Europe Moss was 2nd in the Brussels GP and 7th at Snetterton, despite setting lap records at both courses. Than came April 23, 1962, the day of the 100-mile Glover Trophy race at Goodwood.

In the early going Moss ran the fastest lap—105.37 m.p.h.—in conjunction with Surtees, then pitted. Coming out of the pits, he was 17th, thanks to many minutes spent trying to repair a jammed gearbox. Graham Hill led the race, 3 full laps in front of Moss's car. He worked his way to 9th, but it was apparent that he could not win that day. Stirling was having his "bloody go" anyway. On lap 35 he roared into a right-left job called St. Mary's Corner, much too fast, apparently trying to pass Hill on the outside; actually the car was out of control. It went straight onto the grass, plowed a furrow 150 feet long, hit an 8-foot-high earthen bank, and crumpled into a ditch, a mass of wreckage.

Moss was still inside the car. His face was covered with blood, his uniform stained with it. Moss's ribs were crushed by the steering wheel (which is a prize exhibit in his London home today), the battery wedged between his legs, the gas tank sitting in his lap. His left knee was fractured, his left shoulder torn, two ribs crushed. It required 40 stitches to close his facial wounds. The real damage was internal, in the brain. One eye drooped ominously. He was in a coma, of course. His left side was partially paralyzed, and when he came out of the coma it was slow to react.

But that magnificent will—the will to walk on water, if you remember—was unimpaired, and Moss would not accept any verdict about partial recovery. Two months after the crash, he left the hospital on crutches. A month after that he was walking without crutches, using his left hand to shake hands to strengthen it, headed for Nassau and the sun to rebuild his weakened body. He ran a car on a country road in leisurely fashion, and decided he would drive again after all. The rebuilding job was intensified. He flew around the world, fulfilling some business commitments as well as testing himself in innumerable ways. On May 1, 1963, he again stepped into a racing car, at Goodwood, in a private session. He ran around the deserted, wet circuit for half an hour. When he returned he said simply, "I am retiring."

"I had to think about everything I used to do automatically," he said later. "Brake, downshift, look at the rev counter, and watch the road, too. But I couldn't do it any more, and I couldn't do anything automatically any more. It was evident I wasn't competitive any more. I was at eight-tenths, not nine-tenths where you have to be able to win consistently. Maybe it would have come back more in time; I doubt it. Naturally I have had regrets, especially as motor racing has grown so rich and varied. I made top dollar in my day. Today I'd still make the top sum, but it would be many times as much. Today, with the business involvements that are possible, it would be many, many times more."

But Moss had no money worries, despite his remaining in Britain where the taxes are scandalously high; he had not fled to Switzerland or America as other drivers did. He worked in America regularly as the front man for Johnson Wax's CanAm effort until 1972. All of his income had been built after his retirement, for unlike most top drivers, he was so dedicated to his racing that there were no deals, no garages, no clothing lines, no side businesses while Moss actually was racing. But with the material success, and the restlessness that his enforced retirement brought with it, Moss has had some personal problems. His initial marriage ended in divorce, as did his next. But he was a devoted father, and not all that unhappy to be unattached. He liked his London bachelor house, a gadget-filled home behind the Hilton Hotel, and even enjoyed such things as shopping in the supermarket.

"I doubt that I ever will not regret how things turned out," he said in the early seventies. "Perhaps when I am 60 I might accept the fact that I stopped driving involuntarily; perhaps not. So far there has been nothing that has replaced the life that I once led. No business or other involvement has replaced motor racing in my life. I was very lucky to be a racing driver, of course. Lucky, too, I suppose to have lived through that Goodwood thing. I have travelled all over the world, met all kinds of people, faced all kinds of situations. My life was a series of races and parties in the old days. I was in races to beat other men, not to win championships—and that is not rationalization—for I loved the exhilaration of trying to defeat the other man."

If Monte Carlo, 1961, was his greatest GP race, perhaps the Mille Miglia, 1955, was his greatest sports car race. It was shared with Denis Jenkinson, the British racing journalist. Stirling viewed Denis as the type of navigator he needed for this race over the country roads of Italy: a man who was confident enough in Moss's ability and accustomed enough to speed to keep his mind on a map while the car was speeding over the brows of hills and around blind curves at 170 m.p.h. or more, a man ready to chance placing his entire life in Moss's hands.

Jenkinson was such a man. And like Moss, he was intrigued with the idea of a non-Italian winning this spectacular road race; the only other man ever to do it was Rudi Caracciola, who was German despite his name. It would be impossible to memorize the 1,000 miles of road unless one had driven it 13 years like Taruffi; but a map, drawn laboriously over several practice runs, could fill in the gaps. The driver couldn't follow his race on a map, but a bold navigator could. With hand signals—since they were in an open car, talk was impossible—the navigator could let the driver know whether to go right or left just ahead, even if he couldn't see the road at that instant. Of course, the driver had to have complete confidence in the navigator's ability as well; he was, in effect, placing his life in the map-reader's hands just as much as the navigator was in his driving.

Moss had that kind of confidence in Jenkinson, which built up even further as they practiced together. They constructed a 17-foot-long map of the route that rolled up in a plastic tube and could be played out like aluminum foil from its box. Twice they crashed during practice; once a truck suddenly pulled out of a blind spot and the Moss-Jenkinson car ran smack into it. It was full of bombs for the Italian Air Force, but no explosion followed. After such an adventure, the race almost might be said to be anticlimactic. Moss and Jenkinson won. During the 1,000 miles Denis's glasses were blown overboard, and he had to squint furiously to read the map, but he never once misread the route. He missed a signal only once, when they were pulling away from a refueling depot and an overly filled tank sloshed a pint of fuel down his back. Moss said later, "I might have finished the race without Denis, but I most certainly could not have won without him."

There was a celebration, of course, and when it was over and most people were dragging themselves off to bed, Moss drove another 100 miles or more to Stuttgart, Germany, to pay a courtesy call; then to Cologne to catch a plane back to Britain. Stirling's energy was fabulous, and always on nothing stronger than Coke. Despite his reputation as a playboy, he rarely took alcoholic beverages, rarely smoked, rarely did anything that would interfere with his driving skills. He lived on the fine edge, enjoyed life immensely, wore out people less dedicated than he and less able to keep up with his unique life. Fortunately he didn't wear himself out, off or on the course, and whether he might have viewed Goodwood, 1962, as a good or bad thing, we still have in one piece with us a unique man named Stirling Craufurd Moss.

LOTHAR MOTSCHENBACHER

Lothar Motschenbacher once saw his future in his father's truck repair business in West Germany. He had performed his 1st solo brake job at the age of 11 and was as proud as a boy who had just come in 1st in the town foot race. But at 13 he was apprenticed to Daimler Benz in order to become a master mechanic, and his horizons expanded to racing cars.

"The mechanics who worked in the racing department were heroes to us," the blond Motschenbacher said. "We wanted to be like them and our dream was to be good enough and lucky enough to work in the competition department. We couldn't even conceive of wanting

to be drivers—Juan Fangio, John Fitch, Stirling Moss, Karl Kling, Olivier Gendebien—they were a million miles above our heads. One day Fangio shook my hand, and I worshipped him. I knew some day I was going to be a racing mechanic no matter what, not go back and take over my father's business."

Life was not easy for an apprentice in the truck repair department who at started work at 7:30 A.M. and worked until the work was done, for $15 a month. The training period lasted 42 months, and at the end there was an 8-day test to become a journeyman with papers to prove it. Lothar shifted to passenger cars after 18 months, and for the last 6 months of his apprenticeship received the coveted assignment of working in the 300SL department.

Eventually, however, he went home to work with his father, but the horizons of the young Motschenbacher, born November 19, 1938, in Cologne, already stretched beyond that city. So in July 1958 he came to the United States, unable to speak a work of English, but confident that if there was a Mercedes shop he would succeed. About 5 hours after arriving in Chicago he had a job in Max Hoffman's Mercedes operation and worked there 18 months until he went home when his mother became ill. In those 18 months he learned English and became associated with many SCCA drivers then driving 300SLs while doing their race preparation. They told him that it was mostly sunny and warm in Southern California. That had also been a goal of his—to get someplace where the weather was good. When his mother's health improved, he returned to the States, stopping in Chicago

only to pick up his tools. He was going to Southern California. Again, he was hired at once when he drove into Hollywood Mercedes; he had taken the precaution of taking a course at the factory in automatic transmissions. However, in 6 months he decided to open his own garage and go racing.

Lothar located in Van Nuys, where he specialized in Mercedes service. In 1962 he launched his competition career in the ex-Ken Miles Dolphin Formula Junior. He moved quickly on to a Lotus 22 with which Peter Arundell had just won the European FJ crown. He won 34 races in 54 starts, meanwhile maintaining his Mercedes business. The next step up was brief ownership of a Cobra 427, 2 victories in 4 races, and from there to Group 7 Sports/Racing in the ex-Parnelli Jones King Cobra in 1965 for a private owner, who ran out of money just before Riverside. For 1966 Motschenbacher decided that the only way for him to go was to own his own car, so he ordered a McLaren Mk. II. It was going to be the old hectic task of preparing, maintaining, and driving the car all by himself. He was aided by becoming the 3rd winner of the Tim Mayer Award, and getting the cash that comes with it.

The McLaren began 1966 USRRC competition with Oldsmobile power and scored a victory at St. Jovite in June. Then he added a 2nd place to Bruce McLaren in the Players 200. In mid-season he gained sponsorship from Nickey Chevrolet. But he still had the Olds engine when he won at Mid-Ohio in Lexington, a twisty 2-mile course. It was not an easy victory, for the best Group 7 machinery in the U.S. and most of the best drivers were competing. John Cannon took the early lead over Lothar and Mark Donohue, but Mark jumped Cannon on the 5th of 85 laps, leaving him and Lothar locked in a nose-to-tail battle for 2nd that lasted 20 laps. When Motschenbacher executed a spectacular inside pass into 2nd place 14 seconds off Donohue's Sunoco Lola's pace, Cannon was finished as a challenger. Unable to cut into Donohue's lead, Lothar kept the pressure on. Finally, only 7 laps from the end, it paid off, for Mark pitted with a flat tire and a failing engine. Donohue came back briefly, but dropped out with mechanical problems. Motschenbacher won; Chuck Parsons, the USRRC point leader, inherited 2nd; and Buck Fulp, the wealthy South Carolina cloth manufacturer, took 3rd. At Road America Lothar saved 4th despite shift linkage woes, and finished 4th in the standings.

Nickey sponsorship came in for the CanAm series, but Lothar rewarded his sponsors with only a 5th place at Stardust in Nevada. Switching from the Olds to the Chevy engine for Monterey did not help the effort. Motschenbacher, however, started fast in the USRRC, winning at Laguna Seca in May. With Valvoline sponsorship in 1967 he added a 5th place at Watkins Glen USRRC, then joined the Dana Chevrolet team to get his hands on a Mark III Lola. He was in an older Dana McLaren when a flat tire cost him 2nd place behind

Mark Donohue at Kent. In the Mid-Ohio race he ran off the road, suffering a cracked rib. Motschenbacher finished a distant 2nd to Donohue in the series standings. The CanAm series was not unrewarding for Lothar that year. Beginning with a 5th at Bridgehampton in the Dana Lola, he came in 9th at Mosport, broke down at Laguna Seca, finished 15th at Riverside, and spun out at Stardust. But his 2 points still got him a piece of the Johnson Wax pot of gold for the point leaders.

Motschenbacher now had a new part of his business to think about. He was becoming a Corvette engine specialist and since he was restricting his racing to CanAm and the USRRC Series, there was time to build up the business. In Mexico City in 1968, he was a top qualifier on Ford power—back on his own—but finished 6th in one of the closest USRRC races ever, only 119 seconds behind. In round 2 at Riverside, Lothar ran out of time trying to overtake Donohue who was nursing a sick McLaren Chevvy, and he finished 2nd again to Mark at Laguna Seca in a nose-to-nose battle for 103 of the race's 152 miles. This was a heartbreaker because Motschenbacher finished less than 2 car lengths back, the best showing to that date for Ford-powered Group 7 machinery. Bridgehampton resulted in a blown engine, and at St. Jovite he was 3rd. Lothar bombed at Kent and Watkins Glen, skipped Road America altogether, but came back to finish 2nd to Donohue in the last USRRC race, the Buckeye 200 at Lexington, Ohio.

By then it was CanAm time again, and Lothar started with a 6th at Road America, and got himself some greeting card sponsorship money by Bridgehampton where he took 3rd. He crashed at Edmonton. He then finished 4th in a Laguna Seca rainstorm, switched his power back to Chevrolet and finished 4th in the sunshine at Riverside. In the finale at Stardust, he was running 2nd when a suspension member broke triggering a 59th-lap multiple crash. He suffered minor burns.

Motschenbacher finished 7th in the 1969 series with two 4th places at Bridgehampton and St. Jovite his best showings. But he had the distinction of having started in every CanAm race. The 1970 season was much kinder to him. Lothar had bought "last year's McLaren" from Team McLaren. He finished 2nd at St. Jovite behind Dan Gurney, 3rd at Edmonton, Mid-Ohio, and Atlanta, 6th at Donnybrooke, and 5th at Riverside, the finale in 1970. They added up to 2nd place in the series and an extra $35,000 in point money.

Although his prospects seemed bright at the series's start, 1971 was not nearly as much fun or nearly as profitable for Lothar. Movie actor Paul Newman came in as a sponsor and Motschenbacher entered several cars for the rich series. At Mosport he was 3rd, at St. Jovite 5th, at Road Atlanta 3rd. So far so good, but Watkins Glen and Mid-Ohio were total loses and a 4th at Road America was his best the rest of the way. It all added up to 5th place in the standings. He did keep his every-CanAm-ever-run record going, though; that was some-

thing of which he could be justly proud.

In 1972 the string ended as ailing Lothar missed the Road Atlanta CanAm. That same season he had a spectacular crash at the same track in his F5000 car, then was seriously burned in a garage fire that November. Derek Bell was named Motschenbacher's F5000 driver for 1973, and it was clear Lothar would turn to management primarily.

RALPH MULFORD

The only Indianapolis 500 for which the Speedway does not have a voluminous scoring and timing record is the 1911 event, allegedly won by hometown hero Ray Harroun and his rear-view mirrored Marmon. There are many who say Ralph Mulford won that race, but was the victim of one of the myriad "prearranged results" of the era, occasioned by a timing mixup that strangely never had 1st place in doubt, even though for a crucial period the scoring stands were emptied of timers, and even though Mulford's Lozier was flagged as the winner.

It may have been the Lozier Company's own fault, because, as racing historian Russ Catlin discovered in his article for *Automobile Quarterly*, Mulford was ordered to take 3 precautionary extra laps after the finish flag. By the time he came around for the 3rd time, the Marmon and Harroun were in the victory circle. Then followed an epic timing squabble. Official results were announced 3 times, and Catlin hints that the final result was announced after Lozier public relations director Charlie Emise reached a closed-door accommodation with the AAA. In fact his implication is that no one will ever know the true finish of that race because the timing wire broke twice and because of the unscored laps.

The episode must be viewed against the background of racing at that time. Promoter Carl Fisher had envisioned the 500 as a means of making his huge investment in the Indianapolis Speedway pay off. He had held bloody and disastrous race programs in 1909 and 1910 and only the awesome munificence of a $25,000 prize had lured the citizens of Indiana back once again. Auto racing was truly factory racing then; each manufacturer competed to gain instant fame for his product and, secondarily, to get direct engineering benefits. If something broke, the manufacturer made it stronger. Most cars were still regional products.

Yet, until Joe Jagersburger in a Case hit the judges' stand—where 200 Indianapolis society men were acting as scorers—the race was obviously a battle between Mulford and Fiat's David Bruce-Brown. The Case emptied the stand, careened down pit row, then bounced back onto the track, where the mechanic was left prostrate on the oily bricks. Harry Knight (in his Westcott) swerved to avoid the man, demolishing pit row and an Apperson parked there.

However, by all accounts the Lozier and the Fiat threaded their way through the debris and continued their battle for the lead. The key question to supporters of the AAA-Indianapolis Speedway version came when Mulford passed the methodical Marmon with 24 laps to go. Was he lapping Harroun or was he merely unlapping himself? Bruce-Brown had been taken out of contention by a late stop to repair his car's spark level and finished 3rd. Mulford insisted even unto 1971 that he had won.

But this kind of thing failed to dim the Mulford star. The AAA declared him its National Champion for 1911. Born in 1885, Ralph was already a national hero when Indy began. His Indianapolis career was illustrious, but he never "won" after that although the records state that he was in the top 10 six times in 9 tries. His next best was 3rd in 1916. He finished 7th in 1913, 9th in 1920 and 1921, and 10th in 1912, the year he was a party to the strangest race ever run there. This was the battle that Ralph DePalma lost to Joe Dawson and started a legend, as he pushed his Mercedes into the pits with less than 5 miles left. Fisher had posted prize money for the first 12 cars to finish the race and only 9 had finished when Howdy Wilcox completing the 500 miles some 10 minutes after the checker dropped for Dawson. As Wilcox finished, there was still one car circling the track, Mulford in his Knox. Ralph had had all sorts of mechanical troubles and had made numerous pit stops, including 2 of more than 35 minutes. He had more than 100 miles to go. Starter Fred Wagner wanted to concede him 10th place, but Fisher refused pointing out that he

would get 10th for going less than 400 miles, while De Palma would get nothing for going 495 miles.

Mulford refueled while the discussion went on, then climbed back into his car and resumed his driving round and round. With 17 laps to go, long after even Fisher and Wagner had left, he pitted for a 20-minute pit stop to eat some fried chicken and rest while the crew fitted softer shock absorbers. Almost 9 hours after the official start Mulford finally completed his 500 miles, earning 10th place money. DePalma earned $380.42 for his effort. Mulford led the race in 1913 in a Mercedes before dropping back because he ran out of gas in the backstretch. Paul Stevens, his mechanic, had to run the mile to the pits to get some fuel. Ralph was the first man to run the race on the same set of tires. In 1914, also on Mercedes, he finished 11th. In 1915, switching to a Duesenberg, he suffered gearbox trouble and did not finish; in 1916 on a Peugeot, he finished 3rd. When racing resumed after a break during World War I Mulford returned in a Frontenac. He lasted 37 laps before the driveshaft broke.

His 9th places in the next 2 years were tributes to his sense of pace. He was 46 and had already gone through what was then a fortune. The fact is that Ralph loved cars and racing so much he was easily swindled. After being swindled out of his primary dream (to build a passenger car called the Mulford), after an encounter with 2 sharp bankers called Fry and Bessalian, and after watching Harry Lozier deprived of his company by Detroit money men, Ralph would not speak to anyone even remotely connected with a bank.

Mulford and the Lozier car—one of the finest pre-World War I American vehicles—are inseparable. Ralph came to work for the company because at 16 he already had made a reputation for himself around Asbury Park, N. J., tuning a Lozier boat engine. It was through Lozier and for Lozier that he became a race driver and king of the 24-hour race. And it was on a Lozier that he won the 1911 Vanderbilt Cup in Savannah, Ga. Ralph was in the winning car in the first 24-hour race in which he ever competed at the Point Breeze track, near Philadelphia, Pa., in June 1907. The 23-year-old salesman-engineer shared that ride with Harry Michener. He won 3 of the 11 major Eastern 24-hour races, missing 2 of them and having his car withdrawn once. He also placed 2nd twice and once was 5th.

In the first 24-hour run at Morris Park in New York City on Labor Day 1907, Ralph lasted 13 hours while Richard Smelzer, his teammate, placed 2nd. Smelzer, however, was fatally injured in the next Morris Park race late in September, and Mulford's car was withdrawn. It was not until September 11–12, 1908, at the Brighton Beach track in Brooklyn, N.Y., that Mulford went back into 24-hour action. His Lozier 6 led a 1, 2 finish in an 11-car field. On October 2–3 the great Barney Oldfield was enticed into riding his first 24 for Stearns, but he was never a factor in the race. Mulford

placed 2nd to George Robertson's Simplex as both broke the old 24-hour record, Robertson going 1,177 miles and Ralph 1,125.

On October 15–16—these races started at about 6 p.m.—Mulford again entered the victory circle at Brighton Beach with a new record of 1,196 miles. It was to be Lozier's last appearance in 24-hour racing and Mulford's next to last. On May 13–14, 1910, Ralph placed 2nd to Poole at Brighton Beach. He was riding a Stearns, one of the many marques with which he had short affiliations.

In the Vanderbilt, Grand Prize, and other road races, Mulford had still another mini-career. In the Grand Prize race of November 26, 1908, Mulford had a short-lived 735-cu. in. racing special. "I found that along the fastest stretch down Dale Avenue our new car could do only 100 m.p.h., not fast enough to stay with the huge Fiats of Wagner and Nazzaro or Hemery's Mercedes, so we were practicing constantly to gain time in the bends," Mulford recalled. Ralph led the 1st lap, later replaced the rear 2 cylinders of his car in a workshop on the course, and got back in the race to finish. He had his initial taste of international competition.

On August 27, 1910, the inaugural Elgin, Ill., road race was held over an 8.5-mile course containing 6 corners and one nasty rise that made cars airborne. Mulford won that 305-mile grind, finishing 12 minutes ahead of the National and setting a World Stock Chassis record time of 62.5 m.p.h. Then, in a November program in Atlanta, Ralph saw his erstwhile mechanic Irish Joe Horan win his first 250-mile feature, after himself winning a sprint and placing 2nd in a 200-mile preliminary (by 3 seconds). Mulford won the 1911 AAA championship with his "2nd" at Indy, a class victory at Fairmount Park in Philadelphia (2nd overall behind Erwin Bergdoll in a 730-cu. in. Benz), and a victory in the Vanderbilt Cup race in Savannah.

"It was obvious the DePalma Mercedes was the fastest car there but I wasn't convinced he could do it for 17 consecutive laps. I was right." Mulford took the lead on the 5th lap and held it the rest of the way, setting fast lap for the race on the final go-around. It was perhaps his and Lozier's greatest victory.

The Grand Prize race only 2 days later found a rebuilt Lozier ready to go. It was so cold in usually balmy Savannah that Mulford and his chain-smoking mechanic, Billy Chandler—who once had a cigarette company make him up smokes with a match on the tip so he could light up at 100 m.p.h.—wore long johns. Again Mulford played a waiting game. On lap 17 he finally moved into 2nd, and on lap 22 the Lozier shot into the lead on the strength of a magnificent 36-second pit stop. But on the last lap the Lozier bounced into the air after hitting the street-car tracks on Ferguson Avenue and snapped its driveshaft. Mulford was a DNF and Bruce-Brown won on a Fiat. That was the last race for Lozier.

In 1912 Ralph moved on to the Knox payroll, as much an engineer as a driver, then on to Duesenberg, Mercedes, Peugeot, Hudson, a fling at making his own cars, Paige, Cleveland, and Chandler. He was a freelancer most of the time, his tremendous ability to diagnose what was wrong with an automobile was invaluable. In 1913 he was working with Duesenberg and, as he told it, Fred Duesenberg asked him to use one Edward Rickenbacher (later Rickenbaker) because the kid was going to be competing before home-town fans in Columbus, Ohio. Mulford practiced with the lad, showing him how to drive the track, but was forced to take over and win the race and most of the coveted 25-mile cups when Eddie went on his head. Numerous employers, including Hudson and Paige, asked him to quit driving but he usually had "just a few commitments to fill." In 1918 he won at Omaha, Uniontown, Des Moines, and Tacoma during that war-curtailed season to take his 2nd national title. That was in a Hudson Super Six that he had turned into a potent racing machine a year or so previously in his machine shop near the Sheepshead Bay Race Track in Brooklyn.

His dream of a Mulford passenger car disappeared along with $60,000 invested in 2 prototypes as 2 bankers got themselves hand-built automobiles. He lost another $160,000 in a stock swindle. He worked in 1920 and 1921 for Paige—between races, setting a stock-car record of 102.8 m.p.h. at Daytona Beach in 1921. Finally, after the 1922 racing season, he kept a long-broken pledge to his wife and quit track racing. But he had already found a new speed vocation—mountain climbs. His last race for 5 years was at the Kansas City board track for Duesenberg. He came in 2nd because his car ran out of gas. In 1927 he drove one last race at Des Moines for Duesenberg.

The mountain climbing was for Chandler and Cleveland, as were several cross-country runs. At one time Mulford held the record on Pikes Peak, Mount Washington, and just about every hill that had a road going up it. But if he was a winner in racing and endurance records, he remained a loser in financial matters. When the Chandler Motor Car Company was formed by ex-Lozier people, he refused to join them. All of his ex-cronies ended up millionaires. But he was victimized several more times by financial sharpies and ended up owning a service station in New Jersey during much of the thirties.

In 1938 Mulford founded a boat company, but abandoned it soon after a disagreement with his partner. He spent World War II as a chief inspector at Electric Boat Company's Bayonne, N.J., factory, reportedly adding some 25 m.p.h. to the speed of the PT boats being built there with his suggestions. After the war he became the star salesman for the Elco Yacht Co., which finally gave up the yacht business because it lost money on each boat sold. After that, he went into retirement near Asbury Park where he started, occasionally working on boat engines.

Mulford built 7 cars of his own design, as far as can be ascertained. They were marked by magnificent workmanship and an impeccable choice of the best engineering thinking of the time. One of his best was powered by a 4-cylinder copy of a Duesenberg engine with 4 valves per cylinder. It is interesting to speculate how the auto industry would have reacted if the meticulously prepared Mulford passenger car had indeed reached the market. Such workmanship would have left some kind of ripple on the tide of the American automotive history.

HERBERT MULLER

Some of the scenery at the Canadian-American-Challenge Cup races deserves to be better known in America than it is. It is only when one of these fellows wins a race, as Tony Dean did in 1970 at Road Atlanta, that they emerge as personalities. Herbert Muller never made it, despite some good CanAm performances, such as his 4th place in the Mid-Ohio race in 1971 and 6ths at Road America and Donnybrooke. The answer probably is that Muller basically was a gentleman amateur (despite his high-powered racing program in Europe and America) who spent most of his time in sports cars and prototypes. Had he ever made a serious single-seater attempt, he not only possibly would have been successful but certainly better known.

Muller was a Swiss, born in May 1940 in Lucerne. Motor racing would have been a full-time thing with him; however, when his father died in 1964, young Herbert had to take over responsibility for the family's electroplating factory in the Lucerne suburb of Reinach. By then he already had been competing some 3 years, starting in motorcross events in 1961 on a 500 c.c. Norton motorcycle. Georges Fillipinetti, the Swiss racing entrepreneur, became interested in Muller and became a long-time supporter and sponsor. Car racing was an accident. Buying an old Formula 3 Cooper for its engine, mainly because he had ideas about using it in the cycle, Muller instead raced the car at Hockenheim. His "race" lasted about 300 feet until the engine blew.

The Ollon Villars hillclimb was a bit better. Muller was credited with a time 10 seconds better than that of Jack Brabham himself in a F1 Cooper, and Herbert later dismissed the figure as "a pure mistake, you may be sure." Be that as it may, the feat prompted his father to buy the son a new Cooper with which he promptly recorded three victories in French races. For 1962 his father came up with a Porsche RSK that had been used to record a 2nd in the Swiss Hillclimb Championship the previous season. Filipinetti came up with some interesting machiney for young Herbert to drive, too, like the Ford GT40 at Spa (DNF). At Rossfeld in the new-old Porsche, Muller was narrowly beaten by Edgar Barth in a factory RSK. This led to a factory ride as number 2 driver to Barth in hillclimbs. That was the

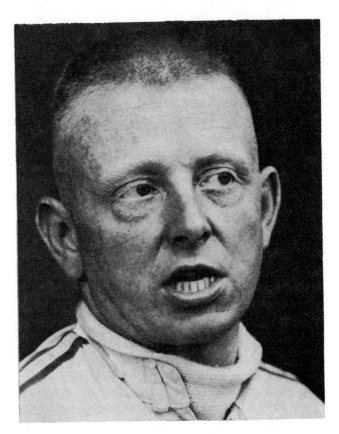

way they finished the season, 1–2, Barth and Muller. In the Nurburgring 1000, Muller's Filipinetti GT40 blew an engine.

Muller's sole F1 ride came in 1963 in a Filipinetti Lotus 24 at Pau. Third most of the race, and 2nd fastest to Jim Clark in fastest-lap calculations, Muller finished 5th when he had to pit for fuel. Filipinetti sold the single-seater soon after, and that ended Muller's F1 racing. Over the next 2 years, there were important races without any important victories or placings. Leading in the Monza 1000, Herbert turned a 4.4-litre Ferrari over to codriver Tommy Spychiger, who promptly ran into a wall and killed himself. At Le Mans, Muller shared a Ford GT40 with Ronnie Bucknum, but they retired early. Muller's racing was interrupted around this time for his compulsary Swiss Army duty, but he managed to get a few races in even during this time.

Muller's initial major race victory came in 1966 when he shared a Targa Florio 1st with Willy Mairesse in a Porsche Carerra 6 when the factory cars fell by the wayside and Filipinetti car prevailed. Later that same season, Muller won the Nurburgring 500 in a factory-entered Fiat-Abarth. Trying for a repeat victory in the 1967 Targa, Muller was leading after 7 laps with a lap record in hand, when the rear axle of his Filipinetti Ferrari P3 broke. Business interfered with racing pretty much in 1968, and Herbert's only start was at Le Mans in a Ferrari LM shared with England's Jonathan Williams. They were running 5th overall when a wheel bearing broke in the morning.

Muller had a Matra factory offer in 1969, but he

chose to stay with Filipinetti. Using a Lola T70-Chevvy, Herbert tried the Targa again, and after a wiring fault put him last at the start, flew over the course to 3rd overall in a single lap, passing some 60 others cars, only to retire later with suspension ills. Matra still liked this driver and handed Muller a car for Le Mans with Johnny Servoz-Gavin; they retired. The Lola was Muller's mount again for Osterreichring, where he finished 2nd to Jo Siffert in a Porsche 917, that model's initial victory. In the Oulton Park Tourist Trophy, Muller set a fastest-lap mark, but retired just before the race ended because of Paul Hawkins's death.

The Interserie is the European equivalent of the CanAm, and Muller initially ran it in 1969, finishing 3rd at Mantorop Park and 2nd at Anderstorp. He was runner up to winner Leo Kinnunen in the series. Beginning in 1971, Muller raced the Ferrari 512 very successfully, including the 512S of 1970 in which he was 4th at the Nurburgring, and 6th at both Monza and the Targa. At Le Mans, codriver Mike Parkes was part of the multi-Ferrari shunt that about eliminated Maranello cars from the race. Selling the cars to Steve McQueen for the Le Mans movie, Filipinetti also lent the Americans Muller as technical adviser. After the film, Herbert bought back the 3 Ferraris and set about getting ready to race them himself in 1971.

At Brands Hatch, Muller and codriver Rene Herzog finished 3rd, at Monza the pair was 6th despite battery trouble, and at Nurburgring they retired after Herzog had three separate accidents on 1 lap. John Wyer offered some Porsche drives, and Muller appeared in a 908/3 with Pedro Rodriguez for the Targa, in which the Mexican broke down on the first lap, and in a 917 with Dickie Attwood at Le Mans, where they finished 2nd overall behind teammates Helmut Marko and Gijs van Lennep. In 1972 there was talk of further Porsche rides in the Interseries, but Kinnunen got the factory car. Muller kept racing his Ferrari 512M in the Interserie, and later in the CanAm. One of the cars was gone, of course; it was one of Herbert's Ferraris in which Pedro Rodriguez met death in late 1971 at the Norisring. Muller also had a de Tomaso Pantera ride in the GT category, with promising, if somewhat unsuccessful results. At Monza he was leading when clipped by a backmarker in the pouring rain, at Spa he was leading again in the GT category when the engine blew. Sports car drivers get used to things like that.

FRANK MUNDY

Lucky Teter's Hell Drivers were in town, and the skinny 17-year-old kid was doing his usual tricks on his used motorcycle to amuse friends and any passers-by. It was 1936 and Atlanta was not exactly Boomtown, U.S.A. Frankie Menendez, half-Irish, had a reputation as a wild man; he wouldn't give an inch in drags on city streets, and he would just as soon race you down Peachtree Street as some back country lane. The others called him Mundy or Mendy because they couldn't pronounce his last name with their Southern drawl, and while they kidded with him, they never dared laugh at him because he was different. Frank grew up with Young Stribling, the boxer, as his hero, and they knew he got what he wanted. They had heard his story of Stribling's big yellow convertible and how he was going to own one some day. The knew he had worked as a Western Union messenger until he saved enough for the motorbike. The word got around that one of the regulars in the Teter thrill show had broken his leg. "Why don't you apply for the job?" said someone. Francis Eduardo Menendez did and made his debut before the home folks at Lakewood Park, crashing through a wall of flaming half-inch thick planks.

Born June 8, 1919, to an Irish mother and a Spanish father, Frank Mundy thus started the road to 2 championships. He spent 7 years with stunt shows, meeting and talking with such greats as Ted Horn, Chet Gardner, and Doc MacKenzie, who drove in the races that sometimes went on the same weekend as the thrill shows. He learned to somersault a car, jump it 120 feet through the air, crash it head on and spin it.

"When I started out stunting," he said later, "I volunteered for the head-on crash because it paid $10 more a week. We crashed junkers, running into each other at 35 m.p.h. The secret was a perfect head-on collision, plus the ability to drive the car from the back seat. You ducked behind a mattress just before impact."

But in 1938, Frank came home with a new ambition —to be a race driver. Stock-car racing in Atlanta in that day was a conglomeration of 75 percent moonshine runners, 20 percent fresh young kids and 5 percent professionals. It was a rough league, but Mundy was never a cream puff. He sometimes beat top pros like the Flock family, Bill France, Glenn Dunnaway, Roy Hall, and Walt Brown, but lost more often then he won. There is no accurate record of who won what in Southern stock-car racing before World War II, but Mundy, who competed when he was not doing thrill show work, won his share.

"I was knocked cold only once on a track and it came in those early days at Lakewood," he recalled. "This was a dirt track, and the stockers kicked up dust so heavy you couldn't see the other cars. Anytime you drive blind you drive scared. I was judging the turns on the backstretch by a clump of trees; when I saw them, I'd turn, count five or six then straighten the car. I was busy counting when I plowed into six other cars who must have been counting, too. I woke up in an ambulance. After they found no broken bones, I raced back, borrowed a car and finished 2nd in the feature."

Mundy jumped back and forth between NASCAR and AAA, and was one of the founders of NASCAR. In 1952, when AAA upped the number of stock-car events from the 3 of 1951 to 15, Mundy had a major disagreement with Bill France and left. He won a race at Springfield, Ill., September 30, his 1st AAA victory. The following year Mundy swept up in a Hudson Hornet, dethroning another NASCAR expatriate, Marshall Teague. Frank repeated in 1955. That 1953 season, however, was the highwater mark of his AAA career. He won 5 races in his Hornet and had the title virtually clinched by July 12. That was also the year that Mundy got a ride at Indianapolis, but he failed to pass his rookie test when the car developed vibration problems in the final phases.

The AAA races with their version of strictly stock cars were hairy affairs in those days, too, for they raced on half-mile tracks. On the night of July 25 at Iliana Speedway near Hammond, Ind., Mundy had a close call. He and his big Hudson Hornet with the No. 7 superimposed on a Confederate flag had won the big Milwaukee race 2 weeks previously, and he was barrelling around the little track with gay abandon. Frank turned and suddenly found himself holding a steering wheel free of its steering column. The runaway car wrecked 5 others in a nearby parking lot, and Mundy suffered only 3 cracked ribs although he was only wearing a lap-type seat belt.

When Mundy saw that the money was better in NASCAR, he applied for reinstatement in 1956. The group required a $1,000 bond of him to ensure he would abide by its rules. He posted the money and piloted a Dodge convertible to a NASCAR 100-mile race record of 81.08 m.p.h. on May 12 on the Raleigh, N.C., mile asphalt. Mundy always flew between races, letting a mechanic make the over-the-road haul. He once arrived in Carroll Speedway near Los Angeles to find his vehicle had broken down en route. He rented a car, watercolored an X on the side and finished 8th without a pit crew, tires, or extra gas. He won $100 while the rental charge was $37, so the net profit was $63.

But the best thing that ever happened to him was meeting Carl Kiekhafer from Mercury Outboard in Fond Du Lac, Wisc. Frank eventually retired to become a salesman for the man who conceived of stock-car racing as both a hobby and a shrewd way to promote outboard boat engines. It was in a Kiekhafer Hornet that Frank won his 1955 crown. And it was with a Kiekhafer Dodge in the convertible circuit that Mundy found that the NASCAR hot dogs were trying just a bit too much for him to stay with them. He did not finish in the top 20 in either the convertible or the Grand National circuits.

JIMMY MURPHY

James Anthony Murphy died at the age of 30 at the height of a racing career that had already stamped him as one of the great drivers of any era. The 5 ft. 7 in.,

145-pound Irishman won 2 AAA national titles when that organization was clearly the major circuit in the United States; he beat the leading European drivers of his day on his own terms, and on theirs, and he won 17 championship races. Born in 1894 in San Francisco and orphaned by the earthquake, he was a shy undersized boy brought up in Vernon, Calif., near Los Angeles by relatives, Judge and Mrs. Martin O'Donnell. Judge O'Donnell did one key thing for him; he gave Jimmy a motorcycle to commute to high school in Huntington Park.

When Murphy found his forte, mechanics, he quit school one year shy of a diploma and opened a garage. He spent free afternoons around the Beverly Hills Speedway watching the drivers and mechanics. He knew he wanted to be connected with racing and, for once, his size was an advantage. He had persuaded Omar Toft to let him be the riding mechanic in the 1916 Corona races, but Toft's car was disqualified the morning of the race. Eddie O'Donnell, however, was looking for a last-minute replacement for his mechanic who was suddenly taken ill. Murphy accepted gleefully; O'Donnell was a Duesenberg team driver. Besides, being 20–30 pounds less, Murphy was a natural: O'Donnell won the 301-mile open road race.

After spending World War I in the Army Air Corps, Murphy rode with O'Donnell, Eddie Rickenbacker, and Tommy Milton during the next several years. At Uniontown, Pa., in 1919 he was given his initial chance to drive. He crashed, injuring his riding mechanic, and Fred Duesenberg was ready to relegate him forever to

the jump seat. But Jimmy was one of the few men with whom Tommy Milton, the tempestuous number one driver, felt friendly. Milton demanded that Murphy be given a another chance, and the chance came when O'Donnell injured an arm just before the beginning of the 1920 season.

Murphy proved himself this time. In the opening race of the 1920 season, his initial full race as a driver, he won the pole, then sped to a wire-to-wire victory in the 250-miler. He ran out of gas on the parade lap with the checkered flag. At Fresno he won again, and this time the rear-axle was within a single thread of the last nut of falling apart. And while he won no other major races that season, he and Ernie Olson, his riding mechanic, were always in contention.

There is no way for us to assess the true nature of the man. Shy during his school days, quiet and close-mouthed but pleasant before strangers, there are only a few clues that seem to point to Jimmy Murphy's single-minded dedication to the proposition that he had to be the best. It was determination that transcended friendship, even physical agony—a determination that cost him his life.

It was at the end of the 1920 season. Tommy Milton had gone to Havana for some of the most relaxed racing ever seen this side of a slow-motion camera. He was due to come back to wrest the Land Speed Record from Ralph DePalma in a car he not only helped to build but which he helped to finance. Duesenberg, however, decided to send Murphy to Daytona to run shakedown trials. Jimmy turned the "trials" into a new LSR of 151 m.p.h. while Milton was on the boat back. He earned the plaudits of the world and the enmity of the man who fought to give him his driving chance. Milton later broke the record, but the rift never healed.

In 1921 Albert Champion, the spark plug tycoon, financed the Duesenberg assault on the French Grand Prix. Ernie Olson was the mechanic and Murphy, who had burned his hand, the driver. The cars were shipped over in parts; it was easier since Indy had just been run. Murphy had been injured (2 broken ribs) in a practice accident and hospitalized. The morning of the race he insisted on competing. Olson and a nurse taped him up; then he was driven to the track and lifted into the car. The road surface was so bad even before racing began that Olson had devised a mesh screen that he could pull up to protect himself and Murphy from flying rocks whenever another car had to be approached from the rear. Murphy knew he had several advantages over the field; his Duesy had 4-wheel brakes, allowing him to drive deeper into corners at speed; the tires, therefore did not take as much of a beating and, with the veteran Olson calling the shots, Jimmy could slipstream other fast cars occasionally.

How Murphy stood 4½ hours of constant pounding no one could ascertain, but he must have been in agony all the way. Yet he even overcame a rock-damaged radiator and a tire blowout in the final 10 miles to beat Ralph DePalma (in a Ballot) and become the first Amer-ican to win a major modern European GP. The shy boy had turned into a man with a need to win so great it could overcome virtually any obstacle.

In 1922 Murphy came to Indianapolis as one of the favorites. He had won the sprints at Cotate, Calif., easily. This was to be the final 2-man car race at the Brick-yard until the Junk Formula of the Thirties. There were more innovative cars in this race. Milton, for instance, entered a vehicle of his own design, the Leach Special, with a transverse spring suspension and the fuel tanks placed so as to lower the center of gravity. The Murphy car was basically a Duesenberg chassis with a Miller engine assembled by Olson. It won the pole and for the first 73 laps of the race was challenged by rookie Harry Hartz in a Duesenberg into setting a record car-killing pace.

Jimmy came in on the 74th lap for his 1st pit stop and returned again on the 75th to finish changing tires and get gas and oil. He was 26 seconds behind Hartz when he took up the chase anew. But on the 78th lap he was back in the pits and dropped to 4th as Hartz and another rookie, Pete DePaolo, fought for the lead. Now it was a battle to move up again, a more difficult battle because by the 90th lap the number of cars on the track had diminished appreciably. But by the 100th lap—half-way—Battling Jimmy had come back to 2nd some 85 seconds off Hartz's pace—or so the scorers said. On the 119th lap Hartz pitted, and Jimmy assumed the lead. In fact, the scorers now declared that Murphy had never lost it, although he and a lot of other drivers had pushed their cars unmercifully because of the scoring error.

At 350 miles Murphy set a pace more than 4 m.p.h. faster than the previous year, and he seemed to be in-creasing his speed. He pitted at 350, changed a tire, took on gas, and was out in 38 seconds. This, in a day when there were no air jacks or quick-change mechanisms, was phenomenal. Murphy continued to speed up be-cause Hartz unlapped himself and now was only a lap behind. On the 180th lap Jimmy was forced in again for tires, the victim of the awesome pace, now 5 m.p.h. faster than the previous year. This time the tire change took 50 seconds, and he was only 200 yards ahead of Hartz as he accelerated out on the track. Driving almost wildly, Jimmy doubled his lead and more over Hartz in the next lap. And he continued the breakneck pace the remaining distance to finish 2 laps ahead of Hartz at 94.48 m.p.h., an average speed almost 5 m.p.h. faster than 1921.

Murphy went on to the 1st of 2 National Champion-ships, winning at Uniontown, Pa., and Tacoma, then, after a crash at Kansas City, he won at Beverly Hills. In 1923 he finished 3rd in the 500 and had what for him was an off season—he failed to win the national title. He was driving for Durant, winning Beverly Hills by 5 feet over Bennett Hill—a rather close finish. After Indiana-polis, he ran 2nd at Kansas City's board track to Durant teammate Hearne, then accepted Harry Miller's offer to compete at Monza in a special car. His brakes failed,

434

but he still managed to finish 3rd. Meanwhile, Eddie Hearne had won Altoona and Fresno to assume the lead for the AAA title. Although Jimmy tried, he could not put together the major victory in the season's closing races to overtake Hearne. For 1924 Murphy was deprived of victory by a late tire change, and he finished 3rd. However, he won Kansas City's last race, won twice at Altoona, and cinched in September at Readville, Mass., in a dirt-track race.

Murphy was 30, and they had even named a dance after him, the Jimmy Murphy Trot. He said it was time to think of retiring and maybe raising a family of his own. But he agreed to race at the dirt track race at the Syracuse, N.Y., Fairgrounds. Murphy did not particularly like dirt tracks, for his was not a broadsliding style of driving. Besides, he had crashed at the same track just the week before. But he had filed an entry, and had to honor his commitment. Jimmy was moving up to take the lead late in the race when a wheel hit an oil slick, and the car slid into the inside rail. Drivers—even Murphy himself—had survived accidents like this innumerable times. But Jimmy Murphy did not. A long wooden splinter was driven into his heart. Tommy Milton was one of those who accompanied the body back to Los Angeles. Murphy had never replied in kind to his public attacks, never had said an unkind word about him. And now the single-sided feud was over.

PAULA MURPHY

Paula Murphy, educated as a schoolteacher at Ohio's Bowling Green University, went to California instead and was married. Then she met an MG and the marriage became secondary. After competing in SCCA racing, William Carroll enticed her to turn professional as part of a team of girls who broke the transcontinental record in a Studebaker Avanti. The same Carroll, then West Coast editor of *Automotive News*, introduced her to Andy Granatelli, who allowed her to come to the Bonneville Salt Flats to drive his special Avanti—161.29 m.p.h., a ladies' record.

But Paula—with a racing helmet on—was no lady. She battled the men in modified stock-car racing in Southern California and took them on again in that fabulous promotion called the Mobil Economy Run. She even took her vacations each year to drive in the Economy Run. In November 1963 she and codriver Barbara Nieland became the 1st women to put their names on the USAC record books as part of a team of Studebaker drivers at Bonneville. And a year later she took Art Arfons's J46 rocket-powered record car out on the Salt Flats and went for a 2-way average of 226.37 m.p.h. Another 1st for her was Indy. She became the 1st woman allowed out on the track in a race car, Andy Granatelli's old Novi. Paula scorched it up past 120 m.p.h. in a exhibition run and managed to terrify Mr. Granatelli who promptly called her in.

In 1965 Ms Murphy—she was divorced by now—espoused drag racing. Eventually she became the 1st woman given a license to drive nitro-methane fuel burning dragsters by NHRA. By then she was a bona fide gate attraction in both AHRA and NHRA racing. Another 1st was shattering the 200-m.p.h. barrier in 1969 at Fort Worth. Prior to that she had competed in the Shell 4000 Trans-Canada Rally.

Paula made an excellent living as "Miss STP," and yearned for a return to road racing. But with all the talk about equal rights no one had come forward with a competitive car as of 1971. All she got were exhibition cars from Andy, and she showed that she still could travel quickly. In June 1971 Paula ran a top speed of 211.76 m.p.h. in a quarter-mile dash at Motion Dragway near Decatur, Ill., an all-time track record there. Her mount that day was a Chrysler-powered STP-Plymouth "funny" car. In August that same year, she smashed the women's closed-course record at Talladega, Ala., with a single-lap average of 171.499 m.p.h. The old mark (1962) had been a mere 147 m.p.h. at Daytona. This time her mount was an STP-Plymouth stock car usually driven by Freddie Lorenzen. The only real racing Paula managed was in runs like the Baja 500 where she was the only woman to finish, using, of all things, a Volkswagen.

LUIGI MUSSO

Luigi Musso was born in Rome, July 29, 1924, youngest of 3 sons of an Italian diplomat who spent many years in China. It was an entire family of sportsmen, with championships shared by several generations in all the manly sports. Luigi himself was a brillant shot, a crack fencer, and champion horseman. He was about 10 when his interest in cars became evident, but he had trouble getting his older brothers to let him drive theirs, so he proceeded to buy an old 750-c.c. Giannini to drive experimentally. He was still using this machine when, on a dare, he entered the 1950 Tour of Sicily.

That first race was momentous only because Musso accidentally crashed into a statue of Garibaldi, causing the car to lose some of its forward gears. The only way Luigi could negotiate some hills, for example, was in reverse. In his next start, in the 1950 Mille Miglia, Musso spun off and crashed without hurting himself, but totalling the car. But it was a point of pride for Musso to run the little racer again, and he rebuilt it for the Tour of Calabria, in which he scored a class victory, and the Naples race, in which he got a handicap victory. In 1951 he again saw discouraging retirements in races like the Tour of Sicily and the Mille Miglia, and the following season his brother Giuseppe (also a driver of some accomplishment) lent Luigi a 750 Stanguellini in which he had some 2nd-place successes; but he never could seem to push across the line on top.

In 1953 Musso was 1 of 3 drivers to get a unique factory ride from Maserati for sports-car racing; each had to buy his own car. He was virtually unbeatable in the 2-litre class in which he raced, and Luigi became the Italian champion in this category. The high spot of the year was a victory in the Perugia Cup at 77.27 m.p.h. More important victories followed in 1954, including the Pescara Grand Prix at 86.7 m.p.h. and the Senigallia race at 86.58. Musso won the Naples GP in a big Maserati, scored a class victory and was 2nd overall to Piero Taruffi in the Targa Florio. In the Mille Miglia he was 3rd overall and 2nd in class. He also scored class victories in the Tourist Trophy and the Buenos Aires 1000. With Jean Behra he won the Supercortemaggiore GP at 109.98 m.p.h. In the Spanish GP, in a Formula 1 car, he finished 2nd to Mike Hawthorn's Ferrari.

By then he was the leading Maserati driver. In 1955 he did not win any major races, but he was 2nd at Bari to Jean Behra and at Caserta, 3rd in the Syracuse GP, the Dutch GP (to Fangio and Moss), and the Tour of Sicily. The following season he had a variety of mounts, including a Lancia with which he won the Argentine GP at 79.38 m.p.h. with Fangio. He also had an OSCA and Ferrari, with which he was 2nd at Sebring with Harry Schell and in the Syracuse GP to Fangio. An accident at Nurburgring shortened Musso's season.

In 1957 he was off to a brilliant start sharing a victory in the Buenos Aires 1000 with Masten Gregory and Eugenio Castellotti in Temple Buell's privately entered 3.5-litre Ferrari at 99.5 m.p.h. Illness prevented a Mille Miglia run, but in the Naples GP he was 2nd, and 2nd again in the British GP at Aintree (that season also de-

signed the European GP) to Tony Brooks and Stirling Moss sharing a Vanwall. Luigi was 2nd in the French GP to Fangio, 3rd at Naples, 2nd once more at Syracuse to Peter Collins, and at Modena to Behra. In the Rheims GP Musso won, nipping Behra, at 123.36 m.p.h. The 1957 season closed with a shared 2nd place with Hawthorn to clinch the sports-car World Championship for Ferrari at the Venezuelan GP. Musso certainly was at his peak in these seasons, for in 1958 his successes continued apace. In the Buenos Aires GP he was 2nd to Fangio's Maserati sports car in the Argentine GP 2nd to Moss by a mere 2.7 seconds with Hawthorn 3rd, and Fangio 4th. In the European opener, the Monaco GP, Luigi was 2nd again to Maurice Trintignant. He was 7th in the Dutch GP and 3rd in the non-title Race of Two Worlds at Monza (to America's Jim Rathmann and Jimmy Bryan) in a car shared with Phil Hill and Hawthorn. Musso finally won the Syracuse GP after so many years of trying, averaging 100.24 m.p.h. In sports cars, at Sebring he shared 2nd with Oliver Gendebien, then won the Targa Florio with the Belgian at 58.91 m.p.h., and was 4th with Hill at the Nurburgring 1000.

He retired with mechanical trouble in the Belgian GP, but returned in good form for the French GP at Rheims. While running 2nd at around 150 m.p.h. to Hawthorn, that season's World Champion, tragedy struck. Just after the 9th lap, Musso's Ferrari ran out of road as he was sliding through a turn. Two other racers, unknowns, had been killed at almost the identical spot in previous years, in precisely the same way, running out of road, hitting a ditch and flipping. Drivers

436

had been asking the circuit owners to fill the ditch, but they had ignored the request, for there was no Grand Prix Drivers Association in 1958. When the dust settled after Musso's spin and flip, he was dead. The ditch was later filled, the corner reworked and a name given it— the Musso Curve—all a bit too late for Luigi.

HERB NAB

One of the best racing mechanics in the world came from Fruits, Colo., and was married in Sho-Sho, Ida. Preposterous? Herbert Nab swore these towns exist, and that he was born on April Fool's Day, 1927. It took 16 years for him to get out of Fruits, but he eventually became a truck driver, then a welder in an Oregon defense plant. He also pitched hay, became a portrait photographer, and combined his experience by becoming a truck driver hauling hay.

In 1952 Herb went to Portland, Ore., with his wife, the former Mary Schine, and entered racing as a mechanic's helper on West Coast hero Bill Amick's Dodge. He had learned about motors earlier, but they were truck motors. This was parttime work, and Herb was working at other jobs in the daytime. In 1956 he made mechanics a full-time job with the Pete DePaolo Ford engineering stock-car setup when that old Indianapolis hero was retained to oversee a major assault on all fronts in late-model stock-car racing. In 1957 all that blew up, and he was back with Amick again.

"In one of the cars I worked over for Bill, he won 3

straight races. That's when people got the idea I was a pretty good wrench man. They actually thought I knew something about what I was doing." Nab knew. In all the years of working in racing, he had learned what would work and what would not. He remembered individual tracks and past problems at them, he was a classic example of the self-taught virtuoso. He knew what to do, but could not tell you his overall plan for a particular car. Nab would show you.

In 1958 he threw in his lot with Holman-Moody, when that organization was a very long gamble to succeed. "I worked on cars for Joe Weatherly, Curtis Turner and others—like Fireball Roberts, Marvin Panch, and Ralph Moody. Then they put me on Freddie Lorenzen's car. Freddie made me look real good from '61 to '64. I just got the car ready to run."

That's not what Lorenzen said. "The man is uncanny how he can interpret what the driver tells him into making the right changes in a car. Sometimes you tell him one thing, and he'll somehow know that what you really want has nothing to do with your suggestion. He is also great for setting up a car to a particular track. Once he gets a reading on the tires and what they'll do, he gets the car handling well as quick as any mechanic I know." The Lorenzen-Nab parting gave rise many rumors of fights and ill will between the 2 men. Nothing could have been further from the truth. Nab was not a racing fan; it was a business to him. When Junior Johnson retired and set up the Holly Farms Poultry racing team, he wanted Nab as his chief mechanic and chassis man. Nab went because, according to his former colleagues at Holman-Moody, he got what he considered a better deal. Johnson was the boss because he owned part of Holly Farms, but Nab had the ultimate responsibility for getting the Holly Farms cars race-ready. Johnson also worked over the engines. Nab moved on to work with others when a better deal arrived.

FELICE NAZZARO

Felice Nazzaro was 42 years old when he returned to Fiat as its racing director in 1922. He had been absent from the racing scene for several years. In the French Grand Prix that year at Strassbourg, the northern Italian entered himself as a driver to the consternation of many. But the "old man", as he was referred to derisively, took the lead at the race's start, yielded it as planned to Pietro Bordino for a time, then retook it to win at an average speed of 79.2 m.p.h. The kind of race he had won can be judged from the fact that only 3 of the 18 starters finished the grind; 4 complete teams—Aston Martin, Ballot, Rolland-Pilain, and Sunbeam—were eliminated, and the other 2 Fiats both suffered broken axles, one of these accidents killing Nazzaro's nephew Biagio outright.

Born in 1880, Nazzaro was the son of a Turin coal merchant. His father apprenticed his tall, quiet, aristocratic-looking son to the small firm of Ceirano at the

age of 15. There Felice came under the direction of Vincenzo Lancia, just a bit older, and the pair became the experimental department of the small carbuilder. When Ceirano was absorbed by the expanding Fabbrica Italiana Automobile Torine (F.I.A.T., later Fiat) in 1899, they continued their experimentation and, in 1900, entered the racing scene.

It was Lancia who gave Fiat its initial competition victory in winning a race to Padua—Nazzaro was 2nd. The following year Felice nabbed his class in the Piombino-Grosseto 50-mile race. In 1905 the 6th and last Gordon Bennett Race was held at mountainous Auvergne, near Clermont-Ferrand, with Nazzaro finishing 2nd. He was also 2nd the following year in the 1st Grand Prix de l'Automobile Club de France, which had begun as a substitute for the Gordon Bennett. That race was won by Franz Szisz in a 12.8-litre Renault at 62.88 m.p.h. in 2 days of daylight racing. In 1907 Nazzaro became an early racing hero by winning 3 major races, the first time that had been done. In the Targa Florio Felice beat 46 other top-flight competitors. Then came the Kaiser Cup, Germany's initial *grand épreuve*, won at 52.6 m.p.h. over the Taunus circuit. Three weeks later, at Dieppe this time, Nazzaro won the French GP at 68.6 m.p.h.

The following year, Nazzaro made his 1st appearance on a track—as compared to the road courses—and became the idol of British motor racing. Selwyn Edge had issued a "world" challenge to all comers to meet his 6-cylinder Napier in a match race at Brooklands. Fiat immediately took up the challenge and rea-

died a special 4-cylinder car that was dubbed Mephistopheles. The Edge Napier, driven by Frank Newton, was called Samson.

The cars started from a rolling start, and Newton took a big lead of better than 300 yards after a couple of laps on the banked Brooklands track. But Felice, who was getting used to the course, then opened up the Fiat and rapidly overtook the Napier. As the crowd and officials gaped, he passed Newton at a speed of 111 m.p.h. A little later, the timers estimated Nazzaro's speed at 120 m.p.h., and at the finish, the Fiat's winning speed was set down as 121.64. Newton's Napier had already retired with a broken crankshaft. Later that season, Nazzaro was leading the French GP once more when his mount's crankshaft failed. But he won the Coppa Florio on the Bologna circuit at 73.2 m.p.h., and he was 3rd in the Savannah Grand Prize race in the United States.

In the spring of 1911, Nazzaro left Fiat to form his own company, in a way following the footsteps of his friend Lancia once more, for Vincenzo already had departed to form the company that still bears his name. Nazzaro as a manufacturer was not as successful as Lancia, although his Nazzaro marque had its moments. In 1913, for example, Felice drove one of his own cars to victory in the Targa Florio around Sicily at 31.04 m.p.h. An interesting feature of that race was the participation of 2 American Fords, but both retired. In 1914 Nazzaro's mount failed to finish the Targa, and his 3-car team retired from the French GP.

Felice was ready to throw in the sponge in 1922, when Senator Agnelli invited him to rejoin Fiat. After his 1922 victory in the French GP, Nazzaro finished 2nd at Bordino in the Italian GP on the new Monza Autodrome driving the same car. A man past 40 cannot race too often, however, and it was a year later, in the initial European GP, that Felice raced again. He came in 2nd, less than a minute behind the winner, Carlo Salamano, in another Fiat. Salamano's victory was the 1st major race won by a supercharged car; the winning speed was 91.1 m.p.h. Nazzaro had led into the last lap, but a broken oil pipe slowed him to a crawl, and Salamano was able to sneak past just before the finish line.

In 1924 Felice appeared for the last time in a major race, retiring after 22 laps of the French GP. When Fiat's racing department was closed soon after, Nazarro moved over to the road experimental department. He continued working there until within a few weeks of his death of natural causes March 21, 1940, in his beloved Turin. In retrospect, Nazzaro was probably the most refined of the early pilots in driving skills. When his competitors shifted gears in the big-engined monsters of his youth, the noise would wake the dead. But Felice had an inborn love of machinery, and he refused to torture it that way; his gear changes were sure but silent. Machines respond to kind treatment, and Nazzaro rarely had to walk back to his pits.

JOCHEN NEERPASCH

"You can only win at Russian roulette so long," said Jochen Neerpasch as he announced his retirement as a racing driver in 1968 at the age of 29. His decision may well have been influenced by a horrendous accident the tall driver had had at the fast Spa course when a Porsche 908 he was sharing with England's Vic Elford was demolished. He came back to race at Le Mans, finishing 3rd with Rolf Stommelen, but quit after the French classic.

After that, however, Jochen Neerpasch, born in Krefeld, Germany, in 1939, still managed to be involved with motor racing. First he became competition director for Ford of Germany, building a winning team within 2 years and making the Ford Capri RS a racing car with which to reckon. During that time, too, he guided the fortunes of many drivers, including Stommelen, whom he steered into Formula 1, and Jochen Mass, whom he shepherded through touring cars and lesser single-seaters toward the Grand Prix trail. Then, in May 1972, Neerpasch dramatically left Ford, spurning a huge raise and other inducements, but parting amicably, to join BMW as worldwide competition manager. His task was even more formidable than that at Cologne: to make BMW a winner after some bad-starts for the Germany builder. BMW had been on its way to the top in F2 and headed toward F1 when it quit racing abruptly in 1970, cutting loose such talents as Jackie Ickx, Jo Siffert, and Dieter Quester. Now it became Neerpasch's challenge to bring the BMW pieces back together again.

He always liked challenges. Jochen's competition career started on a dare back in 1960 when he began racing a Borgward in Grand Touring, saloon, and other forms of competition, and also tried some single-seater races. After 4 years, Neerpasch knew his business, as witness his drive for Carroll Shelby's Cobra team at Le Mans, although his Daytona GT retired late in the race. In those years, too, he was racing a Formula 3 Lotus, which gave him his other serious crash in Argentina, another one from which he walked away. That same season saw Neerpasch's initial major drives for Porsche, where he was to excel and to create his future competitions opportunities.

Sharing a year-old 2-litre Carrera with Gunther Klass, Neerpasch managed a 7th in the tough Targa Florio that year, and the following season saw several Porsche factory starts, with his best placing a 2nd in the Nurburgring 6-hour race with Roy Pierpont—only that was raced in a Ford Mustang. In 1966 Neerpasch scored his initial Porsche victory in a major race, the Circuit of Mugello, near Florence. He and Gerhard Koch drove a 906 to a 66.72 m.p.h. victory. A little later, sharing another 906 with Michel Weber, Jochen won his class at the Monza 1000. He also was 2nd in the German GT championship.

In 1967 Neerpasch won the 84-hour Nurburgring

Marathon, then drove the World Manufacturers Championship series. With Elford in a 910, he scored 3rds at the Nurburgring 1000 and in the Targa, with Stommelen he was 2nd in the Mugello race (a non-title one) and 10th at Le Mans. The year 1968 began with another horrendous crash in practice for the Daytona 24-hour race, but Neerpasch scored his biggest victory there sharing a 907 with Elford (and with 3 other drivers in the closing hours of the race) to win at 106.69 m.p.h. At Sebring he and Elford were 2nd, and at the BOAC 500 at Brands Hatch 3rd. Another 2nd was scored in the Monza 1000 with Stommelen, a 4th with America's Joe Buzzetta at the Nurburgring 1000, still another 4th with Hans Herrmann in the Targa.

After that came Spa, the crash, the return in the Le Mans race, then retirement. At BMW the plan was to get started with saloon and GT racing and not to become involved at first with single-seaters. No one expected that plan to last too long. Surely a Phase 2 that would see BMW F2 and, possibly, F1 cars in action would follow as soon as Neerpasch had the production car racing program in hand. Formula cars would represent a challenge that Jochen could not resist.

NORM NELSON

Norm Nelson was born on January 30, 1923. He was only 17 when thousands packed the Chicago Amphitheater to see the midget racers perform. Nelson had a dirt-track midget and he made a very brief race of it

439

that night. On the first turn of the first lap, he crashed into the wall. He was more embarrassed than injured, and continued driving until the U.S. Army put him into the Signal Corps and sent him to Europe for World War II.

He came back to the midgets after the war, but switched to stock cars when the popularity of the "bugs" declined. For 3 years he drove for other people, Ford, and then the original Rocket Oldsmobile o.h.v.-8 which shook up the stock-car troops when it initially came out. In 1950 he bought his own car and after that, except for a year he drove for Carl Kiekhaefer, he was usually an owner-driver and often an owner-employer too.

The fabulous Kiekhaefer team of Chrysler 300s started out in 1955 in the north and later competed in NAS-CAR. Nelson was one of the original drivers on the team. His 1st race for Kiekhaefer was a 150-miler at Milwaukee. Norm led for much of the last 50 miles but knew his tires were wearing thin. The pressure was intense, but to pit for tires meant dropping completely out of contention. Norm chose to go on to win—but 100 feet past the finish a tire exploded and he hit the wall, demolishing the car. Kiekhaefer did not even mention the car; he congratulated Norm for winning. But Nelson stayed on the team only one year, refusing to turn to NASCAR when the team made a publicity-based decision to compete in the south.

Rugged looking, 6 feet 3 inches with a shock of blond hair, Norm Nelson acquired the nickname Swede when he first went racing professionally in midgets. He was an excellent mechanic and an excellent businessman, as

well as an excellent driver. At one time or other A. J. Foyt, Lloyd Ruby, Jim Hurtubise, and Roger McCluskey all drove on the Nelson team. A Nelson Plymouth—his loyalty to Plymouth began the year after he quit the Chrysler 300 and constituted one of the longest stretches of marque loyalty ever—was a prime ride for amost 2 decades. The difference as the years passed was that later on the contract driver got the faster car, rather than Swede himself.

In 1963, 1965, and 1966, Nelson won the USAC championship in his specialty; he amassed more than 30 victories through the years, making a comfortable enough living to rear 8 children. In 1963, 1965, 1966, and 1968–70 he owned the most successful stock car on the circuit; McCluskey handed him back-to-back titles in the last 2 years.

Such derring-do gave him a stranglehold on all the longevity records in USAC stocks, yet he never had the least desire to switch to single-seater racing again. "I wouldn't be able to do that until my youngest was safely through college," he once quipped. Someone figured this would make him past 60 but nobody is betting that Norm Nelson wouldn't be around and rolling along as usual.

ALFRED NEUBAUER

Manfred von Brauchitsch was leading the German Grand Prix of 1938 in his silver Mercedes, but he was harried by one of his own teammates, Richard Seaman, who was determined to win a GP this season. Brauchitsch was determined, too, but also excitable. Seaman was icy calm. Alfred Neubauer, manager of the Mercedes Benz team, was annoyed and worried. Such dicing on the team gave the crowd a thrill, but was both dangerous and foolish since it could lead to elimination of both cars.

On the 16th lap Neubauer, a giant of a man (they used to say his trousers were made from old zeppelins), signaled Brauchitsch into the pits for fuel and tires—and a chance to cool off. Manfred begged Neubauer to call off Seaman. His face was as red as his helmet, Alfred later recalled. At that moment Seaman also pitted. Neubauer walked over to the Briton. "Please, Dick, do me a favor," he said. "Let Brauchitsch win this race. You should win at Donington." Seaman answered affirmatively, but it was apparent he did not like the order. Neubauer turned back toward Brauchitsch's car and momentarily froze in horror. One of Brauchitsch's fuel tanks was overflowing, and a mechanic was hooking in the electric starter, while Brauchitsch, unaware of the situation, was turning on the ignition.

Alfred's shout was mingled with the roar of the motor and the whoosh of flame as the fuel ignited. The whole tail of the car was in flame in a second. Brauchitsch was struggling to get out of the car, and his coveralls

caught fire. Neubauer leaped at the driver, pulled at the removable steering wheel, and dragged Manfred out of the cockpit. He threw the driver down and rolled him over and over to extinguish the fire on the coveralls. Mechanics meanwhile had the car fire out with the aid of extinguishers. Neubauer caught his breath, then uttered another shout. For there was Seaman sitting in his car watching in a bemused fashion. "Go, go," Alfred yelled, but Seaman pointed out that his order was not to pass Brauchitsch, and Brauchitsch still was in the pit.

Finally he was persuaded to go. Brauchitsch also managed to rejoin the race, but the mechanics had forgotten to fully secure the steering wheel, and at 130 m.p.h. Manfred suddenly was holding a disconnected wheel. He threw it overboard and attempted to steer by holding the naked steering column. But he crashed, and it was Seaman's race after all. Out of a full racing life, it was one of the most unforgettable moments in the life of one of motor racing's most famous team managers.

Alfred Neubauer was born in a northern province of Bohemia (later to become part of Czechoslovakia) on March 29, 1891. He was 7 when he saw his first car, a Benz, and determined then that autos would be his life. In his late teens both his parents died, and Alfred enlisted in the Austrian Army, in the military artillery college at Traiskirchen, near Vienna. With the outbreak of World War I, he went to the front, but he was returned to act as a liaison man at the Austro-Daimler works, where he met the young managing director, Ferdinand Porsche.

At war's end Porsche suggested Neubauer stay on as a production engineer and sometime driver on the factory team. Neubauer's initial outing was the Targa Florio of 1922, in a Porsche-designed 1100-c.c. Sascha. He did not win. The following year Porsche moved over to Daimler-Motoren-Gesellschaft in Stuttgart, and Neubauer went with him. Alfred gave up driving after 1924, a 3rd in that season's Targa his best race ever as a driver. He now concentrated on managing Mercedes racing. His stints covered the periods from 1924 through 1933, from 1938 to 1940, and from 1948 through 1955, when Mercedes left racing. Under his direction drivers blossomed in bunches, the best Caracciola, Lang, Kling, Seaman, Fangio, and Moss.

In 1937 Neubauer captained both the Mercedes and Auto Union teams at the Long Island, N. Y., revival of the Vanderbilt Cup at Roosevelt Raceway. In 1949 he was at Indianapolis as an observer with the idea of racing a Mercedes in the 500-miler in 1951. His procedure was both interesting and revealing. The 1949 race itself seemed to bore him, but immediately afterwards he was out on the track, walking the distance several times, photographing all important points, measuring distances from inner and outer reference points, even digging up and labelling small sample portions of the course at various points. The death of a leading Mercedes executive who had propounded the Indy invasion ended the project.

Neubauer ended his career zealously collecting and guarding Daimler Benz history in the form of data, photographs, and other materials, right on up to the cars that form one of Europe's great historic collections of motor cars. The imperious and often rude man of the early years gave way to a more gracious and patient man, especially with those to whom he took a liking, those who wanted to hear about those glory days when Mercedes *was* racing.

ULF NORINDER

Ulf Norinder, a roly-poly, bearded Swede with an unlimited supply of money to back his racing activities, went into and came out of retirement several times. One thing that kept pulling him back, despite his 220-pounds-plus, his 6-foot 3-inch frame and his need for glasses—all things that scarcely would seem to make him a candidate for the job of racing driver—was the creation, fruition, and spirit of Britain's Formula 5000. It was a form of racing seemingly created for Norinder. The cars were beefier than the usual Formula machines, they were gutsier with a full 5 liters of power, which was one of the major racing lures to Ulf, and they attracted drivers more akin to the older, fun-loving amateur/professional of the old days than the more prim and businesslike pilots of the late sixties and early seventies.

Drivers like Trevor Taylor and Tony Lanfranchi were

extroverts, but the most extroverted of them all was Norinder. At Brands Hatch late in 1969 the drivers had a party following 2 exhausting heats in the final round of the British F5000 championship series at the Hatch. Ulf had finished 7th overall for the season, but you might have thought he had emerged overall victor, for there he was leading the party, in flaming red slacks and a shirt open to the waist, dancing about, singing and coaxing characters like Mike Hailwood into song as well. Later, when the jazz band had about petered out, and the weary waiters and bartender were trying to close the bar and get these crazy racing people on their way, Norinder nearly incited a riot—a friendly one, of course—to keep the bar open.

Ulf was born in Stockholm, Sweden, circa 1934, and educated in the United States. He grew up without any worries about money and added to the kitty himself with real estate transactions from the Bahamas to Switzerland. He moved to Switzerland for tax purposes and also because his house adjoined Jo Bonnier's, and Jo was an old friend from many a race and art auction. Like Bonnier, another well-to-do Swede, Norinder accumulated an outstanding collection of modern art along with a long list of racing and sports cars. The two Swedes had known each other from their teens, and had traveled around to sports car races together in the late fifties. Ulf first raced in 1954, but became really serious—racing became his full-time interest—in 1959. That initial race was in Sweden, on the ice, of course, in an MG TD. Then followed such interesting mounts as a Ferrari Mondial, a 2-litre Maserati, a Porsche RSK, Ferrari GTO, Porsche Carerra 6, a Lola T70 in several forms, even an old Formula 1 Porsche that he drove in the initial F1 race at Karlskoga in 1961, and a Formula Junior Lotus 22, extensively modified to accommodate his rather beefy form.

"It was built for a midget, not a man," he recalled. "But my size gave me one advantage. I was the only man who could use his body as an air brake. Coming down the straight, all I had to do was sit up—had to do that anyway to shift gears—and I could leave my braking points to several seconds later than anyone else because my body tended to brake the car just like an airplane's flaps would."

In 1965 he retired for the 1st time, primarily because an old knee injury was acting up. He took up hunting, went on safari in Africa, roamed the ice in Scandinavia, and was back racing a year later. He tried powerboat racing a few years later as a substitute for cars, but came back to the wheels again. In 1970 he announced a final and irrevocable retirement at the age of 36 at the end of the F5000 season—but there was a new F5000 car ready with his name on it in 1971, a McLaren instead of a Lola, to be raced under the direction of the equally beefy Jackie Epstein. There also were sports car possibilities, although Ulf could never bring himself to concentrate on this form of racing. With Bonnier he drove

some endurance races such as the Sebring 12-hour battle and the Daytona 24-hour race.

What made Norinder so attractive and popular, aside from his "color," was his helping hand, which was extended to whoever needed it. He had plenty of spare power plants in his his well financed operation, and more than one F5000 driver raced on an engine borrowed from Ulf after the driver's own blew in practice. If a driver damaged an airfoil, or ran out of tires, or just needed a spare wrench, everyone in the F5000 circus knew where to go. In his spare time he collected hats and Mercedes motor cars, from a 1937 540K through mint gullwings to the latest offerings from Stuttgart. Norinder had one unfulfilled dream, not so strange when you remember his American upbringing: to race at Indianapolis. He did not make it as a driver, but you can still perhaps expect a Scandinavian invasion of the Brickyard one day.

SAM NUNIS

Floyd Samuel Nunis was one of the old-time racing promoters; part charlatan, part showman, and had there not been a streak of integrity which occasionally overpowered the other forces, automobile racing as we know it might not have been possible. He managed to change and adapt with the times, but was happiest when he remembered the days of his youth on the fair circuit with Ralph Hankinson, a squeaky-voiced giant who controlled much of Eastern U.S. racing. It was fun—not much money, but fun—excitement, showbiz. Sam Nunis had dropped out of the society of Esom Hill, Ala. He ran away at 16 to Birmingham where he played craps with hotel employes, then rode the rails, finally ending in Hamtramck, Mich., where he went to work in a Ford body plant. That was just after World War I and it was in the Detroit area that he 1st saw Hankinson and his wholly-owned racing show.

"When I saw them I knew this was for me," the rail-thin Nunis recalled. "There were 8 or 9 drivers in the troupe, and Hankinson owned the cars. Sometimes they would fill out with locals, but the winner was usually prearranged. Hankinson refused to take me on, so I quit Ford and followed him on my own." Nunis finally wormed his way into the troupe and stayed for 2 years before Hankinson decided to throw in with the AAA Contest Board and run open competition.

Years later, just after World War II when Sam was promoting in old Lakewood Park in Atlanta, he still referred to his days as a racing driver. He told gullible young reporters about how he wheeled a Frontenac-Ford to victory in places like Charlotte, Greensboro, Raleigh, and Atlanta. Decades later he laughed about the stories of driving prowess and noted, "I got my ink, didn't I?" Ink is newspaper space and Nunis was always a master at generating it. However, the story he told of ending his driving career at Concord, N.C., is true. He went through the fence in 1926, landing on a paved road with the car on top of him. It took him 18 months to recover and Hankinson took him on as an assistant promoter, an apprenticeship that was to last a decade. A metal plate in his hip was a souvenir. Once he had made it as a promoter, he began to drive a succession of Lincoln Continentals with built-in heater-massagers on the driver's seat.

There was once a time when Sam thought he could make more money outside racing. He accepted an offer to do sales promotion for the Montgomery Ward mail order house sporting goods line. When the war suspended auto racing, he went into the corporate training program and was assigned to a Baltimore store. He lasted 6 months, then came up to Paterson, N. J., where on impulse he bought the famed Gasoline Alley and the tavern that went with it from driver Joie Chitwood. "I thought it was a good business until I found out that booze was rationed," he recalled. "He took me, fair and square." Sam remained great friends with Chitwood; he admired a deal like that. His life's motto was always *caveat emptor*. Even before Nunis unloaded the tavern late in 1944, he booked Joie's thrill show that—to beat gas rationing—used propane as fuel.

After the war, Nunis went back into race promotion with great gusto. At one time he had race tracks under his wing from Maine to Florida, eventually all AAA Contest Board, and later USAC. He promoted AAA races at Charlotte before the advent of the superspeed-

way and at Salem, N. H., after the old board track was a memory. It was Nunis who gave an assortment of young men the chance to learn the racing promotion business, but his most successful graduate seems to have been Chris Economaki.

Nunis finally settled in at the Trenton State Fairgrounds under the aegis of another promoter, George Hamid. Hamid had the Steel Pier in Atlantic City, one of the wonders of the American entertainment world. Slippery Sam had watched NASCAR absorb part of his empire, and now lung trouble began to dog him. Besides, he used to say, the old days had ended even before the demise of the AAA Contest Board. The only way now was to concentrate on one track if you wanted to have major league shows.

New Jersey proved a gracious host for Nunis, and the Trenton oval was improved several times, the last improvement being an extra loop in the track so that the USAC Trail cars faced new challenges for Sam to ballyhoo. There were many stories about Nunis, most of them with only a grain of truth. But his cadaverous figure and his perpetually pained expression invited such stories. One USAC driver, Eddie Sachs, explained. "Sam has that pained expression because he thinks it's a shame he has to pay us for the fun of racing on his track in 90 degree heat," Sachs said. "I think he has a bad back from sitting on all the money he makes." Nunis never refuted quips like that. After all, it helped the gate. He retired from Trenton, but despite emphysema, was still promoting URC races in 1973.

TAZIO NUVOLARI

Did Tazio Giorgio Nuvolari have a pact with the devil? Was he the greatest driver ever? He was 32 before he won his 1st auto race, then went on to record 70 victories (52 of them outright regardless of class), including 12 World Championship races and 49 Grands Prix. In his career, he finished 130 races, took 2nds 16 times, 3rds 9 times. He began auto racing in 1921 and continued until 1950. This giant talent of the twenties and thirties stood all of 5 feet 5 inches and weighed 130 pounds. He looked like an underfed bookkeeper, and spent his last years as a driver fighting against lung hemorrhages that sent streams of blood coursing down his chest as he manhandled his cars to victory. During his career he was involved in many accidents that cumulatively broke most of the bones in his body at least once, left him minus an index finger, and with one leg an inch and a half shorter than the other.

Nuvolari was born November 16, 1892, in Castel d'Ario in the Province of Mantua, Italy—hence his later *nom de course* of Il Mantovano Volante, the Flying Mantuan. He rode motorcycles first, winning more than his share of 300 races, even when strapped to his machine because of body-long casts from previous in-

juries. When he was 16 a Bleriot airplane crashed near his house and was abandoned. Nuvolari repaired it and attempted to teach himself to fly; he crashed and wiped out the airplane, but sustained only a broken shoulder. In World War I, Tazio was accepted by the Italian Army as an ambulance driver because of his racing background, but his daredevil performance was such that he was transferred with the admonition to give up driving cars before he killed himself.

The thin Italian went back to the motorcycle tracks, rising to the Championship of Italy in 1924. Meanwhile, however, he had started racing automobiles. Nuvolari's 1st auto race was on May 22, 1921, when his Ansaldo was 2nd in the 2-litre class and 4th overall in the Circuit of Garda. During the next 3 years Tazio still rode the 2-wheelers, but slowly built his skills in the 4-wheelers on such mounts as the Chiribin and the Bianchi. It was in the latter car that he won his initial auto race in 1924 at Tigullio. That season he also won the 2-litre class at Savio and Polesine. Then he went back to motorcycles exclusively, not driving in another auto race until March 1927, when he relented to race a Bugatti in the Mille Miglia. That year he won at Garda and Rome (Prix Royal) in Bugattis, was 2nd in class at Montenero and 3rd at Perugia in the same marque.

Bugatti was also Nouvolari's mount in 1928. He really got going then, winning the Tripoli GP, Pozzo, Alessandria, and the Messina Cup unlimited class. He was also 2nd at Cremona and Montenero, 3rd in the European GP at Monza and 4th at Pescara. But the

following year the Italian had trouble finding a suitable mount, and his best efforts were 2nds at Montenero (Alfa) and Monza (Talbot), and a 3rd in the Tripoli GP (Bugatti). Alfa Romeo provided a car in 1930, and Nuvolari provided the talent. He won the Mille Miglia, perhaps the world's most challenging race in those days. He also won the Trieste-Opicina, Maddelena, and Vittorio-Consiglio hillclimbs. He won the RAC's Ulster Tourist Trophy, was 2nd at the Consma Cup hillclimb, and 3rd in the Masaryk GP.

In 1931 Tazio won the Targa Florio for the initial time, added victories in the Italian GP, the Ciano Cup, the Circuit of Tre Province, and 2 hillclimbs. Nuvolari was also 2nd in the Mille Miglia's 3-litre class and in the Belgian GP, and 3rd in the Acerbo Cup. The Targa fell to Nuvolari again in 1932, along with the Monegasque, French, and Italian Grands Prix, the Acerbo and Ciano Cups, Avellino, and a hillclimb. He was 2nd in the German and Marseilles Grands Prix. Then he went on to take the Mille Miglia once more and win the 1933 Le Mans outright (shared with Raymond Sommer), as well as the Tunis GP, Alessandria, the Eifelrennen, and the Nîmes GP, all with Alfas. In an MG Nuvolari won the RAC Ulster Tourist Trophy again. In a Maserati he won the Begian GP and the Ciano Cup, and he was 2nd in the Acerbo Cup and in the Italian GP. In 1934 Nuvolari drove Maseratis to victory at Modena and Naples, was 2nd in the Acerbo, and 3rd in the Spanish and Masaryk races. He drove an Alfa to a Mille Miglia 2nd.

Alfa regained his services full-time in 1935, and the fiery Italian captured Pau, Biella, Turin, the Bergamo and Ciano Cups, the German and Nice Grands Prix, and Modena. He shared 2nd with Rene Dreyfus in the Italian GP, and took another 2nd in the Masaryk GP. He was 3rd in the Penya Rhin.

The German race may have been his finest hour. Some 200,000 Germans expected an easy national victory as a silver fleet took the starting grid—4 Auto Unions and 5 Mercedes Benzes—along with Nuvolari in a worn out Alfa, a good 20 m.p.h. slower than the Germans. When the flag fell, Nuvolari made the middle of the pack at the 1st bend, and was 2nd at the end of the initial lap (just 12 seconds behind Rudi Caracciola's leading Mercedes). He dropped back as far as 6th in the next few laps, then began to move relentlessly ahead again until he took the lead on the 10th lap to the disbelief of the stunned German audience.

Tazio had to pit for fuel on the 12th lap and his untrained, perhaps uninterested Alfa crew took 134 seconds to fill the tank, almost 3 times as long as German pit crews, putting Nuvolari in 6th as he regained the course. In one lap he cut 4 cars out ahead of him and was 2nd to Manfred von Brauchitsch's Mercedes. Relentlessly the Italian pressed the German, forcing Brauchitsch to go faster and faster, cutting corners a bit more sharply, wearing down his tires. A patch of white began to show on one of the Mercedes tires, indicating heavy wear. With Nuvolari only 32 seconds behind, Mercedes could not call in their driver; driver and pit crew both were willing to gamble that the tire would hold for at least the 30 miles or so that remained. But it did not, blowing on the final lap and putting the incredible Nuvolari into the victory circle. If the German crowd was unnerved, the officials were even more so. It was traditional that the driver's national anthem be played as he was presented his award, but no one had thought to learn the Italian anthem. "No matter," said Nuvolari, "I have an answer," and he brought a record to the stand with him, a record carefully wrapped and stored for this occasion. The smile of victory on Nuvolari's gaunt face in the fading photos is one of great satisfaction.

In 1936 Tazio won Penya Rhin, Milan, Modena, the Ciano Cup, and the Hungarian GP. He also won the revived Vanderbilt Cup Race at Roosevelt Raceway on New York's Long Island, leading from start to finish. He was 2nd in the Eiferennen and the Italian GP. In 1937 he won the Mille Miglia once again for Alfa, but his mount in the Vanderbilt Cup caught fire and his other car, taken over from Nino Farina, could do no better than 5th. He drove German Auto Unions to victories in the Italian and Donington Grands Prix in 1938 and was 2nd in the 1939 Eifelrennen. Nuvolari also won the Yugoslovian GP on September 3, 1939, the day Europe went into World War II; it was the last international auto race on the Continent for 7 years. When racing resumed in 1946, Tazio was 54 and hardly regarded as a factor. Yet that year he won the Albi Cup in a Maserati, was 2nd at Mantuna in a Cisitalia, and took 3 other 3rds. In 1947 he won the 1.5-litre class in the Arcangeli GP at Forli and the Circuit of Parma, both drives in Ferraris, and was 2nd overall in the Mille Miglia and 3rd at Lido in Cisitalias.

But the end was near; the competitive grind was finally wearing him out. In 1948 he shared a 7th with Luigi Villoresi in the French GP at Rheims. Tazio's last race was in the Circuit of Monte Pellegrino, in which he took the 1.5-litre class for Cisitalia on April 10, 1950. His hemorrhaging had become worse and worse, doctors could not cure him; his 2 sons were dead. In late July 1953, Nuvolari lapsed into a paralytic coma at his home in Mantua. The Flying Mantuan died August 11.

BARNEY OLDFIELD

Who was the most famous American driver of all time? There is really no contest; it was a stocky, brown-haired, cigar-chomping ex-bicycle rider named Barney Oldfield. He disliked anything but match races, sneered at racing

associations, and felt the only good race promoter was one who was paying him exorbitant money to show up. Thanks to poor reporting and excellent press agentry, Oldfield's 17-year driving career will remain part legend and part reality, the proportions of each to be left to the reader's discretion. He was all showman, as indicated by his recognition of the value of keeping a cigar clenched between his teeth when racing, and using it as a trademark.

Barney actually used the cigar as a shock absorber, because when racing he clenched his teeth so hard they hurt afterward. The poor boy from Wauseon, Ohio, had no formal schooling after the age of 12, but he had charisma. Born June 3, 1878, Bernd Eli Oldfield used to quip that his 1st driving job was in the elevator in the Monticello Hotel in Toledo. By 1894 he had won silver medals and a gold watch in bicycling, and by 1896 he was being paid handsomely by the Stearns bicycle factory to race on its amateur team, as well as selling their bikes. In 1902 a bike-racing acquaintance, Tom Cooper, lent him his 1st gasoline-engined vehicle, a tandem English racing bike, to race in Salt Lake City, then his home base. By then he had already been married and divorced.

Oldfield left Salt Lake City that same year when Cooper wrote that he and a man named Henry Ford were building 2 race cars and that Barney might drive if he came to help on what looked like a sure winner. Oldfield came East on his own money, and thus began his association with the famous 999. He arrived a few days before the cars were to be tested at the Grosse Pointe Track. Neither car would start at the test, and a disgusted Henry Ford sold both, plus the Bagley Avenue workshop, to Oldfield and Cooper for $800 cash.

Cooper and Oldfield, with Spider Huff, an early riding mechanic, continued to work on the cars. They jumped at the chance to bring them to Dayton where an old bike racing promoter and friend, Carl Fisher of Indianapolis and Miami Beach renown (he founded the speedway and the city) promised them 25 per cent of the gate. He was the one who named their red car 999, after a crack NY Central railroad train that had set a mile speed record. The yellow one, Cooper's car, was called the Yellow Arrow. It failed to run at all but they got 999 going for an exhibition run. Oldfield's only contribution was blowing through a tube into the tank to create sufficient pressure to force fuel into the mixing chambers.

It was at the Manufacturer's Challenge Cup, the next exhibition at Grosse Pointe (after Cooper had redesigned the intake manifold for easier starting), that Barney finally got behind the wheel of 999. They had borrowed a horse from a frankfurter wagon to pull the car up to speed on a public road leading to the track. (There was a law banning cars from Detroit streets at that time.) Huff drove and Barney was the mechanic as they circled the track in practice for several laps. But Barney persuaded Huff to let him drive. He drove faster the 1st time out than either of the other partners. The race was to be against Alexander Winton, then American champion, and other hotshots of the day. The promoter was offering $200 if Barney could defeat Winton.

October 25, 1902, was considered by Oldfield his greatest thrill in racing. Ford had come out, counseling caution because, while he was sure of what his engine could take, he was very unsure of Barney's driving capability. But Barney shrugged his advice away, reportedly saying, "I'd rather be dead than broke." The field included Winton on his Bullet, White on his White Steamer, a Geneva Steamer, a smaller Winton called the Pup, and Barney.

Borrowing a page from bicycle racing, Barney was out to get a flying start on the rest by picking up the almost reflex rise of the starter's flag just before it waved down. This caused a false start, then Barney jumped them all and slid and slithered around the track for the 5-mile distance to beat Winton by half a mile. He used the only driving technique he knew, that of bicycle riding. Instead of shutting down for a turn, he powered into it, then steered in the direction of the skid. Ford became more enthusiastic after that and agreed to cooperate in a try for the world's mile record that December on ice. The ice course was necessary because 999 was rigidly suspended and needed a smooth surface. The newly formed AAA was to sanction the run for the record. Barney

drove the mile in the semi-darkness of pre-dawn in 1:01.2 to break Winton's mark, but the AAA disallowed the record for obscure technical reasons. This robbed Oldfield of $250 he had been promised for an official mark by a tire company and probably set the basis for his scorn of AAA. Oldfield and an engineer, Billy Hurlburt, then improved 999. They eliminated the suction intake valves for automatic ones, and changed the ignition system and the suspension.

On Memorial Day 1903 at the Empire City horse track in New York, Oldfield drove a mile in a minute flat in a match race against Charles Wridgeway's Peerless. Camille Jenatzy had done it in 1899 in France in an electric car, but as far as the American public was concerned, Barney was the mile-a-minute man. In June he clipped a second off the mark at Empire City, and in Columbus, Ohio, he lowered it to 0:56.6. On July 15, he wheeled old 999 onto the Empire City track and went down to 0:55.8. That was enough for Alexander Winton, who hired Barney for a $2,500 yearly retainer, with all prize money going to Oldfield alone, plus transportation expenses, mechanics, and free cars.

Ford and Cooper immediately challenged Barney to a match race, with Cooper to drive 999. Barney suffered a tire blowout in the 1st meeting, went through a fence, and killed a spectator. Although the famed Bullet was under repair, Barney said he would beat his old car and colleagues with a smaller, lighter Winton, which he christened the Baby Bullet. He did, easily, and began to name his own price in barnstorming around the country. In November 1903 he broke the 999 record in Los Angeles, going 0:54.4 in the Bullet. Winton brought Barney to Ormond Beach, Fla., where the wealthy raced on the sands, to be matched against William K. Vanderbilt. Henry Ford brought 999 there and in January 1904, Ford himself did a record 0:39.4.

Barney, meanwhile, was making practice runs in the Winton Bullet. However, Vanderbilt stole the headlines later that same month when he lowered Ford's record to 39 seconds flat. The fact that Oldfield beat W. K., Ford, and several others in the finals of the world one-mile straightaway championship was almost obscured.

Soon afterward Oldfield was hired away again, this time by Peerless, for whom he met all comers in the fabulous Green Dragon. To capitalize on the color, he had himself outfitted in a green leather suit. AAA suspended him for "outlaw" racing, but during a period of 18 weeks, appearing on 20 different tracks coast to coast, Oldfield made 4 exhibition runs and won 16 out of 16 against whatever talent was around. The suspensions had no effect on his appeal. He probably did more to popularize the motor car in the United States than any other man. This started with his very first run against Winton. A prosperous coal dealer, Alex Malcomson, was in the crowd, and was convinced by Oldfield's performance that Ford was a good investment. He subsequently put his money where his convictions were to start Henry on his way.

Meanwhile, Oldfield had become as much showman as race driver. Aided by the multi-talented Bill Pickens, he brought joy into the lives of farmers and fair-goers across the length and breadth of America with his interminable record-breaking. Much of it was as phony as a $3 bill, because he paid his alleged opposition and Pickens kept the stop watches. The fair-goers got what they came for, though, a superb show. Oldfield became so expert that he could win or lose by the width of a tire, said one historian, and his histrionic touches were magnificent—like when he reached into the engine of the Peerless Green Dragon, or the Blue Streak, or later, the Golden Submarine or the Blitzen Benz, to turn a coughing rough-sounding power plant into a purring kitten. Of course all he was doing was reconnecting a wire or some such simple adjustment. He always circled the track, waving at the crowd and saying, "You know me, I'm Barney Oldfield."

Oldfield even appeared on the stage occasionally. He and Tom Cooper starred in a success called "Vanderbilt Cup." Barney played a poor mechanic who saved the day. The Green Dragon and Blue Streak were anchored to a treadmill on stage. At the climax Barney opened up the motors and let them roar as the treadmill gave the impression of movement. It was Oldfield's idea to drop dirt on the treadmill, which blew into the audience to give a dusty road effect. By 1908 he was tiring of the fair circuit, and he sold his Peerless cars and retired. However, he stayed retired for only a few months, he came back in 1909 with the 120-h.p. Benz. He was presented with a gold-plated touring car at the opening of Indianapolis Speedway in August of that year for setting the mile record. In 1910 he bought himself another Benz, the famed 200-h.p. Blitzen, and on March 16, at Ormond Beach, he broke all existing speed marks for the mile, 2 miles, and the kilometer. It reestablished him, and even Kaiser Wilhelm sent congratulations. After that he was able to demand as much as $4,000 to enter real races.

Barney was much less successful in organized racing, although he tried. Suspension by the AAA in 1910 (because he engaged in a match race against Jack Johnson, then heavyweight boxing champion of the world) limited him at an age when he should have been at his prime. The suspension, which some claim had overtones of racism because Johnson had tried several times to apply for an AAA license but was refused, increased Barney's contempt for the group and helped foster a flourishing group of rivals. Oldfield later was reinstated and raced at Indianapolis. His best finishes were 5th places in the 1914 and 1916 races. He headed up the Stutz team in the 1914 race and was the top American finisher, 15 miles behind the first 4, all Frenchmen. In the 1915 race he placed his reliance on a Bugatti, but when the car proved underpowered he abandoned it and then failed to get a ride with Maxwell. For the 1916 race he was up on a Delage fitted with dual Miller carburetors, one of 2 dual-carb jobs.

Before the Jack Johnson episode, however, came other exploits that earned him large amounts of money and the scorn of the AAA. In the Green Dragon he staged car verses plane races with Lincoln Beachey in an early Wright airplane. After he sold the Dragon, he raced for Stearns, National, Knox, and then made his Blitzen Benz the major attraction of early IMCA programs. Good press agentry from Bill Pickens continued to put words in his mouth and increase his appearance money. Unfortunately, by the time he decided to play it straight he was past his prime. A look at his record shows his forte to have been road races and sprints. Because he never won an Indianapolis 500 or a championship track event, there is a segment of the racing fraternity that denigrates him. This is not giving the man his due. He ran the first 100-m.p.h. lap in Indy history, and he did it in a front-drive Christie that had defied the greatest drivers of the day. He was a fine road racer, unfortunately going legitimate when road races were on the wane. He won the 1914 Cactus Derby, a 670-mile Los Angeles-to-Phoenix event, in a Stutz, after finishing 2nd and 3rd in the Elgin, Ill., 1914 renewal. Earlier in the year he had lost a 1st at Santa Monica when he took a wrong turn on the final lap, driving for Mercer, and he had finished 5th in the Indy 500. The latter was quite a feat because he was the only American in an American car to crack the top 8 as the French swept up that year.

He drove for Mercer, Stutz, Maxwell, Delage, and Peugeot, and ended his competitive career in the Golden Submarine. But he helped put the Firestone Tire & Rubber Co. on the map. Many senior citizens still remember the slogan " 'Firestone Tires are my only life insurance', says Barney Oldfield, world's greatest driver." The Oldfield tire—backed by Firestone and eventually bought by it—became Firestone's racing division. The Golden Submarine was Barney's final exhibition car and was retired with him in 1918. Barney sensed that even the farmers were too sophisticated to stand for his heroics. Besides he was immersed in the tire business. Until the 1929 crash he was well-to-do. He sold out his tire interests in 1924, toured Europed in 1926. After the crash he was left penniless, but managed to appear in a movie about himself and write his memoirs. He had a dream of a 3,000-h.p. record car to be built by Harry Miller, a dream that was never realized. He finally ended up working at a California country club.

Barney was a leader, too, in the first successful race driver's union, the Automotive Drivers Protective Association. With Earl Cooper, Bob Burman, and Harry Grant, in 1916 he was successful in getting adequate insurance and new safety regulations from the AAA and a minimum purse of $100 per mile. That is the other side of a man who some said was interested only in himself.

In 1945 he remarried his 2nd wife after a separation of 21 years. On October 6, 1946, some 4 months after having been honored by the auto industry and the city of Detroit, he died in Beverly Hills.

JACK OLIVER

According to Jack Keith Oliver's stars—he was born August 14, 1942, at Chaswell Heath, Romford, Essex—Sunday is supposed to be his lucky day. Yet few drivers have suffered more misfortunes on race Sundays than he, and if it were not for his non-Grand Prix drives, Oliver might have been considered one of the leading failures of racing.

Jack's parents were fairly well-to-do, so there was little pressure on him to be conventional. He found school a bore and left at the earliest possible moment, age 17. But engineering and things mechanical obsessed Oliver, and he joined his father's Essex Refrigeration firm. He also built his 1st car, a Ford-engined special that he had some idea of racing. On Boxing Day 1959—the day after Christmas—Oliver went along to Brands Hatch to watch his father's Mercedes 300SL be raced by Sir John Whitmore, and the bug bit him deeply.

The Ford special was not suited to racing, he found, and it was sold for an 850-c.c. Mini, which was quickly

modified for racing. Hillclimbs and some club meets came first, and the Mini gave way in 1962 to a Marcos GT. In 10 races that year, he never placed lower than 3rd, but in the 11th Oliver demolished the wooden wonder rather spectacularly, ending up in a ditch holding a steering wheel while the rest of the car disintegrated around him. Oliver had the wherewithal to purchase the latest Marcos as a replacement, powered by a 997-c.c. engine. For 1963 a 1318-c.c. power plant, again devised by Superspeed, was substituted, and Oliver was able to hold off the onrushing Lotus Elan tide a bit longer.

In 1964 Oliver kept his Marcos until he saw that its course had been run, and that the Elans now were properly sorted out. He immediately bought a Lotus and made his initial start at Brands Hatch in mid-season. The result was a satisfying 3rd behind Peter Procter and Whitmore. After that race, Jack decided it was time to attack racing in a more professional way. He appeared only at races in which he could expect to make enough to maintain his car in a top-class manner. Now thoroughly familiar with the Elan, he swapped it for a Series 2 model for 1965, and the year was generally a good one, the highlight being victory at Montlhéry in the Coupe de Paris. Oliver also borrowed his father's E Jaguar and drove to 3rd overall (and 1st in class) at the Brands Hatch Easter race.

In 1966 he moved into Formula 3 with a Brabham for 3 races, then a "temporary" berth with Team Lotus, which turned into a 3-year contract. Jack's days were also kept busy with a saloon car ride in a D. R. Racing Ford Mustang, and he finished 2nd in the British Saloon Car Championship. But Oliver's heart was in single-seater racing, and the following year he was elated to see that activity increased. Driving a Lotus Components Type 41 Formula 2 car, he managed to do well, including victory in his initial look at Germany's famed Nurburgring. Racing with the Mustang (3 victories and 6 seconds in 10 starts) and with the new Lotus 47 GT car (including victory in the BOAC 500 with codriver John Miles) also continued.

Officially Oliver became number 3 on the Gold Leaf Team Lotus Formula 1 team in 1968, but Jim Clark's tragic death moved him up to number 2. In his 1st start at Monaco, Oliver crashed with Bruce McLaren, but in Belgium he finished 5th. At Zandvoort the Dutch sands fouled Jack's throttle. In the French GP, when leaving the slipstream of 2 preceding cars at speed, his Lotus's wing caught the air and whipped the car backwards in a twinkling, causing Oliver to ram a stone wall at some 150 m.p.h. The car was totalled, but Oliver miraculously walked away without a scratch.

In the British GP he surprised everyone by running the 2nd fastest in practice to team leader Graham Hill, and he actually led the race for 5 laps until Hill took over the lead on team orders. When Hill's car quit about a quarter of the way through the race, Oliver again assumed the lead and continued to pull away from the rest of the field, led by Jo Siffert in a Rob Walker Lotus, until a bearing seized while Jack was 12 seconds ahead. His race—and Team Lotus's—was over.

At the German GP, run under terrible weather conditions, Oliver refrained from pushing his car and finished 11th. Running at Monza for the Italian GP, he set a lap record (2 seconds lower than Clark's time the year previous), but Oliver's mechanical bad luck was continuing, and he dropped out while running 6th. A retirement in the Canadian GP was followed by a practice accident at Watkins Glen, when Oliver's Lotus again was totalled, but he again walked away unscathed; a wheel had broken as he entered a turn. But the season ended on a good note, a 3rd at Mexico behind Hill and McLaren. He had 6 championship points to show for the year's F1 work.

In F2, running as a Lotus driver for the Herts and Essex Aero Club—a deal arranged by Colin Chapman to cut down his racing expenses—Oliver finished 5th, behind the regular Ferrari and Matra team drivers. The expectation was that Oliver would really get going for Lotus in 1969. But Jochen Rindt was a new face on the Lotus scene, and he bumped Oliver clear off the team, since Chapman was still economy minded. BRM offered a spot, and Jack took it. The move was nearly disastrous. Oliver started 10 races, was retired in 8 of them. His finishes were a 6th in Mexico, the year's finale, and a 7th in the South African GP, which had been the season's opener. He had won a single point in the World Championship standings and tied for 16th.

Away from F1, however, Oliver's story was completely different. The long years of Mini, Marcos, Elan, and Mustang driving had paid off. At Sebring Oliver shared a 12-hour endurance race victory with Jacky Ickx in a John Wyer-Gulf Ford GT 40, and the same car and pilots shared victory at Le Mans 3 months later in a neck-and-neck finish. Oliver came back to America that season, too, to drive a new titanium car, the Autocoast Ti22, in the Canadian-American Challenge Cup series, but in 2 starts the car retired twice and finished a poor 13th at Monterey.

There was more of the same in 1970. Starting 12 GP championship races for the Yardley-BRM team, Oliver was retired by mechanical problems in no less than 10 of them. In the Austrian GP he managed a 5th, in the Mexican 7th. His single point of the year was good for a 19th-place tie in the final standings. Jack also retired in the nontitle Race of Champions and was 3rd in the Oulton Park Gold Cup. It was not a completely lost year, however, for in July, in a wedding attended by many of the GP greats, Jack married a young lady named Lynne, who had been a "Personality Girl" for Gold Leaf at the time Jack was driving for that team. That season he also drove the Autocoast CanAm car again and notched 2nds at Mosport and Laguna Seca.

In 1971 Jack looked things over and adopted a new tack—if you can't beat 'em, join 'em—for after watching J. W. Automotive win the World Manufacturers Championship for Porsche in 1970 with complete ease, Oliver switched to that side. The immediate result was victory at Daytona Beach in the 1971 season's 2nd long-distance race of the year, the Daytona 24-hour. He shared a winning Porsche 917K with Mexico's Pedro Rodriguez, a teammate from BRM. With Pedro he also was 2nd in the Buenos Aires 1000, 4th at Sebring, retired at Le Mans after running the race's fastest lap at 151.8 m.p.h. Oliver also won the Monza 1000 and the Spa 1000 with Pedro.

In CanAm racing Oliver took over the new Shadow, backed by UOP, still in its teething stage. There was controversy about his "jumping" J. W. Automotive for the ride, but he rode it out. Then Jackie made a move into Bill France's NASCAR ranks at Texas International Speedway. He was running 7th in the stocker when the engine blew up, but by that time both Oliver and NASCAR knew they wanted to continue this unusual affiliation. So Jackie was in another stocker come the Daytona 500, 1st of some dozen NASCAR appearances that the Briton was to make in 1972, along with his new Shadow drives in the CanAm. In 1973, Oliver returned to Europe for another GP try with the new UOP-supported Shadow, partnered by George Follmer. It wasn't the best F1 ride, but it was something.

ERNIE OLSON

In the days when racing an automobile was a 2-man job, the riding mechanic was the forgotten hero. Unless he turned into a driver, as many did with varying success, his name was doomed to disappear almost with the exhaust of the car. Ernie Olson was an exception. He began his career as a riding mechanic in 1916 and was still connected with racing in 1947 as the man who prepared Lou Moore's Blue Crown Specials for Indianapolis.

His riding mechanic days began almost by happenstance. Born in 1892 in Blairsville, Pa., Ernie worked with Lozier and Hudson—in the experimental engine department of the latter—learning his trade of repairing cars thoroughly. In 1915 he decided he wanted to see the Pan-Pacific International Exposition in San Francisco, so he hitched a ride with a Hudson dealer, A. H. Patterson, driving a car out. It was an uncomfortable 11-day journey by auto in those days. Olson liked the Coast so much he decided to settle in the Los Angeles area.

When he went to watch practice for the 1916 Santa Monica races he met Patterson again. Patterson was preparing the Hudson to race, and he needed a good riding mechanic. Ernie was the natural choice because he knew the car so well. Patterson finished 5th in the Vanderbilt Cup race behind Dario Resta, the winner. In the awesome 403-mile American Grand Prix, the dealer finished a remarkable 3rd, driving the 5 hours without a stop. Olson's efforts were rewarded with a Hudson factory team job, first with Patterson, then with the redoubtable Ira Vail, Hudson's premier driver. There was a hiatus of slightly more than a year for World War I, then in 1919 Ernie returned to Vail in time for the 500. They managed 8th in a Hudson only slightly removed from showroom stock.

It was Vail who developed the art of slipstreaming, and Olson was an important part of the feat of getting behind a faster car and hitching a ride at a speed faster than your own car could go unaided. The mechanic and the driver could not speak to each other because of the noise of racing. Olson guided Vail with hand signals. He told him when to move over to let the faster car pass. Then Vail would drop in right on the other car's tail, taking advantage of the reduced air pressure behind it.

Olson was a great riding mechanic because he was not only an extra pair of eyes, but could also jury-rig in an emergency. In a close race on a board track the throttle spring broke. Ernie devised a "rope" of handkerchief strips, attached it to the accelerator pedal, and thus was able to control the pedal pressure. Another time a fender was partly ripped off and bent toward the wheel making every revolution sound like a boy running a stick down a picket fence. Olson swung out on the hood, ripped the fender loose and tossed it away, then climbed back inside.

Finally, however, he joined Augie and Fred Duesenberg in their Elizabeth, N. J., plant prior to their 1920 invasion of Indy. He was tabbed to ride with Jimmy Murphy. The Murphy-Olson team only finished 4th, but it was the beginning of a relatively successful effort. They repeated their finish in 1921, then left for the French GP at Le Mans. The Duesenberg had a major advantage over the competition, 4-wheel brakes. This permitted Murphy to drive it much deeper into turns before shutting down. The course was in poor condition, the competitors' wheels throwing up fist-sized stones. Injured in practice, Jimmy drove the race in bandages, but with Ernie's expert hand signals he was leading easily—until a rock pierced the radiator 10 miles before the finish. The long lead was welcome then as the team cautiously circled the course for America's 1st GP victory.

Some riding mechanics did not prepare the cars in which they rode. Ernie Olson usually did. When Murphy bought the Duesy race car, Ernie prepared it for the next 500. He installed a new Miller engine instead of the Duesy and removed the front brakes. Olson-Murphy won the pole and the race in 1922. That was the last 2-man Indy until after the 91-c.i. formula expired in 1929. However, in Europe the 2-man cars were still prevalent, and in 1923 Murphy went to Monza for the Italian GP in a Miller. They finished 3rd, despite driving much of the race with only the hand brake for stopping power. Riding in a racing car of that day was not tooling around in comfort. Olson often sat on his leg to cushion himself, and he wrapped himself in gauze to minimize the effects of vibration. Springing was stiff and tire pressures reached 70–75 pounds. Indy was still paved with bricks, and the pounding eventually tired even the strongest of men.

Ernie subsequently rode with Ralph DePalma and the Frenchman Anton Mourre. He became chief mechanic for Bennett Hill in 1926, and through Hill was reunited with Frank Lockhart, a youngster he had refused to employ 7 years before in Beverly Hills. Lockhart won the 500 in a Miller prepared by Olson, then toured the board tracks successfully for 2 years. However, Ernie advised him to try the European circuit instead of the Land Speed Record, and they disagreed violently. Olson was tragically vindicated when Lockhart lost his life in 1928 on the Daytona sands.

In the next several years Ernie worked with Chet Gardner, Shorty Cantlon, and Ralph Hepburn. In 1934 he prepared the Millers that Pete DePaolo and Lou Moore took to the GP of Tripoli. His own active racing career ended in 1939 when he saw defending champ Floyd Roberts killed in a collision with Bob Swanson, who was relieving Hepburn. Olson then worked for the Warner Bros. film company for the next 2 decades; with one exception. In 1947 Lou Moore persuaded him to prepare the 2 Blue Crown Specials for Indy. Mauri Rose and Bill Holland finished 1st and 2nd. Ernie still had the touch.

PAUL O'SHEA

After the death of his close friend, Tommy Cole, in a racing accident, Paul O'Shea temporarily quit sports car racing. He did not return in earnest until he was tempted by the chance to drive a Mercedes-Benz 300SL. The O'Shea success story was made possible by the famed gull-wing car from Stuttgart. The soft-spoken Irishman became a celebrity thanks to the car, giving Daimler Benz racing honors from an entirely unexpected source. When he won his 1st SCCA title, O'Shea was 28 and balding, had a wife and young son, and commuted daily to New York City from suburban Rye, N.Y.

Paul O'Shea was born in Northampton, Mass., in April 1928. As an 11-year-old boy he had built a "racer" using the engine from an old gasoline-powered washing machine. Later he had a midget car powered by a motorcycle engine. Football, however, became a primary interest during school days; he was a small but agile quarterback. The O'Shea competition career began in 1949 when he entered a Simca in a Bridgehampton sports car race. Soon he graduated to a Fiat, powered by a Ford V-8 assembled by John Fitch, who later became a Daimler Benz team driver. He left college, where he was studying law and engineering, and opened a garage. He soon showed definite promise by codriving a Cadillac-Allard with Cole for a victory in a 1951 Vero Beach event. When Cole was killed at Le Mans in 1953, Paul quit temporarily.

He returned in 1955 when Porsche asked him to drive the 1100 at Sebring. "We went down there and we were lucky. Fritz Koster and I took the class. Things broke right for me after that. In 1955 there was this opening at Daimler Benz for an American consulting engineer. They wanted someone to tell them how to put small touches on their cars that the American market likes. They also wanted to know about spark plug wear, timing, and things like that under American driving conditions.

"Naturally I jumped at the chance. I told them they had to make their bumpers higher, and worked on problems of American SL owners," he added. "I got the chance to drive the Mercedes in competition through a personal friend, George Tilp of Short Hills, N.J. He wanted me to campaign his car in competition. Since Daimler Benz agreed, so did I. The first time I took the SL to a race was at the Cumberland, Md., airport in May 1955. The car drove heavy like a production car, yet handled so well I felt confident in driving deeper and deeper into turns."

O'Shea won at Cumberland in 1955 and 1956 and at Thompson, Conn., both those same years, but those courses were too small to let him get the 300SL out of 3rd gear. At the Beverly, Mass., airport in 1955, he failed to finish "because we decided to experiment with different grades and makes of oil." At the next Beverly race he again failed to finish. Still, he won an SCCA national title in 1956 and repeated in 1957, scoring more total points than any other driver in the U.S.

The return to racing seemed the best way to meet the right people for a lucrative auto career. After Beverly, O'Shea began the winning streak that brought him and the 300SL fame. He was 1st overall at Elkhart Lake, home of Road America, after winning at Torrey Pines. In 1955 he won twice at Torrey Pines, swept Hagerstown, Md.; Seattle; Sacramento; and Watkins Glen. He repeated at many of these places the following year (Elkhart, the Glen, Seattle) and added Texas's Fort Worth Airport and 2 hillclimb victories. He hoped to race in Europe, but no offer came.

In 1957 he left Daimler Benz but had much less success with Ferraris and Corvettes. O'Shea returned to the public eye briefly in 1965 as an expert witness for a plaintiff in an early unsuccessful suit against General Motors, alleging the Corvair was an inherently unsafe car. He was neither as entertaining nor apparently as convincing as the GM expert, Stirling Moss. GM won that battle, but eventually lost the war.

NATHAN OSTICH

A Canadian-born general practitioner in Los Angeles, Dr. Nathan Ostich was the first man to bring a jet-powered vehicle to the Bonneville Salt Flats, the "Flying Caduceus," to assault the long-standing reciprocal engine Land Speed Record of England's John Cobb (394.1 m.p.h. in 1947), so his place in automotive history is secure.

Ostich, born in Saskatchewan in 1908, was a United States resident most of his life. He received pre-medical training at the University of Michigan and earned his medical degree at the Los Angeles College of Medical Evangelists. He began practice in 1942 and 7 years later was interested in the automotive speed chase by Ak Miller. First it was drag racing and then Bonneville, which he started visiting in 1950. He set many class records in the years leading up to 1960, when he 1st appeared there to try his hand at the Land Speed Record.

The Caduceus failed to pass the 300-m.p.h. mark in two 1960 appearances. The first time out the vacuum created by his jet engine was so great during static tests it sucked in his air ducts. Modifying the car to eliminate this trouble, he returned, but the Caduceus's rubber ball joints decompressed at high speed and caused the car to shimmy across the salt. Poor course conditions prevented any runs in 1961, but in 1962 the doctor was at Bonneville again and survived a spectacular 331-m.p.h. slide that covered better than a mile and tore off one of his wheels.

"After it was over I was kind of glad it happened," Ostich said later. "I was glad to find out how the car and I would react in such a situation. And we learned that it was impossible to control the car at such high speeds with wheels alone. When it was heading straight down the line, it handled perfectly, but the slightest deviation from the straight, even two degrees, puts many thousands of pounds of pressure on the leading side and there's no way to hold it after that. That's why we added a rudder for 1963."

An estimated $100,000 and 10,000 man hours went into the 1963 edition of the Flying Caduceus. It appeared at Bonneville with an aircraft-like nose cone and vertical fin designed and built by Hanson Brothers Aircraft. The 6,500-pound car was built around a modified Chevrolet chassis. Firestone Tire & Rubber Company equipped the 4-wheeled speedster with specially-built tires capable of performing up to 600 m.p.h., despite the fact that their treads were but 2 hundredths of an inch thick. Firestone also forged the aluminum wheels for the car.

By then Craig Breedove's "Spirit of America," a 3-wheeled jet-powered vehicle, had reached the 407.45 m.p.h. mark, and this was the challenge that faced the 55-year-old doctor when he took to the salt for the last time. He reached 350 m.p.h. and realized that the J47 engine and its 5,200-pound thrust were a little too much for a man of his age to handle on the rough salt flats.

Ostich's dream died there, and his car was retired. But he had set the stage for the subsequent 1964 record derby at Bonneville when no fewer than 3 men assaulted and broke the LSR in similarly jet-powered vehicles, cars that were finally recognized by the sanctioning FIA as true automobiles, not fast motorcycles.

COTTON OWENS

Everett Owens was a skinny boy with white hair that gave him his nickname. He climbed trees outside the Piedmont, S.C., Interstate Fairgrounds to watch the jalopy races, for he knew that if he were to be famous in sports it would be as an auto racer.

His father owned a garage, and Owens grew up in the trade. He was kept in school until he enlisted in the Navy in 1943. When Cotton got out he was still skinny and still wanted to be in racing. A wrecking firm that sponsored Gober Sosbee, one of the titans of early modified stock car racing, offered him a job as a mechanic, and he jumped at it.

A year later, 1947, he got his chance to drive. It was at Hendersonville, N.C., and Sosbee complained that the car did not handle right. Owens asked and received permission to feel it out and amazed everyone with his natural technique through the corners. He drove the car, finished 2nd, and inaugurated a driving career.

With the advent of NASCAR, Cotton remained with the modified division. In 1950–51, he won 54 features, 24 of them in a row, and made his modified Dodge the scourge of the Southeast. Then, at Charlotte, in 1951, came an accident that set him to thinking for a while. He had started well back, but worked his way into the lead in 7 laps. But then a car crashed, and Cotton came around the corner full bore before officials and fans could push it out of the way. It was either hit the people or the car. He drove straight into the car, crushing his cheekbone and injuring an eye.

As he lay on a hospital bed, not knowing whether he was a candidate for a black eye patch, Owens decided that maybe his place was really in the pits. But 90 days later, his sight OK, Owens was charging along as if the crash had never occurred.

Cotton won the 1953 and 1954 modified championships. He ran a service station he had acquired and seemed unlikely to make any serious excursion into the late models. There was no reason to do so; he was doing well piloting modifieds. But in 1950 Owens had accepted a ride for the initial Southern 500 in a Plymouth and finished 7th. That had been about all, until he accepted the driving chores in a new Pontiac for the 1957 Daytona Beach Speed Weeks Classic on the old beach-road course. He won, and soon followed that with a 2nd in the Southern 500.

Convinced the late models were here to stay, Cotton began running more often for Pontiac. But when Daytona Speedway opened in February 1959, he decided that it was time to go into the mechanic business. It was a strange decision at the time, for he was the 1st to go 143 m.p.h. on the big track. The problem was to amass enough money to get another car, or to get a sponsor. He finished 2nd in the initial Atlanta 500 in 1960, and 2nd again in that year's Firecracker 250, setting a Darlington qualifying record.

In 1961 Cotton began to share his car with others, driving the dirt tracks and leaving the big ones for drivers like Bobby Johns, who won the 1961 Atlanta 500 in the Owens Pontiac. In 1962 Junior Johnson and Dave Pearson drove his Pontiac; and in 1963 Cotton Owens finally arrived. He contracted with the Carolina Dodge Dealers Association to maintain a stable of 5 racing Dodges. Johnson, Pearson, and Billy Wade were the original trio. For 1964 the names became Pearson, Bobby Isaac, and then came Charlie Glotzbach, ARCA transferee Earl Balmer, and Buddy Baker. There were others, the latest in 1971, blond Pete Hamilton.

Owens, born May 21, 1924, was married and had 2 children. A skinny, 5-foot 6-incher who weighed 140, he was a quiet, soft-spoken man who has regularly tithed 10 percent of his race winnings to the Baptist church. But he was shrewd, too. He surrounded himself not only with fine young drivers, but with fine wrench twisters, too. Among these were Maurice J. (Pop) Eargle, the 342-pound cigar-smoking strong man who said he worked because of 2 bad habits—eating, and smoking 12 cigars

452

a day—and Louis F. (Bud) Clements, a former Mechanic of the Year, retained to maintain Balmer's car. Owens never officially retired from driving. He just sort of tapered off, driving last in 1962. He had 9 Grand National victories in his career.

AUGIE PABST

The low point in Augie Pabst's racing career was probably the time he drove a car into a motel swimming pool. The high point, internationally, was probably a 4th-place ride at Le Mans, although the 1959 USAC road racing championship and 2 national SCCA Championships sound more important. Americans associate the name Pabst with beer. The blond, blue-eyed August was a member of the family, but until the time he retired from racing in March 1966, to join that firm, he objected to being linked with the brewery. This was not because of any bluenose tendencies, but because Augie felt it irrelevant to his racing career.

In 1956, when he was 21, the minimum age in SCCA, he began racing in a Triumph, then an AC Bristol, and finally bought himself a small Ferrari. "Nothing special," he once said of the Ferrari, "just something to keep the boys in the regional races down." His victories, however, were enough to convince the keeper of the Meister Brauser Scarabs that here was the ideal hero driver. Meister Brauser is another brand of beer, and it amused young Harry Heuer to have a scion of the competition in his camp. Besides, Augie had always

been pleasant to have around—full of jokes, highspirited and good-looking.

Two codrives to victory at the Road America 500 followed, as well as SCCA victories on both coasts. There was a quick assault with the Scarabs upon Europe, with indifferent success. There were Sebring drives for the Briggs Cunningham group, and even a stint in the Chaparral, for Jim Hall. All went smoothly, until the practice session for the 1962 Daytona Continental. Augie was thrown onto the track when his Maserati broke while going 130 m.p.h. It was almost $61,000 in doctors' bills and 6 months later before he was well enough to drive. That was when he became more serious about a foreign-car dealership he had set up in Milwaukee. That was really when he became a pro driver. It was to be 4 more years before Augie Pabst hung up his helmet. He usually had a good ride and he gave a good account of himself. He knew, however, that Dan Gurney, Richie Ginther and all those good boys from USAC were now crowding the road racing scene in America, so he quit. They call the beer Pabst Blue Ribbon, and a man with that name behind him couldn't be satiasfied as an also-ran.

CARLOS PACE

The brothers Fittipaldi were not the only natives of Sao Paulo, Brazil, to have made their mark in Grand Prix racing in the seventies. Another one was Jose Carlos Pace (prounounced Pa-chey), born October 6, 1944, of Italian parentage. Pace's father owned a large cloth making factory, and Carlos was expected to follow his other brothers into the business. He attended college, studying accountancy, but meanwhile harboring the notion to be a racing driver. At 16 he had bought a 125 c.c. go-kart and proceeded to win 6 races and finish 2nd in the Brazilian championships, the same year Wilson Fittipaldi was 4th. In 1961 Pace received a factory go-kart drive for two years, almost always besting Wilson when they met.

In 1963 Pace entered a 1-litre DKW in the inaugural Interlagos race, but did so well in practice that he was offered a Team Willys Dauphine Gordini for the race itself. Carlos finished 3rd after some others were disqualified, with his younger brother, Angeleo, in Pace's own DKW just ahead of him. Then Angeleo was disqualified and Pace found himself 2nd. Such was racing in South America. More Team Willys drives followed, including some class victories and a 5th in the Interlagos 1500. Staying with Team Willys, Pace became Brazil's 1965 saloon class champion.

Among Pace's partners in these varied endurance and saloon car races in 1966 and 1967 were both Fittipaldi brothers, including the then unknown Emerson. Most of the time he drove with Wilson, however, and also went solo on enough occasions to win the 1967 Brazili-

an National Championship with Emerson runner-up in the Fittipaldi-Porsche. He also started racing in Formula Vee, the VW-based single-seater class that was much more popular there than in the U.S. or Europe.

Pace repeated as Brazilian Champion in 1968 in a Team Willy Bino, a prototype loosely based on the Alpine Mk. 2. Then Carlos went over to Alfa Romeo's Jolly Team, driving the 2-litre T33/2. The big victory in this car was the Rio 3-Hour Race. He also won at Bahia before the car was written off at Rio. This kind of action earned Carlos his 3rd consecutive national crown.

The success of Emerson Fittipaldi in Europe caused Pace to make an exploratory trip there in October 1969 and arrange, with Emerson's help, to race a Jim Russell School Lotus 59 in Formula 3 in 1970. The debut race was at Snetterton, where Carlos finished 4th. He was a consistent F3 runner, and the season's end saw Pace crowned the Forward Trust F3 champion. In 1971 he moved up the ladder to Frank Williams's Formula 2 March 712M, thanks to a Brazilian bank sponsorship Carlos brought with him from home. The initial time out in the new car he finished 3rd, but the season gave mostly problems, despite a victory at Imola.

In 1972, though, with his own money and with his sponsorships, Pace found himself in Formula 1, initially in the South African GP. Driving a Williams March 721, he failed to qualify for the race. But in Spain he was 6th, in Monaco 17th. Retired in the British GP, he finished both the German and Austrian races but

was unclassified in both. Another retirement followed in Italy. Scarcely anything like Emerson Fittipaldi's World Championship winning season that same year.

MARVIN PANCH

The 2nd-string driver for Smokey Yunick's awesome Pontiac team for the 1961 Daytona 500 was a square-shouldered man with the face of a boxer who has lost one too many fights. His close-cropped haircut, sleepy eyes, and first wrinkles of impending maturity enhanced the effect. Marvin Panch, born May 28, 1926, in Menominee, Wis., felt he had little chance for the victory in his year-old car when Fireball Roberts, his teammate, was riding in a new, more powerful 1961 car. He was to be the rabbit in this race—set a pace so fast that other contenders would break and Fireball would move in to take over.

But something happened—Roberts's crankshaft snapped, and Panch was suddenly all alone out there in front, the lone hope of the Yunick forces. It was an unexpected assignment; his tachometer, in fact, was broken so that he had no idea how fast he was running. He hung on and won—the 1st of his great superspeedway victories. Marvin Panch was the first Western NASCAR star to succeed when he came East to challenge the big boys in Dixie.

Panch was a realist and a pragmatist. He became a stock-car driver because he found he was good at it. The reflexes he had used in an unsuccessful boxing career, and in high school football and baseball, seemed to make him a natural as a driver. Panch left high school in Minneapolis to help support his widowed mother. It was not long after this that the family moved to Oakland, where he had his short fling in the ring. Days he worked at what he could get, which turned out to be work in a garage. That inevitably lead to exposure to the local automobile racing scene. Marvin decided that it was a good way to make money and began entering a jalopy in the weekly races—as a car owner, until one day his driver failed to show. He ran the car himself, won, and car owner Marvin Panch became driver Marvin Panch. That eliminated splitting the cash. The same year—1949—he ran NASCAR late-model competition for the 1st time at Bay Meadows, finishing 3rd. He won the California NASCAR late-model crown in 1950 and again in 1951. Panch tried his hand at midget racing with mixed success because he was busily trying to build up a business.

He moved south to Gardena, Calif.—where he met his future wife, the daughter of the baker whose shop was adjacent to his garage—and had continued to compete. He was only moderately successful and went into the Army for his 2-year hitch without any great qualms. He got out in time for the 1957 season, and decided to give racing one more chance. He came east to Charlotte, N. C., and, driving a Ford, finished 2nd to Buck Baker in the Grand National point standings, the highest he ever was to rank that season. The next year he moved his family to Daytona Beach, eventually buying a farm on the outskirts of that racing and resort mecca. The move did not help his standings, since he switched to NASCAR's short-lived convertible division with his best a 3rd at Darlington and a 4th at the old Charlotte Fairgrounds. He was spending much of his time selling go-karts, which he felt, as did many others, could not help but sweep the country. Somehow he did not become a millionaire—just as most of the others did not—but he continued to race intermittently. In 1962 he finished among the top 5 in 5 of 8 races.

Marvin Panch joined Ford's 1963 effort to totally dominate NASCAR competition. He was going to devote full time to the business of being a race driver, with a ride in the Wood Brothers' Ford and assorted enduro rides promised in the likes of a Ford-engined Maserati hybrid which was to run at the Daytona Continental and at Sebring. On February 14, 1963, Marvin climbed into the hybrid for a practice run around the high banks of Daytona. The Briggs Cunningham car, entered in the Daytona Continental, had turned 163 m.p.h. laps in morning practice. Now Panch, in a further attempt to learn a road course that included much of the banking, plus a twisty slow infield section, was going to try again. Suddenly the car seemed to slow on the east banking and move sideways up to the guard rail, slamming it and flipping several times before coming to rest on its roof. Friends—Tiny Lund, Steve Patrasek, Bill Wimble, Ernie Graham, and Jerry Rayburn—beat the fire trucks to the wreck, As they got to the car, flames shot out. Undaunted they lifted the wreck and extracted the unconscious Panch. Seconds later, the Maser-Ford was a blazing inferno.

Marvin owed his life to them—and to the fact that for some reason he felt impelled to don a fire protection suit before this practice, although he had hardly ever bothered to take such precautions. He repaid Lund by personally requesting that Tiny take over his Wood Brothers Ford in the Daytona 500, which Lund proceeded to win.

Marvin returned to competition later in the year, winning the North Wilkesboro 250 and finishing in the top 5 in 9 of 12 starts. In 1964 he climbed to 10th in the point standings, running less than half of the Grand Nationals.

In 1965, the combination was the same, Marvin Panch—now 39—and the Wood Brothers. Marvin's record included twelve times in the top 5 in 20 races, 4 victories, and the undisputed rulership of the mean Atlanta International Speedway. A gentleman farmer on his 30-acre spread near Daytona Beach, he was also developing other business interests. On April 11, the

finest drivers in the United States were gathered in Hampton, Ga., a suburb of the metropolis of Atlanta—the finest, that is, except for the Chrysler stars, who were sitting out the season in the periodic engine controversy.

It was a Ford vs. Mercury battle. Darel Dieringer in a Merc stole the lead from Marvin on the 1st lap and led for 40 laps until he had to pit. Then Dieringer's teammate, Earl Balmer, led for 7 laps until he, too, had to pit. Freddie Lorenzen took over. Slowly the race shook down; now it was Lorenzen vs. Panch. The Panch car was involved in the only spectacular mishap of the day, as former SCCA ace J. T. Putney's Chevrolet was nicked by Marvin and spun down the embankment. Putney emerged, safe but fuming, and Marvin motored on. Lorenzen, attempting to win his 4th Atlanta 500 in a row, took advantage of a Panch pit stop to zoom into the lead. But it was short-lived, because Freddie blew a tire and was out of it. Unknown to Lorenzen, Panch had asked for relief on the 212th lap and A. J. Foyt, whose factory Ford had succumbed early to throttle linkage problems, took over.

Foyt had been about to leave the speedway when Glen Wood found him and got him as the relief driver. The victory was credited to Panch, who had handed over with a one-lap lead on Bobby Johns and had led 136 of the 212 laps.

Marvin returned on June 13 to win the Dixie 400 all by himself, outgunning Junior Johnson and Dieringer. On the northern tour he won NASCAR's road race at

Watkins Glen and then captured the Islip, N. Y., quarter-mile track honors. That was it as far as Victory Lane went for 1965, except for his Daytona victory in the Permatex 300.

In 1966 Marvin Panch finished 2nd in the Permatex 300 at Dayona, the World Series of modified racing. He was beaten by a man even older than he, Curtis Turner. In the Daytona 500, he qualified 7th, but was retired by a broken windshield. A piece of tire tread had cracked the windshield as he was running 2nd. At the Peach Blossom at Rockingham, a valve burned; at Bristol, Tenn., the engine blew; and at Atlanta it blew again. Then it was Ford's turn to stay home as both USAC and NASCAR slapped a weight penalty on their s.o.h.c. stock-car engine. That sidelined Panch, among others, but not for long. He switched to the Petty Plymouth reserve car and promptly collaborated with Petty in winning the World 600 at Charlotte. Panch took the lead for the 1st time on lap 302 of the 400-lap race and 18 laps later asked Richard for relief. The burns he had suffered in the fire had begun to ache and he felt it was a good precaution. Richard obliged and the duo raised the track record for the race almost 3 m.p.h., to 135.042. At the Firecracker 400 he managed a 7th place in a year-old car. He was nowhere at Atlanta when Petty won, but he managed a 4th place in the Southern 500, moving up from 14th, and a 6th in Charlotte's National 400, moving up from 12th. That was it, however, for Marvin Panch, race driver. He retired to look after his business interests, enjoy his children, and maybe reminisce about his 17 Grand National victories and about the ones that almost happened.

When he first came into prominence in NASCAR a reporter asked Panch how he came to be a stock car driver. Panch replied bluntly, "I have no idea." After he retired the reporter asked him the same question, reminding him of his previous answer. As he brushed some lint off an expensive coat Marvin replied, "I still have no idea how it happened, but I'm sure glad it did."

JIM PARDUE

They called him Gentleman Jim naturally enough, because James M. Pardue rarely was seen without a smile and always had a pleasant few words for one and all. Pardue, who was born in 1932, used his engaging personality well in his years as an automobile salesman in North Wilkesboro, N.C., until at the age of 29 he succumbed to a long-time ambition to go racing on the late-model stock-car courses in the Southland.

His top finishes in a new Pontiac for the 1962 season were a 3rd at Richmond, Va., and a 4th at Winston-Salem, N.C. He campaigned the same car in 1963 and finished 6th with 22,228 points in the Grand National standings. There was a 3rd at Savannah, a 4th at Richmond and a 5th at Hillsboro, but innumerable finishes

in the top 10. That was good enough to get a Plymouth factory ride. By 1964, he was accepted as one of NASCAR's most consistent performers on the Grand National circuit.

Jimmy Pardue was having quite a year in 1964; he had captured 2nd place in the rich Daytona 500 at Florida's Daytona International Speedway in February, one of 24 top-10 finishes in 50 starts. He had already made better than $35,000 in prize money as he drove out for tire tests at the Charlotte, N.C., Motor Speedway in September 1964. It was a pleasant day in every way save one—it was Gentleman Jim's last.

Pardue's car was travelling at about 140 m.p.h.— a good 10 m.p.h. below the speeds Jim had already reached on the newly paved circuit earlier that day— when, at the 3rd turn of the 1.5-mile course, his right front tire blew out. The '64 Plymouth sailed through the guard rail, covered 300 feet in the air, and crashed down a 75-foot embankment. Pardue was still alive when Darel Dieringer, first to reach the demolished car, pulled him from the wreckage. Rushed to Concord Hospital, Pardue died 2 hours later of massive internal and head injuries.

The tire company's investigations showed that an "external factor" rather than internal failure caused the crash. It was no consolation for the wife, 3 children, mother, brother, and hosts of friends who mourned the loss of Jimmy Pardue.

MIKE PARKES

With his credentials and connections, Michael Johnson Parkes would not have had to work very hard to reach the top in his chosen profession—automobile manufacturing. Certainly he did not have to take up competition driving, right on up to Grand Prix and endurance racing with the demanding Ferrari team, to attract notice. For the quickest results, he could have stayed on his British home grounds instead of traveling to Italy, and then flying about the world as professional drivers must do these days. Was Mike Parkes crazy? Yes, crazy like a fox.

The son of British industrialist J. J. Parkes, former chairman of the Alvis Car and Engineering Company, he liked to do things his own way. A proven automotive engineer and project manager, he was nobody's man but his own.

Born December 24, 1931, near London in Richmond, Surrey, Mike skipped the old school tie, in favor of the much more practical route of a 5-year apprenticeship in engineering with the Rootes Group at Coventry, starting in 1949. He stayed with this through 1962, working on the development of such projects as the Hillman Imp, which is amusing if you knew Mike, who stood 6 feet 4 inches tall. It was during these years, too, that Mike's competition career started, although not by the usual

route. "My first competition car was a 1930 chain-driven Frazer-Nash," he recalled with a grin. "I shared the cost with a couple of other fellows, and we bought that car because that's all we could afford on our apprentice salaries." The Frazer-Nash was raced from 1952 through 1955, in various states of tune, at Vintage Car Club meets.

Following an MG TD (in which he won his 1st race, at Silverstone), Parkes mounts included a Lotus 11 that was acquired in another partnership deal in 1956, a Formula 2 Fry-Climax that was raced from 1957 through 1959, a Formula Junior Gemini, 3.8-litre Jaguar saloons, and a variety of Ferraris, but that's getting ahead of the story. Mike was asked to advise Sir Gawaine Baille on his Lotus 15 early in 1959, and the pair became friends as a result of this chance meeting. They conceived the idea of codriving Baille's Lotus Elite in the Nurburgring 1000 that year and at Le Mans as well. Even after Baille retired from driving, Mike drove the car in British club meets and drove well enough to attract an offer from Tommy Sopwith to join the latter's Equipe Endeavour on a 2-man Jaguar sedan team with Jack Sears. Occasionally, with Sopwith, there would be a ride in a Ferrari Berlinetta. The team's debut was at Snetterton, and Mike won the saloon race in his 3.8-litre Jaguar, Sears coming in 2nd. For the GT race, both drivers practiced with the Ferrari, and Parkes was quicker, so he got the nod; he won that one too. The next weekend at Goodwood, he repeated the double victory.

Parkes drove for Equipe Endeavour in 1960 and 1961 while continuing his work at Rootes. At the Le Mans practice in the latter year, he was testing a Sunbeam when Ferrari invited him to try out a factory car. As a result, Parkes was invited to codrive for the Italians in the actual race, and he accepted, thinking the ride would be in a Berlinetta. Instead Mike was delighted to find himself sharing a 3-litre Ferrari sports car with Willy Mairesse of Belgium; they finished 2nd overall. The same team had the same result in a Berlinetta at Nurburgring in 1962, but retired with an overheated engine at Le Mans that year. Co-driving with John Surtees in a GTO, he was 2nd in the Montlhéry 1000.

On January 1, 1963, Mike Parkes became a full-time member of Ferrari. "My work is divided into two clearcut sections," he said. "I carry out development testing on the prototypes and Formula-1 cars for the racing part of the factory, and then race them. I am responsible for the experimental department of the factory as well, and this entails being involved in a new production car from where it starts on the drawing board to the point where the first prototype is made, developed and tested, and then when the first replicas start to come off the production line. This also involves making spot tests of production cars to ensure that the standards established on the prototypes are being maintained in the production run.

"It is really impossible to compare Maranello with my former Rootes career at Conventry," he added. "In one case I worked for a firm employing 14,000 people and making 4,000 vehicles a week, and now work with 450 people making 17 cars a week. One was big industry; the other is something like a Santa Claus factory making very expensive toys for rich children to play with. Fortunately there are customers who really appreciate the workmanship, time, and energy devoted to the end product at Ferrari, and that, in turn, is derived from the competition experience."

Mike's own Ferrari competition experience continued apace with all this. In 1963 he and Umberto Maglioli of Italy were 3rd at Le Mans, and Parkes alone was 2nd in the Tourist Trophy and in the Coppa Inter-Europa Monza. The following year Mike and Maglioli won the Sebring 12-hour race, and the Briton won the Spa GP, was 2nd with Jean Guichet of France in the Nurburgring 1000, and finished 3rd with Ludovico Scarfiotti of Italy in the Rheims 12-hour race. His Le Mans mount retired, and the season was shortened by an accident at Modena. In 1965, however, Parkes was back at it with Guichet (1st at Monza 1000 kilometers, 2nd at Nurburgring 1000) and Surtees (2nd in Rheims 12-hour race) among others.

A whole new chapter in the Mike Parkes Story opened in 1966. He continued his factory duties, of course, and his long distance racing—winning the Monza 1000 with Surtees, the Spa 1000 with Scarfiotti, and the Paris 1000 with David Piper—but to this was added the challenge of F1. It all started when friction once more tore apart the Ferrari forces, culminating in the June withdrawal of team leader Surtees and elevation of Lorenzo Bandini of Italy to the top spot. Who would fill the number 2 berth? None other than M. J. Parkes, a 34-year-old who had driven F1 cars only on a test track. The car had to be especially adapted for the tall Briton, and Ferrari mechanics complained that they fell out of sight when they had to press down on the pedals. Mike's first F1 race came July 3 at Rheims, and the rookie finished 2nd to Jack Brabham who was on his way to his 3rd World Championship. Mechanical failures and crackups ended his bids at Zandvoort and Nurburgring, but Parkes copped another 2nd at Monza, behind teammate Scarfiotti, in the Italian GP. That was good enough for 12 points in the standings and a tie for 8th place, not bad for only 4 starts.

"F1 races are infinitely preferable to Le Mans and similar starts. The long-distance classics are much more dependent upon luck, and in them, it is much harder to apply the Fangio formula—to win the race at the lowest possible average," said Parkes. "To me, motor racing is a sport, and I drive to enjoy it. Much of my early racing was done because it furthered my curiosity and knowledge about motor cars. Now when I race I give myself a great deal of personal satisfaction, but it is completely selfish, completely egotistical. Of course, creating a motor car is creating something not only useful but, if it's good enough, something that is going to give a great deal of pleasure to a large number of people. And that can be regarded as making a useful contribution with one's life."

Parkes's GP contributions ended abruptly the following season, when after a 5th (good for 2 champion points) at the Dutch GP, he started the Belgian GP at Spa-Francorchamps and was involved in a horrendous accident on the opening lap. He was running 3rd when his Ferrari slid; he overcorrected, causing the car to mount a bank, roll over several times and eventually eject its driver. People who saw the accident thought Parkes must surely have been killed, but he survived with head injuries and a smashed leg.

He never drove GP cars again in competition, and his 1967 long-distance season, which was going well right up until the crash, was ended, too. Parkes and Scarfiotti had teamed for a 2nd at the Daytona 12-hour race, another at Monza for the 1000, and still another at Le Mans, just before Parkes's near-fatal Dutch crash. They also had a 5th at the Spa 1000. After the crash, the Briton tried to regain his touch at various long-distance races, and his extensive experience in such competition has enabled him to get rides with NART and other Ferrari-oriented organizations. But the old touch was elusive.

In 1971 Parkes finally left Ferrari and became team manager for the Swiss-based Scuderia Filipinetti, although he operated out of Modena's old Serenissima factory with a new Fiat 128 stable of cars for European

Group 2 racing. Sports car racing, F1, and GT projects, were also in the offing. Mike would be busy even if he never sat behind the wheel again.

WALLY PARKS

A belly-tank lakester was the ultimate in rodding and the ultimate in streamlining in the days after World War II, when Wally Parks helped to found the NHRA. Parks was editor of *Hot Rod* and NHRA was formed to assist the many rodding clubs around in establishing and maintaining competition in the sport which was only then becoming formalized.

Back in 1934 Parks had become interested in rodding when he went to watch the pioneers of the sport compete on the Muroc Dry Lakes in the desert area of Southern California. In 1937 he joined the Roadrunners, which eventually joined with other Southern California groups to form the Southern California Timing Association, predecessor of the NHRA. Parks, always mechanical, had bought and modified a 1924 Chevrolet 4 from an uncle. His family were Okies, victims of the Dust Bowl, and he had been born in Goltry, Okla., a tiny village almost too small to make the map. Most of his early life, however, had been spent in California.

He found employment in the auto industry as an assembly worker at a General Motors plant, and eventually became a test driver for them. When World War II came, the plant was converted to the production of tanks, and Parks tested them, becoming in fact, part of an exhibition tank drill team. Finally the long arm of the Army grabbed Parks and put him to work—testing tanks, until he saw service in the South Pacific Theater. But the love of rodding had not left him, and Sgt. Parks decided that the world needed a Jeep V-8. He built it with an engine commandeered from an old passenger car, made other modifications and created the world's 1st—and certainly the Philippines' 1st—Jeep rod, open exhaust and all. The Jeep changed his Army career; he became a roving troubleshooter, traveling all over the Philippines in his hot Jeep.

When the war finally ended for him, Wally returned to GM for a short time until he resigned to become business manager of the SCTA. He put together one of the first, if not *the* first, hot rod shows for the rodders to exhibit their machines. It was a rousing success, and the idea of a national organization was already brewing in Parks's imagination. "Hot rod" was an anathema then, referring to the kids who raced illegally on public roads. Parks and his colleagues were determined to change the meaning of the world. It was a long but successful battle. Wally was the first editor of *Hot Rod*, which he encouraged Bob Petersen, a publicity assistant at a movie studio, to start. He eventually ended up as editorial director of a publishing empire before he resigned to devote his full time to the job of president of the NHRA.

It was Parks who supervised the standardization of the sport to a quarter-mile acceleration run from a standing start, between cars classified in the same class or handicapped according to the rating of their class against that of their opponents. The decision to make the quarter mile the standard distance was colored by the fact that the sport had shifted to airport runways and the quarter mile was the distance which allowed enough apron to stop the cars after competing.

The break from Petersen didn't come until 1963, by which time NHRA was organized in every state of the union and had spread the sport overseas. The organization became a member of the Auto Competition Committee for the United States, American representatives to FIA, and Parks became its representative. By this time he had retired from active rodding, something he had carried on throughout his days as *Hot Rod* editor.

Belly tanks from aircraft bombers seemed ideal bodies for lakesters—vehicles intended for competition on the the 1st of 3 straight International Trophy races at 80.56 dry lakes and later at the Bonneville Salt Flats. Moreover, after the war they were very available, very inexpensive, and easy to convert. This was before fiber glass revolutionized rodding construction. Wally created the prototype, or one of the prototypes, of these belly-tank lakesters, and drove it to an assortment of records. He was still running for the record on the beach at Daytona in 1957.

Drag racing, or hot rodding, or more usually rodding, is a highly professional sport that still manages to allow the rankest amateur in his father's car the possibiltiy of competition. Parks presided over the phenomenal growth of the sport throughout the western world and spawned numerous imitators. He was not the sole motivating force; many others in other sections of the country also nurtured the sport. But he was the best organizer and the best politician, joining ACCUS/FIA partly in a move to shut off one of the most potentially dangerous rivals, NASCAR, which once had a burgeoning drag program underway.

In 1972, for the Nationals at IRP, Parks faced the beginning of his greatest challenge. The name fuel drivers, led by Don Garlits himself, boycotted the event. The results were inconclusive since the Indianapolis Raceway Park seemed as crowded as ever. But 1973 came and Wally had made a truce by upping some prize money. At least some of the stars became regulars again.

REG PARNELL

There is a thing about some British drivers. They gain a certain aura, even if they don't exactly accomplish what they set out to do. Stirling Moss, as an example, never won a World Championship, but he never really

had to; his reputation exceeded that of most champions for the obvious reason that he was that good. Reginald Parnell was another case in point; he was a Grand Prix driver who never won a World Championship *grande épreuve,* yet whose reputation as one of the best of his era was firmly established.

Born in 1911 in Derby, England, Parnell started in a classic way, running an MG in club races at Brooklands and at Donington Park in 1935. He won his 1st race in 1937, but the war interfered, and it was 1946 before he started racing seriously. That 1946 season Parnell ran 2 races in a Maserati, coming in 2nd to Prince Bira in the Ulster Trophy and 4th to 3 Alfas at the Grand Prix des Nations at Geneva. In 1947 he won a couple of races in the Swedish GP series in an ERA, won the International Jersey Road Race in the Maser, and came in 3rd to Luigi Villoresi and Louis Chiron in the Nimes GP.

The following season Reg was 3rd in the Jersey race, 2nd in some local hillclimbs, 3rd at the Zandvoort GP behind Bira and Tony Rolt. At Goodwood, Parnell won m.p.h. He was 2nd to Villoresi in the Penya Rhin GP, the first of 3 straight International Trophy races at 80.56, 5th in the Italian GP, his 1st try at a *grande épreuve.* In 1949 most of Reg's action was in a Maser, and there were 3 Goodwood victories, as well as one at Zandvoort. In 1950 he added Alfa Romeo, BRM, and Aston Martin sports car rides, and there were a couple of Goodwood victories, plus a 2nd at Jersey, a 3rd in the European GP at Silverstone and a 4th in the Dunrod running of the RAC Tourist Trophy. His GP start at

Silverstone was in a factory Alfa, making him the only British driver to gain that distinction since Dick Seaman.

Parnell was now at the height of his career, as it was to turn out, although far from its finish. More Goodwood victories, more 2nds including the Thinwall (actually a Ferrari in disguise). He was 5th in the British GP, 7th in the Le Mans 24-hour race for Aston Martin. In 1952 Parnell won only Formula Libre races in Scotland and at Boreham; there were many Aston drives, the best coming at Silverstone and in the Mille Miglia, where Reg recorded 2nds, the latter in the GT class. The next season he and George Abecassis came in 2nd to John Fitch and Phil Walters at Sebring, and a close 2nd to Peter Collins in the Tourist Trophy. In the Mille Miglia he finished 5th, despite a broken throttle cable; Reg just wired the throttle wide open and finished on the ignition key.

There were many more races for Reg Parnell, races that carried all the way to the Tasman races of 1957. He went out like a winner, taking the New Zealand GP at Ardmore in a Ferrari, at 76.94 m.p.h., in January, then the Dunedin GP the following month. After that, Parnell immediately became team manager at Aston Martin, a chore he had occasionally tested himself at as early as 1952 at the Goodwood 9-hour race. A World Championship in 1959 in sports cars and 4 years tracking an elusive World Championship in F1 followed with Aston and its Bowmaker team. In 1963 Bowmaker folded, and Reg Parnell (Racing) Ltd. was born. Chris Irwin and Mike Hailwood were his drivers, but Reg did not live to see either one do well. In January 1964, he died unexpectedly. His son, Tim was there to carry on, but it was not the same.

How good was Reg Parnell? Very good. Without the interference of war, he might well have been one of the best. Even though he was far older than Hawthorn or Collins in the fifties, he could still beat them occasionally. Even though that age difference existed—as well as a considerable experience gap in his opponent's favor— he could duel with Stirling Moss on fairly even terms, although Moss remained a particularly elusive foe as time passed. Parnell's place in racing history was that of leading his country into racing prominence again, and at that he succeeded beyond all expectations.

BENNY PARSONS

Mother's Day 1971 and the South Boston, Va., Speedway were etched indelibly in the mind of Benny Parsons, a balding young man who moved from Detroit to Ellerbe, N.C., to pursue a carreer in NASCAR's Grand National circuit. It was that day and in that locale that Parsons, born July 12, 1941, and yearning for the checkered flag seemingly from birth, bested Richard Petty and James Hylton for his 1st GN victory.

Benny Parsons had been a hero in ARCA, a mid-

western stock car league that annually came down to Daytona for the Vulcan 300 on the Daytona International Speedway. He won the ARCA championship in 1968 and 1969 but even then he was dabbling in NASCAR competition.

In 1970 the opportunity came to campaign what was virtually a factory Ford and Parsons switched to NASCAR. His most lucrative finish was 3rd in the World 600 at Charlotte that year ($11,445) but he did manage 23 top 10 finishes out of 45 races, 12 in the top 5. He earned $52,325 on the season. What would have happened if Ford Motor Co. had continued with all out supporting through Holman-Moody and others was only conjecture for Parsons who felt he had proved himself the equal of most of the NASCAR regulars. Ford didn't; Parsons continued in a 1970 mount for 1971 and won himself $51,720 with 13 top 5 finishes out of 35 races entered.

In 1969 Parsons had won ARCA's 300 miler at Daytona; it was a lucrative victory paying more than $12,000 but Benny said he savored the South Boston victory as much. "It means I'm on the scoreboard. Now I've already done something that three-quarters of the others in NASCAR have never done."

The sparse Mother's Day crowd saw exceptional racing between Parsons and polesitter Bobby Isaac for 247 laps before Bobby broke his engine. Depite a charge by Petty, Parsons won easily.

For 1972 Benny switched to a 1971 Mercury and concentrated even more on the Grand National circuit alone, shunning the South Bostons of the new GN East division. He had a prediliction for 4th place finishes, managing that spot at 6 different tracks. Since most were supertracks the money ranged from $3,400 at Bryan, Tex., $4,730 at Atlanta, $4,175 at Darlington and his biggest payoff, $5,650 for the Daytona 500.

Parsons, son of the owner of a small taxi fleet, was ringing up pretty good fares, considering the equipment.

CHUCK PARSONS

American road racing has had several Grand Old Men. Among these was Charlie Parsons, who at 45 had been rechristened Chuck Parsons in order to get more "with it." Chuck, or Old Charlie, was still chugging along in 1971 in such major series as the Group 7 Canadian-American Challenge Cup. He did not win, but he made life interesting among the back markers.

Parsons hailed from Blue Ridge country in Kentucky, somewhere near Bruin. His limp, so pronounced in later years, wasn't from racing, but from falling off a car when he was 5 years old. They didn't have a doctor, so the smashed bone just healed the way it was. By the time he was 21 (Parsons was born in 1927), Charlie had moved to Southern California. Ten years later, the last race held at Pebble Beach was his first as a spectator. The 150-pound young man was properly impressed. He had saved enough money to buy himself a car, and that turned out to be an Austin-Healey. He began racing in the Healey and in a Porsche, and then went on to a Lotus 15, powered by a Ferrari engine no less. To feed himself, as well as the cars, he founded an imported car dealership in Monterey.

In 1959 Jim Hall sold him what was purported to be the best Birdcage Maserati in the United States. Parsons raced it a year, then sold it, "to recover from the cost." Next came a Sunbeam Alpine, a slightly less hairy car than the Maserati. In 1953 Parsons raced the 1st Lotus 23B twin-cam in the United States. His big victory in this car was at Laguna Seca. In 1964 he was in a 289 Cobra and managed a 5th at Bridgehampton in the Double 500. In 1965 came the Genie-Chevvy Mk. 10 with which he won the United States Road Racing Championship the following season.

By this time Parsons was a triple grandfather, thanks to the 3 daughters of his first marriage. It never showed on the track, however. At Las Vegas he was 2nd, at Riverside 3rd, and at Laguna Seca 2nd again. Coming east he had a bad streak and retired at both Bridge-hampton and at Watkins Glen, although he led the latter for 37 laps. His sponsor decided it was the car, and handed Parsons a new McLaren-Elva Mk. 2. At Mid-Ohio he was 3rd, then 2nd. And old Chuck won the Road America 500 doing a solo act, making the championship his, the hard way.

The CanAm started in 1966, Parsons was in it in his McLaren-Chevvy. A 3rd at Mosport started it all. He was 6th at St. Jovite, 6th again at the Bridge, 16th at

Monterey, 8th at Riverside, and he didn't finish at Las Vegas. The next season he retired at both Mosport and Road America, was 6th at Bridgehampton. On the West Coast he placed 14th, 12th and 10th. They started to write Parsons off for 1968. In a Lola T160 he was 5th at Edmonton, but the car was retired at Road America and Bridgehampton. Monterey was the same story, but there was an 11th at Riverside, and a quite good 4th at Las Vegas. A Lola T163 for 1969 made quite a difference, with Parsons piling up enough points for a 3rd-place finish to the Bruce McLaren-Denis Hulme 1-2 punch. His best showing was a 2nd to Hulme at Riverside. There were 3rds at St. Jovite, Road America, and Monterey, and 5th-place finishes at Mosport, the Glen, and Texas. He completed 9 of 11 starts, his worst position a 7th.

There wasn't much fun in 1970. Parsons started only one of the first 4 races, and in that one, at St. Jovite, he finished 8th. At Mid-Ohio he seemed back in form with a 4th, but this was followed by 3 retirements, a 6th at Moneterey, and a final retirement. Parsons finished a lowly 14th in the standings in the same car he had raced so well in 1969. He didn't have a regular ride in the 1971 CanAm. At St. Jovite, Tony Dean handed him a McLaren M8D, and Parsons finished 4th. At Mid-Ohio, World Racing had a Lola T163 for Parsons, who filled in for Ron Grable, who had suffered a broken leg in another series. Charlie was 5th. At Road America he was classified 14th, with an oil leak holding him in the pits. Paul Newman's McLaren M8D was available at Edmonton and Laguna Seca, and Parsons posted an 8th and a 10th respectively. Parsons drove various high-speed cars in other racing. In 1969, for example, he shared the winning Roger Penske Sunoco Lola Mk. IIIB coupe with Mark Donohue at the Daytona 24-hour race. And in 1972 he still was capable of scoring 3 points in CanAm competition at Road Atlanta. Who says that racing is strictly a young man's game?

JOHNNIE PARSONS

It took 9 years from the time he officially began his racing career in a midget at Los Angeles for Johnnie Parsons to become the USAC National Champion. In his first 2 Indianapolis appearances (1949 and 1950), he finished 2nd, then 1st. Although he seemed to be unbeatable, and he developed into one of the front line drivers of his era, Johnnie Parsons never quite reached the greatness that he had seemed to promise. In fact, he may be remembered for his efforts to encourage late-model stock-car racing on the West Coast as much as for a USAC Championship career that contained 11 victories on the Trail, as well as 4 2nds, and 5 3rds.

That none of these occurred after 1953, although John didn't leave the Trail completely until 1959, would indicate that success really can dull the desire to triumph. In the latter days of his career, a 3rd place in the 1957 Race of Two Worlds at Monza showed that all the skill had not eroded. Parsons never lacked good mounts at Indy. His list of car owners included the Wynn Oil Company, the Belond Equa-Flow people, J. C. Aga-janian, Jim Robbins, and Kurtis-Kraft. He was a good finisher, and was around at the end of 7 of the 10 Indianapolis races in which he competed.

His 2 victories in 1950—at the Indy race flagged at 345 miles because of rain and at the 200-mile race run by AAA on the Darlington banks—were the high points in a career of almost 13 years. All his regional midget championships and his national championship came before then. In an interview with Russ Catlin, Parsons blamed his later lack of success on an inability to get consistently good mounts, something that is moot. Apparently he took his national championship and Indy title very seriously, for he said, "I was determined to make my appearance before the public the best I possibly could. That meant clothes, clothes, and more clothes. I kept fresh changes of clothes for every appearance. I felt that was my price to pay (for being auto racing's champion). Speaking is another thing at which I worked. I would go over and over my speeches, and in time I felt I was improving. I wanted to sell auto racing, and how I tried."

Parsons said that he had made the Championship because Harry Stevens, the chief mechanic who had given him his initial midget ride, had prepared the Walsh car superbly. The 2nd place in the 1949 Indianapolis 500 led to an early 3-cornered championship race among himself, Bill Holland (who won), and Myron

Fohr. Myron led up until the Milwaukee 200, when Parsons broke the battle wide open with victories there and at Syracuse, Springfield and Langhorne. He had also won the opening race of the season at Arlington Downs, Tex. Parsons's initial Championship win had come in 1948, at the 2nd DeQuoin, Ill., 100-miler, when the great Ted Horn lost his life. As the hottest driver in captivity, he was a favorite in the 1950 Indy 500.

"I was determined to win," he said, "but a couple of incidents annoyed me considerably. First, when Harry discovered a crack in the block of my car race day morning and the p.a. announcer made it public, a misconception was set up. When, at the beginning of the race, I came up on my teammate, Freddie Agabashian, and passed him and Mauri Rose early, everyone said I was out to burn up the track and collect all the lap money I could before the engine flew apart. I felt my slow start the previous year had cost me that race. I was merely following the same plan I would have even if there had been no crack in the block. Incidentally, that crack was so minor that the same block was in the car when it finished 2nd in 1951.

"When the race was stopped at 345, people began to ask if I would have won if the race had gone 500 miles. How should I know? Up until then I had raced every car on the track and won. Early in the race, Rose and I went into the first turn together. Rose's front wheel drive was supposed to pull him through faster. But I put it to him as if it were a midget race and he backed off. If he hadn't I already had my seat picked out in about the tenth row of the stands. I felt I earned that lead."

Incredibly, Parsons's car was bought out from under him, and he let emotions rule when he selected the Grancor car to defend his season crown. Making every midget and speaking appearance possible, he had pretty much lost his Trail crown by the time Darlington rolled around. On this stop, he was supposed to get his old car back, but because he missed plane connections, the car was assigned to another driver. There had been much talk that he was washed up anyway. Paul Russo and Ray Nichels gave him their car, however, because Paul had not fully recovered from an accident. Johnnie won by 2 laps and set a new track record.

Parsons once expressed a desire to win the World Championship if he could have an American mount. He was premature by a decade. Born July 4, 1918, Parsons retired before the 1959 Indy 500 and eventually tried to help NASCAR organize a strong West Coast division. A second generation Johnny Parsons, his son, had taken over the USAC driving.

JIM PASCHAL

James Roy Paschal, a quiet, muscular man, allowed himself the luxury of a grin as he drove into the winner's circle of the 1964 Charlotte Speedway World 600. As he wriggled out of the electric blue Petty Team Plymouth, he was sweating, dirty, and tired. He had won the longest NASCAR stocker classic, and he was too tired to laugh and hug people, a 38-year-old man in a sport for young chargers.

It is lucky for the beauty queens that are an integral part of every American post-race ceremony that many drivers tie bandannas across their faces. It makes awarding the traditional kiss of victory less trying, if not always pleasant. Paschal submitted to the tradition with what seemed to be a quiet resignation, although, as a man freed of marital ties, he could have been more enthusiastic. At 5 feet 9 inches tall, he was not much taller than the high-heeled race queens and the girls representing commercial companies who are major supports of NASCAR. Most of all, his attitude revealed that he was tired.

Born December 5, 1926, near High Point, N.C., Jim Paschal was destined never to stray far from there. All he ever sought was a chicken ranch—maybe 100,000 chickens, a few cattle, and enough ground to grow a few things. That, and victory in the Southern 500. He had been in the first Southern 500 when he started racing in 1947, in a modified race at Daytona Beach. A bunch of Carolina boys went down, and Jim joined them. He won a little money, came back, and did a little modified racing back home while working for his father as a furniture refinisher. He intermittently drove in Grand Nationals as early as 1949, but did not join the circuit in earnest until 1953, when he finished 7th overall in the season standings. In 9 of the next 12 years, Paschal finished in the top 10 of each season. In 1958 and 1959 he was in semi-retirement. In much of the rest of that period he had never challenged for the championship because his mounts—Hudsons, Fords, Mercuries, Pontiacs and Plymouths—were non-competitive. He had strings of victories, however. In 1962 he had won 250-milers on consecutive Sundays at Bristol and Nashville, Asheville and Weaverville. All were half-mile, paved tracks, demanding stamina and patience from the winner. In 1963 he made only 32 starts, won 5, and finished in the top 5 in 18 of the others. This is what attracted Lee Petty to him when Lee decided to make some money with his spare car. Lee had driven it a few times, entering it as insurance in case Richard's broke, enabling Richard to switch over. By 1964 the hemi was so reliable that first Buck Baker, and then Jim Paschal were put in the No. 43 Plymouth. It was Paschal's turn for the World 600 in 1964.

It was the kind of warm humid day that drivers hate and cars love. The humidity hung like a shroud that constricted the lungs and made breathing an effort, but it made the engines purr. The favorites were Fred Lorenzen and Richard Petty, with David Pearson possibly coming through for Dodge. Jimmy Pardue has set a new qualifying mark for the 1.5-mile oval of 144.346 m.p.h.; Paschal had qualified 12th.

Pardue soared out in front with Fred Lorenzen (Ford) and Bobby Isaac (Dodge) right on his tail. Suddenly, disaster struck as Junior Johnson's Ford spun on the backstretch, and the Fords, of Fireball Roberts and Ned Jarrett, collided while trying to avoid Junior. Both gas

tanks exploded on impact, Jarrett crawling out of the flames and running to the aid of Fireball. It was too late, however; the accident was ultimately to prove fatal to the great Roberts.

Meanwhile, the Petty forces, Paschal and Richard Petty, were content to let Pardue fight it out with Paul Goldsmith, Lorenzen and Isaac. Pardue led the first 33 laps before Isaac jumped him for the lead, holding out for 15 laps until Goldsmith finally edged in front on the 67th around. Lorenzen, gunning for his 7th straight victory, was waiting just off of the pace. Lee Roy Yarbrough, in a Dodge held the lead for 3 laps while Paul pitted. Goldsmith, however, got it right back keeping it through lap 79, when Pardue took over for 41 laps. Pit time forced 3 quick changes: Goldsmith led a lap, then Yarbrough, and finally David Pearson, in a Dodge, began his 24-lap stint in the lead. All this time Paschal and Petty hung back, watching Lorenzen. Now veteran Buck Baker, in a Dodge, led for 41 laps during which early leaders Isaac and Yarbrough pushed behind the wall with rear-end troubles. While Goldsmith was re-assuming the lead on the 189th lap, fast qualifier Pardue was getting ready to leave the race with a broken oil line. Paschal and Petty were moving up the ladder as much by attrition as anything.

It was a Goldsmith–Lorenzen battle now, with Paul leading through lap 189, Freddie taking charge for 41 laps, then Goldsmith leading until his engine blew. When that happened Freddie looked like a sure winner unless Paschal could catch him. Then fate intervened. Fred ran over a piece of tie rod and spent 9 laps in the pits. For the first time Paschal took 1st place. He kept it to the finish, finally winning by 4 laps over Petty, who had tire woes, and by 7 laps over the Rex White and Fred Lorenzen Fords. The 6th finisher, G. C. Spencer in a Chevvy, was 36 miles behind, and 16 miles ahead of the 7th-place Larry Frank Ford.

Jim almost got his Southern 500 victory that year, driving a Petty Plymouth, but had to settle for 2nd place to Buck Baker. That season he finished 7th over-all, winning more money than he had ever seen before, $54,960 for 22 starts. In 1965, when the Petty forces were paid to sit the NASCAR season out, Paschal showed up in a new Chevrolet of his own. He never made it run well the whole way, but managed 4 top-5 finishes in 10 races for $7,085.

He had bought his farm and he was to buy into a construction business that also prospered. Picking his spots carefully, he won $29,415 in 1966, and then in 1967 shook up the troops again. It was World 600 time, and 41-year-old Jim had qualified 10th in his No. 14 Plymouth, which had been prepared by Bill Ellis. The day of the race was steaming hot, with track temperatures reaching 138 degrees Fahrenheit. Tires would be a problem—that is, if the heat didn't get the driver 1st.

When pole-sitter Cale Yarborough set a torrid pace in the early stages, no one expected Paschal to take out after him. However, along with Darel Dieringer, who

was to exit with a blown engine), there was old No. 14 —not taking it easy in the early stages as usual, but forcing the pace. Paschal assumed the lead for 7 laps, just before the 60-mile mark, and lost it to other con-tenders. He regained it for some 50 miles, then lost it on a pit stop. Slowly the hot shoes were falling out. Paul Goldsmith made what seemed the final challenge, then Paschal was out there all alone from the 161st lap of 400, sailing toward what seemed like certain victory. He might have been too confident, or maybe the heat had gotten to him. Just 58 laps from the end Paschal drove into the guard rail on the 4th turn, bounced sever-al times, mangling his car and flat-spotting the tires. He held a 3-lap lead over Bobby Allison at the time.

He limped into the pits, where the crew worked fran-tically on the machine, thanking their stars that the cau-tion lights had come on and held the field in the same relative positions. Then, 3 laps later, the green flashed, and Paschal limped back into the race–still almost 2 laps over Bobby's Dodge, but with a car that he could no longer push to top speed because of steering prob-lems. Could he hold off Allison and the onrushing David Pearson? Despite the heat, the 75,000 fans were on their feet screaming as lap by lap the challengers whittled away at Paschal's lead. On lap 367 Bobby unlapped himself, and Pearson followed right behind. With only 18 miles to go, Bobby had to pit for gas, removing him as the immediate threat. Paschal's crew was holding up "Gas" sign to him, as well.

The crowd wondered if he would gamble, because Pearson did not need fuel. Jim made his gamble on the speed of his crew. He sped into the pits, took 10 gallons of gas and sped back out before David could completely close the gap. Only 15 miles to go and Pearson was gaining. Paschal made his 2nd gamble. Suddenly he ac-celerated his speed, praying the steering would hold. It did, and James Paschal found himself beside the incredibly voluptuous Winky Louise, who was 2 inches taller and quite a bit cooler in her Miss Firebird cos-tume. He was a winner by the length of a straightaway over Pearson, or 5 seconds on the clock.

The win was his final Grand National feat. Later in the season he switched to an Oldsmobile with little luck, and then came back to Plymouth. It was not his final racing thrill, however. Paschal did not race in 1968 and seemed retired. Then came the opportunity to drive a Javelin in the Grand American (Grand Chal-lenge) NASCAR series. Like an ancient war horse, Jim snapped up the opportunity, gave American Motors its first race victory in more than a decade, and added more in finishing 12 out of 26 in the top 5, for $17,100 in prize money. In 1970 he pressed Tiny Lund all the way, losing the season crown by only 67 points. He won 10 races, finished 21 of 35 in the top 5, and earned $31,367. He curtailed his racing after that, trying Grand American with little success in 1971 and Grand Nation-al East in 1972, earning less than $13,000 for the 2 years combined.

JAS PATTERSON

Back in 1967 someone took a scaled-down version of a Grand Prix racing car chassis and dropped in a 1500 c.c. Cortina engine. By June of that same year, there were enough of these mini-Formula 1 cars around to hold a debut race for Formula Fords, as they were called, at Brands Hatch. The following year F/F moved to the continent initially at Zolder, Belgium. Today F/F cars—now powered by 1600 c.c. engines—are a fixture at race meetings all over Europe, North and South America, Australia and Africa. But it is in Britain where F/F is most popular and most competitive.

Originally conceived as an inexpensive way for the amateur to go single-seater racing, F/F became more expensive as it became more sophisticated and demanding, but still was the least expensive way to get the proper grounding for bigger, more powerful professional classes of racing. To buy a car, properly prepare and maintain it over a full season, and live frugally—the F/F driver's way of life in almost all cases—costs from $5,000 to $15,000 annually if you were lucky and didn't have to buy too many new engines or to repair or replace the car too often.

In Britain perhaps 200 men managed to go F/F racing almost every weekend from March to October. There always was an international flavor to British F/F races . . . Continentals, a few South Americans and Canadians, quite a few Aussies and Kiwis, an occasional American. In 1972, Americans came over in force. There were at least 7 of them, all acting quite independently of each other, all brought by what drew so many non-British nationals to the major F/F championship series and numerous lesser championship series and club events that dotted British race meetings every Saturday and Sunday.

"It's the opportunity for concentrated competition in a very professional atmosphere," said 24-year-old Jas Patterson, one of the more promising of the visiting Americans, who raced a Texaco-supported Wimhurst Mk.4, a British-built F/F car. "In the States you are lucky to race every two or three weeks, unless you keep moving around the country. That can be expensive and very time-consuming. Coast-to-coast it's 3,000 miles, Canada to Mexico it's another 1,000, so we are talking about a large piece of territory.

"And quite frankly, F/F racing in the U.S. is very much on a club level compared to England. In the typical American F/F race, usually there are but 3 or 4 really serious drivers with equipment, talent and determination enough to win. The rest are weekend warriors," said Patterson. "Contrast that with 50 to 75 entries for a Championship F/F race here. Most everyone in a 20 or 30-car starting field wants to win, and 10 to 20 have some kind of a chance."

If Patterson were not typical of the Americans racing in British F/F, he was typical of those with the best chance of making it into richer classifications of racing.

In a few years you might read a capsule biography of the young man that will say this:

JAS PATTERSON. Born 8 January 1948 on Long Island, N.Y., U.S.A. First expressed desire to be a professional racing driver at age 9. Began racing bicycles, switched to go-karts, then motorcycles. Joined SCCA 1968, sponsored by former French GP driver Rene Dreyfus. Began racing with Austin Healey 3000 following year, and won SCCA titles in sports car and endurance races, 1969–70. Drove Daytona 24-hour Race, 1970, in Porsche. Entered single-seater racing with Palliser F/F 1970, SCCA New York Region champion, 2nd in North Atlantic Road Racing Championships, 1971. To the U.K. March, 1972. First European race at Brands Hatch.

Patterson graduated from Colgate University in June 1971, with a degree in economics. In prep school and college he had played soccer and squash, but gave them up for racing, and he gave up skiing, too. In fact, in some ways Patterson started living the life of a motor sport monk once he got to Europe. He woke up in the morning thinking about racing and went to sleep at night with his mind still on the subject. In between he worked at his London garage on his car, practiced at Brands, talked to potential sponsors, raced, of course, sometimes on both Saturdays and Sundays.

"I came over last winter and lived in Chelsea for a month while I scouted about," Jas recalled in 1972. "By the time I went back home, I had located my apartment in Norwood, lined myself up with Len Wimhurst (ex-Brabham and Lola technician and Palliser designer), started the paperwork to get an RAC competition license." Back in the States Patterson built his own crate to ship the racing car, spare parts and special tools to the U.K., made final arrangements and flew back in March. "It was a bit late then, and we had some car problems, so I really got a late start here, but 1972 was my most satisfying year in racing yet.

"We've talked about the concentrated opportunity to practice and race as compared to the States," he said. "There are many other differences in racing here in England, too. In the States you race on special racing tires even in F/F. Here you have so-called 'street' Torino tires, which give the car quite different characteristics. You must use these tires here, but back home they were considered illegal. Most racing in the States is from a running start, whether it's Indianapolis or NASCAR stockers or F/F. In that way it is quite out of step with international racing, which favors standing starts. I've known some American drivers to have great trouble in adapting, and that can be disasterous. A decent start dictates what you are going to be able to do, certainly in F/F in which cars are so evenly matched and opportunities for passing limited. Fortunately, I didn't have any trouble adapting and, in fact, I prefer standing starts," said Patterson.

"Then there's the need the moment you arrive for being ready to qualify for your heat as best you can. In America, usually there are long practice sessions in which you can pace yourself up to a competitive edge. There is time enough to worry about gear ratios, tire pressures, engine adjustments and all the rest during practice and before official qualifying. But here you have a short practice session, and what you do determines your grid position. The British system puts great stress on being race-ready when you arrive at the course, and it makes mid-week practice and work on the car a necessity and not the luxury it is in the States. This system also is closer to the way higher classifications are run and not to the slower pace of the amateur racer so common in America.

"Another major characteristic of racing in Britain is its professionalism. This extends not just to drivers and the way cars are built and prepared, but to officials, who are of a uniformly high quality unlike the States, where you get great disparities in sideline people." Patterson laughed. "I'm sure the SCCA wouldn't like my saying that, but it's true, it understandable. The U.S. is just so large there is little way to properly police every race in Britain is equal to a single area in the U.S., and British officials are dealing with pretty much the same people most of the time. It makes for better work, I think."

"There is a good deal more aggressiveness here. It's more wide open than what U.S. drivers are allowed to do. Many things drivers do here would get them blackflagged, or banned in the States. I suppose it's part of the greater competitiveness in Britain. It's certainly part of learning to be a professional. But the instances of drivers helping each other off course are legion. All of us have stories of how we were helped by British drivers in one way or the other," Patterson said.

Patterson's 1972 F/F season was a successful, albeit not an especially winning one. "It's an accomplishment for an American to last a full F/F season, here," he said. "The competitiveness this year has been especially fierce. Oldtimers around Brands and the other tracks claim it's the roughest, most competitive season they can remember. To win a F/F race now, you almost have to 'drive disconnected.' That's the local way of describing drivers who go all out to win, who drive over anyone who gets in their way, who literally throw their brains away and forget about possible consequences in terms of physical damage, whether to their cars or themselves."

Despite its ferocity, F/F drivers manage to come through the hot-house of single-seater racing fairly well. At least 3 Formula 1 drivers in 1973 were F/F graduates, including the World Champion, Emerson Fittipaldi of Brazil. Others were his one time teammate David Walker, and Tim Schenken and Vern Schuppan, all of Australia, and Jody Scheckter of South Africa. Patterson? He had a number of poles to his credit, still more front-row qualifications and top 3 finishes. And he was a truly polished professional after just a year in British F/F.

In 1973, Jas rose to the increasingly popular Formula Atlantic series in England—comparable to the SCCA's Formula B, using Formula 2 cars with slightly less horsepower. His mount was the Texaco March 722, and a month into the season, Patterson was tabbed the series' "surprise star." The Patterson game plan called for F2, F5000, and, hopefully, a shot at USAC's Championship Trail.

DAVID PEARSON

Dave Pearson, a curly-headed, good-looking youngster, couldn't pay anyone to give him a ride in a Grand National stock car. He had won everything that could be won in NASCAR's minor league—limited sportsmen. He had started racing in a 1940 Ford in an outlaw hobby race at Woodruff, S.C., in 1952. He won $13 for his trouble, but liked the thrill so much he knew that "racing is my life."

This was David Gene Pearson, 3-time NASCAR champion talking: "We didn't know how to prepare that car, we didn't even know how to jimmy the suspension. We did it by getting a bunch of fellas to stand on the left side while we tied it down with chains." Pearson finally bought his own late model in 1960, and assayed the superspeedway circuit—Daytona, Atlanta, Darlington and Charlotte. He spent all of his money, and borrowed most of the rest.

"I went to Daytona that year and stayed with a friend because I couldn't afford my own room. I wasn't

too much better off when I left. My 1959 Chevy couldn't stand the pace and finished 18th. If I had known then what I know now, I never would have bought the car. It had run its course." Pearson's nickname, "Ll'l David," came from his days on the outlaw tracks, when Carolina promoters, faced with dwindling gates because a particular driver was winning everything, would send for him. He would conquer the local Goliath, as likely as not.

Pearson, born December 22, 1934, had a rough time breaking into NASCAR big leagues: "There were some friends of mine in Spartanburg, who tried to use their influence to get me a ride in 1960. It didn't do any good though, and I scraped together the money to buy that Chevvy. I led a few races with it, but it never would stay together long enough to finish a race. In the first World 600 I was second with 54 laps left when my generator came loose. I fastened it with a wire coat hanger and went out again, but I had to make 7 more stops to keep fastening it on. I finished 10th. I got pretty disgusted with late models then and had almost decided to go back to the sportsmen circuit in 1961, when I got a break. Ray Fox and I thought alike. The purpose of a race is to run the car as fast as it will go and win. You've got to have luck, sure, but a well-prepared car and a good race driver can make a lot of the luck you need. With that in mind, we went racing."

It was Pearson's 1st good chance to prove his abilities on the superspeedways. He responded with 3 major victories—the World 600, the Firecracker 250 and the Dixie 400 at Atlanta, making him the 1st man to win on 3 of the NASCAR Big 4 tracks on a single year. "I guess the biggest win was the 600 at Charlotte," said Pearson, who was to shift to a 1965 Dodge owned by Cotton Owens, also of Spartanburg. "That's the longest race on the circuit and everybody wants to win it. It gives the driver and the car a good physical and mental test."

In the Charlotte race he set a qualifying mark of 138.381 m.p.h., then beat Fireball Roberts by 2 laps for the lion's share of the $28,000 purse. In the Firecracker, he lost the pole to Fireball, but won the race at a 154.294 m.p.h. average. Pearson was named Rookie of the Year for NASCAR that season, and became known as a charger, the name every competitive race driver likes to have. He switched over to the Owens Dodge team in 1963, when Chrysler decided to see what its products would do. Again, he failed to win the big ones.

"I guess 1964 would have to be considered a good year," Pearson continued. "I could have won several of the big races, but something always happened when I had a chance. I won 8 races on the short tracks and was fastest qualifier 12 times. It took me a time to get used to all the power the hemi engine generated. But once I did, man, I felt like that Dodge would fly.".

An all-time great by 1971, Pearson took pleasure in his memories. "I'll never forget the feeling I had when I got the checkered flag to win the World 600 in 1961. I forget exactly how much money I won (approximately $20,000), but it didn't enter my mind when I got that flag. It was kind of like I suddenly had made the grade. I had won the Atlanta 500, and a lot of folks thought I was lucky, you know, because I was a rookie and all. That's why it felt so good to win another big race in the same season.

"I learned a lot that year. I learned what it takes to be a real pro. Joe Weatherly and Fireball Roberts probably did more than anybody to teach me. I don't say they taught me the easiest way, either." Pearson remembered one of the biggest lessons of his career. "When we went back to Atlanta for that second race in 1961 (the Dixie 400), I started on the outside front row. Roberts had the pole and Weatherly was starting right behind us. I slipped high in the corner of the first and second turns, and Weatherly came in between me and Roberts. When we got to the third turn, Weatherly and Roberts were already in the groove, and I was high. I thought I could make it through the turn in the high lane, but it was slick, and I crashed into the wall. People said it was because I was a hotshot rookie and they were right. I should have backed off and fallen back in line, but I wanted to lead all the way. Weatherly and Roberts laughed at me about that. I learned my lesson. But if I had to tell about a single thing that hurt me more than any, I guess it would have to be the World 600 in 1962.

"It was a real hot day and Charlotte Motor Speedway at the time was famous for its third and fourth turns, probably the roughest on the circuit. I hadn't won any races that year, and I wanted to win real bad. My car (the Pontiac set up by Ray Fox) was the fastest thing there, and I could drive it anywhere I wanted to go. I led a lot of the race. The heat was tremendous, it must have been more than a hundred degrees. The sweat kept pouring down inside my goggles, and I'd have to wipe it off on the straightaway.

"At the halfway point, when I made a pit stop, it was so hot I thought I was going to pass out sitting in the pits waiting for a tire change. But I knew I could win, and that kept me going. I had begun to think about the victory with about 10 laps to go. Nelson Stacy was about three-quarters of a lap behind, and I knew all I had to do was stroke it and make it to the checkered flag. Everything seemed to be going smooth, and the pit crew was signalling me every lap on how many more laps there were.

"Man, that's a good feeling when you're heading into the tail end of a race with a big lead, and the car is running perfect. There's no way to describe just how good it really does feel. Then, with 7 laps to go, I came off the 4th turn and headed down the straightaway. The car didn't sputter or freeze up or anything—it just flat quit. It didn't smoke—the gauges didn't show any rash change or nothing. It just plain quit. It was the worst feeling I ever had. They never did find out exactly what happened to that engine."

There was another occasion that Pearson probably felt worse about than he did over Charlotte. This day was a Pearson not only didn't like to recall, but wouldn't even speak of. It was Labor Day 1964, and some 80,000 fans gathered at Darlington for the Southern 500. Pearson had qualified his Owens Dodge on the outside pole beside Richard Petty's Plymouth. Again Pearson hadn't won a major race during the season.

The race began, and Pearson and Petty appeared on the verge of having one of the fiercest duels in the history of Darlington's famous old classic. But Pearson's Dodge scraped the retaining wall on the 4th turn and chipped off a pair of lug bolts. While he sat in the pits awaiting a new wheel, tears streaked David's cheeks, and his mouth quivered, holding back the anguish inside. Pearson really wanted that race.

The intense young charger sat out the 1965 season, caught in the middle of the Chrysler-NASCAR controversy. He returned with a vengeance in 1966. Driving for Dodge again, he terrorized the dirt-track stops with 10 of his 15 Grand National victories there, and earned enough points on the superspeedway to win the first of his 3 NASCAR season championships. Then, late in 1967, he startled everyone by switching to Ford. For 1968 former driver Dick Hutcherson became his crew chief and "car owner" in the Holman-Moody scheme of things. Ralph Moody became his overall supervisor.

It was another perfect team. In 1968 Pearson drove the Ford to 16 victories and 36 finishes in the top 5, to earn $118,000 in prize money. David now flew his own plane, and, with his wife Helen (who, by her own admission hated racing) and their 3 boys, moved to a big house in Spartanburg, with a smaller cottage on a private lake. The question now became whether or not Pearson would repeat in 1969, to match the incomparable Lee Petty's back-to-back championships of a decade earlier. Pearson warmed up by becoming the 1st man to break the 190-m.p.h. barrier at Daytona, qualifying his Ford Talladega at 190.029 m.p.h. He then won a 125-mile qualifying race.

In March, at Rockingham, Pearson's blue and gold No. 17 really gained momentum. Scoring a wire-to-wire victory in the Carolina 500, Pearson completed his Grand Slam—victories on each of the South's existing superspeedways. Then he won a 250-mile race at Richmond, Va., and 100-milers at Hampton, Va., and Augusta, Ga.

Everything almost ended at the World 600 at Charlotte. A tire blew and, before he knew it, No. 17 was barrelling toward the inner rail. The Ford bounced off the rail between turns 3 and 4, skidded back up onto the track and leaped onto the outer rail, straddling it, more out of the track than in it. Pearson quipped later, "I just held on because I couldn't steer the car. It's kinda hard to control with 4 wheels off the ground, and since I didn't put that car back on the track, somebody upstairs must have. It would have been all over otherwise."

Undaunted, Pearson returned to the Grand National Trail and a victory in the rain-delayed Yankee 600 at Michigan International Speedway. "It was so dark when I took the checker at Michigan, I could hardly see the flag," Pearson recalled. "Of course, it was partly my fault, because I was so overanxious at the 3rd restart of the day, I forgot to exchange my dark sun goggles for clear ones." He added a victory at the North Wilkesboro 250 in North Carolina, and clinched his championship for the 2nd year in a row by finishing 2nd in the American 500 at Rockingham. In 2 years he had earned some $300,000 in prize money.

Pearson made little effort to defend his title in 1970, concentrating more on the big races. He finished 2nd for the 3rd consecutive year at the American 500, 3 seconds behind Cale Yarborough. He only made 19 starts, but won $87,000, including 1 victory and 9 top-5 finishes. He lost the Daytona 500 to young Pete Hamilton by 3 car lengths, was 3rd at Talladega in the spring, and then won his lone victory, the Rebel 400 at Darlington, by 3 laps. At the Motor State 400 he was 3rd in a wild race, and he looked like a sure winner in the Firecracker 400 when 17 miles to go, a tire blew, and he demolished his front end. He got 4th in both the Talladega 500 and the Southern 500, and was nipped by 3 seconds at Rockingham by Cale Yarborough. For 1971, despite the Ford pullback, he remained with Holman-Moody in its last year as a team. He accomplished little and 1972 found him searching for a new affiliation

After an abortive episode waiting for a Pontiac paid for by Chris Vallo—a mystery moneyed Midwesterner —he found it in the Purolater Mercury vacated by A. J. Foyt. He won the Yankee 400 at Michigan International by a car length over Bobby Allison. In the Firecracker 400 it was even closer—a scant four feet over Richard Petty with Allison in the same car length. He also won Michigan International's Motor State 500, the Rebel 400 at Darlington Delaware's 500 at Dover and the Winston 500 at Talladega as he closed in on 70 Grand National victories during his career, far in excess of anyone else except the incredible Richard Petty. In 1973, in the Woods Brothers Purolator Mercury, he won 3 super-speedway events in a row—Atlanta, Rockingham, and Darlington.

Pearson was asked during one of the slumps in his career why he didn't try single-seater racing. He replied, "I could win at Indianapolis or in Europe and make money if I ever got the right car. But it wouldn't mean as much to me as any little old victory in NASCAR. These people are my fans. They know me."

ROGER PENSKE

"I always set my goals 50 yards farther than they actually should be, then I end up 25 yards nearer the goal," Roger Penske once said. Retired as a driver at 28, and a successful sponsor at 30 with his Sunoco Specials, Penske's goals had a way of being attained successfully and speedily. With all that, this man with a fetish for neatness was among the most level-headed in a sport where desire all too often warps the perspective. Handsome, and seemingly on his way to the top echelon of the world's drivers, Penske quit to become an owner. But Bahamas Speed Week will never forget his driving. Neither will the people who saw him in Puerto Rico at the now extinct Caguas Circuit, or at many of the SCCA locales. "He likes to do things well. He'll rise to a challenge," ex-wife, Lissa, confided one day, "but he won't take that extra step over the line. He's been more than lucky. It's like he sort of dreamed it."

Born February 20, 1937, Penske never had to work, he was just trained that way. His father, J. H. Penske, was vice-president of a warehousing firm and affluent enough to maintain his family in one of the world's richest cities, Shaker Heights, Ohio. But J. H. told Roger early in life, "You can have anything you earn enough money to buy." J. H. would advance the money, but Roger had to earn it back. He started wanting things at 10—and he worked to get them. It was a bicycle initially (for selling newspaper subscriptions), a motorcycle next (when his subscription territory grew too large), and, finally, cars—32 of them in 10 years—on which he made a profit more often than not. The motor-

bike almost killed him and left him with a weak ankle. The cars, MG TD, MG TC, Chevrolet, Oldsmobile, Corvette, Porsche, Jaguar, Cooper, Maserati, and the Zerex Special, became an obsession, fed by visits to the Akron Speedway, and fanned by almost instant success in SCCA racing.

"The first time we went out on a date," said his wife, "we went to a movie, and he fell asleep. I learned later he had spent 5 hours washing his Jaguar before the date. Before we went to a dance or party, we had to wash the car, whether or not it meant being late. He wanted the prettiest car. He was the same with everything. He rarely went out of the house without shining his shoes. When he wore dungarees, they were starched." His driving career began in earnest when Penske was still at Lehigh University, a demanding engineering school. He was an indifferent student, but graduated in 1959 with a BS degree in industrial management. He was working for Houser Chevrolet while going to school, and Ben, the owner got him to go to an SCCA driving school at Marlboro.

Dr. Dick Thompson and Fred Windridge were his teachers at Marlboro, and Roger earned his competition license one long weekend in February, during which he even raced. He competed 3 times more, then sold the car in September when he married the former Lissa Stouffer, heiress to restaurant money. After a quick profit on a gull wing Mercedes-Benz, Roger bought Bob Holbert's old RS Porsche, and had Bob help him prepare it well enough for a 2nd at Marlboro that fall. He was back for the February Marlboro races and ran 2nd

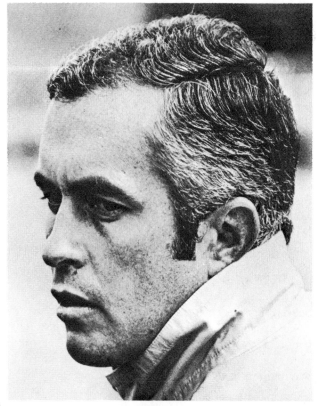

again. Comparing it with the newer machinery at the 1959 Sebring, Penske realized his RS wasn't competitive. He sold it and bought an RSK that Holbert had wrecked, rebuilding it and setting the stage for a Porsche rivalry with Holbert and an SCCA class title, as well as a rebuilding job on an ex-Jim Hall RS 60 Porsche that he raced and sold.

Penske won F Modified in 1960, then bought a Cooper-Monaco and a Type 61 Birdcage Maserati the next year, with the intention of getting a sponsorship deal from DuPont for Telar and Zerex antifreeze. He won 3 nationals in a row with these Zerex Specials, then traded spare Maserati parts to Briggs Cunningham for a Formula 1 Cooper-Climax that Walt Hansgen had crashed at Watkins Glen in 1961. Still, it formed the basis for the Zerex Duralite Special. Molen Ford of Wayne, Pa., helped with the rebuilding of the car, which was badly bent. Roy Gane, Penske's chief mechanic, helped to straighten the frame and reassemble the suspension. The idea of making it into a sports/racer was not original. Roger himself said, "Paul Richards was running a Kel-Cooper with a seat in the center, and Pete Lovely had a Monoposto Cooper on the West Coast. Why shouldn't I build one?" He did, putting on an aluminum body with some aid from his post-college employers, Alcoa. He was building this car for the professional races, and his career as a fast-rising aluminum salesman was now on a collision course with racing. In 1962 he drove Monaco with a Cooper-Climax and Sebring with a Cunningham. In 1963 Penske became D Modified champion, while winning more than $20,000 with the Duralite Special. He also became very friendly with George McKean, who opened a Chevrolet agency in suburban Philadelphia.

There is one other friend in the Penske story who is not often mentioned—John Wyatt III of Richmond, who bankrolled part of the Cooper purchases and acted as business manager until his affiliation in 1964 with the Mecom Racing Team. We are getting ahead of the story, however. One question often raised is, how good a driver was Penske? The answer starts in 1961 when he got the Maserati. That's when he entered the top ranks of American amateurs. Penske's biggest adversary was Hansgen, who, despite a late start due to European commitments, came closest to taking the D Modified crown away from him. The record shows that just about all of Penske's 2nd-place finishes were because of Hansgen, but there was also Peter Ryan.

The 1961 season started with Sebring, where Roger and Holbert drove a superb race to finish 5th overall in the lowest-displacement Porsche entered. Right after Sebring Penske entered the Maserati (now dubbed the Telar Special) at Vineland, N.J., and took his initial overall victory. Skipping the debut National at Marlboro, he appeared at the Virginia International Raceway only to have Hansgen beat him. Then at Cumberland, Ma., with a beautiful lead and a new lap record, Penske blew a piston. He then took races at Elkhart Lake, Lime Rock, and Meadowdale International Raceway, back to back.

At Bridgehampton in August, Hansgen again beat Penske, but only after a nose-to-tail, lead-changing battle. Later that month Roger sold the Maserati and took delivery of one of the 3 Cooper Monacos in the world, and at first it appeared that this new Telar Special would cost him his championship. In its 1st race at Indianapolis, he was leading Hansgen when the magneto sickened, forcing him back to 2nd place. At Watkins Glen, in September, with a 41-second lead, his clutch shaft bearing let go. When the SCCA season ended, though, he had won both the D Modified Championship and the SCCA's Most Improved Driver of the Year award.

With delivery of a Cooper, Penske finished at the Glen Grand Prix, 2nd American driver under the flag (after Dan Gurney); 4th at Riverside, behind Phil Hall and Gurney; 5th at Laguna Seca, with Gurney 2nd; and 2nd in the big Nassau Tourist Trophy race, again behind Gurney.

That was the base on which Roger's driving prowess stood when the Zerex Duralite Special catapulted him into the spotlight of controversy and success—Bahamas Speed Week in 1964. Alcoa had lost him to McKean Chevrolet, where he was heir apparent. Bahamas was mostly fun and games, but when men the caliber of McLaren, Hansgen, Rodriguez, Hall, and Penske get on a race track, even the games get exciting. Perhaps it was the weather, unusually bad for Nassau, or the fact that the likes of Mecom, Hall, and Carroll Shelby had their considerable equipment ready to fight for supremacy, but this Speed Week was one where the racing almost overshadowed the social life.

Penske had a superlight Corvette Grand Sport, laughingly called a prototype, for the Nassau Tourist Trophy and the preceding 5-lap heats. He was there to stop the Cobra march, but instead he stopped the string of Mecom, for whom he had driven the previous season. Hansgen, the Mecom driver, finished 2nd, with Bob Grossman 3rd, both in Ferrari 275LM prototypes. Cobra's top threat, Ken Miles, did not finish. For the Nassau Trophy, the feature of the week's racing, Penske affiliated with Hall to drive one of 3 Chaparrals. Roger seemed through early when he suffered a suspension failure at 31 miles around the crumbling old airport course, but Hap Sharp surrendered his car to Penske at the 102-mile mark in the 252-mile race. The car was 3rd at the time, but Penske took the lead within 87 miles and coasted to a 79-second triumph over McLaren's Olds-McLaren I. Gurney and A. J. Foyt were among the men who chased him and failed to finish. What established Penske as an ace, however, was the Governor's Trophy, in which he duelled Foyt and Hansgen throughout, edging A. J. in the final lap at a record average of 100.12 m.p.h. It seemed as if a new star of the first magnitude had arrived, but they didn't know Roger Penske.

Committed to Chaparral for 1965, Roger suddenly quit as a driver, his star having risen elsewhere; in February Penske bought out McKean Chevrolet, and there was no financial reason to drive and every reason to tend to the car business. Exit Penske the driver, enter Penske the patron. Less than a year passed, and the Sun Oil Company succumbed to Roger's rosy picture of racing publicity. The Sunoco Special was born under the new Roger Penske Racing Enterprises banner. Roger once said, "To succeed, you have to know how to put the right guys together. That's more important than knowing it all by yourself." He picked Mark Donohue, a shy engineer utterly hooked on racing. Donohue, the Chevvy-engined Special, and Roy Gane added up to a USRRC title. Add a Camaro, and you add a TransAm sedan championship. Add a new Lola chassis, and there's a CanAm challenger.

Penske dropped out of CanAm in 1969 when he realized that that series might tax his still relatively small organization even more than all his other racing. Within 2 years, however, Roger was active all over the map again. For example, in 1971 Penske's racing activities included making the American Motors AMX Javelin the TransAm winner, running a Sunoco Ferrari 512M in major endurance races, running a McLaren M19 single-seater for Donohue at Indy and other major USAC races—the year's big victory coming at the Pocono 500—and even an M19 McLaren Grand Prix car, with Donohue 3rd in the 1st Formula 1 race he ever ran and David Hobbs running the United States GP, which conflicted with a postponed Trenton 200 for Mark. For 1972 there was talk of another cutback, because even the "reduced" Penske commitment in 1971 had seemed to strain Donohue, the technical side, and the cars themselves. But 1972's "cutback effort" still saw new challenges as demanding as ever. A new L&M Porsche-Audi for the CanAm; an American Motors Matador for NASCAR racing, something brand new for Penske and Donohue; and USAC, of course, with Gary Bettenhausen partnering Mark in new McLarens. And it saw spectacular Penske Racing victories, too, in the Indianapolis 500 with Donohue, and in the CanAm with George Follmer doing the honors.

Roger, meanwhile, was charging off in many directions, and his holdings in the seventies included automobile dealerships in Philadelphia, Allentown, and even suburban Detroit, his new headquarters. He was also involved in Hertz rental car franchises, insurance, Sunoco gasoline stations, Goodyear tire dealerships, and with Sears Roebuck in a line of Penske high-performance products.

BILL PERKINS

William R. Perkins gained his initial measure of fame in the 1923 Grand Prix de l'Automobile Club de France at Tours, when he was a riding mechanic beside Kenelm Lee Guinness in a 2-litre Sunbeam. Guinness had been going hot and heavy during the race, at speeds of about 110 m.p.h. when the vehicle developed a slipping clutch. Without a moment's hesitation, Perkins slipped off his necktie—drivers and mechanics were a bit more formal in those days—and looped it around the Sunbeam's clutch pedal, pulling on it to increase the pressure on the clutch plates. Recounting the incident later, Henry Segrave recalled that "the strain of holding his head forward against the wind pressure began to tell upon him until, eventually, he had to be helped out of the car and replaced by a fresh mechanic."

Perkins rode with Guinness in all the important Grands Prix in which the Sunbeam and Talbot-Darracqs took part from 1921 through 1924, then retired from riding after another incident, continuing to service Sunbeams until the demise of the Brooklands track and the merger of the marque into the Rootes Group. It was September 1924 when Perkins took the last of his famous rides, this time beside Dario Resta in a supercharged 2-litre car that was scheduled to try for International Class E records at the banked British track. Resta had set several kilometer marks and was on his way to the longer-distance records, when a tire blew while the car was doing in excess of 120 m.p.h. The Sunbeam went out of control, crashed through a retaining fence and landed in a smashed heap which immediately caught fire. Resta was killed instantly, but Perkins was thrown clear. He would never run as a riding mechanic again.

Just 3 weeks later this decision was proven wise when Guinness drove in the Spanish GP at San Sebastian with a mechanic other than Perkins. The course was badly cut up in practice and was repaired by filling in the ruts with dampened clay; it looked good, but was treacherous to drive upon. Taking a corner over such a surface, Guinness skidded off the road and his car turned over 3 times. The driver was seriously hurt and Perkins's replacement was killed.

Bill drove all the big Sunbeam racers himself in testing the cars, and at least once, in 1927, competed in a British hillclimb, recording 3rd fastest time of the day. Kaye Don, Jack Dunfee and many other well-known British drivers came to rely on Perkins's mechanical skills in preparing their Brooklands racers, and even in tuning their road cars. With the passing of Brooklands and the disappearance of an independent Sunbeam marque, Perkins lost his zest for mechanical work. He retired near the old factory that now made trolley cars and was rarely seen except for the annual meetings and rallies of the Sunbeam Register, the owner's club. Perkins died on April 29, 1959.

HENRI PESCAROLO

Medicine's loss was racing's gain in the person of Henri Pescarolo, son of one of France's leading surgeons and a medical student himself until cars got in his way, temporarily at least. Quiet, bearded, and slightly balding, Henri was born in Paris on September 25, 1942, and led a relatively uneventful life until he bought a Lotus 7 in 1965. One thing led to another, especially to a bid from Matra, the French racing car operation, to join its Formula 3 team in 1966.

Pescarolo won the French F3 title that year and moved up to Formula 2 for 1967 in which he raced through the 1970 season with varying success. There were victories like the F2 section of the German Grand Prix of 1969, but there were disheartening things, too, like a serious accident at Le Mans that same season that sidelined Pescarolo for 3 months. Though still suffering from his burns, Henri returned to finish out that season and earn himself not only F2 but Formula 1 starts as well in 1970. His initial F1 drives had come late in 1969 in the Canadian and Mexican Grands Prix. In Canada he lasted 54 laps until his Matra lost its oil pressure, and in Mexico he finished 9th and last of those still running at the race's end.

It was the 1970 season that made Pescarolo's name as a serious driver. He ran all 13 GPs as a factory driver in F1, sandwiched in a few F2 events as part of Bob Gerard Racing's Brabham-FVA BT30 effort, and even managed some sports car and enduro races. In F1, Henri was 7th in South Africa, but retired in the Spanish GP. But at Monaco he was 3rd, his best showing of the year as it was to turn out. In Belgium he was 6th, and in Holland, 8th. In the French GP Pescarolo was 5th, but retired in the British GP. Another 6th in Germany, a 14th in Austria, and retirement in Italy brought the series to North America, where he was 7th in the Canadian race, 8th at Watkins Glen, and 9th in Mexico. The effort added up to 8th World Championship points and 12th place in the GP standings.

In F2 Pescarolo had 2nd at Pau and Barcelona, a 3rd at Zolder, and a 6th at Crystal Palace. Retired at Rouen, the accident came at Paul Ricard in Southern France. By season's end, despite the 3 lost months, he still had earned enough points in the European Trophy series for 10th place. Early in 1970, codriving with Jean-Pierre Beltoise in a Matra 630/650 V-12, Pescarolo had shared a victory in the Buenos Aires 1000 and a 3rd a week later, over the same course, in a 2-heat race. Later in the season, codriving with Johnny Servoz-Gavin, he was 6th at the Monza 1000 and 5th at Sebring. Switching to an Alfa Romeo T33/3 V-8 for the Austrian 1000, Pescarolo and Andrea de Adamich finished 2nd.

If Pescarolo was number 2 to Beltoise on the Matra F1 team in 1970, especially after Servoz-Gavin's retirement, he most certainly would have been number 3 when the French company signed on Chris Amon for 1971. A fiction of 2 number ones was being maintained, but as Jackie Stewart once said, "There is no such thing as 2 number ones for 1 man must lead, must assert himself." The fact that Beltoise was suspended after Buenos

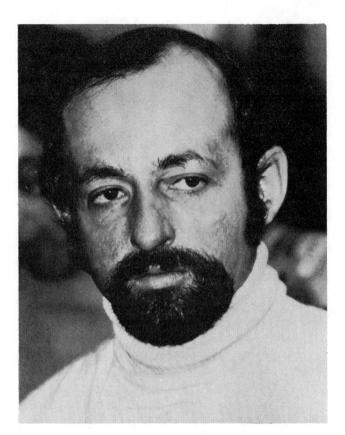

Aires by the French authorities, postponing a showdown and thereby elevating Pescarolo was beside the point.

Therefore, Pescarolo became Frank Williams's driver, with a March 701 to start off with, and a March 711 promised for early in the season. In the nontitle Argentine GP, he finished a strong 2nd to Amon, but in the championship opener, South Africa, Henri was 11th. In Spain the March's rear wing collapsed and he retired after 54 laps. In the nontitle Silverstone Trophy he was 6th. At Monaco Pescarolo was 8th, in Holland 13th, but in his own Frecnh GP he retired again on the 45th lap. Pescarolo's best race of the year, in results at least, turned out to be the British GP, where he was 4th. Retired in Germany, he was 6th in Austria, and ran the race's fastest lap in the Italian GP before being retired once again with a broken gearbox. Pescarolo missed the Canadian GP after a practice crash, and he retired from the U.S. race with a broken camshaft.

Things were better in sports car racing. Henri's big victory came in the BOAC 1000 in an Alfa Romeo T33/3 shared with Andrea de Adamich at 97.17 m.p.h. With de Adamich, Pescarolo was 3rd at Sebring and in the Monza and Spa 1000s. He was 4th at the Buenos Aires and Nurburgring races. With Rolf Stommelen, he retired at the Glen 6-hour race. Medicine would have to wait a while longer. For 1972 Henri decided to concentrate on single-seaters—F1 with Williams and F2 with Motul Rondel racing—except for Le Mans, where he and Graham Hill won in a Matra-Simca MS 670. That victory, and a F2 victory at Enna, were Pescarolo's 1972 high spots.

472

RONNIE PETERSON

For years, Sweden's sole Grand Prix driver was the bearded, dark-haired Jo Bonnier; then in 1970, two more Swedes attained GP status, both tall, blond, and surprisingly experienced for their years. One of these was Reine Wisell, and the other was Ronnie Peterson, who blossomed in 1971.

Born in Orebro on February 14, 1944, Bengt Ronald Peterson jumped from the world of go-karts to full-fledged racing cars after reaching the status of European champion in the kart world in 6 seasons. Part of that time he was a Renault mechanic and built his own Formula 3 car, called the SVVBB, in 1966. The next season he became one of Sweden's top F3 drivers with a Brabham BT18, then took a long and leisurely drive with Wisell from Sweden to Italy, where he purchased an Italian Tecno F3 car (as did Wisell) for the 1968 campaign. With this mount, Ronnie captured 12 of his 26 starts, winning the Swedish title that season, and winning at Monaco and Karlskoga in 1969 in a revamped Tecno-Novamotor sponsored by Vick Scandinavi, the local branch of the cough drop and cold remedy company.

The year 1969 was more memorable for Peterson, however, because he was signed to a 3-year contract by March, the new GP marque that also was racing in F2 and F3. His drives for them led to a 1970 F1 ride, not with March, but with Colin Crabbe's uniquely named Antique Automobiles Team, which used Marches, however. It was shakedown time for the new 701 car, and Peterson's log was nothing to brag about, although he completed 6 of the 9 Grands Prix in which he started. A 7th at Monaco was his best finish, which netted him no championship points. He was 9th in the Belgian, Dutch and British races, 11th in the U.S. race at Watkins Glen, and the retirements came in the French (18th lap, crown wheel and pinion failure), German (11th lap, engine failure) and Italian (36th lap, engine failure) races.

Ronnie also had another bad time in the 1970 Le Mans 24-hour race, while sharing a Ferrari 512S with England's Derek Bell. As he watched from the pits, Bell became involved in a 4-Ferrari crash that ended the team's bid for this international classic. In F2 Peterson had 3 accidents and a retirement, yet managed to capture 5th place in the European Trophy series for the Malcolm Guthrie Racing Team March, with a 3rd at Hockenheim, 4th at Imola, 5th at Tulln-Langenlebarn, and a 6th at both Rouen and Ricard.

In 1971 Peterson was signed as number 1 driver for the STP-March F1 team, and for occasional sports car drives such as his Lola T210 ride at the Buenos Aires 1000. He had 2 spectacular accidents in Argentina, caused, he said, by the rubbish that was left on the circuit. The 1st of these came in an unofficial practice session in Jo Bonnier and Mike Parkes's Ferrari 512S. "I had no less than 5 punctures, and this is what caused the crash. As I was nearing the end of the straight, which is a kilometer or so long, and was running about 180 or 185 m.p.h., a front tire blew and came off, and I ran head on into the Armco barrier. The car was completely destroyed, but I was not hurt at all." Through hard work, mechanics had the car in some semblance of readiness for Bonnier and Parkes to start the 1000.

But Peterson was in the Lola with a local driver. "We were going well in this little car," he said, "and in fact were holding 4th for a time. But on that same straight, doing perhaps 160 m.p.h. in the Lola, I got still another puncture. The car started to slide, then flipped over on its back. The bodywork acted as an airfoil, I guess, because we actually flew a bit and got to an almost vertical position. Then it shuddered like an airplane does when it is about to stall and fell back on its tail. It flipped again and was on its wheels; I passed some trees going backwards that I managed somehow to miss. I thought about driving back to the pits, but I discovered the rear suspension was broken." The Lola was classified 11th in the final standings.

No one could have predicted Peterson's 1971 season. In the South African opener Ronnie was 10th, in Spain he lasted 25 laps until his ignition failed, but at Monaco Peterson was just 25.6 seconds behind Jackie Stewart, and his driving was enough to make a confirmed believer of Stirling Moss. Stewart himself became a Peterson booster. "A seat-of-the-pants driver," Jackie said, "but then I'm one myself." In Holland he was 4th, in France he blew an engine after 20 laps, but in the British GP, Peterson was again headed only by Stewart,

who was 36.1 seconds up on the Swedish driver. In Germany he was 5th, in Austria 8th, in Italy 2nd once again, this time to Peter Gethin in a BRM, by a mere one-hundredth of a second. In Canada he was 2nd a 4th time to Stewart by 38.3 seconds. The season finale was at Watkins Glen, and Peterson finished 3rd. His 33 points gave him 2nd place to Stewart in the driver standings.

Nor was his virtuoisity limited to the big GP cars. In F2 Peterson matched a Jochen Rindt feat by knocking off 5 straight victories in his March 712, and became European champion. In enduro racing, merely as a "demonstration" of his driving, he paired with Andrea de Adamich at the Glen in a 3-litre Alfa Romeo T33/3, and won the 6-hour race at 112.772 m.p.h., beating the 5-litre Porsches and other potent machinery. The year wasn't even over, and Peterson was the most sought-after driver in years. He was still committed to March, however, although he was free to sign a Ferrari contract for 1972 to drive their sports cars in a serious bid for the manufacturers championship. Ronnie's own serious bid would be for the driver's title, and that would come in 1973 with a new GP team, Lotus, partnering the 1972 World Champion, Emerson Fittipaldi of Brazil, in a new John Player Special "super team."

KELLY PETILLO

In 1935 Kelly Petillo was signing lucrative testimonials to Ethyl gasoline. He won the Indianapolis 500 and the AAA national championship that year. He won 2 other races in 1935, at St. Paul and at Langhorne. That was enough to give him the season crown. Born in 1902, Petillo worked in the fruit industry around his native Huntington Park, Calif., and raced as a source of both enjoyment and further income. He first appeared at Indianapolis in 1932 with a midget racing background, finishing 14th in a Miller 4-cylinder car. In 1933 he drove a Lincoln-engined Duesenberg and stalled on the 176th lap, after spinning out.

In 1934 he was back in a Miller 4 and won the pole position, but oil-line trouble doomed him to 11th place. He campaigned in midgets and sprints mostly in the West that year. The next year did not start out auspiciously for Petillo at Indianapolis. The 32-year-old's 1st attempt at qualifying turned out to be a new track record of 121.687 m.p.h., but the effort was disallowed because he used 5/8 of a pint more than the 2.5 gallons of fuel alloted for qualifying. After cleaning out the carburetor, he made a another attempt, but threw a rod through the crankcase. With a patched-up engine he did only 115.-095 m.p.h. on his final attempt.

With the gasoline allowance down 2.5 gallons to 42.5 gallons for the race, the competitors knew they had to average 11.7 m.p.g. or better. The patched-up engine may have helped Kelly. He didn't make the top 10 until after the 30th lap as he babied the car, something alien to his driving style. By the 40th lap he was 4th, and on the 70th lap he led briefly, only to relinquish to Rex Mays. But he had the lead back by the halfway mark, relinquishing only briefly to Wilbur Shaw at the 280-mile juncture for a pit stop.

A light rain late in the race and 2 crashes cut the average speed, but Petillo still drove to a record 106.240 m.p.h. The crash of the Leon Duray-owned Bowes Special on the 9th lap took the lives of Clay Wetherly and his mechanic. This was the same car that, in a May 21 practice, fatally injured 1934 Eastern dirt king Johnny Hannon and his mechanic.

Petillo did well with the Indy title as a lever in making money from endorsements, but he drove less than 20 laps in the 1936 race, taking over the Gilmore Special from Doc McKenzie when it lay 7th and managing to get the car into 3rd. He had less than 2 quarts of fuel left at the finish, but others, like Rex Mays and Harry McQuinn, actually ran out of their 37.5-gallon allotment. In 1937 Petillo tried the difficult role of being both an owner and driver. He had one of the first 318-cu. in. Offenhauser engines, qualified it much more cautiously than usual, but still ran into trouble on the 109th lap, when he ran out of oil. Then Indy played him another trick, making the car and the engine obsolete by adopting the international formula for 1938–40 and eliminating riding mechanics.

He returned in 1938 with a 270-cu. in. Offy. He was riding as high as 2nd place at the halfway mark (after qualifying 21st) when the camshaft seized, eliminating him once more. For 1939 Kelly found a sponsor, Kay Jewelers, but the story was the same. Broken pistons and a balky clutch eliminated him after 140 laps (352 miles). In the Indiana Fur Special Offy, he managed to go 320 miles in 1940.

He left the race on lap 48 in 1941 with a broken connecting rod, but shared a ride with Harry McQuinn for 7th. In all, his career was a record of poor car preparation by people who guessed at fuel mixtures, chassis setups, and carburetion. Petillo's leadfoot driving style was calculated to break poorly prepared cars. His driving was exciting and devil-may-care. In an era of stronger cars, who knows how big he might have struck it? He died in 1970.

LEE PETTY

It seemed so incongruous, that party in a club fronting the St. Johns River. The racing people and the set that travelled with them, or on them, or because of them, were smiling, eating the play foods that waiters brought, and drinking. However, there was a hush about the evening. Bill France came in only briefly, and he was obviously there only because the industrial money-men were. He was somberly correct and he left to go to the hospital where his friend Lee Petty lay seriously injured. They had grown together with stock-car racing; was the track and the sport that had made them now to destory them?

It was 1961 at Daytona Speed Weeks, and the races that day had been the two 100-mile qualifiers. Lee Petty, the man who had won the inaugural Daytona 500 in 1959 by a photo finish, was in the field. Johnny Beau-

champ, the Iowan who had lost it that way, was in the field. In competition the 2 veterans locked cars and hurtled through the guard rail 20 feet to the parking lot below. Beauchamp suffered minor injuries, but Petty's lung was punctured and his left leg so badly smashed that it required 2 operations. Lee walked out of the hospital 4 months later, limping, his driving career effectively over, his team manager career just beginning.

Lee Petty was never much for cocktail parties. He liked his shirt neck open and he favored windbreakers over blazer jackets. He was a family man and racing was better than driving a taxi, or working in a garage, or any of the other jobs that he had had. Racing was 1st a hobby with Lee Petty because he was not like some of the other pioneer NASCAR drivers: he had never run liquor for moonshiners. He had been running occasionally in the dirt tracks around Charlotte, N. C., that year, but the 1st Grand National NASCAR race excited him and he hazarded the family Buick in this strictly stock contest on June 14, 1949, on the old Charlotte Fairgrounds dirt track. He rolled it 4 times, coming out with his pride hurt more than his person. He bought himself a Plymouth and went racing seriously—actually learning by doing, as many stars of that era did. He owned the cars he ran, maintained them, and used boy power like Richard, 12, and Maurice, 10, to make his task easier. Petty was born on March 14, 1914, near Randleman, where the family made its home. Lee was a 3-letter star in high school, but chose to attend King's Business College in nearby Greensboro. The 6-foot 1-inch Petty was very businesslike about racing once he had embraced it. In the 12 seasons of his active career—he started at the age of 35—he never finished lower than 6th in the Grand National standings. He won 3 point championships—in 1954, 1958 (when he also won the short track crown), and in 1959. He finished 2nd in the season twice, 3rd 3 times, 4th 3 times, and closed the 1960 season in 6th place.

In 1959, his best year, he finished 41 of 49 races, was in the top 5 on 31 occasions, and won 12. His $45,570 winnings were an unheard-of amount in NASCAR at that time. There were only 2 superspeedways then—the fantastic new Daytona and Darlington. His victory at Daytona was a classic. It was 3 days later when he was declared the winner.

"Everything seemed to fit together that year. In 1957 and 1958 and a few races in 1959 we ran Oldsmobiles, but I shifted back to Plymouths, which we really knew, and it was much better—Olds was all right when they were a factory operation or you could get parts, but by 1959 there were no more parts. That year was a fine year; even Richard won the Rookie of the Year award.

"When we saw the Daytona Speedway for the first time we knew stock-car racing never was going to be the same again," Lee recalled. "I had won the beach road course at Speed Weeks, but this track was really different, so big it made you wonder about things. It made Darlington look like a shoestring. We figured we'd have to learn how to prepare the car special, just like they prepare cars special for Indianapolis. We studied the rules pretty good to have a strong car; Richard's Oldsmobile convertible was just as strong but we had to learn in the race that an open top car was handicapped."

The Daytona 500 was Lee's greatest personal thrill but he claimed to derive equal satisfaction each time son Richard won. As the years passed he became more and more of a general overseer to the famliy business, taking time off to golf and to relax, as Maurice did the mechanic's work assisted by Richard and a host of cousins, and Richard did the driving. Lee was still in the pits, however—at Daytona, at Darlington, and at tracks that didn't exist when he drove.

By 1972 it was obvious that Lee was all but retired. He had taken up golf and that was his passion now. But that did not change the basic facts about this man, Lee Petty was not only a great driver and manager. He had founded a racing dynasty, and incidentally, still ranked 3rd in total Grand National victories, with 54 as 1973 came.

RICHARD PETTY

Had his father decided to become a champion boat racer instead of a stock-car driver, Richard Petty said he would probably have become a boat racer, too. Had his father decided to try golf, Richard Petty would have tried golf, too. Richard Petty idolized his father and respected him in a manner far beyond that mandated by the Third Commandment. Having a father who turned into a champion stock-car driver after starting in the sport at age 35 didn't hurt the career of the son either. There were many times while he was learning how to race when only the fact that his father owned the car assured Richard of a ride. Richard admitted that he crashed and broke many cars during his learning period, but luckily never injured himself.

Lee Petty was NASCAR's 1st and perhaps best 3-time Grand National champion, driving for Oldsmobile and then for Plymouth. The story of the Petty family—including Maurice, who tried driving but decided he'd rather just work in his brother's pits—was wound up inextricably with one track—Daytona International Speedway. Both Lee and Richard won on other tracks—Richard more than 150 times—but Daytona founded the family fortune.

Richard, born July 2, 1937, was in the 1st Daytona 500, back in 1959, in an Olds convertible. He saw his father come off the final turn to nip Iowan John Beauchamp in a finish so close that it took 3 days of studying pictures to declare an official winner. Richard broke down after 20 miles, but he went on to become NASCAR's Rookie of the Year after a strong 4th in the Southern 500. The Petty family already had an informal tie-in with Plymouth, but the 1960 Plymouth was not the most powerful car on the American road. It

was one of the least powerful at Daytona, much better suited to the half-mile tracks where its handling offset the awesome Pontiac and Ford power.

Lee Petty figured he might outfox the field by utilizing the fact that his cars could go farther on a tank of fuel. They managed to lead 30 laps of the 1960 Daytona 500 despite 10th- and 7th-place starting positions, but a combination of caution flags and Junior Johnson in a '59 Chevvy beat them out. Richard finished 3rd and Lee 4th. Bobby Johns in a Pontiac was 2nd. It was the 1st time Richard ever had topped his father, although at a race in Atlanta he apparently had won, then saw Lee take an extra lap and protest that the scorers had lost a lap. Lee was right, for his wife, who scored, was never wrong, and he took the victory.

In 1961, Lee Petty's career as a driver virtually ended in a severe accident at Daytona, although he was running as late as July 9, 1964, at Watkins Glen. Richard had hurdled the wall in one qualifying race, emerging unscathed. The bumpers of Lee's car and Johnny Beauchamp's hooked late in the other one, and they sailed through the rail. Lee left the hospital the following June with a permanent limp. He became the manager of the family racing team, from the pits instead of the cockpit.

So Richard carried the family colors alone, or in combination with various contract drivers. In 1962 he finished 2nd to Fireball Roberts at Daytona. In 1963 he didn't last at Daytona, but did well enough on the shorter tracks. In 1964 Plymouth finally decided to make a major effort in stock cars, backing Petty and Ray Nichels of Highland, Ind.

That was the year of the hemispherical combustion

chamber engine (hemi) at Daytona and throughout NASCAR's superspeedway circuit. At Daytona Paul Goldsmith, Nichels's driver, went 174.910 m.p.h. to Petty's 174.418 m.p.h. in the preliminary qualifying. In the 50-mile pole position race, Goldsmith set a closed-course mark of 170.940 m.p.h. for the distance, then minutes later Petty broke that mark with 171.919 m.p.h.

In the preliminary 100-milers, Junior Johnson in a Dodge Hemi beat Petty contract driver Buck Baker by an eyelash, with a record 170.777 m.p.h. and in the other, Petty seemed on his way to an easy victory when he ran out of gas on the backstretch of the final lap. On sheer momentum Petty's car rolled toward the final turn, slowing gradually. Meanwhile, pursuers Jimmy Pardue and Bobby Isaac were straining to catch Richard before the finish line. The 3 cars went across almost simultaneously, 2 at 175 m.p.h. and one at 20. After Lee Petty's 1959 victory, a photofinish camera had been set up for just such situations. It "shot" the scene but the film came out blank. Luckily a newsman had also been at the finish, and Isaac had won his 1st Grand National victory.

The 500, however, was another Petty payoff, with Richard a lap up on 2nd-place Pardue and more than 10 miles ahead of Marvin Panch in a Ford. He set what was then a world mark of 154.334 m.p.h. for the distance. Sitting out most of 1965, the Pettys went drag racing, and Richard suffered a nasty accident when the car went out of control and into the crowd. Law suits ensued. But in 1966 Richard was back at the Daytona pay window with another 500 victory, a masterful race in which he beat everyone convincingly.

And in 1971 Petty pulled off a hat trick as neatly as anyone could want, not only winning his 3rd Daytona 500, but having his factory-sponsored cars finish 1st and 2nd as Buddy Baker came across 10 seconds behind Richard in a Petty Enterprises Dodge. With the pullouts of most Detroit factories, the 2 cars were the only factory mounts in the battle. Asked if the factory backing made the difference, Richard said: "The only 2 cars that didn't have trouble today finished one-two. What I'd say is that Petty Engineering did one helluva job preparing these 2 cars." His attitude was backed up by Pete Hamilton's 1970 Daytona victory, which also came in a Petty-prepared car against a full field of factory entries.

The victory was all the sweeter because A. J. Foyt looked like he had the victory sewed up, leading 6 times in the seesaw battle, but ran out of gas on lap 161, and dropped to 8th. Even though he managed to roar back to 3rd in less than 20 laps, he could not get past Richard and Buddy in time, and settled for 3rd. Richard's winning speed of 144.456 m.p.h. was 10 m.p.h. slower than when he initially had won Daytona in 1964, but neither he nor the hysterical Southern stock-car fans could care less. It all seemed like old times.

Considering that Petty had almost 3 times as many victories as his father as the 1973 season progressed, and

that his father was in 3rd place in the all-time listing with 54, Richard Petty won relatively seldom on the superspeedways. His was the skill of the short track racer, where quick reflexes and alertness count for more than the car in many cases. His was the skill of the road course, where he truly seemed to enjoy himself.

Yet Petty had won 20 superspeedway races part way into 1973. At Alabama International Speedway in Talladega, he was shut out, but at Atlanta, Petty won the Dixie 500 in 1966, 1970, and 1971. At Charlotte, he had yet to win, but at Darlington, Richard won the Southern 500 in 1967 and the Rebel 400 in 1966 and 1967. At Daytona, Petty took the 500s in 1964, 1966, 1971, and 1972, the only 4-time winner. At Dover Downs he won the 1971 Delaware 500. Shut out at Michigan, Petty won the 1968 and 1971 American 500s, and the 1967, 1970, and 1971 Carolina 500s at Rockingham, N.C. No victories at Ontario, but two at Riverside's 500, in 1969 and 1972, and its Golden State 400 in 1970. At Texas World Speedway, he won the 1972 Lone Star 500. The rest of his fantastic victory total came on shorter tracks.

Up to 1969, when David Pearson duplicated the feat, Lee Petty had been the only man in NASCAR history to win the season title 3 times—1954, 1958, and 1959. Second in 1960 to Rex White and in 1962 and 1963 to Joe Weatherly, Richard Petty finally broke through in 1964 for his initial NASCAR title. He did it with 9 victories, 5 fewer than the previous year, but with 37 finishes in the top 5. When he returned to action for Plymouth in 1966, he managed a distant 3rd place. However, the Petty family was back in form for 1967.

The season did not start auspiciously. After a series of minor mishaps, Richard's engine blew with 2 laps to go in the Daytona 500. The blue Petty number 43 began rolling at the Asheville-Weaverville, N.C., Speedway the following week, with an easy victory in the Fireball 300. Then there was a dry spell until a month later, when Richard won at Columbia, S. C., and Hickory, N.C. Career victory number 53 came after a wire-to-wire duel with Cale Yarborough at the Virginia 500 and he tied his father's record with a 20-lap triumph over Bobby Allison in the Richmond, Va., 250. The tie-breaker came at the Rebel 400, when Richard survived tire trouble and a late charge by David Pearson for his 55th victory. He had done it in less than 8 full seasons (not counting a few 1958 starts) compared to his father's 16.

After tire trouble at Charlotte's World 600, Petty got back into the winning groove on the half-mile dirt track at Maryville, Tenn., He won Rockingham's Carolina 500 in record time, added Greenville-Pickens to his trophy list, but was again stopped at a superspeedway when he got off one and a half laps late in the Firecracker 400. The NASCAR boys went north, and Richard won the Northern 300 at the Trenton, N. J. Fairgrounds. He won at Fonda, N. Y., but was again stopped, by Bobby Allison, at Oxford, Me. He won his 16th race of the season back in Bristol, Tenn., added his

4th straight Nashville 400 victory for number 17, and then failed again at the Dixie 500 at Atlanta.

At Winston-Salem, N.C., Petty tied the season record of 18 wins set in 1952 by Tim Flock, and at Columbia, S.C., the track where he ran his 1st Grand National, Richard broke it. Although he was leading for the National Championship, and the money crown as well Petty was not finished making records. Savannah, an easy victory in the Southern 500 at Darlington, Hickory, and Richmond followed, and Richard had broken the Fred Lorenzen season money-winning mark of $113,549. Beltsville, Md., Hillsborough, the Old Dominion 500 at Martinsville, and finally the Wilkes 400, and Richard Petty had his 27th victory of the season and an incredible 10 straight!

Ford Motor Company gathered an awesome array of driving talent for the National 500 at Charlotte. No less than 6 USAC stars showed up, 5 of them in Ford products. This was to be the Petty stopper. It was, but not by Ford. Paul Goldsmith in a Plymouth ended Petty chances as a threat in the race when he blew a tire, lost control, and tore off the right side of Petty's car. Richard finally blew his engine and Buddy Baker in a Dodge won.

In the final race of the season, Bobby Allison, driving Fred Lorenzen's Ford, nipped Richard by less than a car length in the Western North Carolina 500 on the Ashville-Weaverville half-miler. It was one of the hardest fought races of that or any other season, as the 2 drivers, along with David Pearson, staged a fender-bumping devil-take-the-loser battle. But it had been a fantastic year for Richard Lee Petty, with $130,270 in prize money and 27 victories out of 48 starts in the toughest stock-car circuit in the world. After that, 1968 was an anticlimax, with only $89,103 coming into the Petty Engineering Inc. treasury from Richard's racing activities. That came from 16 victories—only 1 of them, the American 500 at Rockingham, on a superspeedway. And although the money won went up to $109,180 in 1969, Richard Petty won only 10 out of 50, none on a superspeedway. In his quest to equal his father's 3 NASCAR titles, he finished 2nd to David Pearson who became the 2nd man in that organization's history to turn the hat trick. However, he passed the 100 mark in victories and won the Riverside (Motor Trend) 500.

The year 1969 was remarkable for another reason. The Petty family switched to Fords as Chrysler Corporation decided that it was going to concentrate its effort in NASCAR on Dodge. Ford's director of racing Jacque Passino, was grinning from ear to ear at the announcement. He knew his nemesis was now on his side. The Petty compound in Randleman had spent the winter building new cars from Holman-Moody pieces, and learning the new product's strengths and weaknesses. Yet it was a year of continual experimentation. For 1970, Chrysler had learned its lesson and rehired the Petty family. Number 43 was back on a Plymouth, and, in addition, a young man named Pete Hamilton

from Dedham, Mass., was tabbed to be the contract driver for superspeedway competition.

This was a Petty year. The Petty team took $270,000 in prize money. Pete drove only the big ones, while Richard was sidelined from 5 races with a bad shoulder. It started at Daytona where Hamilton, who led only 13 of the 200 laps, won by 3 car lengths over David Pearson. Petty broke his engine early and took over direction of the Hamilton pit, a rare role for him. There was no thought of his replacing the blond New Engander because Hamilton had worked on building this Plymouth Superbird from the time he was hired in January. He had been coached in driving technique and race strategy by Petty, and most important of all, the Petty family had full confidence in him.

Superspeedway race No. 2 was the Carolina 500, and this time the teacher won an easy 3-lap victory as the pupil, despite having brother Maurice Petty as his crew chief, finished 5th. On the short tracks Petty seemed in top form, too, winning at Savannah, Ga., for the 6th time in the track's history. Could this finally be the year he would win the long-sought 3rd NASCAR crown? At rain-delayed, Atlanta, Hamilton finished 3rd and Richard 5th. Richard won the Wilkesboro 400, then borrowed Jabe Thomas's car to win the Columbia, S. C., Grand National stop. It looked like 1967 all over again as Petty and Hamilton headed for Darlington and the Rebel 400.

It had not been a good week for Petty Engineering at Darlington. Richard had damaged his Superbird in a Wednesday practice accident, and had been forced to qualify the short-track car, the Roadrunner. The whole team had worked long hours to get the car ready for the low-banked, odd-shaped superspeedway.

In the race proper, Petty came from 12th starting position to lead briefly twice. Hamilton's car blew its engine, hit the wall on the 152nd lap, and ground to a halt only after demolishing 10 rugged fence posts. Now it was up to Richard, but disaster descended on the 175th lap. Coming out of the 4th turn into the main straightway, the Roadrunner kissed the inside wall. The car then careened into the foot-thick steel-reinforced concrete barrier guarding pit row, bashing its way almost through. The wreck rode the barrier a short distance, Pety's arm and head dangling gruesomely out the window, then dug into the track surface, flipping end for end and side for side 4 or 5 times before settling near the Junior Johnson-Lee Roy Yarbrough pits. Francis Allen, a Johnson crew member, was diving through the window opening of the upside-down car almost as it came to rest and Lee Roy was not far behind with a Charlie Glotzbach crew member, Buck Bringance. He was out cold and just hanging on his shoulder harness straps," said Allen, who unstrapped Petty. "We worked him out of the car and then he regained consciousness saying, 'my danged shoulder'."

The crowd was silent as the race continued, watching Petty, on a stretcher, being rushed to the track infirmary. Lee and Maurice Petty hurried to the place, there faces white and grim. Richard Petty had suffered what looked like his most serious accident in a career amazingly free of mishap. Moments later Lee emerged grinning. "It's only a dislocated shoulder," he said. When Richard was borne through the pits in the ambulance, he flashed his famous toothy smile and waved his foot. Almost simultaneously the fans learned the news. They gave him a standing ovation, totally ignoring the race. Petty missed 5 races and, with it, probably the chance to win the title. But Hamilton, who had won the Alabama 500 at Talladega, and was to win the Talladega 500, kept things perking.

To start off June, when Petty returned to action, Hamilton lost a disputed decision to Cale Yarborough in the Michigan 400, as Richard exited early.

However, the 1st Falstaff 400 at Riverside, Calif., was a different story. Petty led for virtually the entire race, to give Chrysler its initial victory ever at this road course. And Petty and Hamilton finished 1st and 6th, respectively, at the Dixie 500 in Atlanta. In all, Richard won 18 for $139,000 in prize money, both figures more than champion Bobby Isaac. However, he only finished 4th in the championship lists.

The general constriction of manufacturer support at the end of the 1970 season hit Petty Engineering, yet, at the same time, made it the team to beat in 1971 in NASCAR. Petty Engineering was designated the sole Chrysler representative to NASCAR. It would run 2 cars, Richard's Plymouth and a Dodge, and it would sell Mopar racing components to the independents like Isaac and, officially at least, to Fred Lorenzen's STP Nichels Plymouth. Buddy Baker was signed on for the Dodge, as Hamilton found outside sponsorship, and the Petty family rolled merrily aong, awaiting the day perhaps when Kyle Petty, Richard's son, or another member of the family would take over.

And roll they did. En route to the Winston Cup, emblematic of the NASCAR Grand National championship, Richard won himself 4 Superspeedway events and became the only man to win $1,000,000, in NASCAR purses exclusively. He also became the only NASCAR driver to top $300,000 in a single season and added a total of 18 more Grand National victories to bring his career total to 127. With the championship added to previous victories, Richard having been NASCAR titlist also in 1964 and 1967, Petty put himself in a position to surpass his father's record of being a 3-time king of NASCAR.

The Daytona 500 is perhaps the most prestige-laden of the stock car classics, and Richard, pacing himself magnificently, staved off team-mate Buddy Baker and a hard-charging A. J. Foyt for that win. He also won both 500s at Rockingham, the Dixie 500 at Atlanta, and the Delaware 500 at Dover. That made 17 lifetime supertrack triumphs for another NASCAR standard.

In 1972 Petty was much less of a sure thing . . . . comparatively. He won his 1st victory in a Dodge—he had won for Oldsmobile, Plymouth and Ford—at the Lone Star 500, Boyan, Tex., and he also added Riverside's 500 and 6 other NASCAR victories for $227,015 in earnings and a career total of 148 victories.

Richard was the president of the Professional Drivers Association both during its famed boycott of Talladega in 1969, and when it praised NASCAR safety regulations concerning the speed-cutting adapter plate. Asked once if he would like to try Grand Prix cars, Indy single-seaters, or sports cars, Richard allowed wistfully that he would if he had the time. But he indicated it might never happen. "We make our living running stock cars, and when I retire from stock cars I'll probably be too old to try anything else."

MAURICE PHILLIPPE

Colin Chapman headed Lotus design and engineering right from the moment the first one was assembled in Hazel Williams's garage. However, he also always drew successfully upon the best young brains around—the Mike and Frank Costins, the Keith Duckworths, and the Maurice Phillippes. The last named, in fact, became the basic designer of Lotus racing cars in September 1965, and, aided by quick-sketch suggestions from Chapman (usually done on airline paper napkins as Colin flew from place to place), headed a design team that turned out such cars as the Lotus 39T Tasman car, the 42 Indianapolis car, the 43 Formula 1 car, the 48 Formula 2, the 49 F1 World Championship car of 1968, the 63 4-wheel drive car, and the 72 and 72D World Championship cars.

The name may sound as if it should be with Matra, but Maurice Phillippe was strictly English, born in London in April 1932, brought up in Edmonton, and apprenticed to DeHavilland at the right time. That "right time" was just when several DeHavilland employes, men like Frank Costin, were associated with a new company called Lotus. Phillippe drank all of this in, but he was not one merely to watch and wait. He had some automotive ideas of his own, and in 1954 he started building a rather boxy-looking monocoque 1172 formula sports/racer known as the MPS. The car was, in fact, welded at Lotus, back when the concern was scratching for any kind of engineering work at all.

Maurice started racing the car in 1955 (just as Chapman had started racing the early Lotus designs himself), mostly in club events, but also as "scenery" in filling out the field of some national races as well. The MPS's best finish was a 5th in racing out of its own formula, taking on 1500-c.c. sports cars. Just as he was starting to enjoy his racing, Phillippe recalled later, he was called up to the National Service, despite his DeHavilland job, and posted into the RAF where he got to work on exactly what he had been working on, the Comet. The RAF sojourn lasted 2 years, until 1958 when Maurice went back to the airplane company for want of a better offer.

Phillippe and Brian Hart, a friend from his pre-service days, responded to the then-new Formula Junior craze by building Ford 105E-powered cars. Hart's was given the same name as his sports efforts, Terrier, while Maurice dubbed his Delta. Both were front-engined, space-frame designs, but Phillippe's took longer to build and quicker to write off, thanks to crashes on successive days at Brands Hatch during the Easter weekend of 1958. But the experience was enough to convince Phillippe that his future lay with cars, not aircraft, and he was quick to accept a Ford offer to work as part of a design team in the small passenger car section.

Maurice later became project manager on the development of the Anglia 1200 series, and later moved into Cortina development. All the while, he yearned to go racing again, and tried to buy a Lotus 7 owned by Cosworth, but at first wasn't able to swing the finances. A year later he got the car, and this became his mount for a couple of seasons. In September 1965 came the phone call from Chapman, a talk, a handshake, and Maurice was a member of Lotus as head of the design team under Colin. The "team" was Phillippe. The Tasman car, a Lotus 39T, was the first one, and it had to be ready for shipment by November. That Phillippe creation was a winner at Warwick Farm, 2nd at Levin and Sandown Park, and 3rd at Lakeside.

The Type 43 F1 car was designed to accept a BRM 3-litre H16 engine, and it took at lot of development work before its first race, the Italian GP of 1966. After that, development continued until Lotus had a winner, Jim Clark, in that season's United States GP. Work had

meanwhile started on the Cosworth DFV V-8, sponsored by Ford, with Lotus tabbed as the exclusive user in 1967. Phillippe already had worked with Cosworth on the F2 Type 48, and now he worked furiously to create a Type 49 for F1 racing. Some eyebrows were raised at the idea of using the Cosworth engine as a stressed member of the car, but this was old stuff to aerospace people like Phillippe and Chapman, and that was what they did with the Type 49. If 1967 was a disappointment, it was because of the 49's teething problems. However, 1968 was a World Championship year in this car, both for Graham Hill as driver and Lotus as builder. Jochen Rindt also found this Phillippe design to his liking. In 4 seasons, all highly competitive, Lotus 49 won 17 Grands Prix, as well as setting the fastest lap a dozen times.

Chapman and Phillippe laid preliminary plans to run a 3-car turbine-powered F1 team in 1969, but engine shortages ruined that dream. However, much experience was gained, Maurice felt, with the Type 56 turbines and the Types 62 and 63 Cosworth-powered 4-wheel drive cars of 1969 that resulted from this infatuation with the Indy projects. Type 72, the 1970 F1 car, resulted when Chapman and Phillippe drew up basic specifications independently of each other, then matched their findings and discovered, to their delight, that their basic approach and even some of the details meshed well. Once again, almost as if it were a bad habit, Phillippe participated in designing a World Championship car for Louts and Rindt.

Lotus added some helpers for Phillippe, but the basic design partnership between Chapman and Maurice was expected to remain unchanged as the cigarette-sponsored red and white Team Lotus moved off into the seventies on its inevitable way (it seemed) toward future championship.

At end of 1971, Phillippe faced an almost irresistible offer: to go to the United States and design new cars for the Vel's-Parnelli Jones USAC team that featured such racers as Al Unser, Joe Leonard and, for 1972, Mario Andretti. This was a challenge few men could resist. He left Lotus, and England, for California. And the year saw Phillippe designs win the 1972 World Championship in F1 (Lotus 72D) and National Championship in USAC (Parnelli) for Emerson Fittipaldi and Joe Leonard respectively.

ROY PIKE

Formula 3 in England has often produced top drivers for the Formula 1 scene. One F3 driver who was singled out as a potential winner in F1, but didn't make it, was Roy Giles Pike, a Chequered Flag driver with 7 major F3 victories in 1965. He had also shared honors in that division with the equally well-regarded Chris Irwin.

Pike, born in 1939, was an intense and handsome young man who looked even younger than his years. He was not British, but an American who was born in Pittsburgh and raised in California.

Roy started off in a rather all-American way, driving a used MG TD in gymkhanas and autocrosses on the West Coast in 1959, progressing to racing the following season. For 1961 he built his own 1100-c.c. Formula Junior, purchased from one of the back-of-the-magazine advertisers. He did fairly well in the BMC-powered FJ car, well enough to encourage him to move to England and try his hand at international racing along the FJ route. In an Ausper T3 he made an impressive debut and continued with enough verve to gain an occasional drive for Chequered Flag in a Gemini and in a borrowed Lola.

In 1963 Pike started with a Merlyn factory berth, but never actually raced the car, driving Gemini again instead. His best finish came in the London Trophy Race at Crystal Palace. At Brands Hatch, a crash cost him a broken leg and the rest of that season, but Roy was back the next year in an F3 Brabham and a Cobra, run under Chequered Flag colors. In F3 he won at Oulton Park's Gold Cup and Spring meetings, in Goodwood's Easter Monday Race, Brands Hatch's Guards Trophy, and Silverstone's British Grand Prix. In all but the one at Goodwood, where it was raining, Pike set new lap records.

In the Cobra, Pike had a good year as well; his best showing was a GT class victory and a 6th-overall finish in the Martini Trophy at Silverstone, Roy's favorite course. It was F3 that excited the young American and encouraged him about his future in auto racing. "F3 has done very well in providing a good training ground for young drivers like me," said Pike. "F2 is too expensive and too competitive for youngsters—you never get any real recognition because you can drive really well and still finish 7th or 8th, unless you happen to break from the flag in the leading group.

"In F3 everyone has a pretty fair chance of winning and everyone gets the experience of leading a few cars, even the full field, occasionally. With that goes corresponding experience in reasoning and tactics. That this is a good school for young drivers is borne out, I think, in that somebody like Chris Irwin, my Flag teammate, in practice at Oulton Park and in his first F2 car, was able to make rather fast time in top company. The Cobra? I enjoy driving it, mainly because I have to work hard to get it around the corners, but I prefer the single-seaters, as they are much more precise and responsive to chassis tuning."

Pike's 7 major races in 1965, in the Flag's Brabham-Ford, were at Oulton Park, Goodwood, Pau, Magny-Course, Brand Hatch, and Oulton again. He also took 2nds at Zolder and Silverstone. For 1966 Roy switched to the Charles Lucas Team, signing along with Piers Courage to drive their Lotus 41s. He won at Snetterton and Silverstone, was 2nd at Rheims and Le Mans, and scored 3rds at Brands Hatch, Crystal Palace, and Karlskoga. Pike was also 4th in another Crystal Palace race, 5th at Zandvoort and Goodwood, and 7th at Enna. Late in the year, Pike was scheduled to test-drive the Parnell Team F1, 2-litre Lotus-BRM, but he did not get the chance when Rob Slotemaker cracked it up.

Pike was very much aware of the fine points of preparing a racing car, and liked working on his own cars as much as Jack Brabham, Denis Hulme, or Bruce McLaren. It is an affection that many Britons, native or adopted like Roy, quickly develop. Pike became very much the Briton, especially after marrying Katherine Newman on December 11, 1965, and he continued racing there although prospects for his kind of thing were brightening back in the States. In 1966 through 1968 he continued in F3 with Lucas, driving both the Brabham-Ford BT21 and Titan-Fords. However, that F1 opportunity that he desired so much never came Roy's way.

The next best thing, then, was the new Formula 5000, similar to Formula A in SCCA racing in America, where the cars were just like the GP racers except that they were powered by full 5-litre engines. In 1969 Pike moved into that series with a Leda-Chevrolet in which he often demonstrated that he was as fast as ever.

DAVID PIPER

David Piper of Britain was a familiar figure on European racing circuits for more than a decade, and more recently he has become peripatetic enough to rival even Jim Clark. Piper, a heavy-set, balding man who looked as if he'd been through the mill several times, claimed he had been born in 1930. He was a bit vague about most dates except that one. David also was a bit of a rarity in that he ran as a private entrant much of the time, something not unique but not exactly commonplace either. He has also been, on occasion, the British satellite of Ferrari.

"I started with cycles," he recalled, "and there were about a dozen of them in succession. Then there was an Austin 7 Special that I built on my father's farm in Bedfordshire. Next I found a bullnose Morris sitting up on blocks in a farmyard barn. I almost was paid to take it away, but in all honesty I did pay for it—less than $25 as I remember it. I used that car solidly for two years. Competition? Well, that started in 1953 with an MG J4, an ex-works car. And I did well with it. The next year I even got a factory ride with MG in a 6-hour relay at Silverstone."

Piper's initial international success came in 1955 in the Leinster Trophy Race, when he won with a Lotus 6 fitted with a 750 engine, suitably supercharged. The next year he went to the Targa Florio, sharing a C Jaguar with Danny Margulies, and the car finished a

creditable 4th in its class. About the same time, David purchased a Lotus 11 live-axle model and used it soon after to win at Les Sables d'Olonne. Here he also met Bob Hicks, and the pair formed Team Lotus, long before Colin Chapman was ready for such a move. The team drove matching Lotus 11 cars. Over 3 years Piper won at Montlhéry a couple of times, and at Cosena, among other courses.

That same year Piper started branching out to other cars, codriving Jo Bonnier's Alfa Romeo Disco Volante in the Messina 10-hour race and finishing 4th. He also started ranging farther and farther. In 1957, for example, he started with a victory in Helsinki, followed with a 4th in class at the Nurburgring 1000. His Lotus was wiped out soon after at Saint Etienne; Piper himself was almost wiped out as well. Next Piper bought an uncompleted kit version of a Series 2 Lotus 11, finished it, and raced the car for the rest of 1957 and the full season the following year.

For 1959 he joined forces with Bob Bodle of the Dorchester Service Station chain and formed a partnership that lasted 2 years, until Bodle tired of the effort and the expense involved with battling the factory teams. Piper drove a Lotus 16 Formula 2 car and a Lotus 15 sports/racer during this period, with interchangeable 1500 and 2000 c.c. engines. The extra engine enabled David to drive Formula 1 when he chose. He set lap records both in F1 and F2 competition. For 1960, Piper added an ex-Graham Hill F1 Lotus 16, sometimes called a "Mini-Vanwall." It got its baptism of fire in the New Zealand winter season, his best effort coming at the Lady Wigram, where Piper was just a few seconds behind World Champion Jack Brabham, on Brabham's home grounds.

Back in England, Piper had to concentrate on sports car racing, setting records at Aintree and Brands Hatch, because he was unable to get entries in Grand Prix races, with the exception of the Silverstone battle that year. Maurice Trintignant was driving for Aston Martin then, and their battle still evokes memories on the parts of many old-timers. At the year's end, the Bodle-Piper partnership was dissolved, and the cars sold. Colin Chapman came to the rescue by selling David what he claimed was the initial Lotus 20 Formula Junior car. In this machine Piper won at Dresden in East Germany and placed in many other Continental and British races. A bad crash at Messina ended David's infatuation with FJ racing.

That winter Piper took to buying Lancias in Italy and driving them back to England for resale. With these profits, and those from the sale of British FJ cars in Switzerland, Piper was able to buy a Ferrari GTO that he consistently placed in the top 3 in 1962-63. Both years, for example, Piper won South Africa's Rand 9-hour race, in 1962 with Bruce Johnstone, in 1963 with Tony Maggs. With the latter, incidentally, Piper repeated his Rand victory in 1964 with a 250LM Ferrari. That same year David was 2nd overall in the Daytona 2,000-kilometer race, assisted by Lucien Bianchi; 6th in the Nurburgring 1000; 5th overall and 2nd in the Grand Touring class at Rheims; and 2nd in the Tourist Trophy with the LM. A 4th overall and a 2nd in the GT class at Montlhéry gave Piper a 2nd-place ranking in the Franco-American Trophy chase.

In 1965 Piper, driving mostly a rebuilt 250LM (the car had been badly mauled at Snetterton prior to the 1964 Johannesburg race, which Piper won with a car borrowed from Maranello Concessionaires), won the Rand for the 4th time (in a 365P2 Ferrari); was 2nd at the Spa GP in May and in the Mediterranean GP in August; and 3rd both at Sebring and at Oulton Park's Tourist Trophy. In the Rheims 12 Hours, Piper and Dick Attwood, who shared his South African victory, were 4th.

After that, Piper's drives in international racing became less frequent, although in Continental and British sports car racing he remained quite active. His big appearances included the Spa 1000 in 1969 when he and Pedro Rodriguez copped 2nd in a 3-litre Ferrari 312P. The following season, Piper and Tony Adamowicz drove a similar car to a 5th at the Daytona 24-hour endurance race. Piper's racing temporarily was curtailed by a serious accident later that year, not when he was actually racing, but in the filming of Steve McQueen's motion picture *Le Mans*. Yet he returned late in 1971 to competition status. Whether he would ever race beyond club events was problematical, but he had proven to a medical board he could if he would, despite the loss of the lower part of his right leg. "After 20 years," he said, "it is very difficult to give up racing. I'd really like to have one or two outings a year just for fun. Sort of taper off, you know." He planned to keep his hand in by entering cars in enduros and sports car races no matter what else happened.

ART POLLARD

Art Pollard, a wide-mouthed, pleasant little man from the great northwestern United States, may be remembered as the man who won a Championship Trail race with a Plymouth stock-block-engined car. He may be remembered as the man who campaigned the STP Turbocar, in as frustrating a season as any driver with such tremendous backing could conceive. Unfortunately, he will also be remembered as the man who lost the 1st Ontario 500.

It is seldom that so many race drivers are offered $146,000 on a silver platter, in such a short time, and seldom that so many cannot accept. When Al Unser left a race he had won easily with an engine that failed right after a precautionary pit stop, Lee Roy Yarbrough had only to stroke his way home to the money. He pressed a little too hard, though, and his engine blew. That left the platter full of money to Pollard, the oldest driver in the race, born in 1927. He was in the slowest car still running as well, having qualified 32nd in his QuicKick Special. The 33rd qualifier, Jim Hurtubise, had left hours before. Pollard had only to hold off Jim McElreath, the 2nd oldest driver, to etch his name in history. It was not to be; he made the oldest mistake in the books. Believing McElreath to be a lap behind, he let the Texan by, only to realize his mistake immediately afterward. Pollard hurtled after McElreath and actually caught and passed him for a few seconds on the back straight. But the burst of speed sent him into the 3rd turn too fast to stay in the groove, and McElreath motored past en route to a 2-second victory.

Pollard accepted his $73,000 prize money for 2nd like a man, and never said one thing about leaping off the Rocky Mountains. After all, it was only money. The Pollard story was as American as pizza pie. He married his high school sweetheart and spent his nights—well, some of them—racing modified stock cars, supermodifieds, and eventually sprint cars. "In the Pacific Northwest there are a lot of don'ts about racing. You don't earn much money. You don't face much danger racing, but you sure do have a lot of fun," he said. Medford, Ore., Pollard's home, was well situated to campaign in the tracks where the racing was fun. To the west was Klamath Falls, Coos Bay, and Grants Pass. To the north was Roseburg. It was far to the south of Portland, and was situated in a part of the state that was remote but magnificent.

It took a while to leave such an environment, but

Pollard made it out of the Rouge River National Forest and Crater Lake to go to the pollution-ridden and heavily-populated big time of auto racing. He was just a bit more aggressive and just a bit better salesman than the usual supermodified driver—and just a bit more talented, storming out of the West with a healthy reputation as a charger. Indianapolis was his goal, a goal he reached in 1967 when, in the ThermoKing Special, he got as high as 3rd before fading back to 10th. In 1968 he qualified an STP Turbocar in the 11th spot despite his having had no practice, and some say he was done in only because car owner Andy Granatelli used a popular unleaded gasoline as fuel, instead of kerosene. This may have contributed to the breakdown of a fuel pump drive shaft when he was within challenging distance of 3rd place. In 1969, Pollard was to be the driver of the STP Plymouth in its initial Indy race. He failed to qualify the car, which had gone from the drawing board to the race track much too fast.

Playing nursemaid to a turbine-engined car had been a frustrating experience, because it had so much potential, despite all the efforts to hamstring it. The STP Plymouth was another of the same sort, but here the hamstring came from a tightened pursestring. Soon after Ronnie Householder, the old Ascot charger who was Chrysler's competition director, was allowed to start the Plymouth Indy project, company brass decided that the weakened financial condition of the company dictated a quick return to Chrysler's old excuse for staying away from single-seater racing—"We race what we sell." Not qualifying at Indy had been a key disappointment, because Chrysler felt, correctly, that this was where the maximum public relations benefits lay. It was unfortunate that they couldn't see their way clear to give the car a year's development time for the 1970 race. The short history of the Plymouth would indicate that it had potential . . . at least for the USAC races below the 500-mile level. As it was to develop, USAC later decided to encourage stock-block engines, and had the Plymouth been under development it might have done well.

Pollard had driven almost every race on the 1968 Championship Trail, most of them in the STP Turbocar. He didn't win, and the list of mishaps was excruciating —black-flagged for fuel spillage while leading at Milwaukee; brake failure at Castle Rock; brake failure again, after being on the pole, at the Milwaukee 200; suspension problems at Trenton while 2nd; a broken U-joint while leading Phoenix; and finally, when he was in 3rd place at Riverside and challenging, Andretti crashed into him.

When he signed to drive the Plymouth for 1969 Pollard said, "We don't expect a super-powerful engine, but we do think the Plymouth will provide very dependable power." That was the summary of the year of the MoPar stock block. Pollard proved he had the driving talent to give the Plymouth a good ride when, in STP's Gerhardt Offy, he breezed to an easy victory. But it was necessary to get the wedge shaped MoPar car working.

That came in its 4th outing when, despite churning up only 560 h.p. to the 650 to 700 h.p. generated by the 4-cam Fords and the Offys, Pollard took advantage of its utterly smooth torque range to beat the best that USAC had to offer. The victory came at a new track, the Dover Downs International speedway in Delaware, a high-banked mile track more suited to stock cars. Pollard could only qualify 10th, and he was content to play a waiting game for most of the 1st half of the race, as pole-sitter Bobby Unser blistered himself right out of the contest with a bent valve within 3 laps. Roger McCluskey took over until he used up his tires for an unscheduled pit stop, and finally Al Unser assumed the lead, lapping Pollard on the 64th mile.

By the 115th mile Al was breezing along when Wally Dallenbach crashed into the outside wall, spun, hit the inside wall, and demolished his car. That brought the caution flag out and the field bunched. When the green light flashed Al did not complete another lap; he slammed the wall, and Pollard led Mario. Andretti also tangled with the wall, adding more caution laps, and finally, Pollard was forced to race by the Gordon Johncock Offy for the final 45 miles. He proved equal to the task, and made many Chrysler people very happy.

Meanwhile the Plymouth engine was also in a dirt car for Greg Weld, an automatic transmission road car for USAC events for Sam Posey, among others, and a 4-wheel drive as well. The dirt car was the only one to show acceptable top speed, as Weld won 1 pole position.

The Plymouth did not win again. End of effort.

For 1970, the Art Pollard Car Wash Systems Racing Team was born to promote the franchise operation of the same name. How many cars are cleaner because of Art's efforts no one knows, but the team lost Grant King, the chief mechanic, shifted home base from Indianapolis to Atlanta, and finally lost Art himself when he sought a faster car. Pollard rolled into the 1971 season relentless, still having fun from racing and making a little money, too. In 1972 he finished 7th at Ontario in a Lola Foyt but did not make the field in the other two legs of USAC's Triple Crown.

Pollard was practicing on the first day of qualifying for Indy 1973 when his Cobra-Offy ran into the wall, flipped and burned. He died an hour later. One explanation of the strange crash was that a wind gust had reversed the function of the car's wing, diminishing traction. The controversy was academic for Art Pollard.

FERDINAND PORSCHE

The Porsche racing and sports cars are the epitome of advanced design. In recent years Porsches have been supreme in sports/prototype racing, in hillclimbing, and in amateur and professional road racing. There have been Grand Prix cars, although Porsche, as a company, was never able to match either the bigger factories or the specialized teams that worried only about racing and not about shareowners, customers and the bottom line. Sometimes the name that sits on a car has no other relation to the sport; Mercedes was a girl who perhaps didn't know one end of a car from another. But sometimes the name stands for a man who has contributed much; Ferrari is such name—Porsche is another.

Ferdinand Porsche had a creative lifetime of some 40 years. Like Charles Rolls, of Rolls-Royce, he started as an electrical engineer. Unlike many other automotive designers he was startlingly diversified in his work: cars, trucks, aircraft engines, tanks, and other military vehicles, modern windmills, motorcycles—the list seems endless. Of his more than 70 designs, many stand out, including the Prince Henry Austro-Daimler, the 38/250 Mercedes Benz, the P-wagen Auto Union GP car, the Volkswagen, and the Tiger Tank of World War II.

Porsche (the name is a corruption of Borislav, a Slavic name) was born on September 3, 1875, at Maffersdorf, Bohemia, later a part of Czechoslovakia. His father was a prosperous tinsmith who thought that his 3rd child should follow in that trade. Young Ferdinand worked at tinsmithing for 10 or 12 hours a day devoting his spare time to things mechanical and electrical, which fascinated him. In the end, a compromise was effected, with Ferdinand being enrolled in a technical night school at Reichenberg, the nearest big town.

One night the family was horrified, then mystified, and then elated to find that they had the 2nd electrically

lit structure in town; Ferdinand had built a generator, switchboard, wiring, and bulb all by himself. Since the only other place in town with electricity was the Ginzkey carpet factory, a meeting was arranged with the reigning family, who were duly impressed by the 15-year-old technician and offered to fund his education in Vienna and secure him a position with a friendly electrical firm there.

Enrolled in Vienna Technical College, Porsche found himself head of the factory test shop and chief assistant in the calculating department within 4 years. About this time, the renowned Lohner coachbuilding firm decided the time was right to introduce an electrically driven "carriage" for use by Austro-Hungarian nobility, which they were pleased to serve as official coachbuilders. Ferdinand was offered the job, and he accepted "without a single backward glance," he later recalled. The System Lohner-Porsche was introduced at the Paris Salon of 1900; it was a carriage with a small electric motor in each of its front wheel hubs. The vehicle was notable in several respects; it was the 1st successful front-wheel drive car in Europe, and the 1st to have 4-wheel brakes (since the motors in the front wheels acted as electrostatic brakes and there were drum brakes on the rear wheels). It was the forerunner of many Porsche designs right through World War II, not in the automotive field as such, but in tanks and other military applications.

Soon afterward, Porsche devised a system called the Mixte transmission, another invention that was to have a long life in many Porsche creations. A small gasoline engine was used to generate electric power transmitted via cable to the driving wheels themselves. Its application in a Mercedes (under license) drew praise from Archduke Franz Ferdinand himself when he used it as a staff car, appropriately driven by Porsche as an Army reservist. Since the Mixte system was devised and patented as early as 1897, it is interesting to note that it was still being used by Porsche in World War II, in such little things as the Tiger Tank.

His first military vehicles were developed before World War I, including the Land-Train, a 10-car tractor-trailer rough terrain vehicle that pioneered similar vehicles in use today, and the C-Zug, which transported the heaviest conventional gun ever to travel over roads. It was as much for his military designs as for his automobiles that Porsche was invited to join Austro-Daimler in 1905, succeeding Paul Daimler as managing director. It was fitting, too, that his first design work was on a racing car for the Kaiserpreis race, using a Mercedes engine and the Mixte transmission.

Airplane engines (this was 2 years before Bleriot had flown the English Channel) and a successor to the Maja (the sister of the Mercedes immortalized by Daimler) quickly followed. The revised car went through the 1909 Prince Henry Tour without penalty marks, and the 3-car team earned a special silver medal. Porsche drove a car himself, for he already was famed as a daring, yet steady, competitive driver. He wasn't satisfied merely with outstanding performance; he wanted dominating performance, perhaps setting the tone that has characterized Porsche competition to this day.

At any rate, the Austro-Daimler team in the 1910 Trials finished 1st, 2nd, and 3rd overall, with Porsche and his wife as the lead car's crew. In addition the cars won all the special tests of consequence and demonstrated they were at least 10 m.p.h. faster than their nearest rivals. Capable of nearly 90 m.p.h., these cars had tremendous success in all types of competition, and their engine layout was echoed in the Porsche-designed airplane engines in World War I, considered the best with which to fly against the Allies.

Austro-Daimler was merged with Skoda in 1913 or so, and Ferdinand was put to work designing more military vehicles. The work earned him an honorary doctorate from the Vienna Technical College, which he treasured the rest of his life—even when the Germans laughed at that "rural" degree. With the war's end, Porsche returned to his first love, cars, and especially racing cars. First he designed a strikingly beautiful, architecturally pure 4.4-litre 6-cylinder engine, and then the first of several cars that would be powered by this 60 h.p., s.o.h.c. powerplant: a 2-seat Sasha sports/racing car. In 1922 it was timed at about 90 m.p.h. over a kilometer, and the year 2 of them won their class. A 3rd—driven by a young tester named Alfred Neubauer—was bored out and run against the big cars, finishing 6th. Bigger racing cars were already being built, and that

485

year alone the factory had 43 victories and 8 seconds in a total of 51 racing starts. Then a racing accident caused Porsche to lose his job.

Daimler Benz immediately offered him another job for Paul Daimler, with the extra honor of a seat on the company board. At first the Germans were standoffish with this Czech engineer. But that changed after Porsche redesigned a moderately successful Mercedes 2-litre racer into the car that won the Targa Florio in 1924, and made national heroes of Christian Werner, its driver, and Ferdinand Porsche. Stuttgart Technical College awarded the designer an honorary degree to match the one from Vienna.

Austro-Daimler, meanwhile, was winning on designs Porsche had left behind him. The 2.6-litre ADM won 60 speed trials and rallies, and it was later revised by a Porsche student, Karl Rabe (who later would rejoin the Doctor) into the ADM-R car that made Hans Stuck the European hillclimb champion of 1930. Mercedes couldn't complain, however, for their drivers were winning, too; Rudi Caracciola, for example, won his initial German GP victory in a development of the Porsche Targa car, and later won the Tourist Trophy in a Porsche-designed sports car. The same machines won the Irish GP, the Mille Miglia, and the German GP, as well as many other starts.

Porsche was busy on other things, too—diesel engines, the DB-600 airplane engine, a 500-c.c. BMW motorcycle, and the prototype of the Tiger Tank, built by Mercedes and tested in Russia. Relations at the factory were strained for one reason or another, however, and to get him out, the board sent Porsche on a fact-finding trip to the United States in 1928, moving someone into his place while he was gone. They offered Porsche a consultant's job upon his return, but Steyr offered him leadership of its carbuilding effort, and he accepted. Unfortunately, soon afterward Steyr would be taken over by Austro-Daimler, his old employers, and Porsche wanted no part of that. He set up his own business, Porsche Buro at Kronenstrasse 14 in Stuttgart.

He was not above working for old employers as a consultant, however, and it was for Steyr that he produced his 1st independent design (though numbered No. 7, to suggest that it was not the 1st in the line), the Wanderer, which was notable because it introduced the Porsche independent first suspension concept. He patented it, and because of this, Alfa Romeo, Austro-Fiat, Citroen, Morris, NSU, Standard, Vauxhall, and Volvo, among others, ended up paying royalties to Porsche in order to use the design on their cars.

Stalin invited the designer to Russia, supposedly just to visit (in itself an unusual honor) but actually to feel him out about becoming the Soviet Union's Minister of Technology. There was no racing in Russia, however, and that would never do for Dr. Porsche. He got back to Stuttgart and set about designing a new car for the 1934–36 formula, announced in the fall of 1932. This was the famed 750-kilogram formula, one based almost solely on maximum weight. Porsche's approach was to put the engine in the rear, make a driver's seat of the fuel tank, and generally lay out a car that was strikingly like the racing cars of the sixties and seventies. The car was not all that pretty, but the P-wagen of 1932, which raced for the Auto Union marque, was a pacesetter, and usually the only contender that Mercedes Benz had to face.

Another Porsche Buro design was a People's Car, or Volkswagen, if you prefer. The beetle shape, the general layout, the whole idea, in fact, was laid out by Porsche himself, as early as 1931. The Volkswagen was offered to the government in 1934, given the go-ahead in 1936, tested rather strenuously in 1936–37, and announced in 1938, when orders were taken for the VW at about $400 each. Porsche's income from the project amounted to about $80,000, plus a royalty on each car delivered. The war ended civilian production before many were turned out, and only about 100,000 were built for military use during the war itself. The postwar Beetle and Porsche never really got together financially, and even the money to get him out of a French prison did not come from his fantastically successful design, but from the Cisitalia racing car.

Another prewar project, albeit a secret one that didn't surface until long after its time, was a Land Speed Record car. Tiger Tanks and other wartime machines ended this kind of thing.

At the war's end Porsche found himself in prison. He had been too close to Hitler, but he was not the usual party lackey. While all others referred to him as *Der Führer,* Porsche called him *Herr Hitler.* While everyone from child to octogenarian wore a uniform in Germany, Porsche still dressed in civilian clothes, topped by what was patently a British-made fedora. However, he was a confidant of Hitler's, which not only protected him from the zealots of the Third Reich, but made him jail bait when the war ended with Germany in ruins.

First the Americans had him, and they treated Porsche rather well, respecting his technical abilities. Then the French got him, and, while they attempted to pick his brains for Renault, they treated him very much as a political prisoner. He was in French prisons, including Dijon, for 2 years, but was released (ransomed might be a better word) on August 5, 1947. He came home, but his designing days were about over. Fortunately, Porsche did live to see cars actually bearing his name honored world-wide as fine machines. He suffered a stroke and died on January 30, 1952, in his 75th year, leaving both a son and a grandson to carry on his name and his work.

ALFONSO DE PORTAGO

Don Alfonso Cabeza de Vaca y Leighton, Carvajal y Are, 13th Conde de la Mejorada, 17th Marquis de Portago, better known to his racing friends as Fon, has always been pictured as a Renaissance man, a throwback to the 16th century, a man who would have been more at home fighting Moors, sailing uncharted seas, or having his portrait painted by Goya. True perhaps, but he was also, unknowingly, a prototype for the Now People of the sixties and seventies.

He never had to worry about money. He cared little for law and order of any kind. He came out of the Establishment, but did not choose to be a part of it, using only those parts of it appropriate to the pursuit of his goals. His goals were pleasure and sensations. He was married to one woman, but he knew many women. He was reputedly heir to a vast fortune in American money, as well as what might (or might not) accompany his royal titles, yet he was always in debt. He never really earned a dollar in his entire life, but he never lacked funds, friends, or favors of any kind.

As a racing driver, he was spectacular and sloppy. Despite an adoring clique of writers—one of whom, in particular, was responsible for the legend of Portago—he never won an important race in his life. He was as brutal to cars as he was to people. And when, after a meteoric competition career of some 3 years, he killed himself needlessly and foolishly, he took with him a "best friend" and many innocent lives. With the sugar coating stripped away, his story is scarcely a pretty one.

His father was a poor Spanish nobleman who married Olga Leighton a one-time Irish nurse, the widow and heir of Frank J. Mackey, founder of the Household Finance Company. On October 11, 1928, a son was born to them in London. He was raised in Biarritz, France, while his father went off to side with Franco. Portago's father was more than a vocal supporter, and his escapades earned him time in jail. He died in 1941, about the time that Fon and his mother came to the United States, to live at New York's Plaza Hotel. An attempt to get him a formal education at Lawrenceville, the Ivy League prep school, ended within a month. Private tutors were worn out by the score. After all, Fon already knew 4 languages, how to ride, play polo, and engage in all kinds of other sports, indoors and out. In America he learned only how to fly, then promptly lost his license by flying under a bridge. It was no ordinary bridge, but a low one—20 feet above the water—part of a Florida causewey. Later, he did the same kind of thing in Britain on a British license.

As soon as the war ended, he was back in Biarritz, and became a gentleman jockey until he outgrew the job. He won some 30 races, and was in the Grand National twice, falling from his mount on each occasion. In 1953 he became interested in cars, and his initial experience was serving as ballast for Luigi Chinetti in the Pan American Road Race that year. He immediately bought a 3-litre Ferrari, and with Harry Schell, an American expatriate, he entered the Argentine 1000. The car finished 2nd, with Schell doing all the driving except 4 laps. In that short stint, Portago dropped the car from 2nd to 5th, but Schell was able to regain the

ground. Portago bought a Maserati and blew its engine the 1st time out. He bought an OSCA and flipped it in the German GP in 1954.

He won a Bahamas Auto Club race late in 1954 and had the nerve to ask Ferrari for a team berth. The answer was unprintable. Crash followed crash, with one at Silverstone breaking his leg and putting him temporarily out of his headlong flight to self-destruction. Back he came, however, and in 1955 Nassau Speedweeks he won another race, albeit a minor one, after nearly killing himself and a driver whose car he hit. Portago then tried a new way of killing himself, Olympic bobsledding, teaching himself the sport while practicing and qualifying for the actual Games. Only his political pull got him the berth, but he finished 4th, a remarkable feat.

After the 1955 campaign, in which he drove without much success at Turin, Bordeaux, Pau, Silverstone Nassau, and Argentina, Ferrari finally offered him a team berth, as the 5th man in what was initially a 4-man team, until Eugenio Castellotti was killed in March 1957. He drove the same kind of race he always had, except that Juan Manuel Fangio, Ferrari's number one driver, exercised some control over Portago, and seemed to better his driving somewhat. Fon was at Montlhéry, Castel Fusano, the Tour de France (which he won), Silverstone, Rheims, and Monza. At the Nurburgring, he shaded a 3rd with Phil Hill and Olivier Gendebien. In the British GP he shared a 2nd with Peter Collins behind Fangio, and he won both the Portugese GP and the Rome GP (both minor ones).

Perhaps Portago was finally becoming a race driver by 1957. In the Cuban GP, he was leading the field, including Fangio, when his gas line broke, and he nursed the car to a 3rd behind Juan Manuel and Carroll Shelby. At Sebring, he drove practically all of the 12-hour race and finished 7th. At Montlhéry he set a lap record and a GT track record. Then he accepted an assignment that he did not want, to drive in the 1957 Mille Miglia. It was to be Portago's last race. He shared a car with his friend Edmund Nelson, an American he had met in 1944 in the Plaza Hotel. They started without having once run the course, and despite this handicap, Portago pushed his Ferrari to the limit. More than once he came close to crashing, but pressed on, faster and faster. At the last pit stop before the accident, the Ferrari crew wanted to change the car's tires, but Fon would have none of it. He charged out on the same thinning treads.

At the spot where the road straightens out into the Po Valley, with at most, 30 miles to go for the finish line, his car suddenly appeared in the distance, and the spectators closest to the course pressed forward to see him. As the car came upon this group of spectators, a tire gave way, just as the Ferrari pit crew had feared, and the red car spun into the banking at the roadside, was hurled into the air and safely cleared the spectators closest to the road, but landed with projectile-like ferocity among the more cautious ones at the back of the crowd, killing 9 and injuring 20 others. In the middle of this carnage both Nelson and Portago lay dead.

SAM POSEY

The name on the side of the Mustang Clubs Racing Team Mustang was Peter Revson, but it wasn't the aesthetic-looking, slim Peter climbing into the car this May day; rather it was a solid, round-faced young man with a determined look on his face. The crowd at Lime Rock, Conn., knew this young man, though, for he came from nearby Sharon, and Lime Rock was considered home base for Samuel Felton Posey, called Sam by friends and foes alike.

This was a Trans-American race, an SCCA series for production sedans, held on Memorial Day 1969. The regular stars of this TransAm series—Parnelli Jones, Mark Donohue, George Follmer, Peter Revson—were at Indianapolis on this fine day. Sam Posey wanted to be at Indy, too, for it was one of his dreams, but the Indianapolis officials had decreed that he was not sufficiently experienced even to take a rookie test at the Brickyard. Some said it was because Sam regularly ran the SCCA's Continental Championship series for single-seaters, which competed with USAC's single-seater racers, and USAC ran Indy. Some said that Sam was a bit too opinionated and publicity-conscious to suit the USAC officials, which liked its drivers to know their place. Posey, for example, had recently been the subject of a *Life* picture spread, in which he had suggested that he had an outside chance of winning at Indy in 1969.

Whatever the reason behind the decision, the officials

had told Posey to go away and come back another year, after getting some real racing experience. After all, he had been racing only 4 seasons at this point. Posey was free to borrow Revson's Mustang this day and contest the TransAm for Ford. He captured the pole in qualifying, then won the race rather easily, with Swede Savage (another rising young star) 2nd, and Bob Johnson and John Cannon following in that order. No matter that the field was not exactly star-studded; Sam had risen to a challenge, and he had won. Sam was used to rising to challenges; some people said, in fact, that if he had had a few more challenges in life, he might have been better off.

Sam was born in New York City on May 26, 1944, raised there and in Boca Grande, Fla., Sharon, and other prosperous places. His father, whom he never knew, was killed in World War II. His earliest memories, he later recalled, were of Florida and of a shiny automobile, which he later identified as a Sam Collier MG. Posey, in his own words, "grew up from a fat little rich kid to a fat big rich kid." When he explained it he stayed pretty hard on himself. "When I was 14 years old, I was a 250-pound flunky with no real interest in anything. I was terrible at anything to do with sports—anything. I had a close friend named John Whitman who could beat me at anything, from throwing a ball to riding a horse. John was a natural athlete, and he never thought anything was hard. I just puffed after him."

Laws are pretty lax up in Connecticut's back hills, especially for well-to-do locals. John and Sam began driving cars around when they were far below the legal age. It was then that Sam Posey found something at which he could beat John Whitman. "It was a revelation to me. John was fast, but I was faster. John could drive well, but I drove better. I beat him in a car, not once or twice but consistently. So I conned my mother into buying me a sports car and persuaded a local Swiss-German mechanic that he really didn't want to return to Europe but should work on my car and operate a local garage that I got out of hock."

Sam's grandfather had made money, and his father had added to it. His mother was remarried to a wealthy doctor, and there were absolutely no money worries for Sam. "My mother told me one time that we had quite a lot of money, and she wanted to do things that would give me pleasure. I was to enjoy life and the money, and to do whatever I might want." So the money tree was tapped for a Porsche in 1949, Lime Rock was prevailed upon to open its facilities for Posey practice, and life went its merry way for Sam. The Gunnery School—an exclusive prep school—was followed by the Rhode Island School of Design, from which Posey received a degree in fine arts. He turned out to be a very talented painter and furniture designer. His other tutoring came from John Fitch, in the art at driving sports cars.

When Posey's stepfather saw Sam was serious about racing, he took the young man aside and suggested that 250 pounds spread over 6 feet was a bit much, for racing drivers were athletes just like any other competitors. "I went on a high-protein, low-carbohydrate diet, and went down to 188 pounds," Sam said. "I occasionally go lower, but never higher than 190." A slimmed-down Sam slipped into a single-seater for his initial real race in May 1965, a Lime Rock Formula Vee battle in which he came in 4th. Cars and series followed in profusion, especially after Posey joined another young man, Ray Caldwell, and helped found Autodynamics, a maker of dune buggies and single-seaters (the company later attempted to build Group 7 and TransAm cars for Sam, without great success).

But Posey plugged on, and with his bankroll, anything was possible—at least to participate, to try. He was at Nassau and Daytona in 1966; he was at Le Mans the same year, lasting 4 hours and making 8 pit stops, by his own recollection. In 1966 he scored his initial national sports car victory at Watkins Glen, in a Porsche 904, and won at Marlboro, Md., in an Alfa. The following year he ran the United States Road Racing Championships in the Hudson Wire McLaren, and finished a distant 3rd in the series, thanks to a 2nd at Las Vegas. Mark Donohue had 54 points as the runaway victor that year; Sam had 17 points, with Lothar Motschenbacher in between with 21. Posey ran the CanAm, too. He retired at Elkhart Lake and Bridgehampton, managed a 12th at Mosport and a 13th at Riverside. He ran some TransAms and won the Sebring TransAm race in a Porsche 911s.

The year 1968 saw more of the same. After a 2nd to Jerry Titus in big-car TransAm racing at the Glen, Posey was 2nd in the unusual World Challenge Cup race at Mt. Fuji, Japan. In CanAm racing he drove a Lola-Chevrolet and was 9th in the final standings with $13,-245. Denis Hulme and Bruce McLaren, the winners that year, split $163,000, to put the Posey figure into some perspective. His best finish was a 4th at Edmonton, and he finished 4 of the other 5 races. He ran the USRRC again, too, coming in 3rd at Riverside, for his best showing, in the Caldwell-Chevvy.

The following season was the one of the Indy disappointment and the TransAm victory in Revson's car. Sam ran a complete single-seater series, the SCCA's Continental Championship for Formula A (later Formula 5000) cars, and after dueling for the series lead all year, he finished 3rd behind John Cannon and David Hobbs, a master at F5000 in Europe, who arrived late and started winning big in the U.S. Sam survived a spectacular crash at Riverside and the totalling of not one, but 3 cars that season. Thank God for the family fortune. He had other things to do, too. He tested a TransAm Javelin in the spring; he ran one of Andy Granatelli's Plymouth-engined 4-wheel drive wedges at Indianapolis Raceway Park, coming in 7th and 8th in a 2-heat race; he ran the USRRC again and managed a 2nd to Donohue at the Glen, but flipped at Bridgehampton.

There were some long-distance enduro drives for Ferrari—or rather Ferrari's North American concessionaire, Luigi Chinetti, who ran a little thing called NART, the North American Racing Team. With enough money, you could buy a ride with NART. Sam did just that. He sweated out the non-competitive cars and didn't complain. The cars got a little better, and he still followed team orders—not charging when he wasn't supposed to, turning the car over when ordered. Pretty soon he had top-notch cars and a chance to win his class. Posey proved he could do just that at Sebring in 1969, and then made a few people sit up and notice when he did the same thing at Le Mans in a 4.4-litre Ferrari. That season, in fact, he was the only driver, American or otherwise, who started Sebring, Daytona and Le Mans, the classic enduro races, and finished all 3.

In 1970 he and Mike Parkes were 4th overall at Daytona, and won the 3-litre class. With Ronnie Bucknum, Posey was 5th overall at Le Mans, but 1970 was not a good year for Sam. He had a big-time ride, all right, with his own Dodge Challenger in the rich TransAm series, but Autodynamics was not up to the assignment. Posey didn't get to just drive; he had to worry about mechanical things, sponsors, parts, deals, and every little detail that is usually left to someone else. His Indy jinx hit again. This time Sam passed the rookie test with flying colors, but his Tassi Vatis ride disappeared in a dispute over tires and other things.

The following year, 1971, could have been a disaster. First Dodge pulled out of racing, leaving Posey without a TransAm ride. Then there was a split with Caldwell, sponsorship difficulties, and a slight turn toward a bad press in certain quarters, something Sam had never before experienced. In other words, there was a real challenge to Posey once again, just the kind of thing he liked. He switched to the West Coast to work on new cars. He chose the new SCCA/USAC single-seater racing scene. He continued his Ferrari rides and pointed toward Indy once again. Approaching 27, Posey felt that he had many good years ahead.

"I could never be a hanger-on," he said. "I will race as long as I can with some expectation of success. My goals have always been the same—Indianapolis, and Formula 1. But I have to start winning, or at least consistently placing in the top 2 or 3. My financial resources have given me an advantage, but it is up to me to capitalize upon it now."

Capitalize on it he did, although probably not as much as he would have liked. The problem was that toothy Briton by the name of Hobbs. Without David, Posey might well have dominated the L&M Formula 5000 Continental. As it was he finished 2nd to Hobbs in points and earnings. It was a bit frustrating to look down David's tailpipes so much. In the first 3 races, Sam qualified 2nd fastest to Hobbs. Then Posey qualified on the pole for the next 3 races, but Hobbs came back with 2 more pole-grabs with Sam 2nd. In the races it was equally frustrating. Most Continentals were run in 2 heats (except for the Lime Rock finale). Hobbs won 5 of them, Posey just 1.

At Riverside Sam was 11th in the 1st heat, won the 2nd, and placed 3rd overall. At Laguna Seca he qualified 15th and failed to start, making him 28th overall. At Kent Sam was 2nd in both heats and overall. At Mid-Ohio he trailed Hobbs by a mere two-tenths of a second and won the 2nd heat, making him overall victor. At Road America he was 5th and 22nd, for 13th overall. At Edmonton he won the opening heat and was 15th in the 2nd, placing him 5th. At Donnybrooke the Surtees TS8 was 24th and 27th, making Sam 26th overall. At the single-race Lime Rock battle, he ran 2nd to Hobbs. The year was worth $30,900 to Sam, but money wasn't important, at least not that way.

Often people said that Posey literally bought his rides, as was often true. But Sam prided himself on being a true professional. When he showed up at the United States Grand Prix in October 1971, he was a reserve driver for John Surtees's team. He practiced a few laps and was fast. Surtees gave him a chance, and he capitalized on it for all it was worth. Gijs van Lennep, co-winner at Le Mans, was down for a car, but Sam beat him out of it simply by being 2.76 seconds—almost 3 m.p.h.—faster than the Dutchman. Surtees handed him the car. Some said Posey had bought that ride. "Money did change hands," Sam replied with a dramatic pause. "I am being paid to drive this car." In fact, van Lenneps offered to pay Surtees to leave him in the car, but Sam Posey had seen his chance and seized it. The fact that he finished only 17 laps didn't matter. He drove well.

But a strong and lucrative 5th in the 1972 Indianapolis 500 ($37,411), and a 5th and the Rookie award at Pocono ($13,060) made it seem Posey was on his way to fame as well as fortune. In 1973, though, Sam's busy schedule shrank appreciably, and you couldn't be sure what might happen next.

PAT PURCELL

Born December 3, 1900, at Grand Forks, N.D., James Alexander Purcell, the executive vice-president of NASCAR in its opening decades, was a bluff, bespectacled man with red hair and a pungent wit that could be scathing at times. Purcell's Irish father had wanted him to be a priest, and his Scottish mother hoped for a Methodist minister. He became an express messenger on the railroad instead. In 1919 he joined the *Grand Forks Herald* as a reporter, and became sports editor soon after (he was the entire sports staff as well). Pat took a leave to work as press agent and bill-poster for J. Alex Sloan's IMCA races in western Canada. That was when he became interested in auto racing.

Purcell progressed soon after to the *Fargo Forum* where until 1924 he was sports editor. He covered the Tom Gibbons-Jack Dempsey fight in Helena, Mont., and made friendships that stood him in good stead up to his death in 1966. With time out to marry Agnes Grant in Winnipeg, Manitoba, June 30, 1926, and a brief spell with the *Minneapolis Tribune,* he stayed in Fargo until 1929. Then he decided press agentry was his kind of work. Aside from a few backslides into the sports departments of the *Detroit Mirror* and the *Detroit Times,* he ballyhooed circuses, carnivals, fighters, B. Ward Beam's International Congress of Daredevils, Ralph Hankinson's AAA races, Lucky Teter and his Hell Drivers, and Jimmy Lynch's Death Dodgers, which he developed from one to 6 road units.

World War II settled him down, first as night news editor for the *Chicago Times,* then with the Army War Show. He also worked for *Billboard* and booked circuses, carnivals and Roller Vanities, a roller skating show. During the summer he worked Langhorne and Joie Chitwood's Daredevils. It was from this background that Bill France and Ed Otto persuaded Purcell to become the executive manager of NASCAR. He started work on June 1, 1952, travelled 50,000 miles a year as combination hand-holder for promoters, judge for complaining competitors, and safety inspector. He used to love to recall the old days before loudspeakers when he did the announcing through a huge horn, supported at the big end by some strong-backed local paid by free entry to the race. He enjoyed the ballyhoo and the showbiz of early auto racing, and helped put some of it into NASCAR. When Pat succumbed suddenly to a heart attack, NASCAR found it difficult to find someone to negotiate as skillfully with its promoters.

DIETER QUESTER

One thing that happens when a certain country's national becomes a top Grand Prix driver is that other drivers from his country get a special look and better rides than they ordinarily might. When Juan Fangio was king, half a dozen other South Americans got GP shots and sports car rides. When Jack Brabham came to the fore, literally a score of other Australians and New Zealanders appeared in racing cars in short order. Jo Rindt was an Austro-German, and that led to a resurgence of interest in drivers from these two countries.

One of the Austrians who got his try at Formula 1 was Dieter Quester, born in 1940 and therefore a bit old when he started getting 1st rate rides in 1970. Quester started competition itself rather late by European standards (1965), and it was 1967 before he made more than a ripple on the motoring scene. That season he was 4th in the European Hillclimb Championship, and in 1968 he was 3rd in the same series, while also winning the European Touring Car Championship in a BMW.

More Touring Car titles followed in 1969 and 1970, always in well-prepared factory cars like the BMW 269 and 270. In 1970, too, Quester made a quick transition to top single-seater form, finishing 4th in a tie with Sweden's Ronnie Peterson. Racing a F2 BMW, Quester had his best-ever race at Hockenheim in 1970 when he and Switzerland's Clay Regazzoni had a last-lap duel down to the checker, with Dieter taking the flag. Regge never did get there because his Tecno-Ford flew off the track when Clay got a front wheel sandwiched between

one of Quester's wheels and the BMW body. A couple of weeks later Quester bested Regazzoni again without the aerobatics and learned that BMW was quitting F2 and all other single-seater competition.

Things looked dark until STP-March made an announcement they were signing Quester for F1 with Peterson. That never came about, but meanwhile, Quester returned in a F2 March-BMW. All year different F1 opportunities kept suggesting themselves without ever paying off. One week it was a F1 Surtees, another it was a F1 Tecno. It was not surprising, despite regular sports car drives, that Dieter tired of it all and announced his single-seater retirement early in 1972, although his sports car commitments made him busier than ever, particularly in European 2-litre events, in which he was using the same kind of 16-valve BMW engine that had powered his F2 cars back in 1970.

IAN RABY

Ian Raby was only a club driver, but a determined one, with professional outlook and style. He was born in 1924, and waited until 1949 to begin his racing career, which he spent mostly driving Coopers. One of the high spots of his career came in 1957 when he shared a Le Mans Cooper with Jack Brabham; the pair finished 13th overall. After a string of sports car successes, Raby entered the Formula Junior arena in 1960 and graduated to Formula 1 in 1963, first in a Gilby-BRM and later in the original F1 Brabham-Climax.

In his later years, Raby concentrated on Formula 2. He also operated Ian Raby (Racing) Limited as a team for himself and an expatriate American, Bruce Eglinton, using the Brabham, outfitted with BRM, and a Lotus 27 fitted with a Ford engine in Formula 3. He had a good auto dealership in Brighton, including a section that dealt in used racing machinery, and had 2 of his mechanics working full time on the team cars during the season.

At 43 he was a bit old to still be pushing a car around race tracks. That fact finally caught up with Raby on July 30, 1967, when his F2 Brabham crashed at Zandvoort, Holland, killing one of racing's most professional amateurs.

REID RAILTON

Reid Anthony Railton's accomplishments were many. This painfully lean, bespectacled man who invariably wore suspenders and prescription sunglasses designed and built a complete car of his own; designed "the ultimate car"—a car produced without regard to the costs; designed several Land Speed Record cars; and designed a Water Speed Record Boat. Yet he was a man so in-

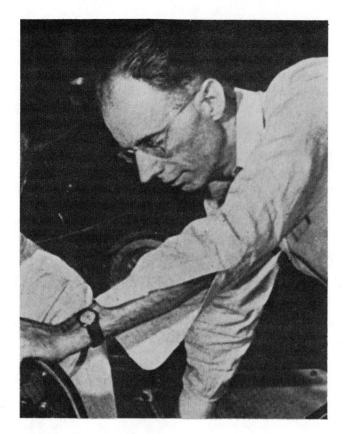

credibly shy, so softspoken, so unpossessed of vanity that his efforts were almost unknown outside the motoring profession until other people started putting Railton's name on some of his creations, thereby gaining him a measure of the public recognition he deserved.

Railton was born June 24, 1895, at Alderley Edge, England, 3 years before the Land Speed Record was officially born, and obtained a Bachelor of Science degree from Manchester University. As a truck design assistant at Leyland Motors Ltd. he worked for none other than John Godfrey Parry Thomas, the Welsh wizard; the thought of these 2 men working on trucks is ludicrous in light of their subsequent achievements. This was 1915, however, and Railton's great achievements were more than a dozen years away.

He left Leyland in 1923 to design and build his own car at Brooklands with Thomas. It was a 2-litre, 4-cylinder, inclined valve o.h.c. design, and by 1927—when Parry Thomas died at the wheel of Babs at Pendine Sands, and Railton gvae up the independent effort—only 10 had been sold. Thomas's old company was restarted as Thomson & Taylor Ltd. in premises that later became the Cooper factory. Railton was T&T's chief designer, his first task to produce a sports version of the Riley 9, introduced in 1926 in its standard form.

Railton also was racing, and in the Brooklands meeting of 1927 he won the one-mile handicap race, in what was to become the Brooklands Riley when replicas were sold. In 1928 he was married, and the following year he initially met Malcolm Campbell who had a 1,400-h.p. Napier Lion airplane engine and needed a car designed for it.

A full-scale model of Railton's design was completed early in 1930 and extensively tested in the Vickers Aircraft wind tunnel. When all the design modifications were completed, the actual building of the car took 36 days and nights; it was delivered in December 1930. The car never was defeated in its 5-year life. By the time it was retired in 1935, other Railtons were in the capable hands of Campbell, based on a 2500 b.h.p. V-12 Rolls-Royce airplane engine. John Cobb's Napier-Railton was so named by Cobb himself, who thus gave Reid credit for his success.

Railton's name was also on an Anglicized version of the American Hudson, starting in 1933, and when production ceased in 1950 some 1,460 of these had been sold. Whitney Straight, the American expatriate who later headed BOAC and served as an aide to King George VI during World War II, had Reid rebuild his 2.5-litre Maserati Grand Prix car around 1933. He was so happy with the results, that he had 3 more Railtonized for his private team. Reid also worked with Raymond Mays and Peter Berthon on the ERA project, based on the Rileys Mays raced, and Reid served as a continuing consultant not only to Riley but to MG.

It was Railton who told Cobb about the Bonneville Salt Flats and started the parade of LSR contenders to the Utah salts (then known as Salduro Salts). The year 1937 was a busy one, for Reid not only designed a Water Speed Record boat for Campbell that went 129.30 m.p.h., but an LSR car for Cobb based on 2 combined 1,250-b.h.p. Napier Lion engines. The Napier-Railton captured the record in 1937, 1938 and 1947, and was the car that held the record longest in history, until the American assaults of the mid-sixties. Reid himself was at these runs; in fact, in 1939 he stayed in America, settling in Berkeley, Calif., and opening his new career by joining Hall-Scott Motor Co., makers of boat engines. He stayed with that concern, working on defense and war projects, through 1945, then quit to become a consultant again. Among his first projects was readying Cobb's prewar car for the 1947 LSR attempt.

In 1948 Reid became a regular Hudson consultant, an association that lasted until 1956. He helped Cobb with the Water Speed Record design in 1949, and was with the burly Britisher when Cobb was killed in a WSR attempt at Loch Ness in 1952. That, plus an aversion to jet propulsion for cars or boats, pretty much ended Railton's involvement with speed.

JIM RATHMANN

Richard R. (Jim) Rathmann, a successful auto dealer in Eastern Florida, looked much more like a salesman than like one of the most talented race drivers of his era. But then, his is a story of paradoxes. He started racing before his older brother, James, and since the rules called for a minimum age of 21, he used his brother's identification and driver's license. When James began racing, he simply reversed the procedure, becoming known as Dick Rathmann. Back in California, where the brothers Rathmann both began, the drivers had an easier way of identifying the two. Dick was "Big" Rathmann and Jim was "Little" Rathmann since the real James was bigger as well as older.

Prematurely balding, blond, slight and bespectacled when he was off the track, Jim was never one of those shove-the-accelerator-through-the-floorboard types. He always favored paved tracks to dirt, since he didn't have the brawn to wrestle a car around some of the hairier clay ovals. And he always drove as much with his head as he did with his heart.

Born in Los Angeles July 16, 1928, Jim Rathmann grew up in an environment in which it would have been difficult not to become a car buff. He did his share of midnight drag racing, but soon gravitated to jalopies and roadsters, racing against men like Troy Ruttman and Andy Linden. After graduation from high school, Jim made up his mind to pursue racing as a business and moved to the Midwest, where he could run with the Hurricane and Mutual associations 7 or 8 times each week. He drove anything—sprints, championship cars, stock cars, midgets—and had his share of spinouts and flips. It was fine training, and while he enjoyed the competition, he always remembered that it was a business.

In 1948 and 1950-51, Jim was Midwest Roadster and Stock Car Association champion, but was prevented from running in the 1951 Indy 500 because of this "outlaw" activity. As an AAA-USAC driver at the height of his career, he compiled an enviable Indianapolis record of 2nd place 3 times (1952, 1957 and 1959) plus the $110,000 winner's share in 1960. He drove the Ken-Paul Watson roadster to a victory over Rodger Ward in that one. Rathmann also won the USAC sortie into Italy, the Race of Two Worlds at Monza, in 1959. He used his share of the Indy purse to advance from a Miami speed shop to a Melbourne, Fla., General Motors dealership. Among other Rathmann career highlights were victories in the 1957 Milwaukee 200 and the only USAC race ever held on Daytona International Speedway (a bastion of NASCAR), the 1959 Daytona 100, which cost the lives of both George Amick and Marshall Teague and terrified the rest of the USAC drivers.

Jim dabbled in sports cars in USAC's short-lived road racing division in 1958 and 1959. He also drove a Corvette at Sebring, finishing 11th overall with Dick Jones, a teammate from the 1953 Mexican road race. In Mexico he started 73rd in an Oldsmobile, Rathmann finishing 5th (behind 4 Lincolns) despite a crash that broke 2 ribs. He won the 1958 Grand Prix de Ramon Balta in Lima, Peru, a 633-mile stock-car road race, codriving with Eddie Pagan and averaging a record 109.258 m.p.h. in the 6-hour race.

Because he increasingly avoided dirt-track races, the best Jim ever did in the USAC national championship

standings was a 2nd in 1957. He never quite retired officially; he just stopped as the money rolled in from the car business. Jim was said to be one of the back doors through which Chevrolet was surreptitiously channeling aid to NASCAR and USAC competitors.

The high point of Rathmann's career must have been the 1960 Indy victory, although he himself thought there were many other races in which he drove better, was braver, or overcame greater handicaps. "Bravery alone doesn't win races," he was quick to point out. "It's good judgment and common sense. If a guy gets carried away, he'll wipe himself out." That didn't mean Jim wasn't brave; that was demonstrated by his greatest victory.

A sensational qualifying period had set the stage for the 1960 Indy thriller. Eddie Sachs was sitting on the pole with a 146.592 m.p.h. average speed, with Jim and defender Rodger Ward right next to him, their cars only fractions of a second slower. Then there was rookie Jim Hurtubise, whose average speed of 149.056 smashed Sachs' qualifying mark to smithereens.

Ward, Sachs, Hurtubise, and Rathmann all traded the lead during the first 100 miles, setting speed records at every juncture. With the superb A. J. Watson pit crew behind him, Ward pitted 1st at the 43-lap mark, confident his stops would be quicker than those of his rivals. He got a 22-second effort but, in his haste to return to the wars, he killed his engine. Rathmann passed, for a 31-second advantage.

Ward drove like a man possessed, and cut Jim's lead to 20 seconds by the 220-mile mark. Although Smokey Yunick and Chick Hirashima of the Rathmann pits directed a 21-second stop, the Watson boys did their job in 15, leaving Jim only 14 seconds to the good as the 2 drivers charged toward the halfway mark. On the 123rd lap, Ward took the lead back and, confident of victory, eased back to 141 m.p.h., expecting Rathmann to make his challenge in the later stages of the race. He also expected to have gained more time by then with quicker pit stops.

But Rathmann knew what he had to do. If the race was to be won in the pits, then Ward had to be forced into the pits an extra time. Rodger had to be short on rubber after his trophy dash to regain the lead, so Rathmann refused to allow the Leader-Card hero to coast at 140. He charged at him and regained the lead in the 128th lap. Ward fell in behind him and ran nose-to-tail for about 14 laps, then charged to the fore before pitting on lap 147.

Jim elected to pit on the same lap and rolled into his pits just as the patented Watson airjack was lifting Ward's car. He lost only a second on the stop, as both men refuelled and took on 3 new tires. He caught Ward 4 laps later and passed him. Biding his time, Rodger stayed right on Rathmann's tail for about 27 miles, then, with less than a 5th of the race left, took the lead on lap 163. They traded the lead back and forth on the 170th and 171st lap, and Rodger, in an effort to save tires, again reduced his speed.

But Jim would have none of this. He charged into the lead with 55 miles to go, and Ward ran 2nd, hoping that Rathmann would cut speed to reduce his own tire wear. He didn't, and on lap 183 Rodger took the lead. Jim caught him on lap 190, and the 2 dashed into the final 25 miles running almost hub to hub, faster each time around. Then one, then the other car would nose forward, and the official leader in the next 7 laps was the one whose nose was ahead at the start-finish line. On the 197th lap, Rathmann achieved a 146.128 m.p.h. average, the fastest lap, in traffic, to that date, and Ward matched him, until he noticed the breaker warning strip on his right front tire leering up at him. Rodger had no choice but to ease off and accept 2nd money. A mere half-minute later, Rathmann got the message that he, too, had to ease off, because his right rear tire had ground off its tread. He did, but won by 13 seconds. Ward and the Leader Card car finished almost 3 laps ahead of 3rd-place Paul Goldsmith in the Demler Special.

Rodger explained the philosophy that motivated Rathmann, and most of the top drivers, when he was asked why he didn't take the chance that the tire would hold up for 7 miles. "It's a lot better to get $45,000 for 2nd the sure way than to risk winding up in the hospital with nothing but doctor bills for your gamble." Jim, the racing businessman, would say amen. His career as a driver ended after the 1963 Indy 500 in which the Florida Chevrolet-Cadillac dealer finished 9th.

BRIAN REDMAN

It isn't often that a top endurance racer retires at a mere 33 years of age, but that is what Brian Redman announced he was doing at the end of the 1970 season. To prove his point, he packed up his family and all his belongings and headed off for a new life in South Africa. No one was betting that he wouldn't be back, although no one could guarantee that he would either. Redman was always an independently minded man who seemed to have all the tools for racing stardom except the dedication that pushes some drivers to the top quickly and keeps them there many years.

Brian Herman Thomas Redman, born in Burnley, Lancashire, March 9, 1937, was the son of a prominent grocery retailer and intended to follow in his father's footsteps. After public school, Brian entered catering college to learn the trade a little better, with every intention of going into the business until the British Army intervened. After being discharged, he actually spent 3 months amid the grocery shelves before moving into the mop business. This sounds strange, but wasn't, for what he did was take over his grandfather's mop factory when the old man died.

"Mops, mops, everywhere mops," said Redman later, "It drove me mad to see all those boring objects. It was only the company MGA that kept me from going crazy." The mop factory was finally sold, and Redman entered the garage business with British rally navigator Mike Wood. This was better, but still not right. Brian still obviously had not settled his mind on a career, and he went back into the family grocery trade for a 2nd hitch.

Redman had started racing on the club level in 1959, with a Morris Minor 1000. He slowly worked his way up the ladder of experience in an XK 120 Jaguar, a Morgan, and other cars. He finally made a name for himself in 1965 in a lightweight E Jaguar, in which he started 17 races and won 16 of them (with a 2nd in the other). In 1966, his E Jag patron, Charlie Bridges, bought Brian a Mark 2 Lola T70 sports car fitted with a 6-litre, Traco-prepared Chevvy engine, in which he starred on the club level and did well in International Group 7 racing.

Charlie Bridges's brother, David, offered Redman still another ride in 1967, a Formula 2 Brabham BT16, and later provided an even more competitive FVA-powered Lola T100. The season's high spot, however, came at the wheel of a Gulf Mirage provided by JW Automotive. Redman and Jackie Ickx shared the car in the Kyalami 9-hour Race—and won. This led to a Wyer team contract, and in 1968 Brian and Ickx shared a winning Ford at the BOAC 500 and the Spa 1000. That same year, Redman debuted in Formula 1, driving a Cooper-Maserati at South Africa, but retiring with engine trouble soon after the start. Later that year he started the nontitle Race of Champions at Brands Hatch in a new Cooper-BRM and finished 5th. He then ran the Spanish GP and copped 3rd.

Redman's 3rd GP of 1968 ended his season. A front wishbone on the Cooper broke while Brian was negotiating a turn at speed and he plowed into the embankment, breaking both bones in his right forearm. An 8-inch steel pin became a souvenier of that accident.

Redman came back as fast as ever, particularly in the sports/racing category. Porsche signed him for a 908 ride in 1969, and after a Daytona 24-hour start with Vic Elford, Brian found his natural partner, Jo Siffert. They won the BOAC 500, the Spa 1000, the Monza 1000, the Nurburgring 1000 and the Watkins Glen 6-hour Race, which clinched the World Manufacturers Championship for the West German factory.

Brian also drove Sid Taylor's Lola 70 in several nontitle events, and tested the new Chevron B16 in its 1st race at Nurburgring. Redman won the 500-kilometer contest. In F1 in 1970, Redman replaced Piers Courage in Frank Williams's de Tomaso effort, but despite his efforts the car proved a disappointment, failing to qualify in the British, French or German Grands Prix. In sports car racing, however, the Redman/Siffert partnership again prospered, their car leading every start, although mechanical problems limited their victories to the Targa Florio and the Spa 1000. In European Sports Car Championship racing, Brian drove both the Chevron B16 and its Spyder version, the same cars that he intended to race in South Africa after his retirement from British and Continental racing.

In January 1971, Redman became sales and marketing director for Richter Motors Limited, one of South Africa's leading BMW dealerships. Just a week before, he had clinched the Springbok series at South Africa's Pietermaritzburg course by winning his 4th consecutive race. His mount was a Richter Motors Chevron-FVC B19 Spyder. What better way for a salesman to get started in his new home territory? But the life of a salesman held no real appeal for Brian after he had tasted it for a few months. That, combined with constant offers of rides—especially tempting ones for single-seater racing in Formula 5000—caused Redman to reconsider his retirement, and the British F5000 opener in March 1971 found Redman sitting in a Castrol-sponsored Sid Taylor McLaren M18. In a test session at Silverstone, Brian had outsped Jackie Oliver for the job. Taylor also provided a BRM P154 CanAm car for the Group 7 Interserie, which brought Redman victories at Imola and Hockenheim, and a 1972 contract to drive Ferrari sports cars.

The determined Redman, seemingly more confident and relaxed in 1972, was fast once more in Ferrari sports car. With Jacky Ickx he shared an Austrian 1000 victory, with Clay Regazzoni he was 2nd at Buenos Aires, 4th at the Daytona 6-Hour Race, 5th at the BOAC

1000. In America, he was driving both CanAm and L&M Continental 5000, with good effect, in a Sid Taylor Chevron. He took a 4th overall at Watkins Glen's double 25-lappers. After winning the 1st heat, his battery failed 8 laps from the finish of the 2nd. And he was 2nd overall at Road Atlanta losing to Bretti Lunger on total time. Though now 35, Redman seems more youthful than that, for this is a whole lot more fun than selling cars in Africa.

ALAN REES

Like many others, Alan Binely Rees was once told that he had no aptitude for his chosen sport—motor racing —and was released from the Cooper Driver's School. Like those others, a list that includes fellow British drivers Peter Arundell and Trevor Taylor, Rees ignored the pronouncement and succeeded both as a driver and, more importantly perhaps, as a major participant in the formation of a new racing marque.

A small man (5 feet 4 inches) built along the lines of America's Richie Ginther, Rees was born near Newport, Monmouthshire, England, on January 12, 1938. He graduated from the University of Swansea in Wales, which has led to the misconception that he was a Welshman. As a youngster his tastes for racing were developed by tales of motorcycle competition from his father and his mother's brother, both of whom had raced. His convictions were cemented by a teenage visit to Goodwood, although in those years he was concentrating on rugby and rifle shooting. At Swansea he bought his initial car, a used Lotus 11, and made his debut at Goodwood in April 1959 in a club meet, finishing 7th.

Rees won 3 races after that, then switched to a 1000-c.c. Lola-Climax with the help of his parents. On Boxing Day, the day after Christmas, he won his inaugural national event, setting the stage for 1960. The Lola was 1st in class in 10 of 16 races entered, and Alan followed the trend by moving into the Formula Junior ranks at the end of the year, thanks to the loan of an older, front-engined Lola FJ by Eric Broadley. He didn't win but was impressive enough to be offered Lotus factory support and a fuel company retainer for 1961, so Rees purchased his own Lotus-Ford 20 FJ car.

In 1961 Alan captured the British FJ title, winning at Crystal Palace and at Goodwood, placing 2nd at Snetterton to Arundell, and taking a 3rd at Silverstone behind Arundell and Taylor. In June of that year, he went to the Continent for the initial time, retiring with brake failure at La Châtre, France (he had had a bad crash at Crystal Palace). Again Rees was impressive, if not all-conquering, and again an offer followed, this time from Colin Chapman, to join the Lotus factory team with Arundell and Bob Anderson, but Rees had to buy his own car. While Peter was the team leader in fact as well as name in 1962, Alan did win once at Mallory Park and twice at Crystal Palace driving a Lotus 22. Among his many 2nds was that at Clermont-Ferrand, when he took over a prototype Lotus 23 after Arundell had crashed in practice.

The next season Alan accepted an offer to drive Lola-Ford Juniors and Lotus-Ford 23B sports cars, for Roy Winkelmann. The team was not well-organized, and it was a poor year all around, despite some good placings at Crystal Palace, Goodwood, and Snetterton. That winter the team was reorganized, with Rees himself becoming managing director of the racing division and of its international express parts service. In 1964, Alan's inaugural as a full-time professional driver, a Brabham-Cosworth as immaculately prepared as any car that year was at his disposal. Alan beat Jack Brabham himself at Rheims and scored at Brands Hatch as well. He was equally impressive, though not a winner, in many other races. For 1965, he shared Winkelmann Racing's Brabham-Cosworth F2 mounts with Jo Rindt, won the Enna GP, and placed at Reims and at Rouen. The next season saw little success for either Rees or Rindt in F2.

Formula 2 continued to be Rees's big interest, and in 1967 he trailed only Rindt at Silverstone, and Rindt and Graham Hill at Snetterton. At Pau and Zandvoort he took 3rds behind Rindt and Hulme, and Jacky Ickx and Chris Irwin, to indicate the kinds of company Alan was keeping. Only Jim Clark, Rindt, and Hill preceded Rees at Keimola, Finland.

A turning point came in 1968, when the Winkelmann F2 team was reorganized yet again, and Rees was given the task of managing it, with Rindt as his chief driver. Under Alan's management the Austrian ace took 6 of the 11 major events that season. Rees established himself as an astute handler of drivers and a meticulous preparer of racing machinery. It was this reputation that led him, in 1969, to an association with Max Mosley, Graham Coaker and Robin Herd—contributing much more than his "AR" initials to the "M—CH" of his partners—to found the successful March marque.

Rees's duties with March were many, principally as the team manager of the factory squad. Of all the directors of the company, he alone got away with test-driving the products, although all of the March men had driving backgrounds of one kind or other. Rees's own serious driving career was over in 1969, but the growing March responsibilities he assumed made it a much easier thing to accept than it would have been a few years before, when he seemed so close to doing something really spectacular on the courses of Europe.

CLAY REGAZZONI

The 1970 Italian Grand Prix at Monza will be remembered for the death of World Champion Jocken Rindt, who was killed in practice, but it also had at least a single pleasant reminder. That's the 1st victory of Gianclaudio Guiseppe (Clay) Regazzoni, a Ferrari team driver, in only his 4th ride in a Formula 1 cockpit. Rindt was dead, but the equally fast defending World Champion, Jackie Stewart, and other Grand Prix drivers like

Denis Hulme, John Surtees, and Jack Brabham—all former World Champions—as well as Chris Amon, Jean-Pierre Beltoise, Jacky Ickx and many others, were contesting as hard as they could for that GP. Starting from the 2nd row of the Monza grid, Regazzoni never slipped lower than 4th, popped into the lead as early as the 10th lap—briefly—then became a serious contender for the victory about lap 32, and never lost it again after the 53rd lap, when Stewart briefly edged in front of Clay's bright red Ferrari.

Victory came at 147.07 m.p.h., almost 6 seconds over Stewart's Matra-Ford, after 68 laps of real duelling. The gap widened with only about 10 laps to go when Regazzoni's long F2 and F3 training came to the fore and he was able to break from the pack. He took the flag amid the hysteria so familiar in Italy when an Italian captures an Italian GP. He was mobbed and carried away from the car atop the shoulders of the spectators.

Regazzoni was not Italian, of course, but Swiss—albeit from the Italian-speaking sector of the Federation—and came not from a racing family, but one that was at least auto-oriented. Clay's father had a large car bodybuilding business. The young Regazzoni was born on September 5, 1939, at Lugano, and started his career by running a Sprite and a Mini. He first squeezed into a real racing car, an F3 de Tomaso, at age 25, when he entered a race driving school at Montlhéry.

His debut race at Imola was nothing spectacular, for the car was not competitive. The much better known Silvio Moser, also a Swiss, lent Regazzoni a Brabham that year, and because of his inexperience Clay soon picked up a deserved reputation as a hairy driver, after numerous spins and a spectacular crash at Monza. Tecno signed Regazzoni for its F3 Temporada team in 1966, and then moved him up to its regular F3 team in 1967. He won at Jarama in his best drive, and drove both F2 and F3 for Tecno in 1968, still learning, and still crashing, at Monaco and Zandvoort.

Ferrari, always looking for fast Italian drivers (even ones from Switzerland), tried Clay out for F2 racing in 1969, but he went back to Tecno when the Modena cars proved to be not as fast as his previous mounts. The parting was amicable, however, and perhaps the Commendatore recognized that Regazzoni's desire for victory was the big thing in the young man's life, even to the extent of walking away from the great Ferrari team. No matter for in 1970 Clay was back in a Ferrari, only this time an F1 car, the goal of all racing drivers. He was not to have a car for every race, but would alternate with another new Ferrari driver, Ignazio Giunti.

In the Dutch GP, his first and a race marred by the death of Piers Courage, Regazzoni finished 4th, directly behind team leader Ickx. In the British GP the story was the same, Clay finishing 4th, and the consensus was that he probably would have been higher with any luck at all; he spent the latter part of the battle driving with almost no brakes. In the Austrian GP it was evident that

Regazzoni would win a GP. He was fastest in 2 of the 3 practices; but in the race he finished 2nd behind Ickx. Then came his Italian victory.

In the 3-race North American series that closed the 1970 season, Regazzoni could not repeat his Italian feat, but he did finish 2nd behind Ickx at both the Canadian and Mexican Grands Prix. At the United States GP, he was placed 14th after his sick car died. For the year, his debut in F1, Clay had amassed 33 championship points. The deceased Rindt had 45, Ickx 40, and then came Regazzoni, followed by Hulme with 27. Small wonder that when the Grand Prix Drivers Association met that winter, Regazzoni's own peers voted him the Wolfgang von Trips Memorial Trophy as top 1970 GP rookie.

The 2nd GP victory proved elusive, even though Clay's Ferrari team was favored to dominate F1 in 1971. Mario Andretti got things going properly with a South African victory, and Clay was 3rd. He did win the nontitle Race of Champions at Brands Hatch, but retired in both the Spanish and Monaco Grands Prix. In another nontitle race Clay was 14th, but in Holland he returned to form with a 3rd. Retirements in France and Germany were frustrations, yet Clay managed another 3rd in Germany before retiring in Austria, Italy, and Canada (the latter due to a crash and fire). He was 6th in the United States, to close the GP season. His 13 points gave him only 7th place in the standings. Clay's sports-car racing with Ferrari wasn't that much better. He managed a 2nd at the BOAC 1000, retired in the Monza 1000, was 8th at Spa's 1000, and retired in the Nurburgring 1000.

Regazzoni in 1972 F1 racing had his ups and downs.

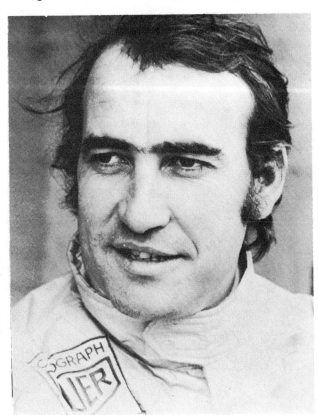

Fourth in Argentina, he was 12th in South Africa. Third in Spain, he retired in Monaco and Belgium. Second in Germany, he retired in both the Austrian and Italian Grands Prix. In Canada he was 4th, in the U.S. GP 8th, for a total of 15 points and a tie for 6th on the season. In Ferrari sports cars, too, there were variations on the winning theme. Regge was 2nd in the Buenos Aires 1000 with Brain Redman, 4th at Daytona, 5th in the BOAC 1000. With Jacky Ickx, easily the best sportscar driver Ferrari had along with Mario Andretti, Clay shared victory at the Monza 1000. At Spa that combo was 2nd, but a soccer accident knocked Clay out of further races. In 1973 Regazzoni switched to the Marlboro-BRM F1 team.

DARIO RESTA

Dario Resta spoke and dressed like an Englishman (although he was born in Milan, Italy, in 1884) because he was raised in Britain from the age of 2. He was quiet, almost withdrawn, off the track, but he drove like a demon. He always planned ahead, and when his new bride demanded he quit racing, he did for a time. Of course, the new Mrs. Resta was the sister of Spencer Wishart, killed racing in 1916; that was one argument. She also possessed several million dollars; that was another.

With it all, Resta may have been a racing immortal, maybe the racing immortal. We shall never know, although he won Indianapolis on his 2nd try in 1916. He won both the Grand Prize and the Vanderbilt Cup at San Francisco in 1915. These were only his 1st American appearances. He won 6 for 6 at Maywood Park in Chicago, and he won the 1916 AAA season crown with 4,100 points, staving off Johnny Aitkin.

Resta drove a Peugeot for Alphonse G. Kaufman, a wealthy New Yorker who had heard about his reputation while in England. Dario had competed since 1907 at places like Brooklands; in a 120-h.p. Mercedes, he set a half-mile mark there of 95.7 m.p.h. His American career—the important part of it—spanned only 2 years, although he did return to Indianapolis as part of the Packard factory team in 1923 (he lasted 88 laps after starting in the front row).

Resta's 1916 victory in the Indianapolis 500 was not his most brilliant, partly because Ralph DePalma was not in the field, having held out for starting money and then had his late-entry refused, and partly because Dario's opposition burned itself out in the early part of the race, letting him get so far ahead that he was able to make a precuationary stop to change tires. His 84 m.p.h. average was 4 m.p.h. slower than he himself had gone the year before, when he and DePalma staged their epic duel. Resta and his Peugeot were fresh from the double victory in the San Francisco road races in February. He was to go on to win the inaugural of his Chicago Auto Derbies and 100-mile invitationals in Chicago and Sheepshead Bay, N.Y. (The 500-mile speed in the 1915 Auto Derby of 97.8 m.p.h. was a record that stood for half a dacade.)

Dario was only one of the favorites in the 1915 Indi-

anapolis field. The formula had been cut to 300 cu.in. from the 450 of the previous year; no one expected the cars to be able to match the previous 82.47 m.p.h. average. It was a cold cloudy day, however, which helped tire wear immensely. Dario led the 1st lap of the race, then relinquished the lead to the Stutz team—1st to Howdy Wilcox for 10 miles, then to Gil Anderson, who set the blistering pace that was to result in the race record. Resta pushed back into the lead on the 82nd mile and held off the Stutz team and the DePalma Mercedes, battling for 2nd behind him.

Now the battle between Resta and DePalma was joined in earnest. Ralph established himself in 2nd place by the 100-mile mark and slowly cut the gap to Resta until, at 175 miles, he put the big German car in front for the 1st time. DePalma held off Dario until the 325-mile mark when he made his scheduled pit stop, then Resta screamed back into the lead. He looked impossible to catch when, coming into the stretch at the 342-mile mark, his right rear tire burst. Magnificently Resta kept the vehicle upright through a wild skid and got it into the pits where he had to change all 4 tires. The great battle was over. Before he could get back, DePalma had lapped him and was pouring on a 90 m.p.h. pace. Dario's steering had worked loose, and so Resta was content to hold second, 3 minutes, 26 seconds behind DePalma, but 5 minutes ahead of 3rd-place Gil Anderson. The average speed was 89.84 m.p.h.

The 1916 classic saw Dario allow Eddie Rickenbacker to set the pace in a Maxwell until his elimination with a broken steering knuckle; he then let Johnny Aitken take the lead in a Peugeot. Resta assumed the lead himself in the 45th mile and was never headed, driving well below his beautifully-prepared Peugeot's capabilities. Actually, his Peugeot, 4 inches shorter in the wheelbase than 3rd-place Ralph Mulford's, was the most modern and fastest car on the track. Wilbur D'Alen finished 2nd in a Duesenberg, also among the short-chassis cars in the race.

Dario apparently had persuaded his wife to let him race after World War I, but his appearances were few, far between, and particularly unsuccessful. He is quoted as saying, "Automobile racing is something one must do consistently or one loses the urge and the ability to compete." In 1923 Dario and Ralph DePalma were mates on the Packard team at the Indianapolis 500. Resta might have taken some solace in the fact that his was the last Packard to go out of the race—with a blown gasket—at 225-mile mark. He died September 2, 1924, in a crash at Brooklands in a Sunbeam, following a tire blowout.

CARLOS REUTEMANN

Following in the footsteps of a Juan Fangio can be pretty harrowing. Trailing along at the same time as an Emerson Fittipaldi doesn't help. Perhaps those statements explain Carlos Alberto Reutemann's basic problem. People may have expected too much of Argentina's favorite driver of the modern age.

Born in the province of Santa Fe April 12, 1942, Reutemann's paternal grandfather was a Swiss-German. His father was an Argentinian, his mother an Italian. At age 7 he began to play with a 1928 Model A Ford his father had at their ranch, but it was 1965 before he got to race a Fiat in a Turismo race. He retired with oil pressure problems. Then a consistent winning streak began that brought Carlos 4 Turismo championships in 2 years. In 1967 he had a de Tomaso (Alessandro de Tomaso, though based in Europe, was an Argentinian) and won a championship with that car. Some changes made the car ready for the 1968 Argentine Formula 1 season (not single-seaters, but GT cars), but more importantly Reutemann started racing in real Formula 2 cars in a series created by YPF, the State-owned oil company.

In 1969 Reutemann won 10 of 12 races in the Argentine F2 season, then did well that winter in the Temporada sports car races. The next season found YPF's racing team in Europe, co-sponsored by a variety of other public and private agencies from the South American nation. Two new Brabham BT30 cars were available, a huge transporter, no less than 8 engines, extensive London raceshops and numerous mechanics. Such was Reutemann's entry into European racing. The year and his career in Europe did not start well. At a wet Hockenheim, Carlos's Brabham tapped Jo Rindt's

499

car, starting a 5-car pile-up that eliminated them, though Reutemann himself managed to stay in the race. Between heats, Rindt came over and expressed himself rather forcibly that Indians ought to stay in jungles and not come to race courses. Carlos was 4th overall in the racing with an excellent 2nd heat, but his ears still were burning even though he only partially got what Rindt had said in English.

Still Reutemann's drives that 1st year were fairly spectacular in other ways. At Nurburgring, no one was faster in the wet practice. Carlos had put in 200 laps round the Ring the week before in a Ford Capri just to ready himself for this race. At Crystal Palace he made the front row alongside Jackie Stewart and François Cevert. At Hockenheim again, only Fittipaldi was faster in practice. Races were another story, for YPF had chosen the wrong engine builder and was operating out of the mainstream, hindered by trying to run the European effort from Argentina and relying too much solely on their own Argentinian mechanics and suppliers.

Reutemann had shown enough, though, for YPF to continue the F2 effort in 1971. All Carlos did in return was finish 2nd overall to sensational Ronnie Peterson in the European series. And he made his Formula 1 debut in the nonchampionship Argentine F1 race, driving Jo Bonnier's old McLaren M7C to a 3rd, thanks to many retirements among the European visitors. In 1972 there was more F2 racing with Rondel Racing, but also a crash in a F2 car at Thruxton that sidelined Carlos a month. There was his F1 championship debut in a Brabham team car, although the year was not one of great accomplishment: 7th in Argentina, retirement in South Africa, a nontitle victory by default over Fittipaldi in the Interlagos GP, 13th in Belgium, 8th in Britain and retirements starting in the German GP.

Fangio hadn't won his 1st World Championship until he was 40, and Carlos Reutemann, the new Fangio, had a while to go yet.

LANCE REVENTLOW

It was hard to feel sorry for the man with the Woolworth five-and-dime millions behind him, but Lance Reventlow—son of the world's richest woman, Barbara Hutton, and a Danish nobleman, Count Kurt von Haugwitz-Reventlow, tried so hard to make the Scarab the first really competitive all-American sports and formula racing machine that you had to feel something when he finally gave up in 1963, after some 5 years of effort.

Lance was born in London on February 24, 1936, and brought to the United States when he was 4. Private schools followed right through to an Arizona prep school, where he was a good, if indifferent, student. He played baseball and football fairly well, was a star swimmer and also managed—away from school—to become

an excellent polo player. He decided to live in Hollywood, so the choice of colleges was limited. He chose Pomona-Claremont, but he was there only a short while; he had discovered something more interesting.

At 19 Lance had discovered racing cars. On Labor Day 1955, he took his street car—a Mercedes 300SL —to a Santa Barbara airport and finished "away back" in 15th. At Salinas, his 2nd start, he took both 2nd overall and class victory. On the way to the race James Dean, idol of young America at the time, flashed by in his Porsche and waved, reminding Reventlow that they were to have breakfast the following morning. Dean didn't make it, dying in a highway accident that day. Bruce Kessler, a friend, joined Lance for the Torrey Pines 6-hour race, and it was Lance who was driving when the car crashed, after Kessler had handed it over in 3rd place The season ended on a happier note, however, with a 3rd at Glendale and a 5th at Pomona.

In 1956 Reventlow bought a pure racing car, a 1100-c.c. Cooper, which he used to win 10 races and collect some 2nds and 3rds. One of the latter was at Elkhart Lake, where Lance and another unknown of those days, Richie Ginther, codrove to 1st in class and 3rd overall. In his initial international event at Nassau, Reventlow retired. He headed for Europe and bought a 2-litre Maserati in 1957. Lance raced at most major European courses, and flipped at Snetterton in his worst accident in racing. Reventlow also drove a Formula 2 Cooper in Britain before returning to the States with the repaired Maserati. Carroll Shelby and Marvin Panch led the Maserati over the line at New Smyrna Beach, Fla. Then

Lance took 2nd in class and 5th overall at Nassau Speed Week.

At this point Lance decided that building his own car would be the key to winning, and he worked out the details with Warren Olsen in the latter's garage in West Los Angeles. Ken Miles did the engineering drawing, and Troutman and Barnes did the chassis design and development. The Scarab design was of space-frame construction, had independent front suspension and a De Dion rear, aluminum disc brakes, Morris Minor rack and pinion steering (suitably modified), a Halibrand quick-change differential, and adjustable rear hubs to get the best possible camber and toe-in for each circuit that would be raced. The Chevrolet Corvette power plant used in the Scarab was bored out to 5562 c.c. and yielded 385 b.h.p. at over 6,000-r.p.m. A 4-speed Corvette geabox controlled this power. Chuck Daigh, who joined the team early, designed a Hillborn fuel injection system especially for the car. After a no-go appearance at Phoenix, the Scarab made its debut at Palm Springs in April, where Lance (still a bit wild as a driver) spun and finished 3rd in the preliminary, cracking a cylinder wall.

On May 4, 1958, the Scarab bearded Briggs Cunningham's Lister-Jaguars, cocks of the American racing walk, for the 1st time and came away with a 3rd and a 5th. A month later, the Scarab won at Santa Barbara, in a California Sports Car Club Formula Libre event. A little later it was leading at Riverside when the differential gave out. Victory over the Lister-Jags finally came in August, at Montgomery, N.Y. on the airport circuit. Daigh scored the victory as Walt Hansgen blew a tire. On Labor Day the Scarabs wiped up the Listers 2 days in a row, then moved into the USAC ranks. Chuck and Lance were 1st and 2nd at Meadowdale. At Riverside Daigh bested the likes of Phil Hill, Jean Behra and Roy Salvadori. A Nevada race saw 2 breakdowns, but the pair won at Laguna Seca, and Lance took the Nassau Cup and Daigh the Nassau Trophy at Speed Week.

That was it for sports cars as far as Reventlow was concerned. He was not through with Project Scarab yet, however. Reventlow was interested in Formula 1, but the resulting car was nothing startling as far as design went. The Achilles' heel proved to be the power plant. Leo Goossen of Offy fame was the design consultant, and so the engine was something approximating a Meyer-Drake, but Leo seemed more interested in his Indianapolis projects, so the 3-litre, F1 car never really had a chance. The learning year was supposed to be 1959, but it was Francorchamps 1960, before a Scarab made a European grid with Reventlow in the cockpit. (Daigh was also there in a 2nd car.) Both retired early— if the engines weren't acting up, the tires were. At Rheims for practice, the Scarabs proved 10 seconds slower than every other car there, and they were snapping connecting rods at a great rate. The formula was

changing to 1.5 litres, and Lance had no interest in going through more frustration. Instead, he placed his bet on the then seemingly firm Intercontinental Formula. Unfortunately for him, it never got off the ground.

The Scarab sports cars were around for many other seasons, but in the hands of other people. Lance Reventlow had had enough, and he never returned to racing. Moreover, his second wife, after he had shed movie starlet Jill St. John, wasn't particularly impressed with auto racing. He joined Briggs Cunningham, another dreamer who hadn't quite made it all the way, in watching Dan Gurney make something of the All-American Eagle. How much he regretted not continuing himself he never said. To compensate Reventlow took up polo and skiing. It was on a private plane trip involving the latter that he was killed in a sudden, heavy thunderstorm July 24, 1972, when the single-engined Cessna 206 in which he was a passenger slammed into a wooded mountainside in the Colorado Rockies.

PETER REVSON

A rookie at the Indianapolis 500 can be anything from a World Champion to a midget driver trying to make the big time. Of course, no "rookie" is ever inexperienced. There are 40 test laps to pass before a driver can even try to make the final field for a 500, a field confined to 33 cars despite entry lists that may total as many as 100 cars. To make the field in your first try is a feat in itself, even when you start from 33rd, and dead last, position.

501

To drive from 33rd to the top 5 finishers is rather good, and it is the kind of driving that puts you in the running for Rookie of the Year honors at Indy.

Peter Jeffrey Revson of New York City made the Indy field his initial try, started 33rd and finished 5th . . . and didn't win rookie honors. But it wasn't surprising, for Revson was so undemonstrative in his Indy debut that he was easily overlooked, particularly by people who didn't know his road-racing credentials, Peter's 1969 Indy heroics were even more impressive because his car, underpowered to say the least and constantly balking through the race, had to be nursed to that finish line. In 1970 he returned with a better mount, but a blown engine after 87 laps ended the slim, handsome 5 feet 11 inch driver's hopes that May. In 1971, though, Peter stole the Brickyard's pole from Mark Donohue, 178.696 m.p.h. to 177.087 and finished 2nd to Al Unser. They knew him at Indy after that race and after his CanAm races later that season.

Revson was the son of Martin Revson, not the brother who founded Revlon and pushed it into an international cosmetic empire, but the brother who came along for the ride and did pretty well too. Born February 27, 1939, in New York City, Revson never had to worry about money. He bounced around the educational trails for a long time, attending Cornell University to study mechanical engineering, Columbia University for liberal arts and the University of Hawaii for surfing and other pastimes. In 1960 he left college and tried his hand at business, 1st as an advertising market research analyst, then as an advertising account executive. By now he was racing. It all started with a Plus 4 Morgan in the SCCA ranks, and included an Austin-Healey and a Taraschi Formula Junior, among others. Peter was 2nd in his debut automobile race on an airport course, and won his next time out.

By 1962 he had had about 4 years of club racing in the United States and 2 years of the advertising business, and he was a bit bored with both, so Revson and an old Cornell classmate named Teddy Mayer—later of Team McLaren—founded the Revson-Mayer FJ Team, using Coopers, and won a race at Mosport and came in 3rd in another in Puerto Rico and still another in Nassau. This was more like it, and Revson decided to turn professional, giving up his advertising connections, taking a $10,000 grubstake and sailing off to Europe. In Britain he founded Revson Racing (America) using a Cooper and a converted English bread van as his rolling headquarters/home. Revson rolled all over Europe in this truck, some 16,000 miles in a summer, racing at the best Continental courses. His big victory was one in the Copenhagen FJ race in 1963.

The following year Peter was offered a spot with Tim Parnell's racing effort, and he drove a Lotus-BRM in the nontitle Oulton Gold Cup Formula 1 race, a Lotus in Formula 2 and a Lotus in Formula 3, where he won at Monte Carlo in a race that included Bob Bonduant

and Roy Pike, other Americans. In 1965 Revson headed back to the U.S. and a berth with the Bill Kay Racing Team in a Brabham BT8, a 2-litre Climax-engined sports car that he raced in the Under-2-Litre Canadian-American race series that used to precede the Group 7 CanAm. But he raced in Europe as well with the Ron Harris Team Lotus F2/F3 forces. In F2 he was 2nd in the Eifelrennen, ran a record 135.2 m.p.h. lap at Enna and finished 2nd to Jo Schlesser. Revson was also 4th at Pergusa and Solitude, 3rd at Dunds and Oulton. He won the F3 Monaco Grand Prix.

In 1966 Peter joined with Skip Scott in the Essex Wire Co. GT40 for sports/prototype racing, and the pair managed 3rd at both Sebring and Spa. He also raced twice in the CanAm in a McLaren-Ford, finishing 4th at Las Vegas and 6th at Riverside. The following season in the Bud Moore Mercury Cougar for the SCCA's Trans-American series. Peter won at both Lime Rock and Bryar. In the Dana Chevrolet McLaren and Sun-Ray DX Lola, another Chevvy-powered car, he raced in the SCCA's United States Road Racing Championship and the CanAm. He had better luck in the former, finishing 2nd to Mark Donohue at Pacific Raceways and 7th overall in the final standings, while in the CanAm Revson's best finishes were a 4th at Mosport and a 10th at Monterey, which gave him a mere 3 points for 6 races. The 1967 season was a bad one in a more personal way when his brother, Douglas, 2 years Peter's junior, was killed in a Spanish F3 racing accident.

Peter drove both TransAm and CanAm again in 1968, 1969 and 1970. In the initial season he had an AMC Javelin and had pairs of 2nds and 3rds for his efforts in TransAm. In CanAm he finished only 2 of 6 starts once again, and got no higher than 4th at Road America. That same year he ran a Shelby Lola-Ford in the USRRC and even journeyed to Japan for the World Challenge Cup at Mt. Fuji Speedway, which proved Revson's big victory of the season. In 1969 the TransAm racing was with a Shelby Boss Mustang, and there were a pair of 3rds, some 4ths and a 5th. In CanAm there were 4 retirements, a 4th at Road America, a 5th at Riverside, a 7th and an 8th. And there was Indy.

In 1970, besides another try at the 500, there was an L&M Lola in the CanAm and Peter's best finish in that series up to then, a 2nd at Mid-Ohio just 76 seconds behind Denis Hulme. But there were also 6 retirements —even at Road America where Revson ran the fastest lap—and 3rds at Donnybrooke and Laguna Seca. Eighth in points, Revson still pocketed at tidy $40,850 in Can-Am winnings. At Indianapolis Raceway Park in a 2-heat USAC race, Revson won handily in a Lola. In TransAm Revson was 2nd at Bryar in the opener, his best finish of the season for the Roger Penske Javelin team that he had joined, but he was to play a season-long 2nd fiddle to Donohue, the Penske team leader, who won 3 races. The season ended at Riverside, where Peter attracted attention by jumping Sam Posey in the pits after the pair had collided on the course and subsequently retired. But they shared a NART Ferrari at Daytona in the beginning of 1971.

The year 1971 was Peter Revson's best in racing. He was given a good car, and he got the most out of it. The series was the CanAm, of course. The team was McLaren, managed by Revson's old buddy, Teddy Mayer. Mounted in the latest McLaren M8F-Chevy, Peter started slowly, finishing 2nd by 9.7 seconds to Denis Hulme, the team leader, at Mosport. Jackie Stewart won St. Jovite in the L&M Lola, Hulme was 2nd, Revson 3rd a lap back of these two. At Road Atlanta Peter won by 17 seconds over Hulme, his initial victory in the CanAm. But not the last by any means. At Watkins Glen Revson won again, with Hulme 2nd by 57 seconds.

At Mid-Ohio Stewart won, with Revson 7th and not running due to suspension problems. At Road America, despite starting dead last, Revson finished a lap over Jo Siffert. Up to now he had never qualified fastest, leaving that to Hulme and Stewart. On the pole at Donnybrooke, Revson won by 47 seconds over Hulme. But his pole position didn't give him any advantage at Edmonton, when the car failed to start; in real British stiff-upper-lip fashion, Revson started 11 laps late, and while Hulme won, Revson finished 12th. His 5th victory came at Monterey, with Peter taking Stewart by 9.23 seconds. He virtually clinched the CanAm title by winning this Laguna Seca race.

Revson got a Formula 1 start at that fall's U.S. GP with Ken Tyrrell's Stewart-François Cevert squad. Ken had a spare car, the original 001 Tyrrell, and Revson found himself among the GP crowd with lots of familiar faces. But the sensation lasted less than a lap when his clutch failed, and he had to walk back to the pits. In 1972 he became a GP regular with Team McLaren, still driving in CanAm when Stewart's ulcer ended the Scotsman's deal with the bright orange cars.

In 1972 Revson intended to concentrate on F1 and give up the CanAm. But this was not to be, for Stewart, who was down to replace him, came up with a bleeding ulcer and was forced to give up the Group 7 series. So Peter found himself back partnering Hulme in more than the McLaren single-seaters. With the challenge of Roger Penske's L&M Porsche-Audi 917-10K, Team McLaren had its problems all season long. There was no champagne for Revson in 1972 in the CanAm, but he could console himself with an excellent showing in F1.

After retiring from the Argentine GP with an engine injesting pebbles, he was 3rd in South Africa, just 26 seconds back on the winner, Hulme, 5th in Spain, 7th in Belgium, then 3rd twice in a row at the British and Austrian Grands Prix, and 4th in Italy. It was a season of great consistency for Revson, and his problems in the CanAm and in the more lucrative 500-mile USAC races, which he preferred to run, were ones, perhaps, more of the car than of the man. After qualifying his Gulf Mc-

Laren on the front row at Indy, he suffered a broken gearbox, in the 23rd lap. At Pocono, the car lasted 7 laps and at Ontario it was front row and quick exit again, this time after 81 laps.

BILL REXFORD

If there ever was a man who profited from the transgressions of others, it was Bill Rexford, NASCAR's Strictly Stock Champion (Grand National) in 1950. Born on March 14, 1927, William J. Rexford came out of Conewango Valley, N.Y., in an Oldsmobile. He couldn't do much when the real hero drivers of those days—Red Byron, Glenn Dunnaway, and the Flocks—were rolling, but then the other heroes were not above trying to circumvent the NASCAR rule book. This was the year Bill France, president and founder, decided to crack down hard. Dunnaway, for example, was once disqualified for spreading his car's front springs to get better handling. Others went the more conventional route of altering the engine or making transmission changes. Rexford won only the Canfield 200, in Ohio, on May 30, 1950. With the shorter schedule and enough top-5 finishes to edge Fireball Roberts, that was enough. He was not even a factor the next year, and his best finish thereafter was a 5th in 1953, as he became an infrequent competitor.

He started in what were then called hot rod races—these were really primitive modifieds—in western New York in 1945. The youngster was not without courage. Modified racing in those days was as much a matter of surviving the numerous crashes as it was of going fast. He caught the eye of NASCAR vice-president Ed Otto, who promoted in that area, and he was encouraged to try the Strictly Stocks after winning a 25-mile feature at Pennroyal Raceway. He picked the right time, for in those days NASCAR had stops at many more Northern and Midwestern tracks—stops which some of the Southern boys didn't bother to make. Bill came South, however, racing for points, and won the crown after amassing 1,959 to Roberts's 1,848.5 and Lee Petty's 1,590.

EDDIE RICKENBACKER

Rickenbacker. The name conjures up many pictures—daredevil American flying ace of World War I; President of the Indianapolis Speedway in the thirties; head of Eastern Airlines; World War II aviation advisor; spokesman for the conservative cause in his later years. He was a geniune American hero. Often forgotten are Rickenbacker's early years, before World War I, when he was a great racing driver, a contemporary—and equal—of Barney Oldfield and Dario Resta.

Born Edward Rickenbacher (he changed the spelling

503

of his name at the outbreak of World War I) in Columbus, Ohio, on October 8, 1890, his boyhood might be called underpriviledged by some, but Rick refused to call it that himself. He started in the auto business at 75 cents a day at the Evans Garage in 1905, took an International Correspondence School course in mechanical engineering, and moved over to the Frayer-Miller automobile plant only 2 blocks away.

Lee Frayer was attracted to this bright youngster and took Rick along with him to Long Island when the 3-car Frayer-Miller team went for the 1906 Vanderbilt Cup races. He ended up as a riding mechanic in Frayer's own car, but the pair failed to qualify for a Vanderbilt berth. Later in the year, when Frayer switched to Clinton Firestone's Columbus Buggy Company, Rickenbacker went along with him. Eventually he learned not only all the mechanical and production aspects of auto building, but the sales side as well, being a driver-demonstrator in Columbus at 1st, and then a factory representative who set up dealerships and made direct sales.

In 1910, Rick started racing the Firestone-Columbus as a publicity stunt in town races in his sales territory, the North Central states. Working at night, he had stripped a regular road car, reinforced its frame, added an extra gas tank, and painted the racer white. Eddie also wore spotless white coveralls. His debut came in a 25-miler at Red Oak, Iowa, over a half-mile horse track. He didn't win (the Firestone-Columbus's right rear wheel collapsed), but in his next outing at the 2-day Aksarben (Nebraska spelled backwards) Week in Omaha he changed all that. In 10 races, of varying lengths, Rickenbacker won 9—5 the 1st day, 4 the next —and he received 1st-place money for the 10th from 2 of the other competitors who had a bet on which of them could win (with Eddie not involved).

He kept winning until a call came from the factory in Columbus from Lee Frayer. Barney Oldfield was scheduled to race in a 100-miler at the local track, and Frayer had a car—the Red Wing Special—ready to do battle with Oldfield. The race strategy was simple: Rick would set the pace in his lighter car, Oldfield would push his Knox to lead him, wearing out his car, and Frayer's Red Wing would end up the winner. That was exactly the way it went.

Rickenbacker's next big race was an historic one, the debut Indianapolis 500 in 1911, in which Eddie and Frayer codrove the Red Wing. They finished 11th, the race being won by Ray Harroun (and his new rearview mirror). The following year, with Frayer retired, Rick had the Red Wing to himself, but a burned crankshaft bearing knocked him out of the race while he was running 4th. That summer Rick quit Columbus and went to work for Fred Duesenberg at the Mason Automobile Company in Des Moines. The company was on the verge of bankruptcy the following year when the 7-man, 3-car team showed up at Sioux City. Rick's teammates were Tom Alley and Ralph Mulford. T. C. Cox, a rival driver, feinted at a turn to let Rick pass, then veered back in front of him. Eddie tried to avoid him and broadsided his car in doing so, but his left front tire hit Cox's left rear. Both Cox and his riding mechanic were killed. Rick pressed on, duelling with Spencer Wishart, who

504

was driving the fastest car in the race. Wishart and Rickenbacker exchanged the lead several times, their tires chucking the surface of the track and throwing bits of it at the man who happened to be trailing. One of these chunks knocked out Rickenbacker's riding mechanic, Eddie O'Donnell, with about 5 laps to go, and Rick had to reach across and operate the oil pump on the straightaways while Eddie lay stunned in his seat. Driving with one hand, Rick managed to edge Wishart by 40 seconds. Tom Alley was 3rd.

For two years, Rickenbacher drove Duesenberg's creations, then switched to the French Peugeot in time for the Corona, Calif., road race. Both here and at Point Loma, the driver and mechanic wore face masks and were connected one to another by speaking tubes; they looked like forerunners of the astronauts or of *Buck Rogers in the 25th Century*. The masks didn't help, and Rick sold the car after its engine quit in both races. Harry Miller bought it and made the Peugeot a winner.

Eddie bounced over to Maxwell to join Oldfield and Billy Carlson. He had many famous races, perhaps the most well-known being on a paved one-mile oval at Providence, R.I., in which Rick and Bill Burman battled it out for most of the race, with Eddie taking the checker after pulling ahead, for the final time, on the 98th lap. His pre-race strategy of switching to heavy tires instead of the expected light ones paid off; Burman had to pit twice to change his light tires, while Rickenbacker made it through the 100 miles on his original shoes. The victory was worth $10,000 to Rick, who now was being publicized by wiley promoters and newspaper writers as Baron von Rickenbacher a Prussian heir; the Dutch Demon; the Big Teuton; and the like.

With his winnings, Rickenbacker approached Carl Fisher and Jim Allison with a plan to operate his own racing ream of four Maxwells. The combine was formed, and 2-car teams were raced at every major event in the United States. Rick, O'Donnell (promoted to driver) and Pete Henderson shared the cockpits; while one pair was being raced, the other pair was prepared and sent to the next race site. Streamlined and heavily reworked, the cars were dubbed Maxwell Specials. Rick had advanced ideas on team management, and they turned out to be a real advantage in those early rough-and-tumble days. Constant practice made his pit crew the best in the business. At Tacoma, Wash., for example, Eddie and Ralph DePalma battled for 300 miles, with Ralph's Mercedes the expected winner because it so outclassed the Maxwell, but at the 225-mile mark Rick picked up almost 30 seconds when he had 4 tires changed in 33 seconds, where Ralph's crew took 62 seconds to switch just one. One of DePalma's unchanged tires blew a lap later and it took another 90 seconds to switch it. Rick won another $10,000 by 30 seconds. All told, in 1916, its last full season, Rick's Maxwell Special team won 7 of the 13 major races it entered.

In the fall Rickenbacker agreed to race a Sunbeam for 1917, after talking over a lucrative proposition with Louis Coatalen. Before sailing for Britain, however, he joined a team of Duesenbergs for the Vanderbilt Cup races, scheduled for California that year. It was before this race, while driving near Riverside, that Rick got his initial airplane ride from a young man by the name of Glenn Curtiss. He didn't win the Vanderbilt, but he won at Ascot Park in Los Angeles. It turned out to be his last auto race, however, his trip to Britain being an abortive one. Rickenbacker was suspected of being a German spy. Soon after his return to the States the war began. Rick was determined to be in it, and to fly if possible. At first, he drove a staff car, not for Black Jack Pershing, as many would have it, but rather for Billy Mitchell, the head of Pershing's military aviation section. At 27 he was transferred to flight school, and after 25 hours he received his wings and a commission. In March 1918 he joined the 94th Aero Pursuit Squadron, and in 7 months became the Ace of Aces, shooting down 26 German planes in 134 air battles.

Rickenbacker formed the Rickenbacker Motor Company in 1921, and cars bearing his name (he acted as sales vice-president of the company) appeared at the New York Automobile Show in 1922. The venture lasted 5 years. The Rickenbacker cars were good machines, but a recession and better-financed competition were too much for the undercapitalized company. In 1927 it went into bankruptcy. After raising $250,000 to pay off his personal debts connected with the company, Rick raised an additional $700,000 and bought the Indianapolis Speedway. He assumed control November 1, 1927, and set about making it a modern track, resurfacing the bricks that gave the Brickyard its name, adding a golf course, and making other improvements.

He joined General Motors the following year, and when GM had to sell Eastern Airlines, Rick managed to come up with the $3.5 million necessary to buy it. His World War II crash and experiences on a raft for 22 days took place in October 1942. He charged back into action after a rest, his services including a mission to Russia. On the race track or in life, Captain Eddie had to be a winner, and he always was. He died in July 1973, at the age of 82, while visiting Switzerland.

JOCHEN RINDT

The time was October 1969; the place was the sweeping Watkins Glen circuit, near Lake Seneca in the Finger Lakes of New York State. The event was the United States Grand Prix. The car was a Ford-powered Team Lotus Formula 1 from Britain. The driver was a German-born self-styled Austrian, with a broken nose that gave him an unusual appearance. Karl Jochen Rindt, then 27, had been driving GP cars for better than 5 years without tasting victory in a championship race. He was fast—for the 6th time in 1969 he was taking the starting

flag from the pole position—but, so far, unlucky. In September Rindt had come his closest to winning, finishing just 8/100ths of a second behind Scotland's Jackie Stewart, who already had clinched the World Championship.

But at this race things were to be different. Jochen led from the flag until lap 12, when Stewart passed him briefly and then yielded once again to Rindt's Lotus. From then on, he never faltered. Stewart dropped out with mechanical problems, Graham Hill crashed, Jacky Ickx spun and washed out his car, Denis Hulme's gearbox gave way, Mario Andretti was struck from behind, all in futile pursuit of the charging Rindt, who took the checker at 126.36 m.p.h. The moment was sweet, but there were to be even sweeter moments ahead, for in 1970, in the space of 83 days, Jo Rindt was to win 5 more Grands Prix, amass 45 championship points, and clinch—as it would turn out by season's end—the World Championship.

Rindt would not know that he had won his championship, however, for within less than a year of that 1st Watkins Glen victory, Rindt would be dead. When the 1970 United States GP rolled around, the race at which the drivers with a chance to overcome, or tie, his 45-point total would fail, he would be 2 months gone.

Rindt was born in Mainz-am-Rhein, Germany, on April 18, 1942. When both his parents were killed in an allied air raid on Hamburg 15 months later, Jo's maternal grandparents took him to live in Graz, Austria, and he grew up there and in Vienna. It was in Graz, in fact, that his automobile career got started. He learned to drive a Volkswagen although still under legal age.

His Austrian school days were interrupted in 1959 for an extended visit to Chichester, England, where Rindt took up the study of English in his usual dedicated way, explaining his later proficiency with the language in both its British and American idioms.

While in England he attended his initial auto race, a Goodwood club meet, and while it was not love at 1st sight, he did start to become fascinated with the sport. What he did fall in love with was the Jaguar, and later he was to drive Jaguar road cars with great satisfaction. Back in Austria, he started working on his grandparents for a car, and soon his grandfather, a lawyer, agreed to the purchase of a Simca to perfect his driving skills enough to gain a license. This gave way to still another Simca that he used for hillclimbs and a few local races. Seeing Innes Ireland, in a Lotus, win the 1.5-litre Formula 1 race at Zeltweg (beating out Jack Brabham in a Cooper and Jo Bonnier in a Porsche), cemented Rindt's desire to be a professional race driver.

Now he needed a better mount, and this turned out to be a fully modified Alfa Romeo Gulietta TI 1300 that Jo purchased in Graz, had race-prepared at the factory, and brought back to Austria, where the local Alfa distributor agreed to keep the car in that condition, if Rindt did well. To keep up his end of the bargaing Jo won his 1st serious race at the Aspern airfield near Vienna, then set off on a season that netted him 8 victories, including the Gaisbergrennen, Timmelsjoch, and Trieste-Oricine events.

In 1963, Rindt sold the Alfa and purchased a year-old Cooper-Ford, in order to go racing in Formula Junior. He teamed with the man who sold him the car, Kurt Bardi-Barry, who was considered an upcoming young driver in those days. Jo had also attracted some early notice. In his first FJ race at Vallelunga, Rindt captured the pole position with the day's fastest time in practice, but his starter jammed at the flag. In his next race, at Cesenatico, though, he won. At Monaco he was 4th in his heat, behind 3 superbly prepared factory cars, and then was running a strong 5th when his engine failed. Rindt's off-course life also was attracting attention, for wherever he went he dressed in red shirts and pink trousers.

Formula 2 was the next mountain to be scaled on Rindt's charge to the top. In characteristic fashion, he did well with a lucky break. It was not lucky for Bardi-Barry, who was killed in a road accident, but the deceased's new sponsor, Ford of Austria, was all primed for a racing season; upon Bardi-Barry's death, the sponsorship was offered to Rindt. Jo grabbed the chance with both hands, and had the Brabham's Ford engine fine-tuned by Cosworth Engineering of Britain, then debuted at the Nurburgring against the world's best. He finished 4th in a F2 car, behind World Champion Jim Clark, Dick Attwood, and Mike Spence, all veterans of single-seater racing.

But it was in Britain that Rindt came to world racing attention. There were two F2 races during a long weekend, the opener at Mallory Park and the 2nd at the Crystal Palace. At Mallory, Rindt's dark blue Brabham found itself in a familiar position—on the pole—but stalled. Rindt had to charge into the field from last, and he was the rawest rookie that day as well. He managed a 3rd, however, behind Clark and Peter Arundell. Then came the Crystal Palace race that set Britain on its ear. In a thrilling duel, he beat World Champion Graham Hill. The victory so shook up the British motoring press, Jo later liked to reminisce, that he was reported as a new Australian driving prospect. "They just couldn't conceive of any young driver coming from anywhere else in those days," he used to say with a laugh.

Offers poured in. From Rob Walker, he received his first F1 drive, in the Austrian GP of 1964. He dropped out however, with what was called "deranged steering." Ferrari stepped forward with a test drive at Le Mans, and Rindt did well enough to be offered a factory contract to drive prototypes in 1965. An existing contract with a fuel competitive to Ferrari's prevented him from signing, and that was just as well, because the single-seater career that Rindt wanted was just ahead. John Cooper appeared and asked Jo to drive a single race, the South African GP at East London, January 1, 1967. Although he again retired early, this time with Cooper's recurrent engine trouble, Rindt was offered a Cooper F1 contract for the rest of the year as a partner to Brabham.

In 3 years he had won just 10 races—8 of those in the Alfa—yet he found himself a factory F1 driver. "It's not just yourself that makes or breaks a career," Rindt said later. "It's a lot of lucky circumstances. I like to motor race. I go as quickly as I can and see what happens. Of course, you must take care of the car—change gears sensibly, watch the instruments, don't overrev—but more than that you just can't worry about. Again it is a matter of luck. If the car breaks, it breaks, and becomes a mechanic's job. Otherwise it's 'press on, regardless.'"

In 1965 F1 racing, Rindt's Climax-powered Cooper was clearly outclassed. For all of his talent and daring, he was 11th in the Belgian-European GP, 14th in the British GP, and 4th in the German GP. At Monza he was 8th, and at Watkins Glen he placed 6th. In 1966, with an improved Cooper-Maserati mount (still overly heavy and underpowered), he placed his cars consistently and ended up 3rd in the final standings for the World Championship, with 22 points. His best performances were undoubtedly 2nds in the rain-soaked Belgian GP to John Surtees (despite a 180 m.p.h. spin while holding the lead at one point) and to Clark in the United States GP. He was also 3rd in the German GP, 4th in the French and Italian races, and 5th in the British GP.

If Rindt's expectations were whetted by the 1966 season, they were not to be fulfilled in F1 racing for a while. Still with Cooper the following season, Jo suffered through frustration after frustration. At South Africa his engine broke down, at Monaco his gearbox failed, and at Holland his suspension gave way. Hope sprang up again when Rindt was 4th at the Belgian GP, but this was followed by engine failure at 3 straight Grands Prix, and an electrical breakdown in the Canadian GP. Another ray of hope, then, when another 4th was registered at the Italian GP, but a broken camshaft ended Rindt's bid at the United States race, and Cooper passed up Mexico. The year's effort yielded but 6 points and a 12th place in the championship standings.

A change of mount seemed the best solution. Jack Brabham offered one with his new marque and Jo signed as Black Jack's number 2 driver. The Repco-Brabham seemed to offer great possibilities, especially when Jo was able to rack up a 3rd in the season opener in South Africa. But it took another 7 Grands Prix before Rindt could complete another race. In Spain his car lost oil pressure; at Monaco he crashed, unhurt; in Belgium his Brabham dropped a valve; while in Holland a damp ignition knocked him out of the race. It was a leaking fuel tank that ended Rindt's French GP, and a fire while running which cost him the British GP. In the German GP, however, Jo captured the pole position and finished 3rd. Engine failures occurred at the Italian and Canadian races, and Jo blew the engine at Watkins Glen. An ignition failure ended the season on the same discouarging note. With 9 points, he was again a 12th in the driver standings.

Cooper had allowed Rindt to race F2 whenever no conflict existed, beginning in 1965, and giving Jo an outlet away from the Grand Prix trail. Driving a Roy Winkelmann-entered car, for example, he won the 192-mile Rheims GP just 2 weeks after sharing a NART Ferrari 275LM with Masten Gregory, to win at Le Mans in the 24-hour endurance race. At one point in the Rheims race, Jo spun off, and was running 11th by the time he regained the course. In 9 laps he regained a chance at the lead, and then for 100 miles he battled Clark, Australia's Frank Gardner, and Alan Rees—F2 veterans all—for the lead that he captured in one of racing's classic close finishes. Just 2 seconds separated the 4 top cars after the nearly 200 miles of dicing. The following season, 1966, featured F2 victories like those at Brands Hatch and the Eifelrennen, despite that season's domination of the class by Honda.

In 1967 Rindt dominated F2 racing, starting with the season opener at Snetterton in which the new 1600 c.c. class debuted in an International Trophy race. For the entire race, he and Graham Hill swapped the lead, the mustachioed Englishman seeming to take it for good on the final lap until Rindt outbraked him in the final turn, squeeking by for the victory in his Repco-Brabham-Cosworth BT23. Victories followed at Silverstone and Pau, at Barcelona he was 2nd to Jim Clark, and then he won the Eifelrennen, Rheims, Rouen-les-Essarts, and Tulln-Langenlebarn. Clark managed a victory again in the Swedish GP, but Rindt won at Brands Hatch to spoil the Scotsman's bid for a long string. Jim then won the Finnish and Albi Grands Prix.

Rindt's domination continued in 1968 with victories in the Thruxton Trophy race, the Linbourg GP, Crystal

Palace, the Rhine Cup, Tulln, and the Mediterranean GP. Occasionally, there was a 2nd, like the one at the Madrid GP, when Jean-Pierre Beltoise managed to sneak past Jo.

To know that he could win in F2, but not F1 was particularly galling to a man with Rindt's temperament. He liked Brabham, but he needed a truly competitive car, so when Colin Chapman offered a place on the Gold Leaf Team Lotus in 1969, once again Rindt leaped at the opportunity to prove his F1 prowess. With the Lotus 49 and its Cosworth-Ford power, Jo quickly demonstrated that he was as much at home in the biggest class of all as he was in F2. That season he captured the pole position 5 times in Championship Grands Prix, and only missed the front row twice.

Jackie Stewart was not to be denied in 1969, and he won 6 Grands Prix. Jo Rindt was not to be denied either, even after fuel pump failure at South Africa. In the Spanish GP he captured his 1st pole start, set a lap record, but crashed when the Lotus airfoil gave way at 150 m.p.h. Rindt missed Monaco; a broken universal joint in Holland gave Jo more rest time than he wanted, and in the French GP he became ill during the race and dropped out. In the British GP Rindt's Lotus was 4th and in the German race he again started from the pole, but his car suffered ignition failure. In the fast Italian GP, however, he again started from the pole and pressed Stewart enough to finish 2nd by a mere 8 seconds. In the Canadian race, he again captured the pole, and finished 3rd. Then came his win at Watkins Glen, and a broken suspension ended Jo's season at Mexico.

In nontitle F1 racing Rindt was 2nd to Jack Brabham in the Silverstone Trophy, and to Jacky Ickx in the Oulton Park International. In the post-season Tasman series in Australia and New Zealand, Jo won the Lady Wigram Trophy at Christchurch and the Warwick Farms International. He was 2nd to Tasman terror Chris Amon in the New Zealand GP and the Sandown Park International. The 7-race standings saw Amon top Rindt. In F2 racing, Jo won at Thruxton, Tulln, Pau and Limbourg, setting the fastest lap time at the first 3. At Albi he set the fastest lap, too, but finished 3rd.

The year 1970 started in the usual Rindt fashion. At South Africa, his engine failed, and in Spain his ignition. At Monaco, the other side of the coin appeared. Jackie Stewart, as everyone expected, led at the start, but dropped out with electrical trouble. Jack Brabham took over the lead, and held it against all comers until the sideslipping Lotus of Jo Rindt suddenly appeared in his rear-view mirrors. The gap closed to 2 seconds, but still Brabham seemed a cinch to win, the narrow streets of Monte Carlo working for a leader who would not yield to a pursurer. At the final hairpin, just before the finish line, Brabham missed his braking point and bumped a barrier. Rindt roared past before Jack could recover, and took his 2nd championship victory, his 1st in Europe.

In the Belgian GP the Lotus's engine failed, but at Holland the new Lotus 72 was sorted out at last, and Rindt won handily, leading from the 3rd lap without real opposition. In fact, he lapped the field, save Stewart. However, Rindt found the sweetness of the victory soured by the death of his closest friend in F1 racing, Piers Courage. In the next race, the French GP, Jacky Ickx's Ferrari grabbed the early lead, but as the Belgian faltered, Rindt passed to win his 2nd GP of 1970. The British GP made it 3 in a row, Ickx again taking the early lead but dropping out, with Rindt taking over. The script had some scary changes, however. Brabham charged up and dogged Rindt until the youngster made a mistake in shifting. The old pro ripped ahead, probably smiling at the poetic justice of it all, and took the lead. He extended that lead at an astonishing rate until, entering the last lap, he led Rindt by 13 seconds. When the winning car returned to cross the line, however, it was Rindt scorching by, followed by a slow Brabham, whose car was all but out of gas.

Seemingly Rindt had his victory, but 1st he had to endure—with astonishingly good grace—a protest, investigation, and meeting regarding his airfoil, which some claimed was above the maximum height allowed by the FIA. In a short while it was over. The height was legal, and Jo was the winner. The 4th in a row came in the German GP, after an intense duel with Ickx on the Hockenheim circuit, which was substituted for the Nurburgring after driver protests. Both drivers pulled ahead of the pack and diced until Jo darted out in front, with 8 miles to go, and crossed the line 7 tenths of a second ahead of his young Belgian rival. At the Austrian GP Rindt was on the pole, but Clay Regazzoni went ahead at the flag, closely followed by Ickx. Chasing the fast Ferraris proved too much for the Lotus this day, and after almost spinning out on spilled oil, Rindt retired with a blown engine while running 4th.

Next came the Italian GP at Monza, and with it Rindt's death. In practice for the race, his Lotus seemed in fine form, and on the parabolic curve at the speedy track, he was doing 190 m.p.h. when a front wheel collapsed and the car swerved into the fencing atop the curve. The Lotus was torn in half, but did not catch fire. Rindt was alive when they reached the wreckage, but then everything that could be done incorrectly was done just that way. Instead of using the superbly equipped Grand Prix Drivers Association mobile hospital—which was equipped for even a major operation—the decision was made to take Jo to a hospital away from the track. The police escort turned left to lead the ambulance to the Modena hospital, 5 minutes away, but the ambulance itself swerved right and headed toward Milan, 40 minutes or more away.

Rindt had severe chest and throat injuries, broken legs and a broken arm. His heart stopped and hand-operated equipment was used to effect resuscitation, but he died en route to the hospital. Could he have been saved? No one will ever know. That his car failed him was particularly ironic. In the year of his death, Rindt said in an interview: "Yes, I get scared, we all get scared, but I get scared that something will happen with the car. It is the cars that break, not the drivers. I am always frightened of something breaking, but while I am frightened, I do not think it will happen. I know I am driving too good a car."

Tall, blond, and athletically built, Rindt was an international man. He spoke a variety of languages in expert fashion, was as at home in Britain as in Austria. He was married to Nina Lincoln, daughter of a famous Finnish racer, and lived in a Lake Geneva chateau next to Jackie Stewart. Though he had sold the family spice business in 1965 to finance his racing efforts and set up other businesses, at the time of his death Ridnt was financially well-fixed with such enterprises as national racing car shows in 5 nations, an Austrian TV show, and the financial management of the Austrian GP. As a lasting tribute, the Austrian GP course has been named for Jochen Rindt, World Champion, 1970.

FIREBALL ROBERTS

The inaugural NASCAR event was run February 15, 1948, on the sands of Daytona Beach, with only 12 of the 50 starters finishing. Among the 38 non-finishers was an athletic-looking hometown boy in car No. 11; his name was Edward Glenn Roberts, Jr. On the 9th lap he missed a turn and his car was damaged beyond immediate repair. Such was the debut of future greatness.

Fireball Roberts was 17 when he made that brief debut in racing. Born January 20, 1931, in the Daytona Beach area, he earned his nickname because of the speed with which he threw a baseball—but not the accuracy. The 5-foot 11-inch youngster attended the University of Florida, but never graduated; neither did he progress very far in baseball. Motor racing was his forte, and, after intermittent forays into the field, he began to campaign the NASCAR circuit in earnest in 1949.

An ironic fate spared him in 1949 at the old Charlotte, N.C., Speedway. He was driving in a modified race on the dirt track, when a wheel hub ripped loose from Buck Baker's car and plunged through the side window of Fireball's car, landing in the seat next to him. Roberts claimed that he didn't realize it was there until after the race, which he won. But fate was only waiting; at Charlotte in 1964 (on the 1.5-mile paved track) Fireball received the burns that led to his death more than a month later. He had never won a race in his "jinx" city, the only venue at which he was shut out in a 15-year racing career.

Roberts stamped himself a fearless man of versatile talents in those 15 years—talents that led to Le Mans in 1963, where he piloted a private Ferrari (with Bob Grossman) into the top 10; talents that made him one of the best-known of American stock car drivers. As a measure of his greatness, he led an unprecedented 1,644 miles in Grand National racing at Darlington alone, nearly twice that of his nearest competitor at the time of his death. He set more than 400 different records at various tracks.

Roberts won the 1959 Firecracker 250 in a Pontiac. He repeated in 1962, averaging 13 m.p.h. faster, and that made him the only man ever to sweep Daytona International Speedway's 2 major stock-car races in the same year, for he had won the 500 earlier in the year. In 1963, he switched to Ford cars and Goodyear tires, and won the inaugural Firecracker 400.

At Atlantia in 1960 Roberts had won the inaugural Dixie 400 in a Pontiac, and even at Charlotte he was fast qualifier in 3 of the 5 years that he essayed the World 600, and in 2 of the 5 National 400s he tried as well. He also had 2 2nd places to his credit for the 1961 World and the 1962 National. But Darlington was Roberts's favorite major track; he won the Rebel 300 in 1957 and 1959 and the Southern 500 in 1958 and 1963. It was here, in 1963, that he drove one of the most perfect races on record—perfect and perfectly dull. His 129.87 m.p.h. record average was to stand for several years. The race average dropped right back down to 117.7 in 1964, but that alone was not what made the feat so perfect.

Painfully injured a month before this race, Roberts began a regimen that brought him to Darlington in perhaps the best physical condition of his life. He had won the pole the 4 previous years, only to see others in the winner's circle; his race plan called for him to start in the pack, maybe about 9th. That meant qualifying on the 2nd day, after the pole and top spots had been allocated. During practice, however, he hit the guardrail with his Holman-Moody Ford and almost washed out, splitting the motor. However, 3 hours of labor by mechanic Eddie Pagan, a former driver, brought Fireball back just before closing time. With only 2 warmup laps, Roberts blasted out a new qualifying mark of 133.819 m.p.h. He had his 9th starting spot.

The driver of the lavender No. 22 Ford was not through surprising the fans, however. When the green flag waved, he did not charge for the lead. He did not even appear in the top 5 until the 20th lap, when he was placed 4th. Roberts was running the most cautious race of his life, and it was 20 laps later when he moved into 3rd, pitted on the 70th lap to leave the top 5, and reappeared on the Darlington scoreboard on the 80th lap. After 10 laps he moved almost unnoticed into 4th place where he was content to stay for 90 laps, when he quietly slipped into 3rd. A pit stop dropped Fireball to 5th but he obviously wanted to stay 3rd, for it took him only 17 miles to reclaim the spot. He moved into 2nd behind Marvin Panch on the 260th lap and now began to charge. On lap 289 the lavender Ford led the pack; there were now only 75 laps left in the race.

When Fred Lorenzen came up to challenge, however, Fireball had the stands moaning in disbelief when he waved Fred by on the 312th lap. What Fireball knew and the fans didn't, however, was that Lorenzen could not finish without one more pit stop. It came on the 330th lap, and from there Roberts cakewalked. Fords filled the top 8 spots, and Roberts led them all. It was to be the last time in a big race, but it made up for previous times, when he was all speed and little stamina.

It is the lot of auto racing journalists to remember fragments and bits of conversations of men who take a far greater risk. When the men die or quit, the fragments remain to the writer—like broken pieces of an old mirror. Roberts once said, "If I get hurt bad in a race, I hope I go quick. But most of all, I hope I don't take anyone with me." Thus the fiery crash that burned Roberts so critically that he never recovered fulfilled one of his fears, while sidestepping the other. According to Glenn Roberts, Sr., Fireball spun his lavender No. 22 Ford intentionally after the cars of Ned Jarrett and Junior Johnson hit and spun down the back stretch. Jarrett's Ford had burst into flames, sending up clouds of smoke. Roberts was following Darel Dierenger's Mercury. He told his father that he felt his best chance to remain in the race was to spin off the banks on to the lower apron. He hit a retaining wall, flipped 30 feet through the air, and landed upside down, flaming. Jarrett, who leaped from his car, dragged Fireball out and, with assistance, removed his scorched "flame-proof" uniform.

The fact that Roberts had not inhaled the flames saved him for the time, although 70 percent of his body was covered with burns. The question, still unanswered, is whether the uniform had been treated with fireproofing on race day. Some drivers take the chance of going without retreatment when the weather gets muggy, because flameproof coveralls make them sweat more. Fireball suffered from asthma, and on a muggy day he never used the flameproofing because he couldn't breathe. May 24, 1964, was a muggy day.

Fireball died of pneumonia, and a blood infection, between preliminary skin graft operations, 37 days after the accident. He left both parents; a wife, Doris; a daughter, Pamela; and many friends. One observer commented, "No man gave his profession more of himself than Fireball. He ran to win, but in a manner that inspired respect as well as excitement."

FLOYD ROBERTS

The story of some drivers is the story of a particular car. That was the case with Floyd Roberts, an alumnus of the Legion Ascot training grounds in Glendale and a resident of Van Nuys, Calif. The car was the blue and red Burd Piston Ring Special, built by Lou Moore to the 1938 Indianapolis formula which allowed either a 3-litre blown engine or a 4.5-litre unblown engine.

Roberts had been a teammate of Moore's in Burd cars in 1936, when Lou made his last Indianapolis appearance as a driver. That was in the era when Indy was still running on a fuel allotment (37.5 gallons) for the 500 miles of racing. That the Burd crew had underestimated the thirst of their engines was obvious, because Roberts went out on the 183rd lap and Moore on the 185th, both out of gas. Floyd had taken 4th place in the 1935 race, giving the Abel Fink car a very steady ride, and, after 1936, he found millionaire Joel Throne would supply a more competitive car for 1937. Unfortunately the car turned sick on race day and he finished 12th.

The 1938 Burd car was entirely conventional for the time, a rear-wheel drive, unsupercharged Miller 4. However, it was put together so well Floyd stamped himself as the man to beat by winning the pole at 125.681 m.p.h. This made the Gulf NoNox gasoline people very happy; as they pointed out that he was getting all of 260 b.h.p., at about 5750 r.p.m., from the d.o.h.c. 270-cu.in. Miller. Floyd was not fooled by his hot qualification speed. He realized that Thorne had excellent supercharged cars with Ronnie Householder and Jimmie Snyder as drivers, that Rex Mays had a very fast Alfa, and that several other cars were capable of an upset. Above all, Floyd was not a charger. He preferred others to take the lead in the early going and pace himself for a late run.

It happened again. Mays blew him off quickly and held 1st until his supercharger quit on the 45th lap.

Floyd moved up only to fall behind Snyder, who was considered Thorne's best hope. Floyd, in the unsupercharged vehicle, had made one less pit stop, the Burd Piston Ring Special was performing magnificently and it seemed, as they went into the final 200 miles of the race, that Roberts was the strongest. Blower troubles put both Snyder and Householder out and Floyd won easily. The tremendous number of points and the short schedule gave Roberts a chance to sweep to the 1938 AAA championship, which he did.

The next year the Burd car had been refined and Roberts was very confident he could once again challenge for the lead. However, there were 6 cars who qualified at a faster time. Floyd was playing his waiting game as best he could when the accident happened. It was the result of a whole chain of events. Ralph Hepburn had been feeling poorly that day, but knew he had a fast car, and Bob Swanson found out the experimental V-16 Sampson was still experimental when it broke after 19 laps. Shortly after the 200-mile mark, Hepburn handed over to Swanson and the youngster decided to charge. On the 107th lap the car skidded tailfirst. Roberts was trying to make up time by driving all out. When Floyd came upon the car, he gambled on trying to squeeze by the still-spinning Sampson. He didn't make it, riding over Swanson and the wall, to die immediately of a broken neck.

The car then was sold to Cliff Bergere, who almost won with it. Cliff was leading at 400 miles when fumes began to leak into the cockpit, sickening him so badly that he quickly faded to 5th, and then collapsed as the race ended. After World War II, the car was refurbished and got Indy winner George Robson as its pilot. At Atlanta's Lakewood Park in September 1946 Robson was moving in on the lead when he lost control. The car was totally destroyed and Robson was dead.

It is a macabre distinction, but the Burd Pison Ring Special killed 2 Indy winners and seriously impaired the performance of another. No other car can claim that dubious honor.

GEORGE ROBERTSON

The name George Robertson is not familiar, like that of Barney Oldfield or Ralph DePalma, yet in its day it evoked almost as emotional a response among racing followers. It belonged to a large, ruggedly-built man who once spent extra time in the pits roasting his crew for sloppy work, won the Vanderbilt Cup, managed Jimmy Murphy's great Duesenberg victory in the 1921 French Grand Prix, and saw the revival of the Vanderbilt Cup at Roosevelt Raceway as the fulfillment of a dream.

Robertson, born in 1884, never lacked for confidence. None of the early drivers did, not Lancia, Lautenschlager nor Oldfield himself. George's active driving career spanned approximately 4 years, and the difference between him and his contemporaries like David Bruce-Brown was that he lived through his accidents, and they did not. The high-speed automobile of the day was a dangerous mechanism, apt to break suddenly in places where modern race cars are as rugged as Gibraltar. It took courage, daring, and flamboyance to drive well then, and Robertson had them all.

His name initially appeared in hillclimbs and some shorter races about 1904, wtih no great consistency as far as victory is concerned. In September 1905 he was chosen to pilot the front-drive Christie in the Vanderbilt Cup eliminations. He was 20 at the time, and he lasted 60 miles until the tires gave out just before the motor, which had been coughing like a consumptive cigarette smoker, died. The year 1906 found him in the Apperson Jackrabbit 60, and a favorite for the U.S. because he was lapping at speeds far in excess of such established drivers as Joe Tracey, Herb Lytle, and Bert Dingley. George looked like a certainty for the 5-car American team when, during a pre-dawn practice on the 30-mile circuit, the steering broke, throwing Robertson and mechanic Arthur Warren clear, but totaling the car.

For 1907 Robertson joined the new Simplex team at the beginning of the season and was teamed with Al Poole, the codriver with whom he had the most success. The 24-hour race was the fad in America then, and the pair was to pilot a Simplex 50 in a whole series of the endurance races that year. Meanwhile, Robertson kept his hand in on sprints by driving a 130 h.p. Hotchkiss, whenever the French car deigned to run. Morris Park, in the Bronx, New York, was a horse racing track converted to auto racing. It had a surface of ordinary dirt, and the heavy cars rutted it quite easily, making steering at relatively high speeds a chancy matter. That was in fair weather. When it rained, the racing chassis appeared to be rolling through an endless bog until the mud fouled something and they halted.

The Robertson-Poole Simplex was painted red on the left side and green on the right, in the manner of nautical tradition. A tradition, incidentally, which proved very appropriate, because soon after the 20 or so racers began their 24-hour enduro, a storm hit with hurricane fury. The Fiat, Darracq, Rolls-Royce, Italia, De Dietrich, Lozier, Motobloc, Matheson, and the Stearns seemingly left Robertson far behind, for the Simplex pitted early and frequently. The Simplex cause seemed hopeless, but big George refused to give up. Hurtling out of his pits, dressed in the oilskins of a clipper ship captain, Robertson forced the competitors to move over with his mad dashes around the course. Actually, Poole's steadier and longer stints at the wheel cut the Simplex deficit just as much; The pair won their class. Al was a much underrated driver who simply disappeared from the records after 1910—as if one day he just decided his racing career was over—but for 3 years, he and Robertson were always contenders, except they were codrivers.

There were 7 such enduro events in 1907, plus innumerable hillclimbs and sprint meetings, mostly under the aegis of the Automobile Club of America. There was, however, no Vanderbilt Cup. The Robertson-Poole combination finished in the top 10 in all of the enduros, which was no small feat. With 1908, stock chassis road racing began in the United States, and Robertson came into his own. The practice of the time was to solicit the car agencies until one found a dealer willing to prepare a racing version in the hopes that the publicity of winning or finishing would bring customers. After all, there were literally hundreds of makes on the market. Robertson finished out of the money in the Briarcliff, N.Y., races, but he finished—all he had expected to do with a Panhard 50-h.p. touring car, heavier and less powerful than his competitors. He took 4th in a Fiat 60 at Lowell, Mass., then finished 5th in the Brighton 24-hour race in Brooklyn, N.Y., with Frank Lescault co-driving. It was 3 weeks later—on the same track, in another 24-hour race with the same codriver—that he drove the Simplex 50 to a record victory, covering 1,177 miles, or, to put it another way, averaging 49.04 m.p.h., including the necessarily long pit stops. A week later, he piloted a Locomobile 40 to a stock-chassis victory at Fairmount Park in Philadelphia.

Now he was an established hero, for he had beaten the likes of Oldfield, DePalma, Mulford, Bob Burman and Montague Roberts. His streak had made him the pre-race favorite for a revived Vanderbilt Cup, to be run on a new course in Long Island, which included 11 miles of the fabulous Motor Parkway.

The facilities—grandstands, pits, parking—were perhaps the finest in the world at the time. The field contained 19 of the finest machines in the world, including a supercharged Chadwick driven by Willie Haupt, an Isotta driven by Lytle, Louis Chevrolet in a Matheson, a Renault, and a Mercedes 120. Robertson had taken over the 120 Locomobile that had set the record lap in the 1906 Vanderbilt, under Joe Tracey. Big George had the veteran Glenn Etheridge as riding mechanic.

It was a cold rainy morning, and the start of the race was delayed. The Locomobile forces kept their car running during the delay, because of the difficulty in starting the car; they paid by losing water as the car overheated. Robertson told his crew chief he would stop at the end of the 1st lap for water, and agreed upon a color system for the filling cans—red cap for gasoline, white for water. Robertson pulled in for a water stop as scheduled after the first lap. To his amazement, the crew chief brought out the red capped gasoline can and started to unscrew the radiator cap. George stopped him in time and berated him and the entire crew, losing time to do it. That allowed Herb Lytle in the Isotta to come up to challenge him by the middle of the race. Once the two of them came up on a slower car, which would not let them pass because the riding mechanic apparently was stone deaf. Robertson lost his temper, unhooked a tire

tool, and let fly at the offender. The hapless mechanic looked around just in time to see George's throwing arm come down and just in time to warn his driver who swerved out of the way.

George pulled away from Lytle very slowly so that he and his riding mechanic were beginning to breathe easy on the 11th and final lap when the tube in the left front tire blew. The men jumped down and set some kind of record—for the time—in changing the tire, then leaped back into the car and blasted full bore down Jericho Turnpike. The speedy tire change may have been the clincher for the race committee announced that Robertson had won by only one minute 48 seconds.

He had promised to have dinner after the race with a New York restaurant owner so he drove into town. He stepped out of the car into a manhole cover, fell and broke his ankle.

Thus Robertson became the initial American to win an international road classic. It was his greatest victory. At Crown Point, Ind., in June 1909, his Locomobile took a 2nd and a 3rd, which he contended would have been victories if the Chicago manager of Locomobile had not refused to release a shipment of a new type of plug that he intuitively felt would not work, despite mechanics' pleas. Back with Simplex and Al Poole for the July Brighton 24-hour track race, Robertson faced new difficulties from a sales official. He and Poole built up a big lead quickly, and were supposed to sit on it. Imagine George's amazement at the 16-hour mark, when the grandstands erupted in frenzied cheering; Poole was repassing everything on the track, running wide open. George ordered Herman Broesel, son of the company owner who had given the "GO-FAST" signal, out of the pits, despite threats of firing, and slowed Poole down for another Brighton triumph. Simplex and Robertson combined for the stock-chassis victories in the Lowell road race and again at Fairmount Park.

The final year of his competition driving career saw the debut of the banked board tracks, and George tried his hand at them briefly. At the inaugural Playa Del Ray, Calif., program, though suffering a severe ear infection, he won a 10-mile open sprint in the new Simplex 90 special that he called, "Zip." He used the same car to beat DePalma and his Fiat Cyclone in every heat in a series of match races at Brighton. Back in 1908, DePalma had won a 3-cornered match with Robertson and Oldfield (Barney never finished). Big George had signed with Benz for the 1910 Vanderbilt Cup; his teammates were to be Eddie Hearne and Bruce-Brown. After setting fast practice times, Robertson was again among the favorites. He was induced to take a sports reporter around the course at speed. It was a bad decision, for this *particular* journalist was definitely not a Denis Jenkinson.

Frightened at the speed, the man panicked completely and grabbed George's arm. The huge Benz screeched off the Motor Parkway onto secondary roads. Out of control, the car flipped, smashing Robertson's back, ribs, and elbow. "As I got to my feet, about to pass out," George recalled, "I saw my adorable passenger. His derby was not even dented." Robertson stayed in competition as a manager. His most amazing exploit was the way he managed to overcome all the roadblocks against foreign entries set by the organizers of the French Grand Prix in 1921. He managed to give Jimmy Murphy and Duesenberg America's sole victory in this classic until modern times. He organized and helped raise the money for the magnificent Roosevelt Raceway, which he managed in 1936. It was the realization of his dream of reviving the Vanderbilt Cup as an international competition, a dream perhaps a generation too early. Robertson died on July 3, 1955, interested in the sport to the very end.

GEORGE ROBSON

The lead driver for the racing team of millionaire Joel Thorne at the 1946 Indianapolis Speedway Classic was supposed to have been Rudi Caracciola, the great German driver who had lived out the years of Nazi domination in Switzerland. Thorne had signed Caracciola when it became apparent that the German's own Mercedes would not make the country in time. Through friends, Rudi had smuggled the car out of Nazi Germany; the Nazis wouldn't let him get one out through normal channels.

Rudi had tested this 91-cu.in. Mercedes near Zurich,

and there is every reason to believe that if it had competed, the 1946 Indianapolis 500 might have turned out differently. However, Caracciola didn't even make the race. He crashed the Thorne Engineering Special, which had an unsupercharged 272-cu.in. 6 cylinder engine, with a 50-gallon gas tank. That left the Thorne hopes squarely on the shoulders of a 37-year-old who had been born in 1909 at Newcastle-on-Tyne, England, and had emigrated to the U.S. from Canada in 1924, where he had arrived in 1917. This was a man who neither smoked nor drank hard liquor, a quiet little man, about 5-feet 6-inches in height, and weighing 145 pounds. George Robson was not the only Robson in that 1946 Indy. His brother Hal, a year younger, had also qualified in the Phillips-Miller Special, an old unsupercharged 8-cylinder car.

George had begun racing in 1930 at a place called Chowchilla, Calif., competing at outlaw meets at Riverside, Santa Maria, and all the old dust bowls of the Depression days. He and his brother had progressed to the paved tracks on the West Coast just before America's entry into World War II, and were winning fairly regularly.

His Indianapolis record before 1946 included no great heroics. In 1940 the 255-cu.in. Offy he was driving lasted 67 laps before retiring with a broken shock. In 1941 his 183 Offy sustained a broken block in the 66th lap. In 1939 he had been unable to qualify the Alfa Romeo entered by Deacon Litz, an old race driver. During the war, the Robson Brothers had operated a tool and die shop in the Los Angeles area, selling the shop and leaving for Indy about 3 weeks prior to the 1946 race. Robson qualified the Thorne Special in 15th spot.

He let the field come back to him and it did, with startling alacrity. Pole-sitter Sam Hanks, Rex Mays, Paul Russo, Shorty Cantlon, Hal Cole, Mauri Rose, George Connor, and brother Hal—whose car exploded on the straight—were out before the race was one fifth through. Then Duke Nalon, Tony Bettenhausen, and Danny Kladis joined them, before George Robson took the lead from Cliff Bergere.

Favored Ralph Hepburn, in the Novi, was the fastest car still on the track, but he had already spent 6 minutes in the pits correcting a leaking brake line. Robson held the lead only 7 laps, then Jimmy Jackson passed him on the 87th lap. George repassed on the 93rd, but 7 laps later had only about 2 car lengths over Jackson, with Hepburn methodically picking off the men in front of him. Ralph was averaging 124 m.p.h., 9 m.p.h. more than the leaders, and it was obvious that at that pace he could make up his huge deficit.

On the 111th lap Jackson pitted for tires and fuel, and was 2 laps behind when he came back on the track. The matter seemed academic, for the 50-year-old Hepburn was closing on the top 2 so fast that the race seemed to be his. But the temperamental Novi stalled in its 121st lap, eliminating Ralph. When George came in for his only pit stop on the 141st lap, there were but 13 cars left in the race. He took on fuel and a right rear tire, and returned to the track still leading.

During most of the last part of the race, Robson's only competition was Jackson, who was less than a minute behind. The Indianapolis sports hero made repeated attempts to close with George, getting as close as 34 seconds at the finish. Only 9 cars were still running, the 9th-place man, Bill Sheffler, about 72 laps back. Sheffler had refused to quit after losing oil pressure early in the race, and had circled the big track at about 90 m.p.h. for the rest of the way. Billy Devore, who actually went farther, was awarded 10th after a deliberate spin on the 167th lap when his throttle stuck.

Robson gave credit to his mechanical crew, which included Eddie Offut (later a car owner) and Chick Hirashima (later an important man in the Ford testing program). He never raced at Indy again. On September 1 at Lakewood Park in Atlanta, near the close of a 100-mile race, Robson and George Barringer, another veteran driver, were injured fatally in a crash.

PEDRO RODRIGUEZ

The 1970 Belgian Grand Prix, temporarily back on the schedule after a year's suspension because of safety problems at the fast Spa course, attracted a reduced Formula 1 field for a number of reasons, but the big stars were there—Jackie Stewart, Jochen Rindt, Jack Brabham, Jacky Ickx, Graham Hill. So was a Mexican driver in the No. 1 Yardley BRM, Pedro Rodriguez, who hadn't won a GP since 1967, driving for a marque that hadn't won since 1966. You could have gotten good odds against his winning, but he did. On a course always noted for separating drivers very nicely into convenient categories—drivers who survived the rigors of the twisty circuit, that is—Pedro set a blistering pace and led most of the race to record his 2nd championship victory and BRM's 1st since Stewart turned that trick for them at Monaco in 1966.

And Rodriguez did it against genuine opposition, despite the slow attrition among the big names due to mechanical difficulties. Chris Amon, not a big name but one of the world's fastest drivers, drove one of the best races of his life only to see his elusive first F1 championship victory slip away once more, this time by a mere 1.6 seconds. Through much of the battle, Amon's March-Ford nipped at Pedro's heels, matching the speedy Rodriguez's lap times. He even set the race's fastest lap, but by that time Rodriguez, who also had been denied by his mount often, would not allow himself to be denied again. Pedro's 149.93 m.p.h. winning average erased Bruce McLaren's old record by more than 2 m.p.h., and only Amon's 3:27.4 (152.07 m.p.h.) lap eclipsed Pedro's fastest, 3:27.9. Both men knew how to go fast, it was evident, but the dice had rolled the Rodridguez way for once.

It was fashionable once to say that Pedro was "less talented" than his kid brother, Ricardo. It was a fiction then, and it later assumed the status of fable. The reason is apparent. Pedro was older (by 2 years), more stoic, and seemingly more inhibited than his colorful younger brother. Don Pedro Rodriguez, father of the Mexican pair, obviously favored his youngest, though Pedro *pere et fils* would deny it. Yet most of Ricardo's important victories were shared with other drivers, and many times the man who shared them was Pedro, who set the pattern that Ricardo chose to follow, perhaps a little too feverishly.

Pedro was born January 18, 1940, in Mexico City. He had an older sister, Conchita, and an even younger brother, Alejandro, born in 1955. He started on motorcycles at 11, won his 1st race the next year, won the Mexican national championship at 14, then retired from the 2-wheeled field, switching to cars, including XK Jaguars and Corvettes, for Mexican races. While Ricardo was blasting around full-time building his early reputation, Pedro was attending an American military school, so his own racing career was suffering a temporary setback at the same time his brother was coming on. From 1957 through 1961, though, they were racing pretty much equally on Don Pedro's money, of which there was an abundance.

Starting in 1962, their rides at places like Le Mans, Sebring and other venues were under the aegis of Luigi Chinetti's NART (North American Racing Team), and it was to the two brothers that Ferrari's offer of a Formula 1 team berth was made in 1962. Pedro was involved in business at the time, and he turned it down, but Ricardo accepted, with tragic results. Pedro started Grand Prix driving at the U.S. race in 1963 in a spare Lotus, and he continued that arragement for several seasons there and in the Mexican GP. He was 5th in the 1965 American race, and 6th, 7th, and 9th in the 1964, 1965, and 1966 Mexican battles.

In the 1967 F1 opener, the South African GP, John Cooper offered Pedro a "trial" drive in a Cooper-Maserati, and he drove the race of his life to score the initial championship victory ever recorded for Mexico in a *grande épreuve*. Luckily the South African band had a copy of Pedro's national anthem to which they could refer at this unexpected moment. And he led the F1 point parade until the next race, of course, the only time Mexico has ever had that distinction as well. Cooper immediately offered him a regular team berth, and he signed and moved to Europe to make a full season of it. The Cooper was not a competitive car, however. He was 5th at Monaco, retired in Holland, 9th in Belgium, 6th in France, 5th in Britain. In the German GP he was 8th. Then a sports car crash broke his foot, and doctors told him it would take a year to heal. But by October, with guts and special exercises, he was in the cockpit again for his national GP, in which he finished 6th even though it was agony to manipulate the pedals. In all, his efforts earned Rodriguez 15 points, tying him with Graham Hill for 6th in the final World Championship standings.

BRM wanted Rodriguez in 1968, and after a tussle, he signed with them instead of Cooper. It took Pedro several races in the Tasman series to sort out his car, but by the time the team returned home, he was ready to race the BRM. At Brands Hatch in a nontitle race he finished 2nd to Bruce McLaren, surging through the field after a poor start. An ignition failure had knocked him out of the South African GP, and accidents cost him the Spanish and Monaco Grands Prix, but he was 2nd in the Belgian race and 3rd in the Dutch. He set the fastest lap time in the French GP, but finished 12th. Timing chain failures in the British and Italian races were wrapped around a 6th in the German race, and a 3rd in Canada and 4th in Mexico encased a suspension failure in the United States GP. Pedro's 18 points were enough for another 6th-place finish in the final standings.

In 1969 Pedro slipped to a 3-way tie for 13th in the standings, driving both privately entered BRM's and factory Ferraris. He was retired from 5 races (South Africa, Spain, and Monaco right at the season's beginning, Britain and Canada later) and could manage only 5th, 6th, and 7th placings at the U.S., Italian, and Mexican Grands Prix. Fortunately, however, he had always done well in long-distance, sports/racing and endurance races of all kinds, and Rodriguez blossomed as a star in these areas.

Take the start of 1970 as a sample of Pedro's skills in this area. His mount was a sexy-looking Porsche 917, running in the light blue colors of the Gulf-Wyer Team. At Daytona, teamed with Finland's Leo Kinnunen for the 1st time, Rodriguez won the 24-hour race at a new record speed of 114.866 m.p.h. Pedro drove for 16 of the 24 hours. It was his 3rd victory at Daytona. Two months later, despite troubles of all kinds, the combination—joined late by Jo Siffert—finished 4th at Sebring. In April at Brands Hatch in the BOAC 1000, the pair won a wet race, and at Monza later in the month they won again with a sizzling 144.4 clocking for the better than 4-hour battle. In May they were 2nd in the Targa Florio. In July the Rodriguez-Kinnunen combination captured the Watkins Glen 6-hour race. Pedro didn't win the Spa 1000, but set an outright lap record of 160.3 m.p.h.

Yardley-BRM provided Rodriguez's F1 mounts again in 1971, and JW Automotive his enduro cars, but now Pedro was teamed with his GP teammate from BRM, Jack Oliver of England. Operating from his Paris and Bray apartments, Pedro looked as if he had many years of fast racing left. No question about his talents any more.

Those talents were directed toward both the GP series and the John Wyer Porsche effort in the last year of the 5-litre World Manufacturers Championship. In F1 Pedro retired in South Africa, was 10th in the nontitle Questor GP, but won the nontitle Oulton Park race. He was 4th in Spain and in the nontitle Silverstone Trophy race. At Monaco he was 9th, in Holland he came close to another F1 victory, trailing Ickx by just 8/100ths of a second despite a bad engine. In France he retired after 28 laps of battling the ultimate winner, Stewart, on even terms.

Meanwhile, things were much better in sports cars. Second at Buenos Aires with Oliver, the pair won Daytona's 24-hour race at 109.203 m.p.h. At Sebring they were 4th, at the BOAC 1000 they retired. But victory came their way again at the Monza 1000 where Pedro's 154.017 m.p.h. lap was fastest of the day. Their winning average was 147.396 m.p.h. Another victory followed at the Spa 1000, and a 2nd at Nurburgring. Retired in the Le Mans 24-hour race, Pedro teamed up with Dickie Attwood in the Austrian 1000. Again he was fastest of the day and again he shared a winning Porsche 917.

July 11, 1971, found Pedro in a Herbert Muller Ferrari 512M. Porsche was about to leave the big series in 1972, and Rodriguez was looking around. The course was Norisring in Germany, a relatively unknown venue. The race was a meaningless (for Pedro) Interserie contest for European Group 7 machines. He qualified 2nd fastest, he led most of the first 12 laps, and then tragedy struck. What happened is still controversial in many quarters. He may have made a mistake and braked too late. He many have had tire trouble. He may have found his way barred by a slower Porsche. Whatever the cause, the result was that his Ferrari hit the Armco barrier tail-first, shot across the course into a wall, then bounced back to the other side and caught fire. It was a long while before they managed to get Pedro out. He was badly burned and had a fractured skull. He was alive when he reached the hospital, but died soon after. Mexico and the Rodriguez family had lost a hero son.

RICARDO RODRIGUEZ

The younger of the two racing Rodriguez brothers of Mexico, Ricardo Valentine Rodriguez de la Vega was born on February 14, 1942. He died, in a 125-m.p.h. crash while practicing for the Grand Prix of Mexico, on November 1, 1962. Between those date he created— or had created for him—a life that few men achieve in lives three or four times as long. He was Mexico's national bicycle champion at age 10. He was the nation's motorcycle champion at 13. He was the automobile racing champion of his country at 15. At 19 he was signed as a full-time driver by a European Formula 1 team. At 20, just before his death, he was declared Mexico's Athlete of the Year, starred in his own motion picture, and was acknowledged by all as one of the 10 or 12 top drivers in the world.

Don Pedro Rodriguez, father of the racing brothers, was a motorcycle champion himself, and by the time he was 22 he had led a team of crack motorcyclists who toured North and South America. Later he became head of Mexico City's motorcycle patrol, and grew to be a sort of secret service chief for Mexican presidents—even learning to drive a locomotive so that he could run presidential trains himself, as a security measure. By being associated with these powerful political figures, Don Pedro's own power, influence and knowledge grew. He wisely purchased real estate upon the recommendations of his friends, and these little parcels turned out to be, like the American joke, in downtown Mexico City and Acapulco, as well as other strategic points. Don Pedro soon was a millionaire. This money went to making his sons happy.

Ricardo spent the early years of his youth chasing Pedro, 2 years older than he, on bicycles, on motorcycles, and, finally, in cars. It started with Ricardo rebuilding an old Fiat Topolino in the family garage and winning some local races, about the same time that Pedro was competing in Jags and Corvettes. His father offered him a better car, and Ricardo chose a bright red 1500-c.c. OSCA. On April 7, 1957, a 15-year-old driver took part (illegally, but with official eyes descreetly closed) in his 1st sports car race, on the twisting Avandaro road circuit. He finished 3rd, behind a powerful Ferrari and a D Jaguar in the hands of highly skilled veteran drivers. The OSCA was traded in, a Porsche

acquired, and a few weeks later on the Puebla airport course Ricardo finished 2nd to Ken Miles, then acknowledged to be one of the best Porsche drivers in the world. In his 3rd try, Ricardo won at Torreon in September, and caused a near riot of adulation by the Mexican fans who almost suffocated the slim (5-feet 5-inches) youth as they carried him to the judges' stand for his prizes.

At the Nassau Speed Week that December, the seemingly inevitable schedule that the Rodriguez brothers had set for themselves went temporarily off the track. Between them, the pair failed to win a single race, despite their high hopes. Ed Crawford, an American Porsche driver, beat Ricardo in 2 different races, and in another, Stirling Moss, Richie Ginther, and John Fitch preceded him across the line. In the major race of the series Ricardo was 8th (although 1st in class when leader Crawford dropped out with a broken axle). Pedro, in that same series, banged up his Ferrari so badly in the opener that he was out of the entire series (understandable, perhaps, since he had been away from competition for almost 2 years while attending an American military school.)

But Ricardo learned from all of this, and his Mexican season saw victory follow victory, even over visitors like Miles who came back expressing amazement at how improved he had become in a short year. Ricardo won the national driving crown easily. At the Nassau races that season, Pedro scored a 2nd in one race and Ricardo won the all-Porsche event. In the 12-hour race at Sebring in the spring of 1959, Ricardo found himself sharing an OSCA with Bruce Kessler, but a crash ended that car. He promptly switched to another OSCA and drove like a madman to finish 2nd in class and 18th overall, behind the Ferraris and Porsche Spyders that dominated the race. However, 1959 was not a happy year for Ricardo or his family. He was 2nd at Avandaro, 13th in his 1st try at the Nurburgring, eliminated at Le Mans in the 4th hour of the 24-hour race by a malfunctioning water pump (in an OSCA shared with Pedro). At Riverside he led, but pushed his car so hard its engine blew. Hope only blossomed at season's end with a 2nd in the Nassau Governor's Cup race in a Dino Ferrari.

The next season was no better. In Cuba for the Havana GP, Ricardo was retired with clutch trouble. At Sebring he and Pedro shared a Ferrari and suffered a similar fate. In the Targa Florio in Sicily the boys brought a battered Ferrari in 7th, after flying off the road 4 times in their vain quest for the lead. At the Nurburgring Ricardo was retired once more by a seized engine. Stung by criticism that his sons were proving temperamentally unsuited to real auto racing, Don Pedro split them up in a pair of 3-litre Ferraris for Le Mans. Pedro never made the race officially, his codriver running out of gas before he even got a chance at the wheel, but Ricardo, teamed with André Pilette, managed to come in 2nd overall, trailing only the veteran Le Mans team of Oliver Gendebien and Paul Frere in a factory Ferrari. The showing buoyed Ricardo; he scored a victory in the Governor's Cup in Nassau and shared 2nd with his brother in Speed Week's main race behind Dan Gurney.

In 1961 Ricardo scored his 1st single-seater victory in a Cooper Formula Junior car (Pedro was 4th) in Mexico City. The brothers again shared cars at Sebring where they led for a time, but settled for 3rd after mechanical troubles. In the Targa, a crackup ended their bid; at Nurburgring they were 2nd, despite a collapsed wheel. At Le Mans they battled for 15 hours, at times wheel to wheel, with Phil Hill and Gendabien in a factory Ferrari, until the Rodriguez car finally gave up the ghost under the constant pounding. It was one of the great Le Mans duels of all time, and if non-finishers can have any measure of glory, Ricardo and Pedro earned it that day. Based on their showing (and with a strong recommendation from his North American representative, Luigi Chinetti) Ferrari allowed both brothers to buy Formula 1 berths. Pedro, concerned about business interests at home, turned his offer down, but Ricardo seized the opportunity and immediately set his sights on taking the World Championship within the year.

Ricardo's initial GP ride was in the Italian race at Monza, in what turned out to be a tragic day. In practice he smashed the suspension of one Ferrari, and there were mutterings once again about the Mexican's inability to drive sophisticated machinery. By the last day of practice, however, Ricardo was running the 6.2-mile course only a second off the time of Wolfgang von Trips, who was battling Phil Hill for the championship that

season. In the race, Ricardo came close to being involved in the melee that killed Trips and 13 spectators. He was running 3rd, ahead of Jim Clark, when Trips came blasting up after an abortive start. If Hill or Trips won this race the championship would be theirs, and Trips was determined it would be he, not the American, who would win this year. He blasted by Clark, intent on passing Rodriguez as well. Instead, Wolfgang's Ferrari brushed Clark's Lotus, and the chain reaction started that converted the Ferrari into a deadly missile.

Rodriguez motored on, partly because he was unaware of what had happened behind him and partly because he was intent on Hill and Ginther, who were ahead of him. But his car was not as powerful as theirs, and in the end it gave up the chase before he did. It was an auspicious GP beginning, and despite the accident and his own failure, Rodriguez could feel some pleasure at his showing. As he went back to sports cars, he looked forward to 1962 with anticipation. In the Canadian GP and at Riverside, he failed to finish, but teamed with Pedro, won the Paris 1000.

In 1962, Ricardo codrove a Ferrari to 2nd—shared with Phil Hill—at Daytona, failed again at Sebring in a car shared with Pedro, and finished 2nd in the nontitle Pau GP. In the Targa Florio in May, Ricardo shared a Ferrari with Willy Mairesse and Gendebien, filling the middle driving assignment in the long race, and the trio shared an impressive victory. His other victory of the year was a repeat at the Paris 1000, again with his brother. In the GP season with Ferrari, Ricardo failed to qualify at Monaco, was 4th in Belgium and 6th in Germany. He retired from the Italian GP. No one was pleased with his performances, least of all Ricardo himself. He was stung by criticisms that said he was undisciplined as a driver and certainly as a team member, his wife of less than a year wanted him to stop racing, for she feared for his life. Supposedly he had agreed to quit—after a final race.

That was the Mexican Grand Prix, in which Ricardo was to drive a Rob Walker Lotus, not a Ferrari. On the 1st day's practice, he drove exceedingly fast—too fast, many said—and he seemed to be doing many things he did not ordinarily do. After turning in some record laps, he seemed finished for the day, but he decided to go out for just one more lap. There are many versions of what happened next. Drivers behind Rodriguez said he was going too fast for the turn. Observers at trackside said the Lotus right rear suspension snapped, causing the right rear wheel to collapse. The car lurched right, then left, on up the steep guard rail. It bounced off one post, the body broke in half, the cockpit portion leaping into the air and catapulting Ricardo through the air for some 50 feet or more (he was not wearing a seat belt). When they reached him he was dead. His skull was fractured, and his torso was almost torn in half. Contrary to some reports, there were no last words. After a day of national mourning, he was buried on Mexico's Day of the Dead. He was not yet 21.

GEORGES ROESCH

In 1871, at the end of the Franco-Prussian War, a young German had the audacity to emigrate to Paris when anti-German feeling was at its height. He found at least one French citizen who did not hate him altogether, and married her. The newlyweds emigrated to Geneva, in Switzerland, and the husband opened a blacksmith shop. Later he became fascinated with bicycles, and in 1896 he even set the Swiss National 100-kilometer record for the 2-wheelers. This Roesch, for that was his name, should be famed really for something else he produced.

A son, Georges Henry Roesch, was born on April 15, 1891, in Geneva. The son would become one of the great automotive designers of history, and a man who created competition cars that have performed rarely-duplicated feats. Young Georges, like his father, emigrated to Paris at the age of 18. There he joined the staff of the Gregoire factory, and in 1911 he moved over to Renault, working directly with Louis Renault himself. A chance meeting with an English visitor at Christmas 1913, fired Roesch up about England, and on February 2, 1914, he landed in Britain with about $50 in his pocket. He found his way to Coventry and got himself a job with Daimler.

In 1916, despite the war and his German name (which had him under surveilance for a whole year, even though he was Swiss, not German), Roesch saw a newspaper ad and landed a job as chief engineer of the Clement Talbot Ltd. factory. At age 25 he had indeed arrived. The war prevented actual motor car production, of course, but Georges's task was to design a car that could be rapidly put into production as soon as the war had ended. What he designed was the A.12, a 3-seater of good design, if we are to believe contemporary observers. Only one ever was built, however, as the man behind Talbot in Britain was killed on the Western Front near the war's end, and the company directors accepted an offer to sell out to a new automobile combine that became known as S-T-D: Sunbeam, Talbot, Darracq.

From chief engineer Georges suddenly found himself reduced to assistant again, albeit to Louis Coatalen, a genius in his own right. This situation lasted from 1920 through 1925. All the while Roesch was designing his own "ideal" car with moving parts that were stiffer, stronger, and yet lighter than anything produced by the still-young industry up to that time. Meanwhile, he was doing rather menial engineering work for S-T-D. Yet Coatalen recognized what he had in this assistant, and when, in 1926, the opportunity presented itself to advance someone to the 1st rank in the engineering department, Louis chose Roesch.

Roesch was a believer in racing performance, even for non-racing cars. He based his designs for a new series of Talbots on S-T-D racing experience—besides, he himself liked nothing better than to speed up, down, and around the Alps on a holiday as much as a Tagra Florio or Alpine Rallyist might. Therefore, "muscle", good handling, braking, and performance had the enthusiast's meaning to this designer. His designs were startlingly modern; the brakes on his 1930 car, for example, brought a 100 m.p.h. car to rest in 5 seconds, or as quickly as modern discs would 30 years later. The Roesch Talbots were quiet, reliable, and the fastest unsupercharged cars of their day, proven in international sports-car racing in the thirties. In only 5 instances in 3 years did a Talbot retire from a race.

In 1930 at Le Mans a Talbot was 3rd overall, 1st in handicap, and 1st in class. The same 90 model won its class in the Irish Grand Prix, the Tourist Trophy, and the Brooklands 500 that same season. Other 90 cars were 2nd and 3rd in class in the same races, and they set 6 British and international speed records. The 105 of 1931 was 1st, 2nd and 3rd in class at the Brooklands Double Twelve, 1st in the unsupercharged class in the Irish GP, 1st in the same class at Le Mans, 1st and 2nd at the Tourist Trophy, and swept the class in the Brooklands 500. A crash ended the Mille Miglia hopes of the 105 in 1932, but it swept its class and overall prizes at the Brooklands 1000, won in class at Le Mans for a 3rd year running, was 1st and 2nd in the Tourist Trophy and the Brooklands 500.

Roesch's 105 design also won the 1932 Alpine Cup team prize, and repeated the feat in 1934. A special belonging to W. M. Couper, a British amatuer driver, dominated almost every Brooklands race it ran in the 1934–38 period. In all, Georges designed the 14/45 and 6 variations of the basic design, the 70 and 75 and 7 variations, the 90 and 2 variations, the 105 and 1 variation, the 95 and 2 variations, and the 110 and 3 variations, one of these being the car Couper raced at Brooklands.

His designs were always well ahead of others. In fact, the modern XK Jaguar series parallels the Roesch designs of 20 years before in many ways, even down to many internal engine dimensions and measurements, and in performance, despite the advantage of modern metallurgy and technology that the later Jags undoubtedly had. In 1932 Georges designed an automatic transmission. The modern claim of twin-cam power from pushrods made by the expert tuner originated on the Roesch drawing board of 1920. In truth, Roesch prolonged the useful life of the pushrod engine 45 or 50 years after its demise was being openly predicted.

To all intents and purposes, the S-T-D combine collapsed early in 1935, and the outbreak of World War II put an end to any hopes that Georges may have had of continuing as a leading automobile designer. Even though he lived until age 78—dying on November 7, 1969—his creative career had ended 30 years before, and his last 3 decades were spent in frustration. More so, for Georges Roesch was obstinate, perverse, demanding, and oblivious to anything outside his world of engines and car design. However, he could be, on occasions, charming, helpful, and considerate, to those to whom he had taken a liking. The shame was that there was no place for this genius in Britain or America, or somewhere in Europe for that matter, after 1939. Age or no age, this was a designer who created things only recently rediscovered in Coventry and Detroit by young, enthusiastic engineers.

ALAN ROLLINSON

When Alan Rollinson won a relatively minor Formula 2 race in February 1971, in the final round of the Columbian Temporada, it got more than the usual attention. It was the initial international F2 race this talented and popular driver had won, after several unlucky seasons in that formula. He did it convincingly, taking the opening heat easily and finishing 3rd, then winning the 2nd heat to pile up enough points to be classified on top of the combined field. His opponents were mainly young, second-string Formula 1 drivers like Rolf Stommelen, Derek Bell, Peter Westbury, and Jo Siffert. There was little doubt that Rollinson would follow them into the top Grand Prix class very soon.

Alan William Rollinson was a Midlander, born in 1943 in the United Kingdom, son of a self-made builder and real estate man. He described himself as "the black sheep of the family" because Rollinson never went beyond the secondary level of schooling—the car bug had bitten him. Alan started serious racing in 1962 after attending a race-driving school. At first his father sponsored the Rollinson Cooper, and then a Cheshire farmer named Frank Lythgoe started picking up the tab, a partnership that continued for many years through F3 and into F2 in 1967. Alan's quest for that first F2 victory started May on 14, 1967, when he finished 5th. Four years is a long time to wait it out; fortunately Rollinson had other series to keep him going during that period.

During 1964 Alan saw a hatful of F3 victories in a Brabham, but disappointments in the F2 McLaren. The F2 jinx continued in 1968, and overflowed in F3 where Alan's Chevron never seemed competitive. Only a great run of early F3 victories in 1969 kept Rollinson driving with backing for his Brabham BT21B. Once again he followed the F2 lure, this season in an Irish Racing Cars BT30, trying a Lotus 59B a few times, as well, but still no victory. Then something new also appeared—Formula 5000 for 5-litre single-seaters—a sort of sidestep from F2, and in this class Rollinson showed he had the skill to win, if not the luck.

In 1969 Alan was 5th in the F5000 standings, taking 2nd at Silverstone in a Brabham-Ford BT30 1.6-litre car, despite giving away all those litres. In a real F5000, a Lola-Chevy T142, he scored 2nds at Koksijde, Oulton, and Brands Hatch, 3rd at Mondello, and 4th at Snetterton. The following year Alan tried 3 different cars in the series, starting with a Lola-Chevy T70, then a Surtees-Chevy TS5A, and finally a Lotus-Ford T70. Retired at the Oulton opener, Rollinson's car bottomed in practice at Brands Hatch, then crashed and broke in 2. He walked away from it, however. He didn't make the Silverstone grid in one race, then retired there in the next. After that came 5th at Thruxton and Silverstone, then 3 more retirements and failures to start. Midseason appendicitis cost Rollinson 2 months of racing, and made for quite a year of frustration.

Still he enjoyed F5000. "I had to learn to drive all over again. It's the only car I've ever driven where I can't use full throttle in some of the corners. In F3, or even F2, there aren't many corners where you can't give the car full boot. In F3 you turn into a corner, give the car full throttle, and get round somehow. But with F5000 there are hardly any corners where you can use full throttle. So I think that it provides the best training for F1, much better than F2, because the cars don't hold the road as well as the F2's and they have this throttle control problem. So it is much more a question of judgment, and that's what real auto racing is all about."

In F2, in an Irish Racing Cars BT30, Rollinson plumbed the depths with a 10th at Crystal Palace, and the heights with a F2 victory at the same place. The following year the Brabham was swapped for a Lotus 69 in Europe. One of these years, in one of those cars, Rollinson would have to get lucky, for he had been storing away that good fortune many a season.

MAURI ROSE

Mauri Rose wouldn't set foot in a midget race car, but he won Indianapolis 3 times—1941, 1947, and 1948. In later years he said that racing, as it was being conducted in the days of his glory, had little to offer in the advancement of automotive engineering. In the post-World War II era he was an engineer who happened to be a race driver, too. Racing was fun and it helped sell the product—Blue Crown Spark Plugs, or Studebaker, or whatever. His proudest accomplishment was not winning America's greatest race 3 times, but the invention of a device that allowed amputees to drive an automobile, one of the 1st, if not *the* 1st, such prosthetic.

Yet, underneath the big mustache, the ever-present pipe, and the talk of engineering, there was the heart of a competitor. The 5-foot, 6-inch Rose started driving about 1927, on the dirt tracks near his home town of Columbus, Ohio, where he was born in 1906. His 1st try at Indianapolis came in 1933, when he was running a modified Studebaker; that attempt ended at the 125-mile mark, with Mauri in 4th place when the car failed. In 1934 he finished 2nd to Wild Bill Cummings and qualified for 10 straight Indianapolis races, starting with that one. In 1936 he finished 4th, but won the AAA national

championship. In 1939 he was 8th, and in 1940 he was 3rd.

The most successful part of Rose's Indy career is inextricably woven together with Lou Moore, a former driver who became one of that unique clan called Indy car owners. In 1941 Mauri's Noc-Out Hose Clamp Special ran with the leaders for 60 laps, then retired with ignition woes. He told Moore—according to Al Bloemker who was Indy's public relations head—he was going to try for a relief ride with someone else. Rather than let that happen, Moore indicated he would pull in Floyd Davis, who was driving his other car, and turn the car over to Mauri. "OK," replied Mauri, "but when we make the change, let's be sure I have enough fuel to go the remaining distance without a pit stop."

Rose computed that the best time to flag Floyd would be at the 180-mile mark. That's what was done, and Rose began charging from 14th position immediately. At 225 miles he was 9th, 4th at 300, and when Wilbur Shaw crashed his Boyle Special Maserati because of a faulty wheel, Marui was challenging Cliff Bergere for what was then 2nd place. He took the lead at 425 miles and was never headed.

In 1946 Rose crashed into the retaining wall and was thrown onto the track in a sitting position. He quickly found out that everything seemed to be in one piece except for that piece upon which he was sitting. Later a piece of concrete was found to be the cause of his discomfort. Rose made no secret of his post-war success formula—the most careful planning and the best equipment. The latter was provided by Moore, who always tried to have some kind of engineering edge for each 500. The planning included an assessment of the opposition and its weaknesses as astute as any in the sport, and a strategy designed to maintain just enough speed to win. Mauri liked to qualify the 1st day, then return only to watch the foes he feared.

The 1947 race was the one which went with a short field (30), because of the tardiness of an agreement between the then newly formed American Society of Professional Automobile Racing and the Speedway. At one time, in fact, 9 cars were on the track qualifying simultaneously. It was also the one in which Rose allegedly "stole" the victory from his sensational rookie teammate, Bill Holland. But there was no doubt about the 1948 triumph.

Rose, Holland, and the Novi hope, Duke Nalon, were content to let Ted Horn and Rex Mays duel for the lead for almost half of the race. When Nalon made his move to the fore, Rose followed him. Better pit work on the next stop gave Mauri the lead over Horn and Nalon, and he outraced every challenge by Duke and the Novi until Duke retired near the end of the race. Holland moved up to the runnerup spot again. In 1949 Rose was running in 2nd place—to Holland—when, with 8 laps to go, the car broke. George Connor, in a 3rd Blue Crown Special, finished 3rd behind John Parsons. In fairness to Rose, he had to drive around the accident when Duke Nalon crashed his Novi into the wall, but he was charging at the end, and there was a magnificent argument afterward because he failed to finish.

The Rose-Moore team broke up after the 1949 race. Moore claimed that Rose ignored pit signals, thus causing the car to retire with a broken magneto strap. For his part, Rose claimed the strap never would have broken if Moore's mechanics had prepared the car properly.

In 1950, with the race shortened by rain, a fire in the pits may have cost Mauri (now driving the Howard Keck Special) his 4th victory. Overflowing fuel splashed on a crew member, and the hot exhaust pipe burst into flames. Unwilling to lose even a second, Rose remained in the car until ordered out of it by the officials. When the fire was out, he climbed in and resumed his chase of Parsons and Holland. The rains came before he had a chance to display one of his patented, finishing bursts of speed.

Rose was under particular strain for the 1950 race, because both his children had contracted polio. He invented an exercising device to help them recover. After the 1951 race in which a wire wheel collapsed, he retired and moved to California. His replacement in the Keck car was Bill Vukovich.

BERND ROSEMEYER

In January on the Frankfurt-Darmstadt Autobahn in Germany, a small group of Germans gather for a simple memorial service at a small stone pillar near the superhighway. The memorial is near a concrete bridge, and it was against this bridge that 28-year-old Bernd Rosemeyer, whose international driving career lasted less than 3 years, crashed to death on January 28, 1938. Thirty-odd years is a long time to remember someone who was merely a racing driver, and whom most of those attending the service never knew, yet Rosemeyer's short life was such that it inspired such memorials.

Rosemeyer was born in Lingen, Lower Saxony, on October 14, 1909, and started his competition career in his teens with motorcycles. The fair-haired cyclist made a name for himself on NSUs and BMWs, and in 1930 he was offered a factory team berth with DKW, part of the recently formed Auto Union group. Auto Union itself, of course, was the auto racing leader of the group, with some of the most powerful cars ever built, those rear-engined, 16-cylinder mounts of 1934. In the debut season, Hans Stuck won the Czech, German, and Swiss Grands Prix, and greater victories lay ahead.

Rosemeyer spent that 1st year winning races, too, although still in the 2-wheel variety. He also kept pestering Auto Union racing officials for a chance to drive their cars. Just why these officials eventually gave in is a mystery, but they did, in November, 1934, and Bernd appeared at Nurburgring for his test run in his best Sunday suit. It befit the occasion, he told the astonished on-

lookers. He spun the squat ugly racer on his initial lap, ending up in a meadow, yet he came back for more. On his 2nd circuit he set a lap mark bettered at that time by only the great Stuck himself. Rosemeyer was immediately signed as a reserve driver.

The year 1935 opened with Stuck, Achille Varzi, and others still piloting the silver Auto Unions around the course—Tunis passed, and then Tripoli. Avus would be next, and the marque's racing officials began to find notes on their desks, and in the mails, "Where is the car for Rosemeyer?"—"Will Rosemeyer drive at Avus?"—"Why is Rosemeyer not racing yet?"—"Rosemeyer *will* drive at Avus!" This persistence once again wore down the supposedly stone-hearted Auto Union officials. Rosemeyer received a car for Avus, although not one of the best. His practice time was the 3rd best among the elite company, but in the race itself, the car failed him, 1st with a thrown tire tread, and then a blown engine. Bernd had driven skillfully, however, even as the tire failed at high speed.

The next race was the Eifelrennen, and this was the race that 1st made Rosemeyer famous. Varzi was ill, Stuck's regular car went bad, and the 3rd Auto Union, driven by Paul Pietsch, was too far back; Rosemeyer was reluctantly given instructions by his pits to go as fast as he could, to try to wear out the leading Mercedes. He responded magnificently, sliding his snarling mount through the corners. Louis Chiron was passed, then Luigi Fagioli; Manfred von Brauchitsch blew his Mercedes engine in a vain attempt to stay ahead of the charging Rosemeyer. Finally, only Rudi Caracciola's Mer-

cedes was ahead of him, and Bernd passed him after a thrilling nose-to-tail chase. The crowd was wild, but as might be expected, in the race's last lap the experienced Caracciola managed to regain the lead, and won by a slight 1.8 seconds.

The day's hero was Rosemeyer, however. The public had a new idol, and the Auto Union team had a new number 3 driver, rather than a mere reserve who had to beg for a car. At Pescara, a particularly difficult course for the big German cars, Bernd managed a 2nd behind Varzi. At one point Rosemeyer's brakes seized and he skidded off the course, flattening a stone kilometer marker, jumping a ditch, and navigating at high speed between a telephone pole and a bridge parapet to regain the course. Afterwards, Dr. Ferdinand Porsche, who had seen the incident, measured the distance between the pole and the bridge through which Rosemeyer had driven so skillfully; it was just an inch wider than the big Auto Union. The fair-haired boy of Germany was 3rd in the Swiss and Italian Grands Prix, then won his 1st GP, the Masaryk in Czechoslovakia, by 6 minutes, beating a field that included such names as Tazio Nuvolari and Luigi Chiron.

It had been a year of learning, really, but 1936 was Rosemeyer's year. After an abortive Monaco, in which the heavy, wheel-spinning Auto Union had spun on a steaming wet street and ended tail-first against a stone wall, Bernd won the fog-shrouded Eifelrennen and the title of *Nebelmeister*, or Master of the Mists. He then took the German, Italian, and Swiss GPs, and the Coppa Acerbo at Pescara, and was awarded the Championship of Europe. He was 2nd in the Hungarian GP, 4th in the Coppa Ciano, and 5th at Barcelona. He won the Freiburg and Feldberg hillclimbs. At Tunis and Tripoli, Rosemeyer's Auto Union caught fire in the blistering heat.

The next season was either a bit harder or a bit unluckier. Mercedes had a newer and faster car, but Varzi and Stuck were past their primes. Rosemeyer was 2nd at Tripoli after a flying tread cost him the lead, and 4th at Avus when his oil pressure failed with victory in sight. He won the Eifelrennen again, however, and he came to the United States to win the Vanderbilt Cup at Roosevelt Raceway on Long Island. Alone, he beat the supposedly better 4-car Mercedes team at Pescara for his 2nd straight Pescara victory. He won the Donington GP in England to the roar of 50,000 British racing fans who had started the race in an anti-German mood. He was 2nd at Capetown, 3rd in the German, Italian and Masaryk races, 4th at Monaco, and 5th in the Swiss and South African Grands Prix.

The Donington race, his 13th in 1936, was his last race ever. That winter, driving an ultra-streamlined Auto Union Special on the Autobahn, he attempted to better the Class B speed figures just set over the same circuit by Carracciola in a Mercedes. The marque was Germany's, yet they were bitter enemies, and Auto Union wanted to beat the 268 m.p.h. clocking even though conditions were not ideal. The clocks showed Bernd at better than 275 m.p.h. when a strong wind hit his car from the side. The car skidded, shed a tire, then somersaulted and piled against the concrete bridge. Rosemeyer was thrown from the car just before the impact, and his body, though thoroughly broken, was unmarked. His face was calm and peaceful. Each year, starting in 1939, and continuing even through World War II, his widow, Elly Beinborn Rosemeyer, the aviatrix, and their son, Bernd, lead a small party to the site to commemorate him.

LLOYD RUBY

Lloyd Ruby liked to give the impression that he was just a pore ol' country boy from Wichita Falls, Tex. However, Wichita Falls had 112,000 not-so-poor country boys in it, and the soft-spoken Ruby was one of the shrewdest and most versatile drivers ever to sit behind the wheel of a race car. With Ruby it could be any kind of race car, too. He was piloting Maseratis with Carroll Shelby when Phil Hill was still making his reputation. Although the main efforts of Ruby's career had been directed at the USAC Championship Trail (with emphasis on the Indianapolis 500), the redoubtable Ruby codrove back-to-back with Ken Miles to victories in the 1965 and 1966 Daytona Continentals and the 1966 Sebring. Just for the record, the man with the prematurely gray sideburns and the white straw cowboy hat was probably the 1st man to wheel a Formula 1 car on a USAC mile track. He did it for promoter Sam Nunis in the 1963 Trenton 100, in Frank Harrison's rebuilt Cooper-Climax. With 2.7 litres of power, he won the pole and led the race until the suspension, fragile for this type of racing, broke.

Born on January 12, 1928, Ruby began competing at 16, first with motorcycles and then in stripped-down Ford roadsters. "We'd race in Texas and Oklahoma five nights a week," Lloyd recalled. "Those cars we had were just like tanks, but they were great to learn in. I was having trouble with this ole boy one night, so I just ran him right through the fence. I went through, too. Taught me a lesson when I stopped feeling good around pay time. You have to be around at the finish to get paid."

Married, with a son and daughter, Ruby became known as a man who was going to finish just about every race he entered. He was the opposite of the famed car-breakers, treating his machinery with finesse and respect that made independent car owners joyous. In fact, that was one reason Shelby-American and the Ford Motor Company went to Ruby for the Continental, the "must" race for their GT project. Lloyd had gone the distance 4 of the first 5 times he competed at Indianapolis, making the top 10 each time he finished. And this was with 5 different mounts. In 1960, Ruby finished 7th in an Agajanian Special; in 1961, he finished 8th in the Autolite Special; in 1962 in the Thompson Industries Special, he again finished 8th; in 1963 he wrecked on the northwest turn on the 126th lap in the Zink Track Burner; and in 1964, in the Bill Forbes Special, Ruby finished 3rd.

Ruby raced independent circuits during the early part of his career. He joined USAC when his friend and sponsor, J. H. (Ebb) Rose, decided to go that route about 1958. His rough jalopy driving was smoothed out by piloting the trucking executive's midgets and sports cars. Ruby liked midget racing and remembered the Tangerine Tournament in Florida (a USAC-brainchild to keep its midget drivers working in the winter) as a key point in his career. "I helped prepare Rose's midgets," Ruby recalled, "and I also drove—against some of the best in the country. Early, I ran into trouble, but we finished pretty good, winning three of four features. I got into road racing because of Rose, too. When USAC started its road racing division, he first owned Corvettes, then switched to Maseratis and Maserati-Corvettes, which he got Micro-Lube to sponsor."

Lloyd's professional Maser baptism, in 1958, was unusual to say the least. At Lime Rock, Ruby was driving a Maserati-Chevrolet which he had helped to build. Suddenly the drive shaft snapped and pushed partly into the cockpit. Lloyd exited the cockpit, and steered the car into the pits with his feet. The next year, in a Maserati, he won a 65-mile feature at Meadowdale, Ill., and ran 2nd to Phil Hill in the Los Angeles Times Grand Prix at Riverside. That was Ruby's most active road-racing year, for he competed in 9 USAC point races, finishing in the top 5 on 7 occasions. He finished as runnerup to Augie Pabst for the season title.

In 1961 Lloyd competed in only 2 of a possible 7, won the inaugural 100-mile heat at Indianapolis Raceway Park, and finished 2nd in the 2nd heat. That was the extent of his road racing success until Daytona, because he was occupied by Championship and stock cars. In the back of his mind, however, he hoped to race in Europe. "But you have to have good equipment," he declared, "that's the thing in racing—any kind of racing. It was never really hard to adjust to road courses. I never really thought about adjusting, but even on a road course I find I can turn left better than right; I feel I have better control."

After Indianapolis in 1964, Ruby campaigned a Lotus 19-based Harrison Special on the Championship Trail and a d.o.h.c. Lotus-Ford sports/racer at selected sports car races. He set a track record in the Harrison Special at Trenton, short-lived, however, when Messrs. Clark and Jones got to work. For 1965 Ruby was contracted to drive a Shrike-Ford for John McManus, a Michigan industrialist.

Victories on the Championship Trail for Ruby were rare, because for many years, he did not make the entire circuit. In 1961, however, at the Milwaukee 200, that combination of well-prepared car and alert driver paid off in victory. Ruby qualified 7th on the mile asphalt track, with a 34.36-second lap in the Zink Trackburner.

On the pole was veteran Don Branson, with a 34.09, and next to him was Parnelli Jones 7/100ths of a second slower. Jones jumped Branson at the green flag, and for 18 miles the two fought a wheel-to-wheel duel. Right behind them were Rodger Ward, the "King of Milwaukee," and Jim Hurtubise. Jones and Branson crashed on the 36th mile, costing Ward his lead, but Ward and Hurtubise took over the wheel-to-wheel duel.

Meanwhile, Ruby was 7th at 10 miles, 6th at 20, 7th again at 30, and had jumped to 3rd behind Hurtubise and Len Sutton by the 40th mile. He, Len, and Eddie Sachs (in the Dean Van Lines car) shuffled between 2nd, 3rd, and 4th for the next 140 miles, while Jungle Jim was setting a record pace in the Autolite car. But Hurtubise dropped all the way to 6th place on the 175th mile, when he was lucky to make his pit on a bald tire.

Sutton dived into the lead for 2 miles, and then Ruby, giving the Zink car its head, streaked past to lead the final 23 miles. Ruby's race strategy and pit work were so perfect that only Sutton was on the same lap with him at the finish. He set a record 101.638 m.p.h. pace. Two races later he parted company with Zink, and drove much of 1962 for his old friend, Rose, then shifted to the Harrison Special in 1963. He car-hopped the 2nd half of the year, although he did drive a Zink car at Indy, crashing it after 126 laps.

In 1964, Lloyd had himself an Indy ride in the Forbes Racing Special out of Chicago, a rear-engined, Offenhauser-powered Shrike. He moved up steadily from the middle of the pack to finish 3rd, behind Foyt and Ward in the same lap. Ruby made the full circuit, even the dirt

523

track races, and finally connected in the last race of the season, moving from 5th qualifying spot to a record victory. That also gave him 3rd place in the USAC standings and a fair living of $61,250. In 1965 Ruby made 11 races, and the best he could do was 3rd place twice. He was running a rear-engined Ford, the DuPont Golden 7 Special. He got up to 5th and was finally credited with 11th place after the car conked out. The 3rds were at Langhorne, Pa., and—for Shelby/Gurney's All American Racers—at the Milwaukee 200.

In 1966 Lloyd was still the AAR Championship Trail man in USAC. His Lotus-Ford dropped out with engine woes at Trenton, but at Indianapolis he came close to his lifelong ambition. He led Indy for 68 laps in a Gurney Eagle-chassised car. His poor Indy luck continued, however, when officials blackflagged him to repair an oil leak, and it was found that an engine part had knocked a hole in the cam cover. From sure victory, he was placed 11th. The luck continued to be mediocre when his private plane crashed on takeoff from Indy after the race, and both he and his chief mechanic, Dave Laycock, were slightly injured. Lloyd's slight spine injury was enough to lose him his Le Mans ride with Miles.

For 1967 Ruby had a new sponsor, Gene White, and a new car, patterned after a Brabham Formula 1 by its builder, Laycock, but with turbocharged Offy power. The initial time out, in the 150-miler at Phoenix, Lloyd won the pole and the race. He was 33rd at Indy when the car dropped a valve on the 4th lap. At Milwaukee he was 6 seconds behind winner Gordon Johncock. Lloyd then dashed off to Le Mans and to partner Hulme in a Ford that led, but eventually retired. When he came back for the Langhorne 100, Laycock had a new Lotus-Ford waiting. Ruby celebrated by breaking the track record for the race by 9 m.p.h. (113.38 m.p.h.), as he circled Al Unser on lap 53 and was never challenged. Ruby cut the fastest race lap at Mosport, and also his tire, costing a minute in the pits, but still finished 4th. He won the pole again at the Hoosier GP, but was not around for the finish. It's nice to have a car owner with money, and Ruby switched back to a Mongoose, with Ford power, to take 3rd in the Labatt 200 at Le Circuit Mont Tremblant. He switched to Offy for a 3rd at Hancock, Calif.

Ruby qualified the Gene White Mongoose-Offy in 5th starting spot in the 1968 Indianapolis 500, and led the race, turning the fastest competitive lap in Indy history (168.666 m.p.h.). A pit stop to change the coil robbed him of all hope for victory, after he had led for 30 laps —he finished 5th. Again he won Milwaukee as he outcharged Mario Andretti on the key 107th lap. Lloyd, now 40, added a 2nd place in the USAC road race stop at Castle Rock, Colo., to try to stave off fast-rising Al Unser. Despite winning the Milwaukee 200, he fell to 4th place in the standings. In the Phoenix 200 he garnered a 2nd place, but he was relieved of his car as Firestone hero Mario Andretti made a vain effort to beat Bobby Unser for the USAC crown.

Of all the years of Indy heartbreak, 1969 was the worst. He seemed an easy winner in his Wynn's Turbo-Offy, and had rolled in for his mandatory pit stop. He pulled away before the refueling hose had been disconnected and destroyed his chance for victory, the car catching fire. He was off to another hard-luck year, the bright spots being a 3rd place in the Milwaukee 200, and a 2nd at Phoenix. For the 1970 Indy, Lloyd qualified 6th fastest, but lasted only 54 laps when the axle case cracked and triggered another fire. He had been 3rd at the time. The 42-year-old driver had won Trenton for the Gene White team as well. It was his best showing, even though he won the pole position for the inaugural Ontario 500 at 177.567 m.p.h. (Ruby blew his engine in the race proper, leading for only 7 laps.)

In 1971, after an 11th at Indy when a gearbox fire in the pits finished him, Ruby had his chance at glory in the California 500, final triple crown event. But he finished fourth two laps behind winner Joe Leonard. Lloyd had moved his car steadily through the field and seemed to have paced himself as only a veteran might. But a combination of tire wear and a less speedy pit crew did him in. In 1972, driving the Wynns Special Lola Foyt, Ruby rolled to a creditable 6th but at Pocono he finished 26th, a DNF, and at Ontario 17th.

PAUL RUSSO

Pudgy Paul Russo, 5 feet 7 inches tall and 190 pounds in his top days, started racing big cars in Chicago in 1932 at the age of 18. He was still around 27 years later, finishing 9th at Indianapolis, and he was making the field as late as 1962. That's not bad for a lad who had to follow in the footsteps of a brother from racing's golden era, Joe Russo. Father of one daughter, Paul was the terror of the Eastern tracks during the period preceding World War II, and won the Eastern crown in 1939. After the war he moved to Hammond, Ind., to race midgets as well as big cars.

The classic Russo anecdote dates from when he built a new car for the 1950 Indy race—in the basement of his home. When he finished, he found he couldn't get it out, so he had to dismantle it, then hastily put the machine together to take 12 practice laps before qualifying easily. This was Basement Bessie, a vehicle that lasted 15 seconds. Paul announced he had not bothered to change the warm-up plugs that came with the engine. A young man by the name of Ray Nichels had helped him build that car, which in later versions lasted for more than a decade. Russo was one of several veteran drivers involved in the Novi saga.

JOHNNY RUTHERFORD

Johnny Rutherford paid for what he earned out of racing. There was the sprint race at Rossburg, Ohio in 1966 where he broke both arms. It was a week before practice for Indianapolis and he had lined up a good ride.

He was sidelined a year. Then in April 1968 he crashed at Phoenix, Ariz., in a championship race, burning his hand severely.

Originally it seemed a smooth path to greatness for John Rutherford of Fort Worth, Texas, born March 12, 1938. The handsome lad began his career in 1959 on the jalopy circuits and moved quickly to USAC in 1962. He was a charger but he had that natural smoothness of style that some drivers instinctively have. He concentrated on sprint cars awhile, becoming USAC sprint champion in 1965. Meanwhile there were occasional Championship Trail rides and stock car rides, but he was never near the winners circle except for one day at Atlanta Speedway. There in the Leader Card Special, Rutherford won the Atlanta 250 miler. But things went downhill after that.

In 1970 the Texan was still trying, getting into the front row at both Ontario and Indianapolis, missing the pole position by eight thousandths of a second at Indy. He was not around at the finish. In 1972 he finished 3rd in the 200-miler at Milwaukee. And then in 1973 he finally seemed to hit his stride. Driving a Gulf McLaren M19C with Offy power, Rutherford won the pole position at Indy. The talk had been of a 200 m.p.h. qualifying speed but a windy day ended that hope. Johnny went 198.413 for his 4-lap average with one lap of 199.071. Then he sat around as driver after driver failed to match his speed, even the king of qualifiers, Bobby Unser, whose speed was .23 m.p.h. slower, about 42 ft. for 10-miles. At 35, Rutherford was a celebrity again, and that had to make him feel that the pain and struggle might have been worth it.

TROY RUTTMAN

Troy Ruttman, 245-pounds and 22 years old, became the youngest ever to win Indy (at the record speed of 128.922 m.p.h.). It happened in 1952 when favored Bill Vukovich broke his steering shaft with Troy in hot pursuit on the 192nd lap. Ruttman's victory his greatest in a career that was to stretch to 1964 (when he retired suddenly during a television interview in Indianapolis), truly was earned the hard way.

Leading after 85 laps, Troy's Seal Fast Offy caught fire during fueling. Chief Mechanic Clay Smith and Ruttman's father were burned. Ruttman went back in 3rd place, behind Vukovich and Jim Rathmann. Rathmann pitted for fuel and tires at 112 laps, and Troy moved to 2nd. Vuky's crew put a tire on backwards during a 134th-lap pit stop, and Troy led again. Ruttman came in on lap 147, and the crew couldn't find new tires. They slammed on rubber he had used during qualification, but Troy lost the lead. He went after it despite the tires, cutting laps at 134 m.p.h. and forcing Vukovich into new records to stay ahead.

By lap 177, Troy was only 30 seconds behind. Then he lost a right wheel-balance weight, and his car began

to shudder and shake on every turn. He refused to back off, charging at Vukovich, nibbling off a second a lap.

When Vukovich parked on the backstretch, the caution lights flashed on, and the cars slackened speed. In the Speedway hospital, his father heard over the loud speaker that Troy was in the lead. In pain from the burns, he leaped off the hospital cot (against doctor's orders) and made his way through thick crowds to Victory Lane. When he saw his son crowned 500 champ, he broke into tears of joy. For Ralph Ruttman must have known that this was the summit for his son who, as a 15-year-old, had been so infatuated with motors that he cut high school back in Lynwood, Calif., to go racing in San Bernardino with the family car.

Born in Mooreland, Okla., on March 11, 1930, Troy was brought West from the dust bowl area of the Depression during the great Okie trek to California. He married early—about the time he headed for Indy—and had 3 children. He had been only in his teens when he became the *enfant terrible* of auto racing. At 16 he was running fender to fender with Vukovitch, Andy Linden, and other West Coast heroes. At 19, with a forged birth certificate, he got his 1st ride at Indy, and was flagged at 151 laps, finishing 12th. In the rain-shorted 1950 race he lasted for 325 of the 345 miles. In 1951 crankshaft trouble sidelined him after 78 laps.

Ruttman also finished 2nd in the national championship in 1952, and won the Raleigh 200. What seemed to be a brilliant career hit a major snag shortly after that race. Troy crashed in a Cedar Rapids sprint-car race, and suffered such a serious arm injury that he was out of racing until 1954, when he placed 4th at Indy. He failed to qualify the Novi in 1955, and was inactive much of the rest of the year. In the 1956 Indy he brought his Zink Heating Special into contention, but spun into the infield on the 22nd lap to avoid an accident. In 1957 he led the race early, but suffered a burned piston in the 13th lap.

Surgery, then "conduct detrimental to racing," finished him off for 1958 and 1959. The "conduct" was too great a love for gambling. The Zink Track Burner was waiting in 1960, and he led for 11 laps but suffered from a faulty rear axle that eventually forced him out on lap 134. In 1961 Troy ended his once-a-year regimen and began to drive both stock cars and sprints. His 91st lap at Indy in the Track Burner (147.589 m.p.h.) was the fastest leading lap up to that time, but he was out at lap 105. He switched allegiance to the Jim Robbins Special, parking, this time, after little more than half the race, with a burned piston. He managed a 3rd in the Syracuse 100, highest he had finished in 10 years.

The Dayton Steel Wheel Special was his new mount for 1963. He drove this Watson-Offenhauser to 12th at Indy, and was piloting a Mercury stock car with enough success to make racing a full-time profession, aside from his very good motorcycle business in Dearborn. In 1964 he went on his head in the Trenton race in April, but returned to action to finish 18th at Indy when his Steel Wheel car spun into the infield after 247 miles.

The announcement of his retirement came suddenly, for he had expected to get a ride in a rear-engined vehicle for 1965. "I discussed this with my wife at some length," he said at the time, "then made the decision quickly. It is just best for me to retire. I love racing—it's been the greatest thing in the world for me—but I just feel that it's time to make way for the younger fellows." The 18-year racing veteran was 34 at the time.

EDDIE SACHS

Born in Bethlehem, Pa., May 28, 1927, Edward Julius Sachs, Jr., died in what was to have been his last Indianapolis 500, the 1964 race, when he crashed into rookie Dave McDonald's car. He apparently was dead of a broken neck before his car, the American Red Ball Special, burned.

He had wanted to win the Indianapolis 500. It was his own personal Mount Everest, even though he told his wife, Nancy, in 1964 that he was ready to settle down to being a moving-firm executive in Detroit. But he had said the same thing the year before, and even had cut his racing schedule appreciably.

Thin and undersized through much of his schooling, Sachs worked as a bellhop, bartender, cab driver—and once as a pole-vault setter—while going as far in school as Edwards Junior College. But he wanted athletic fame, trying 1st in baseball, then in professional football, and finally in racing, after seeing his 1st race in Greensboro, N.C., in 1947.

Initially, Eddie haunted the pits at Dorney Park in Allentown, Pa., and points east, looking for a ride. When he did race on rare occasions, he was all over the track, the least talented man in stock-car racing. After the end of World War II, Lou Heller, at Dorney Park, finally taught him the rudiments of driving. Even then, Sachs was always mindful of public relations. He usually had a few apt quotes before a race, but seldom afterwards—because he hardly ever won.

Practice does make perfect, however; Sachs began to win in sprint cars and midgets. And, finally, he tried the Big One: Indianapolis. In 1956, Eddie passed the rookie driver test after having failed twice before (1953 and 1954), becoming 1st alternate for the race. The following year, Sachs qualified 2nd fastest at 143.822 m.p.h.; he lasted 105 laps until a broken piston relegated him to 23rd overall in the Schmidt Special. He had finished 2nd in the 1956 midwest-sprint title, and 3rd for the national USAC Midget crown.

But there was always something to stop Sachs from attaining his goal at the Brickyard. For example, in 1961, he apparently had the race won. But he decided to take the precaution of pitting on the 198th lap for a right front tire. He lost by 8 seconds to A. J. Foyt, thus becoming the only driver besides Ralph DePalma to lead after 197 laps, and still lose. "I would do the same thing again," Sachs said later. "That tire was down to the threads and could have blown at any moment. It wasn't just my life, but the lives of those other guys, too."

Sachs was one of the 10 American drivers who competed in the Monza Race of Two Worlds in 1957. He finished 7th, although he had led before being sidelined with mechanical troubles. Soon after that race, he suffered facial injuries and a crushed bone in his hand in a midget-car crash at the 16th Street Speedway at Indianapolis.

But Sachs returned in 1958 to win the Midwest title. From 1957 through 1961, he started in the front row at Indianapolis, but finished only in 1961. In 1962 he finished 3rd, having started 28th. In 1963, he was running 3rd when he spun out; in winner Parnelli Jones's oil, he claimed. Sachs made the mistake of repeating this to Jones—who promptly punched him in the jaw. It only enhanced his value as a speaker, once the jaw healed. It was one of the few times that Sachs ended up in the hospital without having been injured in a car crash. No one could question his courage.

Sachs always threatened to become a sports car racer, and once wrote a magazine article about how he was going to set Europe agog. He never quite got around to it.

Championship races won: Trenton 4 times, Indianapolis 100 once, and once at Langhorne, Syracuse, and Atlanta (Lakewood Park).

Sachs once was quoted as saying, "In the long run, death is the odds-on favorite."

BILL SADLER

Born September 3, 1931, in St. Catherines, Ontario, Canada, William George Sadler went through elementary school there and attended St. George's Collegiate School. Sadler's father operated one of Canada's largest auto supply houses and shop facilities there, giving the younger Sadler quite a jump on the usual back-yard car builder. But when he took his bride, Anne, to England on a honeymoon in 1953, the Sadlers were the guests of the Lucas Electric people, for whom Sadler's father was a principal Canadian agent. Part of the entertainment was a day at the Trophy races at Snetterton. "It was love at first sight," Sadler recalled later.

Bill Sadler's initial car was a wedding present, an MG TD that he raced near Ottawa when he returned to Canada. The MG was replaced by a Singer which, in turn, gave way to a Hillman fitted with a Ford V-8 engine. "I learned a lot from that car," said Bill, "about how not to build a car, that is." That winter Sadler acquired a Jowett Javelin, stripped it, and hung its engine, suspension and transmission a home-built, aliminum tubular frame. That was the Sadler Mark I, his initial special.

Mark I debuted at Watkins Glen in 1954, and, during 1954 was raced without much success. It was underpowered, despite modifications to the 1486-c.c. Jowett engine. A year later, Sadler replaced the car's original

body and fenders with a streamlined fiber-glass body; and later dropped in a TR-2 engine and transmission, enhanced by his own fuel-injection system.

But it didn't last long. Sadler purchased a Canadian-built 1956 Corvette engine and replaced the Triumph engine. A home-built radiator was fitted in the space available and an air scoop added to the car's hood to provide carburetor clearance and drive cooling air to it. This became the Sadler Mark II, which Sadler took to England in the fall of 1956, when he joined John Tojeiro's AC staff to help design and build the Tojeiro-Jaguar. Camping in the back of a converted trailer-truck, Sadler managed to compete in several British races with the Mark II that year, scoring a notable surprise by topping 260 entries in the 1956 Brighton Speed Trials with fastest time of the day.

The Sadlers returned to Canada by way of Nassau Speedweeks. The Mark II's biggest date, however, came at Montgomery, N.Y., in 1957, when Sadler briefly took the lead in an SCCA national race ahead of 2 Scarabs and 2 Lister-Jags. A cracked universal joint ended that glory—but the performance, coupled with a Watkins Glen class victory, was enough to attract a patron.

Earl Nisonger, one of the world's largest distributors of automobile parts, approached Sadler, and a deal was made to have Sadler build a new car. The Mark III was the result. It took 8 weeks to build, an incredibly short period of time for a major racing car, especially one as intricate as this one became. The simple, ladder-like, large-tube frame of the Mark II was abandoned in the Mark III for a light, convenient space frame built entirely of square-section seamless tubing, weighing only 83 pounds. A Chevrolet engine was chosen once again, bored and stroked to 327 cu. in. (5340 c.c.)—later a standard size from GM—with a Racer Brown camshaft, Hilborn fuel-injection system as used on Lance Reventlow's Scarabs, and other modifications. Engine and gearbox were mounted about 1.5 inches to the left of the car's centerline, both to increase leg room and, to a certain extent, to balance weight.

About this same time, Sadler moved into the then-active Formula Junior scene with his own front-engined design, using a BMC engine in a multi-tubular frame with aluminum bodywork, independent front suspension, and live rear axle, but few were built before FJ competition faded. FJ competition convinced Sadler that rear-engined cars had it over front-engined cars. Thus, "armed with hacksaw and welding torch," as one writer put it, he proceeded to modify the Mark III into a rear-engined car, the Mark IV. In 1964, there was a Mark V, a start-from-scratch rear-engine design, powered for the first time by a non-Sadler-modified engine. Bill never felt that strongly about his engine conversions, so, when he had a chance to have Doug Duncan, the well-known Canadian stock-car modifier, put together an engine for the Mark V, Sadler jumped at it.

527

Cooper-like in its exterior appearance, the Mark V's similarity ended there. The frame was like that of a box kite, but "scraunched-up," to use a Sadler phrase. One end held most of the car's weight, which was mostly the Chevvy power plant—the other the front suspension, steering, and the driver's legs. It sounds cramped, but it was roomy compared to most of today's competitive sports racing machinery.

Sadler felt strongly about driver accommodations in racing cars: "Your driver becomes so wrapped up in extra-fast driving, trying to stay atop a continually changing situation, that he must not be uncomfortable, if we can help it. Even a small part of his attention should not be diverted by such things as leg cramps, wind buffeting, stiff steering or too-hot cockpit surfaces. And comfort is not all physical; it is psychological, too."

From 1958 through 1961, Sadler designed and built about 30 cars to special order, averaging $9,000 each, except the Austin Healey-powered FJ car which was only $3,000.

"After several years of total involvement in racing," he said later, "I decided that I was building up too many frustrations by feeling too keenly about the treatment of each of my cars, so I decided to cut loose." So he went back into the electronics business and restarted his education, earning a BS from Indiana Tri-State College and a Master's from MIT in electrical engineering. His later career was in the aerospace electronics industry, with companies like General Dynamics and Sperry.

Asked if he ever thought of going back into the car racing end of things again, Sadler replied: "Yes, I really think I'd like to again, but strictly on a for-fun basis. My wife thinks I'd be safer out there, even in a race car, than in piloting my own plane as I now do."

BOB SAID

Born in New York City of Syrian-Russian parents in 1932, Boris (Bob) Said was the first American since World War II to win an European racing victory. He had won at Rouen in 1952, in an OSCA sports car, even though the race was not a major one.

Said started driving when, at 15, he became the owner of an MG TC. He had attempted to enter hillclimbs but was then denied entry because of his age. When finally old enough to qualify in SCCA hillclimbs, he won in class at Mount Equinox, and soon followed with his initial race victory at Allentown, Pa.

Interested in the sport, Said worked in the Jim Pauley Garage where midget and Indianapolis-type cars were prepared for Eastern circuits. Test driving midgets there served to whet his appetite for a better personal mount, and he sold the MG to buy a crashed XK 120 Jaguar, which he rebuilt in the Pauley Garage. Entering

Princeton University, he met Briggs Cunningham, Jr., who in 1952, talked his illustrious father into taking Said to Le Mans in 1952, where Briggs was driving once again. That, and the Rheims race that followed, decided Said on professional auto racing.

Said sold his Jag and purchased a Cisitalia, which had such an unfortunate hunger for valves that it even devoured them in practice. George Moffett hired Said to mechanic his OSCA for a Texas race, but when Moffett crashed in practice, he quit, giving Said permission to race the car if Said could repair it in time. Said did, won the local race, and earned himself a Shell Sportsmanship Award in the process. Jack Frierson, another OSCA booster, was impressed enough to hire Said as his driver for a European sojourn. The Rouen victory followed.

The same OSCA also won at Crystal Palace in England, and was then sold to finance a 2-litre Ferrari Mondial, with the help of Luigi Chinetti. Said did well with this car, and was always in the battle with the more experienced European leaders. In a race at Bari, Italy, he finished 2nd overall, just behind a 3-litre Gordini. Said next drove in the 12-hour Sebring race, and crashed Chinetti's Ferrari Monza into an improperly-parked ambulance while running 2nd and overtaking Mike Hawthorn, the leader. Ferrari's North American representative then asked Said to drive a special 4.5-litre Ferrari Indianapolis car at Daytona Beach, for a record mile on the beach course. Said's 174 m.p.h. return drive, combined with a hesitant 166 m.p.h. 1st run, set a mark of 170 m.p.h. for the 2-way average. The following year, Indy star Bill Holland, driving the same car, managed only 155 m.p.h.

In 1954 Said shared a Tourist Trophy 2-litre Ferrari with Masten Gregory, as the 1st American team in that race, but they finished out of the money. Said retired temporarily from racing about this time to try his hand at real estate speculation, managing to lose almost all of a $100,000 inheritance in a San Pedro, Calif., transaction.

Back racing at Nassau in 1957, he won the 2-litre race and was best overall on handicap in a specially prepared Chinetti Testa Rossa Ferrari. Said continued to push competition machinery around the European circuits with occasional drives on this side fo the ocean (notably in Nisonger-Sadlers) for the next few years.

While so doing in 1960, he met Valerie Witalis, who was competing in an MG. Married in 1962 when he was "dead broke," Bob again quit competitive driving to try his hand again at real estate speculation. With $251 of his own, he borrowed enough to make a down payment of $2,600 on 40 acres in suburban Westchester County, N.Y. In six months, Said had located a buyer who took 36 acres (Bob kept 4 for his own hand-built home) for $130,000. He rode the more than $100,000 profit from this initial deal into real-estate holdings of better than $1 million, headlined a feature story in a December 1964 issue of the *New York Times*: "Auto-Racer, Broke at 30, Tells of Making a Million in 2 Years." After a 2-year hiatus, Bob Said was back in the news.

ROY SALVADORI

Italian in name and looks, Roy Francesco Salvadori was strictly an Englishman. Born May 12, 1922, at Dovercourt, Essex, he was educated at St. Helen's in Brentwood, and, after World War II, he entered the automobile business as a salesman in London. That same year, 1946, Roy also started competing in hill-climbs and sprints in an MG Midget. His 1st road race was May 25, 1947, in the Grand Prix des Frontières at Chimay, France. Salvadori's 2.9-litre Alfa Romeo finished 5th, despite gearbox trouble. Later that year, in the 1st race ever held in Britain on a flat, airport-type circuit, Salvadori scored a 3rd in the Grandsen Lodge Meeting.

In the years that followed, Salvadori drove for a great many marques and almost as many teams, both factory and independent—Maserati, Frazer-Nash, Jaguar, Ferrari, Connaught, BRM, Cooper, Aston Martin, Vanwall, Ecurie Ecosse, Gilby Engineering, Yeoman Credit, and many others. His race history read much like that of Britain itself. In 1953, for example, he raced 4 different cars (Formula 2 Connaught, Ecurie Ecosse, Jaguar, Frazer-Nash, and Aston), scoring 1 victory and 7 2nds. The following year, Roy dropped the Frazer-Nash and drove a Formula 1 Maser in its stead, winning twice, finishing second 4 times, and taking 2 thirds. In 1955 Salvadori won 9 races, then 10 the next season, including the Lavant and Woodcote Cups, the Sussex Trophy, and the Gold Cup at Oulton Park. Spending more time on F1, his victory totals dwindled in 1957, but he scored championship points in the French and British Grands Prix, finishing 5th both times in a Vanwall and a Cooper-Climax respectively.

Salvadori's 1958 F1 season saw a 4th in the Dutch GP, a 3rd in the British race, a 2nd at the German GP and another 4th in the Italian GP. Even greater than his F1 skills, however, was his growing expertise in long-distance racing, including a victory in the 24-hour Le Mans race in 1959, sharing an Aston Martin with Carroll Shelby. The following year, Salvadori's Aston, shared with the then-unknown Jim Clark, was 3rd, but he won 8 other sports and GT races that year and finished 2nd in 2 others to Stirling Moss. In 1961 Salvadori won 1 and placed in 2 of the Tasman Series races and did well the rest of the year, except in World Championship races where he finished with 2 solitary points. He nearly won his initial GP at Watkins Glen that season, but his engine blew as he was closing on the leading Innes Ireland. Still, 1961 had to be a memorable year in the Salvadori

book for his Whitsun International day at Crystal Palace, if for nothing else. There, Roy won the Norbury Trophy in an E-type Jag, took the Green Helmet Trophy in a Cooper-Monaco, and won the London Trophy in a F1 Cooper-Climax.

Two serious crashes in 1962—one at Warwick Farm, Australia, in February when he cracked up a Cooper-Climax at 130 m.p.h., and the other at Oulton Park's Gold Cup in August when his 3.8-litre Jaguar blew a tire and somersaulted into a lake at 90 m.p.h.—caused Salvadori to reduce his racing plans drastically for 1963. He refused a F1 berth and concentrated on sports, GT, and touring-car races from then on. Despite another serious crash, this time at Le Mans when his Jaguar hit an oil patch and spun into a multi-car scramble, it was a good season for Salvadori, and 1964 was even better. He won the Silverstone Trophy and Goodwood Whitsun races in a Cooper-Maserati sports car and the Snetterton Scott-Brown Memorial in a 250 LM Ferrari, was 2nd in the Monza Coppa Europa, and 3rd in the Brands Hatch Guards Trophy and the same venue's Ilford Trophy race. Salvadori cut down his active competition even more in 1965, instead concentrating on a job as team manager for BRM.

Always immaculately dressed, Salvadori was easy-going and a practical jokester throughout his racing career, attributes which he occasionally called upon during his team managing chores, as well. He had became deaf in one ear, but looked remarkably the same as he did 15 years earlier when he was first making a name for himself.

FRANKIE SANDS

If you ever saw Orr, Minn., in the winter you would know why Frankie Sands quit being sheriff there, to turn to race driving for his livelihood, instead of police sirens. There is nothing wrong with Orr in the spring, summer, or early fall, for it is surrounded by picturesque lakes and what used to be good hunting and fishing. But, in the winter, Orr is fit only for polar bears, skiers, and others of similar frigid vein. No wonder Sands decided to travel J. Alex Sloan's IMCA trail from Canada in the summer to Mexico in the winter.

Sands was what was known as a pacemaker. He would shoot out of the pack at a fearful rate of speed, virtually out of control, broadsliding his car wildly across the dirt. But he seldom was around at the finish, for he usually slid into a fence or broke his car. He was thrilling to watch, but the steady drivers like Sig Haugdahl took over to win. Of course, Sands piloted some rather obsolete vehicles, getting speed out of some of them which no one had suspected was still left. He owned a Dreyer when IMCA and Central States Racing Association stalwarts were shifting to Millers, switching to a revamped Peugeot for a 1937 campaign in CSRA.

Little else is known of Frankie Sands. He disappeared from racing during World War II.

ROSCOE SARLES

Handsome, dashing Roscoe Sarles was as daring a race driver as ever trod the boards of a Hollywood film stage or circled the boards of Beverly Hills Speedway. He rode his cars like an Indian scout delivering a do-or-die message, and so he finished high, or broke, or crashed. He seemed to have some guardian angel detailed personally to him until one day in 1922, when the angel must have been looking the other way.

Born in 1894, Sarles had gone to Butler University in his native Indiana to become a mechanical engineer, but he dropped out to seek work in Detroit's budding automobile history. It was at the Velie Motor Car Company that young Sarles was given his initial taste of racing as the company's car tester and pilot of their racing version that campaigned across Michigan in 1915.

In 1916 Sarles shifted his allegiance to the Roamer Company of Kalamazoo, Mich.; a life-long allegiance, even after he left them for more lucrative racing ties, he still promoted their passenger vehicle, using it exclusively. He spent his 1st year primarily as a car tester and mechanic; then, when the firm attempted major-league competition in 1917, he became number 2 pilot to Eddie Hearne. In various places, such as Sheepshead Bay, Omaha, Chicago, and Ascot, young Sarles competed, usually playing the hare to Hearne's hound. He finally settled in a kind of permanent residence near Holly-

wood, because there was work there between races. Hollywood was then going through one of its periodical racing-movie crazes; most of the racing footage was filmed at Ascot. Sarles became friendly with the movie colony; such that contacts added to his income as a racing actor.

His reputation for driving with total abandon was often sustained. At Santa Monica in 1919, at the last road race held on this city's streets, Sarles raced in typical fashion. Roscoe and riding mechanic Ernie Austerburg were among the race favorites in their Roamer. Despite the hot temperatures that day, the crowd was in the tens of thousands. When the starter's flag dropped, Sarles floored the accelerator, sending the car screaming for the lead. One after another, he picked off the cars ahead until he was moving up on 2nd place. Then, in an attempt to shave an outside corner, Sarles lost control, and hurtling into the wire fencing and sand bags isolating the crowds from the course. The barrier did its job admirably. Sarles and his mechanic landed in somebody's front yard unhurt.

Later that year, at Indianapolis, Sarles drove a converted Barney Oldfield Golden Submarine. Its egg-shaped body had been removed, replaced by a conventional 2-seater racing body. Unfortunately, the car lasted only 8 laps. So Sarles returned to the Roamer for the rest of 1919. Two 2nd places were his best finishes that year, in the Elgin, Ill., road races, and in the final Ascot race, after dueling all the way with Joe Boyer. He also finished well up at Sheepshead Bay, N.Y., and at Uniontown, Pa. But this was his last year using the Roamer as his racing mount.

For 1920 Roscoe signed to drive a Frontenac for Louis Chevrolet. In the Washington's Birthday race at Beverly Hills, he started fast again but fell back, just managing to stay in the top 10. The Sarles Frontenac at Indy lasted 58 laps. He did a little better at Tacoma, Wash., and at Uniontown, but still no major victory. He did not finish at Elgin, and in 6 other major starts had crashes that were awesome in their cinematic suddenness. Sarles always emerged virtually unscathed. For instance, in a special race at Indianapolis staged for France's Marshal Foch, Sarles had rolled the car, but managed to walk away.

The month of October, 1920, saw Sarles on the move once again. He joined the Duesenberg team when Tommy Milton switched to Frontenac, taking over Tommy's mount. He placed 2nd in the inaugural race at the Fresno, Calif., board track, setting the stage for his initial major AAA victory. Averaging more than 110 m.p.h. for the 250 miles, Sarles won the Thanksgiving Day Beverly Hills event. It was also a tragedy-ridden contest, in which Eddie O'Donnell, O'Donnell's mechanic, and Gaston Chevrolet died in a crash near the end of the event.

The following year (1921) was to be Roscoe Sarles's

greatest year. Now 27 and married—his wife wanted him to quit competition—Sarles seemed to have developed some sense of pace. A sprint program at Beverly Hills saw Sarles win a semi, and place 2nd to Ralph DePalma in the 75-mile main. In April of the same year, in the Fresno 150-miler, Sarles dogged Joe Thomas, the eventual winner, all the way before finishing 2nd. Then came the Indianapolis 500.

Sarles's Duesy was acknowledged to be one of the fastest cars in the race, but Augie Duesenberg impressed upon him that this must be a team effort. He drove relatively conservatively until, in the final stages of the 500, he lay 2nd behind leader Tommy Milton's fast-fading Frontenac. Now was the time to force the pace, now was the time to make the Frontenac break or wear itself out at an accelerated pace. But Sarles was following orders, circling the Speedway almost sedately. Finally his pit crew began to give the "GO" signal, waving frantically to catch Roscoe's attention. For some reason he failed to understand, or perhaps expected his riding mechanic to watch the pits, but he continued right at the same steady pace into 2nd place, in a classic he could have won.

However, just to prove he was every bit as good a driver as Milton, Sarles later agreed to a match race for both a $10,000 purse and the rights to the title of World Sprint King at Beverly Hills. He won 2 of the 3 25-mile heats, handing Tommy a convincing defeat. In September, Sarles came from far behind to win Uniontown's Universal Trophy 225-miler, then avenged a 3rd-place finish earlier at the Cotati, Calif., board-track inaugural to win there in October's 150-miler. If there ever was a close race, this was it. After the early leaders had burned one another out, Sarles and Joe Thomas emerged as the lead competitors. They raced wheel-to-wheel, 1st one, then the other, assuming the lead. On the last lap, Thomas pulled a car length ahead, making his move early. It was not good enough. Sarles met the challenge and, with a nicely timed burst of speed, flashed across the finish the winner by the width of his front wheels.

There was much talk in the Sarles household that 1922 was to be the final year of competition. Opportunities for the good life seemed possible in a movie career, because Roscoe was good-looking. Then Cliff Durant wanted Sarles to end his Roamer affiliation and become a salesman for the Durant passenger car. Whether Roscoe would eventually have accepted, no one would ever know. After a 3rd place at Beverly Hills, and good finishes at San Carlos, Cotati, and Fresno, Sarles chose to let Ora Haibe run his Duesenberg at Indy, while he ran a Frontenac. Roscoe lasted 88 laps; Haibe finished.

It was apparent that Sarles had cooled his driving style still further, but mechanical woes dogged him all summer. He just could not seem to finish, and now it was September and the opening of the Kansas City board track. Sarles had been scheduled to run the Duesenberg in the rich 300-mile race, but then Durant was called back to Los Angeles. To ensure publicity for his passenger car of the same name, Cliff wanted his Durant racer to run at Kansas City. He sought out Sarles, who agreed to drive it. The car, which had a Miller engine in a Stutz chassis, was very fast but very squirrely. Sarles avoided the early mishaps in this bloody race—Thomas's car crashed into Murphy's car in the worst accident, injuring all 4 men involved—but he was wearing tires at a fearsome rate. Just after making his 2nd tire change, in the far turn, the Durant Special seemed intent upon beating the traffic out of the track. It headed straight through the outer guard rail, then burst into flames. C.V. Pickup, Sarles's mechanic, was thrown clear by the impact, but Sarles himself was trapped in the car by a piece of the wooden railing, burning to death. A wheel from the Durant had struck Pete DePaolo's car, causing it, too, to crash, injuring both DePaolo and his mechanic.

Roscoe Sarles's fabulous luck had finally ended. He was found with his hands before his face, apparently to keep it from the flames, the heavy piece of wood across him like his own tombstone.

SWEDE SAVAGE

The kid was shaggy-haired, blond, and awkward, a teenager who was just becoming a man. He got on his Harley-Davidson, and kicked the starter. It was in 1963 at the Ascot race track in Gardena, Calif., where he looked the youngest by far of the leather-jacketed riders lining up across the start finish line. But when the race started, it was obvious that the youngest was the best. He handled the Harley-Davidson factory machine as if it were a much lighter bike, using its raw power to sweep through the field.

This was David Earle Savage Jr., All-American boy, protégé of a Ford public relations man and Dan Gurney and John Holman and others who watched him handle competition machinery. This was Swede Savage, who had hated the nickname since he was 9 years of age and racing quarter midgets. He was a go-kart racing factory team member at 12, California scrambles champion at age 16 and 17, and an Expert bike rider at 17.

Born on August 26, 1946, he married early, and was an indifferent junior college student. Swede was working in a motorcycle dealership when he met Dan Gurney, part owner. The two rode bikes in the desert and became good friends before Gurney gave him a test in a Group 7 (CanAm type) automobile and became immediately enthusiastic. Swede, Gurney decided, was a natural—a good athlete, a man who wanted to win and who was settled and intelligent enough to work for it.

531

Gurney had wanted Savage, but Monty Roberts had gotten him first. Roberts was a public relations man and Savage was a PR dream—the looks, the catchy name, the ability. Roberts got him to Holman-Moody in Charlotte, N.C., where he languished for several months before Holman sent him to Bondy Long's South Carolina facility to pick out an old Dick Hutcherson car for a race at Hickory, N.C. Swede took the old car and pushed it to 3rd place, against Dixie's finest, before its rear end gave out. There came more good placings in short-track Grand Nationals in the same car, and the Holman-Moody people were predicting ultimate Grand National stardom for Savage.

But, late in 1967, Gurney called to offer Savage a shot at becoming road racer and Indy driver with his All-American Racing organization. Swede accepted. He ran 5 CanAm races for Gurney in a McLaren, with a 4th at Bridgehampton his best finish. He came back to NASCAR for 3 more Grand Nationals, receiving a 3rd at Bristol, a 2nd at Rockingham, and a DNF.

In 1969, the purse strings tightened for the AAR organization; for most races, there was no 2nd AAR car. Ford gave Swede a Mercury at the Daytona 500, but, after qualifying 10th fastest, he lost a wheel and crashed on the 123rd lap while running 4th. He drove 3 USAC Championship Trail road races, an SCCA TransAm, and the Sebring SCCA Continental, where he won pole position from Mario Andretti in an Eagle-Plymouth Formula A, but retired with mechanical ills.

For 1970 Swede had an AAR ride with Gurney in the Plymouth Barracuda TransAm cars, but this was threatened early in the season when Plymouth had to chop its racing budget. However, Gurney gave up his car in order to make sure Savage had a mount. While Savage did not quite justify Gurney's generosity by winning, he was often on the pole in a car that was obviously under development.

In October 1970, Gurney retired as a driver, announcing that Savage would join Bobby Unser, among others, in Dan's 1971 effort. As a tune-up, Unser and Savage were entered in the Bobby Ball 150 at Phoenix the following month, a race that seemed to be pivotal for Savage, there was high drama in this race.

On the front row, the Unser brothers—Al just a shade faster than Bobby—sat awaiting the pace lap. Behind them were A. J. Foyt and Savage. As the pack was waved off, Savage continued to sit on the grid with a dead engine. While the rest of the field moved around the track, the AAR crew worked frantically to get Savage into the race. With the cars returning, they had to push Savage's Eagle-Ford to the inside guard rail. Officials again sent the rest of the field around the circuit, allowing AAR to solve the problem—fuel feed faults. Savage then roared into life, and moved to take his proper place in the 2nd row of the gird.

At the flag, Bobby Unser charged into the lead. After 5 laps, he still led, with brother Al, A. J. Foyt, Lloyd Ruby, Wally Dallenbach, and Savage behind him. Wally and Swede both moved up a place a lap or two later, but the field remained much the same. The Unsers and Foyt were having their own little battle, but back in the pack were Savage, Rutherford, and Dallenbach, some

15 seconds behind the leading trio. Foyt bit the dust on lap 35, Rutherford replacing him in 3rd. Swede battled for 4th, but slipped to 5th, as Roger McCluskey took over 3rd behind Al Unser and Rutherford. Bobby Unser, meanwhile, had been black-flagged, with an oil gusher.

Rutherford lost it on a turn and dropped back several places, with McCluskey assuming 2nd, and Dallenbach and Savage close behind. Al Unser led by half a lap at the 100-lap mark, but, on lap 120, his engine started acting up, and he had to slow, allowing McCluskey to close the gap. Then complete power failure sent Al into the fence, and he had to pit to check out damage. Dallenbach and Savage swept by to take over 1st and 2nd. When Unser returned, he was 3rd and Andretti, who had been lapped, was in his way.

Swede, meanwhile, had his Eagle's nose practically planted in McCluskey's car, and they swept around that way until, coming out of turn 2 on the last lap, Roger's car suddenly slowed, his engine starving for fuel. He drifted high on the banking. With almost 17,000 people roaring from the stands, Savage zipped by the Scorpion-Offy turbocar, followed by Al Unser's Colt-Ford turbo, McCluskey managing to limp in 3rd. Dan Gurney had his initial victory as a team manager, and Swede Savage had tasted victory as a professional for the 1st what everyone was sure would be many times.

But a year later, in 1971, the railbirds were not so sure. There was an accident at the Questor Grand Prix, in which Savage, in a Formula A car, crashed, suffering serious head injuries that were to sideline him for much of the 1971 season. He returned to an assortment of rides, in USAC, on the TransAm, and elsewhere. There were no victories. Savage seemed to have lost that exquisite sense of timing, and was apparently substituting reckless courage. Or it may have been that he was impaired physically. In any event, he crashed several times; each time before he crashed, his car seemed to waver.

Savage accomplished little in 1972's USAC Triple Crown driving a Brabham Offy. He finished 20th at Ontario, Calif., 23rd at Pocono, Pa., and 32nd at Indy. It was too bad. His luck ran out completely in a fiery crash at Indianapolis 1973, in a Patrick Petroleum car. He lingered until July 2, when he succumbed to his injuries and burns.

EVERITT SAYLOR

A fearless sort, born in Brookville, Ohio, October 8, 1909, Everitt Saylor always preferred the slick-oiled dirt banks of the Midwest. But he had dazzled Eastern dirt circles by wearing spotless white knickers when he cleaned up in the area, this earning him the title of "Sissy Britches."

He was a star of IMCA, and of the Central States Racing Association, setting records at Winchester, Ind., and at the old VFW track in Detroit. On his favorite surface, Saylor could compete with the best, including Rex Mays or Duke Nalon. On asphalt, he seemed to be just another driver; maybe less, for, in his only Indianapolis appearance in 1941, Saylor spun on the north straightaway, flipping and injuring himself seriously after 157 laps. Sissy Britches drove a Dreyer d.o.h.c. 8-valve car that made enough noise for an entire field. After World War II interrupted the Indy classics, Saylor did not return to the track, and has not been heard of since.

JACK SCALES

While today's racing enthusiast tends to think of Grand Prix drivers as pretty much an international group, and the signing of one or two Americans or Britons for an Italian racing team like Ferrari as something very natural, this was not always the case, especially in the days before World War I. John E. Scales was the exception, however.

Scales, born in 1886 in England, spent most of his competitive life with Italian marques and a good part of his life living in Italy. He joined the Fiat company as a teenage apprentice about 1904 at their English distributors. Five years later, he moved to Turin, and remained there through World War II in the firm's test department. Known as "Scahless," the closest the Italians could come to pronouncing his name, he began by racing motorcycles for Zenith, another Italian firm. Fiat soon recognized Scales's talent and moved him over to the racing department. One of his first duties was working on the 300-h.p. racer Fiat built for Felice Nazzaro to assault speed records, often serving as the great Italian driver's racing mechanic on these runs. In 1914, Scales was given his first Fiat ride in the French GP at Lyons; he was doing better than the other 2 factory entries when a timing gear broke.

After the war, Scales left Fiat, which had been concentrating on Allied war items such as trucks and airplanes, and returned to England. He and Cyrill Snipe rebuilt 2 staid Eric Campbells into racing cars, entering them in the 1919 Targa Florio. But they had to retire with mechanical problems. He appeared next at Indianapolis for the 500-mile race in 1920, with Albert Guyot, in a 3-litre Gregoire which failed to finish.

The following years, Scales became associated with Amedeo Chiribiri, and helped design the 4-cylinder d.o.h.c., 1500 c.c. Chiribiri voiturette, which was among the 1st entries at the new Monza Autodroma in Italy. In Scales's hands, this car won its class in several important European hillclimbs. Scales moved on to the Sunbeam-Talbot-Darracq marque in Paris as its chief tester, and came into his most productive period as a competition driver. This portion of his career was topped by his 1924 victory in the inaugural race at Montlhéry, the 186-mile Grand Prix de l'Ouverture, in which he nosed out Henry Segrave in a photo finish at an average speed of 100.3 m.p.h.

Returning to England, Scales retired from competition and opened a motoring engineering concern. He continued at that through World War II until a heart condition took him from the automotive scene. When he died on October 23, 1962, at age 76, few of his Surbiton neighbors knew they lived near a famous driver, mechanic, and designer.

LUDOVICO SCARFIOTTI

Ludovico Scarfiotti made September 4, 1966, a day to be remembered even in such scattered places as Akron, Turin, and Monza. That was the day, and Monza was the place when the 33-year-old Turin-born Scarfiotti, piloting a Ferrari equipped with Akron-made Firestone tires, won the 37th running of the Italian Grand Prix. It was Scarfiotti's 1st (and only) *grande épreuve* victory. It was also the 1st GP ever won on Firestone tires, which feat was advertised all over the United States.

Born October 18, 1933, in Turin, Scarfiotti was the grandson of the 1st president of Fiat. Both his grandfather and father had raced as amateurs, so it was natural that Lulu, as he was nicknamed at school, should try the sport in 1955. It was also natural that his 1st mount should be a Fiat 1100 coupe, in which he competed in the American equivalent of club meetings. Scarfiotti's most notable success in his opening years of Fiat racing was a class victory in the 1956 Mille Miglia.

In 1957, Scarfiotti moved into a more exotic Fiat, a Zagato-bodied 2-litre with a V-8 powerplant. The car

stood him in good stead in Italian national competition, giving him both the national hillclimb and circuit titles. Scarfiotti repeated both successes the following year in an 1100-c.c. OSCA Sport. The back-to-back championships earned him a factory berth with OSCA, and he again won both titles with the 1500-c.c. version of the car.

Any Italian who could drive that well attracted the eye of Commendatore Enzo Ferrari. So Scarfiotti was offered a factory ride in a Ferrari sports car for the Buenos Aires 1000 in 1960. Scarfiotti eagerly accepted the codrive with Froilan Gonzales, showing big-car ability until the Ferrari broke down. That same season, he shared Ferraris with Willy Mairesse in the Targa Florio, and with Giorgio Scarlatti in the 24-hour Le Mans and Nurburgring races, but all 3 times without much success.

Ferrari didn't call on him for 1961 drives, forcing Scarfiotti to return to the OSCA, but it was not a successful season. Yet the Commendatore did call for 1962; Scarfiotti was to concentrate on the European Mountain Championship, to do battle with the all-conquering Porsche in this hillclimb series. Scarfiotti responded by winning the championship with his factory-supported, Scuderia Sant-Ambroeus-entered 2-litre Dino. He also drove a few races, his best a 3rd (with codriver Colin Davis of Britain) in the Montlhéry 1000 in a Serenissima-entered Ferrari GTO.

In 1963 Scarfiotti became an official Ferrari team driver. It was a good year. With John Surtees, Lulu shared a big victory at Sebring in an early Ferrari 250P. In the Targa Florio he, Mairesse, and Lorenzo Bandini finished 2nd. At Nurburgring, Scarfiotti and Britain's Mike Parkes won. At Le Mans, he and Bandini were 3rd. At this time, Scarfiotti tried Formula 1 racing, with the Dutch GP at sandy Zandvoort as his 1st try; Ludovico was 6th. In his 2nd event, he smashed himself up pretty well at Rheims in the French GP.

Initially Scarfiotti announced he was retiring, but later he changed his mind. To test himself, he partnered Nino Vaccarella in the 1964 Sebring race, finishing 2nd. The same pair won at Nurburgring. Parkes and Scarfiotti were well-placed at Le Mans that year when their car died. Did he feel up to F1 racing? Scarfiotti said yes, and was given the team's 3rd (and poorest) car, a V-6, while Surtees and Bandini got the new V-8, at the Italian GP. The results were predictable: Surtees won, Bendini was 3rd, Scarfiotti 9th. In the Canadian GP at Mosport (a nonchampionship event), it was Ferrari 1st and 2nd with Pedro Rodriguez and Scarfiotti doing the honors, respectively. In the year's last race, the Montlhéry 1000, Scarfiotti shared a Maranello Concessionaires (Ferrari's British outlet) entry with Scotland's Jackie Stewart, and was running 2nd when the car's steering linkage failed. Repairing it lost them enough time to place them 10th.

Ferrari was boycotting many races in 1965, but Scarfiotti had a ride anyway with Centro Sud's team, using the hand-me-down 1962 BRM. The Brands Hatch Race of Champions was the 1st effort, but a wasted one. In April at Syracuse (Italy), Scarfiotti finished 5th, 2 laps behind winner Jim Clark, then took 2nd with Surtees in the Monza 1000. After a bad Targa Florio, Scarfiotti won the Nurburgring 1000 in a Surtees-shared car. The year was mainly devoted to shaking up European Mountain Championship seekers, however, with a version of his successful Nurburgring 1.6-litre V-6 Dino. In this car, Scarfiotti won every hillclimb he entered but the season's last at Gaisberg, where he drove just fast enough on a storm-torn day to nail down the overall hillclimb championship for himself and Ferrari.

The 1966 season was a success, if for nothing else than that 1st GP victory with the Firestone tires. Scarfiotti started only a single other F1 race, the German GP, but retired with battery trouble after 9 laps. In long-distance racing, however, he was really active, registering a 5th at Sebring and a 2nd at Nurburgring in cars shared with Lorenzo Bandini, and a taste of victory at the Spa GP in Belgium, sharing a winning Ferrari 330P3 coupe with Mike Parkes.

Scarfiotti did virtually nothing in GP in 1967, but managed 2nds with Parkes at both Monza and Le Mans in endurance racing. In the nonchampionship Syracuse GP, he and Parkes finished in a dead heat for the checker, with one of the Italian's 121.82 m.p.h. laps making a course record. In addition to his Ferrari rides, Scarfiotti had tried some GP races in one of Dan Gurney's Eagles, but the car was not really ready that year, and the season was one of frustrations.

Porsche, an old nemesis, signed Scarfiotti for the 1968 hillclimb season, as did Cooper for the GP season. For the latter, Scarfiotti registered a 4th both at Monaco and in Spain; the placings augured a good season. But on June 8, 1968, while practicing for the Rossfeld hillclimb later in the year in Germany, Scarfiotti was killed. His Porsche 910 was speeding at nearly 100 m.p.h., when it veered, brakes smoking, and plunged off the German Alpine road into a group of trees. When the car struck the trees, Scarfiotti was catapulted from the cockpit and thrown another 50 yards. He died in the ambulance of multiple fractures.

Only a few minutes before, another driver had crashed in much the same way at almost the same spot, and had managed to walk away with only a broken arm and hand injuries. In both cases, the cars seemed mechanically perfect. What really happened no one knows.

HARRY SCHELL

Unpredictable, irresponsible, volatile, dynamic, and a thousand more adjectives were used to describe Henry O'Reilly Schell, 1st American to become a full-time professional member of a European Formula 1 team in modern times. He never won a Grand Prix race in a 14-year career, yet left his mark upon the international racing scene with numerous high finishes.

Schell was born June 29, 1921, in Paris, France. Schell's parents were not millionaires but were sufficiently well-to-do to have an apartment in Paris, a villa in Monte Carlo, and a stable of automobiles during the burgeoning European racing era occurring shortly after World War I. Eventually, Schell's parents had also organized and supported the Ecurie Bleu racing team not only on the Continent, but also at Indianapolis in 1940 where 2 Schell 8CTF Maseratis were entered.

Thus it was natural that young Harry, as he moved into his teenage years, became interested in motor racing. He accompanied Luigi Chinetti, Ecurie Bleu team manager in those days, and later Rene Dreyfus and Rene LeBegue, the drivers, to Indy in 1940; and it was at Indy that he caught the racing bug. But World War II interfered; Schell spent part of the war in Monaco and part in the U.S. Army. Discharged in 1946, Harry bought a 1937 supercharged Maser, and made his competition debut in a Riviera race. His next competitive entry was at Indianapolis itself, to which he brought the ancient Maserati and codriver Louie Gerard. Chinetti acted as adviser after he found that he couldn't dissuade Harry from giving the big race a try. Harry was out on the bricks practicing when the car's engine blew, showering him with metal. He escaped unhurt.

Back in Europe, Schell bought a new 1100 c.c. Cisitalia that he raced with indifferent success in 1947. His machine was simply outclassed by the newer Simca-

Gordinis. After that, he purchased both a Formula 2 Cooper-JAP and a 4.5-litre Talbot sports car; the story with these cars was virtually the same as with the Cisitalia. Schell must have shown something, however, because Britain's John Heath signed him up temporarily for his 3-car HWM team. Heath's faith was immediately rewarded when Schell took 2nd at the Naples GP, just behind Alberto Ascari in a formidable Ferrari, and ahead of another Modena car driven by Franco Cortese.

This led to a full-time team berth with Enrico Plate's shoestring Maserati-Plate team. Plate, a skilled Italian mechanic, was attempting to do something with the 1.5-litre supercharged 4CLT Maserati, a very undependable car in its factory configuration. Plate's changes did little for the automobile; Schell still had to find a mount that would allow him to display his prowess. Gordini hired him away from Plate who was then in financial trouble. With Gordini, Schell did well, with a 2nd at Cadours, France, his top 1952 showing. The following season he was 3rd in the Pau GP, behind Ferraris driven by Ascari and Mike Hawthorn, and 4th in the Bordeaux GP. In the Dutch GP his transmission failed; in the Italian GP he was 9th, finishing despite the failure of one of his cylinders midway in the race.

Gordini had money problems by this time, too. With one race left for the Formula 2 cars, Schell's factory Gordini was impounded by creditors in Milan. A torrent of persuasive words freed it for him the day of the Modena race, but only to have the car that was towing the racer break down. The never-say-die Schell drove the GP car the rest of the way to Modena, still on only 5 cylinders. Schell raced that way, too, finishing 5th, even though another cylinder cut out in the final stages. The performance rated near Schell's Le Mans performance earlier that same year when he and Maurice Trintignant finished 1st in the 3-litre class with their 2.5-litre car, 3rd in the Index of Performance, and 6th overall, after actually threatening the leaders a good part of the 24-hour race.

Schell went independent again in 1954, purchasing Juan Fangio's year-old 2-litre Maserati and reworking it into a 2.5-litre car to battle the latest GP cars. The car sported an American flag on its hood, much like the one that Schell wore over his uniform pocket. In the opener, the Argentine GP at Buenos Aires, Schell was 6th. About this time, he also teamed with Alfonso de Portago, the Spanish-nobleman-turned-racing-driver, in a 3-litre V-12 Ferrari. They did well in several races; at Sebring Schell's 1st U.S. road race, the car was up with the leaders before it broke down early in the 12-hour battle.

Returning to Europe, he was 2nd to Stirling Moss's Maserati at the Rome GP with a pit crew that consisted of 2 French movie stars; Schell always had an eye for the ladies. In the European GP at Nurburgring, his Maser quit on the final lap; he pushed the car over the line as several others passed him, but finished 7th nonetheless. In the Pescara, Italy, GP only 3 cars finished;

one of them was Schell's Maserati, 3rd, behind up-to-date factory-prepared Masers. At Aintree, England, he again was 3rd.

In 1954 Harry had also teamed with Moss at Le Mans in a 4.5-litre Maser, his last appearance there, because he felt the race too dangerous. Observers agreed he generally was better in the bigger cars and in smaller fields rather than in the traffic jams of these big sports car races. His father, Laury, had been at Le Mans in 1937; 16 years later, Harry toured the course with Trintignant in his Gordini for a 6th place. In 1955 the pair, now in a 4.4-litre Ferrari, retired with mechanical troubles.

It was at the Spanish GP in October 1954, that Schell became a favorite of European racing fans. After the 1st lap, they had expected to see Fangio and other Mercedes-Benz cars in the lead, with Stirling Moss and his Ferrari and other cars like Schell's blue-and-white Maserati trailing far back. Instead, Harry was leading the initial time around and the 2nd. He lost the lead twice, when he had to pit for gas—part of his strategy was to start with half-filled tanks to better his acceleration—but held it for the most part until the 21st lap, when his old teammate, Trintignant, sneaked past with the lead Ferrari. On the next lap, Hawthorn and Schell had a brush that ended with Schell off the course. By the time he recovered, he was 4th, and could not better that position although he tried. He received the fans' ovation despite retiring with a damaged rear axle.

Soon after, Schell's old mentor, Chinetti, pointed out Schell's improvement to Ferrari. It was seemingly unnecessary, because the factory already was thinking hard about signing Schell to replace Hawthorn, who was moving to Britain's Vanwell. In March 1955, Harry made his Ferrari debut in the Valentino GP at Turin, finishing 5th, the only finisher of 3 Ferraris. At Monte Carlo, that season's European GP site, he had run up from 16th to 8th despite handling problems before the car's engine blew. Hawthorn returned to Ferrari soon after, and Schell moved over to his vacated Vanwall spot. His victories in Tony Vandervell's cars in 1955 included a double at Castle Combe in its Avon Trophy and open formula races, and a single at Snetterton.

The following season Schell won the Caen GP with a Maserati and shared another in a victory at the Nurburgring 1000 with Moss, Jean Behra, and Piero Taruffi. In sports car racing, he and Luigi Musso pushed their Ferrari home 2nd at Sebring. With Vanwall, Schell, at the height of his powers, perhaps, led 6 different Grands Prix only to be retired with blown engines.

In 1957, the story was again the same. At the Caen GP, for example, at which another BRM scored the marque's initial victory, Schell broke the lap record twice, and was leading when his engine again blew. With Maserati, he was 2nd at Pau and 3rd at Pescara (behind Moss and Fangio) and Modena. Teaming up with Moss at Sebring in a 3-litre Maser, Schell shared 2nd place.

BRM signed Schell and Behra for the 1958 season,

and Schell had to suffer with developing machinery once more. He was 5th at Monte Carlo, the 1st time he finished in 4 tries at the twisty course in Monaco; 2nd to Moss's Vanwall in the Dutch GP revival; 5th in the British race; 6th in Portugal; and 5th in the Morocco GP. At Monza, he had a brush with death when Wolfgang von Trips's Ferrari ran up the back of Schell's BRM, wrecking both cars. Schell returned to the pits to display a crash helmet smeared with red from the underpan of Trips's car where it passed over the cockpit.

In 1959, Schell was 3rd at Goodwood's Glover Trophy battle behind Moss and Jack Brabham in Coopers; he once more headed the BRM team with Jo Bonnier replacing Behra. Moss's Cooper edged Schell at the Formula 2 Rouen GP; Schell was 7th in the European GP at Rheims, 4th at Avus in the German race, 5th in the Portuguese GP, 7th at Monza. At Monte Carlo, his car had crashed again. The fatal season was the next one, when Schell switched from BRM to Alfred Moss's and Ken Gregory's Yeoman Credit team of Coopers.

Harry was a superstitious man; in the end his superstition about Friday the 13th proved his undoing. It was at Silverstone, England, in May 1960, in the rain and in practice; rain and practice were 2 things that Schell hated. His Cooper was rounding Beckett's Corner when it hit a monstrous puddle and spun; a low brick wall—only 18 inches high—was ahead but the car failed to smash it. Instead it flipped, landing with Schell underneath. His neck was broken, killing him instantly.

Schell was not a great driver, but he was a great personality. He delighted in extreme statements—in 1958, when FIA announced its new 1.5-litre formula 1 for Grands Prix in 1961, Schell announced he was forming a rival international sanctioning body to oppose the move. The site for his announcement was an ideal one, his own l'Action Automobile bar in Paris, where he spent non-racing hours if he were not at his Deauville villa or abroad his 25-foot cabin cruiser. Another time, after the Levegh holocast at Le Mans, he called the race's organizers "murderers."

He considered himself a cautious driver; so did others. He wanted desperately to win a major GP race, at least in his early years, but he was unwilling to kill himself or someone else to do it. He believed in making his own luck, not in inheriting good or bad luck. "Racing is a drug," he once said; "I am addicted to it."

TIM SCHENKEN

Scratch Jack Brabham. Insert Tim Schenken. It almost went that way. Black Jack raced through 1970, then retired from Formula 1. Tim Schenken came onto the F1 scene late that year in Frank Williams's De Tomaso-Ford 505 to get his feet wet by running a few laps in the Italian, Canadian and United States Grands Prix before retiring in each race. In 1971 he joined the Brabham team behind Graham Hill to continue Australia's F1 representation.

It represented the ultimate a racing fan's dream, for Brabham was Schenken's sports idol. Born in Sydney September 26, 1943, Schenken was 9 years old when he 1st saw Brabham race in the Tasman series in 1953. From that moment on, Schenken wanted to be a racing driver. He grew up in Melbourne, and his 1st car 8 years later (in 1961) was an old Austin A30, which he raced locally. By 1965 he had acquired a Lotus 18, Colin Chapman's 1st rear-engined design, and was running in the Australian version of Formula 2, that is, Formula Junior without the normal FJ weight restrictions. Schenken won 10 of 12 starts in this car, including the Victorian championship, and also won the Australian Hillclimb Championship in a local 500 c.c. car called the "White Special."

In February 1966 Schenken went to Britain, where he eventually signed on as a mechanic on the Chequered Flag team. Over the next year, he had but a single ride in a formula car, "to shut me up," Tim recalled, "because I had been pestering them for six months about it." On a rainy Silverstone track, he finished 7th in one of the Flag's Formula 3 Brabhams. He also managed a few drives in a twin-cam Anglia until the car was sold, but other than these few rides, Schenken's career was stalled. He was eventually able to buy an old Lotus 22 which he and a friend, Charles Beattie, who was to work with Tim from then on, updated with Lotus 41 wheels, better suspension, adjustable sway bars, and other refinements.

Schenken made 22 starts in this rather uncompetitive car before it ended its career against a Crystal Palace fence late in the season, when a wishbone broke. But the drives were not wasted, for Tim's performances were impressive enough for Rodney Bloor to offer him a F3 drive for 1968 with the Sports Motors (Manchester) Ltd. team. Schenken was given a Chevron temporarily, with the idea of replacing it with a Titan later in the season. However, by the time the latter arrived, Tim had so sorted out the original car that the Titan was raced only once (winning at Oulton Park), then sold, while Schenken continued to race the F3 car and his own Formula-Ford Merlyn acquired at the end of 1967.

In 1968, Schenken took 35 FF victories and some 15 more in F3, plus other good placing. It was a record so startling that there was some speculation that it might have been the greatest number of victories scored by a single-seater driver in a season of major racing. Schenken did not confine his racing to Britain; he won 3 Belgian FF events, one at Spa and 2 at Zolder. He managed some Lotus 47 sports-car rides, too, to sharpen his skills for 1969. The lean and lanky Australian became a Brabham team driver for F3 that year, in a BT28. He won at Jarama, Oulton, Barcelona, Crystal Palace, Albi, and Caldwell Park, and finished in a dead heat with Reine Wisell at Montlhéry. Schenken's black and red

Guards Cigarette-supported car also was 2nd at Mallory Park, Hockenheim, Brands Hatch, Karlskoga, Crystal Palace again, Rouen, and Pau, among other placings. His sports-car racing took him as far away as Kyalami for the 9-hour race in South Africa, and he drove a Ford V-6 Capri in the Tour de France and the Marathon de la Route.

Formula 2 beckoned in 1970, with Brabham's Sports Motors team in a BT30, and Schenken finished 4th in the European Trophy series with a 2nd at Paul Ricard, 3rds at Pau and Mantorp Park, and a 5th at Rouen among others. In 13 starts, he finished 9 races, retired 3 times, had a minor accident. Piers Courage's death and Frank Williams's subsequent search for another Grand Prix pilot for his private team led to the three F1 rides for Schenken at the tail end of 1970. Unfortunately, the De Tomaso-Ford 505 still needed sorting out, each race leading to a retirement. The Ford engine gave out after 18 laps in Italy; a rear suspension broke after 62 laps in the U.S. GP; in Canada, it was a general malaise. But Schenken had shown that he could handle the big cars, and there seemed to be little doubt that before 1971 had run its course he would be in the thick of World Championship racing.

Schenken missed the South African F1 opener, but finished 4th in the nonchampionship Race of Champions at Brands Hatch and 5th in another nontitle race, the Questor GP. In Spain, he was 9th; in the nontitle Silverstone International, 3rd. At Monaco, Schenken finished 10th, but in Holland he retired after a shunt with Henri Pescarolo. Twelfth in France, though not running at the race's end, he did the same in the British GP. Sixth in Germany, Schenken did his best 1971 work at the Austrian GP where he finished 3rd behind Jo Siffert and Emerson Fittipaldi. He would have had a 3rd in France and Britain but for late mechanical failures. The year did not end well, with 3 retirements in Italy, Canada, and the U.S. races. Schenken's 5 championship points tied him with Howden Ganley for 14th.

Although he had little sports-car experience, apart from a Matra ride at Le Mans in 1969, Schenken signed on with Ferrari for sports car rides in 1972, partnered with Ronnie Peterson. He had won an F2 race at Cordoba, Argentina, late in November 1971, in a Brabham, and had shared a Ferrari with Peterson for a victory at Buenos Aires. Early in the new year, Tim surprised everyone by leaving Brabham for John Surtees's F1 team. Tim's 5th-place finish in the opening Argentine GP presaged good days ahead, but it turned out to be his best GP of the year.

BILL SCHINDLER

He was a prize fighter but not a very good one, before he ever thought of cars. He stopped fighting "because I always ended up looking worse than the men I beat." That was Bill Schindler, king of the "doodle bugs," the American midget racers. A remarkable man, not only because he raced most of his career with one leg missing, but because of his accomplishments in a difficult racing milieu.

Schindler (born about 1908) began competition at Anderson, Ind., in a Chevrolet-engined sprint car during the Depression. The stock-engined sprints were about the only kind of machinery inexpensive enough to campaign in that era when no one had much money either to watch or to maintain race cars. These cars were Schindler's training grounds from 1931 to 1934, while he was racing out of financial necessity. He competed with only fair success, even after 1934, when he came East for the inaugural midget car meet at Olympic Park in Irvington, N.J., and decided to stay because the race tracks were closer together in the New York-New Jersey-Pennsylvania area. During a 22-year career, which ended abruptly in 1952 in a crash at Allentown, Pa., Schindler raced at Indianapolis, on the AAA championship circuit, and even in late-model stock cars in a Hudson Hornet. But he made his fame mainly in midgets.

There is a turning point in each man's life, whether or not he realizes it at the time. For Broncho Bill Schindler the turning point came at the Mineola, N.Y., Fair in 1936. That spring and summer had been rather eventful for him. In a big-car race, he had rolled and broken his shoulder. In another race, he had collided with the guard rail in avoiding another car which had spun in front of him; he was thrown onto the track, his own car rolling over him. He also had flipped in a midget, was

538

treated in an ambulance for bruises, returned to his car, and won the main event. And in another crash that tore the front end off his car and catapulted Schindler like a man shot out of a cannon, he had suffered head injuries.

The turning point came when he lost his leg at Mineola. Asked years later how it happened, he replied with that slow grin of his: "I was trying to get by, and I thought there was enough room between this guy and the fence. There wasn't as much room as I thought. I tore up the fence, the car and my leg. Doctors took the leg off to stop gangrene from spreading through my system." It was after he came out of the hospital in the winter that he won the U.S. indoor championship and the Jimmy Cagney Trophy. Was it the loss of the leg that spurred him? Contemporaries are inclined to think not, though now he seemed to flower as he literally lived on the circuit—Boston Garden, Providence Arena, Madison Square Garden Bowl, and the Bronx Coliseum in the winter, and Eastern dirt tracks in the summer.

His contemporaries say that the bald Schindler merely matured after learning the hard way just what an automobile can be expected to do. Experience taught him well at places long gone like Castle Hill Speedway in the Bronx, Buffalo, Cedarhurst and Deer Park in New York, Lakeside in Atlanta, and Raleigh, N.C. Surely the man was a born leader. He was president of the American Racing Drivers Club for 6 of the 8 years that he was a member, and because of his handicap he was used extensively during World War II to tour hospitals, showing that loss of a limb need not end productive life.

Racing as much as 7 nights a week in the heyday of the midgets, Schindler had neither the time nor the desire to aspire to Indianapolis. When the so-called AAA hotshots came East, he beat them. This occurred especially on the board tracks in the Boston Garden and at the Nutley, N.J., Velodrome. But the record he set, which may never be surpassed since even midget racing has become a weekend and holiday sport, is 106 midget car victories in 1947 and 1948.

Schindler's reason for not going to Indianapolis sooner than he did was the same as that of another midget hero on the opposite side of America, Bill Vukovich. Asked about it in 1947, he said, "I'm doing all right without making the Indiana haul. Racing around home 7 nights a week for nightly purses of $3,000 makes it possible to win a lot of money without putting all my eggs in one basket. That's what I'd be doing if I took a month off for Indianapolis."

He didn't go until midget purses tapered off when the races became high-speed parades. Schindler had been content with 6 Eastern small-car titles in 8 years. He had finished 2nd the other 2 times. But by then he had family problems, and necessity again forced him to make a move. The man who saved his career was a fabulous little former riding mechanic and AAA official named Frank Del Roy. When Schindler finally said he was available late in 1949, Frankie made a coast-to-coast trip trying to convince car owners of Schindler's ability. But no one wanted a one-legged driver. They all said it would be a handicap in the big cars. Del Roy got only one nibble. Joie Chitwood of thrill-show fame was unable to fill a date to be the movie stand-in for Clark Gable in *To Please a Lady,* which was going to shoot some scenes before the Arlington, Tex., championship race.

Car owner Art Simms said he would let Schindler do this movie part. But Del Roy didn't tell Schindler it was only for the movie, because he hoped to persuade Simms to let Schindler race, too. He did convince Simms, and Schindler ran the race, finishing 2nd to Johnny Parsons, but still there was no Indy mount. Finally with Indy ever closer, Del Roy told Schindler the truth. "I might as well work in a pit crew if they don't want me as a driver," Bill said. But Del Roy didn't give up even at Indianapolis, and when the Chapman Special needed a replacement driver, Frank got Schindler the chance.

The AAA Contest Board was reluctant to permit him to take the rookie test, but his 2nd place at Arlington turned the tide; he steamed around in 132.690 m.p.h., fast for 1950. He didn't finish in the top 10 ever at Indianapolis, but he had proved his ability and had championship mounts from then on.

He won the pole in the December 1950, Darlington 250-mile championship car race and finished 2nd to Parsons again. Mechanical trouble usually dogged him, but he did win at Springfield, Ill., in record time. He was always a fast qualifier, often winning the pole. His fling with stocks, about 8 races, also was dogged by part failures on the Hudson he drove.

During most of his career, Schindler had personal woes. His son suffered from tuberculosis of the spine; Bill devoted every off-track hour to caring for him and his daughter. He was an amateur cook and cake decorator, a fact he kept well-hidden from rivals. He even liked to can peaches, do the ironing, and give his daughter permanents. But on the race track, he would always return to his 1st love, the midgets. At Olympic Park he had begun in the No. 2 Saxon of Bell Lawrence, most of his heyday he spent in the No. 2 Mike Caruso Offy, and in 1952, came the chance to race in the No. 2 Beale Offy. He took it. There was a stirring duel at the Morristown, N.J., track with Paul Russo a week before Allentown. Bill couldn't get past the Indy veteran, though they raced inches apart the entire distance.

The end at Allentown was an anticlimax. The accident was abrupt and unspectacular compared to some he had survived. There was no hanging by one hand on the wireguard rail until a mechanic dragged him to safety as at Nutley. There was no quadruple crash as at Syracuse Fairgrounds. He just seemed to lose control of the car. It flipped and it was all over. Schindler died instantly.

JO SCHLESSER

Jo Schlesser's career went backwards in some sense; as he grew older, he drove more and more exotic machines, including single-seaters, after having spent his earlier career in rally and saloon cars. Sixteen years is a long time to drive, and age 40 is an advanced age for Formula 1 racing.

He was born in Madagascar in 1928. His competition career started on the Continent around 1950, and in a few years he was a regular at the big international rally events, such as the Tour de France. He was at his best in the speed sections of these events, which inevitably led him to road racing and enduro drives, though much later than might be supposed. He emigrated to Europe from Madagascar in 1959, and soon he was splitting his time between the two fast pastimes; for example, in 1964 he shared 2nd with Pedro Rodriguez at the Paris 1000 in a Ferrari GTO and 6th at Sebring in a Cobra, while also running Formula 2 races, and coming in 3rd in the Albi GP with a Brabham-Cosworth.

In 1965, he shared 2nd in a Cobra at Daytona's 24-hour race and 4th in the Sebring 12-hour race with Bob Bondurant. That same year, he and Bondy were 5th at the Rheims 12-hour race. After that Schlesser seemed to want to concentrate on single-seater racing, although he and Guy Ligier, a close friend, continued to race in all kinds of competition together. Perhaps he knew time was running out. At any rate, he ran the F2 trail at Nurburgring, Albi, Rouen, Brands Hatch, Hockenheim, and Crystal Palace. There still were enduro rides, such

as Schlesser's shared 3rd with Joe Buzzetta at Daytona, 1968, in a 2.2-litre Porsche 907, and 2nd with Gerhard Mitter at the Spa 1000 in a similar car. There were non-title and uncompetitive starts in F1 cars such as the one at Oulton Park in 1967 that Jo managed to nurse to a 4th.

The end came on July 7, 1968, in the French GP, with Schlesser at the wheel of what he considered his 1st competitive F1 car, an air-cooled Honda. Schlesser crashed and was killed on the 3rd lap at Rouen in a driving rain. The tragedy robbed everyone of possible delight at Jacky Ickx's 1st *grande épreuve* victory. Ligier quit GP racing soon after, but remembered Schlesser when he named the 1st of his new sports cars, JS1, in Jo's memory. It was the Schlesser crash, coupled with several others (those of Jim Clark, Mike Spence, and Ludovicio Scarfiotti), that started the Grand Prix Drivers Association thinking seriously about circuit safety and racing in bad weather conditions, such as those on the day Jo Schlesser died.

LOUIE SCHNEIDER

All in all, the Indianapolis Motor Speedway was a lucky place for Lou Schneider, a journeyman driver from California. He had made the trip as a mechanic, and alternate relief driver for Frank Elliott in 1927; he ended the trip with his own Miller Special. And while other contemporary drivers may fade into obscurity, Schneider's name will live on because he won the Indianapolis 500 in 1931, through an amazing set of circumstances.

Schneider did not lack competence. He came to prominence just when American racing was ending a golden age. He had to convince the men bankrolling the racing of the late twenties that he was more deserving than veteran drivers searching for a car; he had to have talent. In that 1927 Indianapolis appearance in a Miller Special, Schneider shared the car with L. L. Corum for the 137 laps it lasted, before retiring with a broken timing gear.

In the 1928 Indy, Schneider drove the Armacoast Special spectacularly, rising to 4th at 100 miles, and third at 200 miles, before slowly sinking down to 11th at the finish. Absent in 1929, he returned in 1930, with a sponsoring company which was to continue to support American single-seater racing over a span of more than 40 years, Bowes Seal Fast. His 1930 ride was perhaps more impressive than his famous 1931 drive, though he finished only 3rd in 1930. Louie was in contention all the way and might have bettered 3rd, had it not been for a costly pit stop to wire a damaged shock absorber. Despite the punishment of riding with a wired up shock absorber, he had advanced the car after the pit stop toward the lead.

The 1931 Indianapolis felt the effects of the economic depression then gripping the U.S. Attendance was

down; the entry lists reflected the Speedway management effort to bring back the automobile manufacturers as car sponsors. Yet it was still the converted Miller engines and Duesenbergs that were most competitive. From early in the race on that gray overcast day, the racing designs outshone the semi-stocks. It was defender Billy Arnold fighting other Miller drivers, Paul Bost, Bill Cummings, and Shorty Cantlon, as well as Deacon Litz in a Duesenberg. Schneider in his Miller was 13th after the 1st lap, 10th after 20 laps.

He then began working his way upward, as other contenders dropped out, and the 2 top semi-stock hopes, Tony Gulotta and Russ Snowberger of the Studebaker team fought to stay in the top 10. Lou was 9th at 40 laps, when it began to drizzle. For about 50 miles, the cars ran at 80 m.p.h. under the caution flag. When the green flag came out, it stayed only a short time; Wilbur Shaw and Fred Winnai hurdled the wall. Then the rain returned; the average speed had dropped to 92 m.p.h. Suddenly, the first 10 standings began to shift drastically as Schneider moved to 6th behind the leading Arnold. After 80 laps, he had moved to 3rd, then dropped to 4th 25 miles later, and moved back to 3rd by the halfway mark. At this point, the average speed rose again; the last half of the race promised more excitement. Schneider drove in for his only pit stop of the afternoon, taking on gas, oil, and a new rear tire in only 2 minutes.

Gulotta, running 2nd to the leader Arnold, had been joined in the top 10 by teammates Luther Johnson and Snowberger after 130 laps. Schneider was back in 3rd place again, a position he was to lose to Litz in the next few miles. It seemed as if Billy Arnold was a sure vic-

tor. Arnold, who was to become an Air Force general, had a lead of at least 4 laps on Gulotta, as the field hurtled past the 400-mile mark and the average speed went past 97 m.p.h. Arnold's car owner was flashing signals requesting him to slow down and save the Miller, but Arnold sped on. Five miles later, Arnold's rear axle snapped, causing him to hit the wall. Johnson, in 6th place, rammed into the wreck and was also out of the race.

So a Studebaker, driven by Gulotta, was leading Indy. But not for long; on his 167th lap, Gulotta lost control and wrecked. The fantastic happened: Louie Schneider was leading the Indianapolis 500. Schneider, aided by more caution-flag waving as the Litz car slammed the wall, held on for the victory.

Schneider returned in 1932 with a Miller-engined car for Bowes Seal Fast, placing as high as 3rd before retiring with a broken frame. The next year, in an Edelweiss Special, he stalled on the 1st lap, and was retired.

And that about sums up Louie Schneider's claim to racing immortality.

BENNY SCOTT

"Above all, I want to do well. I want to become a good race-car driver—first of all—and whatever happens after that, happens," said Benny Scott. The words were ordinary, but there was hidden meaning to them, for Benny Scott was black, and there were many eyes watching him. Many people wanted him to do well, some did not. For like a Jackie Robinson in baseball, the 27-year-old Californian was a pioneer in sports.

Auto racing, at least in its big-time sense, was lily-white in its 70-odd years of history. There were black drivers and officials, but in so-called "outlaw" categories, or in all-black situations. Here and there, there were black drivers in the majors, men such as Wendell Scott (no relation to Benny) in NASCAR stock car racing, and officials such as Mel Layton, who was a USAC Indianapolis-type racing official. But there had been no black single-seater racing driver, and single-seaters, whether it be Indianapolis and the 500-mile race, or Grand Prix or even the Continental 5000 series, is where it was at for racing drivers and fans.

Scott was picked in 1972 as the man most likely to make a go in single-seater racing. It was no idle choice. Benny's dad, known as Bullet Scott, was a midget-car racer on dirt tracks in the thirties, but Benny, who was born February 4, 1945, in Los Angeles, never saw his dad race. "Just heard all the stories," he recalled, "and saw some of the clippings and souvenirs, and met some of the other men who had run in that black 'outlaw' circuit. These were the people who were the real pioneers in auto racing for blacks.

"I'm just a lucky guy who happens to be black. I have some talent, and I'm getting a push because I am black, but after that point, it's strictly up to me and what I can do in a race car. There is no carrying a guy in auto racing. He either has it, or he can forget about it."

If Scott sounded like he had no illusions about what he was doing, it was because he already had paid his dues in motor racing. An older brother got him started around 1963, helping out in preparing dragsters. Five years later, Benny began as a racing driver, much as his dad had 30-odd-years before, in short races on dirt and paved ovals. The younger Scott was driving stockers rather than midgets, however. In 1969 Benny won the Southern California championship among the stockers, and the possibility was there to go on in this type of racing, perhaps getting into NASCAR as had Wendell Scott. But he chose instead to go the single-seater route.

The six-foot, 170-pounder had graduated from Long Beach State College with a degree in psychology and was completing his work for a Master's degree in the same field. He later became a psychology instructor at Long Beach State. In mid-1969 he made the big step and joined the SCCA, starting with an inexpensive Austin-Healey Sprite, which he raced it for two seasons.

"Inexpensive is a relative word," Benny said. "Racing in this country below the top-flight professional level had been a leisure-time sport, but it still required fairly large sums of money. Blacks simply didn't have the financial resources to participate until very recently even in so-called amateur sports-car racing. Auto racing's not like baseball, football or basketball, where you put together a few bucks and buy a ball, and maybe a glove or helmet. Nor like track, where all you need is shoes."

Even in the minor-leagues—which was what Benny considered the amateur racing he entered in 1969—you needed more than a little money, or you need not bother even trying: "You have to establish your crentials in any sport, motor racing included," Scott said, "and only then do you have a chance to move up to the big leagues, not on your own money but with someone else's backing."

Benny's backing came in 1971 after he had raced the Sprite and graduated to a Formula B car, a true single-seater, capable of 150 m.p.h. or more, and looking something like the familiar Indy-type of racing car with open wheels, streamlined body and low-slung appearance. Scott was 3rd in the SCCA's Southern California division that year, but his performance happily coincided with a search then going on by a new group called Vanguard Racing. The search was for a black driver who could be groomed—given his native abilities—for possible Indianapolis 500 racing. Vanguard was a group of black and white businessmen and sports-involved men who included Layton; Leonard Miller, a Trenton, N.J. public manpower consultant; Brig Owens, Washington Redskins defensive halfback; Paul Jackson, president of Washington's Jackson & Sanders Construction Co.; R. Sargent Shriver of Peace Corps and French ambassa-

dorial fame; Richard Deutsche board chairman of Connecticut's Harbor Oil Corp.; and race driver John Mahler. All were black, except Shriver, Deutsche and Mahler.

"The way they presented the idea was that I was being picked because I was black, but also because—and perhaps more importantly—because I was potentially an Indy-class driver," said Scott. "There was very little flag-waving or psalm-singing around Vanguard Racing. They were professional men, and we trying to go about the racing thing in a highly professional way." The initial announcements made it sound like they were headed for the 1972 Indy 500, but that wasn't the plan at all, according to Benny. "Look," he said, "I need all the time in a race car I can get. I am relatively inexperienced, compared to all the other drivers who show up at Indy. Even the greatest talent in the world would need experience and polish. I need it just that much more."

The expectation was that rapid advancement could be made if Scott were thrown in top-flight racing, however, and that is why the L&M Continental series was chosen. The cars here were Chevrolet-powered 5000 c.c. single-seaters capable of nearly 200 m.p.h. Some of the better known names in American and international road racing were competing in the rich series, sponsored by the cigarette company.

"We all knew I was not going to win the series," said Scott with a laugh. "The level of racing in this L&M series far exceeded that in club racing, which actually was my background before then. You just don't walk from the amateur ranks into professional racing and take over. I don't care who you are. You pay your dues, and it takes a lot of time. That's another way, perhaps, that auto racing is different from other sports. It demands time, patience, absolute control of yourself in the face of everything. I've gotten into the habit of preparing myself for whatever is ahead, from the best to the worst. I need as much time in this car as possible. That is the real objective this season. Winning comes later."

Benny's Continental car was a British-built McLaren M10A, not the most modern car for the series, but a fairly competitive one. To warm up for the 1972 season, he got his 1st McLaren experience in two SCCA national races at San Diego, Calif., and Phoenix, Ariz. At Phoenix Scott was 2nd, and he won at San Diego. But then reality came to visit. In the L&M series, where such names as David Hobbs, 1971 Continental champion; Sam Posey, a young but veteran Indy and sports car driver; and many other professionals abounded, Scott found himself qualified 28th in the Laguna Seca, Calif., opener. In the race, run in two heats, he finished 19th and 17th and 19th overall. Actually rather good for a 1st, and what must have been nervous, effort. In the 2nd L&M race at Edmonton, Canada, Scott qualified 26th, was 17th and 14th for 15th overall, an improvement in every department over the opener.

"People see only the race, and they forget the long

hours in the shop preparing the car, the hours spent in practicing, both to better know the car and to break in tires and test new tire compounds that might mean an extra second or even fraction of a second in time," Scott said. "If baseball is a game of inches, as they say, auto racing is a game of seconds. We live by the stop watch. It's enough to turn your hair gray."

Scott was black-haired and mustachioed, and not at all gray, despite his feelings on this matter. The Vanguard timetable said that he should get all the preliminary experience he could in the early seventies. Then they would start thinking about Indy, probably starting with shorter USAC (United States Auto Club) races leading up to the famed 500-miler. But after one season, the well-intentioned, but underfinanced Vanguard racing died, and with it, Benny's Indy hopes for 1973. Scott had finished 8 of 10 Continental starts, but boasted only a 10th as his best finish in the slow McLaren. For 1973 Scott bought a Formula Super Vee, quit as a teacher and went racing full time to try to get on the Brickyard on his own. He had no regrets about his Vanguard experience.

"Equipment means the ballgame here as much as driving ability," he said. "That's why Vanguard was so important to me, and why John Mahler, who was as helpful as any man can be, was important, too. He told me how to get the very best out of what equipment I had. When you are a racing driver," added Scott, "you have to put 100 percent of your attention and 100 percent of your effort into your driving, or you could be in serious trouble . . . like crashing, injuring or even killing yourself. So I really don't have the time to be 'another Jackie Robinson,' as it were. So far, and I'm really glad to say this, there doesn't appear to be an necessity for taking what Robinson did, or turning the other cheek or any of that kind of thing. Auto racing, for all of its so-called lily-whiteness, appeared to be color blind to me. It just gets back to that original thing we talked about," said Scott. "A simple matter of money to get started. Now that blacks are getting better off financially, you probably can expect to see more of them in all kinds of racing, and it will be a far better sport for it."

RICHARD SCOTT

Jo Rindt was dead. And with him Jo Rindt Racing, the Formula 2 Lotus Racing Team, died, too. For 1971 a new team, called LIRA, for London International Racing Association, was formed with 2 young drivers. One was Swedish, blond, smiling, the other a Scot, dour, dark, and far less-known than Reine Wisell, the Swede. Richard Scott was born in Aberdeen in 1946, son of a local building contractor. He was through with school in 1964 and immediately went into an apprenticeship program with a BMC distributorship in his native Aberdeen. As part of the program, he was sent for a year's schooling in motor vehicle engineering in Glasgow. He also started racing, not motorcycles or cars, but go-karts, and he had a fairly successful 1965 as a kart racer. In 1966 Scott advanced to a 2-litre Elva-BMW sports/racing car that was raced for 2 seasons, principally on Scottish circuits. At the beginning of 1968 Richard came to a crossroads. First there was the automobile business, represented by BMC; next the sport, represented by the Lotus 41 Formula 3 racing car he was eyeing. The sport won out, after an inner battle, for Scott liked his BMC job.

He set himself up in the used-car business and bought the Lotus. He won numerous hillclimbs in this car, and ran 2nd by a single point in the Formula Libre Lombank Championship in Scotland that season. Another turning point was in evidence. To really succeed, Scott was told, he had to devote himself entirely to racing. He didn't hesitate, but sold his interest in the business and went racing full-time. He sought out Frank Williams, the Piers Courage manager-sponsor, and arranged to use Williams's workshops for Scott's newly acquired Brabham BT21 F3 car. Racing started at Mallory Park, but Richard retired with fuel starvation problems. The following weekend, however, he won the F3 class, set a new F3 record, and was 3rd overall at Ingleton, his home track. On 2 successive weekends, Scott won at Brands Hatch, then followed this with 4ths at Oulton Park and at Mallory.

In Scott's initial international meet, at Silverstone in the rain, he was 9th. His Continental baptism followed quickly at the Paris Grand Prix where the Brabham finished 6th. Back in Britain, victory was his at Brands Hatch. At Rouen he was 6th in his heat, then involved in a chain-reaction accident in his final. The car was relatively unmarked, but it was evident that he was 2 years behind everyone else and was losing precious seconds. The Brabham was sold and a Chevron B15 purchased. The first time out, the new car crashed. In its next 2 appearances, the engine failed on the starting line.

In the Chevron's 4th start at Brands, Scott was running a smooth 5th when he hit an oil patch and spun spectacularly. At Crystal Palace he was 3rd in his heat and 5th overall, then faced more engine failures. In the finale at Oulton Scott dueled other Chevrons the whole race and finished 3rd. At Ingleton he won his F3 class and again set the lap record. At Mallory's finale he was 2nd. In the year's last race, a combined F2–F3 race in Munich, Scott was 2nd still again. The year was a good one, with 6 class or overall victories, and 9 other placings in the top 3.

The year 1970 found Scott back in a Brabham, a BT28 this time, in F3. After 2nds at Thruxton and Snetterton, he won at Thruxton. A 6th at Brands was followed by 4ths at Thruxton and Brands again, and 5ths at Monte Carlo and at Oulton. In F2, racing a Brabham BT30, Scott was 10th at Manthorp Park and 2nd at Phoenix Park. He retired at Hockenheim. Nothing spectacular, yet steady enough to earn him that LIRA berth for 1971. At 25 he stood on the crossroads again. One path led to Grand Prix stardom, the other to lesser racing. His choice was obvious; but it was not to be, at least not soon.

WENDELL SCOTT

The taste of victory was bitter on occasion for Wendell Scott but he survived and went on, the only black man in stock-car racing and one of the few black drivers anywhere. There was, for example, the time at Hagerstown, Md., in his sportsman-modified days when Wendell won an advertised $350 purse. The track official handed him a check for $36, then gave the white winner of the amateur (hobby) races $65. Then there was his lone NASCAR Grand National victory at Jacksonville on December 1, 1963. The crowd knew Scott had won, the other drivers knew Scott had won, but the promoter handed the $1,000 check and trophy to a surprised Buck Baker. Scott protested vehemently, and NASCAR told the promoter it was 1963, not 1763. Scott got the check.

Scott originally became a race driver when the police in his home town of Danville, Va., recommended him to a local promoter who wanted to attract black fans. Borrowing a car, Scott finished 3rd, winning $50, and that was the beginning of a racing career unparalleled for determination and quiet courage. That initial race came in 1947, at a time when racing was definitely a white man's sport in the South. There were tracks where a Jim Crow pit area was created and his wife, Mary, was his entire crew; there were tracks where he had to work on his car in the dark; there were races where the other sportsman drivers used his car like a punching bag. But Scott perservered.

It was not all bad. Earl Brooks was a close friend and fellow NASCAR hopeful. Earl Brooks was white. In 1959, 12 years after he started racing, Scott won the track championship in Richmond, as well as the Virginia State championship. He had a car nicknamed "Old Rusty," and with it, that year, he won 22 races. In 1961, he preceded Brooks into Grand National racing by a year. He earned $3,240 for 23 races that season. His winnings went up every year after that, as did his average purse per race until in 1969, he earned $27,542, with an average take per race of $540.03. With accessory awards and point-fund money, that totalled $47,451.

Born August 29, 1921, Scott came into the major leagues at age 40. He finished 6th in the NASCAR season title race in 1966, 10th in 1967, and 9th in 1968 and 1969. He dropped down to 14th in 1970 when he failed to run the complete circuit. However, he had some satisfactions: he was a celebrity. Rednecked farmers, who a decade previously would have crossed the street to avoid him, sought his autograph.

It made up for that time at Darlington International Speedway when, the morning before the race, the officials threatened disqualification if Scott had a racially mixed pit crew (Frankie and Wendell Jr., his sons, Earl Brooks, and another white friend, Bobby Fleming). He agreed to an all-white crew, but then the officials changed the rookie-deadline rule on him, moving it from 4.30 P.M. to noon. That gave him 75 minutes to have his new car inspected and take the rookie test. No one could do it. He didn't run. But he was back racing there in 1966, and thereafter.

There were other tracks and better promoters. In 1965, Charlotte promoter Richard Howard backed 4 brand-new Chevrolets to halt the Ford domination of NASCAR racing. He chose Scott for one of the cars. Scott was in contention until a drive shaft snapped. That same season, NASCAR champion Ned Jarrett suggested to Ford that Scott was a good candidate for aid. He got a year-old factory machine.

By the beginning of 1973, the 52-year-old Scott still was the only black driver in NASCAR. There was no overt factory support anymore so Wendell was on his own. He had driven over 500 NASCAR events, won 1. That was over 70,000 miles of racing for $2.40 a mile not including expenses. But it must be said that Scott had won respect.

In 1970 at a track in South Carolina, Scott had just finished qualifying and the stands were cheering his time, which was among the 5 fastest despite the presence of factory-backed machinery. "They used to cheer like that, and I knew they were making fun of me," Scott said. "Now they're just cheering my time. That's what feels good. I hope it stays that way from now on."

ARCHIE SCOTT-BROWN

William Archibald Scott-Brown was a short but sturdy, big-mustachioed young man who must have been one of racing's most courageous drivers. He was born without a right hand, but with a forearm that ended in a notched stump with which he held the wheel while shifting gears, and with a short leg, but you never would have known it to see the cheerful young Englishman driving.

Scott-Brown was born in Paisley, England, May 13, 1927. An only child, he was fortunate in having parents who were deep into the racing world, competing in an Alvis (for which his father was a dealer) at Brooklands and other top circuits. He never favored motorcycles, so his mother arranged a 10th-birthday gift of a specially built miniature racing car, powered by a 125 c.c. lawnmower engine. After the usual British schooling, including a still-remembered aggressive cricket career, Scott-Brown failed to get his economics degree, due mostly to his own unwillingness to settle down to classroom regimen, and began a casual job hunt.

He eventually took a position in 1949 as salesman for Dobie's Four Square Tobacco in Cambridge, staying 6 years. Meanwhile, he started to dabble with cars, beginning with 3-wheelers like the BSA and the Morgan. Occasionally, his father, who often travelled to South Africa on business, let him use a BMW, and this whetted his appetite for a regular car to replace the BSAs and Morgans. In 1950 the chance came when a grandmother left him enough money to buy an MG TC. From then on, he tinkered with the MG to obtain as much power from it as possible.

The following year, Scott-Brown was ready to try competition. It took him 2 years before he won his initial race in club meetings; then he ran out of funds. But at the opportune moment, Brian Lister was retiring from active racing, to become a sponsor and builder, eventually choosing Scott-Brown as his protégé. In later years, Scott-Brown remembered it this way: "Something in the way I handled the MG appealed to Brian, and so, despite a certain shortage of essential equipment," Scott-Brown would flap the empty cuff of his blazer at this point, "he asked me to drive for him on an all-expenses paid basis. Of course, I said yes."

Scott-Brown's rival drivers and Lister's fellow sponsors and builders, all friends of both Brian and Scott-Brown, would kid Lister about the economy of having a single-handed driver. The object of their derision enjoyed the seeming cruel joke as much as anyone. In the winter of 1953, the Lister-MG was born, a 1.5-litre car that proved to be underpowered, despite the ministrations of master mechanic Don Moore. Scott-Brown consistently ran 2nd in it at most club meetings.

Lister's answer to that was his Bristol-engined 2-litre model, debuting at Silverstone in May 1954. It won its class and was 5th overall, with Scott-Brown at the wheel. The car and its driver easily dominated the class for the next 2 years until its engine blew up in one of the last 1955 sports car races. Scott-Brown was ready to advance to bigger things, anyway. Soon thereafter, he quit the tobacco company, opened a garage in Cambridge, and was given a single-seater Connaught Grand Prix car to try at the Brands Hatch Boxing Day meeting in December 1955. An easy victory led, in turn, to a Lance Macklin offer, which was quickly accepted, to codrive a factory-entered Austin-Healey in the following March's 12-hour race at Sebring, Scott-Brown's initial visit to the Western Hemisphere.

Unfortunately, at Sebring, the engine acted up and retired car from the race. Flying back to England, Scott-Brown entered the Easter meeting at Goodwood in a Connaught, led Stirling Moss and other good drivers for 12 laps, then retired when his engine blew at the beginning of the 13th. Three straight victories in a Connaught at Brands Hatch started 1956 in the proper fashion; one drive setting a lap record, a feat duplicated later in the season at Snetterton. At Silverstone he finished 2nd to Moss in the up-and-coming Vanwall in May of the same year.

For 1957, Lister decided to have a try at the 3.5-litre class and slipped a Jaguar engine into one of his specials. Scott-Brown won the British Empire Trophy with it, then took 8 more races of the 11 in which he started

545

that year. The following season, Scott-Brown spent 6 weeks in New Zealand and won the Lady Wigram Trophy. Shortly afterward, Briggs Cunningham purchased a Lister-Jag and hired Scott-Brown to codrive it with Walt Hansgen at Sebring under his colors. Cunningham's entry was eliminated on the 4th lap of the airport course when Belgium's Olivier Gendebien drove up the Lister-Jaguar's tail with his Ferrari.

The Ferrari's left-front tire came to rest on Scott-Brown's shoulder; later, he displayed a shirt with the Ferrari's tread tracks clearly discernable near the neck opening. When this happened, both cars spun wildly off the track. Gendebien managed to get his car off the Lister-Jaguar, regaining the race after 35 minutes of frantic hammering on its front end in the pits, but Scott-Brown's car was through for the day. Perhaps the near-miss should have served as a warning to Scott-Brown, but he did not take it. He continued driving and competing, until a sports-car race May 18, 1958, at Spa, Belgium, site of that year's Grand Prix of Europe.

The 31-year-old driver had been around the demanding circuit several times. Scott-Brown was increasing his speed despite wet conditions, when he reached a spot that some say was the same one at which Dick Seaman crashed back in 1939. On the wet, Scott-Brown spun off the course and into the trees. The car immediately, caught fire; he had little chance of getting out.

Those who remember him think of his better days like the one in which he crashed but managed to climb out of the car, bloodstained, with a concussion. First to reach him was a small boy with an autograph album. Scott-Brown had obliged him with a handsome, flourishing signature before quietly passing out.

DICK SEAMAN

Today we are used to professional Grand Prix drivers and even well-paid "amateurs" in sports car ranks. At one time, however, there were real amateurs who went all the way up to the Formula 1 pinnacle. Richard John Beattie-Seaman was probably the last of these; but he may also have been simply the 1st of the modern professionals in GP racing. The son of wealthy parents, he was born February 4, 1913, in Sussex, England. He graduated from Rugby and attended Trinity College, Cambridge, summered in France, and lived a life of splendor in London and at country estates. A chauffeur taught young Dick to drive at his Essex estate in a Daimler, and before going up to Cambridge he had taken part in reliability trials in his own Riley.

In 1931 Seaman entered the Riley in the Shelsley Walsh hillclimb, finishing 2nd behind an equally privileged young man driving another Riley: Whitney Straight. He was an American, who also was entering Cambridge. The two became fast friends, each adopting characteristics of the other. Straight switched to an MG, and so did Seaman, who piloted his Magna as far as the Alpine Trial

of 1932. When Straight acquired a 2.5-litre Maserati and announced he had decided to make auto racing his profession, Seaman was quick to follow by buying a 2-litre unsupercharged GP Bugatti. Whitney had his own plane, and Seaman learned to fly and later purchased a De Havilland Gipsy Moth of his own.

Seaman's dedication was, however, far greater than Straight's, and when Whitney later devoted himself to business, Seaman continued initially as an amateur racer dabbling in professionalism, then as a full-fledged professional racer. His driving abilities were greater than the American's. There were few things that Seaman couldn't do if he put his mind to the task. He turned his back on Cambridge in 1934, soon after acquiring Straight's MG Magnette.

Seaman won the 1100-c.c. class at the 1934 Inter-Varsity Speed Trials, acquired a good knowledge of his car's characteristics at a number of Brooklands races (without winning), then finished 3rd in the Albi GP at Pescara. He took the Prix de Berne, his initial major victory, then was 5th in the 1500-c.c. class at Czechoslovakia's Masaryk GP. At Donington on home soil, he finished 2nd in the Nuffield Trophy Race over a particularly slippery course, attracting considerable attention. The MG marque agreed to lend him a factory-prepared K.3 for the South African 100 Race at the East London course, and he and Straight flew there in the latter's De Havilland Dragon. Whitney won the race in a powerful Maserati; Seaman was 5th in his tiny MG. It was after this race that the American retired to a desk, while the Englishman went on to auto-racing immortality.

In 1935, Seaman acquired a new ERA 1.5-litre racer

that he finished in black and silver, his personal racing colors. ERA agreed to prepare the car, although he provided his own transportation. This followed a 2nd-place finish in a similar factory car at a Donington Club meet, despite brake and other mechanical troubles. Only a powerful 2.3-litre Bugatti managed to finish ahead of Seaman in a well-rounded field of entries. After a number of successful appearances in Britain, Seaman took his ERA to the Continent for the first time in June 1935, but retired early from the Grand Prix des Frontières at Chimay with mechanical trouble. At the Eifelrennen, he was leading the ERA factory cars and the Maserati team when mechanical trouble hit again, and he finished 4th. Several more starts and poor mechanical performances brought him to a parting with ERA, which he charged with preparing his cars poorly in preference to their own team cars.

Seaman hired a full-time racing mechanic and business manager, plunging into professional racing. The soundness of his decision was proven almost at once. At the Grossglockner hillclimb, he was 1st in class and 2nd overall; at Pescara, he won the Coppa Acerbo at 78.99 m.p.h. Seaman then took the Prix de Berne at 82.64 m.p.h., won the Freiburg hillclimb, and averaged 81.4 m.p.h. to win at Brno; at each race, he easily defeated the ERA team. In addition to his own black and silver mount, Seaman found time to drive a factory MG to 10th place in the Tourist Trophy and to share an American Duesenberg single-seater at Brooklands.

Having proved his point with the ERA, Seaman, upon the advice of Earl Howe and Giulio Ramponi, bought one of the complicated 1.5-litre straight-8 Delages designed by Albert Lory around 1925. Working with his personal crew, Seaman rebuilt the 11-year-old car into a lighter, more powerful, and what was to prove eminently more successful form. After a few small meet victories, Seaman took the rebuilt Delage to the Isle of Man and won the RAC's Light Car race at 69.76 m.p.h., once again defeating ERA.

The Delage still needed some adjustments, as indicated by crashes at Nurburgring and Peronne, but Seaman returned to his winning ways for the Coppa Acerbo at Pescara. He took the race at 77.1 m.p.h., defeating a strong Maserati team. At Berne he again bested Maserati (this time entered privately) and the ERA factory forces, winning at 87.86 m.p.h. Seaman then returned to England in time for the Junior Car Club's 200-miler at Donington, and, with the engine still unstripped after 3 races, won at 69.28 m.p.h. when the leader had to pit for fuel, while crafty Seaman nonstopped it. That same year, he borrowed the ex-Whitney Straight 3-litre Maserati from Harry Rose, sleeved down its engine to meet the 2700-c.c. class limit, and won the BRDC's Empire Trophy Race (also at Donington at 66.33 m.p.h.). Once again, he had triumphed over ERA. Revenge was sweet.

At this time, neither Mercedes nor Alfa Romeo would lend him a car fast enough to defend his Star points in the Brooklands Mountain Handicap. Seaman thought of building a more powerful version of the Delage, or even having Dr. Ferdinand Porsche design a Land Speed Record car for a try at Daytona Beach. But Mercedes's refusal was based on thoughts of better ways to use Seaman's talents. Seaman had already demonstrated that his skills were not limited to such cars as MGs. He had shared a 3.8-litre Alfa and won the Donington GP, co-driven a Maserati to a 12th in the German GP, shared a 4th at Spa's 24-hour race in a 4.5-litre Lagonda, and started with an Aston Martin in the Tourist Trophy, from which he retired with mechanical ills. Seaman was surprised and pleased, at the end of the 1936 season, to receive an invitation to join the Mercedes team and pilot one of the world's most powerful racing cars.

He sold the Delage and moved to Germany. Before the 1937 season opened, disaster struck when Seaman crashed at Monza, while practicing with the 1936 Mercedes, and badly burned his legs. He drove the rest of the year wrapped in bandages and spent most of the winter in them after another crash, this time in the 1937 W.125, at the German GP. Between these trials, however, he had been 5th at the Avusrennen, 2nd in the Vanderbilt Cup at America's Roosevelt Raceway, 5th at Pescara, and 4th in the Italian and Masaryk Grands Prix. He was awarded the BRDC's Gold Star.

The following year (1938) was an even better one, for Dick met and married a German girl and won a major *grande épreuve,* the German race, at 80.75 m.p.h. He was 2nd in the Swiss GP behind teammate Caracciola and 3rd at Donington, but war clouds gave the young Englishman cause to worry. After assurances from the British Foreign Office that he would do more for Anglo-German relations by remaining where he was, Dick signed with Mercedes for 1939. After a retirement at the Eifelrennen, Seaman started the Belgian GP on a rainy June 25, 1939, and, driving one of the best races of his career, closed in upon Hans Muller's leading Auto Union, taking the lead at Spa's 22nd lap, 13 laps from the finish. At the La Source turn, Seaman's car skidded into the trees, crashed, and caught fire. Dick Seaman was dead.

Seaman's body was brought back to Putney Vale and buried in English soil. Hitler paid Seaman tribute, sending a wreath to the funeral, set in place by the German ambassador. Mercedes showrooms over the world were stripped of their cars and their windows filled with pictures of Dick, draped in black. Britons and Germans sympathized with each other, but 3 months later they were at war.

JACK SEARS

It seems that British farmers make good racing drivers: Jim Clark, Jackie Stewart, and Jack George Stanley Sears, stock-car champion and rallyist extraordinary, who was not as well known to Americans as he should have been. He was born into a motor-enthusiast family,

February 16, 1930, at Northampton, Norfolk, England. His father, Stanley Sears, was a prewar club racer who took Jack on a tour of the banked Brooklands circuit at 100 m.p.h. in 1939. Given a Morgan for his 17th birthday, Sears made his competition debut in 1948 at a Brighton mud trials. The following year he switched to an MG TC, and went racing for the 1st time in 1950 at Goodwood. Not only did he not win, he spun off the course at the 1st turn.

Well-known as a fast but not particularly predictable driver, Sears, who had switched to an XK 120 Jaguar and MG-Cooper in the intervening years, was learning how to handle a Lister-Bristol properly when the 1st of his children was born in 1955. So he gave up racing, a decision reinforced a few years later when his one-time instructor and close friend, Archie Scott-Brown, died in a crash at Spa. Rallying was something else again, however, and Sears continued to compete as a member of the BMC team. A 2nd child, Suzanne, was born in 1956, and a 3rd, Jennifer, in 1961.

In 1958 he had returned to the race courses, however, as the stock-car craze took hold in Britain, called saloon cars there. He won that season's title in an Austin A105, moved on to Grand Touring competition the following season, and rallied a bit once more. His GT car was an Austin-Healey 3000. Experience improved his consistency, and in 1960 Tommy Sopwith invited Sears to join his team, Equipe Endeavor. Sears's teammates, when he credits with much of his later success, were none other than Graham Hill and Mike Parkes.

For the next 3 seasons he raced with these men in beautifully prepared E Jaguars, 3.8-litre saloons, Aston Martin DB4s, and even Ferrari Berlinettas. In 1962 Sears was 3rd overall in British saloon competition, and the winner of the unlimited class. He was 4th in class at Sebring in an MG A. When Sopwith retired at the end of the season, Sears was considering quitting himself once again. Then a phone call came from the man whom he had bested for the 1958 saloon title, Jeff Uren. Uren offered a berth on the new Willment team, for which Uren now was manager, running Ford Galaxies and Cortinas. The offer was accepted; Sears won his initial Willment race in a Cortina at Oulton Park soon after, despite the fact that he started from the back row of the grid.

In 1963, he won all 8 saloon GT championship races and his 2nd saloon title and set new lap records in 5 of them. Jack also drove all of the other white and red Willment Fords, including a Cortina GT which he and codriver Bob Olthoff took to the U.S., placing 2nd overall and 1st in class in the 12-hour race at Marlboro, Md. Sears also drove for Maranello Concessionnaires, the the British Ferrari distributorship, that season, including a 5th overall and class victory at Le Mans with Mike Salmon. In all, Jack won 18 of 23 races. The total did not include a vintage car race in which he was 1st in a 1914 Sunbeam. The following season was not too happy for Sears, however, since Willment had singled him out to put a Ford Cobra in contention in European and South African racing and the car still needed much sorting out.

HENRY SEGRAVE

When the yellow car pulled up in front of the Clarendon Hotel in Daytona Beach, Fla., a small crowd waiting curiously to see what a genuine British racing hero looked like pressed forward. Henry Segrave was a blue-eyed, red-haired (but balding) young man with ruddy cheeks and an upper-class British accent. He didn't disappoint his Daytona Beach audience.

Henry Segrave's claim to racing immortality came in 1927. Segrave had caught the American Automobile Association by surprise when he had announced in London that he was about to make an assault on Malcolm Campbell's Land Speed Record of 174.88 m.p.h., just set on February 2. He would try later that same year at Daytona Beach, Fla. The AAA only learned about the plan when they read it in the paper. Was he serious? No official Land Speed Record had been set at Daytona since 1910, when Barney Oldfield ran 131.72 m.p.h. in a Benz. There had been other runs, the last one Tommy Milton's in 1920, but no officially recognized records. Brooklands, Arpajon, Southport Sands, and Pendine, lately almost exclusively, had been the sites for record attempts, not Daytona.

But Segrave was serious, having selected Daytona

carefully, using an engineer's analysis and calculations. He had commissioned a new car, the twin-airplane-engined 1000-h.p. Sunbeam, and had made his announcement only when the car was ready. Segrave was thus better prepared than the AAA, which had the problem of accurately timing his runs. For the attempt, a man named Odis Porter had invented an electric timer, which recorded to hundredths of a second. The AAA then ensured the beach course was as swept as humanly possible, enlisting not only the local police but the National Guard to protect the course and keep the expected crowds in check.

A garage and machine shop were built right on the beach, and here the Segrave's Sunbeam with its 2 engines (one would be started by compressed air, which would then start the other one by a friction drive; they were locked together by a dog clutch) was unloaded and made ready. March 28, 1927, Segrave was ready to try his luck. By the time the car was wheeled to the starting point, the dunes overlooking the course were covered with people waiting to see this spectacle. Segrave, who normally lived the life of a monk, was chain-smoking this morning on borrowed cigarettes.

He started from the south end of the beach, heading north. The car didn't roar; rather it hummed, a red streak as it flashed past the crowds. Some said they could see the white crash helmet in the cockpit. Segrave was one of the first men to adopt a real crash helmet, popularizing its use at a time when there were no rules about wearing such protective devices. A few minutes later the red streak passed again, heading south. But the 1000-h.p. Sunbeam had fallen far short of Campbell's time. A check instantly revealed why. The car had been running on only one engine; the rear engine had shut down for lack of air.

With adjustments made overnight, Segrave was on the beach again the following morning, March 29th. This time both engines worked perfectly, and the big car was reached 203.79 m.p.h. Segrave became the 1st man to pass the magic 200-m.p.h. mark.

Henry O'Neal de Hane Segrave was born September 22, 1896, in Baltimore, Md., of an old Leicestershire family that traced itself back 900 years in Britain. Henry was raised in Ireland, and educated at Eton, leaving school in 1914 to enlist in the Army as an infantry officer, but switching to the fledging Royal Flying Corps in 1915. Shot down by antiaircraft fire, his foot was so badly smashed that Segrave was invalided from active air service, but he joined the Air Ministry and was serving as liaison officer in the United States when the war ended.

With Bill Bruce-Brown, the brother of the early American amateur racer David Bruce-Brown, Segrave went to some auto races in the U.S. Eventually, Segrave brought his newly acquired Apperson touring car to race at Sheepshead Bay board speedway on the closed track for his 1st start.

Returning to England, Segrave bought a 1914 Opel 4.5-litre Grand Prix car to go racing. He lost a tire in his debut at Brooklands in 1920, then won that same day, May 20, at 88.5 m.p.h. He won a couple more and finished 2nd twice in other 1920 racing, all at Brooklands. In 1921, driving his own Sunbeam, he won at Brooklands at 94.64 m.p.h., then arranged a deal with the factory to drive No. 10 Sunbeam in the 1921 French Grand Prix if he paid for his own way, his own parts, and any damage that he did to the car. Segrave finished 9th despite mechanical problems. He was signed by the Sunbeam-Talbot-Darracq group to a regular contract.

Segrave was 3rd in the Le Mans Grand Prix des Voiturettes and won the JCC 200-miler at Brooklands at 88.82 m.p.h. in a 1.5-litre Talbot. In 1922, driving one of the previous year's Indianapolis cars fitted with a 4.9-litre engine, he had good success at Brooklands, then did some record-breaking with Lee Guinness in a 350-h.p. airplane-engined Sunbeam. In practice for the RAC Tourist Trophy on the Isle of Man, Segrave made the fastest time (57.7 m.p.h.) in a 3-litre, but retired from the race with magneto trouble. A broken piston knocked him out of that season's French GP while he was running 3rd. In the JCC's Brooklands 200-miler, his car suffered a burnt-out valve seat, but he limped in 3rd, then was 3rd at the Grand Prix des Voiturettes. In the 1922 Coppa Florio, Segrave was 2nd to Andre Boillot. Later, in the Penya Rhin GP, despite several fires in the Talbot engine, he finished 4th.

In 1923, history saw one of Britain's great racing victories, accomplished by Henry Segrave. Driving No. 12

straight-8 Sunbeam, he ran the French GP at Tours and, when the leading Fiat burned out in its dice with Segrave, he won the race at 75.30 m.p.h. It was the initial *grande épreuve* victory for a British car since the GP circus began in 1906, and it was also the only one until 1957 when Vanwall won the British GP. Later in the 1923 season, Segrave won the Grand Prix des Voiturettes at Miramas at 67.22 m.p.h. In 1924, he made the fastest lap time in the French GP at 76.24 m.p.h., but a faulty magneto and a long pit stop of 27 minutes finished the car 5th. Later in the year, he won the San Sebastian GP at 64.12 m.p.h. in a drive so classic that a local paper headlined about "El Maestro Completo." This was to be the last major British driver's victory in GP racing until Tony Brooks won at Syracuse in 1955. Later in the 1924 season, he was 2nd at the Grand Prix de l'Ouverture at Montlhéry with a 109.65 m.p.h. fastest lap and 3rd in the JCC 200.

In 1925, Segrave drove to victory in the Grand Prix de Provence at Miramas in a 1.5-litre Talbot at 78.8 m.p.h., was 3rd in the Grand Prix de l'Ouverture at Montlhéry, retired at Le Mans with clutch trouble. He retired, too, in the French GP with a broken inlet valve, but won the JCC 200-miler at 78.89 m.p.h. The following year he won the Miramas Grand Prix de Provence again at 81.80 m.p.h. and his 3rd JCC 200-miler at 75.56 m.p.h. He was fastest lap setter but 2nd to Albert Divo in the Montlhéry Grand Prix du Salon. Segrave began serious record-breaking at Southport Sands in 1926, setting a flying kilometer Land Speed Record of 152.33 m.p.h. that lasted all of 6 weeks until bested by Parry Thomas. Segrave's record had been set with a V-12 Sunbeam of 4 liters, which set the stage for the invasion of Daytona in 1927.

He officially retired from racing (as opposed to record-setting) after the Essex 6-hour race in 1927, with 31 victories in 49 starts. He joined the Portland Cement Company as a director, lent his name to a car (the Hillman Segrave coupe), and wrote a book called *The Lure of Speed*.

Segrave's 1927 Land Speed Record had fallen less than a year later to Malcolm Campbell, whose mark, in turn, was bested 2 months after that by Ray Keech at 207.55 m.p.h. It was Keech's mark that Segrave bested on March 11, 1929, in the Irving Special, better known as the Golden Arrow, powered by a 12-cylinder Napier Lion airplane engine. Segrave did not fully extend the car when he established a new kilometer Land Speed Record of 231.44 m.p.h., intending to push the record higher, at a later date, but the death of America's Lee Bible while attempting to smash the British ace's record ended Segrave's record-setting for the year. Before returning to Britain, however, Segrave had turned to boat racing, winning the Fischer Cup hydroplane race at Miami, March 21, 1929. When he returned to Britain, he found himself idolized, and the King bestowed upon him a knighthood, on May 27, 1929.

But the fame and honors were not to last long, for Segrave's new infatuation with boats and the Water Speed Record were to have a fatal consequence. At Lake Windermere, June 13, 1930, after setting a new WSR of 98.76 m.p.h. in Miss England II, his boat crashed and exploded, killing a mechanic outright. Segrave and another mechanic were pulled from the water still alive, but Sir Henry was so badly mauled that two and a half hours later he was dead.

The body was cremated in accordance with Segrave's wishes, and Segrave's father took off in a monoplane his son had designed, the Segrave Meteor, and scattered those ashes over the playing fields of Eton.

JOHNNY SERVOZ-GAVIN

In American racing, Johnny Servoz-Gavin would have been known as a flake or a hot dog. He was fast and talented, but he lacked the dedication to make it big. And when he finally became serious about his career, it was too late. Fortunately, he survived his mistakes, and was still young and handsome. He apparently didn't have to worry about his next meal. Others were not quite that lucky.

Georges-Francis Servoz-Gavin was born January 18, 1942, son of a pub owner in Grenoble, France. He went to school only as long as it was necessary; Geo, as his parents called him, was not one for applying himself. He had found that his handsome face and athletic ski prowess could earn him a living without much work. At the age of 20, Geo, or Johnny as the girls of Grenoble now called him, owned a gift shop that gave made him an easy living. He liked to take holidays; there was that time in 1963, after a marriage of short duration soured and he took a trip to forget about it. At Magny-Cours he signed up for the driving course. After a few lessons, he gave it up, claiming he was short of money. It may have been that the discipline demanded in the course was more than Johnny could bear.

But the racing appetite had been whetted. He used some contacts at his gift shop to ride in the 1964 Monte Carlo Rally as codriver to J. C. Ogier in a Citroën. Next, he ran as navigator to J. F. Piot in the Alpine Rally. With this vast experience, he bought a Volvo and announced he was a rallyist extraordinaire. Gavin did well in local rallies and hillclimbs; the local sports car club elected him to drive its Lotus 7 in a series of talent-search races organized by the Ford Company. That settled it.

"I wanted to drive in the worst way," he said later. "Actually I didn't only want to, I *needed* to race. I knew there was no better way to express myself, to find my own limits." But Johnny also continued to enjoy and the good life of France. He wore his hair long, and spent money and time in pursuits far afield from his alleged passion of auto racing.

His 1st single-seater drive was in a contest in Belgium, the prize being a Formula 3 car awarded by the Shell Oil Company. Servoz-Gavin rivals were slower, but more conventional in their approach to racing. He was fastest, but wild and sliding. He didn't win the car. But the drive itself was a turning point. He ordered a F3 Brabham-Cosworth for 1965, setting out to save enough money to pay for it by subletting his apartment and moving in with sympathetic friends. He lived on occasional sandwiches, making him still more handsome, which the girls found even more irresistible. He let his hair grow longer than ever to save barbering costs. He worked at odd jobs at race courses to gain free admission, and slept in a tent or sleeping bag to save on hotel fees.

The car arrived about the same time his bankroll reached the necessary level. But his monk-like existence continued, because racing cost money, too. Servoz-Gavin won a race, then another. At Albi he was 3rd. By year's end, he was 4th in the national F3 standings, which led to an offer for a job as driver for Matra. By 1966, Servoz-Gavin was a winning pro.

The next season he moved up to Formula 2, but during the layoff he had gained too much weight, his endurance weakened by his late hours and other extracurricular activities. He lost races and cars. Jean-Pierre Beltoise and others had arrived on the scene, and the word was that Matra would carry only 3 drivers in 1968, and Johnny probably would not be one of them.

On November 12, 1967, he was given a last assignment by Matra. This was to drive in the Formula 1

Madrid race, testing the F2 car brought up to the minimum weight by adding lead weights. Jim Clark won, trailed by Graham Hill and Jack Brabham, all in true F1 cars, and in 4th place was Johnny Servoz-Gavin in the pseudo-Matra. That saved him; he was rehired by the factory, but only as test driver. He kept quiet. The next thing people knew, Servoz-Gavin had cut his hair and was in training. No more whiskey. He was pleasant to the girls, but stuck to business during the season. From Jean-Claude Killy he learned yoga and began practicing it. He had won some races in the Matra prototype when Jackie Stewart hurt his wrist.

Stewart was unable to drive Ken Tyrrell's Matra-Ford at Monaco. Tyrrell asked the factory for a driver, thinking of Beltoise, but the factory had assigned its own car for that race to Beltoise. They turned to Servoz-Gavin. Fastest in practice on the wet course, Servoz-Gavin found himself on the starting grid next to Graham Hill on race day. Tyrrell's instructions were perfect: "If you find yourself in the lead, go all out. Don't look back. The old pros will shake their fists at you. Ignore them. Just go." For 4 laps he did just that, leading them all, before the Matra died.

In 1969, Tyrrell gave Servoz-Gavin his chance. In F2 he won the European Championship with a 5th at Thruxton, 6ths at Hockenheim and Eifelrennen, 4th at Madrid, 2nd in the Mediterranean GP, and 1st, at last, in the Rome GP at Vallelunga. In nontitle races, he was 2nd at Albi and 4th at Pau. In Formula 1, he started the German GP but blew an engine; in the North American races in Canada, the U.S., and Mexico, he drove the 4-wheel drive Matra and finished 6th, 7th, and 8th. His single championship point tied Servoz-Gavin for 16th in the season standings.

The next season (1970), his engine failed in the South Africa GP; he was 5th in the Spanish race; and he was bumped from the Monaco grid. In mid-season, Servoz-Gavin announced his retirement from racing. He appeared on French television to do it, but neglected to mention what perhaps was the determining factor, blurring vision that had followed an early season incident in which he injured his eye.

WILBUR SHAW

Without Warren Wilbur Shaw, self-taught race-car driver turned Indy executive, the Indianapolis Speedway might have died in 1947. With industrialist Tony Hulman, he saved Indy from being sold as an industrial park; saved Indy where, as a boy, he worshiped the classic Speedway greats—Tommy Milton, Harry Hartz, and Jimmy Murphy.

Still, Shaw would also have been remembered as an Indy driver himself—one of the best.

Born in Shelbyville, Ind., October 13, 1902, Shaw's parents separated when he was quite small. In fact, the

separation came soon after he had won his 1st race, riding a goat at a county fair about the age of 5. He lived mostly with his mother, largely left to his own devices. He idolized his father, who made his living as an insurance salesman but was remembered by Wilbur as an outdoorsman. "He believed in shooting fish," Shaw recalled later; "That way he always got the fish he wanted."

But the time with his father was minimal. Wilbur had little interest in formal education, and used to ride his bicycle 21 miles into Indianapolis or hop freight trains or rough house. "Tommy Milton would want something, maybe clear in town," Shaw said. "I'd jump on my bike and pump my heart out clear over the handlebars running that errand." As soon as possible he quit school, rode the rails to Detroit, and bluffed himself into a job with a storage battery company. He learned enough in 2 hours to keep the job and in a few months was earning $100 a week, a huge salary by 1919 standards. The company transferred him to Indianapolis.

No one ever thought of Shaw as a driving great until nearly the end of his career, a career virtually impossible to duplicate in today's racing milieu. His initial race car was built with the cooperation of a friendly garage owner, Bill Hunt. "It was made of spare parts and other pepole's wrecks and pieces out of the local hardware store," Shaw said. "When we took it to Hoosier Speedway, a half-mile dirt track, the starter, Roscoe Dunning, wouldn't let me drive, saying I'd kill myself in it. This was 1921." Shaw so charmed Dunning with his overwhelming desire to compete that Dunning helped him

build another car. In the practice of the day, the new car fitted Shaw so closely that the steering wheel had to be installed after he put himself into the driver's seat. Old RED (Dunning's initials) made its debut in 1922 and, primarily because Dunning had indeed built a better car, won repeatedly all over the midwestern U.S. Friends sent Shaw an ambulance filled with flowers for his racing debut.

Shaw became a race driver in the same manner that he had become a battery expert. He learned by doing, even when that meant running through fences, flipping cars, and spinning them like gyroscopes. He broke cars because he would not countenance placing 2nd. One of the early owners had even pleaded with Shaw's mother to dissuade her son from racing, afraid Shaw would kill himself. Despite all of this, Shaw won more than he lost, miraculously escaping serious injury for 20 years.

He competed on the board tracks. Once he was standing on the Allentown, Pa., track when the rotted boards gave way, causing him to fall through up to his elbows. In the race itself (after repairs), he received a 4-inch splinter in his nose that vibrated in the wind. Shaw spent half his time getting it out, and the rest of the time steering. Shaw thought of the splinter as an advantage since, in being preoccupied with the splinter, he forgot to be ill from the centrifugal force.

He competed at the Ascot midget track, the American version of a bull ring, before the midget track was eventually closed as being too dangerous. His 2nd wife (the 1st died in childbirth) received her indoctrination watching him spin into the Ascot fence, cracking his ribs. "Dutch Bookman, Louis Schneider and I would deliberately try to run each other off the track. It was brutal," Shaw said. "You figured so many races, so many days in the hospital."

Shaw returned to Indianapolis as a driver in 1927. He placed 4th. His style of driving was unchanged: charge on and trust to luck. The best example of Shaw's style was in the 1931 Memorial Day Race, in a team Duesenberg. Wearing a friend's St. Christopher Medal, though not himself religious, Shaw became bored with holding position according to orders, deciding to sneak a fast move on the back stretch out of sight of owner Fred Duesenberg.

"I came around and there was Shorty Cantlon, then Fred Winnai, Red Shafer, and Ralph Hepburn, whom I passed. I decided to make Hep throttle down for the turn at the end of the straight," Wilbur recalled. "The car got away from me in the turn, and I tried to give her a boot to get hold of her. I was using all the track in front of these guys and heading straight over the wall. I could see the meatwagon [ambulance] coming . . . I and my mechanic went 28 feet into the air, knocking down the telephone wires."

Both Shaw and the mechanic were caught under the cowling when the car landed squarely on its radiator.

The mechanic was hospitalized, but Shaw suffered only scrapes. He returned to the pits waving to his wife and mother in the stands, keeping a respectable distance from Duesenberg because he had just wiped out $25,000 worth of car. But Duesenberg asked him if he were really unhurt, then brought in Jimmy Gleason in the other team car so Shaw could drive.

Shaw immediately started moving the car up from 12th position. "About the 125th lap, we're on the back-stetch with the same 4 boys again—Cantlon, Winnai, Shafer, and Hep. Cantlon sees it's me and throttles down, then Winnai does, then Shafer, and finally Hep. But by this time we're in that same turn, and I—with a strange mechanic—had done a miserable job of getting into it. The car started 'walking' toward that wall again, and I was starting my slide into the basement [under the cowl] when we missed the wall by a thousandth of an inch. My mechanic was dead white. I thought to myself 'Brother, you should have been on the first trip.'" After gaining 6 places, Shaw, glassy-eyed, came in, letting Gleason finish the final 2 laps.

He went back to the garage area where he met Shorty Cantlon. Shorty, a practicing Catholic, took one look at the St. Christopher Medal still hanging around Shaw's neck, and remarked, "I saw you on that turn when you didn't make it. Then I saw you when you almost didn't. Look, Wilbur, don't crowd that saint too much. I don't know much he can stand."

Shaw made a fair living touring the country, driving other people's cars. But 1936 must be considered the turning point in his career. That year was the 1st time he was a major owner of the car he drove in the Indianapolis 500. The name of the car was "The Pay Car"; it was stubby, with a 4-cylinder engine which was an Offenhauser redesign of a Harry Miller creation. Karl Kizer, co-owner and cobuilder, said the chassis was too flexible, but that was the way Shaw wanted it.

In 1936 it placed 7th; Shaw and Kizer rebuilt it. The next year, Shaw won the 500 in it, en route to earnings in the vicinity of $80,000 for the season. But for 24 hours after that 500, he was almost totally exhausted and suffering from a burned foot. It was in late 1937, too, that Shaw went to Europe to compete, becoming the 1st spark in reuniting American and European racing at Indianapolis. He had been impressed by the European machinery at the Roosevelt Raceway revivals of the Vanderbilt Cup, but the Maserati seemed particularly suitable for Indy.

He persuaded Mike Boyle, a Chicago industrialist, to sponsor a Maserati 2GCS. The Maserati was altered for the Speedway; that is, everything was offset to the left. Shaw won with it in 1939 and 1940, and was leading by 5 laps in 1941 when a wheel hub broke. He hit the wall, fracturing 3 of his spinal verterbrae.

By this time, he had given up the dirt tracks that had almost made him a legend. Once he had set a record at Syracuse, N.Y., on a day when the dust at track level was as thick as London fog. He steered by taking his cues from a blimp following the race. Another time, a young driver seemed certain to overhaul him in the stretch; he turned around, waving furiously at the lad, shouting: "No! No!" The boy was bluffed. Shaw's last dirt-track race was at Springfield, Ill., in 1939 at which he won. After the race, a gruelling dangerous grind marred by a serious accident, he was lying on the ground, grimy and tired, and swearing angrily because the purse was only $400—instead of 4 times that as he had thought it would be. At that point, his wife came up and nudged him with her foot. "Well?" she said. That single word decided him; the dirt circuit was no longer worth it. So Shaw joined the ranks of the May drivers, picking and choosing starts other than Indy.

During World War II, Shaw worked as aviation sales manager for Firestone. The routine of being a 9-to-5 worker almost drove him crazy. It may have been partly this factor that spurred his rescue efforts for the old Speedway, when Eddie Rickenbacker lost interest and wanted to use the land as an industrial site. In any case, he persuaded Hulman to buy the plant and, as Speedway president, Shaw struggled to put on the 1946 race. He found the cars and drivers, got the Speedway in reasonable shape, and reorganized the Speedway staff. The 1947 driver's union attempt threatened his labors and only cooler heads saved him. The death of Cantlon in that race sobered everyone.

A handsome, dapper man with a hairline mustache, Wilbur made an excellent front for racing with automotive executives. He realized that the industry had to support the sport much more extensively for it to grow, and he worked toward that end.

When he was killed in a private airplane crash, October 30, 1954, the future of Indianapolis had been assured by Shaw. (Shaw was an expert pilot, having once given flying lessons to movie luminaries.) The memorial to him, a rest stop on the Indiana Turnpike, the Wilbur Shaw Service Area is a final irony. He is honored along with Knute Rockne of Notre Dame, poet James Whitcomb Riley and several governors—a school dropout bracketed with poets, governors, and college men.

CARROLL SHELBY

Carroll Shelby was perhaps the greatest single influence on America's racing posture in the post-1945 period. Here was a man, the son of a Texas mail clerk, who refurbished the image of American drivers in Europe on Europe's own terms. Here was a man with no formal engineering background who built an American-engined marque that challenged and ended Ferrari's domination of the World Manufacturer's Championship. Here was a man who, despite an ailing heart that cut short his driving career, created a sports car that forced the world's largest automobile manufacturer to make the Corvette into the fine automobile it is.

Born in Leesburg, Tex., January 11, 1923, Shelby traveled no easy road to the posh suburbs of Los Angeles, with a 2nd wife, healthy bank balances, and real-estate interests. In between were an Air Force career, 3 children by his high-school-sweetheart 1st wife, 9 or so business failures, 8 years of race driving, and another 8 as a car designer/racing team manager/specialty car manufacturer.

The Shelby family moved to Dallas early where Carroll, who had a heart murmer at age 10, outgrew it, and developed an avid interest in cars and racing. There were an Overland, Dodge, Willys, and Model T and Model A Ford in Shelby's early life. There were visits to tracks, where the likes of Oscar Coleman were the heroes. Shelby graduated from high school, met his 1st wife at a Baptist church social, and was married after he had enlisted in the Army Air Force. He spent World War II at Randolph Field, Tex., and in Denver as a pilot. Returning to Dallas after V-J Day, he made some money owning dump trucks, eventually selling out to work as an oil-field roughneck to learn the business in 1948 and part of 1949. But the pay was low, the work back-breaking, and prospects of turning into a millionaire seemed too distant; Shelby instead became a chicken farmer. His first batch turned a $5,000 profit; the second wiped him out when they died of limberneck disease.

Living on the proceeds of the truck business sale and odd jobs, Shelby returned to automobiles as an avocation, helping a friend work on various versions of the MG. He was 29, and father of 2, when he drove his 1st car competitively—the friend's MG Special—in January 1952, at a drag-racing meet at Grand Prairie Naval Air Station in Texas. It was not until May, at Norman, Okla., that Shelby drove his initial closed-course race in the friend's MG TC. He not only won the SCCA event in class, but then took the XK 120 Jaguar competition too, for instant fame among Southwestern amatuers.

In August 1952, at Okmulgee, Okla., using a borrowed XK 120, he won again, moving into a Cadillac-Allard in November at Caddo Mills, Tex. His path first crossed that of Masten Gregory, a life-long friend, at that race, which he also won. Still strictly amateur, Shelby drove for expenses for all of 1953. He drove Allards for Charlie Brown of Monroe, La., and went 9 for 9 for Roy Cherryhomes of Jacksboro, Tex. It was at a race at Eagle Mountain Naval Air Station in nearby Fort Worth that he 1st wore his famous striped overalls. "I had been working on a farm when I realized I was due to compete. It was a hot day, so I didn't bother to change," Shelby said. "I found the overalls cool and comfortable, and I won the race, too. I became identified with them, so I wore them all the time."

In January 1954, Gentleman Jim Kimberly, the millionaire sportsman who color-keyed his driving costumes to his cars, had donated an amateurs' cup for the Temporada race in Argentina. This was to be Shelby's 1st competition out of the country, becoming quite important in the development of his career. Carroll was able to make the trip only because Cherryhomes, who did not go, donated the car and helped with the expenses. Fortunately, Dale Duncan, his codriver, was an airline pilot, assuring transportation.

During the race, the Allard's carburetors burst into flame on a pit stop. With no other fire-extinguishing apparatus available, Duncan doused the flames by urinating on the engine. He finished even under the clicking of the press photographers' cameras. Anyway, Shelby liked this story. The Shelby/Duncan Allard went on to finish 10th, best of any of the amateur teams, winning the Kimberly Cup for SCCA.

Shelby's driving in this race impressed John Wyer of Aston Martin, whom Carroll met, with Peter Collins and other European stars. Shelby was invited to Europe for a drive with Aston Martin, if he paid his own expenses. He also got himself a Sebring ride for March of that year, expenses paid. The car stayed in contention until the rear axle broke after 77 laps; Shelby and codriver Charlie Wallace sat out the rest of the race. But it was another chance to rub elbows with the international set and the moneyed U.S. hangers-on.

A Texas oil millionaire named Guy Mabee dreamed

of an American sports car that would beat the best that Europe could offer. He asked Shelby to take charge of the effort. Shelby asked his wife whether to take Mabee's offer or the ride with Aston Martin, and they decided to gamble on Europe. However, Shelby attempted to persuade Mabee to buy an Aston Martin on the premise that this would shorten the time to build a good American sports car. Mabee tentatively agreed but continued on his own, as Shelby took off for England.

In April 1954, at Aintree, Shelby finished 2nd in a DBR3 to Duncan Hamilton. This feat got him a Le Mans opportunity codriving with Paul Frere, the Belgian journalist. It was in this Le Mans that Shelby drove his mount into the Aston pits complaining about a wiggly front suspension. The mechanics promptly jacked up the vehicle and the front wheel fell off, its spindle completely sheered.

Two weeks later in the Monza 1000, codriving with Graham Whitehead in a semi-private entry, Shelby made his 1st money, $2,000 for finishing 5th overall in the rain. The European jaunt ended with Shelby participating in a 1-2-3 sweep in the July 17th Silverstone 25-lapper; it was Peter Collins, Roy Salvadori, and Shelby. At this time, Mabee refused to take on the Aston Martin purchase; but Wyer declined Shelby's offer to fulfill the obligation anyway, knowing Carroll's financial condition.

Fortunately, Cherryhomes came to the rescue. He had bought a C Jaguar, which Shelby drove for 2 races before accepting another paid driving effort—Donald Healey's Class D record-setting efforts at the Utah Salt Flats in an assortment of Austin-Healeys. Healey had met Shelby briefly in England, and had apparently been impressed.

The Utah runs were good practice for the Carrera Panamericana in which Shelby was to codrive a factory Healey with Roy Jackson-Moore. At this last Pan-American Road Race, it seemed that the Mexican bureaucracy was fully developed and the Mexican populace fully untamed. When Shelby practiced for this event, and drove the course the wrong way to the starting line, he smashed the car against a road marker 175 miles north of Oaxaca. Then he waited with a badly broken arm. Mexican beer was provided by the residents, and Mexican brandy by 2 Brooklyn girls who saw him crash. Seven hours later, when the road was opened again, the ambulance came through to pick up the debris. The bruised Shelby was feeling no pain, or anything else for that matter, by this time.

Several days later, however, the Mexican authorities refused to let Shelby out of the country, until he could explain what happened to 2 missing Austin-Healey wheels. At the same time, Mexican doctors told him to see a U.S. specialist immediately about his fractured elbow. It was a week later before he could cross the border, and 8 months of operations and a cast before he was reasonably whole again. However, by January 1955, Carroll was back driving, cast and all. He codrove a Ferrari (for Alan Guiberson) with Phil Hill at Sebring, ending up 2nd when a protest was allowed. The manner in which Carroll drove was a monument to determination; he had replaced the plaster cast with a fiber-glass one for the race, with his hand taped to the steering wheel rim for extra support. After the race, it was back to the doctor and a new plaster cast.

Shelby won over 10 races Stateside in 1955; tried a Formula 1 Maserati at Syracuse, Italy, unsuccessfully; and later went to work for Tony Paravano, a West-Coast construction tycoon. Paravano took him to Europe on a car-buying tour, 1st at Ferrari and then at Maserati. Meanwhile, Shelby tried both the 1955 Targa Florio in a Paravano Monza Ferrari—his codriver crashed—and the Tourist Trophy race when it was on the Ards circuit, codriving with Gregory in a Porsche. Shelby and Gregory won in class. Then it was back to the U.S., with a victory in the Seattle Seafair races aboard a 4.9-litre Ferrari, and a disaster at Palm Springs when Shelby rode up the back of an Oldsmobile-powered Special. Both cars were demolished.

While the racing career might have been advancing, his personal life did not. Shelby was growing away from his wife as he savored the foot-loose life of the racing driver. The marriage eventually ended in an amicable divorce, and Carroll was to remarry after he had become financially successful. In 1956, Shelby—backed by Jim Hall's brother, Dick—opened Carroll Shelby Sports Cars in Dallas in an effort to create an independent base for himself. Shelby had become about the most famous road racer ever to come out of the Southwest; had thought the name would bring in business. It might have worked had Shelby spent more time at the place, but he was off driving.

He was, at this time, sponsored by another rich Californian, after Paravano had pulled out. Shelby's new patron was John Edgar, sometimes called the man who made Riverside Raceway. Shelby competed in some 20 races that year, most of them for Edgar, although he also drove in Alfa Veloce Special for the redoubtable Max Hoffman, a man who has handled virtually every major marque imported into the U.S.

Shelby recalled one particular 1956 race, a battle against Alfonso de Portago at the Nassau Speedweeks. It was the next phase of the 70-mile race for the Governor's Cup over the rough-surfaced 3.5-mile circuit at Windsor Field. Windsor Field had to be seen to be believed. It was a deteriorating World War II base, a 9-day construction wonder, still littered with rusted airplanes. Red Crise, the promoter and resident character, had decreed that the race go on despite a late start—certain to cut into that evening's cocktail party. Portago jumped the field of 37 starters before the flag flashed down, but Shelby, driving the big 4.9-litre Edgar Ferrari, caught the Marquis in the straightaway going into the 2nd lap. But soon after, the sun set with subtropical abruptness, the night finding Portago the only contender with headlights.

By the 10th lap, the Marquis was banging the rear bumper of Shelby's car, which somehow was still running at a 100-m.p.h. average in the pitch-black darkness. Shelby let Portago pass, then stayed on the Spaniard's tail, occasionally bashing Portago's rear to let him know Shelby still followed. It was a wild bit of driving because the two often had to take evasive action to avoid slower vehicles, and 8 laps later, Portago was driving blindly, too. With less than 2 laps to go, Carroll moved out in front again, and rolled to victory at a record pace of 99.095 m.p.h. Shelby subsequently broke his shoulder playing football on the beach with a cocoanut, but competed in the final race for the Governors Cup. Unfortunately, the big 4.9-litre Ferrari expired with tire and steering trouble, with Shelby 3rd at the time, and gaining on the leader, Stirling Moss.

Easily America's top road racing star, Shelby was invited to run in the 1st Gran Premio de Cuba, a race run through the streets and down a wide boulevard called the Malecon. It was an exciting time to be in Cuba, with Fidel Castro, then a revolutionary hero, holed up in the Sierra Maestre mountains, and Havana living as if there might not be a next week. The most exciting races were not the Gran Premio, but the stock-car sprints in the morning in which it seemed all the insane Havana taxi drivers had congregated to finish one another off in one grand demolition. Juan Manuel Fangio won the Grand Premio over Shelby.

Carroll, then 34, enjoyed 1957 because it was the acme of his accomplishment as a driver, despite later international victories. He won 19 straight in gathering in his 2nd SCCA title; shared a Maserati with Salvadori at Sebring, which was disqualified for refuelling illegally; and suffered the worst crash of his career in practice at Riverside September 21. Physicians fused 3 of Shelby's vertebrae, and he needed plastic surgery to repair his face. But he was back driving at Riverside in the November 100-mile international race. Shelby spun on the 1st lap, then overtook the entire field to win over Gregory, Dan Gurney, and Walt Hansgen. He had looked forward to a Maserati F1 ride in 1957 as a teammate of Fangio and Moss, but it never came to be.

About this time, Shelby revived the idea of an inexpensive American sports car that could compete with Europe's best. He discussed the idea several times with Harley Earle and Ed Cole, then GM styling vice-president and Chevrolet chief engineer, respectively. Both reportedly were receptive, but top management wasn't. So Shelby put the idea on the back burner, and renewed his association with Wyer and Aston Martin for 1958. At Sebring that year a gearshift lever broke, and Shelby retired. Meanwhile, he cast eyes toward Indianapolis and the really big money.

Indy official Harlan Fengler ended Shelby's Indy career before it started. Jack Ensley, another SCCA driver, had acquired an ex-Pat O'Connor Offy, taking his rookie test in the car with no intention of driving in the race. For that, he wanted Shelby. But Fengler dusted off a little-known rule to block Shelby, to the effect that 2 rookies were not allowed to take driver's tests with the same automobile.

Disappointed, Shelby went back to Europe, where he placed 3rd in a DBRs at Spa. At the Nurburgring 1000, the gearbox broke; and at Le Mans he became ill and had to be relieved by Stewart Lewis-Evans. He accepted an F1 ride from Mimo Dei's Scuderia Centro Sud, driving an outmatched old 250F Maserati. He ran 3 races, finished 2, one of them in 6th place. It was good training for the GP ride that Aston Martin promised him in 1959. Meanwhile, he was talking about his American sports car idea to anyone who would stand still.

The year 1959 was one of great contrasts for Shelby. It was the year that Aston Martin won the World Manufacturers Championship, and Shelby had something to do with that. And it was also the year Aston Martin launched a disastrous F1 bid, and Shelby was involved there, too. Shelby was sick with dysentery the day he and Salvadori shared the winning Aston Martin at Le Mans. However, there was no Sebring win; Shelby was sidelined when the oil pressure blew a seal, seeping into the clutch housing. He did manage a 3rd with Moss and Fairman in an Aston at the Tourist Trophy at Goodwood.

The 1959 F1 Aston Martin attempt was a year too late with its 2.5-litre engine, and too heavy as well. Shelby placed 7th on one magneto in the British GP, and that was his top performance. In their attempts to coax more power from the engine, Wyer got less and less. The engine seized at Zandvoort, there was an 8th at Oporto, Portugal, and a 10th at Monza. With the upcoming German GP scheduled for Avus, the fastest track in Europe, Aston Martin ended the quest.

At Nassau, Shelby drove a Birdcage Maserati for Camoradi, before the suspension gave out. He next tried the New Zealand GP, driving Temple Buell's 250F Maserati with Harry Schell and Jo Bonnier. Shelby got the car into 4th place before handing over to Schell, who had broken down earlier. They placed and took their winnings out of the country in merchandise.

In January 1960, Shelby woke up with a pain in his chest, eventually diagnosed as heart trouble. He drove many races that year with nitroglycerine pills under his tongue, and managed to win the USRRC title. He was DNF at Havana and Sebring and won Castle Rock, Colo., for the Meister Brauser Scarab; then drove Max Balchowsky's Ole Yaller II at Road America, leading until 4th gear broke. He had won the Riverside GP in April, driving a Maserati to take a wide lead, but, as the 1960 season progressed, the pains got worse. In the final 3 races, he managed a 4th and two 5ths.

After the 2nd Riverside GP, Shelby quit driving.

Having retired from driving, Shelby looked for another source of income. The Carroll Shelby School of Driving at Riverside was the answer. A $90 ad had brought in $1,400 worth of requests for a $1 catalog. Earlier, Shelby had become the distributor for Goodyear racing tires, and in the course of his business he met Dave Evans of Ford. He mentioned his American sports car project, but did not press the matter then.

Shelby was, at this time, living in Santa Fe Springs, Calif., and working out of a part of Dean Moon's Speed Shop. His heart trouble had finally been diagnosed as something caused by any overexertion.

In September 1961, Shelby learned that the Bristol engine company was no longer in business, and he dispatched an airmail letter to Derek Hulock of AC in England. The car project was finally taking shape. Shelby 1st thought of the aluminum Buick V-8 or Oldsmobile engines for the car, but then he heard of a new light-weight cast-iron Ford engine. Ford Company's Dave Evans sent him a few of these engines for experiment, through Dean Moon's Speed Shop, and also referred him to Don Frey, one of the few Detroit executives who were truly knowledgeable car buffs.

Shelby was finally at the right place at the right time on 2 continents, a feat never before achieved. Both Ford and AC agreed to the name he claimed he had dreamed —Cobra. Ford also agreed to call the car 1st the Shelby AC Cobra; then the AC Cobra; and finally, when it was successful, the Ford Cobra.

Pete Brock, a refugee from the GM Sting Ray project, was Shelby's 1st employee and test driver, Billy Krause his 1st competition driver. Shelby had to borrow a driving-school student's trailer to get the 1st AC chassis back to Santa Fe Springs. The 260-cu. in. V-8 Ford engine dropped right into place. Frey assigned Ray Geddes to take care of Shelby's accounting, and insisted that the 2nd Cobra be shipped to Dearborn. Shelby sold his 1st Cobra in mid-1962, and about 75 that same year. He had it homologated as a GT at the end of 1962, by which time Krause had started the factory racing effort. Krause led at Riverside until a stub axle broke; and also at Nassau, until the front end went away. Shelby had the right to contact Ford franchises as possible dealers. He was deluged with eager dealers.

The car evolved quickly to a 289-cu. in. engine and rack and pinion steering by the 126th car. It cost $5,995, not exactly everyman's sports car, but reasonable compared with the Corvettes, Maseratis and Ferraris it challenged. Only about 10 percent were being raced, however. Phil Remington joined Shelby's firm early, and soon became "Mr. Everything" at Cobra, which moved to the ex-Reventlow Scarab digs in Venice, Calif., about June 1962.

Factory racing started in earnest for Cobra with the 1963 Daytona Continental, then a 3-hour race. Ford was using Shelby as an extension of its testing facilities, in return for the use of its technical establishment. Three factory Cobras faced the starter—Dan Gurney, Dave McDonald, and Skip Hudson, with an aluminum experimental engine. Hudson crashed early; Gurney led until his ignition went, and this time the defending Continental champion could not use his battery to get the car over the finish line. McDonald finished 4th behind Ferrari's Pedro Rodriguez.

Shelby had switched from overalls to blue jeans with a black cowboy hat, and the back of the blue denim jacket had Cobra written on it. The garb didn't help one bit at Sebring, where the best the 3 Cobras could do was 11th overall (Gurney and Hill, despite bad brakes and electrical woes). The Fireball Roberts-McDonald car succumbed to a rear oil seal leak; the Ken Miles-Lew Spencer car was sidelined when the bolts on the steering gave out. But at Le Mans the Tom Bolton-Ian Sanderson car managed 7th overall.

However, in SCCA racing the Corvette eaters did much better. On July 7 at Lake Garnett, Kans., Bob Johnson, McDonald and Miles pulled a 1-2-3 sweep of the production race; then Miles won the modified race in essentially the same Cobra. Earlier, McDonald and Miles had finished 1st and 2nd at the Dodger Stadium races in Los Angeles; and the Cobra had been 1st, 2nd, and 4th at Laguna Seca. It was a promising beginning for a new sports car. The coupe version was introduced that October, making its racing debut in what was then the 2,000-kilometer Daytona Continental. Bob Holbert and McDonald led the race for 8 hours before an electrical fire finished them, but Johnson and Gurney (in a roadster) took 4th overall, and 2nd in GT, behind a Ferrari GTO.

Sebring was a much more pleasant story. Five factory Cobras and the prototype coupe went down, and, although Miles crashed the coupe in practice, the Cobras shut Ferrari off from points by taking the first 7 places in GT. Cobra led for the manufacturers crown, 18.3 to 16.5, a 1st for an American marque. It was then that the Ford coffers opened, and Carroll Shelby was going overseas again. Gurney took 2nd in GT class, finishing 8th overall in the Targa Florio. At Spa, Hill's coupe set fast time, but Bob Bondurant, Jochen Neerpasch, and Innes Ireland failed. All 4 cars wrecked at Nurburgring, but at Le Mans the story was different. Ferrari went in with a 26-point GT lead only to come out with but 11, as Gurney and Bondurant won in GT class, finishing 4th overall.

The Rheims 12-hour race was a disaster with both the Ireland and Gurney cars failing to finish, as a Ferrari GTO won. As a result, Ferrari led 73.2 - 48.8. But Bondurant won the Freiburg Hillclimb's GT class; then, in the Tourist Trophy at Goodwood, Cobra swept the GT class, led by Gurney in 3rd overall. Ferrari's lead was down to 11 points again, and, with the Coppa de

Europa at Monza to come, was in imminent danger of disappearing. Monza seemed just made for Cobras.

But if the Commendatore couldn't win on the track, he was matchless in the smoke-filled rooms of FIA. He declared he would withdraw his entire entry if his prototypes weren't immediately classified as GT cars. The Monza management was forced to petition FIA for that move because they faced financial fiasco without Ferrari. FIA, of course, refused; the race was cancelled, and Cobra was forced to make a full run at the Tour de France, a race composed of 16 separate events. After winning the first 2, the Bondurant-Neerpasch car suffered a broken crankshaft. Trintignant-Simon won the Rouen leg, but burned a front-wheel bearing. St. Auban-Peron blew a piston in the 4th event. Ferrari clinched, and not even a Cobra sweep in the Bridgehampton Double 500 altered the Ferrari victory at 84.6 to 78.3. m.p.h.

Meanwhile, in the USRRC series, Cobras won 6 of 8. In 3 races, they were 1-2-3 (Augusta, Ga.; Pensacola, Fla.; and Laguna Seca). At Mid-Ohio they were 1-2-3-4; and at Kent they were 1-2. A 4th at Des Moines and a 5th at Meadowdale, Ill., completed the season.

Carroll Shelby was changing, too. The Shelby GT 350 Mustang made its debut in January 1965, and the Cobra operation was downgraded as Shelby-American moved to a new factory near the Los Angeles airport. Carroll was as much the business man as the ex-racer. The costume came out for racing only, and he was now competing to be the performance arm of FoMoCo with Holman-Moody. Ford's battle plan was to wipe Ferrari from the face of racing, after it had failed in attempts to buy out Ferrari. The Ford GT40 Coupe was the news at the Daytona Continental in 1965, but there were Cobra Daytona coupes present to make sure of manufacturers points, too. Luigi Chinetti knew the handwriting on the pit wall when he saw it; he commented that it was inevitable that a good big company would beat a good small company. There were 2 coupes, Miles and Lloyd Ruby in one, Bondurant and Sir John Whitmore in the other. There were 4 factory Cobras. And, to play rabbit, there was Gurney in a Lotus 19. It wasn't a contest for long. Miles-Ruby won overall, and Jo Schlesser-Hal Keck won GT.

For Sebring, Ferrari was officially absent, but his cars were there. Something called the Ferrari Owners Racing Association had quad-cam P-2s. A 10-car assault came from Shelby and Ford—2 GT40s, 4 roadsters, 4 Daytona coupes. A Chaparral won overall, but Schlesser-Bondurant won GT. Ferrari won Monza, Targa Florio, and Nurburgring overall, against token opposition from Ford of England, but Bondurant won 1st in GT at Monza and the Ring, with a 2nd in GT at Spa. Whitmore contributed a victory in GT at Oulton Park, and Bondurant added a GT victory at the Rossfield Hillclimb. The Le Mans entry from both camps was massive, 11 cars each,

and Ford personnel were clearly in command of the operation, with Shelby taking a secondary role.

Ford and Ferrari were both virtually wiped out during the race, but Jack Sears and Dr. Dick Thompson finished 2nd in GT in a Daytona Coupe to help neutralize the Ferrari points. When Bondurant-Schlesser won GT in the Rheims 12-hour race, it was all over. Cobra had become the 1st American-conceived car to win the manufacturers crown. Shelby was happy, but he was pursuing a new dream. With Gurney, he had formed All-American Racers for the express purpose of building an American GP championship car, a car adaptable also for Indianapolis. He was a millionaire now, and Ford-supplied business brains had provided for him for life.

The battle was joined with Holman-Moody and Ford Advanced Vehicles Operations in 1966, the last year the Cobra was produced. Even the Shelby Mustang was going downhill in performance, ruined by over-zealous Ford stylists. A short stint of producing a Ford-engine Sunbeam called the Tiger, had also gone by the boards. The Daytona Continental had 5 Mark 2 GT40s, 2 each from Shelby and Holman-Moody, and one from Roy Lunn's Ford Advanced Vehicles Operations. Shelby won this round by the simple expedient of learning to change the disc brakes quicker. Miles-Ruby were 1st, followed by Grant-Gurney. H-M's lead pair, Hansgen and Mark Donohue, came in 3rd, after losing 10 minutes on the brake change.

There were 13 Ford GTs, but the 2 factory teams were the important ones, plus Graham Hill in the semi-private Alan Mann car. Again it was all Shelby, although he had to stand on the pit wall brandishing a hammer when Miles and Gurney started racing one another at the 3-hour mark. Gurney's car suffered a blown engine when victory was certain, with a few minutes left in the race, so Miles got his 2nd straight victory.

The AAR Eagles, meanwhile, were ready in March 1966. There were 5 to be powered by Ford d.o.h.c. engines; 3 had been sold, with Gurney and Joe Leonard to drive the house cars. Shelby and Gurney were counting on some prize money from Indy to help finance their GP effort. The gruesome first-lap crash finished Dan's car, flat-spotted Leonard's tires. Later, Ruby in a private car was black-flagged for a supposed oil leak while leading; Roger McCluskey also had an oil leak. Leonard got 9th-place money, Jerry Grant 10th, Ruby 11th, and McCluskey 13th. That set back the F1 program money-wise.

Le Mans saw 3 cars each from Shelby and H-M, plus two of Alan Mann's. The Ford 1-2-3 finish followed, with McLaren-Amon designated for the victory over Miles-Ruby.

Late in 1966, the Shelby organization got its feet wet in SCCA TransAm-sedan racing. Two Shelby employees, Don and Gary Pike, had done the job virtually on their own until Jerry Titus was given a Shelby-prepared car with which he won the Green Valley, Tex., enduro, and the title for Mustang. For 1967 Shelby American had a $27,500 TransAm support program, but a Shelby-prepared Mustang team competed through 1969 with an assortment of drivers, including George Follmer, Titus, and Peter Revson, with sporadic success.

Meanwhile, the Cobra died quietly, done in by more comfortable muscle cars that cost less. There were rumors of its revival as a plastic-bodied luxury sports car, but it never happened. The Shelby GT350 and GT500 eventually were produced and assembled in Michigan, leaving Carroll with nothing but money.

For the 1967 Continental it was 3 each again, Shelby versus Holman-Moody. But the entire Ford effort was mousetrapped by gearbox troubles and by the phoenix-like Ferrari effort. Chris Amon and Lorenzo Bandini won, with the top Ford, an old GT40, driven to 6th overall more than 200 miles behind the leader by Dr. Thompson and Jackie Ickx. But Ford was 1st and 2nd at Sebring, with Andretti and McLaren sharing the winning Mk. IV and Foyt-Ruby taking 2nd. Titus won a Trans-Am race to make it a Ford weekend.

Shelby was in complete charge of the early Ford effort at Le Mans, although responsibility was divided for the race proper. The Foyt-Gurney team won it for him, while Donohue's battered GT40 made it to 4th place. Three of the 4 Holman-Moody cars were wiped out just before the 12-hour mark. Gurney won the Belgian GP, meanwhile, to give the Eagle F1 car its initial victory. And the GT350 production shift to Ionia, Mich., was announced near the end of June.

After 1967, the Shelby competition effort seemed to flag. Carroll himself was more at home in a $300 business suit than in sports garb at the track. He appeared periodically to oversee TransAm efforts. Meanwhile, the King Cobra, a Group 7 sports/racer, was crashed by Parnelli Jones and never developed. Carroll turned to a newer Lola chassis for his aluminum Ford 427 engine, and, even with Gurney driving, still had little success. There were too many Ford people involved for him to wield much power. Shelby was out of CanAm and TransAm by 1970; in fact to all intents, after 1970 he seemed out of racing completely.

JO SIFFERT

July 20, 1968, saw the 21st running of the British Grand Prix, an 80-lap 212-mile race at Brands Hatch. It was a dark, cloudy day, but the rain failed to materialize. Graham Hill and Jackie Oliver, both in factory Lotuses, had taken the pole and the 2nd spot on the grid. Chris Amon in a Ferrari completed the top row. Another Lotus 49B, powered by Ford, was in the next row, but this was a private entry of Rob Walker, driven by a slim,

mustachioed Swiss by the name of Jo Siffert.

Siffert was a good, fast driver, and this day he had a good car, spanking new. In fact, he had practiced in an old Tasman car because his original Lotus had been destroyed, along with practically everything else that made up R. R. C. Walker Racing, in a fire that had swept Walker's Dorking garage. When the flag fell, Oliver took an early lead, but yielded to Hill at the 3rd lap. Siffert lay 3rd. On the 27th lap, Hill's universal joint broke, Oliver retaking 1st place, but on lap 43 Oliver's engine failed. That put the thing up to Siffert and to Amon, one of the best, but also a driver who had never won a *grande épreuve* either. Two hungry men, dueling around the Hatch. Chris had to back off, however, when his rear tires were wearing thin. Thus, Jo Siffert, the only Swiss since the Baron de Graffenreid in 1949 in this same race to win a Grand Prix, brought Rob Walker his 9th and, some say, proudest GP victory.

Born July 7, 1936, in Fribourg, Switzerland, just southwest of Berne, Siffert was the son of an automobile dealer. His infatuation with motors came early, and to earn money for a motorcycle, he picked and sold flowers and picked up spent Swiss Army shells to sell to the thrifty military for recycling. He started serious cycle racing in 1957 on a 125-c.c. Gilera, later went through a succession of other marques. He became an expert mechanic in the process, and took the Swiss 350-c.c. Championship in 1959. The following year, Siffert moved over to 4 wheels, entering a Formula Junior in a Stanguellini, but accomplished no great feats. By 1961 he swapped a Lotus 18 for a Lotus 20, and started to attract attention. He won the Circuits of Cesenatico, and Lake Garda, and the Eifelrennen in April. In May he was 3rd in the Grand Prix des Frontières at Chimay, behind John Love and Tony Maggs; then got a Ferrari 2-litre ride for the Nurburgring 1000, in May, finishing 3rd in the under-2000-c.c. class. In June, Jo took Castello-Terramo, was 2nd to Love at Caserta. The next month he was 3rd in the Coupe de Vitesse at Rheims, behind Trevor Taylor and Maggs. In August he won at Enna and at Cadours, then won the Coupe de Paris at Montlhéry.

With Maggs and Taylor, Siffert was joint European FJ champion. Buying a Lotus 22 for FJ racing in 1962, Jo also confidently bought a 4-cylinder Lotus 24 for possible Formula 1 drives. At the Brussels GP, he raced the FJ car fitted with a 1.5-litre Ford-Cosworth engine and finished 6th; then reverted the car to its FJ status, winning at Vienna's Aspern airfield. Siffert's real F1 debut came April 23, 1962, at Pau. Despite gear selector troubles, he finished 6th.

Siffert's initial World Championship event was the Belgian GP that year, in which he placed 10th. Retired in the French GP's 5th lap with clutch trouble, he took 12th in Germany, failed to qualify in Italy. In 1963 Jo continued his berth with Ecurie Filipinetti in a Lotus-BRM, but after coming in 2nd at Imola and winning at

Syracuse, he went completely independent, taking the car with him. He retired at Monaco and Silverstone, crashed in the rain at Spa and finished far back at Rheims, Zandvoort, and in the German race.

In 1964, he joined with Rob Walker in a successful collaboration, even though he was considered number 3 to Graham Hill and John Surtees. That season Siffert was 8th at Monaco, 13th in Holland, retired at the Belgian and French Grands Prix. But he was 11th in Britain, a pleasant 4th in Germany. Retired again in the Austrian GP, he was 7th at the Italian race, then 3rd in the U.S. GP. He retired in Mexico.

In 1965, a 4th in Mexico was the best of the World Championship events for Siffert. Most of his finishes were down in the field, and there were 2 retirements in his Brabham. But there was a sweet victory. This was over World Champion Jim Clark, in the nontitle Mediterranean GP at Enna, where Jo averaged 139 m.p.h. In 1966 after retiring at Monaco, he got a Cooper-Maserati, but crashed it at the Belgian GP. Another retirement in the French GP was followed by a 12th in Britain, and still more retirements, the picture brightening only in the U.S., where Jo was 4th. At the Le Mans 24-hour race that year he shared a 4th in a Porsche Carrera, which was number 1 in the Index of Performance.

While he continued the GP racing in 1967—4th in France and the U.S. his best showings—Siffert stepped up his sports car/enduro activity that season. Joining with Hans Herrmann in a Porsche 910, he was 4th at Sebring and Daytona, 5th at Monza; 2nd at Spa, 6th in

the Targa, and 5th at Le Mans in a 907. In the BOAC 500 with Bruce McLaren, Siffert finished 3rd. The following year saw no change, save for that GP victory in Britain, with retirements galore and some other low placings in F1. But in the enduros, Siffert shared a Porsche 907 and victory at the Daytona 24-hour race with Vic Elford, Rolf Stommelen, Herrmann, and Jochen Neerpasch. Then with Herrmann along, he won Sebring; with Elford in a Porsche 908 he won the Nurburgring 1000; and alone, he won the Austrian 1000.

Grand Prix racing is a bug uneasy to lose, however, and if the temptation was there to concentrate on the sports/prototype type of racing Jo never showed it. In 1969 he still turned out for the GP races and was 4th in South Africa, retired in Spain, 3rd at Monaco, and 2nd in Holland. He could almost taste that 2nd victory, but then came a French GP 9th, a British 8th, a German 5th (although he was in a 13th-lap accident), an Italian 8th, and successive retirements in Canada, the U.S., and Mexico. But in sports car racing, Siffert enjoyed his greatest season—a great season in any sport—with 6 outright victories. In a Porsche 908 shared with Brian Redman, he won at the BOAC 500, Monza, Spa, Nurburgring, and the Watkins Glen 6-hour race. With Kurt Ahrens in a Porsche 917, he won the Austrian 1000. Not content with that showing, Siffert also drove in some Canadian-American Challenge Cup races, starting with Watkins Glen where he was 6th. He was 4th at Mid-Ohio, retired at Road America, 3rd at Bridgehampton, 4th at Michigan, 5th at Laguna Seca, retired at Riverside and 4th at Texas, his points adding up to a 4th-place ranking in the CanAm and a $50,200 purse.

In 1970 there was little diminution of Siffert's activities. Driving for the STP-March team in F1 the usual frustrations were there: 10th in South Africa, failure to qualify in Spain, 8th at Monaco, 7th in Belgium, retirements in 3 straight Grands Prix, 8th in Germany, 9th in Austria, 2 more retirements, 9th in the U.S. GP and a final retirement at Mexico. Contrast that with victories in a Porsche 908/3 Spyder with Redman in the challenging Targa Florio, and at Spa in a Porsche 917 in the series's fastest race. The pair also was 2nd at Daytona in a Porsche 917 and led Le Mans only to have the engine fail. They were 2nd in the Watkins Glen 6-hour race by 44 seconds to teammates Pedro Rodriguez and Leo Kinnunen; then Jo won the Austrian 1000. Siffert ran a single CanAm race that season, coming in 2nd at Watkins Glen to Denis Hulme for 15 points and $10,100.

Siffert drove both GP and endurance races in 1971. He started with March for the former, financed by Porsche, which wanted one of its star drivers happy and was afraid that Ferrari would offer Jo both F1 and enduro rides, but switched to Yardley-BRM before the season opened. Success came again, and early, with Porsche, as Siffert and Derek Bell won the opening Buenos Aires 1000 in a Porsche 917, the race marred by the death of Ignazio Giunti in a shunt with Jean-Pierre Beltoise. At Sebring, Siffert ran the day's fastest lap, but the Porsche finished 5th. In the BOAC 1000, shared with Bell, he was 3rd, at Monza 2nd, at Spa the day's fastest lapper but 2nd again. He scored his 3rd 2nd-place finish in the Nurburgring 1000; then retired in the Targa Florio, Le Mans and Austria. At the Glen, Jo and Gijs van Lennep were 2nd.

In F1, they say it is hard to win one GP and harder still to win another. Yet Siffert accomplished the trick in 1971. Sixth in the nontitle Argentine GP and in the Questor GP, he retired in South Africa, Spain, and Monaco. In Holland he was 6th, in France 4th, in Britain 9th. Retired again in Germany, in the Austrian GP he beat out Stewart for the pole in the final qualifying minutes. Then, as Stewart clinched his 2nd World Championship (because all of his pursuers retired), Siffert led from green flag to checker. He ran the fastest lap at 134.39 and won easily at 132.30 m.p.h., despite a late tire puncture that enabled Emerson Fittipaldi to close on him dramatically but not successfully. Ninth in both Italy and Canada, Siffert came close to another victory in the U.S. GP, finishing 2nd to François Cevert. His 19 championship points tied the Swiss for 4th place in the standings with Ickx.

There was to be a Mexican GP, but it was cancelled, and to celebrate Stewart's championship, an extra F1 race was staged in Britain at Brands Hatch—no points, some money, and maybe some glory. It was run October 24, 1971, and it became Jo Siffert's last race. At better than 130 m.p.h., as a BRM teammate was leading the race, Jo's car skidded, hit an embankment, flipped, and burned. Siffert died in the flames.

DICK SIMON

Born September 21, 1933, Dick Simon was 36 years old before he joined USAC and went to Indianapolis. By that time he had 7 children and was president and board chairman of the Majestic Life Insurance Co. of Salt Lake City, Utah.

That is not to say that Simon, a bald, fit-looking man and a continual bundle of energy, was a total novice. He had started in 1965 in the Canadian-American Modified Racing Association, mainly performing at Salt Lake Fairgrounds, where he was a local favorite, of course. Simon was not a native of the city; he had been born in Seattle, Wash., and attended both high school and junior college out there before moving to Utah to attend the University of Utah, work in a dairy and manage a sporting goods store to earn partial tuition. He earned the rest the hard way, with a skiing scholarship after just a year in the sport.

Simon was very competitive, even in skiing, and it was his aggressiveness that probably cost him a 1960 Olympic berth when he broke an ankle in the Trials. Next he took up skydiving, becoming a national champion in 1965 after winning some 25 major events. The following year he broke his back and both heels when his chute collapsed some 60 feet from the ground: not exactly the way for an insurance man to act. In December 1965, Dick had become a Majestic agent, and despite his hospitalization the next year, he managed to sell $2.8 million in policies personally and establish an agency that averaged $1 million in sales a month. Simon was appointed head of everything at Majestic by April 1968.

That was the same time that Simon started racing a Corvette in SCCA events, moving up the following year into single-seat racing cars in the SCCA's Continental series for Formula A cars (later Formula 5000). In 1970 he joined USAC and raced at both Indy and at Ontario, finishing 14th in the former, despite a lost half-hour to repair a broken supercharger, and 3rd at Ontario. That gave Dick enough points in his Vollstedt-Ford to be 10th in the final point standings for the Championship Trail. Standing proudly alongside him was a Salt Lake department store owner named Fred Auerbach, who had befriended Simon and become involved in what the friend 1st called "squirrel cage" schemes, then helped Simon finance his racing before sponsors like Travelodge and Post Cerals appeared.

Actually the sponsors were sold by Simon, who was a master at selling anything from insurance to the logic of a grandfather (since 1971) going racing to sponsoring a racing car. In 1971 Simon was 17th at Pocono after a fire in the car and 22nd at Ontario after piston problems. He also was 14th again at Indy, again with supercharger ills in the ex-Roger Penske Lola-Ford. More interestingly, perhaps, Dick became involved in a motor sports controversy when he "bumped" rookie John Mahler out of his back-up car when Simon's own car failed to qualify. Mahler had recorded the then-fastest speed ever made by a 1st-year driver and found himself without a ride when Simon took over the car. "I owed it to my sponsors to drive the race. It was as simple as that," Dick said. He proved what he meant two months later when he handed Mahler his spare car after John wrecked his own in practice for the inaugural Pocono 500. Neither man finished, Mahler wrecking Simon's car, Simon escaping a fire in his own mount.

The dream of finishing up high, maybe even winning, at Indianapolis, a dream that had pushed many men forward for a time, kept Simon coming back. In 1972, for instance, he finished 13th at Indy and 16th at Pocono but didn't make the Ontario grid. Unlike most, he had a record of unusual accomplishments, on wheels and off, that made his dream sound a bit more plausible even when you thought about his age, his circumstances, his relative lack of experience in Championship cars. Or maybe you just were being cleverly sold by a master salesman?

JIGGER SIROIS

Frenchy Sirois had a dream for his son: the boy was going to win the Indianapolis 500. When the boy was born April 16, 1935, in Hammond, Ind., Frenchy had named him Leon Duray Sirois, after the racing hero of early U.S. competition. But Leon became known as Jigger, though why, no one could really remember. Frenchy knew what it was like to be with a winning team. He had worked on the pit crews of Lee Wallard, Sam Hanks and Jimmy Bryan in the years they had won at Indy.

Jigger grew up around race cars; in fact, he never knew anything else, making it inevitable that he become a race driver. At an early age, he was competing in stocks at Iliana Speedway, not far from his home town. In 1959 he was Central States Racing Association Rookie of the Year; in 1960, he was Most Improved Driver in the United Auto Racing Association, whose championship he won the following year. In 1963 he became NASCAR midget champ, and his exploits in Midwest midget circles, mostly non-USAC, for several years after that had to make old Frenchy happy. Jigger even won a 100-miler at Milwaukee in 1965, driving a Buick-powered midget.

In 1966, Sirois tried IMCA, driving sprints for 2 years, and finally, in 1968, at the age of 33 he joined USAC. That year he won one of 14 midget races for Weiland Tool and made his Championship Trail debut at Springfield, later managing a 10th in the Central Excavating Special at Michigan International Speedway. In 1969 he passed his rookie test for Indianapolis and it was then that he came close to everlasting notice in the annals of racing. The opening day of official qualifying in 1969 was a blustery rainy day but late in the day it cleared sufficiently for Sirois to go out on the track, the 1st car to attempt to qualify. He got his Quaker State Special up to 161.488 m.p.h., but after 3 of the 4 required laps, owner Myron Cave called him in. Had he taken one more lap and the checker, he would automatically have won the pole position! Before any other driver could be ready to start his try, the rains had come again and stayed, forbidding any more qualifiers.

Had Sirois completed his qualifying for the pole, the resultant controversy might have shaken up the Speedway. Sirois's speed of 161.488 m.p.h. would have been only the 32nd fastest, well below A. J. Foyt's pole-winning 170.568 m.p.h. Sirois could never get the car going even that fast again, and didn't make the race.

Sirois competed less and less after that, never getting the good ride. So Frenchy Sirois's hopes of fathering an Indianapolis 500 winner became just a father's dreams.

J. ALEX SLOAN

There have been only a few giants in the promotional end of auto racing. J. Alex Sloan, prime mover in the founding of the IMCA and partner to the world's greatest publicist, William Pickens, was one of these. Born near Pittsburgh, Pa., Sloan attended Ohio Wesleyan University where he was All-American material in football. After college, he became a sports writer and, later, Sports Editor of the *St. Paul Daily News* in Minnesota. During this period, he had also coached St. Paul Central High School's football team, and on the side, played independent football.

Meanwhile, he was experimenting with the idea of promoting auto races. The Minnesota State Fair was his venue, bringing in such drivers as Barney Oldfield, Bob Burman, Eddie Rickenbacker, and Ralph DePalma. Finally he decided to devote all his time to sports promotion, forming the firm of Sloan and Pickens. One of their 1st steps was to sign Barney to a 3-year pact. Using Oldfield as the nucleus, they set up races almost anywhere a dirt track could be laid out. With Pickens's ability to present the facts at hand in their most favorable light, they made a fortune for themselves and Oldfield, in the process turning cigar-chomping Barney into a household name.

Sloan and Pickens split when Oldfield's pact ended. J. Alex decided there was a more enduring future in developing IMCA, which had been formed by disgruntled major state and country fairs when the AAA Contest Board decided to pick and choose where its Championship Trail would meander. Sloan used IMCA to provide a ready-made circuit for some of his and Pickens's later creations like Leon Duray. But more importantly, he built IMCA until it was at least the equal of AAA in activity 364 days a year. The 365th day, of course, was the day of the Indianapolis 500.

Sloan promoted races and exhibitions almost from the Arctic Circle to the Mexican border, over an area bigger than Europe. At one time he had as many as 5 circuits going, each with its own stars and competition, each playing a different set of towns. Most of these racing teams traveled via private railroad trains, with the pilots in Pullmans and the vehicles themselves in baggage cars. When he died in 1937, his empire was divided among his main aides, Al Sweeney and Frank Winkley, whose organizations promoted IMCA races side by side.

CLAY SMITH

There is a strong likelihood that, had he reached his legal majority in more prosperous times, Clay Smith might never have returned to auto racing. He had wanted to be a petroleum engineer, and he certainly had the brains for it under his red hair, but not the money. In later years, he was able to converse knowledgeably on

562

the most abstruse subject, for he was amazingly well-read.

Born October 24, 1914, in Phoenix, Ariz., Smith was the son of a wholesale grocer who later found it expedient to move his family to Long Beach, Calif. By the time he was in junior high school, Clay was working as a mechanic's helper at the local airport. In school he was a fine student, especially in the physical sciences, but by the time Smith was ready for college, the expression was in full force. Smith gravitated into racing instead of college, driving a self-prepared Ford in AAA Coast racing starting in 1934. But he always hated driving, whether a personal or race car, and he used the swing around the California circuit principally to establish himself as a mechanic.

Several years later, Smith left racing to work almost a decade for an oil company. Because he had an asthmatic condition, the tall, lanky Smith suffered when he left the Southern California climate. What brought him back to racing after World War II was a cam-grinding shop he started with his cousin, Danny (Termite) Jones. He had finally given up on the idea of petroleum engineering at the age of 32.

Smith's garage, on Spring Street, near Signal Hill in Long Beach, was located in one of the great gasoline alleys of America. There were several notable garages clustered there then—besides Smith's, the best-known was Bill Stroppe's of Mercury fame. Stroppe was a lifelong friend and former classmate of Smith's, and it was he who had convinced Clay that the answer to his money problems lay in racing. Clay's cams became fairly popular, but a turning point came one night when he helped Stroppe set up the engine of a V-8 midget. The engine was to have been campaigned by Johnny Mantz against the likes of Bill Vukovich and a wild young half-pint named Walt Faulkner. Mantz, a loser up to then, slaughtered Vuky and Walt, the latter protesting that Mantz's engine was oversize. When the teardown was completed, it was discovered that the engine was not only legal, but actually undersize. Faulkner demanded to know who set up the engine. Mantz indicated the cigar-smoking Smith, and Faulkner went over to congratulate him.

Years later, when he was one of the stars of the J. C. Agajanian stable, Walt Faulkner said: "I was nothing but a cocky so and so, but Clay made a race driver out of me. He told me what it was all about." This was the other side of this unusual man with the "magic wrenches"—his shop became a mecca for race drivers, mechanics, and awestruck kids like Mickey Thompson. He would dispense instruction, philosophy, and aid, to friend and rival alike, with that natural logic whereby he could view a problem as a whole, then dissect it step by step. To the "let's torque it up a little more and see what happens" set that still inhabits parts of the pit area, this made Smith seem like a superman.

It was Mantz who persuaded Agajanian to hire Clay

Smith as the mechanic on his 1948 Indianapolis car, though Smith had never been near Indy's pit area. Mantz was 5th when an oil tank split along the seams. After winning the AAA Pacific title, Mantz went nonstop to finish 7th the following year. Though he worked with Duane Carter and Chuck Stevenson in their glory days, Smith's personal triumph was Faulkner. When Mantz decided to drive stock cars (he won the 1st Darlington 500), Smith persuaded Agajanian to give Walt the Indy ride—straight from the sprints.

Faulkner's record qualification run in 1950 is standard Indianapolis legend now, but Smith was the one who took Walt for his rookie test several weeks previously, sitting with him at the 1st turn even before Walt ever drove the track, explaining the techniques as experienced drivers passed and pointing out deficiencies. The Little Dynamo cut a fine rookie test, but come qualification time he thrilled himself in to a wild spin. It was Smith who talked his confidence back into him for another try that resulted in the record.

It was 1952 that was Smith's greatest year, however. Troy Ruttman won Indy, Stevenson's Smith-prepared Springfield Welding Special won the national title, and the Smith-organized and prepared Lincoln factory team finished 1-2-3 in the stcok-car part of the Pan American Road Race. In 1953 he topped this performance with 1-2-3-4; and, in the car in which he rode, called every shift, almost every turn of the wheel, and the speeds he wanted.

By 1954, Smith was on his way to becoming a wealthy man, but his asthmathic condition was growing worse. He had made arrangements to buy out his partner and settle down in the Long Beach shop, foresaking the racing grind. But he made his annual Midwestern trail tour before that—Springfield, Milwaukee, DuQuoin.

And it was at DuQuoin, Ill., September 6, 1954, that he was killed in a freak pit accident halfway through the 100-mile race. Some say he tried to run from the flipping car, others that he was engrossed in giving Stevenson a pit signal. In any event, the car landed on top of him, killing the 39-year-old Smith instantly. His wife, Ruthelyn, and friends carried on the name in Clay Smith Engineering.

LOUISE SMITH

"My greatest thrill was wrecking Buck Baker's modified No. 7 Dodge at Greenville-Pickens Speedway last July 2," Mrs. Louise Smith told the NASCAR publicity man in 1950. Born July 31, 1916, this distaff daredevil was one of the small coterie of women NASCAR drivers who competed on even terms with their male counterparts.

She, Sara Christian, and Ruby Flock were the best, and many claim Louise could have continued driving long after she stopped for a serious fling at promoting. Mrs. Smith began driving in NASCAR in 1948, and she differed from the rest of the distaff drivers in that she followed the NASCAR circuit religiously. The family owned a parts and wrecking business in Greenville, S.C., then, and apparently had come from the Los Angeles area before that. Mrs. Smith had learned to drive at a Los Angeles school only a year or two previous to her competition debut.

Mrs. Smith was remembered as a doughty campaigner who was totally fearless. She lived in Georgia at last report, but had little interest in viewing the sport after she quit competing herself. "The fun has gone out of it since it became big business," she said.

BILL SMYTH

If there has been any totally democratic racing organization in the world it has been USAC. Formed in 1954 by drivers, car owners, industrialists, and officials who faced the bleak prospect of succumbing to the AAA Contest Board or joining rivals like NASCAR, IMCA or SCCA, USAC has been member-dominated—uncomfortably so in some instances, unfortunately so in others. Car owners wishing to wring more out of their investments in equipment maintained old racing formulas much too long, even to the detriment of their stock in trade—the interest of the crowd in the race. Drivers formed cliques, making it difficult for young talent without a sponsor.

But it was nevertheless democratic, sometimes so fiercely as to balk a member of the Indianapolis 500 establishment. Duane Carter knew the opportunities within USAC's grasp; he implemented his programs across the toes of far too many, never seeing them come to fruition. Henry Banks was perhaps the best-liked man in all of USAC, but he, in turn, did not move fast enough to suit important members.

So Bill Smyth, a smooth, quiet man who had been an SCCA steward, a USAC race official and who had served long years on various AAA Contest Board and USAC committees, was brought in as chief executive officer to propel USAC finally into the days ahead. He did so, with a vengeance, coming as close to supreme power in the organization as anyone else had in its entire history. Nine months after he joined USAC, Smyth became Director of Competition (June 1, 1970), negotiating 2 lucrative contracts for the organization, one with TV and the other with Marlboro, a cigarette company.

Smyth was an example of steady maturity. Born in 1921, he had always been interested in auto racing, but a weak arm precluded either a driver's or mechanic's career. Besides, Smyth was graduated from college into the Internal Revenue Service, which might be called St. Bonaventure University's gift to closer scrutiny of income tax returns. Smyth endured the IRS, surviving the drudgery by frequenting auto races. He volunteered as an official, working his way to the post of Eastern Zone Superviser of the AAA Contest Board. Meanwhile, he departed from the tax business to join Chilton, one of the nation's top publishers of books and magazines for the auto industry. The association with racing was now appropriate to his business, allowing Smyth to openly indulge his pleasure in the sport.

In 1954, when founder Alec Ulmann broke briefly with SCCA, Smyth began a long tenure as Chief Steward of the Sebring, Fla., 12-hour Grand Prix—a tenure ending only in 1968. In 1964, he had left Chilton to become an administrator for John Mecom, Jr., a young oilman who went into racing with unlimited money and won himself the Indianapolis 500 in 1966 with Graham Hill.

Smyth stayed with Mecom even after Mecom found a new interest, the New Orleans Saints professional football team, and left only when the bigger opportunity developed. But all along the way, he had polished his administrative and diplomatic skills until he became the kind of low-key negotiator who could bring both parties to an agreement, or the opponents in an argument to settle, each convinced he had gotten the better of the other.

Determined to make USAC the preeminent racing organization, Smyth was considered the only man in USAC capable of it. A friend described him succinctly, "He dresses like a Hoosier, thinks like a New Yorker, but he has dreams like Alexander the Great." Smyth kept his Texas drawl—not bad for a man from upstate New York. As 1972 came on, he had indeed made USAC a very powerful group.

MOISES SOLANA

Jai-alai is one of the world's fastest games, requiring lightning reflexes, keen eyes, and the nerves of a burglar. Moises Solana, born in Mexico in 1936, had all of these, and became one of the great players in modern jai-alai annals. Since the same characteristics are also useful in other sports, particularly in auto racing, Solana occasionally tried his luck there as well. He concentrated mainly on Mexican competitions, with foreign trips for him being mostly across the Rio Grande.

In Formula 1 championship racing, he managed to find a spare car for the Mexican GP 3 years running—a Cooper-Maserati in 1966, and Lotus-Fords in 1967 and 1968—but retired from each race with mechanical problems. He tried the U.S. race in 1967, again with the same results. But Solana had some talent, qualifying for the latter race 7th fastest in the field of 18. It was in sports car competitions that there was ample proof that he knew what he was doing. Since the 1968 USRRC series opened in Mexico, Solana was on hand, of course. He whipped the field handily. Following that he was 5th at Riverside in another USRRC meet.

His jai-alai winnings turned into cars as often as not, and a visit to Solana would find a McLaren-Chevvy M6B, a Terlingua Mustang, Cobra 427 and a Lola T-70, sometimes driven by his brother, Hernan. Moises

564

competed in everything from quarter midgets to the latest F1 cars, but it was in a rather ordinary machine that he met his death in a rather ordinary Mexican hill-climb July 27, 1969.

RAYMOND SOMMER

One of 3 sons of a wealthy French felt manufacturer, Raymond Sommer was a premier aviator (he held the 6th pilot's license ever issued in his country) who had switched to auto racing at an early age, graduating from amateur ranks into the professionals as a matter of pride, not necessity. Born August 31, 1906, Sommer made his 1st important start in the 1928 Antibes Grand Prix. Four years later, sharing a 2.3-litre Alfa Monza with Luigi Chinetti, he won his 1st major race, Le Mans. It was a feat he repeated in 1933 in another Alfa shared with Tazio Nuvolari, his idol. In the 1932 race, Sommer drove all but 3 of the 24 hours.

Raymond's approach to driving—even after he turned full professional—was to drive anything with 4 wheels that was competitive. Thus, his prewar mounts included such cars as the 2.9-litre Maserati, the Monoposto Alfa, a Chrysler (1931, Le Mans), and the famous Type 158 Alfa. Other Sommer mounts included Ratier, Hotchkiss, Talbot, Cisitialia, BMW, Simca, Bugatti, OSCA, HWM, and Aston Martin. Each car's characteristics were noted down in Sommer's personal diary, every track, every race.

Sommer's prewar victories included the Montreux GP, Comminges, the French GP, and the Spa 24-hour race the same season (1936); Marseilles, the Tunis GP,

and the Circuit des Ramparts at Angoulême. He was French champion in 1937. When mobilization came in 1939, Sommer entered the French Army as a private, and was credited with shooting down an attacking German plane with a hand-held machine gun, à la Victor McLaglen. After a stint in prison camp, he returned to racing in 1945, his best showing a 2nd in the Coupe des Prisonniers. In 1946 he regained the French championship, and became Champion of Europe as well, winning the Montlhéry Coupe du Salon, Forez GP, Lille, Marseilles, and the St. Cloud GP. He also was 2nd at Nice, 3rd in the Brussels and Marseilles sports car races and in the Valentino GP that season.

Sommer was among the Allied racing figures who worked for the release of Dr. Ferdinand Porsche from prison. His own patriotism was evident in his acceptance of a ride in the uncompetitive CTA-Arsenal, the French national car. Switching to Ferraris and other mounts, Sommer regained his winning touch. In 1950 he drove a BRM in its initial appearance, but a broken transmission eliminated the mount from the British GP. It was at the wheel of another British car, a tiny Cooper fitted with a twin-cylinder 1100-c.c. engine, that Raymond drove his last race. He had just been awarded the French Legion of Honor for his accomplishments in auto racing. For a lark, Sommer agreed to try the over-powered Cooper in a minor race, the Grand Prix du Hauté Garonne at the Cadours circuit, September 10, 1950. On a fast curve the car overturned, killing Sommer instantly.

Sommer is not well remembered. He confined his driving largely to the Continent, for one thing. For another, he lacked the ruthlessness that might have pushed his talent into the upper ranks of racing in his day. Yet the battle meant everything to the lean Frenchman; his diary included "credits" he gave himself for a good showing. Often he did not win, yet made the fastest lap. He spoke of the talents of his fellow drivers in terms of the way they battled, never their strings of victories. The nickname pinned on Sommer by several writers in his day told all: Raymond Coeur de Lion.

GOBER SOSEBEE

Called the Wild Injun from Atlanta, Gober Sosebee used to drive an Olds 88 and a Ford modified in early NASCAR racing. Decades later, his name was occasionally among the modified results from the Carolina-Georgia area; he was 36 when he hit his pinnacle by winning the 1950 Speed Weeks modified classic 100-mile race over the Daytona Beach sands, averaging 93.19 m.p.h. Sosebee repeated in 1951 when the race was lengthened to 160 miles. He swapped his 1932 Ford for a 1939, and set the original modified record of 82.37 m.p.h.

Sosebee, a former sailor, was from that era of NASCAR Grand National racing when courage meant as much as savvy. As the experts from the car factories took over; and as the late-model stock car became a more and more esoteric piece of machinery, the ability to stomp on the accelerator was tempered by the necessity of having a mechanical genius in the pits. Sosebee, old for a journeyman race driver anyway, never quite had that kind of aid; he usually prepared his own cars in his Atlanta garage.

So in stock-car racing, he won only at Augusta, Ga., June 1, 1952, in his 1952 Chrysler, and he set 2 marks in 1954 in an Oldsmobile—78.70 m.p.h. for one lap at North Wilkesboro, N.C., a 5/8ths mile track, and 55.41 m.p.h. for 100 miles on the Macon, Ga., half-miler. Then he faded from sight, a relic of the days when a trip with a load of moonshine might bring more than the purse at the cow pasture of the week.

TONY SOUTHGATE

Once it was thought that the normal automobile designer was an older, erudite man, more used to slide rules and drawing boards than to racing his own cars. Since the end of World War II, there has been a new breed. Tony Southgate, born in Coventry, England, May 25, 1940, is an example. Before age 30, Southgate was Chief Designer (Cars) with BRM, designing singleseat racers for Formula 1. And even earlier, he had been associated with Eric Broadley's Lola and Dan Gurney's All-American Racers. Southgate spent his first 21 years in Conventry, including studies at that city's Technical College, before joining an apprentice program with an automotive group. Halfway through that program, Tony realized he wanted racing fulltime, a desire that could have been predicted.

"I was a member of the 750 Motor Club," he recalled, "and I spent half my free time at work either designing or making bits of race cars. In 1961 I designed my first complete car, a 750 Special, but I really didn't know what I was doing. Oh, the engineering side of it was all right, but the suspension geometrics, camber arcs, and things like that weren't too good. I realized it was a very expensive game when the engine blew up after only 4 events. A bloody rod broke." While rebuilding the 750 over the winter, he also started an 1172 Formula design, a rear-engined car. It was at this point that he decided to devote full time to designing.

Southgate took a small pay cut to work for Broadley's Lola factory, joining just in time to become involved with the Bowmaker F1 Lola and the Mark 5 Formula junior car. Broadley would sketch out the broad outline, then left Southgate the task of filling in the rest. In those days, he said, you didn't do quite as much drawing, but made up much of the piping and other things as the car actually was being fabricated. "But on the big Mark 6 GT, I spent 8 months drawing the car; and of course, Ford became interested in that effort— it was the start of the GT/40 project, you will remember

—so all of a sudden we have half a dozen Ford engineers peering over my shoulder. I was still only 23, and after doing so much work on the original GT, it became obvious I was going to get pushed out a bit. So I thought 'bugger this,' and went to work for Ron Tauranac at the end of 1963."

Southgate only stayed with Tauranac 10 months, working on the 1964 1.5-litre F1 cars and the John Zink Track Burner Special for Indianapolis, actually a stretched F1 frame using a number of F1 components. But then Broadley contacted him and asked if he were interested in returning to the fold, since the Ford project was nearing an end. He became involved with the new Lola T60 and T70 F2/F3 single-seaters and sports car respectively. Tony did most of the T60, Eric most of the T70, each backing the other. Next came the T80 and T90 Indy cars, the T100 F2 design and the T120 BMW-powered hillclimber.

Formula A racing in America provided an opportunity for Lola to make up for losses suffered in the revamping of the sports car rules in 1968. Thus was born the T140 model, which brought Southgate new recognition in the U.S. One of those who noted his efforts was Dan Gurney, who was on his way to enlarging his All-American Eagle effort. "I joined them because of F1," Tony said. "To me F1 is the racing formula, bar none. The competition and development are so bloody intense that at times it seems untrue." But his 1st car project was not for F1 but Indianapolis. The 1968 Eagle, a reworking of the 1966–67 design with outboard springs instead of rocker arms, was generally cleaner and lower in profile. Next came an AAR Formula A racer, the Mark 5 Eagle, for none other than Dick Smothers, the American TV personality and racing car driver, and George Wintersteen. Smothers's car was driven by Lou Sell and won the SCCA chase, George 2nd. The Indy car, the Mark 4 Eagle, finished 1st and 2nd at Indy that season with Bobby Unser and Gurney in the cockpits. The Indy Eagle also won at Mosport, Donnybrooke, and Riverside in road races.

In 1969, Southgate redesigned the Indy Eagle as the Mark 6, and changed the Formula A car apparently for the better, since it again ran away with the SCCA title. But the Indy car gave him problems, and even the redesigned version needed shaking down. In the 500 itself, Gurney again finished 2nd in Southgate's creation, and might have won had Lockheed brakes been used. At least, that was Southgate's opinion. Another Southgate project that year was the Mark 7 Eagle for F1, but Gurney chose to forgo the Grand Prix, which meant that Tony had to find another spot for his ultimate ambition to be fulfilled.

Later, in June, John Surtees offered Southgate a job, but by October Tony was with BRM and at work on the 1970 F1 car. Things weren't too good at 1st, but at least the cars were reliable after Spain, and the engines started becoming reliable after Monaco. There were problems, of course, but, at Spa, Pedro Rodriguez won the Belgian GP to give BRM its first *grande épreuve* since Monaco 1966. Later in the year, Rodriguez was 4th in Canada, 2nd in the U.S. GP and might have won if the fuel had been correctly calculated to eliminate a pit stop in the last laps), and 6th in Mexico. No question about Southgate's work here. He had another project in 1970, the P154 BRM Canadian-American Challenge Cup car for Canada's George Eaton. Shakedowns were carried on during racing, but both Eaton and Rodriguez scored 3rds in CanAm racing, not bad for a brand new car, 1st of its type from the marque since 1965. More GP glory, including 2 straight victories at Austria and Italy lay ahead in 1971 for Tony's P160 car.

In 1972, Southgate went to work on a new project— the UOP Shadow DN1, an F1 design for America's Don Nichols and his American sponsor. The car was ready for South Africa 1973, where it was driven by George Follmer and finished 6th in its 1st outing. Southgate apparently hadn't lost his touch for GP machinery that worked well.

ART SPARKS

Art Sparks once took a 150-foot jump with a motorcycle into a small lagoon for a film. Paid $1,000 for the stunt, he was met by the director at the edge of the lagoon. Sparks was asked to try the shot over because the light hadn't been perfect, and was offered $500 for the repeat. The language Art Sparks used on the director will never be repeated in polite company.

The son of a wealthy Kansas innkeeper, Art Sparks was to become one of the finest carbuilders the U.S. racing scene has produced, and later the president of a successful piston company. In between, he was a race driver, a teacher, a college dropout, and appeared as a cinema stunt man in some of the most hare-brained feats ever attempted by a rational human being for almost 11 years.

Among his suicidal stunts were a 300-foot dive from an airplane into the ocean, wearing no protection whatever (he broke every rib but managed to recover in 7 weeks) airplane-to-airplane and airplane-to-automobile transfers, and playing the victim in the dynamiting of a fishing boat. Born in Los Angeles about 1899, Sparks was "discovered" riding his motorcycle after he had returned from a 2nd unsuccessful attempt at college. He never looked at academe again, preferring the $50 a day, and up, of the infant movie industry. During much of his time as stunt man Sparks doubled as a shop instructor at Glendale High School, and was already dabbling in carbuilding.

Uninterested in the waning days of the board tracks, Sparks turned his attention to the so-called outlaw racing, already prospering in Southern California. His very 1st race car was an ingenious mélange of available stock parts. Sparks utilized an Essex chassis with power from a modified flat-head Ford Model T, with the front axle from Chrysler, the rear end from Ford, and a purple paint job applied by Sparks himself. With assistance from Ed Winfield, Art fashioned the engine lovingly with such advanced features for the day as roller tappets, solid-billet crankshaft, and a camshaft with keyed lobes. It took 3 years before the car was finished in 1927.

Art drove 3 races in his purple wonder and led them all. However, in the 3rd he flipped, breaking his collarbone, his jaw, and mostly his desire to drive competitively. When he recovered, he never drove another race —he did some stunts in cars, however—and concentrated upon being a combination car owner and mechanic. Among his early drivers was Lou Moore, but Sparks failed to recognize Moore's potential. Art let the sanctioning associations come to him. His cars raced primarily at the Ascot track in the eastern part of Los Angeles, run by American Legion Post No. 127 and thus called the Legion Ascot track to differentiate it from a famous earlier track. This was a 5/8ths mile macadam oval with extremely wide (130-foot) turns, and racing was so lucrative that the AAA in self-defense gave it a sanction. His cars were successful enough to allow him to graduate from stunt driving to auto racing in 1930. In the depths of the Depression, Sparts had $10,000 in the bank.

Sparks's headquarters were in a small garage in Glendale where his partner, a former hot-rodder named Paul Weirick, was also completely dedicated to racing. (Weirick was later to become quite successful in the plastics fabrication business.) The headquarters became the site of another Ascot superweapon, a very light, 102-inch wheelbased chassis, that using a Miller 16-valve, 4-cylinder engine. The engine used was quite efficient, yielding one horsepower per cubic inch, all without supercharging.

Stubby Stubblefield was installed as the driver, winning 4 straight Ascot mains, before his dislike of Sparks's gruff manner overpowered his desire for a competitive mount. Soon Wild Bill Cummings, one of the few drivers able to stomach Sparks, became the man behind the wheel of what was a forerunner of the famed "Poison Lil", in 1931. Sparks and Weirick had arranged sponsorship from Gilmore Oil Co., a forerunner of Mobil, for the Ascot and Pacific Coast championship races only. Sparks decided that year was the time to prepare for Indianapolis. He designed a car and utilized the Stanford University wind tunnel to test its aerodynamics. The result was the Catfish, a 2-man vehicle with a pointed tail, a huge wing behind the occupants who sat very low in the vehicle and a rounded catfish-like nose.

Its styling was the cleanest of any car at the 1932 Indy 500, and Stubblefield—who obviously had overcome his dislike for Sparks—was lying 6th at 175 laps when an oil leak robbed the car of a finish in the money. At home where Ascot was paying as much as $2,000 to win its feature race, before crowds of 15,000 to 20,000, Kelly Petillo took a turn at winning in Sparks's Gilmore Lionhead Special. Sparks's inevitable argument with Petillo came, reinstalling Cummings in the driver's seat, until Cummings went East early in 1933. Next was Al Gordon, an also-ran until Sparks gave him the ride. When Gordon won the 1933 Pacific Coast crown, Sparks didn't even bother with the 1933 Indy, because he was making too much money at home. Gordon's duels with Ernie Triplett that season became legendary and assured a continuation of the then-current midget boom.

The duel culminated in gory tragedy that was to affect Sparks's career. El Centro, Calif., was a dusty mile track that had been ill-prepared for the scheduled March 100-mile AAA race. As Gordon and Triplett charged out in front in the latest episode in their usual duel, track conditions steadily got worse. A car had stalled in the 4th turn but AAA officials, believing it was no hazard, failed to have it carted away. It was. On the 21st mile, Swede Smith hit it broadside, strewing wreckage across the track. Triplett and Gordon roared out of a dust cloud wheel-to-wheel and found their path blocked. Triplett hit both Smith and a crewman helping Smith out of the wrecked vehicle, killing them both, then sideswiped Gordon, causing both machines to do an end-over-end flip. Triplett was killed, and Gordon, whose car was deflected off a wooden post, was miraculously unhurt, aside from a broken nose and a sore lip.

At this point, the race was stopped and Herb Balmer was declared the winner. Sparks was livid. He filed a protest alleging that Gordon, who was leading at the time of the accident, should have been declared winner.

He then filed an official affidavit, backed by assistant starter Jim Grant and a Sparks's crewman, Joe Petrali, criticizing the handling of the race, the track conditions, and the individual officials.

The accident and the subsequent affidavits made every newspaper in the nation—or so it seemed to the AAA Contest Board. At a closed-door hearing, it banned Sparks from the pits of every one of its race tracks for the next 2 years. Sparks made no comment; he was to work through Paul Weirick that entire period, often shouting instructions from the spectator seats. It was a difficult time for him to be banned. He had just completed an Indy car. He had reworked the engines with his own expensively-made parts which changed the Miller/Offenhauser from 4 to 2 valves per cylinder, and let the engine rev 1,000 r.p.m. higher. Gordon got Poison Lil into second place at Indy after 160 miles, before hitting the wall. Later, Gordon campaigned successfully in the East and Midwest with the car, until, after an argument, Sparks fired him, too.

Ascot had experimented with a half-mile dirt track in an attempt to reduce driver fatalities. The experiment failed and now it was returning to the 5/8ths mile pavement. Sparks picked Kelly Petillo to run for him and Petillo agreed despite the previous ill feelings. He won at Ascot, and in a fog-plagued race at Mines Field in Los Angeles. He quit Sparks, however, at the last minute before the 1935 Ascot season, preferring to invest in his own midget.

In 1935, Sparks gave a new driver, who would be the most successful Ascot driver ever, a chance at the car that would make him a success. Rex Mays, a lanky 23-year-old, was Sparks's choice, and Rex won with such regularity at Ascot that some claim he and Poison Lil killed racing forever at the track in one short year. Mays won everywhere, in fact, except at the 1935 Indy. There he won the pole, led after 300 miles, until the front suspension gave way (the winner was Petillo).

But on January 26, 1936, Ascot died along with Sparks's former ace, Al Gordon, and his riding mechanic, Spider Matlock. The AAA labeled the track unsafe, calling for $10,000 in safety improvement, which the promoters could not raise. In 1936 Sparks and Weirick fielded 2 Indy cars; Mays ran out of the allotted 37.5 gallons of gas while leading. Ray Pixley, in the other car, took 6th. It was not a good year, Mays landing in the hospital several times. Finally, after Rex and Wilbur Shaw crashed in the Vanderbilt Cup race at Roosevelt Field on Long Island, Sparks quit for the remainder of the season. Late in 1936 Weirick bought Sparks out, dissolving the partnership.

For 1937, Sparks decided to build an Indy car from the ground up. He hired Fred Offenhauser and built a 366-cu. in. supercharged twin-cam engine that he called his Big Six. It was the last 2-man car year; Art tapped Jimmy Snyder and Chick Hirashima as his team. Qualifying late, the car started back in the pack although it was the fastest by a full 5 m.p.h. Snyder passed the field in the 1st lap and was running away when the supercharger broke at 65 miles. The performance was not lost, however. Young Joel Thorne, heir to a railroad fortune, had decided to win at Indianapolis. He had been sold 7 refugees from the scrap heap for the 1937 race; now he saw a car he knew had potential. He was camping on Sparks's doorstep when Art and Big Six returned home. He wanted Sparks to build him a 3-car team capable of dominating the 500. After talking to Thorne's lawyers back in New York, Sparks signed one of the strangest contracts in auto racing. Art had a lifetime contract at a low salary, but was to get 10 percent of all winnings. At the age of 75, he was to get a settlement of $50,000. He was in total charge of the operation and was to get as much money as necessary to build an Indianapolis winner. Thorne Engineering Co. was duly founded in Los Angeles and quickly built up a $5,000 payroll, part of which Sparks defrayed with work on aviation components.

In the fall of 1937, the first 4 months' work went down the chute because AAA changed the formula for 1938. The Big 6 had to become a little 6 of 274 cu. in. unsupercharged, or 183 cu. in. supercharged. Sparks tried for one of each, Thorne getting a reworked version of or older car to drive. Ronnie Householder set fast time, but dropped out early in the 1938 race. Jimmy Snyder led at a record pace for about 300 miles before also succumbing to valve-spring woes. Thorne finished 9th. For 1939, Sparks made his own valve springs. Snyder finished 2nd, Thorne 7th, and 2 others dropped out, including Rex Mays.

In 1940, Snyder died in a midget car accident in St. Louis. That year Sparks had not gone to Indy. His relationship with Thorne was increasingly strained, and he was casting about for ways to get out of the lifetime contract. He attempted to enlist in the Marines for World War II but cooler heads prevailed. Art converted Thorne Engineering to war work and was soon earning $1,800 a month from Thorne for running the shop. But in the middle of the war, Lockheed bought out Thorne Engineering. Sparks was supposed to run an Arizona plant for Thorne, but since the eccentric millionaire never paid him, Sparks walked out, eventually not only breaking the contract but also obtaining a $90,000 judgment.

The last hurrah of the Sparks-Thorne liaison was the most successful. In 1946 Art managed to assemble two cars out of the remains of the prewar material, one for Germany's Rudi Caracciola, who demolished it in practice when a bird flew in his face; the other—the unsupercharged 6—for George Robson, who won the Indianapolis 500. After that Sparks pursued an assortment of schemes, including the idea of making racing and automotive pistons out of lightweight forged billets as in aviation practice. He was also partners with Earl (Mad Man) Muntz in several schemes, once preparing

2 very illegal racing Kaiser stock cars for teenager Troy Ruttman and young Rodger Ward to pilot. He prepared a high-performance version of the 265-cu. in. De Soto 6. In 1949, Sparks was asked by the sponsor of the Indianapolis Race Cars, Inc., team to take over the company. Sparks imported some hot-shot motorcycle mechanics from California, and attempted to sort out 2 supercharged 8-cylinder Maseratis and a Miller Special. Fred Agabashian and Lee Wallard qualified the Maseratis, Fred dropping out early, but Wallard worried the favorites by easily taking the lead and pulling away from the field. Unfortunately a gear failure about mile 137 retired him also.

After that Sparks devoted full time to his Forged True Piston Corp., eventually numbering such companies as Porsche, General Motors, Ferrari, Ford, and Chrysler as steady customers.

MIKE SPENCE

Colin Chapman was sitting on the balcony of the Hotel de Paris overlooking Casino Square in Monte Carlo. It was 1962 and a Formula Junior race in which Chapman had only a spectator's interest was being run. But his attention was caught by one of the competitors.

"From there I could see a driver's every movement in the cockpit—the way he turned into a corner, the way he slid the car, every minute correction he made," he said. "I was struck by the very natural style of a particular driver. Now Peter Arundell won that race,

and Peter's a very fine driver, but I could see him fighting his car every inch of the way. The driver of whom I am speaking, on the other hand, was very smooth and completely relaxed. I knew that, with experience, he would develop into a really top driver. You might say that I decided to start grooming Mike Spence for stardom that day."

Michael Henderson Spence, older son of a sliding-door gear engineer, was an unusual man in many ways. He survived a bout with polio at age 6, played cricket well enough to be offered a professional contract, and commanded a British tank crew in Germany during his national service. Born December 30, 1936, in Croydon, Surrey, and educated at Oxford, Spence started competing in automobiles only after he left the Army in 1957. His earliest attempts were rallies in his father's Turner 950, but the following year the Spence family acquired a used AC Ace-Bristol. Mike made his racing debut in this machine at Goodwood in 1958, then competed, mostly in club events, only occasionally. In 1960 he decided to make a concentrated effort at becoming a professional racing driver.

His father, whose Coburn Engineers sliding-door business was doing well, purchased a 998-c.c. Cooper-Austin Formula-Junior car for his son, and Spence won at Snetterton and Silverstone, as well as his Continental debut at Monza, where he captured a 15-lap heat in the Lottery Grand Prix before blowing the engine in the final. He switched to an Emeryson-Ford the following year; the car's fiber glass body was fabricated by a subsidiary company of his father's. But this car suffered numerous mechanical failures before Mike was able to win a 100-lapper at Silverstone, the Commander Yorke Trophy race. He also made his debut in Formula 1, driving to a 2nd at Brands Hatch after retiring while running 7th at Solitude, and in Formula 2, in a Peter Westbury-sponsored Cooper-Climax.

In 1962 Spence joined the newly formed Ian Walker Racing Team, driving his own FJ Lotus-Ford 22, and he competed at 15 different meets in the yellow and green Walker racing colors. He won at Rheims and placed at Monaco, Crystal Palace, Albi, Snetterton, and 4 other races. The following season, when Ron Harris-Team Lotus replaced the former Lotus FJ effort, Spence joined Arundell and John Fenning as a full-fledged member of the team. The Lotus 27 was a long time in becoming competitive, but Spence showed enough for Chapman to offer him a F1 ride in the Italian GP at Monza. He was running 7th, 13 laps from the finish, when his engine quit.

Ron Harris signed Spence for his team again in 1964, this time for the new Lotus 32 F2 cars, and Mike won the opening British event, the F2 section of the Aintree 200, and eventually took the Autocar F2 title. That July he was promoted to the F1 team full-time, seconding Jimmy Clark. His initial go was at Brands Hatch, and following his instructions to finish and nothing else, he

came in 9th in a field that had few dropouts. At Solitude the next weekend, he was running 2nd in the rain when his steering column broke; only the slow speed saved him from a serious crackup. The following week was even worse.

Spence was practicing for an endurance race in Walker's Lotus Elan prototype when the brake bracket snapped just as he slowed for a fast corner. The car climbed a bank, went through the fence, and rolled. Spence was trapped underneath it with almost a full load of fuel—38 gallons. "It was flooding everywhere because the filler cap had been broken open," Spence recalled. "I couldn't even move enough to turn off the ignition, and I sat there listening to everything ticking away. When the marshals arrived, they were smoking! I had to yell mighty loud to get them to put out their cigarettes."

Spence served notice of his F1 prowess at the United States GP at Watkins Glen later in 1964. He was running 2nd in the early part of the race, but Graham Hill, Dan Gurney, and John Surtees soon were ahead of him. Then Jim Clark took the car over after his own had quit on him. At Mexico Spence also ran 2nd a good portion of the race; and at East London for the South African GP, he was leading by 16 seconds over Surtees when the Lotus spun out, costing him 10 of his seconds. Still in the lead, he spun again to avoid a car that blew its engine just in front of him and lost the lead to Surtees and Hill. Finally, in the nontitle Race of Champions, he was 3rd in the opening heat, won the next, and won overall.

Spence came from under Clark's shadow in 1966 with a contract from BRM, although he drove—under loan —for the Parnell Team. He earned 3 points in the World Driver's Championship with 5th-place finishes in the Dutch and Italian Grands Prix in a 2-litre Lotus-BRM. He won the nonchampionship South African GP and also continued to be active in F2 racing. January 15, 1966, Mike married Lynne Condon, moving to Maidenhead, where Mike had showrooms that sold Lotus, Porsche, and Rover cars.

In 1967 Spence put in one of his busiest years: running the noncompetitive H16 BRM in F1, finishing with 9 points and a 10th in the standings; a Chaparral in long-distance races; and a BRM in nonchampionship races. If not a winner because of his car, he was at least consistent a good deal of the time, taking 5ths at the Belgian, Canadian, Italian, and Mexican races, along with a 6th at Monaco, and an 8th in Holland. With Phil Hill as his codriver, Mike won the BOAC 500 at Brands Hatch in a Chaparral, and at Sebring he set the fastest lap time in the 12-hour race before the car suffered mechanical troubles that continued to plague it a good part of the season.

Perhaps it was Spence's versatility that was his downfall. When Clark was killed early in 1968, Spence moved to Chapman's Lotus Indianapolis team. The wedge-shaped, turbine-powered cars were fast, and Spence ran a lap at 169.55 m.p.h. in his own car. Then he settled into another Lotus to sort out its problems, if any, calling upon his mechanical expertise. On the 1st turn at the Brickyard, the car moved higher than usual, and each time around he mintained that higher groove, until a fatal lap in which he entered the turn on a groove ever so slightly higher yet and hit sand and other loose debris that had accumulated there. The Lotus spun and smashed into the wall, demolishing the car, and causing Spence multiple head injuries. Rushed to a hospital, he lingered 4½ hours before succumbing, the 34th driver killed in the history of the Brickyard.

CHUCK STEVENSON

Winning the AAA championship in 1952 took Charles Stevenson, a handsome 6-footer born October 15, 1919, in Sydney, Mont., the entire Championship Trail. He had to do it the hard way, scratching out points to make up the huge lead amassed by Troy Ruttman, who won Indianapolis and Raleigh in succession, then was sidelined by injury.

Stevenson's mount was the Springfield Welding Special and his car owner, Bessie Paoli of Springfield, Ill. Chuck finished 18th at Indianapolis that year and, with two 6ths and a 5th in the ensuing races, could not have been one of the favorites for the crown. But August 24, 1952, at Milwaukee, where he lived, Stevenson's star began to rise. He beat Bill Schindler and Duane Carter for the 400 points offered by the Milwaukee 200, finished third in the Detroit 100, then won at DuQuoin. That put him in a race with Carter, Sam Hanks and Jack McGrath for the title. He won it with consistent finishes in the top 10 and edged Ruttman—who had not turned a wheel the rest of the season—by a mere 50 points.

Chuck switched cars for his title defense in 1953 to J. C. Agajanian's *equipe,* lasting only 42 laps of the Indianapolis 500 in the slightly faster machine, while the previous year he had made 187 laps. Incidentally, he was unique in that he passed 2 driver tests at Indy—in 1951 when, in his rookie ride, his Bardahl Special caught fire on the 93rd lap of the race proper and in 1960 when, after 6 years away from the Brickyard, he was asked to prove his fitness to resume his career. Chuck finally lasted the entire race in the Metal-Cal Special in 1961 for 6th.

Stevenson was never a factor in the 1953 title chase, lasting to win only one race—a repeat in the Milwaukee 200. His next-best finish that year was a 3rd at Springfield. Of course, that was the year that Stevenson went down to Mexico for the Pan American Road Race, scoring one of 2 towering victories on the Lincoln team with the Long Beach crowd of John Mantz, Walt Faulkner, Clay Smith, and Manny Ayulo.

"It was a better buck than I could make on the Trail," Chuck said, "and it looked like fun. It was. But it was a lotta work. Lincoln, our sponsor, wanted to win and made no bones about spending money on the cars. We had some pretty good boys, and we went pretty fast for the kind of car and road.

"I was very close to Clay. When he got killed in 1954 in that freak accident at DuQuoin, I had no desire to race on the Championship Trail anymore," he added. "I became a test driver for Ford and later, when the memory didn't come up every time I turned a wheel, I did a little stock-car racing."

Stevenson was a member of the Leader Card team when he made his comeback as number 3 driver to Rodger Ward. He confined his single-seater activities to Indianapolis, but competed in late-model races occasionally. He still hadn't retired officially when his wavy hair had turned to silver and his son Chuckie was old enough to compete against him, if so minded. Stevenson was briefly involved in the Curtis Turner-Teamsters Union attempt to organize American race drivers soon after his return to racing. He pulled back quickly from the poorly organized effort when he saw it was doomed before it even got under way.

JACKIE STEWART

Jackie Stewart's career may have reached its highest point, so far, in 1970. In one way, 1970 was not particularly a Jackie Stewart year. He yielded his 1969 World Championship to a close friend and neighbor in Switzerland, Jochen Rindt, who was killed in mid-season after clinching the title early with a spectacular series of 5 Grand Prix victories. Stewart was as quick as ever, always having been among the quickest, but Rindt was quicker that one season. Nor did Stewart have any big racing victories in America or Australia or Japan, exotic places at which he had won races before, whether he was winning in Britain and Europe or not.

But in other ways, 1970 was Jackie Stewart's year. A series of small vignettes illustrate how that might be said. Scene one: British Overseas Airways Corporation's Speedbird Club, in a skyscraper off Park Avenue in New York City. Occasion: a press conference to announce BOAC's enlarged participation in the United States Grand Prix that year. Principal attraction: a modishly dressed, long-haired, little Scot with a charming burr, Stewart himself. The room was filled with working newsmen, important visitors, waiters, bartenders, and all the personalities that make up a New York press gathering. Into it walked Jackie Stewart, possibly the smallest man in the room. Yet he dominated. He held that audience, from the most important to the most ordinary, in the palm of his hand. If one day can be singled out as the day Stewart won over the American press, that was it.

Scene 2: Watkins Glen, site of the annual U.S. GP. Again, Stewart was the dominant figure, though surrounded by every other important GP driver in the world. When the race started he charged into the lead. Two men, not Stewart, still had a chance to top or tie Rindt's point total if they could win this day, and Stewart already had indicated that he was out to prevent that if he could. Lap after lap he charged ahead, widening his lead, a study of driving perfection, a pacer wearing out the potential Ferrari contenders following his Tyrrell car. In the end, Stewart's engine gave out. For many laps he drove with smoke bellowing from the car. But he had done it: neither Ferrari was able to win, and the race went to Emerson Fittipaldi in a Lotus. Jackie's car quit on the back of the course, and he walked back to the pits. From the stands they saw him coming and they yelled. He waved, he smiled, he hopped and skipped along, winning the accolades of the watchers again, in a scene reminiscent of his Indianapolis appearance when he had won that crowd, too, by his sportsmanlike attitude after a disheartening mechanical failure. This 1970 day Stewart cemented the American fan's enthusiasm for this overseas driver. And, incidentally, it was Stewart who won the day's BOAC Man of the Race Award, not the winner nor his challengers. It was the 2nd time Jackie accomplished that feat.

Scene 3: Akron, Ohio. Place: the Goodyear Tire & Rubber Company. The other actors: the president and high brass of this major American enterprise. Occasion: the signing of Stewart for continuing association with Goodyear—using their tires in his racing; testing; helping to establish and improve the tire company's name in all aspects of auto enthusiasm, including driver education, films, and the like. Part of Stewart's 1971 activity, he said, would include the Canadian-American Challenge Cup series so long dominated by Bruce McLaren and Denis Hulme. Stewart also had a major contract with L&M Cigarettes for this CanAm work. It was here in the United States, he told his listeners, that he thought racing would expand beyond all expectations.

All in all, 1970 was indeed a Jackie Stewart year. It was a year in which he established himself in racing's richest series. It was a time when he reviewed all his options, including tempting offers from Ferrari and several other marques for lucrative contracts to move over from Ken Tyrrell's private effort to a major factory, and decided what he was doing with Tyrrell was the right way, which proved right with the 1971 World Championship his. It enabled him to consolidate what he had won for a decade of racing effort and to plan for several years in the future. Small wonder that Stewart was quoted early in 1971 as saying that he intended to race at least 3 more years before he would even consider retiring. The seventies were the years in which the still-young Scot would consolidate, and build by still greater totals, the material symbols of his success to ensure his wife and family a prosperous future. He had come a

long way in 30-odd years.

Born at Milton, Dunbartonshire, June 11, 1939, Stewart came from a motoring tradition. His father was a motorcycle racer before establishing a Dumbuck automobile agency and garage, his brother—8 years Jack's senior—raced Jaguars with Ecurie Ecosse and the factory in 1953–54 and at Le Mans in an Aston Martin. Because of Jimmy Stewart's crashes, the family was against Jack's taking to the race courses. But he did so anyway in 1961, using the name A. N. Other, then under his sponsor's name, Barry Filer, using the latter's Porsche, AC Bristol, and eventually, a Ford-engined, wooden-framed Marcos. The following year the family found out about Jackie's racing when he married and the local papers revealed his secret.

Of those days, Stewart said, "I didn't know if I had any real ability at that stage and, as there was very little real opposition up there, it was difficult to get any comparison. That February, however, Jimmy and I took my father's demonstrator E Jaguar to Oulton Park for some testing. I was both surprised and encouraged to find I was quite close to the times Roy Salvadori had set there the previous September."

After a test race at Charterhall in 1961 was won in an Aston Martin, Stewart decided to concentrate on the family Jaguar in 1962, with good success. Rufforth was the scene of his 1st victories of 1963, both in sports car and Grand Touring races in the pouring rain of April 13th. Continued success caused David Murray to invite Jackie to drive one of Ecurie Ecosse's Tojeiro-Buicks at Charterhall's next meeting, and Jackie won this one and

many more for the Scottish crew, including some in its Cooper-Climax Monaco T49. That season Stewart won 14 times, finished 2nd once, 3rd twice and retired in 6 races—23 starts in all.

"I owe David Murray of Ecurie Ecosse an awful lot," Jackie recalled later. "He gave me the opportunity of being seen on the Southern circuits, which would have taken much longer on my own, if indeed, I ever would have travelled much in the South. I must also say that Ken Tyrrell gave me the most wonderful opportunity, letting me drive a single-seater, for at that point nobody knew—including myself—if I'd be any good at it. And the third person I owe very much to is Colin Chapman, of course, who helped me indirectly in many ways, such as remembering my name when someone asked him about a driver for a particular car. Jimmy (Clark) also was in there in that way too."

For 1964 Ecurie Ecosse signed him to a full year's contract for GT races, and he purchased a Lotus Cortina with a friend. Tyrrell's Cooper team added to his driving opportunities with a Formula 3 Cooper-BMC T72 ride after Timmy Mayer's death. At Snetterton, March 14, 1964, just 5 days after he had 1st driven a single-seater, Stewart won his 1st race, again in the pouring rain, which led to a F1 offer 2 days after that. He promptly turned it down. "I wasn't ready for it. To get into a GP car and drive alongside the best men in the world in my very inexperienced state would have led to my making mistakes and to my pushing too hard."

"F3 taught me to drive as smoothly as I possibly could. You must be smooth. If you start being erratic and hairy in the F3 car, you do nothing but slow yourself down. F2 taught me a lot, too, especially about race craft as such—the biding of your time or going all out, for example. In F3 if you slackened up slightly, you could still put the steam on and get back up there. In F2 you couldn't do that. The competition was so strong that, if you slackened, someone would pass you and you just couldn't catch up again unless he slackened. You had to concentrate hard all the time."

The offers came fast and furious after this; Stewart accepted few of them for similar reasons. One he did take was Ian Walker's for a Lotus Elan drive. At Silverstone he spun out after besting Peter Arundell and matching Clark part of the way. At Mallory Park the following week he won, besting Arundell again. He also raced John Coombs's E Jag, a factory Lotus Cortina, and Ecurie Ecosse's Tojeiro-Ford. August 15, 1964, Stewart visited the United States for the 1st time to drive in the Marlboro, Md., 12-hour race. His factory-entered Cortina won. In England he was the year's top F3 pilot, winning 11 or 12 races entered and, in the 12th, in which he lost a clutch, coasting home 2nd. His victories in the Tyrrell car included Monaco, Zandvoort, Rouen, and Rheims.

Stewart started F1 racing late in 1964 when Colin Chapman of Lotus asked him to join Clark in piloting one of the slim green Lotus-Climax 33 cars. At the nonchampionship Rand Grand Prix at Kyalami, Stewart retired in one heat, won the other. For the full 1965 season, Stewart moved over to BRM to act as number 2 driver to Graham Hill. "I placed sixth in my first race in South Africa on New Year's Day in 1965," he recalled, "My third at Monte Carlo after that was fabulous, wonderful and quite exhausting. I was told I made more than 2,500 gear changes in that race." His hands were blistered despite gloves after that one, his shoulder muscles were knotted, and his neck was in pain.

Sorting out courses became a sort of hobby in his rookie big-time year. Driving in the Ardennes at Spa in Belgium, he finished 2nd: "I have no love for this race or its course," he said without a smile. "It is extremely hairy and demands sheer concentration. You speed through forests and over road surfaces that are constantly changing and you must take some turns in excess of 150 m.p.h." Another 2nd in the French GP and a 5th at England's Silverstone were endured, before he found a course and a race to his liking. That was Zandvoort in Holland for the Dutch GP. Recovering from a poor start, the Scotsman bested Dan Gurney and Graham Hill, finishing 2nd to Clark.

"Nurburgring is the end," Jackie once said. "It has 178 corners over its 14 miles once around and you leave the ground—that's right, you fly—at least 22 times a lap. At one point, you leave the ground four times in a row at better than 150 m.p.h. This year I made what can only be called a driver's error; I went six inches or so too far to one side and I had to quit the race, because the underside of my car was almost torn out."

September 12, 1965, at Monza, Stewart accomplished what every F1 rookie dreams about. He won the Italian GP at 130.46 m.p.h. He had tasted victory at Kyalami the December before and again at Silverstone's International Trophy Race in May, but both of these were nontitle races. It was anticlimactic that the U.S. and Mexican Grands Prix ended with retirements, a collapsed suspension in the former and a failing clutch in the latter.

The year 1966 began brightly for Jackie. In New Zealand and Australia, driving his 1965 BRM, which would be obsolete once championship racing got underway, thanks to a change in the engine limits for F1, Stewart won the Lady Wigram and Teretonga Trophy races, added the Sandown Park segment of the Tasman and two Longford starts. He was crowned Tasman Champion. May 22, 1966, in a race expected to be dominated by Ferrari, Stewart and his teammate, Graham Hill, who usually treated Monte Carlo as a home course since he had won more F1 races there than anyone else in history, surprised the GP world by coming in 1st and 3rd. "It was a marvelous thing," Jackie said later, "winning at Monte Carlo, especially when you remember that the year before I made a mistake while leading and wound up 3rd."

The European GP battles were interrupted for Stewart's initial drive at Indianapolis in the 1960 Memorial Day 500. His mount was a Lola, dubbed the Bowes Seal Fast Special. Graham Hill was an opponent for this race in John Mecom's American Red Ball Special, another Lola. Both Britons survived the horrendous start, crash, and restart that marred the 500 that year, finding themselves, with about 100 miles to go, in very good position. Stewart, in fact, was leading by a lap over Jim Clark but his Lola suddenly pulled onto the grass with a scant 20 miles to go as Jackie shut down to avoid blowing his expensive Ford engine, its oil pressure zero. He was a disappointed lad as he walked back to the pits, watching Hill overtake Clark and go on to win, yet he responded to the applause of the crowd—some 300,-000—with a smile and a wave; with that, the applause and cheers rained harder. But the accolades were expensive. Stewart's loss by not winning the race as it seemed he might was about $130,000.

The bad luck from Indy doubled at Spa where Stewart and the F1 circus next gathered. Though still in a 2-litre BRM, as compared to the 3-litre cars of most of the other contenders, Stewart qualified 3rd fastest behind John Surtees and Rindt. Rains pelted the nearly 9-mile course overnight, and some wetness was expected as the starter's flag sent the field on its way. But on the back parts of Spa, the course looked like a river. Four cars went out together at one point; farther down the course all 3 BRMs—Graham Hill, Stewart, and Bob Bondurant—went off together. Stewart got the worst of it. At 150 m.p.h., his car aquaplaned off the course, through 2 stone walls and into a telephone pole.

Stewart was trapped in the car, by its collapsing framework. Fuel poured into the cockpit, with the engine still idling, with no way to turn it off because the dashboard had disintegrated. For 35 minutes, with the fuel eating away at him, Jackie lay inside the car as it resisted all the efforts of Hill—luckily at the site of Stewart's accident—and others to free the Scotsman.

But he was freed, finally, dragged away and stripped of his fuel-soaked clothing. Meanwhile, as Clark looked after Stewart's wife, BRM's Louis Stanley hired a plane to get Stewart to a British hospital, after temporary treatment in Belgium.

From this incident came Stewart's almost fanatical zeal for racing safety, yet he remained as fast and as daring as ever. He would risk all, provided all that could be done to prevent mishaps and aid to an accident victim was properly arranged by course authorities. Rindt's death, a few years later, increased Stewart's determination in these directions, though, he stayed his same, speedy self.

Jackie missed only the French GP, then was back in the British race, still handling his litre-short BRM. There the engine gave up the ghost. At Zandvoort he was 4th, at Nurburgring 5th. The 3-litre BRM P83 finally was ready for Monza, but much sorting out remained. In the

Italian GP a fuel leak retired Stewart, in the nontitle Oulton Park Gold Cup and in the championship U.S. GP, engine failures kayoed him; and in the Mexican finale, the oil leaked once more. Hill moved over to Lotus, attracted by Ford money, and Stewart became number one with BRM in 1967. But the cars still were unsorted, and Stewart's log was filled with disheartening retirements, no matter which BRM he tried. The engine failed in the South African GP; the fuel pump belt and suspension went at the Oulton Park Spring Cup; transmission failures eliminated him in the Silverstone International and the Monaco GP; brakes in the Dutch race.

In the Belgian GP his P83 held together for a 2nd place, in the French his P261 lasted for a 3rd. But then came 7 more retirements—transmission failures at Silverstone and the Nurburgring; sand in the throttle slides at Mosport, Canada; engine again at Monza; the fuel injection drive belt at Watkins Glen; vibration at Mexico. Besides driving the BRM, however, Stewart had been piloting an F2 Matra-Ford MS7 for Tyrrell. In this car he won at Karlskoga, Sweden, and Enna, Sicily, in August, and at Oulton Park and Albi in September. He liked the way this car was put together; and more importantly, he liked working with Tyrrell. When Tyrrell offered him an F1 ride in a Ford-powered Matra for 1968, Stewart took it.

He began the year with 2 more F2 victories, after a retirement in an interim Matra at the South African race. In Britain's nontitle Race of Champions Stewart's Matra was 6th; in the Belgian GP, 4th. Success came again in the Dutch GP with victory in a driving rain. Stewart's arm was in a lightweight cast that day. Back in April, he had broken his right wrist in an F2 start at Jarama, Spain. He was to miss the Spanish and Monegasque Grands Prix and his 3rd Indy bid as a result, driving only at Brands Hatch and Spa with a heavy cast on his wrist. After his Dutch GP victory, Stewart was 3rd in the French race, 6th in the British. Victory came again in the German GP at Nurburgring amid heavy fog and driving rain. The 9 points thus gained moved Stewart to 2nd place in the GP driver standings behind Hill, 26 points to 30. But at Monza engine failure and a Denis Hulme victory tightened the standings. Hulme won again in Canada, Stewart finishing 6th after a long pit stop for suspension repairs. At Watkins Glen, Jackie won easily, "like Jim Clark," he recalled, getting an early lead, building it, then easing off to save the car.

Everything depended upon the Mexican GP. Despite Stewart's missing the early races because of his injury, he now trailed Hill by only 2 points, with Hulme 3 back of Jackie. Hulme retired early in the Mexican GP, bashing a fence. For 38 laps, the lead alternated between Hill and Stewart, before the Matra's fuel system malfunctioned. Stewart had to dropped back. Graham was champion, Stewart was a distant 7th in the race, and 2nd in the season standings.

He would not be denied the title in 1969. In all, he started 14 F1 races, won 7 of them (including one non-title start). He also won 3 F2 starts. At South Africa, he was fastest and won; in the Spanish race, Rindt was fastest, but Stewart still won. After a retirement at Monaco, Stewart won the Dutch GP, and once again ran the fastest lap, feats he repeated in the French race 15 days later. Ten days later, Jackie did the double once more at the Silverstone British GP. Stewart's gearbox failed in the German GP, but he finished 2nd to Jacky Ickx, who was also fastest in lap timing. Jean-Pierre Beltoise won the fastest-lap prize at Monza, but it was Stewart who won the race with a blistering 150.97 m.p.h., and with it, the World Championship.

The North American races were an anticlimax. At Mosport, Stewart and Ickx dueled until Ickx tried to pass him in a tight corner, caught Stewart's wheel, and caused the Scotsman to spin out. The Matra would not restart; Stewart was grim-faced, as he walked back to the pits. At Watkins Glen a duel with Rindt was ended by a rough engine, as Rindt won his 1st *grande épreuve*. Hulme won Mexico; there, Stewart was 4th. The Stewart/Tyrrell/Matra combination seemed likely repeaters for 1970, but the French firm wanted its cars powered by Simca engines, not by Fords. So Stewart went to a new mount, the British March, powered by Ford.

Stewart was 3rd in South Africa, then won in Spain; but in Monaco and Belgium, electrical failure and an engine blow-up ended his bids. In the Dutch GP Stewart was a distant 2nd to Rindt, who otherwise lapped the field. In the French race, he was 9th. In the British, German, and Austrian races, the March failed again and even a 2nd at Monza failed to deter Stewart and Tyrrell from switching to a new, interim car, the Tyrrell, constructed for the 3 remaining North American races. If successful, it would become a prototype for an improved Tyrrell in 1971. On the basis of its race performances, the new mount was not successful. In the Canadian, U.S. and Mexican races, Stewart was retired.

Surprisingly, in 1970, he did not turn a fastest lap all year, yet obviously was as fast as ever. Clearly, it was his equipment—the March, then the interim Tyrrell—that had let him down. Offers poured in for 1971 from 6 factory teams. But Stewart, calling himself "an old woman about switching from something I know," stayed with Tyrrell. If the decision to stick with Ford power had been a mistake in 1970, it could be righted with hard work, despite Ford's dramatic pullout from racing late in the year.

Stewart was not regarded as a sure favorite in 1971; Ferrari, on paper, seemed ready to reassert itself, with a strong team in Ickx, Andretti, and Regazzoni. When Andretti beat Stewart in the South African championship opener, then repeated in the Questor GP, it seemed the experts were right. But in Spain, Stewart won at 97.19 m.p.h. In Monaco, a completely different race, he ran

the day's fastest lap, and won again at 83.49 m.p.h. Maybe the experts weren't wrong, for in the wet Dutch GP, his Goodyears were a problem, and Stewart was 11th, behind 10 Firestone-clad cars. But then, in the French, British, and German Grands Prix, he sewed up the World Championship. His young teammate François Cevert was 2nd in his home GP, where Stewart won at 111.66 m.p.h., running fastest lap. Cevert was 2nd again in Germany while running the fastest lap, but could not catch Stewart's winning car at 114.46 m.p.h. Stewart was fastest in the British GP, too, at 130.48 m.p.h., with Ronnie Peterson 2nd. With 5 in the bag, Stewart thought he might match Jim Clark's figure of 7 season victories, but at Austria—the day he clinched his 2nd title when Ickx dropped out—he retired at 135 m.p.h., when a wheel came off and Stewart went off the road. Then an engine failed in Italy, but he came back to win the Canadian GP at 81.956 m.p.h. in the rain; he led the U.S. race before the car went sour. He nursed it to a 5th, as teammate Cevert won his initial GP.

In the CanAm, success did not come as easily in the L&M Lola, especially when a new element was added to Team McLaren—an element named Peter Revson, who unexpectedly dominated the series. Yet Stewart managed to win at St. Jovite, after retiring at Mosport while leading. He retired at Road Atlanta, and at Watkins Glen after capturing the pole. He won again at Mid-Ohio, despite holding back because he didn't like the course. He retired at Elkhart Lake, was 6th at Donnybrooke, 2nd at Edmonton and Monterey. The car was being sorted out while racing, but Jackie was having a go; he was that kind of driver—a man who generated excitement in others and fought to contain it within himself.

"Excitement is a racing driver's biggest problem," said Stewart once. Believing it can deteriorate a man's performance more than anything else, Stewart always tried to start a race drained of emotion. But it was never easy for him, particularly if someone like Rindt or Ickx were pressing him. That would always be the danger point, Stewart pointed out. "When you try not to make mistakes—try to do things perfectly—that's the time the mistakes come."

No mistakes in 1971, though. Besides the 2nd World Championship, Stewart was honored with an Order of the British Empire (OBE) by the Queen, and earned more than $825,000, perhaps near $1 million—a figure he went past in 1972, thanks to more off-course endorsements, a continuation of his rich Goodyear Tire & Rubber Co. contract of some $335,000 a season, and increased earnings in F1, despite the fact that Stewart's F1 Tyrrell had some problems and Jackie himself had problems, not the least of which was a bleeding ulcer at mid-season. But he charged ahead, in pursuit of young Emerson Fittipaldi in the World Championship series. After taking a whole month off on doctors' orders because of his bleeding ulcer, and after giving up his newest CanAm ride with Team McLaren as a teammate of Hulme, Stewart returned to win the French GP. Fittipaldi's lead was too great, however, and Jackie spent the latter part of 1972 testing a newer Tyrrell-Ford and the latest Goodyear tire compounds anticipating a fast 1973 start. "I had thought about retiring about the time the ulcer hit me," he told a reporter, "I hadn't thought very hard or long about it before deciding I would be back in 1973." And then he started to an all-time record of GP victories, passing Jim Clark's 25 in mid-season, and a possible 3rd World Championship.

ROLF STOMMELEN

The year 1970 was a sort of breakthrough year in Grand Prix racing. A large number of young men got their chances to drive Formula 1 cars; some made good, others fell by the wayside. One who made good, although he never sat in a single-seater until 1969, was Rolf-Johann Stommelen of Cologne, Germany. But he had been a fully experienced driver at speed with 6 years of sports/prototype competition behind him.

Stommelen was born July 11, 1943, in Siegen, Germany, and started active competition at the age of 20 when he had acquired a Porsche 904 GTS. He finished a good 3rd in his 1st start, in a hillclimb near Bitburg. Driving mostly at home and in nearby races and hillclimbs, Rolf first attracted attention in 1965 with some good placings at Nurburgring, and in hillclimbs such as

Ollons-Villars in Switzerland and Gaisburg in Austria. Running the 1966 Le Mans in his own Porsche, Stommelen soon attracted recognition from the German car manufacturer. A year later, in 1967, Stommelen was offered an occasional factory drive at some of the major enduros. His best effort was a victory shared with Paul Hawkins in the Targa Florio. At Daytona Stommelen shared 5th in a Porsche 910 with Jo Siffert; and at Le Mans he and Jochen Neerpasch, 4 years Rolf's junior, nabbed a 6th in another Porsche 910.

The tempo picked up in 1968. With Neerpasch as his partner, Stommelen was 2nd at the Monza 1000 in a Porsche 907, and 3rd at Le Mans in a Porsche 908, after helping Vic Elford and Neerpasch win Daytona. Junior partner to veteran Hans Herrmann, Rolf shared a 2nd at the Nurburgring 1000 in a Porsche 907 and a 3rd at the Spa 1000 in a Porsche 908. In 1969, also in a Porsche 908, their partnership produced a 2nd at Nurburgring, 3rd in the Targa Florio, 4th at Spa, and 6th in the BOAC 500. He led briefly at Le Mans, that year. While Rolf continued to drive an occasional sports car race or hillclimb in 1970, his main activity was in F1 and F2. The German Auto Motor und Sport Publications had decided to sponsor the young driver in F1; at the same time, Stommelen had picked up a Formula 2 sponsor. A determining factor, perhaps, was Rolf's 1st race in a real formula car, in the 1969 German GP when F1 and F2 ran together. Stommelen's Lotus-Ford engine caught fire on the last lap, but he finished the race 8th overall and 4th in his F2 class. The crowd loved it. Before that start, he had only driven in Formula Vee.

His cars in both racing formulas were Brabham, and he even used that marque's F2 car to win the Freiburg hillclimb in July 1970. In F2 racing, however, Stommelen rated about 9th in the unofficial standings at season's end, his best races at Mantorp Park where he finished 2nd, and at Nurburgring where he was 3rd. Third was the best Rolf could accomplish in F1, too, aboard his Brabham-Ford BT33, not bad for learning while competing. Retired in South Africa and Spain, Stommelen was 5th in Belgium, 7th in France, 5th in Germany. Then came a great day for Rolf, the Austrian Grand Prix. Starting from 18th place on the 1st lap, he paced steadily, aided by the attrition that cuts all F1 fields. Late in the race, when Jean-Pierre Beltoise had to pit for fuel because of fuel feeder-line problems, Stommelen was able to steal his way into 3rd, holding it to the checker behind the flying Ferraris of Jacky Ickx and Clay Regazzoni.

The rest of 1970 was anticlimactic. There was another 5th in the Italian GP, a retirement in Canada, 12th in the United States GP, and a retirement in the Mexican finale. Stommelen's 10 points added up to an 11th place in the World Championship standings. At this time, with Jack Brabham's retirement creating an uncertain situation almost until the opening of the 1971 season, Rolf had worries about continuing in GP racing. But these were resolved by an offer, sweetened by the German magazine money, by Eifelland trailers, and BP oil, to drive for the new John Surtees-Rob Walker team and drive a Surtees-Ford T37.

But 1971 was basically unhappy for the bespectacled Stommelen. All season, he had problems with his Surtees-Ford, and at times, he told people, he was risking his life in driving "this terrible machine" at places like Nurburgring. The relationship would end for 1972, but Rolf plugged away through the entire 1971 season. Twelfth in South Africa, Stommelen retired in Spain, but returned with a 6th at Monaco. He was 7th in the Rindt Memorial nontitle race at Hockenheim; retired in Holland when he got a push start, and was disqualified after a spin; in France, 11th; in the British GP, 5th, one of the best Surtees marque placings all season in championship racing. But in his home GP, Stommelen was 10th; in Austria 7th. He retired in Canada, and he refused to run the U.S. GP for medical reasons, giving up the car to Sam Posey as it turned out. Stommelen's whole season netted 3 points, and a tie for 18th, in the world driver standings.

Long-distance racing was better. Driving for Alfa Romeo, he shared a 3rd in the Buenos Aires 1000 and a 2nd at Sebring; was 4th in the Monza 1000; 3rd in the Austrian; while in the Targa, he and Leo Kinnunen retired. He also managed to run a strong 6th in an American stock-car race—his 1st time in such a car and series—at the Talladega 500 before retiring with broken steering, using a 1969 Holman-Moody Mercury. The bug to race the Pettys and Hamiltons got inside Stommelen, and the betting was that he would be back, but serious F1 still was the real goal.

WHITNEY STRAIGHT

An American who became a Briton, Whitney Willard Straight was strictly an amateur who could stay in the running with the best of the professionals. Though his auto-racing career was short, his aviation career a lifetime one, Whiney Straight's name is as well remembered in both fields by those who recall those picturesque years just before World War II.

Although Straight was born in 1912 in the U.S., his antecedents were strictly British. For more than 600 years, his ancestors had been manorial lords in Herefordshire, but a branch of the family had sailed for the Americas early in the seventeenth century. A 12-year-old Whitney came to England in 1925, when his widowed mother remarried an Englishman. At 17, he enrolled at Trinity, and his closest friend, Dick Seaman soon blossomed as one of Britain's great drivers. The following year, Straight started club racing with a Brooklands Riley, placing in 5 of 6 starts.

In 1932 he bought Sir Henry Birkin's 2.5-litre GP Maserati, proceeding to better Birkin's own Brooklands Mountain Circuit record by better than 2 m.p.h. Money being no problem, Straight also purchased a supercharged K3 MG Magnette for voiturette racing, and in this car he won the Coppa Acerbo in 1933 and made more impressive Brooklands showings. In the same Maserati, Straight won the Brooklands Mountain Championships, was 2nd in the Albi Grand Prix, chopped 40 seconds off Rudi Caracciola's Mont Ventoux hillclimb record, and broke Hans Stuck's Shelsley Walsh record. He made 1933 a memorable year for the British; those were days when Britain rarely won on the Continent, which was dominated by the state-supported German teams. Using his own money as a starter, Straight determined to change Continental racing, deciding that the venture had to be self-liquidation, if not money-making. He opened offices in London, and set up garage facilities in Milan, Italy. It was natural, because there he purchased 3 new GP Maseratis from Bologna, one of these the latest 3-litre single-seater. Two of the great mechanical names of the day, Giulio Ramponi and Reid Railton, immediately set about modifying the cars with such niceties as Armstrong Siddeley preselector gearboxes, reworked and more subtly streamlined bodies, and the like. When they were done, Straight's 3 cars could do 170 m.p.h., fast in 1933.

Straight signed Hugh Hamilton and Buddy Featherstonhaugh, as codrivers for his team. The trio had a go at the German teams, but the Mercedes and Auto

Unions were faster. Still, Straight's team was surprisingly successful against these Continental juggernaughts, finishing 4th at Casablanca and Montreux, 2nd in the Vichy GP, and 3rd at Comminges. At Monza, in the Italian GP, only the Auto Unions could best him. Straight attempted to buy an Auto Union, but these were reserved for the German team alone. Would Straight be interested in joining the Auto Union team as a driver? Evidently, his performances in the outclassed Maser were impressive even to the Germans, who were perfectly willing to have Britons win as long as they were in silver cars. Straight accepted the offer, then talked his way out of it when his fiancée expressed strong misgivings about his becoming part of the Auto Union circus.

Whitney determined to leave the field if he had no chance of winning. But, as a last gesture, he did sail the cars to the initial South African GP, then held on a 16-mile Marine Drive Circuit, winning it at 93 m.p.h. His younger brother, Michael, had also entered, finishing 3rd in a Railton-Terraplane at 89 m.p.h. The cars were sold afterwards, the best Maserati going to Prince Bira of Siam, who used it to good effect in his British racing effort. Another of Straight's cars was converted into an unusual sports car, which has since disappeared.

At one time, Straight also owned a 4.3-litre Duesenberg, purchased from Enzo Ferrari with the idea of attacking John Cobb's Brooklands Outer Circuit record of 140.93 m.p.h., set in 1929. Cobb set this mark (which stands today, and since Brooklands is no more, will always stand) in a 24-litre Napier-Railton Special. There was more than a little snickering, when Straight, the new Englishman (having gained British citizenship that same year of 1934), attempted to use an American car with less than a 20 percent the displacement of the record holder, and with less than reliable steering and suspension for Brooklands. But Straight almost pulled the trick off, battling his car all the way to an official speed of 138.78 m.p.h., that did not quite break the overall record. It did become a new Class C Brooklands lap record.

Meanwhile, Straight's competitive eye had settled on aviation. As he withdrew from all-out auto racing, he threw his tremendous energies into the new field, involved, at one point, in some 20 ventures. A pilot since his Trinity days, he joined the Royal Air Force, when World War II came. An aide-de-camp to King George VI in 1944, he also was awarded a CBE. By war's end, he had won many decorations, including the Military Cross and Distinguished Flying Cross.

In 1947, Straight became deputy chairman of British Overseas Airways Corporation, remaining in that post until 1955. He then returned officially to the interests of his youth, taking over as deputy chairman of Rolls-Royce. One wonders if he ever thought of what might have happened if he had gone on to drive with Auto Union.

LEWIS STRANG

In the early days of this century, the classic race-car drivers were Barney Oldfield, Ralph DePalma, Bob Burman, and a man named Lewis Strang. The others are still well-remembered, but Strang has somehow been forgotten. Why that should be is mysterious, because Strang was as big as any of them—in some ways for a time, bigger than any—and he proved that at Atlanta in November 1909, with the Red Devil.

The Red Devil was a car, not a man, a fire-red Fiat with a 200-b.h.p. engine that roared, blew great clouds of smoke, and generally reminded onlookers of the place that preachers warn against. The car, run in England, had been intended as a record-setting mount for the great Ralph DePalma, but it had overturned on him when he tried it out at Bridgeport, Conn., and had broken his leg. So it was that the Red Devil had a new driver this November day, Strang, a hulking man with longish, curled hair, covered by a leather helmet from which streamed a red cloth that presaged the fighter-pilot style of World War I.

The Red Devil obeyed Strang, racing in a cloud of smoke and dust to a new national dirt-track record for the mile of 37.7 seconds, or 95 m.p.h. And a 2-mile record, too, of 1:21.51. It was no fluke, for Strang and the Devil visited the Indianapolis Speedway—then newly paved with bricks—the following December 18th, and, in near-zero weather, set a world quarter-mile record of 8.05 seconds (111.86 m.p.h.). An existing Oldfield record (set before the brick paving) of 43.6 fell to Strang's 40.61-second mile run, a new 5-mile record of 3:17.70 minutes (91.81 m.p.h.) was established before the day was out.

Strang, a nephew of J. Walter Christie, was born in Amsterdam, N.Y., and made his way into auto racing almost prosaically. He started as chauffeur and demonstrator at the H. H. Franklin Company factory in Syracuse, N.Y. One of the Franklin Company's rich customers had hired Strang to chauffeur him around Europe in a Panhard, delivery of same being in France. When Strang returned to the country, now a world traveler and observer of European racing, he became a demonstrator of French Berliet cars, a chauffeur for sugar king H. O. Havemeyer, and a part-time racing driver for some of Havemeyer's friends. Strang's 1st known race was at Long Branch, N.J., racing a Pope on a straight-away track, a sort of 1905-style drag strip.

Strang went to work for his uncle Walter the following year, as head mechanic and back-up driver. Their 1st outing was the 1906 Vanderbilt Cup, where the front-wheel drive Christie car qualified 4th and finished 13th in the main race. In 1907, with Christie injured, Strang took a car on a long Southern tour that ended when the engine exploded. Desiring a more reliable machine, he found it in the new Isotta-Fraschini that John Tyson was importing from Italy. This car was big and powerful, and it suited Strang's personal charging style of driving perfectly. With the Isotta-Fraschini, he scored 3 impressive major American victories back to back, clearly capapulting Strang into the forefront of American racing drivers of the day.

On March 19, 1908, Strang and his Isotta-Fraschini won the 20-lap Savannah Challenge Trophy race along the rugged 17.1-mile course over Georgia wagon roads. On April 24th that same year, he and his car took the 240-mile Briarcliff Trophy race along the equally rugged suburban New York roads. And on September 7 he added the 254-mile Lowell Road Race in Massachusetts to his victory pole. Afterwards, Strang and his friend, the Mercedes driver Emil Strickler, joined forces to co-drive a Renault in a Birmingham, Ala., race. They crashed, and Strickler, whom Strang credited with teaching him successful road-racing techniques, was killed. Strang filled out their contract with Renault by finishing 6th in the Savannah Grand Prize race 10 days later. But he was glad to sever connections with the French marque to join forces with the powerful Buick team in 1909. Here Strang was paired with Burman and Louis Chevrolet.

In his first 2 starts, Strang retired with mechanical failures, but on July 8, 1909, he set a new 75-mile dirt-track record at Columbus, Ohio. In the last days of July, he won all his starts at a 2-day meet in Waco, Tex. The next month, he won the 100-mile G&J Trophy dash at Indy. The call to tame the Red Devil at Indianapolis and Atlanta came soon after that.

That same year, J. I. Case, the farm machinery king, decided to branch out into automobiles. He sensed that racing was one way to get the Case Car name talked about along with the Fords and others. He hired Strang to handle his racing effort, giving him a section of the factory. Strang immediately set about designing racing versions of the basic Case components. The results were fast but tricky machines that took several years to separate from their bugs.

The racing effort got under way in March 1911, at the Pablo Beach near Jacksonville, Fla. Strang finished 3rd in the 300-miler, the race going to Louis Disbrow in a Pope Hummer. Strang and Case signed Disbrow for their team, starting with that year's inaugural Indianapolis 500. Austrian-born Joe Jagersberger, who had built a solid reputation with Mercedes, was also hired to complete the 3-car team.

At the 1911 Indy, none of the Case starters finished. Disbrow was retired from the race when hit by another car. Jagersberger lost a steering knuckle on the 87th lap, in front of the judges' stand, starting a chain-reaction crash that eliminated 4 cars. No one was seriously hurt in that crash; even Jagersberger's riding mechanic, who was thrown onto the track in front of the onrushing field, escaped severe injury. Strang lasted longest, retiring finally in the latter half of the race from a seized piston.

But less than 2 months later, Strang was dead. It happened on the 1911 Wisconsin Reliability Run, which was possibly the safest of all competitions then, while Strang was moving about 10 m.p.h. A farm wagon had bogged down in the mud. After stopping and surveying the situation with Jagersberger and their 2 observers, Strang started to slowly inch around the stalled wagon. But the same rains that had muddied the road had weakened a shoulder. Without warning, the road shoulder gave away under the heavy Case car. Though the 3 passengers were thrown clear, the car rolled over Strang, crushing him to death.

Later, World War I ended the Case racing effort, although the company made cars until 1927.

BILL STROPPE

Born January 15, 1919, in Long Beach, Calif., Bill Stroppe became identified with Clay Smith; both had worked together, and independently. Certainly, both Stroppe and Smith had an important effect on the sport of motor racing as practiced in the United States. Smith was a great Indianapolis mechanic; Stroppe is known for his late-model stock-car and rally exploits. Both started in Long Beach, Calif., a city dwarfed by its next-door neighbor, Los Angeles, shortly after World War II. They started in boat racing, gaining the attention of Mercury executives in 1947, when they entered the Henry Ford Memorial Regatta with a hydroplane powered by a 225-cu. in. Ford 6. Stroppe drove it to victory in 3 events, beating the time of the craft that won the Gold Cup by 2½ minutes.

Stroppe attended Polytechnic High School in Long Beach, playing blocking back on the football team although he worked evenings for the local Ford agency. He was dragging cars on the Southern California dry lakes at the age of 19, while specializing as an engine-repair man in the oil fields. In 1940, he returned to mechanic's work at an auto dealership, but a year later joined the Navy. Assigned to a seaplane tender, Bill spent most of the next 3 years in the South Pacific, earning battle stars at Kwajalein, Eniwetok, Saipan, Tinian, and Guam. He was promoted to Chief Aviation Machinist, a rank that got him a job as a mechanic after the war.

His driving career included Mobil Economy Run class and sweepstakes victories in 1950–51. But, like Clay Smith, he was known for his ability with a wrench. He and Clay Smith came together immediately after the war when Stroppe's midget, driven by Johnny Mantz, was not doing much winning. Smith's ministrations worked wonders. When Clay went with J. C. Agajanian, Stroppe went with him; together with Mantz, they campaigned the Championship Trail in 1948. After Mantz came Chuck Stevenson, then Troy Ruttman as drivers.

In 1950, at Indy, Stroppe handled Jim Bryan's Viking Trailer Special, returning to Smith for the Ruttman 500 victory. It was in the Ruttman pits that Smith and Stroppe told Benson Ford, then Lincoln-Mercury-Division General Manager, they would like backing to enter the Lincoln in the Pan-American Road Races. Ford gave them the go-ahead; Lincoln's swept their division 1, 2, 3, 4 in both 1952 and 1953. Stroppe had copiloted Manty in the 2nd-place Lincoln in 1952 and in the 4th-place Lincoln in 1954. However, only a month before the 1954 event, tragedy struck. Smith was killed by a flying car at DuQuoin, Ill., September 6th.

Stroppe was now chief of one of the biggest racing garages in the country and one of the most sought-after chief mechanics. But he preferred to drive when he could. He hoped, in fact, to make the Kurtis-Kraft chassis into a new American breed of sports car with Mercury engines.

His best year as a driver came in 1953, when he won 8 of 11 starts in a Kurtis-Kraft car, but after Clay Smith died, Stroppe became pitbound, as the business prospered from a large injection of Ford family money. Stroppe-prepared cars were "sanitary"—beautifully painted, clean, shining. His high point came in 1956, as Mercury cars won in both NASCAR and USAC: Elkhart Lake, 2 out of 3 at Milwaukee, Pomona, Phoenix, and the Paramount Ranch, Calif., road race. In 1957, a Mercury convertible prepared by him won the Daytona convertible race on the old beach-road course. Jimmy Bryan won the Northern 500 for Stroppe at Trenton, other Stroppe drivers taking Vallejo and Pomona.

When the mass Detroit exodus from stock-car racing came, Bill spent the next 3 years on special projects for FoMoCo. These included the re-enactment of the 1909 transcontinental race and the introduction of the new Falcon. Stroppe also kept his hand in on Indy cars and boats. In 1961 he handled Autolite performance activities in the West; in 1962, the only time he was away from Ford in those years, he handled special projects for Chevrolet. The Comet's unsuccessful assault on the East African Rally and the run the length of the Western hemisphere on the Pan-American Highway were Stroppe projects. He returned to the stock-car wars for Parnelli Jones's assaults on Pikes Peak and other USAC stops, even venturing on to Daytona. Jones won the USAC title late-model crown in 1964. But it was the 1965 NASCAR-Riverside 500 that retired both Stroppe and Jones from stock-car competition. It was at the Riverside 500, which must have set some kind of high point for Bill's temper, as he and NASCAR tech inspectors went round and round on Jones's car. Jones never ran a NASCAR race after that, and Stroppe was happy when Mercury decided to retire from competition. After this, the West Coast arm of Holman-Moody absorbed Stroppe's business, but left him in charge of his own garage. A great mechanic spawns other greats, among Stroppe's were Verne Houle, an engineer and

transmission expert; Cecil Bowman, Louis Unser, Jr., drag ace Byron Froelich, Jay Lightfoot; and one of the best body men, Al Loya. Les Ritchie also worked for Stroppe on Jones's cars.

HANS STUCK

A man who stood 6 feet 2 inches and who raced nearly 4 decades privately and professionally would be hard to forget; Hans Stuck von Villiez seemed to have been forgotten whenever there is talk of the great drivers of the thirties. Yet Stuck scored a class victory in his debut race at age 24, and kept winning until he captured the German Mountain Championship at the age of 60. He may even have been older when he won that hillclimb title; he claimed December 27, 1900, as his birth date, but that would make him 17 when he was a German artillery officer in World War I. Perhaps, for he was a man of paradox.

Stuck's mother was a French Huguenot, his father a German, and he himself carried an Austrian passport, although he officially was born in Warsaw, Poland. The Stucks were landed gentry who operated an estate farm south of Munich, and Hans's 1st car—a semi-sports Durkopp—was used, supposedly, to carry him to business appointments in the city. He quickly switched to a straight 2-litre sports model in which he won his 1st "competition"—a bet with friends that he could climb a hill faster backwards than they could forward. All Hans did was reverse his gearbox to give him 4 backward speeds.

Stuck's 1st formal competition was the Baden-Baden hillclimb in 1925 in which he won the 2-litre class in his 60-h.p. Durkopp. Fine tuning added 20 more h.p., and soon Hans was winning hillclimbs with a regularity discouraging to his opposition. When the German depression came, the Stuck family farm failed in 1927. The gentleman driver had to turn professional to pay the family bills. He presented himself at Austro-Daimler, where his reputation earned him a factory berth in the 3-litre ADM designed by Dr. Ferdinand Porsche. That 1st season he won 7 runs, scoring fastest time of day, in 4 of the meets. In the next 4 years Stuck won 43 races for the Austrian marque. For himself he won the Swiss mountain championship in 1928, the Austrian title the following year, and the overall European hillclimb crown for racing cars in 1930. He also became adept at ice racing on frozen Bavarian lakes.

In 1931 Stuck left Austro-Daimler, purchasing his own Mercedes Benz SSK at a bargain price from the factory. The factory had also agreed to keep it up to snuff while he raced. He won his 1st big circuit race, the Lemberg GP, then headed for South America for some racing and climbing. There, he refused to race over the poor Argentine roads, but Stuck did agree to enter the world's longest hillclimb, the 37-mile Rio-

Petropolis race. He won, of course. After more hill-climbing glory, including the 1932 International Alpine Championship for sports cars, Stuck joined Auto Union as its number one driver for 1934, the 1st year of the new GP formula.

In March, Hans opened the year by setting international records for 100 miles, 200 kilometers, and 1 hour. Then he went on to 1sts at the Swiss and German Grands Prix and the Masaryk race, 2nds in the Italian GP and the Eifelrennen, and 4th in the Spanish GP. He won 4 hillclimbs, too. Late that same year, Stuck set 5 new records at Avus. There was no doubt he was the best driver in the world that season.

The following season neither Hans nor Auto Union had much racing luck, though Stuck had done better than 200 m.p.h. in a flying-mile test in Italy under the most miserable weather conditions. He did manage a victory in the Italian GP at Monza, and 2nd place in the German GP, but aside from his usual German mountain title, victory eluded Stuck most of the time. Bernd Rosemeyer was the favored Auto Union driver now, and under team orders, he was to win when possible. Hans was 2nd in the German and Tripoli races in 1936, 3rd at Monaco and in the Swiss race. The following year he was 2nd at Rio de Janeiro and Belgium, 3rd in the German GP. In 1938 he was 3rd in the Hungarian GP, in 1939, 1st in the Bucharest race. In these years, Stuck also turned his attention to boat racing, and, using a borrowed racing car engine mounted in a hydroplane, he set a world class record and captured the German hydroplane championship.

Stuck excelled at whatever he tried. He was a 6-handicap golfer and an expert skier, becoming a licensed ski instructor (which in his era was quite an honor). Mercedes Benz, despite its rivalry with Auto Union, hired Stuck as the pilot of its prospective record car, the T80. The T80 never ran because of the war, and now may be seen, engineless, at the Mercedes Benz racing musuem. After the war, Stuck used his Austrian passport to return to racing, again making the winner's circle despite his age (45). He won Germany's initial postwar race, at Hockenheim in an 1100-c.c. Cisitalia, and was 2nd at the Prix de Berne in 1948, won by teammate Piero Taruffi.

A 2-litre *monoposto*, the Alex von Falkenhausen-designed AFM, also occupied his attention in these postwar years. The car, based on a BMW 328, was built in Hans's garage; it was successful whenever it lasted in a race, although it was little more than a sprint car. In 1953, as a favor to his old friend Dr. Porsche, Stuck drove Porsches, principally the 4-camshaft Spyder but also some pushrod models, without any notable success.

Everyone thought Stuck was through, but he returned once more in 1958 with BMW, winning several hill-climbs with the handsome, if overweight and somewhat unwieldy, BMW Type 507. In 1960, driving the 700-c.c. BMW Sport Coupe, Stuck won that last championship,

the German hillclimb title; he also was 1st in class in the Monza 10-hour race.

He continued driving competitively until 1962, when Hans started training his son (born 1952) for the future. The name of Stuck may be in the winner's lists once again—if not Stuck senior, then surely Stuck junior.

SUMMERS BROTHERS

November 12, 1965, the Bonneville Salt Flats echoed to the roar of 4 Chrysler Hemi V-8s as a 32-foot-long, 4-foot-wide, 2-foot 2-inch high special called the Goldenrod ripped down the black line that marked the metered course. A lean, crew-cut young man of 28 named Robert Sherman Summers—he preferred plain Bob or Butch—was in the cockpit. At the end of the morning's work, he held the Land Speed Record for axle-driven automobiles, wresting away a mark that Donald Campbell had won only a bit more than a year before. His times were 409.277 in the mile and 409.695 in the kilometer. The first run had been the fastest at 412 m.p.h.

Art Arfons, Craig Breedlove, and Gary Gabelich were the jet set of the LSR crowd. But the Summers Brothers, Bob and Bill, a year older and a lot heavier, generally are overlooked in all the attention, even though Bob's record has stood longer than anyone's since John Cobb. Perhaps it was because they always were so unassuming.

Bill drove trucks, and Bob was an experimental machinest in the aerospace industry. They were around hot rods all their lives, out in California where they came from. At Bonneville, starting in 1954, Bob practiced driving fast not only in his own cars, but in other people's. In August 1960, Bob piloted the Quincy-Brissette lakester to 264 m.p.h., fastest-ever speed for an open-wheeled vehicle. The following year their Pollywog streamliner was clocked at 302.317 m.p.h., in 1962 at 323 m.p.h. In 1963 Bob set several Class C records with Pollywog. Then, in 1964, the brothers started building Goldenrod on a 7-day, 18-hour-day program, backed by Firestone, Hurst and Chrysler to the tune of $100,000-plus. Mobil Oil joined later. The payoff came that November day. The car has been on the move ever since, visiting auto shows all over the world.

On a practice run the day after record day, by the way, Bob went to 425 m.p.h. one way. The sponsors weren't interested in another unless someone beat the 1965 mark. Almost a decade later, no one had yet, although several had tried.

JOHN SURTEES

The oily grime that clings to the face of a driver after a race in open-cockpit cars, mixing with his sweat to form a speckled mask not unlike that of a coal miner, was particularly heavy on England's John Surtees as he climbed out of his Honda Formula 1 car September 10, 1967, at Monza, Italy. It had been a particularly brutal race on the supertuned machinery and on the drivers as well. Nevertheless, Surtees allowed himself a small smile of satisfaction, like the miner who has dug far more coal than his quota. He deserved it, for he had won the Italian Grand Prix that is still referred to as "the race of the century."

The start of the 38th running of the Italian GP, bearing the honorary title of GP d'Europe that season, had been particularly confused. There were too many officials with flags at the line, and when a minor official had waved his flag too vigorously at someone, the drivers interpreted it as the starting signal. When the real starter waved his flag, it was at the back of the field that was already accelerating past him.

At the end of lap 1, Dan Gurney in his own All American Eagle led, with Jack Brabham, Graham Hill, Jim Clark, Bruce McLaren grouped behind him. Surtees and others formed the next group a little farther back. On lap 5, Clark got past Gurney; on lap 8, the AAR Eagle was done for the day. Around lap 12, Clark's Lotus suffered a rear puncture, pitting on the 13th lap for a wheel change. Denis Hulme, Clark, Hill and Brabham had been in the lead, and behind them a dicing exchange continued among Surtees, Chris Amon—Ferrari's lone entry and the Italian crowd's favorite, of course—, Bruce McLaren, and Jo Rindt.

On lap 18, Hill forced his way into the lead, then Clark—but he was merely unlapping himself since he had just returned from the wheel change. Hill darted into Clark's slipstream and moved away a bit from the other contenders, thanks also to Hulme's overheating engine. Brabham was now a lonely 2nd, and farther back were Surtees, Amon, McLaren and Rindt. Surtees's problems were multiplying; his new, light-weight Honda's fuel injection system, a season-long worry, was again kicking up.

Amon was the 1st of the group to drop out on the 57th lap, after a spin on the previous go-around. Surtees, meanwhile, temporarily had solved his problems and was closing the gap on Brabham, but could take small consolation on that, because Clark was breathing down his pipes. Nine laps from the end—the 59th lap—Hill's Lotus jinx struck. On the parabolic curve, his engine literally exploded; he had to coast into the pits as the others flashed by. Brabham led Surtees by just a bit as they passed the pits, but Clark roared by both of them to take the lead on the 61st lap.

Then Clark suffered a fuel system failure, and his Lotus slowed. Surtees and Brabham passed him on the last lap, but Brabham outbraked the Honda on the last curve, going by on the inside. But he slid wide on the apex, hitting talcum powder that had been spread on oil slicks, and spun broadside. Brabham was quick to

recover, but Surtees, calling on all his skills, slipped by on Brabham's inside to head for the checker. Brabham ducked into Surtees' slipstream and almost rode into his pipes, then slipped out for a slingshot. The car almost edged ahead, but Surtees, overrevving, managed to hold his lead, to win by 2 seconds. Clark came in a relatively distant 3rd.

There is, after all, a slight connection between the mines and the race course. Like the miner, drivers like John Surtees always have accepted certain job liabilities for a chance at some rewards. Sharp-featured, balding, and blessed with a wry wit, Surtees already had his share of rewards. There was the manor house at Surrey, and the MBE from the Queen in recognition of his driving prowess. There were 2 boxer dogs, a beautiful wife, and the income to support this country gentleman's life. Finally, there was the simple knowledge that he, the son of a London motorcycle salesman, had achieved such prominence in life.

Engines and speed were a part of this life almost from the beginning at Tatsfield. He was born February 11, 1934, and at 11 was working part-time for his father, quitting school 4 years later. In 1949, Surtees was already beginning to compete on motorcycles. His 1st race was aboard a 500-c.c. Excelsior B14 at Luton, but soon he switched to a Triumph Tiger. Meanwhile, he signed with the Vincent-HRD Company for a 5-year apprenticeship, which he hoped would lead through the machine shop into engineering. Later, at 21, when he was beginning to win motorcycle races, he joined Ferguson in Coventry, acquiring knowledge of welding techniques and metal-working that would aid him much later.

Between his 1st motorcycle Grand Prix race, the Ulster, and the 1967 Monza victory for Honda, were only 15 years, but what years they were. The 1st factory team offer came from Norton in 1953, but Surtees was disabled in a crash. He rode for Norton in 1954–55 before switching to MV Agusta for the 1st of his 7 motorcycle world championships. Surtees was led into auto-racing competition through a dinner honoring him as Britain's 1958 Sportsman of the Year. Mike Hawthorn and Tony Vandervell (the Vanwall owner) surrounded him. Mike, a cycle enthusiast and auto racer of World Championship caliber, pumped Surtees for cycle tips, meanwhile asking why he didn't give the auto racing a try. Vandervell offered a Vanwall on the spot, but Surtees, thinking the offer not serious, did nothing about it.

The next year, Reg Parnell, always on the lookout for British driving talent, pressed Surtees both at the British and Italian Grands Prix, at which Surtees was a spectator, to try out a car. Though committed to cycling for the season, Surtees finally agreed to drive an Aston Martin DRBI/3000 at Goodwood in October. "As soon as I got into the Aston," Surtees recalled, "I felt the seating position all wrong and had it changed. Then I drove off, only to come in immediately to have

the seat put back into its original position, for I just couldn't drive the car as it was. This, my first racing car, seemed to ride terribly rough. There were noises coming from everywhere, and to a bike man that was strange. After about half a dozen laps, I began to settle down, although the car still felt unsteady. Very soon I had begun to learn how to use this power, and this impression disappeared."

Word of Surtees's Aston Martin tryout spread quickly, and he quickly received a call from Vandervell, who upbraided the youngster for trying out in a car other than a Vanwall. "Then David Yorke, Tony's man, contacted me," Surtees recalled, "and I once more found myself at Goodwood, this time in a full-blooded GP car. I had 3 days there, during which time my confidence and skill increase considerably." (The 3rd day he was circling Goodwood at times several seconds lower than the existing record). "Reg Parnell had offered me a factory berth, but I had determined to try it alone instead, at least for a time." Surtees set about purchasing a Formula 2 Cooper, and at the same time agreed to drive a Ken Tyrell Formula Junior Cooper-Austin in a March 18, 1960, race at Goodwood. Surtees finished 2nd in his 4-wheeler competition debut, behind Clark.

Though committed to finishing the season with MV Agusta, Surtees obtained permission to add auto racing to his schedule whenever there was no conflict with the cycles. At Oulton Park he made his debut in the F2 Cooper, and was 2nd to Innes Ireland. In May he was 4th in the Aintree 200 behind the Porsches of Stirling Moss, Jo Bonnier, and Phil Hill. Colin Chapman of

Lotus, offered Surtees a machine for the next 2 Formula 1 Silverstone meetings. He did well enough for Lotus to provide him a car for the Monaco GP in 1960, his first *grande épreuve*. A failed crown wheel and pinion, however, retired him at Monaco. He returned for the British GP, finishing 2nd to Brabham. Perhaps his best F1 drive that season was the Portuguese GP at Oporto, in which Surtees led from the 11th through the 35th laps, though a fuel tank leaked gasoline into the bottom of his cockpit. Running 24 seconds ahead of Brabham, Surtees's foot slipped off the wet pedals, smashing his car into a curb and splitting its radiator. He was 9th in the final Championship point standings.

After winning 2 World Championships for motorcyclists in 1960, Surtees retired from cycles, concentrating on automobiles. His motorcycle career had included an incredible 7 World Championships and 6 Tourist Trophy victories on the Isle of Man. For 1961, after turning down Chapman because he did not want to rob a driver of a mount, John signed with Parnell's Yeoman Credit team of Coopers, sharing cars with Roy Salvadori. He won his 1st race that year, the Lombank Trophy at Snetterton, and also the Goodwood 100, nipping Stirling Moss in the latter with a lap record speed of 98.18 m.p.h., and an overall average of 95.76 m.p.h. Surtees still was an unpolished driver, however, taking motorcycle-like lines through corners, scaring others with his speed and technique. Though 5th in the Belgian GP, with a lap record there, despite gearbox troubles, he had smashed into a barrier at Brands Hatch when he missed a gear change. After a 4th at Aintree, he dropped a valve at Monaco, was 7th at Zandvoort, and 5th at Spa-Franchorchamps behind 4 more-powerful Ferraris.

A skid on some spilled fuel put Surtees out of the French GP, but he was 2nd to Moss in the Silverstone Intercontinental Race. Bashed by another car at the start of the British GP, Surtees retired in mid-race. He was 5th at Nurburgring, but his car had run up the back of Bonnier's Porsche at Monza, retiring Surtees from the Italian GP. (Bonnier later claimed his helmet bore Surtees's tire marks). Surtees crossed the Atlantic for the U.S. GP at Watkins Glen, but again he retired. The 4 points earned in 1961 had put him 11th on the World Championship table. The learning period was still going on.

For 1962 Surtees again signed with Parnell for the combined Yeoman Credit-Bowmaker Team, this time using an Eric Broadley-designed Lola. The car had teething problems, but a combination of Cooper-Lotus-Lola talent and experience finally sorted out the mount, and Surtees won at Mallory. Further modifications were made in time for the Brussels GP, in which Surtees did well until one of the rubberized fuel tanks became pressurized and lost him valuable time for adjustments. At Rheims, his Lola was leading by 20 seconds when a valve spring broke; at Rouen a shorted plug cost Surtees

2nd, but after regaining his position quickly, his linkage broke. He was 5th in both races. Finally, at the British GP, he finished 2nd to Clark, then repeated the placing in the German GP behind Graham Hill in a BRM.

The rest of the year's races were nothing but frustration again: the Lola holed a piston in the Italian GP; shed a crankcase plug in the U.S. GP, and forced him out of the finale at South Africa with gearbox and engine breakdowns. But 1962 was not completely unsuccessful for Surtees. On February 14, he flew back from the Tasman season to wed Patricia Burke at the Church of St. Cross, Winchester, with Jim Clark at his best man. While on his honeymoon in Australia, Surtees won the Longford, Tasmania, road race. Despite his breakdowns, he was 4th in the Championship point standings with 19.

When Bowmaker could not continue big-time racing in 1963, and since, Coventry-Climax was then considering withdrawing from racing (with all the ramifications that meant for British carbuilders) Surtees finally accepted a Ferrari factory berth, signing a 3-year contract. But it was not the 1st time Surtees's name was associated with Ferrari. In 1962 he had driven a Berlinetta in the Goodwood Tourist Trophy for Bowmaker-Maranello Concessionaires, putting on a good show until a crackup.

Though the Ferrari car had to be sorted out in 1963, Surtees did manage to win his 1st *grande épreuve*, the German GP at Nurburgring, while setting a lap record of 96.88 m.p.h. He had led at Monza until a tappet snapped; then the same car had broken its rear suspension mounting during practice at Watkins Glen. There, he drove an older Ferrari to the lead, but was retired when a piston broke. In Mexico, a rule interpretation disqualified him, and in East London, South Africa, the gearbox acted up. Still, he ended 1963 with 22 championship points, again 4th.

Then came 1964. Surtees won at Syracuse, Italy, in the V-8 Ferrari, was 2nd at Zandvoort, but retired from the next 2 Grands Prix. At Brands Hatch, site of the British and European GP, he was 3rd. Then he won the German race, cracked up at Zeltweg and in a non-F1 go at the Tourist Trophy. Despite the pain of recent injuries, he came back to win at Monza and take 2nds at Watkins Glen and Mexico City to win his 1st World Championship at the age of 30. The GP roulette had finally stopped at his number.

Surtees was 2nd to Clark (his eventual successor as champion) in the 1965 opener at South Africa, 4th at Monaco. The engine of his V-8 Ferrari broke down at Belgium, the European GP in 1965, but he was 3rd in the French and British Grands Prix, the latter the debut of the Ferrari V-12. At Zandvoort he was 7th, at Nurburgring his gearbox broke, and at Monza his clutch went. Surtees had 17 championship points with 2 races remaining—Clark already having cinched his title at Germany—when the Mosport crash ended 1965. In September at Mosport Park in Ontario, Canada, his Lola

T70 Group 7 car shed a wheel during practice at speed. The car ran off a bank, flipped and landed on top of him, fracturing his pelvis, injuring his spinal column and kidneys, and permanently shortening his left leg. Only modern medicine saved him.

For a man given less than an hour to live, he made a strong comeback in 1966. After 7 months on the sidelines, he slipped into a prototype Ferrari GT in a pouring rain at Monza April 25th, and won the 1,000-kilometer race. Then he won the nonchampionship Syracuse GP. In the GP opener at Monaco, Surtees' Ferrari retired after 16 laps with transmission trouble, but he won the Belgian GP in the rain. Then a dispute between Surtees and Eugenio Dragoni, Ferrari team manager, ended the Briton's association with Modena; Dragoni had suggested that Surtees would be replaced late in the Le Mans race by another driver. John would have none of that. For Ferrari he had won the 1964 constructor's title as well as the driving championship, starting 57 races and winning 12. He was 2nd 13 times, 3rd 5 times, 4th once.

Surtees returned to Britain, immediately receiving a berth with Cooper-Maserati for the French GP, designated the European GP that season. Fuel-pump trouble knocked his car out after 5 laps. In the British GP, he lasted 67 laps before the Cooper's suspension failed; at Zandvoort it was ignition. But Surtees doggedly continued, perhaps, spurred as much by some Ferrari snickers as anything else, taking 2nd place at Nurburgring in the German GP, where he had the fastest lap. A fuel leak killed his Italian GP bid, but he was 3rd at Watkins Glen, again setting fast lap.

That year, he won the Mexican GP with World Champion Jack Brabham 2nd, 8 seconds behind. Mexican food had given Surtees's mild food poisoning, but he still had insisted on starting. With Surtees' win, sponsor Cooper thereby gained its 1st F1 victory since 1962, averaging 95.72 m.p.h. Surtees's 1966 championship point-total was 28, second to Brabham's 42.

Perhaps the more ruggedly built Group 7 cars were more suited to his technique than the fragile F1 racers. In 1966, the SCCA, in conjunction with the Canadian Automobile Sport Clubs, inaugurated a rich new series called the Canadian-American Challenge Cup. The series was scheduled for the fall, to avoid conflict with F1. Surtees and his Lola-Chevrolet were immediately placed among the favorites; he won the Cup and more than $58,000. At St. Jovite, Surtees led almost all the way, topping a 2-car McLaren factory team among others. At Bridgehampton he retired as Gurney's Lola-Ford won; at Mosport Park, he retired after a crash at the 1st corner. At Riverside, however, after a failure at nearby Laguna Seca, Surtees won a battle with Jim Hall's Chaparral, and in the finale at Las Vegas he led all the way once more.

The next year (1967) Honda, the Japanese cycle manufacturer, was making a strong effort to bring auto racing laurels to the Far East. Surtees accepted Honda's request to help develop the relatively new marque. The Honda F1 car was big and unresponsive, but its potential seemed enormous. The opening race at South Africa went relatively well, with Surtees finishing 3rd, but then the problems started. At Monaco, Zandvoort, and Spa, the Honda was retired. A piston went in the Monaco GP on the 33rd lap, a throttle slide gave way in the Dutch race's 73rd lap, and in the Belgian GP, a crankshaft broke in the opening lap. A lack of engines canceled the team's appearance for the French GP.

But the cancellation gave Surtees and Honda engineers time to resolve some of the car's difficulties. In the British GP, the car was 6th, in the German 4th. Passing up Canada, Surtees pointed for the Italian race with the new, lightened-chassis car, which became the most important race so far for him. The car was going well in the U.S. GP when, on the 96th lap, the ignition and gearbox both failed. The season ended with a 4th at Mexico, giving Surtees 20 points in the driver standings and a tie (with Amon) for 4th place in the tables.

The new year (1969) promised hope for Honda, but the year disappointed quickly. At South Africa, Surtees was 8th; in Spain, the gear selector gave way in the 74th lap. In the Belgian GP, the rear suspension failed in 11 laps; in the Dutch GP, the alternator quit on lap 50. The year's sole bright spot was the French GP, but tradgedy marred Honda's 2nd-place finish. The race cost Honda its other driver, Jo Schlesser, who was killed when he spun off course and crashed. In the British race, Surtees was 5th, with retirements following in the German (engine), Italian (accident with Amon) and Canadian (gearbox) races. Surtees did take 3rd place (behind Jackie Stewart and Graham Hill) in the U.S. race, but a retirement due to vapor lock in the Mexican finale ended the year. Honda had had enough, withdrawing after that season.

Tied for 7th in the standings with Jo Siffert, with 12 points, Surtees needed sponsorship, choosing BRM, then in one of its dull periods. Surtees made 9 race starts, with the 10th and 11th cancelled in order to rework the uncompetitive car. There were 5 retirements, the most annoying in the Britsh race when the front suspension collapsed on the opening lap. A 3rd in the U.S. GP was the best Surtees had, after a demanding season. He had 6 points and 11th place in the standings.

Surtees had come to what he referred to afterwards as a "cross-roads" in his driving career. "At the time of the Mexican GP in 1969," he said, "I had decided that I must build my own Grand Prix car. I had been in the wilderness too long, I wanted to get really racing again. The options were plain: either join a plain, down-to-earth company, without a lot of boardroom politics going against you, or build your own car. I chose the latter." There already were cars with the Surtees imprint upon them. That same year the initial Surtees Formula

5000/A car, designed by Len Terry, redesigned by Surtees and others, had emerged.

He decided not to develop his car while simultaneously trying to race it. One Surtees car could have been readied for the South African opener of the 1970 season, but Surtees needed some V-8 time in another car, before trying his own V-8. Up to 1970, Surtees had driven mostly V-12 cars, with Ferrari, Maserati, Honda, and BRM. So, at the same time he decided to go ahead with a Surtees F1 car, John also placed an order for a McLaren-Ford M7C. It was in this car that he made South Africa and 3 other 1970 races, retiring in the first 3 outings, and placing 6th in the 4th GP.

At the British race, thereafter, he used his own car, the Surtees-Ford T57, already having won the Oulton Park Gold Cup, a nontitle race, with it. But despite his planning and testing, the car was not yet mechanically ready, and was retired in 4 consecutive Grands Prix. Then came a 5th at Canada, an engine failure in the U.S., and 8th in Mexico. All in all, the season did not fare well (3 championship points and a tie for 17th in the standings), but Surtees felt better than he had in years. The car was his, and he had expected the debut season to be hard. He was seeing better days ahead.

The better driving days were not found in 1971, however. Retired in South Africa after 58 laps, Surtees managed a 3rd in the nonchampionship Race of Champions at Brands Hatch, then an 11th in Spain. Seventh in the Monaco GP, he scored another non-points 3rd in the Rindt Memorial race at Hockenheim; then came a good 5th in the Dutch GP. But it was an 8th in France, a 6th in Britain, a 7th in Germany. Retirements in the Italian and Austrian Grands Prix bracketed another Surtees victory in the nontitle Oulton Gold Cup—his 3rd in a row. He was 11th in Canada and 17th in the U.S. Nor were the other cars he was running doing much better. All the new season really accomplished was to make John a bit grayer and more lined. In 1972 Surtees announced he would not again run a full GP season, but only an occasional lesser race. Soon he wasn't even doing that.

LEN SUTTON

From spinning a Model-A roadster off the dirt track in the 1st turn of the 1st lap in 1945, Len Sutton had come to finish 2nd in the 1962 Indianapolis 500, losing 1st place by 11.52 seconds to teammate Rodger Ward. Born August 9, 1925, in Ains, Ore., Sutton had won some $30,000 with a Watson roadster, and remembered that day when he learned, at age 21, that racing is not all winning. Here at Indianapolis, he had qualified 4th fastest, in 1962, and led the race for some 8 laps. Here in 1956, his rookie year at the world's richest race, he had easily passed his rookie test in a Wolcott Special, but never qualified. The wind had caught the car in the northeast turn during practice, spinning it, then flipping it end over end. His right hand was pulp, his ribs smashed, and there were burns on his body where he had been sandpapered against the track. He remembered his 1st race, when he had won $70 for racing a Model A. "Seventy bucks; I couldn't imagine it coming so easy. I thought I wanted to become an airplane mechanic, but this changed my mind. That spin in my 2nd race changed my mind about it being easy. But I still had the money."

The 1962 payoff was the biggest of his career—a successful one even by American standards. He was a self-taught racer, considering himself fortunate that he did not kill himself while learning. With no drivers' schools for roadster and sprint drivers, Sutton had to learn how to control a car while racing it.

Rolla Vollstedt gave him the kind of roadster that could win a championship in 1948, and then a top sprint car, too. Vollstedt had helped him to a Pacific Northwest midget championship—but when Sutton had the chance at Sacramento in 1955, to try for the big money circuit, he didn't stand in his way. Sutton's ride there led to Indy and the accident. In 1957 Sutton ran in 77 races, 41 of them midget starts, to finish 3rd in the USAC National and Midwest standings, driving the Central Excavating Special to two 4th places in 6 starts.

He won his debut Championship Trail race at Trenton, March 30, 1958, but, though a regular from then on, did not win again until the Milwaukee 200 in 1960 in a Salemi-Watson car that became the Bryant Heating and Cooling Special the next year. Sutton was 4th at Indianapolis in that car, before the transmission failed

at the 110th lap. In 1961 Sutton won 2 stock-car races for Ray Nichels Pontiac. It was after another 1962 jackpot at Milwaukee that he hit a wall, injuring his back and rupturing a lung. Sutton returned to Portland, Ore., for recovery, and to talk with Rolla Vollstedt again.

Vollstedt was building a rear-engined Offy for the Indianapolis 500. The experts said it could not win. At the time, Sutton already had a new Watson for the 1963 Indianapolis race, but it was not fast enough. His 147.392 m.p.h. was bumped by Al Miller, and when he took a Ray Crawford car to 147.620 m.p.h., Ebb Rose, the last qualifier of the day, had bumped him again. That persuaded Sutton to try the Vollstedt machine.

During tire tests at Indianapolis in March 1964, the Vollstedt machine was clocked at an unofficial 154.959 m.p.h. in Sutton's hands, fastest ever at the time. The same car, in November 1963, in its shake-down cruise, had gone only 152 m.p.h. with another driver. Sutton qualified in 8th position, and was running 4th when he pitted for fuel on the 109th lap. Back in the pack in number 6 spot, he moved the Vollstedt Offy to 4th place, charging toward 3rd when mechanical failure forced him out.

Sutton, father of 2 teenage daughters, had been driving winning stockers for Ray Nichels since 1961, and Nichels rated Sutton among the best. "Len drives hard and at the same time is easy on the car," said Ray. "He's smart driver who picks and chooses his spots. He never does anything wild or foolish. You can always tell what he's doing out there."

Sutton compared national championship to late-model stock-car racing this way: "To be the best in national championship driving, you have to drive all the time. If you took a golf leader like Arnold Palmer and let him play his game only once a week, he wouldn't be the champion he is. It's practice, practice and experience, if you're going to be good in your business. There's maybe a dozen national championship races in the year on dirt and asphalt tracks. If you don't drive the circuit, you can't keep the keen edge needed to compete in the 500.

"I don't particularly care to drive dirt, and it's tough for me to run from one end of the country to the other for the asphalt races. With those limitations, you have to find a brand of racing that comes close to the national championship type to keep that edge. Late-model stocks come as close as you can get." He ought to know. He did a lot of both in 20 years of racing.

BOB SWANSON

Sometimes, the difference between racing immortality and oblivion is measured in seconds, for no notice is given to the also-ran no matter how magnificent a job he does with the materials at hand. One such was Bob Swanson, born in Minneapolis, August 20, 1912, who was supposed to become a photoengraver, but who, starting with a Model A roadster, lived for racing.

Swanson's initial rides were in a jalopy owned by Hal and George Robson, the latter to become an Indianapolis winner. Though most of his early experience was on independent tracks, Swanson fitted into midget racing, like a glove. He raced at Motorspeedway in Long Beach, Gilmore, and Legion Ascot in the Los Angeles area.

With Dan Hogan in 1934, Swanson is reputed to have helped build the 2nd Offy midget ever built, then another, which he drove to the Pacific Coast midget championship in 1935. Most of the midgets had 2-cycle engines adapted from outboard motorboats. He picked on these cars by deliberately slowing way down in the turns, causing the 2-cycles to lose revs for the straights where he could easily out-accelerate them. He was so successful in the midgets—he won Gilmore's first 150-lap Thanksgiving Grand Prix and many lesser features —that Earl Gilmore is reputed to have thought up the inverted start just for him. Ronnie Householder, who later would become competition director for Chrysler Corporation, was among his foes. He once shut Swanson off on the outside, after Swanson had made his favorite feint inside before going wide, flipping him.

After he married the widow of driver Ernie Triplett, Swanson decided to try big-car racing. His chance came in a Miller 220 in the March dirt race at El Centro, Calif., but lost to Rex Mays. Mays, with whom Swanson was to stage a series of match races at Legion Ascot, encouraged him to try for Indianapolis. But, in 1936 Indianapolis officials refused to certify him, deciding that he lacked experience in big machinery. But Householder, who preferred his outboard midget, asked Swanson to campaign an Offy midget that he owned.

The Madison Square Garden Bowl in Long Island City, N.Y., was the East's Legion Ascot, only the racing surface was better. Swanson ran 5 features there and won all 5. He competed at Paterson, N.J., Yellow Jacket Speedway, near Philadelphia, and Boston, before returning to Long Island City, where he won the World Championship midget race series on points.

Later, Roosevelt Raceway's 300-mile international race in 1936 attracted Tazio Nuvolari, the Auto Union Germans, the best Americans, and also Swanson. With Dan Hogan, he built a special car for the big purse, stretching a midget chassis 11 inches. But its unsupercharged 98-cu. in. engine, which gave the car a bare 90-m.p.h. speed in the straights, seemed laughable against the Indy monsters and the Alfa Romeos at Roosevelt.

But Swanson was figuring on the stretched midget's maneuverability to compensate for his lack of cubic inches. He is reputed to have passed Nuvolari in practice by sticking the midget's nose inside that of Tazio's Alfa on corners. He qualified at 66.93 m.p.h., 2nd-best of the Americans, with Nuvolari the fastest qualifier at 69.929 m.p.h. During the race, Swanson was riding 4th, but Nuvolari had lapped the field. But when Il Maestro lapped Bob, he swung in behind him and slip-streamed him, or "hitched a ride." The Italian's pit signalled for Nuvolari to get rid of him, but they needn't have worried, As he was towed by the Alfa, Swanson was making lap times several m.p.h. above the capabilities of his engine. So he finally dropped back, content to hold 4th. Unfortunately, a fuel line split on the 71st lap, stranding him out in the boondocks. He manhandled the car back to his pits, but it took so long he could never make up the time, and he finished 23rd. Some magnificent driving went down the drain.

While campaigning midgets, Swanson also managed some nonchampionship sprint experience in the New York-New Jersey circuit, appearing at Ho-ho-kus and Union, N.J., and Mineola, N.Y.

He qualified for Indianapolis in "Poison Lil", a nasty-handling and finicky vehicle, on the last day, putting himself in the 7th row, but worked up to 5th before Lil overheated and otherwise indicated she was through, by the 52nd lap. About the 100th lap, Bud Winfield corralled him as a possible relief driver for Ralph Hepburn. On the 112th lap Ralph pitted, his gimpy leg cramped, his hands blistered, and his face so swollen from the heat that his leather helmet had to be cut off.

When Ralph pitted he was 2nd, but Swanson went out in 4th place. In 8 laps he had the H-&-H Special back in 2nd, and when Wilbur Shaw pitted 2 laps later, Bob was leading the 500. But Hepburn signalled Bob in soon after, and though still suffering from the heat, Ralph was helped into the car for the finish.

Swanson was offered several rides for both the Championship Trail and Indianapolis in 1938. He refused the former to go back to Gilmore, where he was involved in an accident that prevented him from accepting any of the latter. His main foe that year was Sam Hanks, with whom he split honors at the track, drawing as many as 17,000 fans to an arena that seated only 14,000. On May 7 his car flipped, and Swanson suffered crunched legs, a broken collarbone, and a concussion. He had to be helped from crutches into his midget in July, about 9 weeks after the crash, but he returned to midget racing at Gilmore nonetheless. He led the feature, but he was in no condition to hold his advantage, dropping to 2nd. But he did win that year's Thanksgiving GP.

When Swanson signed to drive the Sampson Special at Indianapolis in 1939, he was the envy of West Coast drivers. The Sampson Special seemed to be the answer to the need for more speed for the 500. Riley Brett, one of the better mechanics of the day, had created it, utilizing the blocks from Frank Lockhart's Daytona Beach Stutz Blackhawk record car. Two 91.5-cu. in. Miller engines were mounted in a V position on a common crankcase, creating a 183-cu. in. V-16. With added supercharging, the car should have been the fastest thing then on bricks, but it needed a special fuel mixture. Swanson qualified at just under 130 m.p.h., one of the fastest times, but snapped a driveshaft early.

Once again Hepburn tabbed Bob for relief. This time Swanson spun in the southeast turn, sliding backward toward the outside wall. Defending 500 winner Floyd Roberts tried to squeeze between Swanson and the wall and didn't make it. Roberts's car ran over Swanson's rear wheel and hurtled out over the wall, killing him. Swanson himself was thrown onto the track from the Hepburn car, which caught fire. To avoid running over Swanson, a 3rd driver, Chet Miller, had to veer into the infield. Both Miller (arm injury) and Swanson (cinders in his back and burns on his upper body) were hospitalized.

Swanson should have stayed out of racing until the burns healed completely, but he seemed a man possessed from then on. He insisted on driving midgets right away, and during a July 4th program, he landed on his head, had the track doctor bandage him, and was driving the next night. He won the Gilmore and the unofficial Coast midget championship again and began 1940 with plans to sweep eastward to conquer new worlds. At Indianapolis he drove Alden Sampson's Special to 6th place, then again shunned the dirt Championship Trail for Midwest midget campaigning. It was the wrong decision. On a rutted, hard-packed Toledo track June 12, 1940, he flipped the Harry Stephens midget and was taken to the hospital unconscious. He died the next morning.

It is mere conjecture to suggest that Swanson might have become an all-time great. His 1940 ride in the Sampson showed he had finally found out what Indy was all about. His insistence on returning to midgets may have been based on a lack of confidence with the big cars on one-mile dirt tracks. But it is true that he competed with the best in the world, and his machinery, not his skill, betrayed him.

AL SWEENEY

A white-haired gentleman, reddened by the sun of his adopted Tampa, Albert Joseph Sweeney had a face so innocent-looking that you would trust him with the Sunday church collection. He was not all that innocent. For instance, in 1933, Sweeney decided that indoor midget races at Chicago Stadium would be a crowd-pleaser. Thousands turned out, only to stumble out a few hours later gasping for breath, eyes smarting, and clothes reeking of gas fumes. The air inside became so befouled that the latter part of the program could not be seen.

Sweeney, as of 1970, was one of the two promoters under the IMCA. He began back in 1922 as an exercise boy at Hawthorne Park, a horse track near Chicago. Weighing 106 pounds at the time, he took a turn as a jockey with indifferent success, but it was the only rac-

ing he ever did personally. He never drove a race car, and was not much interested in auto racing until he sensed the promotional possibilities. The sport had everything, according to Sweeney—speed, noise, competition, thrills—everything a crowd could want. He considered auto-racing the best, over pro football, rodeos, boxing, and 6-day bike racing, all of which Sweeney had promoted at one time or another.

However, he confined his promotional efforts to Chicago, and midget racing, until an offer by J. Alex Sloan let him into the big time. The offer was accepted more quickly than Sloan expected; Sweeney's next few cards had been rainouts, separating the promoter from his working capital. "I told Sloan I wanted to learn racing from the ground up," Al said, "and he gave me a broom." But soon Sweeney was touring the length and breadth of the land as an advance man. Much of the job was arranging to put up posters—the paste and the signs came right out of the trunk of Sweeney's car.

Some people looked forward to having that beautiful colorful poster slapped on their buildings. It was the only repair they could make. Sometimes, however, the farmer or the storekeeper demanded and got up to $1 for turning the side of his building into a billboard. Rurals with shotguns were rare, mainly because they didn't consider Sweeney and pal worth the buckshot. There was one town that occupied a special place in Sweeney's heart—Spencer, located in the midst of Iowa's rich corn and hog belt. Sweeney thought he was in trouble when he could only post one bill in the town for the coming races at the fair. But come race day, the people appeared as if by magic, filling the stands to capacity. Sweeney saw his 1st SRO crowd there and the sight hooked him on fair dates.

In 1941 Sweeney formed a partnership with Gaylord White (National Speedways, Inc.), promoting his 1st race at Sioux Falls, S.D. With the great Sloan out of the picture by that time, Sweeney was able to establish his reputation before World War II closed matters down.

Much of IMCA racing is contracted for at the conventions of fair operators. The fair operators contract for attractions—circuses, thrill shows, auto racing, midways, even what are politely known as girlie shows if the law permits. Auto racing is known as a "clean attraction," that is, the fair operator is guaranteed a certain minimum return, usually with a percentage deal in addition.

Sweeney prospered and endeavored to keep the calibre of racing he presented on the highest possible level. His group was considered expert, and emphasized safety, largely because damage suits could be so expensive. At last reports, his partner was Gene Van Winkle, whom he trained. Sweeney also announced occasionally, and always directed the actual racing ("No. 22's steering has a loose nut, either in the suspension or behind the wheel. Get him off the track.") loudly enough so that the crowd in the stands could savour this inside dope. He was singularly disinterested in international racing, except for Canada, which was one of the reasons IMCA didn't join ACCUS.

BOB SWEIKERT

Bayliss Leveritt has been forgotten. But except for this old-time race driver, Robert Sweikert, born in Los Angeles May 20, 1926, might never have become the last champion under AAA Contest Board jurisdiction. Bayliss is credited with turning Bob Sweikert into a professional race driver; he helped Sweikert smooth his driving style, gave him rides, and pointed him straight toward the top. Though the older man never made it in the big time, Leveritt must be remembered as long as Sweikert.

Growing up in Hayward, Calif., Sweikert began by racing roadsters, then graduated to training races in midgets, winning every one. In 1948, Sweikert won the indoor midget championship. Over the next year or so, he established a reputation as a heavy-footed charger. But when Bob decided to go one step further, into the sprints and the championship cars, no one seemed to know him. Leveritt gave him the chance in AAA Pacific Coast competition.

In 1950 Sweikert, a ruggedly good-looking youngster with deep-set gray eyes, passed his rookie test at Indianapolis in the Carter Special. (His car had won the Indianapolis 500 earlier, in 1941, under Mauri Rose and Floyd Davis. Troy Ruttman had driven in 1949, Ruttman's rookie year.) Bob failed to qualify but profited anyway from the trip by getting in as much practice in the Championship cars on the Brickyard as possible and seeing how the race strategy was important.

In 1951, however, after a creditible 7th place in Pacific-AAA sprints, injury sidelined Sweikert for the season. He had been at the bottom of a 4-car pile-up, returning to racing the following year only through great determination. That year, he qualified a McNamara Special at the Indianapolis 500, after being bumped in his 1st attempt. He started 32nd, and was closing on the top 10 when the differential failed. Car-hopping all season, he qualified the Sarafoff Offy on the pole for the Milwaukee 200 and ran in the lead until the car broke down. He ended 46th for the season, but he had gained valuable experience. He was also campaigning sprints in the Midwest—to a 15th-place finish.

The final day of qualifications at Indianapolis in 1953, Sweikert made the field in the Dean Van Lines car, but broke the machine in the race after 151 laps. After that he concentrated on the Midwest sprint circuit, at that time about the toughest oval-track competition in the world. In September, however, the Sweikert star soared in 2 championship races. Al Dean tapped him as his driver for Syracuse, and Robert didn't disappoint him. He shattered the qualifying mark, and led until the 73rd lap when he was eliminated. The following week at the Hoosier 100 may have been Bob's most hard-won victory. Sweikert edged 3 other competitors by less than a second for his initial Championship Trail victory.

Moving his family to Indianapolis in 1954, Sweikert managed a 5th-place finish in the Midwest sprints and a 6th on the Championship Trail that year. He had failed with the Lutes Truck Parks Special at Indianapolis, but won at Syracuse, N.Y.; he also had a 3rd, and twice finished 3rd and 4th, in other races. Sweikert's sprint car was then built by a young man named A. J. Watson. In 1955, John Zink decided to make his team Watson and Sweikert at Indianapolis. It took Sweikert 3 attempts to qualify the new Watson roadster. The circumstances of his 500 victory that year—Vukovich's death and the many cars sidelined by accidents—made Sweikert determined to prove it was no fluke. He was going to be the most active 500 winner in history.

At this time, Sweikert owned 2 sprint cars, one of which he drove; the 2nd was driven by Jerry Hoyt until the latter's death at Oklahoma City, then by others. He campaigned as many of the sprint dates as possible as well as the full Championship Trail. He again won at Syracuse, finishing 2nd 3 times, with a pair of 3rds and a 4th. In the process he accumulated 2,290 points, clinching the 1955 championship long before the season's end, and winning the Midwest title, too.

For 1956, Sweikert, wife Doris and 3 children were installed in a posh new home in Indianapolis. Bob had decided to seek a sponsor who would buy his sprint machines yet let him retain maintenance and pilot chores. He found a sponsor in the D-A Lubricants Com-

pany, of which Tom Binford was president; and at Indianapolis he deserted the Zink forces to drive the D-A Lubricants Special, which brushed the wall and blew a tire, placing him 6th. That year, he managed a 3rd at Milwaukee. Then, in the 4th lap of the June 17th Midwest Spring Feature, his car brushed the outer wall, plunging over the top, crashing and catching fire as it landed. The fire was extinguished immediately and Sweikert was rushed to a hospital—only to die some 3 minutes after being admitted.

PIERO TARUFFI

For the Italian engineer-driver Piero Taruffi, the Mille Miglia was always the race he most wanted to win. For 12 appearances he failed. On the 13th, the last Mille Miglia ever run, he won. Then he retired from racing.

Taruffi was born in 1906. His education extended all the way to a Doctor of Industrial Engineering degree. He was also much more than just a racing driver: an amateur oarsman, a tennis player of international repute, a crack skier, and an Olympic-quality bobsledder (though not an Olympian as is sometimes suggested). As with many European drivers, Piero started with motorcycles in the twenties; he won 22 of the 41 major 2-wheeler races he entered, and broke 38 world records on motorcycles. Taruffi raced or set records on cycles as late as 1939.

By that time he was an outstanding driver of racing cars. Most drivers are closely identified with a single marque or with a very few. But Piero was a jack-in-the-box, frequently riding in the Ferrari camp, but also driving for Mercedes, Lancia, Maserati, Bugatti, Alfa Romeo, Cisitalia, and even General Motors. His 1st 4-wheeled appearances were in Fiats, in 1923 and 1924, when Taruffi ran a Rome-Viterbo race and a hillclimb, but it was mid-1930 before his auto racing career began in earnest. For 9 years he mixed the 2 areas of motor racing quite successfully, beginning with an Alfa victory in the Tunis-Tripoli sports car race in 1930. That same year Taruffi ran the Mille Miglia his initial time, finishing 40th.

Taruffi's 1st major placing in the Mille Miglia came 3 years later, when he was 3rd. He scored the same placing in such other important races as the Eifelrennen and the Acerbo Cup. The following season Piero won his class in the Mille Miglia, finishing 5th overall. He won his class again in 1938, as well as a blistering 109.88-m.p.h. in the Tripoli Grand Prix 1500-c.c. division. Before the war ended racing temporarily, Taruffi also won the Capetown GP in an ERA in 1939, and managed a 2nd overall in the Mille Miglia that same year. He also acted as racing manager for Gilera motorcycles, starting in 1936 until the war intervened.

In 1946, when racing resumed, Piero made a single

start, the Coppa Brezzi, and retired, in a Cisitalia. Some said he did not have it any more. Their error was demonstrated the following season when Taruffi won the Italian 1500-c.c. championship, winning at Caracalla, Vercelli, Sierre-Montana, and Venice on the way. Continuing with Cisitalia, he won the Berne GP in 1948, the 1100-c.c. class in the Pescara GP and the Tour of Sicily. In 1951 he had a particularly outstanding year, sharing a Ferrari with Luigi Chinetti and winning the Pan American Road Race, a 1,000-miler, at 88.07 m.p.h. That same year Taruffi was 2nd in the Tour of Sicily and the Swiss GP (only Juan Fangio beating him out in the latter), 3rd at Bari, and 5th in the German and Italian Grands Prix. He ended 5th in the World Championship standings.

In 1952 Taruffi made it up to 3rd in the standings, winning the Paris GP at 95.25 m.p.h. in a Ferrari, the Swiss GP at 92.78, the Ulster Trophy, and the special Formula Libre section of the British GP preview—the latter 2 in the Ferrari-based Thinwall Special. There were numerous 2nds, too—to Alberto Ascari in the Syracuse GP, to Luigi Villoresi in the Turin GP, to Nino Farina in the Naples GP, to Ascari again in the formal British GP. At the Paris GP and in the Rouen 3-hour race, Taruffi was 3rd. But 1953 was a bit of a disaster; Piero switched to Lancia and ran into 8 retirements in his major starts, including the Mille Miglia, Targa Florio, and Le Mans. But there was a Lancia bright spot; in the Pan American Road Race Piero finished 2nd. In 1954 things got better for Lancia, Taruffi winning the Tour of Sicily at 64.46 m.p.h., the Targa at 55.85, the Syracuse Gold Cup 1100-c.c. class, and others.

A Ferrari provided Taruffi's winning mount in the Tour of Sicily in 1955. He rode a Mercedes to his 2nd-place finish at the Italian GP to Fangio, and to his 4th in the British GP. He drove at Sebring in the 2nd of several appearances there and finished 5th in a Ferrari. Maserati in 1956 took him to victory at the Nurburgring 1000 and 2nds in the Tour of Sicily, Bari GP, and Pescara GP-Acerbo Cup. He was 5th at Sebring again and 3rd in the Targa. But in 1957, at age 51, he finally won the Mille Miglia with a fast 94.84 m.p.h. victory. The winning mount for this 13th attempt was a Ferrari. That same season he had used a Maserati to record a 2nd in the Tour of Sicily and a 4th at the Syracuse GP, as well as a Chevrolet, which was retired at Sebring. He also had his own world record cars, Tarf I and II, twin-boomed specials used for setting 7 marks.

In all, Taruffi won 44 races in 136 starts, an enviable record, and he set 39 international speed records. After "retiring," he still managed to keep busy, running the Italian Mobilgas Economy Run, managing the Camoradi team at Nurburgring, serving as clerk of the course at the Messina 10-hour race, running racing schools, and a few other things. The silver-haired Taruffi never did like rocking chairs and front porches.

RON TAURANAC

When Jack Brabham retired at the end of the 1970 Grand Prix season and headed back to Australia, the man who took charge of his Motor Racing Developments carbuilding and racing effort was the British-born Australian with the French name, Ron Tauranac. The assignment was nothing new to the lean, graying man who once was an RAAF pilot, for it was he who had set up MRD originally and designed the 33 cars that were produced during Brabham's active participation in the company, first at Surbiton, later at Weybridge.

Tauranac was born in England in January 1925, but was in Australia by the time he was 4 when his father, a boilermaker of French ancestry, emigrated there. Ron left school at 14 to be apprenticed to Commonwealth Aircraft; this was at the outbreak of World War II. After the war he worked for a number of engineering firms and discovered motor racing one Sunday afternoon while out for a spin in his Austin 7. "I heard some noises and went to have a look," he recalled. "Just off the road, back in the bush, there was an airstrip and on it people rushing up and down in racing cars. I investigated and got a little bit interested."

Tauranac's little bit of interest involved him in the construction of a 500-c.c. Formula 3 car with the Hooper brothers, Sydney motorcycle dealers. This was followed by the design and construction of his own car, aided by his brother Austin. Taking a 1932 Norton

push-rod engine, Ron built a rear-engined, tubular-framed racer dubbed the Ralt from the brothers' initials. It 1st competed in the Hawkenbury hillclimb in 1949. But the Ralt needed souping up, and Ron set about that task. When Tauranac needed some special welding done, he took it around to a fellow who had been recommended to him, Jack Brabham. In return he modified the suspension on Brabham's Cooper-Bristol.

The relationship continued on friendly terms, even in 1954 when Ron beat Jack in the New South Wales hillclimb championships. The feat brought a generous offer from someone to buy the Ralt, and the car was sold. But Ron immediately laid down a replacement, a 1000-c.c. Vincent-powered car with De Dion suspension in the rear. It took 2 years to build this car, and then it was sold after just 2 races. Obviously Tauranac the driver was already giving way to Tauranac the designer/constructor. The brothers laid down 5 replicas next time, but only 2 of them were finished because Brabham had come home with his initial World Championship and talked Ron into joining him in a prospective racing car business. The idea at 1st was to build cars for other people in the lower levels of racing, and indeed the MRD, Brabham's initial car, was a Formula Junior prototype.

Ron and his wife arrived in Britain during Easter Week of 1960, and he set up shop in Brabham's garage designing a Coventry-Climax version of the Triumph Herald, then a Weber conversion for the Sunbeam Rapier. Meanwhile, working in his bedroom at home, Tauranac designed and constructed some components for the MRD, later renamed BT1. The factory was estab-

lished in quarters rented from Repco, which later made an advertising deal for the cars to be billed as Repco-Brabhams. BT2 was the production version of MRD, and 11 were constructed in 1962. BT3 was the 1st Formula 1 car for Brabham, who had left Cooper in 1961 after winning his 2nd World Championship there the year before. It debuted at the German GP, and interested parties decided it was a workmanlike job, but offered little that was innovative. But the car scored a victory at the Mexican GP that season. Starting in 1963 Dan Gurney and Brabham showed that the "ordinary" cars were competitive.

Tauranac did not mind the critics. "When I was in Australia," he said, "I experimented with design, and it was a hobby. When I came to England it became my livelihood, and I suppose you could say I became a commercial engineer rather than an innovator. I had to earn a living and establish a business. It was a stabilizing influence on the cars I designed."

But he was a quiet innovator. The Tauranac Brabhams introduced such things as adjustable anti-roll bars, airfoils (an introductory honor shared with Ferrari), and the use of lighter, smaller components through combinations such as rubber doughnuts with U-joints in drive shafts. The 1st Tauranac monocoque came at Indianapolis when the regulations for design just about made a monocoque mandatory; the use was resisted in Formula 1 until the regulations there again dictated that form of construction. The 1st GP monocoque was BT33 in 1970.

Ron's designs covered Tasman Specials (BT4, 7A, 11A, 23A, 23B, 23D, 23E, 31), Formula 3s (BT9, 15, 16A, 18A, 21, 21B, 28), Formula 2s (BT10, 16, 18, 18B, 23, 23C, 30), Formula Libre (BT14, 21A, 21C), SCCA Formulas A, B, and C (BT21B, 23F, 23G, 28A, 29), and sports cars (BT5, 8, 17). Then, of course, there were the USAC-Indy cars (BT12 in 1964, BT25 in 1968, BT32 in 1971) and the various F1s (BT3, 7, 19, 20, 24, 26, 33, 34). BT13 was never assigned a job; BT27 was not built.

Tauranac incorporated more and more safety features into his designs in later years. But he was concerned that safety could be carried too far. "If you made the ultimate safe racing car, a car like a box with the driver inside that could not catch fire and was impossible to damage, and ran it round a track between solid Armco barriers, it would be too much like a child's electric slot racing set. If we go too far that way, we might as well have a one-car design for everyone and just run a circus." Ron had other things at hand to worry about, however, with Brabham's retirement. He had become designer-constructor-managing director-team manager all rolled into one.

This situation lasted all of one year. Late in 1971, Bernie Ecclestone, once a driver and later adviser to Jo Rindt and Graham Hill, bought out MRD, although Tauranac temporarily remained as a director and designer. Hill, with whom Ron had had a battle before he left,

returned to replace Tim Schenken, who left for Surtees. Ecclestone already was showing who was boss. It was more than Tauranac could stand, and in February 1972, Ron left MRD.

ANITA TAYLOR

Raven black hair, shiny cobalt-blue eyes, and a driving skill equal to that of most men in saloon races; that about describes the "baby" sister of Trevor Taylor, Anita, who retired in late 1967 at the height of her racing career. Anita was born in December 1942 in a motoring family; besides her brother, there was her father, Raymond, who raced motorcycles when he was younger and who later sponsored a racing team, oldest brother Mike who managed the team, and her mother who did not race, but did drive heavy lorries during World War II.

Like many other Britons, even those not blessed with so many potential driving instructors, Anita started at an early age. "My initial recollection of speed was at Silverstone," she recalled. "It was a meeting, I think it was the first one, held after the end of the war. I can remember swinging on the ropes and watching the big cars." She was a bit older, but not much, when her father allowed her to drive an NSU motor scooter around the pumps at the family's Steering Wheel Garage in Rotherdam; at the earliest possible moment, age 17, she had her driving legalized, and, license in hand, immediately made for the nearest race track. Raymond and his sons faced the inevitable, and they hired Silverstone for a day to give Anita personal racing instruction. Her debut race was at Rufforth in 1961 in a borrowed Lotus Elan. The following year she raced a full season in a Group 2 Anglia, then switched to Minis for a couple of seasons.

In 1966 Anita became the 1st woman to be named a full-time member of the British Ford racing team, and her maroon Broadspeed Group 5 car became a familiar sight among the leaders at Brands Hatch, Crystal Palace, and other courses. "I just loathed those 2 years in Minis," she said later. "I absolutely hated them. I never could get used to the way you had to sling those cars around. And they're so—so forgiving." Several cars did not forgive Anita: she was in at least 4 crackups and had written off 3 Anglias. She was driving one in the 1964 Fast-Lady Trophy Race at Brands Hatch, for example, when one of her tires was slashed by a red-hot piece of someone else's clutch that was flying through the air. The tire blew, the car somersaulted 3 times and went through a fence. One of the fence posts pierced the windshield, another went straight through the radiator into the front seat. Either one could have caught Anita, but luckily neither did. When the would-be rescuers arrived, the indomitable Miss Taylor was arranging her hair.

"I was wearing a driving suit," she laughed, "but I

used to wear skirts. This sounds ridiculous, I know, but the week before I crashed at Rufforth, I'd been driving in a skirt. As I hung there in the car at Rufforth upside down and waiting for the car to be righted, I thought, crikey, thank goodness I'm not in a skirt today." Anita also parted a fence at Aintree and cracked up twice at Brands Hatch. "It's all part of the game," she said. "Frankly, when I was driving, I really got hard-skinned about it. I knew the men in the races took me seriously because I insisted on being taken seriously. I wasn't in racing for a giggle."

A woman is a woman wherever she is, however, and the 1st time David Matthews, a British saloon driver in club events and operator of a garage near that of the Taylors, saw Anita, she was timing Trevor. After that ("I'd been told she was a bit of all right, and she was.") Matthews managed to find occasional business that required his visiting the Steering Wheel Garage. One thing led to another, and Anita became Mrs. Matthews on November 17, 1966. They honeymooned in Nassau, partly courtesy of the Ford Motor Company.

The Americans first noticed Anita's abilities earlier that year and named her a reserve for the Marlboro, Md., 6-Hour Race. She did not get to drive there, but another call resulted in the Nassau Speedweek in November, and the 3-week trip turned into a honeymoon as well as a business trip. Anita's Shelby 350GT Mustang, which she drove for the Ring-Free Oil Racing Team, took 3 silver trophies and brought her the ladies' trophy. Marriage would not affect her racing, she maintained, and to prove it, she codrove at the Daytona 24-

hour race in 1967 and finished 20th out of 80 cars, 5th in her class. That was followed by the Sebring 12-hour race, where she shared 2nd place. Finally, though, she decided home and family came first. But she stayed close to the auto world as a public relations person for Ford of Britain.

GEOFFREY TAYLOR

Few men left their marks on British automobile racing as did Geoffrey Taylor. He built perhaps 100 cars, yet his Alta marque is well-remembered and much-honored; he built an additional 50 or so Alta engines, and the cars they powered—HWMs, Connaughts, Coopers—started Britain back on the road to motoring prominence; he furnished some mounts and helped fashion other mounts that gave a better ride to veterans like Chiron, Bira, Abecassis, and Rolt, and helped the development of Moss, Collins, Schell, and Frere.

The Alta Car & Engineering Company lived from 1930 to 1958, when Taylor retired to spend his last years in the Channel Islands. It had taken Geoffrey 2 years to fashion the prototype Alta, mostly by hand, down to hacking and chiseling its crankcase and conrods from chunks of cold steel. "Old Original," as he called the car in later years, was well-made. As late as 1948 it placed in its class at a Brighton race. Taylor had learned his mechanics and his engineering the hit-and-miss way, starting back at boarding school. Expelled for joy-riding the headmaster's car around the grounds, he moved into the professional end of racing with motorcycles, making and selling hop-up conversions for the 2-wheelers. In 1926 he started to think about building himself a car, and over the next 2 years designed a d.o.h.c. engine with a light alloy block, head, and crankcase, hemispherical combustion chambers, and twin carburetors. The resulting 1074-c.c. power plant developed 49 b.h.p. at 5,200 r.p.m.

Between 1928 and 1930 Taylor turned down handsome offers for "Old Original," but the idea grew upon him to construct replicas, so in 1930, he founded the Alta Company with backing from his father. The name came from a handy World Atlas in Geoffrey's library. He opened it at random and spotted a Canadian lake called Alta and that was it. Next came a factory, built from his own plans by the indomitable Mr. Taylor and 2 unskilled laborers. When he retired in 1958, the Tolworth, Surrey, premises were sold to the HRG factory next door. The original Alta engine was ahead of its time, and a 1934 reworking pushed it even further ahead. Except for minor improvements, that was the last change of any consequence made in the Alta power plant, although 1.5-litre and 2-litre versions were added a little later.

In 1931 Taylor designed a 2-seat, 4-cylinder, sports car, in either a 1074-c.c. regular model or in a d.o.h.c.

1100-c.c. race car model. Taylor's 1486-c.c. single-seat supercharged racing car in 1935 was among the pioneering British models to do away with the conventional radiator front and set it behind a curved wire section. The car did 120 m.p.h. in the hands of people like George Abecassis, considered the best Alta driver of the day. The limited-production 2-litre of about the same time was a good 20 m.p.h. faster with supercharging.

The 1937 1.5-litre single-seat Alta was a major redesign of the chassis and suspension, with Taylor adopting independent suspension front and rear using coil springs and vertical sides. A Roots supercharger brought the top speed up to 130 m.p.h. Two years later, just before World War II, Taylor added torsion bar suspension to his bag of tricks on Alta's last scheduled production sports car, but the war's outbreak caused "production" to cease with just one car finished.

After the war, Geoffrey concentrated more on his real estate business and less on building sports cars, but Grand Prix racing was something special. Taylor had announced a new car in November 1945, that would use his proven Alta engine, but would be constructed in tubular fashion and achieve independent suspension by means of wishbones and rubber blocks in compression. From 1946 through about 1950 he actually built such cars in Roots supercharged 1.5-litre form for the Alta label and in 2-litre unsupercharged form for the John Heath and Abecassis HWM label. Alta's major postwar contributions to the racing scene, however, were in the field of engines, starting in 1952.

Taylor's power plant 1st went into Formula Coopers, then into HWM in the early years of Formula 2 for unsupercharged 2-litre engines. An ultra-light Alta raced by Peter Whitehead served as the prototype for the 2-litres Taylor delivered to the factory carbuilders and was, in turn, an outgrowth of the 1948 GP engine. In 1954 Alta-Connaught engines were born, essentially the same power plant as the 1934 Alta engine, although these late versions were giving upwards of 260 b.h.p.

Often forgotten is the fact that although Taylor's power plants all had 4 cylinders, he actually designed, though never built, 6 and 8 versions. His 6, Taylor claimed, formed the basis for the Jaguar XK series. In 1934 he and another competition machinery expert, Harry Weslake, had formed a consulting partnership that endured for many years and in 1942, according to Geoff, Jaguar gave Weslake and Taylor, Ltd., a commission to design a 6-cylinder power plant. They did just that. Did his design actually form the XK series? There are proponents and opponents on both sides of the question.

Taylor's 8-cylinder engines were designed at 2 different times in his career. The 1st was in 1938, when he planned a supercharged 3-litre Alta that would reach 180 m.p.h., but never had funds to get the project going. The war ended that dream for good. His 2nd "dream-8" came after the war—a proposed 2.5-litre unsupercharged car—but lack of funds also prevented this design from passing the drawing board stage. A drive to provide the means of building the engine was proposed by well-intentioned British motoring enthusiasts, but Taylor—the man who liked to do things for himself—would have none of it. He declined the idea with thanks.

When Tony Brooks drove an Alta-powered Connaught GP car to victory at Syracuse, Italy, in October 1955, it marked the 1st major British victory in such competition since before the war. Whatever Alta and Geoffrey Taylor did after that in the 3 remaining years of the marque was anticlimactic, but the Taylor family was not through with racing. In the early seventies, Geoffrey's son, Mike, was racing in Formula Ford and talking about reopening Alta Engineering, perhaps one day to reenter the carbuilding business.

TREVOR TAYLOR

Formula 5000, first announced in Britain in 1968, brought new life to many drivers; youngsters got bigger and better rides more quickly, and older drivers got a chance to drive powerful single-seaters—in this case 5-litre cars—even if they had been bypassed in Formula 1. One of the "old timers" was a Grand Prix driver who 1st had an F1 ride back in 1961, but who had been missing from the GP ranks for several seasons when F5000 came along. His name was Trevor Taylor.

Trevor Patrick Taylor, born in Wickersley December 26, 1936, was a contemporary of Jim Clark. The 2nd of 3 sons, with a younger sister, Anita, of some automotive repute, Trev gained some of his motor racing interest from his father, Raymond, who was an amateur motorcycle racer as well as a builder. Raymond later quit the building business to join a brother in a garage, which further accelerated the interest of his children in things automotive. Both Trev and Michael, his older brother by a year, learned to drive when they were about 14, and just before Trev turned 17 the pair built their own Ford 8 Special, dubbed "X100." In hillclimbs and sprints, although their homemade car was not really competitive, it soon became apparent that Trev was the more natural and faster driver of the pair, so Michael became mechanic while Trev concentrated on the cockpit.

Early in 1955 the boys were given a Triumph TR 2. That August, Taylor made his 1st circuit appearance at Aintree, but nothing spectacular happened until Trev got into a real racing car. That was a 500-c.c. JAP-engined Staride Formua 3 car. He finished 2nd his initial time out in the car, winning about $25. In the flush of success, the Staride was sold and a Cooper-Norton Mark 8 formerly raced by Stuart Lewis-Evans, of Vanwall fame was purchased. Taylor progressed rapidly, and after the winter was spent in raising the Mark 8 to the latest Mark 10 specifications for 1957, Taylor started placing well consistently. His initial racing victory came in June that season at Mallory Park. This brought notice, as did Trev's sartorial splendor: yellow coveralls and yellow helmet, plus whitewalled tires on the racing car.

By 1958 Taylor was installed in a brand new Cooper Mark 12 with a specially tuned Norton engine. Second in his debut in this powerful car, Trev scored 10 victories in all and won the British F3 Championship that season, and also emerged unscathed from a couple of nasty incidents, including a dive into a lake. With some Shell Oil help, the Taylor family now bought a Formula 2 Cooper for 1959. Trev won a Formula Libre race at Rufforth after several frustrating starts. The 2nd-place car at Rufforth was a Lister-Jaguar driven by Clark, then also on his way up. A Mallory shunt cost Trevor 2 broken ribs and several missed starts, but he had shown enough to cause Colin Chapman to offer the F1 carrot as a future possibility if the Taylors started racing a Lotus.

Accordingly, Trevor was next handed a Lotus 18 Formula Junior car, owned by the family but raced as a Team Lotus car. In his debut at Goodwood, Taylor was 3rd, behind Clark, in an official factory Lotus FJ car, and John Surtees in a Tyrrell Cooper. After 2 more losses to Clark, Trev won the next race when Jim made one of his rare spins in the late stages of the race. Soon Trev won on the Continent at Aix-les-Bains; at Monaco he was 3rd despite a slipping clutch. Save for Clark, he now began winning regularly from everyone else in F3. Taylor and Clark shared the 1960 British FJ title. An F1 Lotus ride did not materialize, although he did get some F2 rides, and in one memorable Crystal Palace meet he won an F2 and 2 FJ races all on the same day.

Chapman handed Taylor a 1960 Lotus F1 car for Crystal Palace and later for Pau and Zandvoort at the start of the 1961 season. But the car was not competitive. Trev decided to concentrate on FJ again, and Chapman provided a Lotus 20 factory car. It was a victory parade all year, and Taylor won his 3rd straight British championship. He was named number 2 to Clark on Lotus's GP team for 1962. At South Africa, he was faster than Clark in practice, then won the Cape GP on January 1, 1962, Trev's initial major victory. In that same Springbok Series, Taylor was 2nd in the Rand GP, retired in the Natal GP when his rear suspension collapsed, and retired in the South African GP when a stone pierced his radiator.

Taylor's best GP performance came that season, a 2nd in the Dutch GP at Zandvoort, giving him 6 World Championship points. The rest of the year was frustration; two 8ths, a 12th, and 5 retirements. In Mexico he was running 3rd when Chapman called Taylor in to hand the car over to Clark whose machine was out of the running; Jim went on to win. In the Belgian and French Grands Prix, the retirements were caused by accidents, one coming when Willy Mairesse cracked into him, the other when Maurice Trintignant spun directly in front of Taylor. He consoled himself by winning the

Natal GP that winter. The next season saw Taylor with Lotus again. At Pau he finished 2nd, but it was a non-title race. Trev's best championship finish was a 6th at Monaco.

In 1964 Taylor left Lotus and joined another ex-Chapman driver, Innes Ireland, in the British Racing Partnership effort, using the BRM. His best effort in these cars was a 6th at the United States GP. At the same time Taylor broadened his driving appearances, making starts in a Porsche 904, Mini-Cooper, and Lotus Cortina GT, among others. But his luck was such that he rapidly solidified his reputation as a hard-luck driver. After 1964 Trev almost disappeared from sight, as far as major racing was concerned, driving only Minis, an F2 Brabham, a Climax in the 1964 British GP (1st to retire), and a private Lotus-47.

Then came F5000. It started in 1969 in Taylor's case. David Hobbs was driving for Team Surtees in F5000, but David also had commitments to JW Automotive. Taylor was tabbed as his substitute at Brands Hatch, where he failed to start after capturing the pole. Again, at Silverstone, he led for several laps, then retired with mechanical problems. From Taylor's drives, however, it was evident that he was at home in the powerful F5000 machines, and when Hobbs decided to go to the U.S. and race in the Formula A Continental series, Taylor was named his replacement in the Team Surtees effort.

Beginning in August, with 6 races already gone, Taylor made a run for the series lead. At Koksijde he won, at Zandvoort he won again, at Snetterton he made it 3 in a row, at Hockenheim 4. But in the last 2 races of the season he suffered engine problems and had a shunt with Peter Gethin. Still, Taylor finished 2nd to Gethin in the final standings. His car, the TS5 of 1969, was replaced the following season by a TS5A, and it suffered all kinds of early-season handling problems. At Brands Hatch Mike Hailwood's Lola piled into both Taylor and Hobbs, kayoing the Team Surtees effort in a few brief seconds. Trev's replacement car was written off at Salzburgring in July, and Surtees quit the series because of financial problems. Taylor quickly arranged a new ride, however, and finished the season in a tie with Reine Wisell for 7th place in the standings. Taylor's only victory in F5000 in 1970 was at Mondello Park in June; he also had a 2nd at Oulton Park, and a 3rd at Mallory. In 1971 he switched over to Leda, another Chevrolet-powered F5000 car, but it did not bring him the new victories he sought.

MARSHALL TEAGUE

There is a continuity about racing that is not unique because it is typical of any ongoing human endeavor. What *is* unique is the relative ease that permits the historian to construct an almost biblical relationship of who begat whom. Marshall Teague, a 5-foot 11-inch Floridian born May 22, 1921, grew up in Daytona Beach on the ocean side of the river. He went to Seabreeze High School and spent his time on the famed beach. He knew how a car could run on the sands because he had run cars there for pleasure and had parked

there to swim all his life. There was never any doubt for Teague: he wanted to work on cars and race them.

Teague is remembered as the man who gave a fellow Seabreeze graduate named Fireball Roberts his chance in stock-car racing. But that is shortchanging him. Marshall Teague never talked much, but he had his own language. According to Red Vogt, one of the all-time great mechanics in NASCAR annals, Teague understood engines intuitively. He could listen to another man's engine and, if given the chance, could fine-tune it so that it not only produced more horsepower, but also was stronger. His driving was equally virtuoso; he would run a track slowly for several laps then pull off to think. When he came back he had usually figured out the fastest way around for his car.

He began racing in 1946, was sidelined a year in 1948 after a serious crash, but in 1949 he won the 200-mile modified classic at Daytona. The NASCAR pioneers knew who he was after that and his garage did good business building and repairing race cars. Marshall and Herb Thomas, an early NASCAR hero, were brought together by the Hudson Motor Car Co. Teague built the cars, and he and Thomas drove them. Thus was the Hudson Hornet era of NASCAR racing inaugurated.

At the 2nd Southern 500 at Darlington, S.C. there were 100 cars hopeful of making the starting line-up; but there was no contest for the pole. A big slab-sided Hornet driven by Teague easily won that with Thomas not far behind. Marshall had won the 1951 Speed Weeks late-model 200 at Daytona, and Thomas was an acknowledged contender for the NASCAR title. When the starter's flag dropped, Teague rumbled into the lead—and kept it until his car went out with a cooling problem. But Thomas in the other Teaguemobile—that's what his competitors called the Hornets—won.

Teague was to win 7 times in all in the Grand National circuit, and after winning twice (including another Speed Weeks beach-road course title) he switched allegiance to the AAA circuit. It was a tremendous coup for the rival organization because Teague had finished 6th in the 1951 Pan American Road Race, too, thereby adding to his fame. The real lure was money—specifically single-seater racing and the Indianapolis 500; but the man who spent 6½ years in the Air Corps as a flight engineer gained his greatest AAA fame in stock-car ranks.

He became AAA stock-car champion in his Hudson for 1952; lost out to Frank Mundy in 1953; but with 5 victories and 11 finishes in the top 3 in 16 races, he regained the title easily in 1954. He had made the starting field of the Indy 500 in 1953 in the Hart Fullerton Offy, but failed in 1954. Teague's best showing at the Brickyard was 7th place in 1957 (starting from 28th). For that feat he was chosen as an American representative for the Race of Two Worlds at Monza, Italy. He never made it, though; car trouble kept him out.

In 1958 it was obvious to Teague that his racing career was stagnating. The day of the Hudson was long past and Teague was just unable to single-handedly battle the hordes of factory technicians and equipment. He returned to Daytona Beach, wondering sometimes if he would have been better off to have stayed with NASCAR. He finished only 5th in USAC stock-car points.

In 1959, however, he had lined up a new Indy ride and was looking forward to it. The Indy cars were also to come to Daytona International Speedway for an April 4 race over a 100-mile distance. It was like coming home for Teague, and although his own mount was not ready, USAC and promoter Bill France both spared no effort to make sure he had a ride. Chapman Root, Jr., his car owner, wheeled out the old vehicle with which Teague had finished 7th in 1957. On February 9 during Speed Weeks, special days were set aside for the Indy cars to parctice on the huge oval.

Bill France hoped that someone would get the world closed-course speed record back from Tony Bettenhausen's Monza 176.818 m.p.h. On February 7 Teague ran the Sumar Special at 171.821. It had been a little squirrelly, but Teague felt the car could go much faster and said so. He tried again on February 11, running a few slow laps to settle in the tires, then standing on it. Suddenly the deep blue car rode right up the west bank and crashed, so quickly that many of the people in the infield missed it. When the rescue crew arrived at the wreck they found Marshall Teague, 37, dead, the front axle of the old car snapped. He left a wife, an adopted daughter, and a record that put him in the Stock Car Hall of Fame.

LEN TERRY

When someone says Lotus its almost automatically brings to mind Colin Chapman and Jim Clark. But there is another name that should also be acknowledged. Len Terry was associated with most of the firm's models, starting with the Mk 7 and ending with the Mk 39. He also helped Dan Gurney get All-American Racers off the ground with Eagles that almost flew, and later created the F5000 Leda cars.

Born in 1923, Terry left school at 14 and got a job as an office boy. At the age of 17, he was the firm's public relations manager, mainly because he had a way with posters. World War II found him in the RAF in India, where his self-taught pen was kept busy doing instructional drawings for trainee mechanics. After the war, he joined Eveready Battery's British subsidiary as a draftsman, and pretty soon Terry found himself in charge of the department.

After 5 years with Eveready, Len jumped at a chance to leave the batteries behind and accepted an opportunity as chief draftsman in the publications department of the Institute of Electrical Engineers. His mind was on bigger things, however, and after a short stint in a design studio working on car styling and design, he met Colin Chapman in 1958 and promptly became part of the infant Lotus organization.

Len had made his 1st car, a special, powered by a Ford 10 engine, in the front room of his house in north London. He always said the chief design consideration of that initial offering was that it be small enough to fit through the room's front window. This was the Mark 1 Terrier that he raced with success in 1957–58. The succeeding model, Mark 2, was raced by Brian Hart, winning 18 of 21 starts in 1959 and often defeating the Lotus, which gave Chapman no end of embarrassment. In the end Terry and Lotus parted company for a time, but Len was kept busy building replicas and designing other cars.

In the next 2 years about 2 dozen Terriers were built, and a Formula Junior Terrier was produced, probably Terry's 1st really unsuccessful car. But he was up to his ears in other areas, as well. In these same years he designed the 1100-c.c. Gilby-Climax sports car, which never placed lower than 3rd in its initial racing season and won a major Formula Libre race in the hands of Peter Arundell. This was followed by Len's 1st attempt at a Formula 1 mount, the Gilby GP, which was impressive in design if not in power.

It was impressive enough for Chapman to phone Terry and ask him if he would like to rejoin Lotus and do some F1 work there, in addition to other things. Terry accepted without hesitation and thus started a successful re-collaboration. His initial 1962 project at Lotus was to work out a better Cortina racing version, but he also started development work on the F1 car that was to bring Clark his 1963 World Championship and provide major assistance on the Indianapolis version that brought Jim in 2nd the same season.

Terry had originally worked on the Lotus Mks. 7, 12, 15, 16, and 17, and now he added the Mk. 23 sports car, 25 F1 car, 27 Formula 2 car, 28 Cortina, 29 Indianapolis car, 31 Formula 3 car, 32 F2 car, 33 F1 car, 34 Indy car for 1964, 35 F2 car, 37, 38 that won with Clark at Indy in 1965, and the 39 Tasman series car. On the day that Clark won at Indy, May 31, 1965, Terry left Lotus to join All-American Racers. Even though Chapman always credited Terry with his share of the success of Lotus, Len felt that he was too far in the background with that marque. Besides, the challenge with Gurney seemed appealing.

The Californian wanted a F1 car of his own, to be called the Eagle, and an Indy version of it, also. The car for the 500, in fact, came 1st, and Lloyd Ruby was riding it merrily along in the 1966 race contending for the big prize when it suffered a massive oil leak. It was classified 11th in the final standings. In F1 the Eagle suffered from lack of a suitable engine through the opening half of the season, relying on Climax power, and then teething troubles once the Weslake Ford power plant was dropped into place, but in 1967 Gurney won both the nontitle Race of Champions at Brands Hatch and the Belgian GP in the car. The following year Indianapolis Eagles were 1st and 2nd with Bobby Unser and Gurney at the wheel. Len Terry had scored again, but he already had gone on his own as consultant.

For 4 months Len designed furniture, then joined Frank Nichols and Carl Haas for a year in a firm called Transatlantic Automotive Consultants. In 1967 he left to form his own company, Design Auto. Among Terry's projects were the King Cobra for Carroll Shelby, the BRM P126 F1 car, a Group 6 Mirage-BMW for John Wyer, a Honda F1 replica for John Surtees, the Indy cars for Gurney, and a new marque called the Leda, which was good enough to win the 1971–72 Tasman series and shake up the 1972 L&M Continental 5000 series for 5-litre single-seaters before being bought out by driver Graham McRae.

HERB THOMAS

On April 6, 1923, tobacco farmer Alton Thomas became the father of the 1st of 5 sons. It would be a while before the world heard about Herbert Watson, newest resident of Barbecue Township, Hartnett County, N.C. Herb attended Ben Haven High in Olivia, N.C., and graduated in 1941. He took up his father's sawmill business, supplying the military with lumber during World War II. A year later he married Helen Perkins, a high school classmate.

It was not until after the war that Thomas discovered racing. He does not remember where or when he ran his 1st race, but it was probably at Greensboro. "A gang of us went up there to see a hot-rod race," he recalled. "After watching, I knew if those drivers could do it, I could do it." After that—despite wifely protests—every minute he could spare, and every dollar, was spent tinkering with rods. He was a car owner 1st, then competed in the wildcat races where, even if you finished in front, you had to catch the promoter before he slipped out the back gate with your purse money. But the stories of his mortgaging farm and business to race are untrue. Thomas grinned and said: "I never mortgaged anything in my life. Our family doesn't believe in owing people."

When NASCAR was organized in 1947 Herb joined at once, going on the Grand National circuit as soon as it was organized 2 years later. He won his 1st GN with a Plymouth at Martinsville, Va., in 1950. A year later Marshall Teague, the Daytona Beach race driver and car owner, talked Thomas into trying a Hudson for the Detroit 250-mile race. The North Carolinian accepted both the offer and the services of Daytona Beach mechanic Smokey Yunick. Herb lost that race, but a month later he took another try at driving Teague's Hudson—this time in the Southern 500. And this time out he won,

and the victory gave him enough points in the GN standings to make him National Champion.

Still running his sawmill business in the time he was willing to spare from racing, he entered the 1952 campaign full of hope. But the circuit was growing, the purses were getting bigger, and with that the competition was getting stronger. Thomas now had a wife and 2 children, as well as the sawmill, and could not make it to all the races. He ran into mechanical troubles at Darlington that year, finished 3rd in the big event, and wound up 2nd to Tim Flock, another Hudson driver, in the national point race.

In 1953, he began driving his own cars. Herb won 12 races in 37 starts, finished 2nd in 8 others, was 3rd in 3 and in the top 10 no less than 32 times for the greatest record ever compiled in Grand National history. It earned him the national championship for a 2nd time, despite the fact that the Southern 500 eluded him again. He was leading with only 5 laps to go when a pit stop for tires dropped him to 5th place.

When 1954 rolled around Thomas made up his mind that racing was his business. He had taken better than $20,000 in prize money in 1953, although the expenses of racing left him with quite a bit less than that. But he had enough to build a comfortable home in nearby Sanford. He also rented a cinderblock garage and machine shop there and moved his cars into it. The sawmill in Olivia was sold. Herb Thomas had become a full-time stock-car driver. He spent all week in that garage—sometimes day and night—preparing his cars for races. Only the inner parts of the engine were left to the nimble fingers of the expert Yunick, who used to fly to every race.

The combination produced a lasting friendship and the best racing team of the mid-fifties. They scored an unprecedented 11 victories in the first 23 races of the 1954 season, and Herb went into the 5th Southern 500 as the favorite. In the time trials Thomas circled the track at a little better than 105 m.p.h., the 2nd-best time. Because of his late appearance for the trials, he earned only 23rd position. But Smokey was in his pits with the race underway. Buck Baker, 1953's winner, took the lead from his pole position and held it for 37 laps at a speed of 108 m.p.h., but he pitted with engine trouble and was, for all practical purposes, out of the race. The lead changed 8 times after that, with Curtis Turner holding the pace for 277 of the 364 laps. Thomas moved up to 5th early in the race and stayed around that position driving steadily as others duelled for the lead. Yunick called Herb into the pits at regular intervals as the others burned themselves out.

Three quarters of the way through Turner pitted, leaving Thomas in the lead. His fans cheered wildly, but his lead lasted only 7 laps. When Yunick beckoned Thomas back to the pits for tires, Turner was in front again. But, in less than a minute, No. 92 was back on the track wearing the last of 14 tires it used that day.

The veteran Turner had a seemingly safe lead of a lap and a half, but with 30 laps to go, he began to slow down, pitting for a quick check. His fuel pump was sluggish, Turner said later, but that was no time to work on a fuel pump. Thomas was only half a lap behind when the Virginian roared back onto the track. Thomas gained steadily until, with 21 laps left, he whizzed by Turner in the 3rd turn, eventually finishing 21 seconds ahead. Lee Petty, who had swapped his Chrysler for Marvin Panch's Dodge, was 3rd. After that it was flash bulbs, congratulations and trophies. He had become the first 2-time winner at Darlington, and his 5:16:01.34 time gave him a record 94.93-m.p.h. average speed. Somebody offered him a beer as an announcer moved in to get the winner's comments. Thomas waved it away. "This is my favorite drink," he said, reaching for a dipper of ice water.

At Shelby, N.C., in 1956, he was seriously injured. He raced again 5 years later in Martinsville, Va., lured back by the huge amounts of money to be had in stock cars. Thomas had been one of the greatest, but despite the ministrations of master mechanic Ray Fox, it was no good this time.

Summing up, the Thomas career showed 2 national championships (1951, 1953) 3 seconds (1952, 1954, 1956) and many mishaps. In 1952 he won a record 9 Grand Nationals, but lost the title to Tim Flock by 106 points. His 1953 record, competing in every one of the 37 championship races, gave him that season. The next year his record was phenomenal again, but retirements made him runner up. Out of 34 races, he won 12,

finished 2nd 4 times, and 5 other times in the top 5. To put it another way, he finished 30 times in the top 10 with his fabled No. 92 Hornet, ending as top money winner with $38,160.55. But Lee Petty won the 1954 championship.

He earned $17,000 in 1955, despite 3½ months on the sidelines after a broken leg at Charlotte Fairgrounds on May 1. Most of it was Darlington 500 money as he gave Chevrolet its 1st triumph in the classic, just as he had won the marque's 1st GN victory earlier in the year at Fayetteville, N.C. Yunick was in his corner once more after a fling with the Kiekhaefer racers. The 1956 season probably broke Thomas's heart, as well as his health. He overhauled Buck Baker late in the season in the National Championship, then suffered his serious mishap at Shelby. Old No. 92 was through.

LARRY THOMAS

Born in 1937, Larry Thomas started racing jalopies and modifieds soon after he graduated from the rural Davis-Downsend High School out in the North Carolina countryside. In 1961 he bought a Dodge and moved up to the GN circuit in a move to better himself. But Thomas really did not have the bankroll that such fast company necessitates, and there were many lean years during which he tore down, patched, and rebuilt that same Dodge engine to keep running in carefully selected races. Between times he fed his wife Emille and 2 children with a Trinity, N.C., garage and speed-shop business. Thomas's best year was 1964 when he started 43 races and finished 27 among the top 10 to rank 8th in the GN championship standings.

Thomas was a favorite of followers of the NASCAR Grand National circuit, and seemed to be making the grade when tragedy struck at age 28, not, as many would expect, on any superspeedway, but on an ordinary road that led toward Daytona Beach. The accident happened near Tifton, Ga., shortly after dawn January 25, 1965, when Thomas's Plymouth Fury struck the rear of a slow-moving car in the early morning fog, swerved off the road and ended, wheels up, in a ravine 35 feet below with Larry dead underneath.

PARRY THOMAS

In April 1969 a controversy suddenly erupted in Britain over a car that had been buried in the ground 42 years. The car was the Thomas Special, better known by a nickname of Babs, and its driver had been John Godfrey Parry Thomas, a parson's son who was a gifted automotive engineer, holder of the Land Speed Record, and bizarre victim of the car in which he died.

Thomas was born at Wrexham on April 6, 1885, and showed early mechanical aptitude growing up in Wales, so no one was surprised when he forsook a possible career in the clergy for technical school and a succession of berths leading to Leyland Motors Ltd. in 1917 as chief engineer. There Thomas designed everything from components like the Thomas piston to entire motor cars like the Leyland 8. He attracted other technical minds like Reid Railton and eventually enough free-lance business to break away from Leyland in 1923 and set up his own consulting/construction business at the Brooklands automotive center.

The burly Thomas often took to the Brooklands oval himself, starting Easter Monday 1922, to test out new ideas, and he soon gained a reputation as a speedster like contemporaries John Cobb, Henry Segrave, and Malcolm Campbell. All, like Thomas, were interested in the LSR. Unlike the rest, Parry had limited funds, and to go record-hunting he needed an existing car rather than a special he could build from the ground up as the others did. The opportunity came in 1925 when Count Louis Zborowski's estate was being settled. The Count, a long-time figure in racing, had been killed the previous year at the Monza Grand Prix, and among the things he left behind was a huge, 27-litre motor car in his Chitty-Chitty-Bang-Bang series, officially called the Higham Special.

The Higham was powered by an American Liberty V-12 airplane engine and was chain-driven. A crude car, it had been expressly built to the Count's orders, and he had raced it a few times at Brooklands, although the rumor was that he envisioned it as an LSR car. Thomas acquired this machine for about $625 and immediately set about modifying it. Parry already had run an LSR attempt at Saltburn Sands in 1924 and failed because his Leyland-Thomas was underpowered, but he had run at Brooklands in the same car within the week and set a new flying mile mark, although missing the flying kilometer that then was used for the LSR. In 1925 the slightly revamped Higham Special was run at the track and also went down to Pendine Sands, but weather conditions and Parry's dissatisfaction with the car's performance had prevented a successful record attempt.

Back at Brooklands, more modifications went into the monster's preparation, including a new aluminum streamlined body, new carbs and Thomas pistons. Someone in the shop started calling the car Babs, and Thomas adopted the name himself, although it was entered as the Thomas Special for most Brooklands races. On March 16, 1926, Segrave ran the LSR to 152.33 m.p.h. at Southport Sands, besting Campbell's 150.87 at Pendine 8 months earlier. Segrave's record would stand only 6 weeks, for Parry Thomas and Babs were ready to do battle, and April 28, 1926, the Welshman averaged 169.30 m.p.h. at Pendine, then came back the following day and raised it further to 171.02 m.p.h., though the engine was misfiring, preventing a hoped-for run of over 180. Pendine had one more successful run on it; the following February Campbell got the LSR up to 174.88 m.p.h.

That set the stage for Thomas again in his 2nd attempt at 180 in March 1927. The weather was poor when he arrived at Pendine, and Thomas's health was no better. He had spent the previous week in bed, getting over the after effects of influenza, and even in the thick sweater he always wore, he was shivering in the damp Welsh air. But things had sufficiently cleared up by March 3 for runs to begin, and Parry was ripping off fast times—past the magic 180 m.p.h. mark, unofficially —when his moment came. On the 3rd pass of the day, just after he left the measured section of the beach, the car was enshrouded in spray and exhaust fumes.

Babs swerved, skidded, and then somersalted. It righted itself, ran in a wide circle as a wheel came off and skipped away. It crunched to a halt as the engine burned fiercely. The crew raced to the car, and could see Thomas slumped in his seat. He was dead, and a grizzly sight met their eyes when they got close. One of Babs's driving chains had snapped, and lashing out had carved away the top of the driver's head from forehead to the back of the neck. He had died instantly, the doctors said later, and he could not have felt the burns inflicted by the fire before the body was pulled from the car.

Thomas's body was carried back to Brooklands, then buried in Byfleet Churchyard. Babs was carried to a garage, inspected, then returned to the beach and buried near where the tragedy had occurred. Later the area was a golf club, and a stone cairn erected in Thomas's memory was knocked down. Then the area was acquired by the British defense establishment as a weapons testing center, and a 9-inch concrete strip covered most of Babs's hidden burial place. But in 1967 a local man came up with the idea of digging up the car, restoring it and placing it in a museum as a memorial to Thomas. For 2 years he battled opposition from those who did not like the idea, and from the British defense people. But in March 1969 he won the right to exhume Babs. The following month a machine tore into the concrete, then scooped 8 feet of dirt away to reveal the remains, and by hand the Parry Thomas car was dug out in a surprisingly good state of preservation, its sparking plugs still alive, patches of blue and white paint clearly showing. Restoration took 2 years.

It was more than a car being restored and polished. The memory of the Wizard of Brooklands was restored, polished, and rightfully put in the place it deserved, no longer overshadowed by the other LSR giants with whom he was the equal in life.

RENE THOMAS

French motorcycle champion René Thomas, also a pioneer aviator (trained by Wilbur Wright himself), was a 1st-rank racing driver for a dozen years and raced for better than 2 decades before going into race management. Like most early European drivers he drove mainly at home, but Thomas did occasionally come to America for the 500-miler at Indianapolis, and it was there—in 1914—that he recorded his greatest major victory.

René turned down the winning car at the 1908 Voiturette Grand Prix at Dieppe in a Canzan-powered Delage, choosing instead a De Dion-Bouton-powered car that finished 5th. Albert Guyot won the race. Thomas recorded 3rds in the Coupe de l'Auto in 1910 and in 1911, and placed in the top 5 in several other races. But he did not do too well in the major European race of that day, the French GP, finishing 9th in 1913, after retiring the year before. In 1914 he took the boat for America with his old adversary and teammate, Guyot, to run as part of a 2-car Delage entry at Indianapolis. Jules Goux, who had won in 1913, was there again with Peugeot teammates Georges Boillot and Arthur Duray. Jean Chassagne was there in a Sunbeam, Ernst Friedrich in a Bugatti, and others challenging America's best.

Earl Cooper, Gil Anderson, and Barney Oldfield were the Stutz team. Caleb Bragg and Spencer Wishart formed the Mercer team. Bob Burman had Specials for himself and Louis Disbrow. Joe Dawson had a Marmon, Howdy Wilcox a Gray Fox. Eddie Richenbacher, his name not yet Anglicized to Rickenbacker, led the Duesenberg forces. But this was not to be an American year. At 250 miles the only question that remained was which French entry would win. Only Wishart made a late rush with

200 miles to go and he was sidelined with a broken camshaft. René Thomas led, followed by Duray, Boillot, and Guyot.

Duray's "baby" Peugeot—only 183 cu. in.—could not overtake Thomas, but his teammate, Boillot, in a full-sized 345-cu. in. Peugeot roared into 2nd and seemed a threat to René until a cracked frame ended his bid. Thomas rolled to an easy 10-mile victory, with Duray 2nd, Guyot 3rd, Goux 4th, and Barney Oldfield, 30 miles behind in 5th, the top U.S. finisher. Thomas's average speed of 82.47 m.p.h. was a new Indy record, but the blasé Frenchman did not seemed overly excited about his $51,675 payoff, a huge amount for those pre-World War I days. He said that he would return for the next race, but that was not until in 1919 when Thomas ran the race's fastest lap at 104.7 m.p.h. but finished a distant 11th.

In 1920 René was angered by the Ballot factory's handing a car over to Ralph DePalma without consulting him. Thomas and Chassagne were the official factory team, and DePalma was acting independently. René vowed to run Ralph "into the ground." In practice this led to an accident that knocked Arthur Chevrolet out of the field, but Thomas and DePalma emerged from it to start. The race quickly developed into a 4-way battle among the 2 verbal opponents, Gaston Chevrolet, and Joe Boyer. Joe was the 1st of the 4 to go, hitting the wall when a faulty steering arm snapped after 300 miles. DePalma looked a sure winner with 14 laps to go when he suffered magneto trouble and had to limp home in 5th place. When Chevrolet's Monroe took the checker, Thomas was 2nd. Tommy Milton and Jimmy Murphy were 3rd and 4th in Duesenbergs. In the garage, Chevrolet's steering arm snapped, but too late for René.

Thomas was at Indy again in 1921 and was classified 10th after dropping out on the 144th lap with a broken water connection. It was René's last major American appearance, but he kept racing and placing fairly well for another 5 years. In 1924, for example, he was 6 in the French GP at Lyon and in 1925 he was 3rd in the San Sebastian GP to teammates Albert Divo and Robert Benoist. Both rides were in Delages, which was Thomas's major car in his closing years. In 1926 he quit driving to turn his attention solely to team management.

ALFRED (SPEEDY) THOMPSON

Racing was a way of life to the Thompson family of Monroe, North Carolina. Bruce Thompson, the father, had once entertained thoughts of going to Indianapolis. His sons, Jimmy and Alfred, each knew how to handle a car before the age of 12. It was Alfred, however, who was left to make the family reputation when NASCAR began to grow; both Jimmy and Bruce were taken by heart attacks.

Born April 3, 1926, Al Thompson first received the

name Speedy from his mother. It was a term of affectionate derision because he was anything but quick in his movements. The nickname stuck but the meaning changed when the 5-foot, 10 inch youngster started mopping up on the short tracks in Virginia and North Carolina. In 1952, for instance, he won 26 of 70 features against the best modified drivers of the era. It was only natural that he also would assay his luck with NASCAR late models or, as they came to be called, the Grand Nationals. But there was a difference between Alfred and his father and brother. They raced much for the fun of racing; to Speedy it was a business—just like the welding shop he opened in Monroe. When the race was over, he would load up his car and, more than likey, go immediately home. Around the track he was friendly enough but he was quiet. Certainly he was not one of the in group in NASCAR.

Yet his NASCAR record shows 19 victories and 4 straight 3rd place finishes in the season points race—in 1956 through 1959. The one and only Carl Kiekhaefer recruited him for that fabulous racing team of Dodges and Chryslers and along with the Flock boys, Speedy was one of the stars. Yet the sport was changing fast and Speedy really did not know whether he liked the change —to superspeedways, high banked, where different skills were needed than on the flat tracks. It was not that the skills were lacking: he had won the 1957 Southern 500 at Darlington for Chevrolet besting Cotton Owens in a Pontiac, Marvin Panch and Jim Reed in Fords and Buck Baker in another factory Chevrolet. But Speedy was not an aggressive driver on a superspeedway. He always seemed uneasy there.

Yet again in 1960 Thompson won the 1st National 400 ever run at Charlotte International Speedway driving a Wood Brothers Ford. But he avoided the superspeedways preferring to concentrate on his welding and his family and some modified racing for the fun of it. It was in 1960 that he learned something about himself. Alfred Speedy Thompson tried to walk away completely from racing, make it a part of his past. But he found that he could not do that. He found that the competition —not for big money on the supertracks but the wheel to wheel competition of modifieds and sportsmen—was as much a part of him as his eyes and ears.

So he went back to his beginnings and there he stayed except for an occasional foray into some NASCAR short track event. And there he was at Charlotte Fairgrounds, a half-miler that ran weekly races, on April 2, 1972. He was piloting a sportsman in the main event and a yellow flag had signalled a caution period during which all cars must stop. He drove the car into his pit and allowed that he had to catch his breath. "This car," he said, "is working me pretty hard." He sat there panting for breath but when the restart was signalled, he drove the car to its position. He made only ¾ of a lap before the car swerved into the rail. Speedy Thompson had died of a heart attack.

DICK THOMPSON

If there is one man who will go down as the master of the Corvette it will be a tall Washington, D.C., dentist named Richard K. Thompson, Jr. He was a monument to what reasonable intelligence, determination, and experience can do for almost any Dartmouth man who skies and plays varsity football. Dick Thompson was not particularly interested in cars before 1951—he was too busy marrying, establishing himself, and drilling holes in people's teeth for fillings. His 1st sports car was an MG TD, for which his wife, Sarah, bought him a mechanic's manual.

He spent evenings in the family basement taking the car apart for the fun of it and learning what made it tick. This car began his racing career—at Sebring in 1952. That was the kind of race where practically anyone with a license could drive if he stayed out of the way of bigger, faster cars and if he were patient. But it was dangerous if a new driver got ambitious. Thompson drove down in the TD, changed the plugs, set down the extra set of tires from a friend's car, and was ready to race. Everyone decided that 12 hours was a long time so pit stops were frequent, long, and leisurely. Yet he finished 8th overall and 6th on index of performance. This so encouraged him that he went into SCCA racing.

In 1953 Thompson bought an original Porsche Super and, despite weird maintenance procedures, won the SCCA national class championship. The Thompson budget could not handle Porsche parts as a steady diet, however, so wherever possible he substituted VW parts. By the end of 1954, in which he also won his class title, he had the most adulterated Porsche in creation. The next year Dick moved to bigger-bore machinery, an XK 140 Jaguar, with which he finished 3rd nationally. That year he also got his first 2 free rides in an XK 140MC, codriving with Charles Wallace at Sebring. When Thompson took over from Wallace, he learned to his horror that the crew had only half-filled the gas tank, so he had to cruise the required 22 laps as if he were in an economy run, and was forced to watch out for MGs and Deutsch-Bonnets roaring past him. He drove 3 hours at 30 m.p.h., the 1st and only man ever to get 25 m.p.g. from a Jaguar in the 12-hour classic. The car finished 10th overall, recording its fastest laps after dark.

The Doc won the production Jaguar event at Nassau Speed Week that year, and in a preliminary race had the pleasure of beating Stirling Moss. Sebring in 1956 found Thompson scheduled to drive a factory-prepared Mercedes 300SL with Paul O'Shea. Unfortunately the car broke down before the race, so he was a spectator, giving him time to watch the 1st Corvette factory effort ever at the Florida Airport course.

Afterwards Chevrolet suggested a deal to Thompson through John Fitch. If he would buy a Corvette and campaign it, the factory would maintain it, checking the car after each race. Thompson would be expected to suggest improvements, if any. Since he had spun a Corvette at Marlboro, Md., already, Dick had plenty of suggestions. His official debut in a Corvette came at Pebble Beach, where the Coast crowd laughed—until he won a preliminary, led the feature, and finished 2nd to a 300SL when he had to slow down because he had run out of brakes. Improvement number one. He won later at Palm Springs, where West Coast writers, accused him of using a limited-slip differential. Dick had not, but he suggested a 4-speed gearbox and the limited-slip differential for 1957. Chevrolet thought up the fuel injection all by itself.

Meanwhile 2 things happened; the flying dentist won SCCA Class B 2 years in a row, and Chevvy shut the door on its original deal, giving him a dealer price, however. Thompson and a friend, Fred Windridge, were asked to enter a Corvette at Sebring in 1958 after Dick won the SCCA title. All they had was a 1957 car beat up in an unfortunate Venezuelan Grand Prix sports-car race, and when Thompson asked for sponsorship, friends all over the country suddenly did not know him. When Dick tried a public solicitation from sports car fans, people yawned. He and Fred finally put the thing on an investment basis, promising $2 for $1, if they won the Grand Touring class prize of $3,000.

They raised $900 of a required $2,000, had $300 in gifts and the use of Chevvy dealer Bob Rosenthal's work space and spare parts. Thompson and Windridge did all the restorative work themselves after office hours, and the car, complete with a free-form, 35-gallon gas tank specially designed for it, arrived at Sebring in fine shape. John Kilbourn, a wealthy Midwesterner, offered to share expenses if he could also share the ride. That helped a great deal. Kilbourn had the first 2-hour stint and roared off yards ahead of the pack. But the fuel injection pump jammed, and he pitted dead last on the 1st lap. Five laps behind, Kilbourn charged out and made up 3 laps before he handed the car to Windridge. Fred was to hold position, allowing the Ferrari Berlinettas to run out of brakes, then Thompson would make up the laps easily before dark.

But when Dick started to up the pace, the Corvette's fan belt broke. Pit examination showed it was from a bent pully that could not stand the strain of all-out campaigning. In all, 14 fan belts were used that race, 8 from Chevvies parked in the pits. One of the belts kayoed the brakes just before sundown, but the trio pressed on. Despite 18 pit stops—still a Sebring record—the car finished 2nd in class. For 1958 Windridge campaigned the Corvette, while Thompson dropped down to Class D and an Austin-Healey 6 for the class championship. The following season Thompson joined forces with GM styling ace Bill Mitchell to campaign the latter's prototype Sting Ray. Mitchell got no aid from the factory, but used his own money. The year was spent—weekends and vacations only, of course—correcting bugs. The Corvette Sting Ray now slithering around the roads, however, is a direct descendent of this Mitchell car. Thompson drives it—for pleasure.

MICKEY THOMPSON

There is no doubt that Marian Lee (Mickey) Thompson deserves a niche in American racing history. But where? The son of Marian Thompson, a captain of detectives in Alhambra, Calif., was restoring life to old Fords and Chevrolets before he could legally drive. Born December 7, 1928, in San Fernando, Calif., he gave promise of things to come by cutting 89m.p.h. in a Model A just a short time after cutting his molars. The unofficial magazine version of his life—which predates the official book version—says that in 1944 he ran a 1936 Ford coupe in a Southern California Timing Association session at 141.65 m.p.h., and over the next several years terrorized the hot-rod fraternity with progressively faster times.

The official version says he met his wife by warning her that there were fuzz (police) about as she pulled away from the local hot-rod eatery. This auspicious beginning eventually led to marriage, which obviously did not sit well with the elder Thompson at the outset, but Mickey settled down, only using money from moonlighting to support his weekend drag meet jaunts. In 1953 he ran his 1st Mexican road race in a Ford—right over a cliff. He was trying to avoid hitting the natives strolling along the road as the race cars passed; when the

car went over, it landed on several anyway, and Mickey was never quite able to explain that he was trying to avoid trouble. It was touch and go, but he got home by sheer serendipity after losing all his money and papers. A Ford minion had spotted him and drove him back.

According to the official version, it was on that race that he met and became fast friends with Piero Taruffi of Italy. They swapped racing information. Mickey has always been friendly that way. The next year he came back with a Ford from the same sponsor—there is the mark of a great salesman—and ran *into* a cliff this time. But he won the 1st lap of the 5-day race before that happened.

Thompson had already begun to build a garage and special parts business and was setting records. Old dragsters say he was the 1st man to take a rod over 120 m.p.h. on a quarter-mile strip; later in the same year (1955) he was the first to exceed 150. This historic juncture in automotive history occurred at the San Fernando strip. Such antics helped business immeasurably, and Thompson next laid claim to the title of Fastest American on Wheels in 1958 with a trip at 294 m.p.h. First America and then the World; Thompson drew a bead on John Cobb's land speed mark of 394.2 set in 1947. He had set the American mark with a dual-engined vehicle; now he went to 4 Pontiac 410-cu. in. engines, running a Mobilgas alcohol-nitro mixture. He pushed the American mark to 330.51, but exceeded Cobb in only one direction (407 plus), crashing on the way back. The car was the famed Challenger I.

However, in 1959, he did eclipse 4 international marks held by Cobb, raising the 5-kilo mark to 345.33, the 5-miler to 340.70, the 10-kilo to 327.59, and the 10-miler to 286.16. On that particular day faulty adjustment of his oxygen mask cost him a shot at the flying mile. The following year, with his Assault, a vehicle built on a slingshot dragster chassis and powered by Pontiac, Thompson lifted the standing kilometer and mile marks from Bernd Rosemeyer of Auto Union. On May 14, 1960, at March Air Force Base in California, he went 132.94 for the kilo and 149.93 for the mile. In this period through 1962, with either Assault, Challenger, or other cars, he set more than 100 international or national class marks.

In November 1960, while testing a speedboat for a possible assault on the WSR, Thompson suffered a broken back. He virtually stormed out of the hospital, was driven home lying on a mattress in the back of a station wagon, and made enough of a recovery to become mobile with orthopedic devices and drive again. His enterprises—and he was one of the finest salesmen in auto racing—included rod and custom shows, high-performance components for American passenger cars and building drag cars.

In 1962 Mickey was ready to turn his talents toward Indianapolis, which he considered ripe for improvement.

He was right, of course, for the Indy cars were obsolete compared with the technical knowledge available in racing. The entire Thompson Indy saga is ringed with legend and uncheckable stories testifying either to his genius, or to his pleading for aid to correct impossible engineering. Dan Gurney drove his Harvey Aluminum Special into the 3rd row on the starting grid, but the Buick-engined vehicle popped its grease seals while in 10th place halfway through the race, retiring.

In 1963, Bill Krause, Duane Carter, and Graham Hill were to be the Indy heroes in Chevvy-engined Thompson vehicles, also called the Harvey Aluminum Specials. Two had steel frames and one used titanium. Krause and Hill pranged their cars early and did not qualify. Al Miller, a 30-year-old rookie, did a fine job with the Krause car, finishing 9th. The veteran Carter ran 100 laps before being sidelined. It was in a Mickey Thompson Sears Allstate Special that Dave McDonald crashed to a fiery death, triggering the 1964 race stoppage. That car was Ford d.o.h.c.-powered. The other Sears car, driven by Eddie Johnson, lasted 6 laps before a fuel pump quit.

Thompson had come to Indy with Allstate tires and a 2-wheel drive system. He abandoned the latter early in shakedown cruises. After the McDonald crash, Mickey announced that he himself would drive in 1965. It was made very unlikely when he collapsed in a record car in the summer of 1964—before the run—then repeated this non-feat 3 times that fall. Thompson's 1965 Indy car, a front-wheel drive, Chevvy-powered Motor Trend/ Challenger Wheel Special, driven by Bob Mathorisey, threw a rod during qualifications and did not make the field of 33 starters. Thompson did not have an entry for the 500 in 1966. There is a story that, to qualify 2 cars, he once used the same chassis and engine, but switched the bodies overnight.

Thompson himself was the 1st to admit that he has never been slow to exhibit a degree of bragadoccio unrivalled outside of fiction. But he also drove himself unmercifully to make his place despite educational and financial limitations. According to Griff Borgeson, his biographer, "there is no personal challenge remotely within reason, which he will not conquer or go down fighting—he is almost pathologically incapable of quitting."

JOEL THORNE

Motor racing always has attracted rich men, who have dabbled in the sport with varying degrees of seriousness. Some of them would have accomplished the same whether they had been rich or not; others accomplished anything only because they had unlimited resources and a willingness to squander them on this particular enterprise for a time. Joel Wolfe Thorne, Jr., definitely was one of the former, not the latter. He had the "hunger" that drives men to do well in sports, at least a modicum of talent and the ability to associate himself with good men who could contribute to the overall success of the racing effort.

Joel Wolfe Thorne Jr., was born in 1914 to a father who was technically heir to a vast banking, railroading, and importnig fortune—not to mention considerable New York suburban real estate—and a mother 13 years his father's junior and a Barnard College professor. Thorne, Sr., was only "technically" heir because after his marriage to the young Irish lady in question, his parents had cut him off. With the birth of a grandson, however, the ice thawed sufficiently to allow the grandfather to hand over $500,000 for medical and incidental expenses.

Thorne's grandfather died 3 years later and left him an outright bequest of $1 million. Around that time Joel, Sr., and his wife divorced, the father getting possession of Joel, Jr., although his grandmother became the person who really worried about him. But when she died, she left father and son the family fortune, all neatly tied up in staggered legacies and untouchable trust funds.

Joel, Sr., also had the problem of finding someone to care for his son. He advertised in the classified and hired a widow who cared for Junior for an $18,000 annual stipend including expenses. When Joel was 10, his father was killed while changing a tire on a lonely Connecticut road, clipped by a passing speeder. Joel, Jr., had seen his father exactly half a dozen times in 5 years, so he had no great sense of loss, apparently. What he did have, now, was a relatively clear title to his life; he sought out his mother, was reunited with her, and set her up in a $60,000 estate near New Rochelle, N.Y. He entered Rutgers University and "majored" in speedboat racing. In 1933 at age 19 Thorne won the American Outboard Association High Point Trophy. To win he spent at least $50,000.

The 3 years at Rutgers were followed by a year at the University of London. Then Thorne got down to more serious business: women, faster boats, and faster cars. He started automobile racing seriously in 1934; by 1935 he was at Indianapolis as a car owner with a ragged old Studebaker 8 driven by Jimmy Snyder. The car finished 22nd; Joel told them he would be back, and was not taken seriously. To learn more about racing, Joel entered the enthusiastically named Grand Prix of the United States, scheduled for June 23, 1935, by the Automobile Racing Club of America, a forerunner of the SCCA.

The "GP" was for sports cars and was being run in Briarcliff, N.Y., with 17 starters. Thorne had a Ford—one especially modified for the 1933 Elgin Road Races run by AAA and was said to develop 120 b.h.p. from its flat-head V-8 engine. He started 15th and made 9th on the 1st lap, climbed to 3rd within 5 laps. At 65 miles he led the race. A pit stop dropped Joel to 2nd, and he finished in that position, even though he equaled the lap record in his rush to regain the lead. Thorne immediately protested, saying the sport crowd was cheating him of his victory, even though he had finished about 10 seconds behind Langdon Quimby and his Willys. His protest was disallowed and Thorne never raced in ARCA again.

That was small potatoes compared to Indy, anyway. In 1936 he was back at the Brickyard with 2 cars, each powered by big 6-cylinder Dodge engines, but entered under the name of a relative, Cliff Thorne, because Joel was engaged in some legal difficulties at the time (and as usual, as it turned out). Joel planned to drive one, and he had Russ Snowberger down for the other. Russ banged the wall, though, and Thorne could not pass the rookie test, so he gave his seat to Dale Evans, who failed to qualify. Snickers were in order, but Thorne's day was coming.

To get seasoning for the Indy race in 1937, Thorne started racing more seriously. His only notable work of the summer was at Pikes Peak where he drove a Miller to 4th. His notable work off-track was to marry a Powers model. In early May 1937, he met and was impressed by Art Sparks. Thorne immediately bought Sparks's new car, a long, narrow job that developed 500 b.p.h. on pump gasoline (an Indy requirement of those days) from a 337-cu. in. supercharged straight-8 engine with d.o.h.c. Snyder again was signed on as driver, and Chick Hirashima was named crew chief.

One car was not enough. Thorne toured Gasoline Alley looking for more equipment. In short order he had added three 4-cylinder Millers, with drivers Floyd Roberts, Al Miller, and Floyd Davis, as well as another ancient Studebaker and Zeke Meyer, and for Thorne himself a 220 front-drive Offy. Snyder did best in qualifying, setting one- and 10-lap records. Roberts, Miller, and Davis made the race, Meyer did not. Joel himself only was fast enough to become 1st alternate. He tried buying the Cliff Bergere car and attempting to dump it so he could start, but track owner Eddie Rickenbacker laid down the law, and Thorne relented, merely adding the car and Bergere to his stable for the race.

When the flag fell, Snyder roared into the lead, and lost it only after 28 laps when the car's transmission broke. Miller lasted 170 laps (and 7 pit stops). Davis crashed in the 190th lap (after 5 pit stops). Roberts, who won the following year, finished 12th. Bergere finished 5th, but Thorne never got credit or purse money; Joel's check had bounced and the car reverted to its original owner. (His monthly allowance had not yet been deposited when the check was presented.)

Joel determined to go about racing more scientifically. He hired Sparks on a lifetime contract, with sweeteners such as $100,000 in free life insurance, 10 per cent of all Indy winnings, 15 per cent of other racing winnings, and 5 per cent of any Thorne Engineering profits. While Art was getting the new company off the ground, Thorne himself went racing again, finishing 5th at Pikes Peak and 6th (highest American driver placing) in the revived Vanderbilt Cup Races held at Roosevelt Raceway on Long Island.

On September 1, 1937, Thorne Engineering Co. was officially open for business at a big former warehouse on Slauson Avenue in Los Angeles, conveniently near the Hollywood studios where Joel would recruit girls as companions for trips to Indy and other places. Sparks set to work to build 3-litre, supercharged racers that would conform to the new 1938 formula. The 2 big 6s that emerged were truly classics in Indy racing and developed 365 b.h.p.

For the 1938 Indy classic, Snyder was given one of the 6s, and all-time midget racing great Ronnie Householder got the other. Billy DeVore got a 4-cylinder, as did Thorne himself. The new cars were fast; both drivers were clocked unofficially through a speed trap at the Raceway at over 174 m.p.h. Householder set an absolute 10-lap qualifying record (still standing since they only do 4 laps now) of 125.769 m.p.h. Snyder was 4th fastest qualifier, Thorne qualified at 120.240 and even DeVore managed to qualify 33rd and last. In the race Snyder and Householder dominated until late when mechanical ills retired both cars with the same failure: hoses connecting the blowers with the intake manifolds separated in the same place. Snyder went out at 375 miles, Householder at 379. DeVore finished 8th, Thorne 9th. The latter had a ham radio (W9XSA) installed in his cockpit and reported happenings to the pits regularly.

In July 1938, Thorne Engineering moved to even bigger quarters on San Fernando Road and a 3rd car was built, similar to the big 1937 cars, but engine displacement was reduced from 337 to 271 cu. in. Blowers were scrapped, and the car was made a single-seater instead of a 2-man racer. This would be Joel's machine. Snyder got one of the blown cars, and Rex Mays replaced Householder. Thorne's 1937 mount was re-equipped with a 270 Offy, and Mel Hansen got the ride. In the 1939 500-miler, Snyder again led at the green, fell to 2nd only when he pitted, but recharged into the lead past the likes of Wilbur Shaw and Lou Meyer with ease, and only fell back again in another pit stop. This time he could not catch Shaw's new Maserati and finished 2nd. Joel was 7th, Mays retired with valve problems, and Hansen slammed a wall in his haste to get back from a pit stop.

Thorne went back to Pikes Peak and finished 3rd. At Milwaukee he was 9th. But then problems arose; Snyder was killed in a midget car race. Sparks and Joel were having problems; there were no new cars for the 1940 race, and Joel ran his 4.5-litre 6 and finished a credible 5th, his highest placing in the 500. In 1941, before the war ended racing, a blown car was readied for Ted

Horn, while Joel again had his usual mount. He retired when 2 cars spun in front of him in the 4th lap, and he hit the wall in trying to elude them. Horn had some problems learning about his new mount, but finished 3rd.

Thorne Engineering became a war-time subcontractor to Lockheed Aircraft, and relations between the boss and Sparks ended in 1943. Relations between the boss and his wife ended the following year, their son later went into NASCAR racing as a sponsor for about a year, but soon tired of it and quit. On top of that Joel charged out of a gas station full tilt on his motorcycle and ran into a truck—multiple fractures. He was still in the cast when he spent 4 days in jail for not sending his wife the alimony checks. Many law suits later, and just before the war ended, Joel dumped Thorne Engineering for $150,000, a fraction of its real worth, but retained the racing cars, selling one to a syndicate so he could ready the other 2 for the 1946 Indy race (there was plenty of money in the Thorne till but he could not touch it).

George Robson was given Thorne's 3-litre car, but Joel managed to break a leg in another motorcycle accident and offered his 4.5-litre car to Rudi Caracciola, the European Grand Prix driver, whose Mercedes-Benz was tied up in customs. Rudi crashed in practice, and only a surplus tank crewman's helmet saved his life. But Robson not only made the race, he surprisingly won it at a modest 114.820 m.p.h. Protests that he had not gotten out of his car during one of his pit stops (then an Indy rule) were disallowed, and the victory stood. There was a last try with one Sparks car in 1948 (another had been sold to get some cash, for alimony and other long-term debts kept Joel's allowance checks very small), but it could not be qualified. He followed with an attempt at a hybrid, dropping the old reliable Sparks 6 into a Mercedes W.163 GP car once raced by Tommy Lee; the car failed to qualify either in 1949 or 1950. Joel ran it once up Pikes Peak in 1951, but failed to finish, and the car was sold.

On July 8, 1951, Thorne created havoc with the rental car people when he took out a Cadillac and ran it in a 150-mile stock-car race at Milwaukee. That was about it for Thorne as an auto racing figure. He talked of several new cars and projects, but none came to pass. On October 17, 1955, Thorne wanted to fly to Las Vegas in his private Beechcraft Bonanza, but it was foul weather, and he had never bothered to get an instrument rating. He took off anyway, lost his way, and flew into the side of a 2-story home, killing not just himself, but 3 other people, and critically injuring 6 more.

JERRY TITUS

"Group 7 racing, you know, CanAm stuff. That's the real thing," Jerry Titus said, as he wiped his forehead with his forearm. He had had another disappointing race at the Bridgehampton road course because his Pontiac Firebird substitute car had not performed at all well. "I wish I could get some kind of a CanAm ride that could lead to something. I have some ideas that I think might cut down that McLaren supremacy. "I never really have had the chance to concentrate on them."

Nobody every learned the ideas. Jerry Titus died August 5, 1970, from injuries sustained when his Firebird crashed at Road America in Elkhart Lake almost a month before. Born in Johnson City, N.Y., October 24, 1928, he was only a few months shy of 42 years old. He had only been racing for 11 years, yet he had managed, despite that late start, to win a Trans-American sedan championship for Mustang and establish himself as a natural driving talent.

There were other talents, too. He was a trumpet player accomplished enough to play professionally in the big-band era. He was a good enough mechanic to spend some years maintaining Maseratis driven by John Fitch and Carroll Shelby. He worked with the fabulous Bill Frick, the man who sired the Fordillac and the Studillac and who turned the wrenches for Phil Walters. And he was a contributor to *Speed Age* and an editor of *Sports Car Graphic*.

Although Jerry, a short (5 feet, 7 inches) man with unruly blond hair, had undoubtedly driven many fast laps testing the work he did on Maseratis, the official start of his racing career did not come until he was 32, when he campaigned a Formula Junior for a Long Island car dealer and also drove go-karts when they seemed likely to become a whole new segment of motor racing. He was 3rd in the 1960 national championships.

The following year Jerry moved to Southern California to become technical editor of *Sports Car Graphic*. His managing editor, W. C. Sheldenham, finally offered him a Sprite to campaign in SCCA. Titus raced it well enough to get a factory Sunbeam. From there he progressed to a Genie-Corvair, a Cheetah, and his 1964 national D Modified championship with a Webster Special. For 1965 Shelby American helped him out with a GT 350 Mustang, and he promptly won the B Production national championship. He simultaneously drove an Elva-Porsche in USRRC.

In 1966 Titus drove a Porsche 911 to the C Production national championship, and Shelby gave him a ride on one of the Mustang TransAm teams. He repaid Carroll by helping Mustang to the title for 2 years. Late in 1968 Canadian Terry Godsall persuaded Titus to try to build his own Shelby-American operation using the Pontiac Firebird as a foundation. Jerry had managed a 6th in the Canadian-American Challenge Cup standings, so he took the gamble. Thus T/G Racing was born. For 1969 the team sold 3 race-prepared Firebirds to customers and campaigned 2, finishing 3rd in TransAm. Titus was chief mechanic, chief tester, chief driver, and one of the most exhausted men you ever saw at the con-

clusion of a racing weekend.

In 1970 Titus felt the Firebird was ready to roll to victory. Because of the late introduction of the TransAm model, SCCA inspectors felt otherwise, and the work of the winter months went for naught. Enough TransAm models had not been built by Pontiac so most of what T/G had done—spoilers, special air scoop—was declared illegal. Frantically Jerry started over, instrumenting the Firebird so he could get more in-cockpit readings. But support was such that only a single car was campaigned—a frustrating campaign right up to Road America. In practice for that race Titus lost control of the car and crashed into a bridge abutment.

FLOYD TREVIS

Floyd Trevis, a resident of Youngstown, Ohio, is, remembered as the builder of one of the most unusual cars ever to show up on an American race track—the Fageol Twin Coach Special. Had the perpetrator of this 2-engined creation, Lou Fageol, persisted, both he and Trevis might have started a new dynasty of vehicles.

The Twin Coach and Trevis arrived at Indianapolis in the same year—1946. The car used 2 supercharged 91-cu.in. engines, one to power the front wheels and the other for the rear. The Roots-type blowers were in the cockpit alongside the driver who, according to contemporary reports, could use either his front screamer, the back one, or both at the same time. The vehicle, in effect, had 4-wheel drive and thus theoretically should have had better traction through the turns. But no special tires were made, and it may have been the victim of stiff "shoes." Russo qualified for a position in the middle of the front row and was in contention when, some 45 miles into the race, he seemed to motor straight into the wall on the northeast turn. He had no explanation for the journey.

Trevis went back to Ohio and was next heard from as a builder of Pete Salemi's Central Excavating Special in 1951 with Bill Vukovich as the pilot. From 1952 until 1960 he found being a chief mechanic more lucrative. Dick Rathmann put his car on the pole in 1958. Floyd went back to carbuilding for the 1960 race with 2 for Jim Robbins. These incorporated several innovations like a built-in exhaust system and a frontal area so low a snake could slither over it. The cars, driven by Eddie Johnson and Bud Tinglestad, finished 6th and 9th, both going the distance. Bowes Seal East came to him for the winning 1961 A. J. Foyt mount, and he built 7 cars in 1963, 2 for the Brickyard.

MAURICE TRINTIGNANT

July 4, 1948, saw the reviving Grand Prix circus at Berne for the Swiss GP. In those days, preliminary races were held at each site, and this day a voiturette race preceded the major event. It was during this preliminary that a 30-year-old French driver, most noted because he came of a racing family, spun when running 2nd and

was hurled out of the light car's cockpit (safety belts and shoulder harnesses were then far in the future). As the hapless driver flew through the air, Raymond Sommer managed to drive underneath him. Maurice Trintignant crashed to the middle of the course unconscious, with the rest of the field bearing down upon him. But quick action by Prince Bira, Giuseppe Farina, and Robert Manzon enabled them to avoid the stricken driver, though each was eliminated by crashing as a result of their evasive actions. Carried to the Berne hospital, Trintignant lingered unconscious for 8 days, then suffered severe internal hemorrhaging. The Frenchman was rushed to the operating theatre, where his heart stopped and the surgeon prounced him dead; but then a heartbeat was faintly heard, then increased, and the operation was carried through. For another 15 days Trintignant lingered at the edge, then began a rapid recovery. His greatest days in auto racing still lay ahead, despite his age and frightful brush with death.

Maurice, always remembered as a dapper, pencil-mustachioed, smallish man, was born October 30, 1917, at Sainte-Cecile-les-Vignes, France, youngest of 5 sons of a prosperous wine merchant and local politician. By the time he was 9, Trintignant was driving a small Peugeot around the family vineyards and vowing to emulate his brothers—or at least 3 of them—as racing drivers.

While still a schoolboy, Maurice was an occasional mechanic with brother René, a rather wild Bugatti driver who had so many accidents that he finally retired, and with Louis, a hillclimb ace and fast Amilcar and Bugatti racer. Another brother was Henri, who raced and drove in hillclimbs before World War II, Raoul, the oldest was the sole non-racing member of the group; but he had a son, Jean-Louis, who became an actor and made several car-oriented motion pictures.

Maurice took up racing seriously in 1938, 5 years after the death of Louis, who was killed while practicing on the Peronne circuit in Picardy. The car in which Maurice made his debut at the 1938 Pau GP was the same 2.3-litre supercharged Bugatti in which Louis died. Maurice finished 5th behind 3 factory Delahayes and a Mercedes codriven by Hermann Lang and Rudi Caracciola. Before the war ended auto racing, Trintignat managed to win the 1938 and 1939 Grands Prix des Frontieres at Chimay, the opening year a Formula Libre race, the next a sports-car event, both times in his Bugatti.

It was in this same car, hidden away for almost 6 years in a barn, that Maurice appeared for the Continent's 1st postwar race, the Coupe de la Liberation of September 1945, held in the Bois de Boulogne. Trint dropped out of the race early with an engine failure. Afterwards, it was discovered that a family of rats had found a home in his fuel tank, and their droppings had mired the petrol filter, causing engine starvation.

After 1946, Maurice traded in the ancient Bug for a supercharged Amilcar with which he won 1947's Avignon GP, and he also drove Delages for the Gersac team, and Simcas for Amedée Gordini. For Simca in 1948 Trintignant won races at Montlhéry and Perpignan before suffering that terrible crash in the Swiss GP. He stayed with Simcas through 1953 with victories in the little blue cars coming at Albi, Angouleme, Cadours, Chimay, Geneva, and Nurburgring. At Le Mans, Maurice and America's Harry Schell shared a class victory. Trintignant was crowned Champion of France.

In 1954 Trintignant became a Ferrari factory driver, joining Farina and Jose Gonzalez. He won outright at Caen, Buenos Aires, and Rouen, shared a 12-hour Hyéres victory with Biotto, and a Le Mans 24-hour victory with Gonzalez. He was 2nd at Bari, Syracuse, and in the Belgian GP. He was 3rd in the Bordeaux and German races, and 4th in the Argentine GP. It added up to a 3rd place in the World Drivers title race. The following year, Trint won his initial *grande épreuve*, the difficult Monaco GP, and shared a Messina 10-hour victory with Eugenio Castellotti. At Monaco his consistency was such that the first 50 laps were run at 1:29.3, the second 50 at 1:29.6, an incredible performance.

Maurice was in Ferraris in 1956, winning at Agadir and Dakar, and at the Swedish GP (with Phil Hill) in Vanwalls. The following season, Trintignant continued to free lance, with a Formula 2 Rheims victory in a Ferrari his best showing. He also put a BRM 3rd in the Moroccan GP and 4th at the British race. Trintignant's 2nd championship victory came in the 1958 Monaco GP when he drove Rob Walker's 1.9-litre Cooper across the finish line ahead of Ferraris driven by Luigi Musso and Peter Collins. He won the Pau GP, was 3rd in the championship German race, and 4th in the Caen GP.

Walker kept giving Trint a good car, and in 1959, the Frenchman was 2nd in the United States GP to Bruce McLaren (the New Zelander's initial championship victory), 3rd at Monaco, and 4th in both the German and Portuguese races. In the U.S. race, which was run at Sebring, Trintignant set the fastest lap. In a Cooper-Borgward, Maurice won at Pau and in Aston Martins he contributed to that team's World Championship in sports car racing, including a 2nd (with Paul Frere) at Le Mans. In 1960 the free-lance efforts continued, with a 3rd in the Argentine GP shared with Stirling Moss for Rob Walker, a Buenos Aires Formula Libre victory, and drives with Porsche and Aston in sports car racing. Driving his own Cooper F2 car, Trintignant won the Prix de Paris, set the day's fastest time in the Mont Ventoux hillclimb, scored 2nds at Syracuse and Pau, and was 3rd at Brussels.

Trintignant was now 33 and finding drives increasingly more difficult to arrange. Yet he plugged on, driving a Cooper-Maserati for Scuderia Serenissima in 1961 and starting 5 championship races without much success. He was 7th at Monaco, retired after 24 laps in the Belgian GP with transmission trouble, and was 13th in the French GP. Maurice was 18th in the German race, and

9th in the Italian. His specialty, as always, was bringing his car home; the Belgian retirement was a rare one. Back in 1954, he had started 21 races, and finished 19 of them.

In 1961 Trintignant won the La Faucille hillclimb, was 2nd in the Auverne 6-hour enduro and at Mont Ventoux, 3rd in the Paris 1000 kilometer race, and 4th in the Targa Florio with Nino Vaccarella in a Maserati. The following season, Trint's consistency started falling off, though probably not completely through his own fault. An accident at Monaco in which he was hit from behind by Richie Ginther (whose throttle stuck wide open) wiped out 4 cars and started a miserable season. At Belgium, Maurice was 8th, at France 7th, followed by retirements at the German, Italian, and U.S. Grands Prix. But he won a nontitle race at Pau for the 3rd time to salve some of his pride.

Trintignant's appearances had become few and far between. Trying for another Pau victory, he retired Rob Walker's Lotus-Climax with gear trouble in 1963. At Monaco his Reg Parnell Lola broke an oil pipe. Parnell had a Lotus-Climax, and in this one, Maurice managed an 8th in the French GP. In a BRM he was 9th in the Italian GP. The following season he retired at Monaco in a BRM, was 11th in the French GP, failed to finish the Italian race, but was 5th in the German GP. That was the last hurrah for Maurice Trintignant, the racing driver; but he did have other interests. There was the family wine business—some 400,000 bottles of 1st grade wine annually—and his political duties. In 1959 the dapper and polished gentleman had become mayor of Vergeze, famous for its Perrier mineral water. Ten miles away in Nimes you occasionally still could find him behind the counter of his wine shop. And he still drove at speed—but in a speedboat.

ERNIE TRIPLETT

Ascot Speedway in Los Angeles spawned far more than its share of great and near great drivers. One historian suggested wryly that in order to survive in this bullring of a track a driver had to be great but many survived and never made their mark elsewhere. So Ernie Triplett was the exception rather than the rule—just as Wilbur Shaw, Bob Carey, Freddie Frame, and others were the exception.

Ernie Triplett was a lanky, prematurely balding dandy who raced in bright red knickers and a neat black bow tie. He was soft-spoken and totally dedicated to automobile racing. He lived and breathed for the sport and seemed to expand when he heard the roar of racing car engines, becoming a different person than his off-track self. Triplett was the 1st king of nighttime automobile racing, a Legion Ascot innovation, and his daring driving style made him a hero to a whole range of West

Coast auto fans. To say this is to equate him with other driving greats of the era because it must be remembered that California, his native state, in itself is larger than all of Scandinavia with a few Benelux countries thrown in for good measure.

Born in 1906 in Belvedere, Calif., Triplett lived a normal middle-class early life, completing high school at age 18 and gravitating toward motor cars just as many of his peers dreamt of being baseball heroes. He did some "outlaw" racing, as competition outside of the AAA Contest Board was known in those days, but when he turned 21, he immediately applied for his AAA license and received it.

His 1st AAA race came at Legion Ascot in February 1928. His Ford Special was not up to the competition, but veterans, including the promoter, and ex-Indy vet Harlan Fengler, tabbed him as a talent. In April 1928 he acquired a Hudson Special for a benefit race at Pleasanton, Calif., just outside Oakland. He made the 75-mile main, and, after some of the prime contenders like Babe Stapp, Freddie Frame, and Mike Moosie fell out, Triplett moved on to his 1st major victory. He won subsequently at Ascot, Banning, and San Jose in 1928, getting himself a ride in the Miller No. 4 for the following season. At 22 Ernie Triplett was the *enfant terrible* of the west coast.

In 1929 Triplett went to Indianapolis where he lasted 48 laps in the Buckeye Duesenberg Special. He took the same car into Altoona, Pa., for the Flag Day 200 on the board track there. It was his 1st, and one of his last, board track races. Late in the race, rookie Red Robinson spun into the guard rail, sending the debris into the steep banking of the turn. Ray Keech, an Indianapolis 500 winner earlier that year, entered the corner too late to see the debris. His car, the Simplex, hit the huge planks, bounded high into the air, and flipped into a flaming funeral pyre for the star. Triplett, who had been closing on the lead, also struck the planks but somehow steered the car down the banking into the safety of the infield. The experience convinced him that board-track racing was not for him. For 1929 Ernie finished 16th in the national standings, which were heavily predicated on Eastern races, but he dominated Ascot.

There were new mounts for both the Pacific Coast AAA circuit and Indianapolis in 1930. The Sinclair Oil Co. sponsored a new Miller for the Ascot wars—Ascot had been regraded and paved with macadam. For the 500 he had the Guiberson Special, named for an oil tycoon. Ernie lost no time in showing that his title of king of Ascot was still relevant. He won the 100-lap season opener over men like Billy Arnold, Wilbur Shaw, Cummings, and Speed Hinkley, and went on from there to master even Gus Schrader, Louis Meyer, Frame, and Moosie. The energetic Triplett campaigned up and down the West Coast, finishing 2nd in the Coast standings. At Indy he lasted 115 laps before mechanical failure did him in.

Now considered a veteran driver, Triplett became indispensable to the western promoters of the era. He developed a personality image, began to wear his famous red knickers and became something of a playboy, albeit one who would not do anything to impair his ability on race day. Night racing was introduced in 1931 to Legion Ascot and Triplett greeted it with 14 straight main event victories. He added daytime victories at San Jose and Bakersfield and wrapped up the West Coast AAA crown early. At Indy he brought in the Buckeye Duesenberg 7th overall. And at the 2 race meetings at the new Oakland Speedway in October and November, Triplett put together back-to-back victories. He totally dominated Lou Schneider, the reigning Indy winner. However, he still refused to go East to make a full try at the national crown because of the Altoona experience—and because he was making more than a good living for those Depression years in his own backyard.

Another form of racing occupied Ernie that year, too. Straightaway runs along the sands at Pismo Beach, Calif., brought out most of the top drivers of the area and even exotica like Bugattis, Frontenac-Fords, and Triplett's own Ford Special. It was great fun for all concerned and Ernie came away with the world Land Speed Record for 4-cylinder automobiles on beach straightaways. He went 135 m.p.h. over the 5-mile course, which was soon to develop different uses as a bathing area for the burgeoning population of the Los Angeles area.

In 1932 Triplett won at Ascot, San Jose, Oakland, Bakersfield, and Fresno for another West Coast cham-

pionship, but away from his stamping grounds again he was relatively ineffectual. He led 8 laps but settled for 9th place at Indianapolis. At the Detroit, Fairgrounds he engaged Bob Carey in a wheel-to-wheel duel in which he led 75 miles only to succumb to engine trouble. In a late Oakland race he again battled Carey only to be sidelined once again for engine trouble. He lost badly to Carey at Oakland in the 2-man championship cars that were used for some races. (Carey won a U.S. title but lost his life at Ascot the next year.)

Triplett had taken on all comers who challenged his West Coast sprint crown. In 1933 a new foil emerged to challenge him, Al Gordon. Gordon was stocky, rowdy, and rough; he owned a night club and had driven outlaw for a year or 2 before the fabled Art Sparks saw something and installed him in a 1st class sprint machine, his "Poison Lil."

Gordon took out after Triplett like a highway patrolman after a speeder. Some of the wildest duels—and the most dangerous—in the history of auto racing followed. Remember that these drivers had no roll bars, no seat belts, and no protective helmets worth mentioning. Yet they regularly bounced off one another, banged fenders, blocked, and slid around until the weekly crowds of almost 20,000 would react with every possible shade of emotion. Often the two would finish inches apart after 100 laps around the banked 5/8ths of a mile, with the 3rd finisher far in the back. The point standings for the AAA Pacific Coast Championship were close all season, partly because Triplett finally wrecked and missed several weeks after fracturing his skull.

The 2 men actually were friendly away from the track, but the rivalry looked much better as a grudge match. That friendship, however, made a difference with Triplett; during his recovery he realized there would always be someone like Al—just a little hungrier for a good ride and the money than he, just a little more reckless and ruthless. He finally lost the 1933 AAA Pacific Coast championship to Al by a few points.

Triplett vowed never to race at Ascot again. In March of 1934 he persuaded his car owner, Bill White, to enter the Imperial Valley Fair races at El Centro, Calif., just over the Mexican border. The track was dirt, improperly prepared, and was certain to become dangerous. The AAA Contest Board relied on the promoter to get it ready properly. But the large purse drew the drivers to this mile track—including Gordon.

From the starter's flag it looked like an Ascot rematch with Triplett and Gordon pulling ahead of the field slowly and surely, battling wheel to wheel. The track surface deteriorated quickly, raising such clouds of dust that people in the pits could not distinguish their own cars. Finally a machine stalled in a corner and stayed there, forcing drivers to swerve around it lap after lap because no official could see it. It was inevitable that another car would hit the abandoned vehicle and strew debris across the entire turn, and one did. A brave mechanic rushed

out to help the driver extricate himself. It was at this moment that the Gordon-Triplett duet bore down upon the new wreck. Al dove inside avoiding the men and the wreckage. Ernie went outside and his rear wheel clipped something, swerving the car into the hapless mechanic and driver, then flipping it end over end, until it hit Gordon. Gordon's car split in two around a heavy post, but he suffered only a broken nose and other facial injuries. Ernie Triplett was dead. The two on the track also died and the crowd was treated to a near-riot between 2 AAA officials—Arthur Pillsbury, regional director, and Jim Grant, assistant starter.

Pillsbury was accused by Grant of not stopping the race soon enough. Grant alleged that he wanted to end it before the fatal accident at the 21st mile. Art Sparks, meanwhile, was protesting that Gordon should be declared the winner instead of Earl Balmer (not the latter day ARCA-NASCAR hero). For his protests Sparks was later banned from the pits for 2 years. Gordon, upon learning of Triplett's death, is said to have gone into town and gotten totally drunk, refusing to race for weeks. Actually Ernie lived until the next day, March 5, 1934, before succumbing to a skull fracture and internal injuries.

It is unlikely that Triplett would have gone much further in racing even had he lived, because he was negotiating the purchase of a resort area. He might have joined the men who used to come annually to Indy to try anew for the Big Apple. Certainly the dangers of the sport might have taken him at some other venue as it did Gordon at Legion Ascot in January 1936, in the race that closed that track once and for all. Both Gordon and mechanic Spider Matlock died in that one. But Ernie Triplett was the kind of talent that always makes one wonder how far he would have gone if he had been born 25 years later.

WOLFGANG VON TRIPS

The car screeched to a halt inches in front of the body on the road. The driver jumped out and dragged the inert form to safety, then raced back to pull from the road some dangerous pieces of the battered and burning car that had careened off the wall moments before. When the ambulance crew came on the scene, they found the 2nd driver waiting beside the injured one, his first aid completed and an improvised shelter erected against the pelting rain. With their appearance, the 2nd driver hopped back into his Ferrari and roared away to do combat once again in the gruelling Le Mans 24-hour race. This was 1958, and the Good Samaritan was Count Wolfgang Graf Berghe von Trips. Some also called him Count von Crash, and the nickname became a prophetic one at Monza several years later.

Trips was born May 4, 1928, in a 50-room family castle near Cologne, Germany. By 1945 he had enough

mechanical knowledge to patch up an Opel 6 and keep the car running another 2 years with baling wire and chewing gum, no doubt borrowed from friendly American soldiers. Then, as later, Trips (nicknamed Taffy) was a frail-looking, hawk-nosed man with a ready smile. He traded the car for a 2500-c.c. JAP British motorcycle on which he started competing in trials and cross-country events. After a spill and a resulting broken arm, the cycle was sequestered by his parents and included in a deal for a surplus U.S. Army Jeep. Wolfgang himself was hustled off to attend an agricultural college so he could properly learn how to manage the family estates. He immediately traded away a number of the niceties of life given him by his parents for another cycle, a BMW that had seen better days, and he returned to competition.

Trips next acquired a battered old Porsche in which he entered a couple of rallies and won one. On the strength of this, the always confident youngster called the Porsche factory to see if they might be willing to give him some parts in return for the publicity value. Instead, Baron Huschke von Hanstein, Porsche's racing director, offered Trips a drive in the 1954 Mille Miglia, "I said, 'Mille Miglia? What's that?' " Trips later recalled. The explanation apparently did not frighten the German because he entered the race, and although he had never done better than 80 m.p.h. before and had never seen the route before, he managed a class victory. Taffy continued driving occasional races for Porsche and Mercedes, meanwhile completing his schooling with honors. His father enrolled him in a Munich bank to learn finance, and other prerequisites for running the family

lands; but the bank made the mistake of giving him a leave of absence to run the 1955 Le Mans race, and he never returned.

Trips did not run the race, being held in reserve, but his practice laps led to a Mercedes sports car ride in the Swedish GP in which his brakes gave out and put his car into a stray bale. He did share a Mercedes that year in the Tourist Trophy and shared Porsche class victories at Le Mans, Avus, Nurburgring, and Sebring, giving him the German Championship. In 1956 the improving pilot won the Berlin GP in a Porsche RS at 126.6 m.p.h. Trips also had his initial Ferrari ride that season, taking a 2nd in the Swedish GP with Peter Collins.

In an expansive moment Enzo Ferrari offered the sports car driver a chance to try a Formula 1 car at Monza. Trips went all out, but just as he was accelerating out of the Curva Grande at 125 m.p.h., the steering arm snapped, sending the car toward the wrong side of of the track into the forest and right at a huge tree. " 'You're dead, Trips,' I said to myself," Wolfgang recalled later, "but the car merely lost one side to that tree and then the other side to another tree. The naked chassis then dug into the ground and flipped end over end. I was thrown clear at the first flip and landed on soft ground. When I could smell the dirt, I said to myself: 'Trips, you're not dead.' "

He was back driving—in Germany—2 weeks later, winning 2 races, although his right arm, badly mauled, was strapped to his side. That kind of courage prompted Ferrari to offer Taffy a GP ride for the rest of 1957. His best showings were 3rd in the Italian and Venezuelan Grands Prix. He was also 2nd in the Mille Miglia, the race in which Alfonso de Portago was killed, ending that series. In 1958 Trips was 3rd in the French GP, Juan Fangio's last race, and shared a 3rd in the Targa Florio and a 2nd in the Argentine 1000. In the Italian GP, he drove his car up the back of Harry Schell's BRM. Harry escaped, but Trips's leg was broken.

In 1959 Trips did not drive for Ferrari, but Porsche offered him cars for a number of races along with his own entries. At Sebring for the 12-hour race, Taffy and Jo Bonnier shared a 3rd, and the same team took a 2nd at the Goodwood version of the Tourist Trophy. Count von Crash's unlikely GP jinx continued in races like Monaco where his Porsche F1 car collided with Cliff Allison's Ferrari, causing both cars to crash. But he won the Berlin GP again at 121.73, to lead a Porsche sweep, and took the Formula Junior Eifelrennen in a Stanguellini.

The following season he demonstrated that he had matured as a driver, taking a 2nd in the German GP, a Formula 2 race, for Porsche and taking a 3rd for Ferrari in a similar class at Modena. His 102.22-m.p.h. average won the Solitude F2 GP for Porsche, and his 100.95 m.p.h. average took Syracuse for Ferrari. Driving a Lotus in the South African GP, he was 3rd, and he shared 2nds with Richie Ginther in the Argentine 1000 and with Phil Hill in the Targa Florio, both rides in Ferraris.

Trips went back on Ferrari's F1 team in 1961, along with Hill, and the pair were to contend for the World Championship for almost the entire year. Except for 2 virtuoso performances by Stirling Moss at Monaco and Nurburgring, the 2 Ferrari pilots dominated the GP circus. Hill won in Belgium at 128.15 m.p.h., Trips taking 2nd. Taffy won in Holland at 96.21 and in Britain at 83.91, Hill taking 2nd in both races. Trips was 2nd to Moss in Germany, Hill 3rd. And Hill was 2nd to Moss at Monaco. Trips's Targa sports car victory, shared with Olivier Gendebien at 64.27, came in between, and going into Monza for the Italian GP September 10, 1961, Trips led Hill 34 points to 33 for the driving title. A victory there would cinch his crown despite what Hill might do at the United States GP, the only race left after Monza.

Hill was beside himself with worry over the race and the title chase, Trips was completely relaxed as he captured the pole. "We may be teammates," he was quoted as saying on the night before the race, "but one has to fight. I love to fight." Then, more philosophically, he added, "So far this year, there have been no crashes. It is pure luck. The line between maximum speed and victory and crashing is so thin—so thin." The day was hazy and hot, the track fast. There were 32 cars at the flag, and only one 6.2-mile lap of the Monza course had been run in the 267-mile battle when tragedy struck.

Trips slowed as he entered a curve, and Lotus's Jim Clark touched his car from behind. Trips lost control, the Ferrari dancing upwards at 130 m.p.h., bouncing off a rail and cutting back across the course and into the crowd. Fourteen spectators died as the Ferrari swept through them before bouncing back onto the course. Trips, too, was dead, his broken body covered by some scattered newspapers until the race was over as Hill had won not only the Italian GP, but the World Championship.

PICKO TROBERG

Born January 1, 1938, in Sundsvall, Sweden, the impressively mustachioed Picko Troberg was an architectural draftsman when he began to take a serious interest in auto racing in 1959. His initial competition drives were in his MG TF road car, but he himself considered his debut real competition machine, perhaps out of national pride, a SAAB in which he entered the 1960–61 ice racing circuit. In 1961 Troberg purchased a Lotus 20 Formula Junior car with which he had limited success, although he did score as high as 2nd at the August Roskilde races.

In 1962 Troberg switched to a Lola Mark 5 for the FJ races and improved noticeably in experience if not

placings. He managed a victory at Monza in July, winning by a mere 8/10 of a second. He was 2nd at Kanonloppet the following month, 3rd at Nurburgring in September's Trips Memorial Trophy Race. In a Mini-Cooper, meanwhile, Picko was winning regularly, and that same year he captured his initial championship, the Swedish title for up-to-1100-c.c. cars. The next year Troberg stayed with the Lola in FJ racing and won at Djurdgardsloppet, Karlskoga, and Budapest. He also was 2nd in the Vienna Grand Prix and 4th in the Lottery GP at Monza. In saloon car racing, the young Swede won several long-distance Swedish and Finnish Grand Touring races and scored 5 outright victories in national races to capture the up-to-1300-c.c. championship.

Troberg's work began to pay off in 1964. That year Picko won Swedish Saloon and GT titles with a dozen victories. In the Targa Florio he drove a Ferrari GTO and placed 2nd in his class and 9th overall. The Swede's 1964 Formula 3 season, his 1st in that Formula 1 incubator, was an impressive start. Picko piloted a Brabham to a 2nd at Caserta, won his heat the next weekend at Monza's Lottery Grand Prix, won at Nuremberg and Trieste-Opicina, and set a lap record (his 1st of 3 that season) at the German venue. At Roskilde he was 2nd, at Zolder 3rd, at Vallelunga for the Rome GP a heat winner and 2nd overall, and at Innsbruck a winner over the equally promising Jonathan Williams in the Tyrol GP.

In 1965 Picko warmed up with a Copenhagen Cup win at Roskilde and a 4th at Chimay in the GP des Frontières for the June Monza Lottery. He then won that race for his 1st major international success by a scant 3 yards in a 5-car-to-the-wire tussle. At Karlskoga soon after, he was 2nd by a mere 6/10ths of a second, setting both a race lap mark and an F3 lap mark at that track of 1:28.4 seconds. In between, the divorced Troborg, who operated a sports car showroom in Stockholm, set up still another showroom across town and established a tuning shop at Helsingfors, Finland. And he still had time, he claimed, for sailing and driving his MGB for pleasure.

While under contract to British Motors Corporation Sweden, AB, for 1966 to drive in all Swedish championship races, he also drove for Juan Manuel Fangio in the Argentinian Temporada races at the start of that year. Pretty far from home to defend his four 1965 championships—ice racing, 2 different saloon car crowns, and F3 —but Treborg thinks that experience is necessary to move up in racing. "F3 is a good training ground," he said, "for Formula One or any advanced series. You only have to remember that there is only a difference of 5 seconds between the F1 and F3 lap records at Monaco. And my ice-racing is excellent, not only for keeping my reflexes up to scratch all the year round, but for furthering my speed-control experience. The spiked tires demand a different kind of technique from that used on a road circuit, of course, but no kind of driving is 'bad' for you, if you really want to be a leading driver."

The "leading driver" won 75 of his 284 career starts in all types of racing, but never advanced beyond F3 in single-seaters, when he retired after the 1971 season. What he did do was inspire the likes of Ronnie Peterson, Reine Wisell, and others. That in itself was no mean accomplishment.

C. F. TROSSI

The Alfa ripped through the countryside, swerved onto a private road and roared toward a castle near the Italian village of Biella. Its horn sounded and an electrical drawbridge hummed into action, lowering a path across a moat. Count Carlo Felice Trossi, known as Didi, first president of Scuderia Ferrari, had arrived at his ancestral home.

Scuderia Ferrari was the Alfa Romeo racing team in 1932, the year that the Count started driving in selected contests. In the Mille Miglia, his 1st appearance, he shared 2nd with Antonio Brivio, another Italian nobleman. The following season Carlo really got going, winning the Florence sports car race at 44.74 m.p.h. and the Pescara-Targa Abruzzo race at 81.39. In the Bordino Grand Prix he was 2nd to Tazio Nuvolari, and again in the Alessandria GP. The Vichy GP fell to Trossi in 1934 at 49.86, the Biella race at 52.11, the Montreaux GP in Switzerland at 63 m.p.h. The Biella was Italy's initial road race, and Carlo drove its fastest lap, as he also did at Montreux. He was 3rd in the French GP and in the Italian GP, and he was 3rd again in the Nice GP when he ran out of fuel 200 yards from the finish and had to push his car across the line.

He had a bad season in 1935 and resigned the following year as Scuderia Ferrari's president, both to concentrate on his driving and also to give the future Commendatore a chance to assume that post. In the Vanderbilt Cup revival on Long Island Trossi was 6th, in the Pescara voiturette race; he trailed only Dick Seaman's Delage. And there were many voiturette victories in the Count's bag that season: the large-engine section of the Eifelrennen at 69.90 m.p.h.; the Lucca race at 56.84 m.p.h.; the Milan race at 55.97 m.p.h.; the Ciano Cup at 67.39 m.p.h., all in Maseratis. Lucca fell again in 1937 at 57.98 m.p.h.; and when the Count rejoined Ferrari's Alfa operation he won the Genoa race at 61.21 m.p.h. Only René Dreyfus beat him across the Florence finish line, but he won at Naples at 61.39. At Valentino he was 3rd and he retired in the Belgian GP.

There were few victories between 1938 and the end of racing with World War II, and the expectation was that Didi's racing days were over. But in 1946 he was back in the cockpit and winning—with the collusion of the Alfa team managers who flagged down Nino Farina and Achille Varzi to allow Trossi a win at 55.59 m.p.h. in the Milan GP. Perhaps they did it because in Europe's 1st great postwar race, the Grand Prix des Nations at

Geneva, Carlo came within 70 seconds of victory without anyone's help and was nipped at the end by Farina. In 1947 he was 3rd in the European GP at Spa to Jean-Pierre Wimille and Varzi, then won the Italian GP at 70.29 m.p.h., this time doing the nipping to Varzi. The Count won going away, with the race's fastest lap at 74.16.

In 1948 Trossi was obviously ill, but he kept driving. The year's bag included a 2nd in the Monza GP to Wimille, then a 90.81 m.p.h. victory over Wimille—by a scant 2 seconds—in that season's European GP. Didi did not drive in 1949, but entered a Milan clinic. Later that year he died of cancer. How good was he? In sports cars very good, and in single-seaters, on the right day, also very good. He was a driver who should be remembered more often.

BOB TULLIUS

The marks where Tullius hit the wall at Daytona International Speedway probably are long gone because he walked away from the crash, one of several unsuccessful rides in a Grand National car. His factory rides for Javelin in what NASCAR now calls its Grand American division were competent but it was Jim Pascal who showed how that car could win. Yet Tullius won SCCA Trans-American races at Sebring and Daytona and took the sedan class in the 12 hours of Marlboro. So it was not because of incompetence that Tullius was not a hero of professional racing.

He merely found out that he could be more successful in racing as an SCCA amateur than as a pro. Many times Tullius had won C Production national honor for British Leyland, one of his sponsors, and for Quaker State, his other major sponsor. Many times his Group 44, Inc., Triumph had been the best in the nation.

The picture should be clear. Group 44 Inc. is a corporation whose president is Bob Tullius. Group 44's chief asset is Bob Tullius. Sponsors pay Group 44 Inc. to campaign their car and their oil. Group 44 lets Tullius do it. Tullius did it quite well considering that his competition was Porsche and Datsun. Born in Rochester, N.Y., in 1935, Tullius was built like a professional fullback and had the looks of a cowboy hero before John Wayne changed the image of what a hero cowboy should look like. An Air Force veteran, Tullius hurt his knee playing football later, and in 1961 at age 26, turned to racing a TR3. The Grand National attempts followed 3 years later, probably too soon for a graduate of amateur road racing, but Tullius looked like a driver to Buck Baker and other Dixie heroes.

But amateur racing is supposed to be for trophies. For Tullius and for other racing team directors like Pete Brock, Bob Sharp, Richie Ginther, and Ray Caldwell it is a professional competition. Sports car makers in the U.S. found that racing sells sports cars even if it may not have the same effect on the people who purchase wheels merely to avoid the necessity of walking. The need is to win. If you do not win, you lose sponsorship.

Thus it is just as necessary for the TR6 of Tullius to win as it is for Richard Petty's Plymouth to win, or Al

Unser's Johnny Lightning Ford, or Jackie Stewart, or anyone. Just as necessary, and maybe more difficult. By 1971 it could be fairly said that the important SCCA amateur races were contests staged as much for the benefit of Madison Avenue advertising people as for the edification of the competitors. The best-prepared cars were competing courtesy of factory money and the factory money was given to allow the word weavers an exciting chance to create favorable images.

At one time Tullius had wanted to progress to Formula 1; then he talked about a top big-bore sports car ride or a NASCAR career. By 1971, a better driver than he had ever been, he now talked mostly about getting enough sponsors of various sorts to make racing truly profitable. It's a funny situation; the top amateurs worry about money more than the top pros. The shades of the Collier brothers and those others who founded SCCA as an organization for gentlemen who race cars *pour le sport*—and not a mention of money—must whirl in dismay.

CURTIS TURNER

The modern auto-racing driver is likely to be a serious young man committed to the proposition that driving racing cars quickly is how he wants to survive in the complex civilization of western man. There may be parties and fun, but they do not interfere with the main passion, automobile racing.

Curtis Turner never let automobile racing interfere with the parties and the fun. In fact, there were times when he went from one of his marathon parties straight to the race track. If the lack of sleep affected his driving perception it was not apparent. Turner was a remarkable man, although he was never quite as remarkable as the legend which grew around him.

The Turner legend flourished because he rose out of the whiskey-running early days of stock-car racing to fender-smashing, broadsliding stardom when NASCAR was organized. Born April 12, 1924, in Floyd, Va., Turner learned 2 vocations early—the lumber business and driving an automobile. There is no recorded proof that he ever drove the modified Fords carrying illegal liquor because he never was booked on police blotters, but legends of his expertise in this respect were too numerous to have no basis in fact. He was certainly a master at controlling an automobile. Once, as much for his own edification as for that of onlookers, he lined up 8 full bottles of liquor on the roadway in a double row barely wider than the Cadillac with which he proposed to execute a tail-sliding 180 degree turn to slide backwards between the bottles. He performed the maneuver, then got out and drawled, "It was easy. I couldn't waste all that good liquor."

Turner was 6 feet 2 inches tall, weighed about 220, and believed implicitly that he could succeed at any-

Lorenzen famous. Curtis and Fearless Freddie came into the final lap neck and neck, fender to fender. Who started the fender banging was forgotten in what looked like a minor demolition derby all around the 1⅜-mile track. Freddie got in the last bash and crossed the finish line on top. On the extra safety lap, Turner plowed into Lorenzen, smashing the front of his own car to bits. He walked back to the pits.

Turner starred for Oldsmobile from 1950 through 1954, then switched to Ford. With Lorenzen, he was a star driver for Holman & Moody when the spirit moved him. Billed originally as the "Blond Blizzard from Virginia," Turner earned the new nickname "Pops" because he popped foes off the track with great abandon. Turner returned to NASCAR competition because he needed the money. He had met his Charlotte obligations even though he had to work for some time merely for the creditors.

Now it was 1965 and old Pops was back to provide copy for the sportswriters. Rockingham, N.C., International Speedway was probably the kind of track Turner should have tried to build—high-banked, a mile long, the shortest and in some ways the toughest of the NASCAR superspeedways. Richard Petty had the pole and Turner, competing despite a broken rib, was back in 4th place in his Glenn Wood Ford, actually the number 2 car for regular Wood driver Marvin Panch.

A broken rib had not cut down Curtis's partying, and he arrived on race day in what he considered the proper condition to race. "If you feel bad enough before you start to race, nothin' that can happen can bother you," he used to say, his sunglasses hiding his eyes. He was in top form. A contender from the beginning, he fought off men whose fathers had once been his competition, giving them a driving lesson, too. If they tried to pass beneath, he would force them too low to retain speed. If they took the high road, he gave them the choice of hitting him or the wall. In fact, he was driving so hard he scraped the outer wall twice himself. Finally it was between the idol of the young, Cale Yarborough, and Turner. Lap after lap the two raced, Pops staying a car-length or less ahead, fighting off every Yarborough probe, every Yarborough feint. It remained thus until 50 laps had passed, then Cale was forced to back off for the last time, and Turner had won his most lucrative victory —$13,090.

He came back the following February to win the Permatex 300, the World Series of modified racing, in a Ford sportsman at Daytona. Then he and Smokey Yunick collaborated on a Chevelle briefly. After Turner had a particularly hair-raising crash at Atlanta, Yunick ended the association, declaring, "I will not build the car that Curtis Turner was killed in." After that, Turner raced infrequently, coming out of what had to pass for retirement when the price was right. The parties still went on, but for the 2nd or 3rd time in his life he had found a woman who meant something to him, and he had

thing. He didn't, but his achievements both in racing and out had a Bunyanesque quality to them. When he failed, he failed big. Turner made and lost and remade several fortunes buying and selling timberlands. Charlotte International Speedway was his idea and somehow, with hardly enough money to cover the cost of the property, he got it built, only to lose it soon afterwards. Convinced, after this sojourn to the owners' side, that the NASCAR drivers were getting a shabby deal, Turner attempted to organize the drivers as a local of the Teamsters Union. He failed utterly and was banished for life by NASCAR, a banishment that was to be rescinded by Bill France after 5 years when NASCAR needed the magic of the Turner name to ride over a rough spot when Chrysler quit. In one of the early Pan American Road races, Turner's driving expertise probably had saved France's and his own life when, faced with a plunge off a cliff, Curtis stopped the car by grinding the frame into the rock.

Seventeen Grand National victories are credited to Turner but, in one year (1956) on the now-discontinued NASCAR convertible circuit, Curtis won 22 and added the Southern 500 for good measure. He was credited with winning some 360 races, in NASCAR and out. During his suspension he tried USAC cars, invariably breaking them. Turner was a fearsome competitor, thinking nothing of forcing a rival into the fence, or spinning him out, or even driving straight into the side of his car.

Perhaps the most famous fender-bashing episode was in the 1961 Rebel 300 when Turner helped make Fred

married her. His new wife wasn't as old as his oldest daughter.

Turner was about to come out for the National 500 at Charlotte when his plane crashed against a mountainside near Punxsutawney, Pa., October 5, 1970, killing him. A passenger, golf pro Clarence King, also died. Friends conjectured that in return for golf lessons, Turner was teaching King, a recovered heart attack victim, how to fly. King, they think, may have been at the controls and suffered a heart seizure. Then Turner failed to regain control of the plane in time. His wife was expecting a child at the time of his death.

STUART TURNER

When the Continent's motoring professionals gathered at the Brussels Show in January 1971, they peered intently at the Ford Motor Company exhibit and shook their heads. For a company whose parent American corporation had renounced racing at the end of 1970, Ford had an attractively-styled and potent-looking new motor car sitting there, and a few moments of study indicated that the GT70, a slightly Opel-like conception, was something more than just a nice looking car. It was a serious rally car for beating out Porsche and Alpine competitors.

The new car was the brainchild of 2 men, both associated with Ford's European operations. One was Jochen Neerpasch, then competition manager for Ford of Germany and no mean long-distance driver himself in Porsches and other machinery for many a year. The other was Stuart Turner, once a leading British rally navigator. He was born January 14, 1933, and grew up to be just an ordinary accountant until his rally skills came to the fore. But that was after Turner's RAF service, during which he learned Russian among other languages, and decided that rallying as a professional not only was more fun but probably a lot more lucrative than accountancy—for in Europe rallying is a big-time sport, not a weekend club diversion as in the United States.

Turner served as navigator and codriver to such luminaries as Erik Carlsson, and became part of the factory teams of Auto Union, Mercedes Benz, Saab, Triumph, and BMC. He wrote a book on rallying and tried his hand with an auto racing newspaper in Britain before he found just the right niche for his talents. That niche was at BMC as competition manager, and he took over that job on October 1, 1961, when the Abingdon-on-Thames effort was at the height of its glory—Monte Carlo Rally, Tulip, Alpine, Liège, BAC, Tour de France, Acropolis, Spa-Sophia-Liège, all the major events fell to Turner's BMC forces.

He left BMC 6 years to the day after he had come, for there were no new worlds to conquer, and the company was retrenching. Castrol Oil needed a publicity and advertising director, but Turner was not happy in a post that far from competition. British Ford came up with a better opportunity, a combination of publicity and rallymaster called competition manager, and he moved over there, rising to the overall Ford of Europe post a few years later. In 1972 Turner became head of Ford's AVO—Advanced Vehicles Operations—at Aveley, England, as well as director of motor sports with European interest in competition of all kinds growing, even American Ford's withdrawal from racing could not stop the competitive urge that produced the GT70 in minds like Stuart Turner's.

KEN TYRRELL

He made it all sound simple. Cut and dried. "I'm a round timber merchant. I buy the trees in their raw state, you see. I work at that from Monday to Thursday, and then I take a long weekend. During my time off, I work at the other thing. One never really interferes with the other."

R. Kenneth Tyrrell was the only private entrant to sponsor a World Champion—Jackie Stewart. And he was the only one to have graduated, as it were, to car construction in the name of keeping his private effort going, as witness the Tyrrell-Ford born in 1970 and World Champion in 1971.

Born March 5, 1924, Ken once raced himself, back in 1952–57. There was a mini-formula back in those days called Formula 3—500-c.c. cars—that featured up-and-coming drivers like Sterling Moss and P. J. Collins, as well as some old fellows out for a last fling like Reg Parnell and Sydney Allard. Tyrrell did not fit either category.

His Cooper-Norton was not remembered so much for its visits to victory lane as for its axe-blade insignia, which may have explained Ken's nickname of Chopper Tyrrell. He did win a couple of Formula Junior races; Karlskoga 1955, for sure. Then there was a stretch in a Formula 2 Cooper-Climax. And an offer to drive Aston Martin sports cars, but he stood aside for Moss. Alan Brown needed a manager for his F2 Cooper team, and Tyrrell was elected. His last race was a dice (that he lost) to Bruce McLaren, who was one of the 1st drivers the manager signed up.

In 1960 Tyrrell started his own FJ team with 2 Coopers. His driver list with Brown's team had been an impressive one—McLaren, Masten Gregory, Jack Brabham, Innes Ireland, Ron Flockhart, Jean Lucas, and even Carrol Shelby. On his own team, the list became equally impressive. John Surtees drove his 1st race in a Tyrrell FJ Cooper.

In those early FJ and F3 days, other Tyrrell drivers included Henry Taylor, Tony Maggs, John Love, Stewart, and Jacky Ickx, much later on. Taylor, who became British Ford's competition manager, won Tyrrell his initial personal team victory at Monaco in 1960 in the FJ race. He had a personal tragedy in those years, too. Tim Mayer, brother of Team McLaren's Teddy, an

American from Philadelphia's Main Line, drove for Tyrrell and, while he never won a race, he was a favorite of Ken's. The sponsor took Tim's death in the 1964 Tasman series very hard.

Fortunately, he had another favorite son at the time, Stewart, who had signed on with a handshake, not a pen, the year before. Jackie cleaned up F3 in Tyrrell's Cooper-BMC's in 1964, moved over to Formula 1 with BRM in 1965, although staying with Ken for F2. It was that season that the winning combination for 1969 was forged. At an awards dinner in Paris, Tyrrell and Matra chief Jean-Luc Lagardere talked informally about a test drive of a new Matra chassis powered by a BRM engine. "I was skeptical at first. I'd seen lots and lots of rather sloppy French cars," Tyrrell later recalled. "But I didn't want to be impolite, and each time I tried to suggest why the test couldn't be carried out, he would come up with a soluion. In the end, he arranged to fly the car, ready to go, to England within the week, and when I got back, I called Jackie and told him I had a car for him to test.

"He asked what it was, and I told him a Matra, a French car. 'Guid God, Ken,' he said, 'what are you getting involved in now? I thought you knew better than that.' But when he tried out the Matra, he raved over it, and I was rather impressed, too." Tyrrell ran the Matra factory F2 team in 1966–67, but Team Brabham, aided by Jochen Rindt in the latter season, dominated the lists, although both Stewart and Ickx won races. In 1968 Jackie joined Ken for F1, Matra having built a chassis just for that purpose to take the Cosworth Ford power plant, although the factory was committed to an all-French F1 car.

Tyrrell might have sponsored the World Champion in 1968, save for Stewart's broken wrist in an F2 race. As it was, the Scot finished 2nd to Graham Hill. He was not denied in 1969 when he dominated F1. Tyrrell and Stewart wanted Ford power again in 1970, and thus they walked away from the Matra chassis for a new March one. But Ken is never one to do things half way. Even before the season's first race, he had visions of his own car, and despite some early Stewart successes in the March, the project moved ahead. When the March started to falter, Tyrrell was ready. By the last 3 races of the 1970 season, an interim Tyrrell car was ready. It was not able to bring Stewart victory again, but 1971 was a different story. Stewart and Tyrrell took their 2nd championship. The long weekends of the round timber merchant are likely to continue for some time to come, with Jackie and François Cevert, Tyrrell's colorful number 2.

RUDI UHLENHAUT

A stocky, pleasant man who is said to have demonstrated several times that he was faster than Juan Manuel Fangio or Stirling Moss, but who never competed in an actual automobile race, was Rudi Uhlenhaut, Director of Engineering (passenger cars) for Daimler Benz, AG, of Stuttgart and previously Mercedes's director of racing. Born in July 1906 in London, of an English mother and German bank-manager father, Rudi and 3 other Uhlenhaut children grew up in Belgium and Germany as his father was transferred from place to place. Thus Rudi spoke perfect German, English and French. "I always knew I wanted to be an engineer," he said later, with a faint smile playing on his lips, "though when I was very young I had things mixed up a bit and thought I wanted to be a locomotive engineer." Things must have been sorted out in his mind early on, however, because he headed straight toward mechanical engineering and, upon graduation with an advanced degree in Munich in 1931, he joined Mercedes.

The Depression had hit Germany and jobs were few and far between, so Rudi's abilities even at the age of 24 must have been outstanding. Mercedes had made an excellent choice. Uhlenhaut moved quickly from engineering production cars to experimental work. By 1934 business had begun to pick up in Germany, and Mercedes felt ready to return to Grand Prix racing, which it once had dominated. Uhlenhaut, however, was not involved in the 1934–35 effort that saw the 3-pointed star of Mercedes flash again in the victory circle. He joined the racing department in the autumn of the following year, after a season that saw Mercedes plummet from its previous successes as its new cars were beaten at almost every turn. At the command of the 30-year-old Rudi were 300

top engineers, technicians and race personnel. In 1937 and the following 2 seasons, when the FIA's formula changed, Mercedes cars won 19 of the 28 GP races held (Auto Union won all the rest but one). Various Uhlenhaut touches had added up to a complete reversal of the disastrous 1936 season.

A major factor in Rudi's success was his decision, just after he took over responsibility for racing, to test the cars himself at the Nurburgring. "I went with a few mechanics," he recalled, "and a couple of the supercharged racing cars. I made my first circuit of the course at a speed slower than I would have driven a passenger car, then drove both machines hard until they broke."

After 2,000 miles of high-speed driving, Rudi said, he had "some idea" of what a racing car was and should be able to do. He continued driving the team cars at top speeds, despite admonitions from the Mercedes management, and often lapped various courses at only fractions of a second slower than Rudi Caracciola and other regular team drivers. But he never wished to participate in an actual race.

"The first time I drove at racing speed I was 30, and that's a bit late to start. Yes, and then it would have been a waste of an engineer. We need engineers as well as drivers, you know. That's the same reason why I never went to my limit, I don't think. I always tried to be on the safe side."

The 1939 season was the last before World War II ended racing for many years. Uhlenhaut stayed at Mercedes during the war, developing cold-weather army vehicles, then managing one of the satellite aircraft engine plants which Daimler Benz developed after Allied bombing began to level their regular Stuttgart and Sindelfingen factories. At the war's end, his command of the English language was put to use when the British Army hired him to work with their engineers on various rebuilding projects.

In 1948 Daimler Benz returned to automobile production and Rudi rejoined the company as chief of its experimental department. It took 3 years of hard work to put the company in a position to go racing again, but when it happened Uhlenhaut was ready.

The introduction of the famous Uhlenhaut-inspired gull-winged Mercedes 300SL in 1952 was a smashing success; the car won 4 of the 5 races that led to the new sports car championship. Attention in the racing department was then turned to GP competition. In 1954 a team of beautifully streamlined cars appeared in the hands of drivers headed by Fangio himself. These won 4 of the 6 races in which they were entered and took the title hands down. The following year, when Moss joined the team, Mercedes swept the GP, sports car and European touring car championships. Rudi, meanwhile, again was testing the cars himself, along with Fangio, Moss and the others, and very nearly matched their best times at most circuits although he was 5 years older than the Argentinian and 25 years older than the Englishman. A few years after Moss had left Mercedes, he said that Uhlenhaut was "among the most brilliant drivers living today."

Americans had only infrequent glimpses of Rudi's driving skills. Some years ago, for example, a group of automotive newsmen were gathered at Daytona International Speedway for a series of demonstrations that included a ride with Rudi in a 1955 Mercedes sports/racing car. Circling the high-banked oval at something like 140 m.p.h., the car suddenly made a frightening lurch. Uhlenhaut, who had been driving as if he were out for a Sunday ride, did not seem overly concerned, but slowed to 80 m.p.h. or so, observing coolly, "One of our tires lost a tread. Wondered about those. Not right for this circuit." He finished the run without mussing a hair, which is more than you could say for the writers in the car.

ALEC ULMANN

It is the Russians' own fault that Leningrad today is not graced with the presence of a remarkable man who was born there June 16, 1903. The city would perhaps have become the site of a race course of world significance—an honor that fell instead to Sebring, Fla., and Road Atlanta, Ga. Alexander Edward Ulmann, known as Alec, was the son of a family that apparently owned one of the 1st motor cars in St. Petersburg. In 1909 the Ulmanns watched Victory Hemery achieve 134.2 m.p.h. in a 14-litre Benz on a special straight section of road near the Czar's summer palace, Krasno Selo. That Ulmann's appetite for adventure might be due in part to heredity was demonstrated when his father insisted upon driving that day, at the risk of his family's life and limb and greatly shocking the chauffeur. The senior Ulmann's 1st exploits behind the wheel apparently caused considerable consternation on the road and, at least to his family, was more thrilling than Hemery's run.

Such exploits may sow seeds that sprout into unforseen dragons. The chauffeur, Vasili, gave Alec lessons on the family Benz Landaulette; by the age of 10 the boy was an accomplished driver. The 1st Cadillac V-8 arrived in St. Petersburg in 1915, equipped with an electric starter motor. This alone convinced Alec that somewhere among the red Indians and cowboys across the ocean there must be wizards of engineering. America, he thought, was certainly the land of the future.

The boy spent several years in a Swiss prep school after the Bolsheviks drove the family from Russia, then attended Harvard and the Massachusetts Institute of Technology, from which he holds a master's degree in aeronautical engineering. Holder of a 1930 pilot's license, he sold aviation products for a variety of concerns, mostly in Europe, and indulged his passion for auto racing, principally as a spectator.

Before World War II Ulmann was a member of the old American Racing Car Association, which staged gentlemen's races at Briarcliff, Alexandria Bay, and Montauk Point, N.Y. After the war he was among the original 200 members of the SCCA and formulated the original book of racing rules. He helped organize and was Chief Steward of the original Watkins Glen, Bridgehampton, Floyd Bennett, and Westhampton road races in New York as well. Then came Sebring, the international endurance contest that he conceived, nurtured, and dominated ever after. Alec split with the SCCA after the 1st event in 1950. The SCCA still clung to the "racing for gentlemen" (i.e. members only) concept at that time, while Ulmann correctly gauged the huge potential of road racing in America and insisted on FIA rules.

In 1939, in England, Alec married Mary Foote, who had organized the Schneider Cup seaplane races of that era. Without this liaison there might have been no Ulmann saga nor any Sebring 12-Hour Race. Mary Ulmann was the financial organizer behind Alec's racing efforts, although the elder of their 2 sons, Edward and Alec, Jr., was involved. She was treasurer of A. E. Ulmann Associates, which deals in aircraft parts.

It is not easy to create, develop, and retain control of an international race, especially one of such exotic appeal as a 12-hour enduro. Ulmann dealt with his problems in 2 ways. First, he built a loyal organization that included Reggie Smith, timer Joe Lane, publicist Fred Kingsbury, Jr., prominent residents of Sebring, and many others. Second, he was, over the years, quite successful in finding commercial backers, such as Martini & Rossi, Alitalia Airlines, various car companies, Castrol, and Amoco.

Over the years, too, Ulmann strengthened his ties within the CSI, sporting arm of the FIA, so that he had at least an even chance in one of his most difficult fights. When the ubiquitous Bill France decided to create the Daytona 2000-Kilometer out of what had been an insignificant Speed Week event, Ulmann sought to ban courses with banking from consideration as championships. He obviously lost but not before what was reported as a bitter battle within the CSI. He made his peace and coexisted with Daytona, and in 1972, when France ended his 24-hour race for a 6-hour affair in overly quick compliance with proposed CSI rule changes, Ulmann held the line and preserved the 12-hour Sebring battle (along with the Le Mans 24-hour event). In the end, then, he may have won after all, but his attention then was on creating a new "Sebring" race at Road Atlanta and vacating the long-criticized airport site of his famed race.

AL UNSER

"Wait until Al gets started; he's the ultimate Unser." That was the family's opinion of the youngest member the famous racing clan. There was a certain preoccupation with Pikes Peak; after all, the family came originally from Switzerland. Al, however, never really made a fetish of the mountain where uncle Louis won 9 times, where another uncle was killed testing a new car for the climb, and where brother Bobby won 11 times in 3 divisions. Al won in 1964 and 1965, but he never really wanted to do anything except beat brother Bobby, who had worked with him and taught him how to drive a race car.

The real track hero of the Unser family might have been brother Jerry Jr., but he was killed at Indianapolis in 1959. Jerry's twin, Louie, who contracted multiple sclerosis, became a competition boat engine builder. Jerry's death affected each of the Unser brothers differently. Bobby punished the cars under him, charging all the time. Al became introspective, studying driving technique as if it were something that could be put under the microscope. He was smooth, a thinker, although Bobby hardly could be called a sloppy driver.

Born May 29, 1939, Al was 5 years younger than Bobby, and the brothers remained very close. For Bobby the training grounds were the roadster circuit; for Al it was Supermodified cars. From 1957 through 1963 he ran the Supermods on weekends, trying to support his

young wife and family during the week with the proceeds of a junk yard his father had bought him. He also moved into USAC midgets in 1964 and for one race in 1965, earning 1.30 points and 144th place in the season standings. Yet it was also in 1965 that he began his climb to the USAC National Championship.

Al had passed his rookie test at Indy in an experimental Maserati which proceeded to blow its only engine in mid-month. A. J. Foyt found him and asked if he would try to qualify the Sheraton-Thompson back-up Lola-Ford. Al's despair turned to ecstasy and, after getting pointers on the car's idiosyncrasies from A. J., he qualified 32nd. He drove steadily to finish 9th overall. For 1965 Al competed in 13 national championship races but won only Pikes Peak.

In 1966, around mid-April, Al heard of a vacancy on the Team Lotus *équipe* for Indianapolis and applied for it. Again he drove a steady race, finishing 12th this time. On the Championship Trail he had three 2nd-place finishes. For 1967 he was 2nd choice to Larry Dickson for the number 2 car to Jackie Stewart on the John Mecom team. Dickson tried out the Lola-Ford and decided he wasn't interested, so Al got the ride. The youngest Unser finished a distant 2nd after miraculously getting through that year's 1st-lap holocaust. But the beginnings of a new phase of his driving career were starting. Al had come under the influence of chief wrench George Bignotti. Under George's direction Al began to diagnose what was lacking in his car, and learned how to tell George about it.

Bignotti worked patiently with Unser all of 1967, knowing that if he could add to his driving ability the skill of helping to make the car mechanically perfect, Bignotti would have the ingredients of a championship team once more. Driving a Lola-Ford in 1968, Al took a 2nd place at Hanford, Calif., then qualified 6th for Indy only to be involved in a wreck when a wheel spindle broke on his 4-wheel drive car. But this was the year he finally won his 1st Championship Trail event, USAC's 1st-ever night race. This wire-to-wire victory was at Nazareth, Pa., a dirt mile oval. He also doubled with victories at IRP and Langhorne.

For a year that ended with a 2nd place in the USAC national title standings, 1969 started inauspiciously. The Bignotti-Al Unser team had joined forces with Vel Miletich and Parnelli Jones, with a little STP money on the side. Al had a 4-wheel drive car ready and waiting for Indy when a bit of foolishness exacted a heavy price. Playing motorcycle games with Parnelli, Al fell, broke a leg, and seemed sure to have lost the whole season. But he returned with a vengeance, winning 5 of the final 6 races and placing 2nd in the other. Pavement, dirt, or road course, it didn't matter—Al was the hot one. He won Milwaukee easily. A broken suspension member failed to stop him at Sacramento, rain failed to stop him at Seattle, a 4-car crash that bunched the field failed to halt him at Phoenix. The 5th victory came at DuQuoin, Ill. And in the Rex Mays 300 at Riverside he finished a close 2nd to Mario Andretti. What turned him on was apparently a monumental feeling of guilt. "I felt I had let the team down with that stupid accident," he said.

For 1970 the element that made Al perhaps the best-known driver since Oldfield was added. Announcement of the Johnny Lightning model car toy sponsorship was held off until the Toy Show and a cartoon debut on TV. Al promptly proved the worth of his contract by winning at Phoenix. Then he took a 2nd at Sears Point Calif. and a 3rd at Trenton. His Indianapolis victory was easily won; he led 190 of the 200 laps. Qualifying at 170.221 m.p.h., he commented, "It's scary," but afterwards, "I drove a conservative race." Al earned $271,698 for the Johnny Lightning team.

Al kept on winning all season on all kinds of tracks to take the national championship with 10 victories out of a possible 18. He won Indianapolis Raceway Park in the rain, took a muddy Springfield dirt track race, and won on the dirt at DuQuoin, Sedalia, and Sacramento, too. He won Milwaukee by 3 laps and had lapped his brother Bobby in the Trenton 300 when it was shortened to 176 miles because of showers. And he was leading the 1st Ontario 500 by a comfortable margin when the turbocharger broke 14 laps from the finish, sidelining him.

Al started the 1971 season south of the border at Rafaela, Argentina by winning the Rafaela 300 easily. He finished 1st in both heats, beating Lloyd Ruby each time. At Phoenix Al came from behind to beat brother Bobby for top money; then, after Trenton went to Mike Mosely, Al won his 2nd Indianapolis 500 in a row.

It was a typical Unser victory. Supremely confident in his Vel's-Parnelli turbocharged Ford, Al never dropped lower than 4th. Mark Donohue had led the first 50 laps only to yield to Joe Leonard, then Bobby Unser before taking the lead back. Al moved into the lead for laps 67 through 72 and Donohue went out; Al found himself battling his teammate Leonard. The lead seesawed back and forth, Lloyd Ruby holding it for a few laps and brother Bobby for 8 more. Leonard had a few more laps in the lead on a caution flag but soon after was out of the race. From there on in the race was Al's as he averaged 157.735 m.p.h for his $283,454 winnings. Then Al edged Leonard the next week at Milwaukee, winning the Rex Mays Classic before a record crowd, but those were his only season victories except for the Hoosier Hundred on a dirt track.

The Vel's-Parnelli team entered 1972 with 3 national champions—Al, Leonard, and Mario Andretti. If the Maurice Phillippe-designed Parnelli Offenhausers were at all potent under the direction of George Bignotti that would be an epic chapter in American racing. But in '72 the victories for Al were inconsistent although he finished 2nd to Leonard for the USAC Trail title.

BOBBY UNSER

The Unser family has a long tradition of racing. Robert William, born February 20, 1934, and brother Al were among the brightest. Bobby was undisputed king of the Pikes Peak hillclimb, winning the championship division in 1956, coming in 5th in 1957, then stringing together 6 straight victories over the twisting road up the mountain. Al then beat him twice in a row before he won again. The boy's father and 2 uncles also raced. One, Louis, was still competing at Pikes Peak in 1967 at the age of 71.

Bobby chose to throw his fortunes in with IMCA and the CRA until late 1962 when he got a USAC ride at Sacramento. He failed to qualify. He dabbled in midget racing, winning 2 of 11 starts in 1963, one of 6 in 1964, before moving to sprints in 1965 for 3rd nationally. He won 3 of 20. Bobby had started by driving modified stocks around his home town, Albuquerque, N.M., when he was 15. In 1950 he won the state's Modified championship, repeated the next year at age 17, then turned to springs and midgets. A wiry 6-footer who looks as if he would be just as much at home bull-riding or steer-wrestling, Bobby drove with a ferocity that often was not matched by the mechanical capabilities of his car.

The Novis, with their screaming supercharged power, seemed the perfect mount, and Bobby drove them well but with bad luck at Indianapolis. The King of the

Mountain spun out of the 1963 Indianapolis race in the Hotel Tropicana Special, after qualifying this Novi at 149.421 m.p.h. He was sidelined in the 2nd-lap tragedy in the 1964 race, thus eliminating his Studebaker Novi-Ferguson 4-wheel drive car.

Pikes Peak was another matter. Hillclimbs have been an exotic tidbit in the American auto sports menu. They are not very good spectator events, for the cars are racing against the clock, one at a time, not against each other. It takes a good sense of timing, a sure hand, and complete fatalism to be a good hillclimb driver. A pair of blinkers may also help. With its wild turns and preciptious drops, the road up Pikes Peak requires long practice and a good memory. Asked once about his hillclimb technique, Unser declared: "I never look down. Besides, I never enter with the idea of falling off." He added that the whole idea was to take each curve in such a way as to set up for the next without losing time.

Actually, Bobby needed to win at the Peak because he said he was afraid of high places. "If I'm on the top floor of a house, I'm scared," he confided. "If I was ever to look down on that ride, I couldn't go on one inch. In 1967 I finished 5th, and I felt ashamed even if I did have a flat. You gotta give credit to Wes Vandervoort and those 3 guys who beat me, but I ran faster than their times years ago. I'll be back with 4 tires next year." He was, and he won.

It took USAC's 1967 foray into Canada to give Bobby his initial Championship Trail victory. Postponed once because of rain, the Telegram Trophy race had drawn 52,000 fans to Mosport to see a pair of heats under lowering skies. Bobby's Shaler Rislone Eagle-Ford was in fast company. He showed he was equal to it by staving off the furious challenge of Lloyd Ruby, the Continental and Le Mans hero, to win the 1st heat by little more than 15 seconds. Ruby, who had been the early leader, had blown a tire when he ran over a piece of metal. He spent a full minute in the pits for repairs, then made up 42 seconds on Bobby to finish 3rd. Roger McCluskey was even closer, barely a car length behind at the finish line.

The 2nd heat started under dark thunderclouds with a pack of very determined drivers. Mario Andretti was starting 21st because he had broken a half-shaft in the opening heat. McCluskey was angry with himself for not catching Bobby. Ruby, Al Unser, A. J. Foyt, and Arnie Knepper all knew they had a shot at victory because they had finished on the same lap as Bobby. But only 2 laps of the 2nd race were run when the rain came and lightening hit one of the course poles. Bobby was at the apex of a tightly bunched 6-car pack when the race was called after 6 laps, and even in that short time Andretti had made up 10 places. Bobby didn't mind at all. His rear end was failing, and it is doubtful whether he could have lasted the second 100. "Sometimes it's better to be lucky than brave," he said. "I guess I was a little of both."

In 1965 Unser was 19th at Indy, the next season 8th, in 1967 he was 9th. And then there was a new year in which everything seemed to come together for Unser on the Trail. With Jud Phillips as his chief wrench and driving a Bob Wilke-owned Leader Car Eagle-Offenhauser, Bobby took 5th in the opening race at Hanford, Calif., then won at the Stardust 150-mile road race at Las Vegas by 2 seconds over Mario Andretti in a close race-long, duel. Bobby continued with a victory in the Phoenix 150, then again beat Mario by 3 seconds at Trenton in what was really an easy race for his turbocharged Offy.

Indianapolis in 1968 was the year of the turbine again. Joe Leonard was the hero driver for STP and Andy Granatelli, and Bobby was among the most outspoken of the anti-progress forces. But Unser's Eagle chassis and the turbocharged Offy engine also showed progress. He could easily run with the turbine, handicapped by new rules. He led the turbine much of the race, until after the 400-mile mark. Ten laps from the finish he had resigned himself to 2nd, because Art Pollard, Leonard's teammate, was blocking him as Joe pulled farther ahead. Then Leonard's turbine gave out and Bobby Unser was an Indianapolis victor, something that had eluded his father, his uncles, his cousins, and his brothers. He received a hero's parade in Albuquerque, and he made $177,523.

Bobby did not run the dirt track stops, and on the paved tracks his usual Trail bad luck seemed to come back with a vengeance. He had seemed a shoo-in for the championship in July. After Trenton he led Andretti by

only 283 points, 3,301–3,018. This lead was cut as Bobby crashed during prerace practice at Sacramento, Calif., and Mario took 4th. The lead disappeared at the opening of the new Michigan Speedway as Mario won on a protest that he—not Bobby driving the Mike Mosely backup car—had finished 2nd to sports car ace Ronnie Bucknum. The score was 3,538 to 3,399 for Bobby. It was all over—or was it?

Hanford's 1.5-mile track, which looks like a zero that was caught in a strong wind, was to be the site of a no-holds-barred race among Leonard in the STP turbine, Foyt, Andretti, and Bobby. Each held the lead at some time. There were some remarkable pace car antics in which the wrong car was picked as leader during a caution period; then the pace car almost precipitated a crash by cruising blithely on after the green had dropped. Foyt sneaked past Unser late in the race. But Bobby held 2nd over Andretti to tighten the championship battle, 3,888–3,806. Both drove relief at Phoenix, and Mario got a 3rd to Bob's 9th. Then came the Rex Mays 300 at Riverside. As Bobby chased Dan Gurney around the road course that Gurney "owned," Mario reenacted the Perils of Pauline in an effort to finish high enough to save the title.

His own car stopped on the 58th lap, but Andretti's back-up car was already retired, so he replaced Leonard in the Parnelli Jones turbine. He quickly wiped out the turbine in a back-straight crash with the other turbine driven by Art Pollard. He leaped out of the car, started jogging toward the infield, but was picked up by Jones for a motorcycle ride back to pit row. Lloyd Ruby, who had a sure 3rd in the championship standings if he continued to run 3rd, was flagged in by crew chief George Bignotti, and his car was turned over to Mario. The diminutive ace had trouble reaching the pedals, but he held 3rd, though it was not good enough. Unser won with a record 4,326 points to Mario's 4,319.2, the closest title race in history. Both beat Dario Resta's 116-point record of 4,100 points.

Unser's 1969 beginning was inauspicious. He had lost 19 races over the 2 seasons before breaking into the victory column once again at the Langhorne 150. The victory marked his return to the Gurney Eagle chassis that had given him so much success the previous year. At Indianapolis he had driven a brand new Lola 4-wheel drive, powered by a turbocharged Offy; he had switched sponsorship from Shaler Rislone to Bardahl, but the car owner still was Bob Wilke and the mechanic Jud Phillips. The Lola suspension and 4-wheel drive were never sorted out. When the car was pushed hard through Indy's low-banked turn the left rear wheel would lift and spin, thus loading the right rear. Yet Bobby qualified 3rd at 169.963 m.p.h. and took 3rd in the race, despite making 2 extra pit stops to change right rear tires.

For Pikes Peak, Bobby moved into the stock-car class for the initial time and won in a Holman-Moody Ford. He took the same car to victory in the Milwaukee 200.

But the next half of the season belonged to brother Al as Bobby's ill luck seemed to have returned with a vengeance. Bobby's best rides were a 2nd to his brother in the Milwaukee 200 championship car race, a 3rd to his brother at Sacramento despite engine trouble, and a 4th at Riverside.

In 1970 Bobby lost the head-to-head duels with his little brother by 3 to 1, but he won the most exciting. It was at Langhorne, and brother Al had seemed an easy victor when a spin brought the caution flag out. The slow laps allowed Bobby's Goodyears to cool and on the 141st lap of the mile track he nipped by to take the lead. He managed to hold off Al's faster Johnny Lightning car for a 1-second victory. Al had beaten him in the USAC season opener at Phoenix by 25 seconds and had been more than a lap ahead of Bobby in the rain-shortened Trenton 300. In the Ted Horn 100, Al nipped Bobby by 6 seconds.

The 1971 season seemed to start the same way. Down in Rafaela, Argentina, Bobby was the king in practice, but Al won the race over the 2.87-mile Rafaela Autodromo. Bobby retired in the 3rd lap with a burned piston. Bobby's Dan Gurney Olsonite Eagle led almost every paved Marlboro Trail stop, including Indianapolis, but something mechanical always seemed to happen. At Indy Unser was 12th, after an 11th in 1970.

The Trenton 200 was different. The Offy-engined car was tuned to perfection, set up to perfection, and so strong that Bobby's flawless ride gave him an easy victory over Mario Andretti. He was more than 2 laps (or 3 miles) ahead, and his 140.771 m.p.h. average bettered the old record by more than 6 m.p.h.

There was no argument from anyone that car owner Dan Gurney had managed to give Bobby the fastest car in USAC in 1972. The trouble was that the Eagle usually wasn't around at the finish despite seven pole positions in a row, a string broken in Milwaukee at State Fair time. Bobby won the season opener at Phoenix and at the Rex Mays 150 in Milwaukee. He lasted 31 laps at Indianapolis, 77 laps at Pocono and 73 laps at Ontario. For 1973, it was a case of Gurney and Bobby figuring out how to keep the car together. If they could, the older Unser might well be USAC's rich man of the year.

NINO VACCARELLA

For true automotive competition, there must not only be a winner and some serious contenders, but a cast of others to round out the field, to provide occasional surprises, and even to assume leading roles from time to time. Nino Vaccarella, born in Palermo, Sicily, March 4, 1933, started as one of these, then became a leading player, especially in the endurance racing world. In Italy, every boy wants to be a racing driver. Vaccarella was one of the lucky ones who made it, which means more than ordinary skills. He became a regular in long-

distance endurance racing and even in Grand Prix competition for a time.

Vaccarella's family had intended him for a career in the law, and he studied at the Instituto Scolastico Oriani, but his mind was always on racing. He was obedient to family wishes until he was 24, when he made his debut in an Italian hillclimb, May 5, 1957. Nino's Lancia 2500 was 8th overall, but 2nd in its class. Two class victories in short traces and a 5th in the 6-hour Esso race followed that year. Vaccarella continued racing and climbing the Lancia until 1959, when he switched to a Maserati and scored 6 outright victories. For the 1st time, Nino contested the Targa Florio and finished 10th and 3rd in class.

In 1960, he dropped out of the Targa, but was 3rd in the Naples Grand Prix and 1st in the Bolzano-Mendola hillclimb. This concentration on GT and climbing events continued over two more seasons and led to his being generally overlooked when young Italian driving talent was being appraised. The Lorenzo Bandinis and Giancarlo Baghettis, who were competing in Formula Junior, were getting all the attention. That changed in April 1961, when Nino finished 4th in the Targa, sharing a Maserati Tipo 63 with Maurice Trintignant, the veteran French driver.

It all happened very quickly after that. Almost at once Vaccarella made his single-seater debut in a non-title Formula 1 event at Vallelunga and came in 3rd in the Coppa Italia. On September 10, 1961, he got his initial championship drive in the Scuderia Serenissima de Tomaso-Osca for the Italian GP. Nino went faster in practice than Bandini, but he retired from the race on

the 13th lap. In his important international sports car debut (the Targa being a "local" race for Vaccarella), Nino shared a 3rd with Trintignant in the Paris 1000, in which they codrove a Ferrari 250GT.

Vaccarella came to America in 1962, but the Maserati Tipo 64 he and Carlo Abate shared at the Sebring 12-Hour Race dropped out with gear linkage troubles. In practice for the Brussels GP, he crashed, but he was back on the starting line in the Pau GP, where he was 6th. In the Targa, Nino and Jo Bonnier, the veteran Swedish driver, shared a brilliant 3rd, employing a 2-litre Porsche that was a factory entry despite its private "sponsorship." He practiced for the Monaco GP, but an accident prevented a start there, and in the Nurburgring 1000, Abate, once again codriving a Ferrari with Vaccarella, damaged their car and ended their bid.

At Le Mans, Vaccarella and Giorgio Scarlatti shared a Ferrari GT and were well up among the leaders when retired at dawn. In the German GP, Nino finished 15th in a Porsche; in the Italian GP he dueled Bandini for much of the race, but the Lotus-Climax engine blew 2 laps from the finish. He was classified 9th on distance. In a Ferrari 3000, he scored a class victory at Clermont-Ferrand and in the Ollon-Villars hillclimb.

In 1963 Nino opened well with a shared 2nd at Sebring with Willy Mairesse in a Ferrari, but crashed in practice for the Targa, then crashed again while practicing for the Nurburgring 1000, badly breaking an arm. It took Vaccarella a while to get back on the track, but in 1964 he shared a Ferrari 275P with various factory drivers, scoring victories at the Nurburgring and at Le Mans, and a 2nd at Sebring once again. The following season, he received another F1 ride in the Italian GP, but his Ferrari was sidelined after 58 laps. On distance he was classified 12th. In endurance racing, however, Vaccarella's successes included an outright victory in the Targa Florio—always his favorite race—in a 275P codriven by Bandini, and a class 2nd (and 4th overall) in the Nurburgring 1000. At Le Mans, partnered by Pedro Rodriguez in a 4.4 Ferrari 365P, Nino shared 7th (but tops in class).

That season was a high spot of his driving career. His activities were self-curtailed after that, although the Vaccarella name continued to pop up in major race results for several years. In 1967 he shared a 5th at Sebring and a 4th at Monza in, respectively, a GT40 Ford and a Ferrari P3/4. At Daytona he was 5th in an Alfa in 1968; at Le Mans he was 5th in a Matra 630. In 1970, Nino was back with Ferrari, and the association was as rich as ever. At Sebring, he and Ignazio Giunti shared victory in a 5-litre 512; at Monza and in the Targa they were 3rd. At Spa there was a 5th, at Nurburgring (with John Surtees) a 3rd.

Vaccarella brought joy to all Italy, and especially to Sicily, in 1971 by winning his 2nd Targa Florio, partnered by Toine Hezemans, a Dutchman. The victory, won at no little effort on his part, broke a string of Porsche parades in the race, and it also was the 1st

Targa Florio victory for Alfa Romeo in 21 years. With Hezemans, too, Nino was 3rd at Sebring, 5th at Monza and in the Nurburgring 1000, and 2nd in the Austrian 1000, all in the Alfa T33/3. In 1972 Ferrari blew just about everybody off the track, Vaccarella included.

IRA VAIL

Brooklyn is a long way from the Oriental Park horse race track in Havana, Cuba. Beverly Hills is even farther. But Ira Vail, the man who gave Hudson one of its greatest victories, travelled that trail and many others. Ira was a man who seized his opportunities. He was a promoter for the AAA Contest Board, then USAC championship races at Syracuse starting in 1925, until, insulted by an undesirable race date, he junked USAC and switched to "outlaw" flat-head stockers in 1963. He still packed in the people.

Vail was born in Brooklyn 6 years before the turn of the century. By 1910 the young man was a motorcyclist of note—and shrewd too. "I found I could sell back the gold medals to the promoter three times a week," he recalled at his winter home in Daytona Beach later. "That was $100 a week when money was worth three times as much as it is now." Vail considered the "slingshot" techniques later used by the late-model stocks at superspeedways old hat. He did it back in 1910 at the old Dexter Bowl Motordrome in Ridgewod. "We called it 'suction riding' in motorcycles, and I took the technique with me when I switched to automobiles. A man would lay back, getting a tow from the leader. Then on the last lap he would dive down and grab the lead going over the finish."

Ira switched to 4-wheelers about 1912 and began to win regularly 2 years later on Eastern dirt track circuits. "It was exciting—I never had any notion of fear. When something went wrong with my car and I spun out, I was more disappointed than anything else," Vail declared. "When someone got hurt or killed, it was too bad, but it was the other fellow. There was a smaller clique of drivers then and we had confidence in each other. The 'squirrels' were known and given a wide berth." Vail's 1st important victory was in the 1961 Sheepshead Bay inaugural; he had qualified a stock Hudson for the race in a unique way. "There was a 90 m.p.h. minimum average, and I knew my car couldn't go 85 m.p.h. on that track by itself," said Ira, "so I asked if I couldn't have Jack LeCaine, a friend of mine and a fine driver, run his new Delage as a pacer for me. They were faced with a short field, so they agreed. I qualified at 91 m.p.h. by having LeCaine tow me in his slipstream. Then I went out and beat all the hotter cars, averaging 86 m.p.h."

Vail never missed a chance to turn a dollar from racing. For the 1916 Indy 500, for example, and for most of the big races that season, he collected $500 from his

tire company and $500 to run Philbrin ignition and (eventually) batteries. Hudson's initial major racing effort was made in the fall of 1916 for the 1917 season. Vail said the Hudsons were all blue cars, and that the firm sponsored the team for only a few races, then sold him his car. He in turn sold it to a Hudson dealer in Barcelona, Spain. Vail next turned to a new Duesenberg 8, called the Philbrin Special, which he drove both on the board tracks and at Indy.

It was with the Philbrin car that Vail was part of a 4- or 5-driver invasion of Cuba for a race meet at which parimutuel betting was permitted. The publicity man for this excursion was the great Bill Pickens, a man of whom Vail was very fond. Pickens was never bothered by inherent lack of color; he manufactured it with publicity that was thrilling reading whether or not it was entirely accurate. He could take the most trival fact, the most offhand remark, and embroider it into a saga that drew people through the gates.

The Cuban gambit was one of his masterpieces. The Stonehams of baseball fame were among the backers of this venture, and John J. McGraw was an official of the corporation. Vail, Louis Chevrolet, Ralph DePalma, Ralph Mulford, Barney Oldfield, and Eddie Hearne were the pilots. Oldfield never raced because he got intoxicated on strange Cuban drinks and tried to remove part of Havana from the map; after insulting Cuban officials at a dinner, he was deported. Hearne ran the Oldfield Golden Submarine.

The Cuban-American Jockey and Auto Club's Grand Carres de Auto took place in early April 1920. There were 5 races per day, none with more than 4 cars, most with 2. All were sprints; Pickens whipped up feuds and David-Goliath situations with gay abandon. Vail was cast as the dirt-track champ; Chevrolet, DePalma, and Mulford the old pro champs, and Hearne the brash young challenger. The newspaper copy flowed like water at Boulder Dam and read like early Gunga Din. Only inclement weather doomed the promotion and the fact that, because of short fields, the Cubans were betting man-to-man instead of through the mutuels.

Vail had a long association with Pickens, touring the hustings with him and later participating in joint promotions, but the Havana adventure he remembered with particular joy—not only because of the nature of the racing but because Cuban and American society took the drivers to its bosom . . . literally. Of his many races in the hinterlands, Ira remembered a contest at North Platte, Neb., with particular glee. Ira had made a deal for 40 percent of the gate on this obscure half-miler. A man named King Riley was the area hero, and to say the crowd was pro-Riley is an understatement.

Ira, who wasn't actually sure where North Platte was, got expense money in advance and showed up the day of the race to find himself confronted with a vigorous challenger. Ira burned up the cow pasture to dethrone King Riley, collected $5,500 from the shellshocked promoter, and "beat it out to the railroad station before the crowd could mob me. I pity those poor race officials."

Beverly Hills Speedway and Legion Ascot in California saw Vail repeatedly, for he went where the money was. At Indianapolis he finished 8th three times—1919,

1922 and 1924—and 7th once—1921. In 1920 he drove a Leach with no success. Also in 1921 he owned and drove the 1st Miller 8. The next year Jimmy Murphy updated the same car and won the race.

But Ira's forte was dirt-track racing. He was in the thick of the AAA dirt-track championship from 1913 through his retirement in 1962. He spent a career clipping split seconds off the world dirt-track records, courtesy of Pickens. He cites a 100-miler in Bakersfield, Calif., as the measure of the Pickens genius. Eddie Hearne, Roscoe Sarles, Tommy Milton, and Barney Oldfield were to be the contestants, but Barney couldn't quite make it from the local pub so Vail substituted. The 3 regulars apparently had bad blood among them, for they staged such a torrid trophy dash that, by 50 miles, only Vail and Sarles had whole mounts. Then, about 75 miles out, Sarles burnt a bearing and left Ira on the track all alone. Unperturbed, Pickens signaled for Ira to speed up each time he passed the grandstands; Ira obeyed. To his amazement he learned that he was going for the world's record for 100 miles. Pickens had whipped the fans up with a steady stream of chatter, so that as Vail powered down for the next-to-last lap, the people were cheering and urging him on. Getting into the spirit of things, Ira went wide on the last turn and broadsided over the finish line to the hysterical shouts of Pickens that he had clipped a full 2 seconds off the mark. The master publicist had turned what might have been a nasty situation into a tour de force and the crowd—completely forgetting it had come to see an auto race—carried Vail off triumphantly.

Ira had been an especial favorite in Syracuse, where Horace P. Murphy, who owned 4 other Eastern tracks, promoted for the Fair Association. When Murphy passed on, the Fair manager asked him to promote the 1925 race. He did, also driving and winning 3rd place. The next year he felt it was unfair to win his own prize money so he negotiated a new deal with the Fair and retired from driving. The Fair and other ventures sustained the Vail family in comfort thereafter.

TONY VANDERVELL

For several years before his death at the age of 68, Guy Anthony Vandervell had been talking of a "comeback" as a constructor of racing cars. Vandervell was no Enzo Ferrari, yet his marque—Vanwall—led Great Britain to its place of eminence on the modern racing scene. The effort cost Vandervell something like $1 million of his own money, much frustration and not a little grief, yet he never wavered in his belief that the effort had to be made, that the goal he sought was worth it all. That goal continued to be achieved in cars like the Lotus, with drivers like Jim Clark, Graham Hill, and Jackie Stewart, on courses like Silverstone and Brands Hatch.

Charles Anthony Vandervell, Tony's father, was an industrialist who pioneered automotive electrical equipment. Tony was born in 1898 into the motor world, as it were, and he raced his 1st motorcycle at the age of 15. Eventually he became a crack Norton racer, then graduated to Talbot and Wolseley cars. In World War I he was a motorcycle dispatch rider, and later was commissioned an officer. Joining his father's electrical business after the Armistice, Vandervell resigned in 1927, a year after CAV was merged with Lucas and Rolax. A few years later he became interested in a new American-developed bearing that carried the trade name Thinwall, and in 1932 he formed Vandervell Products to manufacture the item in Britain under license.

Eventually Vandervell-manufactured Thinwall bearings became one of Britain's hot export items; Vandervell himself became a millionaire strictly on his own, because his father had noted how successful Tony was in business and left the bulk of his estate to others. At Tony's own death, his worth was estimated at about $25 million.

In 1947, Vandervell became involved with the Raymond Mays-inspired BRM project and was one of its earliest active supporters. But he became dissatisfied with the effort's progress and management, and in 1949 he turned to Ferrari, who used Thinwall bearings in his cars, for a Type 125 supercharged V-12 1.5-litre Ferrari racing car that was dubbed the Thinwall Special. Two years later he acquired another Ferrari, a year-old 4.5-litre unsupercharged car in which his drivers dueled BRMs. Vandervell's drivers in this period included such well-known men as Reg Parnell, Mike Hawthorn, Peter Collins, Nino Farina, and Piero Taruffi.

Meanwhile, Tony had started to develop his own car, which emerged in 1953 (although it was 1st raced in 1954). The Vanwall, as the car was known, was a 2-litre Formula 2 car initially, and it owed much to the Ferrari-based Thinwall on which John Cooper modelled its chassis, the engine, though, was far different. There were teething troubles, of course, and it was 1956 before the Vanwall had its 1st big success in the hands of Stirling Moss, who won the International Trophy race at Silverstone in May. The car was tended by the likes of Colin Chapman, Frank Costin, and Harry Weslake.

In July 1957, Tony Vandervell had his proudest moment when his car won the British and European Grand Prix at Aintree, Moss and Tony Brooks sharing the victory. The following year Vandervell won the World Constructors' Championship when Vanwalls took 6 *grande épreuves,* but the pressures proved disastrous to Tony's health. He worried about his drivers, about the cars, about British prestige when things went wrong. In 1959, on doctor's orders, Vandervell disbanded his team.

In 1960 he attempted his 1st comeback, but his health was not up to it. Five years later, Coventry Climax announced its withdrawal from racing. Vandervell tried again but this, too, was defeated by his health. Tony was married for the 3rd time (his other 2 marriages had ended in divorce) in February 1967 to his secretary of 20 years, Marian Moore. A month later, March 1967, he was dead. His most fitting memorial, perhaps, sits in Lord Montagu's auto museum at Beaulieu in England, a big, squat-nosed, almost ugly 2.5-litre Vanwall that led the way in modern British auto racing. A son, Colin, was racing in British Formula Atlantic in the seventies.

GIJS VAN LENNEP

To win Le Mans and to start Formula 1 racing all in one year is quite a project, especially for a small man like Holland's Gijs van Lennep, but he had little trouble accomplishing the feat in 1971. The 1st part—winning Le Mans in a Porsche 917 furnished by Martini Racing and codriven by Helmut Marko, was relatively easy. Even after 3,315.36 miles of racing—over 5,000 kilometers—it was rather easy.

Formula 1 racing was something else again. Van Lennep made his debut in his home race, the Dutch GP at Zandvoort, after his sponsors had "hired" a Surtees TS9 for the blond young man in the wake of his Le Mans victory. He was ill from the flu, but he was determined, and the finish was an acceptable one. But at the United States GP later in the year, where van Lennep expected to drive the Surtees again, an American named Sam Posey outdrove him in practice, and Surtees handed

the car over to Posey. Van Lennep tried to raise the price of his ride, but it was no good. The long trip was for nothing.

Van Lennep had other successful drives in enduros in 1971. He was 9th with Gerard Larrousse in the BOAC 1000, retired in the Monza 1000, was 3rd in the Nurburgring 1000 in a Porsche 908/3, 2nd with Jo Siffert at Watkins Glen's 6-Hour race. His next best ride of the year yielded him 2nd place at the Targa Florio with Andrea de Adamich.

What van Lennep needed in 1972, besides a good ride, was a press agent to make the world better acquainted with his feats and background. Of all the major drivers, enduro and single-seater, he was the least known.

Born March 16, 1942, at Bloemendaal, Holland, Jonkheer Gijs van Lennep learned to drive a Fiat 500 at the age of 11 and built Holland's initial go-kart when he was 15. In 1963 he fitted a Porsche engine into a Volkswagen and went car racing. Soon offered a Formula Vee drive, his performances earned Gijs a drive for Ben Pon's Racing Team Holland in an orange and white Porsche 904 sports cars and he won at Zandvoort 1st time out. Van Lennep also raced Dutch DAF Formula 3 cars fitted with variomatic transmission. But it was his performances in Pon's Porsches and in Porsches entered for him by a Finnish team that earned Gijs a place in the Porsche 917 entered by the Martini team at Le Mans in 1971. Besides his Martini ride, he joined the Gulf-Porsche team late in 1971 to win the Montlhéry 1000, codriving with Derek Bell, and he continued with Wyer in the new Gulf-Mirage M6, partnered by

Derek Bell. In 1972, Gijs also was announced as a Marlboro-BRM driver for the season, but quit before the season had really started, opting for a Formula 5000 ride in a Surtees TS11 with Jackie Epstein's Speed International team.

C. W. VAN RANST

Several years ago *Automotive News*, bible of the American automobile industry, asked a rhetorical question. How many engineers could claim they had worked for and with Louis Chevrolet, Henry Ford, Fred Duesenberg, Charles F. Kettering, and E. L. Cord? There was only one—a man who never received a college education, let alone an engineering degree. His name was C. W. Van Ranst.

Born in 1893, Van Ranst's 1st automotive job was with H. H. Franklin Co. at the age of 15 as a part-time draftsman's assistant while in prep school. After graduation he tested trucks for a while, then developed the 1st motion picture camera for amateurs. Late in 1912 Van Ranst joined U. S. Motors, owners of the Selden Patent that, purporting to be the basic motor car design, required all United States automakers to pay royalties. U. S. Motors included the Columbia, the Stoddard-Dayton, the Maxwell, and the Courier—some of which made cars—but the company folded when Henry Ford, who refused to pay royalties, won the lawsuit that voided the patent and dissolved U. S. Motors in 1913. Van Ranst went back to testing Mack trucks, then left the industry for the final time. Saboteurs blew up his next employer, a firm which made explosives out of reclaimed movie film, late in 1914.

Fred Duesenberg, then up to his ears in racing, hired Van Ranst the following year. He was probably the 1st engine design layout man in motor racing, possibly the 1st in the auto industry. Until then companies had built engines on a "cut and try" basis. C. W.—he never used anything but the initials—learned as much from Fred as he contributed. His early drafting experience, which had stood him in good stead as a layout man, enabled him to think designs through with a clarity that Duesenberg appreciated. Van Ranst became the top engine man in the company.

But he got itchy and quit when a foundry agreed to back him in pursuing a pet theory—a crankcase-driven supercharger. C. W. reasoned that the pressure built up in the crankcase could be utilized to increase the efficiency of the power charge. It was a good idea but, with the materials available at the time, was unworkable in production. The result was a 4-cycle engine with the characteristics of a 2-cycle. The crankcase pressure was carried by a series of rotating valves to the combustion chamber, which increased efficiency but also produced almost equal frictional losses. Van Ranst discarded the idea, but through it met Kettering. Van Ranst had taken his engine to the Delco laboratories in Dayton to use their dynamometer; Kettering and Charles Midgley were simultaneously perfecting the use of iodine to reduce detonation in a farm engine. Van Ranst apparently spent much time with them talking over automotive theory.

C. W. became fascinated with the problems of the racing engine and the conquest of Indianapolis. He worked on the Frontenacs in 1919, when the Speedway accepted almost any kind of vehicle that could be refurbished, but didn't try anything unusual until 1920. Midgley persuaded him to use higher compression pistons and to add lead to the gas to stop the ping. But the pistons failed due to excessive blow-by into the crankcase. Perfect Circle Corporation eventually developed piston rings to correct this condition, the start of a long association by that firm with competition.

Van Ranst was working for Louis Chevrolet at this time, having been commissioned to design a 300 cu. in. engine for Indianapolis. Just as the engine was completed, the AAA Contest Board and the track dropped the 300 cu. in. formula to 183 cu. in. Undaunted, Van Ranst prepared 7 cars for the 1920 race. Although the cars were identical mechanically, 3 of them were called Frontenacs and 4 Monroes, a firm with which Chevrolet had contracted to produce an Indy racing team. The Monroes, however, were painted green and the Frontys burgundy red. Since he was working almost exclusively with stock components, Van Ranst got extra speed by lightening the cars about 300 pounds. He also increased compression ratio to 7:1, fairly high for the day but not as high as in the Midgley experiment. Gaston Chevrolet won the race in a Monroe.

Van Ranst and Chevrolet built the straight-8 engine with which Tommy Milton, a close friend of C. W.'s, won in 1921. Van Ranst ran in this one himself, then finished in 1924 as a driver and co-drove in 1927. In 1922 and 1923 the Frontys finished despite mechanical trouble.

One of Van Ranst's major contributions to racing had nothing to do with Indy or the major-league board tracks. Much of the racing was on dirt tracks where dust quickly wrecked expensive Indy-type engines. Chevrolet reasoned that an inexpensive engine conversion from stock parts would be more suitable and much more saleable. Van Ranst then developed the famed Frontenac head for the Ford Model T engine. Fronty-headed Ts—actually o.h.v. engines with greatly increased breathing capacity—dominated homemade racing cars for a decade and were the basis of the early hot-rodding movement. Fronty-Fords usually retained the Ford engine, frame, and suspension, but fitted a boat-tailed lightweight body.

Shortly before leaving Frontenac Motor Company in 1923 to become a designer for Paige-Detroit, C. W. built a prototype to be sold to Stutz Motor Company, but that car never saw daylight. Van Ranst then formed a firm to produce electric fuel pumps in 1925, but never got it off the ground because AC introduced a cheaper mechanical unit. He designed the "Detroit Special" Indy car for Cliff Durant to drive in 1927 and, when Durant became ill, Milton and Van Ranst codrove the supercharged front drive vehicle for as long as it lasted. E. L. Cord, president of Auburn Motors, was impressed by the car and hired Van Ranst to develop a front-wheel drive passenger vehicle. Thus was the Cord L-29 born.

He designed a similar front-wheel drive for Packard in 1929, but only its 12-cylinder engine was ever used. The prototype was running 31 years later. Van Ranst left Packard in 1936 to open an engineering office. He later developed airplane engines and marine engines, but his Fronty head and his Cord designs earned him his secure place in auto history.

ACHILLE VARZI

The names of Tazio Nuvolari and Achille Varzi are always paired as the leading Italian racing drivers of their day, and in many ways the men were very much alike. Varzi was a perfectionist like Nuvolari, and he certainly was as versatile. Varzi had no preferences as to the kind of car or the type of race in which he would compete. He was at home on the demanding road circuits or on the high speed autodromes, he won the Targa Florio, and he won regularly at Monza. Monte Carlo's twisting streets and low speeds did not find him lacking, nor did the ultra-fast Tripoli Grand Prix of pre-World War II

days. Everywhere he performed almost flawlessly, smoothly, thrillingly; he was not an impetuous showman like Nuvolari, but an ordered stylist.

Born in Calliate, Italy, August 8, 1904, of a wealthy Milanese family, Varzi was slim and blond. Like Nuvolari and Piero Taruffi, Varzi raced motorcycles (in his case the British Sunbeam). He was already an experienced driver when the 1st meeting of the two Italian greats came in the 4-wheelers in 1927 on a wet and windy Verona day. Nuvolari won that race and the rematch at Alessandria, but the 23-year-old Varzi had demonstrated that he was a foe worthy of Nuvolari's best efforts.

In 1928 Varzi purchased his own car, a P.2 Alfa Romeo, and it was in this marque that he was to score his early successes. He bought it from Giuseppe Campari on the eve of the European Grand Prix at Monza and drove the 5-year-old machine to a 2nd behind Louis Chiron's new Bugatti. He tried a Bug in the Tripoli GP and was 3rd, but returned to his Alfa. The next season, driving as an official Alfa pilot, Achille was 3rd in the Mille Miglia, then won the Rome GP, the Circuit of Alessandria, Trieste-Opicina, Ciano Cup and Monza GP for the Championship of Italy. At Monza he had to make up 2 minutes in the final 60 miles after a late pit stop for mechanical trouble, and did so without apparent effort. Varzi was also 2nd in the Spanish Touring Car GP and at Cremona, and 3rd in the Messina Cup.

He repeated as Champion of Italy in 1930, dividing his rides between Alfa and Maserati. Varzi won the Targa, the Coppa Acerbo and the Monza GP again, as well as the Spanish GP and Alessandria, and he was 2nd in the Mille Miglia and 3rd in the Tourist Trophy. Bugatti lured him back in 1931 for a 3-year hitch as a team driver; the opening year he shared a French GP victory with Chiron and won the Tunis GP and Alessandria for himself. He was also 3rd in the German, Monegasque, and Monza Grands Prix and in the Targa.

In 1932 Varzi won the Tunis GP and was 3rd in the Targa, despite seemingly outclassed mounts. In the Rome GP he led the 3-litre class, and he was 2nd at Schauinsland, 4th at Montenero and 5th in the Monza GP. In Achille's final Bugatti season, he outdueled Nuvolari to win the Monaco race, took the Tripoli GP and drove a 4.9-litre Type 54 Bug to victory in the Avusrennen. Varzi was also 2nd in the Belgian GP, and 4th in the Spanish GP and in the Coppa Acerbo.

In 1934, when Enzo Ferrari took over Alfa's racing team after the factory quit the field, Varzi joined Scuderia Ferrari. He was 6th in the Monaco GP while getting used to the Italian cars once again, then posted a streak of victories that led to his 3rd Championship of Italy. Varzi won the Mille Miglia, his 2nd Targa Florio, the Coppa Ciano for the 2nd time, Alessandria for the 5th time, Tripoli for the 2nd year in a row, and the Penya Rhin and Nice Grands Prix. He was also 2nd in the French GP to Chiron, in the Circuit of Biella to Count Trossi, and in the Avusrennen to Guy Moll, all his teammates, and in the Modena GP to Nuvolari, driving a Maserati.

Germany's Auto Union claimed his services for 1935–36, and in the debut season for them, Varzi won Tunis and the Coppa Acerbo, was 2nd at Tripoli and 3rd in the Avusrennen, despite having to adapt himself to a rear-engined car. The following year he won only at Tripoli, was 2nd at Monaco and Berne and in the Circuit of Milan, 3rd in the Coppa Acerbo and in the Hungarian GP. That year he had a serious accident, his Auto Union's rear suspension failing while the car was rounding a corner at about 125 m.p.h. but he came through unscathed. In 1937 his performances were notably poor, and Auto Union dropped him after a 6th in the Italian GP. His best showing was a victory for Maserati in the San Remo GP, but soon after Varzi was in a nursing home for treatment for drug addiction. The strain of racing had caused Varzi to seek relief in drugs.

Achille spent World War II in the home, but when the war ended he presented himself to Alfa once again, a cured man. He was welcomed with open arms and offered a Type 158 Alfa with which he won the Turin GP on the Valentino Circuit and took 2nd in the Milan GP. In 1947 Varzi won the Rosario and Interlagos races in Argentina and Brazil, the Bari GP, and took 2nd in the Peron Cup at Buenos Aires and in the Belgian, Italian, and Swiss Grands Prix. Now 44 but seemingly indestructible, Achille started 1948 with a 2nd at Mar del Plata, Argentina, and won at Interlagos again, both for Alfa. In the new Formula 2 competition, he drove a Cisitalia and captured 3rds at Bari and Mantua.

On June 30, 1948, Varzi was driving a practice lap at Berne. The Bremgarten circuit was soaked by pouring rains, and as Varzi entered a left-hand turn at better than 110 m.p.h., his car skidded sideways. He had started to straighten the machine when its tail hit a pole —the only one on a slight slope banking the course— and overturned on the driver. As usual Achille was wearing only a pilot's helmet made of linen, and he was killed instantly. The manner of his death precipitated the long-overdue requirement for compulsory crash helmets for drivers.

Varzi had always been meticulous about the condition of his cars, the course over which the race would be contested, the styles and performances of the opposing drivers and the characteristics of their cars—about every detail involved in the race. He had never considered a little thing like a more modern headpiece, and it was this little thing that cost him his life.

FRANK VERBECK

A respected Pasadena, Calif., businessman in later years, Frank Verbeck was one of the better Fiat drivers in the very early days of auto racing on the Pacific Coast. But his main claim to fame comes not from his driving but from his role in the ransom of Terrible Teddy Tetz-laff in 1911. Tetzlaff was the most feared driver of his day. When he and Fiat were paired, he automatically became the race favorite.

Just before the Tacoma Montamarathon classic, Terrible Teddy was supposed to come up to make sure that Fiat's sales got a good boost in the Northwest. But a week before the race, Tetzlaff was kidnapped. Rival auto firms and/or gamblers had according to the grapevine, arranged for his abduction by gangsters. Mr. Hewitt, the millionaire distributor of Fiat, indicated he would pay handsomely for his star driver. The gangsters agreed to the double-cross, and the deal was made: Verbeck, then Tetzlaff's teammate, was to be taken to Teddy to bring him to Tacoma in time for the race.

Frank was led to a kind of private club where wealthy patrons were provided with wine, women, and song in a secluded and luxurious mileu, and there was Terrible Teddy, in remarkably good condition for a man who has spent almost a week in such an atmosphere. Verbeck made the final payment, but Tetzlaff categorically refused to leave his kidnappers. Only when the gangsters remarked that from now on he had to pay his own way did he move out and toward the race. Verbeck, later an official of the Mobil Economy Run, alleged that the gangsters had hit on the only thing that could have budged Teddy—money. Otherwise they would have had him on their hands forever.

LEO VILLA

For 45 years, from age 22 to age 67, Leo Villa served the Campbell family. He worked for Sir Malcolm initially, the Land Speed Record king of the twenties and thirties and the Water Speed Record holder as well. After Sir Malcolm's death, his son Donald inherited Villa's talents. Leopoldo Alphonso Villa may not sound very British, but Leo was a Cockney, born within sound of Bow Bells in London on November 30, 1899. His Swiss father, a wine butler, and Scottish mother, a barmaid, expected their son to go into the catering business, but his uncle Ferdinando, a lover of motorbikes and automobiles, was more realistic. When Leo was sacked at age 15 from a restaurant job for hurling an inkwell at a nasty boss, his uncle arranged an interview with Giulio Foresti, Itala's United Kingdom agent.

Villa had taken a night course in drawing at the Castle Street Art School, and a budding interest in cars was reflected in many of his drawings. Foresti didn't need drawings but wanted someone interested enough in cars. Leo started at 15 shillings a week at the racing driver's showroom-garage off Edgeware Road in London. First he cleaned parts, then helped as Foresti rebuilt Count Louis Zborowski's 250 h.p. Itala. He even got to "drive" the monster—under tow—to Higham.

World War I erupted, and Villa joined the RFC. There his preliminary mechanical training was sharpened and put to use as an aircraft mechanic. After the

Armistice, Leo rejoined Foresti as his personal racing mechanic in Giulio's 110 h.p. Austro-Daimler, a Mercedes in disguise. Their main races took place at Brooklands, of course, which was the center of all British racing in those days. It was at Brooklands, too, that Villa met Malcolm Campbell for the first time in 1919.

In Villa's racing mechanic days, his greatest moments came in the Targa Florio with Foresti in an Itala in 1921 when the pair won the 3-litre class, and in a Ballot, in which they were 2nd in the 2-litre class the following season. But in 1922 Leo was badly burned in a garage accident in Paris, where Foresti had transferred his operations. He came home to England to recuperate and was offered a position as Malcolm Campbell's personal mechanic. With Foresti's blessings, Villa accepted.

In those days Campbell was not an LSR man, but a Brooklands regular. He also was a fussy individual, always demanding, sometimes nearly impossible, but strangely content with Villa's work. Campbell ran a varied stable of cars at all times, for street use as well as for the race course, and Villa had the responsibility of caring for them all. Villa was with Campbell throughout the Briton's LSR and WSR days, right up until New Year's Eve 1948, when Sir Malcolm died in bed.

Within the year, Villa was working for the son. Donald Campbell was not as fussy as his father, not as demanding in all things. Some would say he was not as talented either. But he matched his father's feats on water, and only long strings of bad luck—and the advent of jet propulsion—limited his LSR successes. But with each new Donald Campbell Bluebird, Leo Villa was there, as he had been with Sir Malcolm's Bluebirds. He was there, too, at Coniston Water January 4, 1967, when Donald Campbell died in a quest of a new WSR. Later that year Leo was awarded an Order of the British Empire. He joined the Norris Brothers in a jet boat project. But it wasn't the same without a Campbell to serve.

LUIGI VILLORESI

Fiat, Maserati, Ferrari, Lancia, Osca. From the late thirties to the late fifties, these were the honored names in Italian racing, and in world racing, too. One man drove for them all—not only drove, but distinguished himself and the marques. He was seemingly an indestructible man, a man equally at home in single-seaters or in sports cars, a man who drove almost all the Italian races yet did well elsewhere as well.

This was Luigi Villoresi, born May 16, 1909, also known as Gigi, who started racing early in cooperation —and competition—with his brother Emilio, who was to die at Monza in 1939. In 1935, in the Ciano Cup, Luigi's Fiat finished 3rd, a feat he repeated the following season in a Maserati, the marque with which he had his greatest early success. He was a class winner in a

Fiat in the 1936 Monte Carlo Rally, but it was in Masers that he made his earliest major race victories in 1937, winning the Masaryk voiturette race at Brno at 77.60 m.p.h. and taking the Lucca race at 54.74 m.p.h.

In 1938 Gigi won the Albi Grand Prix at 90.20 m.p.h. and at Pescara in the voiturette at 81.48 m.p.h. He was 3rd in the Targa Florio and in 2 South African races, the Grosvenor Cup and the Capetown race. The following season started with a South African GP victory at 99.67 m.p.h., and he won the Targa at 84.78 m.p.h., a record speed for the gruelling road race. But that record stood only a year, until Villoresi himself smashed it in 1940 by wining again, this time at 88.41 m.p.h. There were other races, but these were the high spots of his prewar career.

There would be a completely new career after World War II. It started in 1946, when when Villoresi won the Nice GP at 64.86 m.p.h. and was 2nd to Alberto Ascari at Modena. He raced at Indianapolis and finished 7th in his 3-litre Maser. In 1947–48 he dominated the season-opening Argentine races, winning both heats of the Peron Cup each year. In 1947, too, he won the Alsace GP (68.92 m.p.h.), the Nîmes GP (62.10), the Nice GP (64.05), the Lausanne GP (63.92). Gigi didn't win all the time, though; he was 2nd to Achille Varzi in the Rosario GP in Argentina, 2nd at Vigavano. In 1948 he won again: the British GP at 77.28 m.p.h., Albi, and Comminges (in a Talbot for a change from his Maserati). Ascari nipped Villoresi at the San Remo GP, Jean-Pierre Wimille edged him in the Italian GP. At Garda Gigi was 3rd, and he ranked the same in the European GP at Berne.

Formula 2 was *the* formula in 1949, and Villoresi won F2 races at Garda, Rome, Luxembourg, as well as a Formula 1 race at Zandvoort and the Sao Paula GP. The next year he won a heat at the Peron Cup and won at Posario, as well as the Monza GP at a blistering 101.50 in F2. He was 2nd many times—to Ascari at Bons, Rome, and Luxembourg, to Louis Rosier in the Dutch GP, to Juan Fangio at San Remo. Villoresi was with Ferrari now, and in 1951 his red car with the prancing horse emblem won at Marseilles, Pau and Genoa, and he shared a Mille Miglia victory at 75.72 m.p.h. and won the Inter-Europa Cup at Monza. He was 2nd to Ascari, his recurrent foe, at Monza in the GP, 3rd in the Belgian and European races. But he won again at Syracuse and at Senigallia, in F1 and in sports cars respectively.

The F2 Les Sables d'Olonne GP, a 3-hour grind, fell to Villoresi in 1952, but Ascari won the La Baule GP, and Gigi was 3rd in the Italian and Dutch races. He won at Valentino, however. If the end should have been near, for Villoresi now was 44 years old, it didn't seem so to other drivers. In 1953 Gigi won the Tour of Sicily at 61.05 m.p.h., and won the Monza sports car GP at 109.28 m.p.h. That same season he was 2nd to Ascari in the Bordeaux GP, shared 2nd with his old nemesis (actually one of Villoresi's closest friends) at the Casablanca 12 Hours. In the 3-hour Argentine GP, an F2 race, Gigi was 2nd to Ascari once more; in the Buenos Aires GP he was 2nd to Nino Farina. In the Italian GP he was 3rd.

The year 1954 saw a Lancia victory for Villoresi in the Oporto sports car GP at 92.52 m.p.h. In 1955 he was 3rd at Valentino and Syracuse in Centro Sud team Lancia F1 cars, and in 1956 3rd for Osca in the Tour of Sicily (Villoresi ran many major rallies). It also saw a serious accident at Castel Fusano, which, coupled with Villoresi's continuing sorrow over the death of Ascari, finally drew the curtain on a remarkable driving career.

RED VOGT

It is fitting that Red Vogt has his auto repair business near Daytona International Speedway, for he was one of the midwives in the birth of stock-car racing as an organized major sport. Vogt, an Atlantan, once said wistfully that since stock-car racing had become the biggest business in sport, there was little chance for the independent to build and maintain a competitive late-model stock car. He was the chief mechanic on 2 of the early teams—the Ray Parks cars and the Kiekhafer Outboard Chryslers. Of course, both were independent, but they dominated the field to such an extent they might as well have from factory's efforts.

As a result, Vogt, his freckles still red even if his hair wasn't, continued to dabble in the sport only in the Modified and Sportsman categories. But he could remember when the three Flocks, Red Byron, and Bill France drove for him and Parks: "France was a real good one. He wasn't a charger, but when he saw the chance to go through he went. He drove with his head, not with his nerve." Vogt remembered when France drove his last Beach race. Bill, driving a 1941 Graham Hollywood Supercharged, had a one-lap lead on everyone when a drain screw in the fuel pump fell out. He parked on the back stretch and watched with equanimity. He was co-promoter, too.

Back in the early days of racing Dixie style, the boys often ran on tracks bulldozed out of a cow pasture the previous week. They ran on beaches where the sand would support them, they ran at old horse tracks, and they ran at the few speedways which would have them. Purses were small and uncertain and some promoters unreliable, occasionally downright dishonest. "A man could tow 700 miles for an advertised $2,000 purse and afterward the promoter would pay off maybe $400," recalled Vogt. "You took your share or you didn't get anything. That's what started talk of a new racing association."

There was pre-race inspection of sorts before NASCAR, Vogt said, but the association was formed officially in 1947 after the Atlanta branch of the sport, which included France, Ed Otto, Bill Tuthill, and others, talked about it for a year. Red thought up the name, but France had NASCAR incorporated. The original charter was in Georgia in 1946. NASCAR put the money for purses in the bank beforehand and told the drivers exactly how much money there was.

Vogt could fascinate any listener by recalling NASCAR's early days. He remembered Roy Hall—an almost forgotten name—as one of the greatest natural drivers who ever lived. "He could do things with a car which no car was supposed to do. Red Byron was the only one who could sit on his tail and worry him. I remember one race when Byron came up on his back bumper and stayed there for the whole distance like a car getting towed. Hall did everything he could to shake Red, but he couldn't. After the race he asked Byron why he didn't pass him. 'You were going pretty good,' said, 'I was satisfied.'" Vogt said that if Hall, a North Georgia bootlegger, had been able to "keep his nose clean with the law" he might have been among the all-time greats.

Though he worked with the Flock boys—Bob, Tim and Fonty—Vogt called Byron the greatest driver he ever saw. Red, who showed up in Atlanta after World War II with a bad leg, was equally at home on dirt, asphalt or sand. He could help a mechanic fine-tune a car's suspension and engine like no other driver. Byron retired from driving to become one of racing's top mechanics. Vogt's Kiekhafer days are detailed elsewhere, but after the outboard man got out, Red went back to the garage business. He still occasionally appeared in the Modified race at Daytona Speed Weeks, but the tall redhead was content pretty much to watch and remmeber when stocks were fun for a mechanic.

BILL VUKOVICH

He was a short, stocky, beetled-browed man with sadness—or was it bitterness?—in his eyes. He died when he turned right at Indianapolis on the southeast corner.

A wisp of smoke appeared in the sky—it may have been from the racers in the accident that blocked his path; the people at the party in the Pagoda hardly noticed it then nor did most of the people in the milling crowd infield. Champagne or beer, Indianapolis is party time.

A ferris wheel turned lazily on a field outside the track; the sound of a calliope pierced through the noise of the Glenn Miller orchestra coming over some portable radio or phonograph.

On the track at the southeast corner the right front wheel of the upside down Lindsey Hopkins Special spun lazily in the midst of sudden flames to a halt. Underneath it was all that remained of Bill Vukovich, The Silent Serb who stormed out of the California midget

633

ranks to win two straight Indianapolis 500s was born William Vucerovich in 1919 in Alameda, Calif., and grew up near Fresno. When his father, a carpenter, died and the farm the family had bought a year before was lost, Bill and his brother Eli, 13 and 14 respectively, had to help support their mother and 5 sisters. (An older brother, Mike, had already moved away from home.)

It was 1932 in the middle of the Depression. The boys left school, working at anything they could get—driving trucks, farm work. They took weekly turns at paying for the groceries, according to Eli. It was a harsh time but there was a release—the family's Model T. Bill was driving it around before he reached his teens; the boys chased jackrabbits across fields in it.

Vuky drove his 1st formal race in a Chevrolet-modified owned by Fred Gearhart who then ran a garage in Fresno. He came in 2nd. His 3rd time out, he won; he was 18. Gearhart treated Vukovich like a son, letting him keep all his winnings. Bill cleared $15 on a good week. After several months of modified racing, Gearhart helped the hard, silent youngster to get a midget car ride. In his 1st race in 1938, he locked wheels with another midget, flipped, and broke several ribs and his collarbone. Seven weeks later he was back racing.

Eli began driving midgets then, too. The 1st time they were in the same race, Bill told him, "Don't tangle with me. Out on that track you're just another driver." But the two barnstormed the West Coast the next 2 years, sleeping in the car trailer, driving 15 or 20 heats and races a week, clearing as much as $50 each on the good ones, nothing on the bad ones. It was wild, dangerous racing, the kind where your competitor would drive over you to win if he couldn't pass you. Bill was totally dedicated to it—he didn't smoke or drink, and he ran or bicycled daily to keep fit. He was the fiercest of a California group of drivers who were to dominate Indy for more than a decade after the war. He was so fierce that once, according to Eli, he terrified a Los Angeles crowd into screaming "Stop, stop!" When he pulled in after the race he asked, "What are they yelling about?"

He seemed uninterested in girls until, on a blind date in Fresno, he met a tall brunette named Esther Schmidt, 17. He was so bashful he used to ask her sister to arrange their dates. But 3 months later he proposed; they were married in 1941.

Bill spent the war years repairing Jeeps and trucks and planning for his future racing career. He wanted his own midget. He bought one from Gearhart for $750, working on it nights and weekends until racing resumed in 1945. Vuky painted the car a bright red and named it Old Ironsides. He scarred his hands, broke his shoulders and ribs, suffered concussions, but he was the terror of the midget circuit. On one track he went through the fence at the same place 3 times head first. The last time he said, "I'm going to quit. It's costing too much for crash helmets."

He couldn't bear to lose—especially to his brother Eli. Bill was West Coast midget champ in 1946 and 1947, national midget champ in 1950. And despite his success he earned less than $7,000 a year, even when he won the national title. By 1950 the midget shows were not drawing the fans and such drivers as Walt Faulkner, Andy Linden, and Manny Ayulo had sought greener fields at Indianapolis. Vuky, the best, had rebuffed all prospects of driving a big car up to this point. But he showed up at Indianapolis in May 1950. Walt Faulkner, one of his bitterest competitors in the midgets persuaded him to take the driver's test. He did, successfully, in the Wilbur Shaw Maserati that had won in 1939 and 1940. But the old car couldn't quite qualify for the race.

In 1951 Vukovich returned with a sponsor, Pete Salemi of Cleveland, and a "sled," the Central Excavating Special. He qualified the car but confided before the race to Tony Bettenhausen that he didn't think it would last 30 laps. It lasted 29, then retired with an oil leak. Though he earned only $750 for that race, Vuky earned something more. He had pushed the car into 10th place from far back and when Mauri Rose, 3-time winner of the 500, announced his retirement, Vukovich was tabbed by millionaire sportsman Howard Keck to take his place.

For Vuky, this was the greatest honor possible. Rose was one of the few people of whom he stood in awe. According to contemporary reports Vuky considered him America's greatest racing genius. Vukovich accepted the ride and even retired from midget racing after 1951. He qualified the Keck car 2nd fastest at Indy in 1952, then led from the 32nd lap until a mixup in the pits—they had put a tire on backwards and had to take it off—cost him over 2 minutes. He took the lead back from eventual winner Troy Ruttman and held it until a quarter-inch pin on his steering arm gave on the 192nd lap. He sat out the race on the wall.

"I watched Vuky that day," said Dr. Carlyle B. Bohner, then Speedway medical director, "and I think it began to dawn on him that he had licked Indianapolis."

For a loser, he was amazingly relaxed. He patted Ruttman, a big California youngster, on the back and said, "You're my boy. What you can do once, you can do all the time." He told Keck's chief mechanic Jim Travers, "I should have been here 10 years ago. It's a cinch."

Yet he never hit the Championship Trail, to the promoters' dismay. He was more interested in making sure of the future of his 2 children, Billy and Marlene. He had taken home $7,500 of some $23,000 lap and place money from Indy in 1952 and came back the next year expecting to make it really big. "Nobody's ever going to pass the hat for my family," he said.

The 1953 race was conducted in 130-degree weather more suited to equatorial Africa. Only 5 drivers finished the race without relief; only 19 cars finished at all. Vukovich, completely relaxed, won, leading 195 out of the 200 laps. He even commented to a pitman, "You know, there aren't as many fans in the bleachers this year." His share of an $89,500 purse came to $35,800.

In 1954, after a year of just waiting for Indy, he won easily with a record average of 130.84 m.p.h. With his $29,000 portion of the $75,000 winner's purse, Vuky bought 2 Fresno gas stations, continued to invest soundly, and planned a new home. He worked a full day at one of his stations on a regular basis, spurning almost all offers of big money.

Lincoln invited the olive-skinned speedster to drive the Pan American Road Race in the fall of 1954, and for a change he accepted. His codriver was horrified by the speed at which Vuky took precipitous corners as they wound through the mountains. He protested again and again. When finally the car shot over the bank of a road and dropped 50 feet, Vukovich is reported to have taken his hands off the wheel while the car was still airborne and said, "OK, you drive it." Neither man was seriously hurt.

When Howard Keck decided to drop out of racing in 1955, he released Vuky to Lindsey Hopkins who owned a new roadster. Vuky accepted on the condition his mechanics, Travers and Frank Coon, came with him. Even though he had once hung up a rusty ax labelled "Travers' Tools" in their garage, these 2 had his complete respect.

The late Walt Faulkner said of Vukovich in the weeks before the 1955 Indianapolis race, "All the bounce was gone. He felt he had to win 3 in a row (the hat trick that no one has ever done) because everyone had built him up so much. About a week before the race we were having coffee and he said suddenly, 'I don't think I'll finish.' Then he changed the subject."

On race morning he telephoned his wife to ask what time she was coming to the track. It was the first time he had ever done that. He wore only a T-shirt, white ducks, and bowling shoes as he climbed into the Lindsey Hopkins Special. He put on his gloves and strapped his helmet as he sat waiting for, "Gentlemen, start your engines."

Fifty-five laps later he was leading by 17 seonds after a duel with MacGrath. He waved to the stands where his wife sat. Suddenly ahead of him Rodger Ward's car went out of control with a broken axle. Al Keller, swerving hard to the left to avoid him, headed straight for an abutment and cut right again, spinning into Johnny Boyd's car and knocking it into the 6-foot hole between Ward's overturned car and the wall.

Vukovich went up and over Boyd's right rear wheel, soaring over the wall. His car hit nose 1st, then bounced, spun, bounced again, and crashed flaming upside down. Vuky was dead before the flames reached him.

In death, William Vucerovich, 36, earned more money ($4,300 of a $10,800 purse) than the driver who finished 5th. The Silent Serb had missed the hat trick, but nobody had to pass the hat for his family.

BILLY VUKOVICH

Billy Vukovich prefers not to be called Bill Vukovich, Jr., pointing out that his middle name is John while his father had no middle name. But there never was a time when he did not display complete confidence that he would be among the great drivers of USAC. He quickly tired of the obvious questions put to the son of a two-time Indianapolis winner who died in a flaming wreck. Billy credited his father with only one thing—arousing his interest in automobile racing and showing him that, for a man who was not going on to college, racing was a quicker way to make money than any other thing he could think of. But he inherited his father's temper and his inclination, or need, to make his successes alone.

His father's death must have had some effect on an 11-year-old (born March 29,1944) who heard the news on the radio in Fresno, Calif. However, he claimed he didn't remember his father much because the elder Vukovich wasn't around much when he raced. Naturally, when he announced he was going racing, his mother tried to talk him out of it; he went anyway, starting at 18 in central California and progressing rapidly into Supermodifieds, midgets and sprint cars. Billy started out as a mean rough driver like his father, pushing people out of the way, but as he raced he became more polished, preferring guile.

The Vukovich name did not hurt his career; rather, it made him an instant star. Old auto racing fans strained to see his father's image. When he bumped a competitor, when he shook his fist at an official, they cheered for what they felt was the past reincarnated.

It helped, but Billy himself helped more. In 1964 he was the Clovis track champion and NASCAR's California Rookie of the Year. In 1965 he switched to midgets and became BCRA Rookie of the Year, finishing 3rd overall in his 1st USAC race. In his 1st Championship Trail ride, the Phoenix 200, he came in a creditable 9th. In 1966 he won the BCRA championship and finished 2nd in USAC's Pacific Coast midget circuit. In 1967 he displayed his versatility by running Supermodifieds, winning 8 features; sprint cars with the California Racing Association, winning 6 features; plus 4 BCRA midget victories, 10 USAC midget victories, and one USAC sprint victory. There were also 11 Championship Trail starts. The credentials of 1967 were all Billy needed to move up to top-caliber rides.

His father had also won the 1950 midget championship before he had gone on to Indianapolis, but it was on the strength of Billy's overall record that J. C. Agajanian, the promoter and car owner, gave him a ride in the Wagner Lockheed Special for Indy 1968 and for the entire Trail. It wasn't a bad year, considering Billy was just 23. Most of the Trail drivers don't really hit their stride until much later in life. At Indianapolis Billy started 23rd and finished 7th, winning the Rookie of the Year honors. He added 2 3rds—at Du-Quoin and Nazareth—and finished consistently enough

to take 5th place in the season standings. The future looked bright.

But 1969 was a bummer. Billy broke a connecting rod in the 1st lap at Indianapolis, won only one of 15 midget starts, and did not distinguish himself on the Trail. But Agajanian stuck with him. So did midget car owner Don Carruthers of Anaheim, Calif.—at least for a while. In 1970 he finished 32nd in the point standings. In 6 Trail starts his best was a 3rd on the Sacramento dirt near his hometown of Fresno. At Indy Billy's Suga-Ripe Prune Special lost its clutch after 78 laps. He made 15 midget starts, won 1, finished 2nd three times, and saw Jimmie Caruthers, son of his former car owner, win the national title in his 1st try. But Agajanian continued loyal, and Vukovich continued with a Championship Trail ride for 1971 in which he finished 3rd, earning $101,627, including a 5th in the Indy 500. For 1972, Vukovich teamed with chief "wrench" Judd Phillips to campaign an Eagle Offy. He had but 54 laps at Indy, but then finished 4th at Pocono and 3rd at Ontario.

No one was making comparisons any longer, Bill Vukovich had arrived.

BILLY WADE

A native Texan, Billy Wade got his start in 1950 at age 20, finishing 2nd in a 50-lap Houston feature in his initial outing. At Meyers Speedway there, he won no less than 3 modified championships in a row. Billy joined NASCAR's Grand National circuit in 1962 at the behest of a fellow Texan who sponsored his car in 3 races before he died unexpectedly. Wade was 18th in the Daytona 500 that year, his 1st GN start. He returned to Texas, but had displayed enough talent to find a new sponsor the following year when he became NASCAR's Rookie of the Year.

In 1963 Wade, riding as David Pearson's teammate in a Dodge, finished in the top 10 in 15 of the 31 races in which he started, although he never won one; his best was a 2nd at Nashville. He was 16th in point standings when the season was over. The following year was a different story. Billy jumped both to the Bud Moore Mercury and all the way up to 4th place in points by the time the year was over. His record included 4 wins in a row and 21 other top-10 finishes in 35 races entered. Wade's fellow Texan, A. J. Foyt, stamped this growing great with the tag, "The Mighty Mite." Pretty good for a sophomore who banked nearly $30,000 as a result. The 4 victories were scored in the same high-rise Mercury in which he was to die.

Only 5 feet 7 inches in height and under 150 pounds soaking wet, Billy never considered his diminutive size —which may have contributed indirectly to his death— a handicap. In Houston's Marshall High School, he went out for and made the baseball, football, and gymnastics

teams. In 1964 he had moved from Houston to Spartanburg, S. C., to he nearer the NASCAR circuits and the facilities of Bud Moore, his chief mechanic and car owner. Death came for Billy January 5, 1965, when few people other than professionals were around the Daytona Speedway. But there were tears shed for him that day—there and elsewhere as the sad news was learned from the radio. He was the 5th man to die at Daytona International and the 5th NASCAR driver to die in a 12-month period.

The crash did not look too serious. The 1964 Mercury was all alone on the Daytona International Speedway banking when its tire blew at around 170 m.p.h., and it cracked into the newly-built concrete retaining wall designed to keep a car from hurtling off into space from the 32-degree banked turn. But the car did not burn and the driver, restrained by his seat and shoulder harnesses and protected by helmet and beefed-up chassis, was still sitting at the wheel when the rescuers reached him.

Another NASCAR driver, Darrell Dieringer, had hit the same wall the week before and escaped with minor cuts after similarly pulverising his car. The fact that this car was a wreck today did not appear to mean too much; after all, it was its right side that had smacked the wall 1st. The observers were wrong.

Billy Wade, finally tasting success on the NASCAR circuit, was dead as they lifted him out of the wreckage. He was 34 and left a wife and 4 daughters ranging in age from 4 to 12 years of age. It was a big family for a young man, and that was party the reason why he was out earning an extra $200 a day as a tire tester for the Goodyear Tire & Rubber Company. That and the fact that Billy loved cars.

LOUIS WAGNER

It was all very embarrassing. This powerful man had been apprehended by several New York City policemen after speeding through the city streets in a motor-driven vehicle at a speed in excess of 20 m.p.h. He was a suspicious character if there ever was one. He said his name was Wagner, but he spoke French. And when they had searched him, they had found a deadly weapon—a jacknife. They promptly hustled the fellow off to the Tombs, the old Tombs, a dark, somber place that Wagner later suggested must have been modelled after the Bastille in Paris. How were they to know that he was telling the truth? He was a professional racing driver. He had just won the Vanderbilt Cup of 1906 out on Long Island. The jacknife was an essential tool for the autoist of the day.

Strange things like that always were happening to Louis Wagner. Born at Pre-Saint-Gervais, France, in February 1882, he joined the Darracq company as a sallow teenager and grew up, not only to manhood but to racing stardom with that marque, FIAT, and others. Wagner's earliest notable victory came in the 1903 voiturette (light car) section of the Circuit des Ardennes. He pushed his Darracq around to a winning average of 43.1 m.p.h. He again won the race 2 years later at a 46.7-m.p.h. average speed. In the same race in 1906, he set the fastest lap and finished 4th overall in the main race after again winning the voiturette preliminary.

But Wagner's most notable early victory came in the 1906 Vanderbilt Cup race on Long Island. He averaged 61.4 m.p.h., while beating Vincenzo Lancia and Arthur Duray to the finish line. Small wonder that Louis was enthusiastic as he drove over the New York City border and met up with the police. The Frenchman's association with Darracq ended abruptly the following season. Wagner and Richard Hanriot were driving Darracqs in the rugged Targa Florio when the differentials of both cars broke. But Alexandre Darracq announced—lied would be more accurate—that both drviers merely had driven off the road and wrecked their machines. After all, Darracq reasoned, the manufacturer's reputation was more important than any driver's. Wagner quit on the spot.

Louis took up aviation, as did many of the early race drivers, but he also kept his hand in behind the wheel. There were disappointments, like the French Grands Prix of 1907 and 1908, when Wagner's car failed him. But there were sweet moments, too, such as the Savannah, Ga., Grand Prize races in 1908. Driving a massive FIAT over 400 miles of local streets and country roads, Wagner won after 6 hours and 10 minutes. Victor Hemery was a mere 56 seconds behind. Louis's winning speed was 65.2 m.p.h., and the Savannah police did not arrest him. He tried for repeat victories in the Grand Prize races in 1910 and 1911, but they eluded him. In the former, his FIAT overturned on LeRoche Avenue when it hit a soft spot in the road at 70 m.p.h. and became airborne.

Wagner never seemed able to regain the victory habit either in the few remaining years before World War I, nor after it, but he remained a threat in every race he entered. In the French GP at Dieppe in 1912, for example, his giant 14-litre FIAT roared through 2 days of racing—956 miles—only to finish 2nd to Georges Boillot in a new Peugeot. Two years later, in the same race at Lyon, Wagner was aboard a Mercedes. He might have won, but deferred to the Mercedes team leader, Christian Lautenschlager, to take the checker. Otto Salzer came in 3rd to complete the stunning Mercedes sweep of the last great GP before the war.

Following the war, Wagner appeared less frequently, but like so many of the early drivers kept competing to a fairly advanced age. He was always willing to try something new, like the 1919 Indianapolis 500 race. He had always done fairly well in the United States. But a wheel collapsed on his Ballot on the 44th lap, and Louis had to be content with a 26th placing. In the first few years

of the twenties, Wagner's only outstanding performance came in the 1921 Italian GP at Brescia when he pushed his Fiat to a 3rd behind the Peugeots of Jules Goux and Jean Chassagne.

As the decade wore on, however, he seemed as indestructible as ever. In the 1924 Italian GP, Wagner was 2nd to his Alfa Romeo teammate Antonio Ascari, 4th in the French GP at Lyon. In 1925's French GP, the race in which Ascari died, Louis was 2nd in a Delage to Robert Benoist and Albert Divo in the lead Delage. In the Targa Florio and the Coppa Florio that season, he again scored 2nd, again in a Peugeot. At Le Mans, Wagner was 6th in a 3-litre Aries. In 1926 he tasted victory in a major race for the last time. In the Royal Automobile Club GP at Brooklands, England, he and Robert Senechal shared the winning Delage at 71.61 m.p.h. Later it was again 2nd in the Coppa Floria. There were few races after that, and a couple of seasons later, Louis retired after a quarter of a century of auto racing. During World War II Wagner lost a leg to cancer of the bone, but he continued his association with the sport as supervisor of the Montlhéry course. He lived on with his many memories until 1960 at age 78.

DAVE WALKER

In 1971 Gold Leaf Team Lotus added a couple of new faces for occasional nontitle Formula 1 racing: Tony Trimmer, a lean, longish-haired blond Briton, and Dave Walker, a stocky, close-cropped, gray-sprinkled Austra-

lian very much in the Jack Brabham mold. Dave Walker had been through the mill by the time he was 30 years of age, with a full 2 decades of driving experience.

"I started driving when I was seven," Dave recalled. He was born in Sydney in June 10, 1941, but because of the war was packed off to a safe military school out in the country. By the time he was 12, he was driving 5 miles from home to the railway station to drop off and pick up his elder brother. "Yes, when I was alone, I did imagine myself a racing driver and even spun a few times, but without problems. That's where it all started, I guess."

When he was 17, Dave's architect-turned-farmer father died, and he left school for a trainee appointment as an accountant, attending night school to study economics. But cars were becoming a growing interest, and the family Wolseley went as a down payment on one of the 1st MGA Twin-Cams imported to Australia. "One day a group of people in an MG stopped and asked directions to Corona Hill where there was a climb scheduled. I went along in my car, watched a while, then entered and won. But it was an expensive win, because my car dropped a valve, and I had to be towed all the way home." Then he lost his license for speeding.

Racing drivers have to be incredible optimists, however, even when they are 1st starting out. Brabham and Denis Hulme had gone to Britain and made it, Walker reasoned, so off he went. The 1st job in Britain was with the Chequered Flag as a salesman, no salary, but a commission for each car sold. There were not many sales, but there were a few lessons at the Jim Russell school in a Lotus 18. After a short while Dave decided home was the place to get started, and he and another Australian pooled their resources (about $75) and hitch-hiked their way home.

His mother was happy to see him home, so happy that she helped finance a Brabham Formula Junior car for Walker. The time was May 1963, and David set himself a timetable to see what he could do with this competitive machine. The initial race in the year's schedule was at Warwick Farm, and Walker did well. At Calder, near Melbourne, he finished 3rd, at Oran Park he won 2 weekends in a row. There was no question about Dave's ability at this point, and he put in a happy winter readying for 1964 and becoming a successful Volkswagen salesman. He ran under the BP banner in 1964 with a modified engine, scoring a goodly number of class victories, although his opponents had newer, superior mounts, so they won the overall placings most of the time.

In 1965 at Lakeside, that part of the Walker dream ended in near disaster. At 130 m.p.h. Dave's 2-year-old Brabham suffered a suspension failure, and the car went end over end, demolishing itself and Dave's investment, although the driver walked away without serious harm. It took 6 months to rebuild the car with savings from his job. Then he sold the car, and for the entire year of 1965 his only finish was in a sedan, a Cortina. But those who had supported Walker before, BP and Shell among them, still saw an opportunity for Dave and advised him to try Europe again.

In May 1966, he came to Britain for another shot with about $250 in his pocket, not enough to buy an immediate ride but enough to live a while while scouting about for an opportunity. Good fortune presented the Australian with a Formula 3 test in a Promecon Brabham, which he passed with flying colors. This led to an occasional ride until the team folded. The next season Merlyn offered Walker a special deal for a F3 car. "I borrowed the money for it from friends, spent my nest egg on a VW transporter, and set off for the Continent," Dave recalled. At Imola he was 4th, at Monza he was running 2nd on the last lap until a spin took him out, and at Monthlhéry he was 4th again. Walker won at Opatija, Yugoslavia, a long way from Australia, or even Britain.

For 1968 Alexis offered a complicated deal; Walker would drive the factory Formula Ford—the Yazaki-sponsored MK. 14—and get occasional F3 drives as well as a regular salary. After a few races, Jim Russell got Walker to switch to his Alexis, with the same arrangement, but toward year's end the Colin Chapman-Russell arrangement was made, and Dave found himself in a Lotus. That winter Walker was off to Australia again, but this time in a Vauxhall Ventora on the London-to-Sydney Marathon. He made the trip almost single-handed, survived many mechanical breaks, and finally limped into Sydney.

In the Lotus 61 Dave won the 1969 FF title, got 3 F3 rides in a Lotus 59, finishing 3rd each time out. He

got to America for the 1st time in a Sebring FF race, then learned that Lotus Components had no deal in 1970. Walker was transferred to Gold Leaf Team Lotus in F3, however, and he won the Lombank F3 championship, edging Trimmer and winning 16 races including those at Silverstone, Crystal Palace, Mallory Park, Oulton Park, Caldwell Park, Thruxton, and Mallory Park.

In 1971 Dave won his 3rd and 4th straight championships, both the Super Shell Oil and Forward Trust F3 titles, with 25 victories in tight little cars so evenly matched that *only* driver skill mattered. The victories came at all the British tracks and at Cotinental starts like Monaco and Castellet. Walker also started the non-title Hockenheim Rindt Memorial F1 race in 1971, driving a Lotus 72D; he was 9th. In his only championship F1 start in Holland, he crashed in practice, started the race in a 56B turbine car and crashed that one on the 6th lap. The following season he became a Lotus—John Player Special—regular, backing up Emerson Fittipaldi of Brazil. The arangement ended after 1972 when Colin Chapman signed Ronnie Peterson of Sweden, and David was on the beach as far as F1 was concerned.

MIKE WALKER

In the winter of 1970–71 Mike Walker was one of the most sought-after drivers in British racing. Frank Williams wanted the 25-year-old blond young man for his Formula 1 effort. There was talk of a Church Farm Formula 2 ride. And Lotus went so far as to announce that Walker would drive its Boss-Ford 70 in Formula 5000. But none of these people got Mike, and he himself got nowhere in 1971.

The object of all this attention was born in Birmingham, England, December 18, 1945. He went to Sebright School, following Peter Collins, another graduate who did well at the wheel. In school Mike was a star sprinter, befitting his compact, 5-foot 8-inch physique. He moved into the family's woodworking business at Kidderminster, starting with sweeping up the chips, driving nails, and the like. Next came an assignment as a truck driver. But racing was on his mind, not trucking.

Mike started racing with a 15-year-old Kieft-Norton 500 in 1964, a car bought for a princely $175 or so to go hillclimbing with; it lasted 6 events, and was wiped out in spectacular fashion in the 7th at Shelsley Walsh. That was just a warm-up anyway, for Walker had his sights set on circuit racing. He bought a 3-year-old Mk. 3 Cooper Formula Junior car in 1965, dropped in a 1650-c.c. Ford engine, and went Formula Libre racing. In 30 starts Mike did very little, save interest his father in his racing fortunes. His father was a man of direct action, and in no time Mike was seated in a new Brabham BT18 Formula 3 car, which, once it was properly sorted, proceeded to give him 3 victories, 5 seconds and some other good placings.

In 1967 the BT18 gave way to a BT21 with his father's blessing, but the competition was rather keen that season, and Mike had only one victory to show for his efforts, although he rang up fastest laps at Brands Hatch, Rouen, and Clermont-Ferrand. He also crashed at Crystal Palace and wrote off the Brabham that year. The Chequered Flag came to the rescue for 1968 with an offer putting Mike in the list of Flag drivers that included Clark, Graham Hill, Parkes, Maggs, Stewart, Spence, Irwin, Pike, and others. But the season was not altogether a happy one. Not only was F3 dull, but a few F2 starts in a McLaren also did not go well. And late in the year he was invited to Silverstone to test drive an F1 BRM, waited around 3 days, but never got a chance to get inside the car.

At this low point in his career Warner found a friend. Alan McKechnie offered a 1969 F3 drive combined with a possible F5000 ride if all went well. Mike signed, but F3 was all but forgotten as he concentrated on the Guards F5000 championship in a Lola-Chevvy T142, and proceeded to wrap up 6th place overall, including victories at Silverstone and Oulton Park. His driving won Walker the annual Grovewood Award, and McKechnie provided another F5000 ride in 1970 in a McLaren-Chevvy M10B. Mike won at Oulton and Monza, was 2nd at Anderstrop, but overall he retired in 9 of his 18 starts. Still, his performance caused a storm of activity to sign up what was obviously a good bet for F1 at the still tender age of 25.

Walker hoped that 1971 would be one of his better years, not only for racing, but because he married a long-time girl friend named Jackie. His brother Tony, a Clubman Formula racer in his own right, served as best man. But racing turned sour in 1971 for Walker. His F1 dreams were sidetracked and he did nothing notable on F5000. Walker decided to concentrate on F3 with the Ensign team in 1972, and adding an occasional F2 ride, perhaps with John Surtees's Matchbox team. F1 would have to wait a while.

ROB WALKER

Inside the dark blue confines of his passport, R.R.C. Walker has described his occupation, and has officially been so listed by Her Majesty's Government, as "Gentleman." It is a perfectly valid description. So are about a dozen others: racing manager, team sponsor, classic and vintage car collector, model racer, magazine writer a completely open and friendly figure in the sometimes devious and shark-filled world of motor racing. For Robert Ramsey Campbell Walker *is* Rob Walker, direct descendent of the legendary Johnny Walker who still strides Scotch bottles the world over.

Johnny Walker would not be ashamed of his descendant. Rob was at one time the most respected private entrant in motor racing and one of its most colorful characters. It was not that he was flamboyant, just unusual. For example, he was probably the only racer ever to drive the Le Mans 24-hour race in a business suit (1939). He was probably the only one of the modern Grand Prix entrants who, despite a perpetual lack of racing funds, turned down a $100,000 offer for some his old single-seaters from a collector, then gave the cars to the man on permanent loan for his single-seater museum (Colin Chapman must have quaked at the very thought, Enzo Ferrari would not even have considered seeing the collector, and at least one fellow would have sold the collector some good copies as the original stuff).

Walker never had any active role in the family whisky business, but he never wanted for money either. He lived graciously, bought cars whenever he wanted, and by the time he was 21 (he was born in 1917) reportedly had had 21 cars. One of these was a 3.5-litre Delahaye Type 135 that Walker himself competed in at Brooklands and in the 1939 Le Mans race (8th, codriven by Ian Connell). He got in his 1st stint as a patron rather than driver just before World War II when a special match race was run at Brooklands among his Delahaye, drived by Arthur Dodson, a Darracq, and an Alfa Romeo. The race was held to determine which was the best sports car. Dodson and the Delahaye won.

Walker was what has been described as a "minor educational calamity" at Sherborne and Cambridge. He was an early pilot, once lapped a Tiger Moth round a

steeplechase course, earning a lifetime ban on his flying. World War II put him back in a pilot's seat again, in a Navy airplane, and he spent 6 years at it. Back from the wars, and married, he never raced again; that was one of the conditions under which he successfully wooed his wife. He could get away with an occasional test drive in one of the cars he sponsored, of course.

The cars started out as sports car including one for Prince Bira of Siam. There were Delahayes and Aston Martins galore, but in 1950 two 23-year-old Delages were added to the Walker stable with a view to going Formula 1 racing. Fitted with an ERA engine, one of the cars could at least look competitive. There also followed Porsches, Coopers, and Lotuses. Drivers employed read like a bluebook of racing in those seasons: Brabham, Brooks, Collins, Reg Parnell, Tony Rolt, Trintignant, Bonnier, Salvadori, and Stirling Moss.

It was Moss in January 1958 who raced Walker's St. Andrews blue 2-litre Cooper-Climax to a *grande épreuve* victory in the Argentine Grand Prix against the powerful factory teams of Ferrari and Maserati. Four months later Trintignant gave Walker his 2nd World Championship victory as a sponsor at the Monaco GP, defeating the full might of Ferrari, Vanwall, and BRM, among others. Moss's Argentine victory that year was the initial one for a rear-engined car, and formula car racing with a slightly enlarged engine against an F1 field at that.

Moss also won the 1959 Italian GP for Rob in a Cooper, and the balding Briton also copped the Monaco races of 1960–61 and the German GP of 1961 in Walker-sponsored F1 cars. Moss's terrible crash at

Goodwood in 1962 might have ended the Rob Walker story, but it did not. Walker continued, and Jo Siffert, the Swiss driver, added a new page to the R. R. C. Walker Racing Team log with a British GP victory, the team's 9th.

Rob was always great at lining up sponsors, but even so, the annual racing bill was $30,000 or so in losses (expenses over income). The racing income even included Walker's share of 4 garages, of which he owned 49 percent. The 1st one was acquired in 1947 to ensure proper maintenance of the racing cars. The others followed thanks to Rob's partner, Jack Durlacher, who had earlier been Rob's racing partner. Jack advanced funds and absorbed some of the losses. Durlacher was very much behind the scenes, however, while the tall, slim Walker, usually wearing a cap, his prominent nose a more permanent identifying feature, was out front, timing his racers, commiserating with driver and mechanics, and reflecting on the changing fortunes of the dark blue cars.

Rob had top mechanical help, beginning with veteran wrench Alf Francis. He continued with men associated with or trained by Francis down through the years, right up until more recent times when there was little to do except know how to change engines, which were readied at the independent factories and shipped back and forth to the teams. In the old days the mechanics had to know how to rip the cars apart and put them together again. They even had to resort to psychology on occasion. A famous example was Moss's 1958 Argentine GP victory, won because Stirling had guts enough to race his Cooper to the checker at the rear tires wore down to the 3rd layer of canvas, while Francis fooled the opposition with a big show of getting ready to pit Moss and change tires. Walker did not see that big show; he was back in Britain, but after that he never missed many Grands Prix in which the team raced.

Costs kept soaring, and it looked as if Rob had had it as the seventies opened, but he came up with a new angle to keep the Walker name active in racing. This was the merging of his forces with those of John Surtees's Team Surtees, supported by Brooke Bond Oxo, a British tea distributor that had previously supported Walker and Graham Hill. He had to trade the familiar Walker Lotuses—49C and 72 driven by Hill in 1970—for Surtees mounts. Rolf Stommelen joined on as number 2 driver. The gentleman is still with us.

LEE WALLARD

Determination and courage are common commodities in automobile racing, but there are some men whose determination and whose courage transcend even the milieu of the race track. Lee Wallard was such a man. Athletic, dedicated to auto racing in the U.S. to the extent that he felt it incumbent upon himself to be

641

dressed to the nines whenever he appeared out of uniform, Wallard never feuded with other drivers. Althought the 5-foot 8-inch native of Altamont, N.Y., was a professional, he viewed auto racing as a sport, an athletic endeavor.

Born about 1911, Wallard began racing in jalopy races in southern New York state at the age of 21. He earned what living he could by running a bulldozer. Unlike other competitors in the semipro contests, Wallard took his racing seriously and switched to midget single-seaters. He learned by doing and that was expensive in broken bones as well as in machinery. He was just good enough and just determined enough to hang on and get rides.

Finally, about 1937, Lee switched to the AAA Eastern Sprint circuit. Wallard still wanted to make it big, and that meant Indianapolis. As far as he was concerned winning Indy was the whole show. In 1940 he went out on speculation to Indianapolis. He at least saw the race track. On 1941 he was occupied in healing a broken pelvis after flipping into the 4th row of the grandstands in a New Jersey race.

Wallard returned to racing as determined as ever after service in the Navy during World War II. He came back on the AAA Eastern circuit, running an occasional Eastern Championship race. In 1948 Wallard returned to Indy and got not one but 2 cars. The important one was the Iddings Special. This was a dirt-track car built for the broadsliding of the Trail stops where dirt surfaces still predominated. Other dirt cars had been to the Speedway before, but the general notion was that they were at a great disadvantage. Wallard changed that and in the process discovered a groove that was to last until the rear-engined cars took command.

With just a few hours left to qualify, Wallard rolled out in the Iddings car. His 128.420 m.p.h. lap was 5th fastest, and although he was starting 28th because of his late qualification, Wallard had become the driver to watch. He passed 15 cars in the first 10 laps, then moved into the top 10 at 150 miles. He was passing in the corners—something no one else dared do. He got up to 8th fell back with inept pit work, and charged again, finishing 7th. His drive made Wallard known. He campaigned the Iddings car to win his 1st Championship Trail race at DuQuoin, Ill., the track where Ted Horn, his best friend, was to die later in the season. It is said that Horn's lucky dime fell from his shoe as his body was lifted lifeless from the track; Wallard picked it up and kept it. Lee finished 6th in the Trail standings and 3rd in the Midwest point title race.

In 1949 Wallard inherited Horn's Maserati ride for the 500. He qualified fast but late again, starting 20th. Again he passed and repassed in the first 10 laps to lie 7th. At 20 laps he was 3rd, with only the Novis of Duke Nalon and Rex Mays ahead. And when Nalon crashed, Lee was a single place away from his life's dream. On the 36th lap Mays outsmarted himself, get-

ting caught behind slower traffic, and Wallard cut under him. Lee Wallard was leading the Indianapolis 500! When Mays broke down 12 laps later, things looked especially easy. But joy turns to frustration quickly in racing. Two laps later Wallard himself was sidelined as a gear failed. His best finish in 1949 was 2nd at Del Mar, Calif. The man with the peaked racing helmet did, however, finish in the money 7 times.

For Indianapolis in 1950 Wallard had the 1st car built with him in mind—a Lou Moore Blue Crown Special that could also be used on the dirt tracks. Again Lee was 5th fastest, and again he qualified late. He was in 23rd position. He had advanced to 6th place when rain cut the race short. But then the whole year was frustrating—niggling little things going wrong time and again to thwart him. It was inevitable that Wallard would switch for Indy in 1951.

Murrell Belanger of Crown Point, Ind., had almost the same dream as Wallard. He wanted his car to win the Brickyard. He had spent his money to learn that winning is a team effort. This time the driving member of the team was to be Wallard. All winter the men worked and planned. The Belanger Motors Special No. 99 was the result. It was a small blue car with golden numbers ingeniously painted to look like hammered metal. Its Offenhauser engine had been sleeved down to 241 cu. in. to get more economical fuel consumption. This surprisingly did not affect the speed, because this time Wallard qualified on the 1st day in the middle of the front row (135.039 m.p.h.).

Now 40, Wallard was still a favorite, and had still not realized his ambition. The 1951 Indianapolis 500 had Nalon on the pole and Jack McGrath completing the front row. It was a glorious sunny day and Loretta Young, the race queen, was only one of many celebrities in the famed pagoda watching the spectacle of pre-race activities—the bands and the cars lining up and the last minute activities before "Gentlemen, start your engines" boomed out over the speaker system. Soon 33 snarling machines would be attacking a 40-year-old track and 33 sweating men with visions of fame and fortune would be competing.

When the "GO" flag dropped, McGrath and Wallard leaped ahead of Nalon to begin a trophy-dash duel. It seemed sheer insanity to race wheel to wheel, taking chances to get a slight lead, but that is exactly what Wallard and McGrath did, trading the lead on almost every lap. Finally, on lap 16, the cast changed. Cecil Green charged past McGrath to challenge Wallard, and Walt Faulkner joined the party. Punished by the awesome pace, cars began to break and retire. Green and Wallard made their 1st pit stop almost simultaneously, and Cecil beat Wallard out for the lead (when Jimmy Davies pitted).

The trophy dash continued on and on. Someone had to break, something had to give. It did, Green's tortured engine blowing a piston at 200 miles, and Wallard was rid of one challenger, but only one. Faulkner charged up to rip at his wheels. The field was down to 18 cars by the halfway mark, and Jack McGrath, afflicted by a muscle spasm, drove in for a relief pilot. "They're crazy," Jack gasped. "They're running like it was a dirt-track race." Not long after Faulkner dropped out, and with 175 miles to go, Wallard had his 1st substantial lead—more than a lap over Mike Nazarak. The question now was, could he last? Part of his tail pipe had fallen off and there was obviously something wrong with the suspension. Belanger and Saleh waved the "SLO" sign, but Lee was having none of that. As he passed the pits he would grin and wave like a kid on his 1st merry-go-round ride.

When Nazarak came up to unlap himself, Wallard raced him. At 400 miles there were 9 cars left, all crippled in some way. The real possibility existed that no one would finish. Wallard had obviously lost at least one shock absorber, maybe 2, but he hardly slackened his pace. With 25 miles to go he lost his brakes—it was obvious because he took the corners differently and finally slowed down a little. When the checkered flag finally dropped, Belanger and crew heaved a sigh of utter relief. Duane Carter had come up on Wallard in the last feet of the race. Lee had raced him, dropping inside to go across the line. Wallard rolled past the pit area sitting on the rear cowl of No. 99 waving with both hands to the cheering crowd. He yelled to his crew to meet him in Victory Lane. Then he stood up in the car, turned around and waved like a trick rider. Finally the car rolled almost to a halt but well-wishers pushed him into Victory Lane, a man fulfilled.

Four days later in Reading, Pa., he was hospitalized, fighting for his life. In a sprint-car race, Wallard's mount caught fire. Lee steered the flaming machine past the pit area before leaping out. He had been severely burned on the face, chest, arms, and legs. Months later he finally returned home, having undergone more than 35 skin grafts. A new dream had been born in the pain and agony of the recovery. Lee Wallard wanted to win Indy again. He wanted to come back and show he was not diminished. In 1952, smiling and tanned, he drove a few test laps in a new Belanger, which Carter then finished 4th in the race. Lee exercised and got himself into amaing physical shape considering the intermittent pain the scar tissue afflicted on him.

Finally in 1954 at age 43, Wallard announced his comeback. There was another new Belanger waiting for him. He practiced in the car at the 135-m.p.h. level. He seemed a shoo-in to make the field. But he had seen the new young hot shoes and the new chargers. Lee had watched other drivers in his car and he was a realist. It was a good car and deserved better than a 43-year-old on an ego trip to no one knows where. On the eve of qualification he announced his retirement to accept a position in industry, a position that had been his for after the race as well as before.

Wallard was honored with an official's job, but the extensive scar tissue was slowly killing him. He could not perspire where he was burned and the toxic substances were hard to throw off. On November 28, 1963, Wallard died at age 50. To the last he smiled when anyone mentioned 1951 and the former bulldozer operator standing and waving to the crowd in a slowly rolling blue race car with the 98 in hammered gold, a man supremely happy, a man fulfilled.

PHIL WALTERS

Competition people normally do not much care what Volkswagen dealers have to say about racing, but there was one out on Long Island who was the exception. His name was Phil Walters, or, if you prefer, Ted Tappett. He answered to both names when he was burning up the midget tracks, helping to popularize sports car racing and piloting the Cunninghams that were annual challengers at Le Mans and familiar sights through the adolescent years of road racing in the United States.

Walters was born in New York City (1917) but raised in Manhasset, a Long Island town less than 20 miles away from the big city but a considerable distance from the world's top racing circuits. The curly-haired Walters was not thinking about those places, however, but about local tracks like Freeport and Islip where the midget cars raced. While still in his teens, Phil constructed his own car, a Ford Model A based vehicle in which he was, in his own words, "a street menace." Like most youngsters, Walters thought he was a pretty good driver, good enough, certainly, to compete on the clay and blacktop that comprised the midget circuit.

In 1938 he was unknown, by either of his names. The "Tappett" sobriquet came about when Phil claimed at Freeport that he was a hot-shot from the Midwest in town for a shot at the big time. It took him a while to find anyone willing to give him a chance. Though he was 21, Walters looked barely 17 and seemed evasive about his background. He finally got his chance with a desperate owner late that season. He won his 1st race, a qualifier for a feature, and rode his car from 13th to 6th place in the main event.

In 1939 he won 11 features and finished second 11 times in the 45 top races he entered. The next season, in a better car, he won 26 consecutive races. Now that the boys were watching out for him, things got a bit rougher, and he did not win every time out. Yet in 1941 Walters entered 46 consecutive feature races and never finished lower than 3rd. And he won 22.

With the war, Phil swapped his wheels for wings, but was shot down over Holland. He finished the war in a POW camp, minus about 70 percent of one lung, but with several medals. Coming back, Walters swapped his previous grunt-and-groan, all-out style of driving for a relaxed, fairly calm style to compensate for his lung problem. He proved that he was as good as ever by winning 26 features in a row in 1947. That year he had another string of 47 features in which he never fell lower than 3rd. Midgets were falling into a temporary eclipse then, however, and Ted Tappett started looking for a ride among the modified stock-car racers. He got one from a fellow named Bill Frick, and the combination proved startlingly successful. In 58 races entered in 1948, Walters was 1st or 2nd in all but 5. In those 5 the car conked out on the diminutive driver, whose middle name had become consistency.

The next year Frick-Tappett Motors was founded in Freeport and the Fordillac—Fords powered by Cadillac V-8 power plants—was born soon after. Briggs Cunningham bought a Fordillac for possible racing at Le Mans, where the millionaire sportsman had decided it was time for an all-American try at the endurance race. Cunningham was so taken with the Fordillac that he approached Walters with his long-germinating idea of building the all-American car from scratch. Walters, who later said he had never even heard of Le Mans, let alone the race, was intrigued with the challenge and agreed to join Cunningham.

"The basic design for our sports car would make use of the Cadillac engine," he recalled, " and we were going to select other major components from the various Detroit manufacturers and engineer these into a body design and chassis of our own. Unfortunately, the idea of making the car 100 percent American provided certain inherent handicaps, particularly in such areas as braking and transmissions."

Time ran out on the design team for the 1950 race so Walters took a 3-car stock Cadillac team to France that year for familiarization purposes. In order to go into the design and building business in earnest, operations were moved from Long Island to West Palm Beach, where a large airplane hanger happened to be handy for the Frick-Tappett Motors division of the B. S. Cunningham Company.

At about this time the directors of the Cadillac division of General Motors caught wind of the Fordillac modifications and the proposed Le Mans Cunninghams, and they wanted nothing to do with such matters. No more Cadillac engines were made available to Walters, so the design was shifted to the big Chrysler V-8 power plant. Four cars were finished for the 1951 Le Mans race and arrived just in time to answer the starter's flag. John Fitch and Walters managed an 18th in the race, after reaching as high as 2nd, after 20 hours before a rod bearing gave way. The rest of that season Cunninghams, sometimes driven by Walters, dominated the U.S. racing scene for this class of machinery.

In 1952 C-4s were introduced for the Le Mans assault. They were the fastest things there, but defective valve spring retainers knocked 2 of the 3 entries out of the race, and the 3rd was slowed down to finish 4th, driven 20 of the 24 hours by Cunningham himself.

Again the Cunninghams dominated their class, and the following year the same machines headed for the Sarthe circuit, again with only detail improvements, including a 4-speed gearbox.

The experimental C-5 was entered with Fitch and Walters sharing the wheel, but 1953 was the Jaguar year. Cunninghams were 3rd, 7th, and 10th, but Jaguars won and took 2nd and 4th as well. The Americans were faster, but their drum brakes were no match for the discs on the Jaguars. The C-5 was wiped out 2 weeks later at the Rheims 12-hour race with Fitch driving.

For 1954 Phil again led the Cunningham driver list at Le Mans in a C-4 as he did the next year (the last for the marque), when he also signed to drive for Ferrari in major sports car races and in some Formula 1 competition after Le Mans. Before he ever took a Ferrari wheel, however, the Le Mans tragedy of 1955 caused Phil to reconsider his actions. He retired at the age of 38.

Phil's mark in sports cars, however, remains an impressive one. Walters won at Sebring twice (1953 and 1955) with Fitch in a Cunningham and with Mike Hawthorne in a Cunningham-Jaguar. He also won the Watkins Glen GP twice (1951 and 1954) and the circuit's Seneca Cup, all in Cunninghams, the latter a Cadillac-Healey hybrid.

RODGER WARD

The press called him Rodger the Dodger, and they said it in a tone that made it plain they thought he was a little lower than a flat tire. They were contempuous of of him, but a little afraid, too, because he was capable of going very fast in a race car—if he was in shape. Besides, he owed many people money which he somehow forgot to pay. That had been a long time ago. Rodger Ward became not only a double Indianapolis winner, but also a respected spokesman for the sport. But he remembered those other days. "Many times," he said, "a man's reputation exceeds his activities. That's even more so if one is a loner. I was impressed with my own importance and I was having fun. I was living on racing, not for it."

Born in Beloit, Kans., on January 10, 1921, Rodger Ward made things hard for himself. He could have gone to college but there was no inclination on his part to do so. When the family moved to Los Angeles—where he received most of his schooling—Rodger began tinkering with parts in his father's auto wrecking and junk yard business. He finished a Ford hot rod at 14, and dropped out of high school in his junior year. He was learning something else—to be wary of cops who objected to drag races on city streets at 3 A.M. World War II saved him, turning him into a P-38 fighter pilot. Rodger liked flying so much he seriously thought of making flying his career. When the chance came to learn how to fly a multi-

engined B-17, Ward took it. He was so good he was retained as an instructor in instrument flying. But when the war ended some of the glamour went out of flying.

He was stationed at Wichita Falls, Tex., when a quarter-mile dirt track was built and Rodger's old dream of becoming a race driver was renewed. He saw a few midget races there, and had soon talked his way into a spare-time job maintaining the Ford-engined midgets. When the program was a driver short one night, he volunteered. He did not win, but he was competitive enough to think of trying the sport when he was discharged in 1946 and went home to California.

The United Racing Association then controlled midget racing on the West Coast of the United States. One could race 7 nights a week if he had the stamina and the luck. There was a Blue Circuit for the Offenhauser-powered cars and a Red circuit primarily for Ford 60 machines. The Red circuit was considered a training ground for the faster Offy races, but drivers such as Johnny Mantz, Walt Faulkner, Mack Hellings, and Bill Vukovich, the champ, with his old Drake-powered machine, made competition exciting.

Ward spent the rest of 1946 finishing near the end of the pack. He began to take the machines he could wangle to an ocassional top-5 finish in 1947 and, finally got a ride in a Clay Smith-prepared automobile. He won the San Diego Grand Prix in 1948 and his reckless driving style built him a loyal following. Rodger was graduated by Smith to the Offy the following year. He won often enough to keep his ride; he was also married, and had 2 sons.

In 1950 the popularity of midget racing had peaked, but Rodger added the one feat of which he always remained proud. In a feature at Gilmore Stadium, one of the most difficult of the dirt bullrings where the midgets competed, Ward, in a Ford-powered car, whipped all the Offies in a main event. It was like asking a milk horse to beat Man O' War, but Rodger did it. "I felt ready for Indianapolis after that," Ward said.

Ward took to the AAA stock-car circuit in an Oldsmobile and won the title for 1951. He passed his rookie test at Indianapolis that year and lasted 34 laps in the Deck Manufacturing Special before a broken oil line sidelined him. In 1952 he lasted 130 laps in the Federal Engineering Special, until his oil pressure failed. And in 1953, when he finally talked himself into a ride for the season in the M. A. Walker car, he needed a relief stint from both Andy Linden and Duke Dinsmore, but a faulty ring and pinion did him in after 177 laps. He won his initial Championship Trail races, a rain-shortened 51-lapper at the old Detroit Fairground and the Springfield 100. In 1954 he stalled the Dr. Ray Sabourin Chiropractic Special on Indy's backstretch; there was quite an argument among the press as to whether this was his fault for not coming in for gas. Then in 1955 came the accident at Indy.

Right after the race, Rodger Ward took a long hard look at himself. He was still looking as other teams packed to leave for home or for the next race at Milwaukee. Lights were on high in the Pagoda, where the reporters were wringing the last bit of excitement and the last bit of pathos out of the race—telling how Bob Sweikert had won and how Bill Vukovich had been killed. Ward was struggling with despair and anger at those who intimated he had been responsible for Vuky's death. He felt anew the sickening lurch of his car as it began to loop end for end. He felt the shoulder harness cutting him as the Aristo Blue Special launched itself into the air, hit with a jolt, then bounced up weakly again. The old Offy's front axle had snapped as he had tried to avoid being lapped by Vuky. He had walked away with only a cut on his nose, but some said he was the cause of Vuky's death.

"The fact that I was even involved in the accident that led to Bill's death hit me hard," Ward said. "I knew something was wrong with my car, and yet I drove it because otherwise people would have called me a quitter. Vuky didn't make many friends, but he and I were very close. I admired him. I didn't sleep for 2 or 3 days after that."

The year before at DuQuoin, Ill., Ward had been involved in the freak 88th lap accident that took the life of mechanical great Clay Smith. Ward was running 4th, but had lost his brakes 38 laps earlier. Chuck Stevenson lost control as he tried to pass Rodger, knocking him into Clay who had maintained the midgets in which Rodger had had some of his greatest successes. "I thought of quitting then, too," Ward said. "Clay was another of the few men in racing I really looked up to."

"That night at Indianapolis after Vuky's accident I became a pro," Ward said. "I wasn't a different man the next day, but I was trying. A great many people helped me. Irish Horan of the thrill show for which I worked when not racing; Vuky's oldest brother; Herb Porter, who was the mechanic for Roger Wolcott's cars. Mainly I had to get back not only my own confidence, but my confidence in the human race."

Ward had gone to Milwaukee with the Aristo Blue car, but refused to drive after the kingpin failed and a wheel flopped off in practice. He was fired on the spot. He had a difficult year in 1955; he began to try to pay his debts; he gave up smoking and drinking; he tried to put his life back together. In 1956 at Indianapolis he drove the Filter Queen Special, finishing 8th and finally making the 500 Club for drivers who last the race. "Ed Walsh didn't get the ride he deserved in that car," Ward said. "I drove a terrible race even though it was probably the best I could have done that day."

Later in the 1956 season Porter handed him the Wolcott dirt-track car. It was the beginning of the 1st real team effort Rodger had been involved with since the Clay Smith days. In 1957 at Indianapolis, Ward moved from 24th to 14th in the Wolcott Fuel Injection Special in the first 5 laps. He had begun his 2nd charge upward when the supercharger threw a bearing and that was that after 27 laps. But Wolcott-Porter-Ward was fully prepared for Milwaukee and drove to an easy victory. Of 11 starts on the Trail, Ward led 10 and finished 4. Of those 4, he won 3—adding Springfield, and Sacramento to Milwaukee. In 1958 he was running 4th at Indy when the fuel pump broke and packed him in. He finished 5th in the national point standings, however, winning at Milwaukee and Trenton.

But then Roger Wolcott died, and Ward found himself at liberty. It was soon after that that the famed Triple W team was formed—Ward, premier carbuilder-mechanic A. J. Watson, and greeting card company owner Bob Wilke. Actually Ward was 3rd choice as driver. Watson wanted Jim Rathmann but could not lure him away, then tried to get George Amick who took the Bowes Seal Fast assignment with George Bignotti instead. Finally he turned to Ward, who he felt was getting on in years—and came up with an Indianapolis 500 winner.

The 1959 race must have been doubly satisfying to the erstwhile Rodger the Dodger. He and Rathmann had virtually identical new Watson creations. And then there was Johnny Thompson in a new Racing Associates Special. These 3 and at least 4 others were easily capable of winning. It was a superbly planned race, won as much by Ward's smooth driving as by fast pit work and superior preparation of the machinery. The race hinged on the 2nd pit stop. Thompson went at 84 laps to change tires, and Rathmann followed at 92 laps. Ward built up a 61-second edge on Johnny and 84 on Jim before he,

too, pitted. His own 23-second pit stop was far faster, and he never reliquished the lead. There was a 3rd almost as fast, and Ward coasted home $106,850 richer. He went on to become USAC National Champion, winning also at the Milwaukee 200, DuQuoin, and Indy Fairgrounds.

Both Ward and Rathmann had new Watsons for the 1960 version of the 500, and again they engaged in a monumental duel. "It seems like we traded the lead a million times in the final 120 miles," Rodger recalled. "But I outguessed myself on the 178th lap when I let Jim back in the lead to conserve rubber. Suddenly I realized that if there were an accident we would finish the race under the caution. I had to lead because I had the faster car."

Ward took over on lap 183, Rathmann on 190, and the two were locked in an old-time 20-mile trophy dash, running wheel to wheel. It was Rathmann, then Ward, then with a 146.128 m.p.h. fastest lap, Rathmann surged ahead on the 197th lap. Ward was gaining through the number 3 corner, but then "I noticed out of the corner of my eye the white breaker thread of the tire carcass showing on my right front tire. In the old days I would have taken the gamble just to show I was as brave as anyone. But now I really had no choice but to back off and accept 2nd."

A few seconds later Rathmann suffered the same fate but he was home free, 13 seconds ahead of Ward. Rodger added Trenton and the Milwaukee 100 to his growing string of Championship 1sts in 1960. In 1961 Ward switched to the Sun City Special for Indianapolis, finishing 3rd, but the move away from Leader Card was only temporary. Ward returned full-time for the 1962 season and gave Leader Card its 2nd victory at Indy. He was in total command from lap 126 on and seemed to be unbeatable—or nearly so—whenever the Leader Card cars were running to their potential on the Trail. In a shortened version of the Trail, he won the Milwaukee 200, Trenton 150, and Syracuse 100. He was USAC champion again at the age of 41, a respected and articulate spokesman for automobile racing—and up to that time USAC all-time point leader, an honor subsequently grabbed by A. J. Foyt.

Ward continued on the Trail for 2 more years, but he was done in by a new phenomenon, the rear-engined racing car. Rodger had no trouble adapting. In his Kaiser Aluminum Special he finished 4th in 1963 at Indy, then in 1964, in a rear-engined car, he was 2nd. In 1963 he had added 5 more Trail victories, all 100-milers, at Milwaukee, Springfield, Indy Fairgrounds, Sacramento, and Phoenix, but in 1964 he never broke the top 10 except for the 500.

There had been a simultaneous Ward career in a Bill Stroppe-prepared Mercury in USAC's stock-car races, but although there were victories, they were secondary. Ward was a prosperous businessman when, at the age of 44, he entered the 1966 Indy 500 with a Lola-Ford.

It was his last race; he retired soon after this tragedy-struck race in which he finished 15th. He did not like rear-engined automobiles, and he found—on a very hot day in Trenton, N.J.—that his stamina was no longer there. He retired to his business interests and was shrewd enough to stay retired, a live all-time USAC great, rather than a superannuated driver learning to go fast under new conditions.

BENTLEY WARREN

With the wonderful complexities of the modern single-seater, there are an inordinate number of things that can make a car part of the scenery, while some other driver runs off with the money. Bentley Warren found that out when he switched from the minor leagues of New England racing to the USAC Championship Trail. He was 29 in 1970, his debut campaign, and even managed a 4th in the Milwaukee 200. He found out quickly that the 73 or 74 victories back home were nothing but experience. His 9 years of sportsman and super-modifieds were nothing but experience for "The Flying Fisherman."

A native of Gloucester, Mass., born December 10, 1940, Warren leaped at the chance to drive the cars of Greek ship owner Tassi Vatis. He finished the 1970 season 15th. In 1971 the Vatis team picked up Classic Car Wax as a sponsor and, if the car was not the fastest on the Trail, it was the shiniest—and one of the few with the kind of hydralastic suspension found on the Issigonis-designed BMC transverse-engined passenger cars. That was courtesy of chief mechanic Bill Finley. There were 2 of these, plus a Gurney Eagle for road racing and a Vollstedt chassis dirt car. It did not sound like a scenery operation.

At Rafaela, Argentina, on February 28, 1971, a USAC 300-miler was run on a 2.87-mile oval in 2 heats. Warren had blown an engine at Saturday practice; then on Sunday morning, as he hit the the accelerator to get up to speed, a gush of oil erupted. Bentley brought the car back to his pit, and the crew attacked it desperately. The trouble was a twisted oil hose. The engine had to be pulled, the line repaired and the engine reinserted, with racing only a short time away.

Bentley leapt into the car as the pace car pulled away. He was able to bring the car to 27th position, 17 places below where he qualified, as the pace car completed the 1st of 3 pace laps. But then the car sputtered and the engine stalled. There was no time to adjust the fuel feed balance. Finley raced out to where the car was and brought the engine to life seconds before the green flag dropped. Warren blasted full speed after the pack, but was half a lap behind when racing began officially—and the power was beginning to slack off in his mount again. In desperation he reached behind his right shoulder to flick the fuel feed off-on switch, and the car came to life.

He did this 212 times in the 53 laps of the opening heat, or each time he came to a corner, taking his left hand off the steering wheel while travelling 170 m.p.h. in traffic. Yet he ranged as high as 6th before coasting to a 10th-place finish out of fuel.

Everything was repaired for the 2nd heat, and Warren moved from 10th to 4th place within 3 laps. On the 10th lap he was battling Swede Savage for 3rd. Lloyd Ruby had spun on kerosene dropped by Rick Muther's turbine car, and Savage and Warren were charging wheel to wheel for the same slick spot. Savage got through, but Bentley spun into the wall, rupturing the fuel tank. The car exploded into flame as it rolled down the banking. Warren, shoulder harness off, bailed out like a stunt driver. He suffered only second-degree hand and forearm burns but all he could say was, "I was running as strong as Al Unser. Did that feel good." Warren, after all, did not expect to be in the scenery for very long.

A. J. WATSON

He was called a genius, an American phenomenon who first saw the light of day May 8, 1924, in Mansfield, Ohio, as Abram Joseph Watson. If being able to think a problem through and creating a solution is genius, then the slim, blue-eyed Watson qualified. But A. J. would have been the 1st to disclaim the title. Watson was something better than a genius. He was a success, and one of the most contented successes you'll ever hear about. There was never any doubt about what A. J. would be—there was no chance of his ever becoming a lawyer or a teacher, for instance. His father operated a machine shop, and A. J. grew up with machine tools all around him. He thought in terms of the bits and pieces of metal that turn into chassis (and engines on occasion), just as a mathematician can think in the symbols of his calling. Yet in high school, or in the Air Force, where he spent 1943–46 as a navigator, A. J. was not a budding Da Vinci of the drawing board by any means.

He attended Glendale College in California under the GI Bill after the service. It was there, in his sophomore year, that he found his calling. He met Billy Scully, a hot-rod owner, and with him watched his 1st automobile race in 1947 at Bonelli Stadium, near Los Angeles. They formed a partnership to build and race a jalopy. A. J. helped with the building and the mechanical work and was supposed to drive. His driving career lasted less than one lap—attempting to qualify the car, he spun and that was it. Another driver qualified the car, but it blew up in the consolation race.

But A. J. became a racing mechanic of some repute in roadster circles within the year. In 1948 he was asked to join the Indianapolis crew of Bob Estes, the California Lincoln-Mercury dealer who sponsored cars in the Indianapolis 500 and later in the Carrera Panamericana. The car—a V-8 powered job—did not make the race, so Watson had plenty of time to examine, watch, and learn. A. J. now also owned his own racing jalopy, campaigning successfully in Gardena Stadium and other California tracks. He brought the car into the Midwest later that season, ran it a few times, then sold it to Chicagoan Pat Flaherty, with whom he was to team in the future at Indy. Late in 1949 Dick Rathmann, who had campaigned his car in the Midwest, and A. J. returned to Glendale to a remarkable project.

Joe Mastro was a grocery clerk who was an incurable racing nut. But he also was a very fine promoter. He, Watson, Rathmann, and eventually some of the town's merchants were going to build and run their own Indy car. Even in 1949 a racer cost upwards of $20,000, but Watson, starting his 1st monoposto car, had initially about $2,500 in cash with which to work. Thus began the City of Glendale Special, or as Rathmann dubbed it, the Pots and Pans Special. Watson used discarded parts for much of the Offenhauser engine—only the gear train and cam housings were new. The car barely made it to Indianapolis in time to qualify, and lasted 27 laps when a crankshaft, which under magnaflux had shown an unusual stress pattern, let go. The official reason given was oil line troubles. Rathmann finished 5th in the car at Milwaukee, but at Langhorne the engine disintegrated.

Estes, however, was the gardian angel; he bought the car, hired A. J. as mechanic along with Judd Phillips, and installed Joe James as driver. Watson finished the season a thorough loser and determined to quit racing. His resolve lasted until April 1951, when he came down to wish James and the Estes team farewell as they departed for the Brickyard. He was working as a machinist on Lockheed Aircraft's graveyard shift (midnight to morning), but Lockheed never saw him again and presumably still has his tool box which he has never bothered to collect. James lasted 9 laps in 1951 for 33rd position, then was plagued with mechanical breakdowns in the Estes dirt-track machine until he yielded to another roadster graduate, Jim Rigsby.

Rigsby drove the Estes Championship car to 12th in the 1952 Indianapolis 500, but was fatally injured in a sprint-car accident at Dayton. The next week Watson and Phillips had a new driver, Don Freeland, who finished 5th in the Syracuse 100 and did well on much of the rest of the Championship Trail. But at San Jose, Calif., James returned to the team, winning the pole. Joe had left Estes to win the Midwest sprint title. His return to big cars was fatal—he seemed to be momentarily blinded by the sun—when his car rode over a competitor's rear wheel and flipped.

Watson and Phillips spent the winter building a new Championship car which would be convertible to a dirt machine merely by suspension changes. Freeland finished 27th at the 500 in 1953, spinning on the 76th lap after the axle broke. He did better on the Trail, finishing 7th in the point standings. A. J.'s final season with Estes was 1954. Freeland drove another new Watson Phillips car, a roadster, to 7th at Indianapolis, then finished 10th in the season's standings.

During the next winter A. J. finally decided to strike out on his own, switching allegiance to John Zink, an Oklahoma heating and plumbing executive. He built a dirt car for Bob Sweikert, the Zink driver, and altered a new Frank Kurtis roadster for the Speedway. The pink and white vehicle qualified on its 3rd try, and Sweikert drove it through the pack for a win in 1955, crediting Watson's mechanical ability. Watson was not present; his 18-day-old son had died and he had gone home after explaining to Sweikert how he wanted the car prepared. Bob went on to become the 1st Indy champion to win the Championship Trail since Wilbur Shaw had done it in 1939.

Next came the chance Watson apparently needed. He was commissioned by Zink to build a new Indy car. He had a free hand and all the money necessary. The result was Pat Flaherty's winning car, longer, narrower and lighter than other 1956 Indianapolis mounts, with a new torsion bar suspension and a weight adjustment that allowed changes in load distribution during the race. This feature was even more important in dirt-track machinery. It is this car's background that best explains Watson's success. A. J. knew that Indianapolis Speedway was going to be re-surfaced for 1956; the bricks in the back stretch were going to disappear; the turns would be smoother; speeds had to go up. Obviously tire wear would become more critical, then, unless one of 2 things happened: Firestone would announced a durability breakthrough, or the car itself became lighter. Watson had no hotline to Firestone so he went for lightness, even to the extent of altering the Offy engine.

Watson became the 1st builder at Indianapolis to use magnesium for the top skin of the car and fiber glass in the underpanels. He cut the thickness of the tubing in the chassis, but increased rigidity with a new skeletal design. Whenever possible, light metal took the place of iron and steel. Chick Hirashima, later to work on the Lotus-Ford Engine's race preparation, helped him short-stroke the Offenhauser. The result was a car 200 pounds lighter than anything else in the race, which produced record speeds with no tire problems. Eleven yellow caution periods occurred in the race as others suffered blowouts from overheated and overstrained tires.

When A. J. and Zink chose Pat Flaherty for 1956, the Chicago redhead had a record as a car smasher. His urge to win was so strong, according to printed reports, that he once slammed into another car when both were going at top speed on the off chance that he would ride away from the crash while his foe would be eliminated. He had two 10th places and a dent in the Indy cement outer wall to recommend him.

But that was the kind of driver A. J. had always preferred. Watson left the driving to the driver—even brake-happy Flaherty. It was Zink who told Pat that the key to Indianapolis is accelerating quickest out of the turns, not diving the deepest into them. Flaherty tried it, stayed off the brakes and won. Watson never said a word to Troy Ruttman the next year, either, when Troy hardly practiced though the car was ready. Ruttman put the car on the front row and was in contention when he retired with an overheated engine.

In the winter of 1957 Watson decided to buck the trend to the lay-down engine and also laid the seeds for his eventual split with Zink. He reasoned that a lower center of gravity of itself was not necessarily an advantage. And he proved it when the front row consisted of 2 Zink cars—an old one and a new one and a spare chassis he had built on speculation and sold to Lee Elkins for Dick Rathmann to drive.

The 16-car, 1st-lap accident of 1958 and Ed Elisian's slide limited Watson to Jimmy Reese's 6th. But it had been proved that the Watson cars did not need lay-down engines to run fast. Jim Rathmann drove the patched up Elisian car to a victory in the Race of Two Worlds at Monza only 30 days later. When Jim was ready to order a new Watson, and A. J. was ready to build it, Zink objected, and the association ended. In 1959 began the rise of the Triple W—Watson, Rodger Ward, and Leader Card Racing team owner Bob Wilkie. Watson built 2 roadsters and a dirt track machine. Ward won the 500, and in the other new car Rathmann finished 2nd. Rodger, of course, became USAC champion with 2 dirt-track triumphs (DuQuoin and Hoosier 100) plus the Milwaukee 200 as cornerstones of his title.

For 1960, in an effort to curb Watson's outside activities, Wilkie contracted for 2 new roadsters. Watson overhauled the old LCR cars, built them and 2 more. Jim Rathmann, in one of the outside projects won and Ward finished 2nd. The next year A. J. was limited contractually to the 2 Wilkie mounts, but in 1962 he refused to sign with such a clause, and Wilkie backed away. Four of the first 6 were Watsons. Parnelli Jones set the speed marks in a 1960 model and the LCR boys, Ward and Len Sutton, finished 1st and 2nd. Eight new Watsons came out in 1963, with Ward's 3rd best, but Jones in the antique won it. Watson was very impressed by the Lotus-Fords at this race. He went home to seek his own solution to the rear-engine idea.

Watson returned in 1964 with 2 rear-engined machines, one for Don Branson that was Offy powered, the other for Ward to have a Ford go. The cars were light, with ingenious touches like using the chassis tubing to run water and brake fluid, but A. J. had decided by mid-season that he could do much better for 1965, perhaps with a monocoque car. Nevertheless, the Ward car finished 2nd at Indianapolis in 1964 despite a mixture set too rich, which forced one extra pit stop.

Watson was a Burbank resident in the off-season. He had an abolute insistence on cleanliness in the pits and in the garage, and was impeccably attired in starched linens himself. The prematurely gray A. J. declared that this was not a fetish. "You can see things better if they are clean. It's just common sense." And it's always nice to use common sense, especially if there is creative thinking in the foreground. The Watson-Wilkie alliance was one of the longest lived in the sport, lasting past Bob's death in 1970. Watson continued as general manager and resident genius, preparing anew for 1971. In 1972 Mike Mosely broke his victory drought at Trenton.

JOE WEATHERLY

Oak Grove, Va., in the black-soiled farm country east of Norfolk, is a long way from Riverside International Raceway in California, about a lifetime—the lifetime of Joseph Herbert Weatherly. The son of a chicken farmer who died in a highway mishap when Joe was 9, Joseph Weatherly (born May 29, 1922) grew up in Norfolk where he delivered papers after school to help out his widowed mother. He won a trip to Washington, D. C., as a star carrier boy. In high school in Norfolk, Joe discovered motorcycles. He was a handsome young man then, given to playing practical jokes—rubber snakes, frogs, and other one-dimensional teases. He was called Little Joe because he never grew beyond 5 feet 7 inches, and he loved motorcycles because he could ride tall in the saddle. In 1942 he was drafted to serve with an Engineer Battalion in North Africa. He lost 2 teeth when a sniper shot them out, but came back otherwise unscarred. He began to participate in motorcycle races after the Army, and got himself a Harley-Davidson ride which was about as prestigious as there was in that era.

Weatherly was a winner on the track all summer. In the fall he lay disfigured for life in a hospital after his passenger car's steering failed, and the car hit a tree. His wife-to-be suffered multiple injuries, he crashed through the windshield, and a friend was killed. Because the Buick was green, Weatherly hated the color henceforth. He returned to bike racing, winning 3 American Motorcycle Association national championships before he switched to stock cars in 1950. The switch came when Joe got tired of falling on his head in cycling; he drove his debut race at Chinese Corner Raceway, now a Norfolk shopping center, and he won. He was a natural.

Joe teamed with mechanic Johnny Rhodes and terrorized the independent tracks until they switched their No. 9 modified D Ford to NASCAR racing in 1952. The switch merely expanded the area in which Joe raced. He won 49 of 83 races in 1952 and in 1953 he won NASCAR's modified national crown along with 52 more victories, against the likes of Speedy Thompson and his brother Jimmy, Buddy Shuman, the Flock family, and Cotton Owens. In 1955 his marriage ended, but his racing career took an upward leap—he joined the Ford factory team. It was not the typical divorce. Weatherly never moved his clothes out, came home occasionally as if he were still married and finally—in 1959—remarried his former wife. He also took to flying an airplane and promoting races in 1955. Curtis Turner was his teammate on this factory effort—which blew up in 1957—but the 2 battled in some of the most crowd-pleasing duels ever.

Weatherly continued to campaign steadily, living for the world of late-model stock-car racing, and playing his simplistic practical jokes. He worked hard at being colorful in public; in private he was basically a lonely man who could not bear to be alone for long. He tried promoting races with indifferent success, went back to driving, and won the Rebel 300 at Darlington in 1960 when it was a race for convertibles. In 1961 Little Joe won the National 500 at Atlanta and in 1963 he won Darlington again when the Rebel 300 was split into two 150-mile races. This was the famed "Bear Grease' race which Joe won in his Bud Moore-prepared Pontiac as the factory Fords were sliding and slithering to disaster because the tires they chose had no bite in the corners. Darlington had, as usual, prepared the track with a coating intended to have the opposite effect. It did, for much of the field, including Weatherly.

When track owner Bob Colvin had his idea of running 2 Little Reb races to make up the Rebel 300 he had in mind giving the fans the competition of 2 trophy dashes. Unfortunately his point system tripped him up. The 1st heat was all that any stock-car fan could ask. Fred Lorenzen and Tiny Lund, in the front row, began to bang fenders right from the start. That ended on the 2nd turn when Fearless Freddie spun out after still another love tap by Lund. Little Joe in his Pontiac moved straight into 2nd and outpulled Tiny down the back-

stretch for the lead. But Junior Johnson was there and his Chevrolet gained slowly but surely. Four laps later it was Junior who did the nudging, moving into 1st, with Weatherly and Richard Petty following him like a train.

On the 48th lap, Bob Cooper lost control of his Pontiac and crashed right in front of the Johnson-Weatherly-Petty express. Junior skidded high; Little Joe ricocheted off Junior and passed the Cooper wreck on the low side, nipping into the lead; Petty suffered most: he banged into the railing, rupturing a tire. Almost everyone pitted under the caution flag that followed, Weatherly finding that the right side of his mount had been gashed open. Junior regained the lead and held it until about a mile from the finish when Weatherly's pressure finally paid. The Chevvy's differential broke and Weatherly scooted home a winner over Junior and Fireball Roberts. And that is when Colvin's point system broke down.

Petty steamed out into the lead of the 2nd race as if he were determined to lap the entire field. Weatherly, realizing that all he had to do was finish ahead of Fireball Roberts because Johnson could not repair his car in time for the nightcap, let Petty go and concentrated upon staying in front of Fireball. This he did, finishing 8 seconds behind Petty only because Richard slowed down in the final lap. That was the last major supertrack victory for Weatherly, although he numbered 24 career victories in Grand National competition during his long career. Right after New Year's Day 1964 Weatherly left for Riverside International Raceway in California. He was driving for Mercury now, a new factory ride which he had had with Bud Moore for the last months of the 1963 season, too.

Turn 6 at Riverside is unlike anything in stock-car racing. There is a wall in front of you as you snake quickly off the front of the course. You brake hard and steer for dear life. Weatherly steered but not enough. His car smashed into the wall. He was killed instantly either because his racing harness was not fastened or because it failed to hold. Little Joe Weatherly, with his cut-out gloves, his black and white saddle shoes, and his desperate need to be at the center of things, was just a memory.

JOHN WEBB

Modern motor racing in Britain came about in large part because of John Webb. He rose from press agent to managing director of what was called Motor Circuit Developments, a subsidiary of the Grovewood Securities operation. MCD started when Grovewood, under Webb's urging, acquired Brands Hatch from the 50 or so people who held it. To that start, again under Webb's urging, have been added Mallory Park, Snetterton, Oulton Park and interests in Castle Combe and Ireland's Mondello Park. Webb did not stop at track management.

650

He was the promotional father of Formula Ford, Formula 5000, Formula 100, Formula Atlantic, and, in 1972, a new standard saloon championship in Britain.

Born about 1931, Webb started his own publicity agency in 1951 at age 20. Eventually his client list included Lockheed Aircraft, Silver City Airways, 3M, McAlpines, Air India, Bond, Connaught, and Brands Hatch. It was the latter that commissioned him to find a single owner for the property, and Grovewood was his discovery. He not only sold the Hatch to Grovewood but the idea of his running it. He conceived the idea of the annual Grovewood Awards to the most promising British drivers and racers in cars and cycles. But Webb never won that or any other award for his own racing potential.

His initial "race" came in 1956 when he noticed that the 350-c.c. class at Goodwood had no entries, so he entered one of his client's smaller Anzani-engined Astra vans for the race and won without opposition while garnering a nice lot of publicity. He drove a Ford Consul rental car in his next race and finished 4th in the field of 4. But he was a driver. In 1957 he was driving a Jensen road car and raced it enough to win 19 pieces of silverware. In 1962 he raced his E Jaguar at Brands in a GT race. In 1968 he started a stock-car race at the course, all part of his idea of knowing the problems of the drivers.

Getting to know driver problems and inventing ways of using his clients for fun and profit, Webb invented the original GP charter flights, when the F1 crowd flew from race to race via Webbair. He dismissed it as a hobby.

But the course acquisition and promotion program for Grovewood was no hobby. In 1962 Webb bought up Mallory, and Snetterton came under his wing the next season. Oulton was acquired in 1964, Castle Combe's motor racing rights in 1969, Mendello's rights in 1970. Grovewood had about $2.5 million in racing properties, plus $1.5 million or more in improvements at these courses, in Webb's charge. Making the courses pay was the impetus to his promotion of the various championship and racing series, series that even spilled over to the United States after Webb pioneered them in Britain, or at least popularized them. Without his presence, British racing certainly, and probably international racing, would wear a far different look today.

EDOARDO WEBER

Edoardo Weber, son of a German-speaking Swiss, was born in Turin in 1889. Some say that high-performance carburetion was also born at that time. Weber received a good technical education, joined Fiat as a test driver for a time and, in 1914, became what we would call a service manager for a large Fiat agency. He quit his job 6 years later in Bologna and set himself up in business to cater to the growing number of racing enthusiasts in post-World War I Italy. Edoardo himself was no mean driver in local competition, which gave him an insight into the needs of racing cars.

Late in 1924 Weber introduced a series of modified Fiats in full racing form capable of 90 m.p.h., rather than the factory fresh 40 m.p.h. which most drivers were used to. He even designed his own version of a Roots-type supercharger and, more importantly, his 1st carburetor for gasoline-powered vehicles, a dual-throat affair that was not new in design, but showed great skill nonetheless. A further modification of this carburetor gave it fuel economy that made it a big seller, assuring the future of his tiny enterprise. In 1929 racing again took over Edoardo's attention when the Maserati Brothers, who were industrial neighbors in Bologna, took their carburetion needs to him.

The result was Weber's Type 55-ASS for the Maserati 8C2500. From then on he was the marque's almost-exclusive carburetor supplier, including his 1st true dual-throat model, the 50DCO, introduced in 1931. Scuderia Ferrari was attracted to Weber's products and began using them on its racing Alfas. By 1937, when Webers were standard on all Alfa cars, the company's name was beginning to be known outside of Italy as well. That was the year that Alfa Romeo's Type 158 Alfetta won the Grand Prix crown using special 3-throated Webers. The famous racing mechanic, Alf Francis, brought the word back to England and Webers slowly began to appear there. World War II stopped the product's rise to fame for almost 7 years, and Edoardo himself disappeared without trace near the end of the war in Italy. One story is that communist partisans took him for ransom, but killed him instead. His body never was found.

Fiat, his old company, began to buy pieces of Weber stock, and by 1952 controlled half of its assets. A decision was made in Turin that Weber should be added to the rapidly expanding Fiat empire, and the company bought all the outstanding shares it could find (since then it has acquired almost complete control). Money and brains from the bigger company were poured into the smaller, even at that point really only a good-sized "family" business that turned out a few thousand carburetors a month. For better or worse, mass production methods were introduced (although the quality of Webers remained high) and production by the mid-sixties had reached something in the neighborhood of 100,000 carburetors per month. A decade later, production was up to something over 250,000 carburetors per month, and quality still was high. The design principles of Edoardo Weber, long gone, still were being followed, and his work lived on, more than in name.

BILL WEIGHTMAN

The scion of a pharmaceutical fortune, W. E. (Wild Bill) Weightman will be remembered as the patron of the famed Jimmy Murphy, the only American to win the French Grand Prix, but old-timers also like to remember Wild Bill for his exploits off the race course. Melrose Castle, Casanova, Va., was his home address, and spending money was his real occupation. He ran through a fortune estimated in the millions in a matter of years by such advanced processes as giving diamond rings to young women after a few hours' acquaintance, then forgetting their names the next day. He used to have cars located in garages all over any big city where he stayed for any period of time so that he would not have to wait long for them should he get the urge to drive. Weightman would often move out and leave the cars—machines like Mercedes and Duesenbergs—behind.

Weightman used to travel across country in a private train, following the races and any other matter that happened to catch his fancy. But his classic performance came just before he ran out of that year's allotment of money just after World War I. Wild Bill, who considered himself a rather good amateur driver, was in the city of Los Angeles at the time, both for the races and to back a girlie revue. A motorcycle policeman caught one of his employees doing 60 m.p.h. in a 20-m.p.h. zone, or some such thing, and handed the employee a summons. This was a situation that Wild Bill could not tolerate, for his minions—or he—always proceeded posthaste to or from someplace. He solved the problem with unique methods. Through political connections, he obtained the names of

every one of the 22 motorcycle patrolmen on the Los Angeles Police Force and sent them engraved invitations to a private party in the rooms of one of the posh Los Angeles hotels.

If any motorcycle policeman refused, it is not recorded in the minds of eyewitnesses, for the young women from the revue, who numbered in excess of 22, all seemed occupied. The occasion was marked with great quantities of liquor, great levity, and roast chickens and hams flying through the air. Each gendarme was then transported in his very own private taxi to a dance hall nearby where the jovial atmosphere continued. As dawn crept over the distant mountains, some patrolmen are supposed to have been taxied straight to their motorbikes and enforcement of the traffic laws without fear or favor but with a slight problem with equilibrium.

It would be in the best traditions of Hans Christian Andersen to report that Wild Bill eventually died of liver trouble or some such disease brought on by a full, merry life, but such is not the case. He eventually—when most of his fortune was gone—decided to enter the humdrum world of normality and passed from the auto racing stage. But who knows how many little dress shops were started from the proceeds of the sale of gaily proffered diamond rings? And how many of the nation's lawmen remember with just a touch of pride how it felt to loose a roast chicken in the direction of the chief's noggin?

BOB WELBORN

Bob Welborn of Greensboro, N.C., a man who may have been too logical for his own good, won the 1st NASCAR championship race ever on Daytona International Speedway. He won the 1st of the preliminary 100-mile championships at an average speed of 143.198 m.p.h. in his Chevrolet (Shorty Rollins won the next at 129.500). At Daytona he never won much else.

Welborn came on strong when NASCAR established a separate convertible division; he reasoned that convertibles were going to take over the sport because the fans could see the driver. Bob had also looked around racing and decided it was a good idea to have a Petty in his corner. But it was J. H. Petty, Lee's brother, that he wanted. Bob Welborn got himself a Chevrolet factory ride when that company came into racing, and he saved enough money to put business interests in top condition. However, he reasoned that racing had reached a plateau by 1963 and he quit. Of course the convertible circuit was rendered obsolete because the superspeedways demanded better aerodynamics and convertibles, relatively, were turtles. Whatever his talents at setting up front ends, J. H. proved to be the wrong Petty.

It is difficult to think of Bob Welborn without remem-

track records, only one on a superspeedway. He was logical to the end of his career. When he saw his kind of track disappear one by one, he disappeared from racing too.

LOU WELCH

Since the first day the Winfield Brothers brought their d.o.h.c. supercharged V-8 engines to Indianapolis in 1941, their raw power had intrigued mechanics and car owners. Their eerie scream with the supercharger working had race fans yelling in immediate recognition. Yet despite the fact that they cranked out 700 b.h.p. from 183 cu.in., the Novi never won—because no one was ever able to get that kind of power on to the track for 500 miles.

The word Novi comes from "No. V1," a toll station and later a village in Michigan. The engine did not get the name until Lou Welch took it over in 1946, 5 years after Ed and Bud Winfield 1st ran a car powered by their new engine. They blocked the throttle at half-way to keep the driver from using the engine's full power, and despite a 6-year-old chassis, it ran 4th. The war gap saw manufacturer Welch take over and pour money into the project. He had bankrolled the original engine which, incidentally, was refined by Fred Offenhauser and Leo Goosen working with the Winfields.

For Indy in 1946 Welch had Frank Kurtis build him a chassis and Ralph Hepburn qualified the car at a record 134.449 m.p.h. Starting 19th, Ralph led after 15 minutes and took a long lead by 140 miles, when he pitted. He stayed 9 minutes in the pits with brake trouble. Starting back in 13th he charged up to 2nd, only to retire completely on the 122nd lap when the engine swallowed a valve. Only 7 cars finished.

Cliff Bergere, the Hollywood stunt man turned race driver, was part of a 2-man Novi assault in 1947. His lifelong friend, Ralph Hepburn, had urged him to take the opportunity to drive the new car with an engine built in the shops of Lou Meyer and Dale Drake, who had bought out Offenhauser. The car steered like a truck and Bergere promptly put it in the brook after a spectacular qualification attempt spin. He later said that he had not bothered to come in to have his tachometer repaired. Later the cause of the hard steering was discovered: a mistake in the wheel blueprints had put the rims out of round.

Both Bergere and Doc Williams, a new driver, finally qualified, but the Novi crew accused Doc of not getting maximum potential out of the vehicle. Williams, who had thrilled himself several times, agreed to relinquish the Novi and veteran Herb Ardinger was called back after unusual permission for the driver substitution had been granted. Bergere took the lead from the starting

bering the ever-present cigar in his mouth. That cigar was the key to the man. If it was small and frayed from chewing, Welborn had problems. If it were new and full and he puffed on it, Welborn was doing well. But he was most dangerous when he held it in his fingers because even if he was talking he was also thinking and he had found an edge on you or other adversaries.

Welborn began his NASCAR career driving modifieds at Bowman Gray Stadium. He moved up to Grand National ranks for a few races in 1953 and finished 4th in Grand National point standings in 1955 in a Chevrolet. It was then that he made the decision to concentrate on the convertible division with only occasional sorties into GN. He won the title in 1956, 1957 and 1958, the latter 2 years as an independent operation.

After his 1959 experience at Daytona, he recognized the handwriting on the wall for convertibles and switched back to the Grand Nationals. He won another 100-miler at Speed Weeks in 1960, and after that it was mostly downhill through a succession of cars. In Charlotte's National 400 in 1961, Welborn finished 3rd in a Bud Moore-prepared Pontiac. He campaigned Pontiacs until 1963 when he switched to Dodge, but he did nothing at Speed Weeks. The garage business was going well and Bob had other investments by then, so it was not long after that that he stopped racing. He was 35 by then and his forte had been the small tracks, not the superspeedways which now dominated NASCAR.

He had won 7 Grand Nationals and over 20 convertible races, 10 in 1958 alone. At one time he held 20

flag, pulled out in front, but had to pit inside of 23 laps. He had worn down his right front tire to the cord in 60 miles. Cliff came back 7th, a full lap behind. In 40 miles he unlapped himself and by 150 miles he was gaining on the leader, Mauri Rose, so fast that victory seemed inevitable.

But the Novi engine decided to quit then and the car was through for the day. But Bergere was not. With the leaders 9 laps ahead and the race half over, the Ardinger car was called in and Cliff resumed the chase; he entered the top 10 in 100 miles and had brought the car up to 4th, only 2 laps behind winner Mauri Rose, when the miles ran out.

That was Bergere's last ride in the car. He quit in a huff in 1948 after spinning and putting it into the rail, while merely warming up the car at about 80 m.p.h. The brakes, which he said he had complained of being oil-soaked from a leaky right universal, had grabbed. Welch had remarked that he was "fooling around." It was in the same car several days later that Hepburn was killed. Chet Miller quit the other Novi, but Duke Nalon qualified it, then stayed off the pace until nearly the halfway mark. His pits cost him the lead and then the chance to win, first by slow work that dropped him to 3rd after a fuel stop, then by failing to put enough fuel in his tank. He had to come in 18 laps from the end and even lost 2nd.

Winfield and Jean Marcenac rebuilt the Hepburn racer for 1949, and Rex Mays was persuaded to join Nalon on the team. Nalon took the pole at 132.939 with Mays next to him. The Novis ran 1st and 2nd at a record pace for 23 laps, but on the 24th, Duke's rear axle broke, spinning the car into the northeast wall tail first and rupturing the fuel tank. Nalon, badly burned, escaped, but a wall of fire blocked the track. The caution flag came out but though Mays was the leader he lasted only 24 more laps, stalling with magneto failure.

In 1950, Nalon could not even make the field, but in 1951 he qualified at 136.498, a record until Walt Faulkner blasted it. But the day of the front drive was over and he left early with mechanical troubles. In 1952 Chet Miller raised the records to 139.6 for one lap and 139.034 for the 10 miles. But it was the same old story. Mechanical trouble sidelined both Nalon and Chet.

In 1956 with one Novi missing the chance to qualify, Paul Russo carried the Novi hopes in a crimson car with a tail fin and for 11 laps he looked unbeatable, sending the car hurtling around at 144 m.p.h. laps. On the 12th lap, for the 1st time in his decade of competition, he had the luck to pop a tire, sending the car skidding into the wall. The Novi jinx had struck again. Russo was back in 1957, taking the lead on lap 12 and holding it until Sam Hanks took it away in lap 36. Again it was the new George Salih chassis on the Hanks car that doomed Russo to failure. Paul finished 4th.

At that point Welch was ready to throw in the sponge.

He was only too glad to sell out the Novi project—and its jinx—to the Granatelli brothers in 1961. They had no better luck, so Lou never regretted the decision.

CHRISTIAN WERNER

In Europe it was not unusual for a man to spend his life working for one company. This extended even to glamourous people like racing drivers in the old days. Christian Werner was one of those people. He had been born May 19, 1892, in Stuttgart, so it was natural that Werner should end up in the automobile industry. On December 12, 1911, he joined Daimler-Motoren-Gesellschaft in Untertuerkheim as an engineer-driver, and later became a foreman in the running-in department.

Following World War I he became more and more a competition driver in the renamed Mercedes team, with his 1st great successes coming when he turned 30 in 1922. That year he was 2nd in the Targa Florio, and in the Bucharest Auto Club trials—3 of them—he won 2 and was 2nd in another. One of his runs was a record time and without a single penalty point, causing the BAC to issue him a special silver medal.

In 1923 Werner was at Indianapolis with a Mercedes, finishing 11th at 74.65 m.p.h. A bit slower—41.02—in 1924, he won the Targa and also the concurrent running of the Florio Cup. That year he also won the Semmering race is record time. The next season Werner was 1st in the Robert Batschari race and in the Freiburg and flat-

country races, in 1926 in the Baden-Baden and Bleich-roeder races.

In 1926 Mercedes became Mercedes-Benz, but it was the same Werner story: success in the Grand Prix of Europe, a run in Spain (3rd), victory in the Freiburg and Klausen races. He won Klausen again in 1927, and Freiburg, too. He won the inaugural race at Nurburgring, and was 3rd in the Ring's sports car race that inaugurated the German GP. The next season he won that GP, sharing the car with Caracciola, at 64.51 m.p.h. In 1929 Christian won the Nurburgring ADAC long-distance drive and won the International Alpine Rally as well. He died in Bad Cannstatt, June 17, 1932, still in the employ of Mercedes.

HARRY WESLAKE

Harry Weslake's world lay inside engine cylinder heads. He was the man on the spot when you had a problem making an engine work properly. A secretive man, by necessity in his work, by choice in his private life, very little is known about him, even less about his actual work.

An amateur motorcylist named Gordon Cobbold got Harry started. One day in 1924 he asked Weslake to work on his Sunbeam engine. Weslake did so well that Cobbold was soon beating the factory team. That led to a job offer for this mechanical whiz. Weslake agreed to a consultancy; he did not like working directly for anybody; that it would infringe upon his freedom to hunt, shoot, and fish.

Sunbeam learned a little bit about their new consultant. He was a Devon man. His father was a gas engineer. Harry's love, though, was the breathing of engines. At 17 he designed his 1st carburetor, patented in his father's name because he was a minor. He had a thorough technical background, but preferred to talk plain English, not technical jargon. Like many young men, he scoffed at ideas that came out of books, preferring the practical approach.

Sunbeam got its money's worth. So did W. O. Bentley, his next big client, and the 1st of a long line of automotive marques that would employ the Weslake talents. For Bentley, Harry improved the performance of the Speed 6 Bentley power plant after the factory itself had come perilously close to abandoning the design as a bad idea. The car dominated Le Mans, as well as winning many other races. Jaguar hired him as a consultant, and the XK series owed a lot to Weslake work. In 1971 he was still very much involved in consulting work for Jag and Wally Hassan.

But it was in racing that Weslake was to make his lasting reputation among the laymen. When Tony Brooks won at Syracuse in a Connaught, the Alta engine carried a Weslake cylinder head. Brooks's victory was

the start of something big: British domination of single-seater racing. Vanwall continued the tradition, and won the World Manufacturers Championship in Grand Prix circles. The Vanwall carried Weslake ports, and he had contributed in many other ways to Tony Vandervell's project. Conventry-Climax engines, another Hassan effort, powered Cooper to Formula 1 victory, thanks in no small measure to the Weslake touch. Even in sports car racing with Daimler, Harry tuned the winners to their necessary perfection.

Harry's work was not completely British, though. When Dan Gurney started his F1 effort under the name Eagle, it was first known as Anglo-American Racers, Inc., and Harry Weslake's Rye plant became a Gurney host. Gurney's Eagle power-plant was really a Weslake-designed engine for a Shell research project. While Anglo-American existed, Eagle was a viable operation; later, when chauvinism took over, Dan moved everything to California and Anglo-American became All-American. Eagle deteriorated. The chance for world racing domination might have been tossed away in that decision, but we shall never know for sure.

America also got its Weslake touch in the form of John Wyer's Ford team, which won at Le Mans with Waslake heads, and there have been a couple of 2nd place finishers at Indianapolis with Weslake equipment aboard.

PETER WESTBURY

Felday is a section of Surrey, England, not far from Dorking, and it was here that Peter Westbury started designing and building competition cars while still a student in engineering college. His 1st car, not called a Felday but the MGW Special because it was powered by a 1.5-litre MG engine, was built as a road car but found its way into hillclimbs because of Peter's growing interest in them. The 1958 2-seater, painted a bright blue, was used throughout 1959, then scrapped in favor of an old Formula 2 Cooper-Climax that enabled Westbury to move up in racing class. The following year Peter had the bright idea of swapping the tired Coventry-Climax engine for a 2.5-litre Daimler power-plant, and the resulting Cooper-Daimler started his hillclimb victory string in earnest, after a brief fling on the Continent in a Lotus Elite in regular racing.

Late in 1962 Westbury formed Felday Engineering in the garden of his house at Holmebury St. Mary, and determined that his 1st project would be a car more suitable for hillclimbing than the Cooper-Daimler. The power-plant was still a good one, and around it he created his own spaceframe based chassis, on a prototype Lotus 20, adding a Lotus gearbox and final drive, wheels from Lotus and Cooper, inboard brakes, and a suspension that followed the then-current Grand Prix designs. A Roots-type supercharger was added to the Daimler engine. While the car was dubbed the Felday-Daimler, it eventually became known as Felday 1. The car took less than 11 weeks to build, with Peter starting on January 19, 1963, and its initial racing appearance came on April 7 that same year at Wiscombe Park. Westbury had won his initial MG and Cooper races, and he continued his string with the Felday 1. By year's end, Westbury had won the RAC's Hillclimb Championship and sold the car to Peter Cottrell, the Welsh hillclimber, because a new car had already been taking shape in the designer's head.

Felday 2 was to have been a 2-seater version of the Felday 1, but the project was abandoned, as was another 1964 design dream, Felday 3, a V-8 BRM-engined version of Felday 2. Ferguson Research was responsible, in part, for the abandonment of both of these projects. Westbury was invited to drive the Ferguson P99 4-wheel drive racer in the 1964 RAC. Hillclimb Championship until his new car was finished, and in this mount he charged into the lead for the title once again. He then prevailed upon Ferguson to let him keep the car through the rest of the season with a view to readying his new Felday for the European Mountain Championship, which came later in the season. Peter retained his title with the P99, and his relationship with Ferguson blossomed. Meanwhile, he acquired a Lotus 23B sports car and set about creating Felday 3, when the opportunity to design and build a 4-wheel drive sports car with Ferguson help presented itself. Thus was born his next successful project, Felday 4.

Westbury's design followed Lotus and Ferguson experiments somewhat, but departed in many respects. The 1,000-c.c. engine, for example, was mounted backwards in the car's rear end and Westbury's usual spaceframe design was abandoned for a sheet-steel monocoque design. The car appeared competitively for the 1st time on Britain's Boxing Day 1965, and promptly won, keeping Westbury's record intact. By this time Feldays 5 and 6 were under way. The 5th design was a bigger version of number 4, but powered by a Ford Galaxie engine of 7 litres and destined for Group 7 racing. Its category dried up in Britain, however, so the car became merely a test vehicle for Westbury's effort and for Ferguson. Felday 6, meanwhile, appeared even before Felday 5. It was a hillclimb special, created for Tony Griffiths, but did not feature 4-wheel drive as some early press reports suggested. It was powered by a 4.7-litre Ford engine. Even before these last 2 cars had appeared, the bearded Wesbury, who ran a staff of more than a dozen men at new premises at Forest Green, was thinking about Feldays 7 and 8.

But there is another side to Peter Westbury, the driver side. Born in 1938, he was still a young man when there were (literally) no more hills to conquer by 1966. There had been many circuit drives before then, principally in

Peter's role of tester for Cooper starting in 1961 and later BRM, but also including some British circuit drives like a 2nd in a Boxing Day Brands Hatch race and a victory with the 2-litre Felday-BRM at Snetterton. So no one should have been suprised when Westbury decided to go single-seater racing in a big-time way. He bought 3 Brabham Formula 3 cars, signed on Derek Bell and Mac Dagborn for the other 2 cars, and tucked his own beard into a racing helmet.

They went racing in Formula 2, also; and in the F3 shakedown season Peter scored victories at Silverstone, Chimay, Clermont, Castle Combe (deadheating Bell) and other venues. In 1968 Peter won the F3 championship of France, in 1969 finished 5th overall in the European F2 series. He concentrated on F2 in 1970, but got a Formula 1 shot with the Yardley-BRM team at the United States Grand Prix, although he could not qualify the car. It was a lot more fun than sticking to a drawing board.

DERRICK WHITE

Part-time racer, full-time designer, Derrick White was a quiet South African who came to Britain in 1952 at the age of 23 to join Humber as a technical man. He was one of those people who flitted back and forth from ordinary road cars to competition machines with comparative ease, and left Humber to join Connaught, where he worked on that marque's A and B series single-seaters.

White returned to South Africa for a time, during a period when he built his own sports car, called the Fairway, which raced in Africa. In 1959 he was back in Britain and joining Jaguar. There he developed the independent rear suspension system for the E Jaguar, now standard on all Jags. Eventually Derek became Competition Project Engineer with a team of E Jags running against the GTO Ferraris with some success. It was in this period that he did a considerable amount of racing himself in a 750 Formula car, the Impala, which he had designed.

In 1965 White joined Cooper, and his 1st accomplishment there was the 1966 Cooper-Maserati Type 81, a car that was used by both John Surtees and Jochen Rindt. It won one Grand Prix, was 2nd three times, and 3rd twice in 1966, and it ran the fastest race laps twice. The same car won the South African GP in 1967 for Pedro Rodriguez. That season White's Type 86 was introduced, but he was already making plans to move on to work with Surtees at Honda and Lola.

When he died in the fall of 1970 in a swimming accident in South Africa, he was working for Triumph; his last effort being the all-independent suspension of the Triumph Stag.

REX WHITE

They said that Rex White had learned to drive so carefully and consistently when he had to gather eggs from the farmers around Taylorsville, N. C., and get them undamaged over the rutted treacherous mountain roads to the egg factory. Rex White was only 5-feet 4-inches, counting the brush of stiff blond hair, and he had trouble reaching the pedals in his Chevrolet stock car. But size often breeds competitive spirit. He had come up the hard way—odd jobs, including short order cook, had brought him to Silver Spring, Md., where he began racing at West Lanham Speedway.

In 1954 he had competed in eight sportsman events, faring well enough to win the track crown. So the next year he built his own modified to get a ride. Rex raced at all the Carolina tracks, eventually finishing 16th in NASCAR sportsman standings. In 1956 Rex moved up again to NASCAR Grand Nationals and the short track championships. He got the chance to team with a mechanical whiz named Louis Clements in 1959. Many of his 26 Grand National victories were scored in Chevrolets prepared by Clements, who became his partner in a garage and speed shop enterprise in Spartanburg, S.C.

White moved into NASCAR's top 10 in 1958, finishing 7th. He was running out of Silver Spring, Md., then but his shop was in Spartanburg. There were 2 victories —at Fayetteville and Weaverville, N.C.—and 17 top-10 finishes. In 1957 he had concentrated on NASCAR's short-track division for races on tracks less than half a

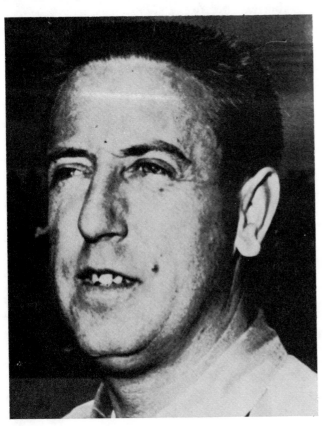

mile in length and had finished 18th, winning 4. In 1959 he was in the short tracks again, losing the championship by 2 points on the final race to Marvin Porter of California.

By this time White had moved to Spartanburg full-time, and he and Clements decided to go for the title. Rex won with consistency, his high finishes overpowering more brilliant and more erratic drivers. It was not until April 5 at a half-mile dirt track at Columbia, S. C., that White finally won. He had a drought until NASCAR's northern tour where Rex won at the Montgomery, N.Y., airport on July 17. He won 2 in August, finished 2nd to Buck Baker in the Southern 500, then won at Martinsville and North Wilkesboro. Already White was so far ahead that he had virtually clinched the title, and the final month did nothing to change the picture.

The title chase in 1961 was close all year but Ned Jarrett edged White out because Ned did better on the superspeedways. Was this Rex's weak spot? It was hard to win without good finishes at the big tracks, and the Chevrolets just did not have the speed to be competitive, not only White's but others, too. That changed in 1962, with White's tire tests in mid-January at Atlanta. His new car ran almost 2 m.p.h. faster than the 1961 record of David Pearson in a Pontiac and a mile faster than Ford tests.

Clements and the White crew were excited again. Clements, a Kentuckian, had come from Owensboro to Spartanburg, S. C., to work with Speedy Thompson and Buck Baker. Louis had gone with Rex shortly after the beginning of the 1959 season began because he was offered a full partnership—half of everything. The Chevvys had been good racers until Ford and Chrysler got serious about the sport. Then there was only consistency to pull the White team through. Daytona was a period of learning, but the 1962 car had done reasonably well. But as the months of the season rolled past, they got longer and harder and more frustrating—blown engines, running over debris, being involved in unnecessary accidents.

By October and the Dixie 400 in Atlanta, Rex and Clements knew they did not have the fastest car any more; they knew that if any of half a dozen cars held together, the White Chevrolet had no chance, even if Rex drove as hard as he knew how. Nowhere else would there be any chance but at Atlanta, because he could run lower through the long Atlanta turns.

In the beginning of the race, Fireball Roberts appeared unbeatable, pulling out front at will. But a wheel stud broke and Roberts had to slow far down and hope he could make the pit before the wheel fell off. That left the lead to Ford's Marvin Panch. It was the latter half of the race. White gambled; he slipstreamed Panch, and he accomplished his purpose. Panch had to pit an extra time for gas and Rex White had finally won a superspeedway classic. Joe Weatherly stole 2nd from Panch.

It was to be the only Superspeedway victory. Rex tapered off in 1963 running only a few races in a Bud Moore Mercury. Then tragedy struck. After the 1964 Pan American road race, the car in which he was a passenger flipped. White suffered a fractured vertebra and did not receive medical clearance to race until March 1965, when he returned to sportsman racing as much to publicize his racing parts supply store as for the purses. The appearances were just an epilogue to a courageous career.

SIR JOHN WHITMORE

A leading British saloon racer and international Gran Turismo competitor, the bearded son of a former Lord Lieutenant of Essex was one of the most engaging competitors on the racing scene, before his retirement in 1967. Sir John Whitmore was known for his flamboyant driving style, and an unpretentious off-track manner. Born in 1937, Sir John started on a military career but eventually found himself invalided out of Sandhurst, England's equivalent of West Point. That left the family acres to farm; Orsett Hall in Essex sits in the middle of 5,500 acres, of which 2,600 are farmed by the Whitmores themselves.

While learning about practical farming in Shropshire, John learned about cars too. "There wasn't much to do in the evenings except go to the local pub." There was a crowd of car enthusiasts there, and we later joined the Hagley club. I started by doing a production car trial and sprint with my Prefect." Early in 1958, John acquired an Austin A-35 and prepared for the annual RAC Rally. One wreck later, he was ready to give it a go with a borrowed A35 with more than 50,000 miles on the clock. Struggling against the collapse of the machine the whole way, John finished 29th. Encouraged by this quite respectable accomplishment, John bought a Lotus 6 powered by an Elva-Ford 1172-c.c. o.h.v. engine.

Using this car and friend Alan Stacey's mechanic, young Whitmore drove in 6 races, the number necessary to get an international competitor's license; he finished 2nd once, and 3rd once. For 1959, he purchased a Lotus Elite—really a pre-production model—again aided by Stacey's influence; Alan was a Lotus team driver at that time. John won with this car in his debut and, still heady from this, proceeded to qualify on the 1st row of the May Silverstone meeting. "There I was with Roy Salvadori in a 3.8 Jaguar, Stirling Moss in a prototype Aston Martin DB4 GT, and Colin Chapman in another Elite," Sir John said. "I really thought I was made, being just a fifth slower than Colin in practice. But he managed to box me in at the start, then got clear himself. I didn't know a thing about tactics, you see."

Chapman must have seen something in the youngster's

style, however. He offered Whitmore a Le Mans drive, with John sharing a Border Reivers Elite with the rising Jim Clark. Despite generator troubles, including an hour and a half in the pits, the pair came in 2nd in their class and 10th overall. "Had we not had the trouble," Sir John wistfully recalled, "we would have won in class, won the Index of Performance and won the Index of Thermal Efficiency—Jimmy and I worked it out afterwards. We would have won thousands of pounds each—it just doesn't bear speaking about."

Money was a problem in those days for Whitmore; his father did not approve of "that other terrible business of yours," and when John wiped out his Elite at Monza after his 12th victory of the year (of 14 starts), there were no funds to replace the car. "My father was born in, and spent nearly half his life in, the Victorian age," Sir John said. "He rode or drove horses nearly all of his life; he never learned to drive a car and very seldom rode in one. He was a very old man by the time I took up racing. His attitude was perfectly understandable to me."

In 1960 Whitmore had to drive other people's cars. First there were Lola drives for Fitzwilliam, then an offer to pilot John Ogier's Tojeiro—a Formula 2 car that never came to pass—and finally an ex-Rob Walker Cooper. There were only 6 races for Whitmore that season, and John won nothing. The following year, however, with money furnished by an oil company, he was scheduled to buy a Lotus 20 Formula Junior chassis to be powered by an engine supplied by still another friend, Don Moore. Instead, on an impulse the young man purchased a little green 850 Mini, and Moore agreed to finance that car as well as the FJ car. The latter did not do well, but with the Mini John became British Saloon Car Champion in 1961.

Based on this success, Sir John made it his business to concentrate on saloon and GT racing; he never regretted this decision. "You have to be exceptionally brilliant like Jimmy Clark to be really good in any sort of a car. I always found it difficult to go from this type of car to the pure racer." In 1962 he joined Ken Tyrrell's Mini-Cooper factory team, where he finished 2nd to John Love. Whitmore also drove a Lotus Elite on occasion, a high spot being a triumph at the Spa Grand Prix in a driving rain.

The 1963 season was a Mini year for John once more, and he came within inches of his 2nd Saloon Championship. Even so, John now was known as the Mini King. "I was sick of that title," he explained, "so I jumped at Stirling Moss's offer to drive an Elan." Stirling was pleased with Whitmore's performance and signed him to a 3-year contract at that season's end. But a generous offer from Ford arrived, and Moss graciously gave Whitmore his release to accept it for 1964. With the Williment Team he drove Galaxies and Cobras. Of the latter, John said: "The Cobra is a tank—but I do like a tank that goes sideways, and this car certainly does." He also drove Lotus Cortinas for Alan Mann, coming in as runner-up for the title.

At the end of 1964 John was invited to test drive the Ford GT at Monza, and did well in the test until the throttle stuck at about 140 m.p.h. The car went off the course, through the trees and hedges, and ended up in pieces. Yet Whitmore was able to get out and walk away, calm and unruffled. A mechanic's error had caused the accident, it was determined afterwards. For 1965 he got the GT for real, a 7-litre Daytona Cobra on occasion, as well as Cortinas for Mann once more. One of his drivers won the manufacturers' title for Carroll Shelby's Cobra factory, and John won the European Touring Car Championship for himself in the Cortina. In 1966 he retained his Cortina title and expanded his GT rides to Sebring, Monza, Spa, and Le Mans.

The reasons for Whitmore's retirement in 1967 were varied. His lovely Swedish wife Gunilla provided one in 1965, when she bore him an heir. His business commitments grew steadily, including an advisory service to farmers, and controlling interests in a general and competition garage, and in a British Ford dealership. England's death duties, should John have been killed in an auto accident, would have wiped out his family estate before he had a chance to provide for his family's future. Also, Whitmore made no secret of the fact that the deaths of several of his friends and one-time teammates —Walt Hansgen and Ken Miles—and accidents to others—Jack Sears, now also retired, and Peter Proctor —also were factors in his retirement.

Whitmore had proved his point anyway; he was as fast as anyone in his racing classes, had earned starting berths in all the major races and had acquitted himself with honor. He moved to Switzerland, where his neighbors were Jackie Stewart and Jochen Rindt.

ROBIN WIDDOWS

For every man who makes the big time in auto racing, there are hundreds who try and fail. There are few regrets for most of them, but once in a while a man quits the grids while his star still shines. Such a man was Robin Michael Widdows, a young Englishman who had the makings of another Graham Hill or Stirling Moss in the eyes of many, but who never quite got that proper chance to show his wares in Formula 1.

Widdows was born in 1942, son of an RAF squadron leader, later Air Commodore, Charles Widdows. He went to Haileybury, the same school attended by Moss and Michael Parkes, but bobsledding, not auto racing, was his main sport until 1964 when Eddie Portman persuaded him to compete in an MG Midget. Widdows was good enough as as sledder, incidentally, to be part of the official British team at the 1965 and 1966 world championships and at the 1964 and 1968 Winter Olympics. The MG was raced regularly at Goodwood and some other club events, and in 1965 Robin switched to Group 7 cars with a 1000-c.c. BRM-engined Formula 2 Lotus 23, in which he won some dozen races or so.

Robin became a full-time racing driver the following year, temporarily retiring from his role as a property

659

developer for which he had studied and begun working after school. Widdows bought a Brabham BT18 Formula 3 car and spent a frustrating year learning without much taste of victory. In 1967, against the advice of many, he continued his go-it-alone ways, but moved up to F2 again, under the banner of his own Witley Racing Syndicate—Witley being Robin's hometown in Surrey —in a brand new Brabham BT23. That season he won the Rhine Cup at Hockenhein and finished 4th in the German Trophy at the same course, among other outstanding performances, despite not really competitive equipment.

For 1968 Widdows signed on with Chequered Flag to pilot an F2 McLaren M4A; he was 2nd at Pau and 3rd at Monza. The cars were suffering teething troubles, however, and the Flag itself had other kinds of troubles, so Robin had his problems. He also drove a Lola T100, and in mid-year, Widdows was offered his first F1 shot in the British Grand Prix in a rather uncompetitive Cooper-BRM that eventually retired with ignition trouble. Just before the Italian GP, Widdows was testing a Mirage-BRM V-12 prototype at Snetterton and crashed, crushing a vertebra and aggrevating an old bobsledding injury.

Back in F2 the following season, he won the Monza Lottery and was 2nd at Rheims in a Brabham BT23C and a Merlyn for Bob Gerard's team. Matra handed Widdows a factory drive at Le Mans, and the 630/650 Spyder he shared with Nanni Galli finished 7th despite fuel pump woes that probably cost the team several places. Widdows was driving a BT30 in the Alistair Walker Team in 1970 when he decided, early in the year, to call it quits. "I am aware," he wrote several British auto writers announcing his retirement, "that I will not realize my ambitions and reach the highest level in motor sport. I am now no longer prepared either to accept second best or continue to take unnecessary risks." The courage he showed in making his decision matched that which he always displayed on the race course.

"WILLIAMS"

He first appeared in 1926 in a Mercedes 28/95 at French courses. He was tall and quiet, ramrod straight, spoke faultless French despite his obvious British background. Soon he was driving Bugattis, 1st privately, then for the factory. The entry list always read "Williams."

He won his 1st big race in 1928—a big one—the French Grand Prix at Comminges at 84.86 m.p.h., and he was 2nd to Louis Chiron in the Antibes GP. In 1929 he again won the French GP, this time at Le Mans, at 82.66, and followed by winning the Monaco GP that year at 48.83 m.p.h. For a man who did not do the full circuit but seemed to disappear at times, only to reappear, Williams did rather well in his driving days. In 1931, 1932, and 1933, for example, he won the La Baule Grand Prix

—his home race, really, for he operated dog kennels at La Baule—in his Bugatti in suprisingly consistent fashion: 89.02 m.p.h., 89.23, and 89.75.

Williams's driving career ended with the rise of Nazism and the impending war. Just after the outbreak he appeared in uniform and under his real name, Capt. William Grover, a member of MI5, the British Intelligence unit. With the fall of France in 1940, Grover went underground, in charge of liaison between the Allies and the Resistance in the area west of Paris. Exactly what happened to him no one really knows. The best that can be pieced together is that Grover and other members of his underground unit were arrested by the Gestapo in 1943. He resisted torture to his death and the body was destroyed. No trace of Williams was left except his record in automotive history.

FRANK WILLIAMS

Motor racing is full of whiz kids in the drivers' seats and in the pits and garages, but the number of "kids" who are patrons for drivers is rather small. Probably the whizziest of these few was Britain's Frank Williams, who became an under-30 version of Enzo Ferrari in 1969, with Piers Courage as his driver.

Williams, born in 1942, set out to be a driver in 1961. Tenacity was one of his more familiar traits. He started his involvement with racing in one of the more familiar ways, hitchhiking to Brands Hatch and other courses almost every weekend when a schoolboy. Once the bug bit, it went deep, and at 17 Frank quit school with the idea of acquiring a car and going racing. It took 3 or 4 years of "bumming around," as he later characterized it, for Williams to save up enough money from odd jobs to buy a used Austin A35, which he promptly destroyed at Mallory Park in its 1st outing.

Williams redoubled his money-making efforts, and with the help of new friends like Jonathan Williams (no relation), he managed to save enough to purchase an A40 that he campaigned in the entire 1962 season without finishing a single race. The following year Williams became Jonathan's mechanic, which gave him a look at most of the European courses. In Britain he lived at Harrow in a room shared with Courage and Charles Crichton-Stuart. Spending little in this arrangement, he saved enough to purchased a Formula 3 Brabham in 1964, which was campaigned again without success, and the story was pretty much the same the next season when Frank switched to an F3 Cooper formerly raced by Graham Hill.

As his own career was sliding along without going anywhere, Courage's was heating up, bringing Williams to a decision. His talents lay elsewhere than in the cockpit, he reasoned, and this fitted in nicely with Courage's own needs, so Williams became a manager. He stopped racing completely at the end of 1966. In addition to masterminding the Courage fortunes, Williams went into

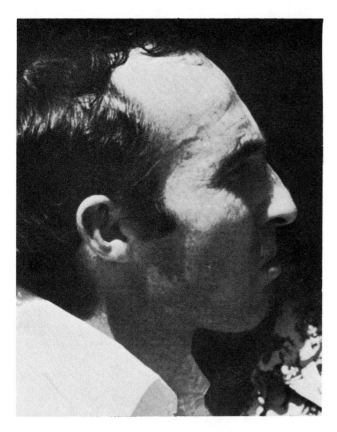

the used racing car business as a full-time occupation. At least that was what he listed as his full-time occupation. Since racing itself filled most of his hours, Frank did most of his car dealing by telephone, which was why a cartoonist once pictured him as having a telephone growing out of his ear.

Because Williams always had admired the way Jack Brabham's cars were designed and built, the Williams-Courage Team equipped itself with an F3 Brabham BT18 for 1967, then switched to an F2 of the same marque for the following season. The big move came in 1969 when Williams decided that Courage was ready Formula 1 and bought a full-blown GP car, a BT26 Brabham-Ford, immaculately prepared and painted a sparkling midnight blue. The team started 10 Grands Prix in 1969 and finished 5 of them, garnering a 10th, two 5ths, and a pair of 2nds. The initial 2nd was on the twisty Monte Carlo course, with Courage finishing just behind the man who owned the Monaco GP, Graham Hill. The other 2nd was in the United States GP at Watkins Glen, where he trailed the man who set the day's fastest time, Jochen Rindt, in a Lotus-Ford. The season saw Courage with 16 championship points to put him 8th, directly behind Hill and tops for a nonfactory entry.

Despite his success with a Brabham, Williams took a big gamble in 1970 that was indicative of the man. He and Courage switched to a brand new GP marque, de Tomaso-Ford, a straightforward design with a fully proven power-plant. It impressed Williams in the same ways that the original Brabhams had, and Alessandro de Tomaso was impressed, too—with both the manager and the driver of the Williams team. That is why the

Italian carbuilder supplied a chassis and an engineer to Williams. Frank supplied the engine and paid for anything else. De Tomaso, who sold impressive mid-engined sports cars, controlled both Ghia and Vignale coachbuilding and had a Mustang-powered, Ferrari-like sports car sold under his own name, recognized the businesslike approach of Frank Williams.

Businesslike it may be, but it also had elements of daring and humor, perhaps the right combination to win a few Grands Prix and who knows what else. "I wanted to go racing," Frank once said, "and I just didn't only talk about it." When Courage was tragically killed in the Dutch GP in 1970, Williams faced another big decision. Characteristically, he met the problem head-on, and went driver-hunting. Frank tried for Emerson Fittipaldi, but by mid-July 1970 when another blue de Tomaso was on the GP grid, his driver was Brian Redman. Later Williams found another driver, France's Henri Pescarolo, and raced his own car, the Moful-Ford. Associating himself with Len Bailey, the freelance designer, for 1972 a new car was born, dubbed (in honor of its French toymaker sponsor) the Politoys-Ford, driven by Pescarolo. Carlos Pace, the Brazilian, also was under contract. Williams was thinking of the future and becoming another Ken Tyrrell, his idol. If anyone could make it to two World Championships privately like Ken, Williams was the man.

JONATHAN WILLIAMS

Some drivers have more than the normal share of crack-ups and incidents, often through no fault of their own. England's Jonathan Williams was one of these. He was undoubtedly one of the better single-seat drivers of his day; if he survived continual crack-ups, he was expected to rise to the top.

Perhaps it was easier to judge future talent in England than elsewhere because it was there that Formula 3—some called it Grand Prix racing on a small scale—had taken greatest hold. If a man did well in F3, he was expected to do reasonably well in Formula 1 as well. Williams did do well in F3, so good things were expected of him.

Born in Cairo, Egypt, on October 26, 1942, J. Jonathan Williams was the son of an RAF bomber pilot. His father took him to some 500 racing at Brands Hatch in 1950 and infected him with the desire to become a racing driver. At the end of the 1960 season Williams started competing in Minis, his inaugural appearance coming at Snetterton. From the start, Jon exhibited versatility. He not only drove the circuits, but appeared in sprints and hillclimbs as well. The following year John switched to an A40 Austin and finished in the top 3 in 12 of the 14 races in which he competed. He also managed a 2nd in the Molyslip Saloon Car Championship.

In 1963 Williams decided he was ready for single-seater racing, and purchased a Merlyn Formula Junior car. In his debut race with the new machine, however, the car's suspension snapped at a crucial point, and it was demolished; Jon was hospitalized for a good length of time. It was the 1st of many such incidents. In August 1963 the young Englishman started racing once more, this time with a Lotus 22 FJ car. In 10 starts, his best effort was a 3rd in the Dresden International meet. The next season, Jon and Piers Courage formed the Anglo-Swiss Racing Team, each piloting a Lotus-Ford F3 car, and started moving up the competition ladder. Among Williams' accomplishments that season were 2nds in the Tyrol Grand Prix at Innsbruck and in a Lottery GP heat at Monza, 3rd at Crystal Palace and at Nurburgring, 4ths at Nurburgring in another start and in the August Bank Holiday race at Brands Hatch, a 5th at Vallelunga, and a 6th at Zolder.

In 1965 Jon joined the Charles Lucas Racing Team, along with Courage, each getting an F3 Brabham for a mount. His debut in these colors was at the delayed March Boxing Day Brands Hatch meet where he was 2nd. The following month at Monza Williams won his heat, but retired in the final. At Goodwood's Easter Monday meeting he was 3rd behind Roy Pike and Courage; at the Zolder GP the next month he not only won his heat, making the fastest lap time in the process, but won the final as well, besting the redoubtable Pike by 5.5 seconds.

A few starts later Williams won the richest F3 race held up to that point, the Viggorelli Trophy at Monza, worth more than $3,500, after taking his heat, again with the fastest lap of the race. At another Monza meet a few days later Jon won his heat and the final again. Misfortune struck again, if lightly, at Chimay in the Grand Prix des Frontières on June 6, 1965. Williams's foot became stuck under his brake pedal while he was in the lead on the final lap and he lost just enough time to lose the race by 8 tenths of a second. In the Lottery GP later in the month, he was 4th, and then came Rheims in July.

Williams was leading the pack when his car went out of control and crashed at near its top speed, pinning him inside. After they extricated the youngster they found both his legs broken, and his back badly battered. Yet, such were Jon's powers of recovery and determination that he was back in an F3 cockpit on September 12 for the starting flag at Monza, just a few days more than 2 months after the crash. And he not only started but lapped the entire field and won his heat, only to have a battery failure at the start of the final; fate was demonstrating that it had something to say about Williams's future.

In 1966 Williams became the de Sanctis's factory's number one F3 driver, and the following season he moved into the big time, he thought, with a Ferrari factory berth. But the real opportunities were limited here. In 1967 John has his first F1 opportunity—and perhaps his only one—when Ferrari handed him a shopworn car

for the Mexican GP. He finished 8th. He also had a Ferrari P4 for a couple of Canadian-American Challenge Cup races, finishing 8th in the Monterey GP and and retiring at Las Vegas. Williams was not with Ferrari in 1968, but with Abarth for sports car racing, and got some Tecno F2 drives, a few in a truly competitive Brabham-FVA BT23C. In the latter he ripped off a 130.08-m.p.h. Lottery GP victory at Monza.

Another switch followed in 1969. Williams took over as the factory test driver for de Tomaso—in whose F1 cars Frank Williams and Piers Courage, Jon's old buddies, were to campaign in 1970 until Piers met his death in one. Jon raced in a Serenissima V-8 Group 6 machine much of the season, but the best he could garner was a 6th in the Tyrol Prize and a 3rd in the Salzburgring race. Serenissima died in 1970, making Williams job-hunt once again; he resigned with Abarth for sports car racing, and his best showing that year was a 4th in the Salzburgring. It looked as if the fast moving racing scene had passed by one its bright lights of just a few years before without even pausing to give him a 2nd chance.

JEAN-PIERRE WIMILLE

Jean-Pierre Wimille was born in 1906, the son of a Parisian newspaperman. He was 25 before he raced, but then it was right into the big time with a 2.3-litre Type 35 Bugatti entered in the Italian Grand Prix at Monza. J-P, as he was always called, and codriver Jan Gaupillat

finished a distant but respectable 4th. Later in the year he failed to finish the French GP at Montlhéry. In 1932 J-P won his initial race, the Oran GP, and North Africa became a favorite venue. That year Wimille also won the Lorraine GP, this time in a 2.3-liter Monza Alfa Romeo.

The following year Wimille's skills began to take on a professional polish, and judgment born of experience tempered the natural fire that had earned him a reputation for wildness. Final proof of his arrival came in 1934 when J-P was invited to join the Bugatti team. The new Type 59 had teething troubles most of that year, however, and it was only at Algiers that Wimille was able to win in one of the Bugatti team's few starts. The following year was a bit more successful, the Frenchman placing at Tunis and Nancy.

In 1936 Wimille took Bugattis as far away as South Africa and America, although he managed home victories in the GP of France as well as the Deauville and Comminges GP's. In South Africa and America, where he competed in the Vanderbilt Cup Race at Long Island's Roosevelt Raceway, J-P garnered 2nds. He was 3rd in the Tunis GP. War clouds were gathering over Europe and North Africa, but there was still time for Wimille to win 3 sports car Grands Prix in France and his 1st Le Mans 24-hour race in 1937.

The 1938 season was a short one for Wimille because of recurring kidney trouble, and his best effort was a 3rd in the Coppa Ciano. But his skills were undiminished, and Mercedes Benz offered Europe's best driver (even if he was not an Aryan) a berth for 1939. J-P refused and rejoined Bugatti instead, despite its absence from all but minor races. He did manage to repeat his 1937 Le Mans victory in a 3.3-litre sports car. During the short time France initially fought in World War II, Wimille served in the Air Force. Then, with the French surrender, he joined the Resistance, as did most French drivers, eventually finding his way to North Africa which he knew so well. When the Allies landed there, Wimille acted as a liaison officer.

With the war's end, Alfa Romeo honored J-P by inviting him to join its 1946 team as its only non-Italian driver. But before he did that, Wimille won Europe's 1st postwar race, the Grand Prix de la Liberation, held in September 1945 on the Bois de Boulogne. He also raced a pre-war Alfa and won 3 races prior to joining the factory team and colleagues Nino Farina, Achille Varzi, and Count Carlo Trossi. It was in this year, too, that Wimille began talking of going into automobile manufacturing. The result was a mid-engined 3-seater bearing his name, with aerodynamic lines, a V-8 engine, and a Cotal electric gearbox.

In 1947 he won the Belgian and Swiss races, the Coupe de Paris, and the new Benoist Memorial Cup, and placed in the Nice and Lausanne GP's. The Nice race was contested in a 1100-c.c. Simca-Gordini that influenced his choice of a mount in many contests in 1948. He won the French and Italian Grands Prix, was 2nd in the Swiss GP, and took 3 other minor prize races. He traveled to South America once again, taking a 3rd in the Mar del Plata Grand Premio prior to the fatal Buenos Aires practice in which he was killed after swerving to avoid an Argentine woman who had run on to the course. His effortless, restrained style lived on, however, in Fangio and the generation of drivers that imitated him.

REINE WISELL

Three drivers were standouts in Formula 3 toward the end of the 1960s, 2 of them Swedes, and all three made it into the Grand Prix circus in 1970. The careers of Ronnie Peterson and Reine Wisell, the two Swedes, were somewhat parallel, though Wisell was almost four years older and Peterson pulled away from the pattern in 1971.

Born September 30, 1941, in Motala, Reine Tore Lief Wisell was a teen-aged motorcycle enthusiast who was also driving a Triumph Herald when the racing bug bit him in 1961. The Herald gave way to a Mini-Cooper, then to other Minis, a Formula Junior-engined Anglia, and an MG Midget. In 1966, he was back to a Mini-Cooper S and captured 2nd place in the Swedish ice-racing championship. That same year, Reine entered F3 with a Cooper, lost out to Picko Troberg in a Brabham BT18, and promptly bought the car for 1967. That season Wisell won 8 races at home for the Swedish Championship and did well on the Continent with 2nds at Vila Real and Jarama.

Since Clay Regazzoni won at Jarama in a Tecno, Wisell decided he wanted one of the Italian cars. Ronnie Peterson agreed, and the 2 Swedes took a long, leisurely drive from home to Italy to pick out a pair for 1968. With his, Wisell became the season's most successful F3 pilot, winning 11 major races and earning a contract to drive for the Chevron factory. While he was supposed to have both B15 (F3) and GT rides, most of Reine's appearances were in the former. He won 6 races overall, including 4 in Britain. In another of his victories (at Pau), Wisell won by 19 seconds, unusually high for a F3 race, but in the 6th (at Montlhéry) he dead-heated with Tim Schenken. Three of his British victories were scored on the last lap, with Schenken the loser each time.

Wisell performed well in most of his limited sports car starts. His best race was the BOAC 500 in which he scored a class victory with John Hine in a Chevron GT. But in the Nurburgring 1000, a skid put the Chevron in a ditch. Wisell also joined forces with Jo Bonnier in the Ecurie Filipinetti effort. He was with the bearded Bonnier at Le Mans, in South Africa, at Spa, and in the Watkins Glen 6-hour Race. Their mounts ranged from a Lola GT to a 7-litre Corvette. Similarly, in 1970, he was with Bonnier again at Le Mans in a Ferrari 512S, and Reine had the misfortune to be driving in the 3rd hour

when an oil line let go and sprayed the car's windshield. He headed toward the pits, but was hit from behind by Clay Regazzoni, who in turn was hit by Mike Parkes and then Derek Bell (in a car shared by Peterson); the 4-Ferrari crash ended the Italian team's bid.

In 1970, Wisell raced Formula 2, Formula 5000, and, finally, F1. In each class he had a team mount: a Chevron in F2, a McLaren in F5000, and a Lotus in F1. If Emerson Fittipaldi had not been running in the US GP at Watkins Glen that fall, Wisell would have been the rage, for in his initial F1 ride the young, long-haired Swede finished 3rd. But Fittipaldi won the race, nipping a fuming Pedro Rodriguez who had run out of fuel near the race's end. That gave Reine 4 points and a tie for 15th place in the season standings. His only other start, in Mexico, ended in a 10th place. He was back in a Lotus for 1971, backing Fittipaldi who had inherited the team lead upon Jochen Rindt's death.

Reine had what would normally regarded as a good initial full season in F1—except Peterson had a sensational season in comparison, finishing 2nd in the driver standings. Wisell won 9 points and tied for 9th place in the standings. Reine was 7th in the non-title Argentine GP tuneup, 4th in South Africa, and 12th in Spain. He was retired at Monaco, 10th in the Hockenheim non-title Rindt Memorial, and disqualified at Holland for reversing into the pits. France saw a 6th place, Britain a 13th (though unclassified), and Germany an 8th. But in Austria he was 4th again and in Canada—Lotus not running the Italian GP—he was 5th. Wisell retired from

the U.S. GP at Watkins Glen. In F2 he had his troubles, and, in fact, had his car impounded in a money dispute late in the season.

SPENCER WISHART

In the days when America's racing greats were more often than not the sons of the wealthy, because only the sons of the wealthy could aspire to the expensive European machinery, Spencer Wishart was one of the most favored. His father, a railroad engineer who amassed a fortune speculating on Wall Street, indulged Spencer in whatever whim money could buy. And money could buy cars.

Before he was 18, Wishart was the terror of Greenwich, Conn., in his red Maxwell runabout. Born in 1890 Wishart literally grew up with the motor car. Apparently he never wanted to be anything but a racing driver. In 1908, for his 18th birthday, his father bought Spence a 90-h.p. Mercedes and accompanied him, beaming, to the AAA Contest Board to get his competition license. Young Wishart spent the year getting acquainted with the Mercedes, winning a few hillclimbs and dirt-track events. In 1909 he entered the Vanderbilt Cup race on Long Island and finished 4th overall, last of the survivors of a 15-car field. In 1910 he managed another finish back in the pack in the Cobe Trophy race at the then unpaved Indy Speedway.

For 1911 there was a radically revised version of the Mercedes as Spence's plaything. Allegedly it cost $63,-000 and its 599-cu.in. 4-cylinder motor was about as fast as any car motor around. With it he finished 4th overall in the 1st Indy 500 and got himself a pro ride on the Simplex team for the Elgin, Ill., road races that year; the car broke down, so Wishart, a thoroughly engaging young man if one could keep him from discussing racing, returned to his Mercedes for the 200-mile race through Philadelphia's Fairmount Park. This set the stage for one of the strange footnotes to history. Wishart apparently had won the race. However, in the final laps, his riding mechanic had been thrown off. Rather than waste time getting him back, Spence picked up a substitute in the pits. He was disqualified on the grounds that his riding mechanic had not been in the car at all times and the victory was awarded to Ralph Mulford. Incensed, Wishart told his father, and they took the matter into court. But money can't buy everything. They lost.

Wishart finished 3rd in the Vanderbilt Cup race in Savannah in 1911, and he was in contention in his Mercedes for Indy in 1912 until a break in the cooling system put the car out. Soon after this, Spencer, now 22, joined the Mercer team. On August 26, 1912, Wishart drove what must have been his greatest race in a 200-mile dirt-track championship in Columbus, Ohio. Spence had never seen the track before; he had never really driven the Mercer at speed. So he started out at a pace which for him was conservative, slowly accelerating as he gathered confidence. At the 65-mile mark Wishart wrestled the lead from Howdy Wilcox, and 10 miles later he was setting what were alleged to be world records for each distance. He won handily. Four days later he was competing in a Mercer at Elgin, and the Wishart jinx had settled back down upon him. He went out with a broken water pipe after spinning off the hay bales when he came into a corner too fast.

Only 8 of the greatest drivers in the country showed for the twin Vanderbilt and Grand Prize races at Milwaukee that October. For this kind of racing Spence returned to his Mercedes. He finished 3rd in the Vanderbilt Cup but it was a tragic week of racing for him. David Bruce-Brown, a Connecticut friend, was killed and Ralph DePalma seemed injured critically in the last lap of the Grand Prize race. For Indianapolis in 1913 Wishart was back in a Mercer. The car finished 2nd but with DePalma doing a relief driving stint. At Elgin Spence led several times, but his driving style precipitated tire trouble, and he eventually finished third.

The Vanderbilt and the Grand Prize races were shifted to Santa Monica, Calif., and Wishart this time stayed with the Mercer team. As customary Spence set some of the fastest laps, and in the Grand Prize race he played hare to burn out the opposition so that teammate Eddie Pullen could drive to victory. He, of course, burned himself out too.

The year 1914 saw war clouds across the Atlantic, and the 24-year-old Wishart wondered for the 1st time whether or not there were other, more permanent, things in life than fast cars. He married right after the Indianapolis 500, where he led until a camshaft broke at 305 miles. And he seemed to have won again on July 4 at Sioux City, Ia., when judges allowed his protest against Eddie Rickenbacker, only to have the protest later disallowed. Wishart and his wife then accompanied DePalma to Germany to pick up Ralph's new Mercedes. They arrived in the U.S. 2 days before war erupted in Europe and not long before the 1914 Elgin Nationals. Wishart led the 301.5-mile Chicago AC Trophy race by a full 10 minutes when the car ruptured its gas tank and put him out.

In the Elgin National Trophy race Spencer dueled Bob Burman's Peugeot for the first 100 miles, assuming a lead of approximately 3 minutes in the Mercer. But soon afterwards, in passing another car, Wishart's rear wheel brushed the other car. The contact was enough to make him lose control at the speed he was going. The car hit a tree and rolled, throwing Spencer and mechanic John Jenter. Both died of internal injuries. Spencer Wishart, millionaire, was dead at 24, but he had done in life what he wanted to do, and that at least is better than never having done anything at all.

WOOD BROTHERS

There are people who come to a race with a stopwatch around the neck, maybe a case of beer and some sandwiches, Polaroid sunglasses to cut the glare, and a big cushion. They yell, they cheer, and they sometimes even scream, and they're not even watching the race much. They're watching the pits. The stopwatch comes up whenever Cale Yarborough, David Pearson, or A. J. Foyt rolls into his position, and the crew comes over the wall like commandos in a war movie to get the car serviced and on its way in the least time possible.

In that league the Wood Brothers of Stuart, Va., are the superstars. In 1965 they went to Indianapolis to crew for Jim Clark of Scotland. In 44.5 seconds total elapsed time they gave him 2 complete pit stops—one of them in 19.8 seconds when he took on fuel, changed 2 tires, got a drink and new goggles, and a verbal enumeration of his competitors.

They went to Riverside to work the pits for Dan Gurney in 4 of his 5 consecutive Motor Trend 500 victories. When they switched to Parnelli Jones for the race, Jones beat Dan. They crewed for Speedy Thompson, Fireball Roberts, A. J. Foyt, Curtis Turner, Joe Weatherly, Marvin Panch, Tiny Lund, Cale Yarborough and David Pearson. They were the super-superstars of pit row.

Stuart is a smallish town in western Virginia where the Wood brothers, their cousins, and their friends grew up. Glen Wood, born there in 1924, brought the family

Glen Wood

665

into motor sports. In 1950 he and a group of friends bought a modified to run the dirt circuit. "It was just for fun and I was nominated as driver," Glen recalled.

At the beginning it may have been just for fun, but the sawmill owner got more serious about it as he continued to drive. In 1954 he was North Carolina state champion in sportsmen; in 1957 he was 3rd on the Grand National convertible division point standings. He was elected most popular NASCAR driver in 1959. In 1960 he won 3 times at Winston-Salem, N. C. By 1964 he had packed up his own racing helmet for good because younger drivers piloted his cars much faster.

For instance, in 1963, with Marvin Panch doing most of the driving, the Wood Brothers became the top car owners, with Ray Lee, an older brother, the owner of record. Glen himself drove the 2 Winston-Salem GN's, with Tiny Lund and Dave McDonald getting assignments when Panch was otherwise occupied. He won one, was 3rd in the other. The Woods were in the top 10 car owners year after year. And Panch was their driver for most of his career.

The Wood Brothers pit crew made their reputation gradually. Originally brother Ray was a crew member, but retired because the Sunday racing interfered with his religious activities. The other three brothers were Leonard, the youngest; Delano, 2nd youngest; and Clay, the oldest. A cousin, Ralph Edwards, and a friend, Ken Martin, completed the 6-man crew that won pit stop contests more often than any other crew around.

A Wood Brothers pit stop was an orchestration of precision. When it was time for their driver to pit, before the car stopped fully, Glen would step in front of it, trailed by Leonard, carrying a 70-pound wheel. Delano, Ralph, and Clay sprint around the rear. Meanwhile, Ken opens the fuel cap. Leonard drops the tire as Clay yanks over an impact wrench for him to change the right front wheel. Meanwhile, Ralph Edwards has brought the right rear wheel over the wall for Clay to change. Delano was in charge of jacking the car. As Clay and Leonard loosened the wheels to be replaced, Delano heaves the car.

Fans with strong field glasses could see that both Leonard and Edwards have a string in their teeth. The string contains lug nuts that they release into the palms of their hands as they refasten the wheels. Meanwhile, Glen checks under the hood, then the left side tires. He watches Ken Martin's feet as Ken and Edwards refuel. He can tell by the movement of the feet within a second or two if he has time to wipe the windshield. Delano, when time permits, gives the driver a drink of water.

On signal, Ralph bangs on the roof with his fist to tell the driver the stop is completed, and the car is away in about 20 seconds. Of course, if 4 tires must be changed, or if there's work under the hood, the 20-second limit is invalid. Then Glen takes over, working with the speed and precision of a surgeon. He allegedly once changed an alternator in 35 seconds. Asked about it, Glen said the old alternator had just about broken loose

from the mounting. Expertise in any area must be respected. The Wood Brothers made pit stops an art unrivaled anywhere in the racing world, even in places where Virginia is unknown.

JOHN WYER

John Wyer, who was JW Automotive along with John Willment and assorted others, is the perfect example for the school that believes that the best team manager is a man who never really raced. There are exponents on the other side, of course, who maintain that only a former driver can really run a successful racing team, and these people maintain that Wyer was a happy exception to the rule.

Either way, "Death Ray," as he was nicknamed for his stern-faced, steely-eyed look about the pits during races, was one of the most successful team managers. Impressario might be a better word than manager, for Wyer always had talented people like gray-haired David Yorke, formerly of Vanwall fame, and bespectacled John Horsman to actually do much of the dirty work in the pits, while Wyer could hold back and take a long view of the proceedings.

The Daytona 24-hour race of 1971 is a perfect example. While his Gulf-Porsches were tooling around the twisty Florida course, with Yorke and Horsman out front in plain sight in the bustling Porsche pits, Wyer—who had done his share of work, you understand—had grabbed a couple of hours of sleep and was now somewhat shielded from the noise (as shielded as you could

ever get at Daytona) by a Gulf-Porsche trailer. He was sipping a Bloody Mary and looking with some satisfaction at a chart that showed one of his cars 56 laps ahead of a Ferrari in 2nd place. Only about a sixth of the race remained, and things looked bloody good.

But an hour later, Wyer was in the pits, as quiet and steely-eyed as ever, while restrained pandemonium reigned. The lead Porsche had a jammed transmission. It was down to one gear, 4th, and had to pit. What to do? Only one choice, rebuild the gearbox, for the rules would not let him merely substitute a new one; small fish could get away with that kind of thing, but not contenders for the World Manufacturers Championship.

For 93 minutes the job went on, and Wyer never once remonstrated with his crew "They were doing their best, which was fine enough," he later said. Jackie Oliver, the driver who was in the car when it happened, was beside himself. Pedro Rodriguez, his codriver, who has been known to be temperamentally affected by problems like this one, or even by a hangnail, was climbing up the pit wall. Finally, the job was done, and Rodriguez hopped into the car and was away. About 3 P.M. when the checker fell, John Wyer's team had won another Daytona and taken still another step toward a World Championship.

Wyer was born in Kidderminster in December 1909. In 1928 he left school to become an apprentice at Sunbeam, the only real racing operation in England at that time. Five years later, his apprenticeship over, he became an engineer, then moved over to Solex Caburettors in 1934. John stayed there until 1947 when an offer he could not resist was made to him: general manager of Monaco Engineering.

Monaco was about the major race-preparation center in Britain in 1947; everybody's race car—from the weekend warrior to the major professional racer—was prepared at Monaco. Wyer got his start as team manager there, when one of Monaco's directors, Dudley Folland, who was racing a 2-litre Aston Martin at places like Spa and Le Mans put John on that job in addition to his other duties. Folland, in fact, almost made a driver out of Wyer in one of the 1st Ferraris imported into Britain, but after a few club meetings, John determined for himself that his talents lay behind the scenes, not in the cockpit.

"My introduction to Le Mans was in 1949," Wyer recalled later. "Dudley Folland ran a pre-war Aston Martin there with Anthony Heal. We didn't win, but at least we were professional about the thing, and this led to an offer from David Brown to become the racing manager of his Aston Martin Lagonda group. The arrangement was to be a temporary one for one year, but after 3 months, he offered me a permanent position as development engineer."

The temporary position lasted almost 13 years. That 1st season they raced only 3 times—Le Mans, the Dunrod version of the Tourist Trophy, and Silverstone in a British Grand Prix preliminary. The cars raced were

ordinary Astons, with certain changes. It was not until 1955 that a special racing car was built; for that reason, Aston's participation, while respectable, was not overpowering. At Le Mans, for example, the marque was 5th and 6th in 1950, then 3rd, 5th, and 7th in 1951. In 1955, Wyer's team was 2nd, a feat repeated in 1956 and 1958. But in 1959 Aston—with John Wyer—won its initial World Championship.

"We had not intended to contest any races but Le Mans that year," Wyer said. "But Stirling Moss, who had won the Nurburgring 1000 in a DBR 1 in 1958, believed he could win again in 1959, and asked us to lend and prepare a car for him for that race. He won, which meant if we could win at Le Mans, we would be in a strong position for the championship, which in those days was the World Sports Car Championship. To make the story short, Roy Salvadori and Carroll Shelby won Le Mans, followed by another of our cars codriven by Maurice Trintignant and Paul Frere."

Another Aston victory at the Goodwood Tourist Trophy gave it the title. Wyer was quick to point out that by this time he had become technical director and general manager of Aston, and much of the credit for the racing success he felt belonged to Reg Parnell, whom he had brought in to help in that area. The situation was probably much like the later days, with Wyer in charge and Parnell around to perform the Yorke-Horsman part. With the championship in hand, Aston Martin withdrew from racing.

Wyer's racing role could have ended right there, but in 1963 a certain American automobile company desired to win a championship. FoMoCo's game plan was always the same: hire the best people, hire the most people, spend whatever it takes, but win. The "best people" had to include Wyer. He was hired to run the Ford Advanced Vehicles Operation at Slough, England. FAVO was a disguise for the GT program, from which sprang John's 2nd World Championship and another Le Mans victory.

Development of the GT40 took almost 4 years, and when the development was about over, Wyer split and formed JW Automotive with John Willment and about 40 others at Slough. Less than 2 years later JW aided by Gulf Oil money, won Le Mans and the World Manufacturers Championship with the GT40. Then in 1969 JW repeated at Le Mans with Jacky Ickx and Jack Oliver (in his 1st Wyer hitch) in a GT40, and developed an offshoot called the Gulf Mirage, a 3-litre prototype. Gulf money was still available in 1970, but the basic car changed from Ford to Porsche. Using 7 cars, including a fearsome thing called the Gulf-Porsche 917K (for kurz, or short tailed version), Wyer's operation won Daytona, the BOAC 500 at Brands Hatch, Monza, the Targa Florio, Spa (in his best race, he said later), the Watkins Glen 6-hours, and Osterreichring. Austrian Porsche Salzburg cars won the other 2 races: Nurburgring and Le Mans, which Wyer considered his worst race ever. Rodriguez went out after only an hour with a defective connecting rod, Mike Hailwood crashed in the rain, and Jo Siffert missed a gear shift and blew an engine. But even without Le Mans, Wyer had his 3rd World Championship, in a 3rd marque.

In 1971 the Gulf-Porsche arrangement continued. Some driver shifts were made, but the end results were much the same, as the sky blue and orange cars dominated major races. In this last year of the 5-litre championship, Wyer and his Porsches won Buenos Aires, Daytona, Monza, Spa, and Austria; while Martini Porsches captured Sebring, Nurburgring, and Le Mans. Alfa Romeo managed to win the BOAC 1000, Targa Florio, and Watkins Glen 6-hour races.

In 1972 the title would go to 3-litre cars running a series of 6-hour or 1000-kilometer races, and Wyer and his Gulf backers were ready with a Mirage for that new ball game. He said it would be an "experimental" season, but it was like any other. Wyer was there, a bit grayer at the temples, perhaps a bit leaner and more lined in the face. A stopwatch hung round his neck, of course, steely-eyed as ever, dominant as ever. The perfect team head.

CALE YARBOROUGH

When they lifted Cale Yarborough from the wreck of his Wood Brothers Mercury Cyclone at Texas International Speedway on December 7, 1969, it did not seem possible that the barrel-chested former semi-professional running back would be back in action by Daytona in February. It was the 5-foot 7-inch Yarborough's

initial serious injury in 12 years of racing; his shoulder was shattered.

But here he was, the pride of Florence County, S.C., a living folk hero, smiling and walking through the pit area at Daytona International Speedway. He went out onto the track in a new Cyclone Spoiler prepared by the Wood Brothers, won the pole position and the $5,000 prize that went with it with a record run of 194.015 m.p.h., and eclipsed his own record set the previous July. The blond Yarborough was 1.5 m.p.h. faster than the next fastest, Buddy Baker. His doctors had said he might never race again.

Cale did not win the 1970 Daytona 500. Pete Hamilton from Massachusetts did. Cale had won a 125-mile preliminary race, then led 11 laps of the 500 itself, took the lead back on the 17th lap, and led until the 32nd lap when his engine blew. It was that kind of year for Yarborough. In the Alabama 500 at Talladega he was challenging for the lead when a fan threw a pop bottle toward the track. It shattered his windshield, forcing 2 extra pit stops. "If that bottle had been a few feet to the left, it would have come through right in my face," he said bitterly after he placed 5th.

Even Cale's initial victory of the year, the Motor State 400 at Michigan International Speedway, was protested by Hamilton. The protest was disallowed, and Cale managed to earn his $100,000 for the year. But when Ford Motor Company announced its withdrawal from racing sponsorships, Cale dropped the shoe. "I'm quitting stock-car racing for 1971 for a shot at the USAC Championship Trail with the Gene White team out of Atlanta," he said. It was like a man voluntarily stepping into the minor leagues. The people who had made him a folk hero really refused to believe it.

William Caleb Yarborough was not always a folk hero, stepping from his private plane into the helicopter that set him down in the infield of the race course and took him away the same way after the race. Born March 27, 1939, in Timmonsville, N.C., he was an unsuccessful turkey farmer, a substitute back on the Sumter, S. C., Generals, a young man who married a girl he met at his uncle's drug store and then failed to support her through either farming or racing as he tried desperately to become a NASCAR star. It was not easy in the early days because the other guys on the track did not care if you were a high school all-state football hero. It was not easy because rides were not easy to get, especially for a kid who falsified his age for 3 years so he could try for Grand National rides.

When he and Betty Jo searched the upholstery of the car to make a 37-cent down payment on a 50-cent bridge toll, he wondered if he should have tried to stay at Clemson College or tried out with the Washington Redskins. He once went to Tennessee because a promoter had offered him $200 appearance money, then practically had to beg for it to have enough to get home. In 5 years there were 12 Grand National starts and a total of $535 in prize money. The sportsman action in

South Carolina kept him alive.

In 1964 he got a break. Herman (The Turtle) Beam had convinced Ford's Jacques Passino to let him run a factory car. Herman picked Cale as his driver, and Cale proceeded to demolish the car while challenging for the lead. That was all right. Ford supplied a new car, but not for long. Beam and Cale failed to check the car thoroughly, and it burned out a wheel bearing, thus losing another race. Cale was back on the farm.

But later that year, Passino offered Yarborough a job as a $1.25-an-hour carpenter at Holman-Moody. Cale came, hoping something would happen to give him a last chance at racing. It happened in 1965; Banjo Matthews and Bob Johns argued, Johns departed for Miami, and Cale got the ride, for the balance of 1965. He earned $25,140 in purses, won once, and finished in the top 10 all of 34 times. For that Passino raised him to $1.75 an hour for the winter. However, the big driver shakeup of 1966 was imminent. And Cale finally caught the brass ring—he drew the assignment with the Wood Brothers.

Glen, Delano, Leonard and Clay Wood, cousin Ralph Edwards, and friend Ken Martin, constitute the finest and fastest pit crew anywhere—certainly the finest through the years in NASCAR. In 20 seconds they can change 2 tires and add 15 gallons of gasoline. That's fast, but if they must they can shave this close to 19 seconds. In a sport where 2 seconds can mean $\frac{1}{4}$ mile on the racetrack a good pit crew is invaluable. In 1966 there were no victories but $23,030 in prize money. In 1967 the legend began to build.

At Britol, Tenn., Cale seemed an easy winner over David Pearson, then still running for Dodge, when he cut his tire on some debris. Even so Glen Wood thought Cale had won it. Unfortunately the scorer disagreed and was upheld by NASCAR. At Atlanta, Cale and his 1967 Ford worked together to win his first 500-mile race easily over Dick Hutcherson with only a brief challenge by USAC's Mario Andretti. His closest call came in practice during the week when veteran Curtis Turner lost control and flipped when Yarborough was close behind. The Turner Chevelle came down barely 12 inches from Cale; Turner walked away and Cale was shaken only by what might have been.

Cale qualified the Bryant Heating Special in the 7th row for the Indianapolis 500, then flew off to win the pole in NASCAR's World 600 at Charlotte. He led 25 laps of the World 600 before his car retired because of steering problems, and at Indianapolis he hit the wall on the 184th lap after getting as high as 4th place. At Rockingham Cale finished 4th, troubled by a faulty transmission. Then came the Firecracker 400 in Daytona. Yarborough had been edged off the pole by Darel Dieringer, but the way this race developed, the pole did not mean much. It was a gray day with rain clouds lowering overhead. The rains finally came at the 260-mile mark, necessitating a 4½ hour wait before the final dash for the trophy. But the cars were blazing hot; the lead changed 44 times. It all came down to the final 20

miles with 4 Ford drivers still in contention—Cale, Darel, David Pearson, and Hutcherson.

The 4 ran close with Pearson 1st, then Hutch, then Dieringer slingshotting off the turns into a short-lived lead only to be corralled once again. Now it was the final lap; Dick, Darel, Cale, and David were running in that order. It became obvious that Pearson was out of contention on the backstretch as the other 3 hurtled through the 3rd turn setting up for the all-important final corner. Hutch dropped down to shut off Dieringer, but not fast enough. Cale sneaked past to steal the race from both and win his 3rd 5-figure purse of the year. He made only 16 appearances, all at superspeedways, had 7 top-5 finishes, and earned $56,685 from NASCAR alone.

But 1968 really was Yarborough's year. The stocky driver won himself $136,786, as he amassed a record 6 superspeedway victories: both Daytona races, the Atlanta 500, and—sweetest of all to a man who grew up next door—the Darlington, S. C., Southern 500. He had switched to Mercury Cyclones, and the change was beneficial to all. The Daytona 500 had been a 1-second victory over Lee Roy Yarbrough, the Southern 500 was a 1-second victory over David Pearson.

Yarborough earned his home-town triumph. Two laps down early in the race, when he switched tire brands, Cale seemed to have the fastest car, but Pearson charged back from a 25-second deficit to take the lead. Then, 50 laps from the end, the 2 leaders slammed into one another, Pearson's car screeching toward the infield as both regained control and pitted for tires. Back on the track, Pearson harried Cale the rest of the way, forcing him into the 1st turn railing no less than 3 times, but somehow Yarborough stayed ahead. That in itself was amazing because, as track temperatures reached 150 degrees, Cale's water jug hose stopped up, and he had scorned a "cool suit" that would have kept his temperature down. "I was about to die," he said as he staggered groggily from his car in victory lane. He lost 12 pounds in what was called the roughest Southern 500 ever.

Cale finished the year by making one of his rare visits to a half-mile track to win the Middle Georgia Speedway 100-miler. In 1969, his outside interests growing, Cale took his Mercury out 19 times and, although he was a contender in every race, misfortune seemed to dog him. There were, however, 2 exceptions. Cale won the Atlanta 500 for the 3rd time in a row, and he added a victory in the Motor State 500 where he and Lee Roy Yarbrough touched fenders on the final turn of the final lap, Lee Roy hitting the wall and Cale winning.

"There's only one way to drive as far as I'm concerned," Yarborough said, "and that's flat out. If you don't charge from the start, there are enough good drivers around who will." The very blond hair was thinning and the barrel chest was slipping southward as he prepared to take a full shot at single-seaters in USAC, but that kind of racing philosophy would make things interesting. It did but it did not assure success. By 1972 Cale

Yarborough was back in NASCAR for 4 top-10 finishes in 5 races. By 1973 he and Junior Johnson had teamed in a Chevvy that seemed sure to add to his 14 GN victories.

LEE ROY YARBROUGH

There never was a driver in NASCAR who had a year like 1969 turned out to be for Lee Roy Yarbrough. Maybe there never will be again because NASCAR racing continues to get more competitive. In 1969 Lee Roy Yarbrough, then 31, won more money and more victories on the Grand National Trail than he had won in 8 previous seasons. He won 7 out of 30 starts and all 7 were on superspeedways (out of 9 superspeedway races in 1969). The best record previously had been 4 in one year by Cale Yarborough and Freddie Lorenzen.

In 1969, as Lee Roy himself said, "everything just fell into place. We didn't do much differently than in 1968, but everything worked." *We* consisted of Junior Johnson, the former driving great who was now a car owner; Herb Nab, who had crewed for Lorenzen in Freddie's glory days; and Yarbrough, a reformed charger who suddenly learned that, even going flat out, there can be race strategy.

Born September 17, 1938, in Jacksonville, Fla., Lee Roy Yarbrough committed himself early to automobile racing—early and totally. He was driving sportsmen and modifieds as soon as he could get into a car, and from the beginning he was a charger. He was 22 before he got his initial Grand National ride and finished 33rd in the 1960 Atlanta 500. But he was a racing veteran by then, having lied about his age at 14 to get his license. He quit school in the 10th grade to racing his own creations. He became so proficient at area dirt tracks that one year he won 52 races and promoters were offering a $500 bonus to any driver who defeated him. He loved racing so much he even had challenge races at night.

"We were racing our old cars down this sandy back country road one night," said Yarbrough, "and I didn't give on a corner. I ran into a tree. I got out and I guess I was so mad at not beating the other guy, I didn't think much about whether or not I was hurt." In 1962 he began to limit himself to NASCAR competition. In GN competition he made the top 10 once in 12 starts; in sportsmen he won 37 races. In 1962 he also discovered the victory lane at Daytona Speedway, 90 miles south of his home town, in a sportsman-modified contest, the Permatex 250. Lee Roy continued to concentrate on sportsman racing, repeating as Permatex 250 king, but in 14 GN races, he made the top 10 five times. He had latched on to a Mercury factory ride in 1963—a very short ride. In Martinsville, Va., he was out of contention, but continued to race his teammates.

Lee Roy was a cocky young man, supremely confident in his own ability to take a 2nd-string automobile and, through sheer muscle and the heaviest foot this side of

motorcycling, turn it into a winner. He had more successful sportsman racing in 1964 and more success on the GN circuit. There were 4 different cars, a Pontiac, a Dodge, and 2 Plymouths, and there were 2 Grand National victories among 11 top-5 finishes in 34 races. He did this after recovering from a fiery wreck in the Permatex 250 where Fred Lorenzen, Larry Frank, and G. C. Spencer had saved his life by pulling him out of the car quickly.

It took an unusual set of circumstances to salvage Yarbrough. Ray Fox had an epic year in 1964 with Junior Johnson in Chevvy, but now, with that factory closing the back door to the parts bin, Fox had switched to Dodge for 1965. Junior never got acclimated, and finally took a better deal with the Holly Farms Poultry Ford. Buck Baker was Fox's next choice and he lasted only about 3 weeks. Fox chose Lee Roy as he had picked David Pearson years earlier, because he was a young, hungry driver with skill and courage. "All he needs is experience," Ray said. (Yarbrough had won the Daytona modified for Fox in the old Pearson Pontiac.)

Yarbrough got experience. He was up among the leaders as long as the car held up and as long as he did not get enmeshed in other people's crashes. No victories in the NASCAR big time, but there was a consolation —a NASCAR version of the world closed-course record.

When Daytona International Speedway opened late in 1958, President William H. G. France posted a $10,-000 bonus for the 1st driver to post laps at over 180 m.p.h. Art Malone, a former drag racer, piloted a strange machine built by Bob Osiecki, a Carolina idea man, a little over 180 m.p.h. The car was a retired Indianapolis roadster with inverted wings to keep it on the ground.

On a windy day early in 1965, Yarbrough and Fox assailed the record again. They waited for the wind to die down, but light was disappearing fast and Yarbrough was impatient to try. He drove his supercharged, specially lightened Dodge onto the course and began to circle faster and faster. He went 181.818 m.p.h., and when he came in, he remarked he could have gone faster. He had done it despite a 20 m.p.h. crosswind. A much more significant run came in July 1966 when he registered 178.660 m.p.h. in a Charger that met all Grand National specifications, to win the pole for the Firecracker 400. He broke his suspension after 126 laps and watched Sam McQuagg take the victory.

Yarbrough had been to Indianapolis in 1965, just managing to pass part of his rookie tests. In 1966 he returned in a machine set up by Jim Rathman, former Indy winner, and sponsored by astronauts Gus Grissom and Gordon Cooper. He asked the sponsors to let a more experienced driver take some laps so he would have some idea of just how fast the car could go. Greg Weld did—and wrecked the car, ending Indy hopes for 1966. So it was back to NASCAR and sportsman racing, a ride in a Dodge and only 2 victories in 3 seasons, one of them—the National 500 at Charlotte in 1966—

his initial superspeedway triumph. It was a victory over the most impressive fields ever assembled for a stock-car race—from USAC, there were A. J. Foyt, Gordon Johncock, and Jim Hurtubise; from IMCA, perennial champ Iggy Katona had come south; and former ARCA champs Jack Bowsher and Earl Balmer were present.

But Yarbrough handled them all with ease after an early race duel with Cale Yarborough. It seemed so easy no one could explain why Lee Roy had not won some of the many superspeedway races he had led in the previous 3 years. Jon Thorne, his car owner, the son of millionaire Joel Thorne who once tried to buy an Indianapolis victory, was overjoyed. It was to be the high point of the Thorne sponsorship because Lee Roy was still the hardest charger in the sport.

In 1968 things were supposed to change. Lee Roy had a full factory ride with the Junior Johnson branch of the Ford NASCAR effort. He was driving a Ford or Mercury instead of a Dodge, but that really did not make much difference, as he had once said. "I'll drive anything if it's got wheels and if it puts me in front." He had Herb Nab as the mechanic, but he himself was a fine wrench twister. Things did change, but he was still the man who just missed. He placed 2nd 3 times. In the Daytona 500, he led most of the way, but not the last second as Cale Yarborough in a twin Mercury Cyclone beat him. Lee Roy made a 2-installment pit stop under the green flag late in the race when he seemed a sure winner. He could not overcome the time lost.

At the Atlanta 500 Cale was the victor again as Lee Roy was black-flagged for long enough to cost him any chance to win, allegedly for passing Cale on a caution flag. He won the pole at Darlington's Rebel 400, but finished 5th because of tire trouble. At the rain-shortened Charlotte World 600, he was 3rd, complaining that the race was not called early enough. He went back to Daytona and another 2nd to Yarborough in the Firecracker.

The Dixie 500 in Atlanta broke the chain of bad luck. Starting from an unaccustomed 5th place and switching tire brands in mid-race, Lee Roy won comfortably. But bad luck returned for the remainder of the year. In 1969, it was the Jacksonville virtuoso's turn. He won the Daytona 500 after losing his back window; he passed Charlie Glotzbach on the 3rd turn of the final lap and crossed a few car lengths ahead. He had won the Permatex 300 the day before.

Then he won the Rebel 400 and the World 600, and qualified in the middle of the 3rd row at Indy for the Memorial Day classic. In the Rebel he somehow weaved through a late-race accident unscathed, but at Charlotte he actually raced off the pace until the final laps, saving his equipment for a superb victory. At Indy the manifold broke, but he finished 23rd overall.

In the Firecracker mechanic Herb Nab made it difficult for anyone to slipstream his driver by moving the exhaust stacks to the rear of the car, thus expelling superheated air toward the radiator of anyone who tried

to draft. Lee Roy made 7 pit stops to 6 by his top 3 competitors, yet managed to nip Buddy Baker by about 4 car-lengths. At the Dixie 500 Lee Roy had demolished his car in practice at midweek. No matter. Nab repaired all, and Lee Roy moved into the victory circle for the record 5th superspeedway victory in a single season. He and the Junior Johnson crew were not yet done.

In the Southern 500, held on a rain-plagued day, a wreck-strewn demolition derby finally boiled down to Lee Roy versus David Pearson in the final 25 miles. Pearson seemed to have it won when Lee Roy hung everything out on an inside pass on the back straight, crossing the finish barely a car-length ahead.

There was another feat left in Yarbrough before being named Driver of the Year. Rockingham, N. C., was the only original big 5 superspeedway that had resisted Lee Roy's onslaught. It fell in the American 500 when Yarbrough won by more than a lap. The real problem again came in practice when he demolished his car. The back-up car was on exhibition in Jacksonville. Nab's boys retrieved it and prepared it in time for Lee Roy to set fast time on the 2nd day of qualifying, then take the race. He had won $188,605 of NASCAR money, another $15,000 from Indy for an all-time money mark for a NASCAR driver. Had there been no PDA boycott at Talladega, Ala., the amount might have gone higher.

After such a year there must be a letdown. Ford made it worse by cutting support money. Johnson and Lee Roy found Jim Robbins, long a USAC car owner, as an emergency sponsor. However, there was not even enough money to make all the superspeedway stops. In any event, Lee Roy finished 9th but running at Daytona, victim of a 7-lap pit stop to replace a faulty ignition coil. In the Rockingham 500 he cut a tire on debris and hit the wall. After qualifying the Jim Robbins Eagle 13th fastest at Indy, Lee Roy came back to an oven-hot Charlotte World 600 to relieve Donnie Allison and win by 2 laps. His own Mercury had burned its clutch out earlier. His engine blew at Daytona, and at the Dixie 500 Charles Glotzbach helped him to a 3rd-place finish. He was 7th in the Michigan 400, skipped Talladega and Darlington, then annexed his 1st victory of the year at Charlotte's National 400 under the caution flag. He earlier had fought off Bobby Isaac and Bobby Allison.

Lee Roy had not lost his desire to race because he still drove sportsman races. But he lived in a mansion in Columbia, S. C., drove a Lincoln Continental, and wore dark sunglasses like a movie star. He was no longer wedded to NASCAR. After leading, he had finished 8th in the Norris Industries Brabham at the debut Ontario, 500. Jack Brabham was interested in putting him in the best single-seater that the Australian could conceive for the new USAC Triple Crown, and there was even talk of some road racing. What can a man who has won 7 superspeedway victories in one season do for an encore? Perhaps win Indianapolis, Ontario, and Pocono. As of 1973 the world was still waiting for that to happen. In 1971 Rocky mountain fever limited his racing and 1972 saw him trying to regain the touch with 9 top-10 finishes in 18 races.

COUNT LOUIS ZBOROWSKI

The owner of some of the most notable airplane-engined specials in the world was the son of an expatriate Pole who himself was killed in 1903 racing a Mercedes up La Turbie. Count Louis Vorow Zborowski, who died in a racing accident at Monza, turned to motor racing for excitement some 6 or 7 years before his death and made racing history at Brooklands, Indianapolis, and on the open road, where his loud black and white checkered linen caps were a trademark.

Zborowski was born in England in 1895 and educated at Eton, so this son of an American mother and a Polish father called England home. His estate at Higham near Canterbury was the site of lavish parties, an elaborate model railroad, and many practical jokes. In later years it housed his carbuilding projects. The 1st and most famous of these was the Chitty-Chitty-Bang-Bang, so called because that's what its huge slow-turning 23-litre Maybach aero engine (from a World War I Gotha bomber) sounded like as it powered the pre-war chain-driven Mercedes chassis with 300 horses. Zborowski's resident engineer, Lt. Clive Gallop, did the engine installation and helped him when he ran the car at Brooklands, the huge 3-mile concrete oval that was about the only track in England where the monster could begin to realize its potential. With about 800 pounds of sand in the tail as ballast, Louis found he could lap Brooklands easily at 110 m.p.h. The engine was turning about 1700 r.p.m.s then, and it is interesting to speculate how fast Louis and the other men with aero-engined cars might have gone if they had had tires that could stay together.

Chitty-Chitty-Bang-Bang faced its 1st match race in 1921 against a V-12 Sunbeam with an 18.3-litre aero engine (also a Maybach). Cupid Hornsted was driving the Sunbeam, which was handily defeated along with a large Vauxhall. After that, A. V. Ebblewhite, Brooklands' official handicapper, imposed a heavy load on Zborowski and his car. Ziggy fooled them, for he then built Chitty II, which was powered by a 19-litre Benz Zeppelin engine. He was to face the Sunbeam and a new aero job in the fall 1921 meeting. Sir Alastair Miller's Viper was powered by a V-8 Hispano-Suiza. Bill Guiness, heir to the stout fortune, won it all in the Sunbeam. These early versions of drag racing were called the Lightning Long Handicap series and were great attention-getters.

It was in Chitty II that Zborowski toured into the Sahara desert, followed by Gallop with the luggage in another car. He got out alive, despite the huge engine's voracious thirst for gas, oil, and attention. It was about this time that Zborowski began to compete in smaller cars in single-seater racing—Aston Martin, in which he had a major financial interest, and Bugatti. In the latter, he lasted 102 miles in the 1923 Indianapolis 500 before a connecting rod sidelined him.

But his real heart was at Brooklands with the big jobs. He commissioned Gallop to create the Higham Special (called Babs by Parry Thomas, a later owner), which was powered by a V-12 Liberty of 27-litre capacity. And old Benz gearbox took the power and with the engine turning 1200 r.p.m., the huge white car was going 100 m.p.h. Zborowski was killed in 1924 at Monza during the Italian Grand Prix before he could run this car.

DENNY ZIMMERMAN

Very few kinds make it to an Indianapolis 500. Denny Zimmerman, a Connecticut rookie at the 1971 500-miler, was 30 when he made the starting field of 33 cars in a 6-year-old car. He looked younger, weighing but 135 pounds, which made him the lightest driver by far, although his sandy hair was getting a bit sparse. He still had a bit of the Soap-Box Derby driver about him, and it was way back in 1954 that Denny had actually driven in that annual competition in his home town of Glastonbury, Conn.

By 1957 Zimmerman was driving for real, starting with a modified stock car at Riverside Park, Mass. He won his initial race the following season with a Ford flat-head. By 1962 Zim was good enough to finish 4th in modified NASCAR stock ranks. In 1964 Denny was Sportsman Champion of both Virginia and Maryland. Zimmerman started driving a sprint car in 1966, won a feature, and finished 5th in the standings. He stayed in

672

the sprints even when he switched over to USAC in 1968, his 1st Championship race the Trenton 200.

Zim's 1st try to make the Indy field came in 1969, but he failed. The story was the same in 1970, although that season he actually tried to qualify (in 1969 he passed his rookie test, but did not attempt to qualify) and registered a 158.912 m.p.h. mark. In 1971 Denny got together with Frank Fiore, a Californian who works for United Air Lines (but who is also enough of a racing bug to run his own Turbo-Offy) for a car called the Fiore Vollstedt Special. The new team 1st ran without success at Rafeala, Argentina, in the 1st USAC race there, a 300 miler. Next came Phoenix where Denny failed to finish, but Fiore had enough faith to keep the combination going for Zim's 3rd Indy try. He not only qualified this time (169.755 m.p.h.), but scored 8th and won Rookie of the Year honors. Distributor failure dumped Zim to 19th in the 1972 Bryant Heating & Cooling Special, however.

JOHN ZINK

John Smith Zink, usually called "Junior" although his father's name actually is John Steele Zink, was an unusual man to be equated with the Indianapolis set. He was always willing to try new ideas, new drivers, new mechanics. He drove competitively with some success, and, unlike many car owners, he regarded the race cars he owned as part of a business. That is not to say Zink was coldblooded about the sport; he probably loved it more than most. But he saw no reason not to make it pay, if possible. The rest of the Zink enterprises—the industrial furnaces and the heaters—all did, and he got enjoyment out of making that part of the business grow, too.

Born in Tulsa, Okla., in 1929, he was the son of an engineer who encouraged his mechanical abilities. At the age of 7 Junior was given a Model T dump truck to dismantle and put together, at first with the aid if his father, then alone. But his mother objected to a dilapidated dump truck in the back yard, and, after about 2 years, she finally decided to have it removed .

In 1937 an uncle took Jack to see a midget race up in Detroit. The little boy contracted a severe case of racing mania and for 4 years saved to buy another Model T. Once he had it, he would beg drained oil from service station owners to save money. The waste oil often contained water which, when it contacted the Ford's hot crankcase, turned to steam and sent the oil gushing. Several times Jack swabbed the cement of station property under the baleful glare of the owner.

In 1941 Jack finished 3rd in the All-American Soap Box Derby, then returned to powered cars. After the Ford came a series of home-built cars, starting with a tiny 2-horse lawnmower engine mounted on a wood frame. It was started by grasping part of the frame and leaning right, tightening the belt to the rear axle. When stopping, one leaned to the left, disengaging the belt. Finally, when he became a high school senior, Jack decided to build his own midget racer. Felix Graves, a former midget driver, owned a garage in Tulsa and let the lad have some space in which to work. Zink built a rail frame, putting on a modified 1937 Ford front end and a Model A rear assembly. He made his own hubs and gas tank, and installed a Ford 60 engine. His father then decided that the boy really was interested in racing, so he offered him money to buy any kind of midget he wanted providing he would not drive it competitively. Jack was disappointed but accepted the terms, ordering an Offy engine and a Kurtis chassis.

Since Buzz Barton, prominent in midget car circles, helped him finish the car, Zink offered him the ride. They won the feature the 1st time out and campaigned successfully with Zink as mechanic the whole summer of 1947. The next year his father stood the gaff for another midget, and Marcel St. Criq and Jack had a fairly good year. Zink, now a student at Oklahoma A & M, spent weekends early in the season driving straight from the Stillwater campus to the race site, sometimes working all night on the cars. In 1949 the team of Barton, Zink, and Tommy Vardeman set Kansas, Colorado, Missouri, Oklahoma, and Texas afire, but success went to both drivers' heads. They left the lad by July, and were replaced by Houston's Cecil Green.

Green edged Vardeman for the Southeast title, but was hurt in a highway accident a few days later. In 1950 a youngster named Jimmy Reece was given his 1st chance in the Zink midget, and he teamed with veteran Bud Camden to terrorize the circuit. Jack received his college degree in mechanical engineering and then finally persuaded his father to let him drive. But it was to be in stock cars. His 1st race at Tulsa was of spectacular brevity; he flipped in the 1st lap, demolishing the Ford sedan he had built. His next race in a Ford coupe launched him on a career good enough to place with the top stock cars in the Tulsa area. He returned to college for graduate work in the winter.

In 1950 oilman M. A. Walker sponsored the 21-year-old Zink's 1st shot at Indianapolis. Green finished 4th, encouraging another try in 1951, and Cecil was leading at 200 miles when a piston broke. A short while later Green was killed at Winchester, Ind. Meanwhile, Reece was winning the Southwest Midget Championship, followed by Camden. Jimmy also beat out the boss for some regional stock-car titles. The following year, the Reece-Zink combination came to Indy with a 4000 series Kurtis towed behind a pickup truck. Jimmy passed his rookie test after Jack stopped the Kurtis' tendency to shed exhaust stacks and rupture gas tanks (5 times). Reece placed 7th in the 500 proper, finishing the entire grind in his rookie try, then finished 8th on the Championship Trail for 1952. Jack did not follow the Trail. He had to begin work in the family business and drove a Chevvy stocker a while around Tulsa and Oklahoma City.

Reece was hired away for 1953, and Zink tried to get Bob Sweikert. When he could not, he gave the Indy ride to Jerry Hoyt, who lasted 60 laps before heat prostration got him. Hoyt won 3rd place at Milwaukee, then wrecked at both Springfield and the Milwaukee 200, and that was the season. With business taking more and more time, Jack had to quit racing himself for 1954, but Gene Hartley was picked to drive the old Zink Kurtis. Gene lasted 400 miles at Indy. Zink's big year was 1955. He got A. J. Watson as his mechanic, Sweikert as driver, and won an AAA championship and the Indy 500.

Always thinking ahead, Zink refused to rest on his laurels. He decided to investigate the many potent overseas engines. He gathered data, consulted such men as Carroll Shelby and Masten Gregory, and ultimately decided to go with the Offy for Indianapolis. His investigations led him into a field he never forgot, however. He read of a turbine-engined racer built by attachés of the Strategic Air Command, and asked General Curtis LeMay, then SAC leader, for permission to try it. He tested the SAC Firebird at Offut AFB and was intrigued by the amount of torque the power plant developed despite only a 180-b.h.p. rating. He filed the information in back of his head, and the Zink Track Burner turbine car appeared some 5 years later. It never did much, but the turbine racing engine grew more feasible with each passing year. The Track Burner was otherwise equipped with Offy power.

For 1956 Zink lost Sweikert as a driver but gained victory in the 500 with Pat Flaherty in a Kurtis-Offy modified by A.J. Watson. Flaherty also won Milwaukee before crashing and sidelining himself for several years. Zink eventually lost Watson to the Leader Card forces, but not before A. J. did the wrench-twisting for the likes of Judd Larson, Reece again, and Troy Ruttman both in the Race of Two Worlds at Monza and at Indy. Ruttman led the 1957 Indianapolis race only to depart with an ailing car on the 12th lap. Zink finished 3rd in the car owners' point standings for 1957. After Larson, however, Zink's interest seemed to drop, and while he continued in the sport with top drivers like Jim Hurtubise, Roger McClusky and Jim McElreath, his business did not permit him the liberty of tending to his racing.

However, Zink contracted with Jack Brabham, former World Champ, to build and run Indy cars in 1964 and 1965. He was joined in this endeavor by the Urschel Corp. of Texas and Earl Slick of Shek Raceway, Inc. The 1964 powerplant was Offy, but for 1965 Ford d.o.h.c., Offy, and Climax all were under consideration. John went with Offy and Jim McElreath the next 3 years, got a 3rd in 1966 and a 5th in 1961. Zink ranked with the great car owners such as Lindsey Hopkins, Al Dean, J. C. Agajanian, and Bob Wilke. And that is saying a great deal, for it is all very well to be a great driver or mechanic, but someone has to put up the money for the enterprise.

PAUL ZUCCARELLI

Paul Zuccarelli was an organizing member of the world's 1st independent racing team in the modern sense, the fastest man at Indianapolis (though never a winner there) and a Grand Prix victor in the days before World War I. He was a Spaniard, and 1st came to attention driving that nation's Hispano Suiza cars, which he not only raced but assisted Marc Birkigt in designing. Zuccarelli's initial major victory was the 1910 Coupe de l'Auto at Boulogne, with Jules Goux and Jean Chassagne 2nd and 3rd in Lion-Peugeots. The Spaniard's winning average was 56.7 m.p.h. But he won more than a race there. Zuccarelli and the 2 Peugeot drivers became close friends, the friendship blossoming into a business proposition for Peugeot.

None of the 3 were technically trained in the formal sense, but all were more than a little familiar with machinery. Zuccarelli was the most familiar, and on that basis, the trio offered themselves to Peugeot as a package. They would design, prepare, and race cars, completely independent of other factory operations, the goal to be, of course, making the French carbuilder's name known beyond France itself. After much soul-searching, the proposal was accepted, and the Charlatan Racing Team was formed by the trio, the 1st autonomous racing team of its kind in the world. A modern counterpart might be JW Automotive of England, which successfully raced "factory" teams for Ford and Porsche, among others.

Even though he was to design the cars and handle other technical matters, Zuccarelli kept driving with Goux and Chassagne. In 1912 he won the 3-litre class in the Grand Prix de France (not to be confused with the French GP, nor the GP de ACF, also being run in those years). His average was 64.87 m.p.h. He raced at Boulogne in the speed trials, climbed Mont Ventoux, and lasted 7 laps in the French GP until the Peugeot's engine failed.

In 1913 Zuccarelli journeyed to America with Goux and their Peugeots to do battle at the Indianapolis 500. Paul lasted 18 laps until a main bearing failed, but he set the race's fastest lap—93.5 m.p.h.—then watched contentedly as Jules won the American classic for the Charlatans at an average speed of 75.93 m.p.h. Back in France, the GP was soon to come, and Zuccarelli took the Peugeots out into the Normandy countryside, where traffic was almost nonexistent and dangers were few, for some speed tests.

They blocked off the road being used for the test at both ends, just to be sure, and a couple of crossroads, but they neglected a donkey track that looked unused. As Zuccarelli was speeding at better than 90 m.p.h. along that road, a small cart, pulled by an old horse and driven by a deaf farmer, popped out from the hidden trail. They collided. The farmer lived, but his horse was killed. So was Paul Zuccarelli.

Photo Credits for "Eighty Years Among the Speed People"

ABC-TV-89
British Leyland Motor Corp.-121
Castrol-100
Chrysler-80
Cunningham Cars-41
Robert A. Cutter-123
Fiat-4, 7, 18
Firestone-76, 102, 115
Ford-8, 38, 61, 63, 64, 74, 77, 81, 107
Ray Fox Engineering-79
Goodyear-85, 116, 117
Hampshire Group-2, 3, 15, 17, 20, 22, 23, 24, 28, 29, 30, 31, 40, 42, 43, 49, 62, 69, 106, 108, 109, 110
Indianapolis Speedway-9, 10, 11, 16, 25, 36, 37
L&M-90, 92
Lime Rock Park-105
London Art Technical-32, 33, 35, 45, 46, 47, 48, 50, 51, 52, 53, 54, 55, 56, 57, 59, 66, 67, 68, 70, 71, 72, 73, 82, 83, 84, 87, 88, 97, 118

Lucas-113
Mercedes-Benz-6, 12, 13, 14, 19, 21, 27, 44
Mobil-39, 60, 112, 114
Bud Moore Engineering-75
Ray Nichels Engineering-65, 101
Penske Racing-94, 95, 96
Porsche-26, 93
Raybestos-Manhattan-103
Renault-1
Rolls Royce-111
SAAB-122
STP-78
Texaco-98, 99, 119, 120
Uniroyal-5
Universal Oil Products-91
Watkins Glen Grand Prix Corp.-34, 58, 86
Wynn's-104

PHOTO CREDITS

Abarth-Taruffi.
Alfa Romeo-Courage, Galli, Kinnunen.
American Gas Association-Gabelich.
Aston Martin-Parnell
Bahamas News Bureau-Foyt, McCluggage, McLaren.
Randy Barnett-Cevert, Revson.
BLMC (British Leyland Motors Corp.)-Eyston, Hopkirk, Makinen, Mims, Salvadori, Tullius.
Bosch-Hall.
Bridgehampton Racing-Fitch.
BOAC (British Overseas Airways Corp.)-Dibley.
BP (British Petroleum)-Donald Campbell.
Castrol-Eaton, Yarbrough
Cunningham Cars-Momo.
Robert A. Cutter-Posey.
Daytona Speedway-Nab.
Dodge-Donnie and Bobby Allison, Buck Baker, Balmer, Bruner, Castles, Dieringer, Eargle, Fox, Garlits, Glotzbach, Goldsmith, Hylton, Isaac, Johnson, Lund, Matthews, McElreath, Nelson, Paschal, Roberts, Sutton, White.
Rene Dreyfus-Dreyfus.
Duckhams-Hailwood.
Esso-Grim.
Fiat-Bonetto, Nazzaro.
Firestone-Arfons, Carter, Pearson.
Ford-Bianchi, Bowsher, Boyd, Bucknum, Clark, Duckworth, Ford, Frank Gardner, Grant, Gurney, Hawkins, Holman & Moody, Jarrett, Johns, Jones, MacDonald, McCluskey, Meyer, Bud Moore, Panch, Bennie Parsons, Ruby, Scott, Titus, Turner, Weatherly, Whitmore, Yarborough.
Ray Fox Engineering-Lorenzen.
Goodyear-Arfons, Gary Bettenhausen, Breedlove, Kenyon.
Harry W. Graff-Portago, Shelby.
Gulf-Attwood, Bell, Hulme, Teddy Mayer, Siffert, Wyer.
Hampshire Group-Anderson, Baghetti, Bandini, Barnato, Barth, Beaufort, Behra, Bergere, Tony Bettenhausen, Birkin, Brilli-Peri, Brooks, Bugatti, Castellotti, Chinetti, Collins, Earl Cooper, John Cooper, Cunningham, Cummings, Dean, DePalma, Duray, Etancelin, Fangio, Farina, Ferrari, Flaherty, Frere, Gendebien, Gonzalez, Goux, Hawthorn, Ireland, Jano, Jarrott, Jenatzy, Junek, Ligier, MacKenzie, Maggs, Maglioli, Mairesse, Maserati Brothers, Tim Mayer, Raymond Mays, Rex Mays, Moll, Jimmy Murphy, Musso, Nuvolari, Oldfield, Parkes, Railton, Reventlow, Ricardo Rodriguez, Schell, Segrave, Spence, Gwenda Stewart, Trevor Taylor, Parry Thomas, Trintignant, Triplett, Trossi, Vaccarella, Varzi, Wimille.
Indianapolis Motor Speedway-Cannon Ball Baker, DePaolo, Hanks, Milton, Mulford, Johnny Parsons, Petillo, Resta, Rose, Ruttman, Shaw, Vail.
Johnson Wax-Chuck Parsons.

Langhorne Speedway-Marshman.
L&M (Liggett & Myers)-Broadley, Cannon, Follmer, Hobbs, Lunger, Matich, McRae, Motschenbacher, Jackie Stewart, Tyrrell.
LAT (London Art Technical)-Bailey, Coppuck, Craft, Eccleston, Derek Gardner, Gerard, Ginther, Giunti, Duncan Hamilton, Hegbourne, Jackson, Lamborghini, Lanfranchi, Marko, Mass, Mieres, Mitter, Moser, Moss, Muller, Neerpasch, Norinder, Pace, Phillippe, Piper, Rees, Reutemann, Rindt, Pedro Rodriguez, Rollinson, Scarfiotti, Schlesser, Scott-Brown, Sears, Servoz-Gavin, Solana, Southgate, Straight, Tauranac, Anita Taylor, Vandervell, Rob Walker, Webb, Widdows, Williams.
Marlboro-Mosely, Al Unser.
Steve Matchett-Matchett.
Mercedes-Benz-Bruachitsch, Caracciola, Fagioli, Herrmann, Lang, Lautenschlager, Neubauer, Rosemeyer, Seaman, Uhlenhaut, Wagner, Werner.
Mobil-Brabham, Cobb, Hurtubise, Mickey Thompson.
NASCAR-Beam, Bill France Jr., Billy France, Friel, Pete Hamilton, Teague, Herb Thomas, Welborn.
National Speed Sport News-Economaki.
Ontario Motor Speedway-Savage, Bobby Unser.
Cotton Owens Garage-Owens.
Page Engineering-Hiss.
Petty Engineering-Lee Petty.
Porsche-Hanstein, Porsche.
Professionals in Motion-Donohue, Penske.
Renoir Racing-Patterson.
SAAB-Erik and Pat Moss Carlsson.
Salt Lake City Chamber of Commerce-Malcom Campbell.
Samsonite-Leonard.
Shelby American-Phil Hill, Miles, Shelby.
SCCA (Sports Car Club of America)-Adamowicz, Amon, Bondurant, Brown, Gethin, Gregory, Grossman, Hansgen, Hayes, Heuer, Holbert, Pabst.
Sports Factor-Guthrie.
STP-Agajanian, Buddy Baker, Granatelli, Lauda, Paula Murphy, Richard Petty, Pollard, Quester, Billy Vukovich.
Texaco-Chapman, Fittipaldi, Dave Walker.
USAC-Amick, Branson, Bryan, Horn, Lou Moore, O'Connor, Rathmann, Schneider, Sweikert, Bill Vukovich, Ward.
Valvoline-Johncock.
Watkins Glen Grand Prix Corp.-Andretti, Beltoise, Bonnier, de Adamich, Elford, Ganley, Graham Hill, Ickx, Larrousse, Oliver, Pescarolo, Peterson, Redman, Regazzoni, Schenken, Stommelen, Surtees, van Lennep, Wisell.
Wood Brothers-Wood.

As soon as cars were invented, people started racing them. With the advance of the twentieth century auto racing became highly organized, and today it is one of the world's favorite spectator sports. Millions each year pack the stands from Indianapolis to Monaco to Nairobi to thrill to the speed and the expertise of the drivers.

Here, in the most comprehensive collection of auto racing biograph: s ever assembled, are the people who made the sport: the drivers, the designers, the mechanics, and the engineers—the winners of every Grand Prix race, every driver who ever scored a world championship point, the speed record holders, and, in fact, anyone who ever made a mark in the field.

This is just a small sampling of the greats who are included: Barney Oldfield, Eddie Rickenbacker, Stirling Moss, Juan Manuel Fangio, Ettore Bugatti, A. J. Foyt, Mario Andretti, Ferdinand Porsche, Jackie Stewart, Swede Savage, the Maseratis. And each of these men has his own amazing story.

More than eight years of research went into compiling the 550 biographies that make up *The Encyclopedia of Auto Racing Greats*. With over 450 photographs taken from every source imaginable, this volume is filled with facts, vignettes, and anecdotes that will delight the racing fan and the racer alike.

(Continued on back flap)